ROAD AT...

SPAIN & PORTUGAL

Contents

Scale 1:300,000
or 4.7 miles to 1 inch

10th edition February 2019

© AA Media Limited 2019

© 2018 MairDumont, D-73751 Ostfildern

A05673

Published by AA Publishing (a trading name of AA Media Limited, whose registered office is Fanum House, Basing View, Basingstoke, Hampshire RG21 4EA, UK. Registered number 06112600).

ISBN: 978 0 7495 8113 8

A CIP catalogue record for this book is available from The British Library.

The contents of this atlas are believed to be correct at the time of the latest revision, it will not contain any subsequent amended, new or temporary information including diversions and traffic control or enforcement systems. The publishers cannot be held responsible or liable for any loss or damage occasioned to any person acting or refraining from action as a result of any use or reliance on material in this atlas, nor for any errors, omissions or changes in such material. This does not affect your statutory rights.

The publishers would welcome information to correct any errors or omissions and to keep this atlas up to date. Please write to the Atlas Editor, AA Publishing, The Automobile Association, Fanum House, Basing View, Basingstoke, Hampshire RG21 4EA, UK.
E-mail: *roadatlasfeedback@theaa.com*

Printed by 1010 Printing International Ltd

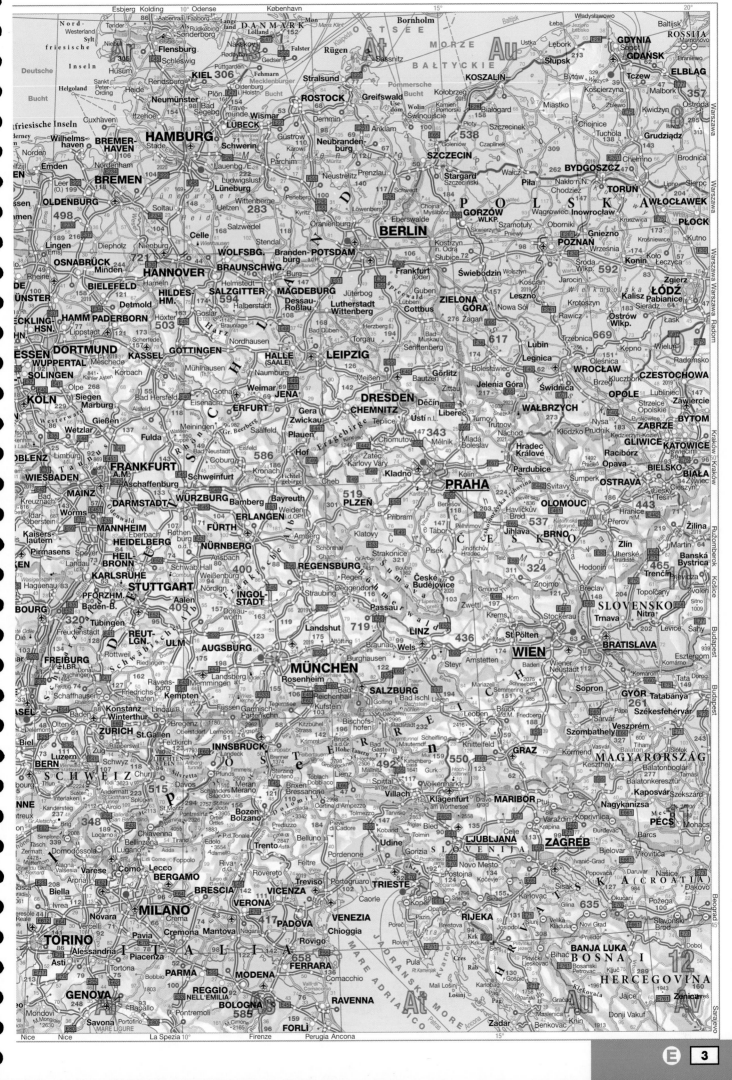

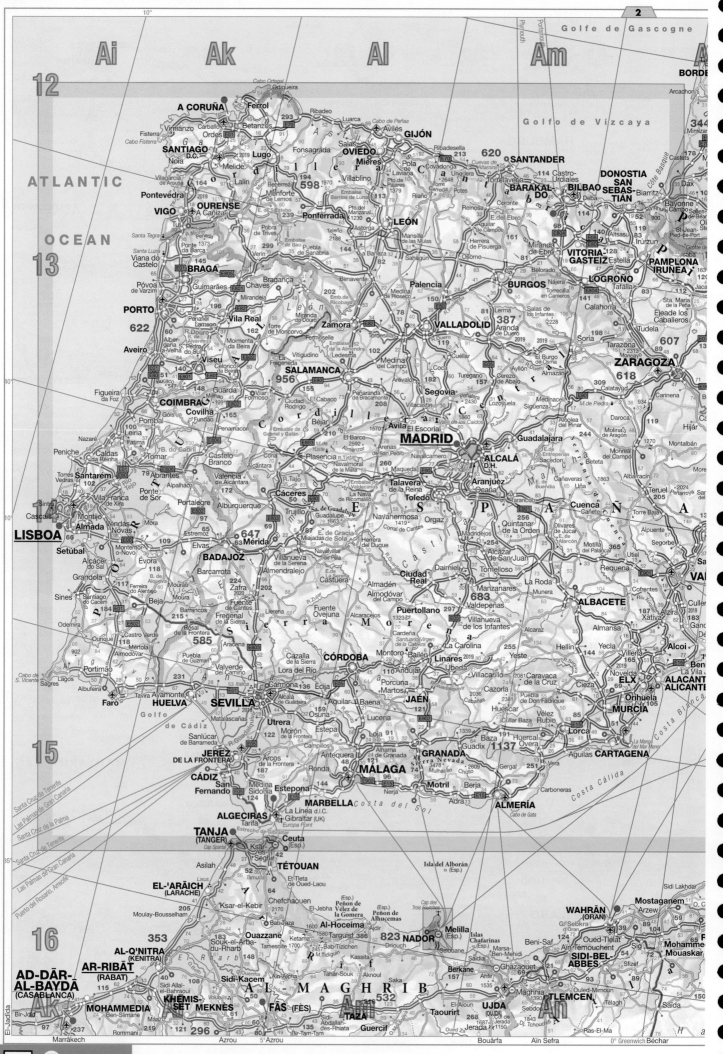

1:300 000

MAPA ÍNDICE	ÍNDICE DE MAPA	BLATTÜBERSICHT	KEY MAP
QUADRO D'UNIONE	CARTE D'ASSEMBLAGE	OVERZICHTSKAART	SKOROWIDZ ARKUSZY
KLAD MAPOVÝCH LISTŮ	KLAD MAPOVÝCH LISTOV	OVERSIGTSKORT	PREGLED LIST

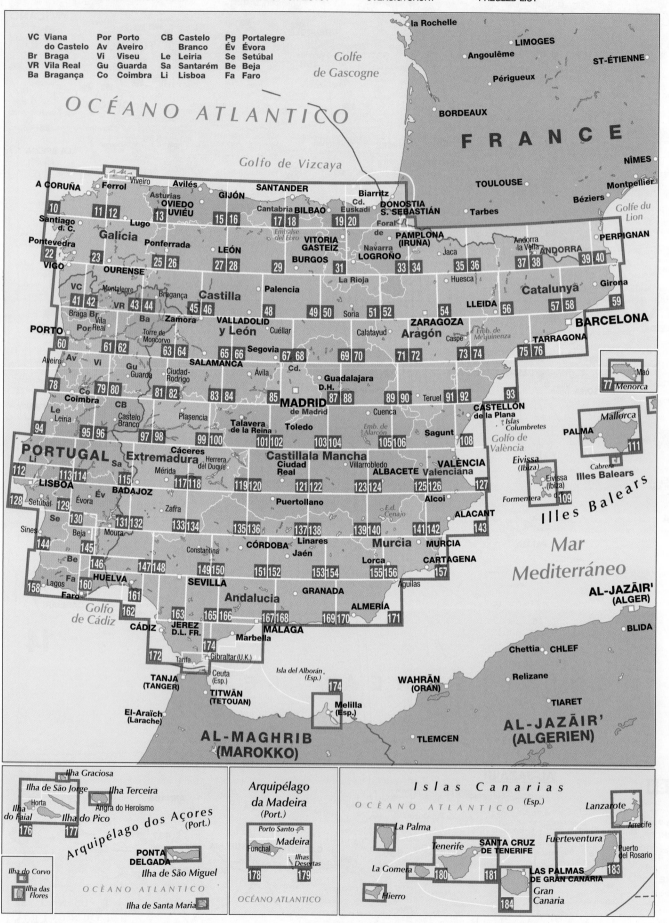

1 : 300 000

Signos convencionales
Sinais convencionais

Zeichenerklärung
Legend

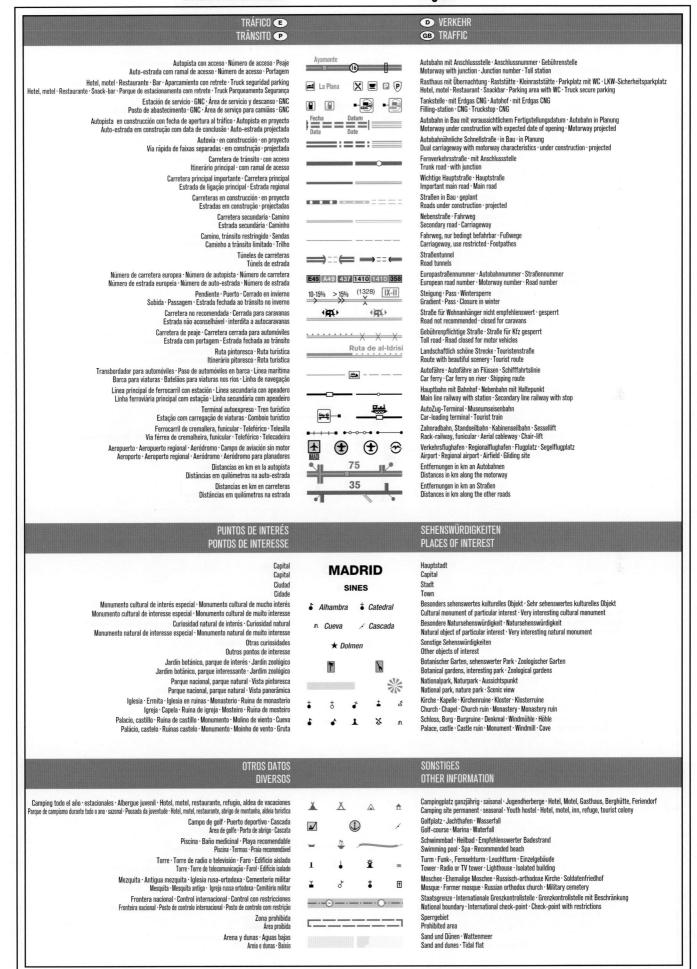

TRÁFICO (E)
TRÂNSITO (P)

(D) VERKEHR
(GB) TRAFFIC

Autopista con acceso · Número de acceso · Peaje / Auto-estrada com ramal de acesso · Número de acesso · Portagem	Autobahn mit Anschlussstelle · Anschlussnummer · Gebührenstelle / Motorway with junction · Junction number · Toll station
Hotel, motel · Restaurante · Bar · Aparcamiento con retrete · Truck seguridad parking / Hotel, motel · Restaurante · Snack-bar · Parque de estacionamento com retrete · Truck Parqueamento Segurança	Rasthaus mit Übernachtung · Raststätte · Kleinraststätte · Parkplatz mit WC · LKW-Sicherheitsparkplatz / Hotel, motel · Restaurant · Snackbar · Parking area with WC · Truck secure parking
Estación de servicio · GNC · Área de servicio y descanso · GNC / Posto de abastecimento · GNC · Área de serviço para camiãos · GNC	Tankstelle · mit Erdgas CNG · Autohof · mit Erdgas CNG / Filling-station · CNG · Truckstop · CNG
Autopista en construcción con fecha de apertura al tráfico · Autopista en proyecto / Auto-estrada em construção com data de conclusão · Auto-estrada projectada	Autobahn in Bau mit voraussichtlichem Fertigstellungsdatum · Autobahn in Planung / Motorway under construction with expected date of opening · Motorway projected
Autovía · en construcción · en proyecto / Vía rápida de faixas separadas · em construção · projectada	Autobahnähnliche Schnellstraße · in Bau · in Planung / Dual carriageway with motorway characteristics · under construction · projected
Carretera de tránsito · con acceso / Itinerário principal · com ramal de acesso	Fernverkehrsstraße · mit Anschlussstelle / Trunk road · with junction
Carretera principal importante · Carretera principal / Estrada de ligação principal · Estrada regional	Wichtige Hauptstraße · Hauptstraße / Important main road · Main road
Carreteras en construcción · en proyecto / Estradas em construção · projectadas	Straßen in Bau · geplant / Roads under construction · projected
Carretera secundaria · Camino / Estrada secundária · Caminho	Nebenstraße · Fahrweg / Secondary road · Carriageway
Camino, tránsito restringido · Sendas / Caminho a trânsito limitado · Trilho	Fahrweg, nur bedingt befahrbar · Fußwege / Carriageway, use restricted · Footpathes
Túneles de carreteras / Túnels de estrada	Straßentunnel / Road tunnels
Número de carretera europea · Número de autopista · Número de carretera / Número de estrada europeia · Número de auto-estrada · Número de estrada	Europastraßennummer · Autobahnnummer · Straßennummer / European road number · Motorway number · Road number
Pendiente · Puerto · Cerrado en invierno / Subida · Passagem · Estrada fechada ao trânsito no inverno	Steigung · Pass · Wintersperre / Gradient · Pass · Closure in winter
Carretera no recomendada · Cerrada para caravanas / Estrada não aconselhável · interdita a autocaravanas	Straße für Wohnanhänger nicht empfehlenswert · gesperrt / Road not recommended · closed for caravans
Carretera de peaje · Carretera cerrada para automóviles / Estrada com portagem · Estrada fechada ao trânsito	Gebührenpflichtige Straße · Straße für Kfz gesperrt / Toll road · Road closed for motor vehicles
Ruta pintoresca · Ruta turística / Itinerário pitoresco · Rota turística	Landschaftlich schöne Strecke · Touristenstraße / Route with beautiful scenery · Tourist route
Transbordador para automóviles · Paso de automóviles en barca · Línea marítima / Barca para viaturas · Batelãos para viaturas nos rios · Linha de navegação	Autofähre · Autofähre an Flüssen · Schifffahrtslinie / Car ferry · Car ferry on river · Shipping route
Línea principal de ferrocarril con estación · Línea secundaria con apeadero / Linha ferroviária principal com estação · Linha secundária com apeadero	Hauptbahn mit Bahnhof · Nebenbahn mit Haltepunkt / Main line railway with station · Secondary line railway with stop
Terminal autoexpreso · Tren turístico / Estação com carregação de viaturas · Comboio turístico	AutoZug-Terminal · Museumseisenbahn / Car-loading terminal · Tourist train
Ferrocarril de cremallera, funicular · Teleférico · Telesilla / Via férrea de cremalheira, funicular · Teleférico · Telecadeira	Zahnradbahn, Standseilbahn · Kabinenseilbahn · Sessellift / Rack-railway, funicular · Aerial cableway · Chair-lift
Aeropuerto · Aeropuerto regional · Aeródromo · Campo de aviación sin motor / Aeroporto · Aeroporto regional · Aeródromo · Aeródromo para planadores	Verkehrsflughafen · Regionalflughafen · Flugplatz · Segelflugplatz / Airport · Regional airport · Airfield · Gliding site
Distancias en km en la autopista / Distâncias em quilómetros na auto-estrada	Entfernungen in km an Autobahnen / Distances in km along the motorway
Distancias en km en carreteras / Distâncias em quilómetros na estrada	Entfernungen in km an Straßen / Distances in km along the other roads

PUNTOS DE INTERÉS
PONTOS DE INTERESSE

SEHENSWÜRDIGKEITEN
PLACES OF INTEREST

Capital / Capital	Hauptstadt / Capital
Ciudad / Cidade	Stadt / Town
Monumento cultural de interés especial · Monumento cultural de mucho interés / Monumento cultural de interesse especial · Monumento cultural de muito interesse	Besonders sehenswertes kulturelles Objekt · Sehr sehenswertes kulturelles Objekt / Cultural monument of particular interest · Very interesting cultural monument
Curiosidad natural de interés · Curiosidad natural / Monumento natural de interesse especial · Monumento natural de muito interesse	Besondere Natursehenswürdigkeit · Natursehenswürdigkeit / Natural object of particular interest · Very interesting natural monument
Otras curiosidades / Outros pontos de interesse	Sonstige Sehenswürdigkeiten / Other objects of interest
Jardín botánico, parque de interés · Jardín zoológico / Jardim botânico, parque interessante · Jardim zoológico	Botanischer Garten, sehenswerter Park · Zoologischer Garten / Botanical gardens, interesting park · Zoological gardens
Parque nacional, parque natural · Vista pintoresca / Parque nacional, parque natural · Vista panorâmica	Nationalpark, Naturpark · Aussichtspunkt / National park, nature park · Scenic view
Iglesia · Ermita · Iglesia en ruinas · Monasterio · Ruina de monasterio / Igreja · Capela · Ruína de igreja · Mosteiro · Ruína de mosteiro	Kirche · Kapelle · Kirchenruine · Kloster · Klosterruine / Church · Chapel · Church ruin · Monastery · Monastery ruin
Palacio, castillo · Ruina de castillo · Monumento · Molino de viento · Cueva / Palácio, castelo · Ruínas castelo · Monumento · Moinho de vento · Gruta	Schloss, Burg · Burgruine · Denkmal · Windmühle · Höhle / Palace, castle · Castle ruin · Monument · Windmill · Cave

MADRID — SINES

Alhambra · Catedral · Cueva · Cascada · Dolmen

OTROS DATOS
DIVERSOS

SONSTIGES
OTHER INFORMATION

Camping todo el año · estacionales · Albergue juvenil · Hotel, motel, restaurante, refugio, aldea de vacaciones / Parque de campismo durante todo o ano · sazonal · Pousada da juventude · Hotel, motel, restaurante, abrigo de montanha, aldeia turística	Campingplatz ganzjährig · saisonal · Jugendherberge · Hotel, Motel, Gasthaus, Berghütte, Feriendorf / Camping site permanent · seasonal · Youth hostel · Hotel, motel, inn, refuge, tourist colony
Campo de golf · Puerto deportivo · Cascada / Área de golfe · Porto de abrigo · Cascata	Golfplatz · Jachthafen · Wasserfall / Golf-course · Marina · Waterfall
Piscina · Baño medicinal · Playa recomendable / Piscina · Termas · Praia recomendável	Schwimmbad · Heilbad · Empfehlenswerter Badestrand / Swimming pool · Spa · Recommended beach
Torre · Torre de radio o televisión · Faro · Edificio aislado / Torre · Torre de telecomunicação · Farol · Edifício isolado	Turm · Funk-, Fernsehturm · Leuchtturm · Einzelgebäude / Tower · Radio or TV tower · Lighthouse · Isolated building
Mezquita · Antigua mezquita · Iglesia rusa-ortodoxa · Cementerio militar / Mesquita · Mesquita antiga · Igreja russa ortodoxa · Cemitério militar	Moschee · Ehemalige Moschee · Russisch-orthodoxe Kirche · Soldatenfriedhof / Mosque · Former mosque · Russian orthodox church · Military cemetery
Frontera nacional · Control internacional · Control con restricciones / Fronteira nacional · Posto de controlo internacional · Posto de controlo com restrição	Staatsgrenze · Internationale Grenzkontrollstelle · Grenzkontrollstelle mit Beschränkung / National boundary · International check-point · Check-point with restrictions
Zona prohibida / Area proibida	Sperrgebiet / Prohibited area
Arena y dunas · Aguas bajas / Areia e dunas · Baixio	Sand und Dünen · Wattenmeer / Sand and dunes · Tidal flat

1 : 300 000

Segni convenzionali
Légende

Legenda
Objasnienie znaków

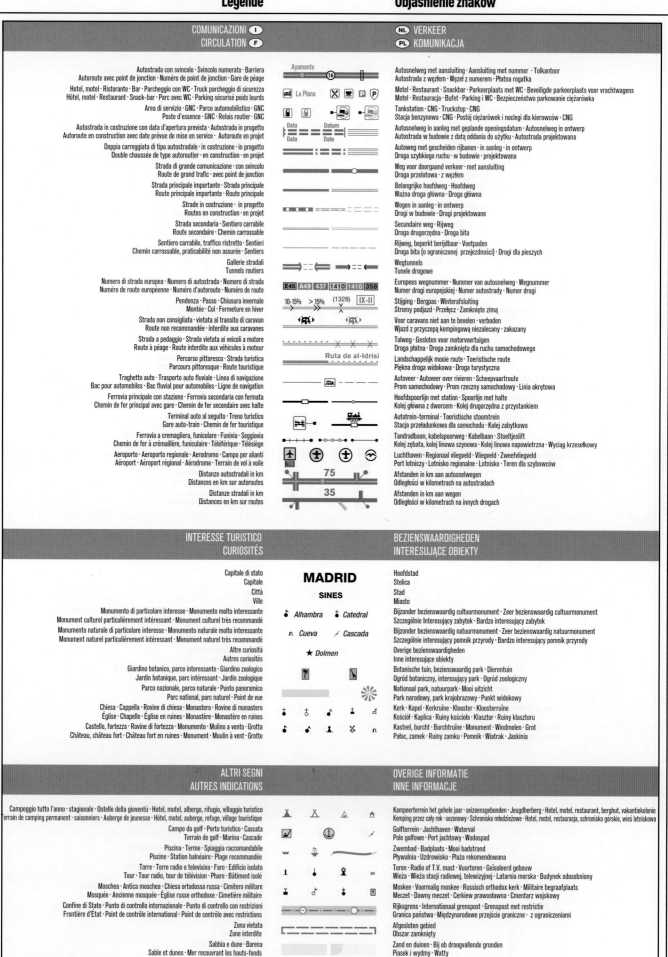

COMUNICAZIONI (I)
CIRCULATION (F)

(NL) VERKEER
(PL) KOMUNIKACJA

Autostrada con svincolo · Svincolo numerato · Barriera
Autoroute avec point de jonction · Numéro de point de jonction · Gare de péage

Autosnelweg met aansluiting · Aansluiting met nummer · Tolkantoor
Autostrada z węzłem · Węzeł z numerem · Płatna rogatka

Hotel, motel · Ristorante · Bar · Parcheggio con WC · Truck parcheggio di sicurezza
Hôtel, motel · Restaurant · Snack-bar · Parc avec WC · Parking sécurisé poids lourds

Motel · Restaurant · Snackbar · Parkeerplaats met WC · Beveiligde parkeerplaats voor vrachtwagens
Motel · Restauracja · Bufet · Parking i WC · Bezpieczeństwo parkowanie ciężarówka

Area di servizio · GNC · Parco automobilistico · GNC
Poste d'essence · GNC · Relais routier · GNC

Tankstation · CNG · Truckstop · CNG
Stacja benzynowa · CNG · Postój ciężarówek i noclegi dla kierowców · CNG

Autostrada in costruzione con data d'apertura prevista · Autostrada in progetto
Autoroute en construction avec date prévue de mise en service · Autoroute en projet

Autosnelweg in aanleg met geplande openingsdatum · Autosnelweg in ontwerp
Autostrada w budowie z datą oddania do użytku · Autostrada projektowana

Doppia carreggiata di tipo autostradale · in costruzione · in progetto
Double chaussée de type autoroutier · en construction · en projet

Autoweg met gescheiden rijbanen · in aanleg · in ontwerp
Droga szybkiego ruchu · w budowie · projektowana

Strada di grande comunicazione · con svincolo
Route de grand trafic · avec point de jonction

Weg voor doorgaand verkeer · met aansluiting
Droga przelotowa · z węzłem

Strada principale importante · Strada principale
Route principale importante · Route principale

Belangrijke hoofdweg · Hoofdweg
Ważna droga główna · Droga główna

Strade in costruzione · in progetto
Routes en construction · en projet

Wegen in aanleg · in ontwerp
Drogi w budowie · Drogi projektowane

Strada secondaria · Sentiero carrabile
Route secondaire · Chemin carrossable

Secundaire weg · Rijweg
Droga drugorzędna · Droga bita

Sentiero carrabile, traffico ristretto · Sentieri
Chemin carrossable, praticabilité non assurée · Sentiers

Rijweg, beperkt berijdbaar · Voetpaden
Droga bita (o ograniczonej przejezdności) · Drogi dla pieszych

Gallerie stradali
Tunnels routiers

Wegtunnels
Tunele drogowe

Numero di strada europea · Numero di autostrada · Numero di strada
Numéro de route européenne · Numéro d'autoroute · Numéro de route

Europees wegnummer · Nummer van autosnelweg · Wegnummer
Numer drogi europejskiej · Numer autostrady · Numer drogi

E45	A49	437	1410	1410	358

Pendenza · Passo · Chiusura invernale
Montée · Col · Fermeture en hiver

Stijging · Bergpas · Winterafsluiting
Stromy podjazd · Przełęcz · Zamknięte zimą

10-15% >15% (1328) IX-II

Strada non consigliata · vietata al transito di caravan
Route non recommandée · interdite aux caravans

Voor caravans niet aan te bevelen · verboden
Wjazd z przyczepą kempingową niezalecany · zakazany

Strada a pedaggio · Strada vietata ai veicoli a motore
Route à péage · Route interdite aux véhicules à moteur

Tolweg · Gesloten voor motorvoertuigen
Droga płatna · Droga zamknięta dla ruchu samochodowego

Percorso pittoresco · Strada turistica
Parcours pittoresque · Route touristique

Landschappelijk mooie route · Toeristische route
Piękna droga widokowa · Droga turystyczna

Ruta de al-Idrisi

Traghetto auto · Trasporto auto fluviale · Linea di navigazione
Bac pour automobiles · Bac fluvial pour automobiles · Ligne de navigation

Autoveer · Autoveer over rivieren · Scheepvaartroute
Prom samochodowy · Prom rzeczny samochodowy · Linia okrętowa

Ferrovia principale con stazione · Ferrovia secondaria con fermata
Chemin de fer principal avec gare · Chemin de fer secondaire avec halte

Hoofdspoorlijn met station · Spoorlijn met halte
Kolej główna z dworcem · Kolej drugorzędna z przystankiem

Terminal auto al seguito · Treno turistico
Gare auto-train · Chemin de fer touristique

Autotrein-terminal · Toeristische stoomtrein
Stacja przeładunkowa dla samochodu · Kolej zabytkowa

Ferrovia a cremagliera, funicolare · Funivia · Seggiovia
Chemin de fer à crémaillère, funiculaire · Téléférique · Télésiège

Tandradbaan, kabelspoorweg · Kabelbaan · Stoeltjeslift
Kolej zębata, kolej linowa szynowa · Kolej linowa napowietrzna · Wyciąg krzesełkowy

Aeroporto · Aeroporto regionale · Aerodromo · Campo per alianti
Aéroport · Aéroport régional · Aérodrome · Terrain de vol à voile

Luchthaven · Regionaal vliegveld · Vliegveld · Zweefvliegveld
Port lotniczy · Lotnisko regionalne · Lotnisko · Teren dla szybowców

MAD

Distanze autostradali in km
Distances en km sur autoroutes

Afstanden in km aan autosnelweg
Odległości w kilometrach na autostradach

75

Distanze stradali in km
Distances en km sur routes

Afstanden in km aan wegen
Odległości w kilometrach na innych drogach

35

INTERESSE TURISTICO
CURIOSITÉS

BEZIENSWAARDIGHEDEN
INTERESUJĄCE OBIEKTY

Capitale di stato
Capitale

MADRID

Hoofdstad
Stolica

Città
Ville

SINES

Stad
Miasto

Monumento di particolare interesse · Monumento molto interessante
Monument culturel particulièrement intéressant · Monument culturel très recommandé

♪ Alhambra   ⚜ Catedral

Bijzonder bezienswaardig cultuurmonument · Zeer bezienswaardig cultuurmonument
Szczególnie Interesujący zabytek · Bardzo interesujący zabytek

Monumento naturale di particolare interesse · Monumento naturale molto interessante
Monument naturel particulièrement intéressant · Monument naturel très recommandé

∩ Cueva   ✗ Cascada

Bijzonder bezienswaardig natuurmonument · Zeer bezienswaardig natuurmonument
Szczególnie interesujący pomnik przyrody · Bardzo interesujący pomnik przyrody

Altre curiosità
Autres curiosités

★ Dolmen

Overige bezienswaardigheden
Inne interesujące obiekty

Giardino botanico, parco interessante · Giardino zoologico
Jardin botanique, parc intéressant · Jardin zoologique

Botanische tuin, bezienswaardig park · Dierentuin
Ogród botaniczny, interesujący park · Ogród zoologiczny

Parco nazionale, parco naturale · Punto panoramico
Parc national, parc naturel · Point de vue

Nationaal park, natuurpark · Mooi uitzicht
Park narodowy, park krajobrazowy · Mooi widokowy

Chiesa · Cappella · Rovine di chiesa · Monastero · Rovine di monastero
Église · Chapelle · Église en ruines · Monastère · Monastère en ruines

Kerk · Kapel · Kerkruine · Klooster · Kloosterruïne
Kościół · Kaplica · Ruiny kościoła · Klasztor · Ruiny klasztoru

Castello, fortezza · Rovine di fortezza · Monumento · Mulino a vento · Grotta
Château, château fort · Château fort en ruines · Monument · Moulin à vent · Grotte

Kasteel, burcht · Burchtruine · Monument · Windmolen · Grot
Pałac, zamek · Ruiny zamku · Pomnik · Wiatrak · Jaskinia

ALTRI SEGNI
AUTRES INDICATIONS

OVERIGE INFORMATIE
INNE INFORMACJE

Campeggio tutto l'anno · stagionale · Ostello della gioventù · Hotel, motel, albergo, rifugio, villaggio turistico
Terrain de camping permanent · saisonniers · Auberge de jeunesse · Hôtel, motel, auberge, refuge, village touristique

Kampeerterrein het gehele jaar · seizoensgebonden · Jeugdherberg · Hotel, motel, restaurant, berghut, vakantiekolonie
Kemping przez cały rok · sezonowy · Schronisko młodzieżowe · Hotel, motel, restauracja, schronisko górskie, wieś letniskowa

Campo da golf · Porto turistico · Cascata
Terrain de golf · Marina · Cascade

Golfterrein · Jachthaven · Waterval
Pole golfowe · Port jachtowy · Wodospad

Piscina · Terme · Spiaggia raccomandabile
Piscine · Station balnéaire · Plage recommandée

Zwembad · Badplaats · Mooi badstrand
Pływalnia · Uzdrowisko · Plaża rekomendowana

Torre · Torre radio o televisiva · Faro · Edificio isolato
Tour · Tour radio, tour de télévision · Phare · Bâtiment isolé

Toren · Radio of T.V. mast · Vuurtoren · Geïsoleerd gebouw
Wieża · Wieża stacji radiowej, telewizyjnej · Latarnia morska · Budynek odosobniony

Moschea · Antica moschea · Chiesa ortodossa russa · Cimitero militare
Mosquée · Ancienne mosquée · Église russe orthodoxe · Cimetière militaire

Moskee · Voormalig moskee · Russisch orthodox kerk · Militaire begraafplaats
Meczet · Dawny meczet · Cerkiew prawosławna · Cmentarz wojskowy

Confine di Stato · Punto di controllo internazionale · Punto di controllo con restrizioni
Frontière d'État · Point de contrôle international · Point de contrôle avec restrictions

Rijksgrens · Internationaal grenspost · Grenspost met restrictie
Granica państwa · Międzynarodowe przejście graniczne · z ograniczeniami

Zona vietata
Zone interdite

Afgesloten gebied
Obszar zamknięty

Sabbia e dune · Barena
Sable et dunes · Mer recouvrant les hauts-fonds

Zand en duinen · Bij eb droogvallende gronden
Piasek i wydmy · Watty

1 : 300 000

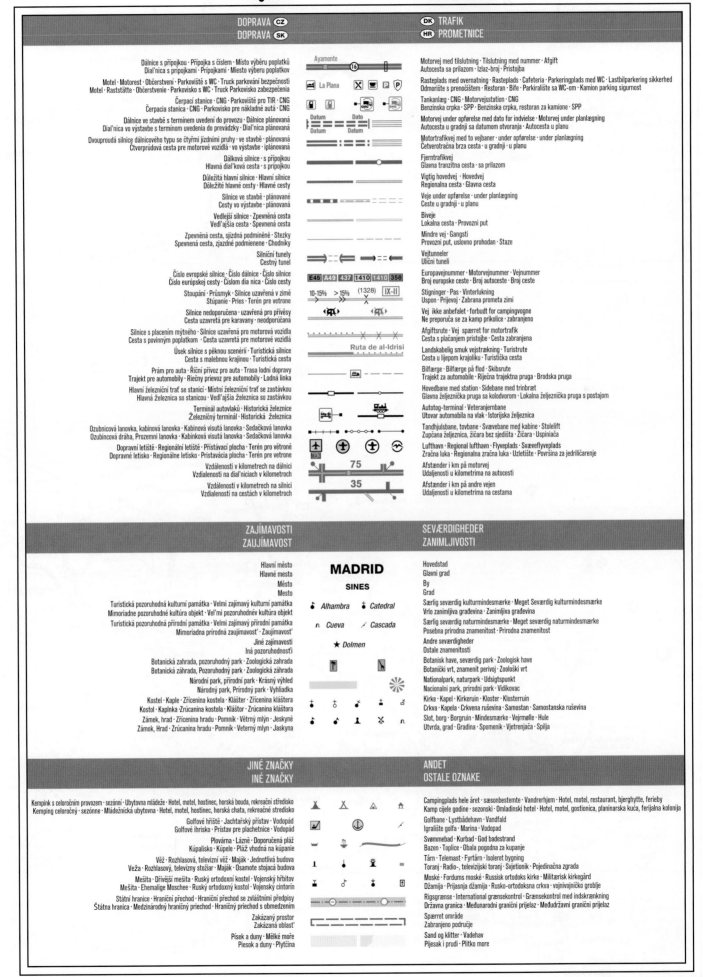

Vysvětlivky
Legenda

Tegnforklaring
Tumač znakova

DOPRAVA (CZ)
DOPRAVA (SK)

(DK) TRAFIK
(HR) PROMETNICE

Dálnice s připojkou · Přípojka s číslem · Místo výběru poplatků	Motorvej med tilslutning · Tilslutning med nummer · Afgift
Diaľnica s pripojkami · Prípojkami · Miesto výberu poplatkov	Autocesta sa prilazom · Izlaz-broj · Pristojba
Motel · Motorest · Občerstvení · Parkoviště s WC · Truck parkování bezpečnosti	Rasteplads med overnatning · Rasteplads · Cafeteria · Parkeringsplads med WC · Lastbilparkering sikkerhed
Motel · Raststätte · Občerstvenie · Parkovisko s WC · Truck Parkovisko zabezpečenia	Odmorište s prenoćištem · Restoran · Bife · Parkiralište sa WC-om · Kamion parking sigurnost
Čerpací stanice · CNG · Parkoviště pro TIR · CNG	Tankanlæg · CNG · Motorvejsstation · CNG
Čerpacia stanica · CNG · Parkovisko pre nákladné autá · CNG	Benzinska crpka · SPP · Benzinska crpka, restoran za kamione · SPP
Dálnice ve stavbě s termínem uvedení do provozu · Dálnice plánovaná	Motorvej under opførelse med dato for indvielse · Motorvej under planlægning
Diaľnica vo výstavbe s termínom uvedenia do prevádzky · Diaľnica plánovaná	Autocesta u gradnji sa datumom otvoranja · Autocesta u planu
Dvouproudá silnice dálnicového typu se čtyřmi jízdními pruhy · ve stavbě · plánovaná	Motortrafikvej med to vejbaner · under opførelse · under planlægning
Čtvorprúdová cesta pre motorové vozidlá · vo výstavbe · iplánovaná	Četverotračna brza cesta · u gradnji · u planu
Dálková silnice · s přípojkou	Fjerntrafikvej
Hlavná diaľková cesta · s prípojkou	Glavna tranzitna cesta · sa prilazom
Důležitá hlavní silnice · Hlavní silnice	Vigtig hovedvej · Hovedvej
Dôležité hlavné cesty · Hlavné cesty	Regionalna cesta · Glavna cesta
Silnice ve stavbě · plánované	Veje under opførelse · under planlægning
Cesty vo výstavbe · plánovaná	Ceste u gradnji · u planu
Vedlejší silnice · Zpevněná cesta	Biveje
Vedľajšia cesta · Spevnená cesta	Lokalna cesta · Provozni put
Zpevněná cesta, sjízdná podmíněně · Stezky	Mindre vej · Gangsti
Spevnená cesta, zjazdné podmienene · Chodníky	Provozni put, uslovno prohodan · Staze
Silniční tunely	Vejtunneler
Cestný tunel	Ulični tuneli
Číslo evropské silnice · Číslo dálnice · Číslo silnice	Europavejnummer · Motorvejnummer · Vejnummer
Číslo európskej cesty · Číslom dia nica · Číslo cesty	Broj europske ceste · Broj autoceste · Broj ceste
Stoupání · Průsmyk · Silnice uzavřená v zimě	Stigninger · Pas · Vinterlukning
Stúpanie · Pries · Terén pre vetrone	Uspon · Prijevoj · Zabrana prometa zimi
Silnice nedoporučena · uzavřená pro přívěsy	Vej ikke anbefalet · forbudt for campingvogne
Cesta uzavretá pre karavany · neodporúčaná	Ne preporuča se za kamp prikolice · zabranjeno
Silnice s placením mýtného · Silnice uzavřená pro motorová vozidla	Afgiftsrute · Vej spærret for motortrafik
Cesta s povinným poplatkom · Cesta uzavretá pre motorové vozidlá	Cesta s plaćanjem pristojbe · Cesta zabranjena
Úsek silnice s pěknou scenérií · Turistická silnice	Landskabelig smuk vejstrækning · Turistrute
Cesta s malebnou krajinou · Turistická cesta	Cesta u lijepom krajoliku · Turistička cesta
Prám pro auta · Říční přívoz pro auta · Trasa lodní dopravy	Bilfærge · Bilfærge på flod · Skibsrute
Trajekt pre automobily · Riečny prievoz pre automobily · Lodná linka	Trajekt za automobile · Riječna trajektna pruga · Brodska pruga
Hlavní železniční trať se stanicí · Místní železniční trať se zastávkou	Hovedbane med station · Sidebane med trinbræt
Hlavná železnica so stanicou · Vedľajšia železnica so zastávkou	Glavna željeznička pruga sa kolodvorom · Lokalna željeznička pruga s postajom
Terminál autovlaků · Historická železnice	Autotog-terminal · Veteranjernbane
Železničný terminál · Historická železnica	Utovar automobila na vlak · Istorijska željeznica
Ozubnicová lanovka, kabinová lanovka · Kabinová visutá lanovka · Sedačková lanovka	Tandhjulsbane, tovbane · Svævebane med kabine · Stolelift
Ozubincová dráha, Prozemní lanovka · Kabínková visutá lanovka · Sedačková lanovka	Zupčana željeznica, žičara bez sjedišta · Žičara · Uspinjača
Dopravní letiště · Regionální letiště · Přistávací plocha · Terén pro větroně	Lufthavn · Regional lufthavn · Flyveplads · Svæveflyveplads
Dopravné letisko · Regionálne letisko · Pristávacia plocha · Terén pre vetrone	Zračna luka · Regionalna zračna luka · Uzletište · Površina za jedriličarenje
Vzdálenosti v kilometrech na dálnici	Afstænder i km på motorvej
Vzdialenosti na diaľniciach v kilometroch	Udaljenosti u kilometrima na autocesti
Vzdálenosti v kilometrech na silnici	Afstænder i km på andre vejen
Vzdialenosti na cestách v kilometroch	Udaljenosti u kilometrima na cestama

ZAJÍMAVOSTI
ZAUJÍMAVOST

SEVÆRDIGHEDER
ZANIMLJIVOSTI

Hlavní město	Hovedstad
Hlavné mesto	Glavni grad
Město	By
Mesto	Grad
Turistická pozoruhodná kulturní památka · Velmi zajímavý kulturní památka	Særlig seværdig kulturmindesmærke · Meget Seværdig kulturmindesmærke
Mimoriadne pozoruhodné kultúra objekt · Veľmi pozoruhodněv kultúra objekt	Vrlo zanimljiva građevina · Zanimljiva građevina
Turistická pozoruhodná přírodní památka · Velmi zajímavý přírodní památka	Særlig seværdig naturmindesmærke · Meget seværdig naturmindesmærke
Mimoriadna prírodná zaujímavosť · Zaujímavosť	Posebna prirodna znamenitost · Prirodna znamenitost
Jiné zajímavosti	Andre seværdigheder
Iná pozoruhodnosťi	Ostale znamenitosti
Botanická zahrada, pozoruhodný park · Zoologická zahrada	Botanisk have, seværdig park · Zoologísk have
Botanická záhrada, Pozoruhodný park · Zoologická záhrada	Botanički vrt, znamenit perivoj · Zoološki vrt
Národní park, přírodní park · Krásný výhled	Nationalpark, naturpark · Udsigtspunkt
Národný park, Prírodný park · Vyhliadka	Nacionalni park, prirodni park · Vidikovac
Kostel · Kaple · Zřícenina kostela · Klášter · Zřícenina kláštera	Kirke · Kapel · Kirkeruin · Kloster · Klosterruin
Kostol · Kaplnka ·Zrúcanina kostola · Kláštor · Zrúcanina kláštora	Crkva · Kapela · Crkvena ruševina · Samostan · Samostanska ruševina
Zámek, hrad · Zřícenina hradu · Pomník · Větrný mlýn · Jeskyně	Slot, borg · Borgruin · Mindesmærke · Vejrmølle · Hule
Zámok, Hrad · Zrúcanina hradu · Pomník · Veterný mlyn · Jaskyna	Utvrda, grad · Gradina · Spomenik · Vjetrenjača · Spilja

JINÉ ZNAČKY
INÉ ZNAČKY

ANDET
OSTALE OZNAKE

Kempink s celoročním provozem · sezónní · Ubytovna mládeže · Hotel, motel, hostinec, horská bouda, rekreační středisko	Campingplads hele året · sæsonbestemte · Vandrerhjem · Hotel, motel, restaurant, bjerghytte, ferieby
Kemping celoročný · sezónne · Mládežnícka ubytovna · Hotel, motel, hostinec, horská chata, rekreačné stredisko	Kamp cijele godine · sezonski · Omladinski hotel · Hotel, motel, gostionica, planinarska kuća, ferijalna kolonija
Golfové hřiště · Jachtařský přístav · Vodopád	Golfbane · Lystbådehavn · Vandfald
Golfové ihrisko · Prístav pre plachetnice · Vodopád	Igralište golfa · Marina · Vodopad
Plovárna · Lázně · Doporučená pláž	Svømmebad · Kurbad · God badestrand
Kúpalisko · Kúpele · Pláž vhodná na kúpanie	Bazen · Toplice · Obala pogodna za kupanje
Věž · Rozhlasová, televizní věž · Maják · Jednotlivá budova	Tårn · Telemast · Fyrtårn · Isoleret bygning
Veža · Rozhlasový, televizny stožiar · Maják · Osamote stojacá budova	Toranj · Radio-, televizijski toranj · Svjetionik · Pojedinačna zgrada
Mešita · Dřívější mešita · Ruský ortodoxní kostel · Vojenský hřbitov	Moské · Fordums moské · Russisk ortodoks kirke · Militærisk kirkegård
Mešita · Ehemalige Moschee · Ruský ortodoxný kostol · Vojenský cintorín	Džamija · Prijasnja džamija · Rusko-ortodoksna crkva · vojnivojničko groblje
Státní hranice · Hraniční přechod · Hraniční přechod se zvláštními předpisy	Rigsgrænse · International grænsekontrol · Grænsekontrol med indskrænkning
Štátna hranica · Medzinárodný hraničný priechod · Hraničný priechod s obmedzením	Državna granica · Međunarodni granični prijelaz · Međudržavni granični prijelaz
Zakázaný prostor	Spærret område
Zakázaná oblasť	Zabranjeno područje
Písek a duny · Mělké moře	Sand og klitter · Vadehav
Piesok a duny · Plytčina	Pijesak i prudi · Plitko more

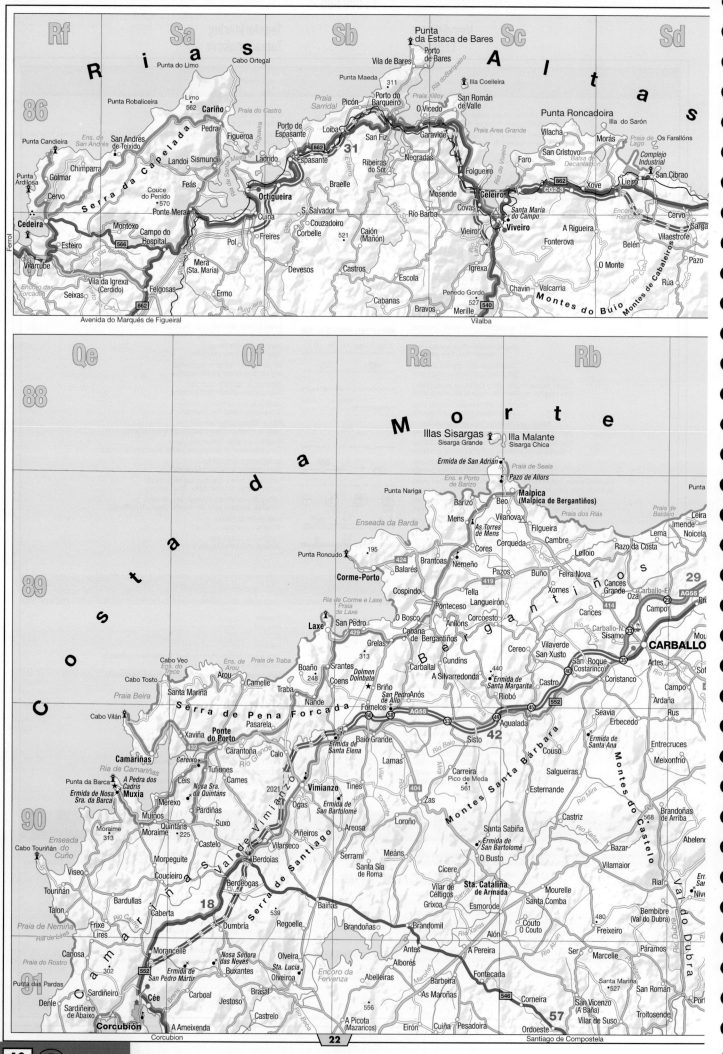

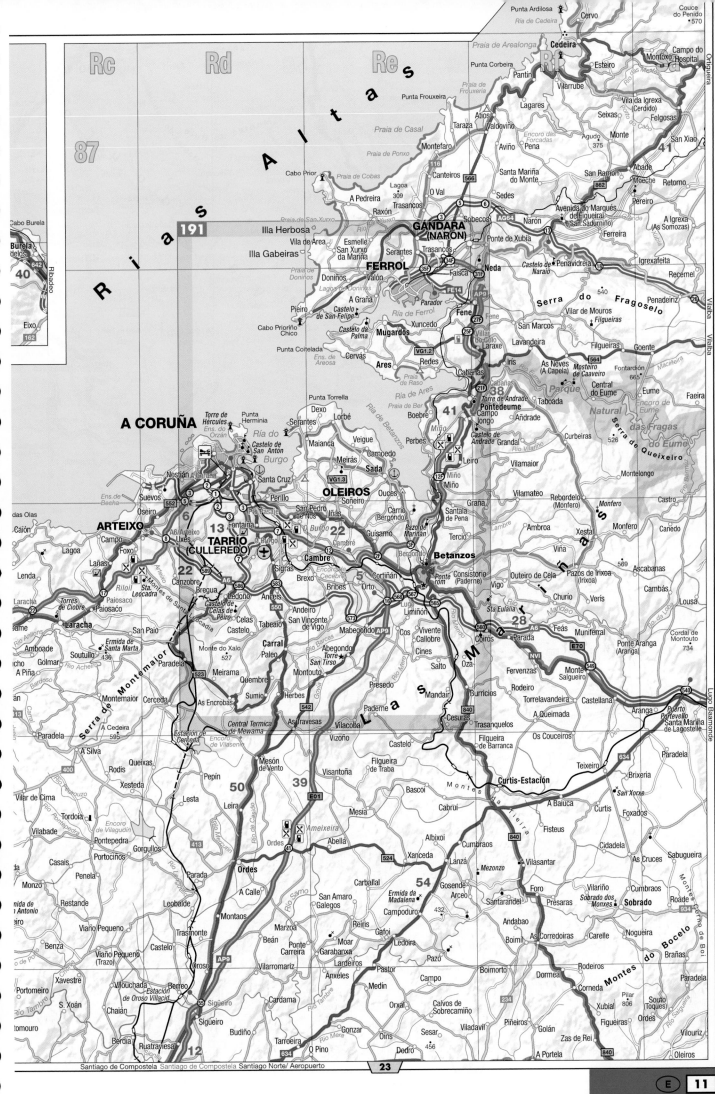

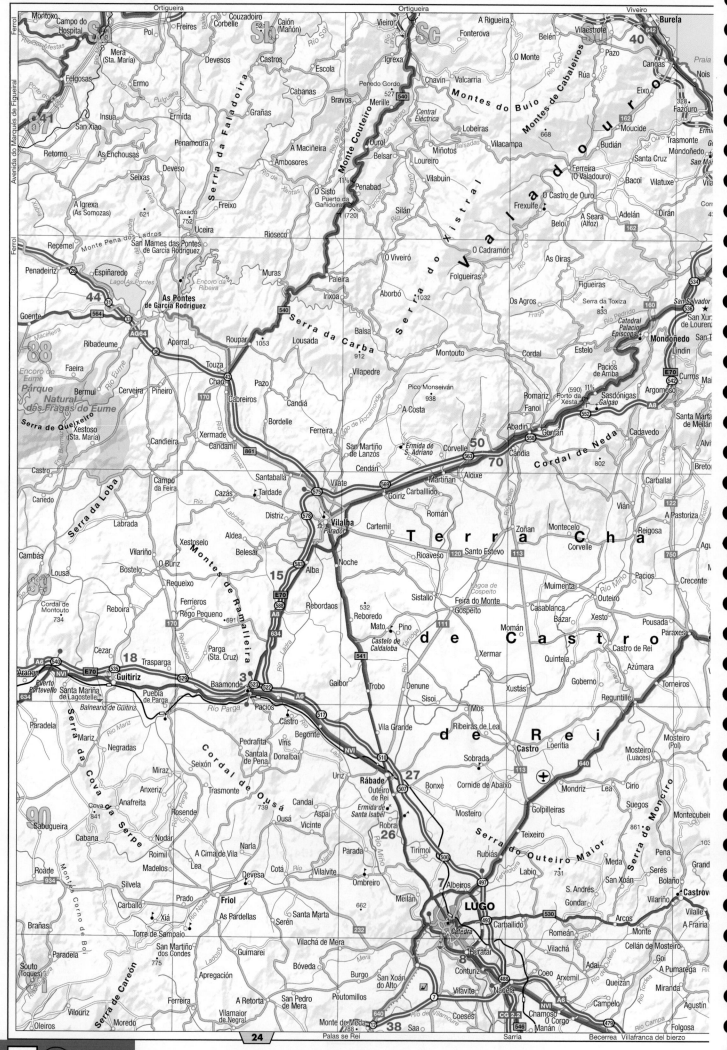

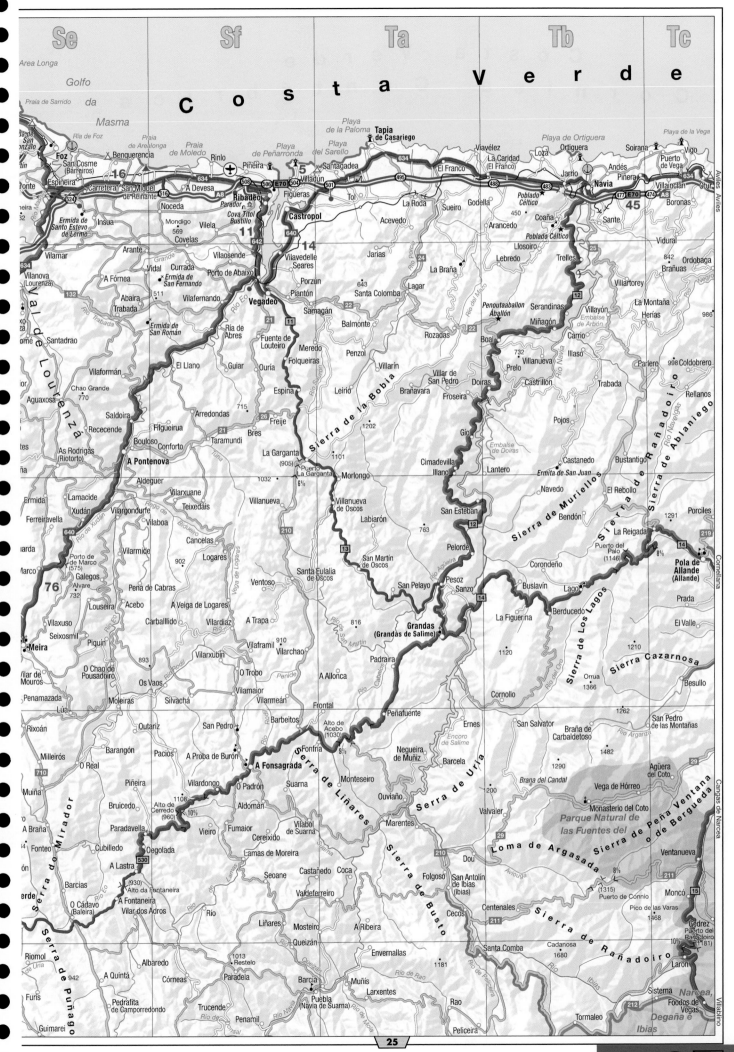

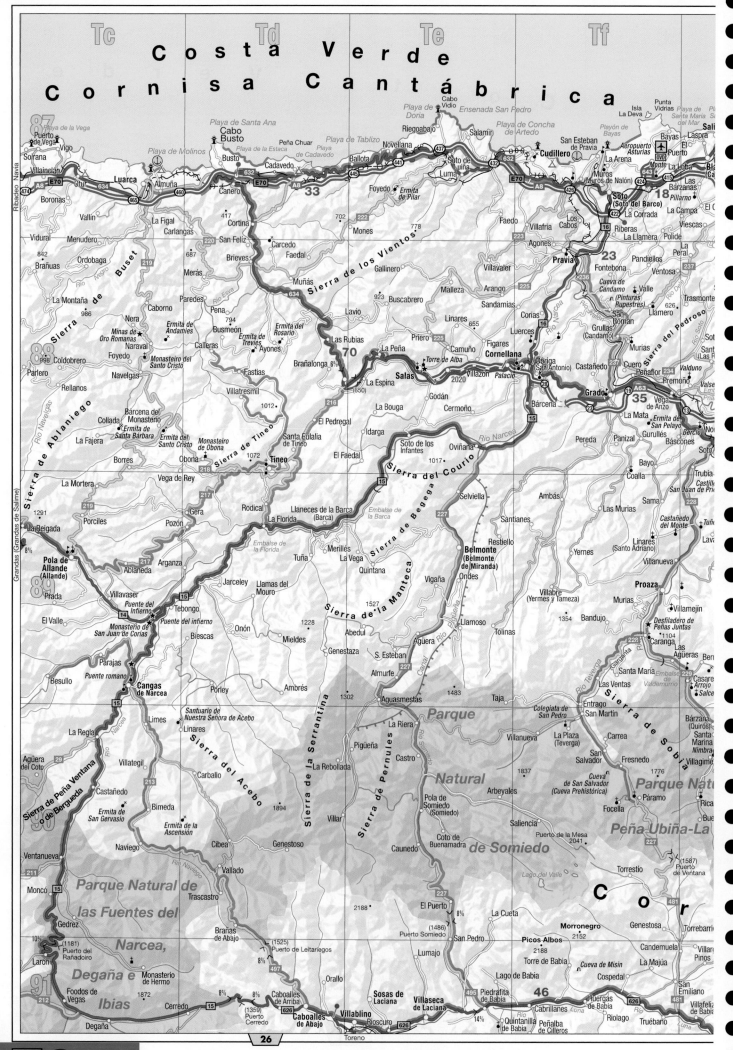

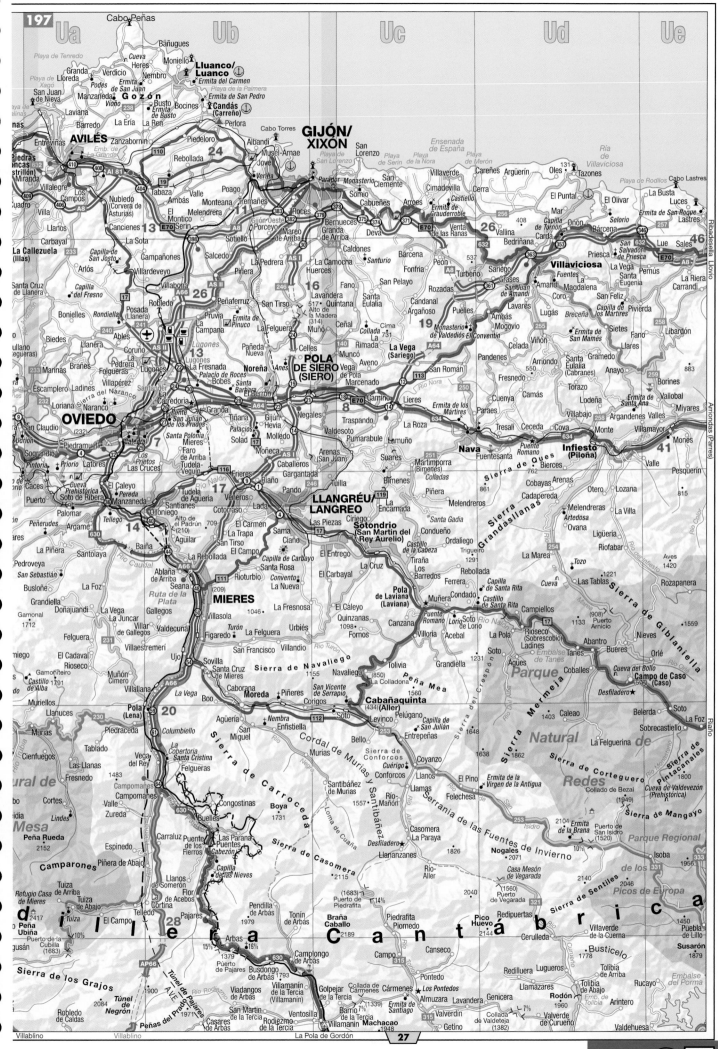

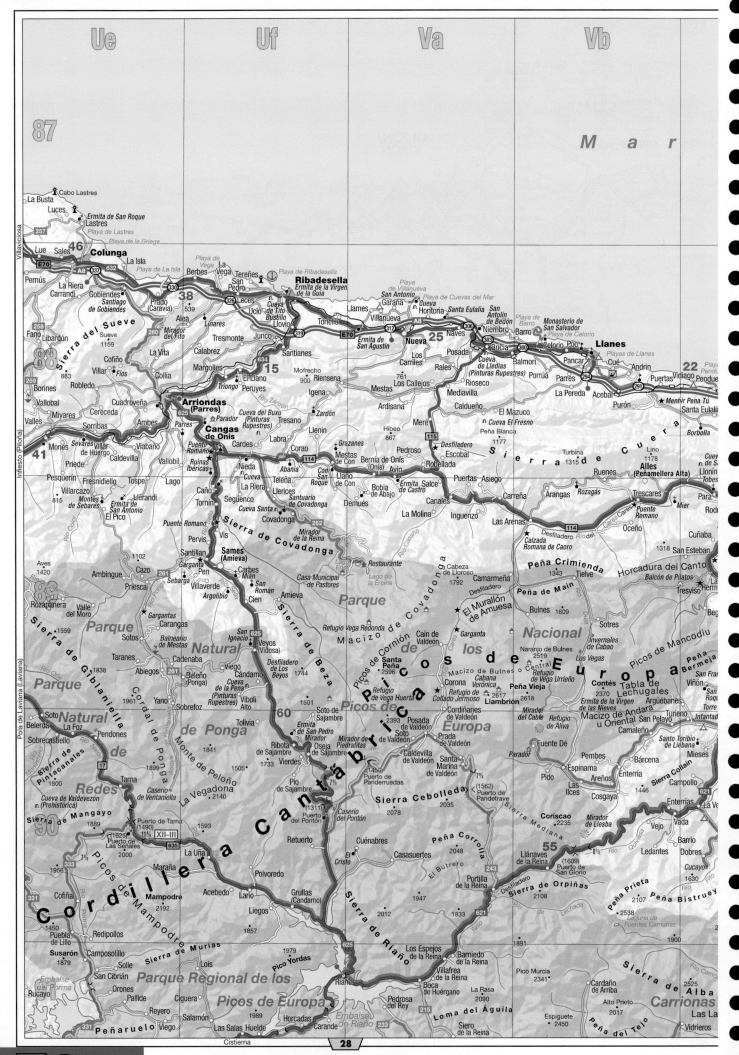

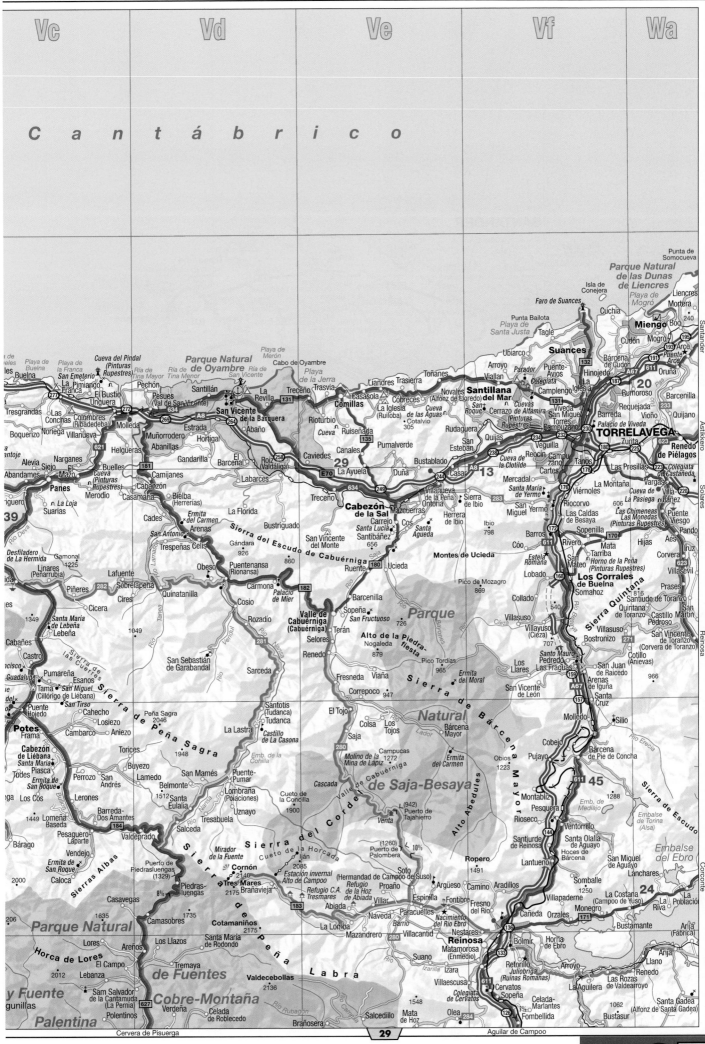

C a n t á b r i c o

Punta de Somocueva
Parque Natural de las Dunas de Liencres
Isla de Conejera
Liencres
Playa de Mogró
Mortera
Faro de Suances
Cuchia
Miengo
Boo
240
Cudón
Mogro
195
Puente Arce
611
Punta Bailota
Playa de Santa Justa
Ubiarco
Suances
132
Bárcena de Cudón
191
Oruña
A67
Tagle
Hinojedo
187
20
Toñanes
Arroyo
Parador
Puente-Avios
Viallan
Camplengo
Rumoroso
Barcenilla
Santillana del Mar (Alfon de Lloredo)
Colegiata
La Iglesia
Requejada
233
Liandres
Trasierra
Novales
San Roque
Cuevas de Altamira (Pinturas Rupestres)
Viveda
Barreda
Vioño
Quijano
Casasola
Cóbreces
La Iglesia (Ruiloba)
Cuevas de las Aguas
San Miguel
Torres
Campuzano
Palacio de Viveda
TORRELAVEGA
623
Cómillas
Cotalvio 305
Rudaguera
230
Veguilla
Zurita
Renedo de Piélagos
Cueva
Ruiseñada
135
San Esteban
Quijas
234
232
Reocín
Campuzano
Riotúrbio
Pumalverde
Bustablado
Duña
238
Cartes
Tanos
180
225
Caviedes
29
La Ayuela
244
Casar
A8
13
Mercadal
178
Las Presillas
223
Colegiata de Castañeda
Abaño
258
Roiz (Valdáliga)
E70
Villanueva de la Peña
Santa María de Yermo
176
Viérnoles
La Montaña
Vargas
220
Treceño
634
249
Ontoria
Sierra de Ibio
283
San Yermo
Riocorvo
Las Caldas de Besaya
La Pasiega
Villa Iñáñez
Cabezón de la Sal
Mazcuerras
Herrera de Ibio
Ibio 798
Barros
611
172
Rivero
Sopenilla
170
Hijas
Pando
San Vincente del Monte
Carrejo
Santa Lucia
Cos
Santa Agueda
Cóo
Mata
Tarriba
Aes
Corvera
Iruz
623
656
Santibáñez
Montes de Ucieda
Estela Romana
San Mateo
Horno de la Peña (Pinturas Rupestres)
Villasevil
San Antonio
Ruente
180
Ucieda
Pico de Mozagro 869
Lobado
168
Los Corrales de Buelna
Prases
182
Barcenilla
Collado
Somahoz
816
Santiurde de Toranzo
Sierra Quintana
Carmona
Palacio de Mier
Sopeña
San Fructuoso
726
Parque
Villasuso
540
Quintana de Toranzo
Castillo Pedroso
San Martín
Valle de Cabuérniga (Cabuérniga)
Terán
Alto de la Piedra-fiesta
Villasuso (Cieza)
707
San Vincente de Toranzo (Corvera de Toranzo)
271
Selores
Nogaleda 879
Pico Tordías 965
Ermita del Moral
Los Llares
Santo Mauro
Pedredo
Las Fraguas
Cotillo (Anievas)
966
Renedo
Fresneda
Viaña 947
Sierra de Bárcena Mayor
San Vicente de León
159
A67
Arenas de Iguña
Correpoco
El Tojo
Colsa
Los Tojos
Natural
Santa Cruz
Molledo
157
Santotis (Tudanca)
Tudanca
Saja
Campucas 1272
Bárcena Mayor
Cobejo
Silio
La Lastra
Castillo de La Casona
280
Molino de la Mina de Lápiz
Ermita del Carmen
Obios 1223
Pujayo
Bárcena de Pie de Concha
Emb. de la Cohilla
Cascada
Valle de Cabuérniga
de Saja-Besaya
Montabliz
611
45
Sierra de Escudo
Puente-Pumar
Lombraña (Polaciones)
Cueto de la Concilla 1900
L (942)
Venta
Puerto de Tajahierro
Pesquera
1288
Emb. de Mediajo
Embalse de Torina (Alsa)
Uznayo
Tresabuela
Salceda
Rioseco
144
Ventorrillo
Sierra del Cordel
(1260)
10%
Santiurde de Reinosa
Santa Olalla de Aguayo
San Miguel de Aguayo
Embalse del Ebro
Mirador de la Fuente
Cueto de la Horcada
Iján
Puerto de Palombera
Soto
Ropero 1491
Lantueno
Hoces de Bárcena
Lánchares
Cornón 2140
Estación invernal Alto de Campoo
(Hermandad de Campoo de Suso)
Refugio C.A. de la Hoz de Abiada
Proaño
Argüeso
Camino
Somballe
1250
La Costana (Campoo de Yuso)
24
Tres Mares 2175
Brañavieja
Refugio C.A. Tresmares
Villar
Espinilla
Fontibre
Aradillos
Villapaderne
La Riva
Piedrasluengas
183
Abiada
Naveda
Paracuelles
Fresno del Rio
Monegro
171
Bustamante
Puerto de Piedrasluengas (1329)
8%
Camasobres 1735
Cotamañiños 2175
La Lomba
Barrio
Nacimiento del Rio Ebro
Nestares
136
Cañeda
Orzales
Ariña (Fábrica)
1635
Santa María de Rodondo
Mazandrero
280
Villacantid
Suano
Reinosa
Bolmir
Horna de Ebro
Arija
Parque Natural
Lores
Areños
Los Llazos
Villaescusa
Izara
Matamorosa (Enmedio)
133
Retorillo
Arroyo
Llano
Renedo
1062
Santa Gadea (Alfonz de Santa Gadea)
2012
El Campo
Lebanza
Tremaya
Valdecebollas 2136
Izarilla
Juliobriga (Ruinas Romanas)
611
Celada-Marlantes
Las Rozas de Valdearroyo
Horca de Lores
y Fuente
Cobre-Montaña
Labra
1548
Colegiata de Cervatos
Cervatos
Sopeña
Olea
284
Fombellida
126
Bustasur
Sam Salvador de la Cantamuda (La Pernia)
627
Verdeña
Celada de Robledo
Rio Rubagón
Salcedillo
Mata de Hoz
Santa Gadea
Palentina
Brañosera
Aguilar de Campoo

Cantábrico

190

CASTRO-URDIALES

Ermita de San Juan de Gaztelugatxe
Ermita de San Pelayo
Arana
Isla de Izaro
Playa de Laga
Gamecho
Elantxobe
Akorda
Ibarrangelu Elejalde (Ibarrangelu)
Natxitua

Bermeo
Torre de Ertzilla
Playa de Laida
Alboniga
Artigas
La Iglesia (Sukarrieta)
Axpe de Busturi (Busturia)
Kanala

San Pelaio
San Miguel
Alto del Sollube (340)
Arrona-tegui
Sta. Elena de Emerando Sollube 663
San Lorenzo de Mesterica
Murueta
Cueva de Santimamiñe
Elexalde-Zeeta (Ereño)
Zelaieta Gabika (Gautegiz Arteaga)
Arteaga

Basigo (Bakio)
Ergoien
Ermita de San Martin
Meñaka
Libano (Arrieta)
Metxika

44
Mungia
San Kristobal
Ermita de Santillandi
Alday (Fruiz)
14
Castillo de Arteaga

Emerando
Zublaur
2101

Playa de Bakio
Fano-Uresaranses
Armintza
Urizar (Lemoiz)
Arteta
I. Biliano
Playa de Armintza
Billabaso
Billela
Ergoien (Gamiz-Fika)
Fruiz
2121
Meaka
Andra-Mari (Morga)
Astelarra
Mendata
Marmiz
Ugarte (Muxika)
Loiola (Arratzu)
2224
Olabe
Berreño

Plentzia
Playa de Plentzia
Elejade (Barrica)
Goieri
Elexalde Auzoa
Andraka
Larrabasterra
Egusquiza
Berango
Gatika
Garai
Fika
Ermita de San Miguel
Goitiolza
Meaca
Flores
Garaiolza
2713
Gorocica Elixalde
Albiz
Gernika-Lumo
2238
Ermita de Santiago Arbacegui y Gernikaiz

Playa de Atxibiribil
Playa de Arrietara
Playa de Azkorri
Sopelana
La Campa
Urduliz
Unbe
634
Zabaloetxe
Lauro
631
Basozabal
Elotxelerri
San Mames
Arteaga-San Martin (Zamudio)
Lezama
Larrabetzu
Ugarte
13
Ibarruri
Urrutxua
Magunas

ALGORTA
Playa de la Arena
Zierbena
639
Las Carreras (Muskiz)
San Pedro de Abanto
126
Portugalete
ELEXALDE (LEIOA)
2704
Aeropuerto Bilbao
BIO
Derio
Arteaga (Derio)
Erandio
Aeropuerto Bilbao (Sondika)
Erbera o San Andres (Etxebarri)
Amorebieta-Etxano
San Martin Amorebieta
Garay (San Miguel)
Ermita de San Cristobal
48
Durango
San Marcos

153 151
147 143
141
145 139 138 136
250 132
130
124
123
119
118
116
115
113
110
109
105 103 100
E70
E80
AP8
E05
634
E80
97

Cueva Peñ del Cuco (Pinturas Rupestres)
Helguera (395)
Samano
Mioño
Ontón
Pobeña
Santurtzi
SANTURTZI
PORTUGALETE
Ortuella
Trapagaran (Valle de Trápaga)
La Reineta
SAN VICENTE DE BARAKALDO (BARAKALDO)
Alonsotegui
Arizgoiti
BILBAO
LA CRUZ (GALDAKAO)
Aguirre
Galdakao
Uransolo
Ermita de San Antolin
Elorriaga
San Antonio
Euba
Bernagoitia
Urtemondo
Orozqueta
DURANGO
Abadiño
Zelaieta
Izarola
Axpe
Mendiola
Irazola

Puerto de la Granja
Santullán
Setares
La Rigada
Otañes
San Juan de Muskiz
Abanto y Ciérvena-Abanto Zierbena
Triano
Basauri
6
A8
7
636
5
Arrigorriaga
Zaratamo
Gutiolo
Elexalde (Bedia)
Ermita de San Marin
Elexalde (Igorre)
Ermita de San Cristóbal Bikarregi
Ugarana (Dima)
Ermita de Aite Oba
1008
Ermita de San Lorenzo
Indusi
Parque Natural
Cueva de Askondo
791
2543
37
Santuario de San Antonio
de Urkiola
Ermita de Santa Bárbara
Alluitz 1034

151
Campo de Ventoso
Ermita de la Trinidad
Trucios-Turtzioz
Alén
Garape
Barrietas
San Miguel de Linares
Traslaviña
630
Beci
San Esteban de Galdames
Cueva de Arenaza
La Aceña
San Pedro
823
Saracho
Zaramillo
873
Ibarra
10
Humarán
Chávarri
Avellaneda
Casa de Juntas
San Martin de Carral
Mimetiz (Zalla)
Güeñes
Sodupe
Emb. de Nocedal
Ganekogorta 1000
Emb. de Artiba
Emb. de Zollo
Zollo
Aguirre
E05
E80
E804
Arrigorriaga
Arrankudiaga
Ugao-Miraballes
Zaratamo
Ermita de San Marin
1
Zelaia (Aranzazu)
Areatza
Zeanuri
Uribe
Alto
Undurraga
2543
Ipiñaburu
Urigoiti
Cueva de Sopelegor 1306
Presa
Otxandio
Parque Natural de Urkiola
9%
Puerto de Barazar (604)
623
Sierra de Arangio
Anteparaluzeta
Olaeta
Mekoleta
49 240
San Juan (Ubide)
2620
Emb. de Albiña
Legutiano
Monumento a la Batalla de Villareal

Abanto
1043
Balmaseda
Peñueco
Burgueño
La Herrera
Pandozales
Regomedo
Herbosa
La Altura
Sollano-Llantada
San Juan de Berbikiz
Zubieta
Akarai
Zudibiarte
Ugalde
Santa Amria de Isasi
Palacio de Zuricalday
Areta
2
Aracaldo
Lodio
Untzeta
3
Llanteno
Murueta
765
San Martin Ibarra
Gallartu
636
624
La Presilla
Caniego
Menamayor
Artieta
Medianas Montiano
Na. Sa. de la Encina
Santa Coloma
Artziniega
Idubaltza 684
Jandiola
Pagolarra 718
Gardea
Llodio
33
33
Gobea
Sierra de Peña
Gorbea
Gorbea
1243
de Gorbea
Cueva de Balzola
Zeanuri
Ermita de San Cristóbal
Natural
de Gorbea

Orrantia
656
Opio
Viérgol
Gordeliz
Abiega
Zuaza
Luiaondo
Monte de Arrola
Jesuri 750
Orozko
Ermita de Garrastatxu
Dólmen
Arbaiza
Torre
Barambio
Echagüen
Cestafe
Elosu
Durango

Entram-basaguas
Cañiego
cejón unte
Villasana de Mena (Valle de Mena)
Santiago de Tudela
Ciella
Medieval
Santa Olaja
1024
Relloso
Santa Olaja
550
Santa María del Llano de Tudela
554
Retes
Menagaray
Beotegui
Torre
Respaldiza (Ayala/Aiara)
Murga
Ermita de San Roque
37
Arbaiza
Torre
Barambio
Areatza
Zeanuri
Uribe
Gopegui (Zigoitia)
Nafarrate
Urrunaga
Ullibarri-Gamboa
13
Urbina

Barruso
Barruso
Sierra de Carbonilla
550
Erbi
Oceca
Menoyo
Izoria
AMURRIO
Mendeica
624
Torre
Saracho
Belandia
Lendoño de Abajo
Inoso
Arexalde (Lezama)
Ciorraga
Ciorraga /Amurrio
4
Igorre
Iñaki
Oketa
1035
San Juan (Ubide)
2620

Peña
Barruso
Encima Angulo
Aro 1185
Aguiñiga
Maroño
Torre
Amurrio
Sierra Salvada
Lastras de la Torre
83
Orduña
Arbieto
706
Uzquiano
Orduña
Sarria
Markina-Xemein Zátrate
Murua
Manurga
Buruaga
Betolaza

Quincoces de Yuso
Cabañes de Oto
Calzada
Robredo de Losa
Lastras de Teza (Valle de Losa)
Teza de Lodosa
Barriga
Villaño
Mijala
Llorengoz
1039
Tertanga
Goba Aundi
Torre
Délica
15%
Torre
Puerto de Orduña (900)
2625
Artomaña
2521
Oyardo
Altube
Altube
Belunza
Izarra
Urkabustaiz
Abecia
Gujuli
Unza
AP68
Autopista Vasco-Aragonesa
Altube
5
22
21
Sarria
Legutiano
Vitoria Gasteiz
19
Murgia
Jugo

Villaluenga
Río Nabón
San Martin de Losa
552
Llorente
Villacián
Zaballa
Castillo Tertanga
556 (900)
Villalambrús
Fresno de Losa
Villaba de Losa (Junta de Villalba de Losa)
Aostri de Losa
Belunza
Izarra
Urkabustaiz
E05
E80
E804
Vitoria Gasteiz
1022
Ermita de Aedo

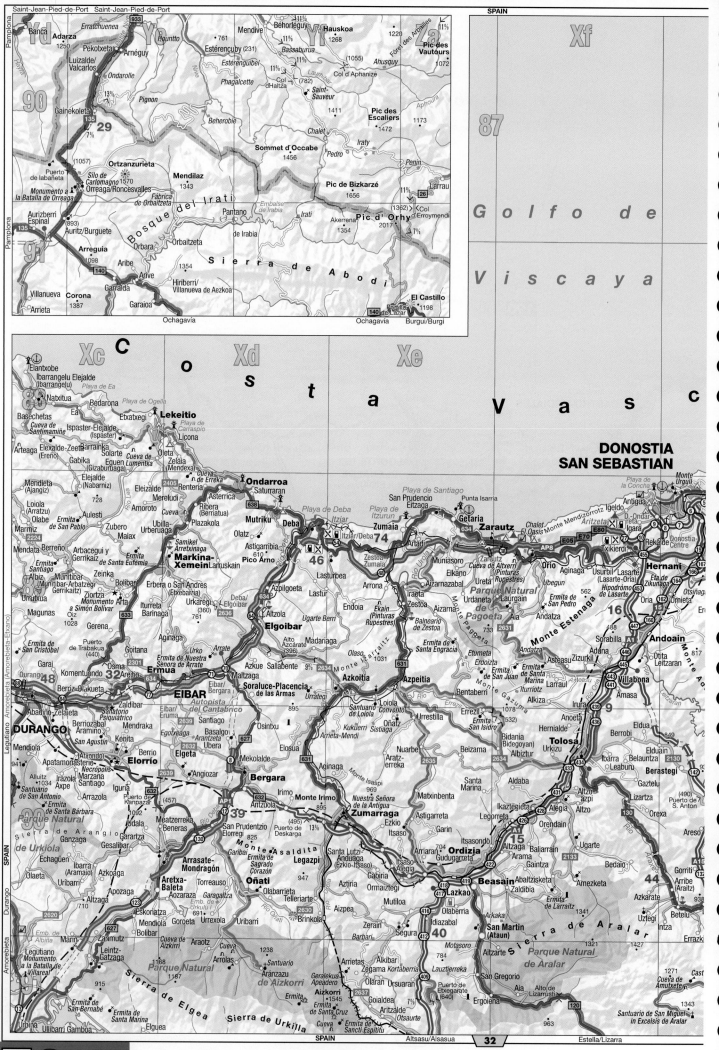

Saint-Jean-Pied-de-Port Saint-Jean-Pied-de-Port

Yd Ya Yl Za Xf

Pamplona
Nive

Adarza 1250
Pekotxeta
Errachuenea
933
Rountto
Mendive
Béhorléguy
11%
Hauskoa 1268
Forêt des Arbailles
1220
11%
Pic des Vautours 1072

Arnéguy
Luizalde/ Valcarlos
Estérencuby (231)
761
Bassaburua
11%
11%
Ahusquy
87

Ondarolle
Estérenguibal
Phagalcette
11%
Col d'Haltza (782)
Laurhibar
Col d'Aphanize

90
13%
Pignon
Beherobie
Saint-Sauveur
1411
Aphoura

Gainékoleta
135
29
7%
(1057)
Ortzanzurieta 1570
Silo de Carlomagno
Orreaga/Roncesvalles
Mendilaz 1343
Chalet
Iraty
Pedro
Pic des Escaliers 1472
1173
Penin

Golfo de

Puerto de Ibañeta
Monumento a la Batalla de Orreaga
Fábrica de Orbaitzeta
Bosque del Irati
Pic de Bizkarzé 1656
Larrau
Col Erroymendi
26
11%

Aurizberri Espinal
135
(893)
Pantano
Embalse de Irabia
Irati
de Irabia
Pic d'Orhy 2017
Akerrena 1354
(1362)
7%

Arreguia 1098
Auritz/Burguete
Orbara
Orbaitzeta
Sierra de Abodi

91
Aribe
1354
Hiriberri/ Villanueva de Aezkoa

140
Garralda
Arive

Villanueva
Corona 1387
Arrieta
Garaioa
El Castillo 1198
140
Portillo de Lazar
Golfo de Viscaya

Ochagavía
Ochagavía
Burgui/Burgi

Xc C o s t a V a s c Xd Xe

Elantxobe
Ibarrangelu Elejalde (Ibarrangelu)
Playa de Ea
DONOSTIA SAN SEBASTIAN

Natxitua
Bedarona
Playa de Ogella
Monte Urgull

Basechetas
Ea
Etxatxegi
Lekeitio
Playa de Carraspio
Licona
Playa de Santiago
Punta Isarria
Playa de la Concha
Antigua

Cueva de Santimamiñe
Ispaster-Elejalde (Ispaster)
Oleta
Zelaia (Mendexa)
San Prudencio Eitzaga
Getaria
Igeldo
D.-Ondarreta
6

Arteaga
Elexalde-Zeet Barrainka (Ereño)
Solarte
Cueva Lumentxa
Playa de Deba
Itziar
Playa de Itzurun
Zarautz
Chalet El Oasis Monte Mendizorrotz
Aritzeta
Igara
Donostia-Centre
9
8
7

Gabika (Gizaburuaga)
Eguen
Renteria
Ondarroa
Saturraran
Itziar/Deba
74
Zarautz
Cueva de Altxerri (Pinturas Rupestres)
E80
AP8
E05 E70
27
10
Rekalde
Ixikierdi
455
19

Mendieta (Ajangiz)
Elejalde (Nabarniz)
2405
Mereludi
Asterrica
Ribera (Berriatua)
Deba
Zumaia
54
Zestoa Zumaia
48
Muniasoro
Elkano
Parque Natural de Pagoeta
Urdaneta
Laurgain
Aginaga
Ermita de San Pedro
Usurbil (Lasarte-Oria)
Lasarte
Hernani
166

Loiola (Arratzu)
Olabe
728
Zubero
Malax
Plazakola
Olatz
Astigarribia
Pico Arno
610
46
Lasturbea
Arrona
Aizarnazabal
Iraeta
Aizarna
Monte Pagoeta 733
2631
Aia
Andatza
Hipódromo de Lasarte
Oria 162
Urnieta
16
453
164

Marmiz
Aulesti
Ermita de San Pablo
2224
Berreño
Arbacegui y Gerrikaiz (Munitibar-Arbatzegi Gerrikaitz)
de Santa Eufemia
Markina-Xemein Larruskain
Erbera o San Andres (Etxebarria)
Deba/ Eibar (360)
2636
Lastur
Endoia
Zestoa
Ekain (Pinturas Rupestres)
Balneario de Zestoa
Ermita de Santa Engracia
Monte Estenaga
Sorabilla 488
447
160
A1
15
Andoain
Otsiñaga

Mendata
Ermita Santiago
Albiz
Zeinka
Munitibar Arta
Iturreta
Urkaregi
761
Altzola
64
Ugarte Berri
Olaso 1031
Monte Zarraitz
631
Etumeta
Erdoizta
817

Albiz (Munitibar-Arbatzegi Gerrikaitz)
Monumento a Simón Bolívar Oiz 1028
Boliar
Barinaga
633
Elgoibar
Alto Azcárate (396)
Madariaga
9%
2634
Monte
Ermita de Santa Marina
Ermita de San Juan
Larraul
Asteasu
Aduna
Zizurkil
446
443
Villabona
Amasa

Uruxa
Magunas
Ermita de San Cristóbal
Goitana
Gerena
Ermita de Nuestra Señora de Arrate
Arrate
Azkue Sallabente
2634
1031
Monte Gazuma
Anoeta
441

Garai
Puerto de Trabakua (440)
Aginaga
Urko
71
70
Maltzaga
Soraluce-Placencia de las Armas
Azkoitia
Azpeitia
Errezil
1078
Monte Iturriotz
439
Tolosa
Urkizu
Eldua
849

Durango
88
18
2301
Ermua
634
EIBAR
Urrategi
895
Santuario de Loiola
Convento
Oñatz
Kukuerri Sistiaga
(532)
Ermita San Isidro
Bidania (Bidegoyan)
Herniale
436
Ibarra
Belauntza
2130

Berriz-Olakueta
64
77
Autopista del Cantábrico
Eibar/ Eruma
2639
Santiago
Osintxu
Elosua
Arrieta-Mendi
Aginaga
Nuarbe
Aratz-erreka
2635
Beizama
Albiztur
2634
Berrobi
Leaburu
Berastegi
Gaztelu
142

Abadino-Zelaieta
DURANGO
Berriozabal
Aramino
Mendraka
Basalgo
627
Egotxeaga Arantzeta Ubera
2632
Mekolalde
631
Monte Isaspi 969
Santa Marina
Elduain
2133
Lizartza
Orexa

Mendiola
San Agustín
Kenita
Berrio
Elgeta
Elgoibar
2639
Angiozar
Bergara
8
Irimo
Nuestra Señora de la Antigua
Matxinbenta
Aldaba
431
Puerto de S. Anton (490)

941
(Atxondo) Necrópolis
Marzana Santiago
Iguria
AP1
632
632
Antzuola
Monte Irimo 895
Zumarraga
Ezkio
Astigarreta
Garin
Ikaztegieta
Alegia
428
Altzo-azpi
130
Areso
A15

Alluitz 1034
Irazola Axpe
Elorrio
(457)
12
39
Itsaso
704
Itsasondo
A1
426
Orendain
Altzo
Ugarte
Gorriti (Araitz)
132

Apatamonasterio
Arrazola
Puerto de Kanpazar 1092
Meatzerreka Beneras
San Prudentzio Elorregi 825
Puerto de Deskarga 13%
(495)
Ermita de Sagrado Corazón
Santa Lutzi-Anduaga (Ezkio-Itsaso)
Aztiria
Gabiria
Arriaran
15
Alegia
Aldaba
Gudugarreta
422
Ordizia
Arama
Gaintza
Baliarrain
Amezketa
44
Azkarate
938

Santuario de San Antonio
Ermita de Santa Bárbara
Parque Natural de Urkiola
Iburri
130
Monte Asaldita
Garibai
Legazpi 947
Olabarrieta Telleriarte
Ormaiztegi
Mutiloa
418
419
Lazkao
417
Beasain
Zaldibia
Ermita de Larraitz 1341
Bedaio
Uztegi

90
SPAIN
Sierra de Arangio
Ganzaga
Gesalibar
Arrasate-Mondragón
Aretxa-Baleta
Aozaraza Garagaltza
Oñati
Aizpea
Zerain
412
40
San Martin (Ataun)
Arkaka
Olaberria
Idiazabal
Aitzarte
784
Segura
Sierra de Aralar
Parque Natural de Aralar
1427
Errazki

Echagüen
Ibarra (Aramaio)
Azkoaga
Uribarri
Altzaga 710
Eskoriatza
Mendiola Bolibar
Goroeta
Urrexola
Uribarri
Aizpea
Barbari
Motasoro
Lauztierreka
Aitzarte
1271
Cast
Cueva de Amutxete
1343

Olaeta
2620
Marin
627
Zarimutz
Cueva de Aizkirri
Araotz
Aránzazu de Aizkorri
Arrolas
1238
Santuario
Arrietas
Alkibar
Zégama Kortaberria
Olaran Ursuaran
409
Puerto de Etxegarate (640)
Ermita de Larraitz
San Gregorio
963
Santuario de San Miguel in Excelsis de Aralar

Emb. de Albiña
Legutiano Monumento a la Batalla de Villareal
Leintz-Gatzaga
915
Parque Natural
1187
Sierra de Elgea
Aizkorri 1545
Geralekua Apeadero 2637
Ermita de Santa Cruz
Goialdea
Aritzalde
7%
Aia
Alto de Lizarrusti
120
Parque Natural de Aralar

13
Urbina
Ermita de San Bernabé
Ermita de Santa Marina
Sierra de Urkilla
Ermita de Sancti Espíritu
Ergoiena
1343

Ullibarri Gamboa
Elguea
SPAIN
Altsasu/Alsasua
32
Estella/Lizarra

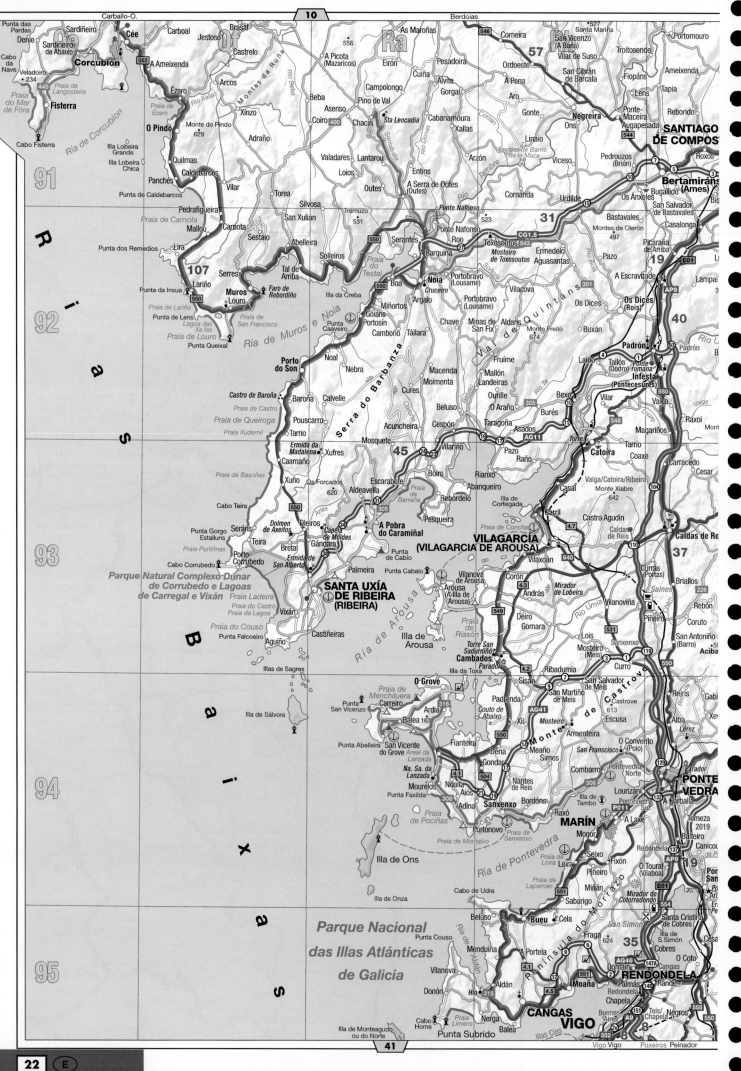

Carballo-O. Berdoias

Punta das Pardas
Denle
Sardiñeiro
Sardiñeiro de Abaixo
Cée
Corcubión
Cabo da la Nave
Veladoiro · 234
552
A Ameixenda
Carboal
Castrelo
Brasal
Jestoso
As Maroñas
Santa Mariña
· 527
Corneira
546
Ra
57
Troitosende
Portomouro
Santiago (A Baña)
San Vicenzo (A Baña)
Vilar de Suso
Fiopáns
Ameixenda
Tapia
Reborido

Praia de Langosteira
445
Praia do Mar de Fóra
Fisterra
Ézaro
A Picota (Mazaricos)
Eirón
Pesadoira
A Pena
Aro
Ordoeste
San Cibrán de Bárcala
Lens
Negreira
Ponte-Maceira
Augapesada
544
Santiago de Compost

Cabo Fisterra
O Pindo
Monte do Pindo
629
Adraño
Campolongo
Beba
Pino de Val
Asenso
Coiro
400
Chacín
Santa Leocadia
Cabanamoura
Gorgal
Gonte
Linaio
Viceso
Ons
Pedrouzos (Brión)
7
Roxos
5
Bertamiráns (Ames)
3
Bi

Ría de Corcubión
Quilmas
Caldebarcos
Panchés
Valadares
Lantarou
Loios
Outes
Entíns
A Serra de Outes (Outes)
Cornanda
Arzón
Tambre
Urdilde
10
Os Ánxeles
San Salvador de Bastavales
Bastavales
Casalonga

91
Illa Lobeira Grande
Illa Lobeira Chica
Punta de Caldebarcos
Vilar
Torea
Silvosa
San Xulián
Tremuzo
531
Ponte Nafonso
523
CG1.5
31
Montes de Olerón
497
Picaraña de Arriba
A Escravitude
19
E01
Lampai
AP9

R
Pedrafigueira
Praia de Carnota
Mallou
Carnota
Sestaio
Abelleira
Praia do Testal
Ponte Nafonso
Roo
27
Toxosoutos
543
Mosteiro de Toxosoutos
Ermedelo
Aguasantas
Pazo
Os Dices (Rois)
Padrón
93
40

92
Punta dos Remedios
Lira
Serres
107
Lariño
Muros
Louro
Solleiros
Boa
550
Noia
Cruceiro
Portobravo (Lousame)
Vilacova
Os Dices
Buxán
Tallós (Dodro)
Laíño
4
Ponte romana
Padrón
Padrón
Río U

Faro de Rebordiño
Illa da Creba
Miñortos
Argalo
Portobravo (Lousame)
Chave
Minas de Aldaris San Fix
Monte Freito
674
Fruíme
Infesta (Pontecesures)
550
Valga
Valga

Punta da Insua
Praia de Lariño
Punta de Lens
Lagoa das Xa fas
Praia de San Francisco
Goiáns
Portosín
Camboño
Tállara
1
Bexo
AG11
Mariños
Raxoi

Praia de Louro
Punta Queixal
Ría de Muros e Noia
Punta Caaveiro
Noal
Nebra
Macenda
Moimenta
Mallón
Landeiras
Ourille
O Araño
305
Burés
10
Torre
Catoira
Tarrio
Coaxe
Carracedo
Cesar

Porto do Son
Cures
Beluso
Cespón
Taragoña
19
Asados
17
Pazo Raño
Valga/Catoira/Ribeira
Monte Xiabre
642
104

R i a s
Castro de Baroña
Baroña
Calvelle
Serra do Barbanza
Acuncheira
45
24
23
Vilariño
Rianxo
Abanqueiro
Casal
Carril
4.7
Castro Agudín
Caldas de Reis
110
37
Caldas de Re

b
Praia de Castro
Pouscarro
Mosquete
Boiro
Illa de Cortegada
640
Vilaxoán
Curras (Portas)
Briallos

a
Praia de Queiroga
Praia Xudemil
Tarrio
Ermida da Madalena
Xufres
Praia de Barraña
Rebordelo
Praia de Concha
Vilagarcia (Vilagarcia de Arousa)
Salnés
226
Rebón
Coruto

i
Praia de Basoñas
Caamaño
Xuño
Os Forcados
620
Escarabote
Aldeavella
305
Pesqueira
4.3
Corón
András
Mirador de Lobeira
Vilanoviña
Piñeiro
San Antoniño (Barro)
Acibal

s
Cabo Teira
550
Oleiros
Aríes
Capela de Moldes
Gándara
A Pobra do Caramiñal
Punta de Cabío
Vilanova de Arousa
Arousa (A Illa de Arousa)
Deiro
Gomara
Lois
531
531
Mosteiro (Meis)
3
1
119
550

93
Punta Gorgo Estalluns
Seráns
Teira
Dolmen de Axeitos
Bretal
38
Ermida de San Alberto
Palmeira
Punta Cabalo
549
Praia de Riasón
Torre San Sadurniño
Cambados
4.2
Ribadumia
7
San Salvador de Meis
Curro

Cabo Corrubedo
Porto-Corrubedo
Parque Natural Complexo-Dúnar de Corrubedo e Lagoas de Carregal e Vixán
Santa Uxía de Ribeira (Ribeira)
Praia Ladeira
Praia do Castro
Praia da Lagoa
Vixán
Praia de Conxa
Ría de Arousa
Illa de Arousa
Parador
Illa da Toxa
9
San Martiño de Meis
Castrove
613
Escusa
Reiris
Alba
Lérez
Xe

Praia Portiñas
Castiñeiras
Illas de Sagres
O Grove
Sisán
AG41
Mosteiro
Armenteira
O Convento (Poio)
129
Parador
Ponte Vedra

94
Praia do Couso
Punta Falcoeiro
Aguiño
Illa de Sálvora
Praia de Menchiluera
Carreiro
Punta San Vicenzo
Ardia
316
Couto de Abaixo
Xil
550
Meaño
Simes
San Francisco
Pontevedra Norte
132
A Carballa

Balea 163
San Vicente do Grove
Na. Sa. da Lanzada
Fianteira
Dena
Gondar
Combarro
308
Lourizán
Pontevedra Sur
P011
A Laxe
Tomeza
2019
Canico

Punta Abelleira
Areal da Lanzada
Mourelos
4.1
504
17
Nantes de Reis
Raxó
Mogán
Marín
Balteiro
137
AP9
9
Po San

Illa de Ons
Noalla
21
Adina
Punta Faxilda
19
Sanxenxo
Bordóns
Illa de Tambo
Seixo
Fixón
Piñeiro
O Toural (Vilaboa)
E01

Praia de Pociñas
Portonovo
Praia de Montalvo
Praia de Sanxenxo
Ría de Pontevedra
Praia de Loira
Loira
Miñán
Sabarigo
551
Mirador de Cotorredondo
554
Santa Cristina de Cobres

Illa de Onza
Cabo de Udra
Praia de Lapamán
San Simón
Illa de S. Simón
Cobres
Cesa

95
Parque Nacional das Illas Atlánticas de Galicia
Beluso
Bueu
Cela
Fraga
624
35
O Coto

Punta Couso
Menduíña
A Portela
9
6
AG46
147A
Cangas
Palmás
Rendondela
148
Rande
555
550

Vilanova
Aldán
Hío
315
Moaña
12
Redondela Chapela
151
Teis/ Chapela
AG46
4.1
4.5

Cabo Home
Praia Limens
Donón
Nerga
Balea
Cangas
Vigo
Buenos Aires
552
8
A9
Negros

Illa de Monteagudo ou do Norte
Punta Subrido
Illas Cíes
41
Vigo Vigo
Puxeiros
Peinador

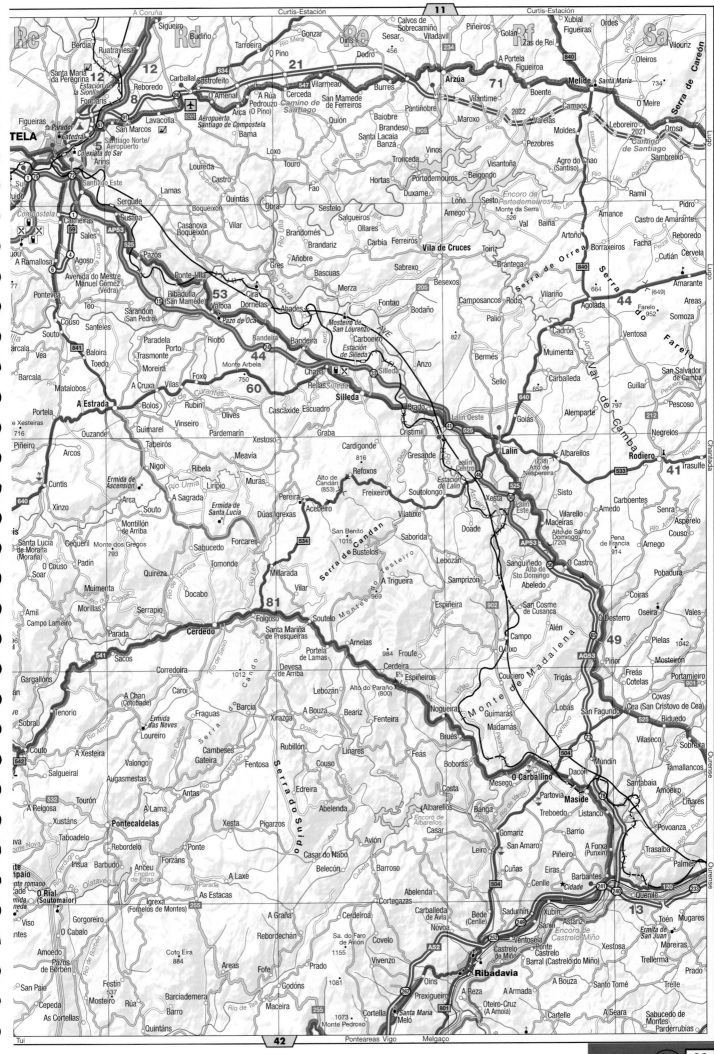

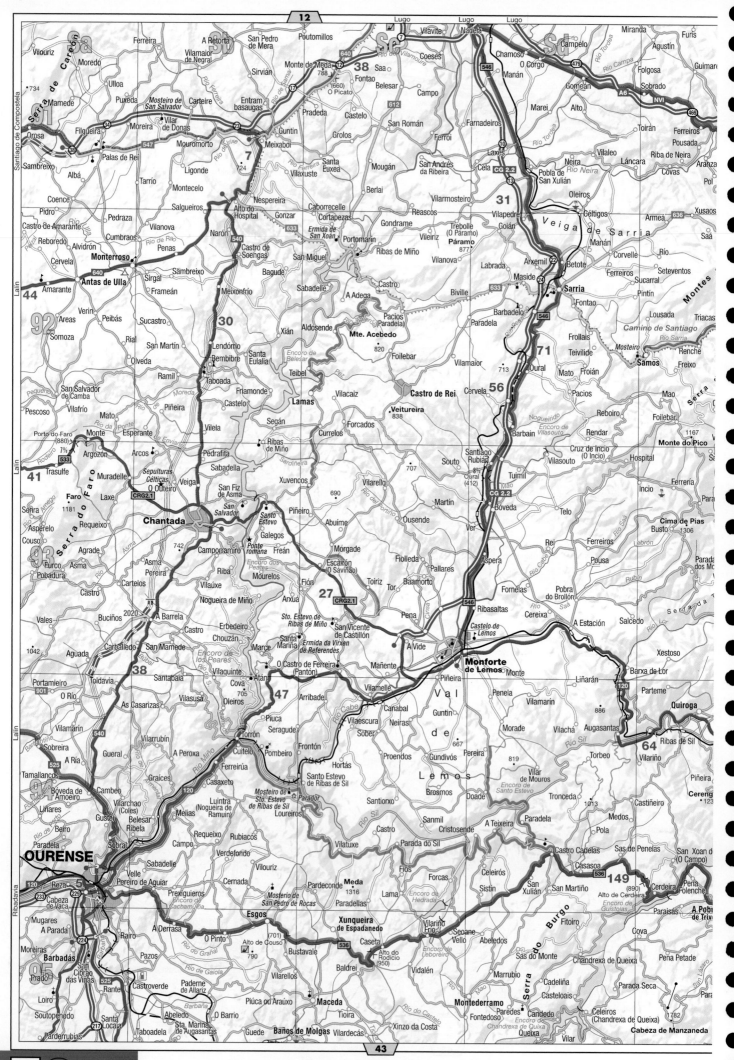

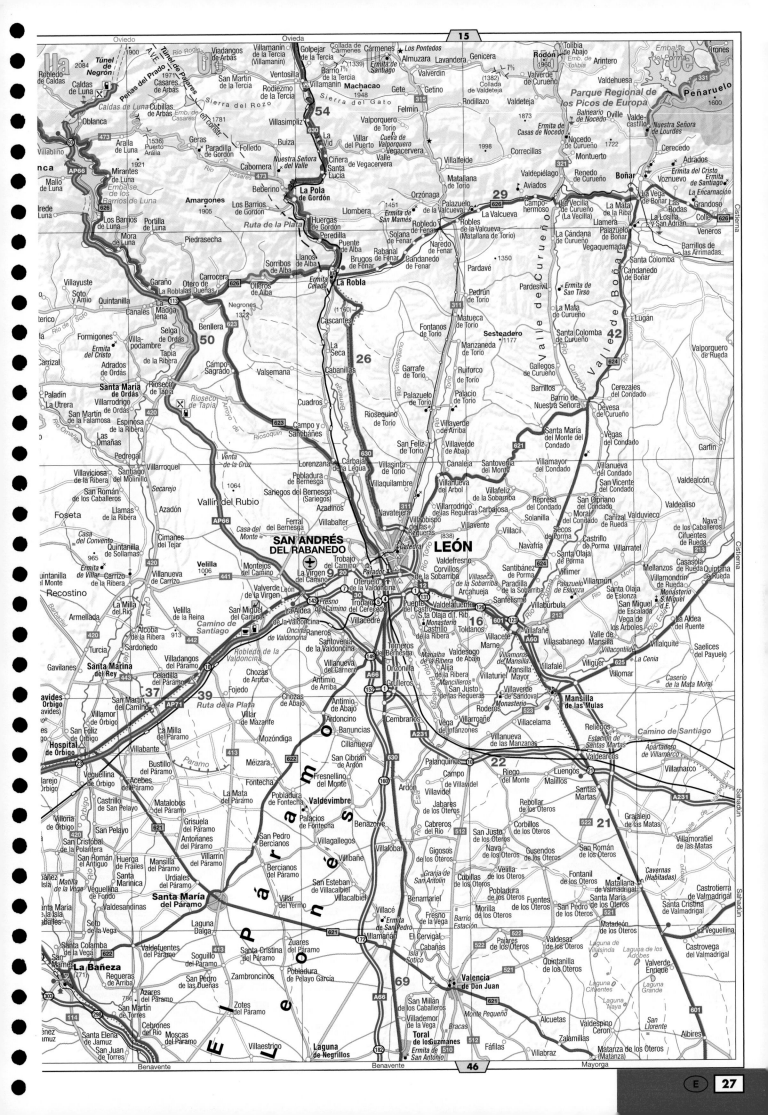

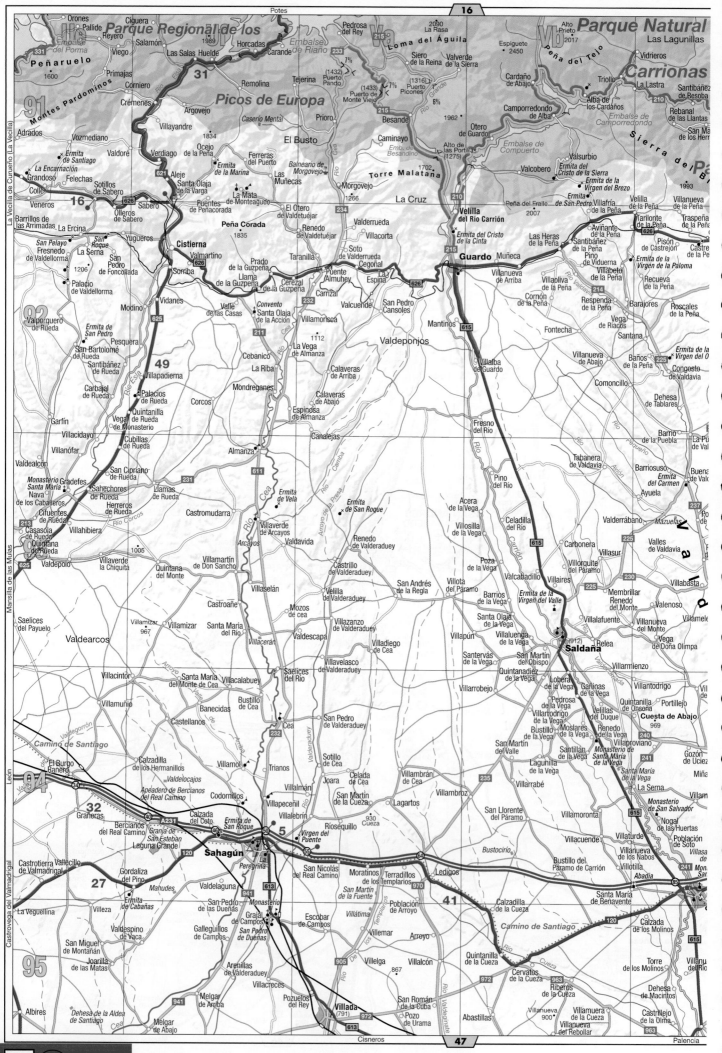

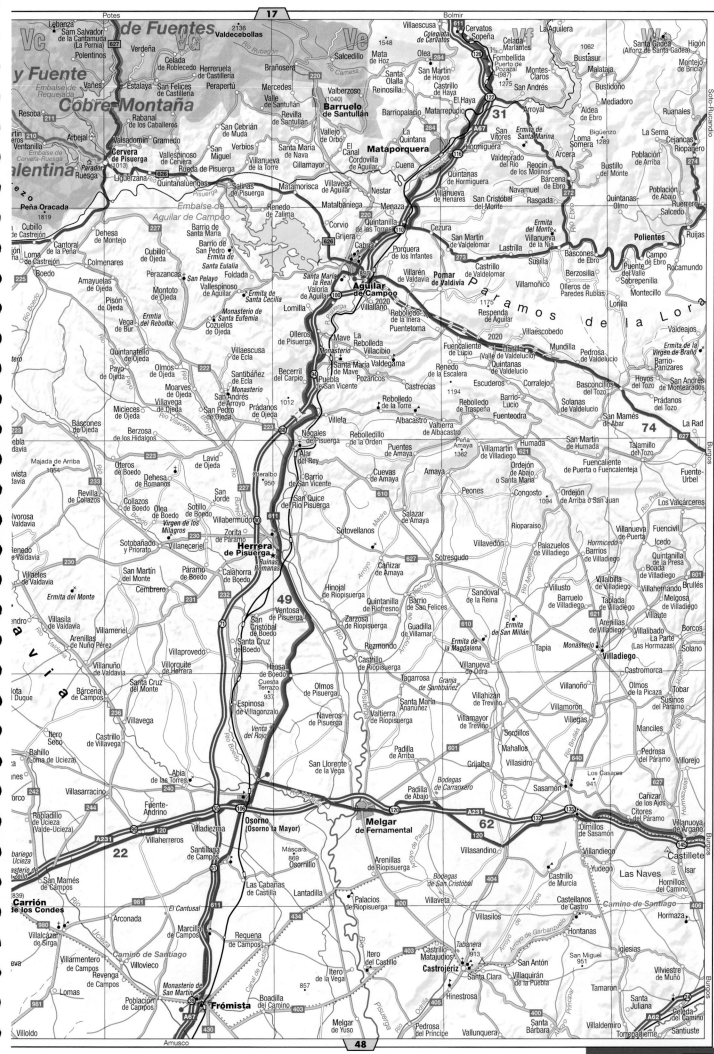

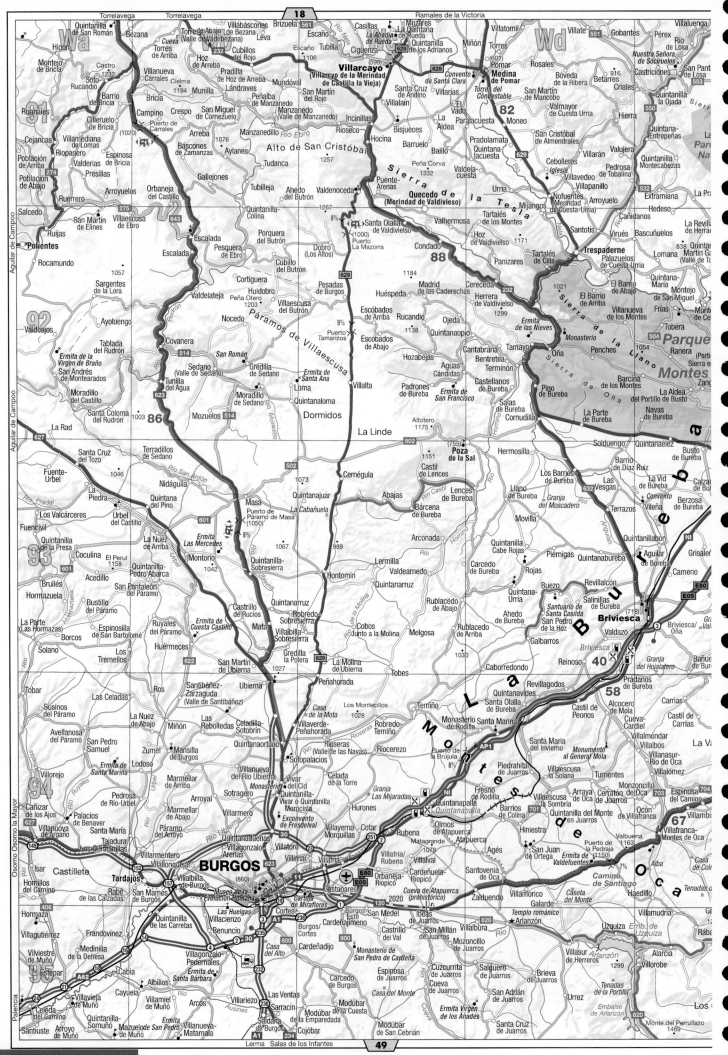

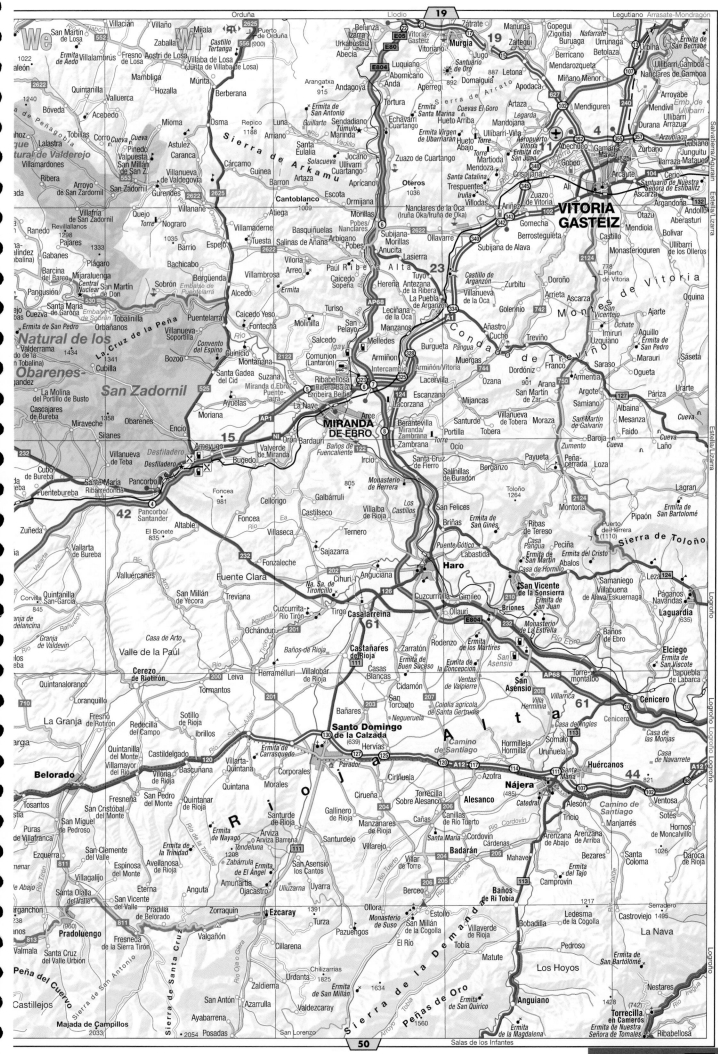

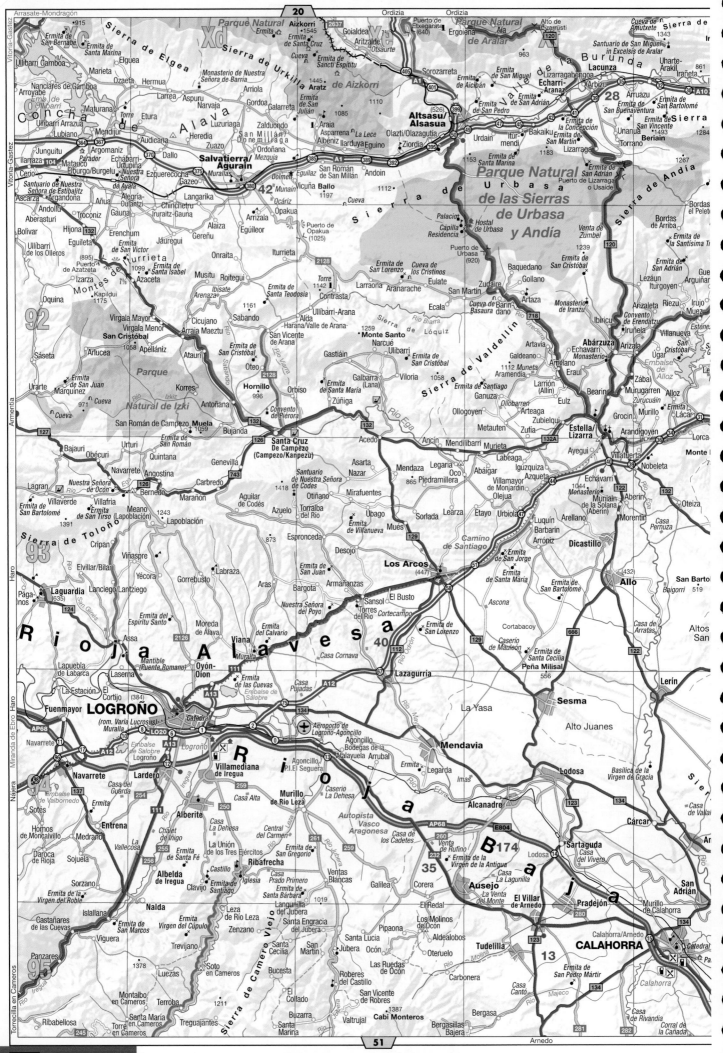

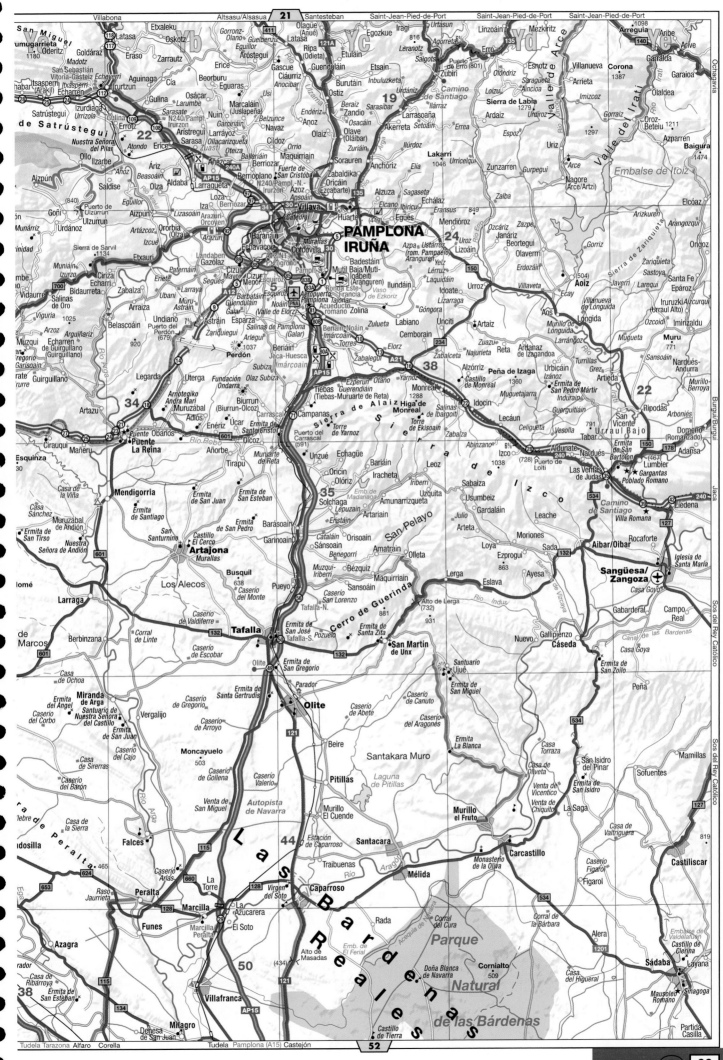

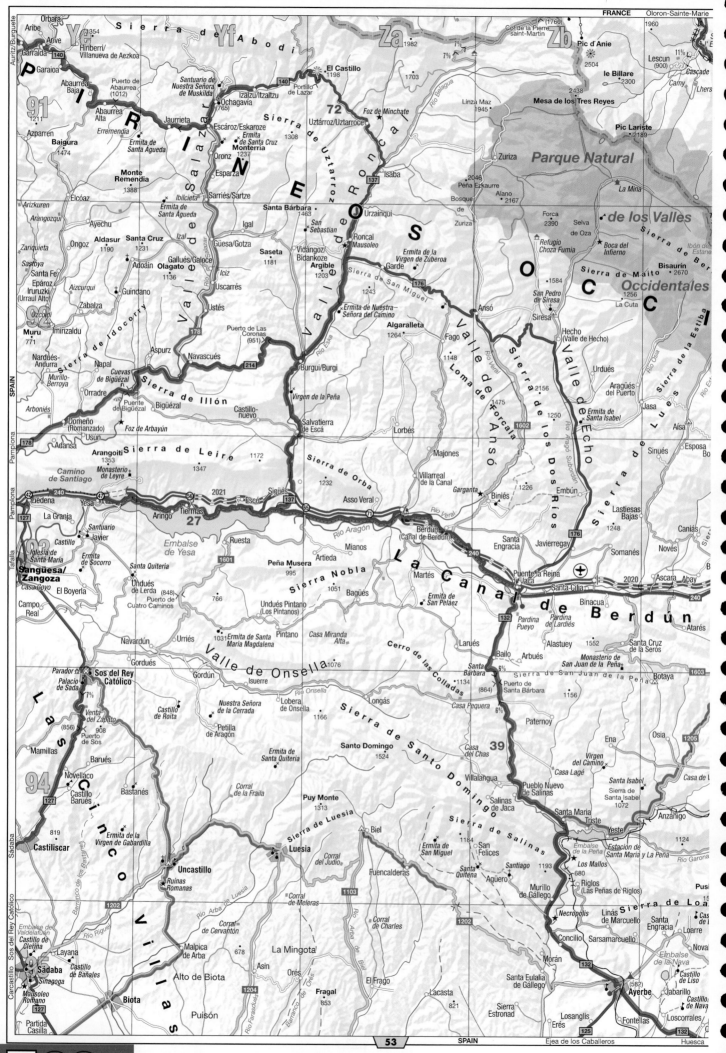

Orbara
Aribe
Arive
Garralda
Garaioa
Abaurrea Baja
Abaurrea Alta
Azparren
Baigura 1474
Monte Remendia 1388
Elcóaz

PIRINEOS

Yc
354
Hiriberri/ Villanueva de Aezkoa
140

Sierra de Abodi
Yf

Santuario de Nuestra Señora de Muskilda
Izalzu/Itzaltzu
Ochagavía (765)
Puerto de Abaurrea (1012)
Portillo de Lazar
140

Escároz/Eskaroze
1308
Ermita de Santa Cruz
Monterria
Oronz 1237
Esparza

Jaurrieta

Sierra de Uztarroz

El Castillo 1198
Foz de Minchate

72

Uztárroz/Uztarroce

Isaba
137

Za
1982
1703

Col de la Pierre saint-Martin (1760)
7%
7%

Zb
Pic d'Anie 2504
le Billare 2300
1960
Lescun (900)
Camy
11%
Lhers
Cascade

Linza Maz 1945
2438
Mesa de los Tres Reyes
Zuriza 2046
Peña Ezkaurre 2167
Parque Natural
La Mina
Pic Lariste 2189

Arizkuren
Arangozqui
Zariquieta
Sastoya
Santa Fe
Epároz
Iruruzki (Urraul Alto)
Ozcoidi
94
Muru 771
Nardués-Andurra
Murillo-Berroya
Arboniés
Domeño (Romanzado)
Usún

Ayechu
Ongoz
Aldasur 1190
Santa Cruz 1231
Adoáin
Olagato 1136
Aizcurqui
Guindano
Zabalza
Imirizaldu

Elcóaz
Izal
Ibilcieta
Ermita de Santa Águeda
Igal
Güesa/Gotza
Iciz
Uscarrés
Ustés
Puerto de Las Coronas (951)
Navascués
214

Santa Bárbara 1463
San Sebastian
Vidángoz/ Bidankoze
Argible 1203
Garde
Ermita de Nuestra Señora del Camino
Burgui/Burgi
Salvatierra de Escá
Lorbés

Roncal Mausoleo
Urzainqui
Ermita de la Virgen de Zúberoa
Sierra de San Miguel 1243

Algaralleta 1264

Forca 2390
Refugio Choza Fumia 1584
San Pedro de Siresa
Siresa
Ansó
Fago 1148
Valle de Ansó

Selva de Oza
Boca del Infierno
Hecho (Valle de Hecho)
Urdués
Aragüés del Puerto
Jasa
Aísa
Sinués
Esposa
Bo

Sierra de Maito 1256
Occidentales
Bisaurín 2670
de los Valles
Sierra de la Estiba
Sierra de Lues

OCCI

Sierra de Idocorry
Valle de Salazar
Napal
Cuevas de Bigüézal
Orradre
Puente de Bigüézal
Bigüézal
Castillonuevo
Virgen de la Peña

Sierra de Illón
Foz de Arbayún

Aspurz
Río Eska
Río Esca

Valle de Roncal

Lomade Forcala 1475
Sierra de Ansó
1250
Sierra de los Dos Ríos
1602
Río Aragón Subordán
Ermita de Santa Isabel
Río Osia
Valle de Echo
Río Es

178
Pamplona
Adansa

178
Arangoiti 1353
Monasterio de Leyre
Camino de Santiago
Sierra de Leire
1172
1347
Sierra de Orba 1232

Majones
Villarreal de la Canal
Garganta
1226
Biniés
Embún
240
176
1248
Lastiesas Bajas
Caniás
Novés
Es

Pamplona
42
240
Liédena
Yesa
47
La Granja
127
Santuario Javier
Castillo
Iglesia de Santa María
Ermita de Socorro
56
2021
Tiermas
Aringo
27
Escó
137
65
Asso Veral
71
Berdún (Canal de Berdún)
Río Aragón
Río Veral
Santa Engracia
Javierregay
176
Puente la Reina de Jaca
Santa Cilia
2020
Somanés
Ascara Abay
240

Embalse de Yesa
Ruesta
Mianos
Artieda
Peña Musera 995
Martés
Ermita de San Peláez

La Canal de Berdún
132
Pardina Pueyo
Pardina de Lardiés
Alastuey 1552
Santa Cruz de la Serós
Atarés

93
Sangüesa/ Zangoza
Casa Goyo
Campo Real
El Boyerla
Undués de Lerda (848)
Puerto de Cuatro Caminos
1601
Santa Quiteria
766
Unduès Pintano (Los Pintanos)
Bagüés
Laruès 1134
Bailo
Arbués
Santa Bárbara
Puerto de Santa Bárbara (864)
Monasterio de San Juan de la Peña
Sierra de San Juan de la Peña
6%
Botaya
1603
1156

Navardún
Urriés
1031
Ermita de Santa María Magdalena
Pintano
Casa Miranda Alta
1076
Cerro de las Colladas
Casa Pequera
6%
Paternoy
Ena
Osia
1205

Las Cinco Villas

Gordués
Isuerre
Río Onsella
Lobera de Onsella
1166
Longás
Sierra de Santo Domingo
Santo Domingo 1524
Casa del Chas
39
Villalangua
Pueblo Nuevo de Salinas
Santa María Triste
Yeste
1124

Parador
Palacio de Sada
Sos del Rey Católico
7%
Venta del Zapato
(856)
908
Puerto de Sos
Castillo de Roita
Nuestra Señora de la Cerrada
Petilla de Aragón
Ermita de Santa Quiteria
Sierra de Luesia
Puy Monte 1313
Sierra de Salinas
Salinas de Jaca
Virgen del Camino
Casa Lagé
Santa Isabel 1072

Mamillas
Baruès
Corral de la Fraila
Biel 1184
San Felices
Santiago 1193
Anzánigo
Santa Isabel

94
Novellaco
Castillo Baruès
127
819
Ermita de la Virgen de Gabardilla
Luesia
Corral del Judío
Fuencalderas
Ermita de San Miguel
Santa Quitena
Agüero
Los Mallos 680
Riglos (Las Peñas de Riglos)
Embalse de la Peña
Estación de Santa María y La Peña

Castiliscar
Uncastillo
Ruinas Romanas
1202
Río Arba de Luesia
Corral de-Meleras
1103
Necrópolis
Linás de Marcuello
Sierra de Loa
Cas
de L

Embalse del Valdelaflón
Río Riguel
Castillo de Clerina
Layana
Malpica de Arba
678
Asín
Orés
La Mingota
Corral de Charles
1202
Concilio
Sarsamarcuello
Morán
Santa Engracia
Loarre
Nova

92
Sádaba
Mausoleo Romano
Sinagoga
127
Biota
Castillo de Bañales
Alto de Biota
Puisón
1204
Fragal 853
Barranco Farasdues
Lacasta
Santa Eulalia de Gállego
821
Sierra Estronad
Losanglis
Erés
Fontellas
132
(582)
Ayerbe
Castillo de Liso
Jabarillo
Castillo de Nava
Loscorrales
132
125

Partida Casilla

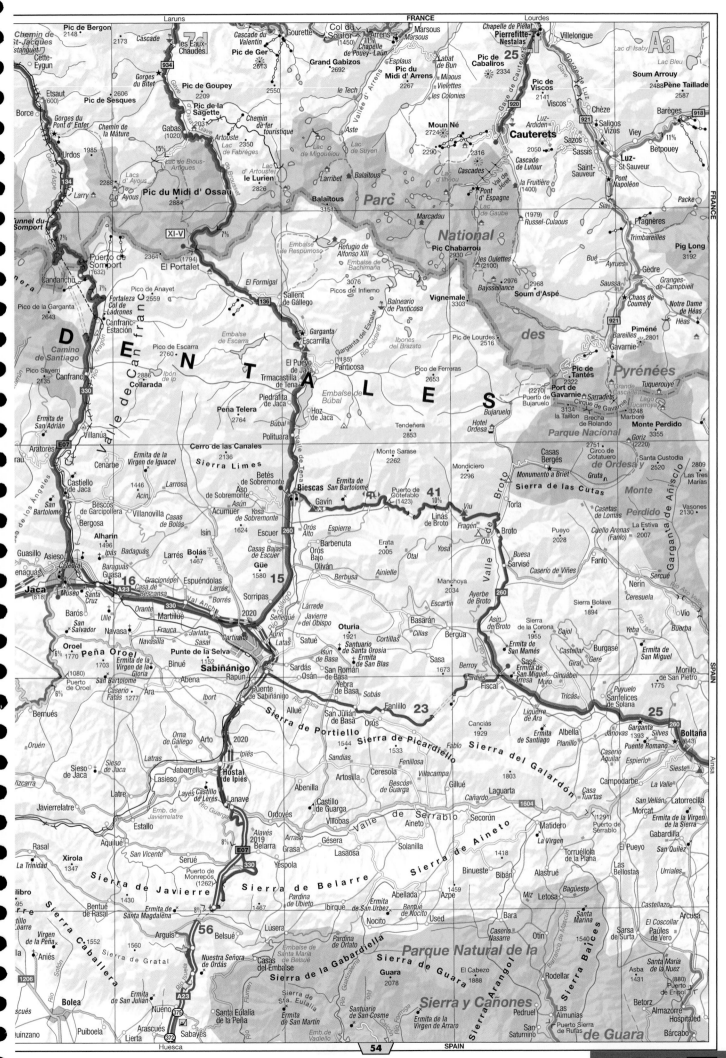

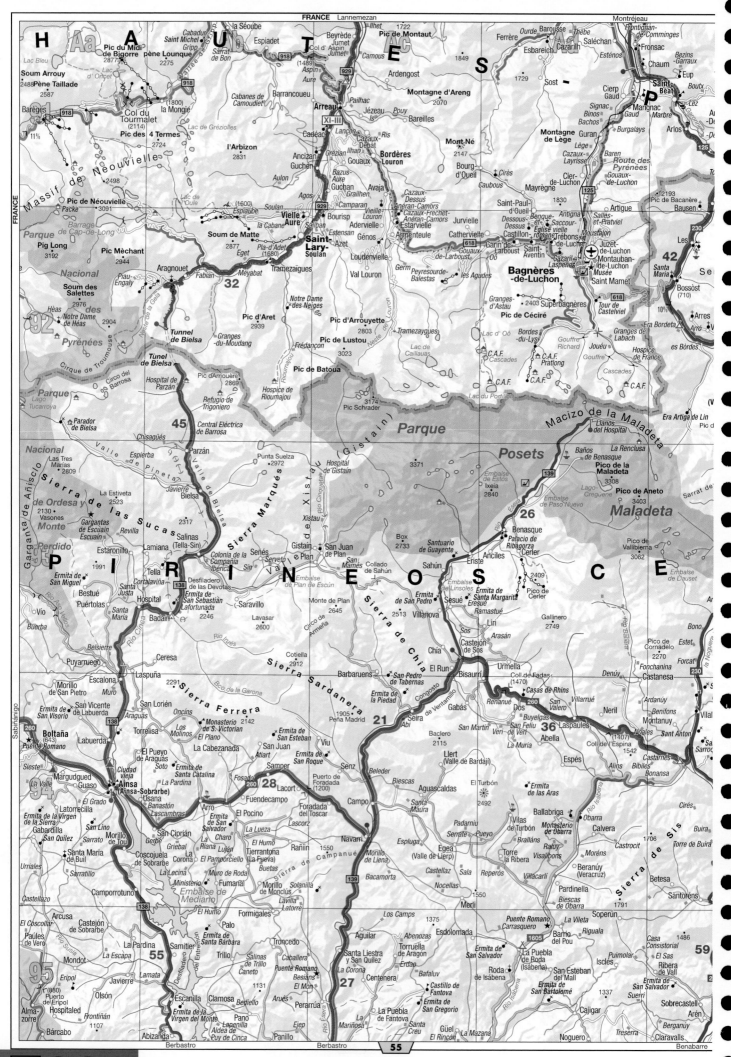

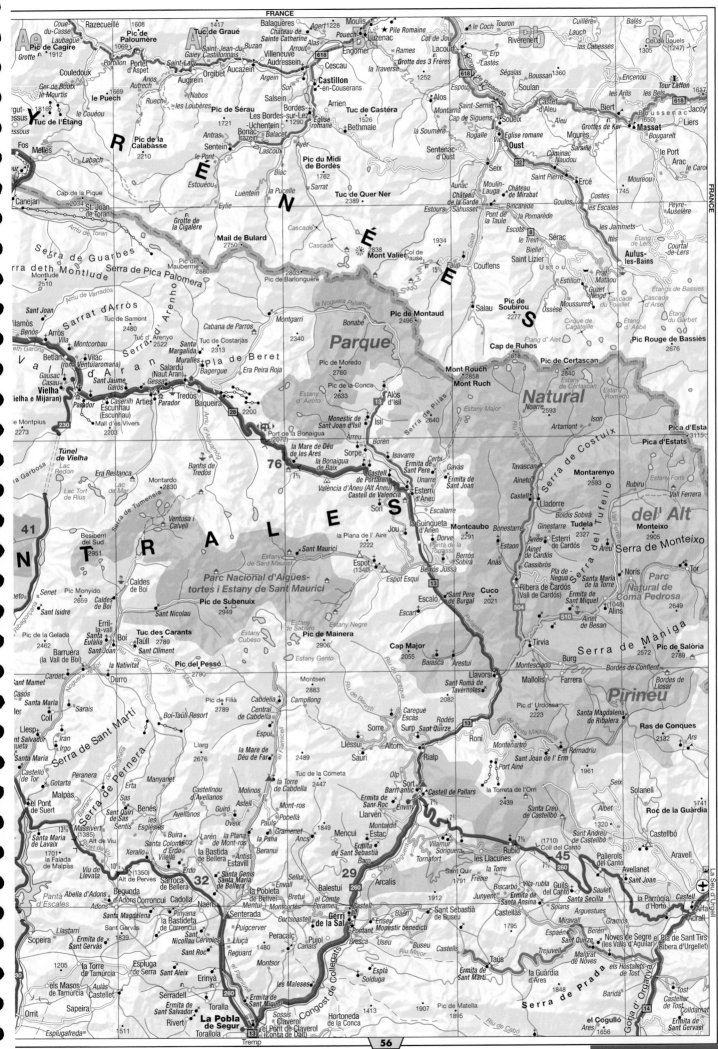

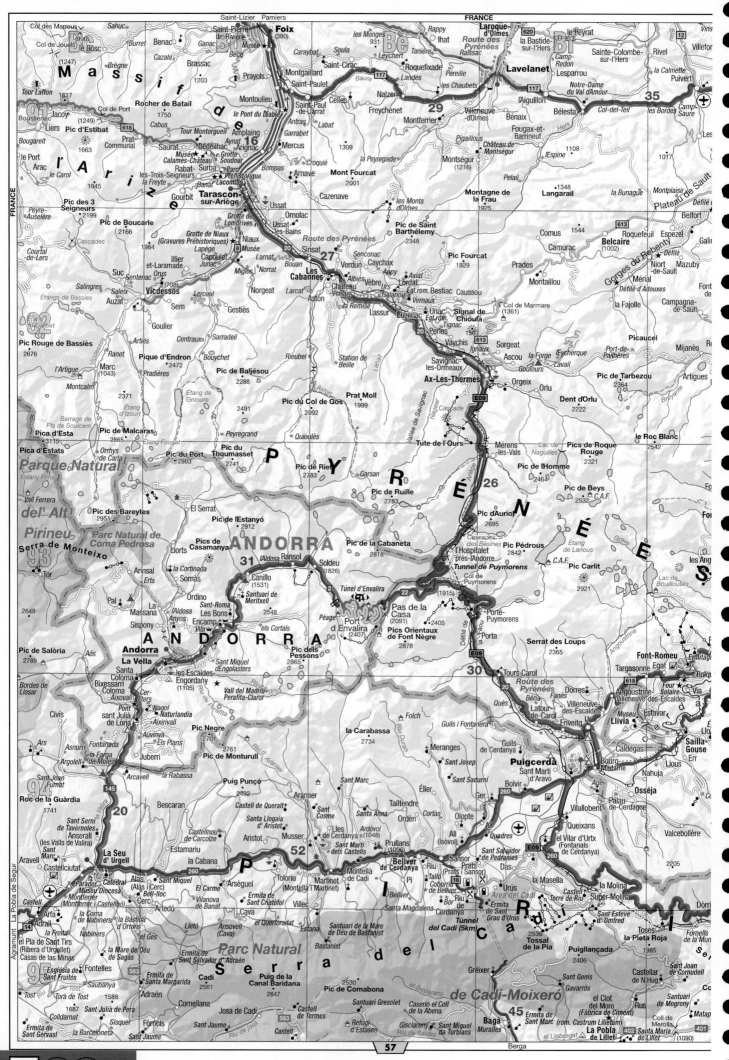

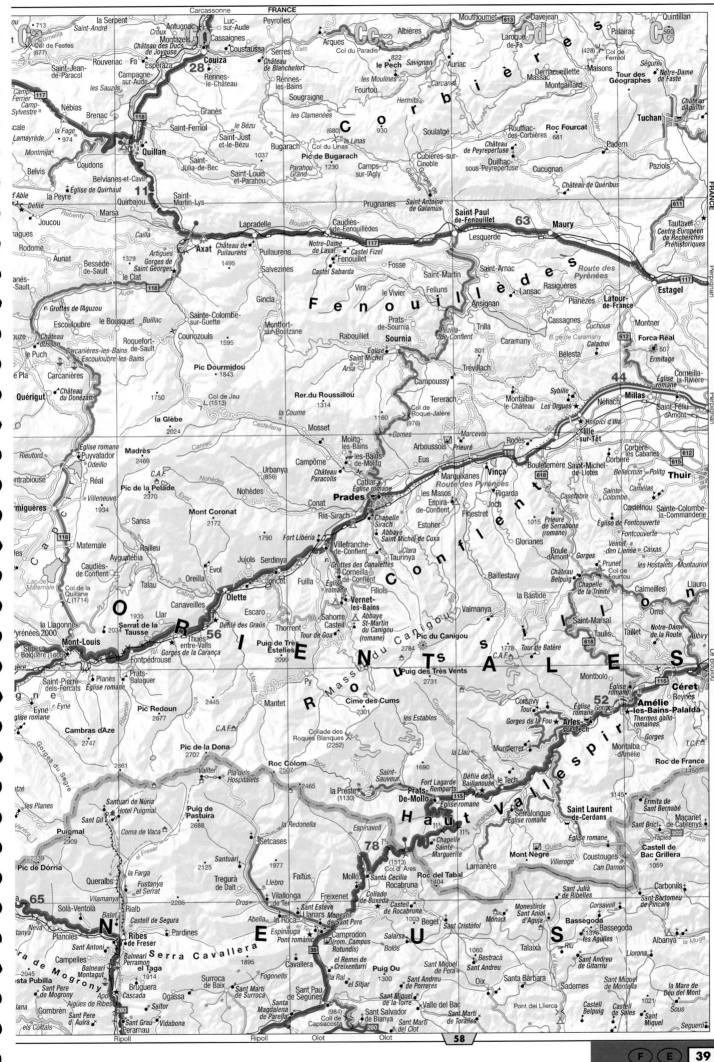

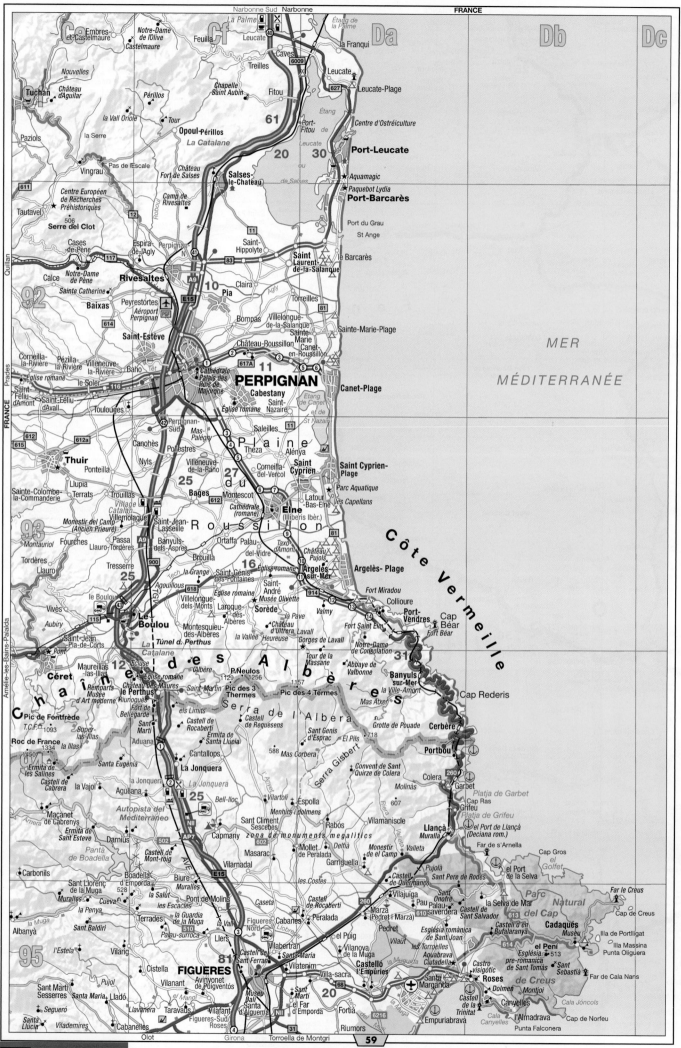

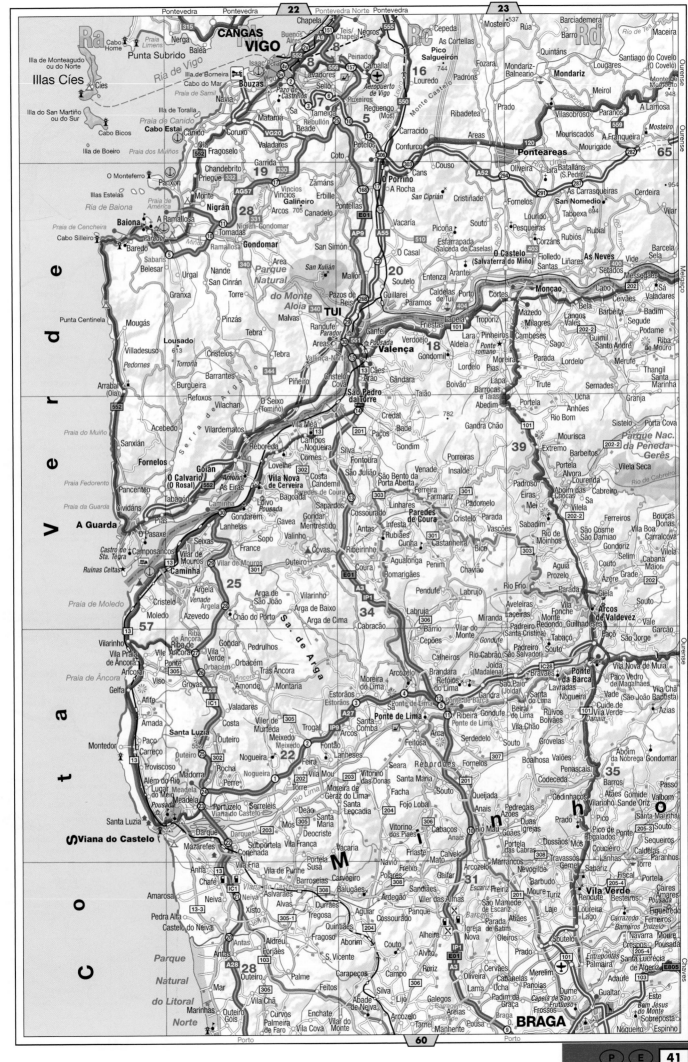

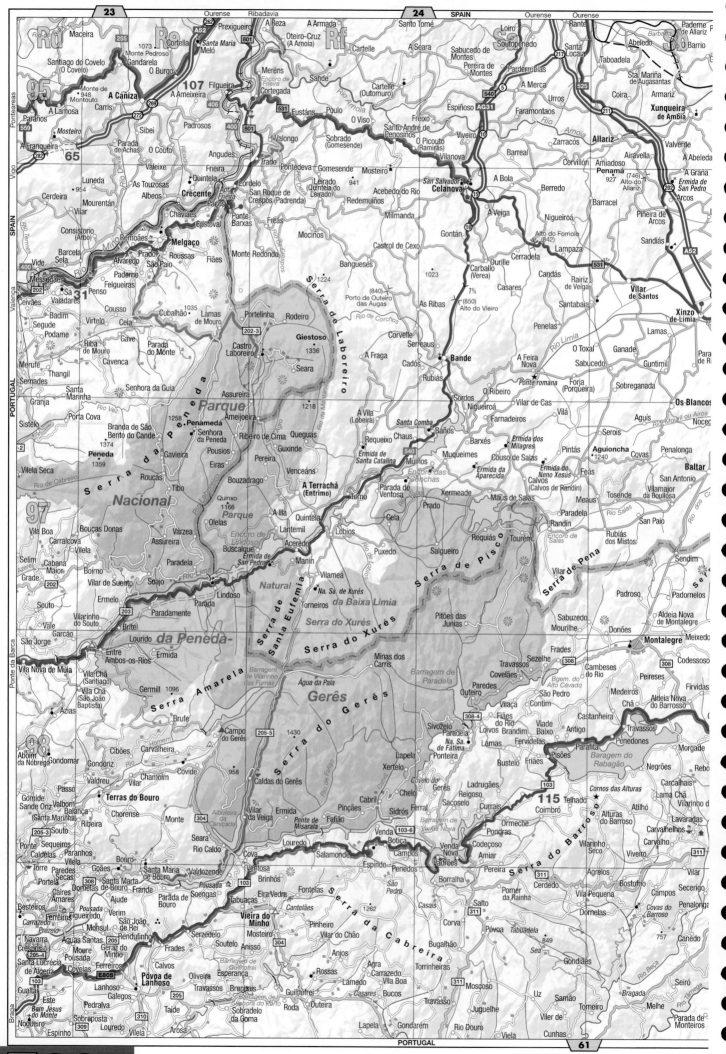

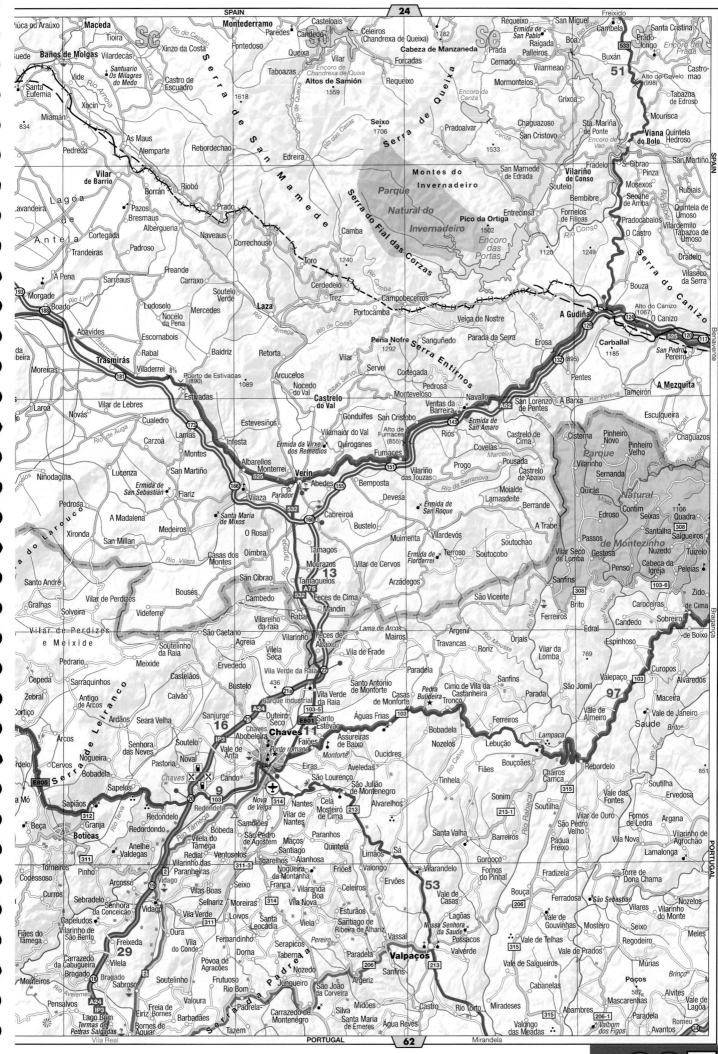

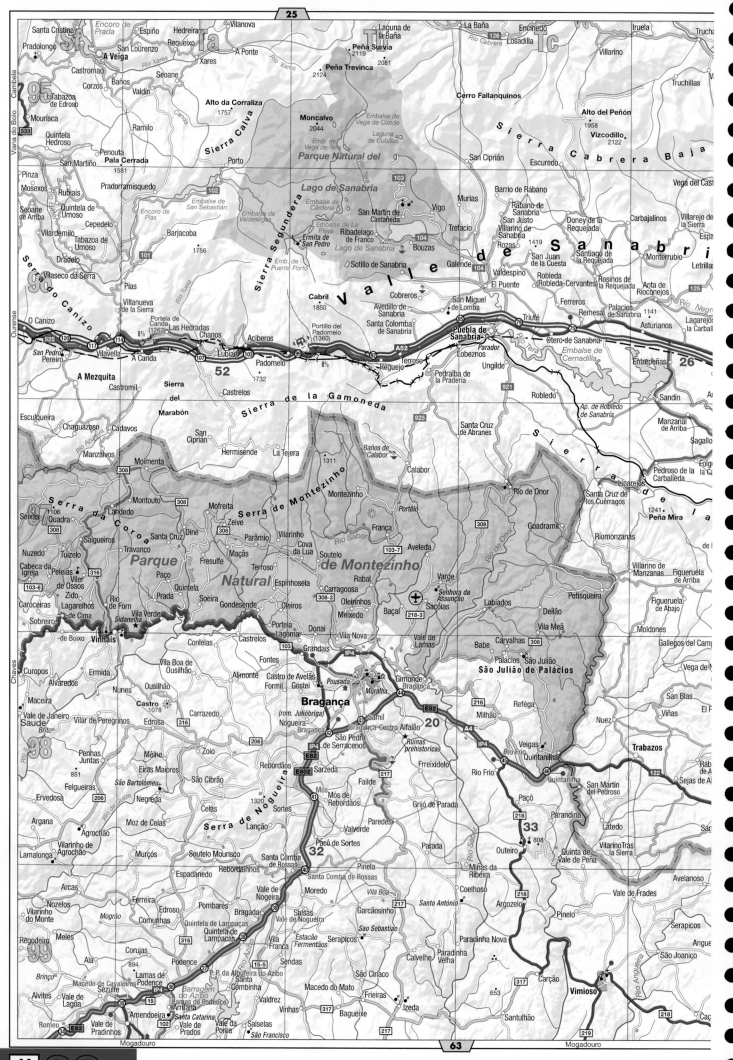

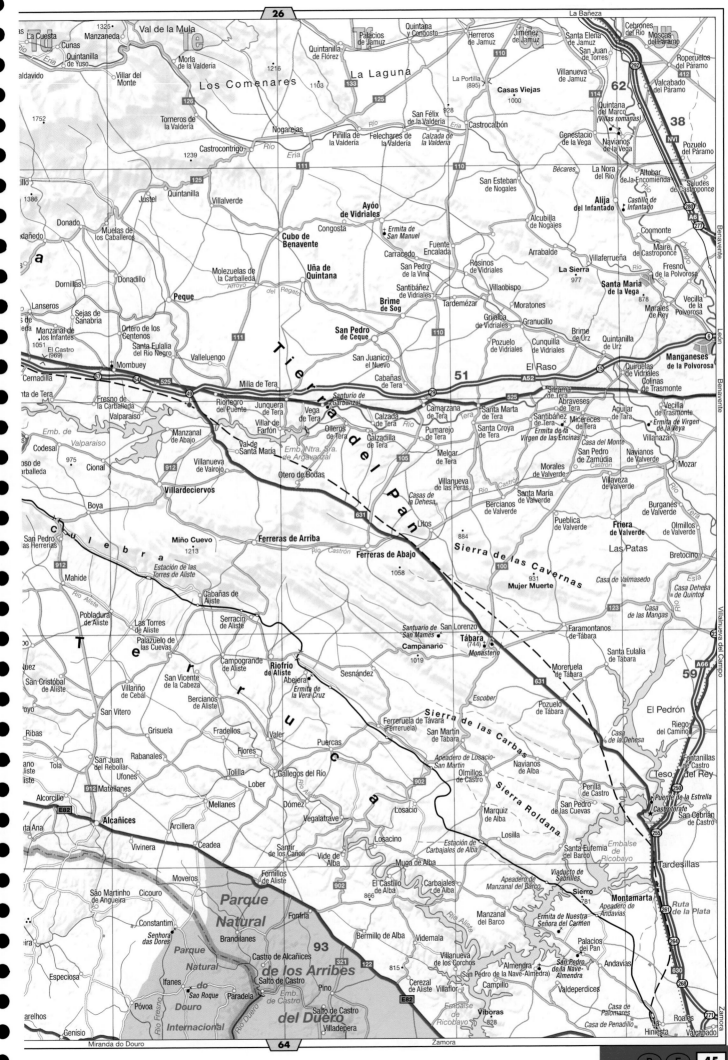

La Cuesta · 1325
Manzaneda
Cunas
Quintanilla
de Yuso
aldavido
Villar del
Monte
Morla
de la Valdería · 1216
Los Comenares
1103
La Laguna
126
1752
133
125
Torneros de
la Valdería
Castrocontrigo · 1239
Nogarejas
Pinilla de
la Valdería
Felechares de
la Valdería
Calzada de
la Valdería
Río
Eria
111
111
125
Justel
1386
Quintanilla
Villalverde
Ayóo
de Vidriales
Congosta
Ermita de
San Manuel
Donado
Muelas de
los Caballeros
andañedo
Donadillo
Molezuelas de
la Carballeda
Cubo de
Benavente
Arroyo
del Regato
Uña de
Quintana
Carracedo
San Pedro
de la Viña
Peque
Lanseros
Sejas de
Sanabria
s de
eda
Manzanal de
los Infantes
Ortero de los
Centenos
Santa Eulalia
del Río Negro
El Castro
(969)
1051
Valleluengo
Santibáñez
de Vidriales
Brime
de Sog
San Pedro
de Ceque
111
110
San Juanico
el Nuevo
Pozuelo
de Vidriales
Cunquilla
de Vidriales
Rosinos
de Vidriales
Villaobispo
Moratones
Grijalba
de Vidriales
Granucillo
Brime
de Urz
La Sierra
977
Santa María
de la Vega
878
Morales
de Rey
Vecilla
de la
Polvorosa
6
Quintanilla
de Urz
Manganeses
de la Polvorosa
Tierra del Pan
Cernadilla
57
54
525
Mombuey
49
Milla de Tera
Cabañas
de Tera
El Raso
51
Sitrama
de Tera
Colinas
de Trasmonte
Quiruelas
de Vidriales
15
a de Tera
Fresno de
la Carballeda
Rionegro
del Puente
Junquera
de Tera
Vega
de Tera
Santurio de
Garbanzal
Calzada
de Tera
Río
Camarzana
de Tera
Santa Marta
de Tera
Abraveses
de Tera
Aguilar
de Tera
Vecilla
de Trasmonte
Valparaíso
Villar de
Farfón
Olleros
de Tera
29
Pumarejo
de Tera
Santibáñez
de Tera
Micereces
de Tera
Ermita de Virgen
de la Veya
Emb. de
Valparaíso
Manzanal
de Abajo
Val de
Santa María
Emb. Ntra. Sra.
de Argavanzál.
Calzadilla
de Tera
105
Melgar
de Tera
Santa Croya
de Tera
Ermita de la
Virgen de las Encinas
Casa del Monte
Villanazar
Codesal
975
Cional
Villanueva
de Vairojo
912
Otero de Bodas
Villanueva
de las Peras
Río
Castron
San Pedro
de Zamúdia
Morales
de Valverde
Navianos
de Valverde
Villaveza
de Valverde
Mozar
oso de
arballeda
Villardeciervos
1213
Miño Cuevo
Santa María
de Valverde
Bercianos
de Valverde
Burganés
de Valverde
Boya
C
u
l
e
b
r
a
Ferreras de Arriba
Río Castrón
Litos
Pueblica
de Valverde
Friera
de Valverde
Olmillos
de Valverde
San Pedro
as Herrerias
912
Estación de las
Torres de Aliste
Ferreras de Abajo
1058
884
931
Sierra de las Cavernas
Las Patas
Bretocino
Esla
Mahide
T
e
r
r
u
Cabañas de
Aliste
Mujer Muerte
100
123
Casa de Valmasedo
Casa Dehesa
de Quintos
Pobladura
de Aliste
Las Torres
de Aliste
Serracín
de Aliste
Santuario de
San Mamés
San Lorenzo
Campanario
1019
Tábara
(744)
Monasterio
Faramontanos
de Tábara
Casa
de las Mangas
Santa Eulalia
de Tábara
Palazuelo de
las Cuevas
Campogrande
de Aliste
Riofrío
de Aliste
Sesnández
631
Moreruela
de Tábara
59
uez
San Cristóbal
de Aliste
Villariño
de Cebal
San Vicente
de la Cabeza
Abejera
Ermita de
la Vera Cruz
Bercianos
de Aliste
Sierra de las Carbas
Pozuelo
de Tábara
El Pedrón
royo
San Vitero
San Juan
del Rebollar
Grisuela
Fradellos
Valer
Ferreruela de Távara
(Ferreruela)
San Martín
de Tábara
Escober
Casa
de la Dehesa
Riego
del Camino
250
Fontanillas
de Castro
ano
liste
Ribas
Tola
Rabanales
Flores
Puercas
Apeadero de Losacio-
San Martín
Navianos
de Alba
Perilla
de Castro
Teso
del Rey
San Juan
del Rebollar
Ufones
Tolilla
Gállegos del Río
902
Olmillos
de Castro
San Pedro
de las Cuevas
Castrotorafe
San Cebrián
de Castro
Alcorcille
912
Matellanes
Lober
Losacio
Sierra Roldana
255
Santa Ana
Alcañices
E82
Arcillera
Mellanes
Dómez
Vegalatrave
Losacino
Marquiz
de Alba
Losilla
Santa Eufemia
del Barco
Embalse
de
Ricobayo
Tardesillas
Vivinera
Ceadea
Samir
de los Caños
Vide de
Alba
Muga de Alba
Estación de
Carbajales de Alba
Sierro
Montamarta
São Martinho
de Angueira
Cicouro
Moveros
Fornillos
de Aliste
902
El Castillo
de Alba
866
Carbajales
de Alba
Apeadero de
Manzanal del Barco
Ermita de Nuestra
Señora del Carmen
Apeadero de
Andavías
261
Ruta
de la Plata
Parque
Natural
Fonfría
Bermillo de Alba
Videmala
Río Aliste
Manzanal
del Barco
Palacios
del Pan
264
Constantim
Brandilanes
93
815
Villanueva
de los Corchos
Almendra
(San Pédro de la Navé-Almendra)
San Pedro
de la Navé-
Almendra
Valdeperdices
630
Senhora
das Dores
Parque
Natural
de los Arribes
321
122
Castro de Alcañices
Salto de Castro
Cerezal
de Aliste
Villaflor
Campillo
Casa de
Palomares
268
Especiosa
Ifanes
do
Sao Roque
Paradela
Pino
Emb.
de Castro
E82
Salto de Castro
Viboras
828
Casa de Penadillo
La
Hiniesta
271
Póvoa
Douro
Internacional
del Duero
Villadepera
Embalse de
Ricobayo
Roales
Valcabado
arelhos
Genísio

Miranda do Douro
Zamora

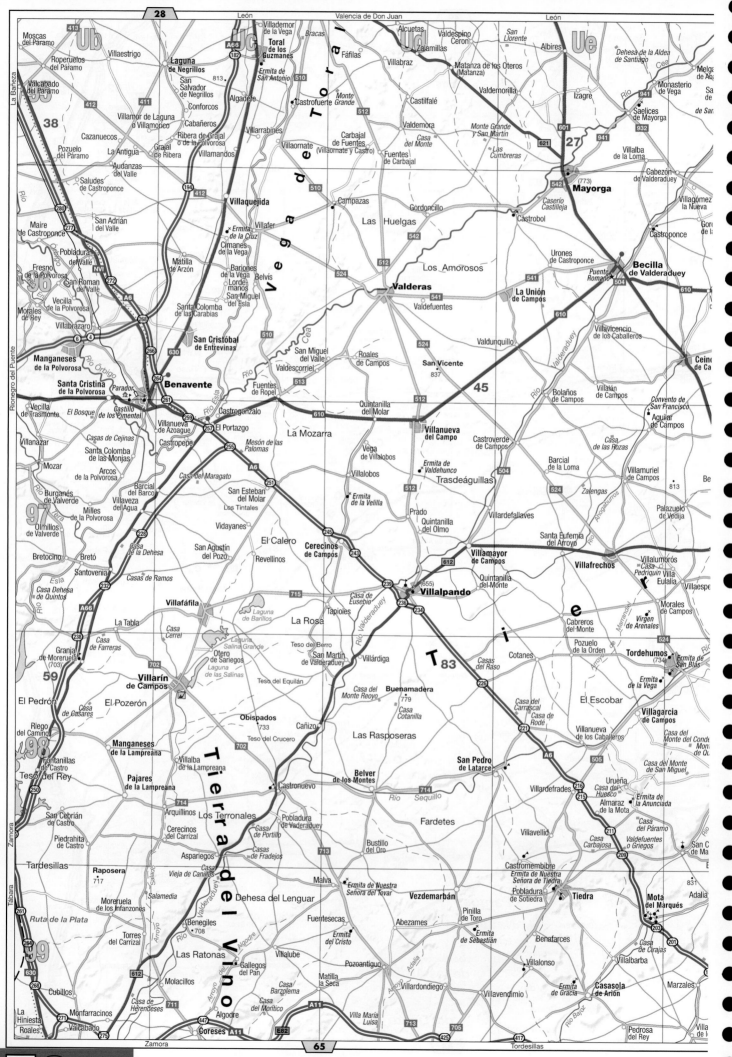

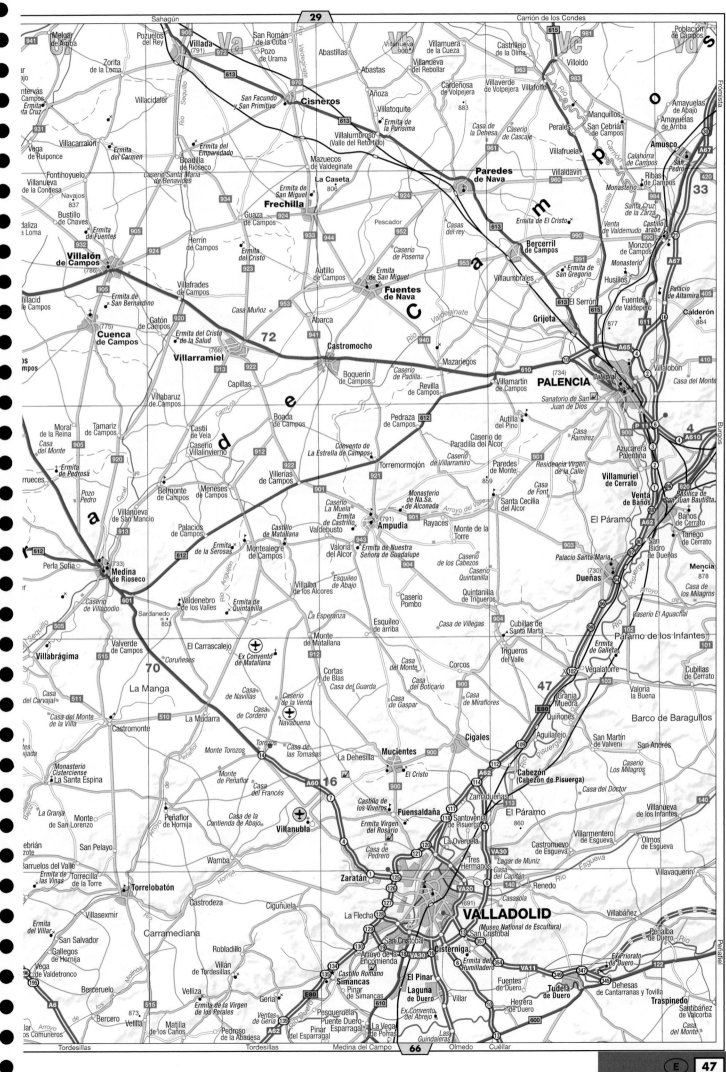

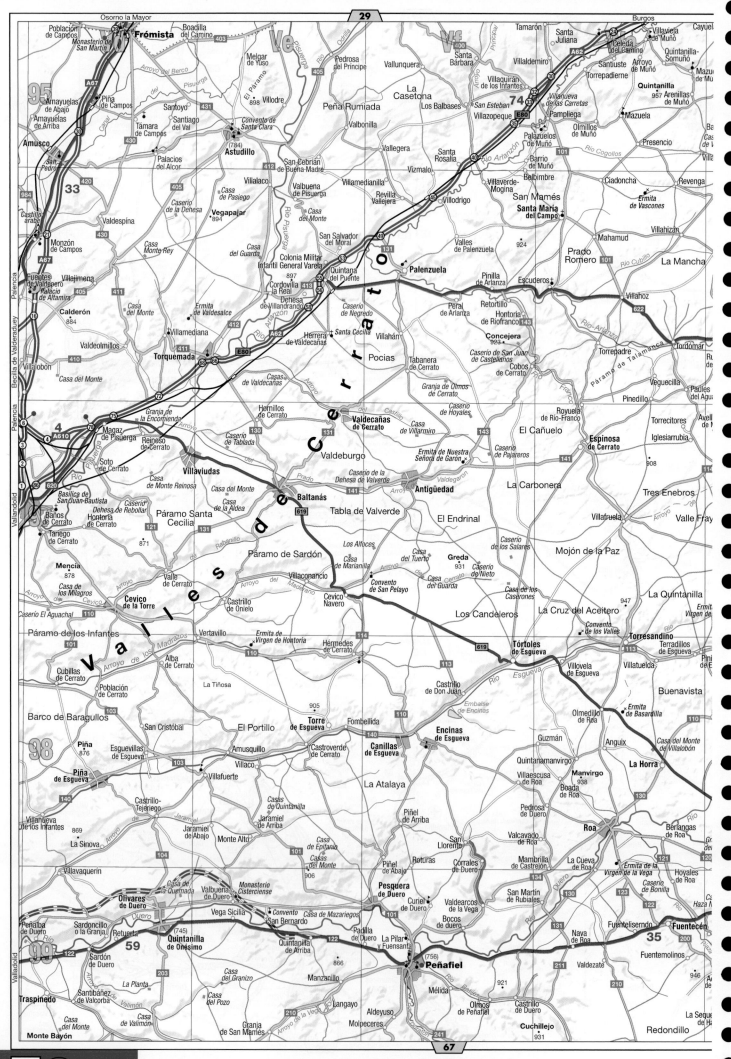

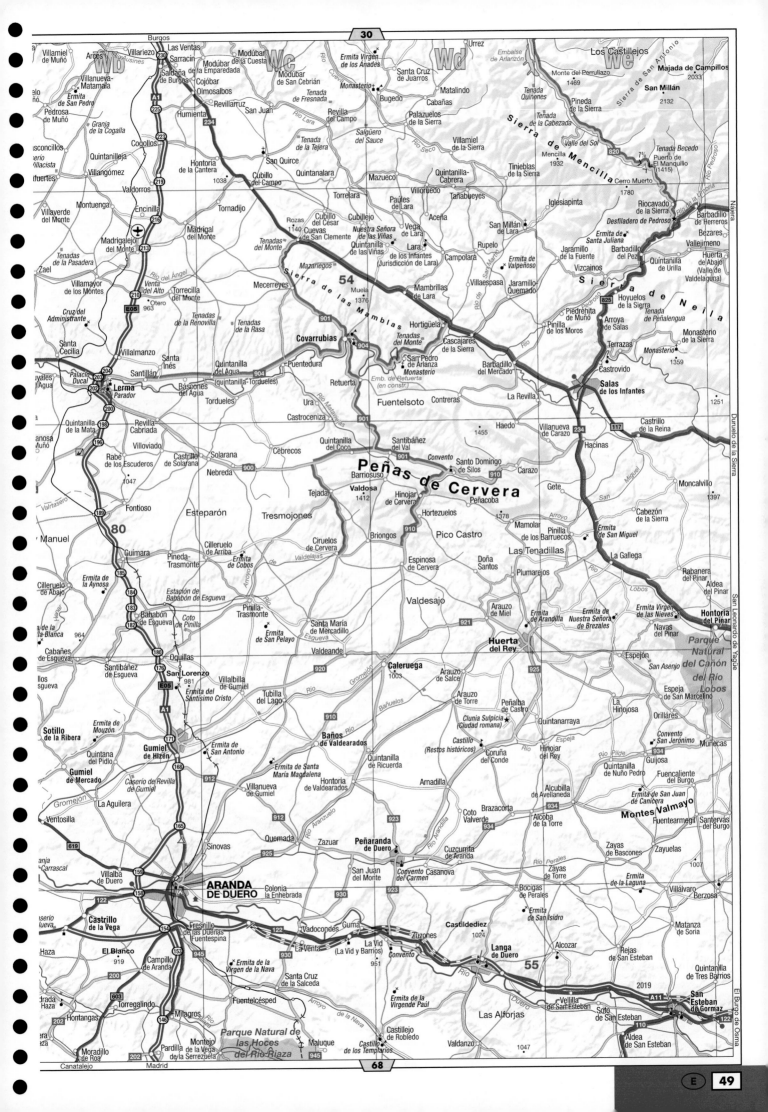

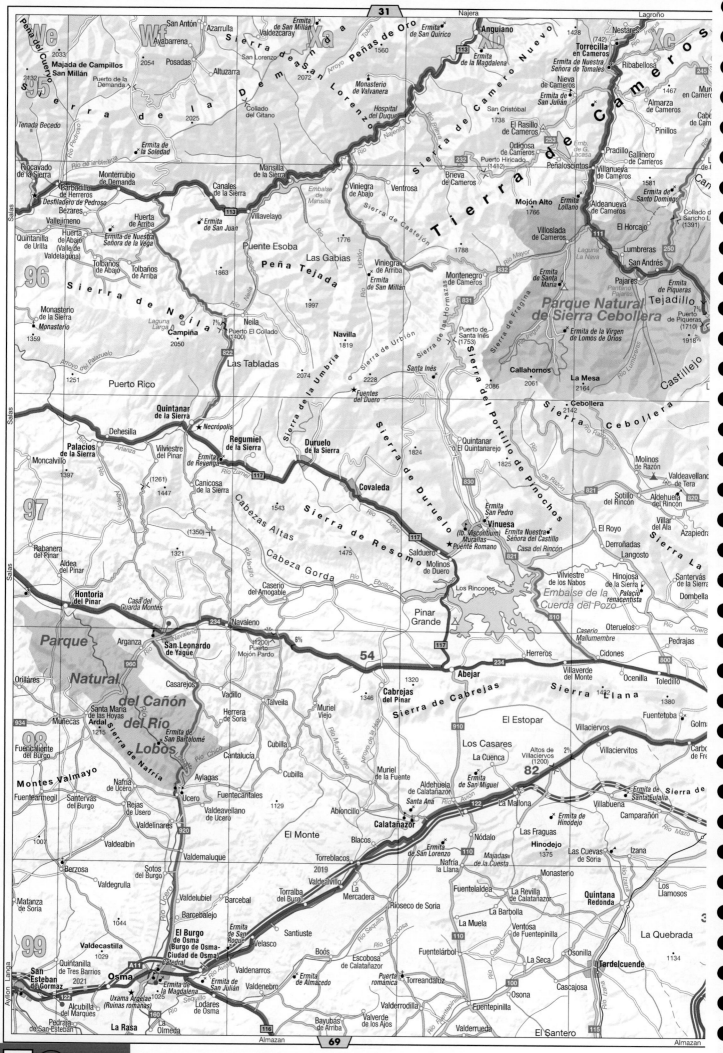

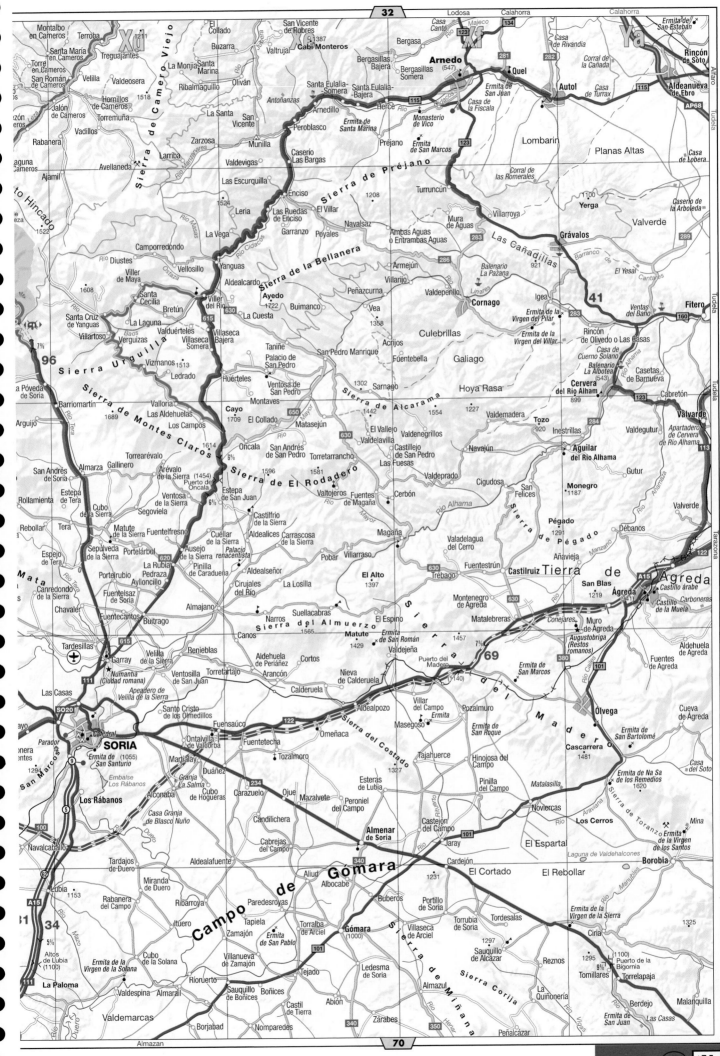

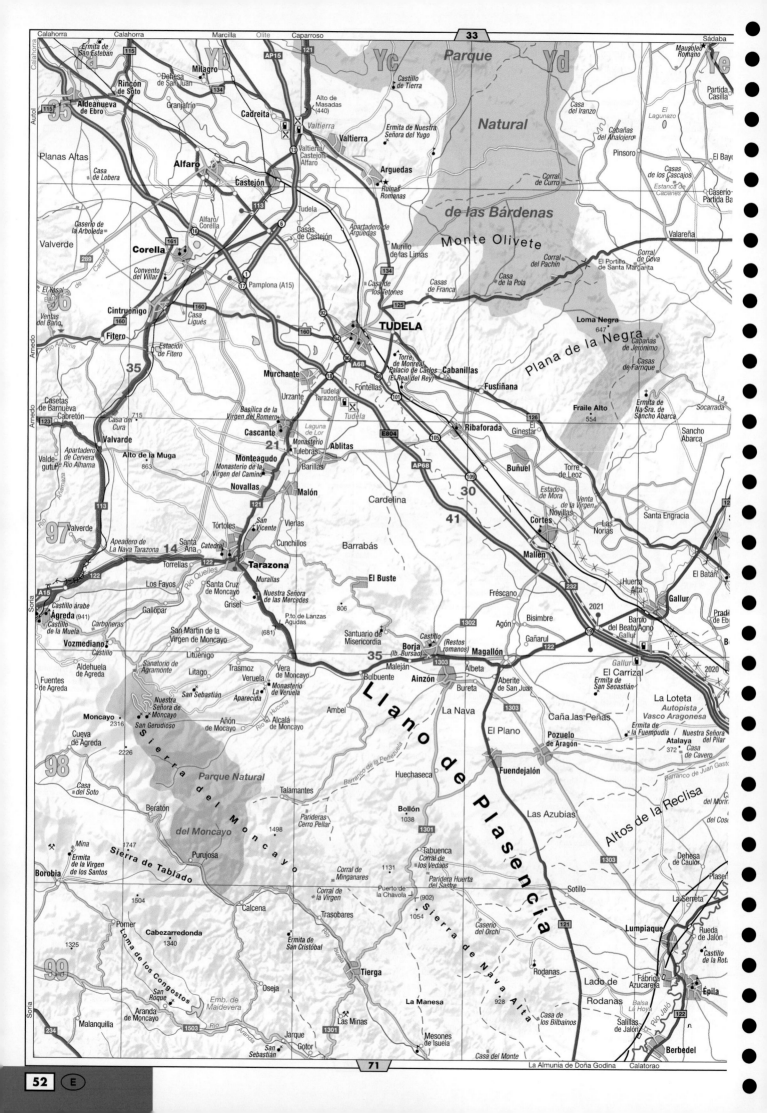

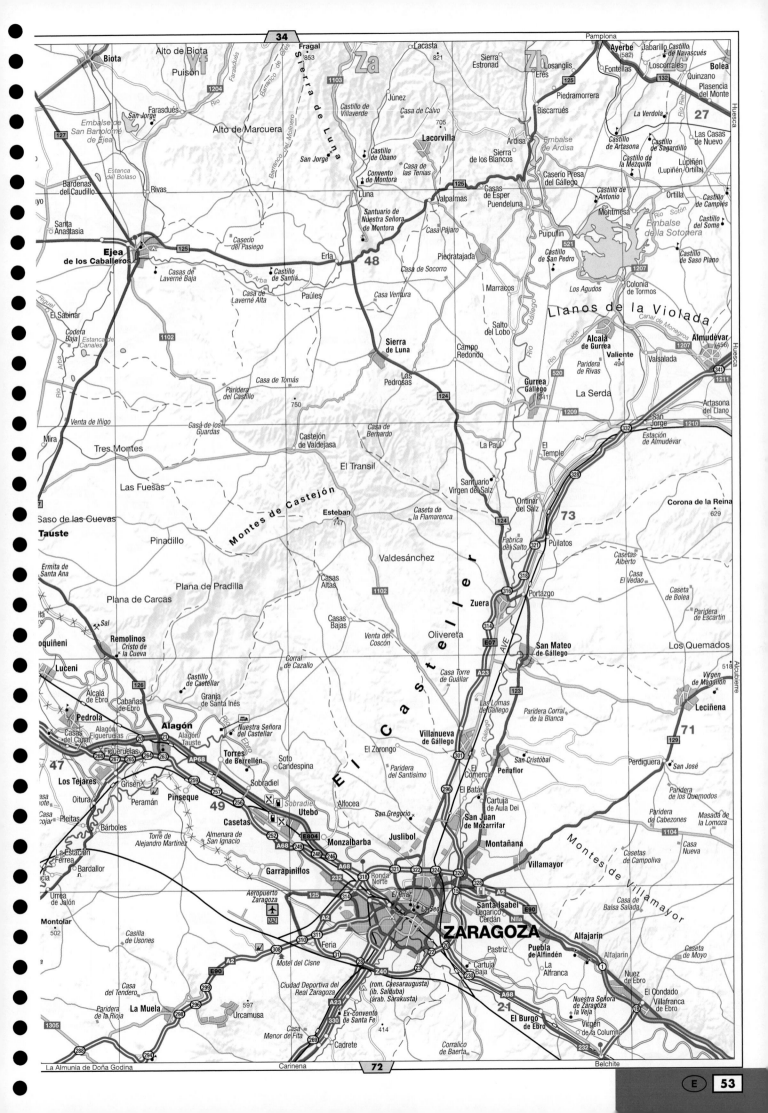

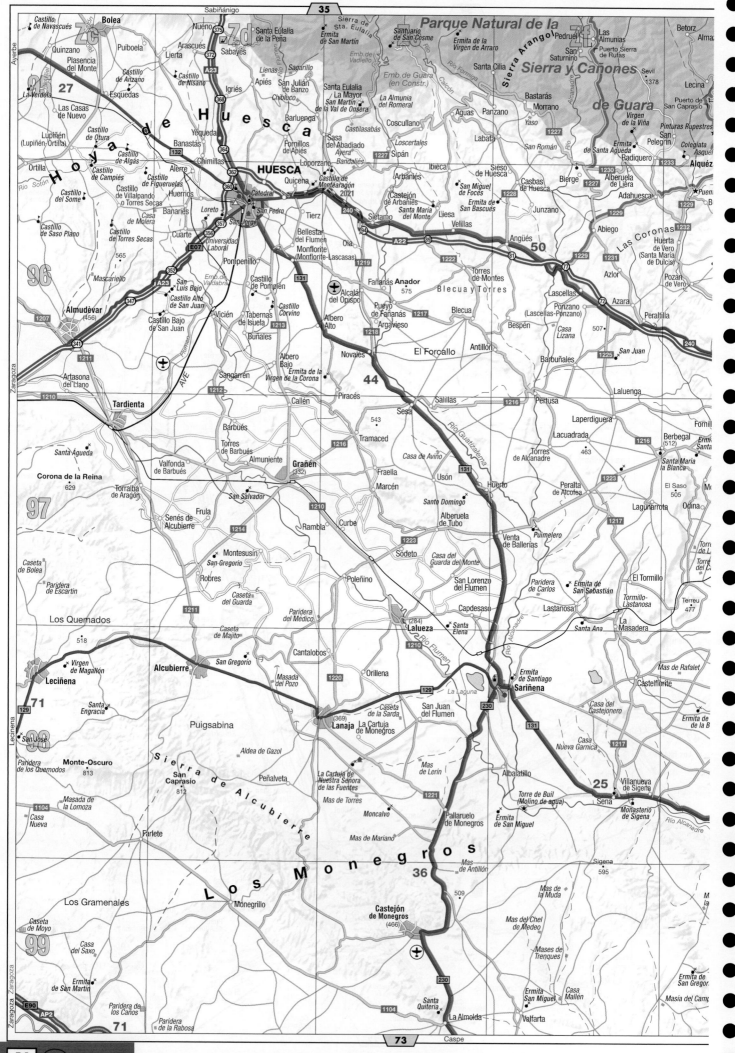

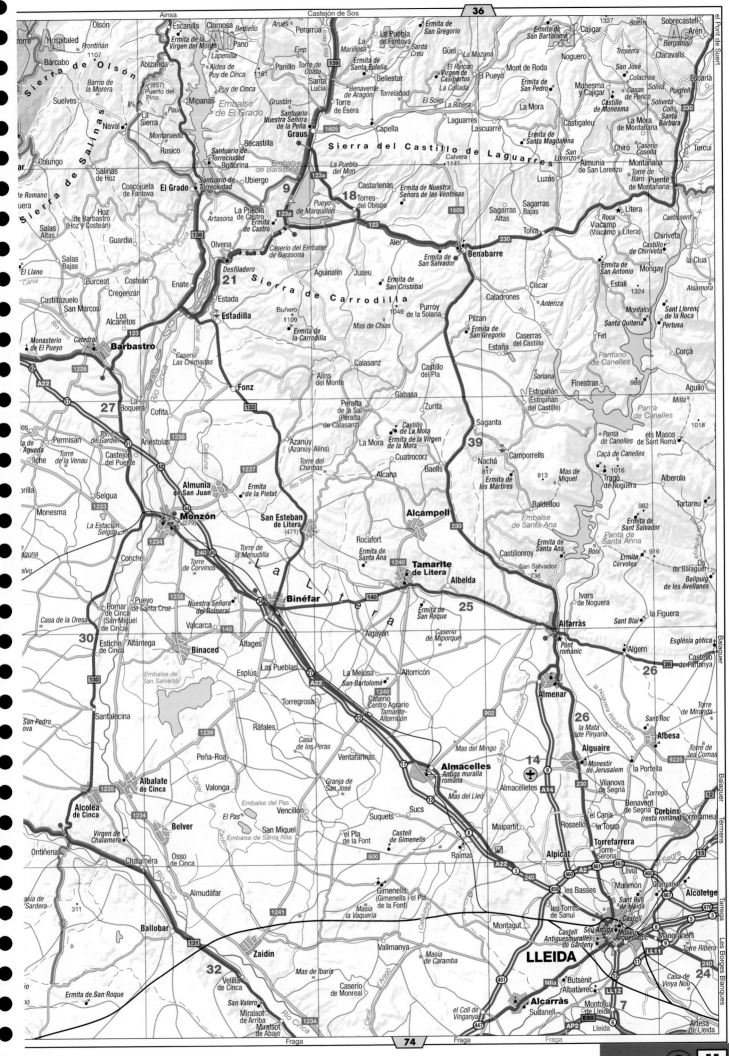

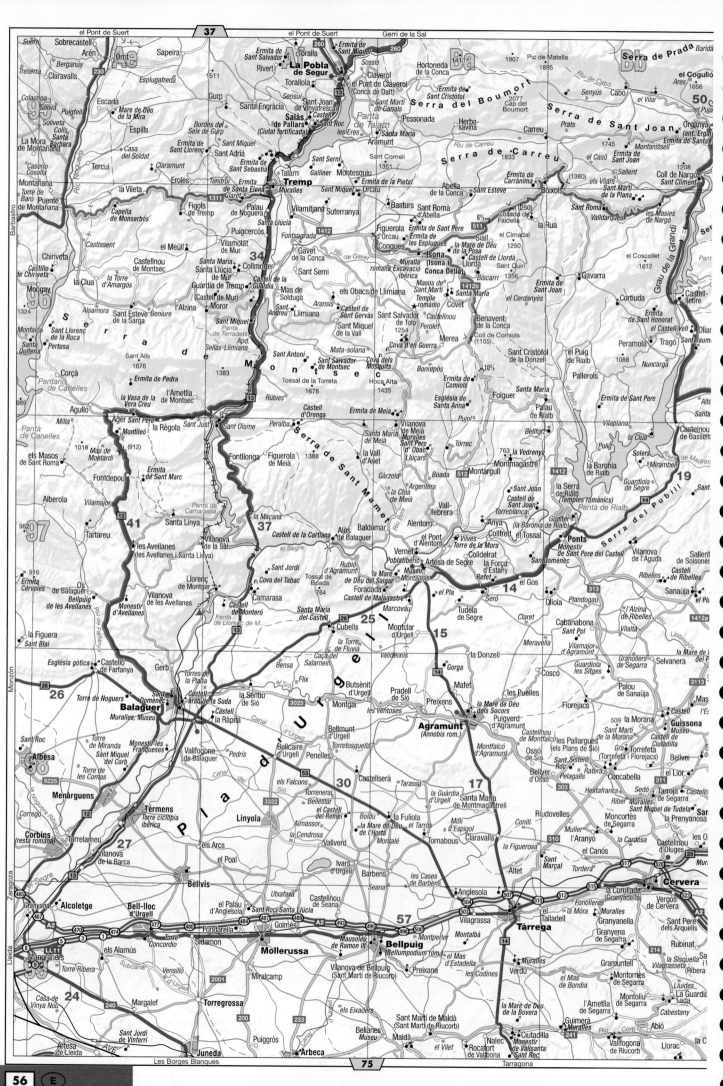

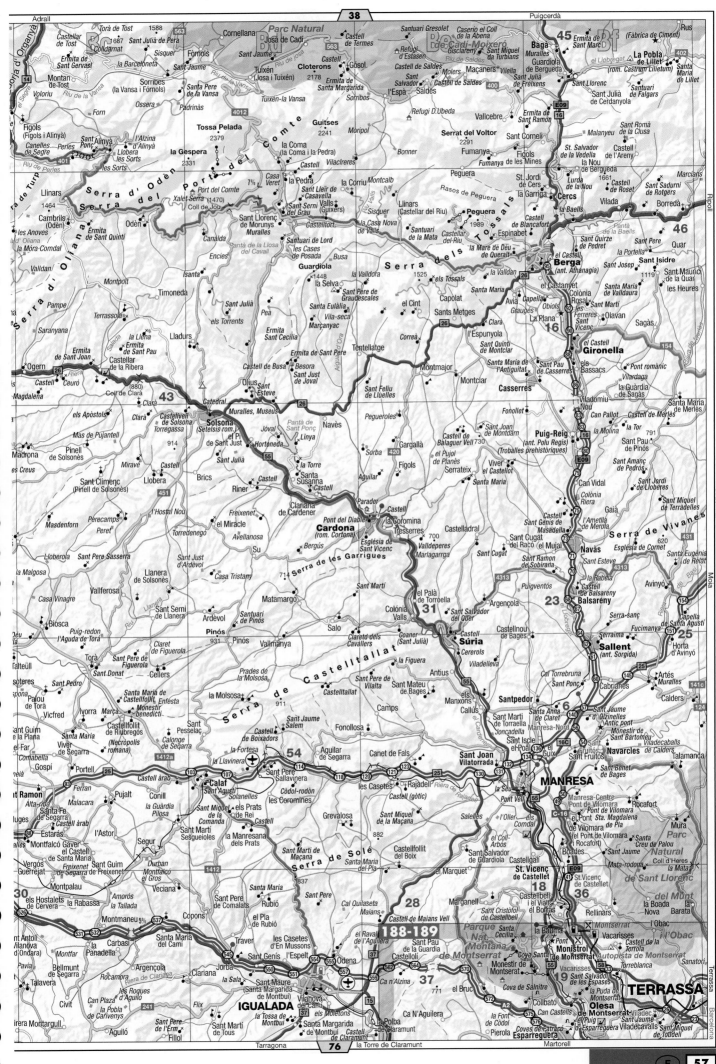

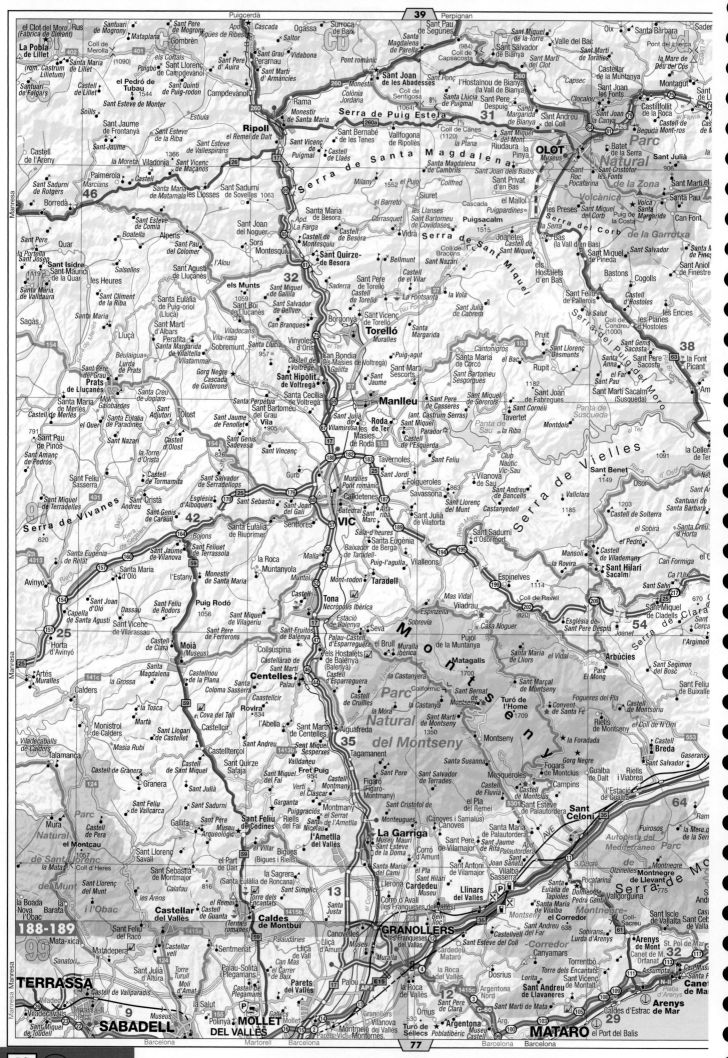

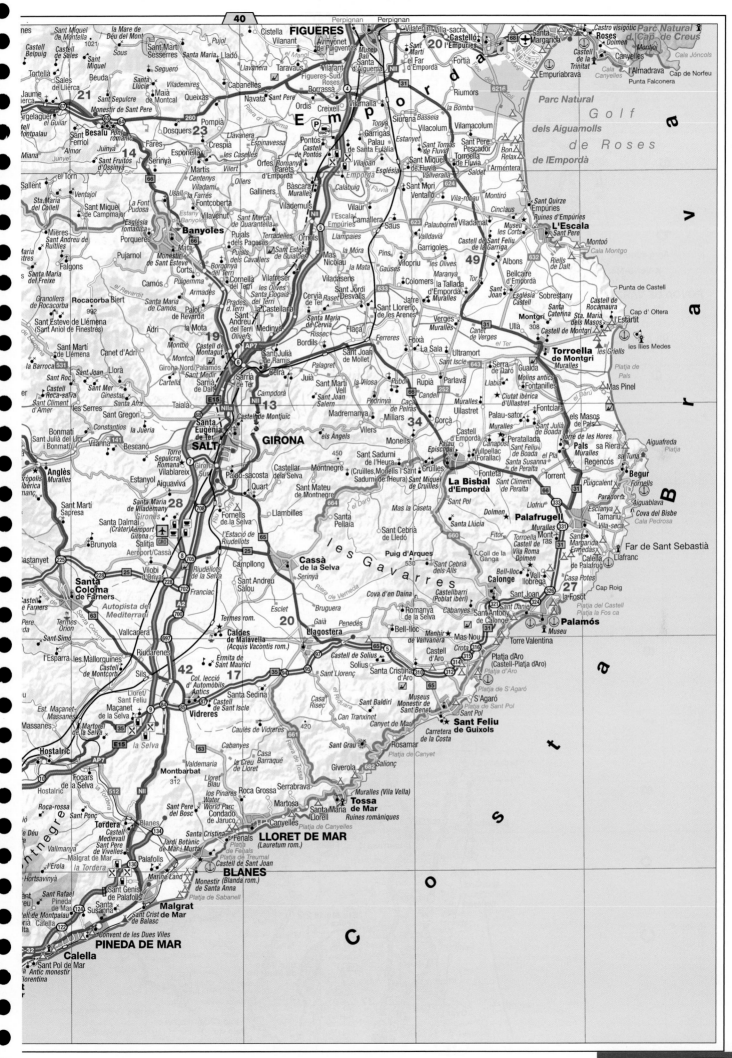

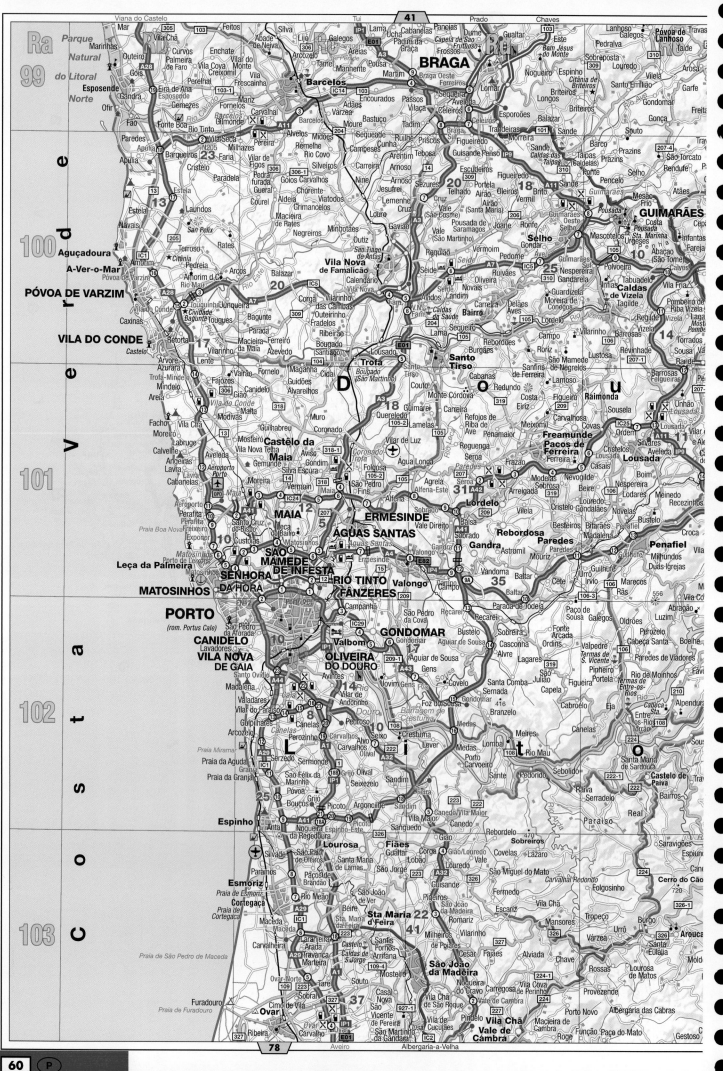

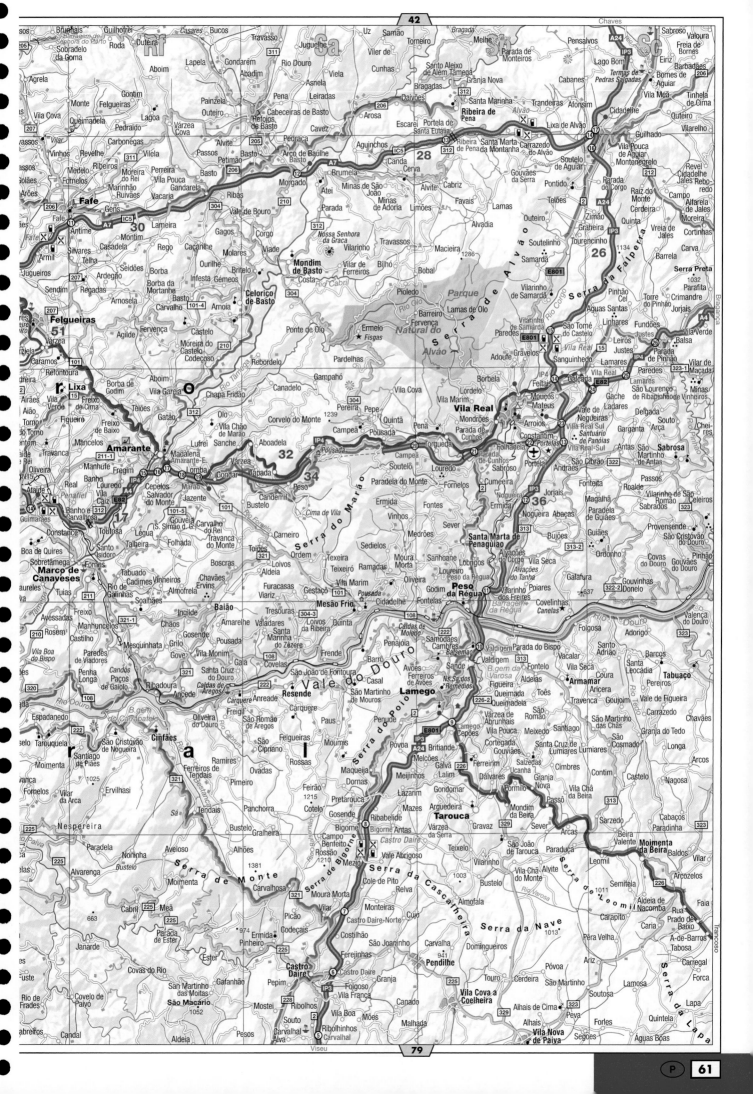

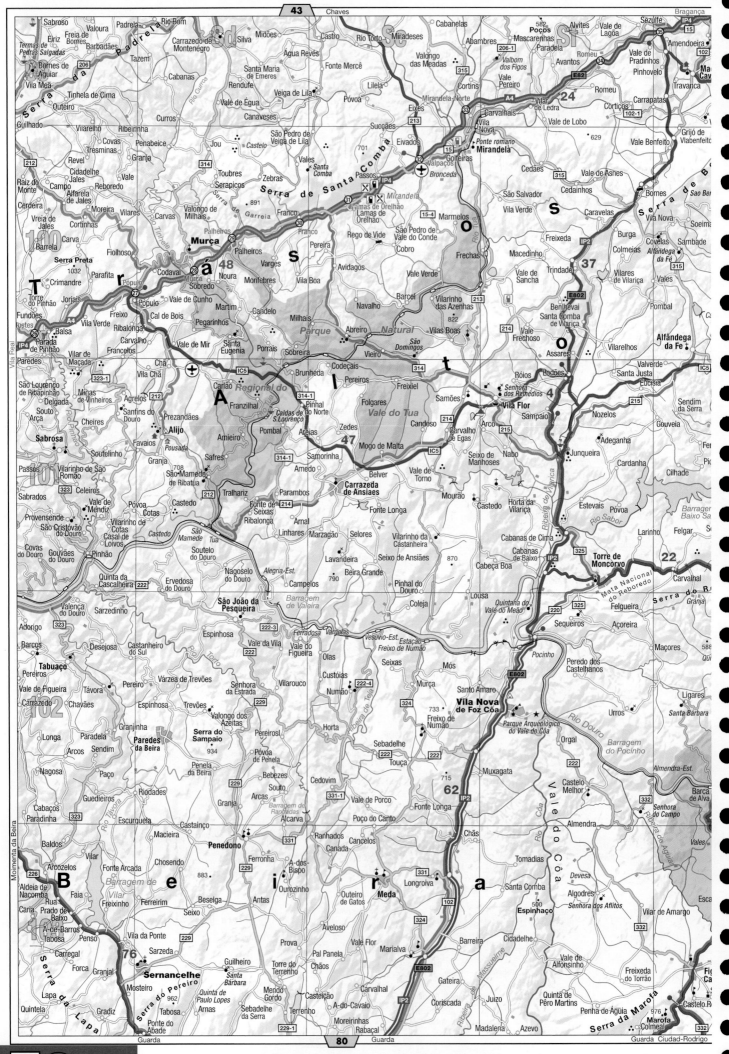

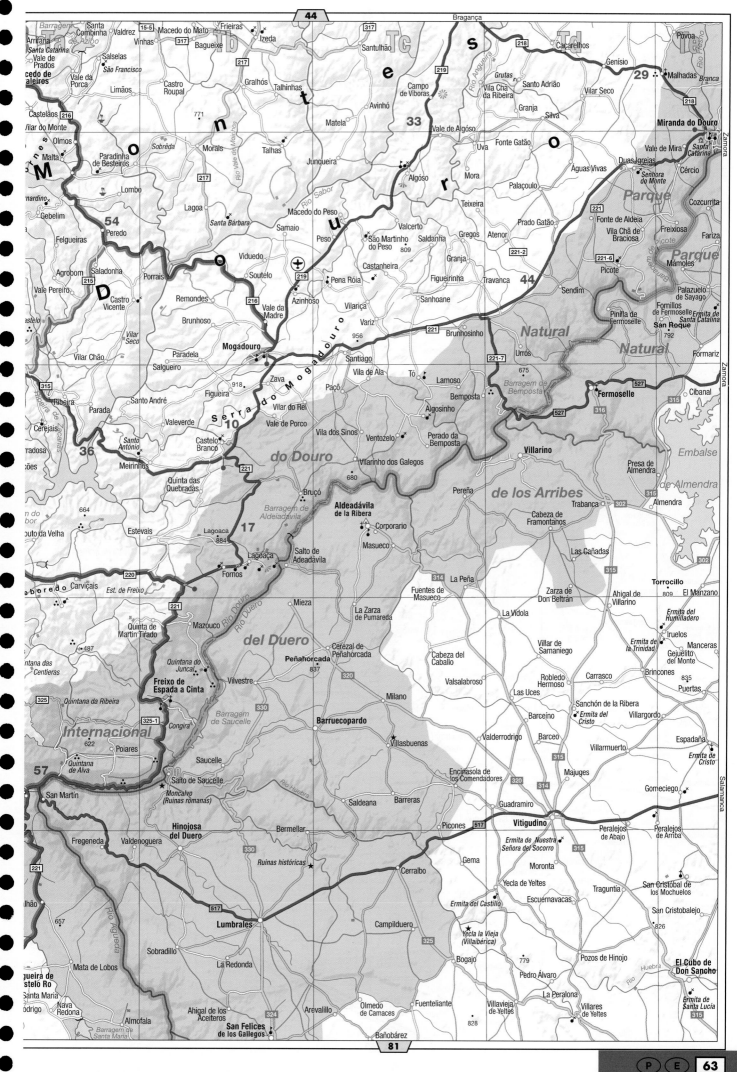

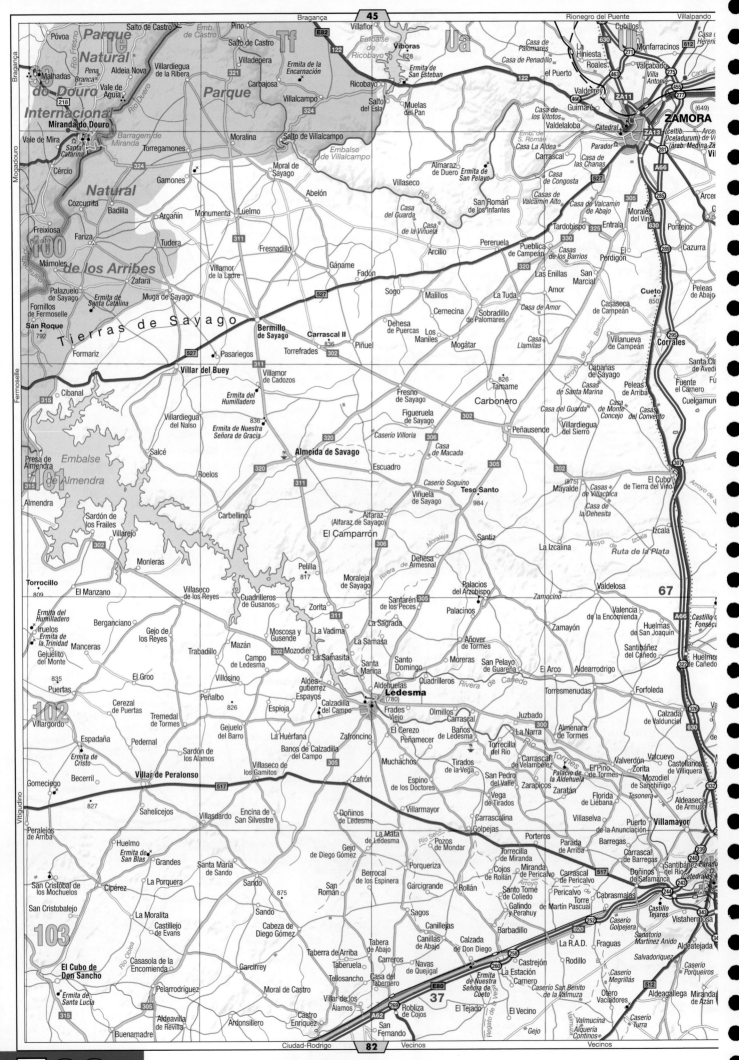

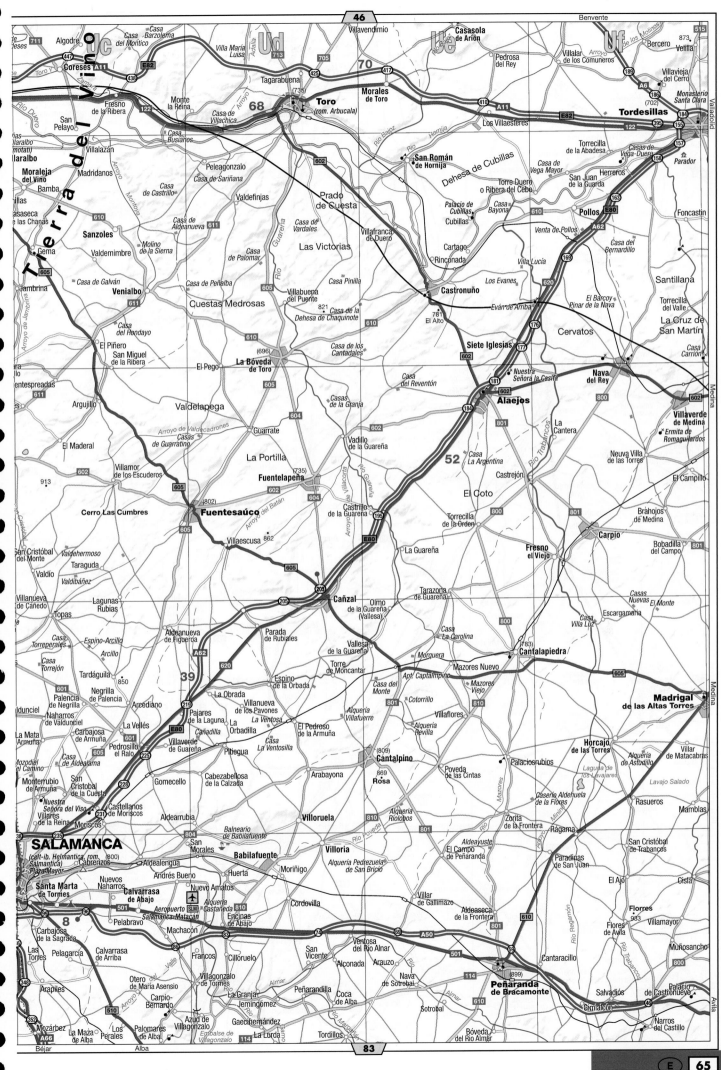

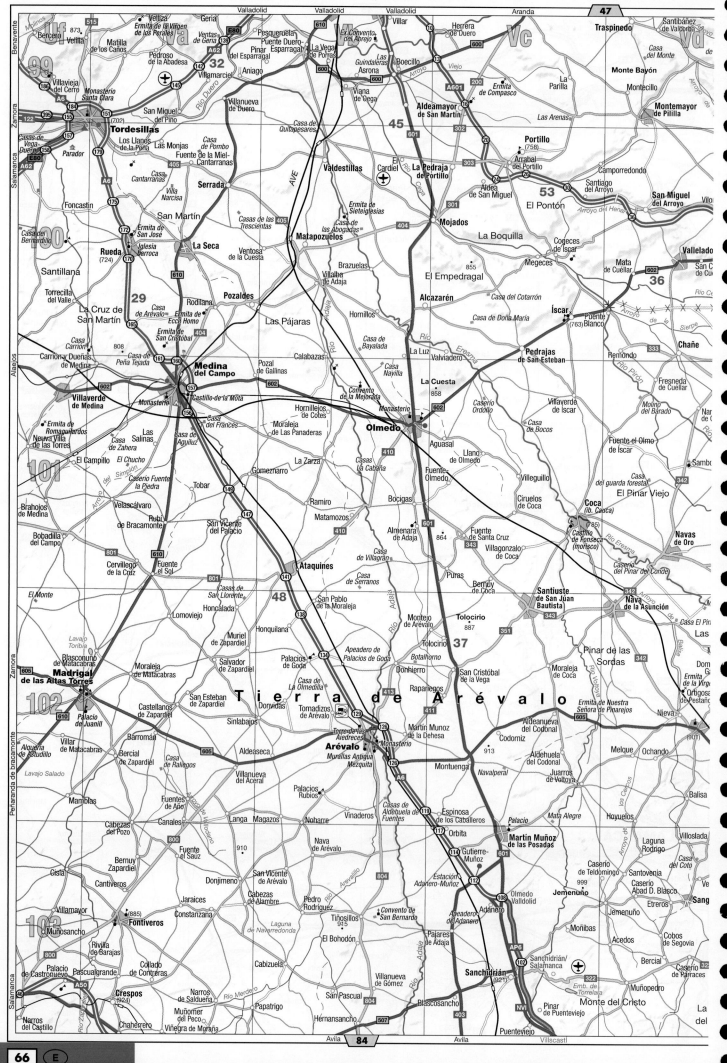

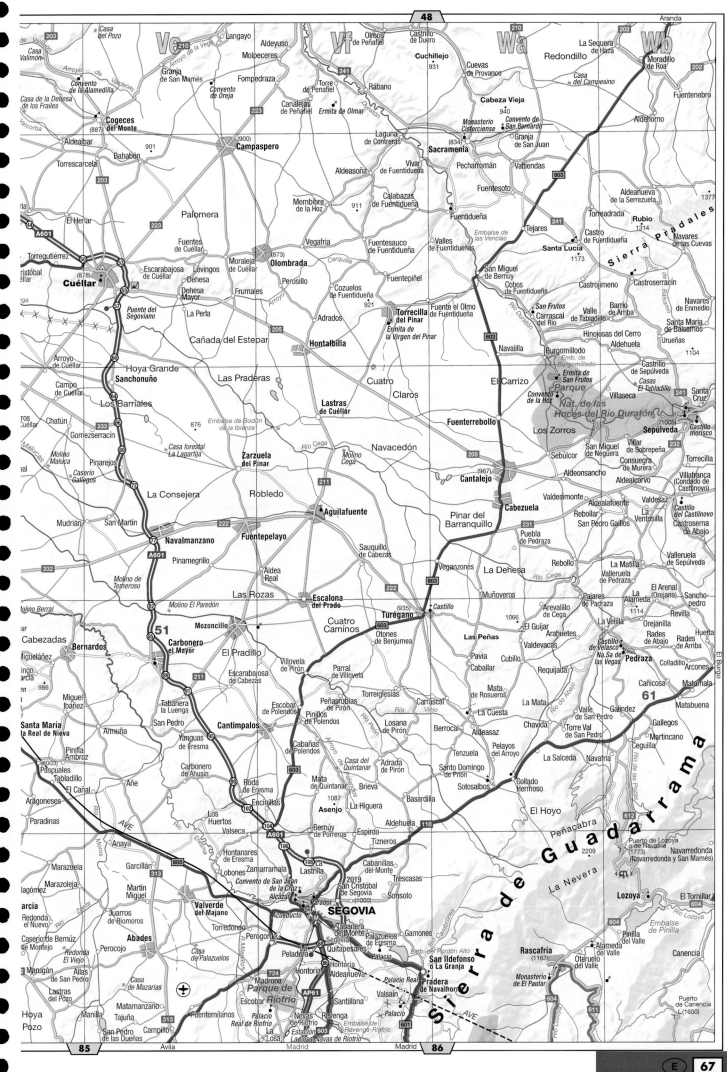

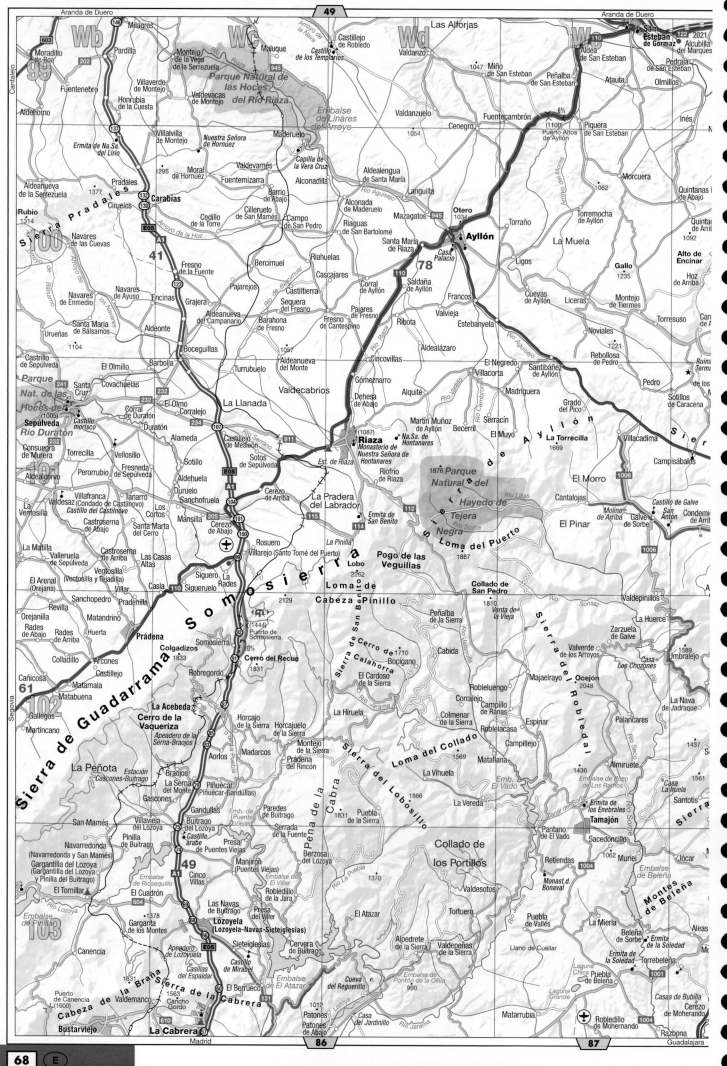

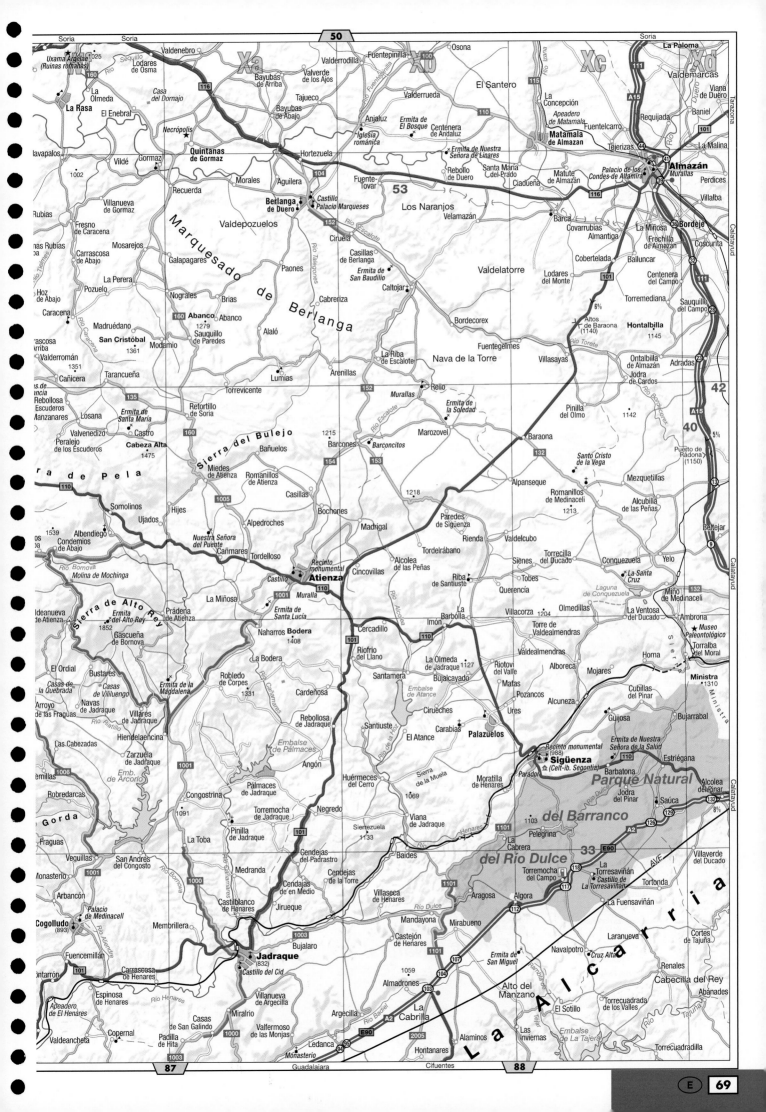

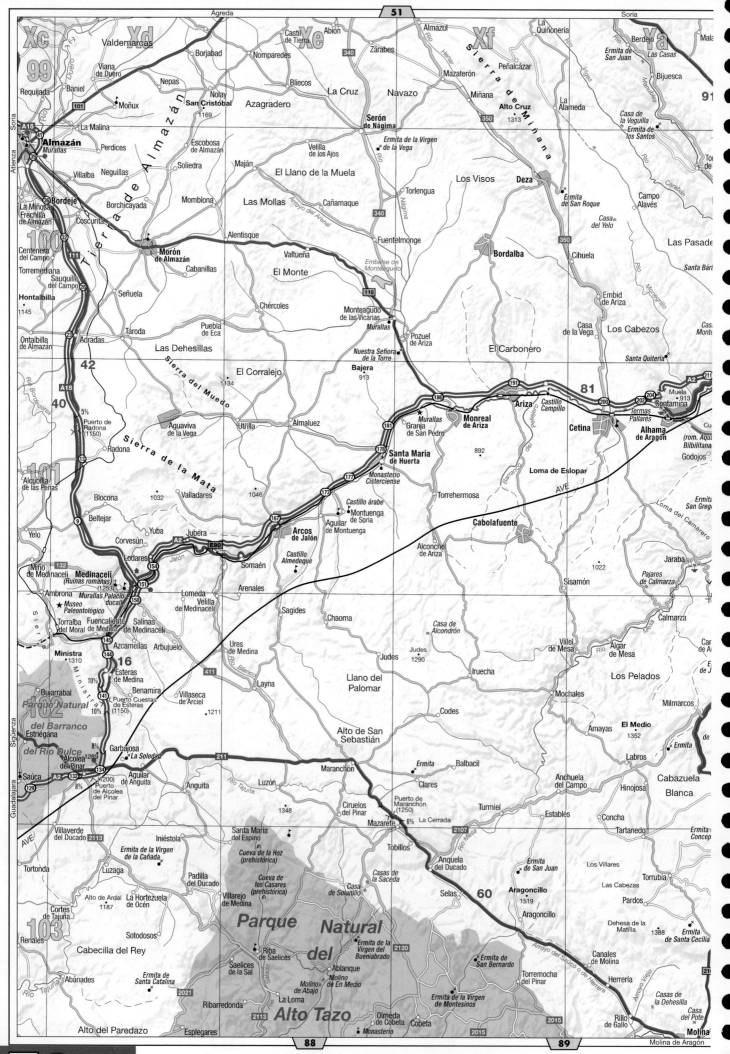

Soria

XC
Xd
Xe
Xf
Ya
99

Valdemarcas
Baniel
Viana
de Duero
Requijada
Moñux
San Cristóbal
1169
Nepas
Nolay
Azagradero
Borjabad
Nomparedes
Castil
de Tierra
Abión
Zárabes
Almazul
La Cruz
Navazo
La
Quiñonería
Berdejo
Ermita de
San Juan
Las Casas
Bijuesca
91

101
Mazaterón
Peñalcázar
Alto Cruz
1313
Miñana
La
Alameda
Casa de
la Veguilla
Ermita de
los Santos
Tor
de

A15
Soria
La Malina
Almazán
Murallas
Perdices
Escobosa
de Almazán
Velilla
de los Ajos
Ermita de la Virgen
de la Vega
Serón
de Nágima
350

Atienza

Bordeje
Villalba
Neguillas
Soliedra
Majá, El Llano de la Muela
Los Visos
Deza
Ermita
de San Roque
Campo
Alavés
La Miñosa
Frechilla
de Almazán
Coscurita
Borchicayada
Momblona
Las Mollas
Cañamaque
Torlengua
Casa
del Yelo
Las Pasade
100
Centenera
del Campo
Morón
de Almazán
Cabanillas
Valtueña
El Monte
Fuentelmonge
340
Bordalba
Cihuela
Santa Bár
Torremediana
Sauquillo
del Campo 28
Señuela
Embalse de
Monteagudo
116
350
Embid
de Ariza
Los Cabezos
Casa
Monte
Hontalbilla
1145
Chércoles
Puebla
de Eca
Monteagudo
de las Vicarías
Murallas
Pozuel
de Ariza
Casa
de la Vega
23
Adradas
Taroda
Las Dehesillas
El Carbonero
Santa Quiteria
42
Sierra del Muedo
El Corralejo
1134
Nuestra Señora
de la Torre
Bajera
913
A2
211
204
Muela
913
Contamina
40
A15
Puerto de
Radona
(1150)
5%
Aguaviva
de la Vega
Utrilla
Almaluez
186
191
81
200
202
Termas
Pallarés
Radona
13
Almácera
Santa María
de Huerta
Muela
Granja
de San Pedro
Ariza
Castillo
Campillo
Cetina
Alhama
de Aragón
101
Alcubilla
de las Peñas
Blocona
1032
Valladares
1046
181
Monreal
de Ariza
892
(rom. Aqua
Bilbilitana)
Godojos
9
Beltejar
Yuba
178
177
Monasterio
Cisterciense
Loma de Eslopar
AVE
Ermita
San Greg
Yelo
Corvesún
Jubera
173
Castillo árabe
Montuenga
de Soria
Torrehermosa
Loma del Camarero
132
Miño
de Medinaceli
Lodares
A2
E90
167
Arcos
de Jalón
Aguilar
de Montuenga
Cabolafuente
Jaraba
Medinaceli
(Ruinas romanas)
(1253)
154
151
Jalón
Somaén
Castillo
Almedeque
Alconchel
de Ariza
1022
Pajares
de Calmarza
Ambrona
Murallas Palacio
ducal
150
Lomeda
Velilla
de Medinaceli
Sisamón
Calmarza
Museo
Paleontológico
Arenales
Sagides
Villel
de Mesa
Algar
de Mesa
Torralba
Fuencaliente
del Moral de Medina
Salinas
de Medinaceli
Chaorna
Casa de
Alcondrón
Los Pelados
Ministra
1310
145
Azcamellas
Arbujuelo
Ures
de Medina
Judes
1290
Iruecha
Mochales
Car
de J
16
144
Esteras
de Medina
10%
411
Río Blanco
Llano del
Palomar
El Medio
1352
Bujarrabal
Benamira
10%
Villaseca
de Arciel
Layna
Codes
Amayas
Ermita
Parque Natural
102
Puerto Cuestas
de Esteras
(1150)
1211
Alto de San
Sebastián
Milmarcos
Estriégana
del Barranco
Garbajosa
8%
La Soledad
211
Maranchón
Ermita
Balbacil
Labros
Cabazuela
Blanca
del Río Dulce
Alcolea
del Pinar
1289
134
Aguilar
de Anguita
Anguita
Luzón
Clares
Anchuela
del Campo
Hinojosa
Saúca
A2
132
129
8%
Puerto
de Alcolea
del Pinar
(4200)
1348
Ciruelos
del Pinar
Puerto de
Maranchón
(1250)
Turmiel
Establés
Concha
Tartanedo
Ermita
Concep
AVE
Villaverde
del Ducado
2113
Iniéstola
Santa María
del Espino
Mazarete
6%
La Cerrada
2107
Tortonda
Luzaga
Ermita de la Virgen
de la Cañada
Cueva de la Hoz
(prehistórica)
Tobillos
Anquela
del Ducado
Ermita
de San Juan
Los Villares
Torrubia
Las Cabezas
103
Alto de Ardal
1187
Padilla
del Ducado
Casas
de la
Saceda
Ermita
de Santa Cecilia
Renales
Cortes
de Tajuña
La Hortezuela
de Océn
Villarejo
de Medina
Cueva de
los Casares
(prehistórica)
Casa
de Solanillo
Selas
60
Aragoncillo
1519
Dehesa de la
Matilla
1388
Cabecilla del Rey
Sotodosos
Parque Natural del
Ermita de la
Virgen del
Bueniabrado
2120
Aragoncillo
Canales
de Molina
Riba
de Saelices
Ermita de
San Bernardo
Herrería
Abánades
Ermita
de Santa Catalina
Saelices
de la Sal
Alto Tazo
2021
Molino
de En Medio
Ablanque
Torremocha
del Pinar
Ermita de la Virgen
de Montesinos
21
Casas
de la
Dehesilla
Alto del Paredazo
Esplegares
Ribarredonda
2113
Molino
de Abajo
La Loma
Olmeda
de Cobeta
Cobeta
Monasterio
2015
2015
Rillo
de Gallo
Casa
del Pote
Molina

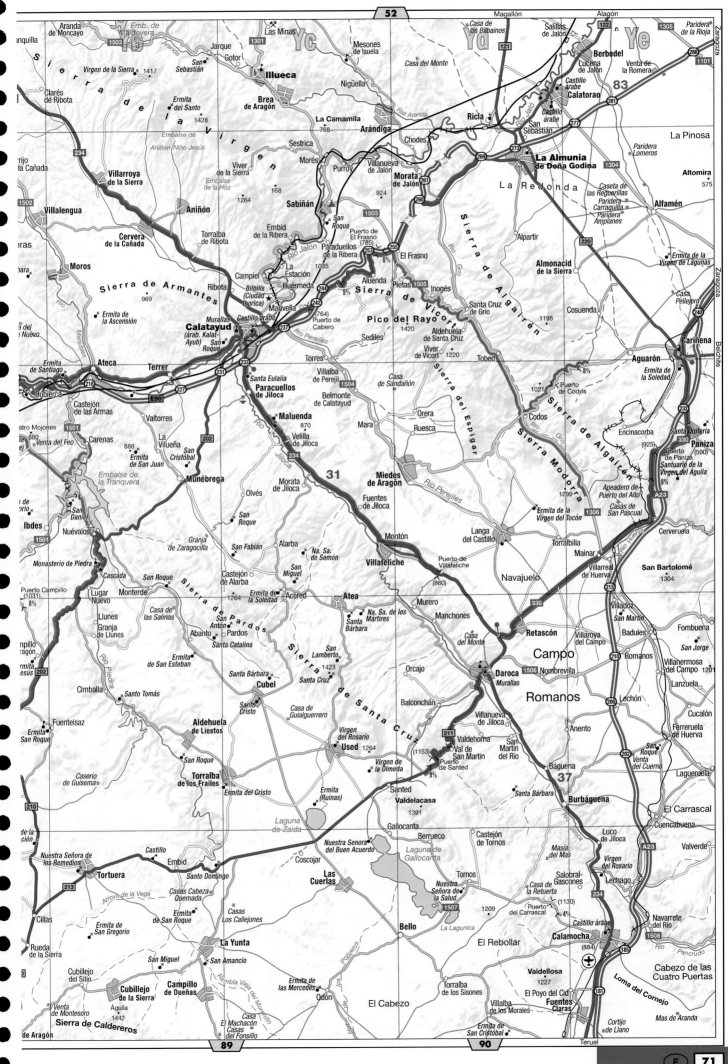

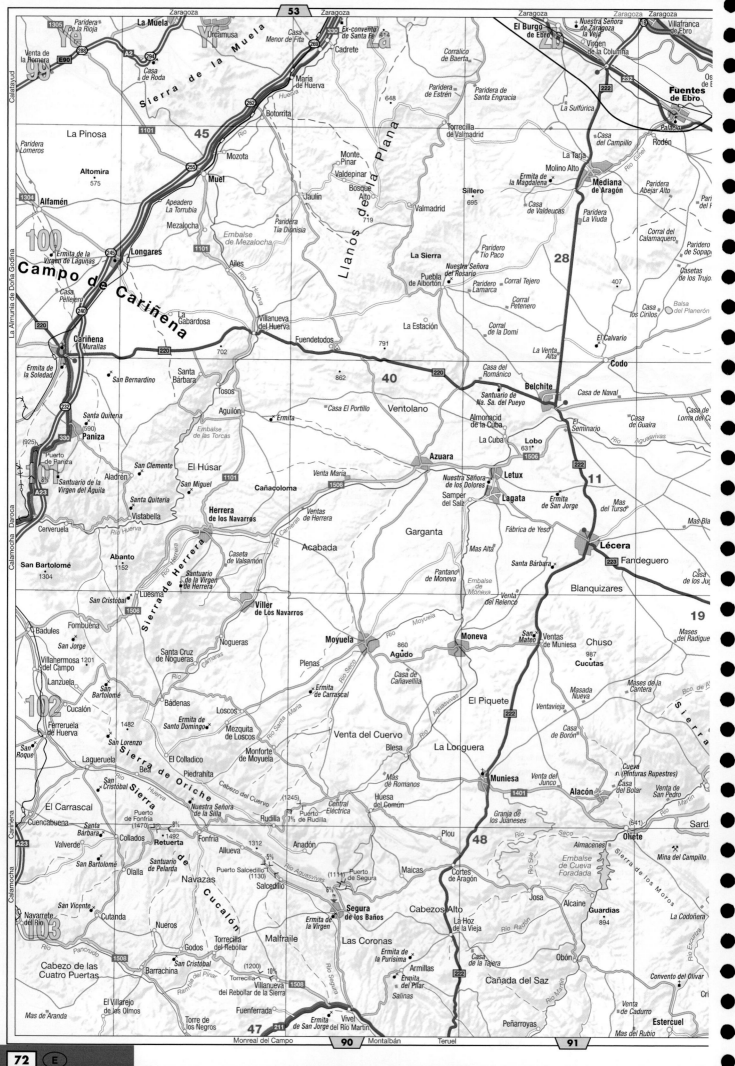

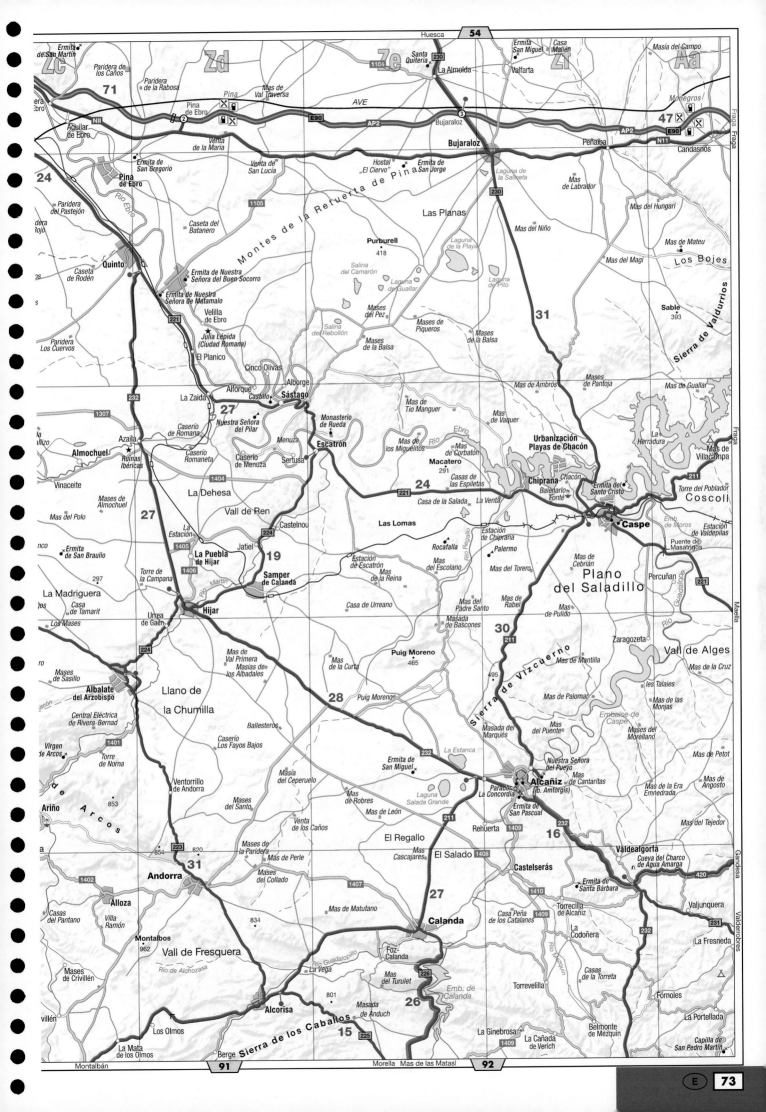

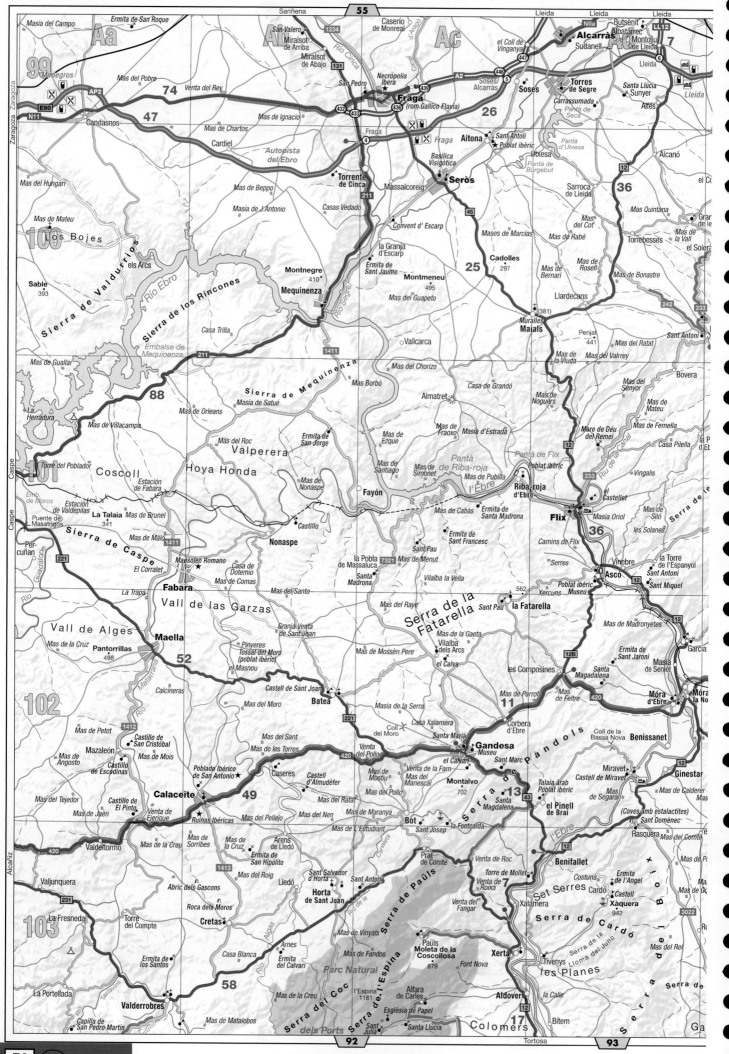

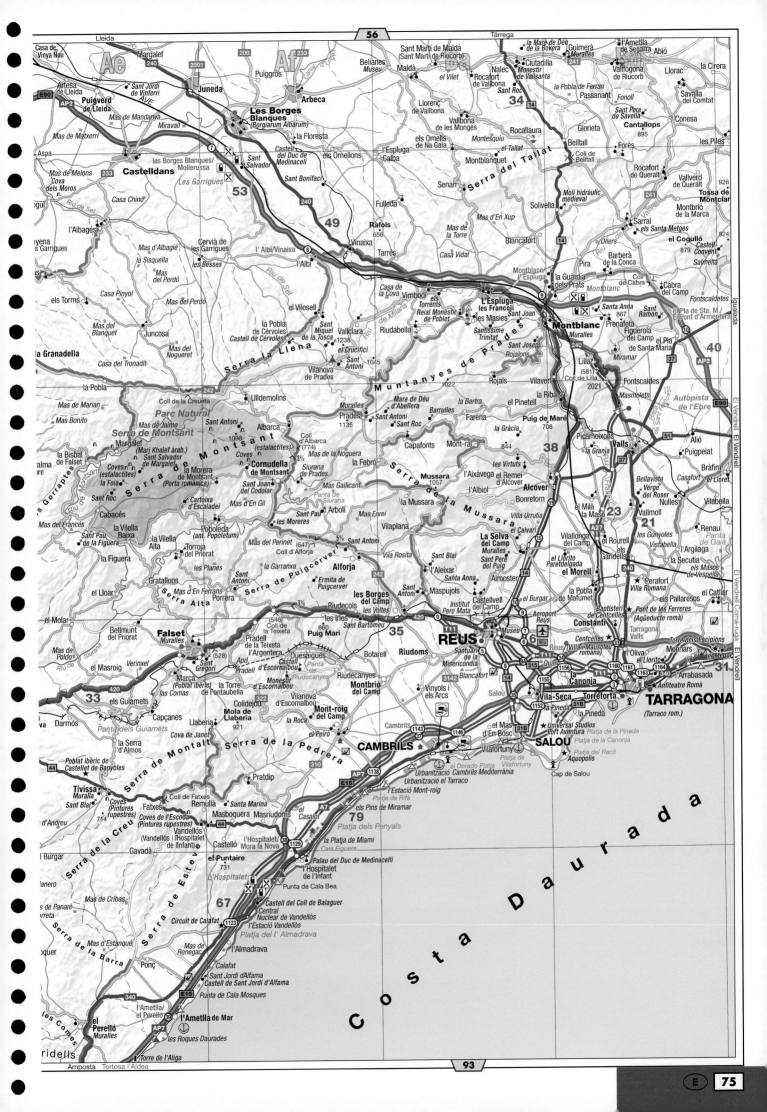

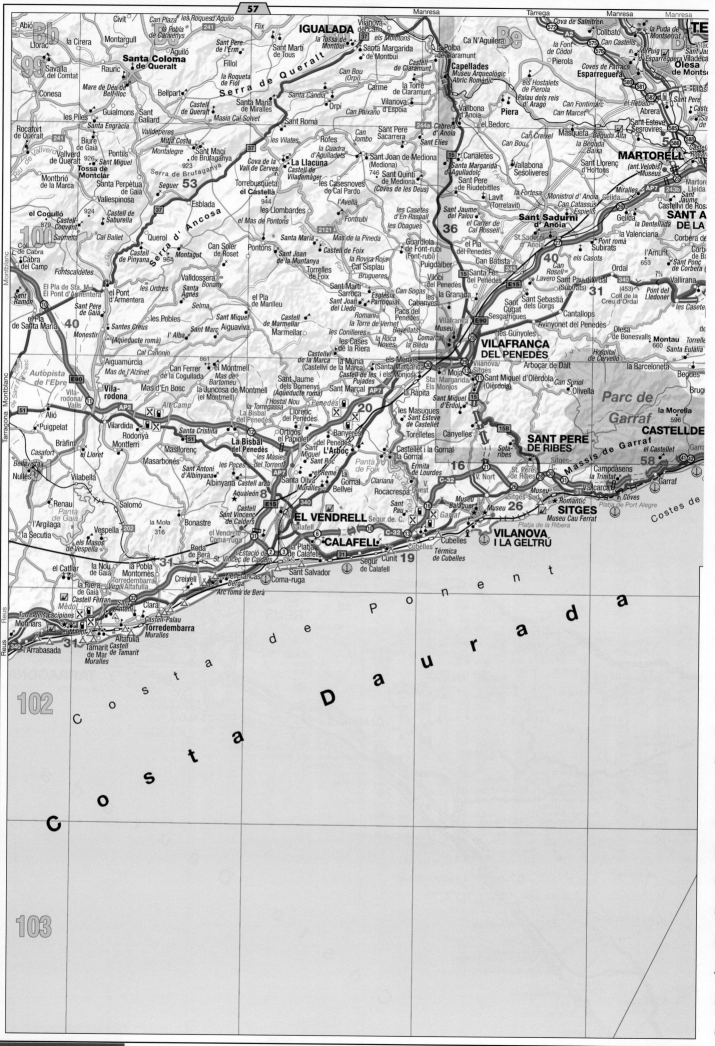

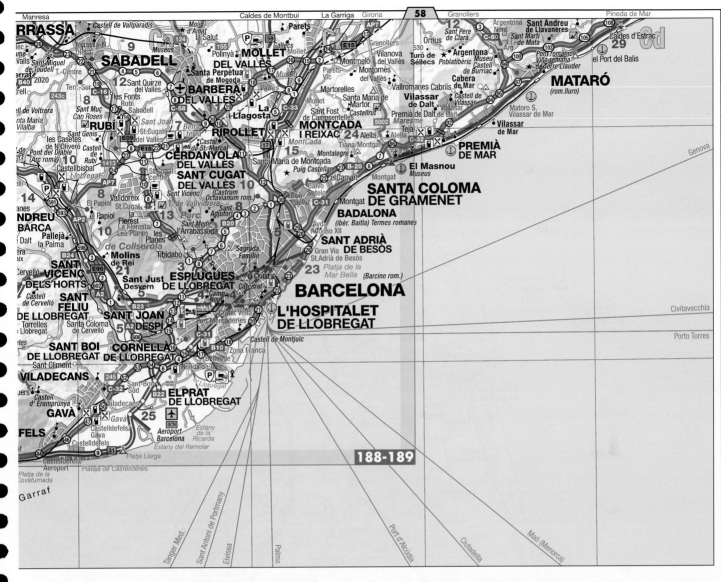

188-189

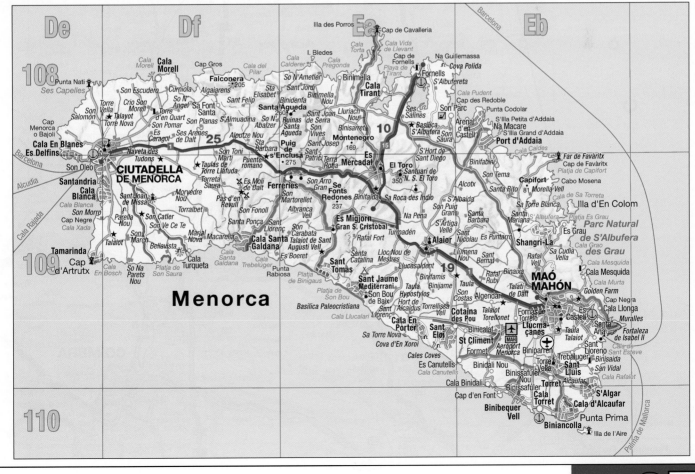

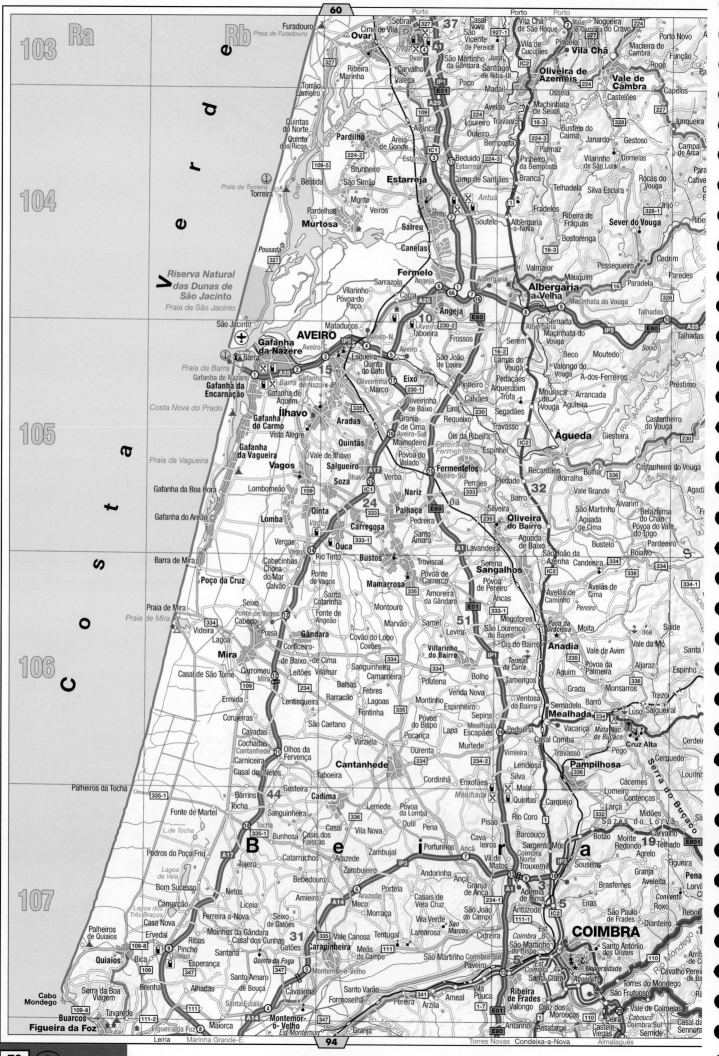

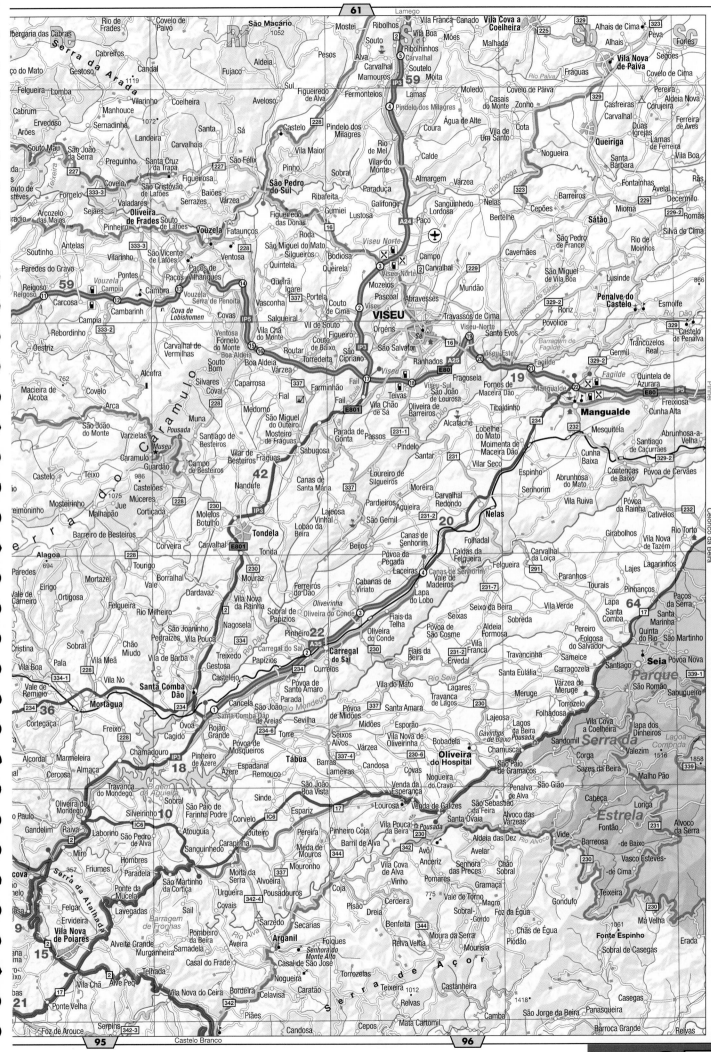

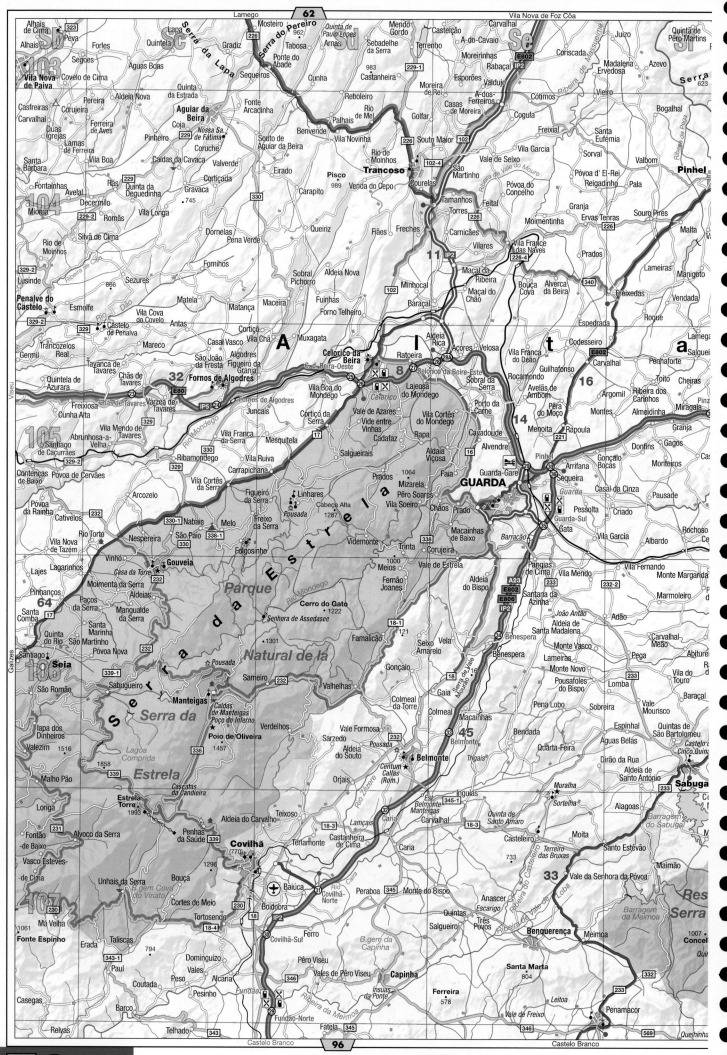

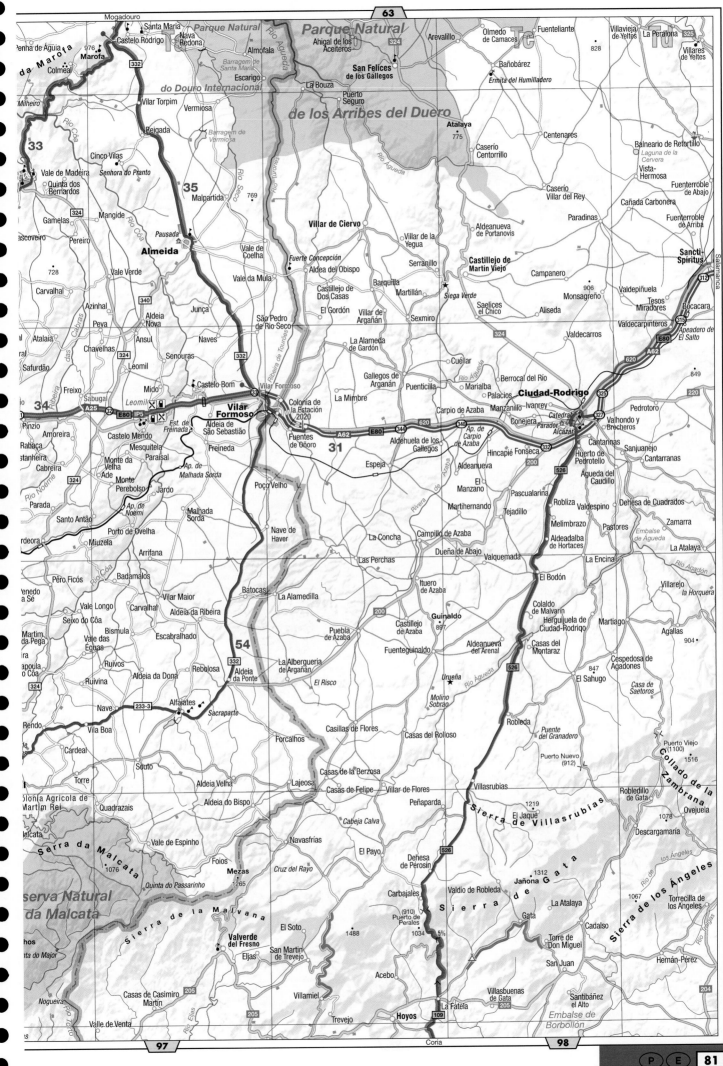

Mogadouro
Santa Maria
Penha de Águia
976
Castelo Rodrigo
Marofa
Colmeal
da Marofa
332
Milheiro
33
Vale de Madeira
Quinta dos
Bernardos
Mascoveiro
324
Gamelas
Mangide
Pereiro
728
Vale Verde
Carvalhal
Azinhal
340
Peva
Aldeia
Nova
Ansul
Atalaia
Chavelhas
324
Naves
Safurdão
Leomil
Senouras
Freixo
34
Mido
Castelo Bom
A25
Sabugal
E80
Leomilho
IP5
Pinzio
32
Amoreira
Castelo Mendo
Rabaça
Mesquitela
anheira
Monte da
Paraisal
Cabreira
Velha
324
Ade
Monte
Perebolso
Jardo
Parada
Ap. de
Noemi
Pêro Ficós
Santo Antão
Porto de Ovelha
enedo
a Sé
Miuzela
rdeora
Vale Longo
Seixo do Côa
Bismula
324
Martim
da Pega
Vale das
Éguas
apoula
o Côa
Ruivos
Ruivina
Rendo
Nave
233-3
Vila Boa
Cárdeal
Souto
Torre
olónia Agricola de
Martim Rei
Quadrazais
malcata
Serra da Malcata
1076
serva Natural
da Malcata
Nogueira
ta do Major

Parque Natural
Nava
Redona
Almofala
332
Escarigo
do Douro Internacional
Vilar Torpim
Vermiosa
Reigada
Rio Côa
35
Malpartida
769
Pausada
Almeida
Vale de
Coelha
Vale da Mula
Junça
São Pedro
de Rio Seco
332
Castelo Bom
Vilar Formoso
33
Vilar
Formoso
Aldeia de
São Sebastião
Est. de
Freinada
Freineda
Ap. de
Malhada Sorda
Malhada
Sorda
Poço Velho
Nave de
Haver
Batocas
La Alamedilla
Vilar Maior
Carvalhal
Aldeia da Ribeira
Escabralhado
54
Rebolosa
Aldeia da Dona
332
Aldeia
da Ponte
Alfaiates
Sacraparte
La Albergueria
de Argañán
El Risco
Casillas de Flores
Forcalhos
Aldeia Velha
Casas de la Berzosa
Lajeosa
Aldeia do Bispo
Casas de Felipe
Casas de Casimiro
Martín
205
El Soto
Foios
Mezas
1265
Quinta do Passarinho
Sierra de la Malvana
Cruz del Rayo
Navasfrías
Valverde
del Fresno
San Martín
de Trevejo
Eljas
205
Villamiel
Treviejo
Valle de Venta

Parque Natural
Ahigal de los
Aceiteros
324
San Felices
de los Gallegos
La Bouza
Puerto
Seguro
de los Arribes del Duero
Atalaya
775
Río Agueda
Villar de Ciervo
Villar de la
Yegua
Fuerte Concepción
Aldea del Obispo
Castillejo de
Dos Casas
Barquilla
Villar de
Argañán
El Gordón
Sexmiro
La Alameda
de Gardón
Ribera de Tourões
Colonia de
la Estación
2020
31
Fuentes
de Oñoro
A62
E80
344
620
Espeja
Aldehuela de los
Gallegos
Aldeanueva
El
Manzano
Campillo de Azaba
La Concha
Dueña de Abajo
Las Perchas
Valquemada
200
Ituero
de Azaba
Guinaldo
897
Castillejo
de Azaba
Puebla
de Azaba
Fuenteguinaldo
Aldeanueva
del Arenal
Uruéña
Molino
Sobrao
Robleda
526
Puente
del Granadero
Casas del Rolloso
Casas del
Montaraz
El Sahugo
847
Villar de Flores
Villasrubias
Puerto Nuevo
(912)
Peñaparda
Cabeja Calva
El Jaque
1219
Sierra de Villasrubias
El Payo
526
Dehesa
de Perosín
Jañona
1312
Sierra de Gata
Carbajales
Valdío de Robleda
La Atalaya
(910)
Puerto de
Perales
1034
5%
1488
Gata
Acebo
Villasbuenas
de Gata
205
Hoyos
109
La Fatela
Coria

Arevalillo
Olmedo
de Camaces
Fuenteliante
Villavieja
de Yeltes
La Peralona
325
828
Villares
de Yeltes
Ermita del Humilladero
Balneario de Retortillo
Laguna de la
Cervera
Centenares
Bañobárez
Caserío
Centorrillo
Vista-
Hermosa
Caserío
Villar del Rey
Fuenterroble
de Abajo
Cañada Carbonera
Paradinas
Fuenterroble
de Arriba
Sancti-
Spiritus
Aldeanueva
de Portanovis
Serranillo
Castillejo de
Martín Viejo
Martillán
Siega Verde
Campanero
906
Monsagreño
Valdepiñuela
Tesos
Miradores
Bocacara
Saelices
el Chico
Aliseda
Valdecarpinteros
312
315
E80
Apeadero de
El Salto
620
A62
849
Valdecarros
324
Cuéllar
Río Agueda
Gallegos de
Argañán
Puenticilla
Berrocal del Río
Palacios
Marialba
220
La Mimbre
Ciudad-Rodrigo
Pedrotoro
Manzanillo
Ivanrey
325
Carpio de Azaba
Conejera
Catedral
327
Valhondo y
Brocheros
344
340
Ap. de
Carpio
de Azaba
Parador
Alcázar
Cantarinas
Sanjuanejo
Hincapié Fonseca
332
200
Huerto de
Pedrotello
Cantarranas
526
Águeda del
Caudillo
Pascualarina
Martihernando
Tejadillo
Robliza
Valdespino
Dehesa de Cuadrados
Melimbrazo
Pastores
Zamarra
Aldeadalba
de Hortaces
La Atalaya
El Bodón
La Encina
Río Agadón
Colaldo
de Malvarín
Villarejo
la Horquera
Herguijuela de
Ciudad-Rodrigo
Martiago
Agallas
904
Cespedosa de
Agadones
Casa de
Saetoros
Puerto Viejo
(1100)
1516
Collado de la Zambrana
Robledillo
de Gata
1078
Ovejuela
Descargamaría
1067
Torrecilla de
los Angeles
Sierra de los Angeles
Río de
Torre de
Don Miguel
San Juan
Cadalso
Hernán-Pérez
Santibáñez
el Alto
204
Embalse de
Borbollón
los Angeles

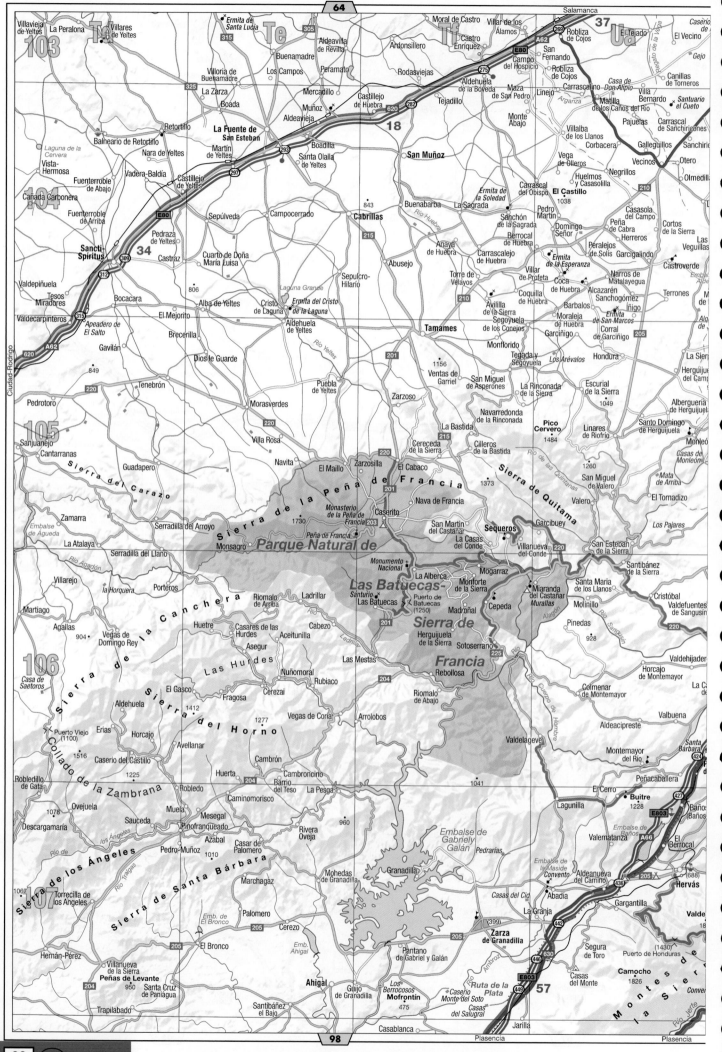

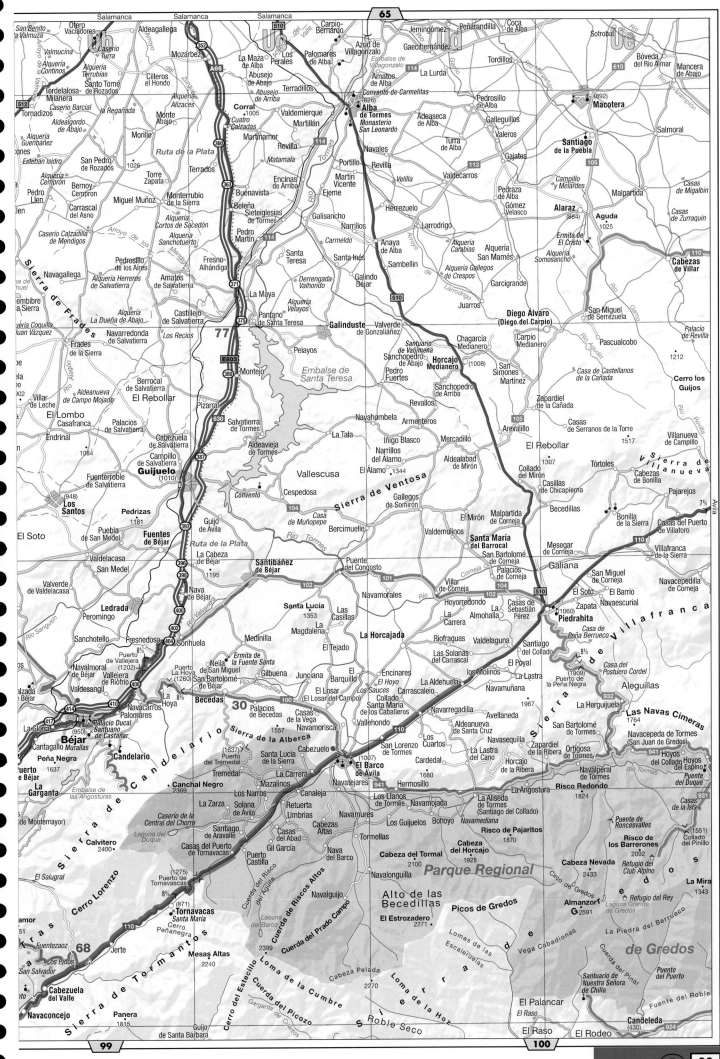

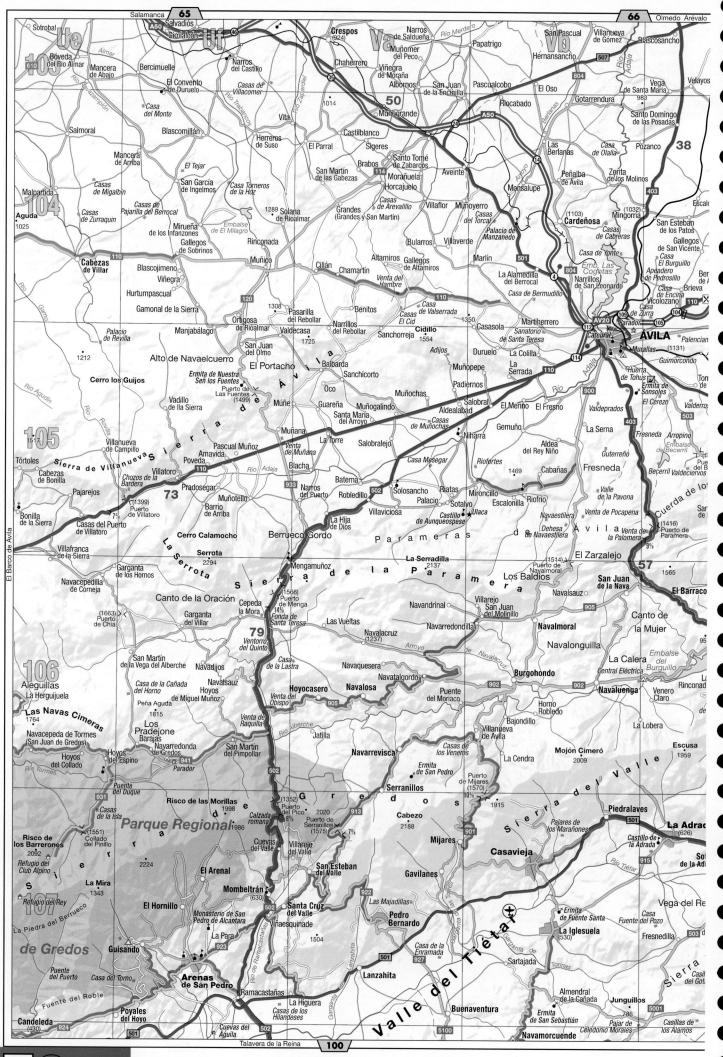

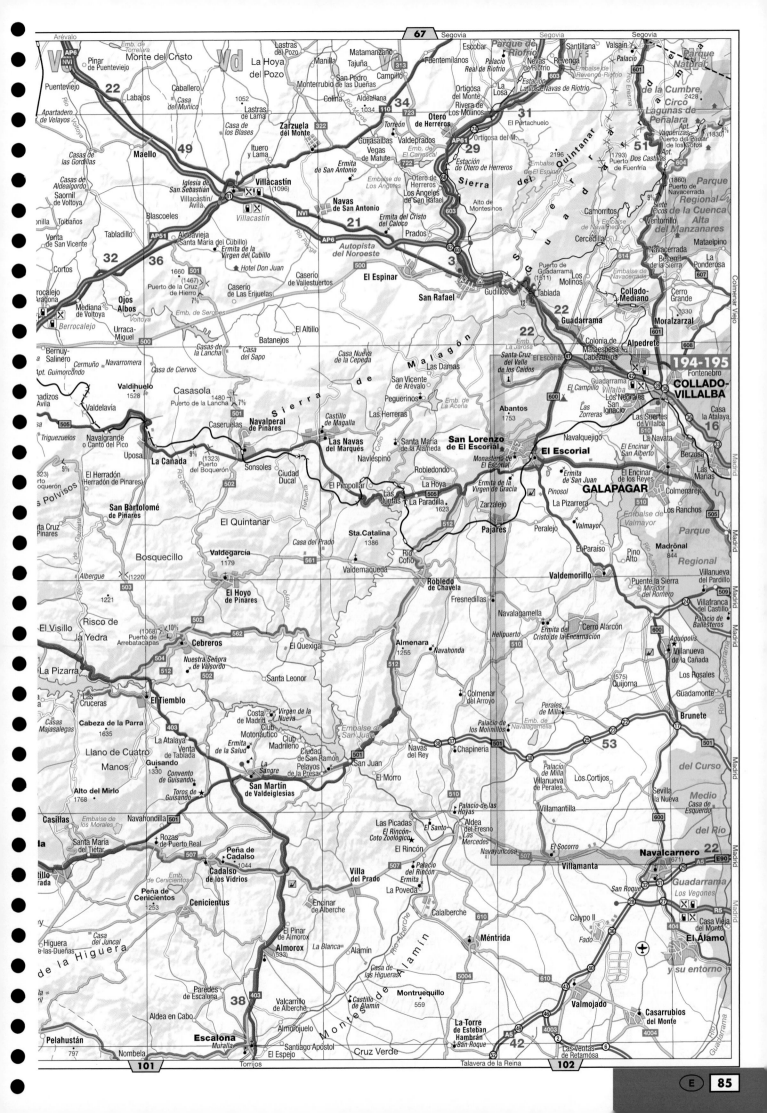

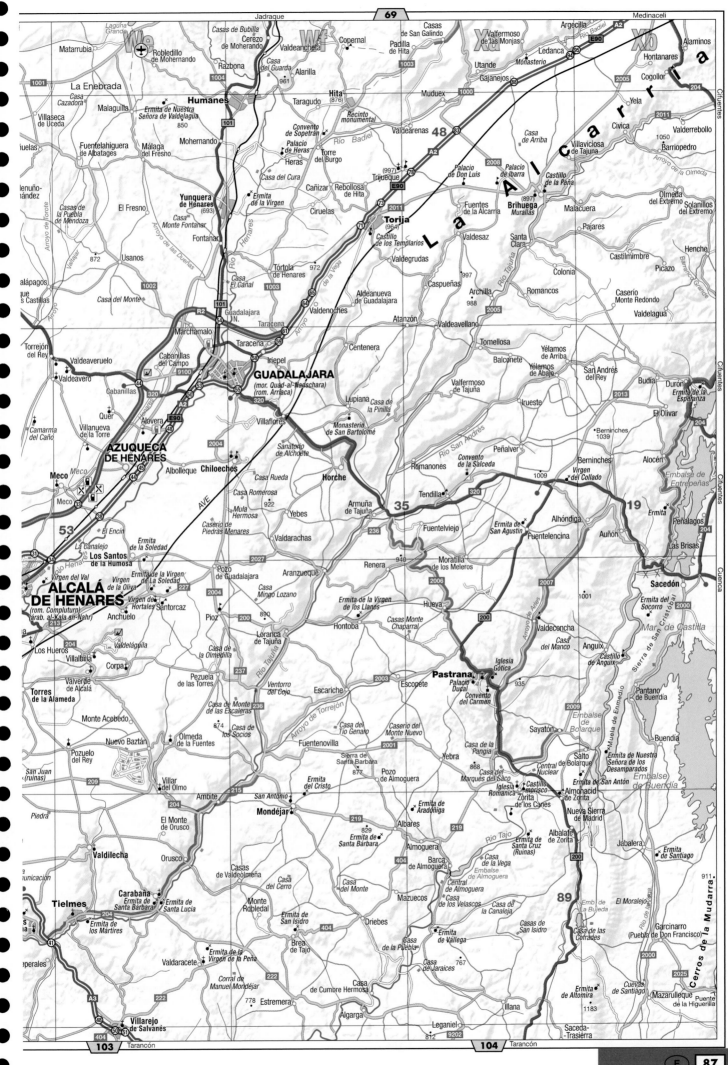

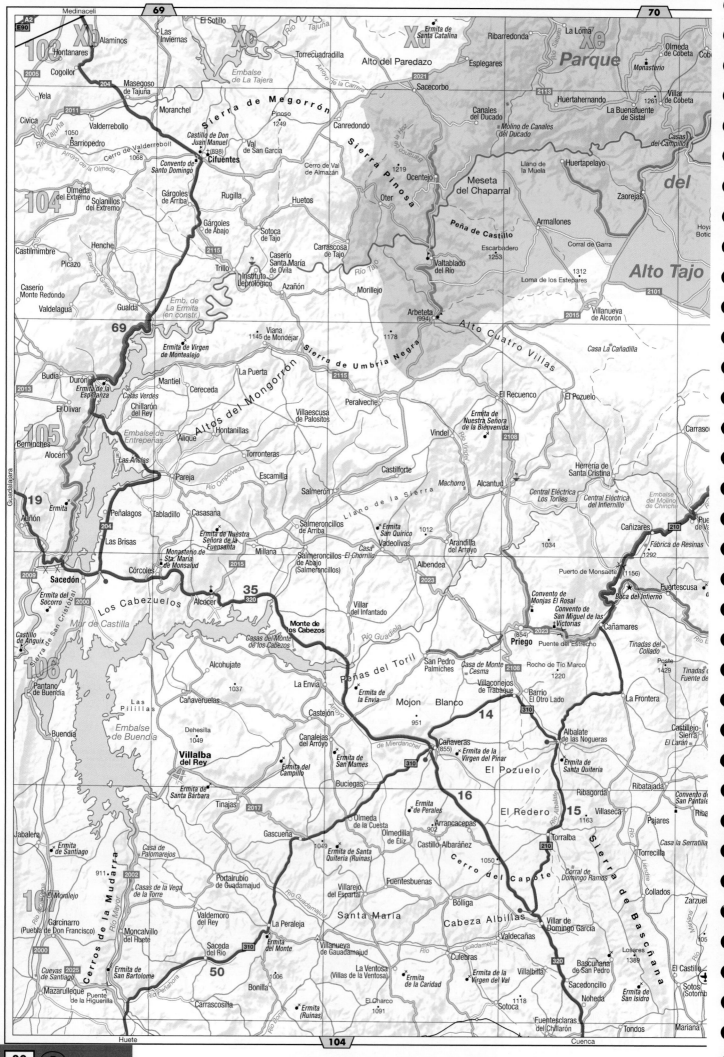

Medinaceli

A2
E90

Xb

103

Hontanares

2005 Cogollor

Yela

2011

Civica

Valderrebollo

Barriopedro

1050

Castilmimbre

Picazo

Caserío
Monte Redondo

Valdelagua

Alaminos

204 Masegoso
de Tajuña

Moranchel

Castillo de Don
Juan Manuel
(898)

Convento de
Santo Domingo

Gárgoles
de Arriba

Gárgoles
de Abajo

Henche

Cifuentes

Rugilla

Sotoca
de Tajo

Trillo

Gualda

El Sotillo

Las Invernas

Torrecuadradilla

Pinoso
1249

Val
de San García

Cerro de Val
de Almazán

Huetos

Caserío
Santa María
de Ovila

Instituto
Leprológico

Azañón

Río Tajuña

Embalse
de La Tajera

Alto del Paredazo

2021

Canredondo

Río Tajo

Carrascosa
de Tajo

Morillejo

Ermita de
Santa Catalina

Sierra de Megorrón

Cerro de Valderreboll
1068

Olmeda
del Extremo

Solanillos
del Extremo

2115

Ribarredonda

Sacecorbo

2113

Esplegares

Canales
del Ducado

Molino de Canales
del Ducado

1219

Ocentejo

Oter

Meseta
del Chaparral

Valtablado
del Río

Escarbadero
1253

La Loma

Xe

Parque

1261

Huertahernando

La Buenafuente
de Sistal

Huertapelayo

Zaorejas

Monasterio

Olmeda
de Cobeta

Villar
de Cobeta

Casas
del Campillo

del

Hoya
Boti

Peña de Castillo

Armallones

Corral de Garra

Alto Tajo

Sierra Pinosa

Arbeteta
(994)

Alto Cuatro Villas

1178

1312

2101

Emb. de
La Ermita
(en constr.)

69

Budia

2013

El Olivar

Berninches

105

Alocén

19

Ermita

Auñón

Duron

Ermita de la
Esperanza

Viana
de Mondéjar
1145

Ermita de Virgen
de Montealejo

Chillarón
del Rey

Calas Verdes

Las Anclas

Embalse de
Entrepeñas

Mantiel

La Puerta

Cereceda

Hontanillas

Alique

Altos del Mongorrón

Torronteras

Peralveche

Villaescusa
de Palositos

Sierra de Umbría Negra

2115

Vindel

Ermita de
Nuestra Señora
de la Bienvenida

Río Vindel

El Recuenco

El Pozuelo

2108

Casa La Cañadilla

Villanueva
de Alcorón

2015

Carrasco

Herrería de
Santa Cristina

Central Eléctrica
del Infiernillo

Embalse
del Molino
de Chincha

204

Peñalagos

Tabladillo

Casasaña

Pareja

Río Ompólveda

Escamilla

Salmerón

Llano de la Sierra

Castilforte

Machorro

Alcantud

Central Eléctrica
Los Toriles

2108

210

Cañizares

Fábrica de Resinas
1292

Pue
de Va

Las Brisas

Ermita de Nuestra
Señora de la
Fuensanta

Millana

Salmeroncillos
de Arriba

Ermita
San Quirico

Vadeolivas

1012

Arandilla
del Arroyo

1034

Puerto de Monsaéte (1156)

Córcoles

Monasterio de
Sta. María
de Monsalud

2015

Salmeroncillos
de Abajo
(Salmeroncillos)

Casa
El Chorrillo

Albendea

2023

Convento de
Monjas El Rosal

Boca del Infierno

Fuertescusa

Convento de
San Miguel de las
Victorias

Cañamares

2009

Sacedón

Ermita del
Socorro

2000

Los Cabezuelos

Mar de Castilla

Alcocer

35

320

Villar
del Infantado

(854)

2023

Priego

Puente del Estrecho

Tinadas del
Collado

Poste
1429

Tinadas d
Fuente de

Castillo
de Anguix

Sierra de San Cristóbal

106

Pantano
de Buendía

Monte de
los Cabezos

Casas del Monte
de los Cabezos

Río Guadiela

Peñas del Toril

San Pedro
Palmiches

Casa de Monte
Cesma

2108

Rocho de Tío Marco
1220

Villaconejos
de Trabaque

Barrio
El Otro Lado

310

La Frontera

Castillejo-
Sierra
El Larán

Alcohujate

1037

La Envía

Mojon

Blanco

951

14

Cañaveruelas

Castejón

Ermita de
la Envía

Ermita de la
Virgen del Pinar

Albalate
de las Nogueras

Ermita de
Santa Quiteria

Ribatajada

Convento
San Pantale

Ri

Buendía

Embalse
de Buendía

Dehesilla
1049

Las
Pilillas

Canalejas
del Arroyo

de Mierdanchel

Cañaveras
(855)

El Pozuelo

Río Albalate

Ribagorda

Villalba
del Rey

Ermita del
Campillo

Ermita de
San Mames

Buciegas

310

16

El Redero

15

Villaseca

Pajares

Ri

Jabalera

Ermita de
Santa Bárbara

Tinajas

2017

Olmeda
de la Cuesta

Ermita
de Perales

Arrancacepas

902

Olmedilla
de Éliz

Castillo-Albaráñez

1163

Torralba

210

Casa la Serratilla

Torrecilla

Sierra de Bascuñana

Ermita
de Santiago

Casa de
Palomarejos

Gascueña

1049

Ermita de Santa
Quiteria (Ruinas)

Villarejo
del Espartal

Fuentesbuenas

1050

Cerro del Capote

Corral de
Domingo Ramos

Collados

Zarzuel

911

2002

Casas de la Vega
de la Torre

Portalrubio
de Guadamajud

Santa María

Bólliga

Cabeza Albillas

Villar de
Domingo García

105

107

El Moralejo

Garcinarro
(Puebla de Don Francisco)

Moncalvillo
del Huete

Valdemoro
del Rey

Río Guadamajud

La Peraleja

Villanueva
de Gauadamajud

Valdecañas

Villalbilla

1118

320

Bascuñana
de San Pedro

Losares
1389

El Castillo

2000

Cuevas
de Santiago

2025

Mazarulleque

Puente
de la Higuerilla

Ermita de
San Bartolome

Saceda
del Río

310

50

Ermita
del Monte

Bonilla

1006

La Ventosa
(Villas de la Ventosa)

El Charco
1091

Ermita de la
Caridad

Ermita de la
Virgen del Val

Culebras

Sotoca

Sacedoncillo

Noheda

Ermita de
San Isidro

Ermita
(Ruinas)

Carrascosilla

Huete

Río Mayor

Cerros de la Mudarra

Río Peñahora

Río Bonilla

Fuentesclaras
del Chillarón

Cuenca

Tondos

Mariana

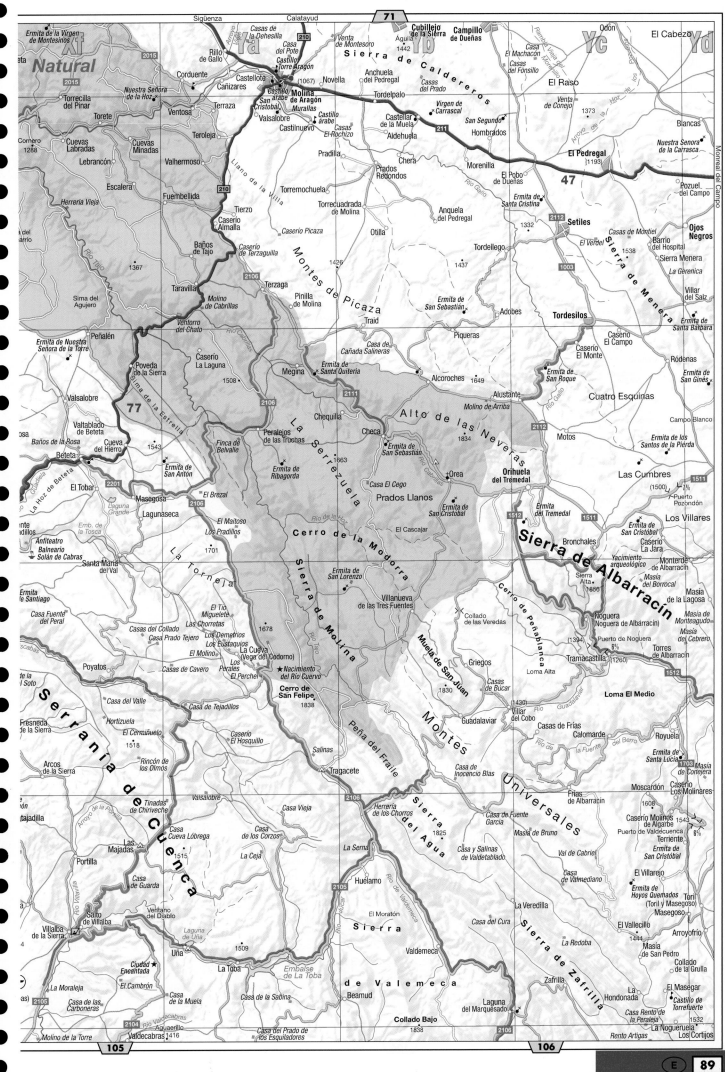

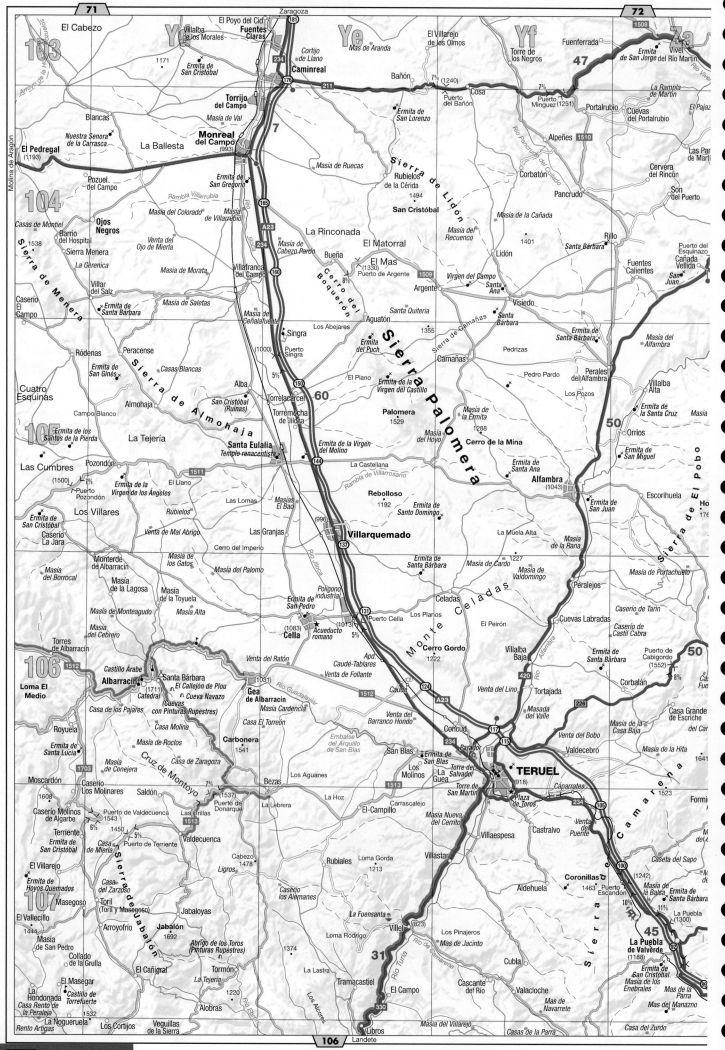

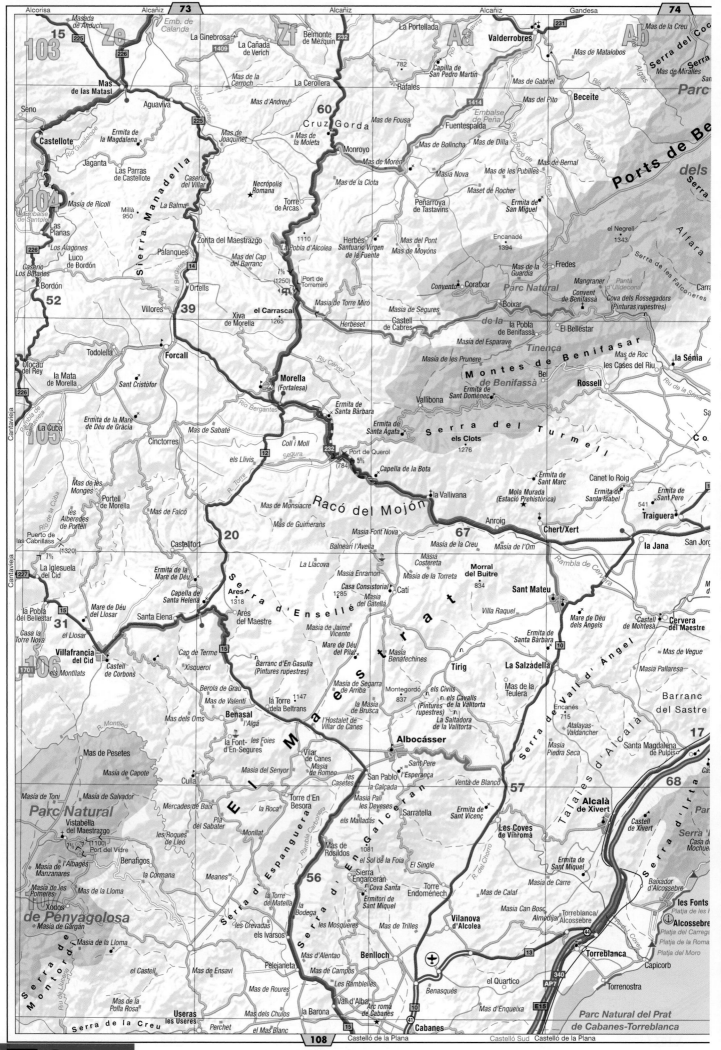

Alcorisa　Alcañiz　Alcañiz　Alcañiz　Gandesa

15
103
225
226

Ze
ZI
Aa
A0

Masada de Anduch
Mas de las Matas
226

Emb. de Calanda
La Ginebrosa
1409
La Cañada de Verich
Belmonte de Mezquin
232
La Portellada
231
Valderrobres
Mas de la Creu

Serra del Coc
Serra de Miralles

Parc

Seno
Aguaviva
225
Mas de la Cerroch
La Cerollera
782
Capilla de San Pedro Martín
Ráfales
Mas de Gabriel
Beceite

Castellote
Rio Guadalope
Jaganta
Ermita de la Magdalena
Mas de Joaquinet
60
Cruz Gorda
Monroyo
Mas de Fousa
Fuentespalda
Mas del Pito
Mas de Bolincha
Mas de Dilla

1414
Embalse de Peña
Mas del Pito

Ports de Be
dels

104
Masía de Ricoll
Las Parras de Castellote
Millà 950
Caserío del Villar
La Balma
Mas de la Moleta
Mas de Morén
Mas de la Clota
Masía Nova
Peñarroya de Tastavins
Mas de les Pubilles
Mas de Bernal
Maset de Rocher
Ermita de San Miguel
el Negrell 1343

Embalse del Santole
Las Planas
52
226
Los Alagones
Luco de Bordón
Caserío Los Bañares
Bordón
Palanques
Zorita del Maestrazgo
Mas del Cap del Barranc
14
Ortells
1110
La Pobla d'Alcolea
Herbés
Santuario Virgen de la Fuente
Mas del Pont
Mas de Moyóns
Encanadé 1394
Mas de la Guardia
Fredes
Convento
Coratxar
Convent de Benifassà
Serra de les Falconeres
Cova dels Rossegadors (Pinturas rupestres)
Carra

Alfara

Olocau del Rey
la Mata de Morella
226
Todolella
39
Villores
Xiva de Morella 1265
el Carrascal
Masía de Torre Miró
Herbeset
Masía de Segures
Castell de Cabres
Masía del Esparave
la Pobla de Benifassà
El Bellestar

7% (1250)
Port de Torremiró

Parc Natural
de la
Tinença
Montes de Benifasar
Serra de les Falconeres
les Cases del Riu
la Sénia

Cantavieja
Forcall
Sant Cristòfor
Morella (Fortalesa)
Rio Bergantes
Ermita de Santa Bàrbara
Ermita de Santa Agata
Masía de les Prunere
Montes de Benifassà
Ermita de Sant Domènec
Vallibona
Serra del Turmell
els Clots 1276
Mas de Roc
Rossell

Cantavieja
La Cuba
105
Ermita de la Mare de Déu de Gràcia
Cinctorres
Mas de Sabaté
Coll i Moll
12
els Llivis
Segura
R. Torre
Port de Querol
232
(784)
5%
Capella de la Bota
la Vallivana
Ermita de Sant Marc
Mola Murada (Estació Prehistòrica)
Ermita de Santa Isabel
Canet lo Roig
541
Ermita de Sant Pere
Traiguera

Mas de les Monges
Portell de Morella
Mas de Falcó
20
Castellfort
Mas de Monsiacre
Mas de Guimeráns
Racó del Mojón
Anroig
Chert/Xert
la Jana
San Jorg

Puerto de las Cabrillass (1320)
7% (1320)
La Iglesuela del Cid
227
la Pobla del Bellestar
31
el Llosar
Casa la Torre Nova
Villafranca del Cid
15
170
106
els Montllats
Castell de Corbons
Mare de Déu del Llosar
Santa Elena
Ermita de la Mare de Déu
Capella de Santa Helena
Ares 1318
Serra d'Ensellé
Arès del Maestre
15
Cap de Terme
Xisquerol
Barranc d'En Gasulla (Pintures rupestres)
La Llacova
Masía Enramon
Casa Consistorial 1285
Masía del Gatellà
Catí
Masía del Pilar
Mare de Déu del Pilar
Masía de Jaime Vicente
Masía Costereta
Masía de la Torreta
Morral del Buitre 834
Villa Raquel
Sant Mateu
Mare de Déu dels Angels
Castell de Montesa
Cervera del Maestre
Masía de Vegue
Masía Pallaresa

El Maestrat
Serra de vall d'Àngel
17

Berola de Grau
Mas de Valentí
Mas dels Oms
Benasal
l'Algà
la Torre de la Beltrans 1147
Masía de Segarra de Arriba
la Masía de Brusca
l'Hostalet de Vilar de Canes
Montegordó 837
els Civils
els Cavalls (Pintures rupestres)
La Saltadora de la Valltorta
Masía Benafechines
Tirig
Ermita de Santa Bàrbara
10
La Salzadella
Mas de la Teulera
Encanés 715
Atalayas-Valdancher
Barranc del Sastre

Mas de Peseets
la Font d'En-Segures
Vilar de Canes
Masía del Senyor
Masía de Romeo
les Casetes
Albocàsser
Sant Pere
l'Esperança
San Pablo
la Calçada
Venta de Blanco
57
Santa Magdalena de Pulpis
Talaies d'Alcalà

Masía de Toni
Masía de Salvador
Mercades de Baix
la Roca
Torre d'En Besora
Masía Pali
les Deveses
els Malladás
Sarratella
Ermita de Sant Vicenç
Alcalà de Xivert
Castell de Xivert
Serra

Parc Natural
Vistabella del Maestrazgo
(1100)
7%
Port del Vidre
Benafigos
les Roques de Lleó
Pla del Sabater
Monllat
Mas de Rosildos
1081
el Sol de la Foia
Sierra Engarcerán
Cova Santa
Torre Endoménech
Mas de Calaf
Masía Can Bosc
Torreblanca/ Alcossebre
Almedíjar
Baixador d'Alcossebre
les Fonts
Platja de les
Alcossebre

Masía de l'Albagés
Manzanares
Masía de les Pomeres
Xoclos
de Penyagolosa
Masía de Gárgán
Meanes
la Cormana
la Torre de Matella
56
la Bodega
les Crevadas
els Ivarsos
les Mosqueres
Emitori de Sant Miquel
Mas de Trilles
Vilanova d'Alcolea
13
el Quartico
Masía de Carre
Ermita de Sant Miquel
Torreblanca
Torrenostra
Capicorb
Platja del Carrega
Platja del Moro

Masía de la Lloma
Masía de la Lloma
el Castell
Mas de Ensavi
Pelejaneta
Mas de Roures
Mas d'Alentao
Mas de Campos
les Ramblelles
Benlloch
Arc roma de Cabanes
41
Benasqués
Vall d'Alba
10
340
AP7
E15
Mas d'Enqueixa
Parc Natural del Prat de Cabanes-Torreblanca

Serra de Montord
Rio de Llucena
Useras les Useres
Perchet
Serra de la Creu
el Mas Blanc
la Barona
15
Cabanes
108
Castelló de la Plana　Castelló Sud　Castelló de la Plana

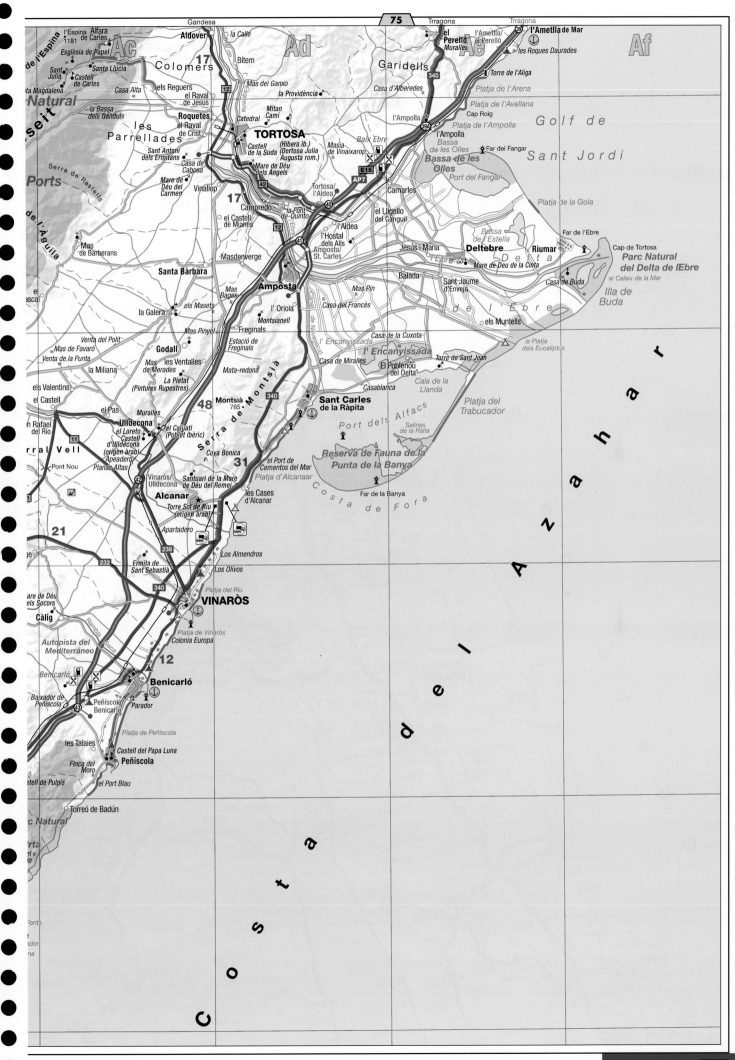

Gandesa

Tarragona · Tarragona

l'Espina · Alfara · de Carles
181
Aldover
la Calle

Església de Papel · Ac · Colomers · 17 · Bítem

Santa Llúcia · Ad · Garidells · el Perelló · Muralles · l'Ametlla · el Perelló · l'Ametlla de Mar
Sant Julià · Castell · de Carles · els Reguers · el Raval · de Jesús · Mas del Ganxo · les Roques Daurades
ta Magdalena · Casa Alta · la Providència · Casa d'Alberedes · 340 · Torre de l'Aliga
Natural · la Bassa · dels Gànduls · Roquetes · Mitan · Camí · Platja de l'Arena
les · Parrellades · el Raval · de Crist · Catedral · Platja de l'Avellana · Cap Roig
Sant Antoni · dels Ermitans · TORTOSA · (Hibera ib.) · Masia · de Vinaixarop · l'Ampolla · Platja de l'Ampolla · Golf de
Seit · Casa de · Cabosa · Castell · de la Suda · (Dertosa Julia · Augusta rom.) · l'Ampolla · Bassa · de les Olles · Sant Jordi
Ports · Mare de Déu del · Carmen · Mare de Déu · dels Angels · E15 · AP7 · Camarles · Bassa de les · Olles · Port del Fangar
Serra de Rastells · Vinallop · 17 · 42 · Tortosa/ · l'Aldea · 40 · el Lligallo · del Gànguil · Platja de la Gola
de l'Àguila · Campredó · la Font · de-Quinto · el Castell · de Mianes · l'Aldea · Bassa · de l'Estella · Far de l'Ebre
Mas · de Barberans · 12 · l'Hostal · dels Alls · Amposta/ · St. Carles · Jesús i Maria · Deltebre · Delta · Riumar · Cap de Tortosa
Masdenverge · 41 · Mare de Deu de la Cinta · d e · l' E b r e · Parc Natural · del Delta de lEbre
Santa Bàrbara · Balada · Sant Jaume · d'Enveja · Casa de Buda · el Calaix de la Mar
Amposta · Mas Pin · Illa de · Buda
la Galera · Mas · Bages · l' Oriola · Casa del Francès · els Muntells
els Masets · Montsianell · Casa de la Cuxota · la Platja · dels Eucaliptus
Venta del Polit · Mas Pinyol · Freginals · l' Encanyissada · Casa de Miralles · l' Encanyissada · Torre de Sant Joan
Mas de Favaró · Godall · les Ventalles · Estació de · Freginals · Casa de Miralles · Cala de la · Llanda
Venta de la Punta · Mas · de Merades · La Pietat · (Pintures Rupestres) · Mata-redona · Casablanca · El Poblenou · del Delta · Platja del · Trabucador
la Miliana · Serra de Montsià · Casablanca
els Valentins · 48 · Montsià · 765 · Sant Carles · de la Ràpita · Salines · de la Ràita
el Castell · Muralles · 340 · Port dels Alfacs
el Pas · Ulldecona · Reserva de Fauna de la · Punta de la Banya
n Rafael · del Rio · el Loreto · Castell · d'Ulldecona · (origen àrab) · el Caluati · (Poblet ibèric) · Far de la Banya
rral Vell · 11 · Apeadero · Planas Altas · Cova Bonica · 31 · el Port de · Cementos del Mar · Platja d'Alcanaar · Costa de Fora
Pont Nou · 42 · Vinaròs/ · Ulldecona · Santuari de la Mare · de Déu del Remei · les Cases · d'Alcanar
21 · Alcanar · Torre Sot de Riu · (origen àrab) · Apartadero
238 · Los Almendros
232 · Ermita de · Sant Sebastià · Los Olivos
Mare de Déu · els Socors · 340 · Platja del Riu
Càlig · VINARÒS
Autopista del · Mediterráneo · Platja de Vinaròs · Colonia Europa
Benicarló · 12
Baixador de · Peñiscola · Benicarló
43 · Peñiscola · Benicarló · Parador
les Talaies · Platja de Peñiscola
Castell del Papa Luna · Finca del · Moro · Peñiscola
Castell de Pulpis · el Port Blau
c Natural · Torreó de Badún
rta
Fonts
dor
na · Costa · del · Azahar

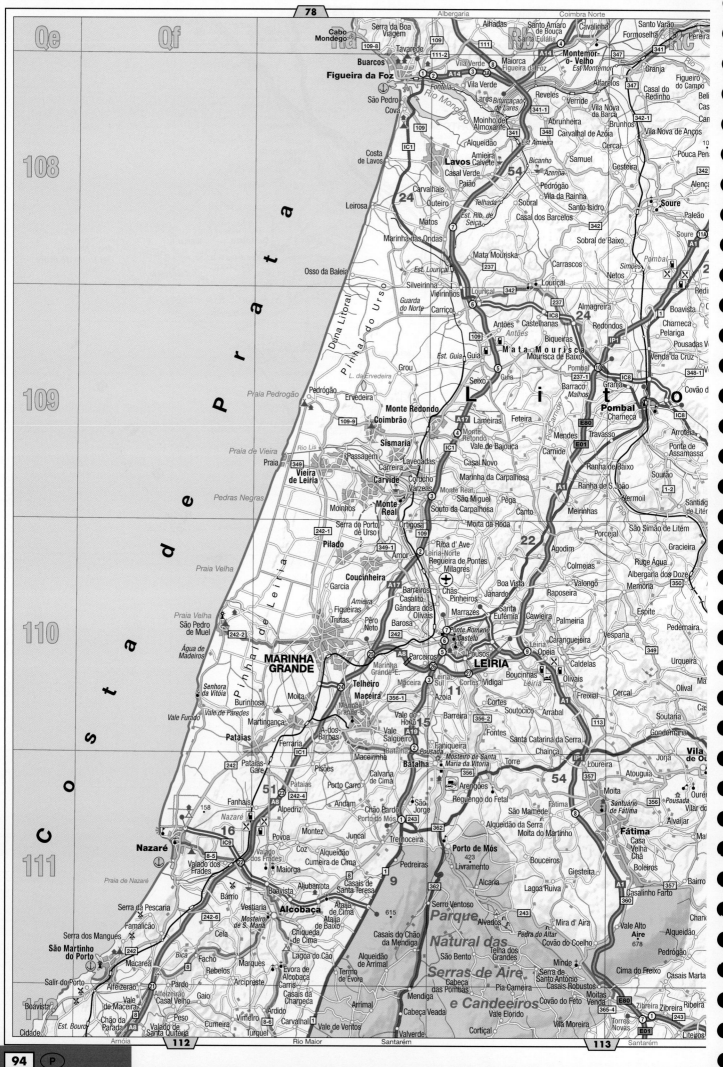

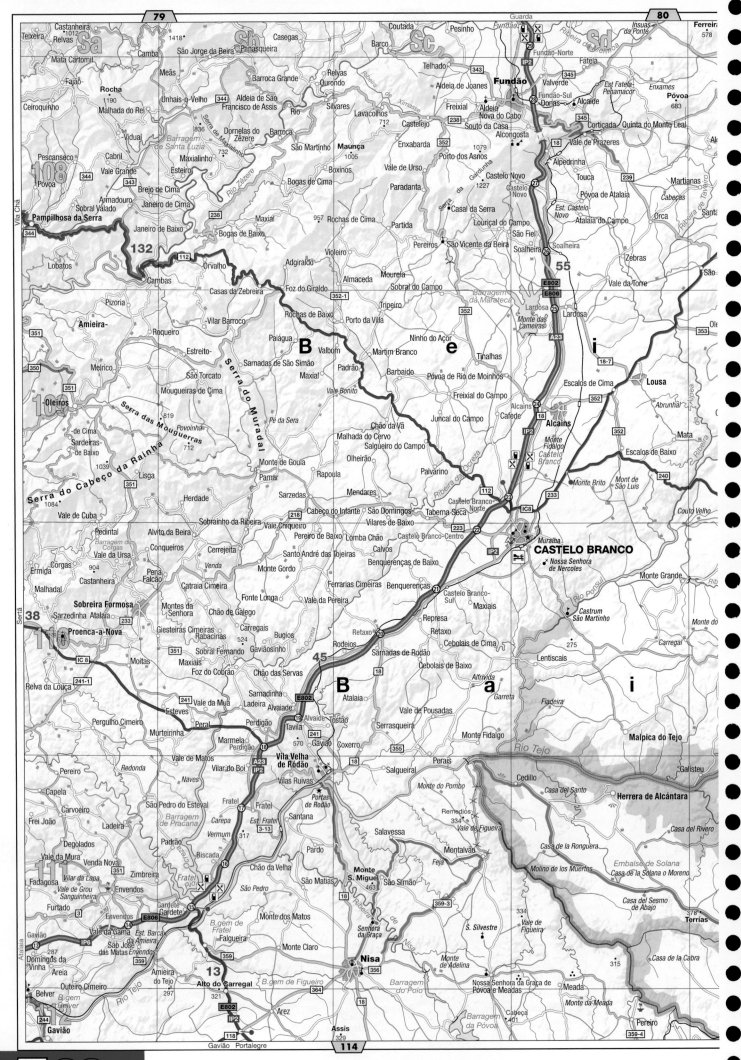

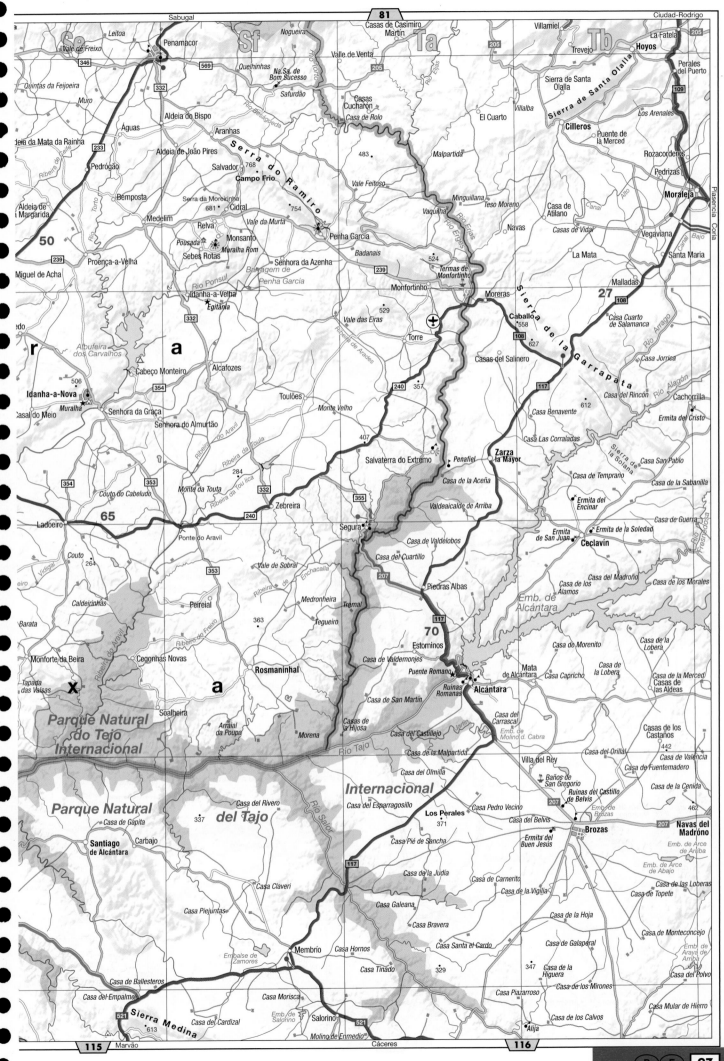

Sabugal · Ciudad-Rodrigo

Casas de Casimiro Martín · Villamiel · La Fatela

Leitoa · Nogueira · Trevejo · Hoyos · 205

Penamacor · Valle de Venta · Sierra de Santa Olalla · Perales del Puerto

Vale de Freixo · 346 · 205 · Villalba · 109

569 · Quelhinhas · Na.Sa. de Bom Sucesso · Sierra de Santa Olalla · Cilleros · Rozacorderos

Quintas da Feijoeira · 332 · Safurdão · Casas Cucharón · El Cuarto · Puente de la Merced · Pedrizas

Muro · Aldeia do Bispo · Casa de Rolo · Plasencia · Coria

Águas · Aranhas · Malpartida · Moraleja

233 · Pedrógão · Salvador · 768 · Serra do Ramiro · 483 · Vale Feitoso · Minguillana · Teso Moreno · Casa de Atilano · Vegaviana

Aldeia da Mata da Rainha · Campo Frio · Vaquilha · Rio Erges · Navas · Casas de Vidal · Santa Maria

Bémposta · Serra da Moreirinha · 681 · 754 · Cidral · 524 · Termas de · Malladas

50 · Medelim · Relva · Vale da Murta · Badanais · Monfortinho · 27 · 108

239 · Monsanto · Senhora da Azenha · 239 · Casa Cuarto de Salamanca

Proença-a-Velha · Pousada · Muralha Rom · Moreras · Sierra de la Garrapata · Casa Jorrica

Miguel de Acha · Sebes Rotas · Rio Ponsul · Barragem de Penha García · Egitânia · Caballo · 558 · 627 · Casa del Rincón · Cachorrilla

Idanha-a-Velha · 332 · 529 · Casas del Salinero · 117 · 612 · Casa del Cristo

r · a · Albufeira dos Carvalhos · Vale das Eiras · Torre · Casa Benavente · Ermita del Cristo

Cabeço Monteiro · 354 · Ribeira de Arades · Casa Las Corraladas · Sierra de la Solana

506 · Alcafozes · 240 · 357 · Penafiel · Zarza la Mayor · Casa San Pablo

Idanha-a-Nova · Toulões · Monte Velho · Casa de la Aceña · Casa de Temprano · Casa de la Sabanilla

Muralha · Senhora da Graça · 407 · Salvaterra do Extremo · Ermita del Encinar · Casa de Guerra

Casal do Meio · Senhora do Almurtão · Valdeaicalde de Arriba · Ermita de la Soledad

354 · 353 · 284 · 355 · Casa del Cuartillo · Ermita de San Juan · Ceclavín

Couto do Cabeludo · Monte da Touta · 332 · Segura · Casa de Valdelobos · Casa del Madroño · Casa de los Morales

65 · Zebreira · 240 · 207 · Casa de la Aceña · Casa de los Alamos

Ladoeiro · Ponte do Aravil · Piedras Albas · Emb. de Alcántara

Couto · 264 · 353 · Vale de Sobral · 117 · Casa de Morenito · Casa de la Lobera

Caldeirinhas · Peireial · Medronheira · 70 · Estorninos · Casa Capricho · Casa de la Lobera

Barata · 363 · Tremal · Tegueiro · Casa de Valdemonjes · Mata de Alcántara · Casa de la Merced · Casas de las Aldeas

Monforte da Beira · Cegonhas Novas · Puente Romano · Alcántara · 442

x · a · Rosmaninhal · Ruinas Romanas · Casa del Orillal · Casa de Valencia

Tapada das Valsas · Soalheira · Casa de San Martín · Casa del Carrascal · Casas de los Castaños

Parque Natural do Tejo Internacional · Arraial da Poupa · Morena · Casas de la Hijosa · Casa del Castillejo · Emb. de Molino d. Cabra · Casa de Fuentemadero

Rio Tajo · Casa de la Malpartida · Villa del Rey · Casa de la Cenida

Parque Natural · Casa del Olmilla · Baños de San Gregorio · 207 · Ruinas del Castillo de Belvis

Internacional · Casa del Rivero · Casa del Esparragosillo · Casa Pedro Vecino · Emb. de Brozas

Casa de Gápita · 337 · del Tajo · Rio Salor · Los Perales · 371 · Casa del Belvis · 207 · Navas del Madroño

Santiago de Alcántara · Carbajo · Casa Pié de Sancha · Ermita del Buen Jesús · Brozas · Emb. de Arce de Arriba

Casa Claveri · Casa de la Judía · Casa de Carnerito · Emb. de Arce de Abajo

117 · Casa Galeana · Casa de la Vigilia · Casa de las Loberas

Casa Piejuntas · Casa Bravera · Casa Santa el Cardo · Casa de Topete

Membrío · Casa Hornos · Casa de la Hoja · Casa de Galaperal · Emb. de Araya de Arriba

Embalse de Zamores · Casa Tinado · 329 · 347 · Casa de la Higuera · Casa de los Mirones

Casa de Ballesteros · 613 · Casa Moriscá · Casa Piazarroso · Casa Mular de Hierro

Casa del Empalme · 521 · Sierra Medina · Casa del Cardizal · Emb. de Salorino · Salorino · 521 · Casa de los Calvos · Casa del Polvo

Molino de Enmedio · Alija

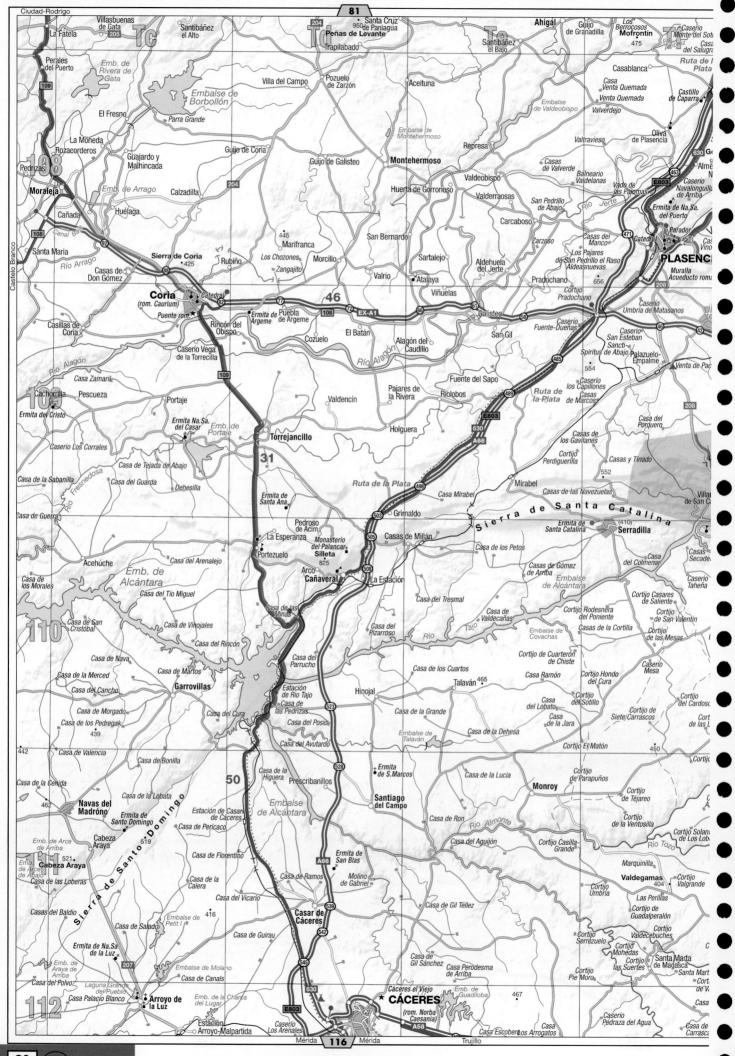

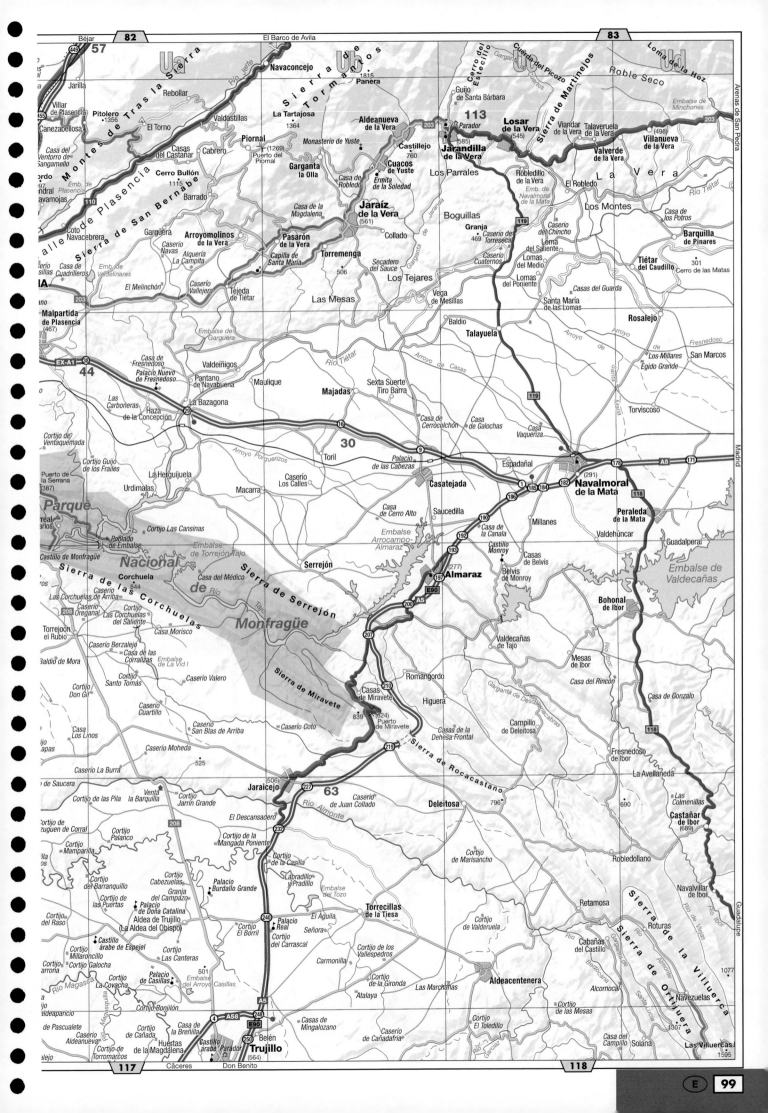

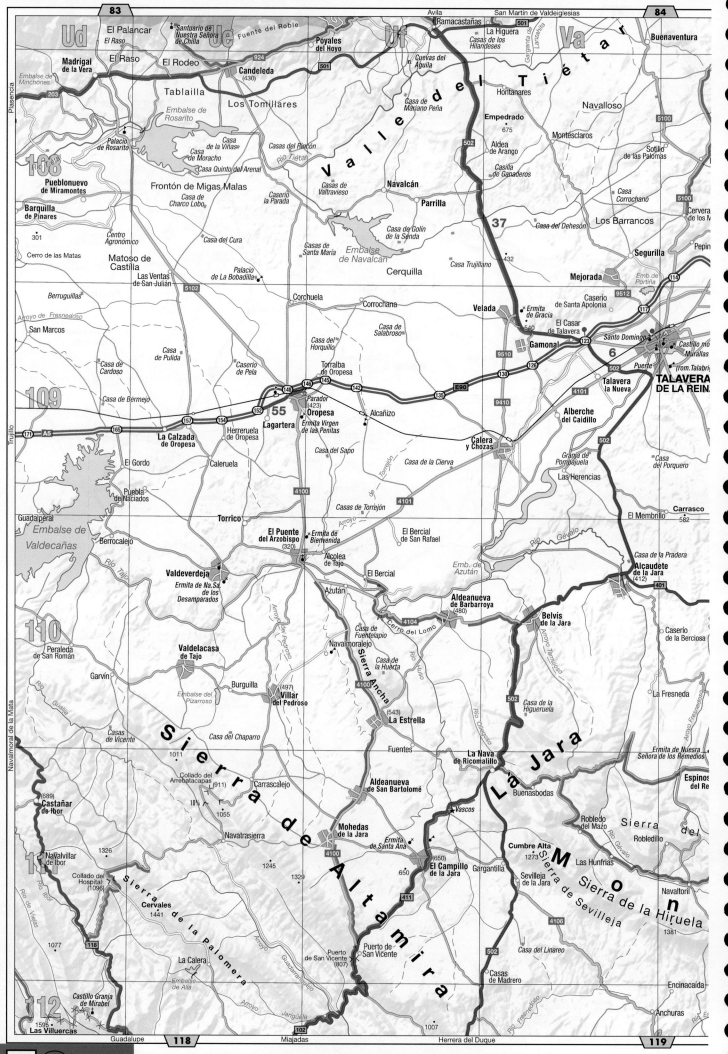

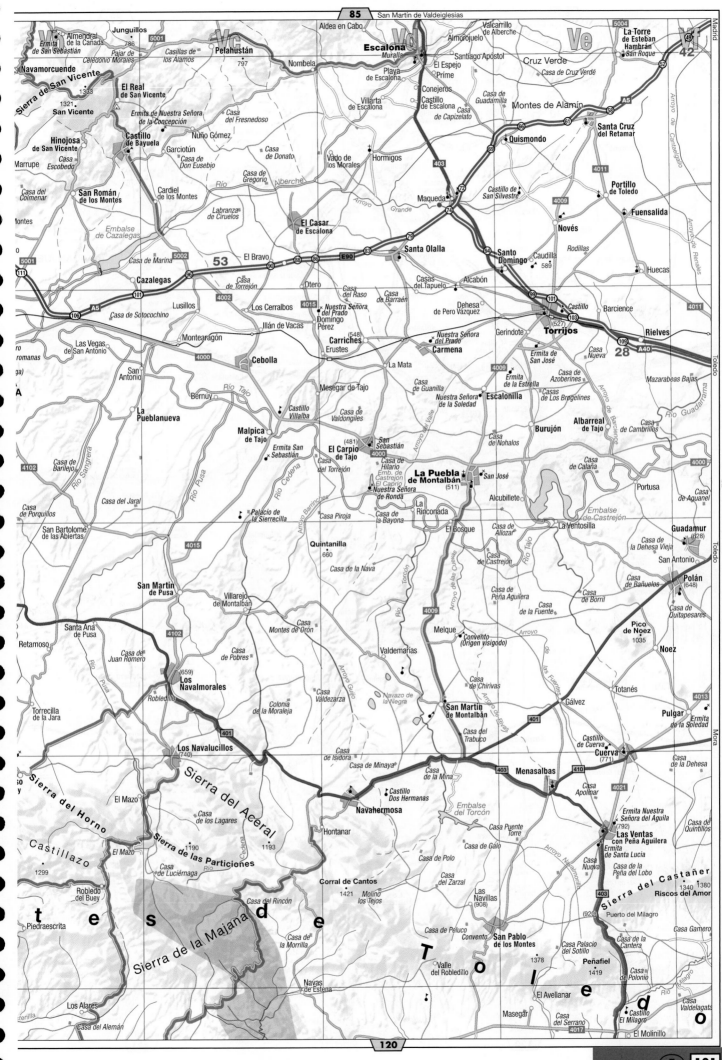

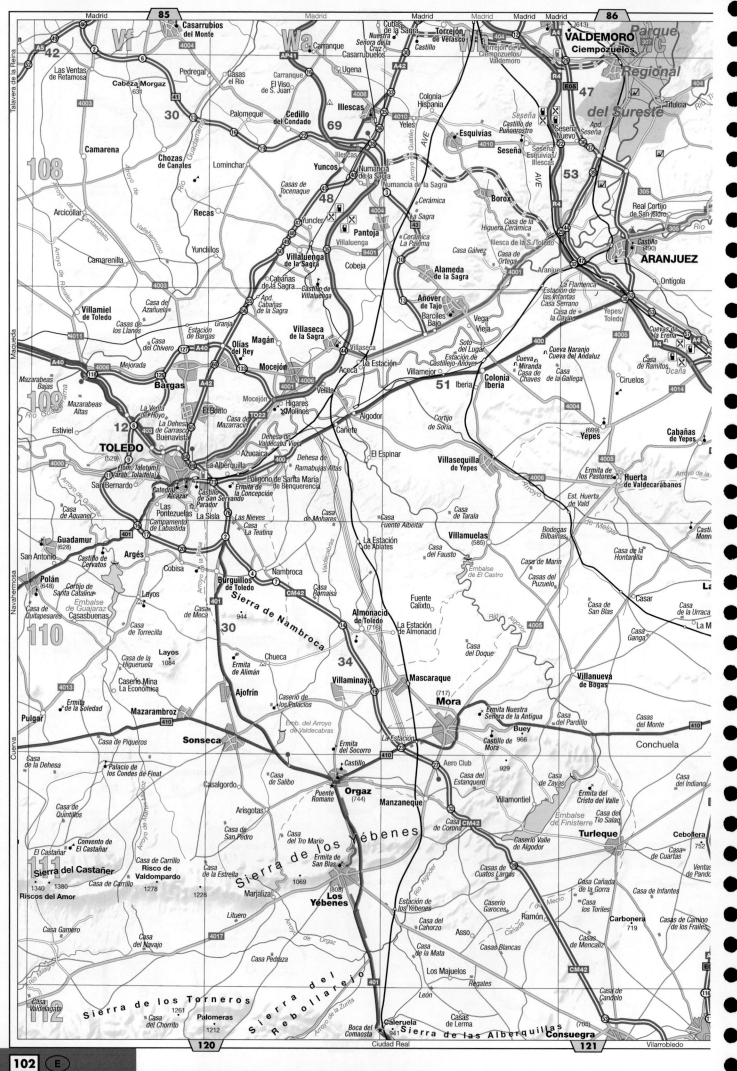

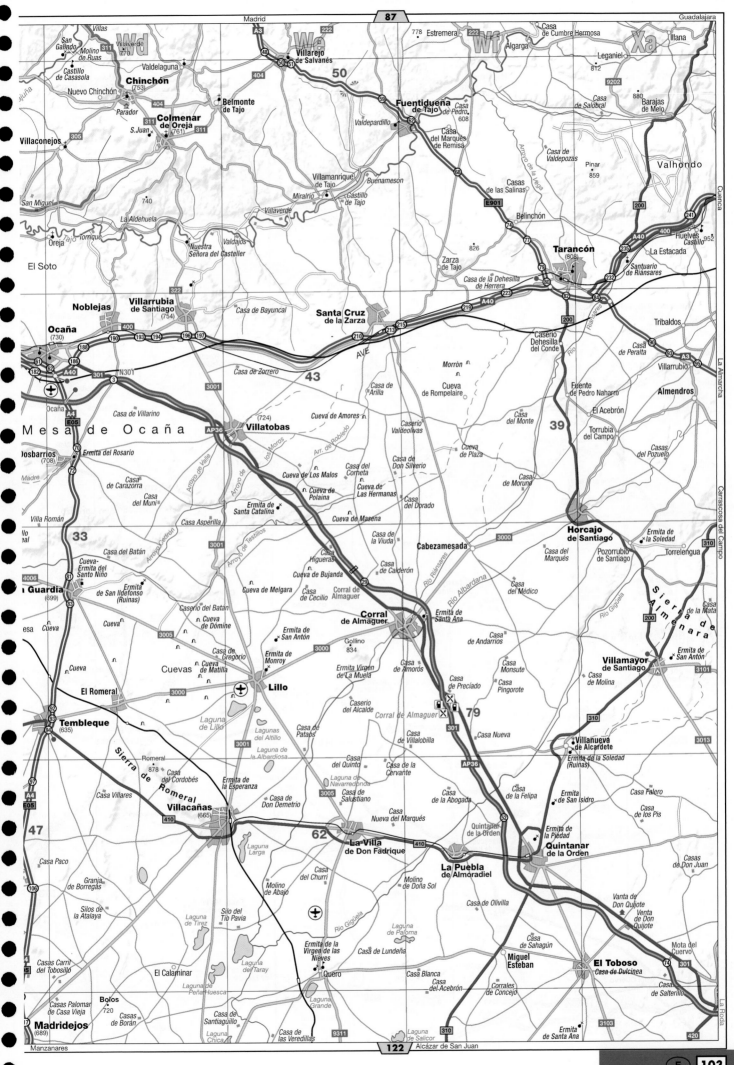

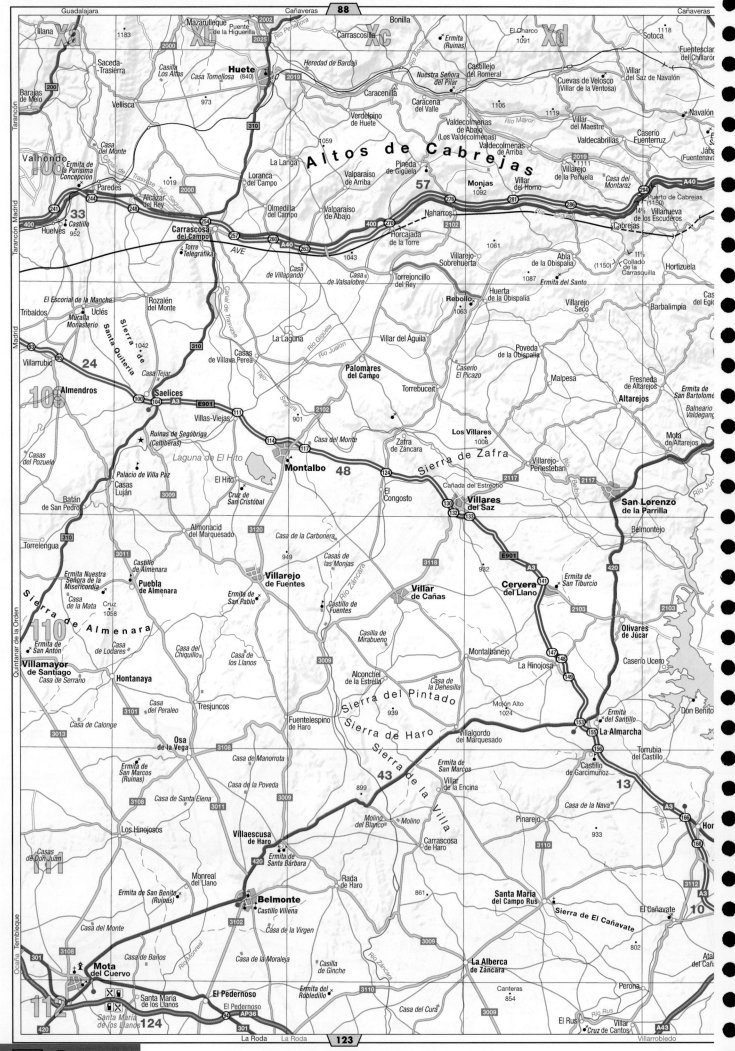

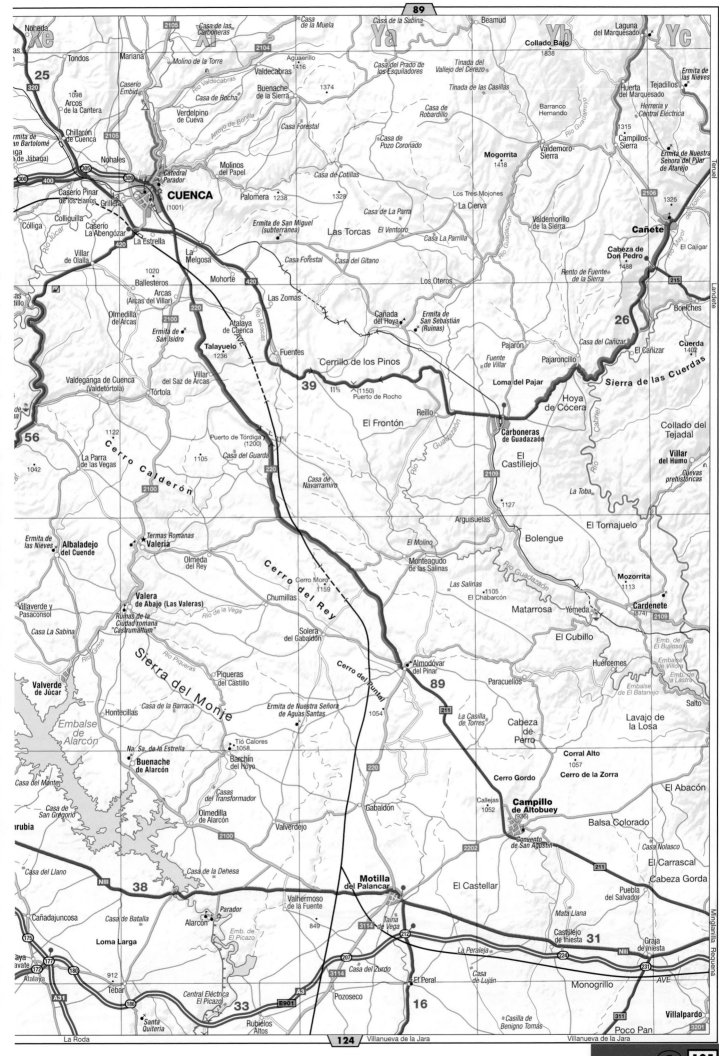

Xe
Xf
Ya
Yb
Yc

25
26
56
39

Noheda
Tondos
Mariana
Casa de las Carboneras
Casa de la Muela
Casa de la Sabina
Beamud
Collado Bajo
1838
Laguna del Marquesado

Molino de la Torre
2105
2104
Aguaerillo
1416
Casa del Prado de los Esquiladores
Tinada del Vallejo del Cerezo
Ermita de las Nieves

1098
Arcos de la Cantera
Caserío Embid
Verdelpino de Cueva
Valdecabras
Buenache de la Sierra
1374
Tinada de las Casillas
Huerta del Marquesado
Tejadillos

320
Chillarón de Cuenca
Casa de Rocha
Río Valdecabras
Casa de Robardillo
Barranco Hernando
Río Guadarroyo
1315
Campillos-Sierra

Ermita de San Bartolomé
de Jábaga)
2105
Nohales
Casa Forestal
Casa de Pozo Coroñado
Mogorrita
1418
Valdemoro-Sierra
Herrería y Central Eléctrica
Ermita de Nuestra Señora del Pilar de Atarejo

300
400
305
309
Catedral Parador
Molinos del Papel
Casa de Cotillas
2106
1325

Caserío Pinar de los Llanos
La Grillera
CUENCA
(1001)
Palomera
1238
1328
Casa de La Parra
La Cierva
Los Tres Mojones
Valdemorillo de la Sierra
Cañete

Cólliga
Colliguilla
Caserío La Abengózar
La Estrella
420
Ermita de San Miguel (subterránea)
Las Torcas
El Ventorro
Casa de La Parrilla
Cabeza de Don Pedro
1488
El Cajigar

Villar de Olalla
La Melgosa
Casa Forestal
Casa del Gitano
Rento de Fuente de la Sierra
215
Boniches

Ballesteros
Mohorte
420
Las Zomas
Los Oteros
Pajarón
Casa del Cañizar
Cuerda

Arcas (Arcas del Villar)
220
Cañada del Hoya
Ermita de San Sebastián (Ruinas)
Fuente de Villar
Pajaroncillo
El Cañizar
1402

Olmedilla de Arcas
2100
Atalaya de Cuenca
Fuentes
Cerrillo de los Pinos
Loma del Pajar
Hoya de Cócera
Sierra de las Cuerdas

Ermita de San Isidro
Talayuelo
1236
11¾
(1150)
Puerto de Rocho
Reillo
Carboneras de Guadazaón
Collado del Tejadal

1122
Villar del Saz de Arcas
Tórtola
El Frontón
El Castillejo
Villar del Humo

1042
La Parra de las Vegas
Cerro Calderón
Puerto de Tórdiga
(1200)
Casa del Guarda
11%
220
2109
La Toba
Cuevas prehistóricas

2100
1105
Casa de Navarramiro
1127
Arguisuelas
El Tornajuelo

Ermita de las Nieves
Albaladejo del Cuende
Termas Romanas
Valeria
Olmeda del Rey
Cerro Moro
1159
El Molino
Monteagudo de las Salinas
Bolengue
Mozorrita
1113

Villaverde y Pasaconsol
Valera de Abajo (Las Valeras)
Chumillas
Río de la Vega
Las Salinas
1105
El Chabarcón
Matarrosa
Yémeda
Cardenete
(874)
2109

Casa La Sabina
Ruinas de la Ciudad romana "Castrumattum"
Solera del Gabaldón
El Cubillo
Emb. de El Bujioso

Valverde de Júcar
Sierra del Monje
Río Piqueras
Piqueras del Castillo
Cerro del Rey
Almodóvar del Pinar
Huércemes
Embalse de Villora
Emb. de la Lastra

Hontecillas
Cerro del Puntal
89
Paracuellos
Embalse de El Batanejo
Salto

Embalse de Alarcón
Casa de la Barraca
Ermita de Nuestra Señora de Aguas Santas
1054
211
La Casilla de Torres
Cabeza de Perro
Lavajo de la Losa

Na. Sa. de la Estrella
Tió Calores
1058
Corral Alto
1057
El Abacón

Valverde de Júcar
Buenache de Alarcón
Barchín del Hoyo
220
Gabaldón
Cerro Gordo
Cerro de la Zorra

Casa del Monte
Casas del Transformador
2202
Callejas
1052
Campillo de Altobuey
(936)
Casa Nolasco

Casa de San Gregorio
Olmedilla de Alarcón
Valverdejo
Convento de San Agustín
El Carrascal

rubia
2100
Casa de la Dehesa
211
El Castellar
Cabeza Gorda

Casa del Llano
NIII
38
Motilla del Palancar
Mata Llana
Puebla del Salvador

Cañadajuncosa
Casa de Batalla
Parador
Valhermoso de la Fuente
3114
Taina de Vega
212
La Peraleja
Castillejo de Iniesta
31

175
Alarcón
Emb. de El Picazo
849
Casa de Luján
224
NIII
Graja de Iniesta
231

177
172
180
912
Tébar
207
Casa del Zurdo
3114
La Paraja
Monogrillo

A31
186
Central Eléctrica El Picazo
A3
E901
33
Pozoseco
El Peral
Casilla de Benigno Tomás
311
Villalpardo
3201

Atalaya
avate
Atalaya
Loma Larga
Santa Quiteria
Rubielos Altos
16
Poco Pan

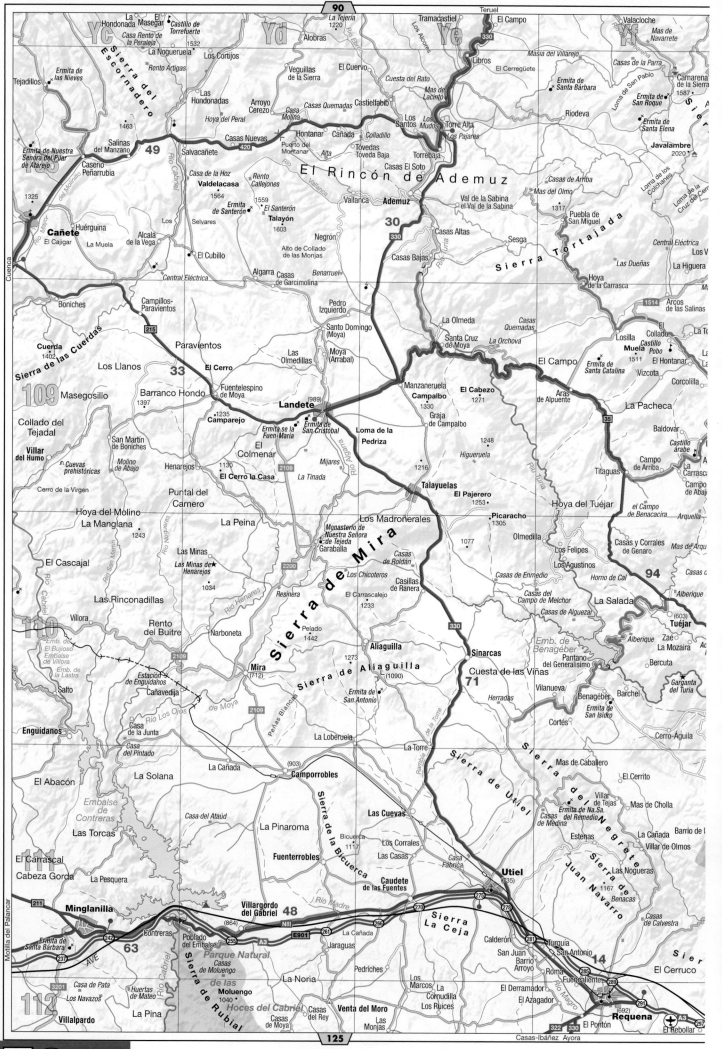

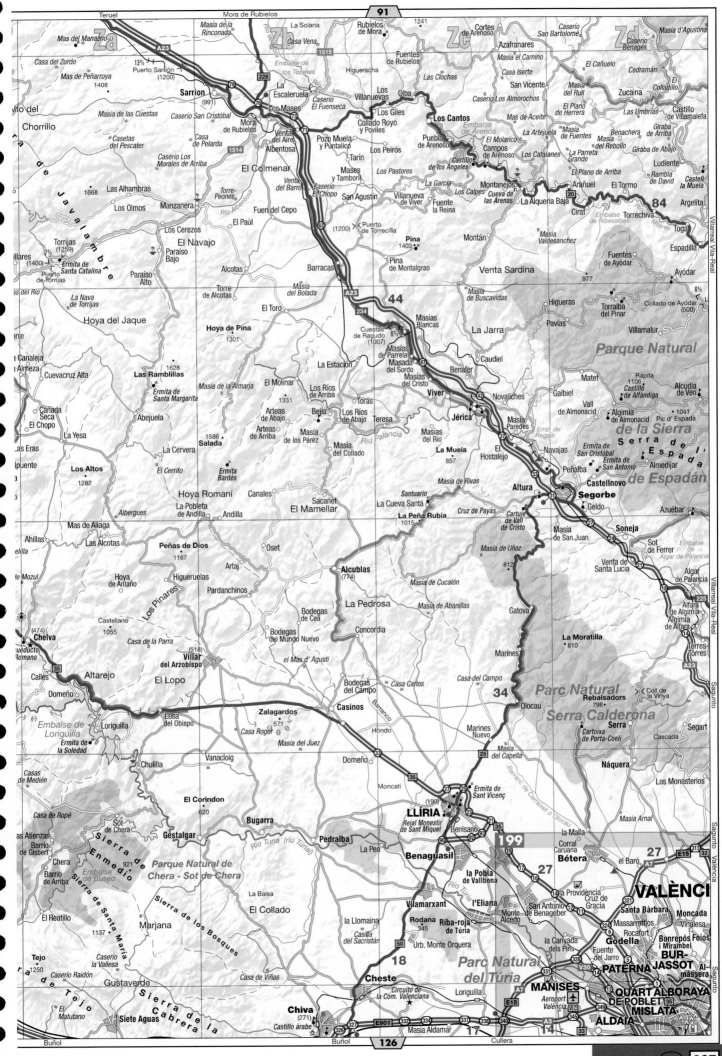

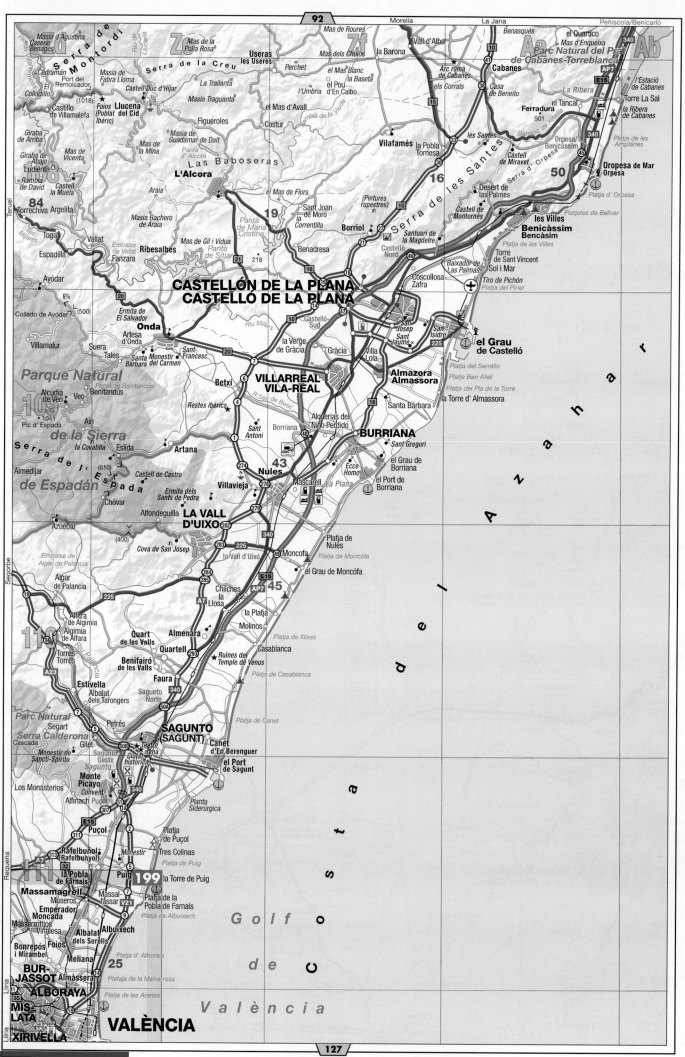

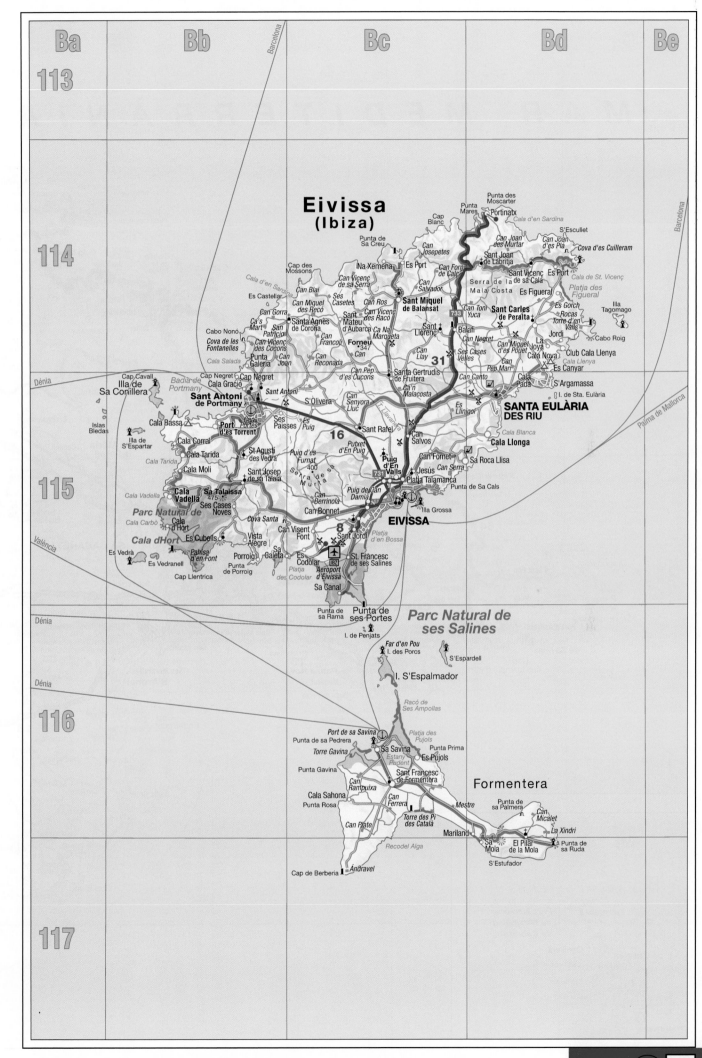

Barcelona

Eivissa
(Ibiza)

114

Punta des
Moscarter

Punta
Mares
Cap
Blanc
Portinatx
Cala d'en Sardina
S'Escullet

Punta de
Sa Creu
Can
Josepetes
Can Joan
des Murtar
Can Joan
d'es Plà
Cova d'es Cuilleram

Na Xemena
Es Port
Can Forn
de Calç
Sant Joan
de Labritja
Sant Vicenç
de sa Cala
Es Port
Cala de St. Vicenç

Cap des
Mossons
Can Vicenç
de sa Serra
Serra de la de sa Cala
Mala Costa
Es Figueral
Platja des
Figueral

Cala d'en Sardina
Can Blai
Ses
Casetes
Can Ros
Sant Miquel
de Balansat
Can Salvador
733
Can Toni
Yuca
Sant Carles
de Peralta
Es Gorch
Rocas
Torre d'en
Valls
Illa
Tagomago

Es Castellar
Can Gorra
Can Miquel
des Recó
Sant
Mateu
d'Aubarca
Can Vicenç
des Racó
Sant
Llorenç
Balafí
Can Negret
Can Miquel
d'es Pouet
La
Joya
Jordi
Cabo Roig

Ca's
Mart
San
Patricio
Santa Agnès
de Corona
Ca Na
Marqueta
Can Llay
31
Ses Cases
Velles
Cala Nova
Club Cala Llenya
Cala Llenya
Es Canyar

Cabo Nonó
Cova de les
Fontanelles
Can Vicenç
des Cocons
Can
Francoll
Forneu
•347
Can
Can Pep
d'es Cucons
Santa Gertrudis
de Fruitera
Can Pep
Mari
Cala
Pada
S'Argamassa

Dénia
Cap Cavall
Illa de
Sa Conillera
Badia de
Portmany
Punta
Galeria
Can
Joan
Can Reconada
Ca'n
Malacosta
Can Canto
I. de Sta. Eulària
Palma de Mallorca

Sant Antoni
de Portmany
Cap Negret
Cap Negret
Sant Antoni
S'Olivera
Can
Senyora
Lluc
SANTA EULÀRIA
DES RIU

Islas
Bledas
Cala Graciò
Cala Bassa
Ses
Paisses
Es
Puig
Sant Rafel
Es
Llinigol
Cala Blanca

Illa de
S'Espartar
Port
d'es Torrent
Putxet
d'En Puig
Can
Salvos
Cala Llonga

Cala Corral
St Agusti
des Vedrà
16
Puig d'es
Furnat
400
Puig
d'En
Valls
731
Can Fornet
Sá Roca Llisa

Cala Tarida
Cala Moli
Sant Josep
de sa Talaia
Serra de se Murtra
Jesús
Can Serra
Platja Talamanca

115
Cala Vadella
Cala
Vadella
Sa Talaissa
•475
Can
Berrinola
Puig de Can
Damià
Illa Grossa
Punta de Sa Cals

Parc Natural de
Cala Carbò
Ses Cases
Noves
Can Bonnet
8
EIVISSA

Cala d'Hort
Cala
d'Hort
Cova Santa
Can Visent
Font
Sant Jordi
Platja
d'en Bossa

Valéncia
Es Cubells
Vista
Alegre
Sa
Caleta
Es
Codolar
St. Francesc
de ses Salines

Es Vedrà
Pahisa
d'en Font
Porroig
Aeroport
d'Eivissa
IBZ

Es Vedranell
Punta
de Porroig
Platja
des Codolar
Sa Canal

Cap Llentrica

Dénia
Punta de
sa Rama
Punta de
ses Portes
Parc Natural de
ses Salines

I. de Penjats
Far d'en Pou
I. des Porcs
S'Espardell

Dénia
I. S'Espalmador

Racó de
Ses Ampollas

116
Port de sa Savina
Platja des
Pujols

Punta de sa Pedrera
Sa Savina
Punta Prima

Torre Gavina
Estany
Pudent
Es Pújols

Punta Gavina
Sant Francesc
de Formentera

Can
Rampuixa
Formentera

Cala Sahona
Can
Ferrera
Mestre
Punta de
sa Palmera
Can
Micalet

Punta Rosa
Torre des Pi
des Català
La Xindri

Can Plate
Mariland
Sa
Mola
El Pilar
de la Mola
Punta de
sa Ruda

Recodel Alga
S'Estufador

Cap de Berberia
Andravel

117

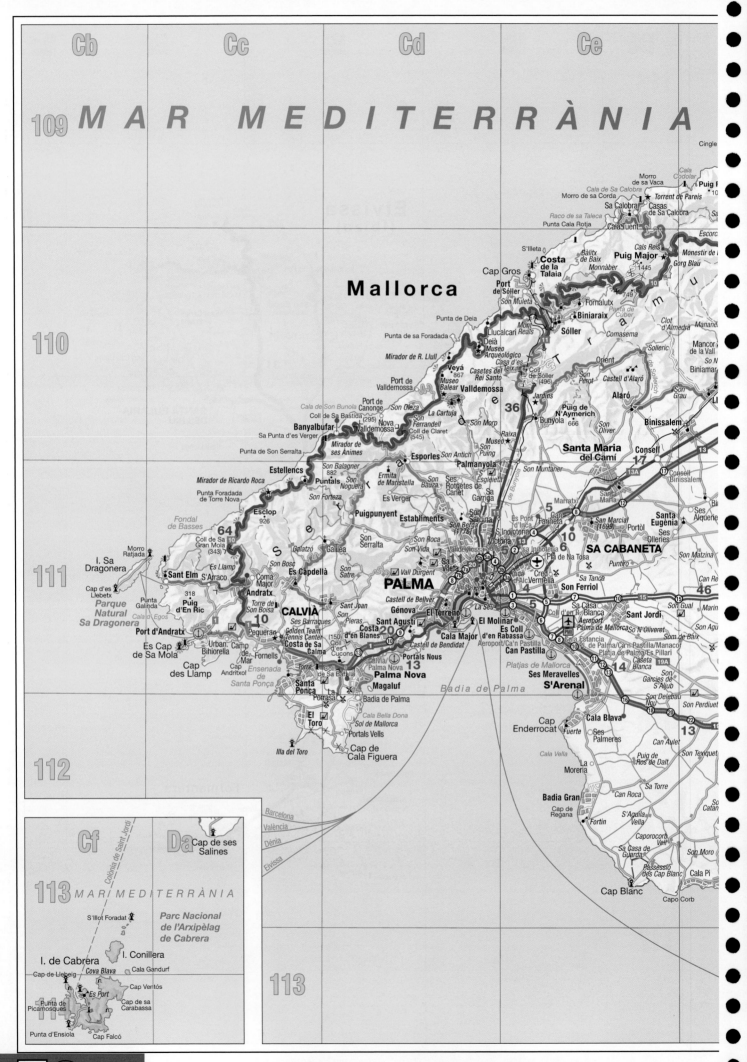

MAR MEDITERRÀNIA

Mallorca

Cingle

Morro
de sa Vaca
Cala de Sa Calobra
Morro de sa Corda
Sa Calobra
Raco de sa Taleca
Punta Cala Rotja

Morro
de sa Vaca
Torrent de Pareis
Casas
de Sa Calobra
Cala Tuent

Puig F

110

S'Illeta
Cap Gros
Costa
de la Talaia
Port
de Sóller
Son Muleta
Fornalutx
Biniaraix
Punta de Deia
Llucalcari
Deià
Museo
Arqueológico
Casa d'es
Teix
Veyá
867
Museo
Balear
Port de
Valldemossa
Valldemossa
Mirador de R. Llull
Punta de sa Foradada
Casetes del
Rei Santo

Bàlitx
de Baix
Monnàber
Puig Major
1445

Sóller
Mont
Reals
Coll
de Sóller
(496)
Son
Perot
Castell d'Alaró
Orient
Jardins
Puig de
N'Aymerich
666
Bunyola
Alaró

Monestir de
Gorg Blau
Escorca

Clot
d'Almedra
Mananell
Comasema
Solleric
Mancor
de la Vall
So N
Biniamar

Son
Grau

LI

Binissalem

Cala de Son Bunola
Coll de Sa Bastida
(295)
Port de
Canonge
Son Oleza
La Cartuja
Son
Ferrandell
Nova
Valldemossa
Coll de Claret
(545)
Banyalbufar
Sa Punta d'es Verger
Punta de Son Serralta
Mirador de
ses Ànimes
Estellencs
Mirador de Ricardo Roca
Punta Foradada
de Torre Nova
Esclop
926
Fondal
de Basses
64
Coll de Sa
Gran Mola
(343)

Son Balanger
882
Puntals
Son
Noguera
Son Forteza
Es Verger
Puigpunyent
Galatzó
Galilea
Son
Serralta
Son Bosc
Es Capdellà
Son
Satre

Son Morp
La Cartuja
Esporles
Ermita
de Maristella
Son Bauza
Ses
Rotgetes de.
Canet
Sa
Garriga
Establiments
Son Roca
Son Vida
Valldemossa
Son
Sardina
Es Pont
d'Inca
Indioteria
Victoria
Indioteria

Museo
Son
Puing
Son Antich
Palmanyola
Son Muntaner
Església
Son Berga
(1776)
5
Ca'n
Fariñeta
8
San Marcial
(1699)
10
6

Santa Maria
del Camí
Consell
17
13A
Consell
Binissalem
13

Marratxi
Santa
Maria

Santa
Eugènia
SA CABANETA

Ses
Olleries
Ses
Alquen

Can Re

Son Matzina

I. Sa
Dragonera
Cap d'es
Llebetx

Morro
Ratjada
Sant Elm
S'Arraco
Es Llamp
Comà
Major
318
Puig
d'En Ric
Andratx
Torre de
Son Boisa
CALVIÀ
Ses Barragues
Peguera
Camp
de
Mar
Costa de Sa
Calma
Torre.

Parque
Natural
Sa Dragonera
Punta
Galinda
Cala d'Egos
Port d'Andratx
Es Cap
de Sa Mola
Cap
des Llamp
Cala d'Egos
Urban.
Bihiorella
Cap
Andritxol
Ensenada de
Santa Ponça
Santa
Ponça
Sa Porrasa
El Toro

Sant Joan
Son
Pieras
Costa
d'en Blanes
(150)
Coll
d'es
Cucons
Calvià/
Palma Nova
Palma Nova
Magaluf
Cala Bella Dona
Sol de Mallorca
Portals Vells

PALMA
Castell de Bellver
Génova
Sant Agustí
13
20
9
Portals Nous
Castell de Bendidat
El Terreno
Cala Major
La Seu

Vall Durgent
Cala Major

Illa del Toro
Cap de
Cala Figuera

Badia de Palma

Barcelona
València
Dénia
Eivissa

Son
Grau

LI

Pla de Na Tosa
Puntiro
Sa Tanga
Son Ferriol
Son Gual
Son Agu
Son Matzina

Can Re

46

Sant Jordi
Marin
Son De Baix
Caseta
Blanca
Ses Cadenes
19A
Caseta
Blanca
14
Son
Garcies de
S'Aljub
Son Delebau
Nou
Son Perdiuet
13
Son Texiquet
19

S'Aguila
Vella
Son Moro
Cala Pi

Sa Casa
Blanca
Aeroport
Palma de Mallorca
PMI
Aeroport/Ca'n Pastilla
Pl. de Palma/Ca'n Pastilla/Manacor
Can Pastilla
Platja de Palma/Es Pillari
Ses Meravelles
Platjas de Mallorca
S'Arenal
Son Ferriol
Es Coll
d'en Rabassa
Es Coll
El Molinar
Cala Estancia
7
8
11
12
13
15
10
22

Cap
Enderrocat
Fuerte
Ses
Palmeres
Cala Blava
Cala Vella
Can Aulet
Can Roca

Badia Gran
Cap de
Regana
Fortin
Caporocorb
Vell
Sa Casa
de Guarda
Passessio
des Cap Blanc

Cap Blanc
Capo Corb

Puig de
Ros de Dalt
La
Moreria
Sa Torre
Son
Cata

Colònia de Sant Jordi
Cap de ses
Salines

MAR MEDITERRÀNIA

Parc Nacional
de l'Arxipèlag
de Cabrera

S'Illot Foradat
I. Conillera
I. de Cabrera
Cova Blava
Cala Gandurf
Cap de Llebeig
Es Port
Cap Veritós
Cap de sa
Carabassa
Punta de
Picamosques
Es Port
Cap Falcó
Punta d'Ensiola

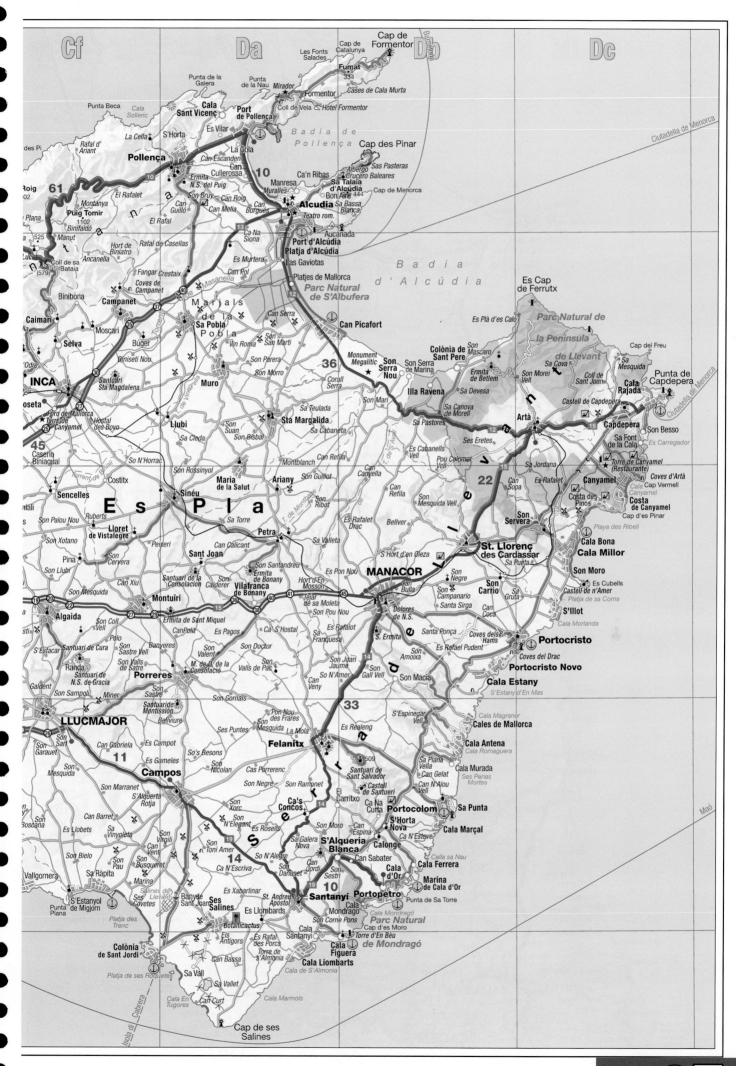

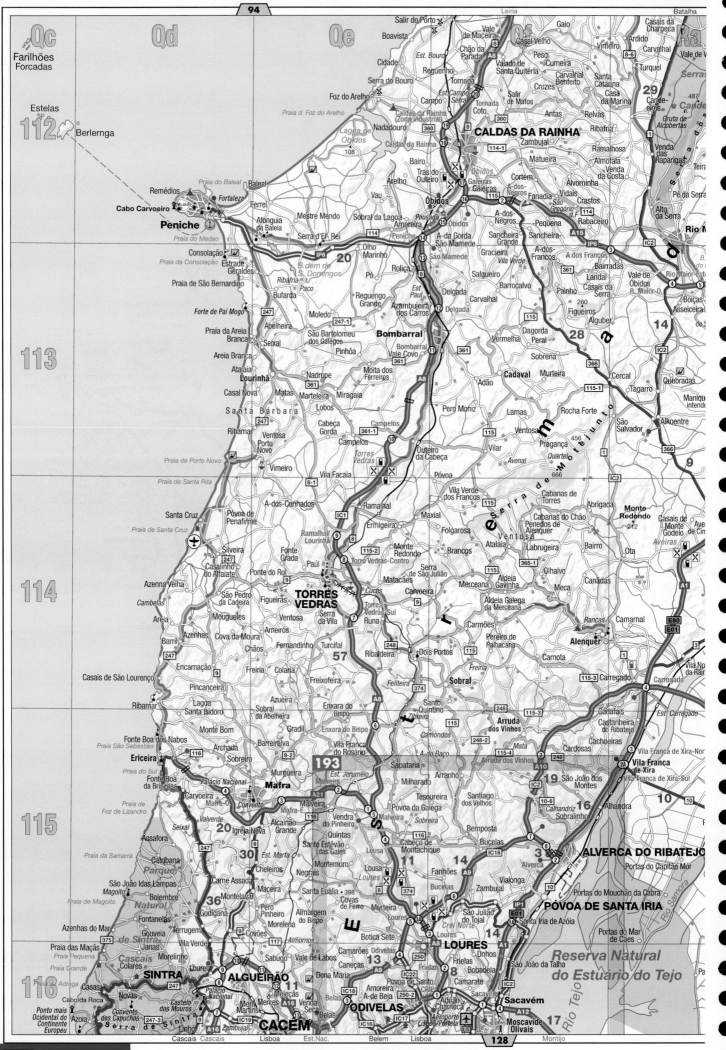

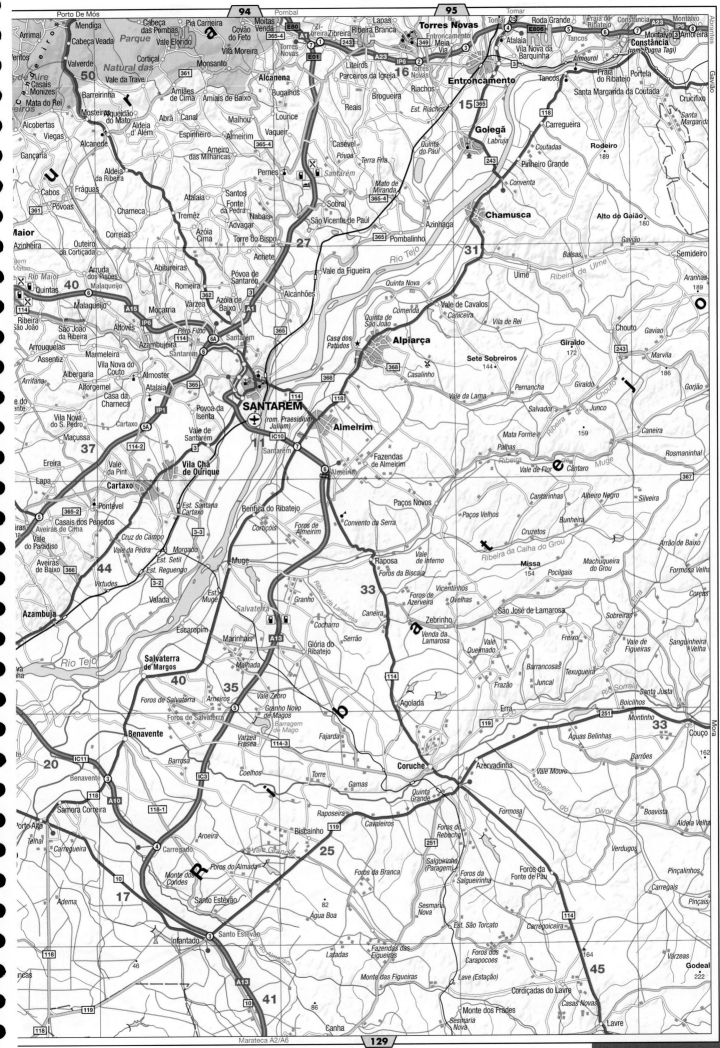

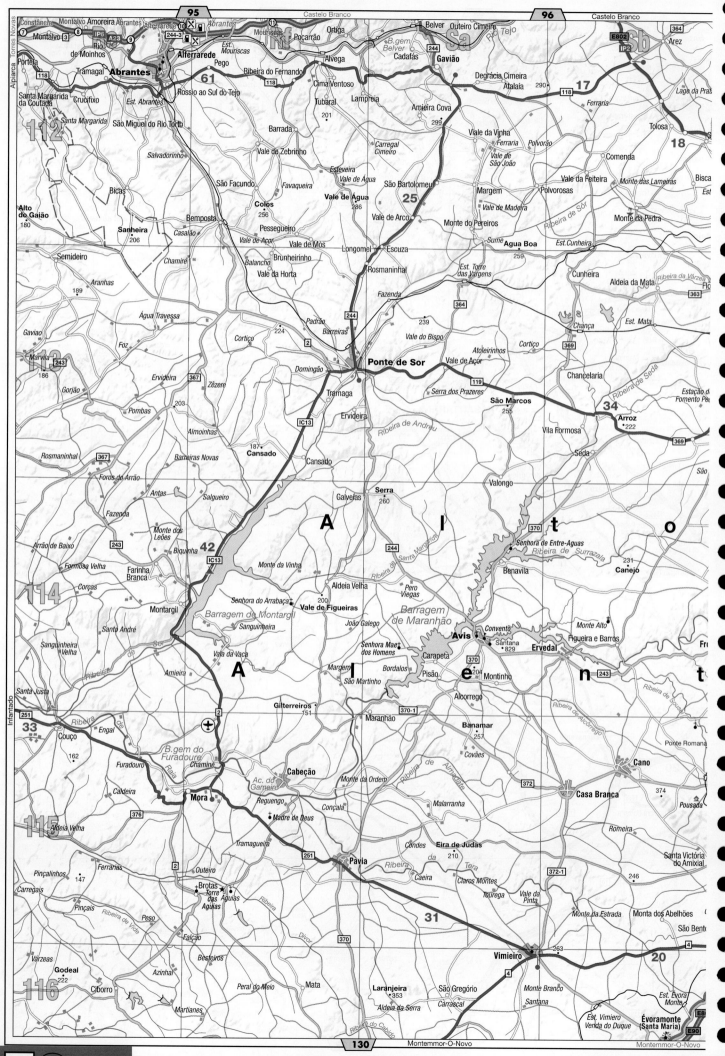

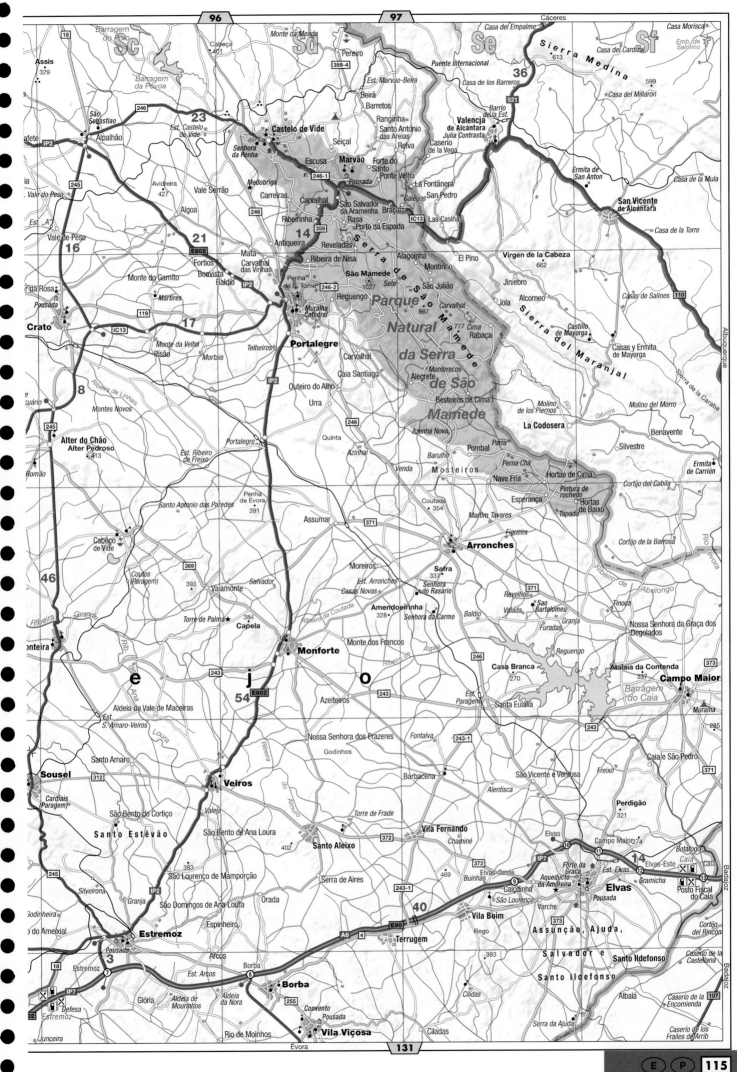

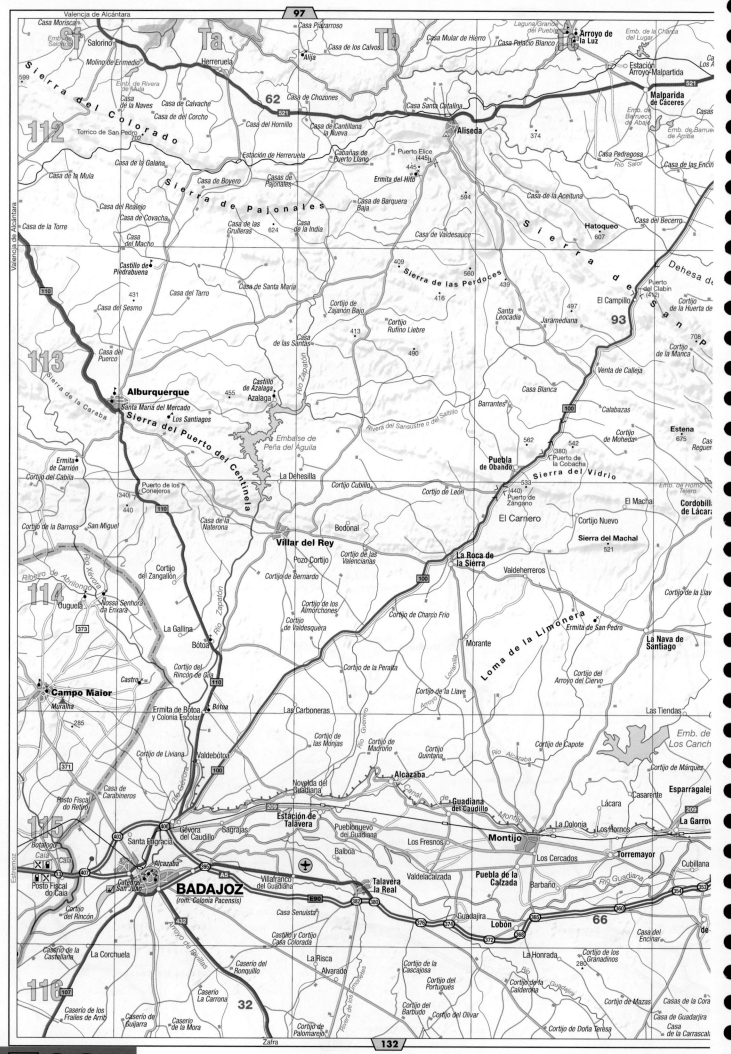

Valencia de Alcántara

Sierra del Colorado

112

Casa Morisca
Salorino
Molino de Enmedio
Herreruela
Emb. de Salorino
599
Sierra
del
Colorado
Torrico de San Pedro
702
Casa de la Naves
Casa de Calvache
Casa del Corcho
Casa de la Mula
Casa de la Galana

Emb. de Rivera de Mula
Estación de Herreruela
521
Casa del Hornillo
Casa de Cantillana la Nueva
Cabañas de Puerto Llano
Casa de Boyero
Casas de Pajonales

62
521
Casa de Chozones
Casa Santa Catalina
Aliseda
Casa Piazarroso
Casa de los Calvos
Casa Mular de Hierro
Casa Palacio Blanco
Puerto Elice (445)
445
Ermita del Hito
374

Laguna Grande del Pueblo
Arroyo de la Luz
Emb. de la Charca del Lugar
Estación Arroyo-Malpartida
521
Malparida de Cáceres
Casas
Emb. de Barrueco de Abajo
Emb. de Barrueco de Arriba
Casa Pedregosa
Casa de las Encin

113

Valencia de Alcántara
110
Casa de la Torre
Casa del Realejo
Casa de Covacha
Castillo de Piedrabuena
431
Casa del Sesmo
Casa del Puerco

Sierra de Pajonales

Casa del Macho
Casa de las Grulleras
624
Casa de la India
Casa del Tarro
Casa de Santa María
Cortijo de Zajanón Bajo
413
Casa de las Santas
Cortijo Rufino Liebre
490

409
Sierra de las Perdoces
416
560
439
Santa Leocadia
Jaramediana
497

Sierra de las Perdoces

Hatoqueo
607
Casa del Becerro
Casa de la Aceituna

Sierra de San
El Campillo
Puerto del Clabín (412)
93
708
Cortijo de la Huerta de
Cortijo de la Manca

114

Sierra de la Caraba
Ermita de Carrión
Cortijo del Cabila
Alburquerque
Santa María del Mercado
Los Santiagos
455
Castillo de Azalaga
Azalaga

Sierra del Puerto del Centinela

Embalse de Peña del Águila
La Dehesilla
Cortijo Cubillo
Cortijo de León

Rivera del Sansustre o del Saltillo
Casa Blanca
Barrantes
562
542
(380)
Venta de Calleja
Cortijo de Moheda
Estena
675
Cas Reguer

Puebla de Obando
Puerto de la Cobacha
Sierra del Vidrio
533
(440)
Puerto de Zángano
El Carnero
Cortijo Nuevo
El Machal
Cordobilla de Lácara

Emb. de Horno Tejero

Sierra del Machal
521

110
Puerto de los Conejeros
(340)
440
110
San Miguel
Cortijo de la Barrosa

114
Ribeiro de Abrilongo
Ouguela
373
Nossa Senhora da Enxara
La Gallina
Bótoa

Casa de la Naterona
Villar del Rey
Pozo Cortijo
Cortijo del Zangallón
Cortijo de Bernardo
Cortijo de las Valencianas

Bodonal
La Roca de la Sierra
Valdeherreros
100
Cortijo de Charco Frío
Morante
Ermita de San Pedro
La Nava de Santiago

Loma de la Limonera
Cortijo del Arroyo del Ciervo
Cortijo de la Llav

115
Campo Maior
Muralha
285
Castro
371
Cortijo del Rincón de Gila
110
Ermita de Bótoa y Colonia Escolar
Bótoa
Cortijo de los Almórchones
Cortijo de Valdesquèra
Cortijo de la Peralta
Cortijo de la Llave

Las Carboneras
Las Tiendas

Emb. de Los Canch

Posto Fiscal do Retiro
Cortijo de Liviana
Valdebótoa
100
Casa de Carabineros

Cortijo de las Monjas
Río Guerrero
Cortijo de Madroño
Cortijo Quintana
Cortijo de Capote
Cortijo de Márquez

Esparragalej
Lácara
Casarente
209
La Garrov

Botalogo
Caia
Cortijo del Rincón
407
403
400
Santa Engracia
Alcazaba
Gévora del Caudillo
Sagrajas

209
Estación de Talavera
Novelda del Guadiana
Alcazaba
Guadiana del Caudillo
La Colonia
Los Hornos

Montijo

Posto Fiscal do Caia
13
Catedral San Juan
BADAJOZ
(rom. Colonia Pacensis)
395
A5
Villafranco del Guadiana
Pueblonuevo del Guadiana
Los Fresnos
Balboa
Talavera la Real
Valdelacalzada
Puebla de la Calzada
Barbaño
Los Cercados
Torremayor
Cubillana

116
107
432
Caserío de la Castellana
La Corchuela
Arroyo de Revillas
Casa Senuista
Castillo y Cortijo Casa Colorada
382
380
E90
376
374
Guadajira
Lobón
372
368
365
66
360
354
353
Río Guadiana
Casa del Encinar
de

32
Caserío del Ronquillo
Caserío La Carrona
La Risca
Alvarado
Cortijo de la Cascajosa
Cortijo del Portugués
Cortijo de la Calderona
La Honrada
Cortijo de los Granadinos
280
Cortijo de Mazas
Casas de la Cora

Caserío de los Frailes de Arrib
Caserío de Guijarra
Caserío de la Mora
Cortijo de Palomarejo
Cortijo del Barbudo
Cortijo del Olivar
Guadajira
Cortijo de Doña Teresa
Casa de Guadajira
Casa de la Carrascala

Zafra

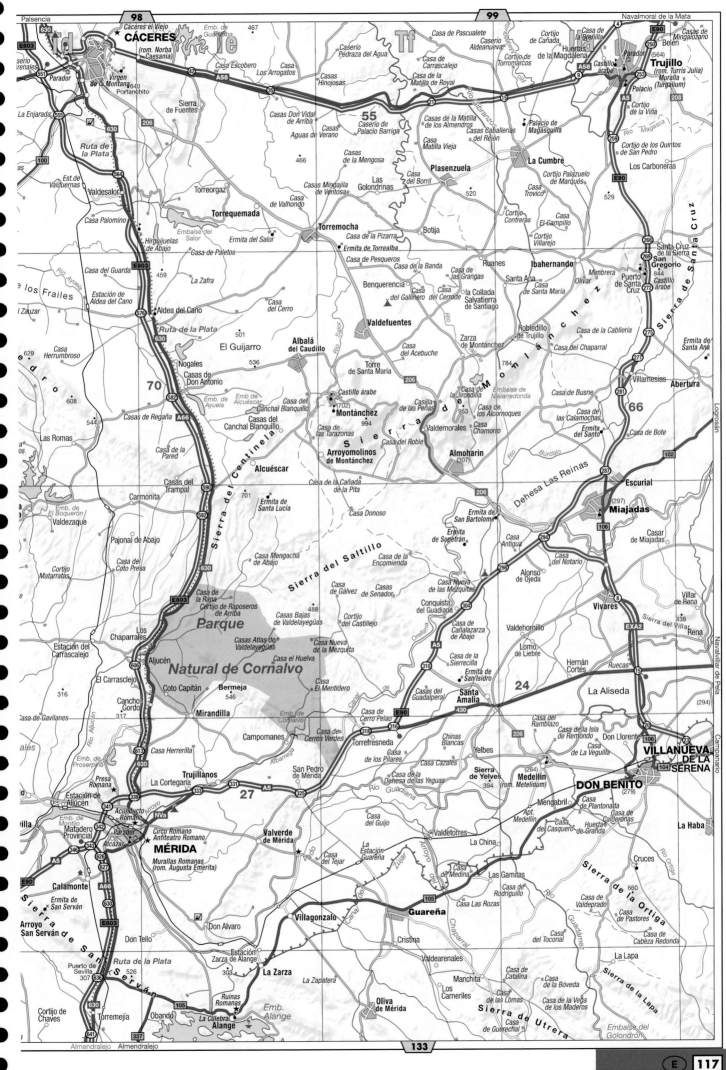

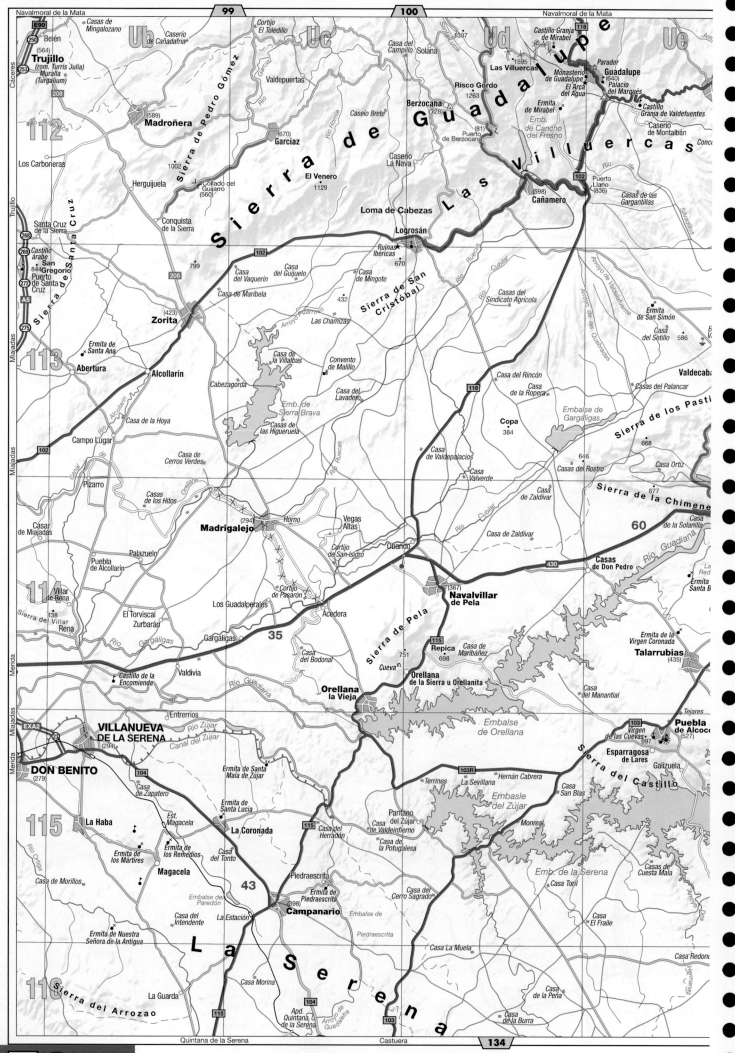

Ub   Uc   Ud   Ue

E90
(250) Belén
Trujillo
(rom. Turris Julia)
Muralla
(Turgalium)
253
Cáceres
Casas de
Mingalozano
Caserío
de Cañadafria
208
(589)
Madroñera
Sierra de Pedro Gómez
Cortijo
El Toledillo
Solana
Casa del
Campillo
Santa Lucia
1307
Castillo Granja
de Mirabel
118
Las Villuercas
1595
Monasterio
de Guadalupe
El Arca
del Agua
Parador
Guadalupe
(640)
Palacio
del Marqués

112

Valdepuertas
Garciaz
(670)
Río Garciaz
Caserío Brete
Berzocana
(728)
Risco Gordo
1263
(81)
Puerto
de Berzocana
Emb.
de Cancho
del Fresno
Ermita
de Mirabel
Castillo
Granja de Valdefuentes
Caserío
de Montalbán
Conce

Los Carboneras
1002
El Venero
Caserío
La Nava
102
(598)
Cañamero
Puerto
Llano (836)
Casas de las
Gargantillas

Herguijuela
Collado del
Guijarro
(560)
1129
Loma de Cabezas

Santa Cruz
de la Sierra
268
Conquista
de la Sierra
Logrosán
Río Ruecas
Cubilar

269 Castillo
árabe
844 San
Gregorio
Puerto
de Santa
Cruz
272
799
102
208
Casa
del Vaquerín
Casa
del Guijuelo
Casa
de Mingote
Ruinas
Ibéricas
670
Sierra de San
Cristóbal
Casas del
Sindicato Agrícola
Ermita
de San Simón
Casa
del Sotillo
586
A5
275
Ermita de
Santa Ana
Casa de Maribela
432
Arroyo de las Quebradas

113
Abertura
Zorita
(423)
Las Chamizas
Pizarro
Arroyo
Convento
de Malillo
Casa del Rincón
Casa
de la Ropera
Valdecab

Alcollarín
Casa de
la Villalbas
Casa del
Lavadero
116
Casas del Palancar

Río Alcollarín
Cabezagorda
Emb. de
Sierra Brava
Casas de
las Higueruela
Copa
384
Embalse de
Gargáligas
Sierra de los Pasti

Casa de la Hoya
Canal de Orellana
Casa
de Valdepalacios
668

Campo Lugar
Casa de
Cerros Verdes
Río Ruecas
Casa
Valverde
Casas del Rostro
646

Casa
de Zaldívar
Sierra de la Chimene
677

Pizarro
Casas
de los Hitos
Horno
Río Cubilar
Casa
de Zaldívar
Casa
de la Solanilla
60

Casar
de Miajadas
(294)
Madrigalejo
Vegas
Altas
Casa de Zaldívar
430
Casas
de Don Pedro
Río Guadiana

Palazuelo
Cortijo
de San Isidro
Obando
La
Red

Puebla
de Alcollarín
114
Villar
de Rena
438
Sierra del Villar
Rena
El Torviscal
Zurbarán
Los Guadalperales
Cortijo
de Pasarón
Acedera
35
Sierra de Pela
(367)
Navalvillar
de Pela
115
Repica
698
Casa de
Maribáñez
751
Ermita de
Santa B
Ermita de la
Virgen Coronada
Talarrubias
(435)

Río Gargáligas
Gargáligas
Casa
del Bodonal
Cueva
Orellana
de la Sierra u Orellanita
Casa
del Manantial

Castillo de la
Encomienda
Valdivia
Río Guadiana
Orellana
la Vieja
Embalse
de Orellana
103
Puebla
de Alcoc
(527)
Virgen
de las Cuevas
697

Entrerríos
Río Zújar
EXA2
23
VILLANUEVA
DE LA SERENA
(294)
Canal del Zújar
103R
Terrines
La Sevillana
Hernán Cabrera
Casa
San Blas
Esparragosa
de Lares
Galizuela
Sierra del Castillo

Mérida
DON BENITO
(279)
104
Ermita de Santa
Maía de Zújar
Pantano
del Zújar
Casa
de Valdeinfierno
Embalse
del Zújar
Monreal
Casa
del Manantial
Casas de
Cuesta Mala

115
La Haba
Est.
Magacela
Ermita de
Santa Lucía
La Coronada
115
Casa del
Herradón
Casa
de la Potugalesa
Casa
El Fraile

Casa
de Zapatero
Ermita de
los Remedios
Casa
del Tonto
Emb. de la Serena
Casa Toril

Ermita de
los Mártires
Magacela
Piedraescrita
Casa del
Cerro Sagrado
Casa
El Fraile

Río Ortiga
Casa de Morillos
Embalse del
Paredón
Ermita de
Piedraescrita
(398)
Campanario
104
Embalse de
Piedraescrita
Casa
de la Peña

Casa del
Intendente
La Estación
Casa La Muela
Casa
Redon

Ermita de Nuestra
Señora de la Antigua
La Serena
Casa Morina
Arroyo
de Guadaefra
Casa
de la Burra
Hermana

116
Sierra del Arrozao
La Guarda
Apd.
Quintana
de la Serena
104
103

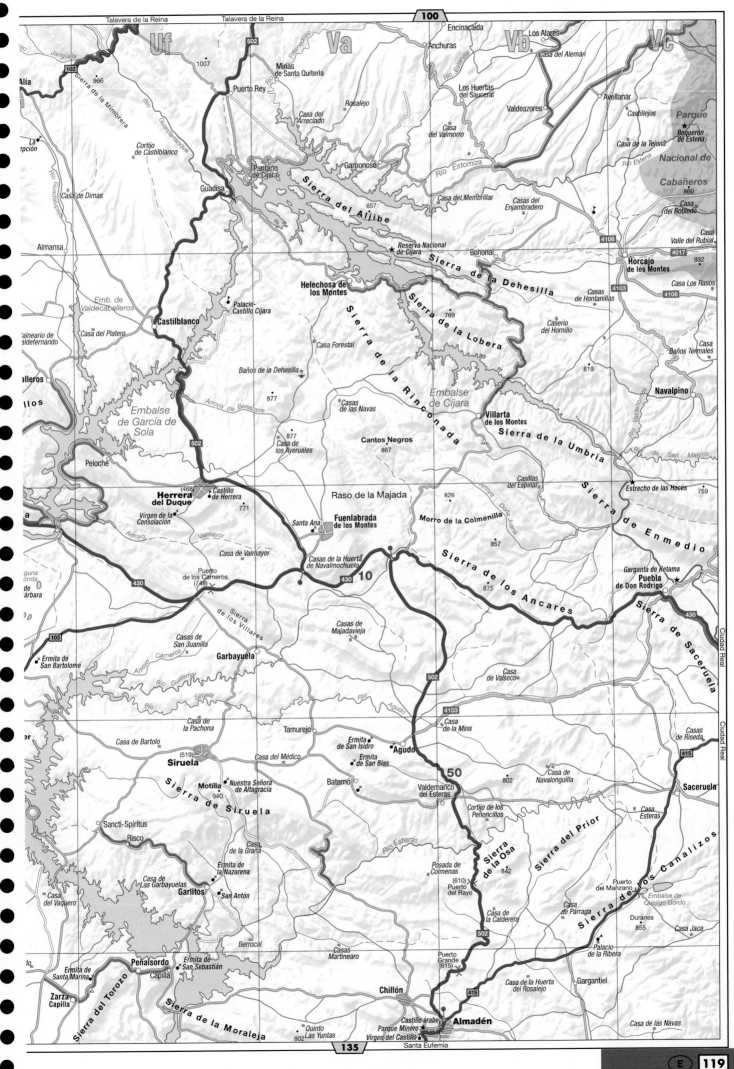

Talavera de la Reina · Talavera de la Reina · Encinacaida

Uf · Va · Vb · Vc

Los Alares
Anchuras · Casa del Alemán
502 · Minas de Santa Quiteria
1007 · Casa de la Tejoná
Castillejos · Parque
Puerto Rey · Avellanar · Boqueron de Estena
Río Estomiza · Nacional de
966 · Casa del Arreciado · Rosalejo · Los Huertas del Sauceral · Valdeazores · Cabañeros · 860
Jarigüela · 102
Sierra de la Mimbrera · Casa del Valmorro · Casa del Robledo
La epción · Cortijo de Castilblanco · Gamonoso · Casa del Membrillar · Casas del Enjambradero · Río Estena
Pantano de Cijara · Sierra del Aljibe · 657 · Casa Valle del Rubial · 4106
Casa de Dimas · Guadisa · 4017
Almansa · Reserva Nacional de Cijara · Sierra de la Dehesilla · Casas de Hontanillas · Horcajo de los Montes · 932
Bohonal · 4103 · Casa Los Rasos · 4106
Emb. de Valdecaballeros · Helechosa de los Montes · Sierra de la Lobera · 819
Palacio-Castillo Cijara · 769 · Caserío del Hornillo · Casa Baños Termales
alleros · Castilblanco · Casa del Platero · Casa Forestal · Sierra de la Rinconada · Embalse de Cijara · Navalpino
Balneario de Valdefernando · Baños de la Dehesilla · 877 · Casas de las Navas · Villarta de los Montes · Sierra de la Umbria
Embalse de García de Sola · Arroyo de Benazaire · 877 · Cantos Negros · 867 · Sierra de San Marcos
a · Casa de los Ayeruales · Casillas del Espinar · Estrecho de las Hoces · 759
Peloché · 502 · Raso de la Majada · 826 · Sierra de Enmedio
laguna onda rbara · Herrera del Duque · 468 · Castillo de Herrera · Morro de la Colmenilla · 857 · Garganta de Retama · Puebla de Don Rodrigo
771 · Virgen de la Consolación · Santa Ana · Fuenlabrada de los Montes · Sierra de los Ancares · 875 · 430
430 · 103 · Puerto de los Carneros 748 · Casa de Valmayor · Valmayor · Casas de la Huerta de Navalmochuelo · 10 · 430 · Sierra de Saceruela · Ciudad Real
Ermita de San Bartolomé · Sierra de los Villares · Casas de Majadavieja · Casa de Valseco
Casas de San Juanillá · 4103 · Casas de Riseda
Garbayuela · Casa de la Mina · 415
er · Carneros · Arroyo · Casa de la Pachona · Tamurejo · Ermita de San Isidro · Agudo · Casa de Navalonguilla · 802
Casa de Bartolo · Río Gualemar · Casa del Médico · Ermita de San Blas · 50 · Saceruela
519 · Siruela · Motilla · Nuestra Señora de Altagracia · Baterno · Valdemanco del Esteras · Sierra del Prior · Casa Esteras
940 · Sierra de Siruela · Cortijo de los Peñoncillos
Sancti-Spíritus · Sierra de la Osa · 842 · Sierra de los Canalizos
Risco · Casa de la Graña · Río Esteras · Posada de Colmenas · Puerto del Manzano · Embalse de Quejigo Gordo
Ermita de la Nazarena · 610 · Puerto del Rayo · Casa de Párraga · Duranes · 855 · Casa Jaca
Casa de las Garbayuelas · Garlitos · San Antón · Casa de la Calderera · 502 · Palacio de la Ribera
Casa del Vaquero · Berrocal · Casas Martineaio · Puerto Grande 615 · Gargantiel
Peñalsordo · Ermita de San Sebastián · Capilla · 415 · Casa de la Huerta del Rosalejo
Ermita de Santa Marina · Sierra del Torozo · Chillón · Casa de las Navas
Zarza Capilla · Sierra de la Moraleja · Quinto Las Yuntas · 802 · Castillo árabe · Parque Minero · Almadén
Virgen del Castillo · Santa Eufemia

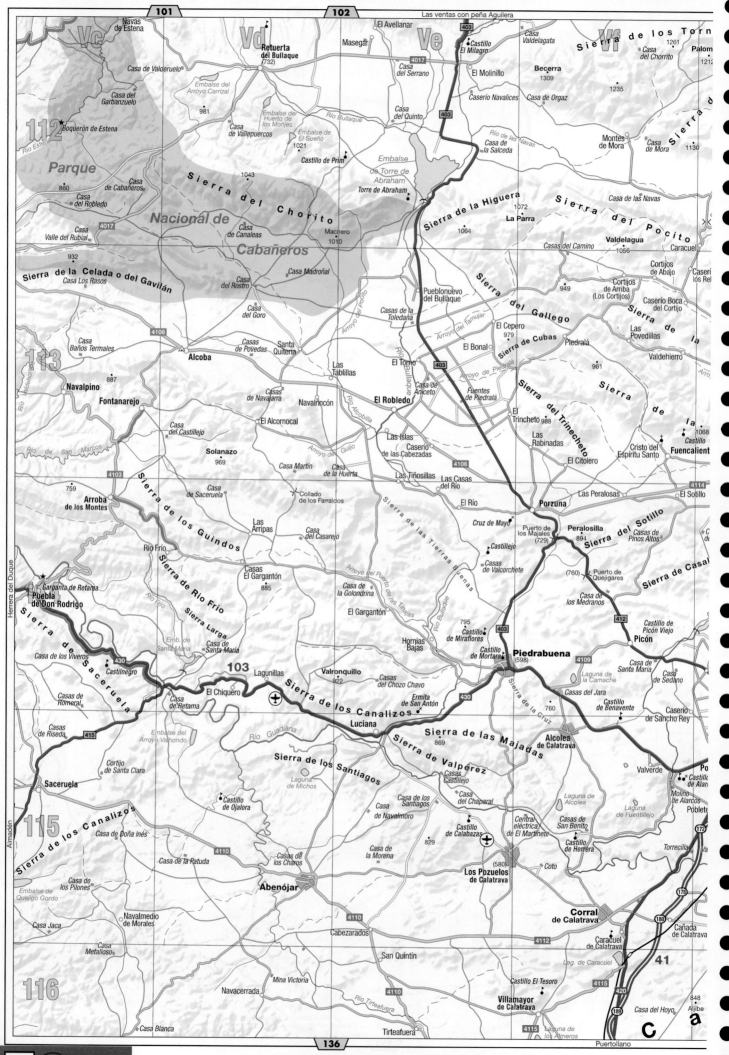

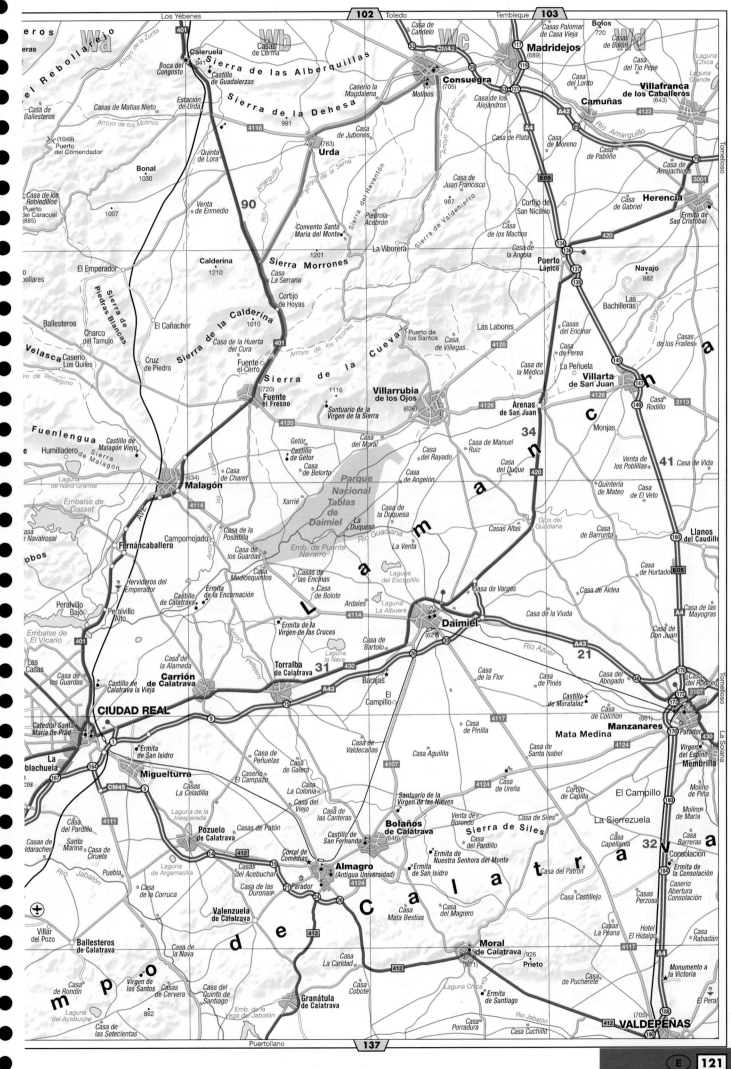

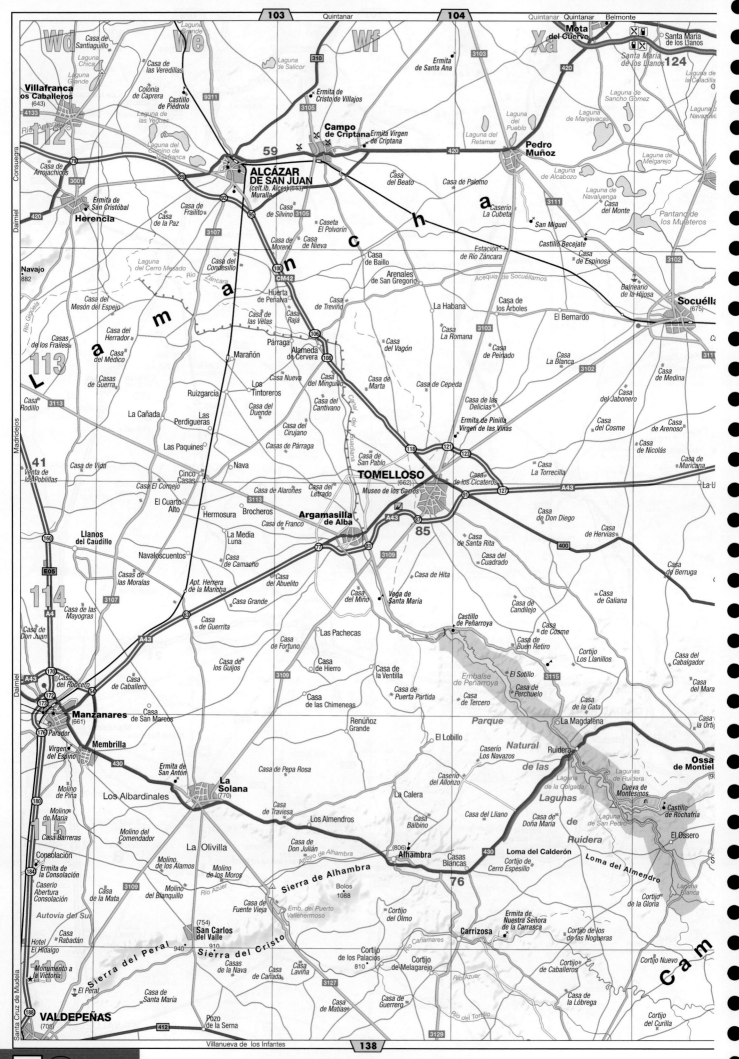

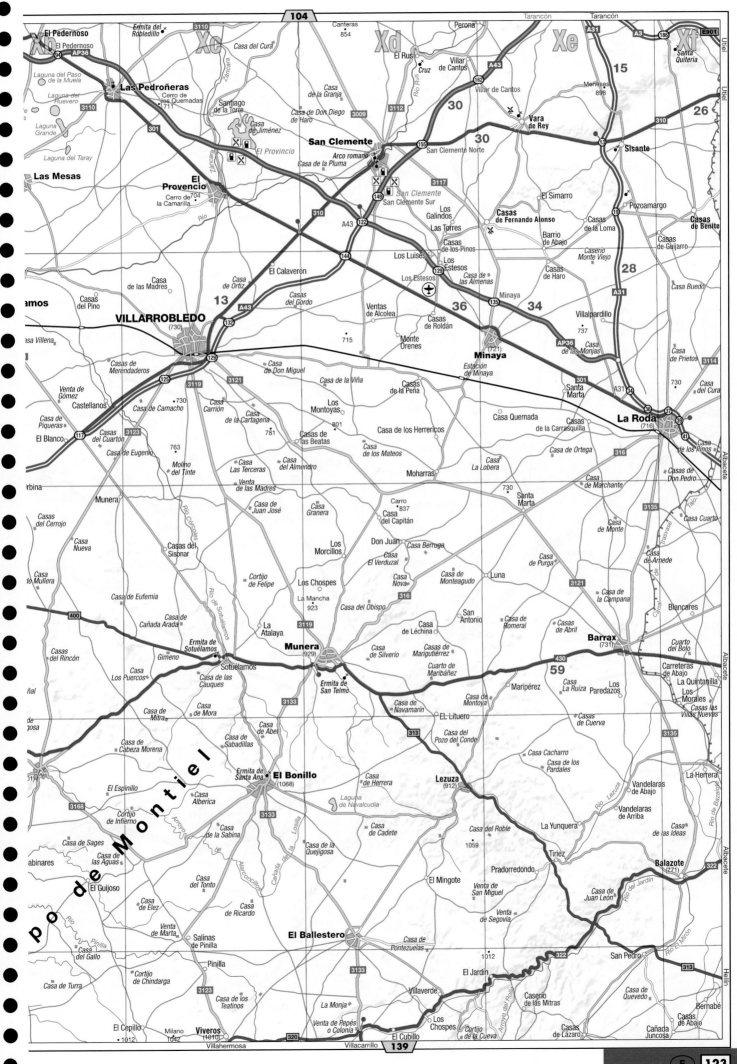

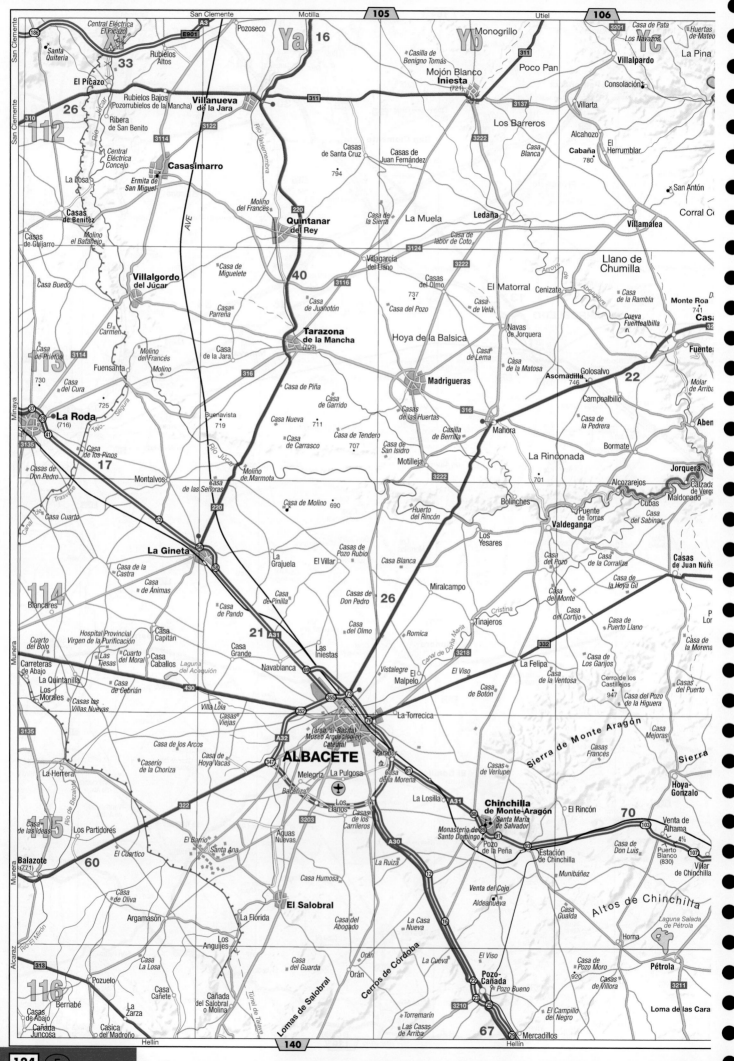

Sierra de Rubial
Moluengo 1040
Casas de Moya
Venta del Moro
Los Marcos
La Cornudilla
Los Ruices
El Derramador
El Azagador
Utiel
Río Magro
Casas del Rey
Las Monjas
La
Requena (692)
Casas de Pradas
Casas de Eufemia
322
El Pontón
291
El Rebollar
A3
297
Siete Aguas
Estación Venta
Mina-Siete Aguas
El Matutano
Sierra de las Cabrillas
Za
302
40
304
306
Venta Quemada
Buñol

Parque Natural
Casas Viejas
Rincón del Toro
Cañada Vieja
Los Cojos
Los Isidros
Casas de Cuadra
Casas de Giménez
Los Duques
Campo Arcis
Valderrama
330
(737)
831 Corral
La Portera
Hortunas de Arriba
Sierra de Malacara 1119
Cerro del Asno
Mijares
Loma Parreta

Los Cárceles
La Zúa
Torrejón
Santa Bárbara
Tamayo
El Retorno
Casas de Penén de Albosa
Albosa
Los Sardineros
Collado de Cruz de Cofrentes
Casas de la Manchega
540
Bultreras 754
Hortunas de Abajo
Juan Vich de-Sotos
Río Magro
Sierra del Asno
Sierra de la Monterilla
57
de las
Hoces del Cabriel

onfite
Tabaqueros
Monasterio
Casas de Cárcel
Baños de Fuente Podrida
Cilanco
Villatoya
Casa Madroñera
Casas de Caballero
Casa El Ciscar
Casas del Río
Pedrones de Arriba
Pedrones de Abajo
Casas de Sotos
Viñuelas
Los Herreros 1086
Martés
Embalse de Forata
63

Cortijo de Patas 742
Casa de ña Anita
3201
as-Ibáñez (707)
Ermita de la Virgen de la Cabeza
Alborea
Casa de la Desesperada
Casa Albarizas 671
Ermita de la Encarnación
Casa de la Lentisosa
Casas del Río
Casa de Penén
Río Cabriel
330
Casa del Cul
Rambla Seca
El Oro
Emb. de Naranjero
Emb. d. Cortes II

Ermita del Calvario
Casa Cendreros
Casas de Ves 703
Barranco
La Rambla
El Viso
Cantoblanco
Balsa de Ves
Casa de la María
Las Casas de Basta
Casas de Alcance
Castillo de Chiret
Cortes de Pallás
Emb. La Muela
3207
3207
albilla
3218
Serradiel
702
Zulema
Casa Sevellar
Casa Carrera
Los Hervideros
Cofrentes
Embalse de Embarcaderos
Los Tejones

Marimínguez
3201
Las Eras
Alcalá del Júcar
Tolosa
Molino de Don Benito 735
Villar de Ves
Barrio del-Santuario
La Pared
Casa Milhombres 895
Casa Peña Maria
Casa del Alcalde
La Muela de Cortes de Pallás

igibre
Antiguo Castillo
Ermita de San Lorenzo
Casa del Cerro
La Gila
Rí Júcar
Casa Tranco del Lobo
Embalse de Cofrentes (Molinar)
Casa de Usero
Jalance (455)
Muela de Jalance 897
El Fresno
Casa de Rosa
La Recueja
era
Casa del Conde
Cruz de la Cueva Alta
Sierra del Boquerón
962
1028
Casa de los Capellanes 987
Juey
Muela de Jalance
Casas del Miñón

Sierra de la Caballa
Casa de Juan Pardo
997
Casas de la Gobernadora
Casas de Juan Gil
Casa de Garijo
Cañada de Arriba
Río
Río Cautabán
Jarafuel (586)
Las Pedrizas 985
Alto de Tona
689
Villavaliente
3227
Casa de Peña Rubia
Villa Juana
Castilla de-Andresón
Casilla del Mamporro
332
Teresa de Cofrentes
869
Caroig 1126
Casa de Cávirá
Benifatal

ez
78
Casa de Conrado
Casilla de Antón
Casilla de Martín
Alatoz
Casa del Hontanar
3201
(902)
Carcelén
La Unde
Sierra Palomera
1260
Casa de Pepín
Río Zarra
Zarra
La Hoz
Ermita de San Roque
Iglesia del Rosario
Ayora (596)
La Muela
Casas de la Molinera

ozo
nte
Casilla de Gaspar
La Herradilla
Caserío Fraguas
Casa del Médico
Muela de Carcelén
Casa de la Florida
Casa de la Ortina
Casa del Medio
La Vega
Montemayor 1108
Ermita de la Virgen de Gracia
Cova del Sordo
Casa Aliaga
Casa de Gachas

Cuerda de la Doblona
Coto de la Milagrosa
1109
Casas de Don Pedro
Casas de la Peña
Las Fuentes
Cueva de la Vieja (Pinturas Rupestres) 1182
Casa de Don Bruno
Rincón del Peñón del Moro
Casa del Campo
de Higueruela
3209
Molatón 1245
Casa de los Bolos
Casas de Torro
La Laguna
Cueva de Venado
Puntal del Ariciseco
Casa del Collado de San Juan 1020
Cueva del Pilar
Casas de Madrona
Solana de Alambín
Cuevas
Casa del Peregrin
991
Cueva
21

Higueruela
Casa Aparicio
Oncebreros
El Royo
Casillas de Marín de Abajo
Alpera (854)
Casa de Delgado
3201
Castillo de Meca
San Benito
Lomas del Mellado
975
Casa del Royo
Sierra
de Enguera
Altos de Salomón 1056
Hoya Redonda
El Puntal
Santig
Navalón de Arriba

Bete
Estación de Villar de Chinchilla
El Salobralejo
Apartadero de Higueruela
Casillas de Marín de Arriba
Estalon de Alpera
Casa de los Altos
El Carrascal
Cueva del Rey Moro
Caserío Los Blancos
El Espino
330
Casa de Alfonso 1073
Casas de Requena
Caserío Corrales de Blay

110 112
(954)
Puerto Los Altos
3½ Casa del Cerro
Casa de Don Fernando
San Rafael
Apeadero de El Mugron
136
Casa del Tostado
140
146
148
Caserío de Sugel
868
Cueva del Gato
Torretallada

Casa de la Almagra
El Ojuelo
Casa de El Bachiller
Bonete (888)
123 124
A31
Embalse de Almansa
ALMANSA (685)
155
El Ventorrillo
9
Loma de Miralcampo
Venta de la Vicenta (692)
Puerto de Almansa

Casato de Higinio
El Casuto de Don Salvador
1089
Casa de los Pinos
Ermita de Belén
Casa Nueva
426
Casa del Rojalero
El Regajo
Casa Rambla d. Campillo
11%
la Font de la Figuera
89

Corral-Rubio
Casa Aguaza
Casa de la Vega
Casa del Torno
412
Botás
Los Pozuelos
Apartadero de Casas del Campillo
Casa de Agua Verde
A31
344
28

Casa de Hueso
3209
39
Fortaleza
Casa de las Minas
Pozo de la Higuera
El Cegarrón
Casa Jodar
Cerro El
Los Pocicos

La Higuera
Montealegre del Castillo (808)
Necrópolis del Llano de la Consolación
Museo Arqueológico Provincial
La Cueva
Yecla
Valencia

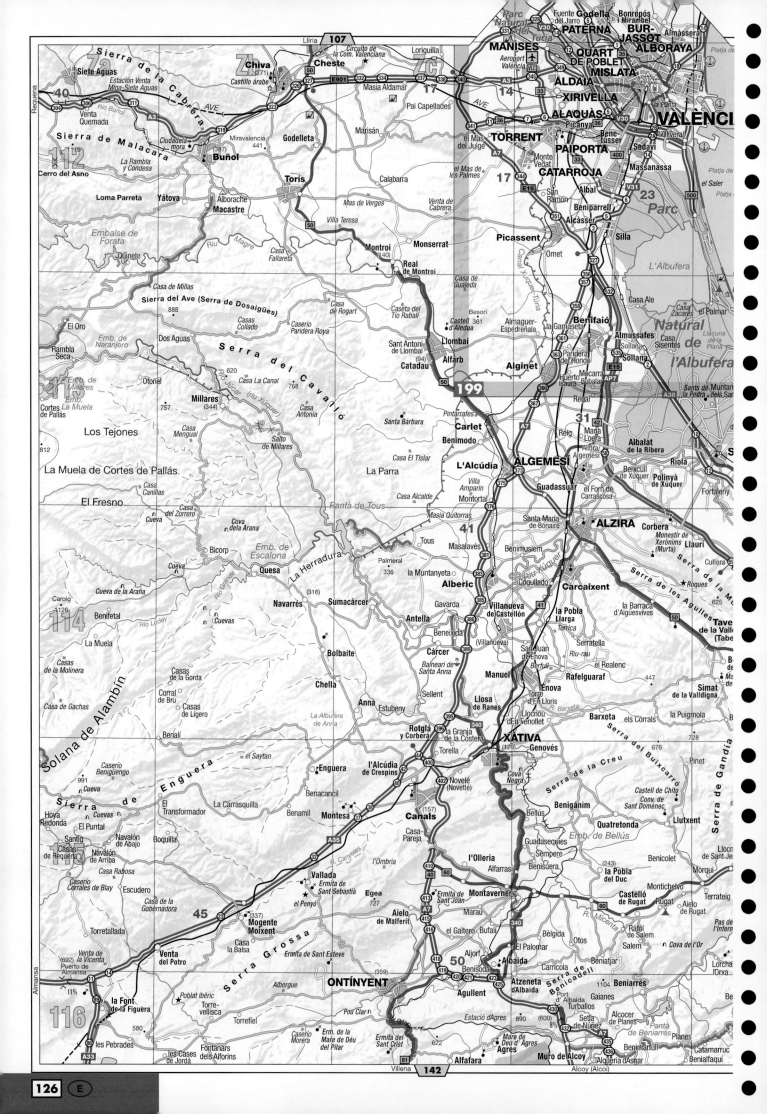

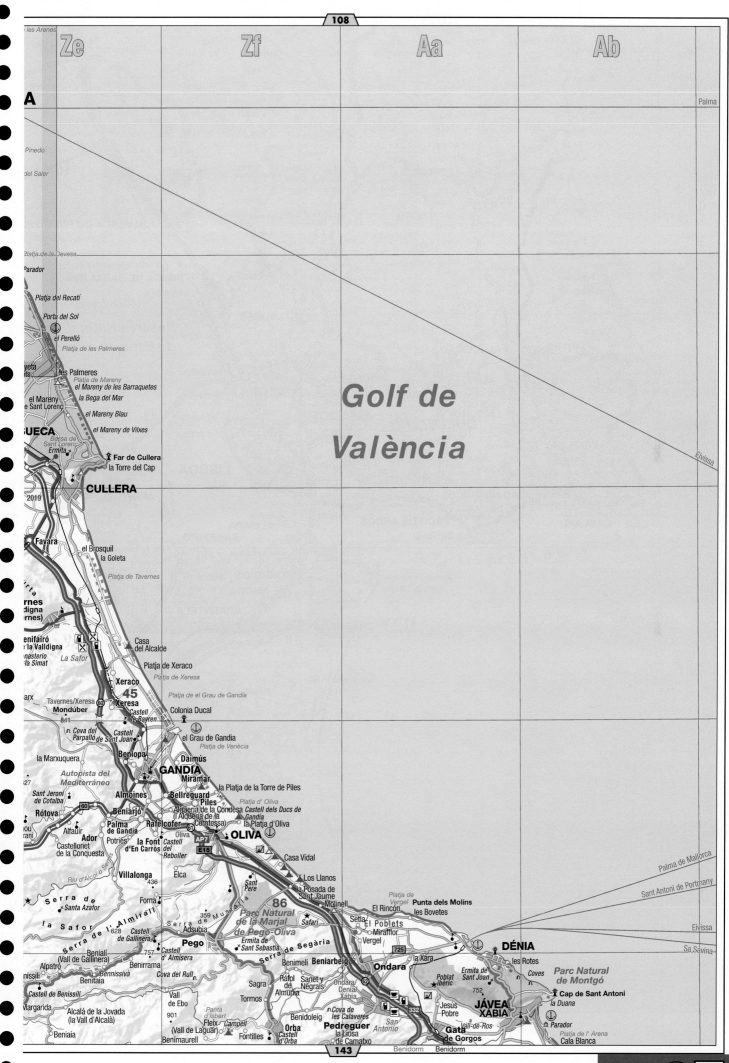

Ze   Zf   Aa   Ab

A   Palma

les Arenes
el Pinedo
del Saler

Golf de

València

Platja de la Devesa
Parador

Platja del Recatí
Porta del Sol
el Perelló
Platja de les Palmeres

les Palmeres
Platja de Mareny
el Mareny de les Barraquetes
la Bega del Mar
el Mareny Blau
el Mareny de Vilxes

yeta
ts
el Mareny
de Sant Lorenç

SUECA
Bassa de
Sant Lorenç
Ermita

Far de Cullera
la Torre del Cap

CULLERA

2019

Favara
el Brosquil
la Goleta

Platja de Tavernes

rnes
digna
rnes)

enifairó
e la Valldigna
nàsterio
la Simat
La Safor

Casa
del Alcalde

Platja de Xeraco

Xeraco
Platja de Xeresa
45
Tavernes/Xeresa 60
Xeresa
Mondúber
841
arx

Platja de el Grau de Gandía

Colonia Ducal

Cova del
Parpalló
Castell
de Bayren
Castell
de Sant Joan

el Grau de Gandia
Platja de Venècia

Benìopa
la Marxuquera
Daimús
GANDÍA
Miramar

Autopista del
Mediterráneo
27

Sant Jeroni
de Cotalba
Almoines
Beniarjó
Rótova
60
Palma
de Gandía
Rafelcofer
Oliva
Alfauir
Ador
Potries
Castellonet
de la Conquesta
la Font
d'En Carrós
61
Castell
del
Reboller
AP7
E15

Bellreguard
Piles
la Platja de la Torre de Piles
Platja d' Oliva
Alqueria de la Condesa
(l'Alqueria de la
Comtessa)
Castell dels Ducs de
Gandía
la Platja d'Oliva

OLIVA

Casa Vídal

Villalonga
436
Elca

Los Llanos
la Posada de
Sant Jaume
Molinell

Palma de Mallorca

Sant Antoni de Portmany

Eivissa

Sa Savina

Forna
Sant
Pere

Serra de
Santa Azafor
la Safor
Serra de l'Almirall
628
359
Adsubia
Serra de Mustalla
Safari
Platja de
Vergel
El Rincón
Setla
Punta dels Molíns
les Bovetes
Miraflor
Vergel

Parc Natural
de la Marjal
de Pego-Oliva

86

El Poblets

DÉNIA
les Rotes
Coves

Parc Natural
de Montgó

Castell
de Gallinera
Pego
757
Castell
d' Almisera

Serra de Segària

Ondara
725
la Xara

Ermita de
Sant Joan
752

Benialí
(Vall de Gallinera)
Alpatró
nissili
Castell de Benissili
Benirrama
Bennissivà
Benitaia
Cova del Rull
Margarida
Alcalá de la Jovada
(la Vall d'Alcalà)
Beniaia

Ermita de
Sant Sebastià

Benimeli
Sagra
Ráfol
de
Almúnia
Tormos

Beniarbeig
Sanet y
Negrals

Ondara

62

Ondara/
Denia/
Xàbia

Poblat
iberic
Jesús
Pobre

Cap de Sant Antoni
la Duana

JÁVEA
XÀBIA
332

Vall de Ebo
901
Fleix
Benimaurell
(Vall de Laguar)
Campell
Fontilles

Orba
Castell
d'Orba
la Llosa
de Camatxo

Benidoleig
Cova de
les Calaveres
Pedreguer

San
Antonio

Gata
de Gorgos
Vall-de-Ros

Parador
Platja de l' Arena
Cala Blanca

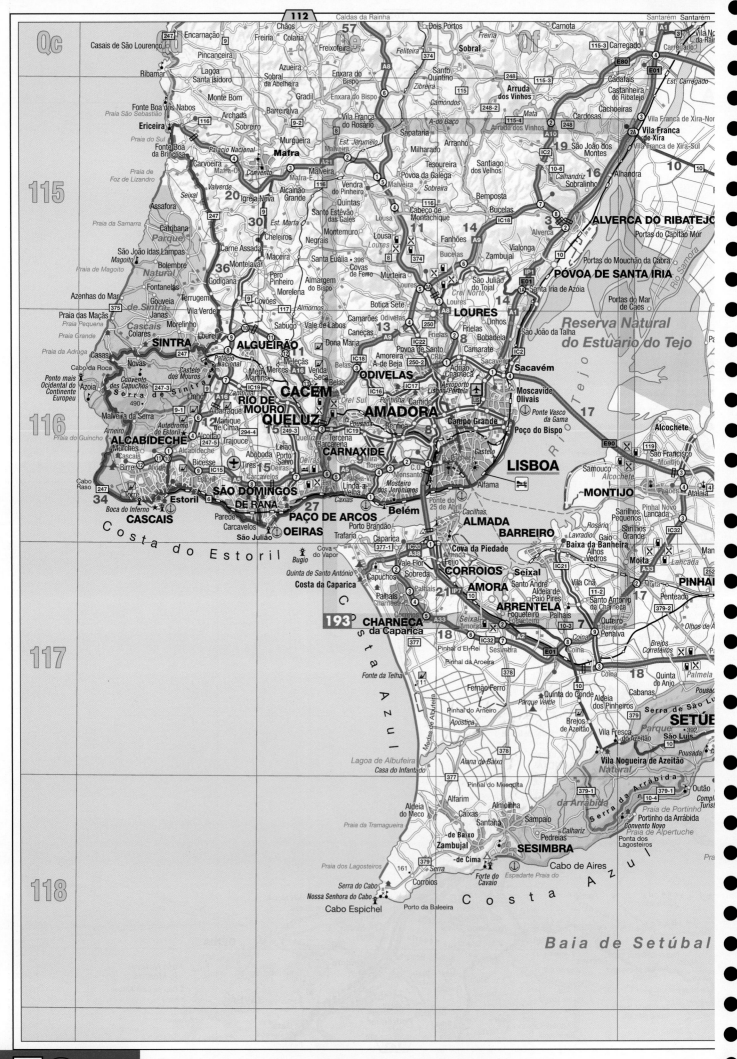

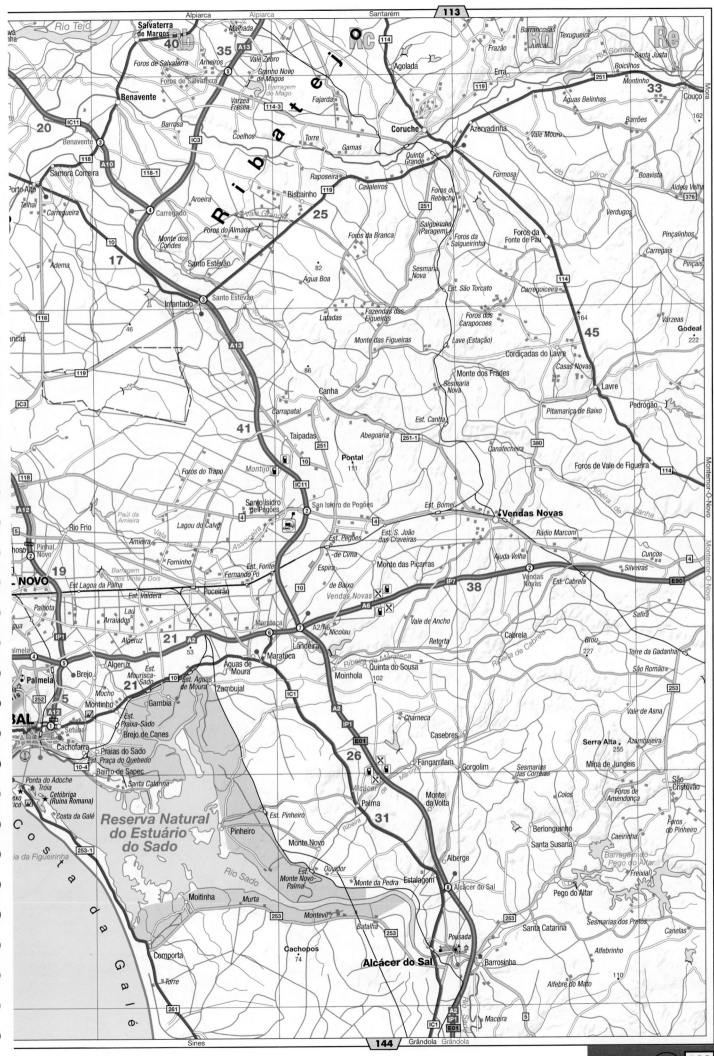

Rio Tejo · Alpiarca · Alpiarca · Santarém

Salvaterra de Magos · Malhada · **40** · **35** · A13 · Barrancosas Juncal · Texugueira · Re

Foros de Salvaterra · Arneiros · Vale Zebro · Frazão · Santa Justa · Erra · Rio Sorraia · Boicilhos

Foros de Salvaterra · Granho Novo de Magos · 119 · 251 · Montinho · **33**

Benavente · Fajarda · Águas Belinhas · Couço

114-3 · Vãrzea Fresca · Barrões · 162

20 · IC11 · Barrosa · Coelhos · Torre · Coruche · Azervadinha · Vale Mouro · Boavista

Benavente · 3 · Gamas · Quinta Grande · Formosa · Ribeira do Divor · Aldeia Velha

118 · A10 · Samora Correira · Aroeira · Raposeira · Foros do Rebacho · 376

Porto Alto · Telhal · 4 · Carregado · Bisrainho · 119 · Cavaleiros · 251 · Verdugos

Carregueira · Foros do Almada · **25** · Foros da Branca · Salgueirinha (Paragem) · Foros da Salgueirinha · Foros da Fonte de Pau · Pinçalinhos

Monte dos Condes · Santo Estêvão · 10 · **17** · Est. São Torcato · Carregais · Pinçais

Adema · Santo Estêvão · 82 · Sesmaria Nova · Carregoiceira · 114

Água Boa · Latadas · Fazendas das Figueiras · Foros dos Carapocoes · 164 · Várzeas · **Godeal** 222

118 · Infantado · 3 · Santo Estêvão · A13 · Monte das Figueiras · Lave (Estação) · **45**

Canha · 86 · Cordiçadas do Lavre · Casas Novas

119 · Carrapatal · Monte dos Frades · Lavre

41 · Taipadas · Abegoaria · 251-1 · Sesmaria Nova · Pitamariça de Baixo · Pedrógão

Foros do Trapo · Montijo · 251 · Pontal 111 · Canafecheira · 380 · Foros de Vale de Figueira · 114

IC11 · 10 · San Isidro de Pegões · Est. Bomel · Rádio Marconi · Cuncos

118 · Santo Isidro de Pegões · 2 · 4 · Vendas Novas · Silveiras · 4

A12 · Paúl da Amieira · Lagou do Calvo · Est. Pegões · Est. S. João das Craveiras · Ajuda Velha · 2 · Vendas Novas · E90

Rio Frio · Amieira · -de Cima · Monte das Piçarras · IP7 · **38** · Est. Cabrela

5 · Forninho · Espira- · Vendas Novas · Vale de Ancho · Safira

Pinhal Novo · **19** · Est. Fonte Fernando Pó · de Baixo · A6 · Retorta · Cabrela · Grou 227 · Torre da Gadanha

2 · -NOVO · Est. Lagoa da Palha · Barragem dos Vinte e Dois · Poceirão · Vendas Novas · A2/A6 · São Romão

Est. Valdera · 10 · Maratéca · 7 · Nicolau · 253

Palhota · Lau Arraiados · 6 · Landeira · Ribeira de Maratéca · Quinta do Sousa · Vale de Asna

IP1 · Algeruz · **21** · A2 · 53 · Moinhola 102 · Charneca · Serra Alta 255 · Azambujeira

4 · 5 · Algeruz · Aguas de Moura · Casebres · Mina de Jungeis

Brejo · Est. Mourisca-Sado · 10 · Est. Aguas de Moura · Zambujal · Sesmarias das Correias · São Cristóvão

Palmela · Mocho · **21** · Gambia · IC1 · Fangarrifam · Gorgolim · Colos · Foros de Amendonça

252 · **5** · Montinho · A2 · **26** · Monte da Volta · Berlonguinho · Foros do Pinheiro

BAL · A12 · 1 · Setúbal · Est. Praixa-Sado · Brejo de Canes · IP1 · Palma · Santa Susana · Caeirinha

Cachofarra · Praias do Sado · Est. Praça do Quebedo · Bairro de Sapec · Santa Catarina · E01 · **31** · Barragem do Pego do Altar · Freixial

10-4 · Ponta do Adoche · Tróia · Cetóbriga (Ruina Romana) · Costa da Galé · Est. Pinheiro · Pinheiro · Monte Novo · Alberge · Pego do Altar

Reserva Natural do Estuário do Sado · Rio Sado · Est. Monte Novo-Palma · Ouvidor · Monte da Pedra · Estalagem · 8 · Alcácer do Sal · Santa Catarina · Sesmarias dos Pretos · Canelas

253-1 · ia da Figueirinha · Moitinha · Murta · 253 · Montevil · Batalha · Pousada · Alfebrinho

Costa da Galé · Cachopos 74 · 253 · **Alcácer do Sal** · Barrosinha · Alfebre do Mato · 110

261 · Comporta · Torre · 253

Sines · A2 · IP1 · E01 · IC1 · Maceira · 5 · Rio Sado · Grândola · Grândola

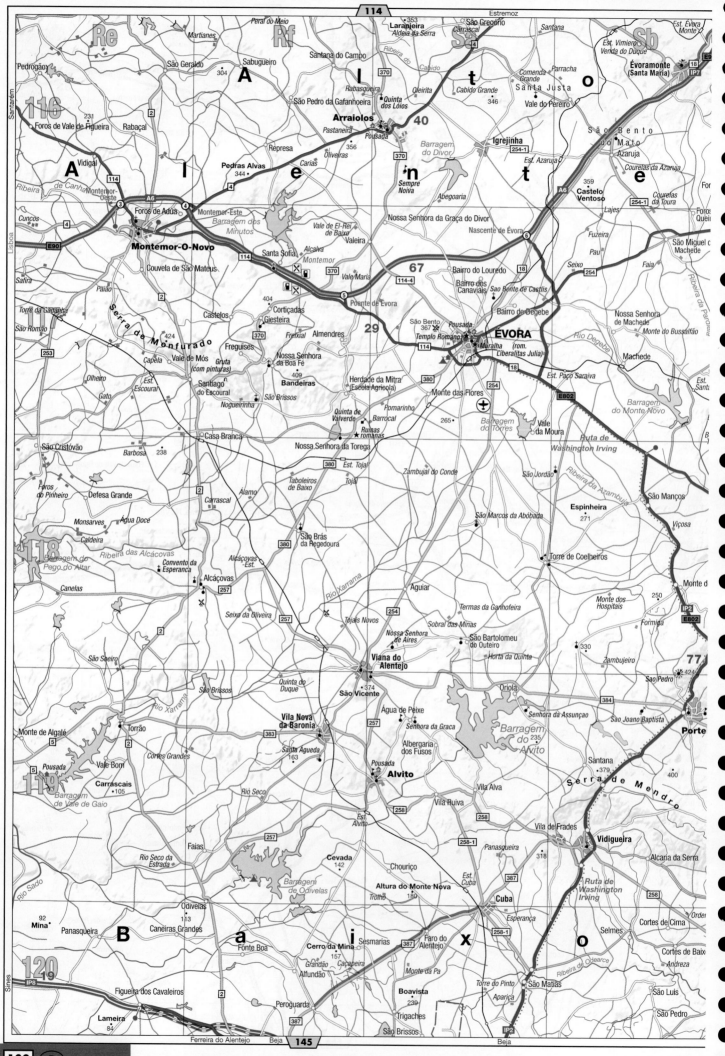

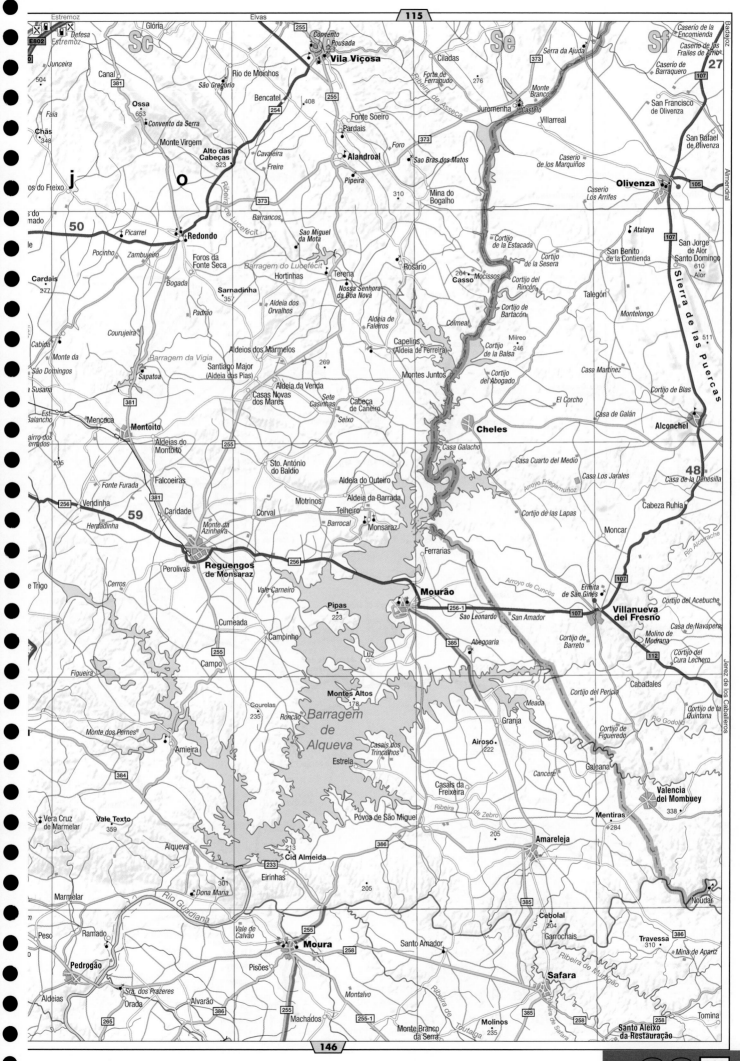

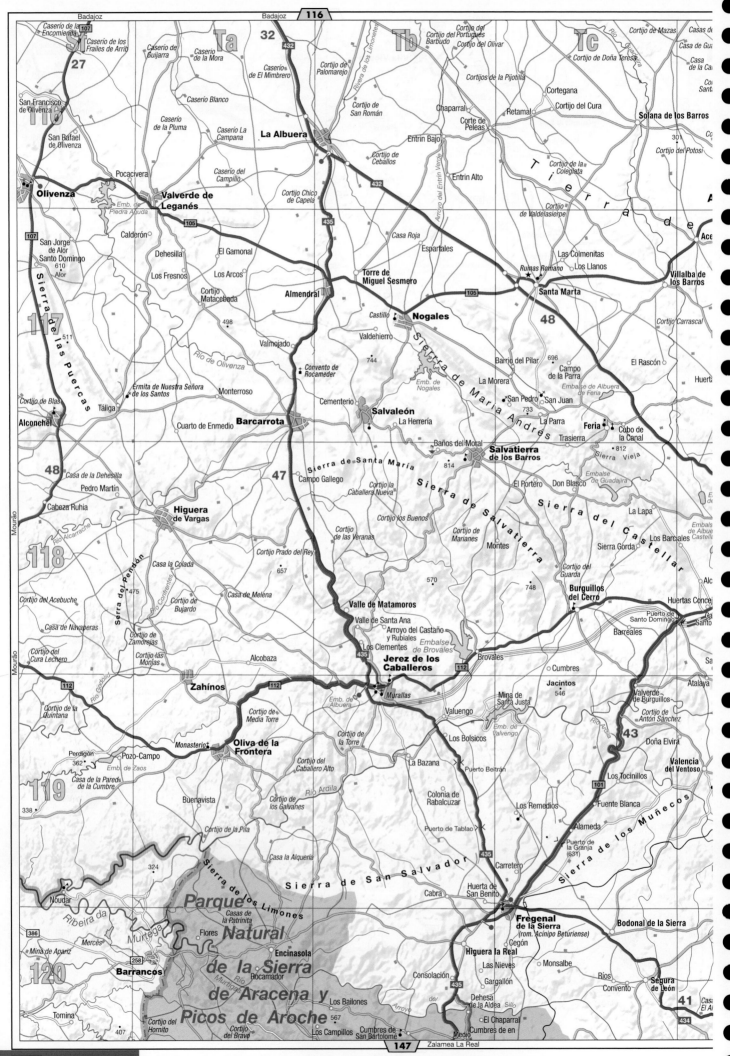

Badajoz   Badajoz

Ta   Tb   Tc

32

Caserío de la Encomienda
Caserío de los Frailes de Arrib
Caserío de Guijarra
Caserío de la Mora
27
San Francisco de Olivenza
San Rafael de Olivenza
Caserío Blanco
Caserío de la Pluma
Caserío La Campana
Pocacivera
Olivenza
Valverde de Leganés
Emb. de Piedra Aguda
Caserío del Campillo
La Albuera
Cortijo de Palomarejo
Cortijo de San Román
Cortijo de Ceballos
Cortijo del Portugués
Cortijo del Olivar
Cortijo de Doña Teresa
Cortijo de Mazas
Casas de
Casa de Gua
Casa de la C
Co
Sant
Cortijo del Barbudo
Cortijos de la Pijotilla
Chaparral
Cortegana
Cortijo del Cura
Solana de los Barros
Retamal
Corte de Peleas
Entrin Bajo
Entrin Alto
301
Cortijo del Potosí
Cortijo de la Coleglata
Tierra de
A

San Jorge de Alor
Santo Domingo
610
Alor
107
Calderón
Dehesilla
El Gamonal
Los Arcos
Los Fresnos
Cortijo Matacebada
498
Almendral
Cortijo Chico de Capela
Casa Roja
Espartales
Ruinas Romano
Las Colmenitas
Los Llanos
Santa Marta
Villalba de los Barros
Ace
Cortijo de Valdelasierpe
48

Sierra de las Puercas
511
Cortijo de Blas
Táliga
Ermita de Nuestra Señora de los Santos
Monterroso
Convento de Rocameder
Valmojado
744
Castillo
Nogales
Valdehierro
Sierra de María Andrés
Emb. de Nogales
La Morera
Barrio del Pilar
696
Campo de la Parra
El Rascón
Embalse de Albuera de Feria
Huerta
San Pedro
733
San Juan
Cementerio
Salvaleón
La Herrería
La Parra
Feria
Cubo de la Canal
Cortijo Carrascal
Trasierra
117

Alconchel
Cuarto de Enmedio
Barcarrota
Baños del Moral
Salvatierra de los Barros
814
Sierra Vieja
812
48
Casa de la Dehesilla
Pedro Martín
Cabeza Ruhia
Sierra de Santa María
Campo Gallego
Cortijo la Cabrera Nueva
Cortijo los Buenos
Sierra de Salvatierra
El Portero
Don Blasco
Embalse de Guadajira
La Lapa
Sierra del Castellar
Los Barciales
Sierra Gorda
Embals de Albue Castella
E
d
47

Higuera de Vargas
Río Alcarrache
118
Mourão
Cortijo del Acebuche
Casa de Navaperas
475
Casa la Colada
Cortijo de Bujardo
Casa de Melena
Cortijo Prado del Rey
657
Cortijo de las Veranas
Cortijo de Marianes
Montes
570
748
Cortijo del Guarda
Burguillos del Cerro
Huertas Conce
Alc
Puerto de Santo Domingo
Ga
Santo

Serra del Pendón
Río Godolid
Mourão
Cortijo del Cura Lechero
Cortijo de Zamorejas
Cortijo las Monjas
Alcobaza
Valle de Matamoros
Valle de Santa Ana
Arroyo del Castaño y Rubiales
Los Clementes
Embalse de Brovales
Jerez de los Caballeros
Brovales
Cumbres
Barreales
Mina de Santa Justa
Jacintos
546
Valverde de Burguillos
Cortijo de Antón Sánchez
Atalaya
112

Zahínos
112
Cortijo de la Quintana
Cortijo de Media Torre
Monasterio
Oliva de la Frontera
Cortijo de la Torre
Emb. de Albuera
Murallas
Valuengo
Emb. de Valvengo
Los Bolsicos
La Bazana
Puerto Beltrán
43
Doña Elvira
Valencia del Ventoso

119
Perdigón
362
Pozo-Campo
Emb de Zaos
Casa de la Pared de la Cumbre
338
Buenavista
Cortijo del Caballero Alto
Río Ardila
Cortijo de los Galvanes
Colonia de Rabalcuzar
Puerto de Tablao
Los Remedios
Alameda
Los Tocinillos
Fuente Blanca
101
Sierra de los Muñecos

Nóudar
324
Ribeira da
Murtega
Parque
Natural
Sierra de los Limones
Casas de la Patrinita
Flores
Casa la Alquería
Sierra de San Salvador
Carretero
Puerto de la Granja
(631)
435
Huerta de San Benito
Cabra
386
Mercês
Mina de Apariz
258
Barrancos
120
de la Sierra
Encinasola
Rocamador
Río Murtigas
Los Bailones
Consolación
Higuera la Real
Cegón
Las Nieves
Gargallón
Monsalbe
Ríos
Convento
Fregenal de la Sierra
(rom. Acinipo Beturiense)
Bodonal de la Sierra
Dehesa de la Aldea
Sillo
El Chaparral
Segura de León
41
Casa El A
434
Tomina
Cortijo del Hornito
407
Cortijo del Bravo
de Aracena y
Picos de Aroche
567
Los Campillos
Cumbres de San Bartolomé
Cumbres de en
Medio

432
432
105
435
105
435
435
112
435
101

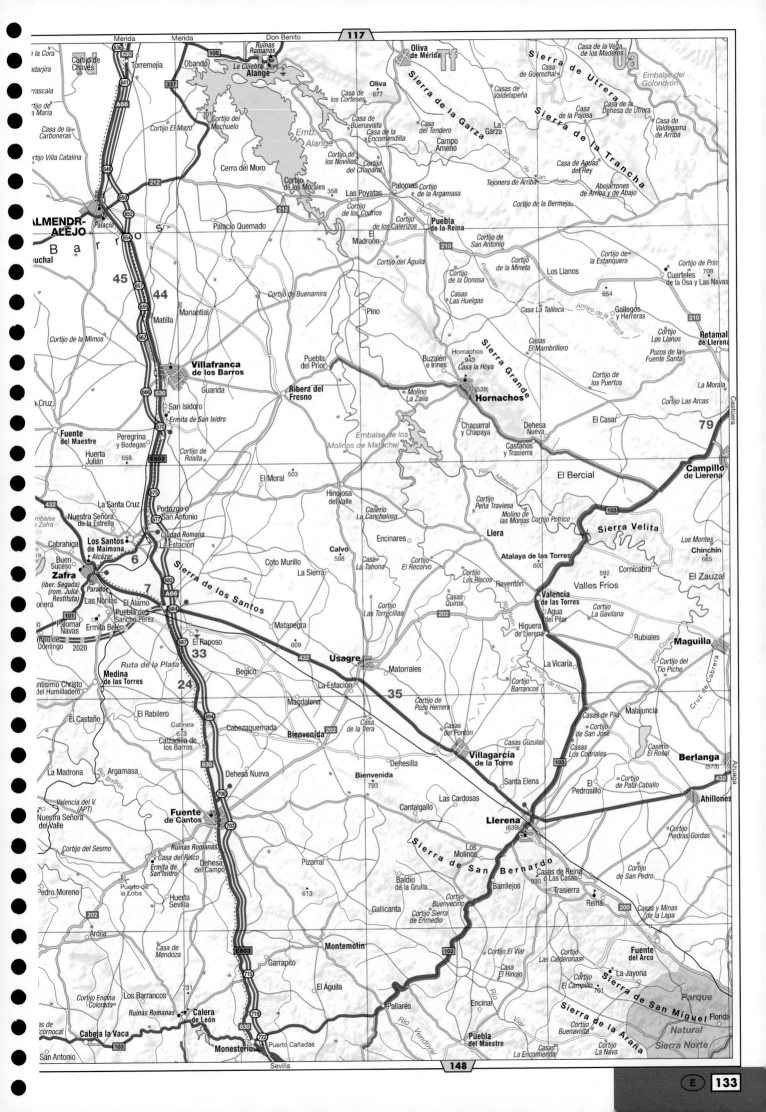

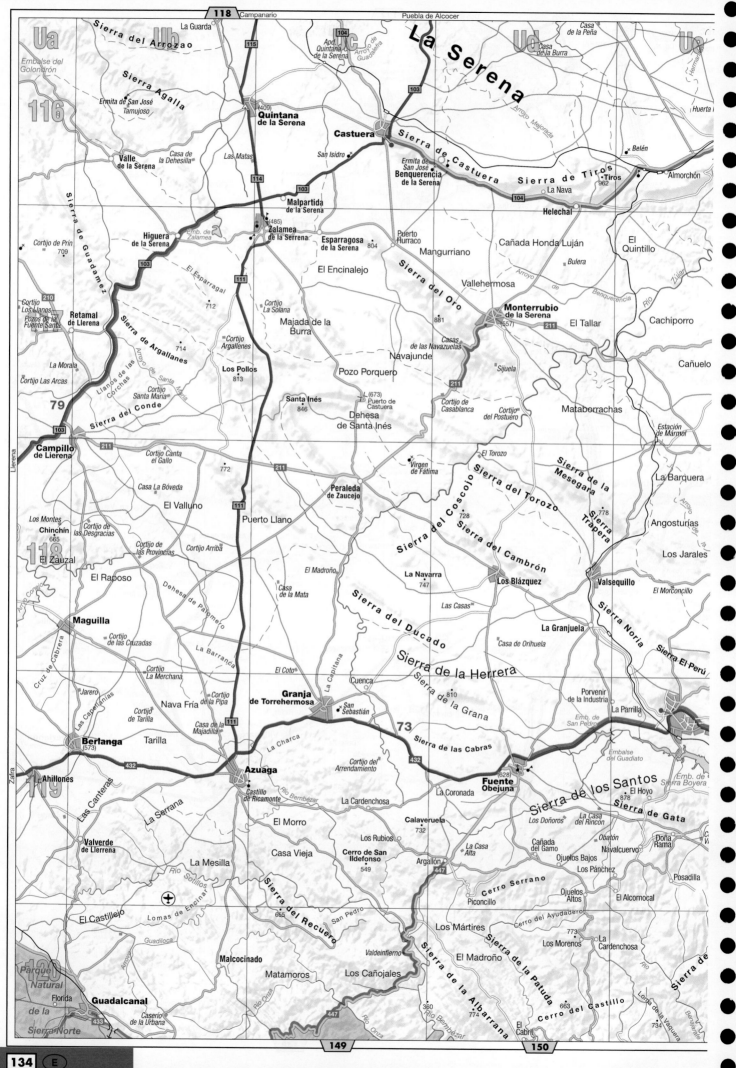

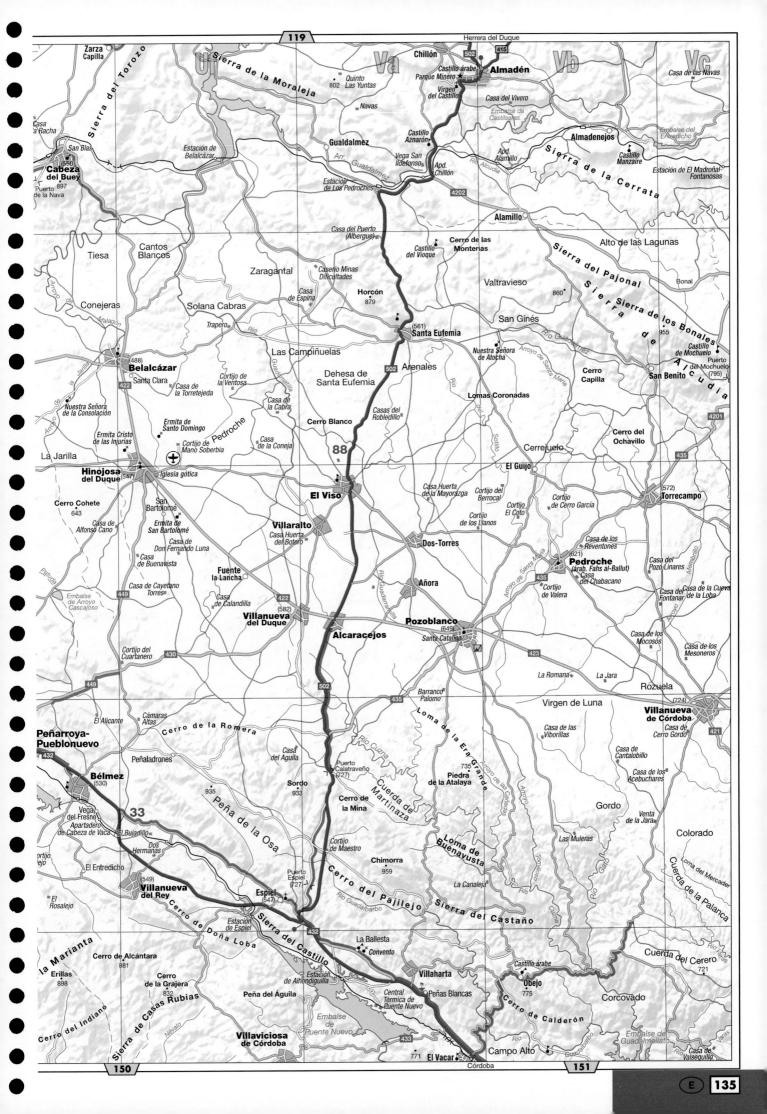

Herrera del Duque

Zarza
Capilla

Sierra del Torozo

Sierra de la Moraleja

Chillón

502

415

Castillo árabe
Parque Minero ★
Virgen
del Castillo

Almadén

Va

Vb

Vc

Casa de las Navas

Quinto
Las Yuntas
802

Navas

Casa
la Racha

San Blas

**Cabeza
del Buey**
(550)

Puerto
de la Nava
897

Tiesa

Cantos
Blancos

Zaragantal

Estación de
Belalcázar

Gualdalmez

Arr.
Gualdalmez

Vega San
Ildefonso

Castillo
Aznarón

Apd.
Alamillo

Apd.
Chillón

Río Alcudia

Embalse de
Castilseras

Almadenejos

Castillo
Manzaire

Embalse del
Entredicho

Estación de El Madroñal-
Fontanosas

Sierra de la Cerrata

Estación
de Los Pedroches

4202

Alamillo

Alto de las Lagunas

Conejeras

Solana Cabras

Casa del Puerto
(Albergue)

Caserío Minas
Dificultades

Casa
de Espina

Horcón
879

Trapero

Río

Cerro de las
Monterías

Castillo
del Vioque

Valtravieso

860

Sierra del Pajonal

Sierra de los Bonales

Bonal

Malagón

Arroyo de

(488)
Belalcázar

Santa Clara

422

Casa de
la Torretejeda

Cortijo de
la Ventosa

Las Campiñuelas

Dehesa de
Santa Eufemia

(561)
Santa Eufemia

502

Arenales

Nuestra Señora
de Atocha

San Ginés

Río Guadalmez

Arroyo de Santa María

955

Cerro
Capilla

Castillo
de Mochuelo

Puerto
del Mochuelo
(795)

Sierra de Alcudia

San Benito

4201

Guadamatilla

Guachanilla

Nuestra Señora
de la Consolación

Ermita Cristo
de las Injurias

Ermita de
Santo Domingo

Cortijo de
Mano Soberbia

Casa de
la Cabra

Casa de
la Coneja

Casas del
Robledillo

Lomas Coronadas

Río

Sotillo

Cerrejuelo

Cerro del
Ochavillo

435

La Jarilla

Cortijo de
Pedroche

Cerro Blanco

88

El Viso

El Guijo

Casa Huerta
de la Mayorazga

Cortijo del
Berrocal

(572)
Torrecampo

**Hinojosa
del Duque**
(547)

Iglesia gótica

San
Bartolomé

Ermita de
San Bartolomé

Villaralto
Casa Huerta
del Botero

Cortijo
El Coto

Cortijo
de los Llanos

Cortijo
de Cerro García

Casa de los
Reventones

Cerro Cohete
643

Casa de
Alfonso Cano

Casa de
Don Fernando Luna

Dos-Torres

(621)
Pedroche
(árab. Fahs al-Ballut)

Casa del
Pozo Linares

Patuda

Casa de
Buenavista

**Fuente
la Lancha**

Casa
de Buenavista

Casa de Cayetano
Torres

449

Embalse
de Arroyo
Cascajoso

Casa de
Calandilla

(582)
**Villanueva
del Duque**

422

Río Guadarramilla

Añora

435

Casa
del Chabacano

Cortijo
de Valera

Arroyo de Santa María

Casa de la Cueva
de la Loba

Casa del
Fontanar

Pozoblanco
(649)
Santa Catalina

423

Casa de los
Mocosos

Casa de los
Mesoneros

Cortijo del
Cuartanero

430

Alcaracejos

502

435

Barranco
Palomo

La Romana

La Jara

Rozuela

449

Cámaras
Altas

Cerro de la Romera

Virgen de Luna

(724)
**Villanueva
de Córdoba**

El Alicante

Casa de las
Viborillas

Casa de
Cerro Gordo

421

**Peñarroya-
Pueblonuevo**

432

Peñaladrones

Casa
del Águila

Río Cuzna

Puerto
Calatraveño
(727)

Loma de la Era Grande

Arroyo de las Cañadas

735

Piedra
de la Atalaya

Casa de
Cantalobillo

Casa de los
Acebuchares

Bélmez
(530)

Vega
del Fresno

Apartadero
de Cabeza de Vaca

El Bujadillo

Sordo
933

Cerro de
la Mina

Cuerda de
Martinaza

Gordo

Venta
de la Jara

33

Dos
Hermanas

935

Peña de la Osa

Cortijo
de Maestro

Loma de
Buenavista

Las Muleras

Colorado

El Entredicho

Cortijo
viejo

El Rosalejo

(549)
**Villanueva
del Rey**

Cerro de Doña Loba

Puerto
Espiel
(727)

Chimorra
959

La Canaleja

Río

Tamujoso

Loma del Mercader

Cuerda de la Palanca

la Marianta

Cerro del Indiano

Erillas
898

Cerro de Alcántara
881

Cerro
de la Grajera
832

Sierra de Casas Rubias

Névalo

Espiel
(547)

Estación
de Espiel

Sierra del Castillo

432

Cerro del Pajilejo

Sierra del Castaño

Río Guadalbarbo

Cuerda del Cerero

721

Peña del Águila

Estación
de Alhondiguilla

La Ballesta

Convento

Río Guadalmellato

Corcovado

Central
Térmica de
Puente Nuevo

Villaharta

Peñas Blancas

Castillo árabe
Obejo
775

Cerro de Calderón

Embalse
de
Puente Nuevo

**Villaviciosa
de Córdoba**

433

771
El Vacar

Campo Alto

Córdoba

Guadalmellato

Río Varas

Embalse de
Valsequillo

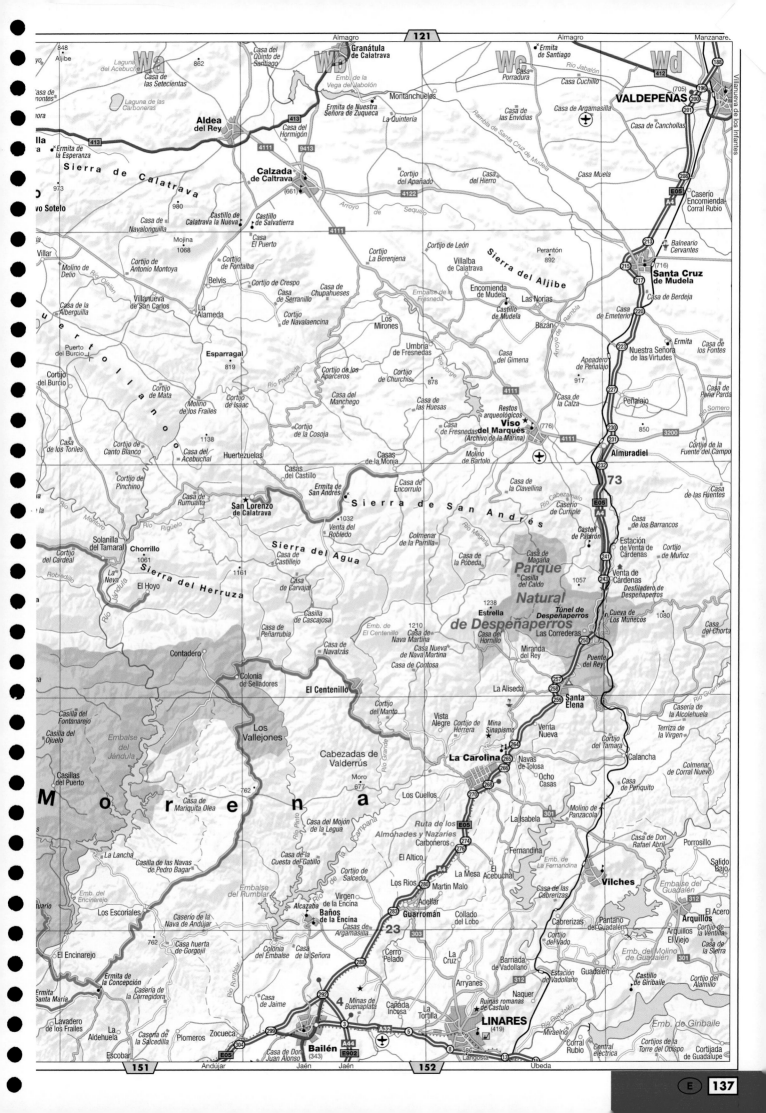

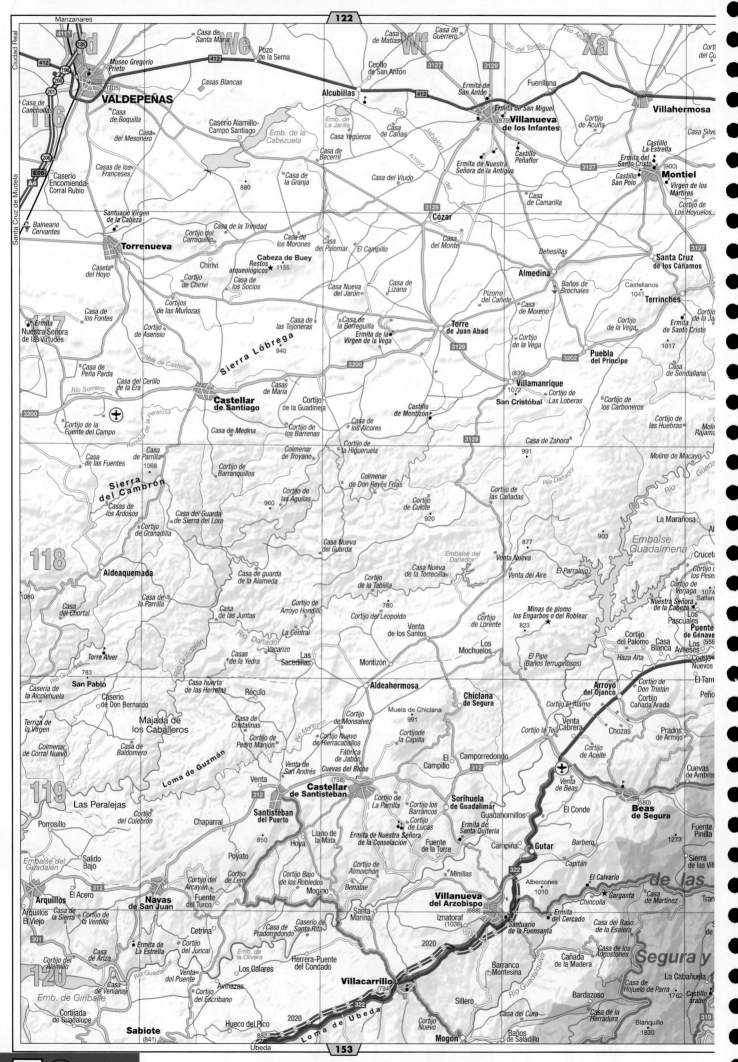

Manzanares

Ciudad Real

Santa Cruz de Mudela

4117 Vd

185

412

412 We

Wf

Xa

196
200
201

412

Museo Gregorio Prieto

(705)

VALDEPEÑAS

E05

A4

Casa de Canchollas

Caserío Encomienda-Corral Rubio

Casa de Boquilla

Casa del Mesonero

Caserío Alamillo-Campo Santiago

Casas Blancas

Casas de los Franceses

Casa de Santa María

880

Pozo de la Serna

Casa de la Granja

Emb. de la Cabezuela

Emb. de La Jarilla

Casa de Becerril

Casa Yegüeros

Casa de Matías

Cerillo de San Antón

Alcubillas

Río

Casa de Cañas

Casa del Viudo

3127

Casa de Guerrero

Ermita de San Antón

412

Ermita de San Miguel

879 Villanueva de los Infantes

Castillo Peñaflor

Ermita de Nuestra Señora de la Antigua

3129

Fuenllana

Río del Torllo

Río Azuel

3129

Cortijo del Cu

Xb

Villahermosa

Cortijo de Acuña

Casa Silve

Castillo La Estrella

Ermita del Santo Cristo

(900)

Montiel

Castillo San Polo

Virgen de los Mártires

Cortijo de los Hoyuelos

Santuario Virgen de la Cabeza

Balneario Cervantes

Caseta del Hoyo

Torrenueva

Chirivi

Cortijo de Chirivi

Cabeza de Buey
Restos arqueológicos ★ 1155

Casa de la Trinidad

Casa de los Morones

Cozar

Almedina

3129

Santa Cruz de los Cáñamos

Casa de los Socios

Casa del Palomar

El Campillo

Casa del Monte

Dehesillas

Baños de Brochales

Castellanos 1041

Terrinches

Cortijos de las Muñozas

Casa Nueva del Jarón

Casa de Lizana

Pizorro del Cañete

Casa de Moreno

Cortijo de la Vega

Ermita de Santo Cristo

1017

Cortijo de la Vega

Ermita Nuestra Señora de las Virtudes

Casa de los Fontes

Cortijo de Asensio

Casa de las Tejoneras

Casa de la Borreguilla

Ermita de la Virgen de la Vega

Torre de Juan Abad

Cortijo de la Vega

3202

Puebla del Príncipe

Casa de Sendallana

Sierra Lóbrega 940

3200

(830)

Villamanrique

Cortijo de las Loberas

Cortijo de los Carboneros

Cortijo de las Huebras

Casa de Peña Parda

Casa del Cerillo

Casa de la Era

Río Somero

Rambla de Castellar

3200

Cortijo de la Fuente del Campo

Castellar de Santiago

Casas de María

Casa de Medina

Cortijo de la Guadineja

Cortijo de los Bárrenas

Casa de los Alcores

Castillo de Montizón

1072

San Cristóbal

Casa de Zahora

3129

991

Molino de Macayo

Río

Molí Rajama

Sierra del Cambrón

Casa de Parrilla 1068

Cortijo de Barranquillos

Casa del Guarda de Sierra del Loro

Casa de las Fuentes

Colmenar de Troyano

Cortijo de la Higueruela

Colmenar de Don Reyes Frías

Cortijo de las Cañadas

Cortijo de Culote 920

La Marañosa

Cortijo d los Pese

Embalse Guadalmena

Cortijo de Verjaga 1074

Salfarr

Aldeaquemada

Casas de los Ardosos

Cortijo de Granadilla

960

Cortijo de las Águilas

Casa Nueva del Guarda

Embalse del Dañador

877

903

Venta Nueva

El Parralejo

Nuestra Señora de la Cabeza

Los Pascuales

Crucet

118

1080

Casa del Chortal

Casa de la Parrilla

Casa de guarda de la Alameda

Cortijo de Arroyo Hondillo

Casa de las Juntas

Cortijo de la Tablilla

780

Casa Nueva de la Torrecilla

Venta del Aire

Cortijo de Lorente

Minas de plomo los Engarbos o el Roblear

823

El Pipe (Baños ferruginosos)

Haza Alta

Puente de Génave

Los (555 Aviesos

Cortijo del Palomo

Casa Blanca

Cortijo Nuevos

El-Tam

Torre Alver 783

La Central

Río Dañador

Vacarizo

Casas de la Yedra

Las Sacedillas

Cortijo del Leopoldo

Venta de los Santos

Los Mochuelos

Montizón

Caseria de la Alcolehuela

San Pablo

Río Guarrizas

Caserío de Don Bernardo

Casa huerta de las Herreras

Réculo

Aldeahermosa

Cortijo de Monsalvez

Muela de Chiclana 991

Chiclana de Segura

Cortijo El Álamo

Venta Cabrera

Chozas

Prados de Armijo

Arroyo del Ojanco

Cortijo de Don Tristán

Cortijo Cañada Arada

Peño

Cuevas de Ambros

Terriza de la Virgen

Majada de los Caballeros

Casa de Cristalinas

Cortijo de Pedro Manjón

Río Montizón

Cortijo Nuevo de Hierracaballos

Cortijo de la Capilla

Cortijo la Teja

Cortijo de Aceite

Colmenar de Corral Nuevo

Casa de Baldomero

Venta de San Andrés

Fábrica de Jabón

Cuevas del Biche

El Campillo

Camporredondo

312

Beas de Segura (580)

119

Las Peralejas

Porrosillo

Cortijo del Culebrón

Chaparral

(758)

Castellar de Santisteban

Santisteban del Puerto

850

Hoya

Cortijo de La Parrilla

Cortijo los Barrancos

Cortijo de Lucas

Sorihuela de Guadalimar

Guadahornillos

Ermita de Santa Quiteria

Campiña

Gutar

Venta de Beas

El Conde

Barbero

Capitán

El Calvario 1010

Chincolla

Garganta

1273

Fuente, Pinilla

Sierra de las Vill

Casa de Martínez

Tran

Embalse del Guadalén

Salido Bajo

El Acero

312

Arquillos

Arquillos El Viejo

Casa de la Sierra

Cortijo de la Ventilla

Navas de San Juan

Cortijo del Arcayán

Cortijo de Lero

Cortijo Bajo de los Robledos

Mogino

Benatae

Llano de la Mata

Ermita de Nuestra Señora de la Consolación

Fuente de la Torre

Cortijo de Almorchón

Minillas

322

Albercones 1010

Villanueva del Arzobispo (688)

Santuario de la Fuensanta

Ermita del Cercado

Cañada de la Madera

Casa de los Angostones

de las

Segura y

La Cabañuela

301

Cortijo del Alamillo

Casa de Ariza

Ermita de La Estrella

Cortijo del Juncal

Fuente del Turco

Cetrina

Emb. de la Olivera

Caserío de Pradorredondo

Santa Marina

Casa de Santa Rita

Iznatoraf (1036)

2020

Barranco Montesina

Casa del Raso de la Esalera

La Cabañuela

120

Emb. de Giribaile

Casa de Venianaj

Venta del Puente

Avinazas

Cortijo del Escribano

Río Guadalén

Los Calares

Herrera-Puente del Condado

322

Villacarrillo (794)

Sillero

Loma de Úbeda

Casa del Cura

Cañada de la Madera

Rio Guadalquivir

Bardazoso

Casa de la Herradura

Segura y

319

Cortijada de Guadalupe

Casa de Guadalupe

Sabiote (841)

Hueco del Pico

882

2020

Mogón

Cortijo Nuevo

Baños de Saladillo

Blanquillo 1830

Castillo árabe

1762

Úbeda

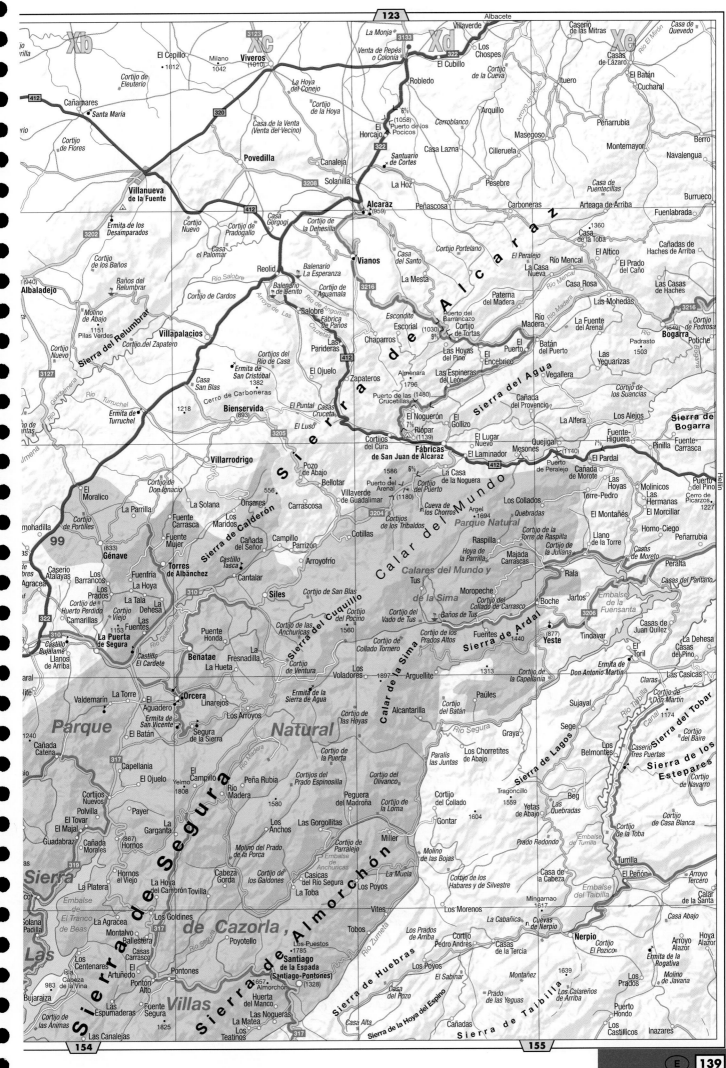

Xb · Xc · Xd · Xe

El Cepillo · Milano 1042 · Viveros (1010) · 1012 · La Monja · 3133 · Villaverde · Albacete · Caserío de las Mitras · Casa de Quevedo

3123 · Venta de Pepés o Colonia · Los Chospes · Casas de Lázaro

Cortijo de Eleuterio · La Hoya del Conejo · El Cubillo · Cortijo de la Cueva · El Batán · Cucharal

Cañamares · 412 · 320 · Cortijo de la Hoya · Robledo · Arquillo · Ituero

Santa María · Casa de la Venta (Venta del Vecino) · 6% (1058) · El Horcajo · Puerto de los Pocicos · Cerroblanco · Masegoso · Peñarrubia · Montemayor · Berro

Cortijo de Flores · 322 · Santuario de Cortes · Casa Lazna · Cilleruela · Navalengua

Povedilla · Canaleja · La Hoz · Pesebre · Casa de Puentecillas · Burrueco

Villanueva de la Fuente · 412 · 3208 · Solanilla · Alcaraz (959) · Peñascosa · Carboneras · Arteaga de Arriba · Fuenlabrada

Ermita de los Desamparados · 3202 · Cortijo Nuevo · Cortijo de Pradogallo · Casa Górgogi · Cortijo de la Dehesilla · Casa del Santo · 1360 · Casa de la Toba · El Altico · Cañadas de Haches de Arriba

Casa el Palomar · Vianos · Casa del Santo · El Peralejo · La Casa Nueva · El Prado del Caño · Las Casas de Haches

Cortijo de los Baños · Reolid · Balenario La Esperanza · Río Mencal · Casa Rosa · 3216

Albaladejo (940) · Baños del Relumbrar · Cortijo de Cardos · Balenario de Benito · Cortijo de Aguamala · Río Mencal · Paterna del Madera · Las Mohedas

Molino de Abajo · 1151 Pilas Verdes · Salobre · Fábrica de Paños · Escondite · Puerto del Barrancazo · (1030) 9% · Cortijo de Tortas · Río Madera · La Fuente del Arenal · 3216 · (649) Cortijo de Pedrosa

Cortijo Nuevo · Villapalacios · 3127 · Cortijo del Zapatero · Escorial · Chaparros · Las Parideras · El Puerto · Batán del Puerto · Las Yeguarizas · 1503 · Bogarra · Potiche

Sierra del Relumbrar · Cortijos del Río de Casa · 412 · Las Hoyas del Pino · El Encebrico · Vegallera

Ermita de San Cristóbal 1382 · El Ojuelo · Zapateros · Almenara 1796 · Las Espineras del León · Cortijo de los Suancias

Casa San Blas · Cerro de Carboneras · 1218 · Bienservida (893) · Casas Cruceta · El Puntal · El Noguerón 7% · Puerto de las Crucetillas (1480) · Sierra del Agua · Cañada del Provencio · Los Alejos · Sierra de Bogarra

Ermita de Turruchel · El Lusó · El Gollizo · El Lugar Nuevo · La Alfera · Fuente-Higuera 7% · Pinilla · Fuente-Carrasca

3205 · Villarrodrigo · Pozo de Abajo · Cortijos del Cura · Fábricas de San Juan de Alcaraz · Ríopar (1139) · Mesones · Quejigal (1140) · El Pardal

Bellotar · 6% · La Casa de la Noguera · El Laminador · 412 · Puerto de Peralejo · Cañada de Morote · Las Hoyas · Puerto del Arenal

El Moralico · Cortijo de Don Ignacio · 556 · Villaverde de Guadalimar · Puerto del Arenal (1180) · Cortijo del Puerto · 1586 · Cueva de los Chorros · Argel 1694 · Los Collados · Torre-Pedro · Molinicos · Las Hermanas · El Morcillar · Cerro de Picarzos 1227

La Parrilla · La Solana · Onsares · Carrascosa · 3204 · Cortijos de los Tribaldos · Parque Natural · Quebradas · El Montañés · Homo-Ciego · Peñarrubia

Fuente Carrasca · Los Maridos · Cañada del Señor · Campillo · Parrizón · Cotillas · Calar del Mundo · Raspilla · Cortijo de la Torre de Raspilla · Llano de la Torre · Casas de Moreto

99 · Génave · (833) · Castillo Tasca · Arroyofrío · Hoya de la Parrilla · Cortijo de la Juliana · Peralta

Caserío Atalayas · Fuenfría · Torres de Albánchez · Cantalar · Calares del Mundo y Tus · Majada Carrascas · Rala · Embalse de la Fuensanta · Casas del Pantano

Los Barrancos · La Hoya · 310 · Siles · Cortijo de San Blas · de la Sima · Moropeche · Cortijo del Collado de Carrasco · Boche · Jartos · Casas de Juan Quílez

Los Prados · La Tala · La Dehesa · Cortijo del Pocino · Cortijo de las Anchuricas · 1560 · Cortijo del Vado de Tus · Baños de Tus · 3206 · La Dehesa Casas del Pino

Cortijo de Huerto Perdido · 322 · Cortijo Viejo · Las Fuentes · Sierra del Cuquillo · Fuentes de Ardal · 1440 · Yeste (877) · Tindavar · El Toril

Camarillas · 1153 · 310 · Puente Honda · Cortijo de Ventura · Cortijo de Collado Tornero · Cortijo de los Prados Altos · Sierra de Ardal · Ermita de Don Antonio Martín · Claras · Las Casicas

Castillo Bujálame · La Puerta de Segura · Benatae · La Fresnadilla · Los Voladores · 1897 · Arguellite · 1313 · Cortijo de la Capellanía · Cortijo de Don Martín · Sierra del Tobar

Llanos de Arriba · Castillo El Cardete · La Hueta · Ermita de la Sierra de Agua · Alcantarilla · Paúles · Sujayal · Cortijo del Baire · Sierra de los Estepares

La Torre · Valdemarín · El Aguadero · Orcera · Linarejos · Cortijo de las Hoyas · Cortijo del Batán · Sege · Caserío Tres Puertas · Cortijo de Navarro

Parque · Ermita de San Vicente · Segura de la Sierra · Los Arroyos · Natural · Graya · Los Chorretites de Abajo · Sierra de Lagos · Los Belmontes · Cortijo de Casa Blanca

1240 · El Batán · Cortijo de la Puerta · Paralís las Juntas · Tragoncillo · Beg

Cañada Catena · Capellanía · El Ojuelo · El Campillo · Peña Rubia · Cortijos del Prado Espinosilla · Cortijo del Olivanco · Cortijo del Collado · 1559 · Yetas de Abajo · Las Quebradas · Embalse de Turrilla

Cortijos Nuevos · Yelmo 1808 · Río Madera · 1580 · Peguera del Madroña · Cortijo de la Loma · 1604 · Prado Redondo · Cortijo de la Toba

Polvilla · Payer · La Garganta · Los Anchos · Las Gorgollitas · Miller · Molino de las Bojas · Embalse del Taibilla

El Tovar · El Majal · 319 · Cañada Morales · (867) Hornos · Molino del Prado de la Porca · Cortijo de Parralejo · Casicas del Río Segura · La Muela · Cortijo de los Habares y de Silvestre · Casa de la Cabeza · El Peñón · Arroyo Tercero

Guadabraz · Sierra · La Platera · Hornos el Viejo · La Hoya del Cambrón · Tovilla · Los Poyos · La Toba · Mingarnao 1617 · Turrilla · Cálar de la Santa

Las · Cabeza Gorda · Cortijo de los Galdones · Vites · Los Morenos · La Cabáñica · Cuevas de Nerpio · Casa Abajo

Embalse de El Tranco de Beas · La Agracea · Los Goldines · Tobos · Los Prados de Arriba · Pedro Andrés · Casas de la Tercia · Nerpio · Cortijo El Pozico · Arroyo Alazor · Hoya Alazor

Solana Padilla · Montalvo · Ballestera · 317 · Río Segura · Poyotello · Los Puestos 1785 · Sierra de Huebras · Los Poyos · Montañez · 1639 · Los Calareños de Arriba · Los Prados · Molino de Javana

983 · Isla Cabeza de la Viña · Casas Carrasco · El Artuñedo · Pontones · Santiago de la Espada (Santiago-Pontones) (1328) · Almorchón 657 · Casa del Pozo · Prado de las Yeguas · Puerto Hondo

Bujaraiza · Las Espumaderas · Ponton Alto · Villas · Huerta del Manco · Sierra de la Hoya del Espino · Cañadas · Los Castillos

Cortijo de las Ánimas · Las Canalejas · Fuente Segura 1825 · Las Nogueras · La Matea · Los Teatinos · 317 · Sierra de Taibilla · Inazares

Sierra de Cazorla, Sierra de Segura · Sierra de Almorchón · Hellín

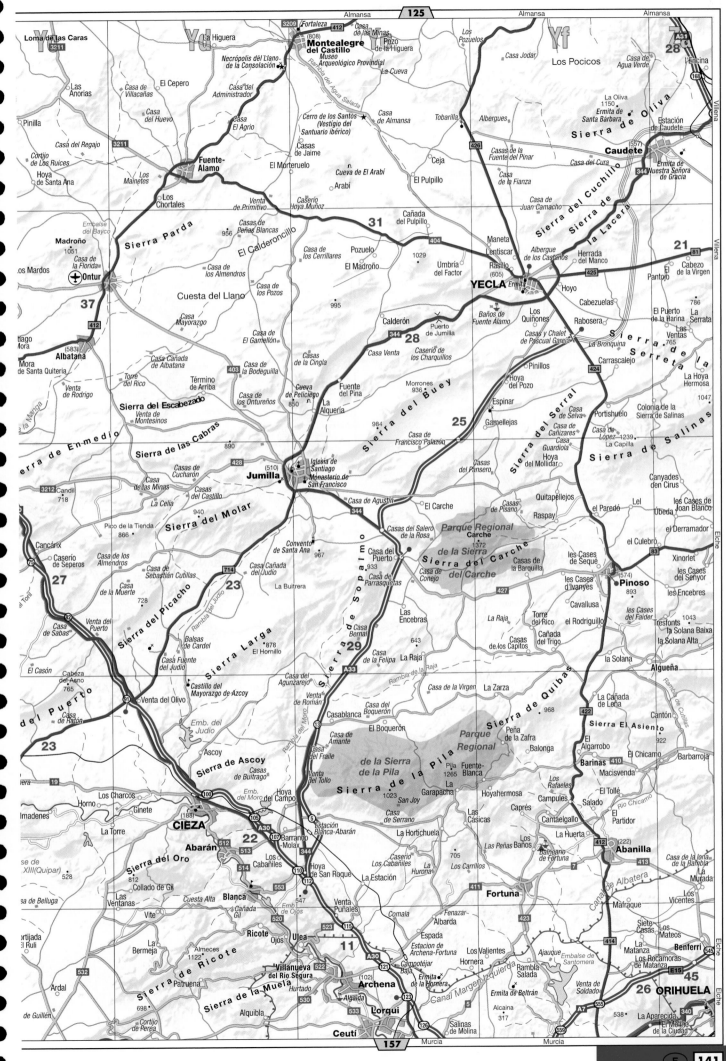

Almansa Almansa Almansa

Loma de las Caras
3211

Yd

Yf

Los Pozuelos

Yf

7a
28

L'Encina
A31

Vilena

La Higuera

3209 Fortaleza
412

Casa de las Minas

Pozo de la Higuera

Casa Jodar

Los Pocicos

Casa de Agua Verde

168

Las Anorias

Montealegre del Castillo
Museo Arqueológico Provincial

La Cueva

La Oliva
1150

Ermita de Santa Bárbara

Estación de Caudete

Sierra de Oliva

Pinilla

Necrópolis del Llano de la Consolación

El Cepero

Casa del Administrador

Casa de Villacañas

Casa del Huevo

Casa El Agrio

Cerro de los Santos (Vestigio del Santuario ibérico)

Casa de Almansa

Tobarilla

Albergues

Casas de la Fuente del Pinar

Casa del Cura

Caudete

Ermita de Nuestra Señora de Gracia

344

557

Casa del Regajo
3211

Cortijo de Los Ruices

Hoya de Santa Ana

Casa de Jaime

Casa de la Fianza

Casa de Juan Camacho

Sierra del Cuchillo

Sierra de la Lacera

Madroño
1051

Casa de la Florida

Ontur

Los Mardos

El Morteruelo

Venta de Primitivo

Caserío Hoya Muñoz

Cueva de El Arabí

Arabí

El Pulpillo

Maneta

Lentiscar

Albergue de los Castaños

Herrada del Manco

21

81

Cabezo de la Virgen

Embalse del Bayco

Sierra Parda

Los Chortales

Casas de Peñas Blancas
956

El Calderoncillo

Casa de los Cerrillares

Pozuelo

El Madroño

1029

Rasillo

425

404

El Pantojo

786

La Serrata

Las Ventas

La Hoya Hermosa

37

412

Cuesta del Llano

Casa de los Almendros

Casa de los Pozos

995

Umbría del Factor

YECLA

Ermita

Hoyo

El Puerto de la Harina

Sierra de la Serreta

Santiago de Mora

583

Albataná

403

Venta de Rodrigo

Término de Arriba

Casa Cañada de Albatana

Torre del Rico

Casa de la Bodeguilla

Cuesta del Gamellón

Casas de la Cingla

Fuente del Pina

Calderón

344

28

Puerto de Jumilla

Casa Venta

Caserío de los Charquillos

Baños de Fuente Alamo

Los Quiñones

Rabosera

Casas y Chalet de Pascual García

La Bronquina
765

Carrascalejo

424

Mora de Santa Quiteria

Venta de Montesinos

Sierra del Escabezado

Cueva de Peliciego
850

La Alquería

Morrones
936

984

Casa de Francisco Palazón

Pinillos

Hoya del Pozo

Espinar

Gamellejas

Sierra del Buey

Sierra del Serral

Casa de Selva

Casa de Cañizares

Portishuelo

Colonia de la Sierra de Salinas

1047

Sierra de Enmedio

Sierra de las Cabras
890

428

Jumilla
510

Iglesia de Santiago

Monasterio de San Francisco

25

Casas del Pansero

Casa Guardiola

Casa de López 1239

La Capilla

Sierra de Salinas

3212 Candil
718

Casa de las Minas

Casas de Cucharón

Casa del Castillo

La Celia

940

Pico de la Tienda
866

Sierra del Molar

Casa de Agustín

344

El Carche

Casas del Salero de la Rosa

Parque Regional Carche de la Sierra del Carche
1372

Casas de Pisano

Raspay

Quitapellejos

el Paredó

Canyades den Cirus

les Cases de Joan Blanco

el Derramador

El Culebró

Xinorlet

Elche

Cancárix

75

Caserío de Seperos

27

Casa de los Almendros

Casa de Sebastián Cutillas

714

Convento de Santa Ana
967

Casa Cañada del Judío

Casa del Puerto
933

Sierra del Carche

Casas de la Barquilla

les Cases de Sequé

les Cases d'Ivanyes

574

Pinoso

893

83

les Cases del Senyor

la Muerte
728

23

La Buitrera

Casa de Parrasquetas

Casa de Conejo

Cavallusa

el Rodriguillo

les Encebres

Tresfonts
1043

82

Venta del Puerto

Sierra del Picacho

Rambla del Judío

Balsas de Cardel

El Hornillo
878

Sierra Larga

Las Encebras

La Raja

Torre del Rico

Casas de los Capitos

Cañada del Trigo

la Solana Baixa

la Solana Alta

Casa de Sabas

El Casón

Casa Fuente del Judío

643

La Raja

la Solana

Algueña

Cabeza del Asno
765

Castillo del Mayorazgo de Azcoy

Casa del Agunzarejo

Casa Bernal

Casa de la Felipa

29

A33

Rambla de la Raja

Casa de la Virgen

La Zarza

Sierra de Quibas

968

422

La Cañada de Leña

Cantón

del Puerto

23

Casa de Ratón

91

Venta del Olivo

Venta de Román

Casablanca

Rambla del Moro

13

Casa del Boquerón

Peña de la Zafra

Parque Regional de la Sierra de la Pila

Sierra El Asiento

922

El Algarrobo

El Chicamo

Barbarroja

19

Emb. del Judío

Ascoy

Sierra de Ascoy

Casas de Buitrago

Casa del Fraile

Casa de Amante

El Boquerón

Balonga

Barinas
410

Macisvenda

de Bellusa

Los Charcos

Ginete

100

Emb. del Moro

Hoya del Campo

Venta del Tollo

de la Sierra de la Pila

Pila
1265

Fuente-Blanca

La Garapacha

Los Rafaeles

Hoyahermosa

Caprés

Campules

El Tollé

Salado

El Partidor

412

222

Abanilla

Casa de la Ioña de la Rambla

La Murada

Horno

La Torre

CIEZA
188

105

Abarán
512

22

513

107 Barranco-Molax

Estación Blanca-Abarán

5

Casa de Serrano

San Joy
1023

La Hortichuela

Caserío los Cabañiles

La Hurona

705

Las Cásicas

Las Peñas Baños

Balneario de Fortuna

7

413

Sierra del Oro
812

514

344

Los Cabañiles

110

Hoya de San Roque

112

La Estación

Los Carrillos

La Huerta

Canal de Albatera

Los Vicentes

528

Collado de Gil

Cuesta Alta

553

Blanca
547

Fortuna

411

Mafraque

532

Las Ventanas

Cañada Gil

520

Emb. de Ojos

Venta Puñales

Comala

Fenazar-Albarda

423

La Matanza

Siete Casas

Los Mateos

de Belluga

Vite

Ricote

523

115

Espada

Estación de Archena-Fortuna

Ajauque

Embalse de Santomera

414

La Matanza

Los Rocamoras de Matanza

E15

Benferri
545

La Bermeja

Álmeces
1122

Sierra de Ricote

Ojós

Ulea

11

A30

121

Villanueva del Río Segura

522

102

Archena

Campotéjar Baja

Los Valientes

Los Hornera

Ermita de la Hornera

Rambla Salada

26

ORIHUELA
340

Ardal

Patruena

Sierra de la Muela

Alquibla

698

530

Hurtado

Algaida

123

533

Lorquí

126

Alcaina
317

Ermita de Beltrán

Canal Margen Izquierda

5

559

A7

555

538

La Aparecida

El Molino de la Ciudad

de Guillén

Cortijo de Perea

Ceutí

Salinas de Molina

Murcia Murcia Murcia

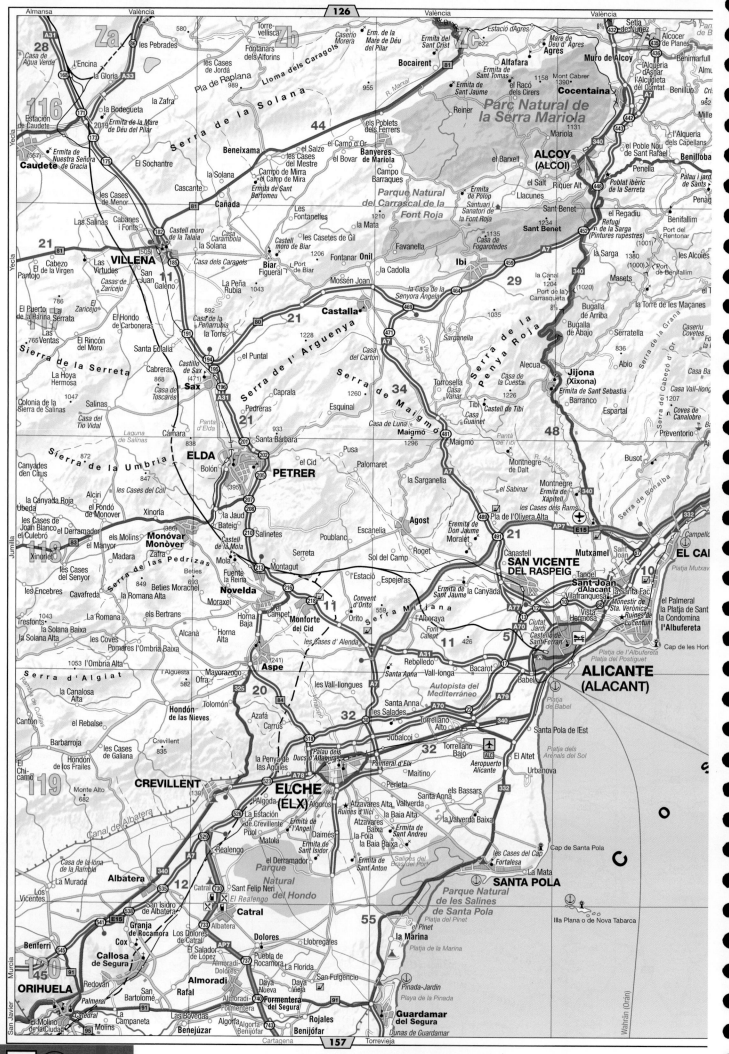

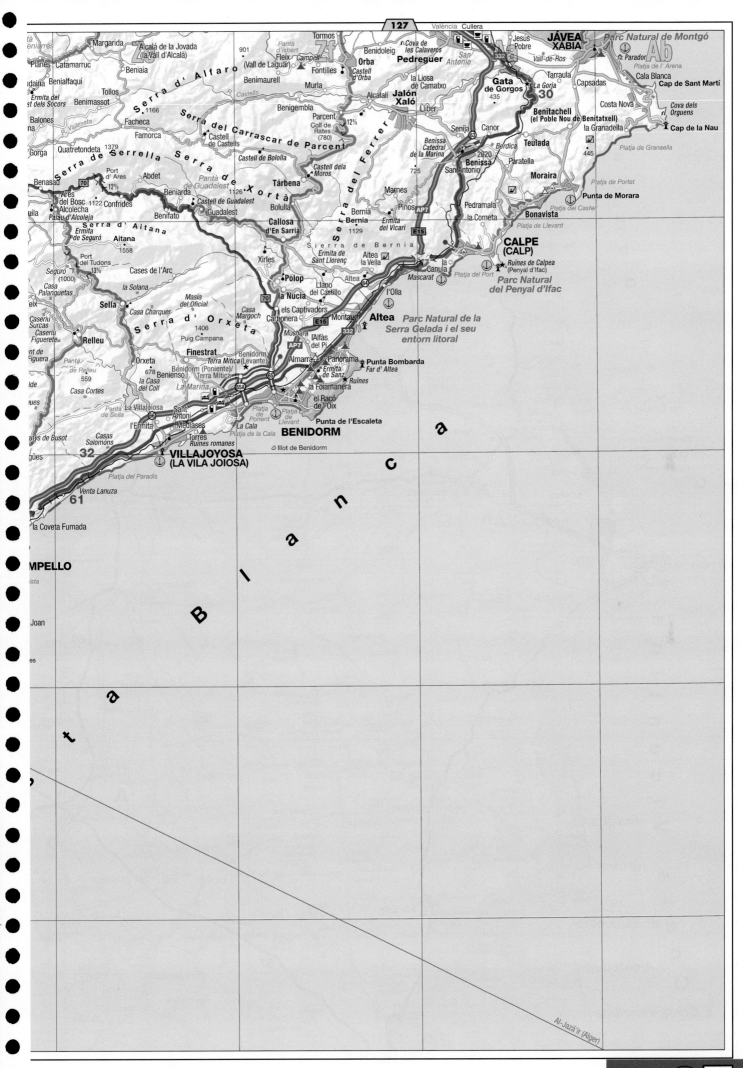

València Cullera

Margarida
Alcalá de la Jovada (la Vall d'Alcalà)
Planes Catamarruc
901
Pantà d'Isbert
Fleix Campell
Tormos
Benidoleig
Cova de les Calaveres
JÁVEA
XABIA
Parc Natural de Montgó
Parador Ab

Beniaia
Orba
Pedreguer
San Antonio
Vall-de-Ros
Platja de l' Arena

daina Benialfaquí
Benímaurell
Murla
la Liosa de Camatxo
Gata de Gorgos
435
La Gorja
Tarraula
Capsadas
Costa Nova
Cala Blanca
Cap de Sant Martí

Ermita del st dels Socors
Benimassot
Serra d' Alfaro
Benigembla
Castells
Alcalalí
Jalón Xaló
30
Benitachell (el Poble Nou de Benitatxell)
Cova dels Orguens

Balones
Facheca
1166
Serra del Carrascar de Parcent
Parcent
Coll de Rates (780)
12%
Lliber
Senija
Canor
Benissa Catedral de la Marina
Teulada
Bérdica
445
Cap de la Nau

na
Gorga
Quatretondeta
1379
Castell de Castells
Castell de Bolulla
Castell dela Moros
2020
Benissa
San Antonio
Paratella
Platja de Granaella

Benasau
Serra de Serrella
Port d'Ares
12%
Abdet
Tárbena
1126
Serra de Xortà
725
Moraira
Platja de Portet

Ares del Bosc
Alcolecha
70
1122
Beniarda
1558
Castell de Guadalest
Guadalest
Bolulla
Marnes
Pedramala
la Cometa
Bonavista
Punta de Morara
Platja del Castell

Palau d'Alcoleja
uila ila
Confrides
Benifato
Callosa d'En Sarrià
Serra del Ferrer
Bernia
1129
Piños
Ermita del Vicari
AP7
E15
Platja de Llevant

Serra d' Aitana
Ermita de Seguró
Aitana
1558
Port del Tudons
13%
Xirles
Sierra de Bernia
Ermita de Sant Llorenç
Altea la Vella
E15
la Canula
CALPE (CALP)
Ruïnes de Calpea (Penyal d'Ifac)
Parc Natural del Penyal d'Ifac

Seguró (1000)
Casa Palanquetas
la Solana
Pólop
la Nucia
Llano del Castillo
Altea
64
l'Olla
Mascarat
Platja del Port

Sella
Casa Charquer
Masia del Oficial
Casa Margoch
els Captivadors
Carbonera
E16
Montaud
Altea
332
l'Alfàs del Pi
Parc Natural de la Serra Gelada i el seu entorn litoral

Caseriu Surcas Caseriu Figuerete
Relleu
1406
Puig Campana
678
Mushara
AP7
Panorama
Punta Bombarda
Far d' Altea

ent de Figuera
Pantà de Relleu
559
Orxeta
Benienso
Finestrat
Terra Mítica (Levante)
Benidorm (Poniente)/ Terra Mítica
65A
Almarra
Ermita de Sanz
Ruïnes

Casa Cortes
la Casa del Coll
La Marina
65
65A
la Foiamanera
el Racó de l'Oix

Pantà de Sella
l'Ermita
Sant Antoni
Mediases
66
Platja de Ponent
Platja de Llevant
Punta de l'Escaleta

anys de Busot
Casas Salomóns
Torres Ruïnes romanes
La Cala
BENIDORM

gües
32
VILLAJOYOSA (LA VILA JOIOSA)
Platja de la Cala
Illot de Benidorm

Platja del Paradís

MPELLO
Venta Lanuza
61

la Coveta Fumada

Joan

Costa Blanca

Al-Jazà'ir (Alger)

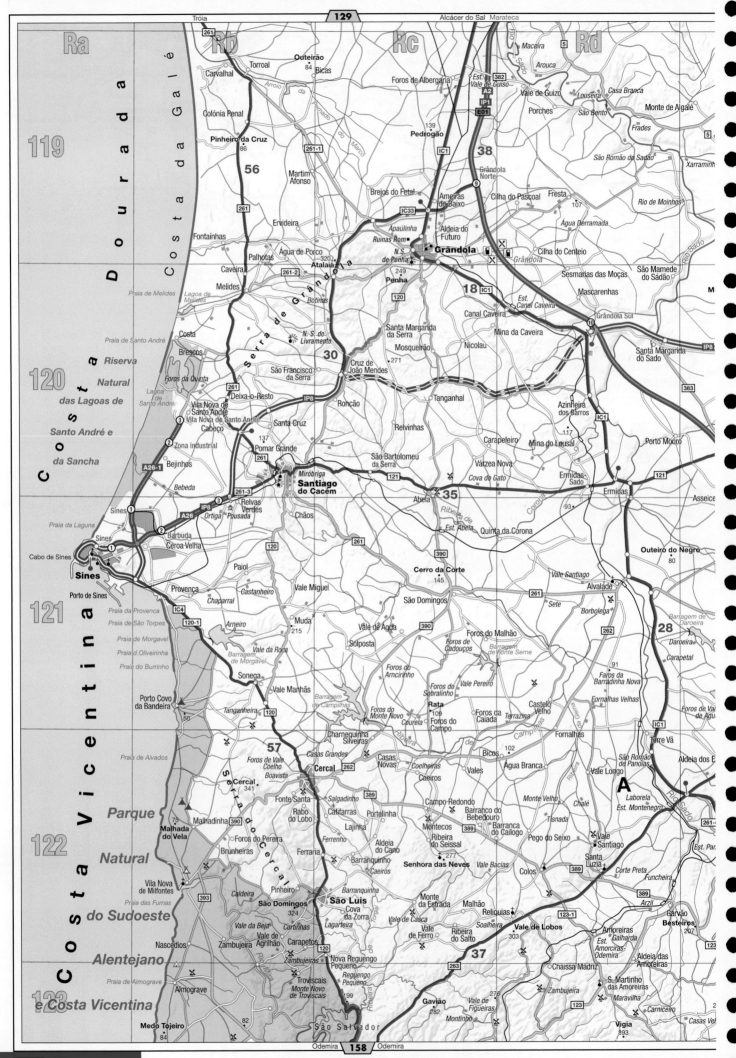

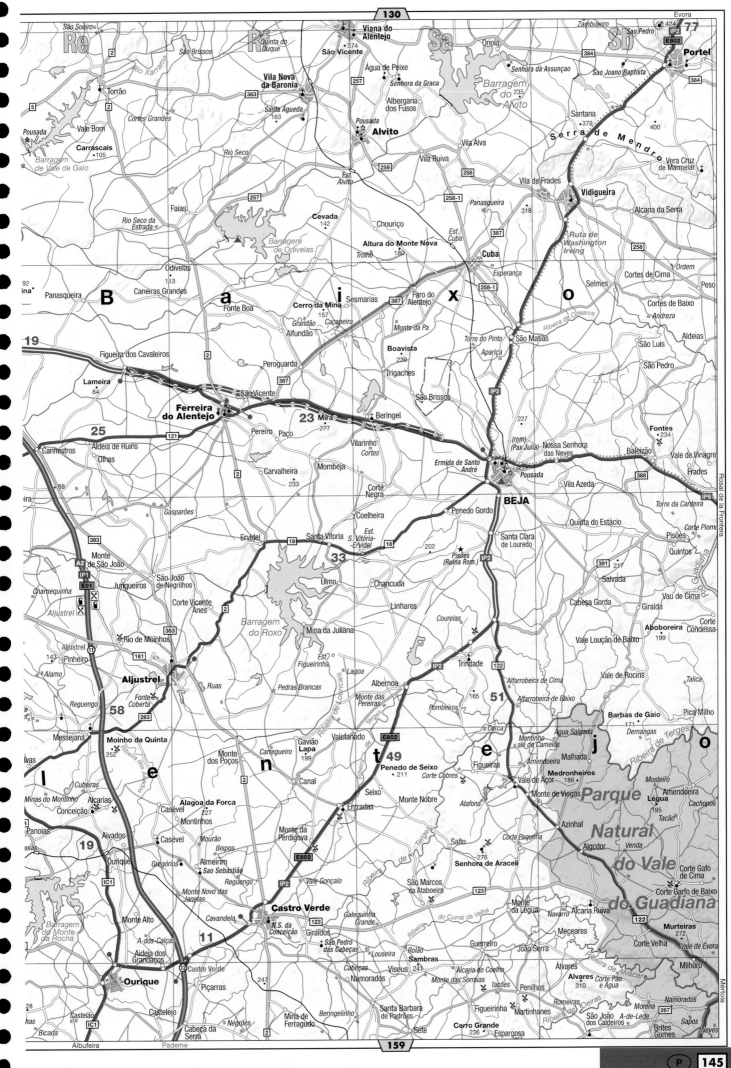

Evora

São Soeiro
Quinta do Duque
Viana do Alentejo
São Vicente
São Pedro
Zambujeiro
424
E802
Portel

Quinta do Duque
São Brissos
374
Oriola
Sao Joano Baptista
384

Rio Xarrama
2
Água de Peixe
Senhora da Assunçao
379
Santana
400

Vila Nova
da Baronia
383
Senhora da Graca
Albergaria dos Fusos
235
Vera Cruz
de Marmelar
384

Torrão
Cortes Grandes
Santa Águeda
163
Pousada
Alvito
Barragem
do Alvito
Vila del Frades
Vidigueira
Alcaria da Serra

Vale Bom
Rio Seco
258
Vila Alva
318
Panasqueira
258-1
258

Pousada
Carrascais
105
Rio Seco da
Estrada
Faias
257
Est.
Alvito
258
Vila Ruiva
258
Ruta de
Washington
Irving
258

Barragem
de Vale de Gaio
Barragem
de Odivelas
Cevada
142
Chouriço
Est.
Cuba
387
Esperança
Cortes de Cima
Ordem

92
Odivelas
113
Altura do Monte Nova
180
Cuba
258-1
Selmes
Peso

ina
Panasqueira
B
Caneiras Grandes
a
i
Sesmarias
387
Faro do
Alentejo
x
Ribeira de Odearce
o
Cortes de Baixo
Andreza

Fonte Boa
Cerro da Mina
157
Cacapeira
Monte da Pa
Torre do Pinto
São Matias
Aparica
São Luis
Aldeias

19
Figueira dos Cavaleiros
2
Grandão
Alfundão
Boavista
239
Trigaches
São Pedro

Lameira
84
Peroguarda
387
IP2
227

São Vicente
São Brissos
Fontes
234

25
Ferreira
do Alentejo
121
23 Mira
277
Beringel
Vilarinho
Cortes
(rom)
(Pax Julia)
Nossa Senhora
das Neves
Baleizão

Canhestros
Aldeia de Ruins
Olhas
Pereiro
Paço
Ermida de Santo
André
Pousada
Vila Azeda
388
Frades

88
Carvalheira
233
Mombeja
Corte
Negra
BEJA
IP8

Gasparões
383
Coelheira
Penedo Gordo
Quinta do Estácio
Torre da Cardeira
Corte Piorna
Pisões

A2
Monte
de São João
Ervidel
18
Santa Vitoria
S. Vitória-
Ervidel
18
202
Pisões
(Ruina Rom.)
IP2
Santa Clara
de Louredo
391
217
Quintos

IP1
E01
Junqueiros
São João
de Negrilhos
Corte Vicente
Anes
2
Ulmo
Chancuda
Salvada
Cabeça Gorda
Giralda
Aboboreira
199
Corte
Condessa

Charnequinha
Aljustrel
Rio de Moinhos
383
Barragem
do Roxo
Linhares
Courelas
Vale Loução de Baixo
Talica

Aljustrel
161
Mina da Juliana
Est.
Figueirinha
Trindade
122
Vale de Rocins

143
Pinheiro
Ruas
Lagoa
IP2
Albernoa
165
51
Alfarrobeira de Cima
Alfarrobeira de Baixo
Pica Milho

Alamo
Reguengo
58
263
Pedras Brancas
Monte das
Pereiras
Pombeiros
Cerca
Montinho
alé de Camelos
Malhada
Barbas de Gaio
171
Demangas
Ribeira de Terges

Messejana
Moinho da Quinta
252
Carregueiro
Gavião
Lapa
199
Valefanado
E802
t 49
e
Figueiras
Amendoeira
Vale de Acor
Medronheiros
186
Mosteiro
j
o

l
Cubeiras
e
n
Monte
dos Poços
Canal
Penedo de Seixo
211
Corte Cobres
Monte de Viegas
Parque
Amendoeira
Légua
195
Cachopos
Tacão

Minas do Montinho
Conceição
Alcarias
Casével
Montinhos
Alagoa da Forca
227
Seixo
Entradas
Monte Nobre
Atafona
Azinhal
Natural
do Vale
Corte Gafo
de Cima

Panoias
Aivados
Casével
Mourão
Bispos
Monte da
Perdigova
Salto
276
Corte Pequena
Algcdor
Venda
Tacão
Corte Garfo de Baixo

noias
19
Gregórios
Almeirim
Sao Sebastião
Reguengo
E802
IP2
Vale Gonçalo
Senhora de Araceli
São Marcos
da Ataboeira
123
Monte
da Légua
Navarro
Alcaria Ruiva
do Guadiana

Ouriqui
IC1
Monte Novo das
Janelas
Castro Verde
N.S. da
Conceição
123
Galequinha
Grande
Giráldos
do Curral da Velha
Meçeares
122
Murteiras
272

Monte Alto
Cavandela
123
São Pedro
das Cabeças
Rolão
Guerreiro
João Serra
Álvares
Corte Velha
Vale de Evora

Barragem
do Monte
da Rocha
11
A-dos-Calças
Aldeia dos
Grandaços
12 Castro Verde
Picarras
247
Cabeças
Viseus
241
Sambras
Alcaria do Coelho
Monte das Sorraias
Tacões
Penilhos
310
Alvares
Milhôro

28
has
Bicada
IC1
Castelão
Castelejo
Cabeça da
Serra
2
Negrões
Mina de
Ferragudo
Beringelinho
Sete
Santa Barbara
de Padrões
Figueirinha
Martinhanes
São João
dos Caldeiros
A-de-Lede
Romeiras
Morena
267
Námorados
Sapos
Brites
Gomes
Neves

Cerro Grande
236
Espargosa

Albufeira
Pademe

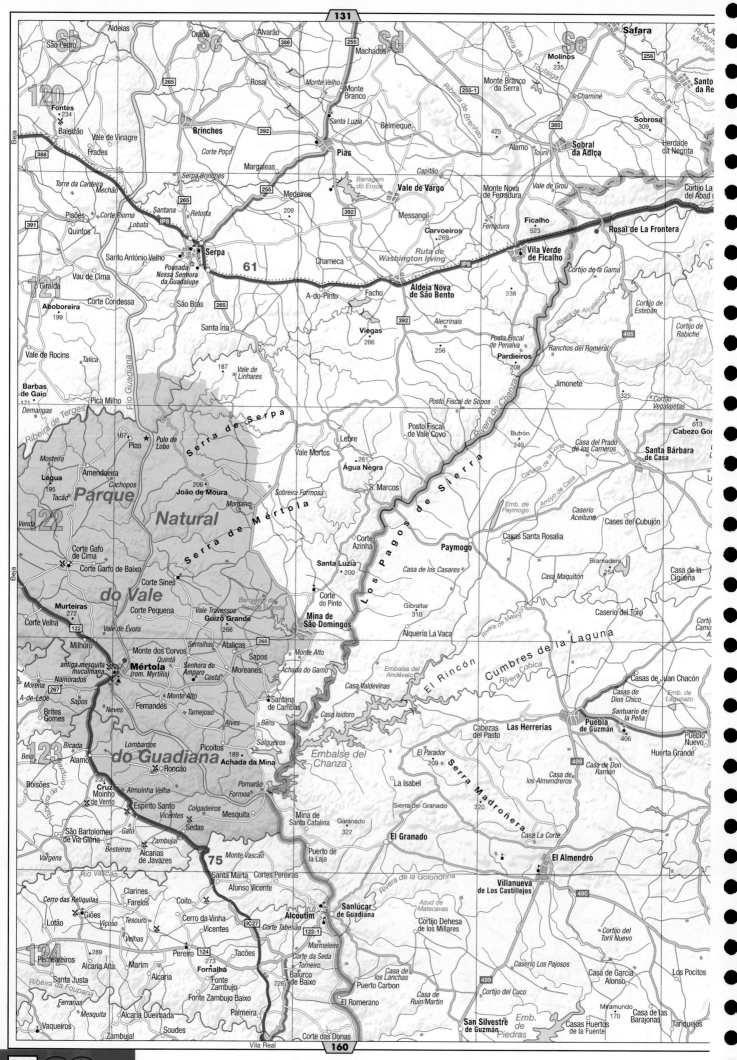

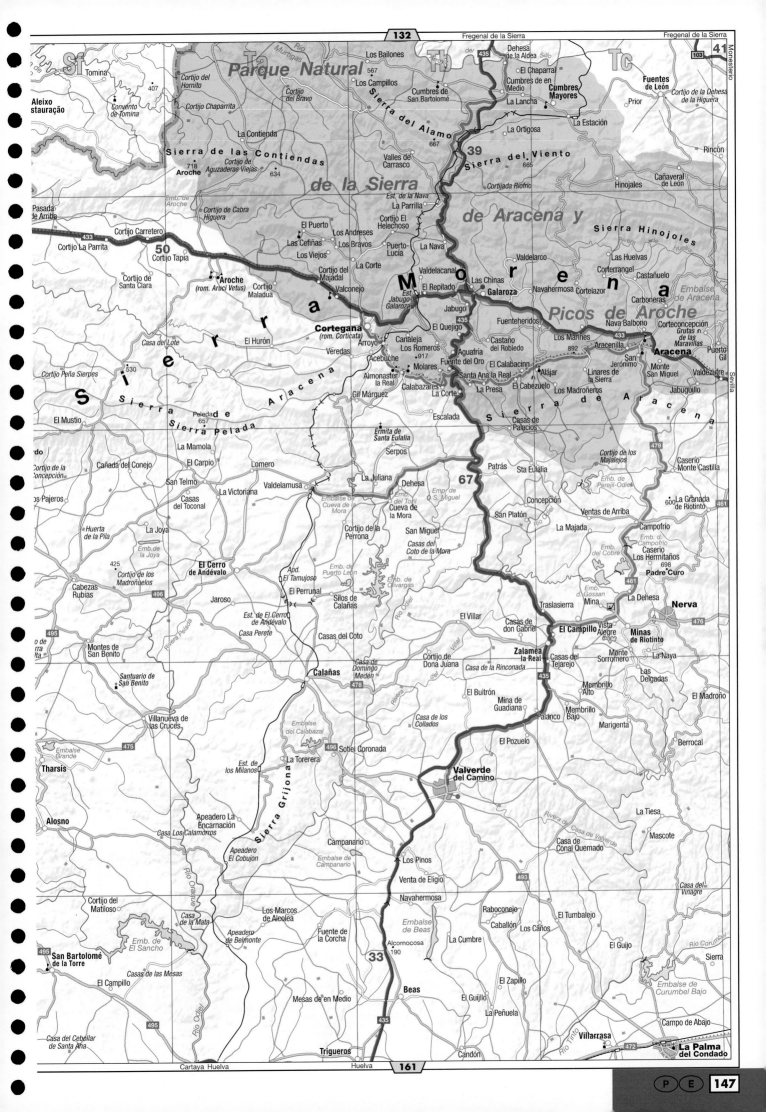

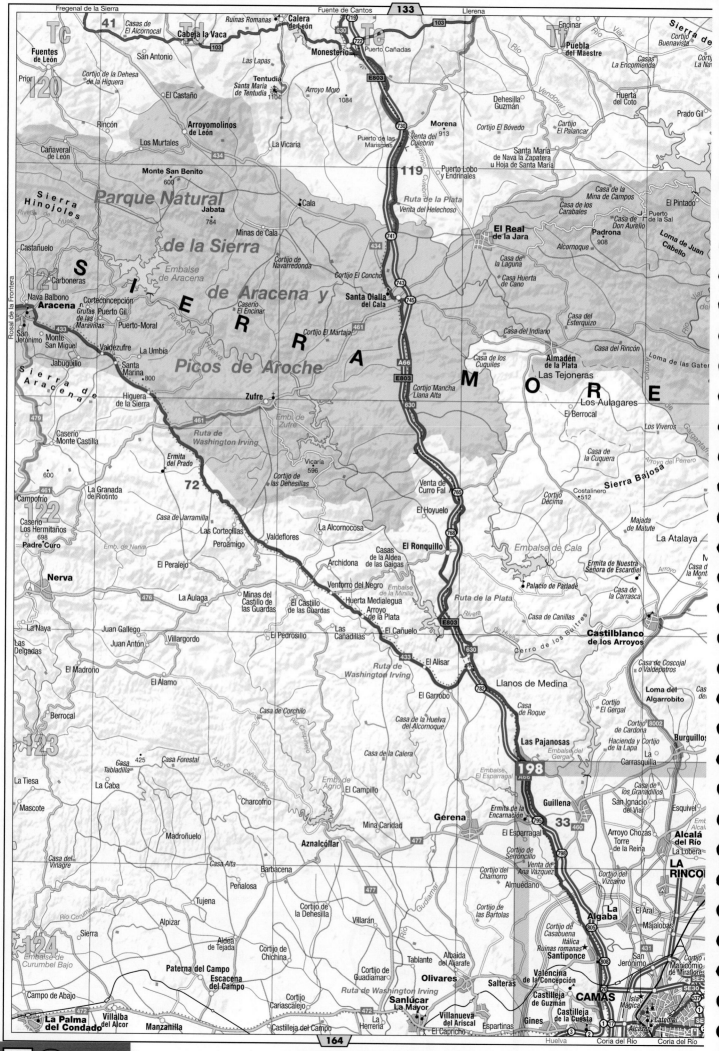

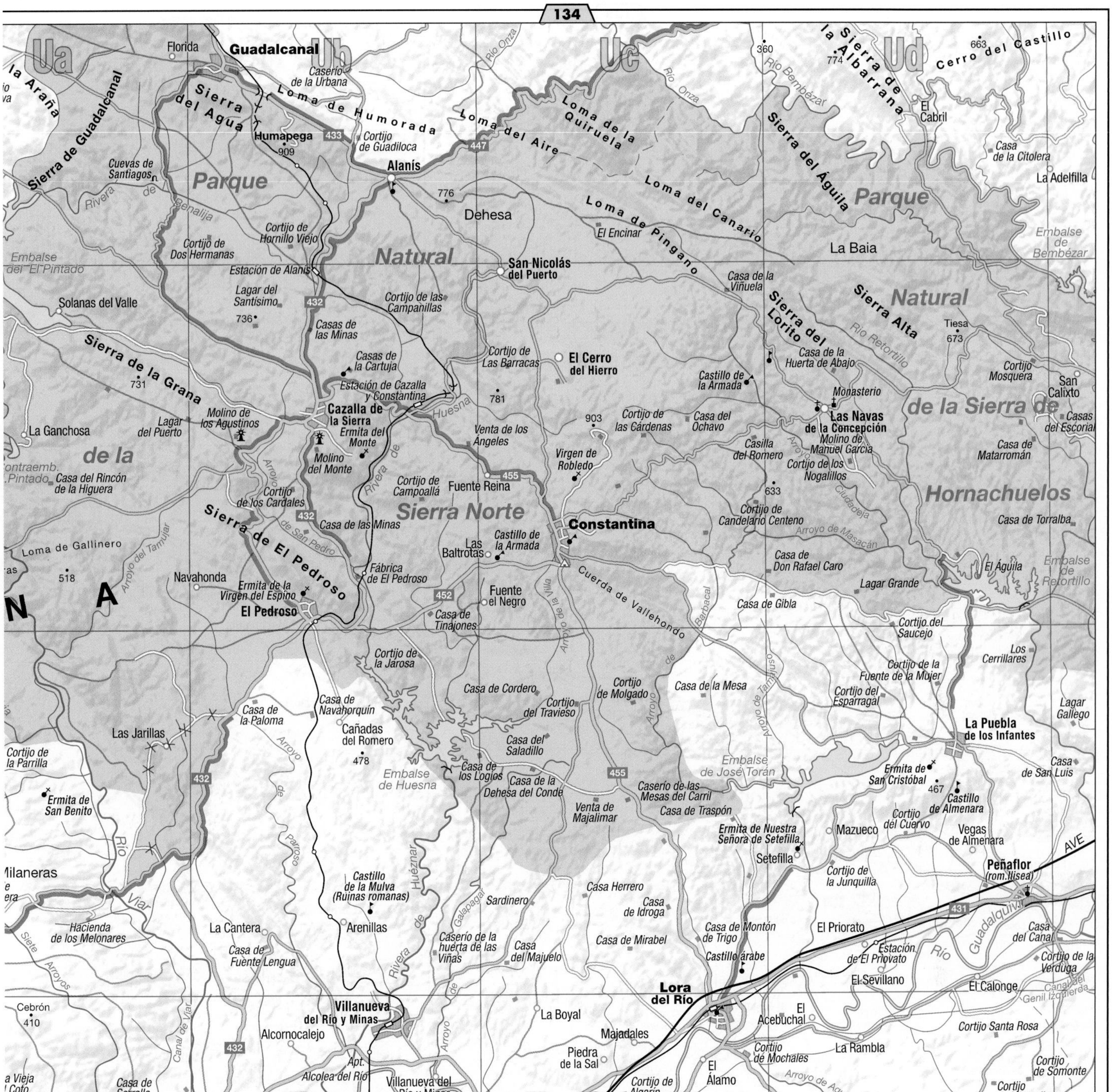

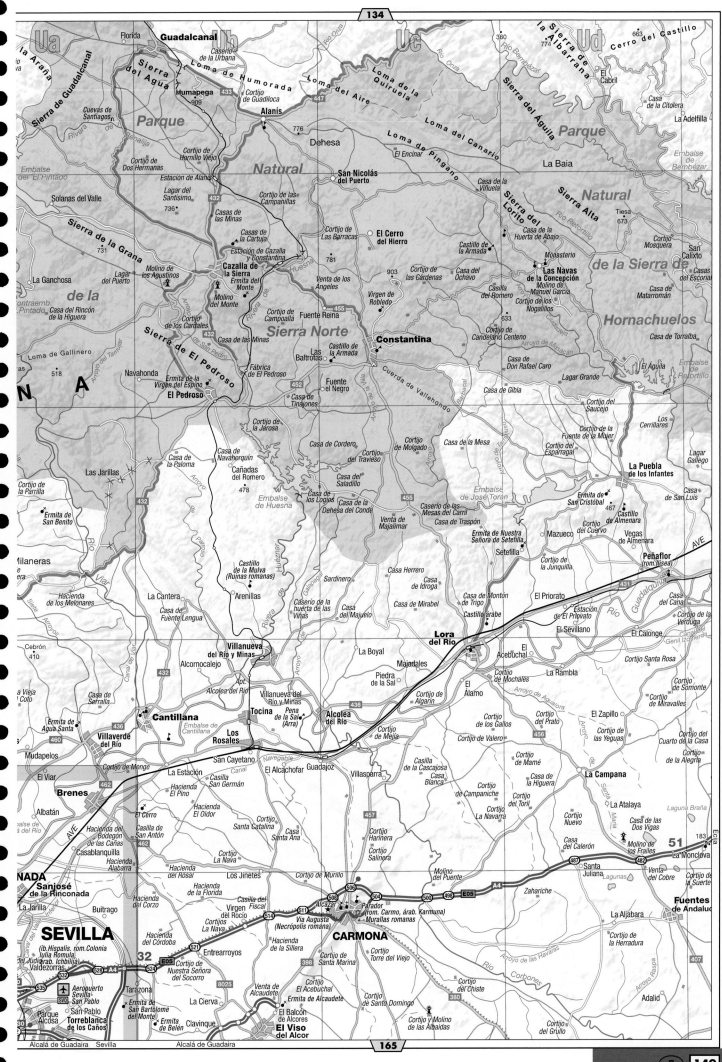

Ua
Ub
Uc
Ud
Florida
Guadalcanal
Caserío de la Urbana
Sierra del Agua
Loma de Humorada
Loma del Aire
Loma de la Quiruela
Sierra de la Albarrana
Cerro del Castillo
El Cabril
Sierra de Guadalcanal
Humapega
Cortijo de Guadiloca
Alanís
Cuevas de Santiagos
Parque
Natural
Dehesa
San Nicolás del Puerto
Loma del Canario
Loma de Pingano
El Encinar
Sierra del Águila
Casa de la Citolera
La Adelfilla
Embalse de Bembézar
La Baia
Cortijo de Hornillo Viejo
Cortijo de Dos Hermanas
Embalse del El Pintado
Estación de Alanís
Lagar del Santísimo
Solanas del Valle
Cortijo de las Campanillas
Casa de la Viñuela
Sierra del Lorito
Sierra Alta
Tiesa
Casas de las Minas
Casas de la Cartuja
Estación de Cazalla y Constantina
Sierra de la Grana
Cortijo de Las Barracas
El Cerro del Hierro
Casa de la Huerta de Abajo
Castillo de la Armada
Monasterio
Cortijo Mosquera
San Calixto
Cazalla de la Sierra
Ermita del Monte
Molino de los Agustinos
Lagar del Puerto
La Ganchosa
de la
Venta de los Ángeles
Cortijo de las Cárdenas
Casa del Ochavo
Las Navas de la Concepción
Molino de Manuel García
de la Sierra de
Casas del Escorial
Casa de Matarromán
Virgen de Robledo
Casilla del Romero
Cortijo de los Nogalillos
Contraemb. Pintado
Casa del Rincón de la Higuera
Molino del Monte
Cortijo de Campoallá
Fuente Reina
Hornachuelos
Cortijo de los Cardales
Sierra Norte
Cortijo de Candelario Centeno
Casa de Torralba
Casa de las Minas
Constantina
Loma de Gallinero
Sierra de El Pedroso
Las Baltrotas
Castillo de la Armada
Arroyo de Masacán
Casa de Don Rafael Caro
El Águila
Embalse de Retortillo
Navahonda
Fábrica de El Pedroso
Lagar Grande
A
N
Ermita de la Virgen del Espino
El Pedroso
Fuente el Negro
Cuerda de Vallehondo
Casa de Gibla
Casa de Tinajones
Cortijo del Saucejo
Los Cerrillares
Cortijo de la Jarosa
Cortijo de la Fuente de la Mujer
Casa de Cordero
Cortijo del Travieso
Cortijo de Molgado
Casa de la Mesa
Cortijo del Esparragal
Lagar Gallego
Casa de Navahorquín
Casa de la Paloma
Las Jarillas
Cañadas del Romero
Casa del Saladillo
La Puebla de los Infantes
Cortijo de la Parrilla
Embalse de Huesna
Casa de los Logíos
Casa de la Dehesa del Conde
Embalse de José Torán
Ermita de San Cristóbal
Casa de San Luis
Ermita de San Benito
Caserío de las Mesas del Carril
Casa de Traspón
Venta de Majalimar
Castillo de Almenara
Cortijo del Cuervo
Ermita de Nuestra Señora de Setefilla
Mazueco
Vegas de Almenara
Setefilla
Milaneras
Castillo de la Mulva (Ruinas romanas)
Casa Herrero
Peñaflor (rom. Ilisea)
Cortijo de la Junquilla
Sardinero
Casa de Idroga
Hacienda de los Melonares
La Cantera
Arenillas
Casa de Montón de Trigo
El Priorato
AVE
Casa de Fuente Lengua
Caserío de la huerta de las Viñas
Casa del Majuelo
Casa de Mirabel
Castillo árabe
Estación de El Priovato
Casa del Canal
Cortijo de la Verduga
Lora del Río
El Sevillano
El Calonge
Canal del Genil Izquierda
Cebrón
Villanueva del Río y Minas
La Boyal
El Acebuchal
Cortijo Santa Rosa
Alcornocalejo
Majadales
Piedra de la Sal
Cortijo de Mochales
La Rambla
Cortijo de Somonte
Apt. Alcolea del Río
Cortijo de Algarín
El Álamo
Cortijo de Miravalles
Casa de Serralla
Villanueva del Río y Minas
Arroyo de Aguafora
El Zapillo
Ermita de Agua Santa
Cantillana
Tocina
Pena de la Sal (Arra)
Alcolea del Río
Cortijo de los Gallos
Cortijo del Prato
Cortijo de las Yeguas
Cortijo del Cuarto de la Casa
Villaverde del Río
Embalse de Cantillana
Los Rosales
Cortijo de Mejía
Cortijo de Valero
Mudapelos
Cortijo de la Alegría
Cortijo de Monge
San Cayetano
Navegable
Cortijo de Mamé
El Viar
La Estación
Canal
El Alcachofar
Guadajoz
Villasparra
Casilla de la Cascajosa
Casa Blanca
Casa de la Higuera
La Campana
Brenes
Hacienda El Pino
Casilla San Germán
Cortijo de Campaniche
Cortijo del Toril
La Atalaya
Laguna Braña
Albatán
El Cerro
Hacienda El Oidor
Cortijo La Navarra
Cortijo Nuevo
Casa de las Dos Vigas
Hacienda del Bodegón de las Cañas
Casilla de San Antón
Cortijo Santa Catalina
Casa Santa Ana
Cortijo Harinera
Casa del Calerón
Molino de los Frailes
Écija
Casablanquilla
Cortijo Salinera
La Monclova
Hacienda Alabarra
Cortijo La Nava
Santa Juliana
Lagunas
Venta del Cobre
Cortijo de la Suerte
Hacienda del Rosal
Los Jinetes
Cortijo de Murillo
Molino del Puente
Zaharíche
Sanjosé de la Rinconada
Hacienda de la Florida
Hacienda del Corzo
Casilla del Fiscal
Alcázar
Parador (rom. Carmo, árab. Karmuna)
Fuentes de Andalucía
La Jarilla
Buitrago
Virgen del Rocío
Murallas romanas
Cortijos La Nava
Vía Augusta (Necrópolis romana)
La Aljabara
SEVILLA
(ib. Hispalis, rom. Colonia Iulia Romula, árab. Ichbiliia)
Hacienda del Córdoba
CARMONA
Cortijo de la Herradura
Hacienda de la Sillera
Valdezorras
Entrearroyos
Cortijo de Santa Marina
Cortijo Torre del Viejo
Arroyo de las Havaras
Corbones
Cortijo de Nuestra Señora del Socorro
Aeropuerto Sevilla-San Pablo
Tarazona
Venta de Alcaudete
Cortijo El Acebuchal
Ermita de Alcaudete
Cortijo del Chiste
Adalid
Parque Alcosa
San Pablo
Ermita de San Bartolomé del Monte
La Cierva
Cortijo de Santo Domingo
Torreblanca de los Caños
Ermita de Belén
Clavinque
El Balcón de Alcores
El Viso del Alcor
Cortijo y Molino de las Albaidas
Cortijo del Grullo

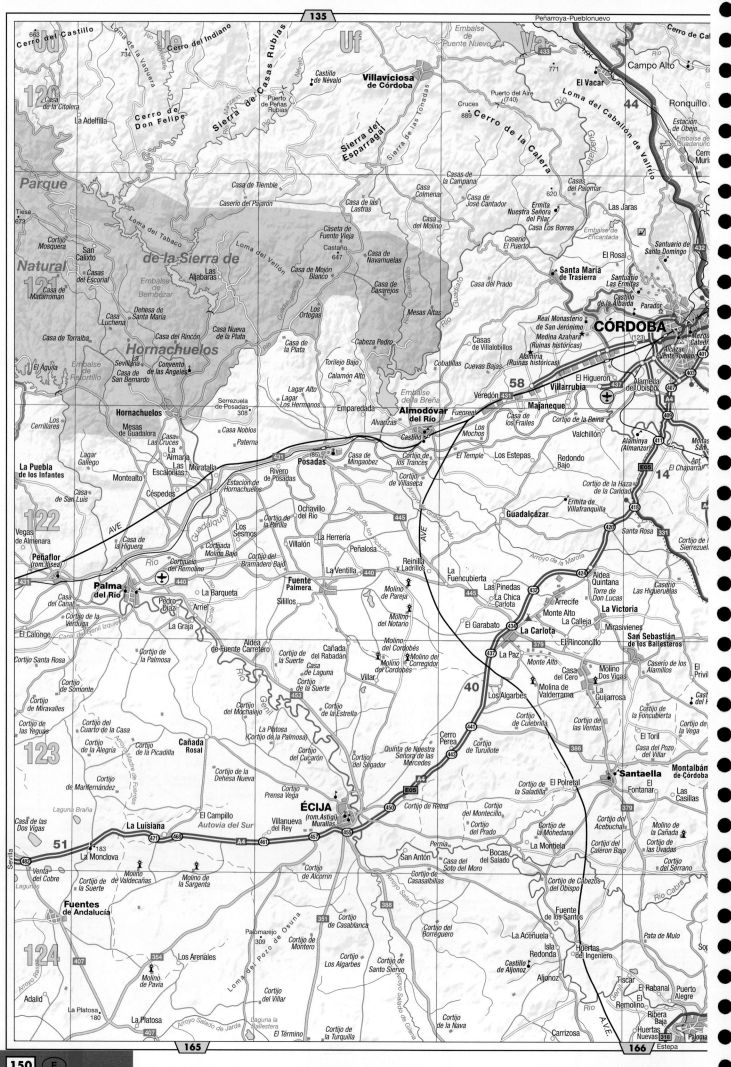

Cerro del Castillo
663
Ud
Cerro del Indiano
Uf
Sierra de Casas Rubias
Peñarroya-Pueblonuevo
Cerro de Cal
Embalse de Puente Nuevo
Vac
Loma de la Vaquera
734
Casa de la Citolera
120
Río Guadiato
433
Campo Alto
El Vacar
771
La Adelfilla
Sierra de Don Felipe
Puerto de Peñas Rubias
Castillo de Névalo
Villaviciosa de Córdoba
Sierra del Esparragal
Sierra de las Tobadas
Puerto del Aire (740)
Loma del Caballón de Valfrío
44
Ronquillo
Estación de Obejo
Cruces
889
Cerro de la Calera
Embalse de Guadanuño
Cerro Muri
Parque
Casa de Tiemble
Casa de la Campana
Casas del Palomar
620
Las Jaras
Tiesa 673
Casa de la Citolera
Caserío del Pajarón
Casa de las Lastras
Casa Colmenar
Casa de José Cantador
Casa del Molino
1143
Ermita Nuestra Señora del Pilar
Casa Los Borres
Embalse de Encantada
Santuario de Santo Domingo
Cortijo Mosquera
San Calixto
Casas del Escorial
Loma del Tabaco
Caseta de Fuente Vieja
Castaño 647
Casa de Navamuelas
Caserío El Puerto
El Rosal
Natural
121
Casa de Matarromán
de la Sierra de
Loma del Vellón
Las Aljabaras
Casa de Mojón Blanco
Santa María de Trasierra
Santuario Las Ermitas
Embalse de Bembézar
Dehesa de Santa María
Casa Nueva de la Plata
Los Ortegas
Casa de Casarejos
Mesas Altas
Casa del Prado
Castillo de la Albaida
Parador
Casa Luchena
Casa del Rincón
Cabeza Pedro
Real Monasterio de San Jerónimo
CÓRDOBA
Casa de Torralba
Hornachuelos
La Sevillana
Convento de las Ángeles
Casa de la Plata
Torilejo Bajo
Calamón Alto
Cobatillas
Cuevas Bajas
Medina Azahara (Ruinas históricas)
(123)
Mezq Catedr
El Águila
Embalse de Retortillo
Casa de San Bernardo
Embalse de la Breña
Casas de Villalobillos
Alamiria (Ruinas históricas)
El Higuerón
437
Alcázar Puente romano
401
Los Cerrillares
Hornachuelos
Serrezuela de Posadas 308
Casa Noblos
Emparedada
Almodóvar del Río
Fuenreal
58
Veredón
431
Villarrubia
Majaneque
Alameda del Obispo
A4
403
407
409
Mesas de Guadalora
Las Cruces
Casa La Almaria
Paterna
Rivero de Posadas
Posadas
85
Casa de Mingaobez
Castillo
Alvarizas
Los Mochos
Casa de los Frailes
Cortijo de la Reina
Valchillón
Alaminya (Almanzor)
411
E05
14
La Puebla de los Infantes
Lagar Gallego
Montealto
Las Escalonias
Moratalla
431
Estación de Hornachuelos
Ochavillo del Río
Cortijo de la Parilla
Cortijo de los Trances
El Temple
Los Estepas
Cortijo de Villaseca
Redondo Bajo
El Chaparral
Apt.
Cortijo de la Haza de la Caridad
418
122
Casa de San Luis
Céspedes
Guadalquivir
Los Sesmos
Villalón
La Herrería
445
Ermita de Villafranquilla
Guadalcázar
Santa Rosa
331
420
Cortijo de Sierrezuel.
Vegas de Almenara
AVE
Casa de la Higuera
Río
Cortijada Molino Bajo
Cortijo del Bramadero Bajo
La Ventilla
440
Peñalosa
Reinilla y Ladrillo
AVE
La Fuencubierta
Las Pinedas
La Chica Carlota
424
Aldea Quintana
Torre de Don Lucas
Caserío Las Higueruelas
Peñaflor (rom.Ilisea)
431
Cortijuelo del Remolino
Canal
La Barqueta
Fuente Palmera
Silillos
Molino de Pareja
El Garabato
432
Arrecife
Monte Alto
La Calleja
La Victoria
Mirasivienes
San Sebastián de los Ballesteros
Palma del Río
Pedro Díaz
Arriel
La Graja
Canal del Genil Izquierda
Aldea de Fuente Carretero
Cañada del Rabadán
Molino del Cordobés
Molino del Corregidor
Molino del Notario
434
La Carlota
379
El Rinconcillo
Monte Alto
Casa del Cero
Molino Dos Vigas
Caserío de los Alamillos
El Privil
Casa del Canal
Cortijo de la Verduga
El Calonge
Cortijo Santa Rosa
Cortijo de la Palmosa
Cortijo de la Suerte
Casa de Laguna
Villar
Cortijo de la Suerte
453
Cortijo de la Estrella
437
La Paz
Los Algarbes
Molina de Valderrama
La Guijarrosa
Cortijo de la Foncubierta
Cast del H
Cortijo de Somonte
Cortijo de Miravalles
Cortijo del Cuarto de la Casa
La Platosa (Cortijo de la Palmosa)
Cortijo del Mochalejo
Cortijo del Cucarón
Cortijo del Segador
Quinta de Nuestra Señora de las Mercedes
Cerro Perea
441
Cortijo de Culebrilla
Cortijo de Turullote
El Toril
Cortijo de la Vega
Casa del Pozo del Villar
123
Cortijo de las Yeguas
Cortijo de la Alegría
Cortijo de la Picadilla
Cañada Rosal
Cortijo de la Dehesa Nueva
443
El Polretal
Cortijo de la Saladilla
Santaella
El Fontanar
Montalbán de Córdoba
Las Casillas
Cortijo de Marifernández
Laguna Braña
Cortijo Prensa Vega
ÉCIJA (rom.Astigi) Murallas
A4
E05
450
Cortijo de Reina
Cortijo del Montecillo
Cortijo del Prado
Cortijo de la Mohedana
Cortijo del Calerón Bajo
Cortijo del Acebuchal
Molino de la Cañada
Cortijo de las Uvadas
Casa de las Dos Vigas
El Campillo
Autovía del Sur
Villanueva del Rey
455
461
457
Pernía
San Antón
Casa del Soto del Moro
Bocas del Salado
La Montiela
Cortijo de Cabezos del Obispo
Cortijo del Serrano
51
Sevilla
482
183
La Monclova
471
468
A4
Cortijo de Alcorrín
Cortijo de Casasalbillas
Arroyo Saladillo
La Aceñuela
Río Cabra
Pata de Mulo
Venta del Cobre
Lagunas
Molino de Valdecañas
Cortijo de la Suerte
Molino de la Sargenta
368
Cortijo de Casablanca
Cortijo del Borréguero
Isla Redonda
Huertas del Ingeniero
Fuente de los Santos
Aljonoz
407
Fuentes de Andalucía
Palomarejo 309
Cortijo de Montero
351
Molino de Pavía
354
Los Arenales
La Platosa 180
La Platosa
407
Arroyo Salado de Jarda
Laguna la Ballestera
El Término
Cortijo de los Algarbes
Cortijo de Santo Siervo
Cortijo del Villar
Arroyo Salado de Guena
Cortijo de la Nava
Cortijo de la Turquilla
Castillo de Aljonoz
Carrizosa
Tiscar
El Rabanal
El Remolino
Ribera Baja
Huertas Nuevas
318
Paloma
Adalid
124

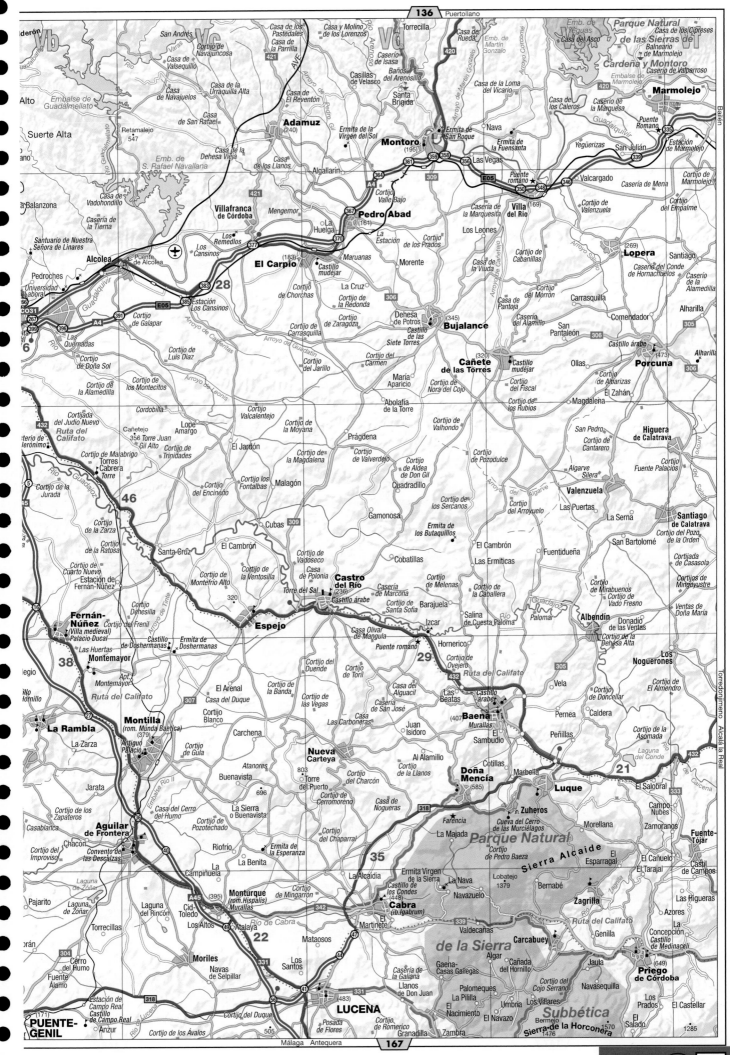

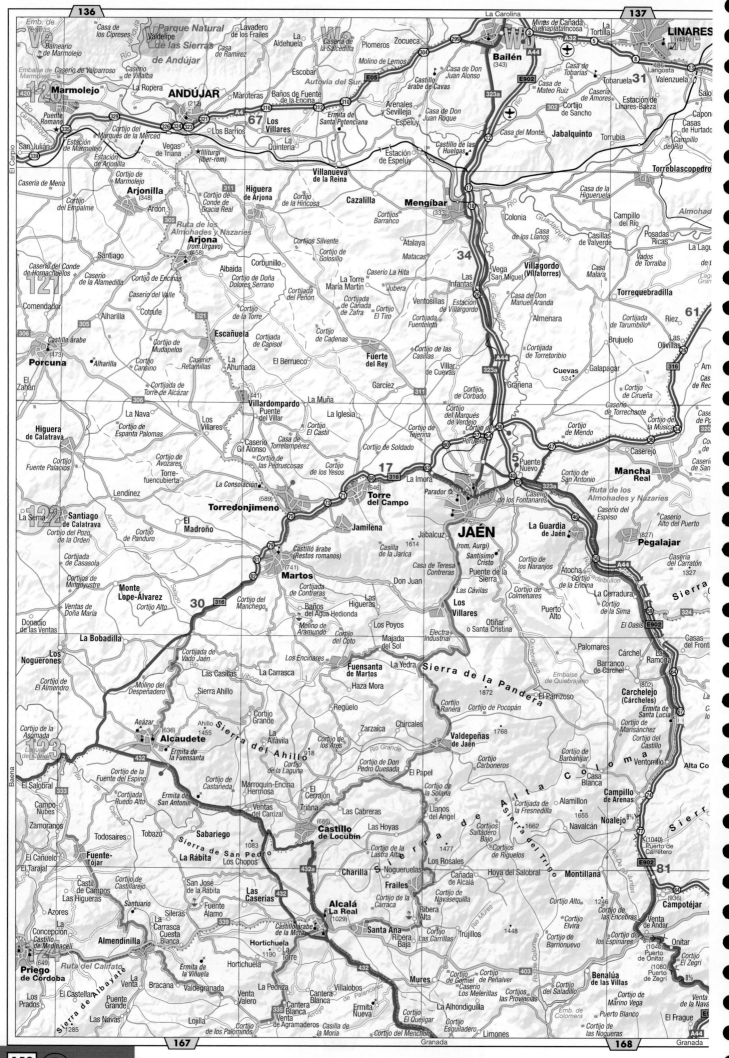

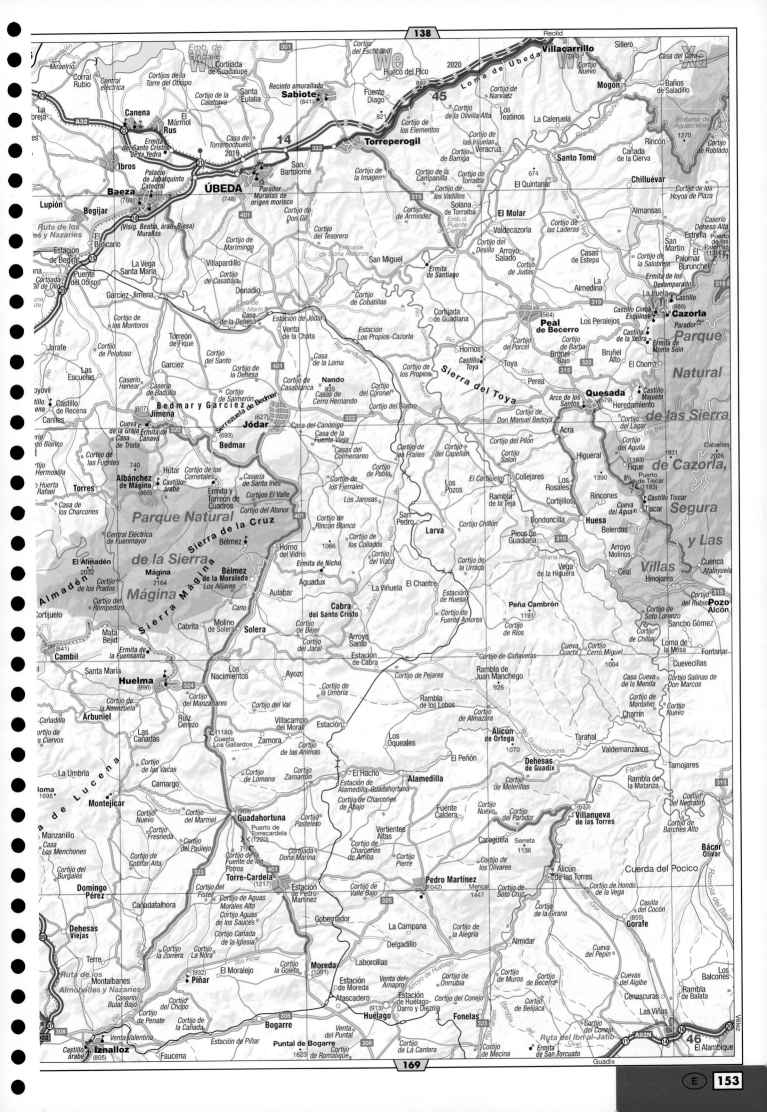

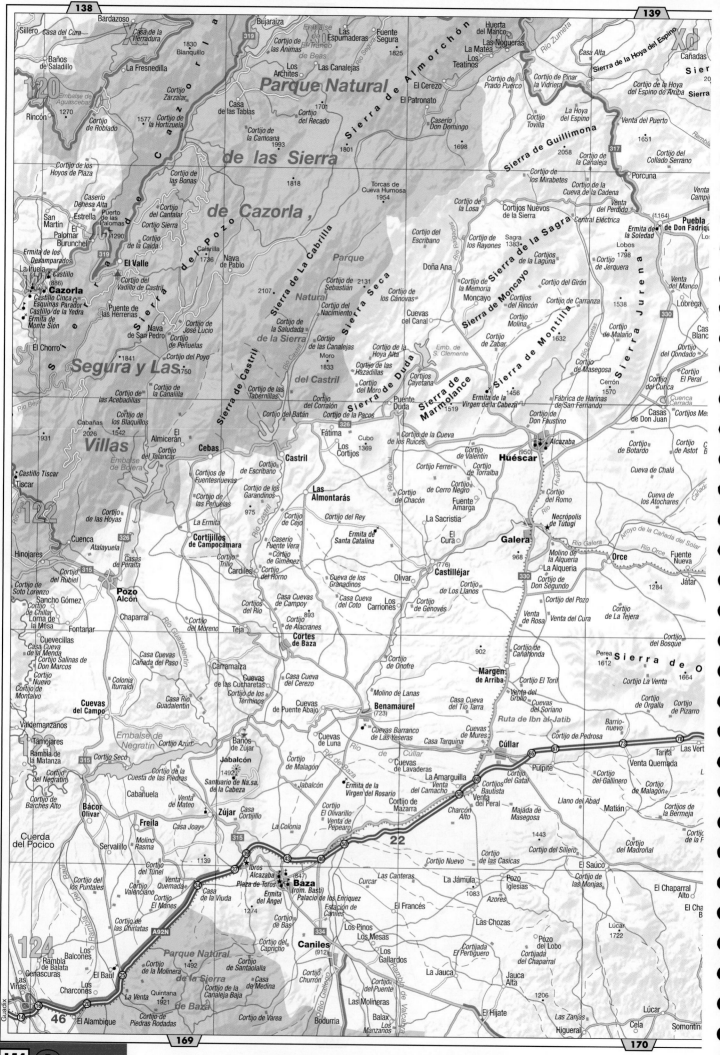

Sillero
Casa del Cura
Bardazoso
Casa de la Herradura
Bujaraiza
Embalse del Tranco de Beas
Las Espumaderas
Fuente Segura
Huerta del Manco
Las Nogueras
La Matea
Los Teatinos
Casa Alta
Río Zumeta
Cañadas
Xd
Sier

Baños de Saladillo
La Fresnedilla
1830
Blanquillo
Cortijo de las Ánimas
Los Archites
Las Canalejas
1825
Cortijo de Pinar la Vidriera
Sierra de la Hoya del Espino
Sierra

120
Embalse de Aguascebas
Rincón
1270
Cortijo de Roblado
La Fresnedilla
Parque Natural
El Cerezo
El Patronato
Cortijo de Prado Puerco
Cortijo de la Hoya del Espino de Arriba
Sierra

Cortijo de los Hoyos de Plaza
1577
Cortijo de la Hortizuela
Cortijo Zarzalar
Casa de las Tablas
1701
Cortijo del Recado
Caserío Don Domingo
1698
La Hoya del Espino
Venta del Puerto
1651

Caserío Dehesa Alta
Estrella
Puerto de las Palomas
Cortijo del Cantalar
Cortijo Sierra
1993
Cortijo de la Camoana
de las Sierra
1801
Sierra de Guillimona
2058
Cortijo de la Canaleja
317
Cortijo del Collado Serrano

San Martín
El Palomar
Burunchel
(1290)
Cortijo de la Caida
1818
de Cazorla,
Torcas de Cueva Humosa 1954
Cortijo de los Mirabetes
Cortijo de la Cueva de la Cadena
Porcuna
Venta

Ermita de los Desamparados
La Iruela
319
El Valle
Calarilla
1736
Nava de Pablo
Parque
Cortijo del Escribano
Cortijo de los Rayones
Sagra 1383
Cortijos Nuevos de la Sierra
Central Eléctrica
Venta del Perdido
(1.164)
Puebla de Don Fadriqu
Los

Castillo (886)
Cazorla
Castillo Cinco Esquinas Parador
Cortijo del Vadillo de Castril
2107
Sierra de La Cabrilla
Natural
Cortijo de Sebastián
2131
Cortijo de los Cánovas
Cortijo de los
Moncayo
Sierra de la Sagra
Lobos 1798
Ermita de la Soledad
Venta del Manco
Lóbrega

Castillo de la Yedra
Ermita de Monte Sión
Nava de San Pedro
Cortijo de José Lucio
Cortijo de Peñuelas
Sierra de la Cabrilla
Cortijo del Nacimiento
Cortijo de los Cánovas
Cortijo de la Memoria
Moncayo
Sierra de Moncayo
Cortijos del Rincón
Cortijo del Girón
330
Venta
Cortijo de Jerquera

El Chorro
1841
1750
Cortijo del Poyo
Cortijo de la Saludada de la Sierra
Cortijo de las Canalejas Moro 1833
Cortijo de la Hoya Alta
Cortijo de las Hazadillas
Emb. de S. Clemente
Cortijo de Zabar
Cortijo de Carranza
1538
Cortijo de Malaño
Cas Blanc

Segura y Las
1931
Cortijo de las Acebadillas
Cortijo de la Canalilla
Cortijo de las Tabernillas
del Castril
Cortijo del Moro
Cortijos Cayetana
Sierra de Marmolance
Cortijo Molina
1632
Sierra de Montilla
Cortijo de El Peral
Cortijo del Condado

Río Bejar
Cabañas
Castillo Tiscar
Tiscar
2026 1542
de los Blaquillos
El Almicerán
Cortijo del Talancar
Cebas
Cortijo del Batán
Cortijo de la Pacos
Sierra de Duda
Puente Duda
1519
Ermita de la Virgen de la Cabeza
1456
Cerrón 1570
Fábrica de Harinas de San Fernando
Cortijo del Curica
Cuenca Cerrada

122
Cuenca
Atalayuela
Casas de Peralta
Cortijos de Fuentesnuevas
Cortijo de Escribano
Castril
Fátima
326
Cubo 1369
Los Cortijos
Cortijo de la Cueva de los Ruices
Cortijo de la Cueva de los Ruices
Alcazaba
Cortijo de Don Faustino
Casas de Don Juan
Cortijos Mes

Hinojares
315
Cortijo del Rubiel
Cortijo de las Hoyas
La Ermita
Cortijo de los Garandinos
975
Las Almontarás
Cortijo del Rey
Cortijo de Chacón
Cortijo de Valentín
Cortijo de Torralba
Huéscar (950)
Cortijo del Romo
Cortijo de Botardo
Cortijo de Astot
Cueva de Chalá

Cortijo de Soto Lorenzo
Sancho Gómez
Cortijo de Chillar Loma de la Mesa
Fontanar
Cortijillos de Campocámara
Caserío Fuente Vera
Cortijo de Giménez
Cortijo del Cejo
Ermita de Santa Catalina
El Cura
La Sacristia
Fuente Amarga
Cortijo de Cerro Negro
Necrópolis de Tútugi
Cueva de los Atochares

Cuevecillas
Casa Cueva de la Menda
Cortijo Salinas de Don Marcos
Cortijo Nuevo
Cortijo de Montalvo
Chaparral
Cortijo del Moreno
Teja
Cardiles
Cortijo del Horno
Cortijo Trillo
Cueva de los Granadinos
Olivar
Castilléjar
Cortijo de Los Llanos
Galera
968
330
Molino de la Alquería
La Alquería
Orce
Río Galera
Fuente Nueva
Játar
1284

Pozo Alcón
Casas Cueva Cañada del Paso
Cortijos del Río
893
Cortijo de Alacranes
Cortes de Baza
Casa Cuevas de Campoy
Casa Cueva del Coto
Los Carriones
Cortijo de Genovés
(776)
Cortijo de Don Segundo
Venta de Rosa
Venta del Cura
Cortijo de La Tejera
Cortijo del Bosque

Valdemanzanos
Tamojares
Carramaiza
Colonia Iturraldi
Guevas de las Cucharetas
Cortijo de los Términos
Casa Cueva del Cerezo
Molino de Lanas
Cortijo de Onofre
902
Cortijo de Cañahonda
Cortijo El Toril
Perea 1612
Sierra de O
1664
Cortijo La Venta
Cortijo de Orgalla
Cortijo de Pizarro

Cuevas del Campo
Casa Río Guadalentín
Cuevas de Puente Abajo
Benamaurel (723)
Casa Cueva del Tío Tarra
Margen de Arriba
Venta del Grullo
Cuevas del Soriano
Barrio-nuevo

Embalse de Negratín
Cortijo Azúr
Baños de Zújar
Cuevas de Luna
Cuevas Barranco de Las Yeseras
Cuevas de Mures
Casa Tarquina
Ruta de Ibn al-Jatib
Cúllar
Cortijo de Pedrosa
73
78

Cuerda del Pocico
315
Cortijo Seco
Jabalcón
1492
Cortijo de Malagón
de Cúllar
Río
Cuevas de Lavaderas
65
67
Pulpite
Las Vert
Tarifa
Venta Quemada

Cortijo del Negratín
Cabañuela
Santuario de Na.sa. de la Cabeza
Cortijo de la Cuesta de las Piedras
Jabalcón
Ermita de la Virgen del Rosario
La Amarguilla
Venta del Camacho
60
Cortijos Bautista
Venta del Peral
Cortijo del Gatal
Llano del Abad
Matián
Cortijos de la Bermeja

Cortijo de Barches Alto
Bácor Olivar
Freila
Venta de Mateo
Zújar
Casa Cortijillo
Cortijo El Olivarillo Venta de Pepearo
Cortijo de Mazarra
Charcón Alto
58
Majada de Masegosa
1443
Cortijo del Sillero
Cortijo del Madroñal

Servalillo
Molino Rasma
Casa Joay
La Colonia
315
Cortijo Nuevo
Las Casicas
El Saúco
Cortijo de las Monjas

39
43
45
50
22
El Francés
Pozo Iglesias
El Chaparral Alto

Las Viñas
Genascuras
Rambla de Balata
Los Balcones
El Baúl
25
37
34
Ibros Alcazaba
Plaza de Toros
Baza (rom. Basti)
(847)
Palacio de los Enríquez
Estación de Caniles
Las Canteras
Curcar
La Jámula
1083
Azores
Las Chozas
El Cha B

124
Rambla de Balata
Cortijo del los Puntales
Cortijo Valenciano
Cortijo El Manes
A92N
Casa de la Viuda
1274
Ermita del Ángel
Cortijo de Bas
334
Los Pinos
Los Mesas
Los Gallardos
La Jauca
Cortijada El Pertiguero
Lúcar 1722
Lúcar

Cortijo de las Chirlatas
Parque Natural
Cortijo de la Molinera
1492
Cortijo de Santaolalla
Cortijo del Capricho
Caniles (912)
Cortijo Churrón
Cortijo del Puente
Jauca Alta
Pozo del Lobo
Cortijada del Chaparral
1206
El Chaparral

16
20
46
El Alambique
El Baúl
La Venta
Quintana 1921
Cortijo de Piedras Rodadas
de la Sierra
de Baza
Casa de Medina
Cortijo de la Canaleja Baja
Bodurria
Las Molineras
Balax Los Manzanos
El Hijate
Higueral
Las Zanjas
Cela
Somontin

Guadix
14

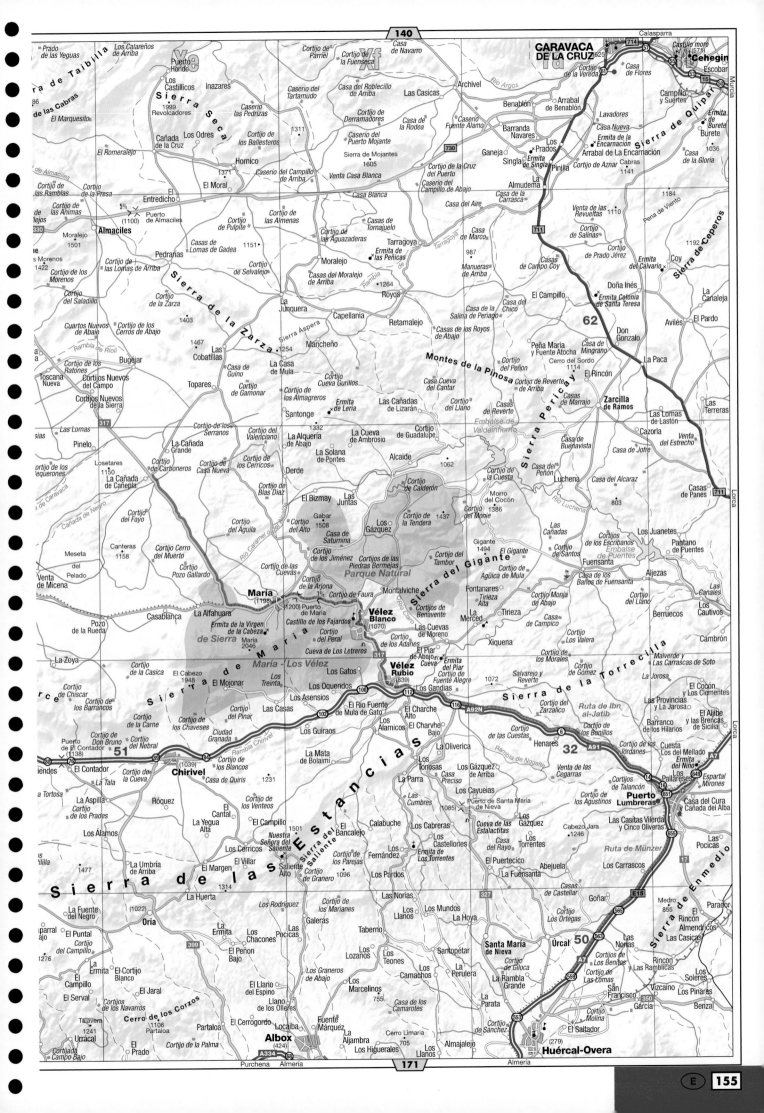

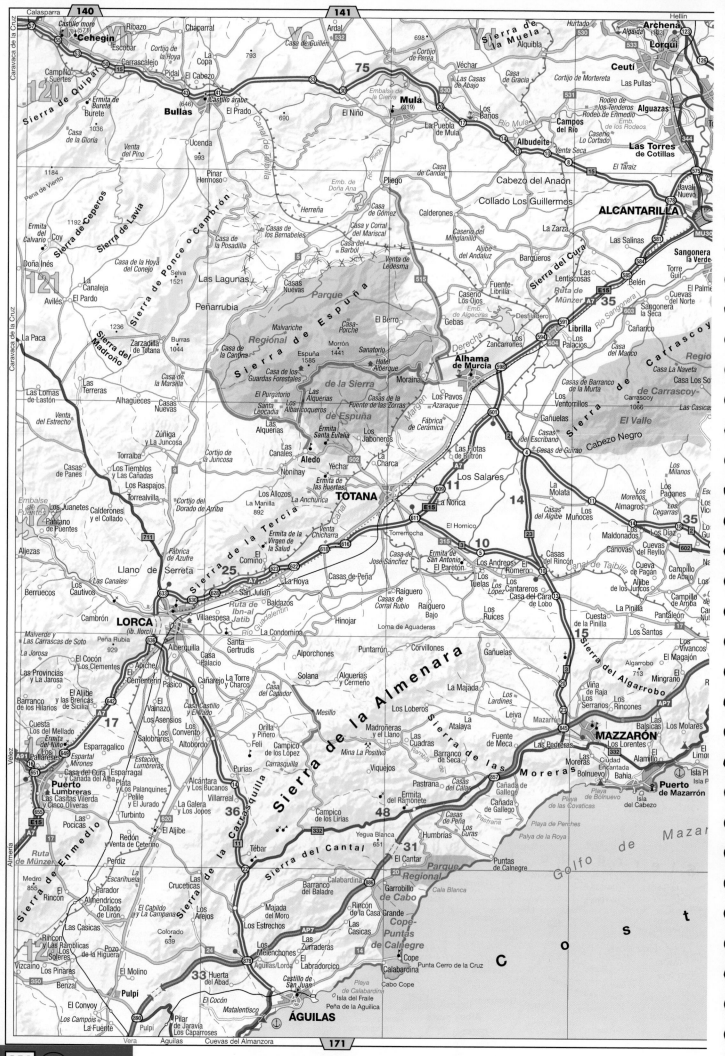

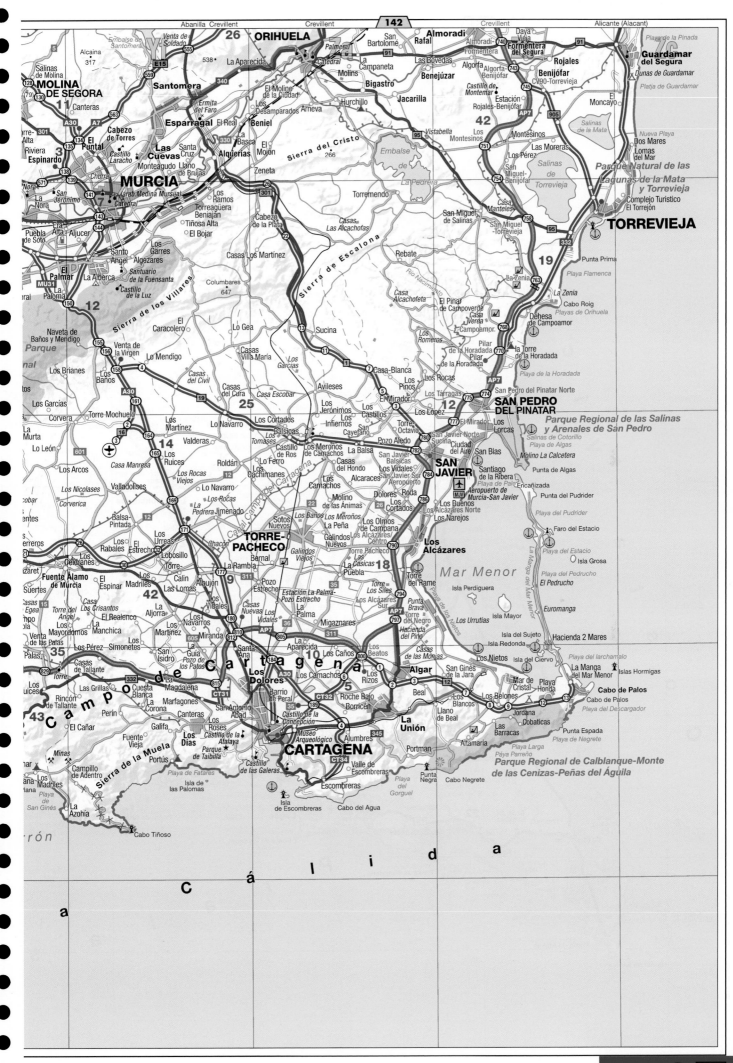

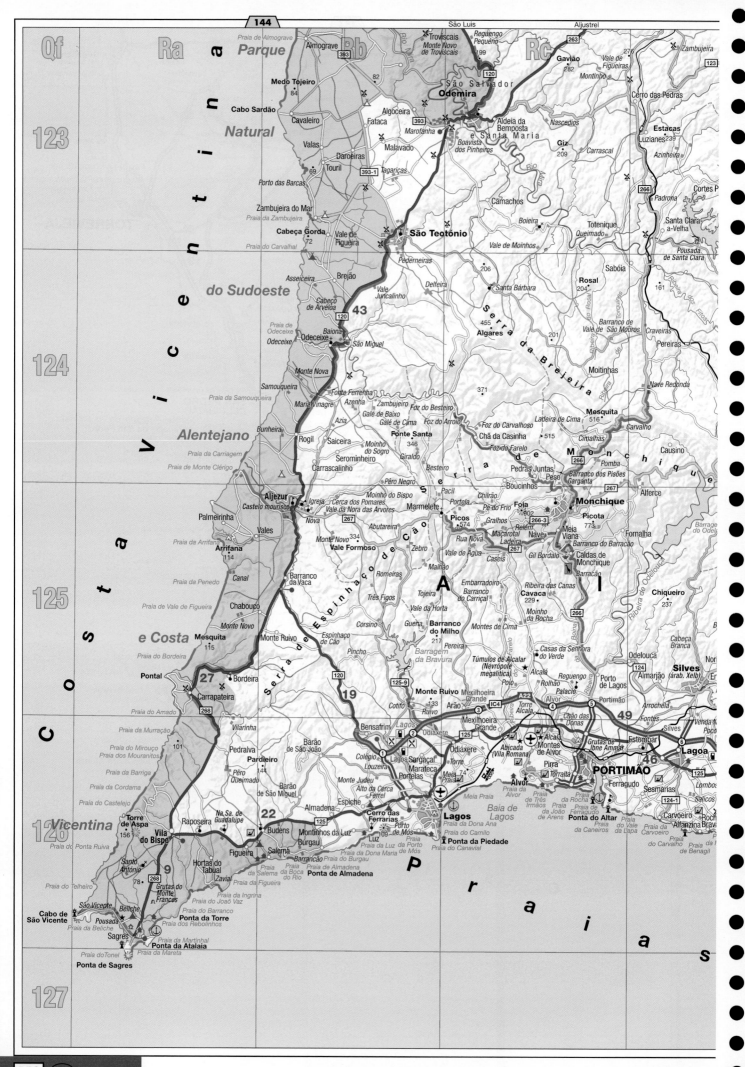

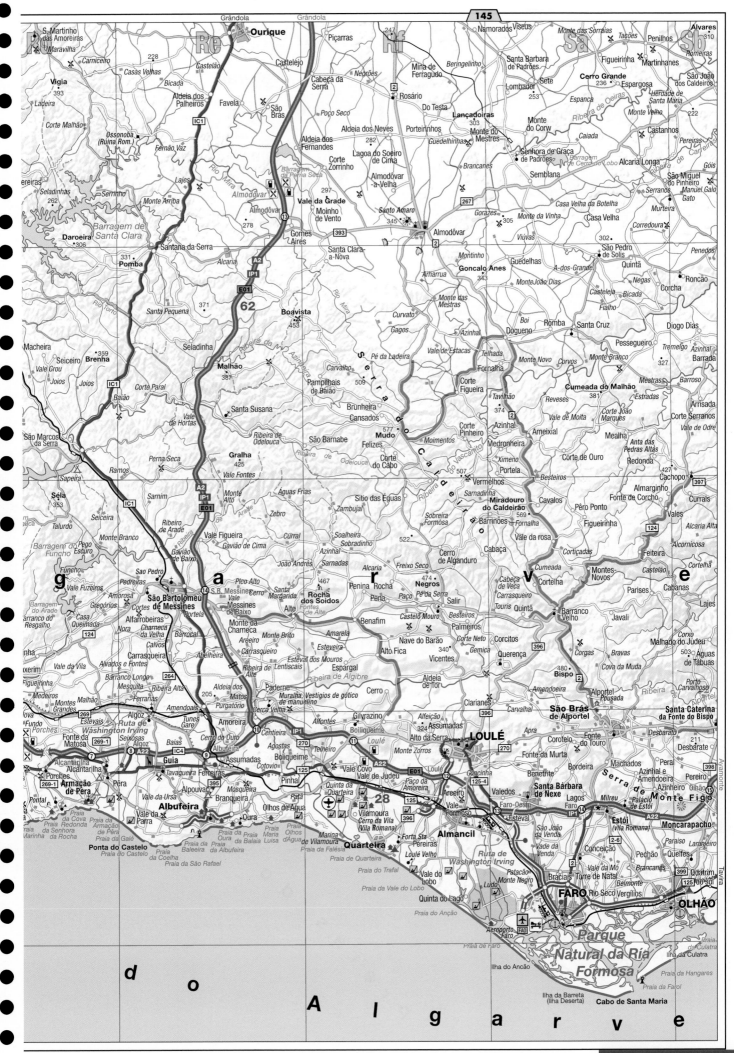

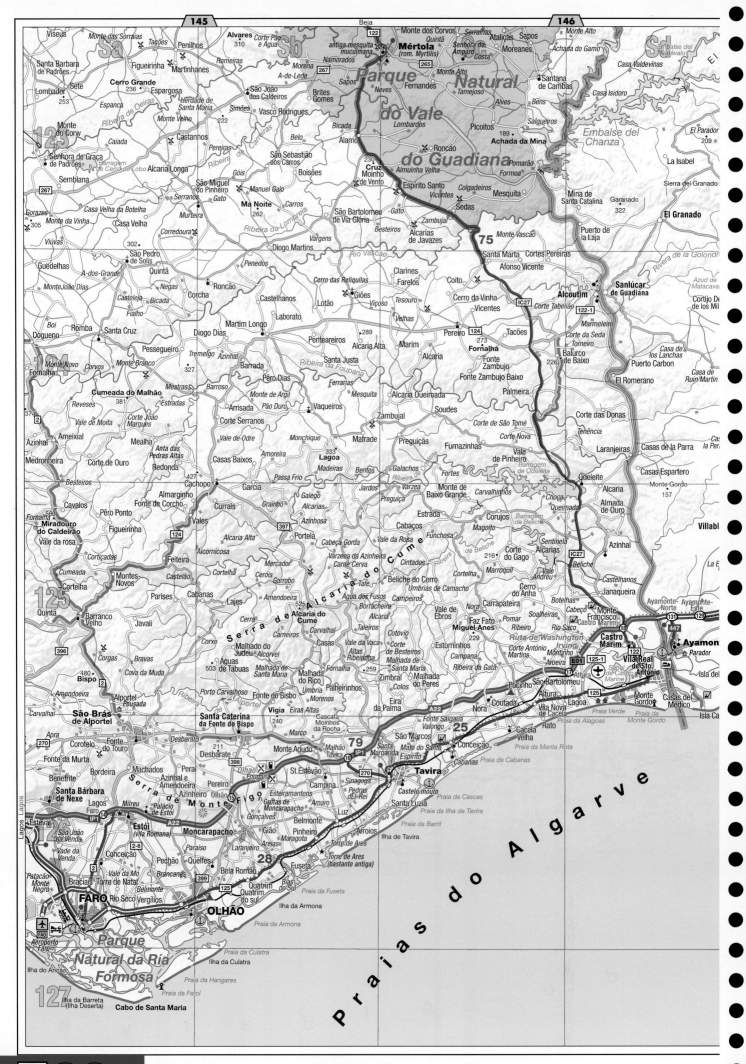

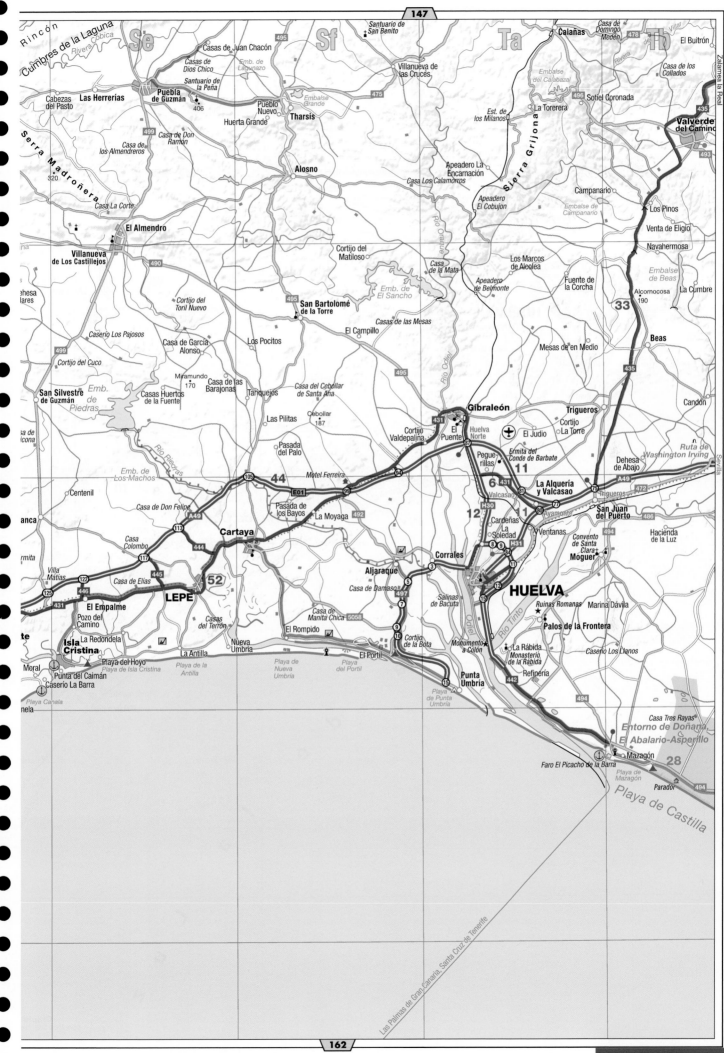

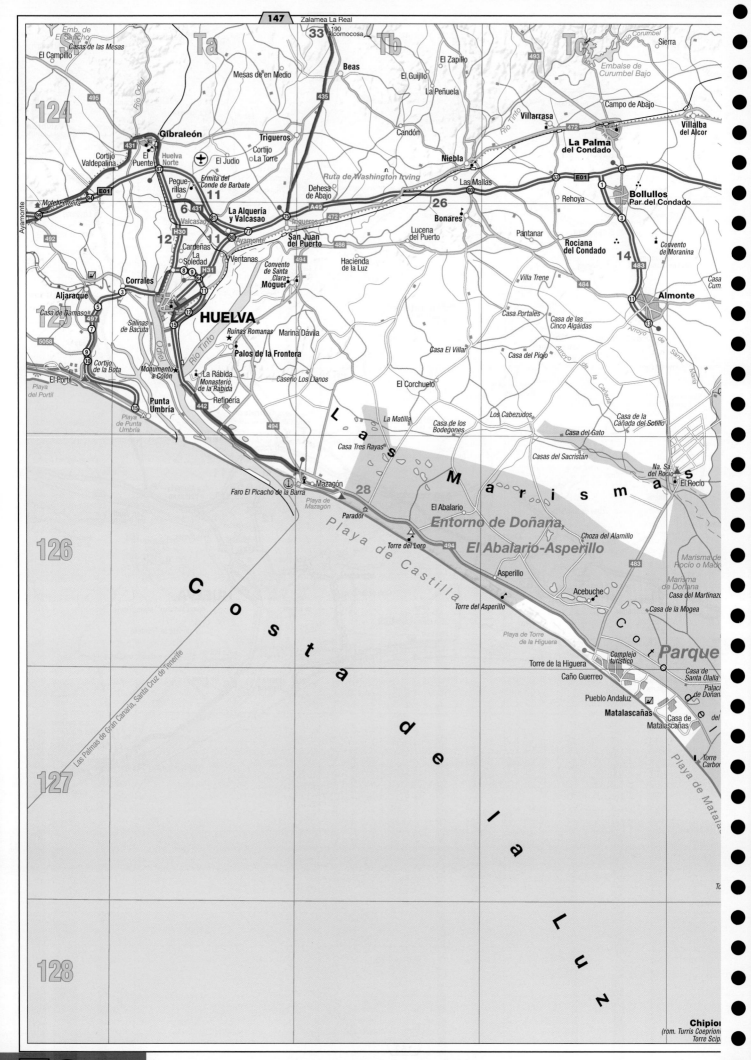

Zalamea La Real

33 Alcornocosa

El Campillo

Emb. de
El Sancho

Casas de las Mesas

Ta

Tb

Tc

Sierra

Río Corumbel

El Zapillo

El Guijllo

La Peñuela

493

Embalse de
Curumbel Bajo

Campo de Abajo

El Judío

Beas

Mesas de en Medio

435

Candón

Río Tinto

Villarrasa

472

Villalba
del Alcor

124

495

Río Odiel

Gibraleón

Triguueros

Cortijo
La Torre

La Palma
del Condado

Cortijo
Valdepalina

431

El
Puente

Huelva
Norte

El Judio

Niebla

Las Mallas

60

53

E01

48

1

Bollullos
Par del Condado

Convento
de Moranina

Pequerillas

Ermita del
Conde de Barbate

11

Ruta de Washington Irving

Rehoya

3

Motel Ferreira

94

E01

6

431

Valcasao

81

La Alquería
y Valcasao

75

472

26

Bonares

Pantanar

Rociana
del Condado

483

Casa
Cum

99

492

12

11

H30

80

77

Ayamonte

San Juan
del Puerto

486

Lucena
del Puerto

484

14

Cardeñas

La
Soledad

Ventanas

494

Hacienda
de la Luz

Villa Trene

11

Almonte

Corrales

8

9

H31

Convento
de Santa
Clara

Moguer

Casa Portales

Casa de las
Cinco Algáidas

13

Aljaraque

84

11

12

HUELVA

Ruinas Romanas

Marina Dávila

Casa El Villar

Casa del Piojo

Arroyo de la Cañada

125

5

497

3

Casa de Damaso

Salinas
de Bacuta

15

Palos de la Frontera

El Corchuelo

9

Odiel

Río Tinto

Caserío Los Llanos

Los Cabezudos

Casa de la
Cañada del Sotillo

10

Cortijo
de la Bota

Monumento
a Colón

La Rábida
Monasterio
de la Rábida

El Portil

El Portil

Punta
Umbría

442

Refinería

La Matilla

Casa de los
Bodegones

Casa del Gato

Na. Sa.
del Rocío

El Rocío

15

494

L

Casa Tres Rayas

a

s

M

a

r

i

s

m

a

s

Playa
de Punta
Umbría

Faro El Picacho de la Barra

Playa
de Mazagón

Mazagón

28

El Abalario

Casas del Sacristán

Marisma de
Rocío o Madr

Parador

Entorno de Doñana,
El Abalario-Asperillo

Choza del Alamillo

Marisma
de Doñana

Playa de Castilla

Torre del Loro

494

Asperillo

483

Casa del Martinazo

Acebuche

Casa de la Mogea

126

C

o

s

t

a

Torre del Asperillo

Playa de Torre
de la Higuera

C

Torre de la Higuera

Complejo
turístico

Parque

Caño Guerrero

Casa de
Santa Olalla

d

e

l

a

Pueblo Andaluz

Palaci
de Doñan

Matalascañas

Casa de
Matalascañas

del

L

u

z

Playa de Matala

127

Torre
Carbon

Las Palmas de Gran Canaria, Santa Cruz de Tenerife

128

Chipioi
(rom. Turris Coeprioni
Torre Scip

To

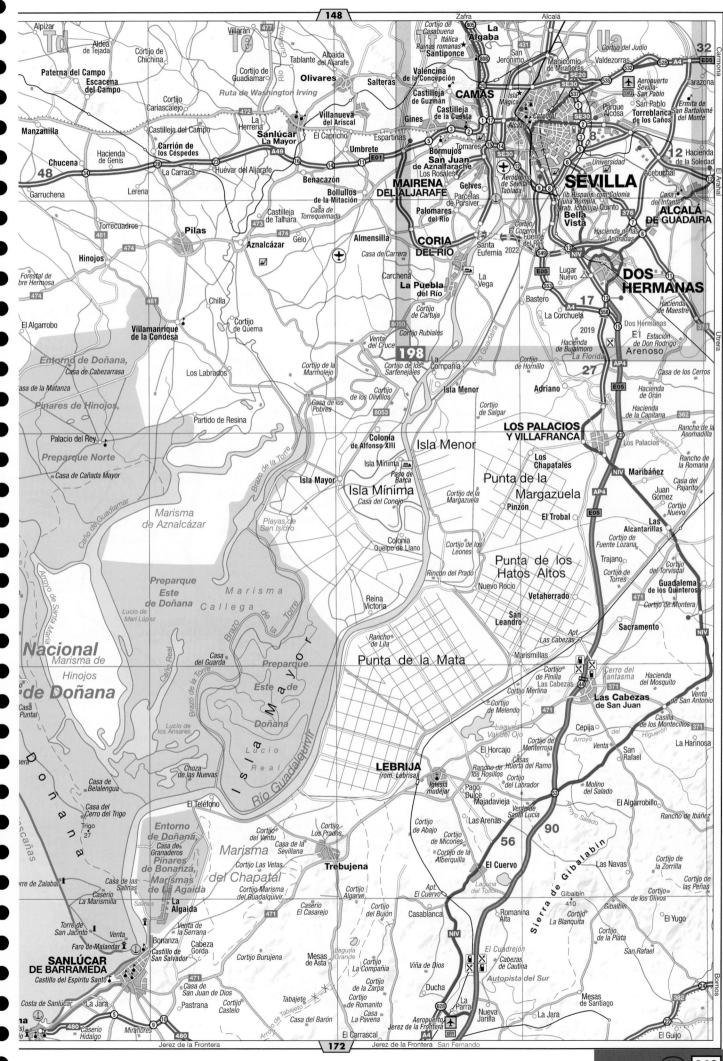

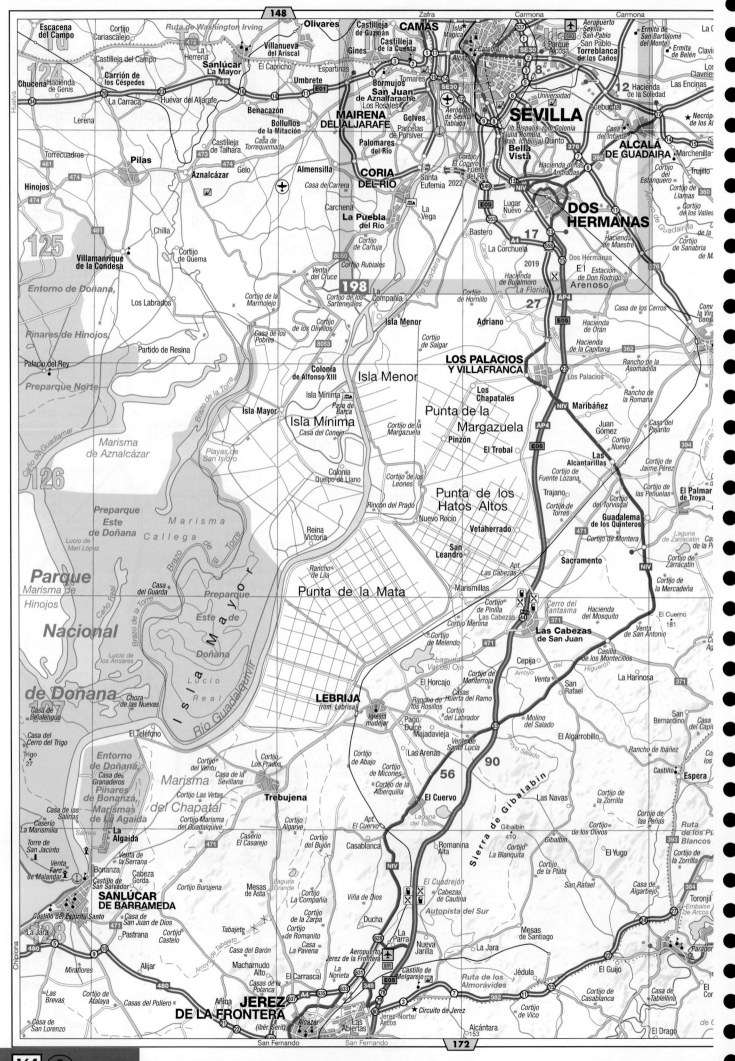

Escacena del Campo
Cortijo Cariascalejo
Castilleja del Campo
Carrión de los Céspedes
Chucena
Hacienda de Genís
La Carraca
Lerena
Huévar del Aljarafe
Torrecuadros
Pilas
Hinojos
Aznalcázar
Gelo
Villamanrique de la Condesa
Cortijo de Quema
Chilla
Palacio del Rey
Los Labrados
Partido de Resina
Entorno de Doñana,
Pinares de Hinojos,
Preparque Norte
Ruta de Washington Irving
Olivares
Villanueva del Ariscal
Sanlúcar La Mayor
La Herrería
El Capricho
Umbrete
Espartinas
Benacazón
Bollullos de la Mitación
Castilleja de Talhara
Casa de Torrequemada
Almensilla
Casa de Carrera
Carchena
La Puebla del Río
Cortijo de Cartuja
Venta del Cruce
Cortijo Rubiales
Cortijo de la Marmolejo
Cortijo de los Sartenejales
Cortijo de los Olivillos
Cortijo de los Pobres
Casa de los Pobres
Colonia de Alfonso XIII
Isla Minima
Paso de Barca
Isla Mayor
Isla Mínima
Casa del Conejo
Casa de Granaderos
Cortijo Las Vetas
Cortijo de la Margazuela
Colonia Quelpo de Llano
Cortijo de los Leones
Rincón del Prado
Reina Victoria
Rancho de Lila
Preparque Este de Doñana
Callega
Marisma
Lucio de Mari López
Parque
Marisma de Hinojos
Nacional
Preparque Este de Doñana
Isla Mayor
Lucio Real
Río Guadalquivir
Brazo de la Torre
Caño de Guadiamar
Marisma de Aznalcázar
Playas de San Isidro
de Doñana
Casa del Cerro del Trigo
Trigo 27
El Teléfono
Choza de las Nuevas
Casa de Belalengua
Lucio de los Ánsares
Casa del Guarda
Entorno de Doñana
Marisma del Chapatal
Pinares de Bonanza,
Marismas de La Agaida
Casa de las Salinas
Caserío La Marismilla
Torre de San Jacinto
La Algaida
Bonanza
Venta Faro de Malandar
Castillo de San Salvador
SANLÚCAR DE BARRAMEDA
Castillo del Espíritu Santo
La Jara
Pastrana
Cortijo Castelo
Tabajete
Alijar
Miraflores
Las Brevas
Cortijo de Atalaya
Casas del Pollero
Casa de San Lorenzo
Añina
JEREZ DE LA FRONTERA
(ibér. Serit)
Alcázar
Macharnudo Alto
Casas de la Polanca
El Carrascal
La Norieta
Mesas de Asta
Laguna Grande
Cortijo La Compañía
Cortijo de la Zarza
Cortijo de Romanito
Casa del Barón
Cortijo de la Pavena
Casa La Pavena
Aeropuerto de Jerez de la Frontera
Castillo de Melgarejo
Nueva Jarilla
La Parra
Ducha
Cortijo Burujena
Cortijo Marisma del Guadalquivir
Cortijo Marisma del Guadalquivir
Caserío El Casarejo
Cortijo Algarve
Cortijo del Bujón
Casablanca
Cortijo del Ventu
Cortijo Los Prados
Casa de la Sevillana
Trebujena
Cortijo de Abajo
Cortijo de Micones
Cortijo de la Alberquilla
El Cuervo
LEBRIJA
(rom. Lebrisa)
Iglesia mudéjar
Pago Dulce
Majadavieja
Venta de Santa Lucía
Rancho de los Rosillos
Cortijo del Labrador
Casas Huerta del Ramo
Las Arenas
Apt. El Cuervo
Laguna del Tollón
Romanina Alta
El Cuadrejón
Cabezas de Cautina
Viña de Dios
Autopista del Sur
Gibalbín
Sierra de Gibalbín
San Rafael
Las Navas
Molino del Salado
El Algarrobillo
Rancho de Ibáñez
Castillo
Espera
Cortijo de la Zorrilla
Cortijo de las Peñas
Ruta de los Pueblos Blancos
Cortijo de la Zorrilla
Toronjil
Casa de Tablellina
El Drago
El Yugo
Casa de Algarbejo
San Rafael
Cortijo de la Plata
Cortijo La Blanquita
Gibalbín
Mesas de Santiago
El Guijo
Jédula
Paradór
Cortijo de Casablanca
Cortijo de Vico
Alcántara
Circuito de Jerez
Jerez-Norte/Arcos
Las Abiertas
San Fernando
San Fernando

CAMAS
Castilleja de Guzmán
Castilleja de la Cuesta
Gines
Tomares
Bormujos
San Juan de Aznalfarache
Los Rosales
MAIRENA DEL ALJARAFE
Gelves
Parcelas de Porsiver
Palomares del Río
Coria del Río
Santa Eufemia 2022
La Vega
Isla Magica
Catedral
Alcázar
SEVILLA
(lb. Hispalis, rom. Colonia Julia Romula, árab. Ichbilija) Quinto
Universidad
Aeródromo de Sevilla Tablada
Bella Vista
Casa del Infante
Cortijo El Copero
Fuente del Rey
Lugar Nuevo
La Florida
Bastero
La Corchuela
Dos Hermanas
Arenoso
Aeropuerto Sevilla-San Pablo
Parque Alcosa
San Pablo
Torreblanca de los Caños
Acebuchal
Hacienda de la Soledad
ALCALÁ DE GUADAIRA
Marchenilla
Cortijo del Estanquero
Trujillo
Cortijo de Llamas
Ermita de San Bartolomé del Monte
Ermita de Belén
Las Encinas
Hacienda de las Andrádas
DOS HERMANAS
Hacienda de Maestre
Estación de Don Rodrigo
Hacienda de Bujalmoro
Cortijo de Hornillo
Isla Menor
Adriano
Cortijo de Salgar
LOS PALACIOS Y VILLAFRANCA
Los Chapatales
Punta de la Margazuela
Pinzón
El Trobal
Maribáñez
Juan Gómez
Cortijo Nuevo
Las Alcantarillas
Cortijo de Fuente Lozana
Trajano
Cortijo del Torvisçal
Punta de los Hatos Altos
Cortijo de Torres
Nuevo Rocío
Vetaherrado
Guadalema de los Quinteros
San Leandro
Marismillas
Apt. Las Cabezas
Punta de la Mata
Cortijo de Pinilla
Las Cabezas
Cortijo Merlina
Cortijo de Melendo
Las Cabezas de San Juan
Cepija
El Horcajo
Cortijo de Monterroja
Laguna Val del Ojo
Cerro del fantasma
Hacienda del Mosquito
El Cuerno 181
Venta de San Antonio
Casilla de los Montecillos
La Harinosa
San Rafael
San Bernardino
Casa del Capi
Hacienda de Orán
Hacienda de la Capitana
Casa de los Cerros
Rancho de la Asomadilla
Rancho de la Romana
Casa del Pajarito
Cortijo de Jaime Pérez
El Palmar de Troya
Laguna de Zarracatin
Cortijo de Montera
Sacramento
Cortijo de Zarracatin
Cortijo de la Mercadeña
El Palmar
Necrópolis de los Al

Chipiona
San Fernando

198

172

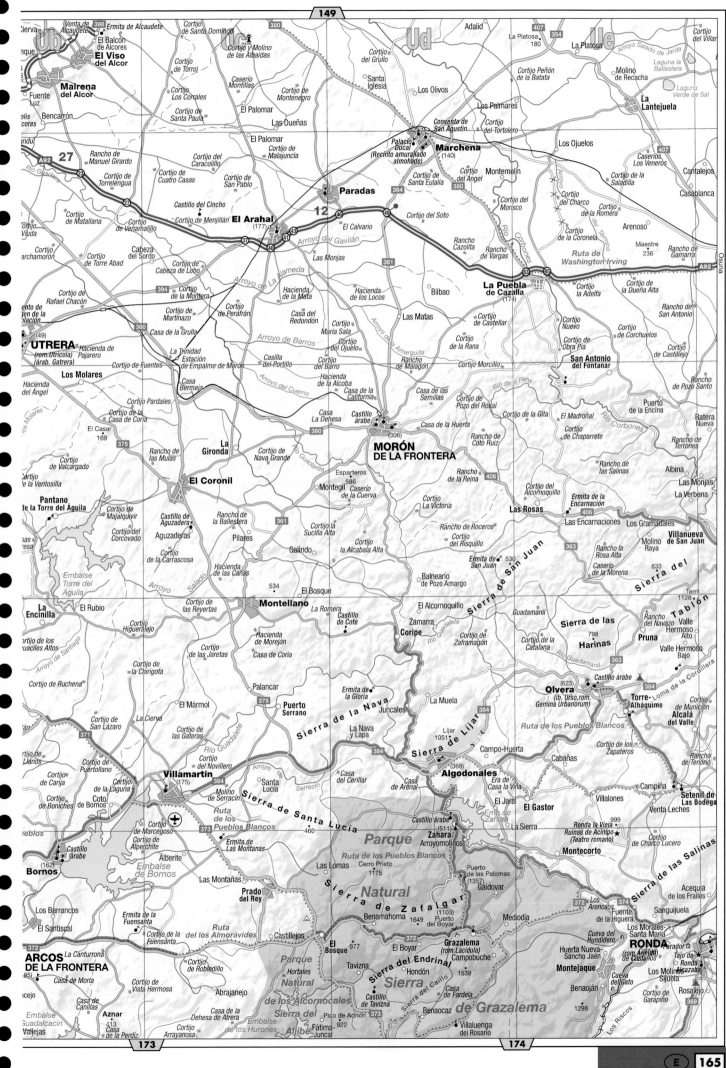

Sierra
Venta de
Alcaudete
398 Ermita de Alcaudete
El Balcón
de Alcores
El Viso
del Alcor
Cortijo de Santo Domingo
Cortijo y Molino
de las Albaidas
380
Adalid
La Platosa
180
407 354
La Platosa
Arroyo Salado de Jarda
Cortijo
del Villar
Ub Ud lle
Mairena
del Alcor
Fuente
Luz
Bencarrón
Cortijo
del Grullo
Santa
Iglesia
Los Olivos
Molino
de Recacha
Laguna la
Ballestera
Laguna
Verde de Sal
La
Lantejuela
A92 27
Rancho de
Manuel Girardo
23
Río Guadaira
27
Cortijo
de Matallana
Cortijo de
Venamalillo
Cabeza
del Sordo
Cortijo de
Cabeza de Lobo
Cortijo de Torroi
Cortijo de
Montenegro
El Palomar
Las Dueñas
El Palomar
Cortijo de
Malajuncia
Cortijo de
Santa Paula
Cortijo del
Caracolillo
Castillo del Cincho
Cortijo de
Cuatro Casas
Cortijo de
San Pablo
Cortijo de Menjillán
El Arahal
(177)
43
41
40
37
12
46
Paradas
364
49
Cortijo del Soto
Convento de
San Agustín
Palacio
Ducal
(Recinto amurallado
almohade)
Marchena
(140)
Cortijo
del Tortolero
Los Palmares
Los Ojuelos
Cortijo Peñón
de la Batata
Molino
de Recacha
Caseríos
Los Veneros
Cantalejos
Casablanca
Cortijo de
la Saladilla
407
Cortijo del
Morisco
Cortijo del
Charco
Cortijo
de la Romera
Arenoso
Maestre
236
Rancho de
Gamarra
A92
Osuna
El Calvario
Arroyo del Gavilán
Las Monjas
361
Cortijo de
Santa Eulalia
380
Cortijo
del Ángel
Montemolín
Rancho
Cazolita
Rancho
de Vargas
63
65
Ruta de
Washington Irving
Cortijo
la Adelfa
Cortijo de
la Dueña Alta
Cabeza de
Marchamorón
Cortijo de
Torre Abad
394
Cortijo
de la Montera
Arroyo de La Alameda
Hacienda
de la Mata
Hacienda
de los Locos
Bilbao
La Puebla
de Cazalla
(174)
Cortijo
Nuevo
Cortijo de
Obra Pía
Cortijo de
Corchuelos
Rancho de
San Antonio
onto de
en de la
ación
Cortijo de
Rafael Chacón
360
Cortijo de
Martinazo
Casa de la Grulla
Cortijo
de Perafrán
Casa del
Redondón
Cortijo
Maria Sala
Arroyo de Barros
Las Matas
Cortijo de
Castellar
Cortijo de
la Rana
Cortijo de
Castilleja
UTRERA
49
(rom. Utricola)
(árab. Gatrera)
Hacienda de
Pajarero
La Trinidad
Estación
de Empalme de Morón
Casilla
del-Portillo
Cortijo
del Ojuelo
Arroyo de la Amarguilla
Río de la Peña
Cortijo de
San Antonio
del Fontanar
Los Molares
Hacienda
del Ángel
Cortijo Pardales
Casa
Bermeja
Cortijo
del Barro
Hacienda
de la Alcoba
Cortijo
del Barro
Casa de la
California
Rancho
de Málagón
Cortijo Morcillo
Casa de las
Semillas
Cortijo de
Pozo del Rosal
Arroyo del Cuerno
Casa de la
Huerta
Rancho de
Pozo Santo
Puerto
de la Encina
Ratera
Nueva
El Casar
169
Cortijo de la
Casa de Coria
375
360
Casa
La Dehesa
Castillo
árabe
(306)
MORÓN
DE LA FRONTERA
Casa de las
Semillas
Rancho de
Coto Ruiz
Cortijo de la Gita
El Madroñal
Cortijo
de Chaparrete
Río Corbones
Rancho de
Terrones
Albina
Cortijo
de Valcargado
Cortijo de
la Ventosilla
La
Gironda
El Coronil
Cortijo de
Majalquivir
Castillo de
Aguzadera
375
Rancho de
las Mulas
Cortijo de
Nava Grande
Río Guadairilla
Rancho de
la Ballestera
Pilares
Esparteros
586
Montegil
Caserío
de la Cueva
406
Rancho
de la Reina
Cortijo
La Victoria
Cortijo del
Alcornoquillo
Ermita de la
Encarnación
406
Las Rosas
Las Monjas
La Verbena
Rancho de
las Salinas
Las Encarnaciones
Los Gramadales
Villanueva
de San Juan
Pantano
de la Torre del Águila
Cortijo del
Corcovado
Cortijo
de la Carrascosa
361
Galindo
Cortijo la
Sucilla Alta
Cortijo la
Alcabala Alta
Cortijo
del Risquillo
363
Ermita de
San Juan
530
Rancho de
Roceros
Rancho la
Rosa Alta
Molino
Raya
Caserío
de la Morena
833
Sierra del
esa
Embalse
Torre del Águila
Arroyo Salado
534
El Bosque
Hacienda
de las Cañas
Balneario
de Pozo Amargo
El Alcornoquillo
Sierra de San Juan
Sierra de las
Guadamanil
798
Terril
1128
La
Encinilla
El Rubio
Cortijo de
las Reyertas
Montellano
La Romera
Zamarra
Coripe
Río Guadalete
Cortijo de
Zaframagón
Cortijo de la
Catalana
Harinas
Rancho
del Navazo
Valle
Hermoso
Alto
Pruna
Valle Hermoso
Bajo
Rancho la
Cortijo de los
Guaciles Altos
Cortijo de
Higueralejo
Castillo
de Cote
Hacienda
de Morejón
Casa de Coria
Tablón
Cortijo de
Ruchena
Cortijo de
la Chirigota
Cortijo de
las Jaretas
Palancar
Ermita de
la Gloria
La Muela
(623)
Olvera
(ib. Urso, rom.
Gemina Urbanorum)
Castillo árabe
384
Torre-
Alháquime
Loma de la Cordillera
Cortijo
de Munición
Alcalá
del Valle
El Mármol
375
Puerto
Serrano
Ermita de
la Nava
Juncales
Sierra de la Nava
La Nava
y Lapa
Líjar
1051
Sierra de Líjar
(368)
Campo-Huerta
Ruta de los Pueblos Blancos
Cabañas
Cortijo de los
Zapateros
Puerto
de la Encina
Rancho
del Tenorio
Campiña
Cortijo de
San Lázaro
371
La Cierva
Cortijo de
las Gateras
Arroyo
Río Guadalete
384
Casa
del Cerillar
Algodonales
Era de
Casa la Viña
El Gastor
Villalones
Setenil de
Las Bodegas
Venta Leches
Cortijo de
Puertollano
Villamartín
(175)
384
Molino
de Serracín
Arroyo
Serracín
Sierra de Santa Lucía
460
Casa
de Arenal
El Jaral
La Sierra
Ronda la Vieja
999
Ruinas de Acinipo
(Teatro romano)
Cortijo
de Charco Lucero
Cortijo de
Carija
Cortijo de
la Laguna
Coto
de Bornos
373
Ruta de los
Pueblos Blancos
Cortijo
de Marcegoso
Santa
Lucía
Castillo árabe
(511)
Zahara
Arroyomolinos
Emb. de
Zahara
Montecorto
Cortijo de
Boniches
Cortijo de
Alperchite
Alberite
Ermita de
Las Montañas
Parque
Ruta de los Pueblos Blancos
Natural
Las Lomas
Cerro Prieto
1175
Puerto
de las Palomas
(1357)
Gaidovar
372
Los
Arenosos
374
Sierra de las Salinas
Acequia
de los
Frailes
ueblos
Castillo
árabe
(162)
Bornos
Las Montañas
Prado
del Rey
Sierra
de
Zafalgar
Benamahoma
1649
(1103)
Puerto
del Boyar
Mediodía
372
Fuente
de la Higuera
Sanguijuela
Los Barrancos
El Santiscal
Ermita de la
Fuensanta
Cortijo de la
Fuensanta
Castillejos
Ruta
de los Almorávides
El
Bosque
977
El Boyar
Grazalema
(rom. Lacidula)
Campobuche
Huerta Nueva-
Sancho Jaén
Cueva del
Hundidero
RONDA
(rom. Arunda)
Parador de
Ronda
Tajo de
Ronda
ARCOS
DE LA FRONTERA
(85)
La Canturraña
Casa de Morla
Cortijo de
Robledillo
Parque
Tavizna
Hondón
1539
Sierra del Endrinal
Sierra
Montejaque
Cueva
del Gato
Cortijo de
Garapiño
369
aucejo
Casa de
Canillas
Aznar
413
Casa
de la Perdiz
Cortijo de
Vista Hermosa
Abrajanejo
Natural
Sierra del
Aljibe
Hortales
Cortijo de
Arrayanosa
Castillo
de Tavizna
Pico de Adrión
922
Fátima-
Juncal
373
de los Alcornocales
Casa la
Dehesa de Atrera
Embalse
de los Hurones
Sierra
Benaocaz
Casa
de Fardela
de Grazalema
Villaluenga
del Rosario
Benaoján
1298
Los Riscos
Los Molinos
Sijuela
Rosalejo
Embalse
Guadalcacín
Vallejas

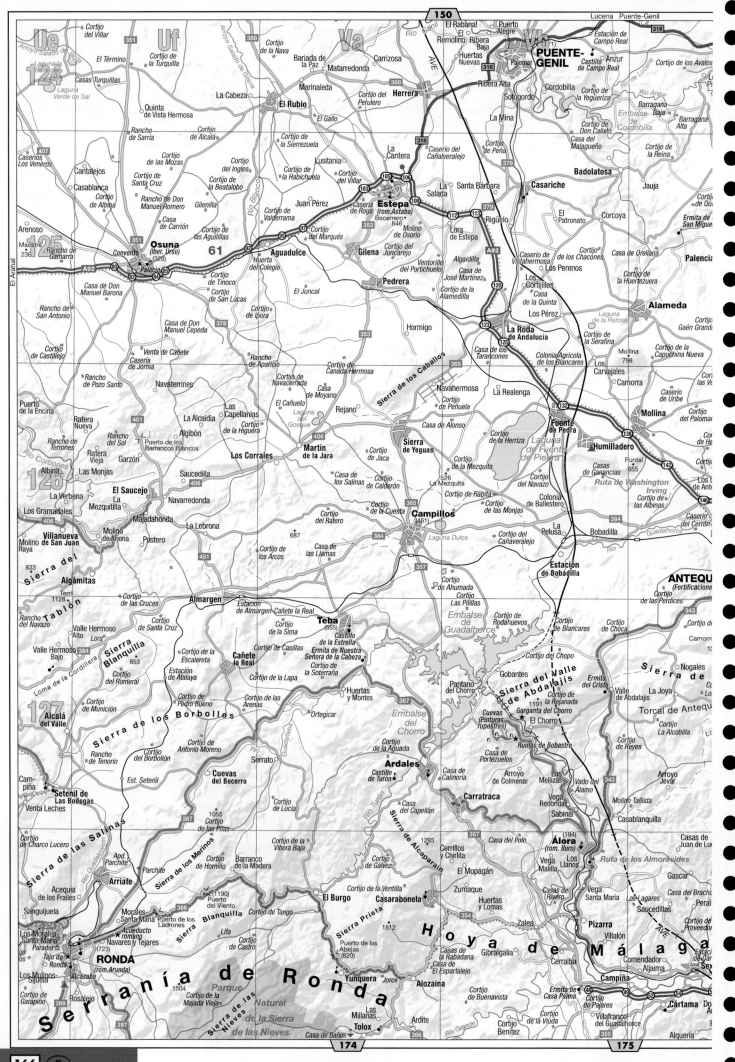

Ue
124

Uf

Va

Vb

Lucena   Puente-Genil

318

Arroyo Salado del Vega
Laguna la Ballestera
Cortijo del Villar
351
El Término
Cortijo de la Turquilla
388
Cortijo de la Nava
Bariada de la Paz
Matarredonda
Carrizosa
Río Genil
El Rabanal
El Remolino   Ribera Baja
Estación de Campo Real
318

El Arahal
Casas Turquillas
Laguna Verde de Sal
Casas de la Turquilla
La Cabeza
Marinaleda
388
Cortijo del Perulero
Herrera
Huertas Nuevas
318
Puerto Alegre
Palomar
PUENTE-GENIL
171
Anzur
Castillo de Campo Real
Cortijo de los Ávalos

407
Caseríos Los Veneros
Cortijo del Villar
Quinta de Vista Hermosa
El Gallo
La Cantera
Ribera Alta
Cordobilla
Sotogordo
Embalse de Cordobilla
Barragana Baja
Barragana Alta

Cantalejos
Casablanca
Cortijo de Santa Cruz
Cortijo de las Mozas
Gilenilla
Cortijo del Ingles
Cortijo de la Beatalobo
Lusitania
Cortijo de la Habichuela
Cortijo del Villar
105
106
318
Caserío del Cañalveralejo
Cortijo de Peña
379
La Salada
Santa Bárbara
Badolatosa
Casariche
Jauja
Cortijo de Qu
Ermita de San Migue

125
Maestre 236
Arenoso
Rancho de Gamarra
Cortijo de Albina
Rancho de Don Manuel Romero
Gilenilla
Juan Pérez
103
Estepa (rom. Astaba)
Becerrero 846
109
112
113
379
Rigüelo
El Patronato
Corcoya
Palencia

351
Osuna (Iber. Urso)
61
(328)
Casa de Carrión
Cortijo de las Aguilillas
97
95
92
Cortijo del Marqués
353
Caseria de Roga
Molino de Osorio
Lora de Estepa
A92
Algaidilla
Caserío de Vistahermosa
Los Perenos
Cortijo de los Chacones
Casa de Orellana

80
Convento
82
Palacio
85
84
Huerta del Colegio
Aguadulce
Gilena
Pedrera
Ventorillo del Portichuelo
Casa de José Martínez
120
Los Cortijillos
Casa de la Quinta
Los Pérez
Cortijo de la Huertezuera

Casa de Don Manuel Barona
Cortijo de Tinoco
Cortijo de San Lucas
El Juncal
378
Cortijo de Ipora
Hormigo
Cortijo de la Alamedilla
123
125
La Roda de Andalucía
Laguna de la Ratosa
Alameda
Gaén Grande
Cortijo de

Rancho de San Antonio
Casa de Don Manuel Cepeda
353
Venta de Cañete
Caseria de Jornia
Rancho de Aparicio
Cortijo de Canada Hermosa
Casa de los Tarancones
Colonia Agrícola de los Blancares
Los Carvajales
Mollina 798
Cortijo de la Serafina
Cortijo de la Capuchina Nueva

Cortijo de Castillejo
Navaterrines
La Alcaidia
Cortijo de Navacerrada
Laguna del Gosque
Rejano
Sierra de los Caballos
Navahermosa
365
La Realenga
132
Camorra
Caserío de Uribe
Mollina
Cortijo del Palomar

Puerto de la Encina
Ratera Nueva
Rancho del Sol
Las Capellanias
Algibón
Cortijo de la Higuera
El Cañuelo
Cortijo de Peñuela
Casa de Alonso
526
Fuente de Pedra
Laguna de Fuente de Piedra
138
Humilladero

451
Rancho de Pozo Santo
Ratera Vieja
Garzón
Saucedilla
406
Martín de la Jara
Cortijo de Jaca
Sierra de Yeguas
Cortijo de la Herriza
La Mezquita
Cortijo de la Mezquita
Cortijo de Rábita
Cortijo del Navazo
Casas de Ganancias
Puntal 655
Ruta de Washington Irving
142
Los L de Ant

126
Albina
Río Corbones
Las Monjas
La Mezquitilla
Navarredonda
406
Casa de los Salinas
Cortijo de Calderón
365
Cortijo de la Cuesta
Campillos (461)
Cortijo de Rábita
Cortijo de las Monjas
Colonia de Ballestero
La Pelusa
Bobadilla
384
Caserío del Cerrón
146

La Verbena
Los Gramadales
El Saucejo
Majadahonda
La Lebrona
687
Cortijo del Ratero
Casa de las Llamas
384
Laguna Dulce
Cortijo del Cañaveralejo
Estación de Bobadilla
Guadalhorce
Río

Villanueva de San Juan
Molino de San Juan Raya
Molino de Arjona
Postero
451
Cortijo de los Arcos
357
Cortijo de Ahumada
ANTEQU
(Fortificacione

833
Sierra del
Algámitas
Terril 1128
Tablón
Cortijo de las Cruces
Almargen
Estación de Almargen-Cañete la Real
Cortijo de la Sima
Teba (655)
Cortijo de las Pililas
Embalse de Guadalborce
Cortijo de Rodahuevos
Cortijo de Blancares
Cortijo de Choca
343
Camorro
Cortijo de las Perdices
Cortijo de

Rancho del Navazo
Valle Hermoso Alto
Lora
384
Sierra Blanquilla 853
Cortijo de Santa Cruz
Cortijo de Casillas
Castillo de la Estrella
Ermita de Nuestra Señora de la Cabeza
Cortijo del Chopo
Gobantes
Cortijo de Rodahuevos
Sierra del Valle de Abdalajís
Ermita del Cristo
Sierra de
Nogales
Camorro

Valle Hermoso Bajo
Loma de la Cordillera
Cortijo del Romeral
Cortijo de la Escalereta
Estación de Atalaya
Cañete la Real
Cortijo de la Lapa
Cortijo de la Soterraña
Pantano del Chorro
1191
Cortijo de la Rejanada
Gargantar del Chorro
Valle de Abdalajís
La Joya
Torcal de Antequ

127
Alcalá del Valle
Cortijo de Munición
Sierra de los Borbollos
Cortijo de Antonio Moreno
Cortijo de Pedro Bueno
Cortijo de las Arenas
Huertas y Montes
367
Ortegicar
Embalse del Chorro
Cuevas (Pinturas rupestres)
El Chorro
Ruinas de Bobastro
Cortijo de Reyes
Cortijo la Alcobilla
Arroyo Jevar

Rancho de Tenorio
Cortijo del Borbollón
Est. Setenil
Cuevas del Becerro
Serrato
Río Guadalteba
Cortijo de la Aguada
Ardales
Castillo de Turón
Casa de Portezuelos
Casa de Calinoria
Arroyo de Colmenar
Las Mellizas
Vado del Álamo
343
Molino Tallista
Casablanquilla

Campiña
Setenil de las Bodegas
Venta Leches
Cortijo de Lucía
Río Turón
Carratraca
Casa del Capellán
Sierra de Alcaparain
1293
357
Casa del Polo
Álora (rom. Iluro) (194)
Ruta de los Almorávides
Casas de Juan de Lu
Gascar
Cortijo del Bracho
Peral

Cortijo de Charco Lucero
Sierra de las Salinas
Apd. Parchite
Parchite
Sierra de los Merinos
1055
Cortijo de las Pilas
Cortijo de la Vibora Baja
Barranco de la Madera
Cerrillos y Chirlita
El Mopagán
Zumaque
Vega Malilla
Los Llanos
Vega Santa María
Saucedillas
Cortijo de Proveedor

Acequia de los Frailes
Arriate
Río Guadalcorcín
366
Cortijo de Hornillo
(1190) Puerto del Viento
Cortijo de la Ventilla
El Burgo
Casarabonela
Huertas y Lomas
Casas de Rivero
Los Lagares
AVE
Villalón
Pizarra

Sanguijuela
Morales-Santa María
Aquicludo romano
Navares y Tejares
(723)
RONDA (rom. Arunda)
Alcazaba
Sierra Blanquilla
Lifa
Cortijo de Tango
Sierra Prieta
1512
Puerto de las Abejas (820)
354
Zalea
Gibralgalía
Cerralba
Comendador
Aljaima
Campina
48
Cártama
Do

369
Tajo de Ronda
Los Molinos Sijuela
Cortijo de Garapiño
Rosalejo
Parque Natural de la Sierra de las Nieves
Cortijo de la Majada Vieja
397
Sierra de las Nieves
1504
Yunquera
Jorox
Alozaina
Hoya de Málaga
Casa de la Rabadana
Casa de El Espartalejo
Cortijo de Buenavista
Ermita de Casa Palma
Cortijo de Pajares
Villafranco del Guadalhorce
355
Alquería
49
52
54

Las Millanas
Tolox
Ardite
Casa de Baños
366
Cortijo de la Viuda
Cortijo Benítez

Serranía de Ronda

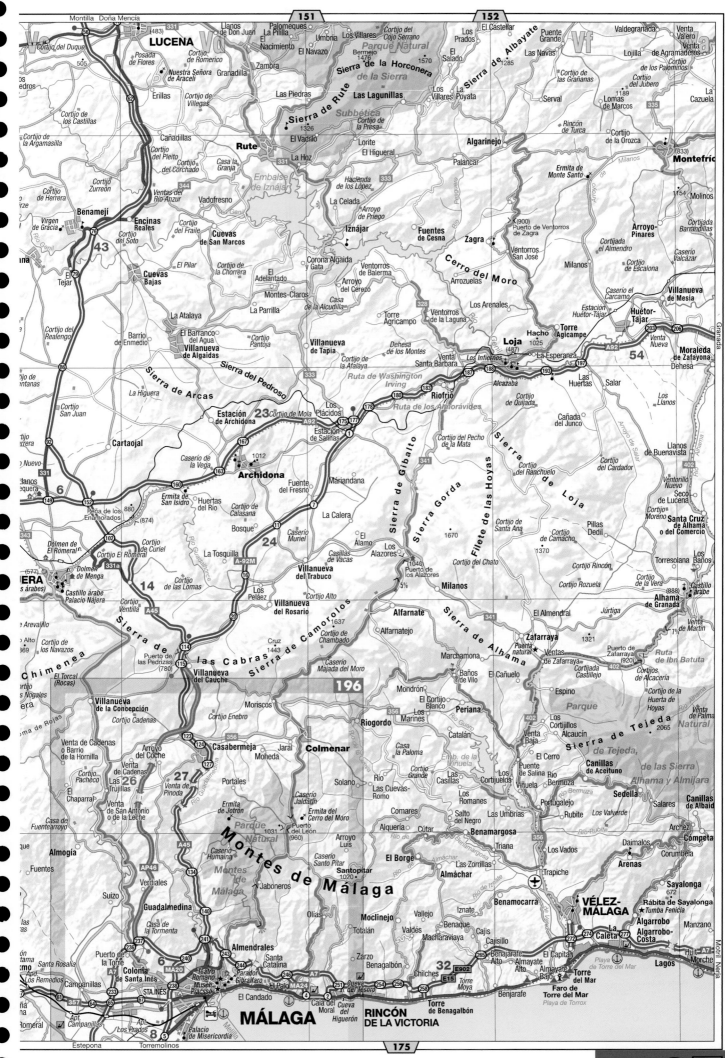

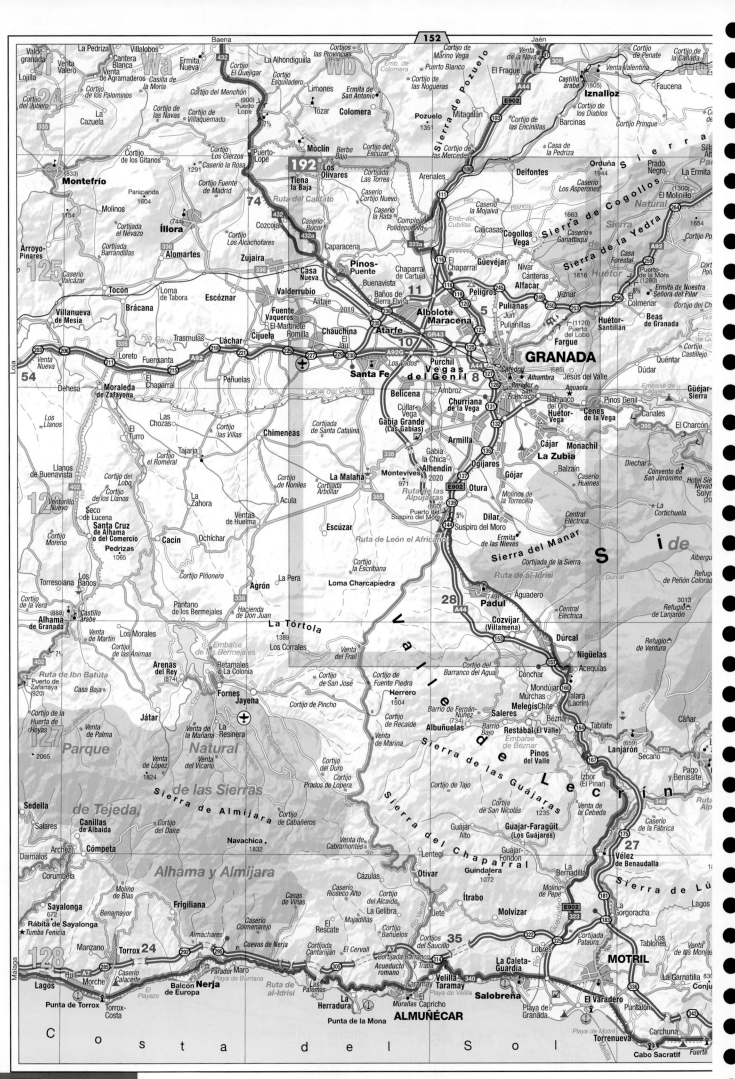

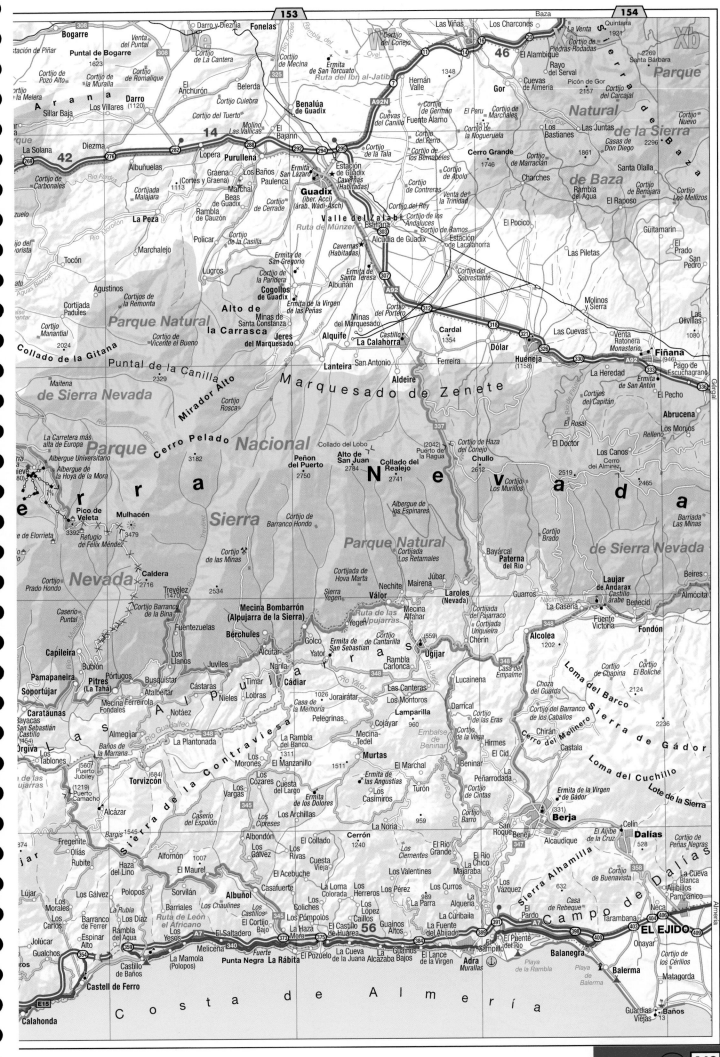

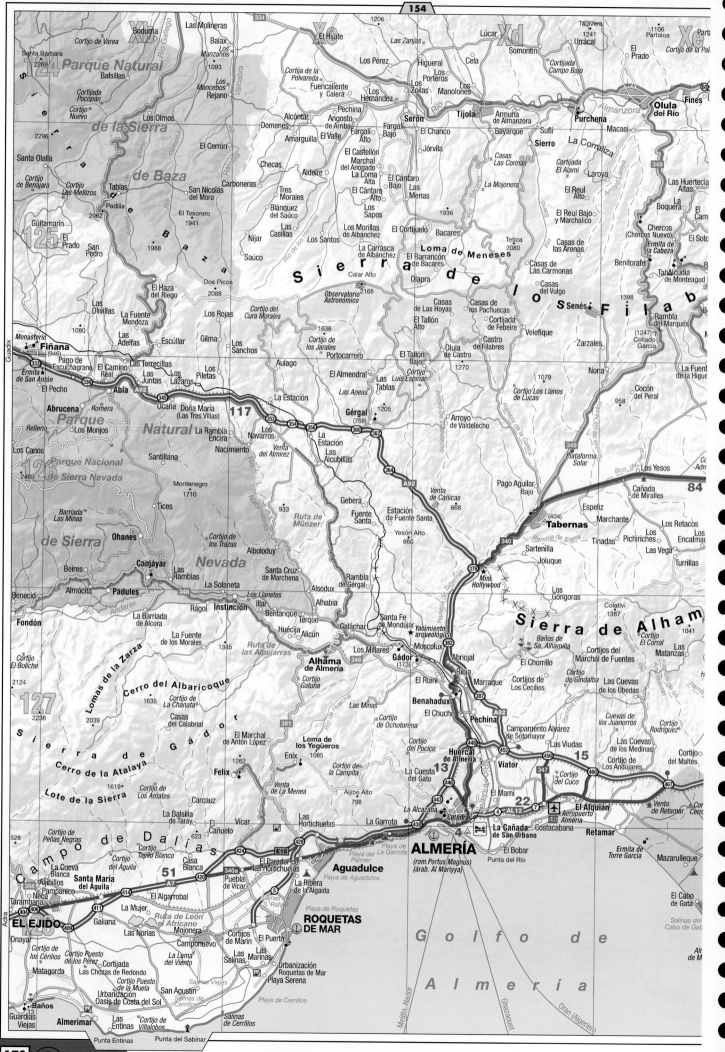

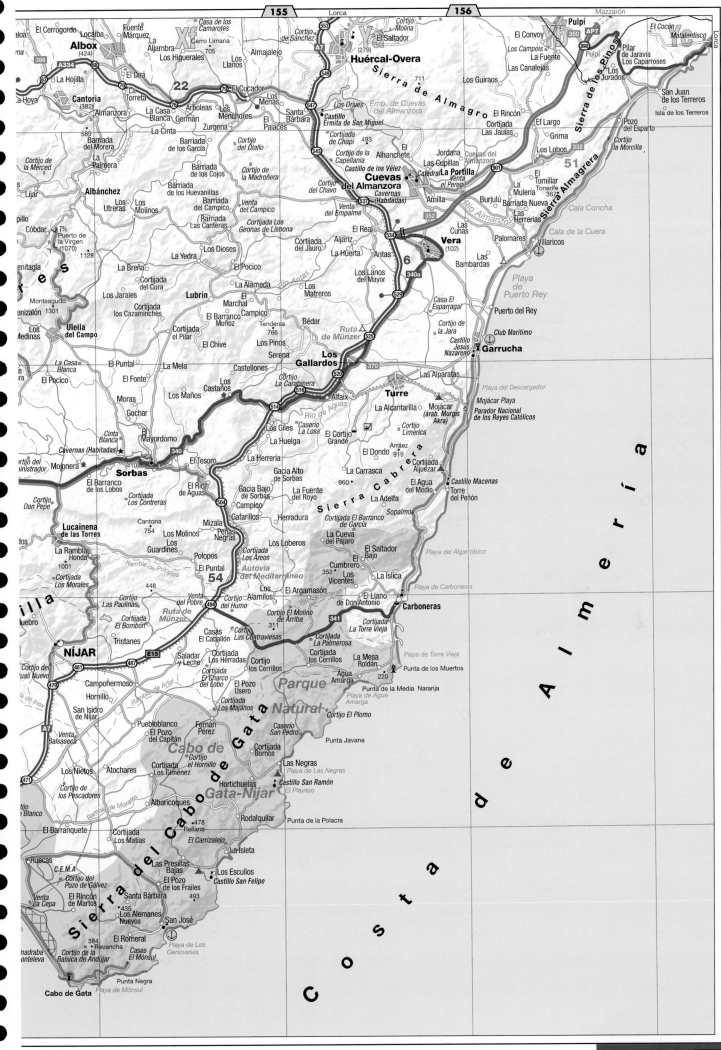

Mazzarón

Lorca

Pulpí

El Cerrogordo
Locaiba
El Cocón
Matalentisco
Fuente
Márquez
Casa de los
Camarotes
Cortijo
de Sánchez
Cortijo
Molina
El Convoy
AP7
Lorca
Albox
(424)
La
Aljambra
Cerro Limaria
Almajalejo
El Saltador
350
Pulpí
890
Los Campois
La Fuente
Pilar
de Jaravia
Los Higuerales
705
Huércal-Overa
Las Canalejas
Los Caparroses
A334
68
El Dirá
Los
Llanos
549
711
Los Guiraos
San Juan
de los Terreros
399
63
La Hojilla
70
La
Torreta
79
El Cucador
Los
Menas
547
Los Orives
Emb. de Cuevas
del Almanzora
El Rincón
Los
Jurados
Isla de los Terreros
a-Hoya
Cantoria
(382)
76
Arboleas
Germán
Los
Menchores
Santa
Bárbara
Castillo
Ermita de San Miguel
Cortijada
Las Jaulas
El Largo
Grima
332
Pozo
del Esparto
Almanzora
La Casa
Blanca
El Palacés
La Cinta
543
Cortijada
de Chapi
493
Cortijo de la
Capellanía
El
Alhanchete
Jordana
Las Cupillas
Cuevas del
Almanzora
Los Lobos
Cortijo
la Morcilla
589
Barriada
del Morera
Barriada
de los García
Cortijo
del Ollalo
Castillo de los Vélez
Catedral
La Portilla
El
Tomillar
367
51
Cortijo
de la Merced
Zurgena
La Palmera
Barriada
de los Cojos
Barriada
de la Madroñera
Cortijo
del Chavo
Cuevas
del Almanzora
Cavernas
(Habitadas)
Venta
el Peregil
Arnilla
901
La
Mulería
Tonerife
Barriada Nueva
Sierra de Almagro
Albánchez
Los
Utreras
Los
Molinos
Barriada
del Campico
Barriada
Las Canteras
Venta
del Campico
637
Venta
del Empalme
Burjulú
Las
Herrerías
Cala Concha
7%
Puerto de
la Virgen
(1070)
Cóbdar
1128
La Yedra
Cortijada Los
Gironas de Lisbona
El Real
340a
534
Aljariz
La Huerta
Antas
Vera
(102)
Las
Cunas
Río Almanzora
Cala de la Cuera
La Breña
El Pocico
Cortijada
del Jauro
Las
Bambardas
Palomares
Villaricos
enitagla
Monteagudo
enizalón 1301
Los
Jarales
Cortijada
del Cura
La Alameda
Río Antas
Los
Matreros
Los Llanos
del Mayor
Playa
de
Puerto Rey
Los
Medinas
Uleila
del Campo
Lubrín
El
Marchal
El
Campico
Béder
529
Casa El
Esparragal
Puerto del Rey
La Casa
Blanca
Cortijada
los Cazaminches
El Barranco
Muñoz
Tenderas
766
Ruta
de Münzer
525
Cortijo de
la Jara
Castillo
Jesús
Nazareno
Club Marítimo
El Pocico
era
El Puntal
Cortijada
el Pilar
El Chive
Los Pinos
Serena
Los
Gallardos
370
Garrucha
La Mela
Castellones
520
Las Alparatas
Playa del Descargador
El Fonte
Los
Castaños
Cortijo
La Carabinera
516
Alfaix
Turre
Mojácar
(árab. Murgis
Akra)
Parador Nacional
de los Reyes Católicos
Moras
Gochar
514
Los Giles
Caserío
La Losa
Río de Aguas
La Alcantarilla
Mojácar Playa
Cinta
Blanca
El
Mayordomo
La Huelga
El Cortijo
Grandé
Cortijo
Limérica
340
Cavernas (Habitadas)
El Tesoro
La Herrería
Gacia Alto
de Sorbas
El Dondo
Arráez
919
Cortijada
Aljuézar
Sierra Cabrera
ortijo del
inistrador
Mojonera
(410)
Sorbas
El Río
de Aguas
504
Gacia Bajo
de Sorbas
Campico
La Carrasca
960
El Agua
del Medio
Castillo Macenas
El Barranco
de los Lobos
Cortijada
Los Contreras
La Fuente
del Royo
La Adelfa
Torre
del Peñón
Cortijo
Don Pepe
Cantona
754
Gafarillos
Herradura
Cortijada El Barranco
de García
Sopalmo
Lucainena
de las Torres
Mizala
Peñas
Negras
Los Loberos
La Cueva
del Pájaro
La Rambla
Honda
1001
Los Molinos
Los
Guardines
352
Cumbrero
El Saltador
Bajo
Playa del Algarrobico
Cortijada
Los Morales
Ramble de Polopos
Polopos
Cortijada
Los Áreos
Autovía
del Mediterráneo
54
El Puntal
Los
Vicentes
La Islica
Playa de Carboneras
448
311
Los
Alamilos
El Argamasón
illa
uebro
Venta
del Pobre
494
Cortijo
del Humo
Ruta de
Münzer
Cortijo El Molino
de Arriba
El Llano
de Don Antonio
Carboneras
Tristanes
341
Cortijada
La Torre Vieja
NÍJAR
487
E15
Casas
El Caballón
Cortijo
Las Contraviesas
Cortijada
La Palmerosa
481
Saladar
y Leche
Cortijada
Los Hérradas
Cortijo
los Cerrillos
Cortijada
los Cerrillos
Playa de Torre Vieja
479
Cortijo del
uali Nuevo
Campohermoso
Cortijada
El Charco
del Lobo
El Pozo
Usero
Agua
Amarga
La Mesa
Roldán
220
Punta de los Muertos
Hornillo
Ramble de Artal
Cortijada
Los Majanos
Parque
Punta de la Media Naranja
Playa de Agua
Amarga
San Isidro
de Níjar
Pueblóblanco
El Pozo
del Capitán
Fernán
Pérez
Caserío
San Pedro
Cortijo El Plomo
Venta
Balsaseca
Cabo de
Cortijada
Bornos
Punta Javana
471
Los Nietos
Atochares
Cortijo
el Hornillo
Gata
Natural
Las Negras
Cortijo de
los Pescadores
Cortijada
Los Giménez
Playa de Las Negras
Gata-Níjar
Castillo San Ramón
El Playazo
Albaricoques
Ramble de Morales
478
Rellana
Rodalquilar
Punta de la Polacra
El Barranquete
Cortijada
Los Matías
El Carrizalejo
La Isleta
Ruecas
C.E.M.A
Las Presillas
Bajas
Los Escullos
Cortijo del
Pozo de Gálvez
El Pozo
de los Frailes
Castillo San Felipe
Venta
La Cepa
El Rincón
de Martos
Santa Bárbara
493
435
enadraba
onteleva
384
Revancha
Los Alemanes
Nuevos
San José
Cortijo de la
Balsica de Andújar
El Romeral
Casas
El Mónsul
Playa de Los
Genoveses
Punta Negra
Cabo de Gata
Playa de Mónsul

Sierra del Cabo de Gata

Costa de Almería

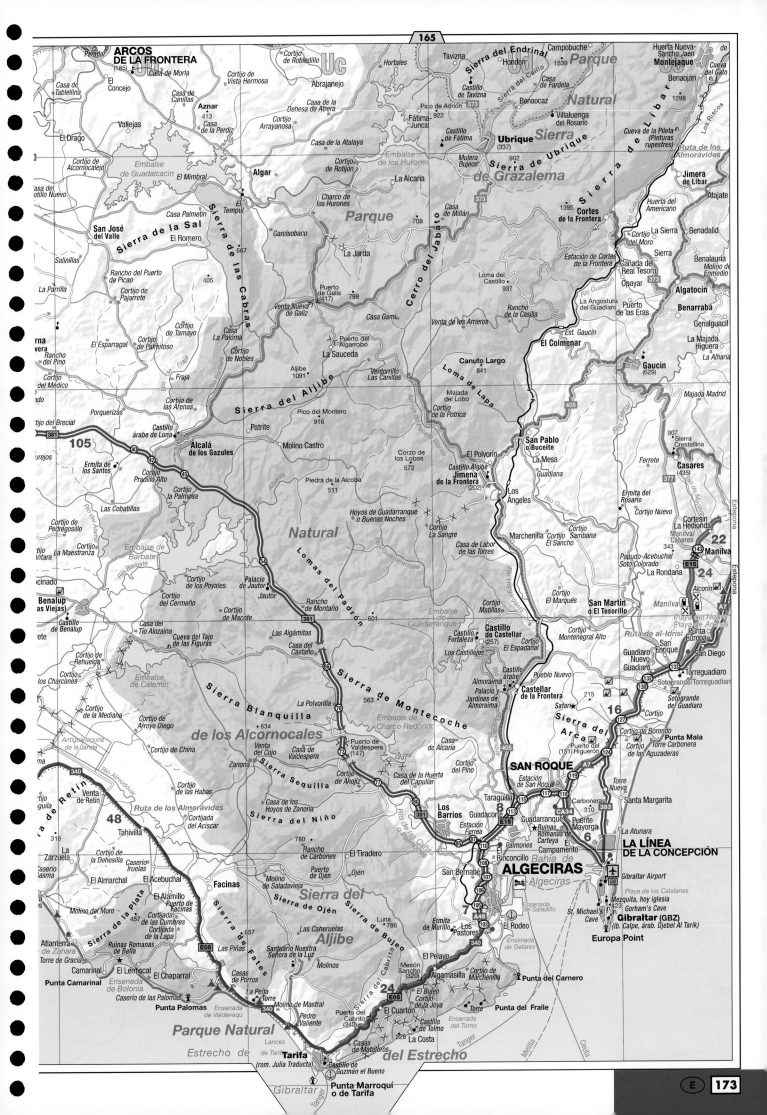

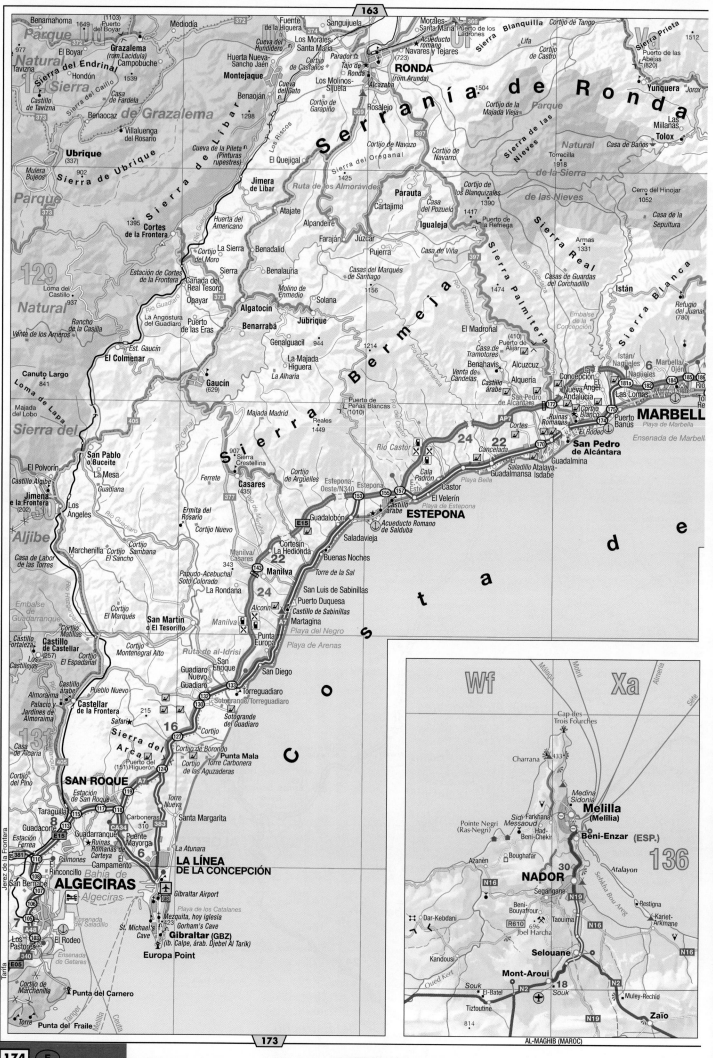

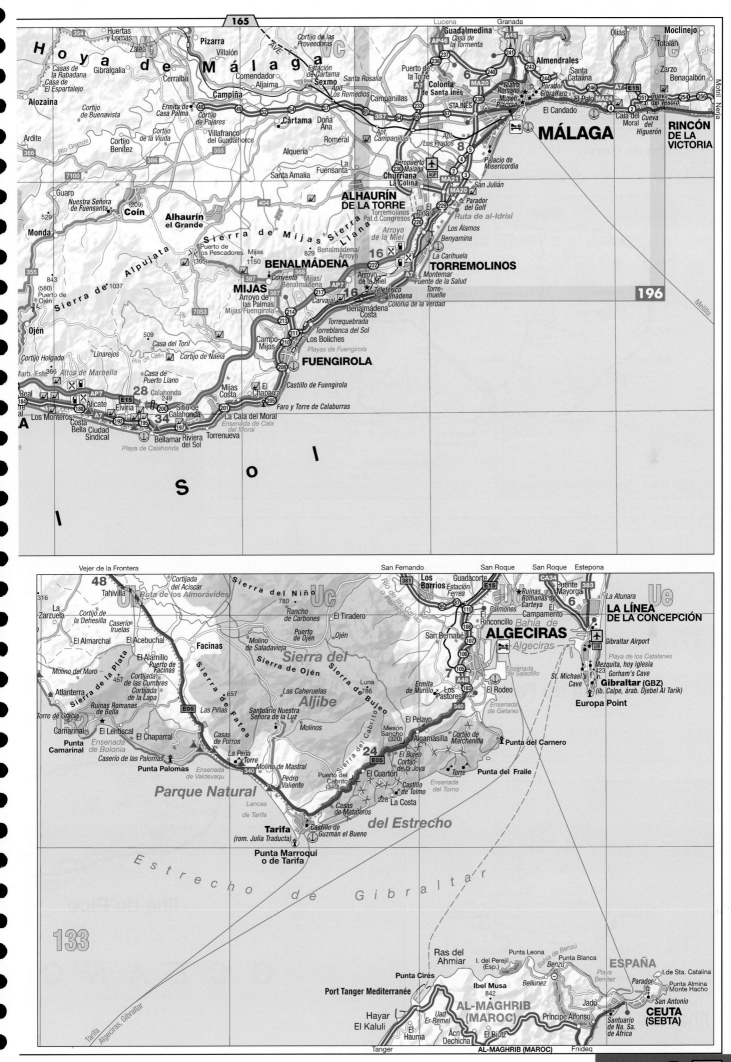

H o y a   d e   M á l a g a

Huertas y Lomas
Zalea
354
Pizarra
Villalón
Cortijo de las Proveedoras
Lucena
Guadalmedina
Granada
Olías
Moclinejo
Totalán

Casas de la Rabadana
Casa de El Espartalejo
Gibralgalia
Cerralba
Comendador
Aljaima
Estación de Cártama
Sexmo
Santa Rosalía
Apt. Los Remedios
Puerto de la Torre
Colonia de Santa Inés
AP46
237
Casa de la Tormenta
236
A45
241
Almendrales
Santa Catalina
Zarzo
Benagalbón

Alozaina
Cortijo de Buenavista
Campiña
48
49
52
54
57
Campanillas
233
357
MA20
238
6
240
244
243
Teatro Romano
Museo Picasso
246
251
El Palo
254
256

Ardite
Cortijo de Pajares
Cártama
Doña Ana
61
64
65
67
STA.INES
239
Palacio de Misericordia
Parador Gibralfaro
MA24
4
2
Cueva del Tesoro

Nuestra Señora de Fuensanta
209
Coín
Villafranco del Guadalhorce
355
Alquería
La Fuensanta
Apt. Campanillas
Aeropuerto
230
Málaga
AGP
3
8
5
San Julián
El Candado
Cala del Moral
Cueva del Higuerón
MÁLAGA
RINCÓN DE LA VICTORIA

529
Monda
Guaro
Alhaurín el Grande
Alhaurín de la Torre
Santa Amalia
Churriana
La Colina
MA21
MA20
Parador del Golf
229

843
(580)
Puerto de Ojén
1037
Sierra de Mijas
Puerto de los Pescadores
305
Mijas
1150
Benalmádena/Arroyo
El Pinar
Torremolinos
Pal.d.Congresos
228
Arroyo de la Miel
Los Álamos
Benyamina
La Carihuela
196

Ojén
Sierra de Alpujata
387
MIJAS
Convento
Mijas/Benalmádena
222
Arroyo de la Miel
A7
Montemar
Fuente de la Salud
Torre-muelle
TORREMOLINOS

Casa del Toril
Arroyo de las Palmas Mijas/Fuengirola
AP7
217
16
Teleférico
Benalmádena
Colonia de la Verdad

Cortijo Holgado
509
214
213
Carvajal
Benalmádena Costa
Torrequebrada
Torreblanca del Sol

Linarejos
Casa de Puerto Llano
211
210
Campo-Mijas
Los Boliches
Playas de Fuengirola

Cortijo de Naela
208
FUENGIROLA

Marb.-Este
366
Altos de Marbella
28
Calahonda
249
Mijas Costa
El Chaparral
Castillo de Fuengirola

Real
184
Alicate
E15
188
200
Sitio de Calahonda
205
Faro y Torre de Calaburras

Los Monteros
192
195
34
197
La Cala del Moral
201
Ensenada de Cala del Moral

Costa Bella Ciudad Sindical
Bellamar Riviera del Sol
Torrenueva
Playa de Calahonda

S o l

Vejer de la Frontera
San Fernando
San Roque
San Roque
Estepona

48
Tahivilla
Cortijada del Aciscar
Sierra del Niño
Uc
381
Los Barrios
Estación Ferrea
E15
CA34
Puente Mayorga
383
Ue
La Atunara

316
La Zarzuela
Cortijo de la Dehesilla
Caserío Iruelas
780
Rancho de Carbones
El Tiradero
Guadacorte
Ruinas Romanas de Carteya
El Campamento
LA LÍNEA DE LA CONCEPCIÓN

El Almarchal
El Acebuchal
Facinas
Molino de Saladavieja
Puerto de Ojén
Ojén
85
87
110
Palmones
Rinconcillo
Bahía de
Gibraltar Airport

Molino del Moro
El Alamillo
Puerto de Facinas
Cortijada de las Cumbres
Sierra del
Luna
786
San Bernabé
108
107
106
ALGECIRAS
Algeciras
Playa de los Catalanes
Mezquita, hoy iglesia

Atlanterra
457
Cortijada de la Lapa
Sierra de Fates
Las Cañeruelas
Santuario Nuestra Señora de la Luz
Sierra del Bujeo
Ermita de Murillo
105
Los Pastores
103
El Rodeo
340
St. Michael's Cave
423
Gorham's Cave
Gibraltar (GBZ)

Torre de Gracia
Camarinal
Ruinas Romanas de Bella
El Lentiscal
El Chaparral
657
Las Piñas
Aljibe
Molinos
A48
Ensenada de Getares
Europa Point

Punta Camarinal
Ensenada de Bolonia
Casas de Porros
Sierra del Cabrito
Mesón Sancho
320
Algamasilla
Cortijo de Marchenilla
Punta del Carnero

Caserío de las Palomas
La Peña Torre
El Bujeo
Cortijo de la Joya
Torre
Punta del Fraile

Punta Palomas
340
Molino de Mastral
Pedro Valiente
Puerto del Cabrito
340
24
E05
El Cuartón
Castillo de Tolmo
Ensenada del Tomo

Parque Natural
Lances de Tarifa
228
La Costa
Casas de Matatoros
del Estrecho

Tarifa
(rom. Julia Traducta)
Castillo de Guzmán el Bueno

Punta Marroquí o de Tarifa

E s t r e c h o   d e   G i b r a l t a r

133

Ras del Ahmiar
Punta Leona
Punta Blanca
Bahía de Benzú
Benzú
ESPAÑA
I.de Sta. Catalina

Punta Cirés
Ibel Musa
842
Beliunez
Playa Benítez
Punta Almina Monte Hacho
Parador

Port Tanger Méditerranée
Uad Er-Remel
Príncipe Alfonso
San Antonio

Hayar El Kaluli
El Haouma
Âcn Dechicha
El Biutz
Santuario de Na. Sa. de África
CEUTA (SEBTA)

AL-MÁGHRIB (MAROC)

Tanger
AL-MAGHRIB (MAROC)
Fnideq

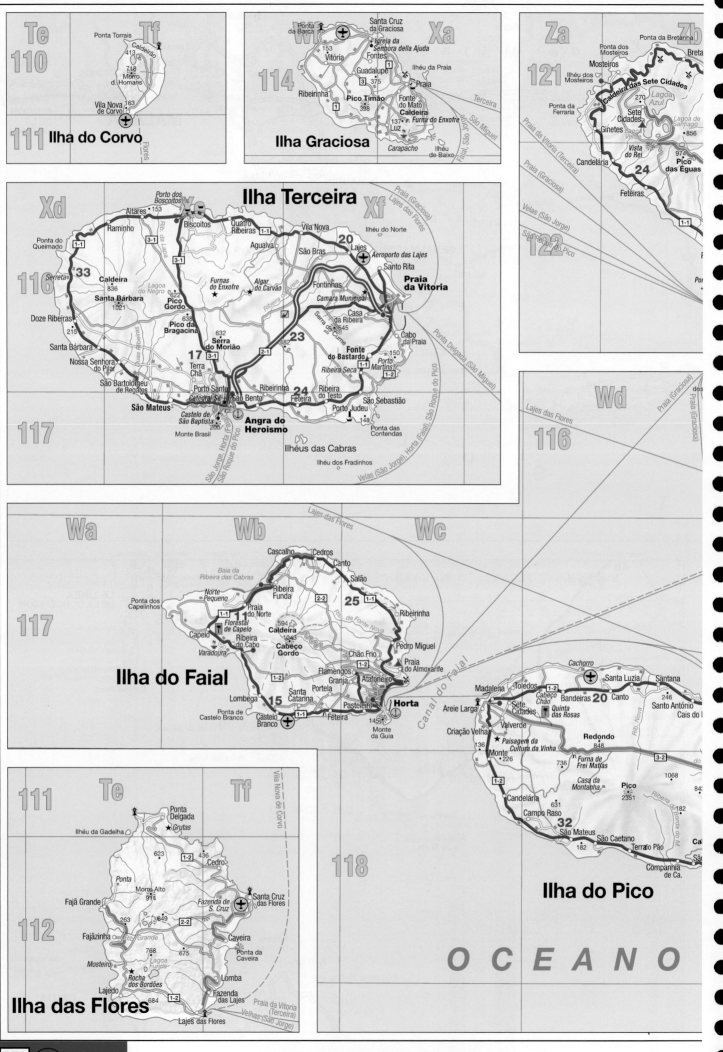

Te **Tf**
110

Ponta Torrais
Caldeirão 413
718
Morro d. Homans

Vila Nova 163
de Corvo

111 Ilha do Corvo

Wf **Xa**

Ponta da Barca
Santa Cruz da Graciosa
Igreja da Senhora della Ajuda
153 Fontes
Vitória
Guadalupe 1
114 3 375 Ilhéu da Praia
Ribeirinha Praia
Pico Timão Fonte do Mato
1 398 **Caldeira**
137 *Furna do Enxofre*
Luz
Carapacho Ilhéu de Baixo

Ilha Graciosa

Za **Zb**
121
Ponta dos Mosteiros Ponta da Bretanha Breta
Ilhéu dos Mosteiros Mosteiros
Caldeira das Sete Cidades 270 *Lagoa Azul*
Ponta da Ferraria Sete Cidades *Lagoa de Santiago*
Gínetes 856
Vista do Rei 974
Candelária **Pico das Éguas**
24
Feteiras
1-1

Xd Porto dos Boscoitos **Ilha Terceira** **Xf**
Altares 153
Raminho Biscoitos Quatro Ribeiras Vila Nova 1-1
1-1 3-1 Agualva São Brás **20** Lajes Ilhéu do Norte
116 3-1 Furnas do Enxofre Fontinhas Aeroporto das Lajes
33 *Lagoa do Negro* Algar do Carvão Santo Rita
Caldeira 836 622 **Pico** *Câmara Municipal* **Praia da Vitória**
Santa Bárbara **Gordo** Casa da Ribeira
1021 638 545 Cabo
Doze Ribeiras **Pico da Bragancia** **23** Fonte da Praia
215 632 **Serra** do Bastardo 150
Santa Bárbara **do Morião** 482 Porto
Nossa Senhora **17** 3-1 *Ribeira Seca* Martins
do Pilar **Terra** 2-1 1-1
São Bartolomeu **Chã** Ribeirinha **24** Ribeira 1-2
de Regatos Porto Santo Feteira do Testo São Sebastião
São Mateus *Catedral Sé* São Bento Porto Judeu 148
Castelo de **Angra do** Ponta das
São Baptista 208 **Heroismo** Contendas
Monte Brasil
117 **Ilhéus das Cabras**
Ilhéu dos Fradinhos

Wd
116

Wa **Wb** **Wc**
117
Cascalho Cedros
Canto
Salão
Baía da Ribeira das Cabras Ribeira
Norte Funda 2-2 **25** 1-1
Ponta dos *Pequeno* Praia Ribeirinha
Capelinhos do Norte 594
1-1 **11** *Florestal* *Rio da Fonte Nova*
de Capelo **Caldeira** Pedro Miguel
Capelo Ribeira **Cabeço** 1043 Praia
do Cabo **Gordo** Chão Frio do Almoxarife
Varadoura 1-2
Flamengos Atafoneiro
Ilha do Faial *Granja* 1-2
Portela Pasteleiro **Horta**
Lombega **15** Santa Catarina Areie Larga
Ponta de *Feteira* 1451 *Canal do Faial*
Castelo Branco Castelo 1-1 *Monte*
Branco da Guia

Cachorro
Madalena *Cabeço* Toledos 1-2 Santa Luzia Santana
Chão Bandeiras **20** Canto 246
Sete Cidades *Quinta* Santo António
Areie Larga *das Rosas* Cais do
Criação Velha
Valverde
Paisagem da **Redondo**
136 *Cultura da Vinha* 848
Monte *Furna de*
226 736 *Frei Matias* 3-2
111 **Te** **Tf** *Casa da* 1068
Montanha **Pico**
Ponta Delgada 1-2 2351 182
Grutas Candelária 843
Ilhéu da Gadelha 631 *Ribeira* 182
623 1-2 436 Campo Raso Companhia
Ponta Cedro **32** de Ca.
Morro Alto São Mateus São Caetano
914 Terrado Pão
Fajã Grande Fazenda de 182
Ponta S. Cruz **Ilha do Pico** Companhia
Fajãzinha 263 Santa Cruz de Ca.
349 das Flores
Mosteiro 2-2
768 Caveira
Rocha 675
Lajedo *dos Bordões* Ponta da
Lagoa Caveira
Funda Lomba
684 Fazenda
112 1-2 das Lajes
Ilha das Flores Lajes das Flores

118 O C E A N O

Ilha de São Miguel

Ilha de São Jorge

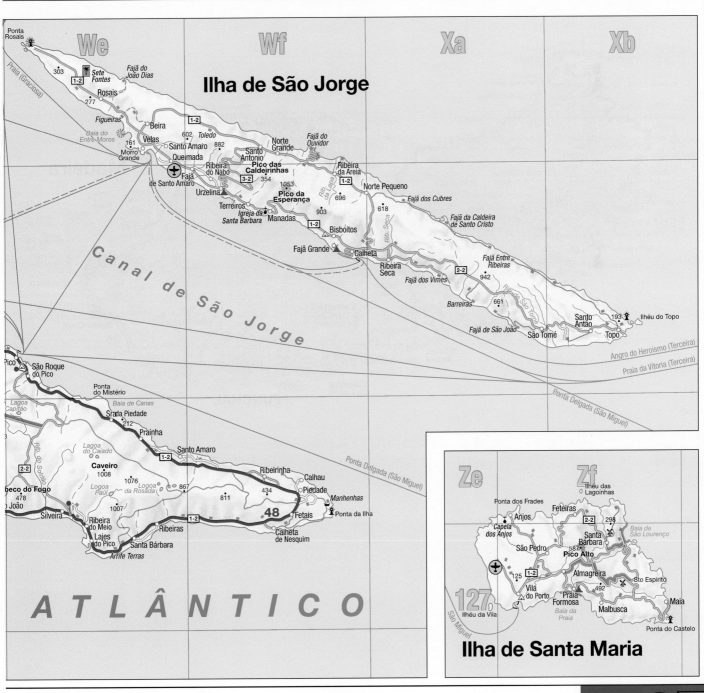

Canal de São Jorge

ATLÂNTICO

Ilha de Santa Maria

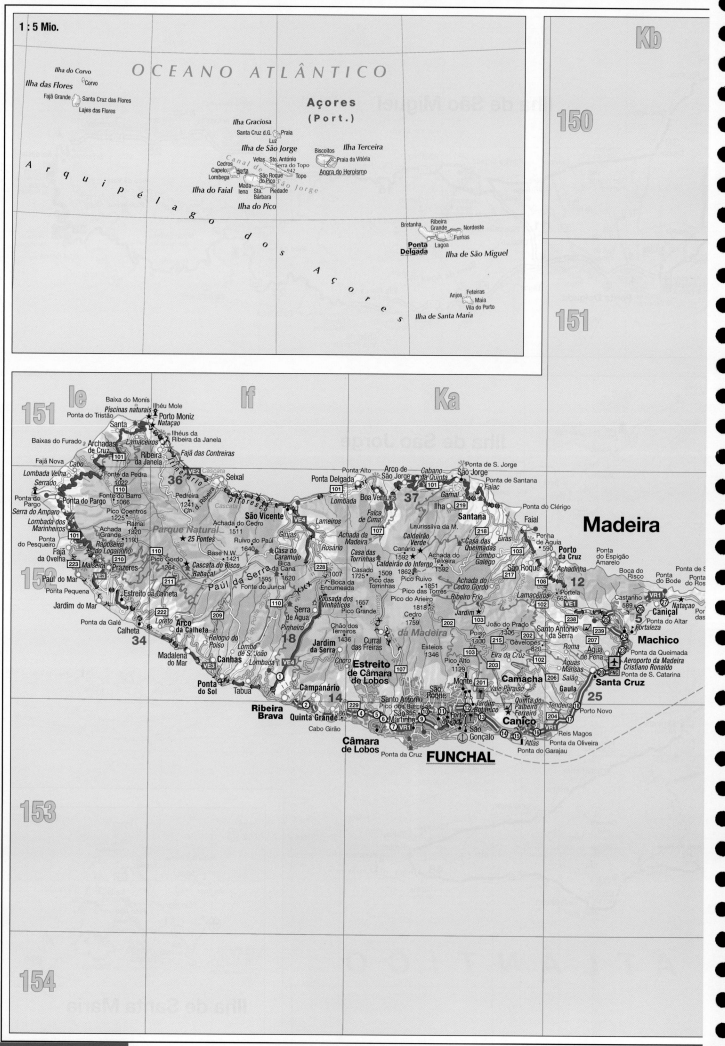

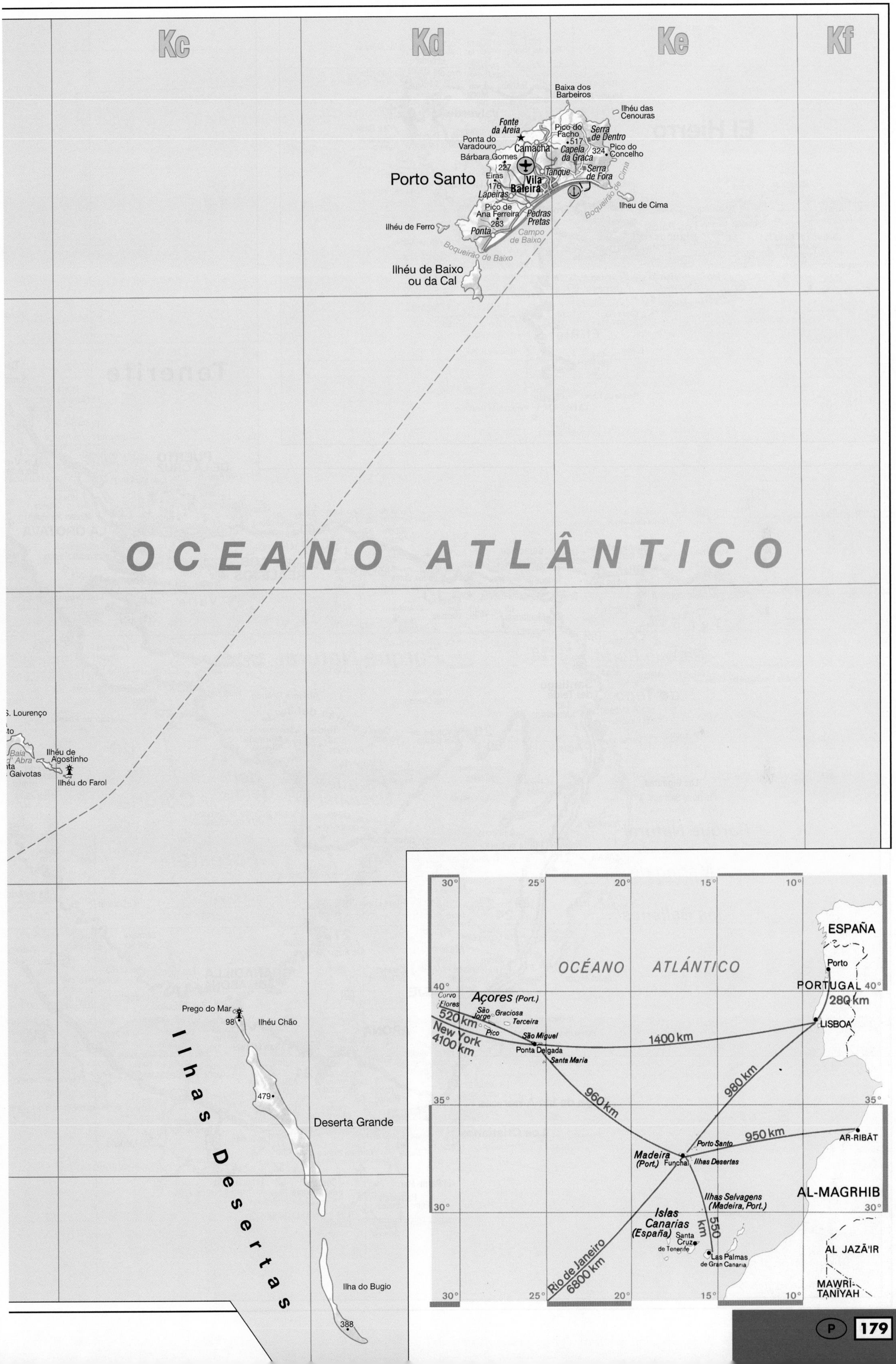

Baixa dos
Barbeiros

Ilhéu das
Cenouras

Fonte
da Areia

Pico do
Facho

Serra
de Dentro

Ponta do
Varadouro

•517

Pico do
Concelho

Camacha

324

Bárbara Gomes

Capela
da Graça

Porto Santo

227

Tanque

Serra
de Fora

Eiras

176

Vila

Lapeiras

Baleira

Ilhéu de Cima

Pico de
Ana Ferreira

Pedras
Pretas

283

Ilhéu de Ferro

Ponta

Campo
de Baixo

Boqueirão de Cima

Boqueirão de Baixo

Ilhéu de Baixo
ou da Cal

OCEANO ATLÂNTICO

S. Lourenço

Baía
d'Abra

Ilhéu de
Agostinho

Gaivotas

Ilhéu do Farol

Prego do Mar

98 •

Ilhéu Chão

479 •

Deserta Grande

Ilhas Desertas

Ilha do Bugio

388 •

Inset map

30°	25°	20°	15°	10°

OCÉANO   ATLÁNTICO

ESPAÑA

Porto

40°   PORTUGAL 40°

280 km

Corvo
Flores

Açores (Port.)

São
Jorge   Graciosa

New York
4100 km

520 km

Terceira

Pico

São Miguel

1400 km

LISBOA

Ponta Delgada

Santa Maria

960 km

980 km

35°   35°

Porto Santo

950 km

AR-RIBÁT

Madeira
(Port.) Funchal

Ilhas Desertas

AL-MAGRHIB

Ilhas Selvagens
(Madeira, Port.)

30°   30°

Islas
Canarias
(España)

Santa
Cruz
de Tenerife

550 km

AL JAZÃ'IR

Rio de Janeiro
6800 km

Las Palmas
de Gran Canaria

MAWRĪ-
TANIYAH

30°	25°	20°	15°	10°

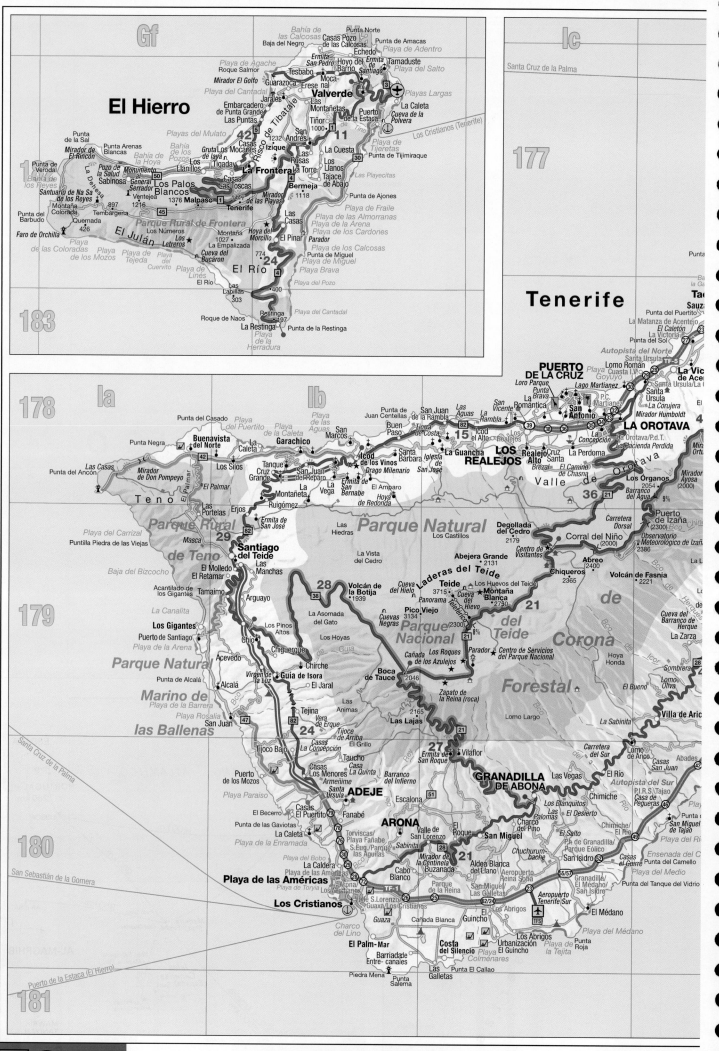

El Hierro

Gf

Bahía de las Calcosas
Punta Norte
Casas Pozo de las Calcosas
Baja del Negro
Punta de Amacas
Playa de Adentro
Playa de Agache
Ermita San Pedro
Hoyo del Barrio
Ermita de Santiago
Tamaduste
Playa del Salto
Roque Salmor
Tesbabo
Echedo
Mirador El Golfo
Moca
Guarazoca
Erese nal
Playa del Cantadal
Jarales
Valverde
Playas Largas
Embarcadero de Punta Grande
Las Montañetas
La Caleta
Las Puntas
Tiñor 1000
Puerto de la Estaca
Cueva de la Polvera
1232
San Andrés
Izique
Casas Los Mocanes
Las Rosas
La Cuesta
Playa de Tijeretas
Gruta de Jaya
Tigaday
La Torre
Los Llanos
Punta de Tijimiraque
Los Llanillos
La Frontera
Tajace de Abajo
Las Playecitas
Casas Las Toscas
Bermeja
Los Palos Blancos
1376 **Malpaso**
1118
Mirador de las Playas
Punta de Ajones
Tenerife
Playa de Fraile
Playa de las Almorranas
Las Casas
Playa de la Arena
Montaña 1027
Hoya del Morcillo
El Pinar
Playa de los Cardones
La Empalizada
Parador
Playa de los Calcosas
774
Punta de Miguel
Playa de Miguel
El Julán
Los Letreros
Cueva del Bucaron
El Río
Playa Brava
El Río
Las Lapillas 303
400
Playa del Pozo
Roque de Naos
197
La Restinga
Playa del Cantadal
La Restinga
Punta de la Restinga
Playa de la Herradura

Punta de la Sal
Punta Arenas Blancas
Mirador de El Rincón
Bahía de los Pozos
Punta de Verodal
Bahía de los Reyes
Pozo de la Salud
Sabinosa
Monumento al General Serrador
Santuario de Na Sa de los Reyes
Ventejís
Montaña Colorada
897
Tembárgena
1216
Quemada
426
Faro de Orchilla
Playa de las Coloradas
Playa de los Mozos
Playa de Tejeda
Playa del Cuervito
Playa de Liñes
Parque Rural de Frontera

Tenerife

Ic

Santa Cruz de la Palma

177

183

---

la
178

Punta del Casado
Playa del Puertito
Playa de la Caleta
Playa de las Aguas
Ib
Punta de Juan Centellas
Buen Paso
San Juan de la Rambla
Las Aguas
San Vicente
La Rambla
La Romántica
Puerto de la Cruz
Loro Parque
Punta Brava
Lago Martianez
Playa Cuesta I.W.
Goyuyo
Lomo Román
Autopista del Norte
Santa Úrsula
La Matanza de Acentejo
El Caletón
La Victoria
Punta del Sol
La Vic de Acer
Santa Úrsula/La C
La Corujera

Buenavista del Norte
La Caleta
Garachico
San Marcos
San Juan de la Rambla
Icod de los Vinos
Santa Bárbara
Iglesia de San José
La Guancha
P.C. Martianez
San Antonio
Mirador Humboldt
LA OROTAVA
La Concepción
La Orotava/P.d.T.
La Hacienda Perdida
Realejo Alto
Cruz Santa
La Perdoma

Punta Negra
Las Casas
Mirador de Don Pompeyo
Punta del Ancón
42
Los Silos
Tanque
Cruz Grande
San Juan del Reparo
La Vega
Drago Milenario
El Amparo
LOS REALEJOS
Realejo Bajo
El Camino de Chasna
Brezal
Los Órganos
Mirador Ayosa (2000)
2054
Barranco del Agua
9%

Teno
El Palmar
La Montañeta
Ermita de San Bernabé
Hoya de Redonda
Valle de Orotava
Carretera Dorsal
36
21
Puerto de Izaña

Erjos
Ruigómez
Las Hiedras
Parque Natural
La Vista del Cedro
Los Castillos
Degollada del Cedro
2179
Centro de Visitantes
Corral del Niño (2000)
Observatorio Meteorológico de Izaña
2386

179
Mirador de Don Pompeyo
Parque Rural
Masca
29
Ermita de San José
Abejera Grande
2131
Laderas del Teide
Los Huevos del Teide
Abreo 2400
Volcán de Fasnia
2221

Playa del Carrizal
Puntilla Piedra de las Viejas
de Teno
82
Santiago del Teide
Las Manchas
28
38
Volcán de la Botija
1939
Cueva del Hielo
Teide 3715
Cueva del Hievo
Panorama
Montaña Blanca 2730
Chiqueros 2365
21
del Teide
de

Baja del Bizcocho
El Molledo
El Retamar
Tamaimo
Arguayo
La Asomada del Gato
Los Hoyos
Pico Viejo 3134
Cuevas Negras
Teleférico (2300)
8%
Corona

Acantilado de los Gigantes
La Canalita
Los Gigantes
Puerto de Santiago
Playa de la Arena
Los Pinos Altos
Chío
Chiguergue
Chirche
Guía
Parque Nacional
Cañada de los Azulejos
Los Roques de los Azulejos
Parador
Centro de Servicios del Parque Nacional
Cueva del Barranco de Herque
La Zarza
Hoya Honda

Parque Natural
Punta de Alcalá
Virgen de la Luz
GUÍA DE ISORA
El Jaral
Boca de Tauce 2046
Zapato de la Reina (roca)
Sombrera
El Bueno
Lomo Oliva
28

Alcalá
Marino de
Playa de la Barrera
Tejina
Las Ánimas
2165
El Río
Lomo Largo
La Sabinita
Villa de Aric

Playa Rosalía
San Juan
47
82
Vera de Erque
24
Las Lajas
21

las Ballenas
Tijoce de Arriba
El Grillo
Casas La Concepción
Forestal
Carretera del Sur
Lomo de Arico
Abades
42

Tijoco Bajo
Taucho
Casa La Quinta
27
Ermita de San Roque
Vilaflor
Las Vegas
El Río
Casas San Juan
180
Santa Úrsula
Casas Los Menores
Armeñime
Barranco del Infierno
GRANADILLA DE ABONA
Los Blanquitos
Las Palomas
Chimiche
P.I.R.S. Tajao
Casa de Pegueras
46

Puerto de los Mozos
Playa Paraíso
El Becerro
El Puertito
79
Fanabé
Escalona
51
El Desierto
Chimiche/El Río
San Miguel de Tajao
49
Playa del Ri

Casas La Enramada
Punta de las Gaviotas
La Caleta
78
76
ADEJE
Santa Úrsula
ARONA
Valle de San Lorenzo
El Roque
Chuchurumbache
Aldea Blanca del Llano
San Isidro 52
Ensenada del C
Punta del Tanque del Vidrio

Playa del Bobo
30
29
La Caldera
Cabo Blanco
San Miguel
Playa de las Américas
Playa de las Américas
28
72
Mirador de la Centinela
Buzanada
Parque de la Reina
Aeropuerto Reina Sofía
Granadilla/El Médano/San Isidro
23
Aeropuerto Tenerife Sur
TFS
El Médano
Punta Roja
Playa del Médano

Los Cristianos
Playa de Torvia
Valle S. Lorenzo
26
25
Guaxa/Los Cristianos
Los Abrigos
Guaza
Cañada Blanca
El Guincho
180
San Sebastián de la Gomera
Charco del Lino
Guaza
62/24
Urbanización El Guincho
Los Abrigos
Playa de la Tejita

181
Puerto de la Estaca (El Hierro)
El Palm-Mar
Costa del Silencio
Playa Colmenares
Punta del Callao
Barriada de Entre-canaies
Piedra Mena
Las Galletas
Punta Salema

OCÉANO

ATLÁNTICO

SAN CRISTÓBAL DE LA LAGUNA (LA LAGUNA)

SANTA CRUZ DE TENERIFE

CANDELARIA

Punta del Hidalgo
Bajamar
Tejina
Tegueste
Vega de las Mercedes
El Rosario
La Esperanza
La Matanza de Acentejo
Güímar
Fasnia
Arico/Poris de Abona

Parque Rural de Anaga

Faro de Anaga

La Palma

Gf   Ha   Hb

176

177

178

Santo Domingo de Garafía
Barlovento
Los Sauces
Puntagorda
La Tricias
Tijarafe
Los Llanos de Aridane
Tazacorte
Puerto Naos
El Paso
San José
Santa Cruz de la Palma
San Pedro de Breña Alta
Malpaíses
Monte de Luna Fuego
Los Canarios
Fuencaliente de la Palma
Volcán de Teneguía
Faro de Fuencaliente
Punta de Fuencaliente

Parque Nacional de la Caldera de Taburiente

Parque Natural de Cumbre Vieja

OCÉANO

ATLÁNTICO

Parque Natural del Archipiélago Chinijo

Punta Mosegos
Punta Grieta
Caleta de Morro Alto
Punta de los Mosquitos
La Caldera
52
Faro de Alegranza
Alegranza
Alegranza
Punta Delgada
Punta de la Mareta
El Caletón
Punta Trabuco

Roque del Oeste
Punta de la Camella
Montaña Clara
256
Caleta de Gu'zman
Punta Gorda
Baja de las Majapalomas
Punta del Aqua
157
Playa Lampra
Playa de las Conchas
Pedro Barba
Punta de Pedro Barba
O de la Sonda
La Baja del Ganado
Las Agujas
La Baja del Ganado
Graciosa
266
Caleta de Pedro Barba
Punta del Bajío
Caleta de Burro
Punta Fariones
Caletón de las Huertas
Caleta del Sebo
Caleta de Arriba
Playa de la Canteria
Charca de la Laja
Playa Francesa
La Punta
Orzola
El Arco
Caletón Blanco
El Río
Casas La Breña
El Arco
Caleta del Mojón Blanco
Mirador del Río
Ye
Punta Prieta
La Caleta
La Bahía
Guinate
Los Molinos
Casas Las Escama
C. del Guincho

Los Lomillos
Mágues
Cueva de los Verdes
Punta Escamas
C. de las Aulagas
Lanzarote
22
Haria
Punta Usaje
Jameos del Agua
Los Caletones
Punta Guerra
Las Bajas
Faja
451
Arrieta
Los Picachos
Punta de Mujeres
Caleta del Caballo
Playa de Famara
Tabayesco
Caleta de Campó
Boca de Abajo
Punta Prieta
Bajamar
Cortijo de Don Juan Feo
Playa de la Garita
La Isleta
La Caleta de Famara
10
Mirador de Haria
El Roque
Casa del Molino
Urbanización Famara
Mala
Playa del Serfio
La Santa
Sóo
293
Ermita del Valle
Charco del Palo
Piedra Mansa
Urbanización Vista Graciosa
Las Laderas
Los Valles
Caletón de las Ánimas
El Jable
Eremita de San Sebastián
Guatiza
Teneza
El Cuchillo
Tinajo
Ermita de San Rafael
Teguise
El Mojón
Urbanización Los Cocoteros
368
20
Muñique
33
Playa de Cho Gregorio
Islotes de Punta Gaviota
Castillo de Guanapay
Tresequite
Playa del Tio Joaquin
Punta Gaviota
Tiagua
1
Volcán Nuevo
Mancha Blanca
La Vegueta
46
Tao
Urbanización Oasis de Nazaret
Playa de la Madera
Punta del Paletón
Casas del Islote
Ermita de los Dolores
Nazaret
Urbanización Las Cabreras
30
Caleta de la Ensenada
El Volcán
Las Cañas
458
Monumento al Campesino
Mozago
10
Corona
235
Ensenada del Banco
Parque Nacional de Timanfaya
56
Casas de la Florida
San Bartolomé M.Mina
Tahiche
321
Punta de Tierra Negra
Natural
Montaña Negra
510
Casa del Rincón
444
Fundación César Manrique
Tahiche
Bonanza Cumplida
517
Pico Partido
Argana
Las Salinas
Playa del Paso
Ruta de los volcanes
26
Montaña Blanca
11
Costa Teguise
Casas de El Golfo
Islote de Hilario
de
35
Punta de Tope
Ensenada de la Gorrina
Punta del Jurado
Montañas del Fuego
Conil
Güima
Playa Bastián
El Golfo
30
67
Vegas de Tegoyo
Puerto del Carmen
Aeropuerto
LZ20
Ensenada de las Caletas
Playa de Montaña Bermeja
Los Volcanes
Tías
3
Los Hervideros
Mácher
LZ2
Castillo de San José
Yaiza
Uga
23
Punta del Volcán
2
ACE
Castillo de San Gabriel
Salinas de Janubio
Casas de la Degollada
Urbanización Los Pocillos
Aeropuerto Lanzarote-Arrecife
Playa de Janubio
Las Casitas de Femés
Urbanización Playa Honda
18
Pico Naos
Cortijos Viejos
Casa de los Majones
Arrecife
Caletón del Río
Atalaya de Femés
415
Urbanización San Antonio
Caleta Piedra Alta
Las Breñas
608
Femés
Playa Quemada
Hoyas Hondas
Casas de Masión
Los Rostros
La Puntilla
Puerto del Carmen
Punta Ginés
Hacha Grande
Playa de la Arena
Urbanización Atlante del Sol
560
Urbanización Montaña Baja
Bahía de Avila
La Capagna
Punta Gorda
(Ruinas)
Punta Limones
Playa Blanca
Punta del Águila
Punta del Papagayo
Caleta Larga
Punta Pechiguera
Punta del Mujeres
Playa Mujeres
Caleta del Congrio
Corralejo

Cádiz

Las Palmas de Gran Canaria, Santa Cruz de Tenerife, Santa Cruz de la Palma

1 : 4.8 Mio.
OCÉANO ATLÁNTICO

Islas Canarias
Islas Canarias (Esp.)

P.N. de la Caldera de Taburiente
2426
La Palma
San Andrés y Sauces
Lanzarote
Haria
Parque Nac. de Timanfaya
Arrecife
Los Llanos de Aridane
Santa Cruz de la Palma
Playa Blanca
Tias
Fuencaliente de la Palma
Garachico
S. CRISTÓBAL DE LA LAGUNA
Corralejo
Santiago
3718
P.N.
Puerto de la Cruz
d.T. P. de Teide del Teide
SANTA CRUZ DE TENERIFE
Fuerteventura
La Gomera
Vallehermoso
Gáldar
Puerto del Rosario
P.N. de Garajonay
San Sebastián de la Gomera
1487
La Aldea de San Nicolás
1949
Tuineje
Frontera
1501
Los Cristianos
LAS PALMAS DE GRAN CANARIA
Telde
Gran Tarajal
Valverde
San Bartolomé de Tirajana
Tenerife
Taibique
El Hierro
Maspalomas
Gran Canaria
Morro Jable

Lc Ld
180

Playa de Barlovento de Jandía

El Islote
Casa de Agua Melianes
Casa Pecene
Playa de Cofete
Punta Pesebre
Caleta de la Madera
Punta de Barlovento
Jandía
Casas de Mal Nombre
Casas de Esq
Punta Cofillo
O de Cachorros
Montaña Aguda
435
Cofete
(Abandonada)
El Golfo
Fraile
683
Casas de Gran Valle
Jandía
Playa de Tigre
Casas Cueva de la Negra
Casas de Jorós
Úrban. Marabu
Casería Puerto de la Luz
Casas de Butihondo
Punta de Jandía
Playa de los Pilas
Playa de Juan Gomez
Casas del Matorral
Morro Jable
Punta de Matorral (o Morro Jable)
Playa del Mato

Santa Cruz de Tenerife
Las Palmas de Gran Canaria

Fuerteventura

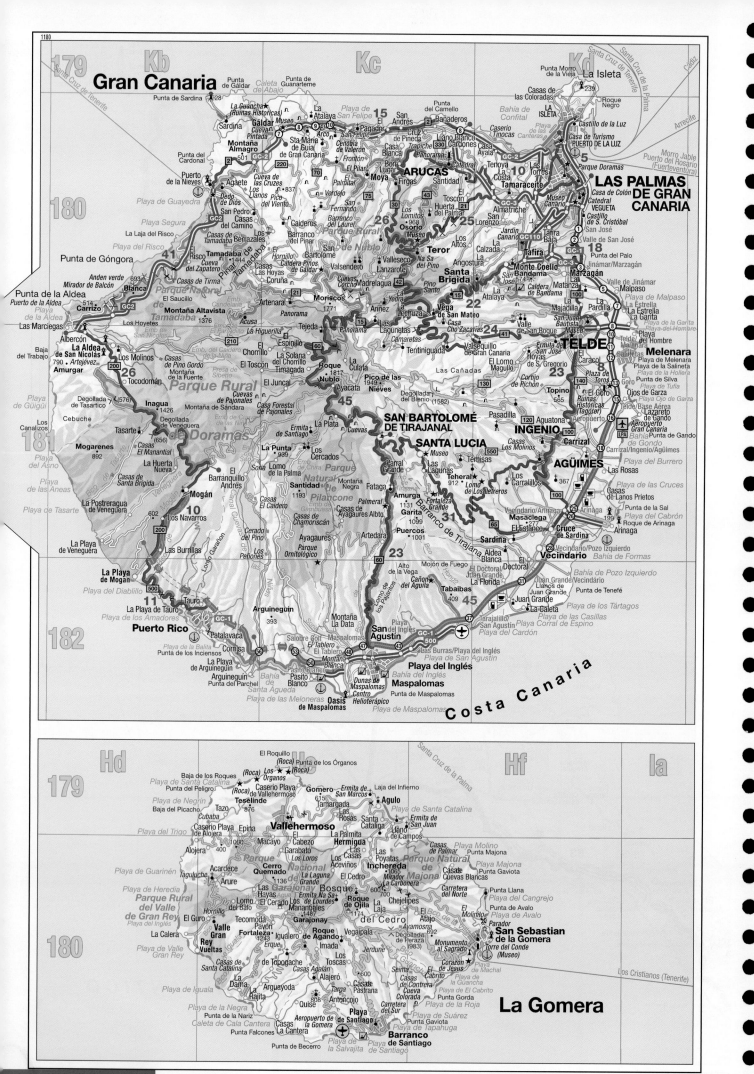

Distancias en kilómetros · Distâncias em kilómetros · Entfernungen in Kilometer · Distances in kilometres
Distanze in chilometri · Distances en kilomètres · Afstanden in kilometer · Odległości w kilometrach
Vzdálenosti v kilometrech · Kilométertávolság · Afstænder i kilometer · Kilometerangivelse

ESPAÑA (E)

Distance matrix between Spanish cities (distances in km).

	Zaragoza	Zamora	Vitoria	Valldolid	Valencia	Toledo	Teruel	Tarragona	Soria	Sevilla	Segovia	Santander	San Sebastián	Salamanca	Pontevedra	Pamplona	Palencia	Oviedo	Ourense	Murcia	Málaga	Madrid	Lugo	Logroño	Lérida	León	Jaén	Huelva	Guadaljara	Granada	Girona	Cuenca	Córdoba	Ciudad Real	Castellón	Cádiz	Cáceres	Burgos	Bilbao	Barcelona	Badajoz	Ávila	Almería	Alicante	Albacete	A Coruña
A Coruña	781	395	599	438	948	665	895	1014	619	922	527	454	641	460	759	133	692	440	286	173	994	591	98	614	928	315	921	943	654	1009	1166	759	987	794	1014	1042	662	487	546	1088	654	518	1140	1015	852	
Albacete	391	512	598	449	187	246	220	419	448	503	365	692	473	872	569	498	705	759	146	253	757	940	548	654	596	306	596	282	603	141	372	200	235	625	506	485	638	510	504	688	356	168				
Alicante	484	679	744	616	413	318	432	551	595	517	832	639	1027	662	665	871	926	82	472	419	940	654	666	558	762	407	692	448	351	617	308	383	383	642	672	652	787	524	688	622	658					
Almería	756	803	901	739	499	591	704	769	413	640	984	996	1150	934	789	995	1049	218	552	206	1048	868	225	509	602	168	889	496	366	555	443	676	789	942	796	622	328									
Ávila	424	179	357	119	465	131	414	657	253	498	364	452	109	528	450	169	373	427	566	670	421	404	566	464	1104	264	310	92	538	691	1026															
Badajoz	718	358	450	414	661	367	708	952	632	210	392	657	745	292	465	743	462	607	566	670	421	404	566	464	1104	264	310	92	538	691	1026															
Barcelona	313	825	567	728	351	692	428	100	467	996	663	708	571	845	1109	437	691	896	1057	589	997	624	402	477	170	784	799	1090	564	888	102	541	865	693	282	1118	601	606	610							
Bilbao	302	377	62	280	611	468	475	536	230	861	352	101	397	614	155	243	285	609	783	921	482	410	481	136	450	336	723	943	401	811	648	552	789	596	554	981	601	158								
Burgos	300	225	118	127	315	380	533	142	709	200	181	213	244	211	90	296	456	631	768	410	569	134	533	183	570	790	248	659	685	399	443	552	828	449												
Cáceres	611	268	559	323	629	260	602	845	525	267	302	567	655	201	652	372	516	526	651	478	297	569	575	844	408	433	358	521	997	440	321	449	876													
Cádiz	965	649	940	704	776	614	785	1025	878	124	683	948	1035	682	899	1033	752	897	568	650	236	650	956	1151	788	332	213	294	686	263	449	876														
Castellón	309	676	569	612	144	433	187	376	719	513	710	573	1035	487	555	868	922	311	720	419	920	241	759	522	812	383	610	372	263	416																
Ciudad Real	510	458	555	394	352	117	361	601	326	295	639	651	817	585	444	650	704	361	344	206	702	523	657	541	419	256	259	786	267	195																
Córdoba	700	582	745	584	521	344	530	770	485	829	613	796	775	634	840	841	476	159	397	713	847	731	120	234	447	202	955	633	431																	
Cuenca	289	422	510	358	179	147	448	270	564	259	578	517	382	432	400	614	668	286	165	667	369	555	231	861	641	979																				
Girona	390	903	645	805	443	769	520	192	544	1088	740	638	785	922	1247	563	768	974	1134	680	1089	701	1072	555	231	1181	641	979																		

PORTUGAL (P)

	Aveiro	Beja	Braga	Bragança	Caia e São Pedro	Castelo Branco	Coimbra	Évora	Faro	Fátima	Galegos/Marvão	Guarda	Leiria	Lisboa	Portalegre	Porto	Quintanilha	São Gregório	São Leonardo	Santarém	Segura	Setúbal	Valençax do Minho	Viana do Castelo	Vila Real	Vila Real de Santó Antonio	Vila Verde de Ficalho	Vila Verde de Raia	Vilar Formoso	Viseu

I←→I km
10 km = 6.2 miles

1:150 000

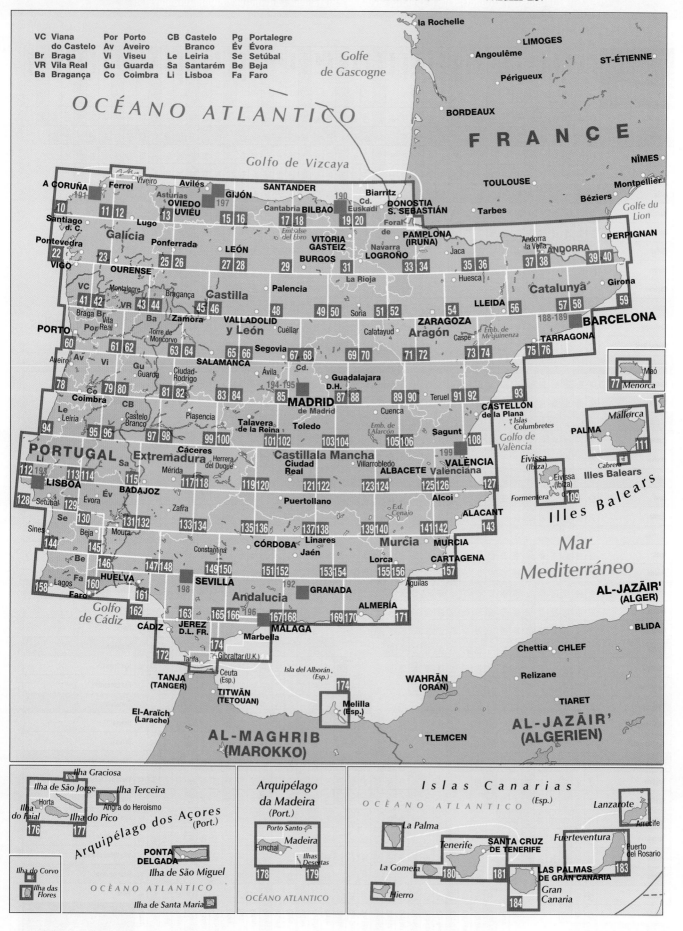

1 : 150 000

Signos convencionales Legenda (E)	Sinais convencionais Objaśnienia znaków (P)	Zeichenerklärung Vysvětlivky (D)	Legend Legenda (GB)	Segni convenzionali Tegnforklaring (I)	Légende Tumač znakova (F)
Autopista con acceso y número de acceso	Auto-estrada com ramal e número de acesso	Autobahn mit Anschlussstelle und Anschlussnummer	Motorway with junction and junction number	Autostrada con svincolo e svincolo numerato	Autoroute avec point de jonction et numéro de point de jonction
Estación de peaje, Carretera de peaje	Portagem, Estrada com portagem	Mautstelle, Gebührenpflichtige Straße	Toll station, Toll road	Stazione a barriera, Strada a pedaggio	Gare de péage, Route à péage
Autopista en construcción, Autopista en proyecto	Auto-estrada em construção, Auto-estrada em projecto	Autobahn in Bau, Autobahn in Planung	Motorway under construction, Motorway projected	Autostrada in costruzione, Autostrada in progetto	Autoroute en construction, Autoroute en projet
Autovía, Autovía en construcción	Vía rápida de faixas separadas, Vía rápida em construção	Schnellstraße, Schnellstraße in Bau	Dual carriageway, Dual carriageway under construction	Superstrada, Superstrada in costruzione	Chaussée double, Chaussée double en construction
Carretera federal	Estrada federal	Bundesstraße	Federal road	Strada statale	Route nationale
Carretera principal con nombres de calles, Carretera de tránsito con nombres de calles	Estrada principal com os nomes das ruas, Estrada de trânsito com os nomes das ruas	Hauptverbindungsstr. mit Str.-Namen, Durchgangsstr. mit Str.-Namen	Main road with street names, Thoroughfare with street names	Strada principale con i nomi delle strade, Strada di attraversamento con i nomi delle strade	Route principale avec des noms des rues, Route de transit avec des noms des rues
Número de autopista, Número de carretera europea	Número de auto-estrada, Número de estrada europeia	Autobahnnummern, Europastraßennummern	Motorway numbers, European road numbers	Numero di autostrada, Numero di strada europea	Numéro d'autoroute, Organismes européens
Transbordador para automóviles, Transbordador para pasajeros	Balsa para viaturas, Barca de passageiros	Autofähre, Personenfähre	Car ferry, Passenger ferry	Traghetto per auto, Traghetto passeggeri	Bac pour automobiles, Bac pour piétons
Ferrocarril, Tráfico de larga distancia con estación	Linha ferroviária, Tráfego de longa distância com estação	Eisenbahn, Fernverkehr mit Bahnhof	Railway, Long-distance traffic with station	Ferrovia, Traffico a lunga percorrenza con stazione	Chemin de fer, Le trafic grandes lignes avec gare ferroviaire
Área de servicio	Area de serviço	Autobahnraststätte	Service area	Area di servizio	Station service
Estación de servicio	Estação de serviço da estrada	Autobahntankstelle	Service station	Stazione di servizio	Station d'essence d'autoroute
Auto-estrada aparcamiento	Auto-estrada Parque de estacionamento	Autobahnparkplatz	Motorway parking place	Autostrada Parcheggio	Autoroute Parking
Aeropuerto	Aeroporto	Verkehrsflughafen	Airport	Aeroporto	Aéroport
Puntos de interés	Locais de interesse	Sehenswürdigkeiten	Tourist attractions	Interesse turistico	Curiosités
Zona edificada	Área urbana	Bebauung	Built-up area	Caseggiato	Zone bâtie
Aguas	Águas	Gewässer	Waters	Acque	Eaux
Frontera nacional	Fronteira nacional	Staatsgrenze	National boundary	Confine di Stato	Frontière d'État

(NL)	(PL)	(CZ)	(SK)	(DK)	(HR)
Autosnelweg met aansluiting en aansluitingnummer	Autostrada z węzłem i numerem węzła	Dálnice s přípojkou a přípojka s číslem	Diaľnica s prípojka s prípojka číslo	Motorvej med tilkørsel og tilkørsel med nummer	Autocesta sa prilazom, a Izlaz-broj
Tolkantoor, Tolweg	Płatna rogatka, Droga płatna	Místo výběru poplatků, Silnice podléhající poplatkům	Miesto výberu poplatkov, Cesta s povinným poplatkom	Vejafgiftsstation, Afgiftsrute	Vámház, Dijellenében használható út
Autosnelweg in aanleg, Autosnelweg in ontwerp	Autostrada w budowie, Autostrada projektowana	Dálnice ve stavbě, Dálnice plánovaná	Diaľnica vo výstavbe, Diaľnica plánovaná	Motorvej under opførelse under planlægning	Autocesta u izgradnji, Autocesta u planu
Autoweg met gescheiden rijbanen, Autoweg in anleg	Droga, Droga ekspresowa w budowie	Rychlostní komunikace, Rychlostní komunikace ve stavbě	Diaľnice, Diaľnice vo výstavbe	Motortrafikvej, Motortrafikvej under anlæg	Brza cesta, Brza u izgradnji
Rijksweg	Droga państwowa	Státní silnice	Hlavná diaľ ková cesta	Primærvej	Glavna tranzitna cesta
Hoofdweg, Weg voor doorgaand verkeer	Droga główna, Droga przelotowa	Hlavní silnice, Průjezdní silnice	Hlavná cesta, Priechodná cesta	Hovedvej med gadenavne Gennemfartsvej med gadenavne	Glavna veza, Glavna cesta
Motorvejnummer, Europees wegnummer	Numer autostrady, Numer drogi europejskiejs	Číslo dálnice, Číslo evropské silnice	Číslo diaľ nice, Číslo európskej cesty	Motorvejnummer, Europavejnummer	Broj autoceste, Broj europske ceste
Autoveer, Personenveer	Prom samochodowy, Prom pasażerski	Trajekt pro auta, Osobní přívoz	Trajekt pre automobily, Prievoz	Bilfærge, Passagerfærge	Trajekt za automobile, Osobe trajekt
Spoorweg, Langeafstandsverkeer met station	Kolej, ruchu dalekobieżnego z stacją	Dálková dopravní se stanici	Železnica, Draha pre diaľ kovú dopravu so stanicou	Jernbanelinie, Fjerntrafik med banegärd	Željeznica, Glavna tranzitna s stanica
Verzorgingsplaats	Miejsce obsługi podróżnych	Odpočívka	Motorest	Motorvejsrasteplads	Restoran
Autosnelwegbenzinestation	Stacja benzynowa przy autostradzie	Čerpací stanice na dálnici	Diaľnica benzínová pumpa	Motorvej tankstation	Benzinska crpka
Parkeerplaats	Autostrada parking	Významné zajímavosti	Parkovisko	Motorvej parkeringsplads	Parkiralište
Luchthaven	Port lotniczy	Dopravní letiště	Dobravné letisko	Lufthavn	Zračna luka
Bezienswaardigheden	Interesujące obiekty	Významné zajímavosti	Zaujímavosti	Seværdigheder	Znamenitosti
Bebouwing	Obszar zabudowany	Zastavěna plochna	Zastavená plocha	Bebyggelse	Zgrada
Wateren	Wody	Vodstvo	Vodstvo	Vande	Vode
Rijksgrens	Granica państwa	Státní hranice	Štátna hranica	Statsgrænse	Državna granica

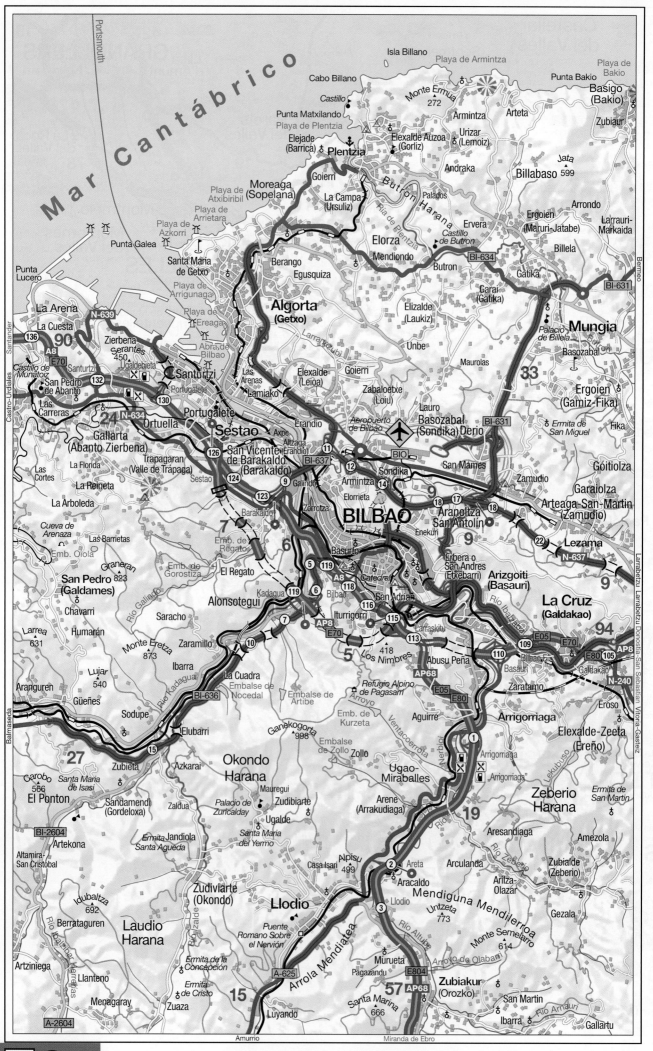

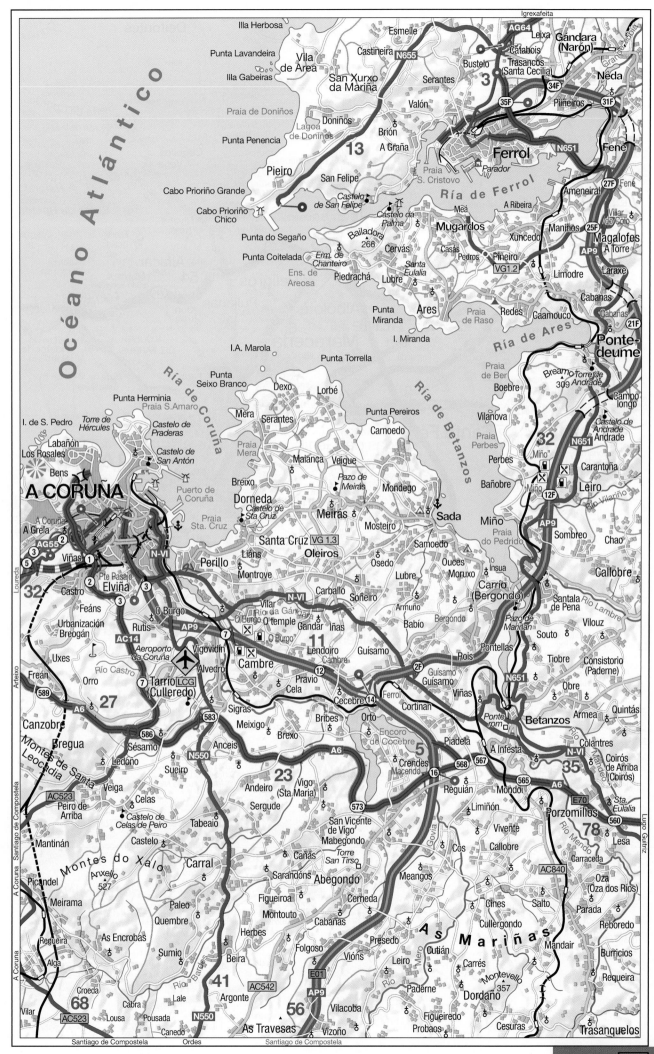

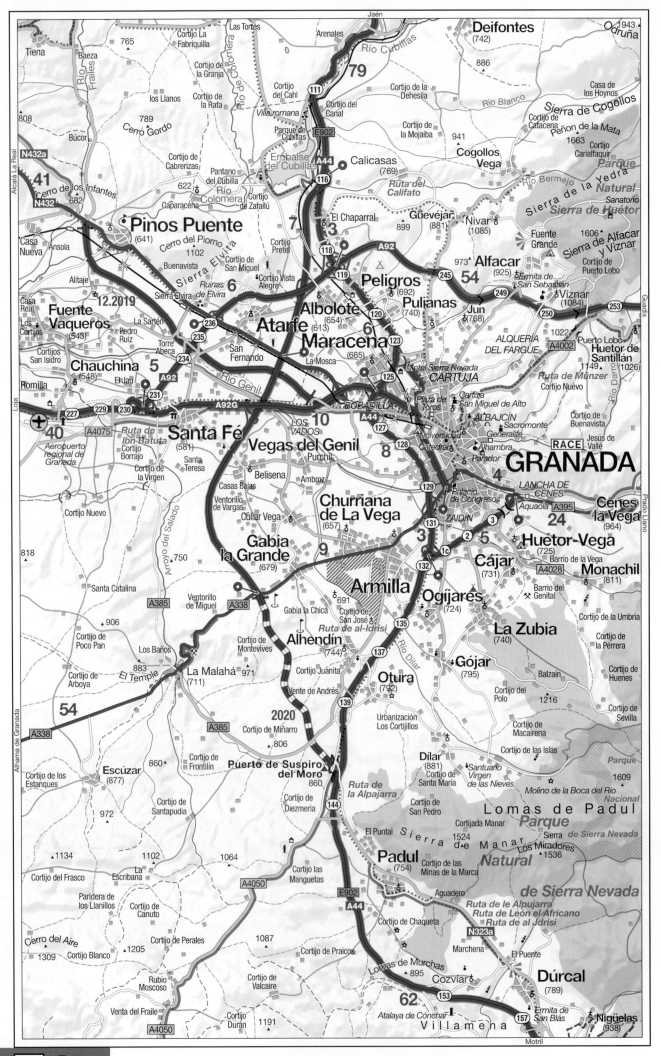

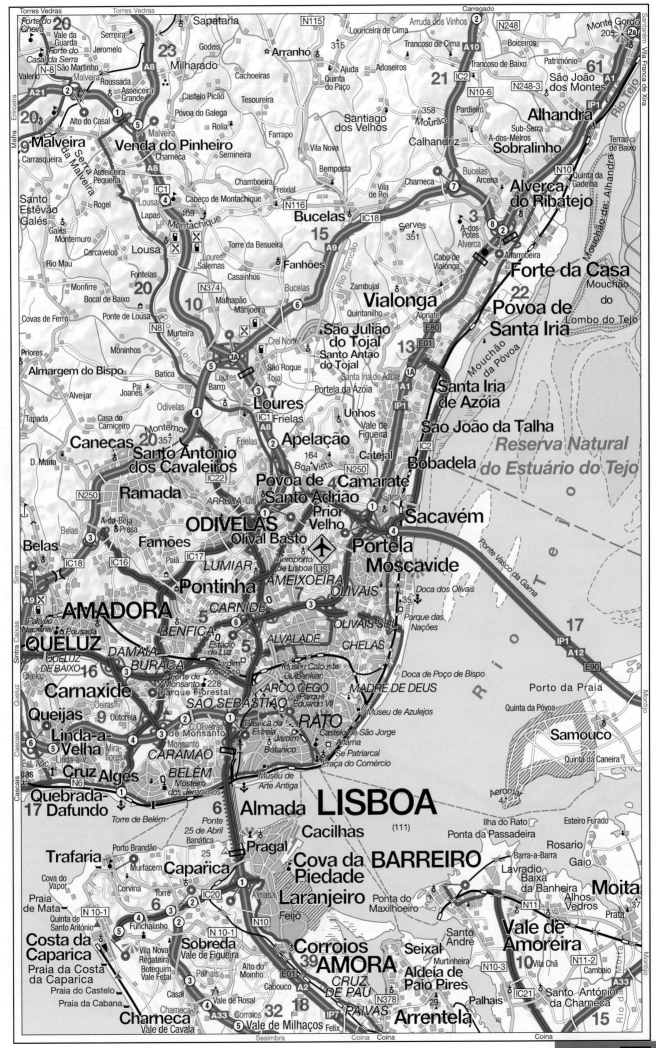

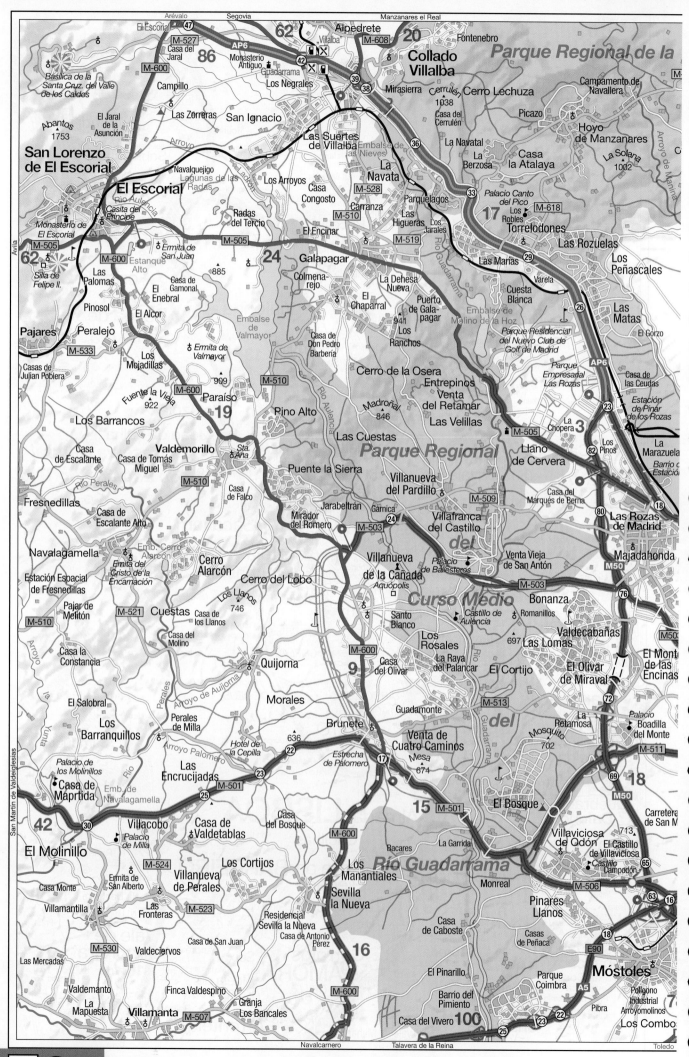

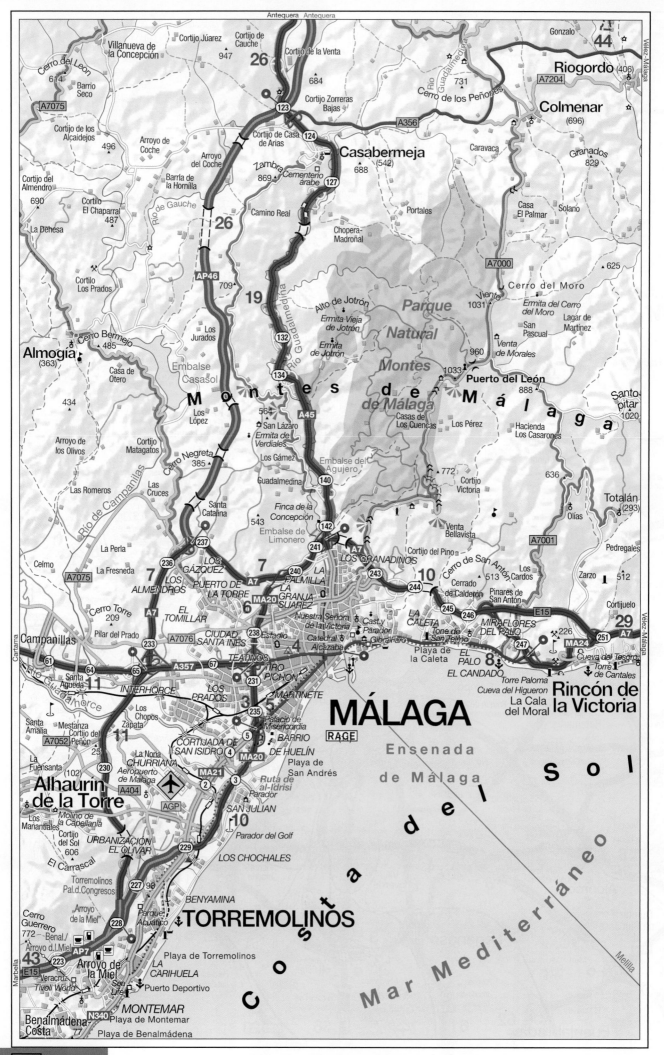

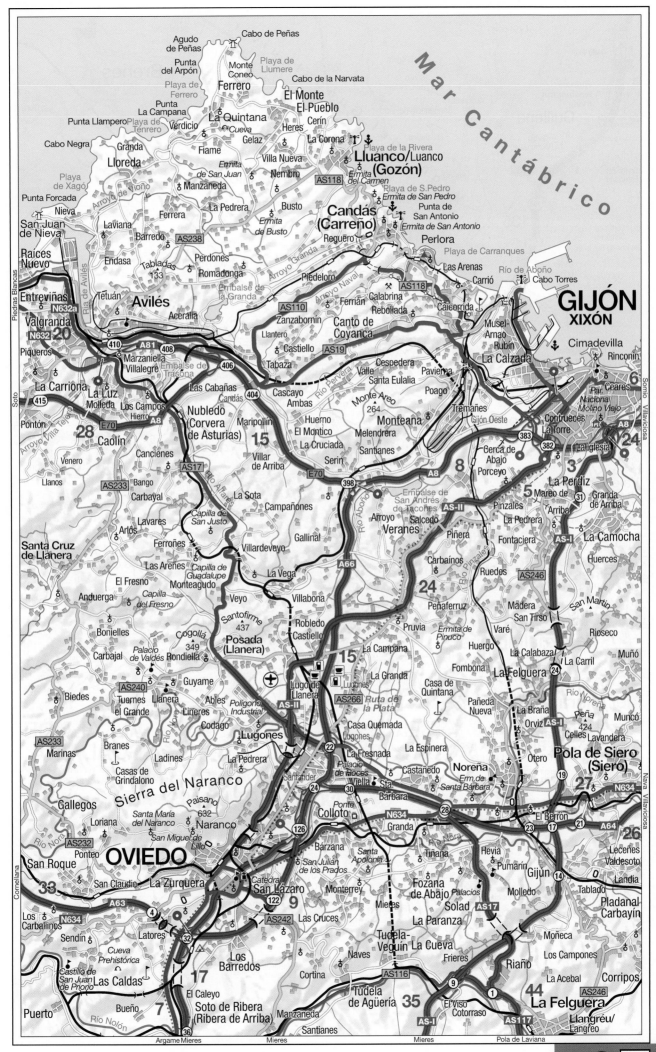

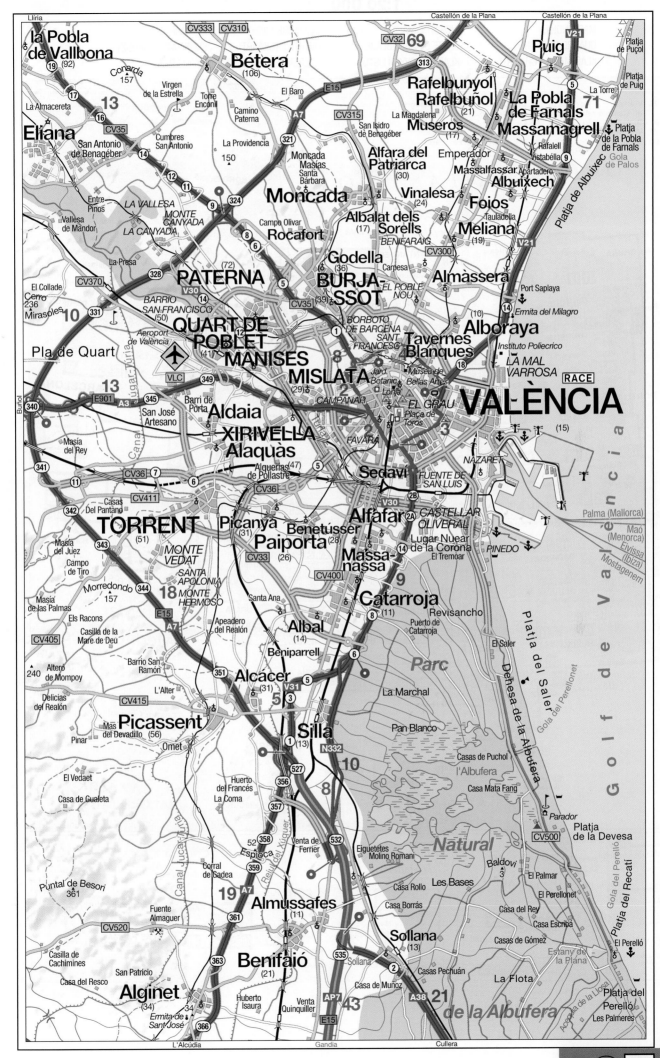

1:20 000

MAPA ÍNDICE   ÍNDICE DE MAPA   BLATTÜBERSICHT   KEY MAP
QUADRO D'UNIONE   CARTE D'ASSEMBLAGE   OVERZICHTSKAART   SKOROWIDZ ARKUSZY
KLAD MAPOVÝCH LISTŮ   KLAD MAPOVÝCH LISTOV   OVERSIGTSKORT   PREGLED LIST

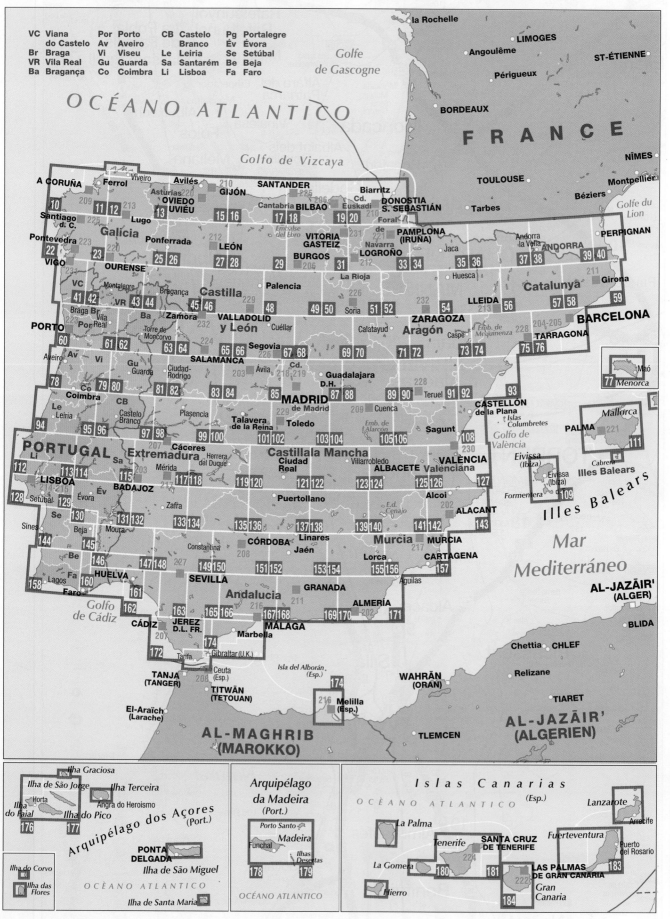

1 : 20 000

Signos convencionales / Legenda — Sinais convencionais / Objaśnienia znaków — Zeichenerklärung / Vysvětlivky — Legend / Legenda — Segni convenzionali / Tegnforklaring — Légende / Tumač znakova

E	P	D	GB	I	F
Autopista	Auto-estrada	Autobahn	Motorway	Autostrada	Autoroute
Carretera de cuatro carriles	Estrada com quatro faixas	Vierspurige Straße	Road with four lanes	Strada a quattro corsie	Route à quatre voies
Carretera de tránsito	Estrada de trânsito	Durchgangsstraße	Thoroughfare	Strada di attraversamento	Route de transit
Carretera principal	Estrada principal	Hauptstraße	Main road	Strada principale	Route principale
Otras carreteras	Outras estradas	Sonstige Straßen	Other roads	Altre strade	Autres routes
Calle de dirección única - Zona peatonal	Rua de sentido único - Zona de peões	Einbahnstraße - Fußgängerzone	One-way street - Pedestrian zone	Via a senso unico - Zona pedonale	Rue à sens unique - Zone piétonne
Información - Aparcamiento	Informação - Parque de estacionamento	Information - Parkplatz	Information - Parking place	Informazioni - Parcheggio	Information - Parking
Ferrocarril principal con estación	Linha principal ferroviária com estação	Hauptbahn mit Bahnhof	Main railway with station	Ferrovia principale con stazione	Chemin de fer principal avec gare
Otro ferrocarril	Linha ramal ferroviária	Sonstige Bahn	Other railway	Altra ferrovia	Autre ligne
Metro	Metro	U-Bahn	Underground	Metropolitana	Métro
Tranvía	Eléctrico	Straßenbahn	Tramway	Tram	Tramway
Autobús al aeropuerto	Autocarro c. serviço aeroporto	Flughafenbus	Airport bus	Autobus per l'aeroporto	Bus d'aéroport
Comisaria de policia - Correos	Esquadra da policía - Correios	Polizeistation - Postamt	Police station - Post office	Posto di polizia - Ufficio postale	Poste de police - Bureau de poste
Hospital - Albergue juvenil	Hospital - Pousada da juventude	Krankenhaus - Jugendherberge	Hospital - Youth hostel	Ospedale - Ostello della gioventù	Hôpital - Auberge de jeunesse
Iglesia - Iglesia de interés	Igreja - Igreja interessante	Kirche - Sehenswerte Kirche	Church - Church of interest	Chiesa - Chiesa interessante	Église - Église remarquable
Sinagoga - Mezquita	Sinagoga - Mesquita	Synagoge - Moschee	Synagogue - Mosque	Sinagoga - Moschea	Synagogue - Mosquée
Monumento - Torre	Monumento - Torre	Denkmal - Turm	Monument - Tower	Monumento - Torre	Monument - Tour
Zona edificada, edificio público	Área urbana, edifício público	Bebaute Fläche, öffentliches Gebäude	Built-up area, public building	Caseggiato, edificio pubblico	Zone bâtie, bâtiment public
Zona industrial	Zona industrial	Industriegelände	Industrial area	Zona industriale	Zone industrielle
Parque, bosque	Parque, floresta	Park, Wald	Park, forest	Parco, bosco	Parc, bois

NL	PL	CZ	SK	DK	HR
Autosnelweg	Autostrada	Dálnice	Diaľnica	Motorvej	Autocesta
Weg met vier rijstroken	Droga o czterech pasach ruchu	Čtyřstopá silnice	Stvorprúdová cesta	Firesporet vej	Cesta sa četiri traka
Weg voor doorgaand verkeer	Droga przelotowa	Průjezdní silnice	Prejazdná cesta	Genemmfartsvej	Tranzitna cesta
Hoofdweg	Droga główna	Hlavní silnice	Hlavná cesta	Hovedvej	Glavna cesta
Overige wegen	Drogi inne	Ostatní silnice	Ostatné cesty	Andre mindre vejen	Ostale ceste
Straat met eenrichtingsverkeer - Voetgangerszone	Ulica jednokierunkowa - Strefa ruchu pieszego	Jednosměrná ulice - Pěší zóna	Jednosmerná cesta - Pešia zóna	Gade med ensrettet kørsel - Gågade	Jednosmjerna ulica - Pješačka zona
Informatie - Parkeerplaats	Informacja - Parking	Informace - Parkoviště	Informácie - Parkovisko	Information - Parkeringplads	Informacije - Parkiralište
Belangrijke spoorweg met station	Kolej główna z dworcami	Hlavní železnice s stanice	Hlavná železnica so stanicou	Hovedjernbanelinie med station	Glavna željeznička pruga sa kolodvorom
Overige spoorweg	Kolej drugorzędna	Ostatní železnice	Ostatné železnice	Anden jernbanelinie	Ostala željeznička traka
Ondergrondse spoorweg	Metro	Metro	Podzemná dráha	Underjordisk bane	Podzemna željeznica
Tram	Linia tramwajowa	Tramvaj	Električka	Sporvej	Tramvaj
Vliegveldbus	Autobus dojazdowy na lotnisko	Letištní autobus	Letiskový autobus	Park+Ride	Autobus zračnog pristaništa
Politiebureau - Postkantoor	Komisariat - Poczta	Policie - Poštovní úřad	Polícia Poštový úrad	Politistation - Posthus	Policijska postaja - Pošta
Ziekenhuis - Jeugdherberg	Szpital - Schronisko młodzieżowe	Nemocnice - Ubytovna mládeže	Nemocnica - Mládežnícka ubytovňa	Sygehus - Vandrerhjem	Bolnica - Omladinski hotel
Kerk - Bezienswaardige kerk	Kościół - Kościół zabytkowy	Kostel - Zajímavý kostel	Kostol - Pozoruhodný kostol	Kirke	Crkva - Znamenita crkva
Synagoge - Moskee	Synagoga - Meczet	Synagoga - Mešita	Synagóga - Mešita	Telemast - Fyrtårn	Sinagoga - Džamija
Monument - Toren	Pomnik - Wieża	Pomník - Věž	Pomník - Veža	Mindesmærke - Tårn	Spomenik - Toranj
Bebouwing, openbaar gebouw	Obszar zabudowany, budynek użyteczności publicznej	Zastavěná plocha, veřejná budova	Zastavaná plocha, verejná budova	Bebyggelse, offentlig bygning	Izgradnja, javna zgradna
Industrieterrein	Obszar przemysłowy	Průmyslová plocha	Priemyselná plocha	Industriområde	Industrijska zona
Park, bos	Park, las	Park, les	Park, les	Park, skov	Park, šuma

Alicante (Alacant)

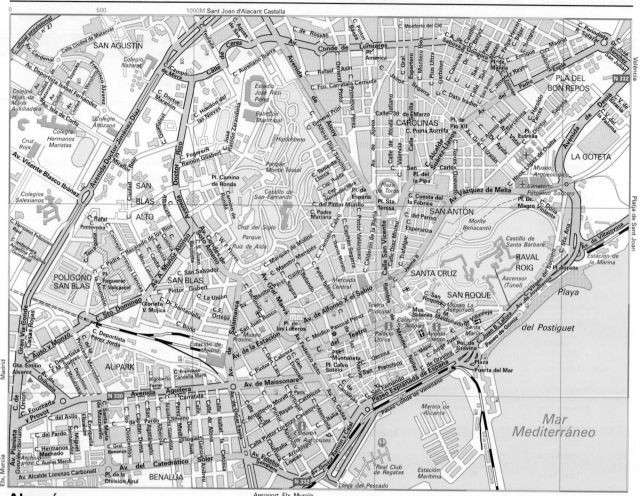

Almería

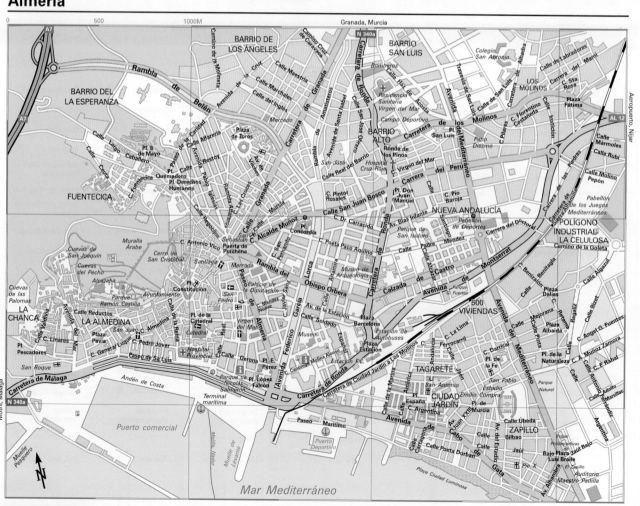

Ávila

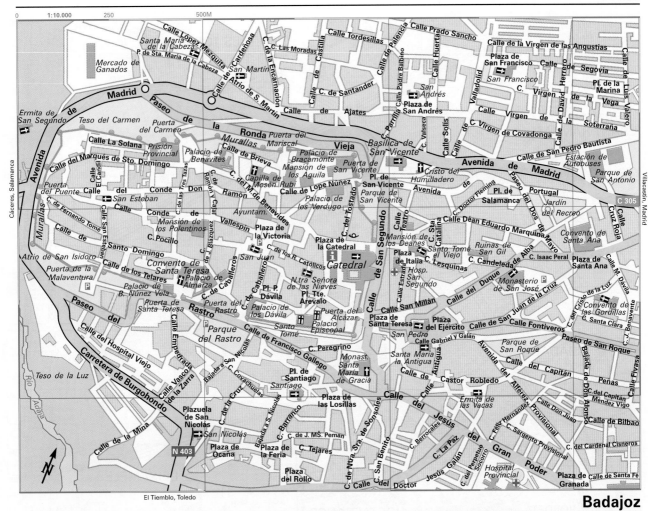

Badajoz

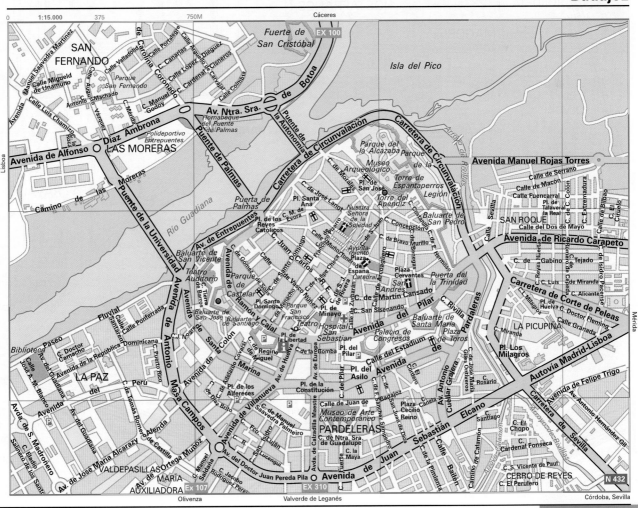

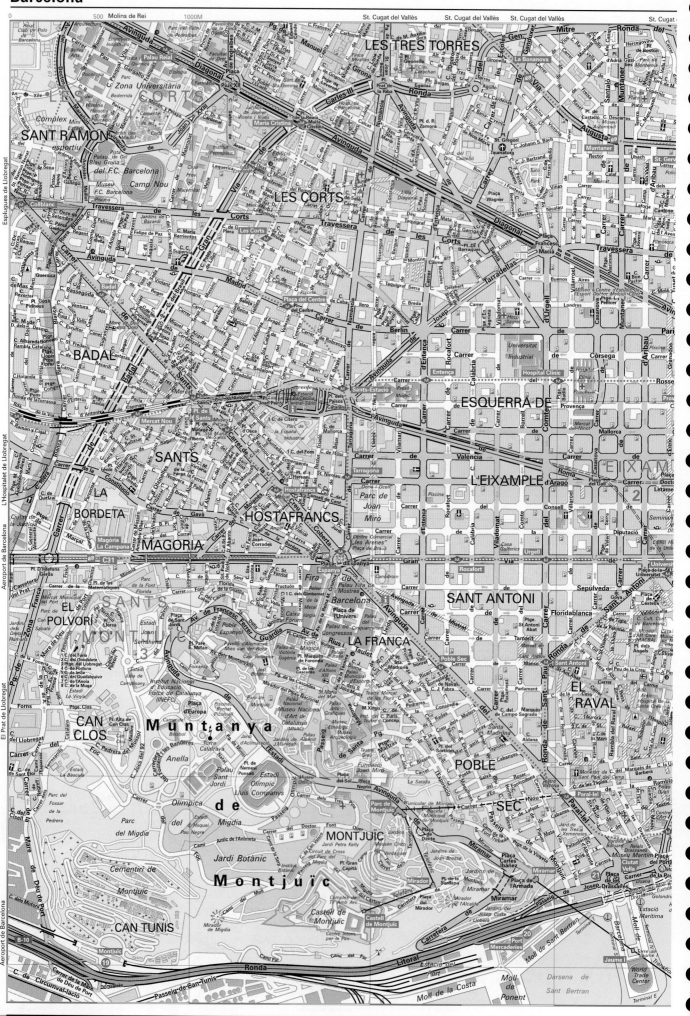

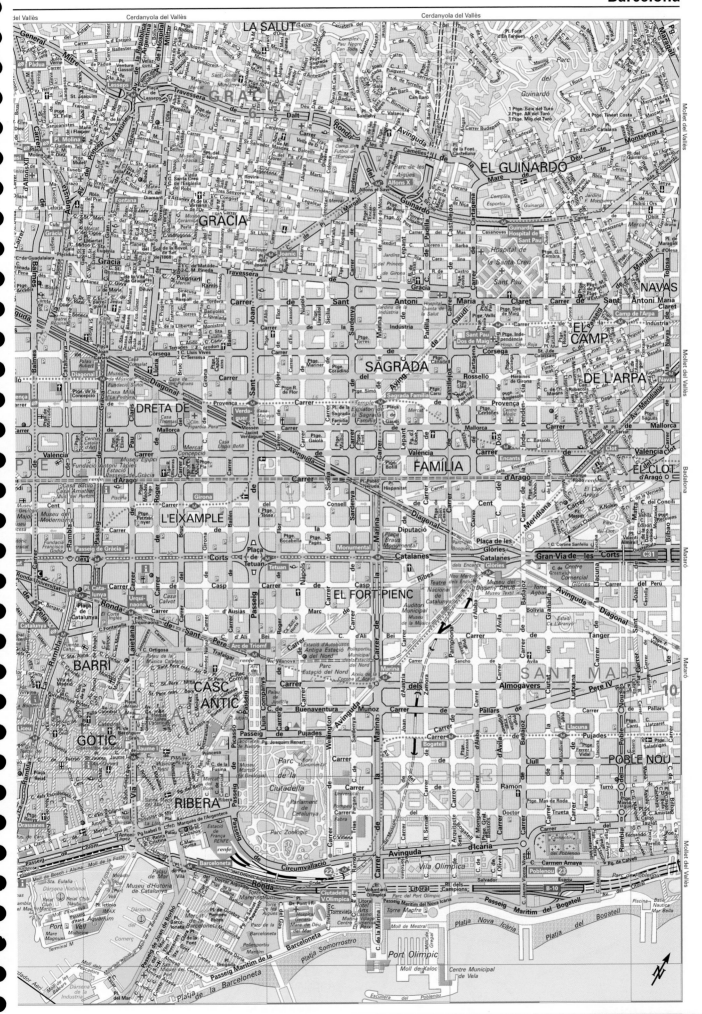

Bilbao

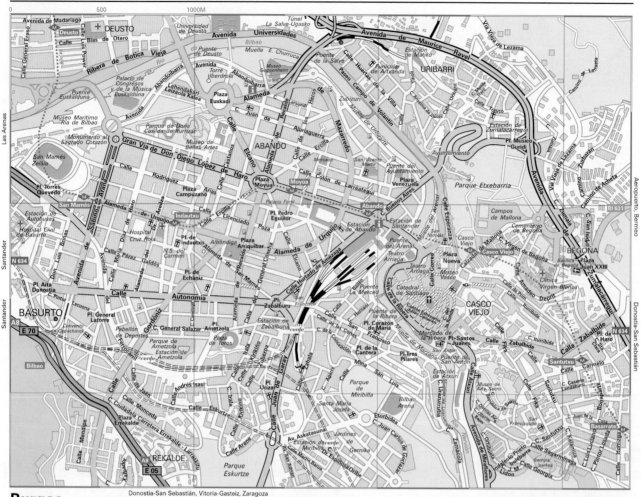

Burgos

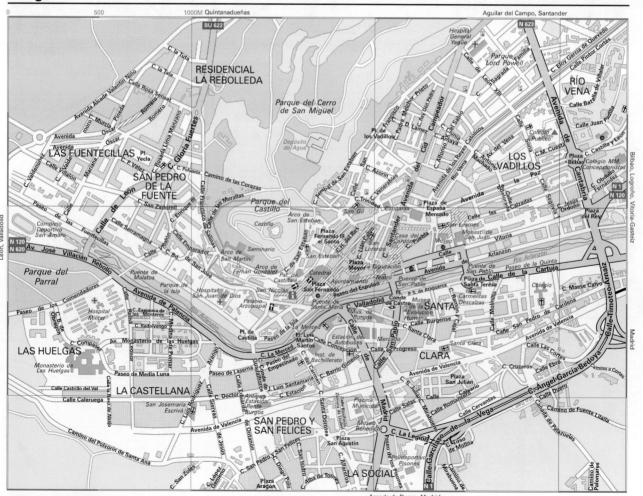

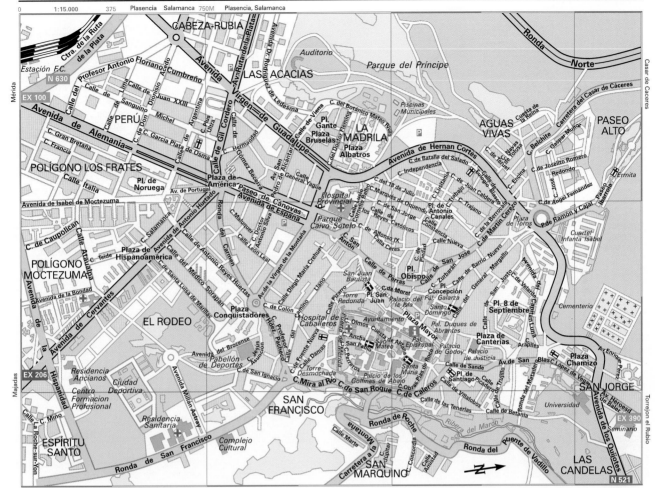

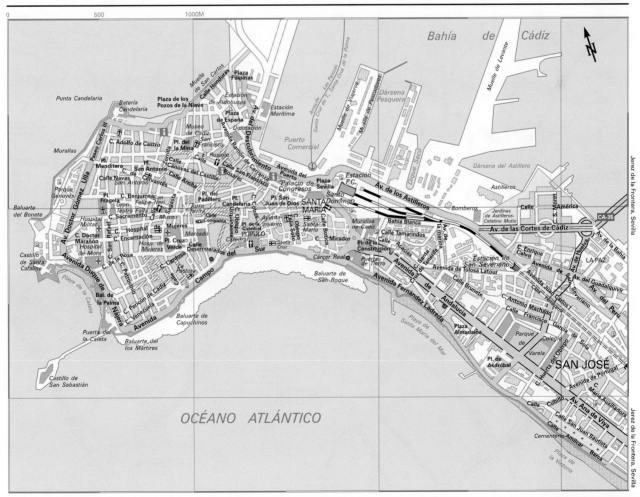

Ceuta

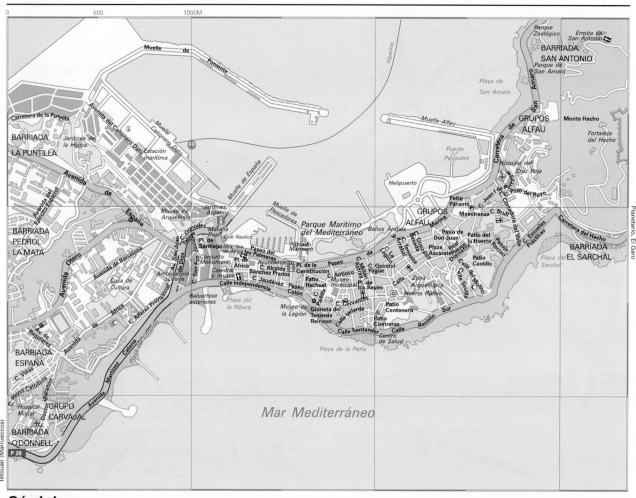

Córdoba

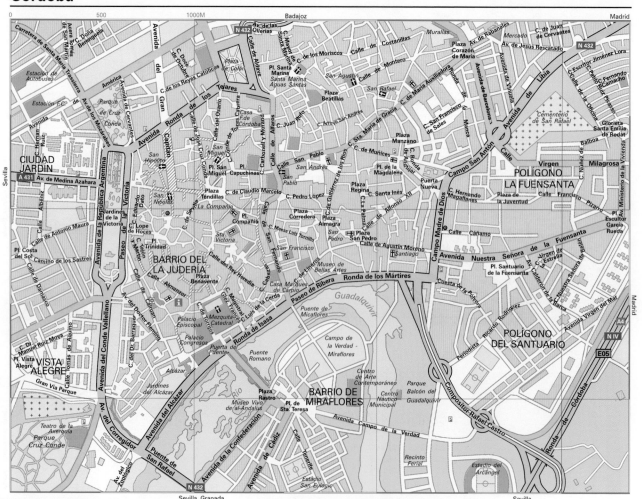

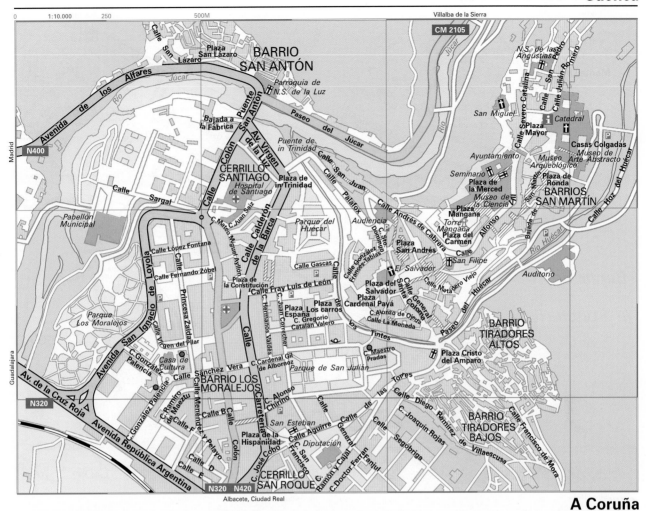

Cuenca map labels:
1:10.000
250 — 500M
Villalba de la Sierra
CM 2105
N.S. de las Angustias
N.S. de las Angustias
Calle San Lázaro
Plaza San Lázaro
BARRIO SAN ANTÓN
Calle San
Río Júcar
Avenida de los Alfares
Madrid N400
Parroquía de N.S. de la Luz
Puente San Antón
Bajada a la Fábrica
Paseo del Júcar
Av. Virgen de la Luz
Puente de in Trinidad
Calle San Juan
Calle San Pedro
Calle Severo Catalina
Calle Julián Romero
San Miguel
Plaza Mayor
Catedral
CERRILLO SANTIAGO
Hospital de Santiago
Plaza de in Trinidad
Calle Palafox
Colón
Calle Sargal
Calle
C. Mateo Miguel Ayllón
Calle Calderón de la Barca
Ayuntamiento
Museo Arqueológico
Casas Colgadas
Museo de Arte Abstracto
Parque del Huécar
Calle Andrés de Cabrera
Seminario
Plaza de Ronda
Calle Martín
Pabellón Municipal
Calle López Fontana
Plaza de la Merced
Museo de la Ciencia
BARRIOS SAN MARTÍN
Calle Fernando Zóbel
Calle Gascas
Audiencia
Calle Sto. Domingo
Plaza Mangana
Torre Mangana
Plaza del Carmen
Río Huécar
Calle Hoz del Huécar
Parque Los Moralejos
Av. San Ignacio de Loyola
Princesa Zaida
Plaza de la Constitución
Calle Fray Luis de León
C. Juan Correcher
C. Hermanos Valdés
Plaza San Andrés
C. González Francés-tablas
El Salvador
Calle San Filipe
Plaza del Salvador
Plaza Cardenal Payá
Calle General Santa Coloma
Calle Mota
otero Viejo
Auditorio
Calle Virgen del Pilar
Casa de Cultura
C. González Palencia
Sánchez Vera
Plaza España
Plaza Los carros
C. Gregorio Catalán Valero
C. Alonso de Ojeda
Calle La Moneda
Paseo del Huécar
BARRIO TIRADORES ALTOS
Guadalajara
N320
Av. de la Cruz Roja
C. Ramiro de Maeztu
Calle B
Menéndez y Pelayo
C. Ramiro
BARRIO LOS MORALEJOS
Calle Menéndez y Pelayo
C. Cardenal Gil de Albornoz
Parque de San Julián
los Tintes
Maestro Pradas
Plaza Cristo del Amparo
C. Alonso Chirino
Calle de las Torres
N320 Av. González Palencia
Calle C
Calle C
San Esteban
Calle Aguirre
Calle General
Calle Diego Ramírez de Villaescusa
BARRIO TIRADORES BAJOS
Calle Francisco de Mora
Avenida República Argentina
Plaza de la Hispanidad
C. José Cobo
FC San Francisco
Calle Diputación
C. Joaquín Rojas
Calle Segobriga
Calle D
Calle E
CERRILLO SAN ROQUE
C. Doctor Ferran Fanjul
Ramón y Cajal
N320 N420
N320 N420
Albacete, Ciudad Real

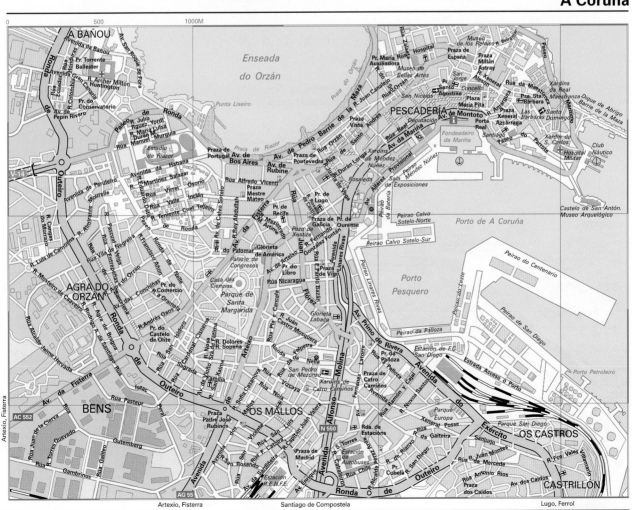

A Coruña map labels:
500 — 1000M
Enseada do Orzán
A BAÑOU
Avenida da Bañou
Pr. Torrente Ballester
R. Archer Milton Huntington
Ronda de Monelos
Av. San Roque de Fora
Museo de los Reloxes
Pr. María Ruaza
Praza de España
Praza Millán Astray
Paseo
Pr. María Ruaza
Hospital
Museo de Bellas Artes
R. Juan Canalejo
Rúa da Maestra
Xardins da Real
Maestranza Dique de Abrigo
San Jorge
San Nicolás
Rúa Orzán
Concello
Plaza María Pita
Santo Agostiño
Praza Santa Bárbara
Santa Domingo
R. Colombia
Av. de Pepín Rivero
Paseo de Ronda
Punta Liseiro
Praia do Orzán
PESCADERÍA
R. Juan Canalejo
Santiago
Porta Real
Av. de Montoto
Diputación
Fondeadeiro da Mariña
Barrie de la Maza
Praza Vista
Rúa Orzán
Santo André
Rúa Real
Praza Xeneral Azcárraga
Paseo do Parrote
Estadio de Riazor
Praza de Portugal
Praia de Riazor Av. de Bos Aires
Av. de Pedro Barrie de la Maza
Praza de Pontevedra
Av. de Rubine
Rúa da Mariña
Xardins de Méndez Núñez
Santiago
Xardín de S. Carlos
Club Náutico
Av. da Habana
Rúa
Rúa Durán Loriga
Peirao Provisional
Hospital Militar
Av. Martínez Salazar
Osorio
Rúa Juan Flórez
Sala de Exposicións
Castelo de San Antón Museo Arqueológico
R. Manuel Murguía
Praza Mestre Mateo
Pr. de Lugo
Peirao da Batería
Porto de A Coruña
R. Eduardo Dato
Rúa Valle Inclán
Pr. de Recife
Peirao Méndez Núñez
V-14 Outeiro
R. Teniente Chel. Tejeiro
Ronda de
Pr. de Galicia
Praza de Pr. de Ourense
R. Maxia Arume
Peirao Calvo Sotelo-Norte
R. Canosa rio Monrazo
Av. R. Rey Abdullah
Pazo de Xustiza
R. Fernando González Fontán
Peirao Calvo Sotelo-Sur
Porto Pesquero
R. Luís de Camoéns
Rúa Vila de Negreira
Glorieta do Patomar
Glorieta de América
Av. de Arteixo
Pr. do Libro
Praza Eloido Vigo
Peirao Linares Rivas
Peirao do Centenario
R. Francisco Añón
Palacio de Congresos
Rúa Nicaragua
Avenida Linares Rivas
Peirao de San Diego
R. Mosteiro de Caaveiro Rodrigo A. de Santiago
Casa das Ciencias
Praza Bazán
R. Andrés Gaos
Parque de Santa Margarida
Av. Primo de Rivera
AGRA DO ORZÁN
Pr. do Castelo de Olite
Glorieta Labaca
Florida
Peirao da Palloza
R. Alcalde Jaime Hervada
Pr. do Comercio
R. Nosa Sra. de Fátima
R. Juan Castro Mosquera
Carrola
Estación de F.C. San Diego
Estrada Acceso a Porto
Rúa da Cervantes
R. Dolores R. Sopena
San Pedro de Mezonzo
Molina
Pr. da Palloza
R. Juan Montes
Rúa Alcalde Juan Montes
BENS
AC 552
Familia Sagrada
Praza de Catro Camiños
Parque San Diego
OS CASTROS
Rúa Pasteur
Peral
Isaac
Mallos
Vizcaya
Praza de Catro Camiños
Avenida
Parque Europa Posse
R. Novoa Santos
R. de Rianxo
R. Fcor. Vales Villamarín
Av. da Cierva
Rúa Torres Quevedo
Rúa Galileo
Gutemberg
OS MALLOS
Nola
Nelle
R. da Gaiteira
Rúa Antonio Ríos
Rúa Gambrinus
Praza Padre José Rubinos
Rúa F. Cantoira
Rúa Vicente
San Pedro de Mezonzo
N550 Alfonso
Alfonso Molina
Santuirio
R. San Diego
Praza dos Caídos
CASTRILLON
AG 55
Praza de Madrid
Estación de Autobuses
Santander
Estación R.E.N.F.E.
Capitán Juan Varela
Ronda de Outeiro
R. San Rosendo
R. Cubela
Rúa Chile
Av. dos Caídos
Artexio, Fisterra
Santiago de Compostela
Lugo, Ferrol

Donostia-San Sebastián

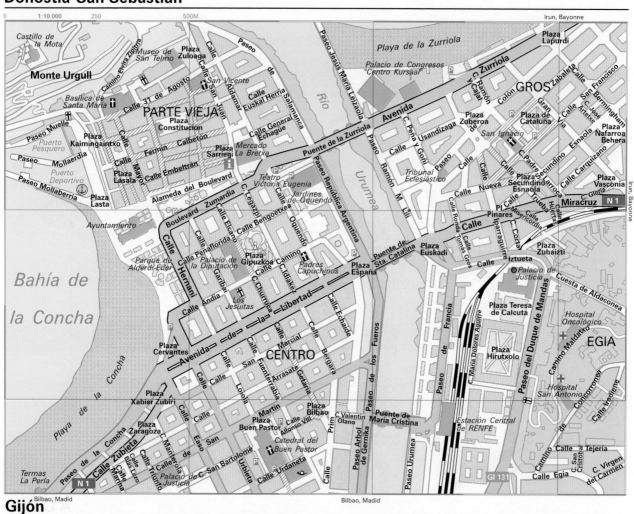

Gijón

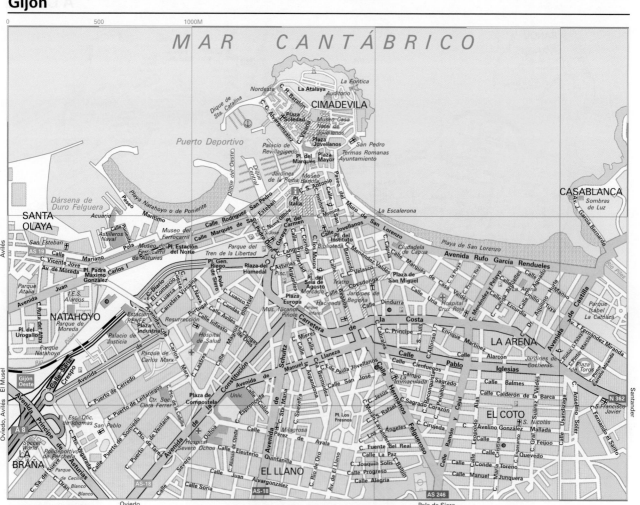

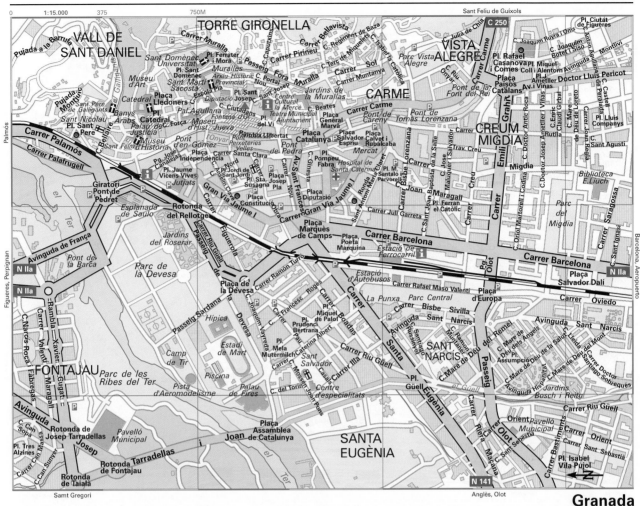

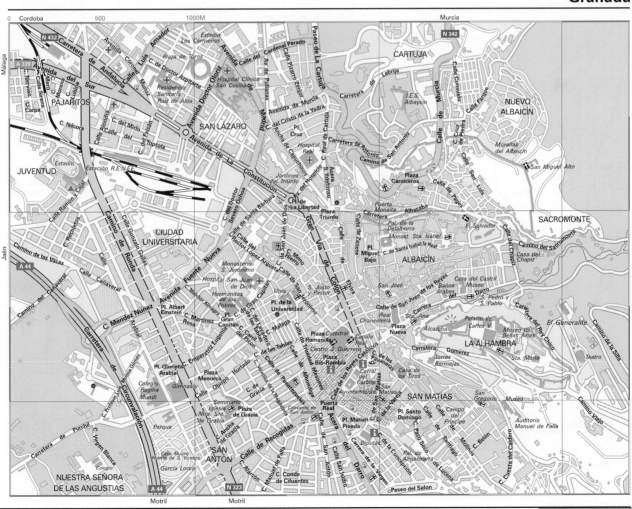

León

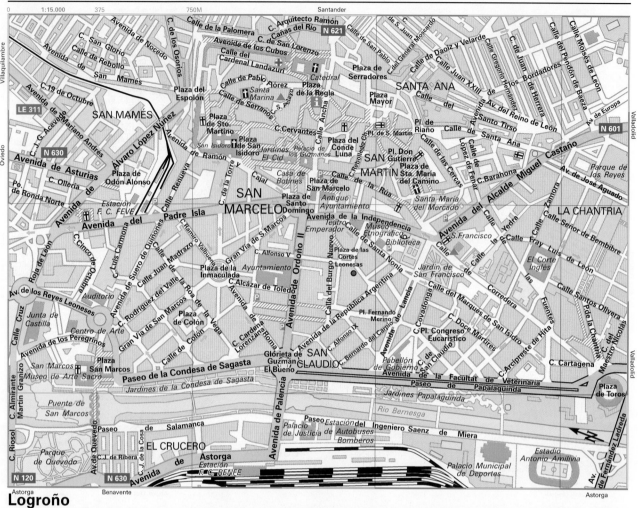

Logroño

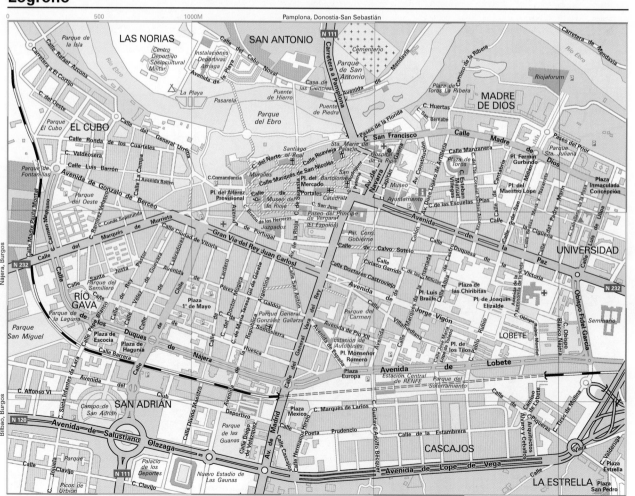

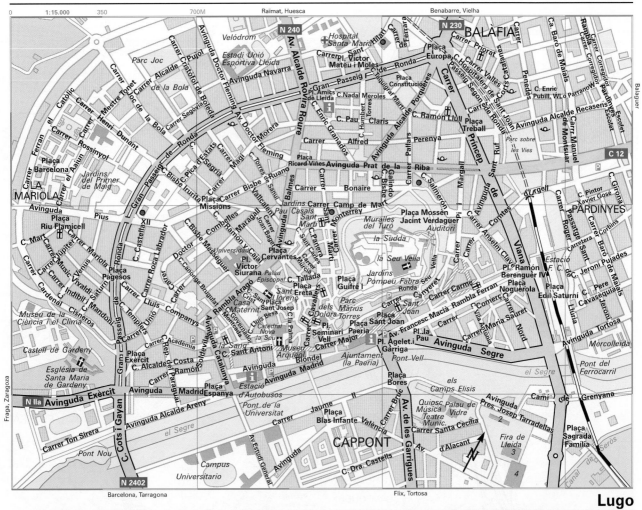

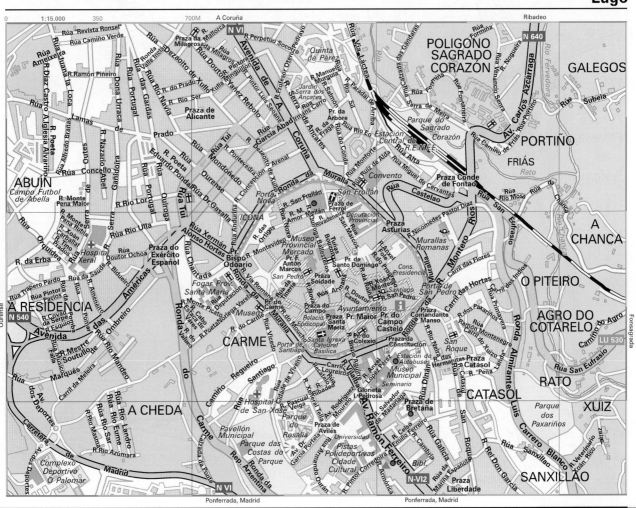

Lisboa

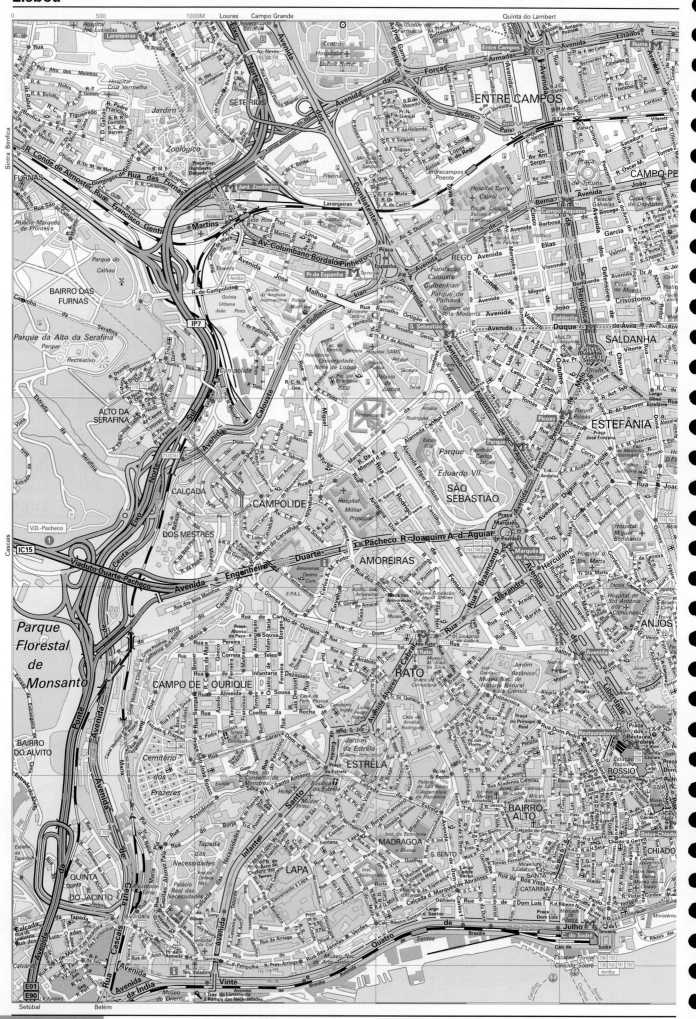

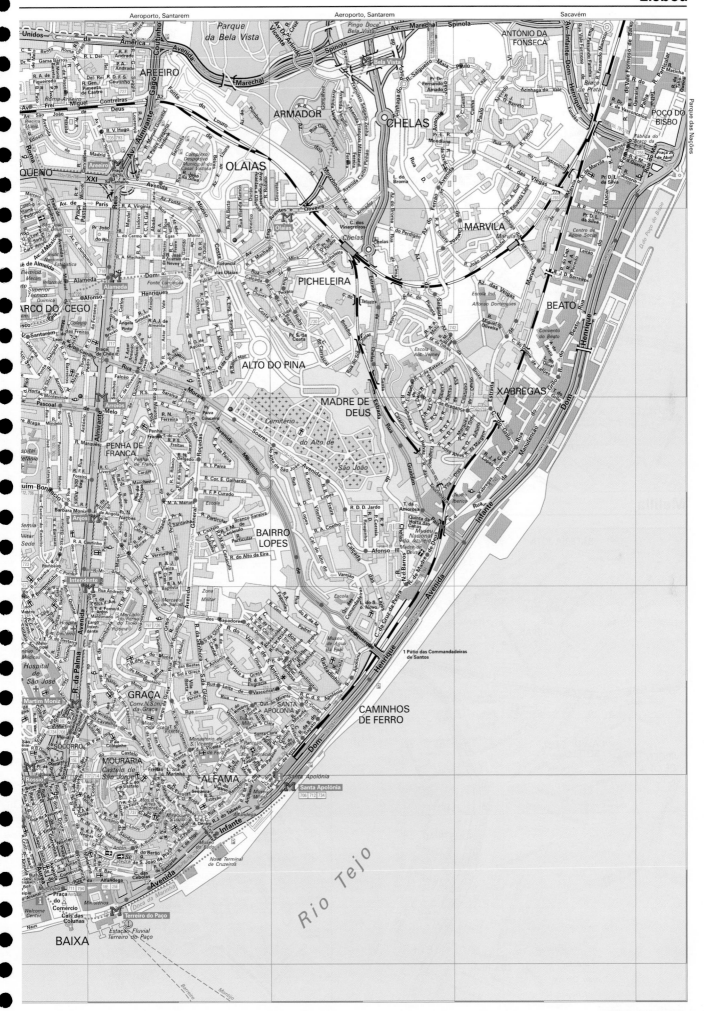

Málaga

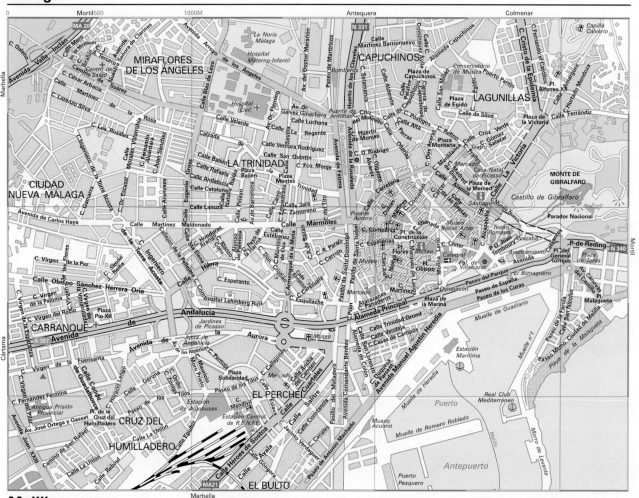

Melilla

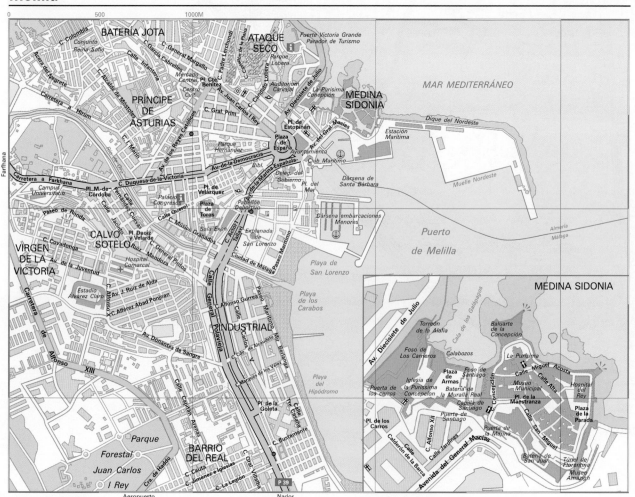

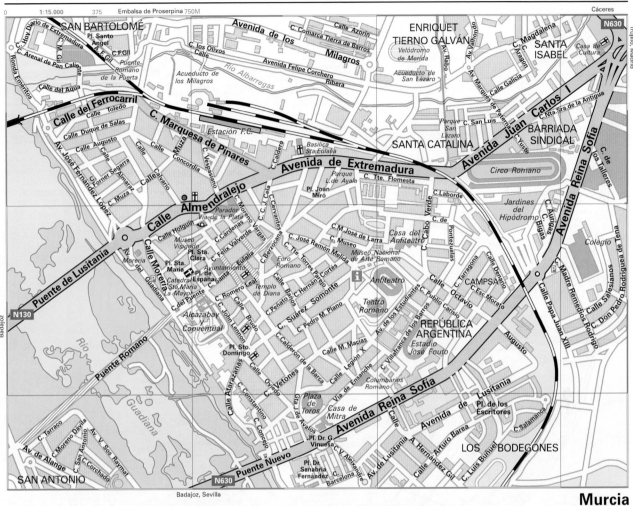

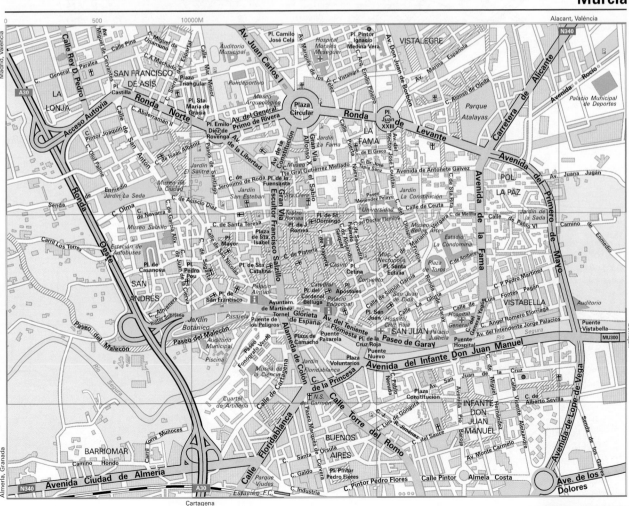

Madrid

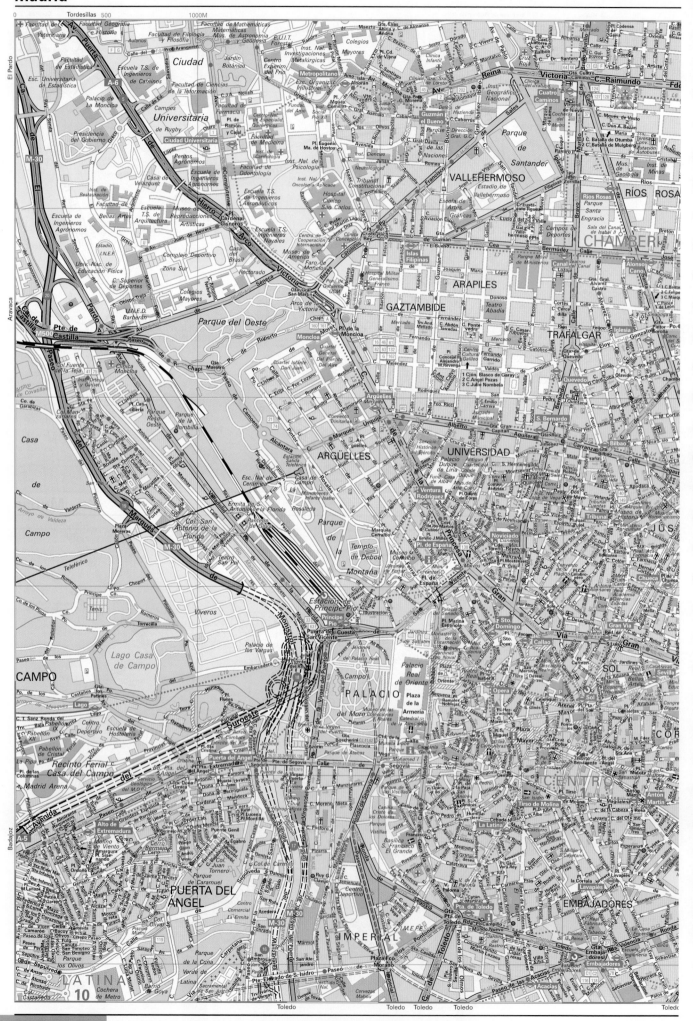

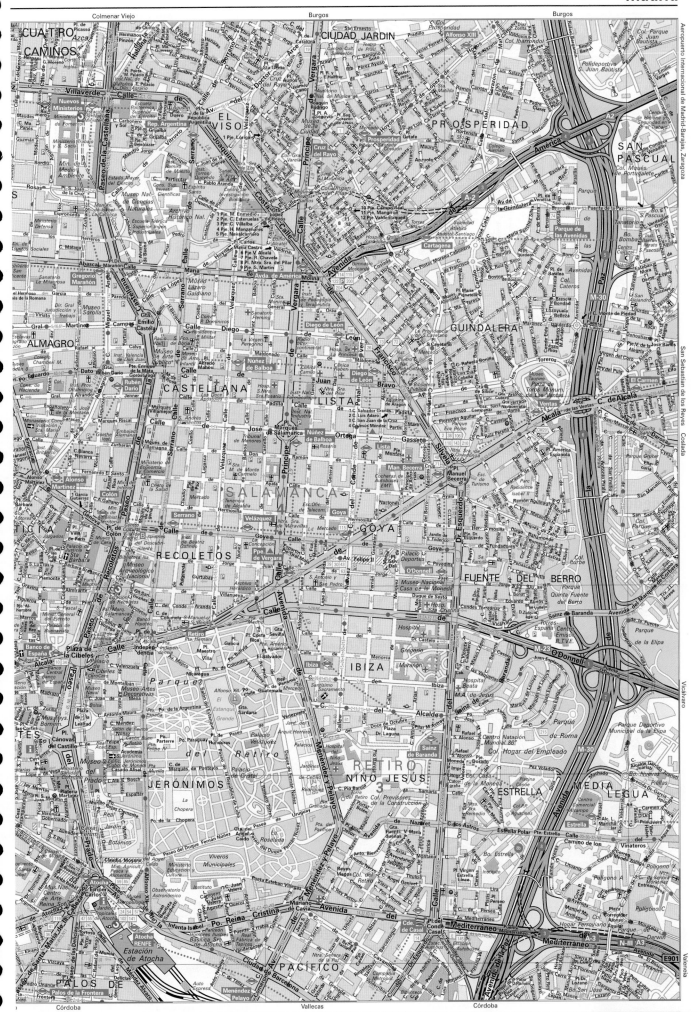

Ourense (Orense)

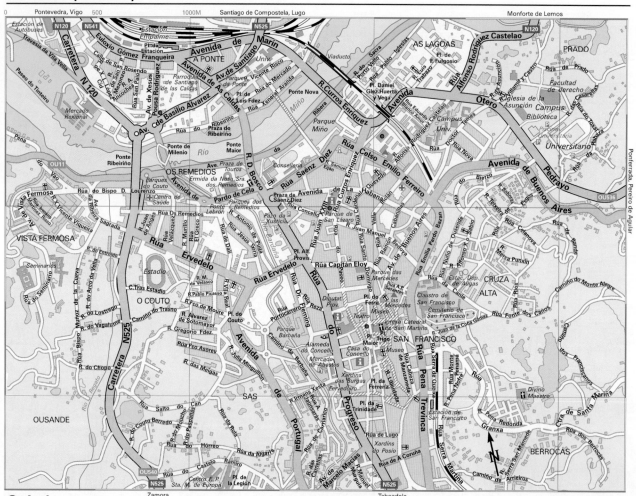

Oviedo

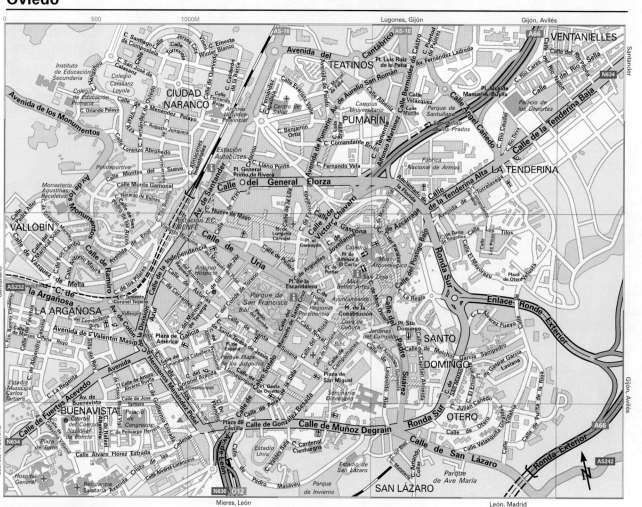

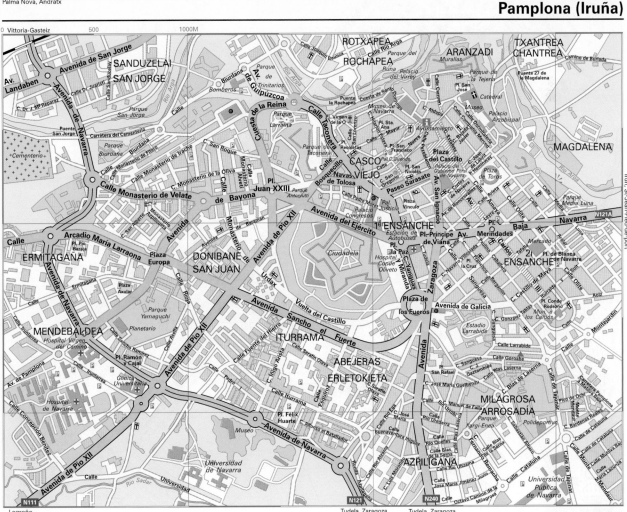

Las Palmas de Gran Canaria

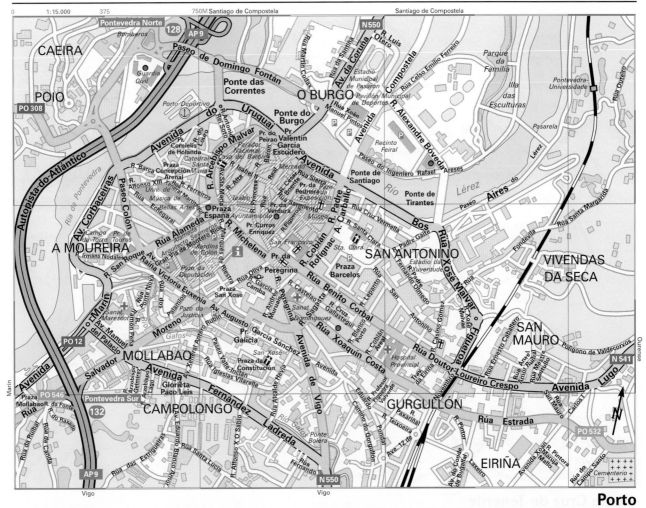

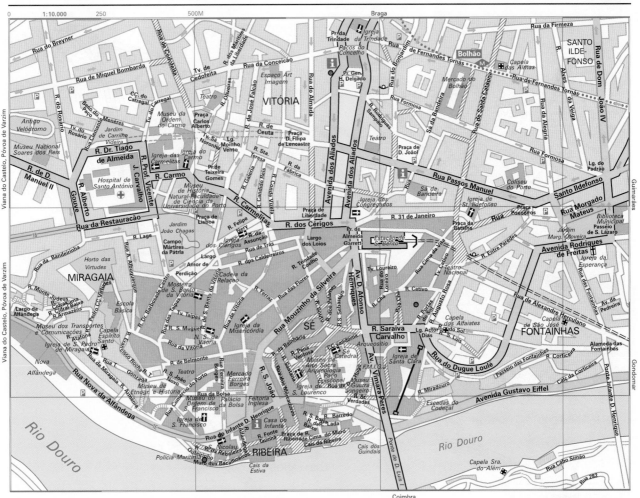

Salamanca

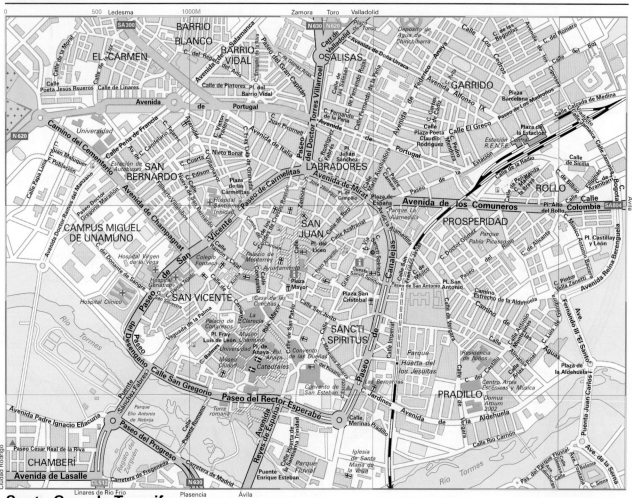

Santa Cruz de Tenerife

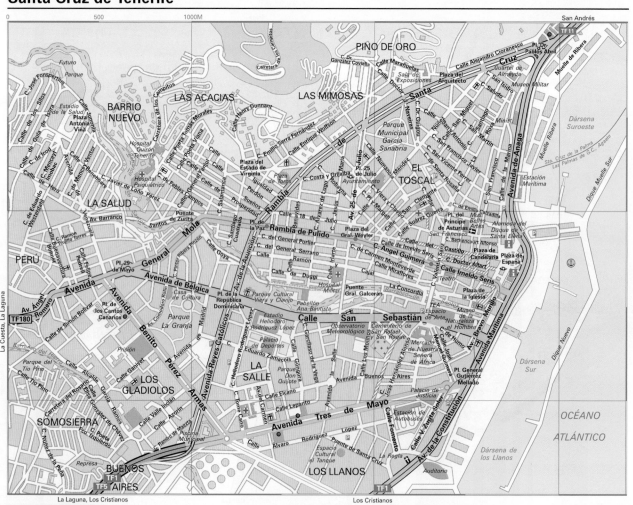

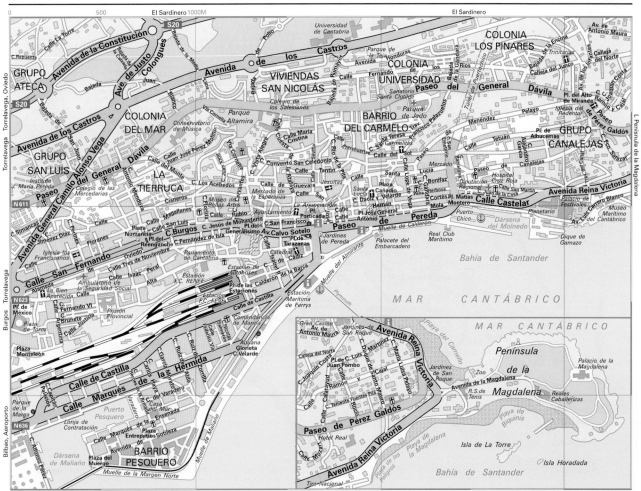

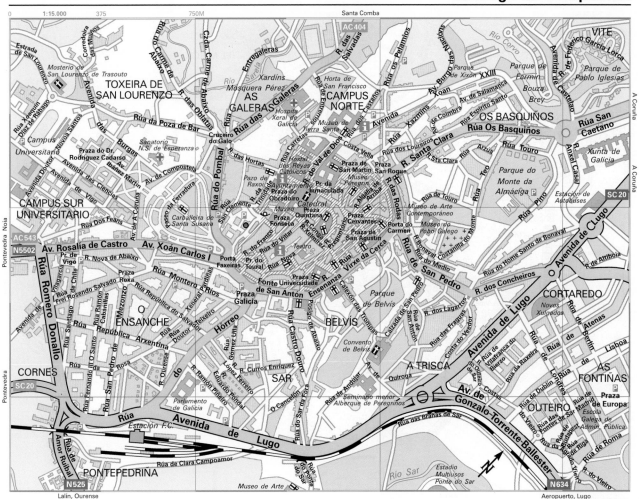

Segovia

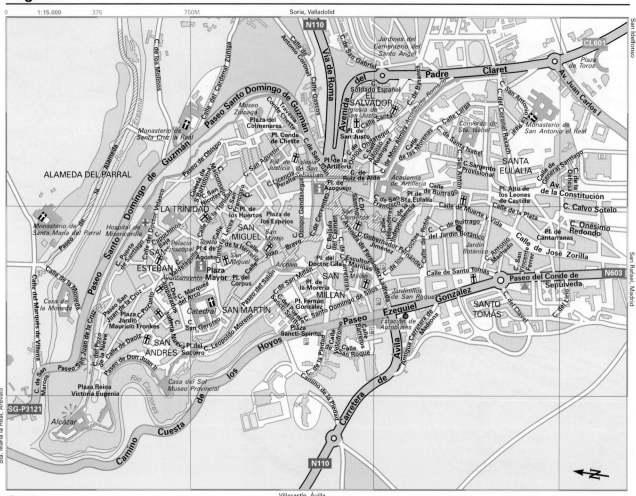

Soria

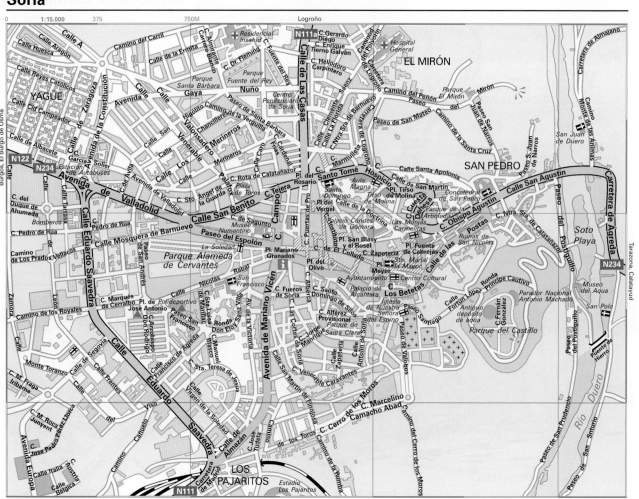

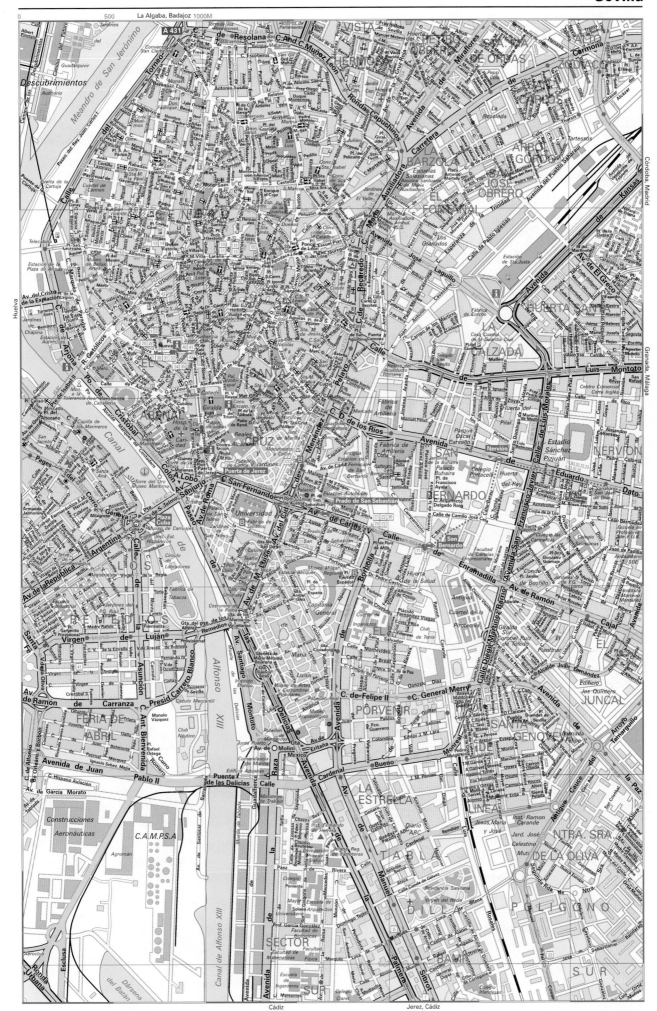

Tarragona

Teruel

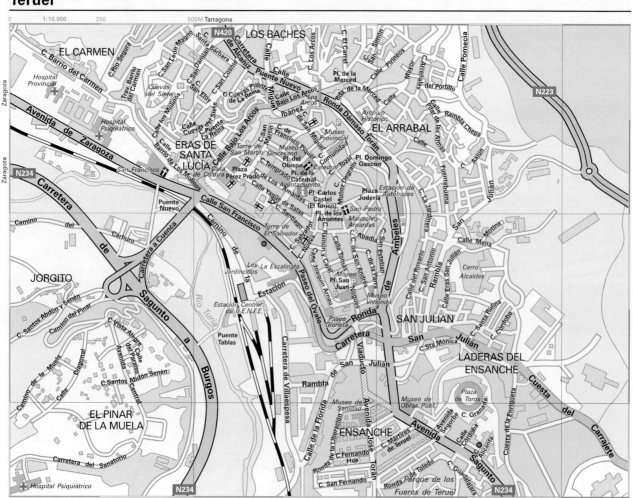

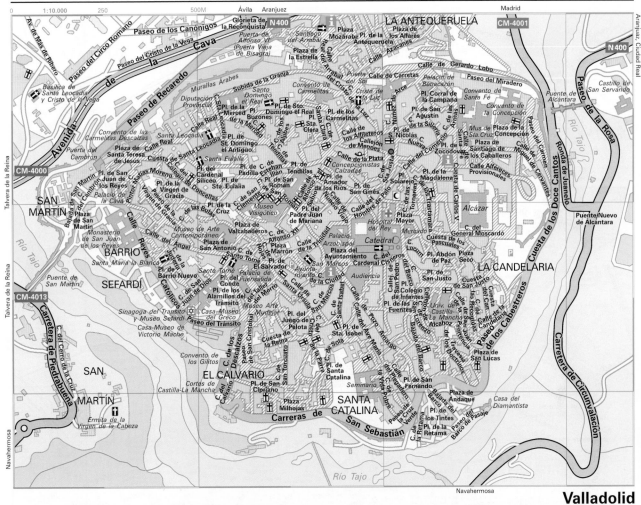

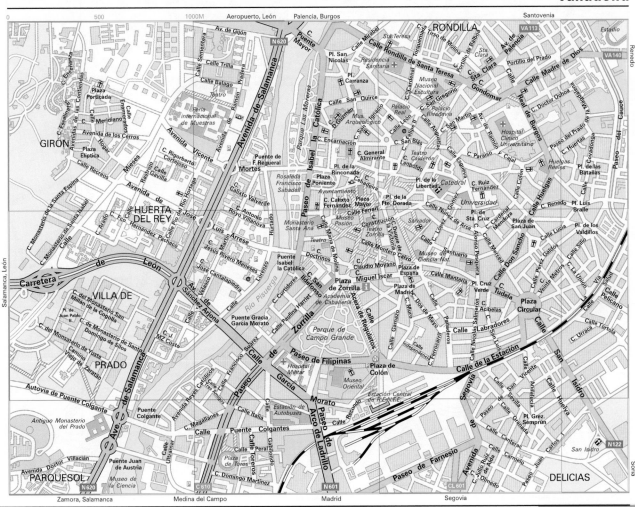

Valencia

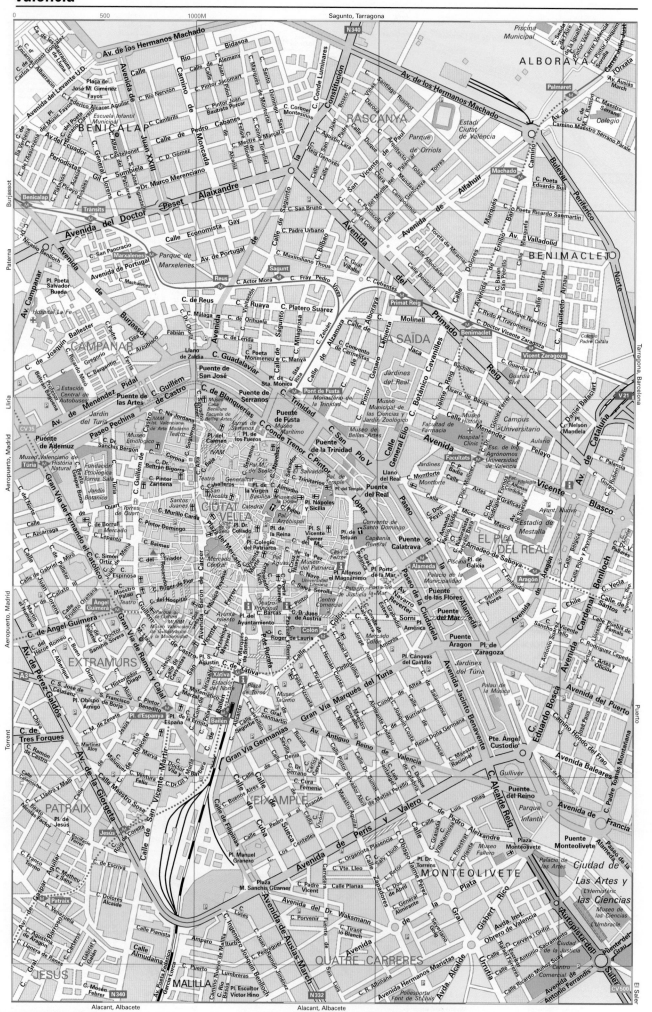

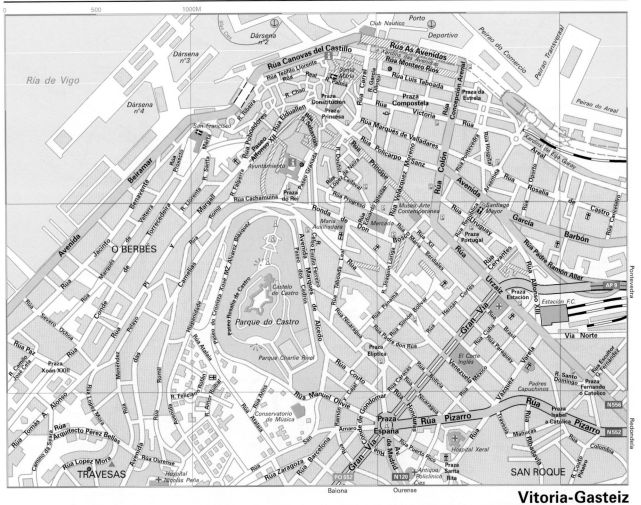

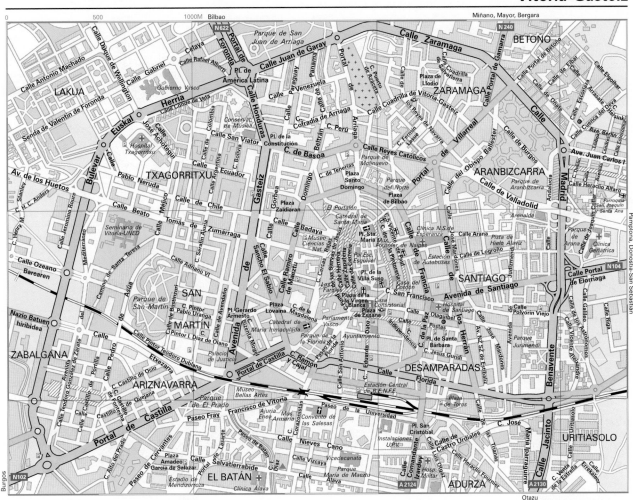

Zamora

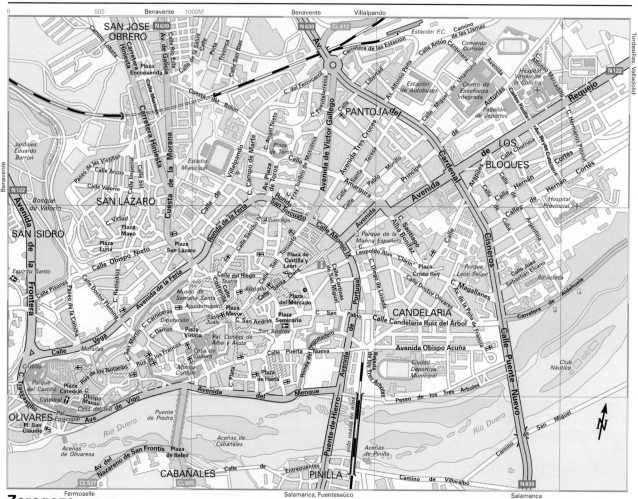

Zaragoza

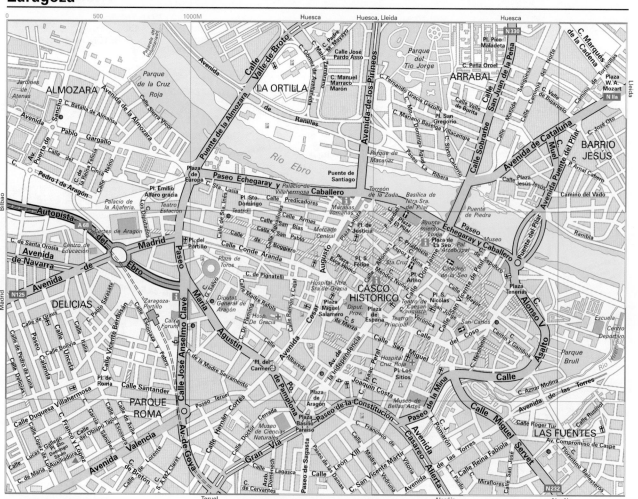

ESPAÑA

km/h				
	50	90	100	120
	50	90	100	120
	50	70	80	80 / 90
	50	80	90	100
	50	80	90	100
	50	70	80	90

 504 645 km²   46 300 000   Madrid 3 200 000   112   112   **SOS** 112

 SPA   +34   🕐 +1h Greenwich Mean Time (GMT)   ✓   ✓   ✗   0,5‰

 1 Euro (EUR) = 100 Cent   **i** Instituto de Turismo de España – Turespaña +34 91 3 43 35 00 www.tourspain.es   ✓   24h +34 900 11 22 22 RACE

PORTUGAL

km/h				
	50	90	100	120
	50	90	100	120
	50	70	80	100
	50	80	90	110
	50	80	90	90
	50	80	80	80

 92 345 km²   10 600 000   Lisboa 545 000   112   112   **SOS** 112

 POR   +351   🕐 Greenwich Mean Time (GMT)   ✓   ✓   ✓   ✗   0,5‰

 1 Euro (EUR) = 100 Cent   **i** Turismo de Portugal +351 211 14 02 00 www.turismodeportugal.pt   ✓   24h 707 509 510 ACP

233

OCÉANO ATLÁNTICO
F
AND
ANDORRA LA VELLA
P
E
MAR MEDITERRÁNEO
DZ
MA

	km/h				
		50	90	–	–
		50	90	–	–
		50	90	–	–
		50	80	–	–
		50	80	–	–
		50	70	–	–

468 km²   78 000   Andorra la Vella 22 000   110   116   SOS 118

CAT   +376   +1h Greenwich Mean Time (GMT)   ✗   ✗   ✗   0,5‰

1 Euro (EUR) = 100 Cent   **i** Ministeri de Turisme e Medi Ambient +376 87 57 02 www.visitandorra.com   ✓   24h +376 80 34 00 Automòbil Club d'Andorra

---

✈ | | Code | | |
|---|---|---|---|
| Ⓔ Aeropuerto de Alicante | ALC | www.aena.es | 142 Zc 119 |
| Ⓔ Aeropuerto de Almería | LEI | www.aena.es | 170 Xd 127 |
| Ⓔ Aeropuerto de Asturias | OVD | www.aena.es | 14 Tf 87 |
| Ⓔ Aeropuerto de Barcelona-El Prat | BCN | www.aena.es | 77 Ca 101 |
| Ⓔ Aeropuerto de Bilbao | BIO | www.aena.es | 19 Xa 89 |
| Ⓔ Aeropuerto de Fuerteventura | FUE | www.aena.es | 183 Ma 178 |
| Ⓔ Aeropuerto de Gerona | GRO | www.aena.es | 59 Ce 97 |
| Ⓔ Aeropuerto de Gran Canaria | LPA | www.aena.es | 184 Kd 181 |
| Ⓔ Aeropuerto de Ibiza San José | IBZ | www.aena.es | 109 Bc 115 |
| Ⓔ Aeropuerto de Jerez | JRZ | www.aena.es | 172 Tf 128 |
| Ⓔ Aeropuerto de Lanzarote – Arrecife | ACE | www.aena.es | 182 Mc 175 |
| Ⓔ Aeropuerto de Madrid – Barajas | MAD | www.aena.es | 86 Wc 106 |
| Ⓔ Aeropuerto de Málaga | AGP | www.aena.es | 175 Vd 128 |
| Ⓔ Aeropuerto de Menorca | MAH | www.aena.es | 77 Eb 109 |
| Ⓔ Aeropuerto de Murcia-San Javier | MJV | www.aena.es | 157 Zb 122 |
| Ⓔ Aeropuerto de Pamplona-Noáin | PNA | www.aena.es | 33 Yc 92 |
| Ⓔ Aeropuerto de Reus | REU | www.aena.es | 75 Ba 102 |
| Ⓔ Aeropuerto de Salamanca | SLM | www.aena.es | 65 Du 103 |
| Ⓔ Aeropuerto de San Sebastián | EAS | www.aena.es | 21 Yb 88 |
| Ⓔ Aeropuerto de Santa Cruz de La Palma | SPC | www.aena.es | 181 Hb 177 |
| Ⓔ Aeropuerto de Santander | SDR | www.aena.es | 18 Wb 88 |
| Ⓔ Aeropuerto de Santiago de Compostela | SCQ | www.aena.es | 13 Rd 91 |
| Ⓔ Aeropuerto de Sevilla | SVQ | www.aena.es | 149 Ua 124 |
| Ⓔ Aeropuerto de Son Sant Joan | PMI | www.aena.es | 110 Ce 111 |
| Ⓔ Aeropuerto de Tenerife Norte | TFN | www.aena.es | 181 Id 178 |
| Ⓔ Aeropuerto de Tenerife Sur Reina Sofía | TFS | www.aena.es | 180 Ic 180 |
| Ⓔ Aeropuerto de Valencia | VLC | www.aena.es | 126 Zd 112 |
| Ⓔ Aeropuerto de Zaragoza | ZAZ | www.aena.es | 53 Yf 99 |
| Ⓔ Aeropuerto Región de Murcia | RMU | www.airm.es | 157 Yf 122 |
| Ⓟ Aeroporto de Faro | FAO | www.ana.pt | 159 Sa 126 |
| Ⓟ Aeroporto Francisco Sá Carneiro – Porto | OPO | www.ana.pt | 60 Rb 101 |

✈ | | Code | | |
|---|---|---|---|
| Ⓟ Aeroporto Humberto Delgado Lisboa | LIS | www.ana.pt | 128 Qf 116 |
| Ⓟ Aeroporto da Madeira – Cristiano Ronaldo | FNC | www.anam.pt | 178 Kb 152 |
| Ⓟ Aeroporto João Paulo II – Ponta Delgada (Azores) | PDL | www.ana.pt | 177 Zb 122 |

✈ | | Code | | |
|---|---|---|---|
| Ⓔ Aeropuerto de Albacete | ABC | www.aena.es | 124 Ya 115 |
| Ⓔ Aeropuerto de Badajoz | BJZ | www.aena.es | 116 Tb 115 |
| Ⓔ Aeropuerto de Burgos | RGS | www.aena.es | 30 Wc 94 |
| Ⓔ Aeropuerto de Córdoba | LEB | www.aena.es | 150 Va 121 |
| Ⓔ Aeropuerto de El Hierro | VDE | www.aena.es | 180 Ha 182 |
| Ⓔ Aeropuerto de Granada – Jaén | GRX | www.granada.es | 168 Wb 125 |
| Ⓔ Aeropuerto de La Coruña | LCG | www.aena.es | 11 Rd 89 |
| Ⓔ Aeropuerto de Madrid | MCV | www.aena.es | 86 Wb 106 |
| Ⓔ Aeropuerto de Melilla | MLN | www.aena.es | 175 Xa 131 |
| Ⓔ Aeropuerto de Sabadell | QSA | www.aena.es | 77 Ca 99 |
| Ⓔ Aeropuerto de Valladolid | VLL | www.aena.es | 47 Va 98 |
| Ⓔ Aeropuerto de Vigo | VGO | www.aena.es | 41 Rc 95 |
| Ⓔ Aeropuerto de Vitoria | VIT | www.aena.es | 31 Xb 91 |
| Ⓔ Aeropuerto de Huesca | HSK | www.aena.es | 54 Zd 96 |
| Ⓔ Aeropuerto de La Gomera | GMZ | www.aena.es | 184 He 180 |
| Ⓔ Aeropuerto de León | LEN | www.aena.es | 27 Ub 93 |
| Ⓔ Aeropuerto de Lleida | ILD | www.aena.es | 55 Ad 98 |
| Ⓔ Aeropuerto de Logroño | XRY | www.aena.es | 32 Xe 94 |
| Ⓟ Aeródromo da Graciosa (Azores) | GRW | | 176 Wf 114 |
| Ⓟ Aeródromo de Espinho | | www.accv.pt | 60 Rc 103 |
| Ⓟ Aeródromo de São Jorge (Azores) | SJZ | www.ana.pt | 177 We 117 |
| Ⓟ Aeródromo do Corvo (Azores) | CVU | www.ana.pt | 176 Tf 111 |
| Ⓟ Aeródromo Municipal de Bragança | BGC | www.aerovip.pt | 44 Tb 97 |

✈

		Code		
Ⓟ	Aeródromo Municipal de Cascais		www.aerodromo-cascais.pt	128 Qd 116
Ⓟ	Aeródromo Municipal de Coimbra	CBP	www.aeroclube decoimbra.com	95 Rd 107
Ⓟ	Aeroporto da Horta (Azores)	HOR	www.horta-hor.airports-guides.com	176 Wb 117
Ⓟ	Aeroporto das Flores (Azores)	FLW	www.ana.pt	176 Tf 112
Ⓟ	Aeroporto de Santa Maria (Azores)	SMA	www.ana.pt	177 Ze 127
Ⓟ	Aeroporto do Pico (Azores)	PIX	www.ana.pt	176 Wd 117
Ⓟ	Aeroporto do Porto Santo (Porto Santo)	PXO	www.anam.pt	179 Id 150

◉ UNESCO World Heritage

ⒶⓃⒹ	Madriu-Perafita-Claror, Vall del	2004	38 Bd 94
Ⓔ	A Coruña (Tower of Hercules)	2009	11 Rd 88
Ⓔ	Alcalá de Henares (University and Historic Precinct)	1998	86 Wd 106
Ⓔ	Almadén (Heritage of Mercury)	2012	119 Va 116
Ⓔ	Altamira, Cuevas de	1985	17 Vf 88
Ⓔ	Aranjuez, Cultural Landscape	2001	86 Wc 108
Ⓔ	Atapuerca, Cueva de	2000	30 Wc 94
Ⓔ	Ávila	1985	84 Vb 104
Ⓔ	Baeza	2003	153 Wd 121
Ⓔ	Barcelona (Palau de la Música Catalana and Hospital de Sant Pau, Sagrada Familia)	1997	77 CA 100
Ⓔ	Burgos Cathedral	1984	30 Wb 94
Ⓔ	Cáceres (Old Town)	1986	117 Td 112
Ⓔ	Calatayud (Mudejar Architecture of Aragon)	1986	71 Yc 100
Ⓔ	Córdoba (Historic Centre)	1984	150 Vb 121
Ⓔ	Cuenca (Historic Walled Town)	1996	105 Xf 108
Ⓔ	Doñana National Park	1994	164 Td 126
Ⓔ	Elx / Elche, Palmeral	2000	142 Zb 119
Ⓔ	Garajonay National Park	1986	184 He 180
Ⓔ	Granada, Alhambra, Generalife and Albayzín	1984	168 Wc 125
Ⓔ	Guadalupe (Royal Monastery of Santa María)	1993	118 Ue 112
Ⓔ	Ibiza, Biodiversity and Culture = Eivissa	1999	109 Bc 115
Ⓔ	Las Médulas	1997	25 Tb 94
Ⓔ	Lugo (Roman Walls)	2000	12 Sc 90
Ⓔ	Madrid, El Escorial	1984	86 Vf 105
Ⓔ	Mérida, Archaeological Ensemble	1993	117 Td 115
Ⓔ	Monte Perdido / Mont Perdu	1997	35 Aa 92
Ⓔ	Oviedo (Monuments of Oviedo and the Kingdom of the Asturias)	1985	15 Ua 88
Ⓔ	Poblet, Reial Monestir de	1991	75 Ba 100
Ⓔ	Rock Art of the Mediterranean Basin on the Iberian Peninsula = Arte Rupestre	1998	
Ⓔ	Salamanca (Old City)	1988	65 Uc 103
Ⓔ	San Cristóbal de La Laguna	1999	181 le 178
Ⓔ	San Millán Yuso and Suso Monasteries	1997	31 Xa 95
Ⓔ	Santiago de Compostela (Old Town)	1985	23 Rc 91
Ⓔ	Santiago de Compostela (Route of) = Camino de Santiago	1993	
Ⓔ	Segovia (Old Town, Aqueduct)	1985	67 Vf 103
Ⓔ	Serra de Tramuntana	2011	110 Cc 111-Cf 109
Ⓔ	Sevilla, Cathedral, Alcázar and Archivo de Indias	1987	163 Ua 124
Ⓔ	Tarragona (Archaeological Ensemble of Tárraco)	2000	75 Bb 102
Ⓔ	Teide National Park	2007	180 Ic 179
Ⓔ	Toledo (Historic City)	1986	102 Vf 109
Ⓔ	Úbeda	2003	153 Wd 120
Ⓔ	València, La Lonja de la Seda	1996	127 Zd 112
Ⓔ	Vall de Boí (Catalan Romanesque Churches)	2000	37 Ae 93
Ⓔ	Vizcaya Bridge = Puente de Vizcaya	2006	19 Wf 89
Ⓟ	Alcobaça, Mosteiro de Santa Maria	1989	94 Ra 111
Ⓟ	Alto Douro Wine Region = Região do Vinho do Alto Douro	2001	61 Sb 102
Ⓟ	Batalha, Mosteiro de Santa Maria da Vitória	1983	94 Rb 111
Ⓟ	Coimbra, Universidade	2013	78 Rd 107
Ⓟ	Convento de Cristo (Tomar)	1983	95 Rd 111
Ⓟ	Elvas	2012	115 Sf 115
Ⓟ	Évora	1986	130 Sa 117
Ⓟ	Guimarães	2001	60 Re 100
Ⓟ	Lisboa, Mosteiro dos Jerónimos etc.	1983	128 Qf 116

◉ UNESCO World Heritage

Ⓟ	Porto	1996	60 Rb 102
Ⓟ	Sintra (Kultur Landscape)	1995	112 Qd 116
Ⓟ	Vale do Côa	1998	62 Sf 102

🌳

		km²		
Ⓔ	Parque Nacional Caldera de Taburiente	46,9	www.gobiernode canarias.org/parques nacionalesdecanarias/de	181 Ha 176
Ⓔ	Parque Nacional d'Aigüestortes i Estany de Sant Maurici	141,19	www.aiguestortes.info	37 Af 93
Ⓔ	Parque Nacional de Cabañeros	389,96	www.visitacabaneros.es	120 Vc 112
Ⓔ	Parque Nacional de Doñana	542,52	www.donana reservas.com	164 Td 126
Ⓔ	Parque Nacional de Garajonay	39,86	www.gobiernode canarias.org/parques nacionalesdecanarias/de	184 He 180
Ⓔ	Parque Nacional de la Sierra de Guadarrama	339,6	www.parquenacional sierraguadarrama.es	86 Wa 104
Ⓔ	Parque Nacional de l'Archipiélago de Cabrera	100,2	www.mapama.gob.es/es/ red-parques-nacionales/ nuestros-parques	110 Cf 13
Ⓔ	Parque Nacional de las Islas Atlánticas de Galicia	83,33	www.parquenacional illasatlanticas.com	22 Ra 94
Ⓔ	Parque Nacional de los Picos de Europa	646,6	www.parquenacional picoseuropa.es	16 Uf 89
Ⓔ	Parque Nacional de Monfragüe	178,62	www.parque demonfrague.com	99 Tf 109
Ⓔ	Parque Nacional de Ordesa y Monte Perdido	155,08	www.ordesa.net	35 Zf 92
Ⓔ	Parque Nacional de Sierra Nevada	862,08	www.mapama.gob.es/es/ red-parques-nacionales/ nuestros-parques	169 Wd 126
Ⓔ	Parque Nacional de Tablas de Daimiel	19,28	www.lastablasde daimiel.com	121 Wb 113
Ⓔ	Parque Nacional de Teide	189,9	www.gobiernode canarias.org/parques nacionalesdecanarias/de	180 Ic 179
Ⓔ	Parque Nacional Timanfaya	51,07	www.gobiernode canarias.org/parques nacionalesdecanarias/de	182 Mb 174
Ⓟ	Parque Nacional da Peneda-Gerês	702,9	www.icnf.pt	42 Re 97

🎡

Ⓔ	Aqualand Maspalomas	35100	Maspalomas	www.aqualand.es/ grancanaria	184 Kc 182
Ⓔ	Aquapark Cerceda	15185	Cerceda	www.cerceda.es	11 Rd 89
Ⓔ	Fort Bravo	04200	Tabernas	www.fortbravooficial.com	170 Xd 126
Ⓔ	Gnomo Park	17310	Lloret de Mar	www.gnomo-park.com	59 Ce 98
Ⓔ	Hidropark	07400	Puerto Alcudia	www.hidropark alcudia.com	111 Da 109
Ⓔ	Holiday World Maspalomas	35100	Maspalomas	www.holidayworld maspalomas.com	184 Kc 182
Ⓔ	Illa Fantasia	08339	Vilassar de Dalt	www.illafantasia.com	77 Cc 99
Ⓔ	Isla Mágica	41092	Sevilla	www.islamagica.es	164 Tf 124
Ⓔ	Jungle Park	38640	Las Águilas del Teide	www.aguilasjungle park.com	180 Ib 180
Ⓔ	Palmitos Park	35109	Maspalomas	www.palmitospark.es	184 Kc 182
Ⓔ	Parc d'atraccions del Tibidabo	08035	Barcelona	www.tibidabo.cat	77 Ca 100
Ⓔ	Parque Acuático Mijas	29640	Mijas	www.aquamijas.com	175 Vc 129
Ⓔ	Parque de Atracciones de Madrid	28011	Madrid	www.parquede atracciones.es	86 Wb 106
Ⓔ	Parque de Atracciones de Zaragoza	50007	Zaragoza	www.atraczara.com	53 Za 99
Ⓔ	Parque de Atracciones del Monte Igueldo	20008	San Sebastián	www.monteigueldo.es	21 Ya 89
Ⓔ	Parque Temático del Mudéjar de Castilla y León	47410	Olmedo	www.olmedo.es/ pasionmudejar	66 Va 101
Ⓔ	Parque Temático Dinópolis	44002	Teruel	www.dinopolis.com	90 Yf 106
Ⓔ	Parque Warner Madrid	28330	San Martín de la Vega	www.parquewarner.com	86 Wc 107
Ⓔ	Pola Park	03130	Santa Pola	www.polapark.com	142 Zd 119
Ⓔ	PortAventura	43840	Vila-seca	www.portaventura.es	75 Ba 102
Ⓔ	Rancho Texas Park Lanzarote	35510	Puerto del Carmen	www.ranchotexas lanzarote.com	182 Mc 175

Ⓔ Senda Viva	31513	Arguedas	www.sendaviva.com	52	Yc 95
Ⓔ Siam Park	38660	Costa Adeje	www.siampark.net	180	Ib 180
Ⓔ Sioux City Western Theme Park	35107	San Bartolomé de Tirajana	www.spain-grancanaria.com	184	Kc 182
Ⓔ Terra Mitica	03502	Benidorm	www.terramiticapark.com	143	Zf 117
Ⓔ Tivoli World	29631	Benalmádena	www.tivoli.es	175	Vc 129
Ⓔ Western Park Magaluf	07182	Magaluf	www.western-park.com	110	Cd 111
Ⓟ Aqualand Algarve – The Big One	8365-908	Alcantarilha	www.aqualand.pt	159	Rd 126
Ⓟ Aquashow Park	8125-303	Quarteira	www.aquashowpark hotel.com	159	Rf 126
Ⓟ Badoca Safari Park	7501-909	Vila Nova de Stº André	www.badoca.com	144	Rb 120
Ⓟ Jamor Adventure Park	1495-751	Cruz Quebrada	www.adventurepark.pt	128	Qe 116
Ⓟ Magikland	4560-221	Penafiel	www.magikland.pt	60	Re 101
Ⓟ NaturWaterPark	5000-037	Vila Real	www.naturwaterpark.pt	61	Sc 101
Ⓟ Parque aquático Norpark	2450-065	Nazaré	www.norpark.com	94	Qf 111
Ⓟ Parque aquático Scorpio	4835-235	Guimarães	www.ezportugal.com/ waterparks-portugal	60	Re 100
Ⓟ Pena Aventura	4870-110	Ribeira de Pena	www.penaaventura.com.pt	61	Sb 99
Ⓟ Portugal dos Pequenitos	3040-256	Coimbra	www.portugaldospe quenitos.pt	78	Rd 107
Ⓟ Slide & Splash	8401-901	Lagoa	www.slidesplash.com	158	Rd 126
Ⓟ Visionarium	4520-153	Santa Maria da Feira	www.visionarium.pt	60	Rc 103
Ⓟ Zoomarine Albufeira	8200-864	Albufeira	www.zoomarine.pt	159	Re 126

①	②	③	④	⑤
28001*	Madrid	M	86	Wb 106
3800-000*	Aveiro	AV	78	Rc 105
AD500	Andorra La Vella	▫ AND	38	Bd 93
GI	Gibraltar	▫ GBZ	174	Du 132

	①	*
Ⓔ (Cast.)	Código postal	Código postal más bajo en lugares con varios códigos postales
Ⓔ (Cata.)	Codi postal	Codi postal més baix en localitats amb diversos codis postals
Ⓔ (Eusk.)	Posta-kodea	Posta-kode bajuena posta-kode ugariko lekuetan
Ⓔ (Gale.)	Código postal	Código postal menor nos lugares con mais dun código postal
Ⓟ	Código postal	Código postal menor em caso de cidades com vários códigos postais
Ⓓ	Postleitzahl	Niedrigste Postleitzahl bei Orten mit mehreren Postleitzahlen
ⒼⒷ	Postal code	Lowest postcode number for places having several postcodes
Ⓘ	Codice postale	Codice di avviamento postale riferito a città comprendenti più codici di avviamento postale
Ⓕ	Code postal	Code postal le plus bas pour les localités à plusieurs codes posteaux
ⓃⓁ	Postcode	Laagste postcode bij gemeenten met meerdere postcodes
ⓅⓁ	Kod pocztowy	Najniższy kod pocztowy w przypadku miejscowości z wieloma kodami pocztowymi
ⒸⓏ	Poštovní směrovací číslo	Nejnižší poštovní směrovací číslo v městech s vicenásobnými poštovními směrovacími čísly
ⓈⓀ	Poštovné smerovacie číslo	Najmenšie poštové smerovacie číslo v miestach s viacerými poštovými smerovacími číslami
ⒹⓀ	Postnummer	Laveste postnummer ved byer med flere postnumre
ⒽⓇ	Poštanski broj	Najniži poštanski broj u mjestima sa više poštanskih brojeva

	②	③	④	⑤
Ⓔ (Cast.)	Nombre	Provincia/Distrito	Número de página	Coordenadas de localización
Ⓔ (Cata.)	Nom	Província/Districte	Nombre de página	Coordinada de localització
Ⓔ (Eusk.)	Izen	Probintzia/Barruti	Orri zenbakia	Bilaketa eremua sartu
Ⓔ (Gale.)	Nome	Provincia/Distrito	Número de páxina	Rueiro
Ⓟ	Nome	Provincia/Distrito	Número da página	Coordenadas de localização
Ⓓ	Name	Provinz/Distrikt	Seitenzahl	Suchfeldangabe
ⒼⒷ	Name	Province/District	Page number	Grid reference
Ⓘ	Nome	Province/Distretto	Numero di pagina	Riquadro nel quale si trova il nome
Ⓕ	Nom	Province/District	Numéro de page	Coordonnées
ⓃⓁ	Naam	Provincie/District	Paginanummer	Zoekveld-gegevens
ⓅⓁ	Nazwa	Prowincja/Dystrykt	Numer strony	Współrzędne skorowidzowe
ⒸⓏ	Název	Provincie/Okres	Číslo strany	Údaje hledacího čtverce
ⓈⓀ	Názov	Provincie/Okres	Číslo strany	Udanie hľadacieho štvorca
ⒹⓀ	Navn	Provins/Distrikt	Sidetal	Kvadratangivelse
ⒽⓇ	Ime	Pokrajina/Kotar	Broj stranica	Koordinatna podjela

Ⓔ (Cast.) = Castellano   Ⓔ (Cata.) = Català   Ⓔ (Eusk.) = Euskera   Ⓔ (Gale.) = Galego

Ⓔ A–B–C ...
A – B – C – D – E – F – G – H – I – J – K – L – M – N – Ñ – O – P – Q – R – S – T – U – V – W – X – Y – Z

Ⓟ A–B–C ...
A – B – C – D – E – F – G – H – I – J – L – M – N – O – P – Q – R – S – T – U – V – X – Z

A	Alicante/Alacant	GI	Girona	RI	La Rioja
AB	Albacete	GR	Granada	SA	Salamanca
AL	Almería	GU	Guadalajara	SE	Sevilla
AS	Asturias	H	Huelva	SG	Segovia
AV	Ávila	HS	Huesca	SO	Soria
B	Barcelona	IB	Illes Balears/	SS	Guipúzcoa/Gipuzkoa
BA	Badajoz		Islas Baleares	T	Tarragona
BI	Bizkaia/Vizkaya	J	Jaén	TE	Teruel
BU	Burgos	L	Lleida	TF	Santa Cruz de Tenerife
C	A Coruña	LE	León	TO	Toledo
CA	Cádiz	LU	Lugo	V	Valencia/València
CB	Cantabria	MA	Málaga	VA	Valladolid
CC	Cáceres	MC	Murcia	VI	Alava
CE	Ceuta	MD	Madrid	Z	Zaragoza
CO	Córdoba	ML	Melilla	ZA	Zamora
CR	Ciudad Real	NC	Navarra		
CS	Castellón/Castelló	OR	Ourense	◻	
CU	Cuenca	P	Palencia	AND	Andorra
GC	Las Palmas	PO	Pontevedra	GBZ	Gibraltar

A

44155 Ababuj TE 91 Zb 105
15563 Abade C 11 Rf 87
36589 Abades PO 23 Re 92
40141 Abades SG 67 Ve 103
10748 Abadía CC 82 Ua 107
27730 Abadin LU 12 Sc 88
31280 Abáigar NC 32 Xf 93
27765 Abaira LU 13 Se 88
09141 Abajas BU 30 Wc 93
21760 Abalario, El H 162 Tb 126
26339 Ábalos RI 31 Xb 93
20269 Abaltzisketa SS 20 Xf 90
19432 Abánades GU 69 Xd 103
42368 Abanco SO 69 Xa 100
33579 Abandames AS 17 Vc 89
30640 Abanilla MC 141 Yf 119
39549 Abanillas CB 17 Vd 88
24397 Abano LE 26 Tf 93
15938 Abanqueiro C 22 Ra 93
50375 Abanto Z 71 Yb 102
48500* Abanto y Ciérvana BI
 19 Wf 89
48500* Abanto-Zierbena BI 19 Wf 89
33994 Abantro AS 15 Ud 89
39549 Abaño CB 17 Vd 88
30550 Abarán MC 141 Yd 119
34338 Abarca P 47 Va 96
31178 Abárzuza NC 32 Xf 92
34307 Abastas P 47 Vb 95
34307 Abastillas P 28 Vb 95
31692 Abaurrea Alta NC 34 Ye 91
31692 Abaurrea Baja NC 34 Ye 91
32695 Abavides OR 43 Sc 96
22713 Abay HU 34 Zc 93
03517 Abdet A 143 Ze 116
01013 Abechuco VI 31 Xb 91
01449 Abecia VI 19 Xa 91
32615 Abedes OR 43 Sd 97
33844 Abedul AS 14 Te 89
15318 Abegondo C 11 Re 89
42146 Abejar SO 50 Xb 98
06475 Abejarrones de Arriba y de
 Abajo BA 133 Ua 116
49591 Abejera ZA 45 Tf 98
02439 Abejuela AB 140 Xf 118
04691 Abejuela AL 155 Ya 123
44422 Abejuela TE 107 Za 109
32679 Abeledo A OR 43 Sb 95
32690 Abeledo OR 42 Sb 95
36518 Abeledo PO 23 Rf 93
32790 Abeledos OR 24 Sd 95
15873 Abelenda C 11 Rc 90
32520 Abelenda OR 23 Re 94
32520 Abelenda OR 23 Re 94
24145 Abelgas de Luna LE 26 Ua 91
17869 Abella GI 39 Cb 95
22427 Abella HU 36 Ad 94
15685 Abellá C 11 Re 90
08592 Abella, L' B 58 Cb 98
22622 Abellada HU 35 Ze 94
25556 Abella d'Adons L 37 Ae 94
25651 Abella de la Conca L 56 Ba 96
15290 Abelleira C 22 Qf 92
15258 Abelleiras C 10 Ra 91

49254 Abelón ZA 64 Tf 100
22620 Abena HU 35 Zd 94
02250 Abengibre AB 124 Yc 113
22621 Abenilla HU 35 Ze 94
13180 Abenójar CR 120 Vd 115
22437 Abenozas HU 36 Ac 95
02500 Abenuj AB 140 Yb 117
01193 Aberasturi VI 31 Xc 92
31264 Aberin NC 32 Xf 93
50529 Aberite de San Juan Z
 52 Yd 98
10262 Abertura CC 117 Ub 113
49834 Abezames ZA 46 Ud 99
22463 Abi HU 36 Ac 94
39210 Abiada CB 17 Ve 90
34491 Abia de las Torres P 29 Vd 94
01477 Abiega VI 19 Wf 90
22143 Abiego HU 54 Zf 96
33557 Abiegos AS 16 Ue 89
11405 Abiertas, Las CA 172 Tf 128
31473 Abínzano NC 33 Yd 93
03100 Abio A 142 Zd 117
43427 Abió T 75 Bb 99
42127 Abión SO 51 Xe 99
42193 Abioncillo SO 50 Xa 98
39639 Abionzo CB 18 Wb 89
22392 Abizanda HU 55 Ab 95
04510 Abla AL 170 Xb 126
16195 Abla de la Obispalía CU
 104 Xd 108
33875 Ablaneda AS 14 Tc 89
19442 Ablanque GU 70 Xe 103
33618 Ablaña de Arriba AS 15 Ub 89
33424 Ables AS 15 Ua 88
31523 Ablitas NC 52 Yc 97
14029 Abolafia de la Torre CO
 151 Vd 121
27837 Aborbó LU 12 Sc 88
01449 Abornicano VI 31 Xa 91
11630 Abrajanejo CA 173 Uc 128
49624 Abraveses de Tera ZA
 45 Ua 97
08630 Abrera B 76 Bf 99
38618 Abrigos, Los TF 180 Ic 180
04260 Abriojal AL 170 Xd 127
04520 Abrucena AL 169 Xb 126
27546 Abuíme LU 24 Sc 93
37640 Abusejo SA 82 Tf 104
37891 Abusejo de Abajo SA
 83 Uc 103
37891 Abusejo de Arriba SA
 83 Uc 104
02511 Abuzaderas AB 140 Yb 116
38892 Acardece TF 184 He 180
33986 Acebal AS 15 Uc 89
33509 Acebal AS 16 Vb 88
28755 Acebeda, La MD 68 Wc 102
24996 Acebedo LE 16 Uf 90
36779 Acebedo PO 41 Rb 97
01427 Acebedo VI 31 Wf 91
32815 Acebedo do Río OR 42 Rf 96
36556 Acebeiro PO 23 Re 93
24357 Acebes del Páramo LE
 27 Ua 94
10857 Acebo CC 81 Tb 107
24413 Acebo LE 26 Td 94
27243 Acebo LU 13 Se 89

39549 Acebosa, La CB 17 Vd 88
16412 Acebrón, El CU 103 Xa 109
41500 Acebuchal SE 164 Ua 124
11391 Acebuchal, El CA 173 Ub 132
23211 Acebuchal, El J 137 Wc 119
41440 Acebuchal, El SE 149 Ud 123
21342 Acebuche H 147 Tb 121
 Acebuche H 162 Tc 126
18770 Acebuche, El GR 169 Wf 128
45292 Aceca TO 102 Wa 109
06730 Acedera BA 118 Uc 114
09129 Acedillo BU 30 Wa 93
31282 Acedo NC 32 Xe 92
40145 Acedos SG 66 Vd 103
10879 Acehúche CC 98 Tc 110
10666 Aceituna CC 98 Td 108
10627 Aceitunilla CC 82 Te 106
21570 Aceituno H 146 Se 122
09640 Aceña BU 49 Wd 96
48191 Aceña, La BI 19 Wf 89
41563 Aceñuela, La SE 150 Va 124
29400 Acequia de los Frailes MA
 165 Uf 128
18657 Acequias GR 168 Wc 127
34111 Acera de la Vega P 28 Vb 93
50347 Acered Z 71 Yc 101
32870 Acerdo OR 42 Rf 97
23240 Acero, El J 138 Wd 119
06207 Aceuchal BA 132 Td 117
33747 Acevedo AS 13 Ta 87
38439 Acevedo TF 180 Ib 179
38890 Aceviños, Los TF 184 He 180
49574 Aciberos ZA 44 Ta 96
22710 Acin HU 35 Zd 93
23488 Acra J 153 Wf 122
42174 Acrijos SO 51 Xe 96
18131 Acula GR 168 Wb 126
22612 Acumuer HU 35 Zd 93
15937 Acuncheira C 22 Ra 92
35350 Acusa GC 184 Kb 180
22147 Adahuesca HU 54 Zf 96
27162 Adai LU 12 Se 91
39761 Adal CB 18 Wd 88
47129 Adalia VA 47 Uf 99
41620 Adalid SE 150 Ud 124
14430 Adamuz CO 151 Vc 120
05296 Adanero AV 66 Vc 103
31454 Adanso NC 34 Ye 93
27611 Adega, A LU 24 Sc 92
38670 Adeje TF 180 Ib 180
27773 Adelán LU 12 Sd 87
14978 Adelantado, El CO
 167 Vd 125
04639 Adelfa, La AL 171 Ya 126
23210 Adelfar J 137 Wb 119
04510 Adelfas, Las AL 170 Xb 125
14749 Adelfilla, La CO 149 Ue 120
46140 Ademuz V 106 Ye 108
05520 Adijos AV 84 Va 105
36979 Adina PO 22 Ra 94
31153 Adiós NC 33 Yb 92
31448 Adoáin NC 34 Ye 92
19325 Adobes GU 89 Yb 104
25556 Adons L 37 Ae 94
46729 Ador V 127 Ze 115
04770 Adra AL 169 Wf 128
05430 Adrada, La AV 84 Vc 107

09462 Adrada de Haza BU 49 Wb 99
40192 Adrada de Pirón SG 67 Vf 102
42216 Adradas SO 69 Xd 100
24859 Adrados LE 27 Ue 91
40354 Adrados SG 67 Vf 100
24277 Adrados de Ordás LE
 27 Ua 92
25717 Adraén L 38 Bd 95
25797 Adrall L 37 Bc 95
15293 Adraño C 22 Qf 91
17199 Adri GI 59 Ce 96
41728 Adriano SE 163 Ua 125
03786 Adsubia A 127 Zf 115
20150 Aduna SS 20 Xf 89
39670 Aés CB 17 Wa 89
35489 Agaete GC 184 Kb 180
37510 Agallas SA 81 Td 106
25692 Àger L 56 Ae 96
09199 Agés BU 30 Wd 94
20600 Aginaga SS 20 Xf 89
20710 Aginaga SS 20 Xe 90
20170 Aginaga SS 20 Xf 89
36520 Agolada PO 23 Rf 92
50560 Agón Z 52 Yd 97
26150 Agoncillo RI 32 Xe 94
33129 Agones AS 14 Tf 88
31639 Agorreta NC 21 Yc 91
15883 Agoso C 23 Rc 92
03698 Agost A 142 Zc 118
02409 Agra AB 140 Yb 117
23369 Agracea J 139 Xb 118
23291 Agracea, La J 139 Xb 120
27513 Agrade LU 24 Sa 93
02490 Agramón AB 140 Yc 118
25310 Agramunt L 56 Ba 98
03837 Agres A 126 Zc 116
15808 Agro do Chao (Santiso) C
 23 Rf 91
18132 Agrón GR 168 Wb 126
04149 Agua Amarga AL 171 Ya 127
32101 Aguada OR 24 Sa 93
35638 Agua de Bueyes GC
 183 Lf 178
04638 Agua del Medio, El AL
 171 Ya 126
06444 Agua del Pilar BA 133 Ua 118
18640 Aguadero GR 168 Wc 126
23370 Aguadero, El J 139 Xb 119
41550 Aguadulce SE 166 Va 125
23569 Aguadux J 153 We 122
21342 Aguafría H 147 Tb 121
38359 Agua García TF 181 Id 178
15148 Agualada C 10 Rb 90
27248 Aguarda LU 12 Se 89
36780 A Guarda = La Guardia PO
 41 Ra 97
50408 Aguarón Z 71 Ye 100
22141 Aguas HU 54 Ze 95
38428 Aguas, Las TF 180 Ic 178
47418 Aguasal VA 66 Vc 101
02449 Agua Salada AB 140 Xf 117
30439 Agua Salada MC 140 Yb 120
15282 Aguasantas C 22 Rb 92
22451 Aguascaldas HU 36 Ac 94
09593 Aguas Cándidas BU 30 Wc 92
33842 Aguasmestas AS 14 Te 89
02049 Aguas Nuevas AB 124 Ya 115

44382 Aguatón TE 90 Ye 104
35259 Aguatona GC 184 Kd 181
44566 Aguaviva TE 92 Ze 104
42258 Aguaviva de la Vega SO
 70 Xd 101
27743 Aguaxosa LU 13 Se 88
13410 Agudo CR 119 Va 115
22282 Agudos, Los HU 53 Zb 96
37594 Águeda del Caudillo SA
 81 Td 105
33844 Agüera AS 14 Te 89
48880 Agüera BI 19 We 89
09569 Agüera BU 18 Wd 90
33814 Agüera del Coto AS 13 Tc 90
33118 Agüeras, Las AS 14 Tf 89
27678 Agueria LU 25 Sf 92
33679 Agüeria LU 15 Ub 90
22808 Agüero HU 34 Zb 94
33993 Agües AS 15 Ud 89
11500 Agüica CA 172 Te 129
06291 Águila, El BA 133 Te 120
10252 Águila, El CC 99 Ub 111
14749 Águila, El CO 150 Ud 121
40340 Aguilafuente SG 67 Vf 101
33619 Aguilar AS 15 Ub 89
22461 Aguilar HU 36 Ac 95
44156 Aguilar de Alfambra TE
 91 Zb 105
19204 Aguilar de Anguita GU
 70 Xd 102
09249 Aguilar de Bureba BU
 30 We 93
34800 Aguilar de Campoo P
 29 Ve 92
47814 Aguilar de Campos VA
 46 Ue 97
31228 Aguilar de Codés NC
 32 Xd 93
50175 Aguilar de Ebro Z 73 Zc 99
14920 Aguilar de Frontera CO
 151 Vc 123
26530 Aguilar del Río Alhama RI
 51 Ya 97
42259 Aguilar de Montuenga SO
 70 Xe 101
08256 Aguilar de Segarra B
 57 Bd 98
49624 Aguilar de Tera ZA 45 Ua 97
47281 Aguilarejo VA 47 Vc 98
30880 Águilas MC 156 Yc 124
42366 Aguilera SO 49 Xa 100
09370 Aguilera, La BU 49 Wb 98
39213 Aguilera, La CB 17 Vf 91
09216 Aguiló BU 31 Xc 92
43429 Aguiló T 76 Bc 99
50155 Aguilón Z 72 Yf 101
35260 Agüimes GC 184 Kd 181
31867 Aguinaga NC 33 Yb 91
22588 Aguinalín HU 55 Ac 96
01479 Aguíñiga VI 19 Wf 90
15965 Agüiño C 22 Qf 93
48480 Aguirre BI 19 Xa 89
48960 Aguirre BI 19 Ac 95
32634 Aguis OR 42 Sb 97
17707 Agullana GI 40 Cf 94
46890 Agullent V 126 Zc 116
25692 Agulló L 55 Ae 96

38830 Agulo TF 184 He 179
27143 Agustín LU 12 Se 91
18160 Agustinos GR 169 Wd 125
46177 Agustinos, Los V 106 Yf 110
41760 Aguzaderas SE 165 Uc 126
39849 Ahedo CB 18 Wd 89
09247 Ahedo de Bureba BU 30 Wd 93
09551 Ahedo del Butrón BU 30 Wb 91
10650 Ahigal CC 98 Te 107
37248 Ahigal de los Aceiteros SA 81 Tb 103
37173 Ahigal de Villarino SA 63 Td 102
46176 Ahillas V 107 Za 110
06940 Ahillones BA 134 Ua 119
23659 Ahumada, La J 152 Vf 121
20809 Aia SS 20 Xf 89
01476 Aiara, Ayala VI 19 Wf 90
01476 Aiara/Ayala VI 19 Wf 90
31460 Aibar = Oibar NC 33 Yd 93
46812 Aielo de Malferit V 126 Zc 115
46812 Aielo de Rugat V 126 Zd 115
17255 Aiguablava GI 59 Db 97
08591 Aiguafreda B 58 Cb 98
17255 Aiguafreda GI 59 Db 97
43815 Aiguamúrcia T 76 Bc 101
17181 Aiguaviva GI 59 Ce 97
43714 Aiguaviva T 76 Bd 100
03569 Aigües A 142 Zd 118
50152 Ailes Z 72 Yf 100
12222 Aín CS 108 Zd 109
31697 Aincioa NC 33 Yd 91
25572 Ainet de Cardós L 37 Bb 93
22623 Aineto HU 35 Ze 94
25577 Aineto L 37 Bb 93
22636 Ainielle HU 35 Ze 93
22349 Ainsa-Sobrarbe HU 36 Aa 94
50570 Ainzón Z 52 Yc 98
36990 Aiós PO 22 Ra 94
32666 Airavella OR 42 Sb 95
01120 Airraia Maeztu VI 32 Xd 92
22860 Aísa HU 34 Zc 92
25182 Aitona L 74 Ac 100
20211 Aitzarte SS 20 Xf 91
43364 Aixàvega, L' T 75 Ba 101
AD600 Aixirivall □ AND 38 Bd 94
AD500 Aixovall □ AND 38 Bc 94
20749 Aizarna SS 20 Xe 89
20749 Aizarnazabal SS 20 Xe 89
31448 Aizcurqui NC 33 Ye 92
20214 Aizpea SS 20 Xe 90
31172 Aizpún NC 33 Ya 91
31171 Aizpún NC 33 Yb 92
39806 Aja CB 18 Wc 89
28864 Ajalvir MD 86 Wd 105
26133 Ajamil RI 51 Xd 96
39728 Ajanedo CB 18 Wb 89
48320 Ajangiz BI 19 Xc 89
09216 Ajarte BU 31 Xc 92
30628 Ajauque MC 141 Yf 120
39170 Ajo CB 18 Wc 88
05370 Ajo, El AV 65 Va 103
45110 Ajofrín TO 102 Wa 110
35628 Ajuy GC 183 Lf 178
31698 Akerreta NC 33 Yc 91
48311 Akorda BI 19 Xc 88
03000* Alacant = Alicante A 142 Zd 118
44549 Alacón TE 72 Zb 102
50481 Aladrén Z 72 Yf 101
47510 Alaejos VA 65 Ue 101
50630 Alagón Z 53 Yf 98
10691 Alagón del Caudillo CC 98 Te 109
44563 Alagones, Los TE 91 Ze 104
07730 Alaior IB 77 Ea 109
01207 Alaiza VI 32 Xd 92
21340 Alájar H 147 Tc 121
38812 Alajeró TF 184 He 180
14857 Al Alamillo CO 151 Vd 123
28723 Alalaya Real MD 86 Wc 104
42368 Alaló SO 69 Xa 100
28130 Alalpardo MD 86 Wd 105
18170 Alambique, El GR 169 Xa 124
06340 Alameda BA 132 Tc 119
29530 Alameda MA 166 Vc 125
40311 Alameda SG 68 Wc 101
04271 Alameda, La AL 171 Xf 125
13379 Alameda, La CR 137 Wa 117
40176 Alameda, La SG 67 Wb 102
42126 Alameda, La SO 70 Xf 99
13690 Alameda de Cervera CR 122 Wf 113
37497 Alameda de Gardón, La SA 81 Tb 105
45240 Alameda de la Sagra TO 102 Wb 108
14193 Alameda del Obispo CO 150 Vb 121
28749 Alameda del Valle MD 67 Wa 103
28042 Alameda de Osuna MD 86 Wc 106
18520 Alamedilla GR 153 We 123
37554 Alamedilla, La SA 81 Tb 106
05160 Alamedilla del Berrocal, La AV 84 Vb 104
04828 Alamicos, Los AL 155 Xf 123
13413 Alamillo CR 135 Vb 116
11391 Alamillo, El CA 173 Ub 132
30868 Alamillo, El MC 156 Ye 123
23130 Alamillon J 152 Wb 123
04149 Alamillos, Los AL 171 Xf 127
45909 Alamín TO 85 Ve 107
19490 Alaminos GU 88 Xb 103
05154 Álamo, El AV 83 Ud 105
06310 Álamo, El BA 133 Td 118
29313 Álamo, El MA 167 Ve 126
28607 Álamo, El MD 85 Wa 107
41898 Álamo, El SE 148 Td 123
41440 Álamo, El SE 149 Uc 123
04811 Álamos, Los AL 155 Xe 123
29620 Álamos, Los MA 175 Vd 129
38715 Álamos, Los TF 181 Hb 176
25221 Alamús, Els L 56 Ae 99
41380 Alanís SE 149 Ub 120
46970 Alaquàs V 126 Zd 112
37312 Alaraz SA 83 Ue 104
50345 Alarba Z 71 Yc 101
09199 Alarcia BU 30 We 95
16214 Alarcón CU 105 Xf 111
34480 Alar del Rey P 29 Ve 93
45138 Alares, Los TO 101 Vb 112
19227 Alarilla GU 87 Wf 103
07340 Alaró IB 110 Ce 110
25718 Alàs L 38 Bd 94
22311 Alastrué HU 35 Zf 94
22760 Alastuey HU 34 Zb 93
02152 Alatoz AB 125 Yd 114
22621 Alavés HU 35 Zd 94
18314 Alazores, Los GR 167 Ve 126
27813 Alba LU 12 Sb 89
36152 Alba PO 22 Rc 94
44395 Alba TE 90 Yd 105
27204 Albá LU 24 Sa 91
34492 Albacastro BU 29 Ve 92
02001* Albacete AB 124 Ya 115
11406 Albadalejo Alto CA 172 Tf 128
34219 Alba de Cerrato P 48 Vd 98
34888 Alba de los Cardaños P 28 Vb 91
37800 Alba de Tormes SA 83 Uc 104
37478 Alba de Yeltes SA 82 Te 104
12135 Albagés, L' CS 91 Ze 107
25155 Albagés, L' L 75 Ae 100
23760 Albaida J 152 Vf 121
46860 Albaida V 126 Zc 115
41809 Albaida del Aljarafe SE 148 Tf 124
09216 Albaina BU 31 Xc 92
46470 Albal V 126 Zd 112
06011 Albalá BA 115 Sf 116
10187 Albalá de Caudillo CC 117 Te 113
13340 Albaladejo CR 138 Xb 117
16111 Albaladejo del Cuende CU 105 Xe 110
46687 Albalat de la Ribera V 126 Zd 113
46135 Albalat dels Sorells V 108 Zd 111
46591 Albalat dels Tarongers V 108 Zd 110
22534 Albalate de Cinca HU 55 Aa 98
44540 Albalate del Arzobispo TE 73 Zc 102
16841 Albalate de las Nogueras CU 88 Xe 106
19117 Albalate de Zorita GU 87 Xa 107
22220 Albalatillo HU 54 Zf 98
04857 Albánchez AL 171 Xe 125
23538 Albánchez de Mágina J 153 Wd 122
33492 Albandi AS 15 Ub 87
17733 Albanyà GI 39 Ce 95
43360 Albarca T 75 Af 101
30627 Albarda MC 141 Ye 120
27130 Albaredo LU 13 Se 91
32514 Albarellos OR 23 Rf 94
32618 Albarellos OR 43 Sd 97
36516 Albarellos PO 23 Rf 93
19112 Albares GU 87 Wf 107
24310 Albares de la Ribera LE 26 Td 93
30850 Albaricoqueros, Los MC 156 Yc 122
04116 Albaricoques AL 171 Xf 127
44100 Albarracín TE 90 Yd 106
45522 Albarreal de Tajo TO 101 Ve 109
41200 Albatán SE 149 Ua 123
02653 Albatana AB 141 Yc 117
25171 Albatàrrec L 55 Ad 99
03340 Albatera A 142 Za 119
27004 Albeiros LU 12 Sc 90
22558 Albelda HU 55 Ac 97
26120 Albelda de Iregua RI 32 Xd 94
22371 Albella HU 35 Zf 94
16812 Albendea CU 88 Xd 106
19275 Albendiego GU 69 Wf 101
14859 Albendín CO 151 Ve 122
01208 Albéniz VI 32 Xe 91
44477 Albentosa TE 107 Zb 108
36429 Albeos PO 42 Re 96
30150 Alberca, La MC 157 Yf 121
37624 Alberca, La SA 82 Tf 106
16620 Alberca de Záncara, La CU 104 Xd 111
45695 Alberche del Caudillo TO 100 Va 109
35479 Albercón GC 184 Kb 181
12318 Alberedes de Portell, Les CS 91 Ze 105
07400 Albergo Crucero Baleares IB 111 Db 109
18152 Albergue de Elorrieta GR 168 Wd 126
18160 Albergue de la Hoya de la Mora GR 169 Wd 126
30510 Albergue de los Castaños MC 141 Yf 117
18494 Albergue de los Espinares GR 169 Wf 126
32622 Alberguería OR 43 Sc 96
37555 Alberguería de Argañán, La SA 81 Tb 106
37762 Alberguería de Herguijuela SA 82 Ua 105
46176 Albergues V 107 Za 109
46260 Alberic V 126 Zc 114
46177 Alberique V 106 Yf 110
46312 Alberique V 106 Yf 110
11650 Alberite CA 165 Uc 128
22112 Albero Alto HU 54 Zd 96
22255 Albero Bajo HU 54 Zd 96
25611 Alberola L 55 Ae 97
30811 Alberquilla MC 156 Yb 123
30442 Alberquilla, La MC 140 Ya 119
45006 Alberquilla, La TO 102 Wa 109
22147 Alberuela de Liera HU 54 Zf 96
22212 Alberuela de Tubo HU 54 Ze 97
25712 Albet L 37 Bb 94
50549 Albeta Z 52 Yd 98
25450 Albi, L' L 75 Af 100
31877 Albiasu NC 21 Ya 90
09239 Albillos BU 30 Wb 95
41659 Albina SE 166 Ue 126
43716 Albinyana T 76 Bc 101
43479 Albiol, L' T 75 Ba 101
24293 Albires LE 27 Ue 95
15685 Albixoi C 11 Re 90
48382 Albiz BI 19 Xc 89
20495 Albiztur SS 20 Xf 90
42132 Albocabe SO 51 Xe 99
12140 Albocàsser CS 92 Aa 106
19160 Albolleque GU 87 We 105
04531 Alboloduy AL 170 Xc 126
18220 Albolote GR 168 Wb 125
18708 Albondón GR 169 We 128
48370 Alboniga BI 19 Xb 88
17136 Albons GI 59 Da 96
46369 Alborache V 126 Zb 112
02513 Alborajico AB 140 Yc 117
46120 Alboraya V 108 Zd 112
02215 Alborea AB 125 Yd 113
19264 Alboreca GU 69 Xc 102
15258 Alborés C 10 Ra 91
50781 Alborge Z 73 Zd 101
05358 Albornos AV 84 Va 103
04800 Albox AL 171 Xf 124
07750 Albranca Vell IB 77 Ea 109
30190 Albudeite MC 156 Yd 120
06170 Albuera, La BA 132 Tb 116
03550 Albufereta, L' A 142 Zd 118
46550 Albuixech V 108 Ze 111
30330 Albujón MC 157 Yf 122
18518 Albuñán GR 169 Wf 125
18700 Albuñol GR 169 We 128
18659 Albuñuelas GR 168 Wc 127
18180 Albuñuelas GR 169 We 125
11170 Alburejos, Los CA 172 Ua 130
06510 Alburquerque BA 116 Sf 113
45523 Alcabón TO 101 Vd 108
41359 Alcachofar, El SE 149 Ub 123
02410 Alcadima AB 140 Xf 117
02124 Alcadozo AB 140 Ya 117
16290 Alcahozo CU 124 Yc 112
04830 Alcaide AL 155 Xf 122
14940 Alcaidía, La CO 151 Vd 124
41657 Alcaidía, La SE 166 Uf 126
44792 Alcaine TE 72 Zb 103
38686 Alcalá TF 180 Ib 179
50691 Alcalá de Ebro Z 53 Ye 98
41500 Alcalá de Guadaira SE 164 Ua 124
22282 Alcalá de Gurrea HU 53 Zb 96
28802 Alcalá de Henares MD 86 Wd 106
44432 Alcalá de la Selva TE 91 Zb 106
16315 Alcalá de la Vega CU 106 Yc 108
02214 Alcalá del Júcar AB 125 Yd 113
22135 Alcalá del Obispo HU 54 Ze 96
11180 Alcalá de los Gazules CA 173 Ub 130
11693 Alcalá del Valle CA 166 Ue 127
50591 Alcalá de Moncayo Z 52 Yb 98
12570 Alcalà de Xivert CS 92 Ab 107
23680 Alcalá La Real J 152 Wa 124
03728 Alcalalí A 143 Zf 116
22560 Alcampell HU 55 Ac 97
22513 Alcana HU 55 Ac 97
03669 Alcanà A 142 Za 118
26509 Alcanadre RI 32 Xf 94
43530 Alcanar T 93 Ac 105
22300 Alcanetos, Los HU 55 Aa 96
25162 Alcanó L 74 Ad 100
11593 Alcántara CA 172 Ua 128
10980 Alcántara CC 97 Ta 110
30813 Alcántara y Los Bucanos MC 156 Yb 123
02489 Alcantarilla AB 139 Xd 119
30820 Alcantarilla MC 156 Ye 121
04638 Alcantarilla, La AL 171 Ya 126
41727 Alcantarillas, Las SE 164 Ua 126
16812 Alcantud CU 88 Xd 105
49500 Alcañices ZA 45 Td 98
44600 Alcañiz TE 73 Zf 102
45687 Alcañizo TO 100 Uf 109
14480 Alcaracejos CO 135 Va 118
30592 Alcaraces MC 157 Za 122
02300 Alcaraz AB 139 Xd 117
11580 Alcaria, La CA 173 Uc 129
25180 Alcarràs L 74 Ad 99
46290 Alcàsser V 126 Zd 112
29711 Alcaucín MA 167 Vf 127
23660 Alcaudete J 152 Vf 123
45662 Alcaudete de la Jara TO 100 Va 110
04769 Alcaudique AL 169 Xa 128
07710 Alcaufar IB 77 Eb 109
31780 Alcayaga NC 21 Yb 89
06182 Alcazaba BA 116 Tb 115
04778 Alcazaba, La AL 169 Wf 128
06300 Alcázar BA 133 Td 118
18710 Alcázar GR 169 Wd 127
16464 Alcázar del Rey CU 104 Xb 108
13600 Alcázar de San Juan CR 122 We 112
37607 Alcazarén SA 82 Ua 104
47238 Alcazarén VA 66 Vb 100
30710 Alcázares, Los MC 157 Za 122
39680 Alceda CB 18 Wa 89
01423 Alcedo VI 31 Wf 92
03649 Alciri A 142 Za 118
13116 Alcoba CR 120 Vd 113
24393 Alcoba de la Ribera LE 27 Ub 93
42351 Alcoba de la Torre SO 49 Wd 98
06380 Alcobaza BA 132 Ta 118
28109 Alcobendas MD 86 Wc 105
19125 Alcocer GU 88 Xc 106
03841 Alcocer de Planes A 126 Zd 116
09258 Alcocero de Mola BU 30 Wd 94
16537 Alcohujate CU 88 Xc 106
03801 Alcoi = Alcoy A 142 Zd 116
03815 Alcoies, Les A 142 Zd 117
04480 Alcolea AL 169 Xa 127
14610 Alcolea CO 151 Vb 121
13107 Alcolea de Calatrava CR 120 Vf 115
22410 Alcolea de Cinca HU 55 Aa 98
19260 Alcolea del Pinar GU 69 Xd 102
41449 Alcolea del Río SE 149 Uc 123
Alcolea del Río, Apt. SE 149 Ub 123
45571 Alcolea de Tajo TO 100 Uf 110
03814 Alcolecha A 143 Ze 116
25660 Alcoletge L 55 Ae 99
10135 Alcollarín CC 118 Ub 113
42134 Alconaba SO 51 Xd 98
37329 Alconada SA 65 Ud 103
40529 Alconada de Maderuelo SG 68 Wd 100
40529 Alconadilla SG 68 Wd 100
06131 Alconchel BA 132 Sf 117
42269 Alconchel de Ariza Z 70 Xf 101
16433 Alconchel de la Estrella CU 104 Xc 110
06393 Alconera BA 132 Td 118
04897 Alcóntar AL 170 Xc 124
12110 Alcora, l' CS 108 Ze 108
03699 Alcoraya, L' A 142 Zc 118
49517 Alcorcillo ZA 45 Td 98
28921 Alcorcón MD 86 Wb 106
29691 Alcorrín MA 173 Ue 130
44550 Alcorisa TE 73 Zd 103
10515 Alcorneo CC 115 Se 113
10373 Alcornocal CC 99 Uc 111
14249 Alcornocal, El CO 134 Ue 119
13100 Alcornocal, El CR 120 Vd 113
41359 Alcornocalejo SE 149 Ub 123
41899 Alcornocosa, La SE 148 Te 122
41250 Alcornoque SE 148 Tf 121
41780 Alcornoquillo, El SE 165 Ud 127
19310 Alcoroches GU 89 Yb 105
12579 Alcossebre CS 92 Ab 107
44422 Alcotas TE 107 Zb 108
46176 Alcotas, Las V 107 Za 110
07740 Alcotx IB 77 Eb 109
43460 Alcover T 75 Bb 101
03801 Alcoy = Alcoi A 142 Zd 116
42320 Alcozar SO 49 We 99
02249 Alcozarejos AB 124 Yc 114
22251 Alcubierre HU 54 Zd 98
42351 Alcubilla de Avellaneda SO 49 We 98
42213 Alcubilla de las Peñas SO 70 Xc 101
42391 Alcubilla del Marqués SO 69 Wf 99
49696 Alcubilla de Nogales ZA 45 Ua 96
13391 Alcubillas CR 138 Wf 116
04558 Alcubillas, Las AL 170 Xc 126
45516 Alcubillete TO 101 Ve 109
46172 Alcublas V 107 Zb 110
07400 Alcudia IB 111 Da 109
46250 Alcúdia, L' V 126 Zc 113
46690 Alcúdia de Crespins, l' V 126 Zc 115
18511 Alcudia de Guadix GR 169 Wf 125
04276 Alcudia de Monteagud AL 170 Xe 125
12222 Alcudia de Veo CS 108 Zd 109
03829 Alcudieta del Comtat, l' A 142 Zd 116
10160 Alcuéscar CC 117 Te 113
24207 Alcuetas LE 27 Ud 95
19264 Alcuneza GU 69 Xc 102
18451 Alcútar GR 169 We 127
29679 Alcuzcuz MA 174 Uf 129
01117 Alda VI 32 Xe 92
31892 Aldaba NC 33 Yb 91
20267 Aldaba SS 20 Xf 90
46960 Aldaia V 107 Zd 112
36945 Aldán PO 22 Rb 95
15215 Aldaris C 22 Rb 92
31878 Aldatz NC 21 Ya 90
48120 Alday BI 19 Xb 88
27813 Aldea LU 12 Sb 89
43896 Aldea, L' T 93 Ad 104
09554 Aldea, La BU 30 Wc 91
35119 Aldea Blanca GC 184 Kd 181
38628 Aldea Blanca del Llano TF 180 Ic 180
10251 Aldeacentenera CC 99 Uc 111
37718 Aldeacipreste SA 82 Ua 106
48891 Aldeacueva BI 18 Wd 89
37520 Aldeadalba de Hortaces SA 81 Tc 105
37250 Aldeadávila de la Ribera SA 63 Tc 101
45620 Aldea de Arango TO 100 Va 108
39419 Aldea de Ebro CB 29 Vf 91
41400 Aldea de Fuente Carretero SE 150 Uf 123
22250 Aldea de Gazol HU 54 Zd 98
24391 Aldea de la Valdoncina, La LE 27 Ub 93
10163 Aldea del Cano CC 117 Te 113
28620 Aldea del Fresno MD 85 Ve 107
37488 Aldea del Obispo SA 81 Tb 104
10291 Aldea del Obispo, La CC 99 Ua 111
09660 Aldea del Pinar BU 50 We 97
09211 Aldea del Portillo de Busto, La BU 30 We 92
24920 Aldea del Puente, La LE 27 Ue 93
13380 Aldea del Rey CR 137 Wa 116
05197 Aldea del Rey Niño AV 84 Vb 105
22439 Aldea de Puy de Cinca HU 55 Ab 95
42345 Aldea de San Esteban SO 68 We 99
47160 Aldea de San Miguel VA 66 Vc 100
35470 Aldea de San Nicolás, La GC 184 Kb 181
21880 Aldea de Tejada H 148 Td 124
10291 Aldea de Trujillo CC 99 Ua 111
45908 Aldea en Cabo TO 101 Vd 107
37187 Aldeagallega SA 83 Ub 103
37116 Aldeagutiérrez SA 64 Tf 102
23267 Aldeahermosa J 138 Wf 119
05520 Aldealabad AV 84 Va 105
05154 Aldealabad del Mirón AV 83 Ud 105
40389 Aldealafuente SG 67 Wb 101
42134 Aldealafuente SO 51 Xe 98
40513 Aldealázaro SG 68 Wd 100
47313 Aldealbar VA 67 Vd 100
42173 Aldealcardo SO 51 Xe 96
40389 Aldealcorvo SG 67 Wb 101
37350 Aldealengua SA 65 Uc 103
40555 Aldealengua de Santa María SG 68 Wd 100
37183 Aldealgordo de Abajo SA 83 Ub 104

Aldealgordo de Abajo | 239

E

42180 Aldealices SO 51 Xe 97
40153 Aldeallana SG 85 Ve 103
26145 Aldealobos RI 32 Xe 95
42112 Aldealpozo SO 51 Xe 98
42180 Aldealseñor SO 51 Xe 97
47162 Aldeamayor de San Martín VA 66 Vc 99
02691 Aldeanueva AB 124 Yb 115
37497 Aldeanueva SA 81 Tc 105
40195 Aldeanueva SG 67 Vf 103
19244 Aldeanueva de Atienza GU 69 Wf 102
45661 Aldeanueva de Barbarroya TO 100 Uf 110
26123 Aldeanueva de Cameros RI 50 Xc 96
37767 Aldeanueva de Campo Mojado SA 83 Ub 105
26559 Aldeanueva de Ebro RI 52 Ya 95
37429 Aldeanueva de Figueroa SA 65 Uc 102
19152 Aldeanueva de Guadalajara GU 87 Wf 104
37540 Aldeanueva del Arenal SA 81 Tc 106
40532 Aldeanueva de la Serrezuela SG 67 Wb 100
10440 Aldeanueva de la Vera CC 99 Ub 108
10740 Aldeanueva del Camino CC 82 Ua 107
40568 Aldeanueva del Campanario SG 68 Wc 100
40462 Aldeanueva del Codonal SG 66 Vc 102
40517 Aldeanueva del Monte SG 68 Wc 100
37592 Aldeanueva de Portanovis SA 81 Tc 104
45575 Aldeanueva de San Bartolomé TO 100 Uf 111
05580 Aldeanueva de Santa Cruz AV 83 Ud 106
23215 Aldeaquemada J 138 Wd 118
14191 Aldea Quintana CO 150 Va 122
40292 Aldea Real SG 67 Vf 101
37110 Aldearrodrigo SA 64 Ub 102
37799 Aldearrubia SA 65 Ud 102
40181 Aldeasaz SG 67 Wa 102
05212 Aldeaseca AV 66 Vb 102
37870 Aldeaseca de Alba SA 83 Ud 104
37189 Aldeaseca de Armuña SA 64 Ub 102
37317 Aldeaseca de la Frontera SA 65 Ue 103
40235 Aldeasoña SG 67 Vf 100
37187 Aldeatejada SA 64 Ub 103
15948 Aldeavella C 22 Ra 93
05193 Aldeavieja AV 85 Vd 104
37493 Aldeavieja SA 82 Te 104
37779 Aldeavieja de Tormes SA 83 Uc 105
37493 Aldeavilla de Revilla SA 82 Te 103
37317 Aldeayuste SA 65 Ue 103
27728 Aldeguer LU 13 Se 89
40530 Aldehorno SG 67 Wb 99
10638 Aldehuela CC 82 Td 106
19354 Aldehuela GU 89 Yb 104
40160 Aldehuela SG 67 Vf 102
40317 Aldehuela SG 67 Wb 100
40311 Aldehuela SG 68 Wc 101
44192 Aldehuela TE 90 Yf 107
44192 Aldehuela TE 91 Zb 104
05593 Aldehuela, La AV 83 Ud 106
23747 Aldehuela, La J 137 Wa 120
28380 Aldehuela, La MD 103 Wd 108
42107 Aldehuela de Ágreda SO 52 Ya 98
42193 Aldehuela de Calatañazor SO 50 Xb 98
37460 Aldehuela de la Bóveda SA 82 Tf 103
40462 Aldehuela del Codonal SG 66 Vc 102
50374 Aldehuela de Liestos Z 71 Yb 102
10671 Aldehuela del Jerte CC 98 Te 108
37497 Aldehuela de los Gallegos SA 81 Tb 105
42180 Aldehuela de Periáñez SO 51 Xe 98
42166 Aldehuela de Rincón SO 50 Xc 97
50324 Aldehuela de Santa Cruz Z 71 Yd 100
37639 Aldehuela de Yeltes SA 82 Te 105
37100 Aldehuelas SA 64 Tf 102
42173 Aldehuelas, Las SO 51 Xd 97
04897 Aldeire AL 170 Xc 125
18514 Aldeire GR 169 Wf 126
40380 Aldeonsancho SG 67 Wa 101
40531 Aldeonte SG 68 Wb 100
47313 Aldeyuso VA 67 Vf 99
27843 Aldixe LU 12 Sc 89
27116 Aldomán LU 13 Sf 90
AD400 Aldosa, l' ◘ AND 38 Bd 93
AD100 Aldosa, l' ◘ AND 38 Bd 93
27611 Aldosende LU 24 Sc 92
43591 Aldover T 93 Ad 103
31480 Aldunate NC 33 Yd 93
33345 Alea AS 16 Uf 88
19237 Aleas GU 68 Wf 103
03100 Alecua A 142 Zc 117
30859 Aledo MC 156 Yc 122
20260 Alegia SS 20 Xf 90
35540 Alegranza GC 182 Mc 172
01240 Alegría-Dulantzi VI 32 Xc 91
43381 Aleixar, L' T 75 Ba 101
24960 Aleje LE 28 Uf 91
02448 Alejos, Los AB 139 Xe 117
08328 Alella B 77 Cb 100
04117 Alemanes Nuevos, Los AL 171 Xf 128
32705 Alemparte OR 43 Sc 95
36511 Alemparte PO 23 Rf 92
48870 Alen BI 19 We 89
32138 Alén OR 23 Rf 93
42225 Alentisque SO 70 Xe 100
25736 Alentorn L 56 Ba 97
22588 Aler HU 55 Ac 96
50670 Alera Z 33 Yd 95
22194 Alerre HU 54 Zd 96
26324 Alesanco RI 31 Xb 94
26315 Alesón RI 31 Xb 94
33579 Alevia AS 17 Vc 88
18170 Alfacar GR 168 Wc 125
03838 Alfafara A 126 Zc 116
22511 Alfages HU 55 Ab 98
04830 Alfahuara, La AL 155 Xe 122
04288 Alfaix AL 171 Ya 126
50172 Alfajarín Z 53 Zb 99
44160 Alfambra TE 90 Yf 105
50461 Alfamén Z 71 Ye 100
22416 Alfántega HU 55 Aa 98
46594 Alfara de Algimia V 108 Zd 110
43528 Alfara de Carles T 93 Ac 103
49177 Alfaraz ZA 64 Tf 101
49177 Alfaraz de Sayago ZA 64 Ua 101
46195 Alfarb V 126 Zc 113
29194 Alfarnate MA 167 Ve 127
29194 Alfarnatejo MA 167 Ve 127
26540 Alfaro RI 52 Yb 95
25120 Alfarràs L 55 Ad 97
46893 Alfarrasí V 126 Zd 115
03580 Alfàs del Pi, L' A 143 Zf 117
46725 Alfauir V 127 Ze 115
23614 Alfávila, La J 152 Wa 123
02448 Alfera, La AB 139 Xe 117
25161 Alfés L 74 Ad 99
46500 Alfinach V 108 Zd 111
50120 Alfocea Z 53 Za 98
34240 Alfoces, Los P 48 Ve 97
12609 Alfondeguilla CS 108 Ze 109
43365 Alforja T 75 Af 101
18710 Alfornón GR 169 We 128
50783 Alforque Z 73 Zd 101
27774 Alfoz LU 12 Sd 87
39526 Alfoz de Lloredo CB 17 Ve 88
09571 Alfoz de Santa Gadea BU 17 Wa 91
50195 Alfranca, La Z 53 Zb 99
12160 Algá, L' CS 92 Zf 106
41980 Algaba, La SE 148 Tf 124
24238 Algadefe LE 46 Uc 95
07769 Algaiarens IB 77 Df 108
07210 Algaida IB 111 Cf 111
11549 Algaida, La CA 163 Te 127
14978 Algaida y Gata Corona CO 167 Vd 125
41560 Algaidilla SE 166 Vb 125
30420 Algaidón, El MC 140 Yb 119
14439 Algallarín CO 151 Vd 121
11200 Algamasilla CA 175 Uc 132
41661 Algámitas SE 166 Uf 126
11179 Algámitas, Las CA 173 Uc 131
11639 Algar CA 173 Uc 129
14811 Algar CO 151 Vd 124
30366 Algar, El MC 157 Za 123
14100 Algarbes, Los CO 150 Va 123
19332 Algar de Mesa GU 70 Ya 102
46593 Algar de Palancia V 108 Zd 110
19116 Algarga GU 103 Wf 107
18280 Algarinejo GR 167 Vf 125
16338 Algarra CU 106 Yd 108
04710 Algarrobal, El AL 170 Xb 128
41730 Algarrobillo, El SE 163 Ua 127
29750 Algarrobo MA 167 Vf 128
21730 Algarrobo, El H 163 Td 125
30648 Algarrobo, El MC 141 Yf 119
29751 Algarrobo-Costa MA 167 Vf 128
14670 Algarve CO 151 Ve 122
29491 Algatocín MA 173 Ue 129
22559 Algayón HU 55 Ac 98
44562 Algecira, La TE 91 Zd 104
11203 Algeciras CA 174 Ud 132
46680 Algemesí V 126 Zd 113
07712 Algendar IB 77 Eb 109
25130 Algerri L 55 Ad 98
30157 Algezares MC 157 Yf 121
41650 Algibón SE 166 Uf 126
46148 Algimia de Alfara V 108 Zd 110
12414 Algimia de Almonacid CS 107 Zd 109
46230 Alginet V 126 Zd 113
03296 Algoda, L' A 142 Zb 119
11680 Algodonales CA 165 Ud 127
28310 Algodor MD 102 Wa 109
49539 Algodre ZA 65 Uc 99
19268 Algora GU 69 Xb 103
03169 Algorfa A 157 Zb 120
03296 Algorós A 142 Zb 119
48940 Algorta BI 19 Xa 88
25125 Alguaire L 55 Ad 98
30560* Alguazas MC 156 Ye 120
03668 Algueña A 141 Yf 118
04567 Alhabía AL 170 Xc 127
30800 Alhagüeces MC 156 Yb 121
04400 Alhama de Almería AL 170 Xc 127
50230 Alhama de Aragón Z 70 Ya 101
18120 Alhama de Granada GR 167 Wa 126
30840 Alhama de Murcia MC 156 Yd 121
13248 Alhambra CR 122 Wf 115
44423 Alhambras, Las TE 107 Za 108
04619 Alhanchete, El AL 171 Ya 125
29492 Alharia, La MA 174 Ue 129
23790 Alharilla J 151 Vf 121
29130 Alhaurín de la Torre MA 175 Vc 129
29120 Alhaurín el Grande MA 175 Vb 129
18620 Alhendín GR 168 Wc 126
19132 Alhóndiga GU 87 Xb 105
01010 Ali VI 31 Xb 91
10137 Alía CC 118 Ue 112
44150 Aliaga TE 91 Zb 104
16313 Aliaguilla CU 106 Ye 110
03000* Alicante = Alacant A 142 Zd 118
14240 Alicante, El CO 135 Ue 119
29600 Alicate MA 175 Vb 129
04409 Alicún AL 170 Xc 127
18539 Alicún de las Torres GR 153 Wf 123
18538 Alicún de Ortega GR 153 Wf 123
24199 Alija de la Ribera LE 27 Uc 93
24761 Alija del Infantado LE 45 Ua 96
11400 Alijar CA 172 Te 128
23568 Alijares, Los J 153 Wd 122
25574 Alins L 37 Bb 93
22421 Alíns del Monte HU 55 Ac 96
25794 Alinyà L 57 Bc 95
43813 Alió T 76 Bb 101
19129 Alique GU 88 Xc 105
41889 Alisar, El SE 148 Te 123
39720 Alisas CB 18 Wc 89
10550 Aliseda CC 116 Tb 112
37500 Aliseda SA 81 Tc 104
23213 Aliseda, La J 137 Wc 118
05630 Aliseda de Tormes, La AV 83 Ud 107
18240 Alitaje GR 168 Wb 125
42132 Aliud SO 51 Xe 99
41420 Aljabara, La SE 149 Ud 124
14730 Aljabaras, Las CO 150 Ue 121
29580 Aljaima MA 166 Vc 128
04814 Aljambra, La AL 171 Xf 124
21110 Aljaraque H 162 Sf 125
04629 Aljariz AL 171 Ya 125
30890 Aljezas y El Llano MC 156 Ya 122
35640 Aljibe GC 183 Ma 177
04750 Aljibe de la Cruz, El AL 169 Xa 127
30178 Aljibe del Andaluz MC 156 Yd 121
30335 Aljibe de los Juncos MC 156 Ye 122
30813 Aljibete, El MC 156 Yb 123
30811 Aljibe y las Brencas de Sicilia, El MC 156 Yb 123
04715 Aljibillos AL 170 Xa 128
41567 Aljonoz SE 150 Va 124
46860 Aljorf V 126 Zc 115
30390 Aljorra, La MC 157 Yf 122
02512 Aljube AB 140 Yc 117
06894 Aljucén BA 117 Td 114
30152 Aljucer MC 157 Yf 121
20215 Alkibar SS 20 Xe 91
20494 Alkiza SS 20 Xf 89
31797 Alkotz NC 21 Yb 90
17539 All GI 38 Bf 94
33889 Allande AS 13 Tc 89
32660 Allariz OR 42 Sb 95
40130 Allas de San Pedro SG 67 Ve 103
39798 Allendelagua CB 19 We 88
44145 Allepuz TE 91 Zb 106
33578 Alles AS 16 Vb 89
31290 Allín NC 32 Xf 92
31262 Allo NC 32 Xf 93
27113 Allonca, A LU 13 Ta 89
31292 Alloz NC 32 Ya 92
44509 Alloza TE 73 Zc 103
30859 Allozos, Los MC 156 Yc 122
22610 Allué HU 35 Zd 94
44492 Allueva TE 72 Yf 103
25100 Almacelles L 55 Ac 98
25109 Almacelletes L 55 Ad 98
44548 Almacenes TE 72 Zb 103
29718 Almáchar MA 167 Ve 128
29788 Almachares MA 168 Wa 128
18820 Almaciles GR 155 Xd 121
13400 Almadén CR 119 Va 116
41240 Almadén de la Plata SE 148 Tf 121
13480 Almadenejos CR 135 Vb 116
30530 Almadenes MC 141 Yc 119
11520 Almadraba CA 172 Td 129
04150 Almadraba de Monteleva AL 171 Xe 128
11100 Almadraba Esparola CA 172 Te 130
17480 Almadrava, L' GI 59 Db 95
43860 Almadrava, L' T 75 Af 103
19490 Almadrones GU 69 Xb 103
24374 Almagarinas LE 26 Te 92
13270 Almagro CR 121 Wb 115
30333 Almagros MC 156 Ye 122
46450 Almaguer-Espedreñals V 126 Zd 113
04692 Almajalejo AL 171 Ya 124
42180 Almajano SO 51 Xd 97
11500 Almajar CA 172 Te 129
42258 Almaluez SO 70 Xe 101
31796 Almandoz NC 21 Yc 90
02640 Almansa AB 125 Yf 115
10137 Almansa CC 119 Ue 112
23479 Almansas J 153 Wf 121
42212 Almantiga SO 69 Xc 100
24170 Almanza LE 28 Uf 93
04815 Almanzora AL 171 Xe 124
42191 Almarail SO 51 Xd 99
10350 Almaraz CC 99 Ub 110
49180 Almaraz de Duero ZA 64 Ua 100
47861 Almaraz de la Mota VA 46 Ue 98
16740 Almarcha, La CU 104 Xd 110
11393 Almarchal, El CA 173 Ub 132
29330 Almargen MA 166 Uf 126
14749 Almarja, La CO 150 Ue 122
03503 Almarrà A 143 Zf 117
42169 Almarza SO 51 Xd 97
26111 Almarza de Cameros RI 50 Xc 95
46132 Almàssera V 126 Zd 111
25261 Almassor L 56 Af 98
12550 Almassora = Almazora CS 108 Zf 109
25187 Almatret L 74 Ac 101
35018 Almatriche GC 184 Kd 180
29749 Almayate Alto MA 167 Vf 128
29749 Almayate Bajo MA 167 Vf 128
42200 Almazán SO 70 Xc 100
02439 Almazarán AB 140 Xf 118
24398 Almázcara LE 26 Tc 93
12550 Almazora = Almassora CS 108 Zf 109
22148 Almazorre HU 35 Aa 95
42126 Almazul SO 51 Xf 99
12570 Almedíjar CS 92 Aa 107
12413 Almedíjar CS 107 Zd 109
13328 Almedina CR 138 Xa 117
23470 Almedina, La J 153 Wf 121
18438 Almegíjar GR 169 We 127
49210 Almeida de Sayago ZA 64 Tf 101
25126 Almenar L 55 Ad 98
12590 Almenara CS 108 Ze 110
23009 Almenara J 152 Wb 121
47419 Almenara de Adaja VA 66 Vb 101
50191 Almenara de San Ignacio Z 53 Yf 98
37115 Almenara de Tormes SA 64 Ub 102
42130 Almenar de Soria SO 51 Xe 98
14812 Almendinilla CO 152 Vf 124
37176 Almendra SA 64 Td 101
49183 Almendra ZA 45 Ua 99
06171 Almendral BA 132 Tb 117
10667 Almendral CC 98 Tf 108
04559 Almendral, El AL 170 Xc 126
18128 Almendral, El GR 167 Vf 127
45631 Almendral de la Cañada TO 101 Vb 107
06200 Almendralejo BA 133 Td 116
29013 Almendrales MA 167 Vd 128
30893 Almendricos MC 155 Yb 124
21593 Almendro, El H 161 Se 123
16420 Almendros CU 104 Xa 109
13248 Almendros, Los CR 122 Wf 115
12500 Almendros, Los CS 93 Ad 105
28500 Almendros, Los MD 86 Wd 107
41111 Almensilla SE 163 Tf 125
04001* Almería AL 170 Xd 127
04711 Almerimar AL 170 Xb 128
46178 Almeza, La V 107 Za 109
23479 Almicerán, El J 154 Xa 122
18515 Almidar GR 153 Wf 124
02437 Almirez AB 140 Ya 118
19225 Almiruete GU 68 We 102
44591 Almochuel Z 73 Zc 101
04458 Almócita AL 170 Xb 126
13580 Almodóvar del Campo CR 136 Ve 116
16215 Almodóvar del Pinar CU 105 Ya 110
14720 Almodóvar del Río CO 150 Uf 122
29150 Almogía MA 167 Vc 128
19115 Almoguera GU 87 Xa 107
23392 Almohadilla J 139 Xb 118
44369 Almohaja TE 90 Yd 105
05515 Almohalla, La AV 83 Ud 106
10132 Almoharin CC 117 Tf 113
46723 Almoines V 127 Zf 115
50178 Almolda, La Z 73 Ze 99
50133 Almonacid de la Cuba Z 72 Zb 101
50108 Almonacid de la Sierra Z 71 Ye 100
16431 Almonacid del Marquesado CU 104 Xb 110
45420 Almonacid de Toledo TO 102 Wa 110
19118 Almonacid de Zorita GU 87 Xa 107
21350 Almonaster la Real H 147 Tb 121
18816 Almontarás, Las GR 154 Xb 122
21730 Almonte H 162 Tc 125
17850 Almor GI 59 Cd 95
03160 Almoradí A 142 Zb 120
11350 Almoraima CA 173 Ud 131
06614 Almorchón BA 134 Ue 116
45910 Almorojuelo TO 101 Vd 107
45900 Almorox TO 85 Vd 107
43393 Almoster T 75 Ba 101
22531 Almudáfar HU 55 Ab 99
03827 Almudaina A 143 Zd 116
30410 Almudema, La MC 155 Ya 120
22270 Almudévar HU 54 Zc 96
41909 Almuédano SE 148 Tf 124
50100 Almunia de Doña Godina, La Z 71 Yd 100
22141 Almunia del Romeral, La HU 54 Ze 95
22420 Almunia de San Juan HU 55 Ab 97
22587 Almunia de San Lorenzo HU 55 Ad 96
22144 Almunias, Las HU 35 Zf 95
22255 Almuniente HU 54 Zd 97
33700 Almuña AS 14 Tc 87
18690 Almuñécar GR 168 Wb 128
13760 Almuradiel CR 137 Wd 117
33843 Almurfe AS 14 Te 89
46440 Almussafes V 126 Zd 113
24838 Almuzara LE 15 Uc 91
44134 Alobras TE 106 Yd 107
19133 Alocén GU 87 Xb 105
38852 Alojera TF 184 He 180
18350 Alomartes GR 168 Wa 125
15846 Alón C 10 Rb 90
10109 Alonso de Ojeda CC 117 Ua 114
48810 Alonsotegui BI 19 Xa 89
39649 Aloños CB 18 Wa 89
29500 Álora MA 166 Vb 128
25737 Alòs de Balaguer L 56 Af 97
25586 Alòs d'Isil = Alòs de Gil L 37 Ba 92
21520 Alosno H 161 Sf 123
08586 Alou, L' B 58 Ca 96
19208 Alovera GU 87 We 105
29567 Alozaina MA 175 Va 128
29460 Alpandeire MA 174 Ue 129
42213 Alpanseque SO 69 Xb 101
04638 Alparatas, Las AL 171 Ya 126
50109 Alpartir Z 71 Yd 100
03788 Alpatró A 127 Ze 116
28430 Alpedrete MD 85 Vf 105
19184 Alpedrete de la Sierra GU 68 Wd 103
19276 Alpedroches GU 69 Xa 101
08587 Alpens B 58 Ca 96
44721 Alpeñes TE 90 Yf 104
02690 Alpera AB 125 Ye 115
25110 Alpicat L 55 Ad 98
21880 Alpizar H 148 Td 124
30816 Alporchones MC 156 Yc 123
46178 Alpuente V 106 Yf 109
18450 Alpujarra de la Sierra GR 169 Wf 127
07769 Alputze Nou IB 77 Df 108
29195 Alquería MA 167 Ve 127
29679 Alquería MA 174 Uf 129
29130 Alquería MA 175 Vc 128
04779 Alquería, La AL 169 Wf 128
18840 Alquería, La GR 154 Xc 122
30528 Alquería, La MC 141 Ye 117
37796 Alquería Alizaces SA 83 Ub 104
12448 Alquería Baja, La CS 107 Zc 108

240 | Aldealices

37865 Alquería Carabias SA 83 Ud 104
37350 Alquería Castañeda SA 65 Ud 103
37453 Alquería Cemprón SA 83 Ub 104
37453 Alquería Continos SA 83 Ub 103
37766 Alquería Coquilla de Juan Vázquez SA 82 Ua 105
37788 Alquería Cortos de Sacedón SA 83 Ub 104
03829 Alqueria d'Asnar, l' A 126 Zd 116
04830 Alquería de Abajo, La AL 155 Xf 122
05298 Alquería de Astudillo AV 65 Uf 102
46715 Alquería de la Condesa, l' = Alquería de la Comtessa V 127 Zf 115
03810 Alqueria dels Capellans, L' A 142 Zd 116
37865 Alquería Gallegos de Crespos SA 83 Ud 104
37453 Alquería Gueribáñez SA 83 Ub 104
37788 Alquería Herreros de Salvatierra SA 83 Ub 104
10410 Alquería La Campita CC 99 Ua 108
37458 Alquería La Dueña de Abajo SA 83 Ub 104
21550 Alquería La Vaca H 146 Sd 122
37320 Alquería Pedrezuela de San Bricio SA 65 Ud 103
37405 Alquería Revilla SA 65 Ue 102
37317 Alquería Riolobos SA 65 Ue 102
30580 Alquerías MC 157 Yf 120
30850 Alquerías, Las MC 156 Yc 121
30850 Alquerías, Las MC 156 Yc 122
37789 Alquería Sanchotuerto SA 83 Ub 104
37312 Alquería San Mamés SA 83 Ud 104
12539 Alquerías del Niño Perdido CS 108 Zf 109
37312 Alquería Somosancho SA 83 Ue 104
30835 Alquerías y Cermeño MC 156 Yc 123
37453 Alquería Terrubias SA 83 Ub 103
37787 Alquería Velayos SA 83 Uc 104
37405 Alquería Villafuerte SA 65 Ud 102
21610 Alquería y Valcasao, La H 162 Ta 125
22145 Alquézar HU 54 Aa 95
04130 Alquián, El AL 170 Xd 127
30611 Alquibla MC 141 Yd 120
18518 Alquife GR 169 Wf 125
40510 Alquité SG 68 Wd 101
25632 Alsamora L 55 Ae 96
31800 Alsasua = Altsasu NC 32 Xe 91
04568 Alsodux AL 170 Xc 126
09219 Altable BU 31 Wf 93
43893 Altafulla T 76 Bc 102
30385 Altamaría MC 157 Zb 123
48350 Altamira San Kristobal BI 19 Xb 88
05141 Altamiros AV 84 Va 104
25589 Alt Àneu L 37 Ba 93
16780 Altarejos CU 104 Xd 109
25215 Alta-riba L 57 Bc 98
03590 Altea A 143 Zf 117
03599 Altea la Vella A 143 Zf 117
25289 Altés L 56 Bb 96
25350 Altet L 56 Ba 98
03195 Altet, El A 142 Zc 119
02139 Altico, El AB 139 Xe 117
23210 Altico, El J 137 Wb 119
40400 Altillo, El SG 85 Vd 104
48144 Alto BI 19 Xb 90
27164 Alto LU 24 Sd 91
24792 Altobar de la Encomienda LE 45 Ub 96
30813 Altobordo MC 156 Yc 123
12225 Alto del Pinar CS 107 Zd 109
32137 Alto de Santo Domingo OR 23 Rf 93
27212 Alto do Hospital LU 24 Sb 91
25567 Altorn L 37 Ba 94
22540 Altorricón HU 55 Ac 98
09559 Altos, Los BU 30 Wb 92
14930 Altos, Los CO 151 Vc 124
35018 Altos, Los GC 184 Kc 180
31800 Altsasu = Alsasua NC 32 Xe 91
01139 Altube VI 19 Xa 91
12410 Altura CS 107 Zc 109
39880 Altura, La CB 19 We 89
26289 Altuzarra RI 50 Wf 95
20015 Altza SS 21 Ya 89
20248 Altzaga SS 20 Xf 90
01169 Altzaga VI 20 Xc 90
20180 Altzibar SS 21 Ya 89
20268 Altzo SS 20 Xf 90
20268 Altzoazpi SS 20 Xf 90
20870 Altzola SS 20 Xd 89
50322 Aluenda Z 71 Yc 100
30351 Alumbres MC 157 Za 123
19320 Alustante GU 89 Yc 105
06170 Alvarado BA 116 Tb 116
14720 Alvarizas CO 150 Uf 122
27579 Alvidrón LU 24 Sa 92
15838 Alvite C 22 Ra 91
27287 Alvites LU 12 Se 88
25632 Alzina, L' L 56 Ae 96
25794 Alzina, l' L 57 Bc 95
25749 Alzina de Ribelles, l' L 56 Bb 97
46600 Alzira V 126 Zd 114
31422 Alzórriz NC 33 Yd 92
31486 Alzuza NC 33 Yc 91
31715 Amaiur/Maya NC 21 Yd 89
36527 Amance PO 23 Rf 92
33311 Amandi AS 15 Ud 88
27576 Amarante LU 24 Sa 92
04897 Amarguilla AL 170 Xc 125
20150 Amasa SS 20 Xf 89
37890 Amatos de Alba SA 83 Ud 103
37792 Amatos de Salvatierra SA 83 Ub 104
31395 Amatrain NC 33 Yc 93
05560 Amavida AV 84 Uf 105
09136 Amaya BU 29 Vf 93
19332 Amayas GU 70 Ya 102
34429 Amayuelas de Abajo P 47 Vd 95
34429 Amayuelas de Arriba P 47 Vd 95
34485 Amayuelas de Ojeda P 29 Vd 92
33826 Ambás AS 14 Tf 89
33438 Ambás AS 15 Ub 87
33312 Ambás AS 15 Ud 88
26586 Ambas Aguas o Entrambas Aguas RI 51 Xe 96
24524 Ambasmestas LE 25 Ta 92
50546 Ambel Z 52 Yc 98
33557 Ambingue AS 16 Ue 89
28580 Ambite MD 87 We 107
15145 Amboade C 11 Rc 89
27836 Ambosores LU 12 Sb 87
33819 Ambrés AS 14 Td 89
15313 Ambroa C 11 Rf 89
42230 Ambrona SO 70 Xc 102
18102 Ambroz GR 168 Wc 126
36516 Amedo PO 23 Rf 93
36885 Ameixeira, A PO 42 Re 95
15870 Ameixenda C 22 Rc 91
15298 Ameixenda, A C 22 Qf 91
15821 Amenal, O C 23 Rd 91
17170 Amer GI 58 Cd 96
15220 Ames C 22 Rc 91
08480 Ametlla del Vallès, L' B 58 Cb 98
43860 Ametlla de Mar, L' T 93 Ae 103
25692 Ametlla de Montsec, L' L 56 Ae 96
25217 Ametlla de Segarra, L' L 56 Bb 99
09219 Ameyugo BU 31 Wf 93
20268 Amezketa SS 20 Xf 90
48499 Amezola BI 19 Xa 90
32665 Amiadoso OR 42 Sb 95
33558 Amieva AS 16 Uf 89
33558 Amieva AS 16 Uf 89
36669 Amil PO 23 Rc 93
31290 Amillano NC 32 Xf 92
36840 Amoedo PO 23 Rc 95
32170 Amoeiro OR 23 Sa 94
49173 Amor ZA 64 Ub 100
48340 Amorebieta-Etxano BI 19 Xb 89
25271 Amorós L 57 Bc 99
48289 Amoroto BI 20 Xc 89
43895 Ampolla, L' T 93 Ae 104
43870 Amposta T 93 Ad 104
34191 Ampudia P 47 Vb 97
39840 Ampuero CB 18 Wd 88
35611 Ampuyenta, La GC 183 Ma 178
31395 Amunarrizqueta NC 33 Yc 93
26270 Amunartia RI 31 Wf 94
08757 Amunt, l' B 76 Bf 100
01470 Amurrio VI 19 Wf 90
34420 Amusco P 47 Vd 95
47177 Amusquillo VA 48 Ve 98
44212 Anadón TE 72 Za 103
27229 Anafreita LU 12 Sa 90
25572 Anàs L 37 Bb 93
40121 Anaya SG 67 Ve 103
37863 Anaya de Alba SA 83 Ud 104
37465 Anaya de Huebra SA 82 Tf 104
33534 Anayo AS 15 Ud 88
07315 Ancanella IB 111 Cf 110
15181 Anceis C 11 Rd 89
36829 Anceu PO 23 Rd 94
31699 Anchóriz NC 33 Yc 91
23294 Anchos, Los J 139 Xc 119
19287 Anchuela del Campo GU 70 Xf 102
19350 Anchuela del Pedregal GU 89 Yb 103
28818 Anchuelo MD 87 We 106
13117 Anchuras CR 100 Va 112
30850 Anchurica, La MC 156 Yc 122
18181 Anchurón, El GR 169 We 124
22469 Anciles HU 36 Ad 93
31281 Ancín NC 32 Xe 93
11500 Ancla, El CA 172 Te 129
19128 Anclas, Las GU 88 Xb 105
01439 Anda VI 31 Xa 91
15816 Andabao C 11 Rf 90
01439 Andagoya VI 31 Xa 91
24127 Andarraso LE 26 Tf 92
20809 Andatza SS 20 Xf 89
49162 Andavías ZA 45 Ua 99
15669 Andeiro C 11 Rd 89
33719 Andés AS 13 Tb 87
46162 Andilla V 107 Zb 109
24722 Andiñuela LE 26 Te 94
20140 Andoain SS 20 Xf 89
01260 Andoin VI 32 Xe 91
01193 Andollu VI 32 Xc 92
44500 Andorra TE 73 Zd 103
AD500 Andorra La Vella ◘ AND 38 Bd 93
31261 Andosilla NC 32 Ya 94
48620 Andraka BI 19 Xa 88
48115 Andra-Mari BI 19 Xb 89
36628 András PO 22 Rb 93
07150 Andratx IB 110 Cc 111
07860 Àndravel IB 109 Bc 117
30858 Andreos, Los MC 156 Yd 122
37181 Andrés Bueno SA 65 Uc 103
21239 Andreses, Los H 147 Ta 121
33596 Andrin AS 16 Vb 88
23740 Andújar J 152 Vf 120
04559 Aneas, Las AL 170 Xc 126
50369 Anento Z 71 Yd 102
22487 Aneto HU 37 Ae 93
29660 Ángel, El MA 174 Va 129
11339 Ángeles, Los CA 173 Ud 130
28223 Ángeles, Los MD 86 Wb 106
40424 Ángeles de San Rafael, Los SG 85 Ve 104
20578 Angiozar = Anguiozar SS 20 Xd 90
17160 Anglès GI 59 Cd 97
25320 Anglesola L 56 Ba 99
19245 Angón GU 69 Xa 102
39788 Angostina CB 18 We 88
01118 Angostina VI 32 Xd 93
04897 Angosto de Arriba AL 170 Xc 124
05631 Angostura, La AV 83 Ud 106
35310 Angostura La GC 184 Kd 180
26210 Anguciana RI 31 Xa 93
36428 Angudes PO 42 Re 95
22123 Angüés HU 54 Zf 96
26322 Anguiano RI 31 Xb 95
02140 Anguijes, Los AB 124 Ya 115
19283 Anguita GU 70 Xd 102
09313 Anguix BU 48 Wa 98
19119 Anguix GU 87 Xb 106
26288 Anguta RI 31 Wf 94
47239 Aniago VA 66 Va 99
22162 Aniés HU 35 Zc 95
39451 Anievas CB 17 Vf 89
39571 Aniezo CB 17 Vc 90
50313 Aniñón Z 71 Yb 100
31796 Aniz NC 21 Yc 90
42366 Anjaluz SO 69 Xb 99
24488 Anllares del Sil LE 26 Tc 91
24488 Anllarinos del Sil LE 26 Tc 91
15110 Anllóns C 10 Ra 89
46820 Anna V 126 Zc 114
31799 Anocíbar NC 33 Yb 91
20270 Anoeta SS 20 Xf 90
02512 Anorias, Las AB 141 Yc 116
15149 Anós C 10 Ra 89
31172 Anoz NC 33 Yb 91
31194 Anoz NC 33 Yc 91
19287 Anquela del Ducado GU 70 Xf 103
19357 Anquela del Pedregal GU 89 Yb 104
12370 Anroig CS 92 Aa 105
25798 Anserall L 38 Bc 94
22728 Ansó HU 34 Zb 92
31195 Ansoáin NC 33 Yb 91
25722 Ansovell L 38 Bd 95
49349 Anta de Rioconejos ZA 44 Td 96
49317 Anta de Tera ZA 45 Td 96
04628 Antas AL 171 Ya 125
36839 Antas PO 23 Rd 94
27570 Antas de Ulla LU 24 Sa 92
46266 Antella V 126 Zc 114
22589 Antenza HU 55 Ad 96
48210 Anteparaluzeta BI 19 Xc 90
29200 Antequera MA 167 Vc 126
15258 Antes C 10 Ra 91
01220 Antezana de la Ribera VI 31 Xa 92
07640 Antigors, Els IB 111 Da 113
35630 Antigua GC 183 Lf 178
20008 Antigua SS 20 Xf 89
24796 Antigua, La LE 46 Ub 95
34248 Antigüedad P 48 Vf 97
21449 Antilla, La H 161 Se 125
22133 Antillón HU 54 Zf 96
24251 Antimio de Abajo LE 27 Uc 94
24391 Antimio de Arriba LE 27 Uc 93
25513 Antist L 37 Af 94
08262 Antius B 57 Be 98
38813 Antoncojo TF 184 He 180
01128 Antoñana VI 32 Xd 92
24281 Antoñán del Valle LE 26 Ua 93
24357 Antoñanes del Páramo LE 27 Ub 94
26589 Antoñanzas RI 51 Xe 95
20577 Antzuola SS 20 Xd 90
01428 Anucita VI 31 Xa 92
31798 Anué NC 21 Yc 91
15688 Ánxeles C 11 Re 91
27229 Anxeriz LU 12 Sa 90
25738 Anya L 56 Ba 97
22830 Anzánigo HU 34 Zc 94
36512 Anzo PO 23 Re 92
14512 Anzur CO 166 Vb 124
01426 Añana = Salinas de Añana VI 31 Xa 92
09215 Añastro BU 31 Xb 92
42108 Añavieja SO 51 Ya 97
15609 Andrade C 11 Rf 88
40492 Añe SG 67 Ve 102
01477 Añes VI 19 Wf 90
31195 Añézcar NC 33 Yb 91
11400 Añina CA 172 Te 128
36587 Añobre PO 23 Re 92
50590 Añón de Moncayo Z 52 Yb 98
14450 Añora CO 135 Va 118
31154 Añorbe NC 33 Yb 93
37111 Añover de Tormes SA 64 Ua 102
34307 Añoza P 47 Vb 95
31430 Aoiz NC 33 Yd 92
28755 Aoslos MD 68 Wc 102
31481 Aos NC 33 Yd 92
25788 Aós L 38 Bc 93
09511 Aostri de Losa BU 19 Wf 91
20550 Aozaraza SS 20 Xd 90
03311 Aparecida, La A 157 Yf 120
30395 Aparecida, La MC 157 Za 122
15327 Aparral C 12 Sb 88
31500 Apartadero de Arguedas NC 52 Yc 96
14249 Apartadero de Cabeza de Vaca CO 135 Ue 119
02640 Apartadero de Casas del Campillo AB 125 Yf 116
26528 Apartadero de Cervera de Rio Alhama RI 52 Ya 97
02694 Apartadero de Higueruela AB 125 Yd 115
24345 Apartadero de Villamarco LE 27 Ue 94
48291 Apatamonasterio BI 20 Xc 90
29590 Apeadero Campanillas MA 175 Vc 128
49162 Apeadero de Andavias ZA 45 Ua 99
21500 Apeadero de Belmonte H 147 Ta 124
Apeadero de Carpio de Azaba SA 81 Tc 105
02691 Apeadero de El Mugron AB 125 Ye 115
37593 Apeadero de El Salto SA 81 Td 105
49540 Apeadero de Losacio-San Martin ZA 45 Tf 98
49163 Apeadero de Manzanal del Barco ZA 45 Ua 99
05215 Apeadero de Palacios de Goda AV 66 Vb 102
13738 Apeadero de Peñalajo CR 137 Wc 117
50490 Apeadero de Puerto del Alto Z 71 Ye 101
Apeadero de Robledo de Sanabria ZA 44 Tc 97
21309 Apeadero El Cobujon H 161 Ta 123
21309 Apeadero La Encarnación H 161 Ta 123
50450 Apeadero La Torrubia Z 72 Yf 100
29590 Apeadero Los Prados MA 175 Vd 128
29591 Apeadero Los Remedios MA 175 Vc 128
29394 Apeadero Parchite MA 166 Uf 128
01129 Apellániz VI 32 Xd 92
01139 Aperregi VI 31 Xa 91
30811 Apiche MC 156 Yb 123
22195 Apiés HU 54 Zd 95
01138 Apodaca VI 31 Xb 91
20530 Apotzaga = Apozaga SS 20 Xc 90
20530 Apozaga SS 20 Xc 90
27235 Apregación LU 12 Sb 91
01439 Apricano VI 31 Xa 91
22625 Aquilué HU 35 Zd 94
22620 Ara HU 35 Zd 94
37418 Arabayona SA 65 Ud 102
25712 Arabell = Aravell L 37 Bc 94
30510 Arabí MC 141 Ye 116
48498 Aracaldo BI 19 Xa 90
21200 Aracena H 147 Tc 121
21200 Aracenilla H 147 Tc 121
39212 Aradillos CB 17 Vf 90
38550 Arafo TF 181 Id 178
19344 Aragoncillo GU 70 Xf 103
40123 Aragoneses SG 67 Vd 102
19294 Aragosa GU 69 Xb 103
22338 Araguás HU 36 Aa 94
22731 Aragüés del Puerto HU 34 Zb 92
41600 Arahal, El SE 165 Uc 125
40173 Arahuetes SG 67 Wa 102
12110 Araia CS 108 Ze 108
01250 Araia VI 32 Xe 91
31891 Araitz NC 20 Ya 90
31797 Araizotz NC 21 Yc 91
31850 Arakil NC 33 Ya 91
41989 Aral, El SE 148 Ua 124
24146 Aralla de Luna LE 27 Ua 91
20248 Arama SS 20 Xf 90
01169 Aramaio VI 20 Xc 90
31290 Aramendía NC 32 Xf 92
25518 Aramunt L 56 Af 95
48370 Arana BI 19 Xb 88
09215 Arana BU 31 Xb 92
31271 Aranarache NC 32 Xe 92
33756 Arancedo AS 13 Tb 87
42180 Arancón SO 51 Xe 98
09400 Aranda de Duero BU 49 Wb 98
50259 Aranda de Moncayo Z 52 Yb 99
50266 Arándiga Z 71 Yd 99
31292 Arandigoyen NC 32 Ya 93
16812 Arandilla del Arroyo CU 88 Xd 105
15317 Aranga C 11 Rf 89
33554 Arangas AS 16 Vb 89
33128 Arango AS 14 Te 88
31448 Arangozqui NC 33 Ye 92
31192 Aranguren NC 33 Yc 92
28300 Aranjuez MD 102 Wc 108
31754 Arano NC 21 Ya 89
25726 Arànser L 38 Bd 94
27714 Arante LU 13 Se 88
36458 Arantei PO 41 Rc 96
31790 Arantza NC 21 Yb 89
20567 Arantzaau SS 20 Xd 91
48140 Arantzazu BI 19 Xb 90
20690 Arantzeta SS 20 Xd 90
25212 Aranyó, L' L 56 Bb 98
27689 Aranza LU 24 Se 91
19141 Aranzueque GU 87 Wf 106
15984 Araño, O C 22 Rb 92
12232 Arañuel CS 107 Zd 108
20567 Araotz SS 20 Xd 91
20567 Araoz = Araotz SS 20 Xd 91
37796 Arapiles SA 65 Uc 103
22466 Arasán HU 36 Ad 93
22193 Arascués HU 54 Zd 95
46179 Aras de Alpuente V 106 Yf 109
31239 Aras o Tres Aras NC 32 Xd 93
22860 Aratorés HU 35 Zc 93
20738 Aratzerreka SS 20 Xe 90
37850 Arauzo SA 65 Ue 103
09451 Arauzo de Miel BU 49 Wd 97
09451 Arauzo de Salce BU 49 Wd 98
09451 Arauzo de Torre BU 49 Wd 98
28023 Aravaca MD 86 Wb 106
38540 Araya TF 181 Id 178
31170 Arazuri NC 33 Yb 92
48381 Arbacegui y Gerrikaiz BI 20 Xc 89
48419 Arbaiza BI 19 Xa 90
19237 Arbancón GU 69 Wf 103
22121 Arbaniés HU 54 Ze 96
24690 Arbás LE 15 Ub 91
25140 Arbeca L 75 Af 99
34846 Arbejal P 29 Vc 91
19492 Arbeteta GU 88 Xd 104
33840 Arbeyales AS 14 Te 90
01420 Arbigano VI 31 Xa 92
31839 Arbizu NC 32 Xf 91
36430 Arbo PO 42 Rd 96
08793 Arboçar de Dalt B 76 Be 100
04660 Arboleas AL 171 Xf 124
43365 Arbolí T 75 Af 101
31454 Arboniés NC 33 Ye 92
43720 Arbós = Arboç, L' T 76 Bd 101
43720 Arbós, l' = Arboç T 76 Bd 101
17401 Arbúcies GI 58 Cd 98
22760 Arbués HU 34 Zb 93
42240 Arbujuelo SO 70 Xd 102
23193 Arbuniel J 153 Wc 123
15821 Arca C 23 Rd 91
36684 Arca PO 23 Rd 93
36690 Arcade PO 22 Rc 94
24227 Arcahueja LE 27 Uc 93
25593 Arcalís L 37 Ba 94
16123 Arcas CU 105 Xf 109
16123 Arcas del Villar CU 105 Xf 109
01192 Arcaute VI 31 Xc 91
25799 Arcavell L 38 Bc 94
24171 Arcayos LE 28 Uf 93
09218 Arce BU 31 Xa 92
39478 Arce CB 17 Wa 88
37429 Arcediano SA 65 Uc 102

Arcediano | 241

49151 Arcenillas ZA 64 Ub 100
49159 Arceñas de Villaralbo ZA 64 Ub 100
15818 Arceo C 11 Re 90
39419 Arcera CB 29 Vf 91
30600 Archena MC 141 Ye 120
29755 Archez MA 168 Vf 127
29300 Archidona MA 167 Vd 126
41899 Archidona SE 148 Te 122
19411 Archilla GU 87 Xa 104
18492 Archillas, Los GR 169 Wf 127
23478 Archites, Los J 154 Xb 120
30195 Archivel MC 155 Xf 120
45182 Arcicóllar TO 102 Vf 108
49514 Arcillera ZA 45 Te 98
37429 Arcillo SA 65 Uc 102
49272 Arcillo ZA 64 Ua 100
10828 Arco CC 98 Td 110
37110 Arco, El SA 64 Ub 102
09592 Arconada BU 30 Wc 93
34449 Arconada P 29 Vd 95
40164 Arcones SG 68 Wb 102
09195 Arcos BU 30 Wb 95
15258 Arcos C 22 Qf 91
27142 Arcos LU 12 Sd 90
27518 Arcos LU 24 Sb 93
32348 Arcos OR 25 Sf 94
32693 Arcos OR 42 Sb 96
36677 Arcos PO 23 Rc 93
36389 Arcos PO 41 Rb 96
06010 Arcos, Los BA 132 Ta 117
30329 Arcos, Los MC 157 Ye 122
31210 Arcos, Los NC 32 Xe 93
42250 Arcos de Jalón SO 70 Xe 101
16191 Arcos de la Cantera CU 105 Xe 108
11630 Arcos de la Frontera CA 164 Ub 128
49699 Arcos de la Polvorosa ZA 46 Ub 97
16141 Arcos de la Sierra CU 89 Xf 106
44421 Arcos de las Salinas TE 106 Yf 109
22520 Arcs, Els HU 74 Aa 100
25144 Arcs, Els L 56 Ae 98
32621 Arcucelos OR 43 Sd 96
22149 Arcusa HU 35 Aa 95
31697 Ardaiz NC 33 Yd 91
30170 Ardal MC 141 Yc 120
13250 Ardales CR 121 Wb 114
29550 Ardales MA 166 Va 127
31421 Ardanaz de Izagandoa NC 33 Yd 92
22474 Ardanúy HU 36 Ad 94
15109 Ardaña C 10 Rb 89
25287 Ardèvol L 57 Bd 97
36989 Ardia PO 22 Ra 94
06270 Ardila BA 133 Td 120
50614 Ardisa Z 53 Zb 95
33507 Ardisana AS 16 Va 88
29108 Ardite MA 175 Va 128
23760 Ardón J 152 Vf 121
24232 Ardón LE 27 Uc 94
24251 Ardoncino LE 27 Uc 94
37460 Ardonsillero SA 82 Tf 103
25727 Ardòvol L 38 Be 94
36389 Area PO 41 Rb 96
27578 Areas LU 24 Sa 92
36873 Areas PO 23 Rd 95
36711 Areas PO 41 Rb 96
36861 Areas PO 41 Rc 95
48143 Areatza-Villaro BI 19 Xb 90
38789 Arecida TF 181 Ha 176
48269 Areitio BI 20 Xc 89
30889 Arejos, Los MC 156 Yb 124
31263 Arellano NC 32 Xf 93
22583 Arén HU 36 Ae 95
33125 Arena, La AS 14 Tf 87
39627 Arenal CB 18 Wb 89
05416 Arenal, El AV 84 Uf 107
14830 Arenal, El CO 151 Vc 123
40176 Arenal, El SG 67 Wb 101
07740 Arenal d'en Castell IB 77 Eb 108
02449 Arenalejo AB 140 Xf 118
18220 Arenales GR 168 Wc 125
42257 Arenales SO 70 Xe 102
10896 Arenales, Los CC 97 Tb 108
18312 Arenales, Los GR 167 Vf 125
41400 Arenales, Los SE 150 Ue 124
13619 Arenales de San Gregorio CR 122 Wf 113
23710 Arenales y Sevilleja J 152 Wa 120
48190 Arenao BI 19 Wf 89
33936 Arenas AS 15 Uc 88
33538 Arenas AS 15 Ud 89
39553 Arenas CB 17 Vd 89
29753 Arenas MA 167 Vf 128
33555 Arenas, Las AS 16 Vb 89
41740 Arenas, Las SE 163 Tf 127
47160 Arenas, Las VA 66 Vc 99
39450 Arenas de Iguña CB 17 Vf 89
18126 Arenas del Rey GR 168 Wa 127
13679 Arenas de San Juan CR 121 Wc 113
05400 Arenas de San Pedro AV 84 Uf 107
01129 Arenaza VI 32 Xd 92
41350 Arenillas SE 149 Ub 122
42368 Arenillas SO 69 Xa 100
09239 Arenillas de Muñó BU 48 Wa 95
34477 Arenillas de Nuño Pérez P 29 Vc 93
09107 Arenillas de Riópisuerga BU 29 Ve 94
34473 Arenillas de San Pelayo P 28 Vc 93
24329 Arenillas de Valderaduey LE 28 Uf 95
09133 Arenillas de Villadiego BU 29 Wa 93
38520 Arenitas, Las TF 181 Id 178
41640 Arenoso SE 166 Ue 125
29400 Arenosos, Los MA 165 Ue 128
44622 Arens de Lledó TE 74 Ab 103
32500 Arenteiro OR 23 Rf 94
08350 Arenys de Mer B 58 Cd 99
08358 Arenys de Munt B 58 Cd 99
26311 Arenzana de Abajo RI 31 Xb 94
26312 Arenzana de Arriba RI 31 Xb 94
39582 Areños CB 16 Vb 90
34849 Areños P 17 Vd 91
15126 Areosa C 10 Ra 90
15624 Ares C 11 Re 88
25794 Ares L 56 Bb 95
48499 Aresandiaga BI 19 Xa 89
03814 Ares del Bosc A 143 Ze 116
12165 Ares del Maestre CS 92 Zf 106
31876 Areso NC 20 Ya 90
01476 Arespalditza = Respaldiza VI 19 Wf 90
25595 Arestui L 37 Ba 93
20550 Aretxabaleta SS 20 Xc 90
01450 Aretxalde VI 19 Xa 90
05153 Arevalillo AV 83 Ud 105
37292 Arevalillo SA 81 Tc 103
40185 Arevalillo de Cega SG 67 Wa 102
05200 Arévalo AV 66 Vb 102
42161 Arévalo de la Sierra SO 51 Xd 97
37607 Arévalos, Los SA 82 Ua 105
25713 Arfa L 38 Bc 95
14298 Argallón CO 134 Ud 119
15213 Argalo C 22 Ra 92
06240 Argamasa BA 133 Td 119
13710 Argamasilla de Alba CR 122 Wf 114
13440 Argamasilla de Calatrava CR 136 Vf 116
02328 Argamasón AB 124 Xf 115
04149 Argamasón, El AL 171 Ya 127
33163 Argame AS 15 Ua 89
35509 Argana GC 182 Mc 175
28500 Arganda MD 86 Wd 107
33539 Argandenes AS 15 Ue 88
01193 Argandoña VI 32 Xc 91
33875 Arganza AS 14 Td 89
24546 Arganza LE 25 Tb 93
42141 Arganza SO 50 Wf 98
49251 Argañín ZA 64 Te 100
33314 Argañoso AS 15 Uc 88
22135 Argavieso HU 54 Ze 96
19196 Argecilla GU 87 Xb 103
17853 Argelaguer GI 59 Cd 95
12230 Argelita CS 108 Zd 108
08251 Argençola B 57 Be 97
08717 Argensola = Argençola B 57 Bc 99
44165 Argente TE 90 Yf 104
25736 Argentera L 56 Ba 97
43773 Argentera, L' T 75 Af 102
08310 Argentona B 77 Cc 99
45122 Argés TO 102 Vf 110
43765 Argilaga, L' T 76 Bb 101
17421 Argimon, l' GI 58 Cd 97
25799 Argolell L 38 Bc 94
01192 Argomaniz VI 32 Xc 91
09572 Argomedo BU 18 Wb 91
39626 Argomilla CB 18 Wa 89
27748 Argomoso LU 12 Sd 88
39197 Argoños CB 18 Wd 88
09217 Argote BU 31 Xb 92
24989 Argovejo LE 28 Uf 91
27511 Argozón LU 24 Sa 93
38690 Arguayo TF 180 Ib 179
38869 Arguayoda TF 184 He 180
39586 Argüébanes CB 16 Vc 89
31513 Arguedas NC 52 Yc 95
02484 Arguellite AB 139 Xd 118
33314 Argüerín AS 15 Ud 87
39212 Argüeso CB 17 Ve 90
25795 Arguestues L 37 Bb 95
42169 Arguijo SO 51 Xc 97
35120 Arguineguín GC 184 Kb 182
31176 Arguiñano NC 32 Ya 92
31174 Arguiñariz NC 33 Ya 92
22150 Arguis HU 35 Zd 95
16360 Arguisuelas CU 105 Yb 109
49716 Argujillo ZA 65 Uc 101
07529 Ariany IB 111 Da 111
31671 Aribe NC 20 Ye 91
38589 Arico = Villa de Arico TF 180 Id 179
24132 Arienza LE 26 Tf 92
22417 Ariéstolas HU 55 Ab 97
09570 Arija BU 17 Wa 91
09570 Arija (Fábrica) BU 18 Wa 91
48499 Arilza-Olazar BI 19 Xa 90
35118 Arinaga GC 184 Kd 181
50682 Aringo Z 34 Yf 93
15892 Aríns C 23 Rc 91
AD400 Arinsal ◘ AND 38 Bc 93
24845 Arintero LE 15 Ud 91
01195 Ariñez VI 31 Xb 92
35349 Ariñez GC 184 Kc 180
44547 Ariño TE 72 Zc 102
45109 Arísgotas TO 102 Wa 111
25722 Aristot L 38 Bd 94
31892 Arístregui NC 33 Yb 91
20215 Aritzalde SS 20 Xe 91
31798 Aritzu NC 21 Yc 91
31671 Arive NC 20 Ye 91
31892 Áriz NC 33 Yb 91
50220 Ariza Z 70 Xf 101
31177 Arizala NC 32 Ya 92
31177 Arizaleta NC 32 Ya 92
48011 Arizgoiti BI 19 Xa 89
31713 Arizkun NC 21 Yd 89
31439 Arizkuren NC 33 Ye 92
23760 Arjona J 152 Vf 121
23750 Arjonilla J 152 Vf 121
20247 Arkaka SS 20 Xf 90
24319 Arlanza LE 26 Td 93
09199 Arlanzón BU 30 Wd 95
31191 Arlegui NC 33 Yb 92
33427 Arlós AS 15 Ua 88
01216 Arlucea VI 32 Xc 92
32822 Armada, A OR 23 Rf 95
17844 Armadàs GI 59 Ce 96
19461 Armallones GU 88 Xe 104
31228 Armañanzas NC 32 Xe 93
32678 Armariz OR 42 Sb 95
27693 Armeá LU 24 Se 92
42174 Armejún SO 51 Xe 96
24284 Armellada LE 27 Ua 93
36192 Armenteira PO 22 Rb 94
17472 Armentera, L' GI 59 Da 95
37755 Armenteros SA 83 Ud 105
09215 Armentia VI 31 Xb 92
38678 Armeñime TF 180 Ib 180
27649 Armesto LU 25 Se 92
18100 Armilla GR 168 Wc 126
44742 Armillas TE 72 Za 103
48620 Armintza BI 19 Xa 88
01220 Armiñon VI 31 Xa 92
40494 Armuña SG 67 Ve 102
04888 Armuña de Almanzora AL 170 Xd 124
19135 Armuña de Tajuña GU 87 Wf 105
24567 Arnadelo LE 25 Ta 93
09410 Arnadilla BU 49 Wd 98
24568 Arnado LE 25 Sf 93
26589 Arnedillo RI 51 Xe 95
09571 Arnedo BU 18 Wa 91
26580 Arnedo RI 51 Xf 95
36599 Arnego PO 23 Rf 92
36511 Arnego PO 23 Sa 93
32520 Arnelas OR 23 Re 93
17720 Arnera GI 40 Ce 94
03312 Arneva A 157 Za 120
04619 Arnilla AL 171 Ya 125
32417 Arnoia, A OR 23 Rf 95
31133 Arnotegiko Andra Mari NC 33 Yb 92
39195 Arnuero CB 18 Wc 88
15838 Aro C 22 Rb 91
33546 Arobes AS 16 Ue 88
21240 Aroche H 147 Ta 121
38640 Arona TF 180 Ib 180
31867 Aróstegui NC 21 Yb 91
15121 Arou C 10 Qf 89
36626 Arousa PO 22 Ra 93
46178 Arquella V 106 Yf 109
49126 Arquillinos ZA 46 Uc 98
02314 Arquillo AB 139 Xd 116
23230 Arquillos J 137 Wd 119
23230 Arquillos El Viejo J 137 Wd 119
31880 Arquisquil NC 21 Ya 90
36794 Arrabal = Oia PO 41 Ra 96
49696 Arrabalde ZA 45 Ua 96
30410 Arrabal de Benablón MC 155 Ya 120
30410 Arrabal de La Encarnación MC 155 Ya 120
47160 Arrabal del Portillo VA 66 Vc 100
43007 Arrabasada, L' T 76 Bb 102
08035 Arrabassada, l' B 77 Ca 100
31794 Arraioz NC 21 Yc 90
31797 Arraitz NC 21 Yc 90
31174 Arraiza NC 33 Yb 92
16855 Arrancacepas CU 88 Xd 107
48498 Arrankudiaga BI 19 Xa 89
31866 Arrarats NC 21 Yb 90
20500 Arrasate-Mondragón SS 20 Xd 90
22622 Arraso HU 35 Zd 94
20600 Arrate SS 20 Xd 89
48383 Arratzu BI 19 Xc 89
09292 Arraya de Oca BU 30 Wd 94
30440 Arrayán MC 140 Ya 119
48291 Arrazola BI 20 Xc 90
09572 Arreba BU 30 Wb 91
14191 Arrecife CO 150 Va 122
35509 Arrecife GC 182 Mc 175
33775 Arredondas AS 13 Sf 88
39813 Arredondo CB 18 Wc 89
01426 Arreo VI 31 Xa 92
25551 Arres L 36 Ae 92
22372 Arresa HU 35 Zf 94
25587 Àrreu L 37 Ba 93
01439 Arriano VI 31 Xa 91
20218 Arriaran SS 20 Xe 90
29350 Arriate MA 166 Uf 128
27437 Arribade LU 24 Sc 94
31891 Arribe NC 20 Ya 90
14700 Arriel CO 150 Ue 122
48114 Arrieta BI 19 Xb 88
09215 Arrieta BU 31 Xb 92
35542 Arrieta GC 182 Md 174
31438 Arrieta NC 20 Yd 91
20710 Arrieta-Mendi SS 20 Xd 90
20215 Arrietas SS 20 Xe 91
48480 Arrigorriaga BI 19 Xa 89
01208 Arriola VI 32 Xd 91
33540 Arriondas AS 16 Ue 88
33310 Arriondo AS 15 Ud 88
13100 Arripas, Las CR 120 Vd 114
01207 Arrizala VI 32 Xd 92
22336 Arro HU 36 Ab 94
25551 Arró L 36 Ae 92
13193 Arroba de los Montes CR 120 Vc 114
33314 Arroes AS 15 Uc 87
20567 Arrolas SS 20 Xd 91
10623 Arrolobos CC 82 Tf 106
20749 Arrona SS 20 Xe 89
48370 Arronategui BI 19 Xb 88
48100 Arrondo BI 19 Xa 88
31243 Arróniz NC 32 Xf 93
05196 Arropino AV 84 Vc 105
25537 Arròs L 37 Ae 92
25571 Arròs L 37 Bb 93
01520 Arroyabe VI 31 Xc 91
41889 Arroya de la Plata SE 148 Te 122
09131 Arroyal BU 30 Wb 94
39419 Arroyal CB 29 Vf 91
02437 Arroyo AB 140 Ya 118
39360 Arroyo CB 17 Vf 88
39213 Arroyo CB 17 Vf 91
21342 Arroyo H 147 Tb 121
34347 Arroyo P 28 Va 95
30413 Arroyo Alazor MC 140 Xe 120
46140 Arroyo Cerezo V 106 Yd 108
41200 Arroyo Chozas SE 148 Ua 123
02610 Arroyo de Alarconcillos AB 123 Xc 115
29500 Arroyo de Colmenar MA 166 Vb 127
40215 Arroyo de Cuéllar SG 67 Vd 101
28170 Arroyo de Galga MD 86 Wd 104
45290 Arroyo de Guatén TO 102 Wb 108
47195 Arroyo de la Encomienda VA 47 Vb 99
10900 Arroyo de la Luz CC 98 Tc 112
29631 Arroyo de la Miel MA 175 Vc 129
13739 Arroyo de la Rambla CR 137 Wc 117
19238 Arroyo de las Fraguas GU 68 Wf 102
29650 Arroyo de las Palmas MA 175 Vc 129
06380 Arroyo del Castaño y Rubiales BA 132 Tb 118
29239 Arroyo del Cauche MA 167 Vd 127
14978 Arroyo del Cerezo CO 167 Ve 125
23340 Arroyo del Ojanco J 138 Xa 119
09239 Arroyo de Muñó BU 48 Wa 95
14979 Arroyo de Priego CO 167 Ve 125
09615 Arroyo de Salas BU 49 We 96
06850 Arroyo de San Serván BA 116 Td 115
01427 Arroyo de San Zardornil BU 31 We 91
04550 Arroyo de Verdelecho AL 170 Xd 126
23380 Arroyofrío AB 139 Xc 118
44122 Arroyofrío TE 89 Yd 107
29500 Arroyo Jevar MA 166 Vc 127
29193 Arroyo Luis MA 167 Ve 128
23487 Arroyo Molinos J 153 Wf 122
11688 Arroyomolinos CA 165 Ud 128
28939 Arroyomolinos MD 86 Wa 107
10410 Arroyomolinos de la Vera CC 99 Ua 108
21280 Arroyomolinos de León H 148 Td 120
10161 Arroyomolinos de Montánchez CC 117 Tf 113
06260 Arroyo Moro BA 148 Te 120
18270 Arroyo-Pinares GR 168 Vf 125
23499 Arroyos, Los J 139 Xc 119
23470 Arroyo Salado J 153 Wf 121
23550 Arroyo Santo J 153 We 122
30441 Arroyo Tercero MC 140 Xe 119
47162 Arroyo Viejo VA 66 Vc 99
23100 Arroyovil J 152 Wc 121
09549 Arroyuelo BU 30 Wd 91
39232 Arroyuelos CB 30 Wa 91
18312 Arrozuelas GR 167 Ve 125
31840 Arruazu NC 32 Xf 91
26151 Arrubal RI 32 Xe 94
31878 Arruitz NC 21 Ya 91
23700 Arryanes J 137 Wc 120
25799 Ars L 37 Bc 94
25722 Arseguell = Arsèguel L 38 Bd 94
48278 Arta BI 20 Xc 89
07570 Artà IB 111 Dc 110
20759 Artadi SS 20 Xe 89
31422 Artaiz NC 33 Yd 92
46162 Artaj V 107 Zb 110
31140 Artajona NC 33 Yb 93
25577 Artamont L 37 Bb 92
12527 Artana CS 108 Ze 109
31395 Artariain NC 33 Yc 93
22390 Artasona HU 55 Ab 96
22283 Artasona del Llano HU 54 Zc 96
31290 Artavia NC 32 Xf 92
31272 Artaza NC 32 Xf 92
01428 Artaza VI 31 Xa 91
01196 Artaza VI 31 Xb 91
31173 Artázcoz NC 33 Yb 92
31109 Artazu NC 33 Ya 92
48170 Arteaga BI 19 Xa 89
48314 Arteaga BI 20 Xc 88
31241 Arteaga NC 32 Xf 92
02137 Arteaga de Arriba AB 139 Xe 117
48170 Arteaga-San Martin BI 19 Xa 89
12430 Arteas de Abajo CS 107 Zb 109
12430 Arteas de Arriba CS 107 Zb 109
35108 Artedara GC 184 Kc 181
25718 Artedó L 38 Bd 94
15142 Arteixo C 11 Rd 89
35479 Artejévez GC 184 Kb 181
12125 Artejuela, La CS 107 Zc 108
48192 Artekona BI 19 Wf 90
35350 Artenara GC 184 Kc 180
15109 Artes C 10 Rb 89
08271 Artés B 58 Bf 98
25150 Artesa de Lleida L 75 Ae 99
25730 Artesa de Segre L 56 Ba 97
12220 Artesa d'Onda CS 108 Ze 109
48112 Arteta BI 19 Xa 88
31491 Arteta NC 33 Yd 93
31480 Artieda NC 33 Ye 92
50683 Artieda Z 34 Za 93
25599 Arties L 37 Af 92
09588 Artieta BU 19 We 90
48370 Artigas BI 19 Xb 88
31754 Artikutza NC 21 Yb 89
22620 Arto HU 35 Zd 94
01468 Artomaña VI 19 Xa 91
36528 Artoño PO 23 Rf 92
22623 Artosilla HU 35 Ze 94
23291 Artuñedo, El J 139 Xb 120
31754 Artzan NC 21 Ya 90
01478 Artziniega VI 19 Wf 90
35400 Arucas GC 184 Kc 180
22460 Arués HU 36 Ab 95
38892 Arure TF 184 He 180
26270 Arviza o Arviza Barrena RI 31 Wf 94
27168 Arxemil LU 12 Sd 91
27619 Arxemil LU 24 Sd 92
27548 Arxuá LU 24 Sb 93
32616 Arzádegos OR 43 Se 97
15839 Arzón C 22 Ra 91
31291 Arzoz NC 33 Ya 92
01520 Arzubiaga VI 31 Xc 91
15984 Asados C 22 Rb 92
31282 Asarta NC 32 Xe 93
15313 Ascabanas C 11 Rf 89
22715 Ascara HU 34 Zc 93
09215 Ascarza BU 31 Xb 92
01193 Ascarza VI 31 Xc 91
43791 Ascó T 74 Ad 101
31243 Ascona NC 32 Xf 93
30535 Ascoy MC 141 Yd 119
13597 Asdrúbal CR 136 Vf 117
10628 Asegur CC 82 Te 106
30813 Asensios, Los MC 156 Yb 123
15238 Asenso C 22 Ra 91
33555 Asiego AS 16 Va 89
22713 Asieso HU 35 Zc 93
50619 Asín Z 34 Yf 95
22372 Asín de Broto HU 35 Zf 93
27513 Asma LU 24 Sa 93
27519 Asma LU 24 Sb 93
25799 Asnurri L 38 Bc 94

242 | Arcenillas

40517 Barahona de Fresno SG
68 Wc 100
31879 Baraibar NC 21 Ya 91
05635 Barajas AV 84 Uf 106
13250 Barajas CR 121 Wc 114
28042 Barajas MD 86 Wc 106
16460 Barajas de Melo CU
103 Xa 108
34878 Barajores P 28 Vb 92
14850 Barajuela CO 151 Vd 122
48901 Barakaldo = San Vicente de
Barakaldo BI 19 Xa 89
27680 Baralla LU 25 Se 91
01450 Barambio VI 19 Xa 90
09569 Baranda BU 18 Wc 90
27244 Barangón LU 13 Se 90
31160 Barañáin NC 33 Yb 92
42213 Baraona SO 69 Xc 101
31395 Barásoain NC 33 Yc 93
08230 Barata, La B 58 Bf 99
41870 Barbacena SE 148 Td 124
32890 Barbadás OR 24 Sa 95
27616 Barbadelo LU 24 Sd 92
37440 Barbadillo SA 64 Ua 103
09615 Barbadillo de Herreros BU
50 We 96
09613 Barbadillo del Mercado BU
49 Wd 96
09614 Barbadillo del Pez BU
49 We 96
27341 Barbain LU 24 Sd 92
16196 Barbalimpia CU 104 Xe 109
37607 Barbalos SA 82 Ua 104
32459 Barbantes OR 23 Rf 94
32140 Barbantiño OR 23 Sa 94
06499 Barbaño BA 116 Tc 115
20214 Barbari SS 20 Xe 90
31243 Barbarin NC 32 Xf 93
03689 Barbarroja A 141 Za 119
22464 Barbaruens HU 36 Ac 93
22300 Barbastro HU 55 Aa 96
31180 Barbatáin NC 33 Yb 92
11160 Barbate CA 172 Ua 131
19262 Barbatona GU 69 Xc 102
15837 Barbeira C 10 Ra 91
27113 Barbeitos LU 13 Sf 90
25262 Barbens L 56 Ba 98
22637 Barbenuta HU 35 Ze 93
43422 Barberà de la Conca T
75 Bb 100
08210 Barberà del Vallès B 77 Ca 99
23280 Barbero J 138 Xa 119
50297 Bárboles Z 53 Ye 98
40530 Barbolla SG 68 Wb 101
19269 Barbolla, La GU 69 Xb 102
42291 Barbolla, La SO 50 Xb 99
36826 Barbudo PO 23 Rd 94
22255 Barbués HU 54 Zd 97
22132 Barbuñales HU 54 Zf 96
33879 Barca AS 14 Td 89
42210 Barca SO 69 Xc 100
11150 Barca, La CA 172 Ua 131
22148 Bárcabo HU 55 Aa 95
19115 Barca de Almoguera GU
87 Xa 107
11570 Barca de la Florida, La CA
172 Ua 129
36683 Barcala PO 22 Rc 92
36683 Barcala PO 23 Rc 92
06160 Barcarrota BA 132 Ta 117
42318 Barcebal SO 50 Wf 99
42318 Barcebalejo SO 50 Wf 99
37217 Barceíno SA 63 Td 102
27113 Barcela LU 13 Ta 90
36435 Barcela PO 41 Re 96
08002 Barcelona B 77 Cb 100
08859 Barceloneta, La B 76 Bf 100
25717 Barceloneta, La L 57 Bc 95
33858 Bárcena AS 14 Tf 88
33314 Bárcena AS 15 Uc 88
33316 Bárcena AS 15 Ud 87
39582 Bárcena CB 16 Vb 90
39809 Bárcena CB 18 Wd 89
09592 Bárcena de Bureba BU
30 Wc 93
34477 Bárcena de Campos P
29 Vd 94
39790 Bárcena de Cícero CB
18 Wc 88
39312 Bárcena de Cudón CB
17 Wa 88
39419 Bárcena de Ebro CB 29 Vf 91
33874 Bárcena del Monasterio AS
14 Tc 88
39420 Bárcena de Pie de Concha CB
17 Vf 90
09569 Bárcena de Pienza BU
18 Wd 90
39850 Bárcena de Udalla CB
18 Wd 89
39549 Barcenal, El CB 17 Vd 88
39518 Bárcena Mayor CB 17 Ve 90
09566 Bárcenas BU 18 Wc 90
39513 Barcenilla CB 17 Ve 89
39477 Barcenilla CB 17 Wa 88
09568 Barcenilla de Cerezos BU
18 Wc 90
37217 Barceo SA 63 Td 102
46176 Barchel V 106 Yf 110

16118 Barchín del Hoyo CU
105 Xf 111
27658 Barcia LU 13 Ta 91
36837 Barcia PO 23 Rd 94
36878 Barciademera PO 23 Rd 95
47674 Barcial de la Loma VA
46 Ue 97
49760 Barcial del Barco ZA 46 Uc 97
06393 Barciales, Los BA 132 Td 118
27278 Barcias LU 13 Se 90
45525 Barcience TO 101 Ve 109
45250 Barciles Bajo TO 102 Wb 109
09212 Barcina del Barco BU
31 We 92
09593 Barcina de los Montes BU
30 We 92
18550 Barcinas GR 168 Wc 124
32300 Barco, O = O Barco de
Valdeorras OR 25 Ta 94
05600 Barco de Ávila, El AV
83 Uc 106
32300 Barco de Valdeorras, O = O
Barco OR 25 Ta 94
42368 Barcones SO 69 Xb 101
47500 Barco y Pinar de la Nava, El
VA 65 Uf 100
50296 Bardallor Z 53 Ye 98
09219 Bardauri BU 31 Xa 92
23330 Bardazoso J 138 Xa 120
50694 Bardenas del Caudillo Z
53 Ye 95
15124 Bardullas C 10 Qe 90
36300 Baredo PO 41 Ra 96
39170 Bareyo CB 18 Wc 88
45593 Bargas TO 102 Vf 109
31229 Bargota NC 32 Xe 93
41569 Bariada de la Paz SE
166 Va 124
31396 Bariáin NC 33 Yc 93
25794 Bardías L 37 Bb 95
46758 Bárig = Barx V 126 Ze 114
31523 Barillas NC 52 Yc 97
48278 Barinaga BI 20 Xd 89
30648 Barinas MC 141 Yf 119
31272 Baríndano NC 32 Xf 92
24239 Bariones de la Vega LE
46 Uc 97
15113 Barizo C 10 Ra 89
49582 Barjacoba ZA 44 Ta 96
24521 Barjas LE 25 Ta 93
38726 Barlovento TF 181 Hb 176
22192 Barluenga HU 54 Zd 95
24913 Barniedo de la Reina LE
16 Va 91
25593 Baro L 37 Ba 94
46117 Baró, El V 107 Zd 111
01211 Baroja VI 31 Xb 93
12193 Barona, La CS 108 Zf 107
25747 Baronia de Rialb, La L
56 Bb 97
15979 Barosa C 22 Qf 92
22712 Barós HU 35 Zc 93
30179 Barqueros MC 156 Yd 121
14700 Barqueta, La CO 150 Ue 122
37488 Barquilla SA 81 Tb 104
10318 Barquilla de Pinares CC
99 Ud 108
05692 Barquillo, El AV 83 Uc 106
15210 Barquiña C 22 Ra 92
46600 Barraca d'Aigüesvives, La V
126 Zd 114
12420 Barracas CS 107 Zb 108
30085 Barracas, Las MC 157 Zb 123
32655 Barracel OR 42 Sb 96
44220 Barrachina TE 72 Yf 103
44400 Barrachinas, Las TE
91 Zb 107
05110 Barraco, El AV 84 Vc 106
10696 Barrado CC 99 Ua 108
14911 Barragana Alta CO
166 Vc 124
14911 Barragana Baja CO
166 Vc 124
48288 Barrainka BI 20 Xc 88
32430 Barral OR 23 Rf 95
25529 Barranc de Peranera L
37 Ae 94
03100 Barranco A 142 Zd 117
23191 Barranco de Cárchel J
152 Wc 123
18711 Barranco de Ferrer GR
169 Wd 128
29310 Barranco del Agua, El MA
167 Vd 125
29400 Barranco de la Madera MA
166 Uf 128
30889 Barranco del Baladre MC
156 Yc 124
35421 Barranco del Laurel GC
184 Kc 180
18190 Barranco del Oro GR
168 Wc 126
30890 Barranco de los Hilarios MC
155 Yb 123
04270 Barranco de los Lobos, El AL
171 Xe 126
35457 Barranco del Pinar GC
184 Kc 180
38810 Barranco de Santiago TF
184 He 180

30876 Barranco de Seca MC
156 Yd 123
38109 Barranco Hondo TF
181 Id 178
46174 Barranco Hondo V 107 Zb 110
30550 Barranco-Molax MC
141 Yd 119
23330 Barranco Montesina J
138 Wf 120
04271 Barranco Muñoz, El AL
171 Xf 125
04889 Barrancón de Bacares, El AL
170 Xd 125
14450 Barranco Palomo CO
135 Va 118
06292 Barrancos, Los BA
133 Td 120
11630 Barrancos, Los CA
165 Ub 128
23391 Barrancos, Los J 139 Xb 118
30412 Barranda MC 155 Ya 120
04117 Barranquete, El AL
171 Xe 127
35128 Barranquillo Andrés, El GC
184 Kb 181
10550 Barrantes CC 116 Tb 113
36749 Barrantes PO 41 Rb 96
09587 Barrasa BU 18 We 90
02639 Barrax AB 123 Xe 114
32812 Barreal OR 42 Sa 95
06670 Barreales BA 132 Tc 118
39313 Barreda CB 17 Vf 88
39572 Barreda-Dos Amantes CB
17 Vc 90
33417 Barredo AS 15 Ua 87
33970 Barredos, Los AS 15 Uc 89
37129 Barregas SA 64 Ub 103
27792 Barreiros LU 13 Se 87
27520 Barrela, A LU 24 Sb 93
37256 Barreras SA 63 Tc 102
17515 Barretó, El GI 58 Cb 96
04450 Barriada de Alcora, La AL
170 Xb 127
38631 Barriada de Entre-canales TF
180 Ib 180
04271 Barriada del Campico AL
171 Xf 125
04850 Barriada del Morera AL
171 Xf 125
04850 Barriada de los Cojos AL
171 Xf 125
04850 Barriada de los García AL
171 Xf 125
04850 Barriada de los Huevanillas AL
171 Xf 125
23713 Barriada de Vadollano J
137 Wc 120
04271 Barriada Las Canteras AL
171 Xf 125
04458 Barriada Las Minas AL
169 Xb 126
04618 Barriada Nueva AL
171 Yb 125
44760 Barriada Obrera del Sur TE
91 Za 104
18710 Barriales GR 169 We 128
38769 Barriales, Los TF 181 Ha 177
48650 Barrica BI 19 Xa 88
24394 Barrientos LE 26 Ua 94
48870 Barrietas, Las BI 19 We 89
09511 Barriga BU 19 Wf 91
06900 Barrilejos BA 133 Tf 119
24151 Barrillos LE 27 Ud 92
24877 Barrillos de las Arrimadas LE
27 Ue 92
39957 Barrio CB 16 Vb 90
39210 Barrio CB 17 Ve 90
32453 Barrio OR 23 Rf 94
01423 Barrio VI 31 Wf 92
02328 Barrio, El AB 124 Ya 115
05514 Barrio, El AV 83 Ue 106
32112 Barrio, O OR 24 Sb 95
46390 Barrio Arroyo V 106 Yf 111
18659 Barrio Bajo GR 168 Wc 127
16611 Barrio de Abajo CU
123 Xe 112
24412 Barrio de Abajo LE 25 Tc 93
40552 Barrio de Abajo SG
68 Wc 100
09213 Barrio de Abajo, El BU
30 Wd 92
05560 Barrio de Arriba AV 84 Uf 105
40331 Barrio de Arriba SG
67 Wb 100
46350 Barrio de Arriba V 107 Za 111
09213 Barrio de Arriba, El BU
30 Wd 92
09572 Barrio de Bricia BU 30 Wa 91
09249 Barrio de Díaz Ruiz BU
30 Wd 93
29250 Barrio de Enmedio MA
167 Vd 125
18659 Barrio de Fernán-Núñez GR
168 Wb 127
46350 Barrio de Gisbert V
107 Za 111
10500 Barrio de la Estación CC
115 Se 112
22320 Barrio de la Morera HU
55 Aa 95

34470 Barrio de la Puebla P
28 Vc 92
24133 Barrio de la Puente LE
26 Tf 92
46350 Barrio de las Atienzas V
107 Za 111
24689 Barrio de la Tercia LE
15 Uc 91
50650 Barrio del Beato Agno Z
52 Ye 97
44313 Barrio del Hospital TE
90 Yc 104
06176 Barrio del Pilar BA 132 Tc 117
22483 Barrio del Pou HU 36 Ad 95
02213 Barrio del Santuario AB
125 Ye 113
10629 Barrio del Teso CC 82 Te 106
09226 Barrio de Muñó BU 48 Vf 95
24150 Barrio de Nuestra Señora LE
27 Ud 92
30300 Barrio de Peral MC
157 Za 123
49358 Barrio de Rábano ZA 44 Tc 96
09135 Barrio de San Felices BU
29 Ve 93
34810 Barrio de San Pedro P
29 Vd 92
34810 Barrio de Santa María P
29 Vd 92
34815 Barrio de San Vicente P
29 Ve 93
32311 Barrio e Castelo OR 25 Ta 94
16860 Barrio El Otro Lado CU
88 Xe 106
24223 Barrio Estación LE 27 Uc 94
24526 Barrio las Lamas LE 25 Ta 92
09127 Barrio-Lucio BU 29 Vf 92
42169 Barriomartín SO 51 Xd 97
11149 Barrio Nuevo CA 172 Tf 130
18891 Barrionuevo GR 154 Xd 123
02511 Barrio Nuevo, El AB
140 Yb 116
39418 Barriopalacio BU 29 Ve 91
09126 Barrio-Panizares BU
29 Wa 92
19490 Barriopedro GU 87 Xb 104
11370 Barrios, Los CA 175 Ud 131
23740 Barrios, Los J 152 Vf 120
09249 Barrios de Bureba, Los BU
30 Wd 93
09199 Barrios de Colina BU
30 Wd 94
24609 Barrios de Gordón, Los LE
27 Ub 91
34111 Barrios de la Vega P 28 Vb 93
24148 Barrios de Luna, Los LE
27 Ua 91
24368 Barrios de Nistoso, Los LE
26 Tf 92
09124 Barrios de Villadiego BU
29 Vf 93
09553 Barriosuso BU 18 Wc 91
09618 Barriosuso BU 49 Wd 97
34470 Barriosuso P 29 Ve 93
33595 Barro AS 16 Vb 88
36875 Barro PO 23 Rd 95
36190 Barro = San Antoniño (Barro)
PO 22 Rc 93
05229 Barromán AV 66 Va 102
01428 Barron VI 31 Xa 91
39408 Barros CB 17 Vf 89
11139 Barrosa, La CA 172 Te 130
24521 Barrosas LE 25 Sf 93
32520 Barroso OR 23 Re 94
37255 Barruecopardo SA 63 Tc 102
09554 Barruelo BU 30 Wc 91
34820 Barruelo de Santullán P
29 Ve 91
09124 Barruelo de Villadiego BU
29 Vf 93
47129 Barruelos del Valle VA
47 Uf 98
25527 Barruera L 37 Ae 93
09553 Barruso BU 19 We 90
11130 Bartivas CA 172 Tf 130
35421 Bartolomé San GC
184 Kc 180
43415 Bartra, La T 75 Ba 101
50596 Barués Z 34 Ye 94
46758 Barx V 126 Ze 114
32372 Barxa, A OR 25 Sf 94
32545 Barxa, A OR 43 Se 97
27328 Barxas LU 25 Se 93
03818 Barxell, El A 142 Zc 116
32897 Barxés OR 42 Sa 97
46667 Barxeta V 126 Zd 114
27391 Barxo de Lor LU 24 Sd 93
33117 Bárzana AS 14 Ua 90
33456 Bárzanas, Las AS 14 Ua 87
31866 Basabúrua NC 21 Yb 90
20570 Basalgo SS 20 Xd 90
22372 Basarán HU 35 Ze 93
40180 Basardilla SG 67 Vf 102
30580 Basca, La MC 157 Yf 120
17483 Bàscara GI 59 Cf 96
15685 Bascoi C 11 Re 90
09339 Basconcillos BU 49 Wb 95
09126 Basconcillos del Tozo BU
29 Wa 92
33825 Báscones AS 14 Tf 88

39250 Báscones de Ebro P 29 Vf 92
09347 Báscones del Agua BU
49 Wb 96
34406 Báscones de Ojeda P
29 Vc 92
09146 Báscones de Zamanzas BU
30 Wb 91
36580 Bascuas PO 23 Re 92
09259 Bascuñana BU 31 Wf 94
16191 Bascuñana de San Pedro CU
88 Xe 107
09213 Bascuñuelos BU 30 Wd 92
48314 Basechetas BI 20 Xc 88
12193 Baseta, La CS 108 Zf 108
48130 Basigo BI 19 Xa 88
48100 Basozabal BI 19 Xa 88
48180 Basozabal BI 19 Xa 89
01420 Basquiñuelas VI 31 Xa 92
08680 Bassacs, Els B 57 Bf 96
43527 Bassa dels Ganduls, La T
93 Ac 104
03195 Bassars, Els A 142 Zc 119
17734 Bassegoda GI 39 Cd 95
17469 Basseia GI 59 Da 95
25198 Basses, Les L 55 Ad 99
50680 Bastanes NC 34 Ye 94
25725 Bastanist L 38 Be 95
22141 Bastarás HU 54 Zf 95
15280 Bastavales C 22 Rb 92
41100 Bastero SE 164 Ua 125
18870 Bastianes, Los GR
169 Xa 124
37621 Bastida, La SA 82 Tf 105
25555 Bastida de Bellera, La L
37 Af 94
25715 Bastida d'Ortons, La L
38 Bc 95
25556 Bastideta de Corroncui, La L
37 Af 95
17714 Bastons GI 58 Cd 96
25655 Basturs L 56 Ba 96
36448 Batalláns = San Pedro PO
41 Rd 96
02329 Batán, El AB 139 Xe 116
10692 Batán, El CC 98 Td 109
23293 Batán, El J 139 Xb 119
50660 Batán, El Z 52 Ye 97
50830 Batán, El Z 53 Zb 98
38294 Batán de Abajo TF 181 Ie 177
02137 Batán del Puerto AB
139 Xe 117
16420 Batán de San Pedro CU
104 Xa 109
40409 Batanejos SG 85 Vd 104
43786 Batea T 74 Ab 102
03600 Bateig A 142 Zb 118
05130 Baterna AV 84 Va 105
06659 Baterno BA 119 Va 115
17534 Batet GI 39 Cb 95
17812 Batet de la Serra GI 58 Cd 95
28976 Batres MD 86 Wa 107
37624 Batuecas, Las SA 82 Tf 106
18800 Baúl, El GR 154 Xa 124
08296 Bauma, La B 57 Bf 99
25549 Bausen L 36 Ae 91
18410 Bayacas GR 168 Wd 127
04479 Bayárcal AL 169 Xa 126
04888 Bayarque AL 170 Xd 125
33457 Bayas AS 14 Tf 87
33119 Bayo AS 14 Tf 88
50694 Bayo, El Z 52 Ye 95
24137 Bayos, Los LE 26 Te 91
42366 Bayubas de Abajo SO
69 Xa 99
42366 Bayubas de Arriba SO
69 Xa 99
18800 Baza GR 154 Xb 124
10697 Bazagona, La CC 99 Ua 109
13739 Bazán CR 137 Wc 117
06389 Bazana, La BA 132 Tb 119
15847 Bazar C 10 Rb 90
27258 Bazar LU 12 Sd 89
44492 Bea TE 72 Yf 102
36312 Beade PO 41 Rb 95
30382 Beal MC 157 Za 123
16152 Beamud CU 105 Yb 107
15689 Beán C 11 Rd 90
31179 Bearin NC 32 Xf 92
32520 Beariz OR 23 Re 94
21630 Beas H 161 Tb 124
20200 Beasain SS 20 Xe 90
18184 Beas de Granada GR
168 Wd 125
18516 Beas de Guadix GR
169 We 125
23280 Beas de Segura J 138 Xa 119
31892 Beasoáin NC 33 Yb 91
14850 Beatas, Las CO 151 Vd 123
15258 Beba C 22 Qf 91
24608 Beberino LE 27 Ub 91
24761 Bécares LE 45 Ua 96
05610 Becedas AV 83 Uc 106
05153 Becedillas AV 83 Ue 105
44588 Beceite TE 92 Ab 104
27640 Becerreá LU 25 Sf 91
05196 Becerril AV 84 Vc 105
37148 Becerril SA 64 Te 102
40510 Becerril SG 68 Wd 101
28490 Becerril de la Sierra MD
85 Wa 104

34487 Becerril del Carpio P 29 Ve 92
48870 Beci BI 19 We 89
20268 Bedaio SS 20 Xf 90
04288 Bédar AL 171 Ya 125
48287 Bedaroa = Bedarona BI 20 Xc 88
20268 Bedayo = Bedaio SS 20 Xf 90
32431 Bede = Cenlle OR 23 Rf 95
48390 Bedia BI 19 Xb 89
22438 Bediello HU 36 Ab 95
23537 Bedmar J 153 Wd 122
23537 Bedmar y Garcíez J 153 Wd 121
09568 Bedón BU 18 Wc 90
08784 Bedorc, El B 76 Be 99
33315 Bedriñana AS 15 Ud 88
02536 Beg AB 139 Xe 119
46419 Bega del Mar, La V 127 Ze 113
39580 Beges CB 16 Vc 89
17867 Beget GI 39 Cc 95
06250 Begico BA 133 Te 118
23520 Begíjar J 153 Wc 121
27373 Begonte LU 12 Sb 90
17857 Begudà GI 58 Cd 95
08782 Beguda Alta B 76 Bf 100
08782 Beguda Baixa, La B 76 Be 100
08859 Begues B 76 Bf 101
25556 Begunda d'Adons L 37 Ae 94
17255 Begur GI 59 Db 97
15808 Beigondo C 23 Rf 91
31753 Beintza-Labaien NC 21 Yb 90
31393 Beire NC 33 Yc 94
04458 Beires AL 169 Xb 126
32981 Beiro OR 24 Sa 94
20739 Beizama SS 20 Xe 90
37700 Béjar SA 83 Ub 106
12430 Bejís CS 107 Zb 109
12512 Bel CS 92 Aa 105
14280 Belalcázar CO 135 Uf 117
48460 Belandia BI 19 Wf 90
22622 Belarra HU 35 Zd 94
31174 Belascoáin NC 33 Yb 92
20491 Belauntza SS 20 Xf 90
20491 Belaunza = Belauntza SS 20 Xf 90
09226 Belbimbre BU 48 Vf 96
50130 Belchite Z 72 Zb 101
32520 Belecón OR 23 Re 94
22450 Beleder HU 36 Ac 94
10292 Belén CC 99 Ua 112
27889 Belén LU 10 Sd 87
30834 Belén MC 156 Ye 121
37789 Beleña SA 83 Uc 104
19237 Beleña de Sorbe GU 68 We 103
33557 Beleño AS 16 Uf 89
33996 Belerda AS 15 Ue 90
18515 Belerda GR 169 We 124
23489 Belerdas J 153 Wf 122
27814 Belesar LU 12 Sb 89
27188 Belesar LU 24 Sc 91
32950 Belesar OR 24 Sb 94
36307 Belesar PO 41 Rb 96
46868 Bèlgida V 126 Zd 115
25266 Belianes L 75 Ba 99
18101 Belicena GR 168 Wb 125
16470 Belinchón CU 103 Wf 108
29604 Bellamar MA 175 Vb 130
07769 Bellavista IB 77 Df 109
41704 Bellavista SE 163 Ua 125
43887 Bellavista T 76 Bb 101
17141 Bellcaire = Bellcaire d'Empordà GI 59 Da 96
17141 Bellcaire d'Empordà GI 59 Da 96
25337 Bellcaire d'Urgell L 56 Af 98
22436 Bellestar HU 55 Ac 95
25335 Bellestar L 56 Af 98
12599 Bellestar, El CS 92 Ab 105
22196 Bellestar del Flumen HU 54 Zd 96
17708 Bell-lloc GI 40 Cf 94
17245 Bell-lloc GI 59 Cf 97
25220 Bell-lloc d'Urgell L 56 Ae 99
43738 Bellmunt de Ciurana = Bellmunt del Priorat T 75 Ae 102
25213 Bellmunt de Segarra L 57 Bc 99
25336 Bellmunt d'Urgell L 56 Af 98
33681 Bello AS 15 Uc 90
44232 Bello TE 71 Yd 103
22149 Bellostas, Las HU 35 Zf 94
02460 Bellotar AB 139 Xc 118
43421 Bellpart B 76 Bc 99
25250 Bellpuig L 56 Ba 99
46714 Bellreguard V 127 Zf 115
43413 Belltall T 75 Bb 99
46839 Bellús V 126 Zd 115
43719 Bellvei T 76 Bd 101
25212 Bellvel L 56 Bb 98
07500 Bellver IB 111 Db 111
25721 Bellver L 38 Be 94
25720 Bellver de Cerdanya L 38 Be 94
25318 Bellver d'Ossó L 56 Bb 98
07260 Bellviure IB 111 Cf 112
23568 Belmez J 153 Wd 122
14240 Bélmez CO 135 Ue 119
23568 Bélmez de la Moraleda J 153 Wd 122
39557 Belmonte CB 17 Vd 90
16640 Belmonte CU 104 Xb 111
50332 Belmonte de Calatayud Z 71 Yc 101
34304 Belmonte de Campos P 47 Va 97
44642 Belmonte de Mezquín TE 92 Zf 103
33830 Belmonte de Miranda AS 14 Te 89
28390 Belmonte de Tajo MD 103 Wd 108
16779 Belmontejo CU 104 Xd 110
02487 Belmontes, Los AB 139 Xe 119
27774 Beloi LU 12 Sd 87
30385 Belones, Los MC 157 Zb 123
09250 Belorado BU 31 We 94
27865 Belsar LU 12 Sc 87
22363 Belsierre HU 36 Aa 93
22150 Belsué HU 35 Zd 95
42248 Beltejar SO 69 Xd 101
01449 Belunza VI 19 Xa 91
15990 Beluso C 22 Ra 92
36939 Beluso PO 22 Rb 95
22533 Belver HU 55 Ab 98
49830 Belver de los Montes ZA 46 Ud 98
13379 Belvis CR 137 Wa 117
24236 Belvis LE 46 Uc 96
28862 Belvis de Jarama MD 86 Wc 105
45660 Belvís de la Jara TO 100 Va 110
10394 Belvís de Monroy CC 99 Uc 110
31193 Belzunce NC 33 Yb 91
15873 Bembibre C 10 Rb 90
24300 Bembibre LE 26 Td 93
27556 Bembibre LU 24 Sb 92
43592 Bemboire OR 43 Sf 96
32617 Bemposta OR 43 Sd 97
22580 Benabarre HU 55 Ac 96
30410 Benablón MC 155 Ya 120
46810 Benacancil V 126 Zb 115
46351 Benacas V 106 Yf 111
41805 Benacazón SE 164 Te 124
12123 Benachera CS 107 Zd 108
29493 Benadalid MA 173 Ue 129
12190 Benadresa CS 108 Zf 108
47880 Benafarces VA 46 Ue 99
12449 Benafer CS 107 Zc 109
12134 Benafigos CS 92 Ze 107
29738 Benagalbón MA 167 Ve 128
46173 Benagéber V 106 Yf 110
22713 Benaguás HU 35 Zc 93
46180 Benaguasil V 107 Zc 111
04410 Benahadux AL 170 Xd 127
29679 Benahavís MA 174 Uf 129
29749 Benajarafe Alto MA 167 Ve 128
29491 Benalauría MA 174 Ue 129
46811 Benalí V 126 Zb 114
29630 Benalmádena MA 175 Vc 129
29639 Benalmádena MA 175 Vc 129
18510 Benalúa de Guadix GR 169 Wf 124
18566 Benalúa de las Villas GR 152 Wb 124
11190 Benalup CA 173 Ub 130
11190 Benalup-Casas Viejas CA 173 Ub 130
11679 Benamahoma CA 165 Ud 128
29718 Benamargosa MA 167 Ve 127
24234 Benamariel LE 27 Uc 94
18817 Benamaurel GR 154 Xb 123
29770 Benamayor MA 168 Wa 128
14910 Benamejí CO 167 Vc 125
46810 Benamil V 126 Zb 115
42230 Benamira SO 70 Xd 102
29719 Benamocarra MA 167 Vf 128
30410 Benamor de Abajo MC 140 Ya 120
11612 Benaocaz CA 173 Ud 128
29370 Benaoján MA 174 Ue 128
29791 Benaque MA 167 Ve 128
29490 Benarrabá MA 173 Ue 129
16337 Benarruel CU 106 Yd 108
12160 Benasal CS 92 Zf 106
03814 Benasau A 143 Zd 116
22440 Benasque HU 36 Ad 93
12181 Benasqués CS 108 Aa 107
23260 Benatae J 138 Wf 119
23390 Benatae J 139 Xc 118
25658 Benavent = Benavent de la Conca L 56 Ba 96
25132 Benavent de Segrià L 55 Ad 98
06519 Benavente BA 115 Sf 113
49600 Benavente ZA 46 Ub 96
22436 Benavente de Aragón HU 55 Ac 95
24280 Benavides de Órbigo LE 27 Ua 93
24233 Benazolve LE 27 Uc 94
41510 Bencarrón SE 165 Ub 124
27329 Bendilló LU 25 Se 94
33888 Bendón AS 13 Tb 89
04479 Benecid AL 170 Xa 127
49123 Benegiles ZA 46 Uc 99
31395 Benegorri NC 33 Yc 93
03460 Beneixama A 142 Zb 116
46293 Beneixida V 126 Zc 114
04760 Benejí AL 169 Xa 127
03390 Benejúzar A 157 Za 120
25555 Benés L 37 Af 94
46017 Benetúser = Benetússer V 126 Zd 112
46017 Benetússer = Benetúser V 126 Zd 112
03316 Benferri A 141 Za 120
03786 Beniaia A 127 Ze 116
30579 Beniaján MC 157 Yf 121
03828 Benialfaquí A 143 Zd 116
03788 Benialí A 127 Ze 115
03778 Beniarbeig A 127 Zf 116
03517 Beniardá A 143 Ze 116
46722 Beniarjó V 127 Ze 115
03850 Beniarrés A 126 Zd 116
46844 Beniatjar V 126 Zd 115
12580 Benicarló CS 93 Ac 106
12560 Benicasim = Benicàssim CS 108 Aa 108
12560 Benicàssim = Bencàsim CS 108 Aa 108
46838 Benicolet V 126 Zd 115
46689 Benicull de Xúquer V 126 Zd 113
03759 Benidoleig A 127 Zf 116
03501*Benidorm A 143 Zf 117
30130 Beniel MC 157 Za 120
03509 Benienso A 143 Ze 117
46450 Benifaió V 126 Zd 113
46791 Benifairó de la Valldigna V 126 Ze 114
46511 Benifairó de les Valls V 108 Ze 110
43512 Benifallet T 74 Ad 103
03816 Benifallim A 142 Zd 117
03517 Benifato A 143 Ze 116
46450 Benifayó = Benifaió V 126 Zd 113
46825 Benifetal V 126 Za 114
22474 Benifons HU 36 Ae 94
46830 Beniganim V 126 Zd 115
03794 Benigembla A 143 Zf 116
38129 Benijo TF 181 Ie 177
03178 Benijófar A 157 Zb 120
03810 Benilloba A 142 Zd 116
03827 Benillup A 142 Zd 116
03827 Benimarfull A 126 Zd 116
03812 Benimassot A 143 Ze 116
03791 Benimaurell A 127 Zf 116
03769 Benimeli A 127 Zf 116
46291 Benimodo V 126 Zc 113
46611 Benimuslem V 126 Zd 114
04769 Benínar AL 169 Wf 127
46703 Benipoa V 127 Ze 115
46469 Beniparrell V 126 Zd 112
03788 Benirrama A 127 Ze 116
43747 Benisanet = Benissanet T 74 Ad 102
46181 Benisano V 107 Zc 111
46869 Benisoda V 126 Zc 116
03720 Benissa A 143 Aa 116
03788 Benissili A 127 Ze 116
46839 Benisuera V 126 Zd 115
14940 Benita, La CO 151 Vc 123
03726 Benitachell = Poble Nou de Benitatxell, el A 143 Aa 116
04276 Benitagla AL 170 Xe 125
03788 Benitaia A 127 Ze 116
12222 Benitandús CS 108 Zd 109
04275 Benitorafe AL 170 Xe 125
05141 Benitos AV 84 Va 104
25632 Beniure L 56 Ae 96
04276 Benizalón AL 170 Xe 125
29749 Benjarafe MA 167 Ve 128
24123 Benllera LE 27 Ub 92
12181 Benlloch CS 92 Aa 107
03788 Bennissivà A 127 Ze 116
25551 Benòs L 36 Ae 92
10135 Benquerencia CC 117 Tf 113
27792 Benquerencia LU 13 Se 87
06429 Benquerencia de la Serena BA 134 Ud 116
25617 Bensa L 56 Af 98
20737 Bentaberri SS 20 Xe 89
04569 Bentarique AL 170 Xc 127
31750 Bentas NC 21 Yb 90
09593 Bentretea BU 30 Wd 92
22622 Bentué de Nocito HU 35 Ze 94
12150 Bentué de Rasal HU 35 Zc 94
24389 Benuza LE 25 Tb 94
29620 Benyamina MA 175 Vd 129
15686 Benza C 11 Rc 90
04647 Benzal AL 155 Yb 124
51002 Benzú CE 175 Ud 133
15113 Beo C 10 Ra 89
31193 Beorburu NC 33 Yb 91
31483 Beortegui NC 33 Yd 92
01477 Beotegui VI 19 Wf 90
31780 Bera = Vera de Bidasoa NC 21 Yb 89
31799 Beraiz NC 33 Yc 91
31869 Beramendi NC 21 Ya 91
39730 Beranga CB 18 Wc 88
48640 Berango BI 19 Xa 88
01211 Berantevilla VI 31 Xa 92
01211 Beranturi = Berantevilla VI 31 Xa 92
25510 Beranui L 37 Af 94
22484 Beranúy HU 36 Ad 94
20492 Berastegi SS 20 Ya 90
42107 Beratón SO 52 Yb 98
18248 Berbe Bajo GR 168 Wb 124
50294 Berbedel Z 71 Ye 99
22131 Berbegal HU 54 Aa 97
11500 Berben CA 172 Te 129
09511 Berberana BU 31 Wf 91
33346 Berbes AS 16 Uf 88
31252 Berbinzana NC 33 Ya 93
22636 Berbusa HU 35 Ze 93
09569 Bercedo BU 18 Wd 90
26327 Berceo RI 31 Xa 94
47115 Bercero VA 66 Uf 99
34310 Bercerril de Campos P 47 Vc 96
47115 Berceruelo VA 47 Uf 99
18451 Bérchules GR 169 We 127
40144 Bercial SG 66 Vd 103
45571 Bercial, El TO 100 Uf 110
45571 Bercial de San Rafael, El TO 100 Uf 110
05229 Bercial de Zapardiel AV 66 Va 102
49592 Bercianos de Aliste ZA 45 Te 98
24252 Bercianos del Páramo LE 27 Ub 94
24325 Bercianos del Real Camino LE 28 Uf 94
49333 Bercianos de Valverde ZA 45 Ua 97
40550 Bercimuel SG 68 Wc 100
05380 Bercimuelle AV 84 Uf 103
37750 Bercimuelle SA 83 Ud 105
46312 Bercuta V 106 Yf 110
50316 Berdejo Z 70 Ya 99
15151 Berdeogas C 10 Qf 90
15884 Berdía C 11 Rc 91
03720 Berdica A 143 Aa 116
15128 Berdoias C 10 Qf 90
33887 Berducedo AS 13 Tb 89
25795 Berén L 37 Bb 95
46666 Berfull V 126 Zd 114
08600 Berga B 57 Bf 96
37159 Berganciano SA 64 Te 102
22583 Berganúy HU 36 Ae 95
01212 Berganzo VI 31 Xb 93
20570 Bergara SS 20 Xd 90
26588 Bergasa RI 51 Xf 95
26588 Bergasillas Bajera RI 51 Xf 95
26588 Bergasillas Somera RI 51 Xf 95
44556 Berge TE 91 Zd 103
01423 Bergonda = Bergüenda VI 31 Wf 92
15166 Bergondo C 11 Re 89
22714 Bergosa HU 35 Zc 93
22373 Bergua HU 35 Ze 93
31191 Beriáin NC 33 Yc 92
04760 Berja AL 169 Xa 127
27186 Berlai LU 24 Sc 91
05162 Berlanas, Las AV 84 Vb 104
06930 Berlanga BA 133 Ub 119
42360 Berlanga de Duero SO 69 Xa 100
24438 Berlanga del Bierzo LE 25 Tc 92
09316 Berlangas de Roa BU 48 Wa 98
30610 Bermeja, La MC 141 Yd 120
37291 Bermellar SA 63 Tb 103
48370 Bermeo BI 19 Xb 88
36517 Bermés PO 23 Rf 92
33118 Bermiego AS 14 Ua 89
49168 Bermillo de Alba ZA 45 Tf 99
49200 Bermillo de Sayago ZA 64 Tf 100
38729 Bermudez TF 181 Hb 176
15329 Bermui C 12 Sa 88
02327 Bernabé AB 123 Xf 116
14880 Bernabé CO 151 Ve 124
18615 Bernadilla, La GR 168 Wc 128
48290 Bernagoitia BI 19 Xb 89
30700 Bernal MC 157 Za 122
48891 Bernales BI 18 Wd 89
13630 Bernardo, El CR 122 Xa 113
40430 Bernardos SG 67 Vd 102
01118 Bernedo VI 32 Xd 93
03599 Bernia A 143 Zf 116
33556 Bernia de Onís AS 16 Va 88
19133 Berninches GU 87 Xb 105
37453 Bernoy-Cemprón SA 83 Ub 104
33394 Bernueces AS 15 Uc 87
22711 Bernués HU 35 Zc 94
45693 Bernúy TO 101 Vc 109
40460 Bernúy de Coca SG 66 Vc 101
40190 Bernúy de Porreros SG 67 Vf 102
05195 Bernúy-Salinero AV 85 Vc 105
05211 Bernuy Zapardiel AV 66 Va 103
12160 Berola de Grau CS 92 Zf 106
12160 Berola de Grau CS 92 Zf 106
32617 Berrande OR 43 Se 97
35489 Berrazales, Los GC 184 Kc 180
32812 Berredo OR 42 Sa 96
48381 Berreño BI 19 Xc 89
15687 Berreo C 11 Rd 91
48710 Berriatua = Ribera BI 20 Xd 89
01138 Berrícano VI 19 Xb 91
48230 Berrio BI 20 Xc 90
31195 Berrioplano NC 33 Yb 91
48230 Berriozabal-Aramiño BI 20 Xc 90
31013 Berriozar NC 33 Yb 91
48240 Berriz = Berriz-Olakueta BI 20 Xc 89
31790 Berrizaun NC 21 Yb 89
48240 Berriz-Olakueta BI 20 Xc 89
02329 Berro AB 140 Xe 116
30848 Berro, El MC 156 Yd 121
20493 Berrobi SS 20 Xf 90
06612 Berrocal BA 119 Uf 115
21647 Berrocal H 148 Tc 123
40181 Berrocal SG 67 Wa 102
10700 Berrocal, El CC 82 Ua 107
41240 Berrocal, El SE 148 Tf 122
37609 Berrocal de Huebra SA 82 Ua 104
37130 Berrocal de la Espinera SA 64 Tf 103
37592 Berrocal del Río SA 81 Tc 105
37795 Berrocal de Salvatierra SA 83 Ub 105
10392 Berrocalejo CC 100 Ud 110
05194 Berrocalejo de Aragona AV 85 Vc 104
10665 Berrocosos, Los CC 98 Tf 107
31796 Berroeta NC 21 Yc 90
33186 Berrón, El AS 15 Ub 88
25588 Berròs Jussà L 37 Ba 93
25588 Berròs Sobirà L 37 Ba 93
01194 Berrosteguieta VI 31 Xb 92
22373 Berroy HU 35 Zf 93
47813 Berrueces VA 47 Uf 97
50373 Berrueco Z 71 Yd 103
23649 Berrueco, El J 152 Wa 121
28192 Berrueco, El MD 68 Wc 103
30800 Berruecos MC 155 Yb 122
10318 Berruguillas CC 100 Ud 109
15220 Bertamiráns C 22 Rc 91
31720 Bertizarana NC 21 Yc 90
03669 Bertrans, Els A 142 Za 118
31866 Berute NC 21 Yb 90
10129 Berzocana CC 118 Ud 112
28420 Berzosa MD 85 Wa 105
42351 Berzosa SO 49 Wf 99
09245 Berzosa de Bureba BU 30 We 93
28194 Berzosa del Lozoya MD 68 Wc 103
34485 Berzosa de los Hidalgos P 29 Vd 92
39250 Berzosilla P 29 Vf 92
17850 Besalu GI 59 Ce 95
24885 Besande LE 28 Va 91
17162 Bescanó GI 59 Ce 97
25719 Bescaran L 38 Bd 94
22623 Bescós de Guarga HU 35 Ze 94
36598 Besexos PO 23 Re 92
22133 Bespén HU 54 Zf 96
27328 Bessarredonda LU 25 Sf 93
22362 Bestué HU 36 Aa 93
33815 Besullo AS 13 Tc 89
35637 Betancuria GC 183 Lf 178
14449 Betán de los Canos CR 136 Vc 117
15319 Betanzos C 11 Re 89
09512 Betarres BU 30 Wd 91
02694 Bete AB 125 Yd 115
31890 Betelu NC 20 Ya 90
46117 Bétera V 107 Zd 111
22583 Betesa HU 36 Ae 94
22638 Betés de Sobremonte HU 35 Zd 93
16870 Beteta CU 89 Xf 105
03640 Beties A 142 Zb 118
25537 Betlan L 37 Ae 92
01510 Betolaza VI 19 Xb 91
22148 Betorz HU 35 Aa 95
27617 Betote LU 24 Sd 92
12549 Betxí CS 108 Ze 109
17850 Beuda GI 59 Ce 95
08515 Beulaigua B 58 Ca 96
31867 Beunza NC 21 Yb 91
15982 Bexo C 22 Rb 92
09572 Bezana BU 18 Wa 91
09615 Bezares BU 49 Wf 96
26312 Bezares RI 31 Xb 94
44121 Bezas TE 90 Ye 107
18660 Béznar GR 168 Wc 127
31395 Bézquiz NC 33 Yc 93
03410 Biar A 142 Zb 117
22311 Bibán HU 35 Zf 94
22486 Bibiles HU 36 Ae 94
12124 Bibioj CS 91 Zd 107
46825 Bicorp V 126 Zb 114
20496 Bidania SS 20 Xe 90
31174 Bidaurreta NC 33 Ya 92

A
B
C
D
E
F
G
H
I
J
K
L
M
N
Ñ
O
P
Q
R
S
T
U
V
W
X
Y
Z

Bidaurreta | 245 E

20496 Bidegoyan SS 20 Xf 90
27632 Biduedo LU 25 Se 92
32141 Biduedo OR 23 Sa 94
15895 Biduido C 22 Rc 91
33190 Biedes AS 15 Ua 88
50619 Biel Z 34 Za 94
39550 Bielba CB 17 Vd 89
22350 Bielsa HU 36 Ab 93
02360 Bienservida AB 139 Xc 117
06250 Bienvenida BA 133 Te 119
13596 Bienvenida CR 136 Vc 117
33539 Bierces AS 15 Ud 88
22144 Bierge HU 54 Zf 96
17199 Biert GI 59 Ce 96
33816 Biescas AS 14 Td 89
22630 Biescas HU 35 Ze 93
22451 Biescas HU 36 Ac 94
22484 Biescas de Obarra HU 36 Ad 94
03380 Bigastro A 157 Za 120
08415 Bigues i Riells B 58 Cb 98
31454 Bigüézal NC 34 Yf 92
50316 Bijuesca Z 70 Ya 99
48141 Bikarregi BI 19 Xb 90
01309 Bilar = Elvillar VI 32 Xc 93
48001*Bilbao BI 19 Xa 89
41530 Bilbao SE 165 Ud 125
48001*Bilbo = Bilbao BI 19 Xa 89
48112 Billabaso BI 19 Xa 88
48100 Billela BI 19 Xa 88
01195 Biloda = Villodas VI 31 Xb 92
33818 Bimeda AS 14 Tc 90
33527 Bimenes AS 15 Uc 89
22510 Binaced HU 55 Ab 98
22791 Binacua HU 34 Zb 93
07712 Binaixa IB 77 Eb 109
22500 Binéfar HU 55 Ab 97
07143 Biniali IB 110 Cf 111
07369 Biniamar IB 111 Cf 110
07713 Biniancolla IB 77 Eb 110
07101 Biniaraix IB 110 Ce 110
07711 Binibequer Vell IB 77 Eb 110
07314 Binibona IB 111 Cf 110
07712 Binicalaf IB 77 Eb 109
07712 Binidali Nou IB 77 Eb 109
07750 Binidenfa IB 77 Ea 108
22773 Biniés HU 34 Zb 93
07740 Binifabini IB 77 Eb 109
07749 Binifaida IB 77 Ea 109
07315 Binifaldó IB 111 Cf 109
07730 Binifamis IB 77 Ea 109
07730 Binijame IB 77 Ea 109
07748 Binimella IB 77 Ea 108
07748 Binimella Nou IB 77 Ea 108
07711 Biniparren IB 77 Eb 109
07720 Binisaida IB 77 Eb 109
07748 Binisarret IB 77 Ea 108
07300 Biniseti Nou IB 111 Cf 110
07711 Binissafúler IB 77 Eb 110
07711 Binissafúler Nou IB 77 Eb 109
07350 Binissalem IB 110 Cf 110
22620 Binué HU 35 Zd 93
22622 Binueste HU 35 Zf 94
25752 Biosca L 57 Bc 97
50695 Biota Z 34 Ye 95
22470 Bisaurri HU 36 Ad 94
43372 Bisbal de Falset, La T 75 Ae 101
43717 Bisbal del Penedès, La T 76 Bc 101
17100 Bisbal d'Empordà, La GI 59 Da 97
25795 Biscarbó L 37 Bb 94
22807 Biscarrués HU 53 Zb 95
22710 Biscós de Garcipollera HU 35 Zc 93
50561 Bisimbre Z 52 Yd 97
09554 Bisjueces BU 30 Wc 91
43510 Bítem T 93 Ad 103
17723 Biure GI 40 Cf 94
43428 Biure de Gaià T 76 Bc 100
31398 Biurrun NC 33 Yb 92
27612 Biville LU 24 Sc 92
AD600 Bixessarri ◘ AND 38 Bc 94
04830 Bizmay, El AL 155 Xf 122
05140 Blacha AV 84 Va 105
42193 Blacos SO 50 Xa 98
30540 Blanca MC 141 Yd 119
28630 Blanca, La MD 85 Vd 107
43411 Blancafort T 75 Ba 100
43330 Blancafort T 75 Ba 102
02328 Blancares AB 123 Xf 114
44314 Blancas TE 89 Yd 104
02600 Blanco, El AB 123 Xb 113
30382 Blancos, Los MC 157 Zb 123
17300 Blanes GI 59 Ce 98
04897 Blánquez del Saúco AL 170 Xc 125
38600 Blanquitos, Los TF 180 Ic 180
05193 Blascoeles AV 85 Vd 104
05147 Blascojimeno AV 84 Uf 104
05146 Blascomillán AV 84 Uf 102
05299 Blasconuño de Matacabras AV 66 Va 102
05290 Blascosancho AV 84 Vc 103
14208 Blázquez, Los CO 134 Ud 118
22133 Blecua HU 54 Ze 96
22133 Blecua y Torres HU 54 Ze 96
08731 Bleda, La B 76 Bd 100
44790 Blesa TE 72 Za 102
42128 Bliecos SO 70 Xe 99
42248 Blocona SO 70 Xd 101
15218 Boa C 22 Ra 92
32375 Boa OR 25 Se 95
32375 Boa Cambela OR 25 Sf 95
25736 Boada L 56 Ba 97
37290 Boada SA 82 Te 104
34305 Boada de Campos P 47 Va 97
09314 Boada de Roa BU 48 Wa 98
09125 Boada de Villadiego BU 29 Wa 93
08299 Boada Nova, La B 58 Bf 99
17723 Boadella d'Empordà GI 40 Cf 95
08297 Boades B 57 Bf 98
37208 Boadilla SA 82 Te 104
34468 Boadilla del Camino P 29 Vd 95
28660 Boadilla del Monte MD 86 Wa 106
34349 Boadilla de Rioseco P 47 Va 95
32631 Boado OR 43 Sb 96
33720 Boal AS 13 Tb 88
28413 Boalo, El MD 86 Wa 104
15118 Boaño C 10 Qf 89
29540 Bobadilla MA 166 Vb 126
26321 Bobadilla RI 31 Xb 95
23669 Bobadilla, La J 152 Vf 123
47462 Bobadilla del Campo VA 66 Uf 101
29540 Bobadilla Estación MA 166 Vb 126
04120 Bobar, El AL 170 Xd 128
25178 Bobera = Bovera L 74 Ad 101
33429 Bobes AS 15 Ub 88
33556 Bobia de Abajo AS 16 Va 89
32514 Boborás OR 23 Re 94
37593 Bocacara SA 82 Td 104
24913 Boca de Huérgano LE 16 Va 91
46880 Bocairent V 142 Zc 116
41563 Bocas del Salado SE 150 Va 123
40560 Boceguillas SG 68 Wc 100
02486 Boche AB 139 Xe 118
19276 Bochones GU 69 Xa 101
19223 Bocígano GU 68 Wd 102
47419 Bocigas VA 66 Vb 101
42329 Bocigas de Perales SO 49 Wd 99
33449 Bocines AS 15 Ub 87
09553 Bocos BU 18 Wc 91
47317 Bocos de Duero VA 48 Ve 99
36598 Bodaño PO 23 Re 92
24860 Bodas, Las LE 27 Ue 91
12182 Bodega, La CS 92 Zf 107
45740 Bodegas Bilbaínas TO 102 Wb 110
09109 Bodegas de Carranxero BU 29 Ve 94
46160 Bodegas de Cea V 107 Zb 110
26150 Bodegas de la Atalayuela RI 32 Xe 94
46160 Bodegas del Campo V 107 Zb 110
46160 Bodegas del Mundo Nuevo V 107 Zb 110
09109 Bodegas de San Cristóbal BU 29 Ve 94
03408 Bodegueta, La A 142 Za 116
19278 Bodera, La GU 69 Xa 102
37520 Bodón, El SA 81 Tc 106
06192 Bodonal BA 116 Tb 114
06394 Bodonal de la Sierra BA 132 Tc 120
18810 Bodurria GR 170 Xb 124
15608 Boebre C 11 Re 88
47151 Boecillo VA 66 Vb 99
34859 Boedo P 29 Vc 92
15826 Boente C 23 Rf 91
07749 Boeret, Es IB 77 Ea 109
42216 Bordejé SO 70 Xc 100
24312 Boeza LE 26 Te 92
39692 Bofetán CB 18 Wa 88
37291 Bogajo SA 63 Tc 103
18562 Bogarre GR 169 Wd 124
10990 Bohio y Casas de la Hinojosa CC 97 Sf 110
05165 Bohodón, El AV 66 Vb 103
06692 Bohonal BA 119 Vb 113
10320 Bohonal de Ibor CC 99 Ud 110
05690 Bohoyo AV 83 Ud 107
25528 Boí L 37 Ae 93
15816 Boimil C 11 Rf 90
15818 Boimorto C 11 Rf 91
15930 Boiro C 22 Ra 93
24717 Boisán LE 26 Te 94
25528 Boí-Taüll Resort L 37 Af 94
25122 Boix L 55 Ad 97
12599 Boixar CS 92 Aa 104
25652 Bóixols L 56 Ba 95
30570 Bojar, El MC 157 Yf 121
08273 Bojons B 58 Ca 97
32812 Bola, A OR 42 Sa 96
27122 Bolaño LU 12 Se 90
13260 Bolaños de Calatrava CR 121 Wc 115
47675 Bolaños de Campos VA 46 Ue 96
46822 Bolbaite V 126 Zb 114
25571 Boldís Sobirà L 37 Bb 93
25332 Boldú L 56 Ba 98
22160 Bolea HU 35 Zc 95
48278 Bolibar BI 20 Xc 89
29640 Boliches, Los MA 175 Vc 129
02150 Bolinches AB 124 Yb 114
01194 Bolívar VI 31 Xc 92
01194 Bolívar = Bolibar SS 20 Xc 90
39681 Bollacín CB 18 Wa 90
16843 Bólliga CU 88 Xd 107
41110 Bollullos de la Mitación SE 164 Tf 124
21710 Bollullos Par del Condado H 162 Tc 124
39213 Bolmir CB 17 Vf 91
30877 Bolnuevo MC 156 Ye 123
32373 Bolo, O OR 25 Sf 95
03600 Bolón A 142 Zb 118
36681 Bolos PO 23 Rd 92
17867 Bolòs GI 39 Cc 95
06389 Bolsicos, Los BA 132 Tb 119
22340 Boltaña HU 35 Aa 94
22439 Bolturina HU 55 Ab 96
03518 Bolulla A 143 Zf 116
17539 Bolvir GI 38 Bf 94
17474 Bomba, La GI 59 Da 95
04617 Bombardas, Las AL 171 Yb 125
25586 Bonabé L 37 Ba 92
25586 Bonaigua de Baix, La L 37 Ba 93
07400 Bon Aire IB 111 Da 109
13129 Bonal, El CR 120 Ve 113
22486 Bonansa HU 36 Ad 94
43816 Bonany T 76 Bc 100
11540 Bonanza CA 163 Td 128
28669 Bonanza MD 86 Wa 106
21830 Bonares H 162 Tb 125
43884 Bonastre T 76 Bc 101
03724 Bonavista A 143 Aa 116
25572 Bonestarre L 37 Bb 93
02691 Bonete AB 125 Yd 115
16311 Boniches CU 105 Yc 109
33426 Bonielles AS 15 Ua 88
16540 Bonilla CU 88 Xc 107
05514 Bonilla de la Sierra AV 83 Ue 105
02610 Bonillo, El AB 123 Xc 115
35431 Bon Lugar GC 184 Kc 180
25716 Bonner L 57 Be 95
22487 Bono HU 36 Ae 93
17470 Bon Relax GI 59 Da 95
25638 Bonrepòs L 56 Ba 96
46131 Bonrepós i Mirambel V 126 Zd 111
43479 Bonretorn T 75 Ba 101
AD200 Bons, Les ◘ AND 38 Bd 93
27153 Bonxe LU 12 Sc 90
24850 Boñar LE 27 Ue 91
42218 Boñices SO 51 Xe 99
33675 Boo AS 15 Ub 89
39478 Bóo CB 17 Wa 88
42313 Boós SO 50 Xa 99
15881 Boqueixón C 23 Rd 92
04859 Boquera, La AL 170 Xe 125
22300 Boquera, La HU 55 Aa 96
34305 Boquerín de Campos P 47 Vb 96
33590 Boquerizo AS 17 Vc 88
30559 Boquerón, El MC 141 Ye 119
46811 Boquilla V 126 Zb 115
50641 Boquiñeni Z 52 Ye 97
22860 Borau HU 35 Zc 93
42223 Borchicayada SO 70 Xd 100
09133 Borcos BU 30 Wa 93
50229 Bordalba Z 70 Xf 100
31176 Bordas de Arriba NC 32 Ya 92
31172 Bordas el Peletón NC 32 Ya 91
42367 Bordecorex SO 69 Xb 100
42216 Bordejé SO 70 Xc 100
27830 Bordelle LU 12 Sb 88
25551 Bòrdes, Es L 36 Ae 92
25788 Bordes de Conflent L 37 Bb 93
25799 Bordes de Llosar L 37 Bc 94
25636 Bordes del Seix de Gurp L 56 Af 95
17462 Bordils GI 59 Cf 96
44563 Bordón TE 91 Ze 104
36966 Bordóns PO 22 Rb 94
25586 Borén L 37 Ba 93
29718 Borge, El MA 167 Ve 128
25400 Borges Blanques, Les L 75 Af 99
43350 Borges del Camp, Les T 75 Ba 101
08573 Borgonyà B 58 Cb 96
17844 Borgonyà del Terri GI 59 Ce 96
33583 Borines AS 15 Ue 88
50540 Borja Z 52 Yc 98
42218 Borjabad SO 70 Xd 99
02249 Bormate AB 124 Yc 113
41930 Bormujos SE 164 Tf 124
11640 Bornos CA 165 Ub 128
42138 Borobia SO 52 Ya 99
33792 Boronas AS 13 Tc 87
45222 Borox TO 102 Wb 108
32636 Borrán OR 43 Sc 96
08296 Borràs, El B 57 Bf 99
17770 Borrassà GI 59 Cf 95
36625 Borraxeiros PO 23 Rf 92
08619 Borredà B 58 Bf 96
24443 Borrenes LE 25 Tb 94
33878 Borres AS 14 Tc 88
22612 Borrés HU 35 Zd 93
30351 Borricén MC 157 Za 123
12190 Borriol CS 108 Zf 108
15115 Bosco, O C 10 Ra 89
29314 Bosque MA 167 Vd 126
11670 Bosque, El CA 165 Uc 128
12127 Bosque, El CS 91 Zc 107
28670 Bosque, El MD 86 Wa 106
41770 Bosque, El SE 165 Uc 126
45516 Bosque, El TO 101 Vd 110
49620 Bosque, El ZA 46 Ub 97
50430 Bosque Alto Z 72 Za 100
25550 Bossòst L 36 Ae 92
27307 Bostelo LU 12 Sa 89
39451 Bostronizo CB 17 Vf 89
43785 Bot T 74 Ac 102
40469 Botalhorno SG 66 Vb 102
43772 Botarell T 75 Af 102
22711 Botaya HU 34 Zc 94
23520 Boticario, El J 153 Wc 121
10188 Botija CC 117 Tf 112
06510 Bótoa BA 116 Ta 114
50441 Botorrita Z 72 Yf 99
33891 Bouga, La AS 14 Te 88
27720 Bouloso LU 13 Se 88
32613 Bousés OR 43 Sc 97
32520 Bouza OR 23 Re 94
32563 Bouza OR 43 Sf 96
32430 Bouza, A OR 23 Rf 95
37488 Bouza, La SA 81 Tb 103
32868 Bouzadrago OR 42 Rf 97
24414 Bouzas LE 26 Tc 94
36209 Bouzas PO 41 Rb 95
49361 Bouzas ZA 44 Tb 96
03850 Bovar, El A 142 Zb 116
27233 Bóveda LU 12 Sb 91
27340 Bóveda LU 24 Sd 93
01427 Bóveda VI 31 We 91
32172 Bóveda de Amoeiro OR 24 Sa 94
09512 Bóveda de la Ribera BU 30 Wd 91
37316 Bóveda del Río Almar SA 84 Ue 103
49155 Bóveda de Toro, La ZA 65 Ud 100
03160 Bóvedas, Las A 142 Za 120
03700 Bovetes, Les A 127 Aa 115
49561 Boya ZA 45 Td 97
41449 Boyal, La SE 149 Uc 123
11679 Boyar, El CA 165 Ud 128
31400 Boyeral, El NC 34 Ye 93
28339 Boyeriza, La MD 86 Wc 107
09219 Bozoo BU 31 Wf 92
05357 Brabos AV 84 Va 104
14813 Bracana CO 152 Vf 124
18381 Brácana GR 168 Wa 125
24200 Bracas LE 27 Uc 95
15339 Braelle C 10 Sb 86
43812 Bràfim T 76 Bb 101
47461 Brahojos de Medina VA 66 Uf 101
22483 Bralláns HU 36 Ad 94
36585 Brandariz PO 23 Re 92
15819 Brandeso C 23 Re 91
49511 Brandilanes ZA 45 Te 99
36685 Brandomés PO 23 Re 92
15859 Brandomil C 10 Ra 90
15859 Brandoñas C 10 Ra 90
15684 Brandoñas de Arriba C 10 Rb 90
36524 Brántega PO 23 Rf 92
15110 Brantoas C 10 Ra 89
33758 Braña, La AS 13 Ta 88
33815 Braña de Carbaldetoso AS 13 Tb 90
33887 Braña del Candal AS 13 Tb 90
33877 Brañalonga AS 14 Td 88
15806 Brañas C 11 Sa 90
33818 Brañas de Arriba AS 14 Td 90
33728 Brañavara AS 13 Ta 88
39210 Brañavieja CB 17 Vd 90
33194 Brañes AS 15 Ua 88
34829 Brañosera P 17 Ve 91
33717 Brañuas AS 13 Tc 88
24360 Brañuelas LE 26 Te 93
28737 Braojos MD 68 Wc 102
15151 Brasal C 10 Qf 91
45542 Bravo, El TO 101 Vc 108
27867 Bravos LU 12 Sc 87
21239 Bravos, Los H 147 Ta 121
09490 Brazacorta BU 49 Wd 98
13450 Brazatortas CR 136 Ve 117
47238 Brazuelas VA 66 Vb 100
24716 Brazuelo LE 26 Tf 94
50246 Brea de Aragón Z 71 Yc 99
28596 Brea de Tajo MD 87 Wf 107
33310 Breceña AS 15 Ud 88
37478 Brecerilla SA 82 Te 105
17400 Breda GI 58 Cd 98
15199 Bregua C 11 Rd 89
41310 Brenes SE 149 Ua 123
04271 Breña, La AL 171 Xf 125
38713 Breña Alta = San Pedro de Breña Alta TF 181 Hb 176
38712 Breña Baja = San José TF 180 Hb 177
35570 Breñas, Las GC 182 Mb 175
33775 Bres AS 13 Sf 88
25592 Bresca L 37 Ba 95
32636 Bresmaus OR 43 Sc 96
15969 Bretal C 22 Qf 93
49751 Bretó ZA 46 Ub 97
49698 Bretocino ZA 46 Ub 97
27286 Bretoña LU 12 Se 88
25591 Bretui L 37 Ba 94
42173 Bretún SO 51 Xd 96
11520 Brevas, Las CA 172 Td 128
15669 Brexo C 11 Re 89
38411 Brezal TF 180 Ic 178
16878 Brezal, El CU 89 Ya 105
36658 Briallos PO 22 Rc 93
30153 Brianes, Los MC 157 Ye 121
42368 Brías SO 69 Xa 100
15659 Bribes C 11 Re 89
33594 Bricia AS 16 Va 88
09572 Bricia BU 30 Wb 91
25287 Brics L 57 Bd 97
05194 Brieva AV 84 Vc 104
40180 Brieva SG 67 Vf 102
26322 Brieva de Cameros RI 50 Xb 96
09198 Brieva de Juarros BU 30 Wd 95
33784 Brieves AS 14 Td 88
19400 Brihuega GU 87 Xa 104
24719 Brimeda LE 26 Tf 94
49629 Brime de Sog ZA 45 Tf 96
49622 Brime de Urz ZA 45 Ua 96
37217 Brincones SA 63 Td 102
20220 Brinkola SS 20 Xd 90
26290 Briñas VI 31 Xa 93
15119 Briño C 10 Ra 89
15865 Brión C 22 Rb 91
26330 Briones RI 31 Xb 93
09610 Briongos BU 49 Wc 97
19128 Brisas, Las GU 88 Xb 105
09240 Briviesca BU 30 We 93
15310 Brixeria C 11 Rf 90
09557 Brizuela BU 18 Wb 91
13720 Brocheros CR 122 We 114
44367 Bronchales TE 89 Yc 105
10660 Bronco, El CC 82 Te 107
30510 Bronquina, La MC 141 Yf 117
27422 Brosmos LU 24 Sc 94
46409 Brosquil, El V 127 Ze 114
22370 Broto HU 35 Zf 93
06389 Brovales BA 132 Tb 118
10950 Brozas CC 97 Tb 111
08294 Bruc, El B 57 Be 99
32521 Brués OR 23 Rf 94
24648 Brugos de Fenar LE 27 Uc 92
17533 Bruguera GI 39 Cb 95
17240 Bruguera GI 59 Cf 97
08731 Brugueres B 76 Bd 100
08850 Bruguers B 76 Bf 101
27135 Bruicedo LU 13 Se 90
23009 Brujuelo J 152 Wb 121
08553 Brull, El B 58 Cb 98
09129 Brullés BU 29 Wa 93
28690 Brunete MD 85 Wa 106
17441 Brunyola GI 59 Ce 97
23488 Bruñel Alto J 153 Wf 121
23489 Bruñel Bajo J 153 Wf 121
22665 Búbal HU 35 Ze 92
42132 Buberos SO 51 Xe 99
50239 Bubierca Z 71 Ya 101
18412 Bubión GR 169 Wd 127
26132 Bucesta RI 32 Xd 95
16851 Buciegas CU 88 Xd 106
27529 Buciños LU 24 Sa 93
19133 Budía GU 87 Xb 105
27779 Budián LU 12 Sd 87
15821 Budiño C 11 Rd 91
33116 Bueida AS 14 Ua 90
33694 Buelles AS 15 Ub 90
33579 Buelles AS 17 Vc 88
33598 Buelna AS 17 Vc 88
37208 Buenabarba SA 82 Tf 104
16114 Buenache de Alarcón CU 105 Xf 111
16192 Buenache de la Sierra CU 105 Xf 108
19443 Buenafuente del Sistal, La GU 88 Xe 104
37209 Buenamadre SA 82 Te 103
28590 Buenamesón MD 103 We 108
45673 Buenasbodas TO 100 Va 111
29693 Buenas Noches MA 174 Ue 130
45634 Buenaventura TO 100 Va 107
11150 Buena Vista CA 172 Ua 131
28006 Buena Vista MD 86 Wb 106
06120 Buenavista BA 132 Ta 119
14550 Buenavista CO 151 Vc 123
18330 Buenavista GR 168 Wb 125
37789 Buenavista SA 83 Uc 104
45005 Buenavista TO 102 Vf 109
38713 Buenavista de Arriba TF 181 Hb 176

246 | Bidegoyan

07750 Cala Santa Galdana IB 77 Df 109
07659 Cala Santanyí IB 111 Da 113
07469 Cala Sant Vicenç IB 111 Da 109
22514 Calasanz HU 55 Ac 96
30420 Calasparra MC 140 Yb 119
19128 Calas Verdes GU 88 Xb 105
42193 Calatañazor SO 50 Xb 98
07830 Cala Tarida IB 109 Bb 115
50300 Calatayud Z 71 Yc 100
07748 Cala Tirant IB 77 Ea 108
50280 Calatorao Z 71 Yd 99
07711 Cala Torret IB 77 Eb 110
07315 Cala Tuent IB 110 Ce 109
07769 Cala Turqueta IB 77 Df 109
07830 Cala Vadella IB 109 Bb 115
24170 Calaveras de Abajo LE 28 Va 92
24170 Calaveras de Arriba LE 28 Va 92
02600 Calaverón, El AB 123 Xc 113
43817 Cal Ballet T 76 Bc 100
12140 Calçada, La CS 92 Zf 107
43815 Cal Canonjo T 76 Bc 100
50268 Calcena Z 52 Yb 99
50710 Calcineras Z 74 Aa 102
39460 Caldas de Besaya, Las CB 17 Vf 89
24146 Caldas de Luna LE 27 Ua 91
36650 Caldas de Reis PO 22 Rc 93
15295 Caldebarcos C 22 Qf 91
36721 Caldelas PO 41 Rc 96
14880 Caldera CO 151 Ve 123
38660 Caldera, La TF 180 Ib 180
38758 Caldera, La TF 181 Ha 176
35649 Caldereta GC 183 Ma 177
06130 Calderón BA 132 Ta 117
30510 Calderón MC 141 Ye 117
46390 Calderón V 106 Ye 111
30178 Calderones MC 156 Yd 121
30800 Calderones y el Collado MC 156 Yb 122
08275 Calders B 58 Bf 98
42112 Calderuela SO 51 Xe 98
25528 Caldes de Boí L 37 Af 93
17455 Caldes de Malavella GI 59 Ce 97
08140 Caldes de Montbui B 58 Cb 99
08393 Caldetes = Caldes d'Estrac B 77 Cd 99
33584 Caldevilla AS 16 Ue 88
24914 Caldevilla de Valdeón LE 16 Va 90
33391 Caldones AS 15 Uc 88
33507 Caldueño AS 16 Va 88
33995 Caleao AS 15 Ud 90
08370 Calella B 59 Cd 99
17210 Calella de Palafrugell GI 59 Db 97
10137 Calera, La CC 100 Ue 111
13248 Calera, La CR 122 Wf 115
29313 Calera, La MA 167 Ve 126
38879 Calera, La TF 184 Hd 180
06292 Calera de León BA 133 Td 120
45686 Calera y Chozas TO 100 Va 109
09451 Caleruega BU 49 Wd 98
45589 Caleruela TO 100 Ue 109
23312 Caleruela, La J 153 Wf 120
07688 Cales de Mallorca IB 111 Db 112
35107 Caleta, La GC 184 Kd 182
29751 Caleta, La MA 167 Vf 128
38910 Caleta, La TF 180 Ha 182
38479 Caleta, La TF 180 Ib 178
38678 Caleta, La TF 180 Ib 180
Caleta de Famara, La GC 182 Mc 174
35540 Caleta del Sebo GC 182 Mc 173
18680 Caleta-Guardia, La GR 168 Wc 128
38740 Caletas, Las TF 181 Hb 177
38370 Caletón, El TF 180 Id 178
33172 Caleyo, El AS 15 Ua 89
33957 Caleyo, El AS 15 Uc 89
39727 Calgar CB 18 Wb 88
18290 Calicasas GR 168 Wc 125
12589 Càlig CS 93 Ac 106
30331 Calin MC 157 Yf 122
08506 Calldetenes B 58 Cb 97
15689 Calle, A C 11 Rd 90
43510 Calle, La T 93 Ad 103
14540 Calleja, La CO 150 Va 122
48890 Callejo, El BI 18 Wd 89
38730 Callejones TF 181 Hb 177
33507 Callejos, Los AS 16 Va 88
22255 Callén HU 54 Zd 97
33873 Calleras AS 14 Td 88
46175 Calles V 107 Za 110
33411 Callezuela, La AS 14 Ua 88
15389 Callobre C 11 Re 89
03510 Callosa d'En Sarrià A 143 Zf 117
03360 Callosa de Segura A 142 Za 120
08262 Callús B 57 Be 98
50238 Calmarza Z 70 Ya 102
15129 Calo C 10 Qf 90
39572 Caloca CB 17 Vc 90
44126 Calomarde TE 89 Yc 106
17251 Calonge GI 59 Da 97
07660 Calonge IB 111 Db 112
14709 Calonge, El CO 150 Ud 122
03710 Calpe A 143 Aa 117
12428 Calpes, Los CS 107 Zc 108
08711 Cal Quilaseta B 57 Bd 99
39728 Calseca CB 18 Wb 89
08731 Cal Sisplau B 76 Bd 100
07315 Cals Reis IB 110 Ce 110
42367 Caltojar SO 69 Xb 100
33390 Caltorrebruna B 57 Be 98
17445 Ca l'Uix GI 58 Cd 97
41610 Calvario, El SE 165 Ud 125
36770 Calvario, O PO 41 Rb 97
37181 Calvarrasa de Abajo SA 65 Uc 103
37191 Calvarrasa de Arriba SA 65 Uc 103
15979 Calvelle C 22 Ra 92
22485 Calvera HU 36 Ad 94
07184 Calvià IB 110 Cd 111
32648 Calvos OR 42 Sa 97
15819 Calvos de Sobrecamiño C 11 Re 91
45950 Calypo II TO 85 Vf 107
39766 Calzada, La CB 18 Wc 89
37714 Calzada de Béjar, La SA 83 Ub 106
09244 Calzada de Bureba BU 31 We 93
13370 Calzada de Caltrava CR 137 Wb 116
37448 Calzada de Don Diego SA 64 Ua 103
24760 Calzada de la Valdería LE 45 Tf 95
24342 Calzada del Coto LE 28 Uf 94
34129 Calzada de los Molinos P 28 Vc 95
45580 Calzada de Oropesa, La TO 100 Ue 109
49332 Calzada de Tera ZA 45 Tf 97
37797 Calzada de Valdunciel SA 64 Ub 102
02249 Calzada de Vergara AB 124 Yc 113
35018 Calzada La GC 184 Kd 180
10817 Calzadilla CC 98 Tc 108
34309 Calzadilla de la Cueza P 28 Vb 95
37114 Calzadilla del Campo SA 64 Tf 102
06249 Calzadilla de los Barros BA 133 Te 119
24343 Calzadilla de los Hermanillos LE 28 Uf 94
49331 Calzadilla de Tera ZA 45 Tf 97
04692 Camachos, Los AL 155 Xf 124
30592 Camachos, Los MC 157 Za 122
30369 Camachos, Los MC 157 Za 123
39587 Camaleño CB 16 Vb 90
17465 Camallera GI 59 Cf 96
17463 Camañas TE 90 Yf 105
03600 Cámara A 142 Za 117
25613 Camarasa L 56 Af 97
14240 Cámaras Altas CO 135 Uf 119
45180 Camarena TO 102 Vf 108
44459 Camarena de la Sierra TE 106 Yf 108
45181 Camarenilla TO 102 Vf 108
35329 Camaretas GC 184 Kc 181
18561 Camargo GR 153 Wd 123
23360 Camarillas J 139 Xb 118
44155 Camarillas TE 91 Zb 105
11391 Camarinal CA 175 Ub 132
15123 Camariñas C 10 Qe 90
43894 Camarles T 93 Ae 104
28816 Camarma de Esteruelas MD 86 Wd 105
33554 Camarmeña AS 16 Va 89
49332 Camarzana de Tera ZA 45 Tf 97
41900 Camas SE 163 Tf 124
33529 Camás AS 15 Ud 88
34849 Camasobres P 17 Vd 90
32621 Camba OR 43 Sd 96
36630 Cambados PO 22 Rb 93
39571 Cambarco CB 17 Vc 90
15317 Cambás C 11 Sa 89
32100 Cambeo OR 24 Sa 94
36839 Cambeses PO 23 Rd 94
23120 Cambil J 153 Wc 122
15216 Camboño C 22 Ra 92
15111 Cambre C 10 Rb 89
15660 Cambre C 11 Rd 89
25283 Cambrils L 57 Bc 96
43391 Cambrils T 75 Ba 102
10629 Cambrón CC 82 Te 106
30800 Cambrón MC 156 Yb 122
14820 Cambrón, El CO 151 Vc 122
14850 Cambrón, El CO 151 Vd 122
16146 Cambrón, El CU 89 Xf 107
10629 Cambroncino CC 82 Te 106
15121 Camelle C 10 Qf 89
09245 Cameno BU 30 We 93
39594 Camijanes CB 17 Vd 89
24883 Caminayo LE 28 Va 91
33519 Camino AS 15 Uc 88
39212 Camino CB 17 Ve 90
38312 Camino de Chasna, El TF 180 Ic 178
10620 Caminomorisco CC 82 Te 107
04510 Camino Real, El AL 170 Xb 126
44350 Caminreal TE 90 Ye 103
43750 Camins de Flix T 74 Ac 101
33390 Camocha, La AS 15 Uc 88
29532 Camorra MA 166 Vb 126
28470 Camorritos MD 85 Vf 104
17834 Camós GI 59 Ce 96
33456 Campa, La AS 14 Ua 87
48610 Campa, La BI 19 Xa 88
28024 Campamento MD 86 Wb 106
11314 Campamento, El CA 175 Ud 131
04240 Campamento-Álvarez de Sotomayor AL 170 Xd 127
45122 Campamento de Labastida TO 102 Vf 110
28240 Campamento de Navallera MD 86 Wa 105
33423 Campana, La AS 15 Ub 88
18530 Campana, La GR 153 We 124
41429 Campana, La SE 149 Ud 123
06460 Campanario BA 118 Uc 115
21609 Campanario H 161 Tb 123
31397 Campanas NC 33 Yc 92
37479 Campanero SA 81 Tc 104
30440 Campanero, El MC 140 Ya 119
07310 Campanet IB 111 Cf 110
03325 Campaneta, La A 142 Za 120
29590 Campanillas MA 175 Vc 128
11130 Campano CA 172 Tf 130
33470 Campañones AS 15 Ub 88
42290 Camparañón SO 50 Xc 98
47310 Campaspero VA 67 Ve 100
24221 Campazas LE 46 Ud 96
08872 Campdàsens B 76 Bf 101
07157 Camp de Mar IB 110 Cc 111
03314 Camp de Mirra = Campo de Mirra, el A 142 Zb 116
17530 Campdevànol GI 58 Cb 95
03459 Camp d'Or, El A 142 Zb 116
17461 Campdorà GI 59 Cf 96
03791 Campell A 127 Zf 116
17534 Campelles GI 39 Ca 95
03560 Campello A 142 Zd 118
03560 Campello, El A 142 Zd 118
27163 Campelo LU 12 Sd 91
03660 Campet, El A 142 Zb 118
01110 Campezo/Kanpezu VI 32 Xd 92
04271 Campico AL 171 Xf 125
04277 Campico AL 171 Xf 126
30889 Campico de las Lirias MC 156 Yc 123
30835 Campico de los López MC 156 Yc 123
50299 Campiel Z 71 Yc 100
33993 Campiellos AS 15 Ud 89
37273 Campilduero SA 63 Tc 103
19223 Campillejo GU 68 We 102
02462 Campillo AB 139 Xc 118
04870 Campillo AL 155 Xd 124
39696 Campillo CB 18 Wb 89
40153 Campillo SG 85 Ve 103
49183 Campillo ZA 45 Ua 99
04825 Campillo, El AL 155 Xe 123
04779 Campillo, El AL 169 Xa 128
04859 Campillo, El AL 170 Xe 125
11520 Campillo, El CA 172 Td 129
10550 Campillo, El CC 116 Tc 113
13250 Campillo, El CR 121 Wc 114
13344 Campillo, El CR 138 Wf 117
21650 Campillo, El H 147 Sf 124
21650 Campillo, El H 147 Tc 122
23269 Campillo, El J 138 Wf 119
23293 Campillo, El J 139 Xc 119
30420 Campillo, El MC 140 Yb 119
30410 Campillo, El MC 155 Ya 121
28292 Campillo, El MD 85 Vf 105
28500 Campillo, El MD 86 Wd 107
41870 Campillo, El SE 148 Te 123
41439 Campillo, El SE 150 Ue 123
44121 Campillo, El TE 90 Ye 107
47460 Campillo, El VA 66 Uf 101
30335 Campillo de Abajo MC 156 Ye 122
30868 Campillo de Adentro MC 157 Yf 123
16210 Campillo de Altobuey CU 105 Yb 111
50214 Campillo de Aragón Z 71 Ya 102
09493 Campillo de Aranda BU 49 Wb 99
23130 Campillo de Arenas J 152 Wc 123
30335 Campillo de Arriba MC 156 Ye 122
37550 Campillo de Azaba SA 81 Tb 105
10329 Campillo de Deleitosa CC 99 Uc 110
19360 Campillo de Dueñas GU 89 Yb 103
45578 Campillo de la Jara, El TO 100 Uf 111
02511 Campillo de las Doblas AB 140 Yb 116
02129 Campillo de la Virgen AB 140 Ya 116
06443 Campillo de Llerena BA 133 Ub 117
02510 Campillo del Negro, El AB 124 Yb 116
30439 Campillo de los Jiménez MC 140 Yb 120
Campillo del Río J 152 Wc 120
Campillo del Río J 152 Wc 121
09587 Campillo de Mena BU 18 Wd 90
19223 Campillo de Ranas GU 68 We 102
37778 Campillo de Salvatierra SA 83 Ub 105
29320 Campillos MA 166 Va 126
21386 Campillos, Los H 147 Tb 120
44400 Campillos, Los TE 91 Zb 107
16311 Campillos-Paravientos CU 106 Yc 109
16316 Campillos-Sierra CU 105 Yb 108
37311 Campillo y Melardes SA 83 Ue 104
30438 Campillo y Suertes MC 155 Yb 120
09572 Campino BU 30 Wb 91
08470 Campins B 58 Cc 98
11692 Campiña CA 166 Ue 127
23270 Campiña J 138 Xa 119
29570 Campiña MA 166 Vc 128
14940 Campiñuela, La CO 151 Vc 124
19275 Campisábalos GU 68 Wf 101
38767 Campitos, Los TF 181 Ha 177
17457 Campllong GI 59 Ce 97
25515 Campllong L 37 Ba 94
24699 Camplongo de Arbás LE 15 Ub 91
15100 Campo C 10 Rb 89
15109 Campo C 10 Rc 89
15144 Campo C 11 Rc 89
15819 Campo C 11 Re 91
22450 Campo HU 36 Ac 94
24414 Campo LE 15 Uc 91
27181 Campo LU 24 Sc 91
32537 Campo OR 23 Rf 93
32161 Campo OR 24 Sb 94
33628 Campo, El AS 15 Ua 90
33614 Campo, El AS 15 Ub 89
34847 Campo, El P 17 Vc 91
44131 Campo, El TE 106 Ye 107
50217 Campo Alavés Z 70 Ya 100
02251 Campoalbillo AB 124 Yc 113
06475 Campo Ameno BA 133 Tf 116
46352 Campo Arcis V 125 Ye 112
03850 Campo Barraques A 142 Zc 116
32626 Campobecerros OR 43 Se 96
11610 Campobuche CA 174 Ud 128
37494 Campocerrado SA 82 Te 104
30410 Campo Coy MC 155 Ya 121
27826 Campo da Feira LU 12 Sa 89
22348 Campodarbe HU 35 Aa 94
21700 Campo de Abajo H 162 Tc 124
46178 Campo de Abajo V 106 Yf 109
46178 Campo de Arriba V 106 Yf 109
46176 Campo de Benacacira, El V 106 Yf 109
33990 Campo de Caso AS 15 Ud 89
13610 Campo de Criptana CR 122 Wf 112
40242 Campo de Cuéllar SG 67 Vd 101
39250 Campo de Ebro CB 29 Wa 92
06176 Campo de la Parra BA 132 Tc 117
24415 Campo de las Danzas LE 25 Tb 94
37140 Campo de Ledesma SA 64 Tf 102
37450 Campo del Hospicio SA 82 Tf 103
03314 Campo de Mirra, el = Camp de Mirra A 142 Zb 116
37317 Campo de Peñaranda, El SA 65 Ue 103
40551 Campo de San Pedro SG 68 We 100
06393 Campo de Santo Domingo BA 133 Td 118
27328 Campo de Val LU 25 Se 93
24225 Campo de Villavidel LE 27 Uc 94
15359 Campo do Hospital C 10 Sa 87
28679 Campodón MD 86 Wa 106
15686 Campoduro C 11 Re 90
21668 Campofrío H 147 Tc 122
06160 Campo Gallego BA 132 Ta 118
49592 Campogrande de Aliste ZA 45 Te 98
04110 Campohermoso AL 171 Xf 127
24849 Campohermoso LE 27 Ud 91
11680 Campo-Huerta CA 165 Ud 127
04647 Campois, Los AL 171 Yb 124
36110 Campo Lameiro PO 23 Rc 93
09650 Campolara BU 49 Wd 96
39577 Campollo CB 16 Vc 90
15614 Campo Longo C 11 Re 88
15838 Campolongo C 22 Ra 91
10134 Campo Lugar CC 118 Ub 113
33620 Campomanes AS 15 Ub 90
06800 Campomanes BA 117 Te 115
29650 Campo-Mijas MA 175 Vc 129
13160 Campomojado CR 121 Wb 114
24410 Camponaraya LE 25 Tb 93
14814 Campo-Nubes CO 151 Vf 123
30334 Campo Nubla MC 156 Ye 122
04745 Camponuevo AL 170 Xb 128
39292 Campoo de Yuso CB 17 Wa 90
28510 Campo Real MD 86 Wd 106
50689 Campo Real Z 33 Ye 93
22280 Campo Redondo HU 53 Za 96
27514 Camporramiro LU 24 Sb 93
23269 Camporredondo J 138 Wf 119
42172 Camporredondo SO 51 Xd 96
47165 Camporredondo VA 66 Vc 100
34888 Camporredondo de Alba P 28 Vb 91
22570 Camporrells HU 55 Ad 97
46330 Camporrobles V 106 Yd 111
22395 Camporrotuno HU 36 Aa 94
15809 Campos C 23 Rf 91
07630 Campos IB 111 Da 112
44158 Campos TE 91 Zb 104
33416 Campos, Los AS 15 Ua 87
37209 Campos, Los SA 82 Te 103
42173 Campos, Los SO 51 Xd 97
24123 Campo-sagrado LE 27 Ub 92
36596 Camposancos PO 23 Rf 92
36788 Camposancos PO 41 Ra 97
12448 Campos de Arenoso CS 107 Zc 108
39716 Camposdelante CB 18 Wc 88
30192 Campos del Río MC 156 Yd 120
43781 Camposines, Les T 74 Ad 102
24857 Camposolillo LE 16 Ue 91
07260 Campot, Es IB 111 Cf 112
18565 Campotéjar GR 152 Wc 124
30627 Campotéjar Baja MC 141 Ye 120
24610 Campo y Santibáñez LE 27 Uc 92
43897 Campredó T 93 Ad 104
17867 Camprodon GI 39 Cc 95
26311 Camprovín RI 31 Xb 94
08259 Camps B 57 Be 98
22437 Camps, Los HU 36 Ac 95
30648 Campules MC 141 Yf 119
39300 Campuzano CB 17 Vf 88
45720 Camuñas TO 121 Wd 112
33867 Camuño AS 14 Te 88
07816 Can IB 109 Bc 114
27425 Canabal LU 24 Sc 94
07669 Ca Na Curta IB 111 Db 112
36414 Canadelo PO 41 Rb 96
08784 Ca N'Aguilera B 76 Be 99
34829 Canal, El P 29 Ve 91
39630 Canal, La CB 18 Wa 89
22773 Canal de Berdún HU 34 Za 93
16555 Canal de Trasvase Tajo-Segura CU 104 Xb 109
02312 Canaleja AB 139 Xc 116
05693 Canaleja AV 83 Uc 106
21342 Canaleja H 147 Tb 121
24197 Canaleja LE 27 Uc 93
11170 Canaleja, La CA 172 Ua 130
14400 Canaleja, La CO 135 Va 119
30812 Canaleja, La MC 155 Yb 121
46178 Canaleja, La V 106 Yf 109
24170 Canalejas LE 28 Va 92
04647 Canalejas, Las AL 171 Yb 124
23291 Canalejas, Las J 154 Xb 120
16857 Canalejas del Arroyo CU 88 Xd 106
47311 Canalejas de Peñafiel VA 67 Vf 99
28870 Canalejo, La MD 87 We 105
33555 Canales AS 16 Va 89
05212 Canales AV 66 Va 102
39507 Canales CB 17 Ve 88
12469 Canales CS 107 Zb 109
18160 Canales GR 168 Wd 126
24120 Canales LE 27 Ub 92
30800 Canales, Las MC 155 Yb 122
30859 Canales, Las MC 156 Yc 122
26329 Canales de la Sierra RI 50 Wf 96
19432 Canales del Ducado GU 88 Xd 104
19343 Canales de Molina GU 70 Ya 103

248 | Cala Santa Galdana

22210 Casa de Aviño HU 54 Ze 97	
45593 Casa de Azañuela TO 102 Vf 109	
45518 Casa de Azoberines TO 101 Ve 109	
13610 Casa de Baillo CR 122 Wf 113	
13590 Casa de Baldomero CR 136 Ve 117	
23240 Casa de Baldomero J 138 Wd 119	

22210 Casa de Aviño HU 54 Ze 97
45593 Casa de Azañuela TO 102 Vf 109
45518 Casa de Azoberines TO 101 Ve 109
13610 Casa de Baillo CR 122 Wf 113
13590 Casa de Baldomero CR 136 Ve 117
23240 Casa de Baldomero J 138 Wd 119
10500 Casa de Ballesteros CC 97 Se 111
45470 Casa de Ballesteros TO 121 Wa 112
50172 Casa de Balsa Salada Z 53 Zb 99
16639 Casa de Baños CU 104 Xb 111
44559 Casa de Baños TE 91 Zd 104
45161 Casa de Bañuelos TO 101 Ve 110
45690 Casa de Barilejo TO 101 Vb 109
10550 Casa de Barquera Baja CC 116 Tb 112
45530 Casa de Barraén TO 101 Vd 109
13200 Casa de Barrunta CR 121 Wd 114
06650 Casa de Bartolo BA 119 Uf 115
16710 Casa de Batalla CU 105 Xe 111
47238 Casa de Bayalada VA 66 Vb 100
45360 Casa de Bayuncal TO 103 We 109
21760 Casa de Belalengua H 163 Td 127
30170 Casa de Belluga MC 140 Yc 119
13670 Casa de Belorto CR 121 Wb 113
12180 Casa de Beneito CS 108 Aa 108
11579 Casa de Ber CA 172 Ua 129
13730 Casa de Berdeja CR 137 Wd 117
45580 Casa de Bermejo TO 100 Ud 109
05140 Casa de Bermudillo AV 84 Vb 104
50800 Casa de Bernardo Z 53 Za 97
02600 Casa de Berruga AB 122 Xb 114
22714 Casa de Bescansa HU 35 Zd 93
40219 Casa de Bocos SG 66 Vc 101
13250 Casa de Bolote CR 121 Wb 114
10940 Casa de Bonilla CC 98 Tc 111
13300 Casa de Boquilla CR 138 Wd 116
44780 Casa de Borón TE 72 Zb 102
45161 Casa de Borril TO 101 Ve 110
10133 Casa de Bote CC 117 Ua 113
02156 Casa de Botón AB 124 Yb 114
06500 Casa de Boyero BA 116 Ta 112
06475 Casa de Buenavista BA 133 Te 116
14270 Casa de Buenavista CO 135 Uf 118
30810 Casa de Buenavista MC 155 Ya 122
13710 Casa de Buen Retiro CR 122 Xa 114
10263 Casa de Busne CC 117 Ua 113
13200 Casa de Caballero CR 122 We 114
13194 Casa de Cabañeros CR 120 Vc 112
02610 Casa de Cabeza Morena AB 123 Xb 115
06400 Casa de Cabeza Redonda BA 117 Ua 115
21740 Casa de Cabezarrasa H 163 Td 125
43517 Casa de Cabosa T 93 Ac 104
02610 Casa de Cadete AB 123 Xd 115
14270 Casa de Calandilla CO 135 Uf 118
45522 Casa de Calaña TO 101 Ve 109
45880 Casa de Calderón TO 103 We 110
06400 Casa de Calderonas BA 117 Ua 115
16415 Casa de Calonge CU 104 Xa 110
10570 Casa de Calvache CC 116 Ta 112
50615 Casa de Calvo Z 53 Za 95
02600 Casa de Camacho AB 123 Xc 113
13720 Casa de Camacho CR 122 We 114

13320 Casa de Camarilla CR 138 Xa 116
45522 Casa de Cambrillos TO 101 Ve 109
30890 Casa de Campico MC 155 Ya 122
13116 Casa de Canaleas CR 120 Vd 112
10900 Casa de Canals CC 98 Tc 111
13300 Casa de Canchollas CR 137 Wd 116
30193 Casa de Candal MC 156 Yd 120
45700 Casa de Candelo TO 102 Wc 112
13710 Casa de Candilejo CR 122 Xa 114
11638 Casa de Canillas CA 173 Ub 128
41219 Casa de Canillas SE 148 Tf 122
14440 Casa de Cantalobillo CO 135 Vb 119
10560 Casa de Cantillana la Nueva CC 116 Tb 112
13390 Casa de Cañada CR 122 We 116
30420 Casa de Cañadaberosa MC 140 Yb 119
21740 Casa de Cañada Mayor H 163 Td 126
19310 Casa de Cañada Salineras GU 89 Ya 105
06410 Casa de Cañalazarza de Abajo BA 117 Tf 114
13320 Casa de Cañas CR 138 Wf 116
44790 Casa de Cañavellila TE 72 Za 102
30510 Casa de Cañizares MC 141 Yf 117
45910 Casa de Capizelato TO 101 Vd 108
06007 Casa de Carabineros BA 116 Sf 115
45311 Casa de Carazorra TO 103 Wd 109
45580 Casa de Cardoso TO 100 Ud 109
10270 Casa de Carrascalejo CC 98 Tf 112
02100 Casa de Carrasco AB 124 Ya 113
41111 Casa de Carrera SE 164 Tf 125
45126 Casa de Carrillo TO 102 Vf 111
41640 Casa de Carrión SE 166 Uf 125
02600 Casa de Cartagena AB 123 Xc 115
23214 Casa de Carvajal J 137 Wb 118
14729 Casa de Casarejos CO 150 Uf 121
49130 Casa de Casares ZA 46 Ub 98
05154 Casa de Castellanos de la Cañada AV 83 Ue 105
13779 Casa de Castillejo CR 137 Wb 118
45161 Casa de Castrejón TO 101 Vd 110
49880 Casa de Castrillo ZA 65 Uc 100
06400 Casa de Catalina BA 117 Ua 116
50690 Casa de Cavero Z 52 Ye 98
46622 Casa de Cavirá V 125 Za 114
14270 Casa de Cayetano Torres CO 135 Uf 118
02328 Casa de Cebrián AB 124 Xf 114
45880 Casa de Cecilio TO 103 We 110
13700 Casa de Cepeda CR 122 Wf 113
10390 Casa de Cerro Alto CC 99 Ub 109
10520 Casa de Cerrocolchón CC 99 Ub 109
14440 Casa de Cerro Gordo CO 136 Vc 119
06470 Casa de Cerro Pelao BA 117 Tf 115
06470 Casa de Cerros Verdes BA 117 Tf 115
10135 Casa de Cerros Verdes CC 118 Ub 113
45567 Casa de Charco Lobo TO 100 Ue 108
13420 Casa de Charet CR 121 Wb 113
45313 Casa de Chaves TO 102 Wb 109
45165 Casa de Chirivas TO 101 Vd 110
10560 Casa de Chozones CC 116 Ta 112

13370 Casa de Chupahueses CR 137 Wb 117
05195 Casa de Ciervos AV 85 Vd 105
47120 Casa de Cirajas VA 46 Ue 99
13200 Casa de Colchón CR 121 Wd 114
09257 Casa de Colmenar BU 30 We 94
35001 Casa de Colón GC 184 Kd 180
21600 Casa de Conal Quemado H 147 Tc 123
30529 Casa de Conejo MC 141 Ye 118
49281 Casa de Congosta ZA 64 Ub 100
02154 Casa de Conrado AB 125 Yd 114
23214 Casa de Contosa J 137 Wb 118
41870 Casa de Corchilo SE 148 Td 123
41450 Casa de Cordero SE 149 Ub 122
47639 Casa de Cordero VA 47 Va 98
41770 Casa de Coria SE 165 Uc 127
45400 Casa de Corona TO 102 Wb 111
41230 Casa de Coscojal o Valdepotros SE 148 Tf 123
13710 Casa de Cosme CR 122 Xa 114
06500 Casa de Covacha BA 116 Sf 112
23250 Casa de Cristalinas J 138 We 119
45909 Casa de Cruz Verde TO 101 Ve 108
10600 Casa de Cuadrilleros CC 99 Tf 108
45780 Casa de Cuartas TO 102 Wc 111
11595 Casa de Cuéllar CA 172 Tf 129
26520 Casa de Cuerno Solano RI 51 Ya 96
19116 Casa de Cumbre Hermosa GU 103 Wf 107
21500 Casa de Dámaso H 161 Sf 125
11593 Casa de Dehesa CA 172 Ua 129
02690 Casa de Delgado AB 125 Ye 115
10137 Casa de Dimas CC 119 Ue 112
21649 Casa de Domingo Medén H 161 Ta 123
37450 Casa de Don Alipio SA 82 Ua 103
45917 Casa de Donato TO 101 Vc 108
41250 Casa de Don Aurelio SE 148 Tf 122
46620 Casa de Don Bruno V 125 Ye 115
45860 Casa de Don Demetrio TO 103 We 111
13700 Casa de Don Diego CR 122 Xa 114
16600 Casa de Don Diego de Haro CU 123 Xc 112
45643 Casa de Don Eusebio TO 101 Vc 108
21440 Casa de Don Felipe H 161 Se 125
02691 Casa de Don Fernando AB 125 Yd 115
14270 Casa de Don Fernando Luna CO 135 Uf 118
13200 Casa de Don Juan CR 121 Wd 114
23710 Casa de Don Juan Alonso J 152 Wb 120
23710 Casa de Don Juan Roque J 152 Wa 120
13240 Casa de Don Julián CR 122 Wf 115
02691 Casa de Don Luis AB 124 Yc 115
23639 Casa de Don Manuel Aranda J 152 Wb 121
41659 Casa de Don Manuel Barona SE 166 Uf 125
41659 Casa de Don Manuel Cepeda SE 166 Uf 125
02600 Casa de Don Miguel AB 123 Xc 113
23220 Casa de Don Rafael Abril J 137 Wd 119
41450 Casa de Don Rafael Caro SE 149 Ud 121
21559 Casa de Don Ramón H 161 Se 123
45370 Casa de Don Silverio TO 103 We 109
02200 Casa de Doña Anita AB 124 Yc 113

11595 Casa de Doña Benita CA 172 Ua 129
13180 Casa de Doña Inés CR 120 Vc 115
13248 Casa de Doña María CR 122 Xa 115
47410 Casa de Doña María VA 66 Vc 100
50794 Casa de Dotemio Z 74 Ab 101
02512 Casa de El Apedreado AB 140 Yc 116
02695 Casa de El Bachiller AB 125 Yd 115
29567 Casa de el Espartalejo MA 175 Va 128
30528 Casa de El Gamellón MC 141 Yd 117
14430 Casa de El Reventón CO 151 Vc 120
02142 Casa de El Rinconcito AB 140 Ya 117
13210 Casa de El Veto CR 121 Wd 114
13730 Casa de Emeterio CR 137 Wc 117
05194 Casa de Encina AV 84 Vc 104
13768 Casa de Encorrulo CR 137 Wb 118
47315 Casa de Epifanio VA 48 Ve 98
30410 Casa de Eras MC 140 Xf 119
14491 Casa de Espina CO 135 Va 117
13630 Casa de Espinosa CR 122 Xa 113
28670 Casa de Esquerdo MD 85 Wa 106
02600 Casa de Eufemia AB 123 Xb 114
02600 Casa de Eugenio AB 123 Xb 113
49630 Casa de Eusebio ZA 46 Ud 97
11612 Casa de Fardela CA 174 Ud 128
49741 Casa de Farreras ZA 46 Ub 98
10190 Casa de Florentino CC 98 Tc 111
30410 Casa de Flores MC 140 Ya 120
34005 Casa de Font P 47 Vc 97
13200 Casa de Fortuno CR 122 We 114
30520 Casa de Francisco Palazón MC 141 Ye 118
13710 Casa de Franco CR 122 We 114
13770 Casa de Fresnedas CR 137 Wc 117
10697 Casa de Fresnedoso CC 99 Ua 109
29150 Casa de Fuentearroyo MA 167 Vc 127
44126 Casa de Fuente García TE 89 Yb 107
45573 Casa de Fuentelapio TO 100 Uf 110
41350 Casa de Fuente Lengua SE 149 Ub 122
10950 Casa de Fuentemadero CC 97 Tb 111
13390 Casa de Fuente Vieja CR 122 We 115
13640 Casa de Gabriel CR 121 Wd 112
46620 Casa de Gachas V 125 Za 114
06131 Casa de Galán BA 131 Sf 117
10950 Casa de Galaperal CC 97 Tb 111
13270 Casa de Galera CR 121 Wb 115
13630 Casa de Galiana CR 122 Xa 114
45121 Casa de Galo TO 101 Vd 111
10520 Casa de Galochas CC 99 Uc 109
49151 Casa de Galván ZA 65 Uc 100
10161 Casa de Gálvez CC 117 Tf 114
10510 Casa de Gapita CC 97 Se 111
21540 Casa de García Alonso H 161 Se 124
46623 Casa de Garijo V 125 Ye 114
02100 Casa de Garrido AB 124 Ya 113
47194 Casa de Gaspar VA 47 Vb 98
06800 Casa de Gavilanes BA 116 Td 104
41450 Casa de Gibla SE 149 Uc 121
10004 Casa de Gil Sánchez CC 98 Te 111
10004 Casa de Gil Téllez CC 98 Te 111
45569 Casa de Golín de la Senda TO 100 Uf 108
30176 Casa de Gómez MC 156 Yc 121
10340 Casa de Gonzalo CC 99 Ud 110

30191 Casa de Gracia MC 156 Yd 120
11549 Casa de Granaderos CA 164 Te 127
43790 Casa de Grandó T 74 Ac 101
45917 Casa de Gregorio TO 101 Vc 108
45870 Casa de Gregorio TO 103 Wd 110
45910 Casa de Guadamilla TO 101 Ve 108
06800 Casa de Guadarjia BA 116 Td 116
50130 Casa de Guaira Z 72 Zb 101
46195 Casa de Gualeda V 126 Zc 113
45531 Casa de Guanilla TO 101 Vd 109
16142 Casa de Guarda CU 89 Xf 107
06478 Casa de Guerechal BA 117 Ua 116
10870 Casa de Guerra CC 97 Tb 110
13248 Casa de Guerrero CR 122 Wf 116
13200 Casa de Guerrita CR 122 We 114
50376 Casa de Guialguerrero Z 71 Yc 102
30170 Casa de Guillén MC 140 Yc 120
04839 Casa de Guino AL 155 Xe 121
10005 Casa de Guirau CC 98 Tc 111
49121 Casa de Herendeses ZA 46 Ub 99
02610 Casa de Herrera AB 123 Xd 115
13630 Casa de Hervias CR 122 Xa 114
49148 Casa Dehesa de Quintos ZA 45 Ub 97
45533 Casa de Hilario TO 101 Vd 109
13710 Casa de Hita CR 122 Wf 114
23330 Casa de Hojuelo de Parra J 138 Xa 120
13593 Casa de Hontanar-Gordo CR 136 Vf 118
26338 Casa de Hornillo RI 31 Xb 93
02328 Casa de Hoya Vacas AB 124 Xf 115
02695 Casa de Hueso AB 125 Yd 116
13200 Casa de Hurtado CR 121 Wd 114
41440 Casa de Idroga SE 149 Uc 122
45710 Casa de Infantes TO 102 Wc 111
44114 Casa de Inocencio Blas TE 89 Yb 106
45150 Casa de Isidora TO 101 Vd 110
23710 Casa de Jaime J 137 Wb 120
19119 Casa de Jaraices GU 87 Xa 107
21210 Casa de Jarramilla H 148 Td 122
16670 Casa de Jiménez CU 123 Xc 112
30800 Casa de Jofré MC 155 Ya 122
14300 Casa de José Cantador CO 150 Va 121
41560 Casa de José Martínez SE 166 Va 125
30850 Casa de José Sánchez MC 156 Yc 122
30510 Casa de Juan Camacho MC 141 Yf 117
45710 Casa de Juan Francisco TO 121 Wc 112
02600 Casa de Juan José AB 123 Xc 114
02161 Casa de Juan León AB 123 Xe 115
02100 Casa de Juanotón AB 124 Ya 113
02153 Casa de Juan Pardo AB 125 Ye 114
45140 Casa de Juan Romero TO 101 Vb 110
45700 Casa de Jubones TO 121 Wb 112
45840 Casa de la Abogada TO 103 Wf 111
10550 Casa de la Aceituna CC 116 Tc 112
10880 Casa de la Aceña CC 97 Ta 109
13150 Casa de la Alameda CR 121 Wa 114
13597 Casa de la Alberguilla CR 137 Vf 117
14978 Casa de la Alcudilla CO 167 Ve 125
34240 Casa de la Aldea P 48 Ve 97
28180 Casa de la Aldehuela MD 86 Wc 104
02695 Casa de la Almagra AB 125 Yc 115

45720 Casa de la Angola TO 121 Wc 113
11580 Casa de la Atalaya CA 173 Uc 128
28760 Casa de la Atalaya MD 86 Wa 105
10185 Casa de la Banda CC 117 Tf 113
16114 Casa de la Barraca CU 105 Xf 110
45533 Casa de la Bayona TO 101 Vd 109
11510 Casa de la Bedora CA 172 Tf 129
30528 Casa de la Bodeguilla MC 141 Yd 117
02140 Casa del Abogado AB 124 Ya 115
13200 Casa del Abogado CR 121 Wd 114
16238 Casa de labor de Coto CU 124 Yb 112
11330 Casa de labor de las Torres CA 173 Ud 130
13344 Casa de la Borreguilla CR 138 Wf 117
06400 Casa de la Bóveda BA 117 Ua 116
10291 Casa de la Breñilla CC 99 Ua 112
13710 Casa del Abuelito CR 122 Wf 114
06420 Casa de la Burra BA 118 Ud 116
10280 Casa de la Caballería CC 117 Ua 113
02536 Casa de la Cabeza AB 139 Xe 119
10500 Casa de la Cabra CC 96 Sd 111
14280 Casa de la Cabra CO 135 Uf 117
13412 Casa de la Calderera CR 119 Vb 115
11595 Casa de la Calera CA 172 Tf 129
10190 Casa de la Calera CC 98 Tc 111
41860 Casa de la Calera SE 148 Te 123
41530 Casa de la California SE 165 Ud 126
13738 Casa de la Calza CR 137 Wc 117
02639 Casa de la Campana AB 123 Xe 114
10394 Casa de la Canala CC 99 Uc 109
19117 Casa de la Canaleja GU 87 Xa 107
45127 Casa de la Cantera TO 101 Ve 111
30177 Casa de la Cantina MC 156 Yc 121
02600 Casa de la Cañada Arada AB 123 Xc 114
10161 Casa de la Cañada de la Pita CC 117 Te 113
05635 Casa de la Cañada del Horno AV 84 Uf 106
21750 Casa de la Cañada del Sotillo H 162 Tc 125
11520 Casa de la Capitana CA 172 Td 128
16433 Casa de la Carbonera CU 104 Xb 110
06200 Casa de la Carboneras BA 133 Td 116
30410 Casa de la Carrasca MC 155 Ya 121
41230 Casa de la Carrasca SE 148 Tf 122
06800 Casa de la Carrascala BA 116 Td 116
02110 Casa de la Castra AB 124 Xf 114
28312 Casa de la Cavina MD 102 Wb 109
45830 Casa del Acebrón TO 103 Wf 111
13779 Casa del Acebuchal CR 137 Wa 117
10186 Casa del Acebuche CC 117 Tf 113
10930 Casa de la Cenida CC 97 Tb 111
45850 Casa de la Cervanta TO 103 We 111
45686 Casa de la Cierva TO 100 Uf 109
21580 Casa de la Cigüeña H 146 Sf 122
14749 Casa de la Citolera CO 150 Ud 120
13768 Casa de la Clavellina CR 137 Wc 118
14280 Casa de la Coneja CO 135 Uf 117
47190 Casa de la Contienda de Abajo VA 47 Va 98

02151 Casa de la Corraliza AB 124 Yc 114
13195 Casa de la Corruca CR 121 Wa 115
43430 Casa de la Cova T 75 Ba 100
03100 Casa de la Cuesta A 142 Zc 117
23711 Casa de la Cuesta del Gatillo J 137 Wb 119
02434 Casa de la Cueva AB 140 Xe 119
14410 Casa de la Cueva de la Loba CO 135 Vc 118
41240 Casa de la Cuquera SE 148 Tf 122
43549 Casa de la Cuxota T 93 Ad 105
10193 Casa de la Dehesa CC 98 Te 110
16214 Casa de la Dehesa CU 105 Xf 111
23509 Casa de la Dehesa J 153 Wd 121
34300 Casa de la Dehesa P 47 Vc 95
45125 Casa de la Dehesa TO 102 Ve 111
49148 Casa de la Dehesa ZA 45 Ua 98
49760 Casa de la Dehesa ZA 46 Ub 97
11630 Casa de la Dehesa de Atrera CA 173 Uc 128
06410 Casa de la Dehesa de las Yeguas BA 117 Tf 115
41450 Casa de la Dehesa del Conde SE 149 Uc 122
47313 Casa de la Dehesa de los Frailes VA 66 Vd 99
06400 Casa de la Dehesa de Utrera BA 133 Ua 116
14430 Casa de la Dehesa Vieja CO 151 Vc 120
45160 Casa de la Dehesa Vieja TO 101 Ve 110
06131 Casa de la Dehesilla BA 131 Sf 118
06430 Casa de la Dehesilla BA 134 Ub 116
16434 Casa de la Dehesilla CU 104 Xc 110
16470 Casa de la Dehesilla de Herrera CU 103 Wf 108
49718 Casa de la Dehesita ZA 64 Ub 101
02212 Casa de la Desesperada AB 125 Ye 113
23748 Casa de la Disea J 136 Vf 119
02650 Casa del Administrador AB 141 Yd 116
13250 Casa de la Duquesa CR 121 Wc 114
06476 Casa de la Encomendilla BA 133 Tf 116
10132 Casa de la Encomienda CC 117 Tf 114
05460 Casa de la Enramada AV 84 Va 107
30529 Casa de la Felipa MC 141 Ye 118
45800 Casa de la Felipa TO 103 Wf 111
30510 Casa de la Fianza MC 141 Yf 116
26580 Casa de la Fiscala RI 51 Xf 95
13250 Casa de la Flor CR 121 Wc 114
02690 Casa de la Florida AB 125 Ye 114
02652 Casa de la Florida AB 141 Yc 117
45161 Casa de la Fuente TO 101 Ve 110
23592 Casa de la Fuente Vieja J 153 We 122
06500 Casa de la Galana BA 116 Sf 112
45313 Casa de la Gallega TO 102 Wb 109
13249 Casa de la Gata CR 122 Xa 114
30439 Casa de la Gloria MC 155 Yb 120
02211 Casa de la Gobernadora AB 125 Yd 114
46640 Casa de la Gobernadora V 126 Za 115
13100 Casa de la Golondrina CR 120 Ve 114
11510 Casa de la Granadina CA 172 Tf 129
10192 Casa de la Grande CC 98 Td 110
13344 Casa de la Granja CR 138 We 116
16600 Casa de la Granja CU 123 Xd 112
06656 Casa de la Graña BA 119 Uf 115

41600 Casa de la Grulla SE 165 Uc 125
10291 Casa del Aguijón CC 98 Ta 111
14250 Casa del Águila CO 135 Uf 119
13590 Casa del Águila CR 136 Ve 117
41400 Casa de Laguna SE 150 Uf 123
30529 Casa del Agunzarejo MC 141 Yd 119
02434 Casa de la Herrada AB 140 Xf 119
23300 Casa de la Herradura J 138 Xa 120
10940 Casa de la Higuera CC 98 Td 111
14749 Casa de la Higuera CO 150 Ue 122
41429 Casa de la Higuera SE 149 Ud 123
45222 Casa de la Higuera TO 102 Wb 108
23519 Casa de la Higueruela J 152 Wb 121
45660 Casa de la Higueruela TO 100 Va 110
45114 Casa de la Higueruela TO 102 Vf 110
10950 Casa de la Hoja CC 97 Tb 111
45311 Casa de la Hontanilla TO 102 Wc 110
10134 Casa de la Hoya CC 118 Ub 113
02151 Casa de la Hoya Gil AB 124 Yc 114
16318 Casa de la Hoz CU 106 Yd 108
41860 Casa de la Huelva del Alcornoque SE 148 Te 123
13114 Casa de la Huerta CR 120 Vd 113
41530 Casa de la Huerta SE 165 Ud 126
45574 Casa de la Huerta TO 100 Uf 110
41460 Casa de la Huerta de Abajo SE 149 Ud 121
11370 Casa de la Huerta del Capullar CA 173 Uc 131
13680 Casa de la Huerta del Cura CR 121 Wb 113
13400 Casa de la Huerta del Rosalejo CR 119 Vb 116
06510 Casa de la India BA 116 Ta 112
03315 Casa de la Iona de la Rambla A 141 Za 119
30412 Casa del Aire MC 155 Xf 121
06400 Casa de la Isla de Remondo BA 117 Ua 115
02100 Casa de la Jara AB 124 Ya 113
10194 Casa de la Jara CC 98 Te 110
13450 Casa de la Javiera CR 136 Ve 117
10189 Casa de la Jirondilla CC 117 Tf 113
10980 Casa de la Judia CC 97 Ta 111
16393 Casa de la Junta CU 106 Yc 110
41250 Casa de la Laguna SE 148 Tf 121
05123 Casa de la Lastra AV 84 Uf 106
46624 Casa del Alcalde V 125 Yf 113
46770 Casa del Alcalde V 127 Ze 114
30800 Casa del Alcaraz MC 155 Ya 122
45138 Casa del Alemán TO 101 Vb 112
02214 Casa de la Lentisosa AB 125 Ye 113
14850 Casa del Alguacil CO 151 Vd 123
02600 Casa del Almendro AB 123 Xc 113
10940 Casa de la Lobata CC 98 Tc 111
10980 Casa de la Lobera CC 97 Tb 110
10980 Casa de la Lobera CC 97 Tb 110
13332 Casa de la Lóbrega CR 122 Xa 116
23592 Casa de la Loma J 153 We 121
44591 Casa de la Loma del Callizo TE 72 Zc 101
14600 Casa de la Loma del Vicario CO 151 Ve 120
09001 Casa del Alto BU 30 Wb 95
10193 Casa de la Lucia CC 98 Te 111
02410 Casa de la Luz AB 140 Xf 117
10400 Casa de la Magdalena CC 99 Ub 108

06920 Casa de la Majadilla BA 134 Ub 119
10980 Casa de la Malpartida CC 97 Ta 110
46625 Casa de la María V 125 Ye 113
30814 Casa de la Marsilla MC 156 Yb 121
06910 Casa de la Mata BA 134 Uc 118
13230 Casa de la Mata CR 122 We 115
16415 Casa de la Mata CU 104 Xa 110
21520 Casa de la Mata H 147 Ta 124
45700 Casa de la Mata TO 102 Wb 111
21740 Casa de la Matanza H 162 Td 125
10270 Casa de la Matilla del Royal CC 117 Tf 112
02246 Casa de la Matosa AB 124 Yb 113
13679 Casa de la Médica CR 121 Wc 113
18440 Casa de la Memoria GR 169 We 127
10181 Casa de la Mengosa CC 117 Tf 112
10980 Casa de la Merced CC 97 Tb 110
41450 Casa de la Mesa SE 149 Uc 122
13410 Casa de la Mina CR 119 Vb 115
45150 Casa de la Mina TO 101 Vd 111
41250 Casa de la Mina de Campos SE 148 Tf 121
14447 Casa de la Mina de San Cayetano CO 136 Vd 119
21760 Casa de la Mogea H 162 Tc 126
41230 Casa de la Montera SE 148 Ua 122
16640 Casa de la Moraleja CU 104 Xb 111
02049 Casa de la Morena AB 124 Yb 115
02151 Casa de la Morena AB 124 Yc 114
13180 Casa de la Morena CR 120 Ve 115
13194 Casa de la Morilla CR 101 Vc 111
09591 Casa de la Mota BU 30 Wc 94
16146 Casa de la Muela CU 105 Ya 107
02499 Casa de la Muerte AB 141 Yd 118
10500 Casa de la Mula CC 115 Sf 112
06510 Casa de la Naterona BA 116 Ta 114
13270 Casa de la Nava CR 121 Wa 116
16622 Casa de la Nava CU 104 Xd 111
45516 Casa de la Nava TO 101 Vc 110
10570 Casa de la Naves CC 116 Sf 112
02459 Casa de la Noguera, La AB 139 Xd 118
05215 Casa de La Olmedilla AV 66 Vb 102
28812 Casa de la Olmedilla MD 87 We 106
22413 Casa de la Oresa HU 55 Aa 97
02611 Casa de la Ortigosa AB 122 Xb 115
46620 Casa de la Ortina V 125 Ye 114
06650 Casa de la Pachona BA 119 Uf 115
06400 Casa de la Pajosa BA 133 Ua 116
41360 Casa de la Paloma SE 149 Ub 122
19111 Casa de la Pangía GU 87 Xa 106
10160 Casa de la Pared CC 117 Te 113
16340 Casa de La Parra CU 105 Ya 108
46174 Casa de la Parra V 107 Za 110
14430 Casa de la Parrilla CO 136 Vc 120
23215 Casa de la Parrilla J 138 Wd 118
13180 Casa de la Patuda CR 120 Vc 115
13600 Casa de la Paz CR 118 Vb 113
02253 Casa de la Pedrera AB 124 Yc 113
18570 Casa de la Pedriza GR 168 Wc 124

06600 Casa de la Peña BA 118 Ud 116
45127 Casa de la Peña del Lobo TO 101 Ve 111
11638 Casa de la Perdiz CA 173 Ub 128
21591 Casa de la Pericona H 160 Sd 124
19142 Casa de la Pinilla GU 87 Wf 105
10184 Casa de la Pizarra CC 117 Tf 112
14730 Casa de la Plata CO 150 Uf 121
16600 Casa de la Pluma CU 123 Xc 112
13768 Casa de la Póbeda CR 137 Wc 118
31500 Casa de la Pola NC 52 Yd 96
06460 Casa de la Portugalesa BA 118 Uc 115
13250 Casa de la Posadilla CR 121 Wb 114
30177 Casa de la Posadilla MC 156 Yc 121
16640 Casa de la Poveda CU 104 Xb 111
45662 Casa de la Pradera TO 100 Va 110
19119 Casa de la Puebla GU 87 Wf 107
02124 Casa de la Quebrada AB 140 Xf 117
02610 Casa de la Quejigosa AB 123 Xc 115
47359 Casa de la Quemada VA 48 Vc 99
41599 Casa de la Quinta SE 166 Vb 125
44700 Casa de la Rabosa TE 91 Zb 104
02247 Casa de la Rambla AB 124 Yc 113
06800 Casa de la Rana BA 117 Te 114
10883 Casa de la Arenalejo CC 98 Tc 110
44230 Casa de la Retuerta TE 71 Yd 103
21647 Casa de la Rinconada H 147 Tb 123
30195 Casa de la Rodea MC 155 Xf 120
10513 Casa de la Ronguera CC 96 Sd 111
10120 Casa de la Ropera CC 118 Ud 113
45672 Casa del Arreciado TO 119 Va 112
10870 Casa de la Sabanilla CC 97 Tb 109
02610 Casa de la Sabina AB 123 Xc 115
16192 Casa de la Sabina CU 105 Ya 107
47230 Casa de las Abogadas VA 66 Vb 100
02610 Casa de las Aguas AB 123 Xb 115
50792 Casa de la Salada Z 73 Ze 101
13194 Casa de la Salceda CR 120 Ve 112
30411 Casa de la Salina de Periago MC 155 Xf 121
16610 Casa de las Almenas CU 123 Xd 113
21540 Casa de las Barajonas H 161 Se 124
23220 Casa de las Cabrerizas J 137 Wc 119
10133 Casa de las Calamochas CC 117 Ua 113
13270 Casa de las Canteras CR 121 Wb 115
16146 Casa de las Carboneras CU 105 Xf 107
02612 Casa de las Cauques AB 123 Xc 114
49027 Casa de las Chanas ZA 64 Ub 100
13248 Casa de las Chimeneas CR 122 Wf 114
21750 Casa de las Cinco Algáidas H 162 Tc 125
14600 Casa del Asco CO 136 Ve 120
19117 Casa de los Cofrades GU 87 Xa 107
10694 Casa de las Corralizas CC 99 Ua 110
13700 Casa de las Delicias CR 122 Xa 113
41429 Casa de las Dos Vigas SE 149 Ud 123
13270 Casa de las Duronas CR 121 Wb 115
10195 Casa de las Encinas CC 116 Td 112
13350 Casa de las Envidias CR 137 Wc 116

03420 Casa de la Senyora Ángela, La
A 142 Zc 117
23711 Casa de la Señora J
137 Wb 120
29110 Casa de la Sepultura MA
174 Va 129
11560 Casa de la Sevillana CA
163 Te 127
13344 Casa de las Fuentes CR
137 Wd 118
06657 Casa de Las Garbayuelas BA
119 Uf 115
44409 Casa de las Golondrinas TE
91 Za 107
10189 Casa de las Grangas CC
117 Tf 113
06500 Casa de las Grulleras BA
116 Ta 112
45909 Casa de las Higueras TO
85 Ve 107
13770 Casa de las Huesas CR
137 Wb 117
02320 Casa de las Ideas AB
123 Xe 115
16236 Casa de la Sierra CU
124 Ya 112
23230 Casa de la Sierra J
138 Wd 120
31370 Casa de la Sierra NC
33 Ya 94
06410 Casa de la Sierrecilla BA
117 Tf 114
23250 Casa de las Juntas J
138 We 118
14300 Casa de las Lastras CO
150 Uf 121
29327 Casa de las Llamas MA
166 Va 126
10950 Casa de las Loberas CC
97 Tc 111
06478 Casa de las Lomas BA
117 Ua 116
02600 Casa de las Madres AB
123 Xc 113
49148 Casa de las Mangas ZA
45 Ub 97
13200 Casa de las Mayorgas CR
122 Wd 114
02650 Casa de las Minas AB
125 Ye 116
10820 Casa de las Minas CC
98 Td 110
30528 Casa de las Minas MC
141 Yd 118
41370 Casa de las Minas SE
149 Ub 121
41360 Casa de las Minas SE
149 Ub 121
02512 Casa de las Monjas CU
123 Xe 113
26350 Casa de las Monjas RI
31 Xc 94
02511 Casa de las Monjas de
Pozo-Cañada AB 140 Yc 116
13591 Casa de las Morras CR
136 Ve 117
13414 Casa de las Navas CR
119 Vc 116
45470 Casa de las Navas TO
120 Vf 112
28339 Casa de las Niñas MD
86 Wc 107
10512 Casa de la Solana o Moreno
CC 96 Sd 111
06640 Casa de la Solanilla BA
118 Ue 114
10940 Casa de las Pedrizas CC
98 Td 110
11149 Casa de las Peñuelas CA
172 Tf 131
47814 Casa de las Rozas VA
46 Ue 97
11549 Casa de las Salinas CA
164 Td 127
50375 Casa de las Salinas Z
71 Yb 102
06510 Casa de las Santas BA
116 Ta 113
41530 Casa de las Semillas SE
165 Ud 126
02110 Casa de las Señoras AB
124 Ya 114
13270 Casa de las Setecientas CR
121 Wa 116
23478 Casa de las Tablas J
154 Xb 120
10170 Casa de las Tarazonas CC
117 Te 113
13344 Casa de las Tejoneras CR
138 We 117
50615 Casa de las Tenias Z 53 Za 95
47639 Casa de las Tomasas VA
47 Va 98
13690 Casa de las Velas CR
122 We 113
13600 Casa de las Veredillas CR
103 We 112
14400 Casa de las Viborillas CO
135 Vb 119

16393 Casa del Ataúd CU
106 Yc 111
44791 Casa de la Tejera TE
72 Zb 103
13110 Casa de la Tejona CR
119 Vc 112
11510 Casa de la Tinaja CA
172 Tf 129
02137 Casa de la Toba AB
139 Xe 117
29011 Casa de la Tormenta MA
167 Vd 128
10500 Casa de la Torre CC
115 Sf 112
13344 Casa de la Trinidad CR
138 We 117
45760 Casa de la Urraca TO
102 Wc 110
14430 Casa de la Urraquilla Alta CO
151 Vc 120
02693 Casa de la Vega AB
125 Yd 115
19115 Casa de la Vega GU
87 Xa 107
50239 Casa de la Vega Z 70 Ya 100
06400 Casa de la Vega de los
Maderos BA 117 Ua 116
06400 Casa de la Veguilla BA
117 Ua 115
50316 Casa de la Veguilla Z
70 Ya 99
02312 Casa de la Venta AB
139 Xc 116
13710 Casa de la Ventilla CR
122 Wf 114
02156 Casa de la Ventosa AB
124 Yb 114
06250 Casa de la Vera BA
133 Te 119
50610 Casa de Laverné Alta Z
53 Yf 96
11500 Casa de la Vicuña CA
172 Te 129
10950 Casa de la Vigilia CC
97 Ta 111
10130 Casa de la Villalbas CC
118 Uc 113
02600 Casa de la Viña AB
123 Xd 113
31130 Casa de la Viña NC 33 Ya 93
45569 Casa de la Viñas TO
100 Ue 108
41380 Casa de la Viñuela SE
149 Uc 121
49272 Casa de la Viñuela ZA
64 Ua 100
16640 Casa de la Virgen CU
104 Xb 111
30529 Casa de la Virgen MC
141 Ye 119
14650 Casa de la Viuda CO
151 Vd 121
13250 Casa de la Viuda CR
121 Wc 114
18800 Casa de la Viuda GR
154 Xa 124
45880 Casa de la Viuda TO
103 We 110
10191 Casa del Avutardo CC
98 Td 110
02400 Casa de la Zarzuela AB
140 Yb 117
30177 Casa del Barból MC
156 Yc 121
11400 Casa del Barón CA
164 Te 128
45760 Casa del Batán TO
103 Wd 110
11595 Casa del Beato CA 172 Tf 129
13610 Casa del Beato CR
122 Wf 112
13391 Casa del Becerril CR
138 We 116
10550 Casa del Becerro CC
116 Tc 112
10960 Casa del Belvis CC 97 Ta 111
47500 Casa del Bernardillo VA
65 Uf 100
06730 Casa del Bodonal BA
118 Uc 114
44549 Casa del Bolar TE 72 Zb 102
30559 Casa del Boquerón MC
141 Ye 119
10271 Casa del Borril CC 117 Tf 112
47270 Casa del Boticario VA
47 Vb 98
29570 Casa del Bracho MA
166 Vc 128
02611 Casa del Cabalgador AB
122 Xb 114
45700 Casa del Cahorzo TO
102 Wb 111
41429 Casa del Calerón SE
149 Ud 123
09316 Casa del Campesino BU
67 Wa 99
10129 Casa del Campillo CC
99 Uc 112
50135 Casa del Campillo Z
72 Zb 100

46150 Casa del Campo V
107 Zc 110
46620 Casa del Campo V 125 Yf 114
14709 Casa del Canal CO
150 Ud 122
10170 Casa del Canchal Blanquillo
CC 117 Te 113
10980 Casa del Cancho CC
97 Tc 110
02434 Casa del Cano AB 140 Xf 119
23592 Casa del Canónigo J
153 Wd 121
13720 Casa del Cantivano CR
122 Wf 113
16390 Casa del Cañizar CU
105 Yb 109
30815 Casa del Capador MC
156 Yc 123
29550 Casa del Capellán MA
166 Va 127
02612 Casa del Capitán AB
123 Xd 114
02328 Casa del Capitán AB
124 Xf 114
11648 Casa del Capitán CA
164 Ub 127
47012 Casa del Capitán VA 47 Vc 99
30858 Casa del Cara de Lobo MC
156 Yd 122
10500 Casa del Cardizal CC
97 Sf 112
10950 Casa del Carnerito CC
97 Ta 111
10980 Casa del Carrascal CC
97 Ta 110
47850 Casa del Carrascal VA
46 Ue 98
03420 Casa del Cartón A 142 Zb 117
11510 Casa del Carvajal CA
172 Tf 129
47820 Casa del Carvajal VA 46 Uf 98
13100 Casa del Casarejo CR
120 Vd 114
06413 Casa del Casquero BA
117 Ua 115
11370 Casa del Castaño CA
173 Uc 131
22231 Casa del Castejonero HU
54 Zf 98
10980 Casa del Castillejo CC
97 Ta 110
13193 Casa del Castillejo CR
120 Vd 113
21510 Casa del Cebollar de Santa
Ana H 161 Sf 124
11680 Casa del Cerillar CA
165 Ud 127
13344 Casa del Cerillo de la Era CR
138 Wd 117
14547 Casa del Cero CO 150 Va 123
02211 Casa del Cerro AB
125 Yd 113
02695 Casa del Cerro AB
125 Yd 115
10184 Casa del Cerro CC 117 Te 113
28596 Casa del Cerro MD 87 Wf 107
10189 Casa del Cerro de la Collada
CC 117 Tf 113
14550 Casa del Cerro del Humo CO
151 Vc 123
11595 Casa del Cerro del Inglés CA
172 Tf 129
21760 Casa del Cerro del Trigo H
163 Td 127
06420 Casa del Cerro Sagrado BA
118 Uc 115
14412 Casa del Chabacano CO
135 Vb 118
28950 Casa del Champiñón MD
86 Wa 107
10269 Casa del Chaparral CC
117 Ua 113
13191 Casa del Chaparral CR
120 Ve 115
10331 Casa del Chaparro CC
100 Ue 110
22761 Casa del Chas HU 34 Za 94
30411 Casa del Chico MC
155 Ya 121
16422 Casa del Chiquillo CU
104 Xb 110
45593 Casa del Chivero TO
102 Vf 109
45470 Casa del Chorrito TO
102 Vf 112
23215 Casa del Chortal J
138 Wd 118
45860 Casa del Churri TO
103 We 111
13720 Casa del Cirujano CR
122 Wf 113
46620 Casa del Collado de San Juan
V 125 Ye 115
10530 Casa del Colmenar CC
98 Tf 110
45646 Casa del Colmenar TO
101 Vb 108
02211 Casa del Conde AB
125 Yd 113

13600 Casa del Condesillo CR
122 We 113
41140 Casa del Conejo SE
163 Tf 126
24271 Casa del Convento LE
27 Ua 93
10570 Casa del Corcho CC
116 Ta 112
35613 Casa del Cordobés GC
183 Ma 177
45870 Casa del Cordobés TO
103 Wd 111
45370 Casa del Corneta TO
103 We 109
02150 Casa del Cortijo AB
124 Yc 114
50690 Casa del Coscojar Z 52 Ye 98
13630 Casa del Cosme CR
122 Xa 113
47430 Casa del Cotarrón VA
66 Vc 100
40449 Casa del Coto SG 66 Vd 103
06800 Casa del Coto Presa BA
117 Td 114
13700 Casa del Cuadrado CR
122 Xa 114
10990 Casa del Cuartillo CC
97 Ta 110
46199 Casa del Cul V 125 Yf 113
02630 Casa del Cura AB 123 Xf 113
02660 Casa del Cura AB 141 Yf 116
10940 Casa del Cura CC 98 Tc 110
16317 Casa del Cura CU 89 Yb 107
16620 Casa del Cura CU 104 Xc 112
19226 Casa del Cura GU 87 Wf 104
23300 Casa del Cura J 154 Wf 120
26528 Casa del Cura RI 52 Ya 97
45580 Casa del Cura TO 100 Ue 108
30890 Casa del Cura y Cañada del
Alba MC 155 Yb 123
45622 Casa del Dehesón TO
100 Va 108
02246 Casa de Lema AB 124 Yb 113
04480 Casa del Empalme AL
169 Xa 127
10500 Casa del Empalme CC
97 Se 112
06850 Casa del Encinar BA
116 Td 115
10980 Casa del Esparragosillo CC
97 Ta 111
45400 Casa del Estanquero TO
102 Wb 111
41240 Casa del Esterquizo SE
148 Tf 121
45749 Casa del Fausto TO
102 Wb 110
14410 Casa del Fontanar CO
135 Vb 118
30559 Casa del Fraile MC
141 Ye 119
13600 Casa del Frailito CR
122 We 112
47639 Casa del Francés VA 47 Va 98
47400 Casa del Francés VA
66 Va 101
43549 Casa del Francès T 93 Ad 104
45917 Casa del Fresnedoso TO
101 Vc 108
35639 Casa del Frontón GC
183 Ma 178
10189 Casa del Gallinero CC
117 Tf 113
02610 Casa del Gallo AB
123 Xb 115
13194 Casa del Garbanzuelo CR
120 Vc 112
21750 Casa del Gato H 162 Tc 125
13739 Casa del Gimena CR
137 Wc 117
16192 Casa del Gitano CU
105 Ya 108
13116 Casa del Goro CR 120 Vd 113
47313 Casa del Granizo V 48 Vd 99
02140 Casa del Guarda AB
124 Ya 116
10882 Casa del Guarda CC
98 Tc 109
10164 Casa del Guarda CC
117 Td 113
16216 Casa del Guarda CU
105 Xf 109
19229 Casa del Guarda GU
87 Wf 103
34259 Casa del Guarda P 48 Ve 96
34246 Casa del Guarda P 48 Vf 97
26375 Casa Del Guarda RI 32 Xc 94

41849 Casa del Guarda SE
163 Te 126
47194 Casa del Guarda VA 47 Vb 98
49272 Casa del Guarda ZA
64 Ua 100
23260 Casa del Guarda de la
Alameda J 138 We 118
22212 Casa del Guarda del Monte
HU 54 Ze 97
23250 Casa del Guarda de Sierra del
Loro J 138 We 118
40480 Casa del guarda forestal SG
66 Vd 101
42140 Casa del Guarda Montes SO
50 Wf 97
06470 Casa del Guijo BA 117 Tf 115
10130 Casa del Guijuelo CC
118 Uc 113
06460 Casa del Herradón BA
118 Uc 115
13720 Casa del Herrador CR
122 We 113
13710 Casa del Hierro CR
122 Wf 114
13350 Casa del Hierro CR
137 Wc 116
50670 Casa del Higueral Z 33 Yd 95
49715 Casa del Hondayo ZA
65 Uc 100
02152 Casa del Hontanar AB
125 Yd 114
13370 Casa del Hormigón CR
137 Wb 116
10560 Casa del Hornillo CC
116 Ta 112
13450 Casa del Hornillo CR
136 Ve 117
23213 Casa del Hornillo J
137 Wc 118
45569 Casa del Horquillo TO
100 Uf 109
13440 Casa del Hoyo CR 120 Vf 116
47862 Casa del Huesco VA 46 Ue 98
02651 Casa del Huevo AB
141 Yd 116
41240 Casa del Indiano SE
148 Tf 121
45780 Casa del Indiano TO
102 Wc 111
41500 Casa del Infante SE
163 Ua 125
26223 Casa del Inglés RI 31 Xb 94
06468 Casa del Intendente BA
118 Ub 115
50670 Casa del Iranzo Z 52 Yd 95
13344 Casa de Lizana CR
138 Wf 117
13630 Casa del Jabonero CR
122 Xa 113
45170 Casa del Jaral TO 101 Vb 109
19187 Casa del Jardinillo GU
86 Wd 103
11170 Casa del Judío CA 172 Tf 130
28650 Casa del Juncal MD
85 Vc 107
11130 Casa del Lanchar CA
172 Tf 130
10120 Casa del Lavadero CC
118 Uc 113
13710 Casa del Letrado CR
122 Wf 114
45671 Casa del Linareo TO
100 Va 111
13248 Casa del Llano CR
122 Xa 115
16730 Casa del Llano CU
105 Xe 111
10194 Casa del Lobato CC
98 Te 110
45720 Casa del Lorito TO
121 Wd 112
21240 Casa del Lote J 147 Sf 121
06500 Casa del Macho BA
116 Ta 112
10870 Casa del Madroño CC
97 Tb 110
13260 Casa del Magrero CR
121 Wc 115
41350 Casa del Majuelo SE
149 Uc 122
41570 Casa del Malagueño SE
166 Vb 125
06630 Casa del Manantial BA
118 Ud 114
13779 Casa del Manchego CR
137 Wb 117
19132 Casa del Manco GU
87 Xa 106
30849 Casa del Manco MC
156 Ye 121
49660 Casa del Maragato ZA
46 Uc 97
02611 Casa del Marañal AB
122 Xb 114
50690 Casa del Marinote Z 52 Ye 98
16410 Casa del Marqués CU
103 Wf 110
19119 Casa del Marqués del Saco
GU 87 Xa 106

28595 Casa del Marqués de Remisa
MD 103 Wf 108
29461 Casa del Marqués de Santiago
MA 174 Ue 129
21760 Casa del Martinazo H
162 Tc 126
02152 Casa del Médico AB
125 Ye 114
06650 Casa del Médico BA
119 Va 115
10528 Casa del Médico CC
99 Ua 110
13720 Casa del Médico CR
122 We 113
45890 Casa del Médico TO
103 Wf 110
46620 Casa del Medio V 125 Yf 114
13720 Casa del Mesón del Espejo
CR 122 Wd 113
13300 Casa del Mesonero CR
138 Wd 116
10500 Casa del Millaron CC
115 Sf 112
13690 Casa del Minguillo CR
122 Wf 113
13710 Casa del Miño CR 122 Wf 114
12598 Casa del Mochuelo CS
92 Ab 107
23711 Casa del Mojón de la Legua J
137 Wb 119
14300 Casa del Molino CO
150 Uf 121
35558 Casa del Molino GC
182 Mc 174
16195 Casa del Montaraz CU
104 Xd 108
02150 Casa del Monte AB
124 Yb 114
05380 Casa del Monte AV 84 Uf 104
09194 Casa del Monte BU 30 Wc 95
13345 Casa del Monte CR
138 Wf 117
16411 Casa del Monte CU
103 Wf 109
16465 Casa del Monte CU
104 Xa 108
16630 Casa del Monte CU
104 Xa 111
16440 Casa del Monte CU
104 Xc 109
16730 Casa del Monte CU
104 Xe 111
16630 Casa del Monte CU
122 Xa 112
19182 Casa del Monte GU
87 We 104
19116 Casa del Monte GU
87 Wf 107
23712 Casa del Monte J 152 Wb 120
24191 Casa del Monte LE 27 Ub 93
24206 Casa del Monte LE 46 Ud 95
34419 Casa del Monte P 47 Vd 96
34239 Casa del Monte P 48 Vd 96
34465 Casa del Monte P 48 Ve 96
34249 Casa del Monte P 48 Ve 97
37405 Casa del Monte SA 65 Ue 102
47813 Casa del Monte VA 47 Uf 97
47270 Casa del Monte VA 47 Vb 98
47331 Casa del Monte VA 66 Vd 99
50360 Casa del Monte Z 71 Yd 102
50266 Casa del Monte Z 71 Yd 99
49624 Casa del Monte ZA 45 Ua 97
28812 Casa del Monte de las
Escaleras MD 87 We 106
47820 Casa del Monte de la Villa VA
47 Uf 98
47840 Casa del Monte del Conde VA
46 Ue 98
47862 Casa del Monte de San Miguel
VA 46 Ue 98
09311 Casa del Monte de Villalobón
BU 48 Wa 98
50200 Casa del Monte Nuevo Z
70 Ya 100
49630 Casa del Monte Reoyo ZA
46 Ud 98
49530 Casa del Montico ZA 65 Uc 99
13670 Casa del Moral CR
121 Wb 113
45310 Casa del Muni TO
103 Wd 109
40145 Casa del Muñico SG
85 Vd 103
13194 Casa del Navajo CR
102 Vf 111
02511 Casa del Nordal AB
140 Yb 116
10109 Casa del Notario CC
117 Ua 114
41450 Casa del Ochavo SE
149 Uc 121
16421 Casa de Lodares CU
104 Xa 110
10980 Casa del Olmillo CC 97 Ta 111
02155 Casa del Olmo AB 124 Ya 114
30510 Casa de López MC 141 Yf 117
10950 Casa del Orillal CC 97 Tb 110
14440 Casa de los Acebuchares CO
135 Vb 119

10870 Casa de los Alamos CC
97 Tb 110
13343 Casa de los Alcores CR
138 Wf 117
10189 Casa de los Alcornoques CC
117 Tf 113
45710 Casa de los Alejandros TO
121 Wc 112
21559 Casa de los Almendreros H
161 Se 123
02499 Casa de los Almendros AB
141 Yc 118
30528 Casa de los Almendros MC
141 Yd 117
23330 Casa de los Angostones J
138 Xa 120
13700 Casa de los Árboles CR
122 Xa 113
02328 Casa de los Arcos AB
124 Xf 115
06670 Casa de los Ayeruales BA
119 Va 113
13760 Casa de los Barrancos CR
137 Wd 118
10500 Casa de los Barreros CC
115 Se 112
50270 Casa de los Bilbaínos Z
52 Yd 99
40150 Casa de los Blases SG
85 Vd 104
21760 Casa de los Bodegones H
162 Tb 125
02690 Casa de los Bolos AB
125 Yd 115
26144 Casa de los Cadetes RI
32 Xe 94
14600 Casa de los Caleros CO
151 Ve 120
10950 Casa de los Calvos CC
97 Tb 112
04660 Casa de los Camarotes AL
155 Xf 124
49155 Casa de los Cantadales ZA
65 Ud 100
02213 Casa de los Cañizos AB
125 Ye 114
46623 Casa de los Capellanes V
125 Yf 114
41250 Casa de los Carabales SE
148 Tf 121
21560 Casa de los Casares H
146 Sd 122
09310 Casa de los Caserones BU
48 Vf 97
30528 Casa de los Cerrillares MC
141 Ye 117
41710 Casa de los Cerros SE
163 Ub 125
23540 Casa de los Charcones J
153 Wc 122
13700 Casa de los Cicateros CR
122 Xa 113
23770 Casa de los Cipreses J
136 Vf 120
21600 Casa de los Collados H
161 Tb 123
35649 Casa de los Coroneles GC
183 Ma 177
06475 Casa de los Corteses BA
133 Te 116
16150 Casa de los Corzos CU
89 Ya 107
10192 Casa de los Cuartos CC
98 Te 110
41240 Casa de los Cuquiles SE
148 Tf 121
13344 Casa de los Fontes CR
138 Wd 117
14711 Casa de los Frailes CO
150 Va 122
02156 Casa de Los Garijos AB
124 Yc 114
02409 Casa de los Grajos AB
140 Yb 118
41209 Casa de los Granadillos SE
148 Tf 123
13196 Casa de los Guardas CR
121 Wa 114
13250 Casa de los Guardas CR
121 Wb 114
50612 Casa de los Guardas Z
53 Yf 97
30850 Casa de los Guardas
Forestales MC 156 Yc 121
13200 Casa de los Guijos CR
122 We 114
02600 Casa de los Herrericos AB
123 Xd 113
11370 Casa de los Hoyos de Zanona
CA 173 Uc 131
44540 Casa de los Jugos TE
72 Zc 101
45138 Casa de los Lagares TO
101 Vc 111
21595 Casa de los Lanchas H
146 Sd 124
14430 Casa de los Llanos CO
151 Vc 120
16432 Casa de los Llanos CU
104 Xb 110

23630 Casa de los Llanos J
152 Wb 121
41450 Casa de los Logios SE
149 Ub 122
45710 Casa de los Machos TO
121 Wc 112
35571 Casa de los Majones GC
182 Mb 175
02600 Casa de los Mateos AB
123 Xd 113
13196 Casa de los Medranos CR
120 Vf 114
14440 Casa de los Mesoneros CO
135 Vc 118
34218 Casa de los Milagros P
47 Vd 97
10950 Casa de los Mirones CC
97 Tb 112
14440 Casa de los Mocosos CO
135 Vb 118
10879 Casa de los Morales CC
98 Tb 110
44143 Casa de los Morcos TE
91 Zc 105
13344 Casa de los Morrones CR
138 We 117
02409 Casa de los Niños AB
140 Yb 118
30528 Casa de los Ontureños MC
141 Yd 117
44100 Casa de los Pajares TE
90 Yc 106
02160 Casa de los Pardales AB
123 Xe 115
14600 Casa de los Pastedales CO
136 Vd 120
10940 Casa de los Pedregak CC
98 Tb 110
22535 Casa de los Peras HU
55 Ab 98
02409 Casa de los Peruelos AB
140 Yb 118
10592 Casa de los Petos CC
98 Te 110
06470 Casa de los Pilares BA
117 Tf 115
13180 Casa de los Pilones CR
120 Vc 115
02630 Casa de los Pinos AB
123 Xf 113
02640 Casa de los Pinos AB
125 Ye 115
45800 Casa de los Pis TO
103 Xa 111
41130 Casa de los Pobres SE
163 Te 125
10318 Casa de los Potros CC
99 Ud 108
30528 Casa de los Pozos MC
141 Yd 117
13592 Casa de los Quemados CR
136 Vf 117
14412 Casa de los Reventones CO
135 Vb 118
45470 Casa de los Robledillos TO
121 Wa 112
29320 Casa de los Salinas MA
166 Va 126
13191 Casa de los Santiagos CR
120 Ve 115
13344 Casa de los Socios CR
138 We 117
28580 Casa de los Socios MD
87 Wf 106
41590 Casa de los Tarancones SE
166 Vb 125
02310 Casa de los Teatinos AB
123 Xc 116
31500 Casa de los Tetones NC
52 Yc 96
13592 Casa de los Toriles CR
137 Vf 117
19115 Casa de los Velascos GU
87 Xa 107
49193 Casa de los Vitotos ZA
64 Ua 99
41710 Casa del Pajarito SE
163 Ua 126
13344 Casa del Palomar CR
138 We 117
47862 Casa del Páramo VA 46 Ue 98
13195 Casa del Pardillo CR
121 Wa 115
13350 Casa del Pardillo CR
121 Wc 115
45410 Casa del Pardillo TO
102 Wb 110
06692 Casa del Parrilla BA
119 Vb 112
10820 Casa del Parrucho CC
98 Td 110
13450 Casa del Pastor CR
136 Vd 117
13300 Casa del Patrón CR
121 Wc 115
30810 Casa del Peñón MC
155 Ya 122
16421 Casa del Peraleo CU
104 Xb 110

46620 Casa del Peregrín V
125 Za 115
16393 Casa del Pintado CU
106 Yc 111
21750 Casa del Piojo H 162 Tc 125
10592 Casa del Pizarroso CC
98 Td 110
06689 Casa del Platero BA
119 Uf 113
29500 Casa del Polo MA 166 Vb 128
10950 Casa del Polvo CC 98 Tb 112
10590 Casa del Porquero CC
98 Tf 109
45663 Casa del Porquero TO
100 Va 109
10191 Casa del Posio CC 98 Td 110
05631 Casa del Postuero Cordel AV
83 Ue 106
19300 Casa del Pote GU 89 Ya 103
02150 Casa del Pozo AB 124 Yb 114
02534 Casa del Pozo AB
139 Xd 120
16236 Casa del Pozo CU 124 Yb 113
47313 Casa del Pozo VA 48 Vd 99
02696 Casa del Pozo de la Higuera
AB 124 Yc 114
14547 Casa del Pozo del Villar CO
150 Vb 123
14410 Casa del Pozo Linares CO
135 Vb 118
29440 Casa del Pozuelo MA
174 Uf 129
14710 Casa del Prado CO
150 Va 121
28295 Casa del Prado MD 85 Vd 105
21570 Casa del Prado de los
Carneros H 146 Se 122
16192 Casa del Prado de los
Esquiladores CU 89 Ya 108
06510 Casa del Puerco BA
116 Sf 113
02511 Casa del Puerto AB
140 Yc 116
14491 Casa del Puerto CO
135 Va 117
30529 Casa del Puerto MC
141 Ye 118
21760 Casa del Puntal H 162 Td 127
40392 Casa del Quintanar SG
67 Vf 102
13194 Casa del Quinto CR
120 Ve 112
45489 Casa del Quinto TO
103 We 111
13380 Casa del Quinto de Santiago
CR 121 Wb 116
06411 Casa del Ramblazo BA
117 Ua 115
45530 Casa del Raso TO 101 Vd 109
23330 Casa del Raso de la Esalera J
138 Xa 120
13670 Casa del Rayado CR
121 Wc 113
04693 Casa del Rayo AL 155 Ya 123
06500 Casa del Realejo BA
116 Sf 112
41600 Casa del Redondón SE
165 Uc 125
02512 Casa del Regajo AB
141 Yc 116
47510 Casa del Reventón VA
65 Ue 101
10818 Casa del Rincón CC
97 Tb 109
10940 Casa del Rincón CC
98 Tc 110
10340 Casa del Rincón CC
99 Uc 110
10120 Casa del Rincón CC
118 Ud 113
14749 Casa del Rincón CO
150 Ue 121
35572 Casa del Rincón GC
182 Mc 175
41240 Casa del Rincón SE
148 Tf 121
42153 Casa del Rincón SO 50 Xb 97
45159 Casa del Rincón TO
101 Vc 111
14249 Casa del Rincón, La CO
134 Ud 119
41370 Casa del Rincón de la Higuera
SE 149 Ua 121
06240 Casa del Risco BA
133 Td 119
10512 Casa del Rivero CC 96 Sd 111
02161 Casa del Roble AB
123 Xd 115
10170 Casa del Roble CC 117 Tf 113
30440 Casa del Roble MC
140 Yb 119
30195 Casa del Roblecillo de Arriba
MC 155 Xf 120
02640 Casa del Rojalero AB
125 Yf 116
50130 Casa del Románico Z
72 Zb 101
02160 Casa del Romeral AB
123 Xe 114

13200 Casa del Roncero CR
122 Wd 114
13116 Casa del Rostro CR
120 Vd 113
46620 Casa del Royo V 125 Yf 115
23748 Casa del Rozalejo J
136 Vf 119
02151 Casa del Sabinar AB
124 Yc 114
41450 Casa del Saladillo SE
149 Uc 122
02212 Casa del Salado AB
125 Ye 113
25737 Casa del Salarnein L 56 Af 98
38729 Casa del Salto TF 181 Hb 176
02359 Casa del Santo AB
139 Xd 117
10513 Casa del Santo CC 96 Sd 111
40409 Casa del Sapo SG 85 Vd 105
45560 Casa del Sapo TO 100 Uf 109
50174 Casa del Saxo Z 54 Zc 99
03400 Casa dels Caragols, La A
142 Za 117
13194 Casa del Serrano CR
101 Ve 112
06510 Casa del Sesmo BA
116 Sf 113
10512 Casa del Sesmo de Abajo CC
96 Sd 111
25637 Casa del Soldat L 56 Ae 95
06770 Casa del Sotillo BA
118 Ue 113
11580 Casa del Sotillo Nuevo CA
172 Ua 129
42107 Casa del Soto SO 52 Ya 98
41563 Casa del Soto del Moro SE
150 Va 123
37130 Casa del Tabernero SA
64 Ua 103
06500 Casa del Tarro BA 116 Ta 113
06470 Casa del Tejar BA 117 Te 115
06475 Casa del Tendero BA
133 Tf 116
50196 Casa del Tendero Z 53 Yf 99
11190 Casa del Tío Alozaina CA
173 Ub 131
19119 Casa del Tío Genaro GU
87 Wf 106
45450 Casa del Tío Mario TO
102 Wa 111
10828 Casa del Tío Miguel CC
98 Tc 110
45730 Casa del Tío Pepe TO
121 Wd 112
45789 Casa del Tío Salao TO
102 Wc 111
06400 Casa del Toconal BA
117 Ua 115
02610 Casa del Tonto AB
123 Xc 115
06469 Casa del Tonto BA
118 Uc 115
29650 Casa del Toril MA 175 Vb 129
02640 Casa del Torno AB
125 Ye 115
05419 Casa del Torno AV 84 Ue 107
45692 Casa del Torrejón TO
101 Vc 109
02640 Casa del Tostado AB
125 Ye 115
45128 Casa del Trabuco TO
101 Vd 110
10592 Casa del Tresmal CC
98 Te 110
25165 Casa del Tronadit L 75 Ae 100
34248 Casa del Tuerto P 48 Vf 97
45138 Casa de Luciérnaga TO
101 Vc 111
45840 Casa de Ludeña TO
103 We 111
16240 Casa de Luján CU 105 Ya 111
03109 Casa de Luna A 142 Zb 117
13610 Casa del Vagón CR
122 Wf 113
16878 Casa del Valle CU 89 Xf 106
13118 Casa del Valmorro CR
119 Vb 112
10130 Casa del Vaquerín CC
118 Uc 113
06600 Casa del Vaquero BA
119 Ue 115
10729 Casa del Ventorro de
Sangamello CC 98 Tf 108
10005 Casa del Vicario CC 98 Tc 111
13270 Casa del Viejo CR
121 Wb 115
21880 Casa del Vinagre H
148 Tc 123
13345 Casa del Viudo CR
138 Wf 116
13400 Casa del Vivero CR
135 Vb 116
31589 Casa del Vivero NC 32 Xf 94
42126 Casa del Yelo SO 70 Ya 100
45121 Casa del Zarzal TO
101 Vd 111
44123 Casa del Zarzoso TE
90 Yd 107
46825 Casa del Zorrero V
126 Zb 114

A
B
C
D
E
F
G
H
I
J
K
L
M
N
Ñ
O
P
Q
R
S
T
U
V
W
X
Y
Z
Ⓔ

14280 Casa de Torretejeda CO 135 Uf 117
29679 Casa de Tramotores MA 174 Uf 129
41440 Casa de Traspón SE 149 Uc 122
13240 Casa de Traviesa CR 122 We 115
13610 Casa de Treviño CR 122 Wf 113
23530 Casa de Trista J 153 Wc 122
02610 Casa de Turra AB 123 Xb 116
26560 Casa de Turrax RI 51 Ya 95
19184 Casa de Uceda GU 86 Wd 103
44520 Casa de Urreano TE 73 Ze 101
46624 Casa de Usero V 125 Ye 113
14310 Casa de Vadohondillo CO 151 Vb 121
10990 Casa de Vaidemojones CC 97 Ta 110
49170 Casa de Valcamín de Abajo ZA 64 Ub 100
10592 Casa de Valdecañas CC 98 Te 110
13270 Casa de Valdecañas CR 121 Wb 115
06400 Casa de Valdegama de Arriba BA 133 Ua 116
06460 Casa de Valdeinfierno BA 118 Uc 115
10990 Casa de Valdelobos CC 97 Ta 110
10120 Casa de Valdepalacios CC 118 Ud 113
16460 Casa de Valdepozas CU 103 Wf 108
06400 Casa de Valdeprado BA 117 Ua 115
13194 Casa de Valderuelo CR 120 Vc 112
10550 Casa de Valdesauce CC 116 Tb 112
11370 Casa de Valdespera CA 173 Uc 131
50135 Casa de Valdeucas Z 72 Zb 100
45534 Casa de Valdongiles TO 101 Vd 109
10930 Casa de Valencia CC 97 Tb 111
10181 Casa de Valhondo CC 117 Te 112
47331 Casa de Valimón VA 67 Vd 99
31579 Casa de Vallaliebre NC 32 Ya 94
13194 Casa de Vallepuercos CR 120 Vd 112
13450 Casa de Valmaseda CR 136 Ve 117
49141 Casa de Valmasedo ZA 45 Ua 97
06690 Casa de Valmayor BA 119 Uf 114
44126 Casa de Valmediano TE 89 Yc 107
23748 Casa de Valquemado J 136 Ve 119
16161 Casa de Valsalobre CU 104 Xc 108
13410 Casa de Valseco CR 119 Vb 114
14430 Casa de Valsequillo CO 151 Vc 120
05141 Casa de Valserrada AV 84 Va 104
50696 Casa de Valtriguera Z 33 Yd 94
49882 Casa de Vardales ZA 65 Ud 100
13250 Casa de Vargas CR 121 Wc 114
47520 Casa de Vega Mayor VA 65 Ue 100
02246 Casa de Vela AB 124 Yb 113
23413 Casa de Venianaji J 138 Wd 120
13720 Casa de Vida CR 122 Wd 113
02651 Casa de Villacañas AB 141 Yd 116
49881 Casa de Villachica ZA 65 Ud 99
47419 Casa de Villagrán VA 66 Vb 101
45880 Casa de Villalobilla TO 103 Wf 110
16555 Casa de Villapando CU 104 Xb 108
45300 Casa de Villarino TO 103 Wd 109
34248 Casa de Villarmiro P 48 Vf 97
13670 Casa de Villegas CR 121 Wc 113
47280 Casa de Villegas VA 47 Vb 97
10940 Casa de Vinojales CC 98 Tc 110
25001 Casa de Vinya Nou L 56 Ad 99
29440 Casa de Viña MA 174 Uf 129
46370 Casa de Viñas V 107 Zb 111
22624 Casa de Vizcarra HU 34 Zc 94
05194 Casa de Yonte AV 84 Vb 104
47460 Casa de Zahera VA 66 Va 101
13343 Casa de Zahora CR 138 Xa 117
06630 Casa de Zaldívar BA 118 Ud 114
06630 Casa de Zaldívar BA 118 Ud 114
30170 Casa de Zambrana MC 140 Yc 120
06700 Casa de Zapatero BA 118 Ub 115
44122 Casa de Zaragoza TE 90 Yd 106
45400 Casa de Zayas TO 102 Wb 111
45310 Casa de Zorrero TO 103 We 109
05194 Casa de Zurra AV 84 Vb 104
10161 Casa Donoso CC 117 Tf 114
02651 Casa El Agrio AB 141 Yd 116
05194 Casa El Burguillo AV 84 Vc 104
10280 Casa El Campillo CC 117 Ua 112
19193 Casa El Cañal GU 87 Wf 104
19310 Casa El Cego GU 89 Yb 105
16813 Casa El Chorrillo CU 88 Xd 105
13720 Casa El Cornejo CR 122 We 114
04620 Casa El Esparragal AL 171 Ya 125
06600 Casa El Fraile BA 118 Ue 115
06909 Casa El Hinojo BA 133 Tf 120
06800 Casa el Huelva BA 117 Te 114
19360 Casa El Machacón GU 89 Yb 103
06800 Casa El Mentidero BA 117 Te 114
02312 Casa el Palomar AB 139 Xc 117
40450 Casa El Pinar SG 66 Vd 102
50155 Casa El Portillo Z 72 Za 101
13370 Casa El Puerto CR 137 Wb 117
46269 Casa El Tislar V 126 Zc 113
44110 Casa El Torreón TE 90 Yd 106
50160 Casa El Vedao Z 53 Zb 97
02612 Casa El Verduzal AB 123 Xd 114
02612 Casa El Verduzal AB 123 Xd 114
21830 Casa El Villar H 162 Tb 125
30590 Casa Escobar MC 157 Za 121
45645 Casa Escobedo TO 101 Vb 108
10181 Casa Escobero CC 98 Te 112
13414 Casa Esteras CR 119 Vc 115
28524 Casa Eulogio MD 86 Wc 107
46300 Casa Fábrica V 106 Ye 111
45810 Casa Falero TO 103 Xa 111
46389 Casa Fallareta V 126 Zb 112
44147 Casa Folios TE 91 Za 106
06670 Casa Forestal BA 119 Va 113
16192 Casa Forestal CU 105 Ya 108
16192 Casa Forestal CU 105 Ya 108
18183 Casa Forestal GR 168 Wd 125
21870 Casa Forestal H 148 Td 123
38712 Casa Forestal TF 181 Hb 177
21730 Casa Forestal de Cumbre Hermosa H 162 Td 125
35368 Casa Forestal de Pajonales GC 184 Kb 181
40240 Casa forestal La Lagartija SG 67 Ve 101
43887 Casafort T 76 Bb 101
37767 Casafranca SA 83 Ub 105
45490 Casa Fuente Albeitar TO 102 Wa 109
16890 Casa Fuente del Peral CU 89 Xf 106
05427 Casa Fuente del Pozo AV 84 Vb 107
18770 Casafuerte GR 169 We 128
06131 Casa Galacho BA 131 Se 118
10980 Casa Galeana CC 97 Ta 111
45222 Casa Gálvez TO 102 Wb 108
13194 Casa Gamero CR 102 Vf 111
11580 Casa Gami CA 173 Uc 129
45760 Casa Ganga TO 102 Wc 110
02312 Casa Gorgogi AB 139 Xc 117
31411 Casa Goya NC 33 Ye 93
31400 Casa Goyo NC 33 Ye 93
02007 Casa Grande AB 124 Ya 114
13200 Casa Grande CR 122 We 114
44193 Casa Grande de Escriche TE 90 Za 106
02600 Casa Granera AB 123 Xd 114
42191 Casa Granja de Blasco Nuño SO 51 Xd 98
03109 Casa Guainet A 142 Zc 117
02691 Casa Gualda AB 124 Yc 115
30510 Casa Guardiola MC 141 Yf 118
06800 Casa Herrerilla BA 117 Te 115
41440 Casa Herrero SE 149 Uc 122
10199 Casa Herrumbruso CC 117 Td 113
45880 Casa Higueras TO 103 We 110
10570 Casa Hornes CC 97 Sf 111
41250 Casa Huerta de Cano SE 148 Tf 121
23749 Casa huerta de Gorgojil J 137 Wa 120
14460 Casa Huerta de la Mayorazga CO 135 Va 118
23250 Casa huerta de las Herreías J 138 We 118
14270 Casa Huerta del Botero CO 135 Va 118
06600 Casa Huerta la Racha BA 134 Ue 116
02140 Casa Humosa AB 124 Ya 115
32337 Casaio OR 25 Tb 94
15684 Casais C 11 Rc 90
12126 Casa Iserte CS 107 Zc 108
21550 Casa Isidoro H 160 Sd 123
13180 Casa Jaca CR 119 Vc 115
11158 Casa Jandilla CA 172 Ua 131
18811 Casa Joay GR 154 Xa 123
02640 Casa Jodar AB 125 Yf 116
10818 Casa Jorrica CC 97 Tb 109
36618 Casal PO 22 Rb 93
36475 Casal, O PO 41 Rc 96
49193 Casa La Aldea ZA 64 Ua 100
06389 Casa la Alquería BA 132 Ta 119
47510 Casa La Argentina VA 65 Ue 101
28248 Casa la Atalaya MD 86 Wa 105
46640 Casa la Balsa V 126 Zb 115
13630 Casa La Blanca CR 122 Xa 113
06443 Casa la Bóveda BA 134 Ub 118
46198 Casa La Canal V 126 Zb 113
19460 Casa La Cañadilla GU 88 Xe 105
13360 Casa La Caridad CR 121 Wb 116
37400 Casa La Carolina SA 65 Ue 102
06132 Casa la Colada BA 132 Ta 118
13270 Casa La Colonia CR 121 Wb 115
21593 Casa La Corte H 161 Se 123
26130 Casa La Dehesa RI 32 Xd 94
41530 Casa la Dehesa SE 165 Uc 126
22822 Casa Lagé HU 34 Zb 94
14960 Casa la Granja CO 167 Vd 125
19237 Casa La Iruela GU 68 We 102
26513 Casa la Lagunilla RI 32 Xf 94
02639 Casa La Lobera AB 123 Xe 113
02327 Casa La Losa AB 124 Xf 116
06420 Casa La Muela BA 118 Ud 116
30153 Casa La Naveta MC 156 Ye 121
11180 Casa La Paloma CA 173 Ub 129
29718 Casa la Paloma MA 167 Ve 127
16340 Casa La Parrilla CU 105 Ya 108
11400 Casa la Pavena CA 164 Tf 128
38677 Casa La Quinta TF 180 Ib 180
13700 Casa La Romana CR 122 Wf 113
26230 Casalarreina RI 31 Xa 93
02639 Casa La Ruiza AB 123 Xe 114
16100 Casa La Sabina CU 105 Xe 110
11130 Casa las Canteruelas CA 172 Tf 130
14857 Casa las Carboneras CO 151 Vd 123
14749 Casa las Cruces CO 150 Ue 122
45480 Casa La Serrana TO 121 Wb 113
16146 Casa la Serratilla CU 88 Xe 107
06470 Casa Las Rozas BA 117 Tf 115
02600 Casa Las Terceras AB 123 Xc 113
06290 Casa la Tahona BA 133 Tf 118
06228 Casa la Tallisca BA 133 Tf 117
45006 Casa La Teatina TO 102 Wa 110
13630 Casa La Torrecilla CR 122 Xa 113
37410 Casa La Ventosilla SA 65 Ud 102
13390 Casa Laviña CR 122 Wf 116
02314 Casa Lazna AB 139 Xd 116
12150 Casa le Torre Nova CS 92 Zd 106
45109 Casalgordo TO 102 Wa 111
31592 Casa Ligués NC 52 Yb 96
22132 Casa Lizana HU 54 Zf 96
49173 Casa Llamilas ZA 64 Ua 100
47680 Casa Llorente LE 27 Ue 95
15866 Casalonga C 22 Rc 92
10004 Casa Los Arrogatos CC 98 Te 112
14029 Casa Los Borres CO 150 Va 121
21520 Casa Los Calamorros H 147 Sf 123
19238 Casa Los Chozones GU 68 We 102
50130 Casa los Cirilos Z 72 Zc 100
30320 Casa Los Crisantos MC 157 Yf 122
06131 Casa Los Jarales BA 131 Se 118
10694 Casa Los Linos CC 99 Tf 110
18561 Casa Los Menchones GR 153 Wc 123
02612 Casa Los Puercos AB 123 Xb 114
13193 Casa Los Rasos CR 119 Vc 113
30153 Casa Los Sotos MC 156 Ye 121
45789 Casa los Toriles TO 102 Wc 111
43891 Casalot, El T 75 Af 102
14749 Casa Luchena CO 150 Ue 121
13115 Casa Madroñal CR 120 Vd 113
46354 Casa Madroñera V 125 Yd 112
23638 Casa Malara J 152 Wb 121
22231 Casa Mallén HU 73 Zf 99
30154 Casa Manresa de Corvera MC 157 Yf 122
03193 Casa Manteles A 157 Zb 121
21560 Casa Maquitón H 146 Se 122
03520 Casa Margoch A 143 Zf 117
39551 Casamaría CB 17 Vc 89
06460 Casa Marina BA 118 Uc 116
13100 Casa Martín CR 120 Vd 113
06131 Casa Martínez BA 131 Se 117
13270 Casa Mata Bestias CR 121 Wc 115
10270 Casa Matilla Vieja CC 117 Tf 112
30528 Casa Mayorazgo MC 141 Yd 117
13250 Casa Mediosquintos CR 121 Wb 114
02696 Casa Mejoras AB 124 Yc 115
10161 Casa Mengacha de Abajo CC 117 Te 114
46199 Casa Mengual V 126 Zb 113
50012 Casa Menor de Fita Z 72 Yf 99
05198 Casa Mesegar AV 84 Va 105
24844 Casa Mesón de Vegarada LE 15 Ud 90
13180 Casa Metalloso CR 120 Vc 116
46624 Casa Milhombres V 125 Ye 113
02410 Casa Mina AB 140 Ya 118
19139 Casa Mingo Lozano GU 87 Wf 106
10829 Casa Mirabel CC 98 Te 109
50685 Casa Miranda Alta Z 34 Yf 93
44100 Casa Molina TE 90 Yd 106
46140 Casa Molina V 106 Yd 108
45810 Casa Monsute TO 103 Wf 110
19290 Casa Monte Fontanar GU 87 We 104
34419 Casa Monte Rey P 48 Vd 96
45179 Casa Montes de Orón TO 101 Vc 110
10570 Casa Morisca CC 97 Sf 112
10694 Casa Morisco CC 99 Ua 110
13300 Casa Muela CR 137 Wc 116
10950 Casa Mular de Hierro CC 97 Tb 112
33556 Casa Municipal de Pastores AS 16 Uf 89
34338 Casa Muñoz P 47 Va 96
47238 Casa Navilla VA 66 Vb 101
12127 Casa Negra CS 91 Zc 107
14749 Casa Noblos CO 150 Ue 122
17406 Casa Noguer GI 58 Cc 97
16372 Casa Nolasco CU 105 Yb 111
02612 Casa Nova AB 123 Xd 114
09490 Casanova BU 49 Wd 98
15881 Casanova Boqueixón C 23 Rd 92
25285 Casa Nova de Valls, La L 57 Bd 96
02600 Casa Nueva AB 123 Xb 114
02100 Casa Nueva AB 124 Ya 113
02640 Casa Nueva AB 125 Yf 115
02691 Casa Nueva AB 140 Yc 116
13720 Casa Nueva CR 122 We 113
18291 Casa Nueva GR 168 Wb 125
30410 Casa Nueva MC 155 Ya 120
45518 Casa Nueva TO 101 Ve 109
45127 Casa Nueva TO 101 Ve 111
45810 Casa Nueva TO 103 Wf 110
50172 Casa Nueva Z 53 Zc 98
02140 Casa Nueva, La AB 124 Yb 115
02136 Casa Nueva, La AB 139 Xe 117
28296 Casa Nueva de la Cepeda MD 85 Ve 105
06800 Casa Nueva de la Mezquita BA 117 Te 114
14749 Casa Nueva de la Plata CO 150 Ue 121
06410 Casa Nueva de las Mezquitas BA 117 Tf 114
23265 Casa Nueva de la Torrecilla J 138 Wf 118
23260 Casa Nueva del Guarda J 138 We 118
13344 Casa Nueva del Jarón CR 138 We 117
45850 Casa Nueva del Marqués TO 103 We 111
23214 Casa Nueva de Nava Martina J 137 Wb 118
22231 Casa Nueva Garnica HU 54 Zf 98
14840 Casa Olivar de Mangula CO 151 Vd 122
06640 Casa Ortiz BA 118 Ue 113
45780 Casa Paco TO 103 Wc 111
50615 Casa Pájaro Z 53 Za 96
30818 Casa Palacio MC 156 Yb 123
10550 Casa Palacio Blanco CC 98 Tc 112
45127 Casa Palacio del Sotillo TO 101 Ve 111
03578 Casa Palanquetas A 143 Zd 117
11580 Casa Palmetín CA 173 Ub 129
10164 Casa Palomino CC 117 Td 112
44559 Casa Palomitas TE 91 Zd 105
26339 Casa Pangua RI 31 Xb 93
46650 Casa-Pareja V 126 Zc 115
02100 Casa Parreña AB 124 Ya 113
45470 Casa Pedraza TO 102 Wa 111
10550 Casa Pedregosa CC 116 Tc 112
47810 Casa Pedriquín VA 46 Ue 97
10980 Casa Pedro Vecino CC 97 Ta 111
50400 Casa Pellejero Z 72 Ye 100
44630 Casa Peña de los Catalanes TE 73 Zf 103
46624 Casa Peña María V 125 Yf 113
22761 Casa Pequera HU 34 Za 94
21300 Casa Pereta H 147 Ta 122
31264 Casa Pernuza NC 32 Ya 93
10004 Casa Perodesma de Arriba CC 98 Te 111
10950 Casa Piazarroso CC 97 Ta 112
10980 Casa Pié de Sancha CC 97 Ta 111
10580 Casa Piejuntas CC 97 Sf 111
43370 Casa Pilella T 74 Ad 101
45810 Casa Pingorote TO 103 Wf 110
49882 Casa Pinilla ZA 65 Ud 100
25165 Casa Pinyol L 75 Ae 100
45533 Casa Piroja TO 101 Vc 109
30177 Casa-Porche MC 156 Yc 121
13350 Casa Porradura CR 121 Wc 116
21720 Casa Portales H 162 Tc 125
17230 Casa Potes GI 59 Da 97
26130 Casa Prado Primero RI 32 Xd 94
04827 Casa Preciso AL 155 Xf 123
45128 Casa Puente Torre TO 101 Ve 111
31230 Casa Pujadas NC 32 Xd 94
02620 Casa Quemada AB 123 Xe 113
28048 Casa Quemada MD 86 Wb 106
45567 Casa Quinto del Arenal TO 100 Ue 108
39591 Casar CB 17 Ve 88
32428 Casar OR 23 Re 94
45760 Casar TO 102 We 110
06443 Casar, El BA 133 Ua 117
13310 Casa Rabadán CR 122 Wd 115
29566 Casarabonela MA 166 Va 128
46640 Casa Rabosa V 126 Za 115
13690 Casa Rajá CR 122 Wf 113
02640 Casa Rambla del Campillo AB 125 Yf 115
34005 Casa Ramírez P 47 Vc 97
10530 Casa Ramón CC 98 Te 110
10190 Casar de Cáceres CC 98 Td 111
45542 Casar de Escalona, El TO 101 Vc 108

256 | **Casa de Torretejeda**

10109 Casar de Miajadas CC
118 Ua 114
10640 Casar de Palomero CC
82 Te 107
19170 Casar de Talamanca, El GU
86 Wd 104
45614 Casar de Talavera, El TO
100 Va 109
32520 Casar do Nabo OR 23 Re 94
06600 Casa Redondo BA
118 Ue 116
10199 Casa Regueros CC
117 Td 113
42148 Casarejos SO 50 Wf 98
06489 Casarente BA 116 Tc 115
16318 Casa Rento de la Peraleja CU
106 Yc 107
33117 Casares AS 14 Ua 89
29900 Casares MA 173 Ue 130
32813 Casares OR 42 Sa 96
24688 Casares de Arbás LE
15 Ub 91
10628 Casares de las Hurdes CC
82 Te 106
41580 Casariche SE 166 Vb 125
18811 Casa Río Guadalentín GR
154 Xa 123
17240 Casa Risec GI 59 Cf 98
32151 Casarizas, As OR 24 Sb 94
13640 Casa Rodillo CR 121 Wd 113
46170 Casa Roger V 107 Zb 110
06172 Casa Roja BA 132 Tb 117
45420 Casa Romaisa TO
102 Wa 110
19139 Casa Romerosa GU
87 Wf 105
02137 Casa Rosa AB 139 Xe 117
45950 Casarrubios del Monte TO
102 Vf 107
28977 Casarrubuelos MD
102 Wb 107
19139 Casa Rueda GU 87 Wf 105
04829 Casas, Las AL 155 Xe 123
14208 Casas, Las CO 134 Ud 118
13196 Casas, Las CR 120 Wa 114
42190 Casas, Las SO 51 Xd 98
38914 Casas, Las TF 180 Ha 182
38480 Casas, Las TF 180 Ia 178
38890 Casas, Las TF 184 He 180
46313 Casas, Las V 106 Ye 111
50316 Casas, Las Z 70 Ya 99
38812 Casas Agalán TF 184 He 180
10181 Casas Aguas de Verano CC
117 Tf 112
13670 Casas Altas CR 121 Wc 114
46147 Casas Altas V 106 Ye 108
50120 Casas Altas Z 53 Za 97
40165 Casas Altas, Las SG
68 Wb 101
19129 Casasana GU 88 Xc 105
02360 Casa San Blas AB
139 Xc 117
06620 Casa San Blas BA
118 Ud 115
31131 Casa Sánchez NC 33 Ya 93
10870 Casa San Pablo CC
97 Tb 109
41410 Casa Santa Ana SE
149 Ub 123
10550 Casa Santa Catalina CC
116 Tb 112
10980 Casa Santa el Cardo CC
97 Ta 111
06800 Casas Atlas de Valdelayegüas
BA 117 Te 114
46146 Casas Bajas V 106 Ye 108
50120 Casas Bajas Z 53 Za 97
22636 Casas Bajas de Escuer HU
35 Ze 93
10161 Casas Bajas de Valdelayegüas
CC 117 Te 114
22376 Casas Bergés HU 35 Zf 93
13248 Casas Blancas CR
122 Xa 115
13300 Casas Blancas CR
138 We 116
26291 Casas Blancas RI 31 Xa 94
44369 Casas Blancas TE 90 Yd 105
38129 Casas Blancas TF 181 If 177
45700 Casas Blancas TO
102 Wb 111
45124 Casasbuenas TO 102 Vf 110
10270 Casas Caballerías de Rejón
CC 117 Tf 112
19361 Casas Cabeza Quemada GU
71 Yb 103
23291 Casas Carrasco J 139 Xb 120
45710 Casas Carril del Tobosillo TO
103 Wc 111
13191 Casas Castillejo CR
120 Ve 115
46198 Casas Collado V 126 Zb 113
02316 Casas Cruceta AB
139 Xc 117
10890 Casas Cucharón CC
97 Ta 108
35625 Casas Cueva de la Negra GC
182 Ld 180
30400 Casas Cueva de Valero MC
140 Ya 120

35628 Casas de Abaise GC
183 Lf 178
02326 Casas de Abajo AB
123 Xf 116
30193 Casas de Abajo, Las MC
156 Yd 120
02639 Casas de Abril AB 123 Xe 114
38139 Casas de Afur, Las TF
181 Ie 177
02410 Casas de Alcadozo AB
140 Ya 117
46625 Casas de Alcance V
125 Yf 113
05289 Casas de Aldealgordo AV
85 Vc 104
30849 Casas de Algibe MC
156 Yd 122
46177 Casas de Alguezar V
106 Ye 110
05357 Casas de Arevalillo AV
84 Va 104
23711 Casas de Argamasilla J
137 Wb 119
46140 Casas de Arriba V 106 Yf 108
02511 Casas de Arriba, Las AB
124 Yb 116
10895 Casas de Atilano CC
97 Tb 108
35108 Casas de Ayagaures Albto GC
184 Kc 181
13250 Casas de Bartolo CR
121 Wb 114
10394 Casas de Belvís CC
99 Uc 110
16707 Casas de Benítez CU
123 Xf 112
22612 Casas de Bolás HU 35 Zd 93
45730 Casas de Borán TO
103 Wd 112
19229 Casas de Bubilla GU
87 We 103
44114 Casas de Búcar TE 89 Yb 106
30530 Casas de Buitrago MC
141 Yd 119
35626 Casas de Butihondo GC
182 Ld 180
46354 Casas de Caballero V
125 Ye 113
05320 Casas de Cabreras AV
84 Vb 104
46351 Casas de Calvestra V
106 Yf 111
45710 Casas de Camino de los
Frailes TO 102 Wc 111
46354 Casas de Cárcel V
125 Yd 112
10890 Casas de Casimiro Martín CC
97 Ta 107
31500 Casas de Castejón NC
52 Yb 96
04691 Casas de Castellar AL
155 Ya 123
16878 Casas de Cavero CU
89 Xf 106
49620 Casas de Cejinas ZA
46 Ub 97
23592 Casas de Cerro Hernando J
153 We 121
13270 Casas de Cervera CR
121 Wa 116
35109 Casas de Chamoriscán GC
184 Kc 181
13195 Casas de Ciruela CR
121 Wa 115
38811 Casas de Contrera TF
184 He 180
30850 Casas de Corral Rubio MC
156 Yc 122
46352 Casas de Cuadra V
125 Ye 112
45700 Casas de Cuatos Largos TO
102 Wb 111
30520 Casas de Cucharón MC
141 Yd 118
02639 Casas de Cuerva AB
123 Xe 115
06600 Casas de Cuesta Mala BA
118 Ue 115
38800 Casas de Cuevas Blancas TF
184 Hf 180
21550 Casas de Dios Chico H
146 Se 123
10162 Casas de Don Antonio CC
117 Te 113
18870 Casas de Don Diego GR
169 Xa 125
21640 Casas de Don Gabriel H
147 Tb 122
10818 Casas de Don Gómez CC
98 Tc 108
16417 Casas de Don Juan CU
103 Xa 111
18820 Casas de Don Juan GR
154 Xd 122
02630 Casas de Don Pedro AB
123 Xf 115
02155 Casas de Don Pedro AB
124 Ya 114
02690 Casas de Don Pedro AB
125 Yd 114

06770 Casas de Don Pedro BA
118 Ue 114
30334 Casas de Egea MC
156 Ye 122
06270 Casas de El Alcor BA
132 Td 120
35638 Casas de El Cortijo GC
183 Ma 178
35570 Casas de El Golfo GC
182 Mb 175
02499 Casas de El Tesorico AB
140 Yc 118
46320 Casas de Enmedio V
106 Ye 110
35639 Casas de Escaque GC
183 Ma 178
14449 Casas de Escorial CR
136 Vd 117
50614 Casas de Esper Z 53 Zb 95
35626 Casas de Esquinzo GC
182 Le 180
23470 Casas de Estepa J
153 Wf 121
46352 Casas de Eufemia V
125 Ye 112
35629 Casas de Ezquén GC
183 Ma 179
31500 Casas de Farrique NC
52 Yd 96
37541 Casas de Felipe SA
81 Tb 106
16610 Casas de Fernando Alonso CU
123 Xe 112
49124 Casas de Fradejos ZA
46 Uc 98
31500 Casas de Franca NC 52 Yc 96
44126 Casas de Frías TE 89 Yc 106
29540 Casas de Ganancias MA
166 Vb 126
16338 Casas de Garcimolina CU
106 Yd 109
46352 Casas de Giménez V
125 Ye 112
10592 Casas de Gómez de Arriba CC
98 Te 110
35625 Casas de Gran Valle GC
182 Ld 180
49719 Casas de Guarratino ZA
65 Uc 101
13720 Casas de Guerra CR
122 Wd 113
16708 Casas de Guijarro CU
123 Xf 112
30849 Casas de Guirao MC
156 Yd 122
02139 Casas de Haches, Las AB
140 Xe 117
16611 Casas de Haro CU
123 Xe 113
13110 Casas de Hontanillas CR
119 Vb 113
23519 Casas de Hurtado J
152 Wc 120
35639 Casas de Jacomar GC
183 Ma 179
02650 Casas de Jaime AB
141 Ye 116
35625 Casas de Jorós GC
182 Ld 180
21550 Casas de Juan Chacón H
146 Se 123
29150 Casas de Juan de Luque MA
166 Vc 128
16236 Casas de Juan Fernández CU
124 Yb 112
02153 Casas de Juan Gil AB
125 Ye 114
02151 Casas de Juan Núñez AB
124 Yc 114
02487 Casas de Juan Quílez AB
140 Xe 118
41899 Casas de la Aldea de las
Gaigas SE 148 Te 122
05693 Casas del Abad AV 83 Uc 107
03659 Casas de la Barquilla MC
141 Yf 118
37541 Casas de la Berzosa SA
81 Tb 106
38779 Casas de la Bombilla TF
181 Ha 177
14300 Casas de la Campana CO
150 Uf 121
13460 Casas de la Canaleja CR
136 Vd 116
35629 Casas de la Cañada de
Teguital GC 183 Ma 179
02630 Casas de la Carrasquilla AB
123 Xe 113
41370 Casas de la Cartuja SE
149 Ub 121
13179 Casas del Acebuchar CR
121 Wb 115
30528 Casas de la Cingla MC
141 Ye 117
06800 Casas de la Cora BA
116 Td 116
10530 Casas de la Cortilla CC
98 Te 110
35570 Casas de la Degollada GC
182 Mb 175

49334 Casas de la Dehesa ZA
45 Tf 97
10359 Casas de la Dehesa Frontal
CC 99 Ub 110
19300 Casas de la Dehesilla GU
89 Ya 103
35558 Casas de la Florida GC
182 Mc 174
35629 Casas de la Florida GC
183 Lf 179
30848 Casas de la Fuente de las
Zorras MC 156 Yc 121
30510 Casas de la Fuente del Pinar
MC 141 Yf 116
46822 Casas de la Gorda V
126 Zb 114
49420 Casas de la Granja ZA
65 Ud 101
35639 Casas de la Guirra GC
183 Ma 178
02400 Casas de la Higuera AB
140 Ya 117
06660 Casas de la Huerta de
Navalmochuelo BA
119 Va 114
05634 Casas de la Isla AV 84 Ue 107
05193 Casas de la Lancha AV
85 Vd 105
16708 Casas de la Loma CU
123 Xe 112
46355 Casas de la Manchega V
125 Yf 112
38788 Casas de la Mata TF
181 Ha 176
10270 Casas de la Matilla de Los
Almendros CC 117 Tf 112
13459 Casas de la Molina CR
136 Vd 117
13770 Casas de la Monja CR
137 Wb 118
13247 Casas de la Nava CR
122 We 116
35118 Casas de Lanos Prietos GC
184 Kd 181
21400 Casas de la Parra H
160 Sd 124
44459 Casas de la Parra TE
90 Yf 108
21390 Casas de la Patrinita H
132 Ta 120
30420 Casas de la Pelota MC
140 Yb 119
02600 Casas de la Peña AB
123 Xd 113
02690 Casas de la Peña AB
125 Ye 114
11400 Casas de la Polanca CA
172 Te 128
11400 Casas de la Pollero CA
172 Te 128
41710 Casas de la Presa SE
164 Ub 126
19182 Casas de la Puebla de
Mendoza GU 87 We 104
19244 Casas de la Quebrada GU
69 Wf 102
29566 Casas de la Rabadana MA
175 Va 128
02139 Casas de la Rambla AB
140 Ya 117
13189 Casas de la Retamosa CR
136 Vd 116
19286 Casas de la Saceda GU
70 Xe 103
10980 Casas de las Aldeas CC
97 Tb 110
04275 Casas de las Arenas AL
170 Xd 125
02600 Casas de las Beatas AB
123 Xc 113
04212 Casas de Las Carmonas AL
170 Xd 125
35009 Casas de las Coloradas GC
184 Kd 180
13250 Casas de las Encinas CR
121 Wb 114
50792 Casas de las Espiletas Z
73 Ze 101
10137 Casas de las Gargantillas CC
118 Ue 112
05291 Casas de las Gordillas AV
85 Vc 104
10110 Casas de las Higueruela CC
118 Uc 113
04212 Casas de Las Hoyas AL
170 Xd 125
02230 Casas de las Huertas AB
124 Yb 113
21500 Casas de las Mesas H
147 Sf 124
25796 Casas de las Minas L
38 Bc 95
16432 Casas de las Monjas CU
104 Xc 110
30366 Casas de las Monjas MC
157 Za 123
06670 Casas de las Navas BA
119 Va 113

06427 Casas de las Navazuelas BA
134 Ud 117
10530 Casas de las Navezuelas CC
98 Te 109
16470 Casas de las Salinas CU
103 Wf 108
47492 Casas de las Trescientas VA
66 Va 100
02534 Casas de la Tercia AB
139 Xd 120
13194 Casas de la Toledana CR
120 Ve 113
44642 Casas de la Torreta TE
73 Zf 103
05692 Casas de la Vega AV
83 Uc 106
16520 Casas de la Vega de la Torre
CU 88 Xb 107
50600 Casas de Laverné Baja Z
53 Yf 96
23250 Casas de la Yedra J
138 We 118
02329 Casas de Lázaro AB
123 Xe 116
10950 Casas del Baldío CC
98 Tb 111
30849 Casas del Barranco de la
Murta MC 156 Yd 121
11170 Casas del Berrueco CA
172 Tf 130
04728 Casas del Calabrial AL
170 Xb 127
30876 Casas del Calar MC
156 Yd 123
13194 Casas del Camino CR
120 Vf 112
35489 Casas del Camino GC
184 Kb 180
19495 Casas del Campillo GU
88 Xe 104
46320 Casas del Campo de Melchor
V 106 Ye 110
50690 Casas del Canal Z 53 Ye 98
10160 Casas del Canchel Blanquillo
CC 117 Te 113
10616 Casas del Castañar CC
99 Ua 108
13779 Casas del Castillo CR
137 Wb 118
30520 Casas del Castillo MC
141 Yd 118
02600 Casas del Cerrojo AB
123 Xb 114
13100 Casas del Chozo Chavo CR
120 Ve 114
10711 Casas del Cid CC 82 Tf 107
30590 Casas del Civil MC 157 Yf 121
16890 Casas del Collado CU
89 Xf 106
16890 Casas del Collado CU
89 Xf 106
23592 Casas del Colmenareo J
153 We 122
02511 Casas del Conde AB
140 Yb 116
37650 Casas del Conde, La SA
82 Tf 105
49706 Casas del Convento ZA
64 Ub 101
21300 Casas del Coto H 147 Ta 122
21330 Casas del Coto de la Mora H
147 Tb 122
02600 Casas del Cuartón AB
123 Xb 113
30590 Casas del Cura MC
157 Yf 121
42313 Casas del Dornajo SO
69 Wf 99
16196 Casas del Egidillo CU
105 Xe 109
22150 Casas del Embalse HU
35 Zd 95
13650 Casas del Encinar CR
121 Wd 113
06692 Casas del Enjambradero BA
119 Vb 112
45700 Casas de Lerma TO
102 Wb 112
14749 Casas del Escorial CO
149 Ue 121
30849 Casas del Escribano MC
156 Yd 122
19360 Casas del Fonsillo GU
89 Yb 103
23193 Casas del Frontil J
152 Wc 123
13591 Casas del General CR
136 Ve 117
02125 Casas del Ginete AB
140 Xf 117
02600 Casas del Gordo AB
123 Xc 113
06470 Casas del Guadalperal BA
117 Tf 114
10318 Casas del Guarda CC
99 Uc 108
29611 Casas del Guarda del
Corchadillo MA 174 Uf 129
30592 Casas del Hondo MC
157 Za 122

35630 Casas del Hospinal GC
183 Lf 178
30170 Casas del Hoyo MC
140 Yc 120
46811 Casas de Ligero V 126 Zb 114
35560 Casas del Islote GC
182 Mb 174
13107 Casas del Jara CR 120 Vf 114
10600 Casas del Manco CC
98 Te 108
35625 Casas del Matorral GC
182 Le 180
21409 Casas del Médico H
160 Sd 125
46622 Casas del Miñón V
125 Za 114
37510 Casas del Montaraz SA
81 Tc 106
10730 Casas del Monte CC
82 Ua 107
45780 Casas del Monte TO
102 Wc 110
47315 Casas del Monte VA 48 Ve 98
19125 Casas del Monte de los
Cabezos GU 88 Xc 106
30412 Casas del Moralejo de Arriba
MC 155 Xf 121
16238 Casas del Olmo CU
124 Yb 113
30414 Casas de Lomas de Gadea
MC 155 Xe 121
02691 Casas de los Altos AB
125 Ye 115
35640 Casas de Los Apartaderos GC
183 Ma 177
23250 Casas de los Ardosos J
138 Wd 118
49722 Casas de los Barrios ZA
64 Ua 100
30177 Casas de los Bernabeles MC
156 Yc 121
45521 Casas de los Brogelines TO
101 Ve 109
03659 Casas de los Capitos MC
141 Yf 118
02049 Casas de los Carrileros AB
124 Ya 115
50694 Casas de los Cascajos Z
52 Ye 95
10950 Casas de los Castaños CC
97 Tb 110
13180 Casas de los Charos CR
120 Vd 115
13640 Casas de los Frailes CR
122 Wd 113
13300 Casas de los Franceses CR
138 Wd 116
10590 Casas de los Gavilanes CC
98 Te 109
05491 Casas de los Hilandeses AV
100 Uf 107
10134 Casas de los Hitos CC
118 Ub 114
45593 Casas de los Llanos TO
102 Vf 109
13200 Casas de los Morales CR
122 We 114
04212 Casas de los Pachuecas AL
170 Xd 125
16612 Casas de los Pinos CU
123 Xd 113
44414 Casas de los Raimundos TE
91 Zc 107
30411 Casas de los Royos de Abajo
MC 155 Xf 121
05114 Casas de los Veneros AV
84 Vb 106
06770 Casas del Palancar BA
118 Ue 113
14300 Casas del Palomar CO
150 Va 121
30510 Casas del Pansero MC
141 Yf 118
02486 Casas del Pantano AB
140 Xe 118
44509 Casas del Pantano TE
73 Zc 103
02600 Casas del Pino AB
123 Xb 113
02434 Casas del Pino AB
140 Xe 118
06950 Casas del Pontón BA
133 Tf 119
02160 Casas del Pozo del Conde AB
123 Xd 115
16420 Casas del Pozuelo CU
103 Xa 109
19328 Casas del Prado GU
89 Yb 103
02694 Casas del Puerto AB
124 Yc 114
05621 Casas del Puerto de
Tornavacas AV 83 Uc 107
05571 Casas del Puerto de Villatoro
AV 84 Ue 105
45750 Casas del Puzuelo TO
102 Wb 110
49630 Casas del Raso ZA 46 Ud 98
38769 Casas del Remo TF
181 Ha 177

34300 Casas del Rey P 47 Vb 96
46310 Casas del Rey V 106 Yd 112
02611 Casas del Rincón AB
123 Xb 114
05480 Casas del Rincón AV
100 Ue 108
30858 Casas del Rincón MC
156 Yd 122
02420 Casas del Río AB 140 Yb 118
46356 Casas del Río V 125 Yf 113
13128 Casas del Río, Las CR
120 Ve 114
10580 Casas del Rivero CC
97 Sf 111
14470 Casas del Robledillo CO
135 Va 117
37540 Casas del Rolloso SA
81 Tb 106
13414 Casas del Romeral CR
120 Vc 114
21750 Casas del Sacristán H
162 Tc 126
35639 Casas del Saladillo GC
183 Ma 179
30529 Casas del Salero de la Rosa
MC 141 Ye 118
10880 Casas del Salinero CC
97 Ta 109
10720 Casas del Salugral CC
98 Tf 107
10120 Casas del Sindicato Agrícola
CC 118 Ud 113
02600 Casas del Sisonar AB
123 Xc 114
45530 Casas del Tapuelo TO
101 Vd 109
21640 Casas del Tejarejo H
147 Tc 123
21440 Casas del Terrón H
161 Se 125
21330 Casas del Toconal H
147 Ta 122
05357 Casas del Torcal AV
84 Vb 104
10160 Casas del Trampal CC
117 Te 113
16118 Casas del Transformador CU
105 Xf 111
04212 Casas del Vulgo AL
170 Xd 125
45672 Casas del Madrero TO
100 Va 111
46621 Casas del Madrona V
125 Yf 115
35639 Casas de Majada Blanca GC
183 Ma 178
06660 Casas de Majadavieja BA
119 Va 114
Casas de Majanicho GC
183 Ma 176
05278 Casas de Majasalegas AV
85 Vc 106
35626 Casas de Mal Nombre GC
182 Ld 180
10590 Casas de Marcos CC
98 Tf 109
13343 Casas de María CR
138 We 117
02160 Casas de Marigutiérrez AB
123 Xd 114
30810 Casas de Marrajo MC
155 Ya 121
35570 Casas de Masión GC
182 Mb 175
35627 Casas de Matas Blancas GC
183 Le 179
11380 Casas de Matatoros CA
173 Uc 132
45470 Casas de Matías Nieto TO
121 Wa 112
46350 Casas de Medién V
106 Yf 111
46312 Casas de Medina V
106 Yf 111
45700 Casas de Mencaliz TO
102 Wc 111
02600 Casas de Merendaderos AB
123 Xb 113
05148 Casas de Migalbín AV
84 Ue 104
10592 Casas de Millán CC 98 Te 110
10292 Casas de Mingalozano CC
99 Ub 112
10360 Casas de Miravete CC
99 Ub 110
02612 Casas de Mitra AB
123 Xc 115
46317 Casas de Moluengo V
106 Yd 111
37765 Casas de Monleón SA
82 Ua 105
44313 Casas de Montiel TE
89 Yc 104
02486 Casas de Moreto AB
139 Xe 118
46310 Casas de Moya V 106 Yd 112
46176 Casas de Mozul V 106 Yf 110
05520 Casas de Muñochas AV
84 Va 105

13114 Casas de Navajarra CR
120 Vd 113
22810 Casas de Nuevo, Las HU
53 Zc 95
05146 Casas de Pajarilla del Berrocal
AV 84 Ue 104
06510 Casas de Pajonales BA
116 Ta 112
21359 Casas de Palacios H
147 Tb 122
38820 Casas de Palmar TF
184 Hf 180
30800 Casas de Panes MC
155 Yb 122
13720 Casas de Párraga CR
122 We 113
38811 Casas de Pastrana TF
184 He 180
13179 Casas de Patón CR
121 Wb 115
35626 Casas de Pecenescal GC
182 Le 180
46352 Casas de Penén de Albosa V
125 Ye 112
30816 Casas de Peña MC
156 Yc 122
30876 Casas de Peña MC
156 Yd 123
30528 Casas de Peñas Blancas MC
141 Yd 117
23485 Casas de Peralta J
154 Xa 122
22587 Casas de Perico HU 55 Ad 95
06445 Casas de Pila BA 133 Ua 119
35368 Casas de Pino Gordo GC
184 Kb 181
13140 Casas de Pinos Altos CR
120 Vf 114
30510 Casas de Pisano MC
141 Yf 118
11391 Casas de Porros CA
175 Ub 132
13115 Casas de Povedas CR
120 Vd 113
35639 Casas de Pozo Negro GC
183 Ma 179
02155 Casas de Pozo Rubio AB
124 Ya 114
46310 Casas de Pradas V
125 Yd 112
02314 Casas de Puentecillas AB
139 Xe 116
47182 Casas de Quintanilla VA
48 Ve 98
49750 Casas de Ramos ZA 46 Ub 97
10199 Casas de Regaña CC
117 Td 113
06960 Casas de Reina o las Casas
BA 133 Ua 119
46811 Casas de Requena V
126 Za 115
30810 Casas de Reverte MC
155 Ya 121
29569 Casas de Rivero MA
166 Vb 128
16321 Casas de Roldán CU
106 Ye 110
16612 Casas de Roldán CU
123 Xd 113
07315 Casas de Sa Calobra IB
110 Ce 109
06500 Casas de Salines BA
115 Sf 113
13190 Casas de San Benito CR
120 Vf 115
19246 Casas de San Galindo GU
87 Xa 103
19117 Casas de San Isidro GU
87 Xa 107
06690 Casas de San Juanilla BA
119 Uf 114
47219 Casas de San Llorente VA
66 Va 101
50368 Casas de San Pascual Z
71 Ye 101
35478 Casas de Santa Brigida GC
184 Kb 181
38869 Casas de Santa Catalina TF
184 Hd 180
16234 Casas de Santa Cruz CU
124 Ya 112
45569 Casas de Santa María TO
100 Ue 108
49709 Casas de Santa Marina ZA
64 Ua 101
05515 Casas de Sebastián Pérez AV
83 Ud 106
10132 Casas de Senador CC
117 Tf 114
05154 Casas de Serranos de la Torre
AV 83 Ue 105
46199 Casas de Sotos V 125 Yf 113
35649 Casas de Taca GC 183 Lf 177
30398 Casas de Tallante MC
157 Yf 123
35489 Casas de Tamadaba GC
184 Kb 180
35627 Casas de Tamaretilla GC
183 Lf 179

35489 Casas de Tirma GC
184 Kb 180
45214 Casas de Tocenaque TO
102 Wa 108
30412 Casas de Tornajuelo MC
155 Xf 121
45686 Casas de Torrejón TO
100 Uf 109
02690 Casas de Torró AB
125 Ye 115
49170 Casas de Valcamín Alto ZA
64 Ua 100
13195 Casas de Valdaraches CR
121 Wa 115
34230 Casas de Valdecañas P
48 Ve 96
06470 Casas de Valdelapeña BA
117 Tf 116
19110 Casas de Valdeolmeña GU
87 Wf 107
19244 Casas de Valiluengo GU
69 Wf 102
45569 Casas de Valtravieso TO
100 Uf 108
10672 Casas de Valverde CC
98 Te 108
47100 Casas de Vega-Duero VA
65 Uf 100
02520 Casas de Verlupe AB
124 Yb 115
02212 Casas de Ves AB 125 Ye 113
10332 Casas de Vicente CC
100 Ud 110
10895 Casas de Vidal CC 97 Tb 108
49718 Casas de Villachica ZA
64 Ub 101
05370 Casas de Villacomer AV
84 Uf 103
14729 Casas de Villalobillos CO
150 Va 121
16555 Casas de Villava Perea CU
104 Xb 109
02215 Casas de Villena AB
125 Yd 113
02691 Casas de Villora AB
124 Yc 116
29787 Casas de Viñas MA
168 Wb 128
35629 Casas de Violante GC
183 Lf 179
03409 Casas de Zaríceio A
142 Za 117
05148 Casas de Zurraquín AV
84 Ue 104
10181 Casas Don Vidal de Arriba CC
117 Te 112
32613 Casas dos Montes OR
43 Sc 97
49708 Casaseca de Campeán ZA
64 Ub 100
49151 Casaseca de las Chanas ZA
64 Ub 100
35611 Casas El Almácion GC
183 Lf 178
04114 Casas El Caballón AL
171 Xf 127
35128 Casas El Caidero GC
184 Kb 181
05141 Casas El Cid AV 84 Va 104
46352 Casas El Ciscar V 125 Ye 113
13100 Casas El Gargantón CR
120 Vd 114
38612 Casas el Guirre TF 180 Ic 180
35478 Casas El Manantial GC
184 Kb 181
06228 Casas el Membrillero BA
133 Tf 117
04118 Casas El Mónsul AL
171 Xf 128
35660 Casas El Puertito GC
183 Ma 176
38678 Casas El Puertito TF
180 Ib 180
45215 Casas el Río TO 102 Wa 108
19352 Casas El Rochizo GU
89 Ya 104
46140 Casas El Soto V 106 Ye 108
40317 Casas El Tabladillo SG
67 Wb 101
06140 Casa Senuista BA 116 Ta 115
28312 Casa Serrano MD
102 Wb 109
21400 Casas Espartero H
160 Sd 124
02214 Casa Sevallar AB 125 Ye 113
02696 Casas Francés AB
124 Yc 115
06445 Casas Guzulas BA 133 Tf 119
10004 Casas Hinojosas CC
117 Tf 112
02439 Casas Hoya-Nevada AB
140 Xf 118
44559 Casas Hoya Vidales TE
91 Zc 104
41740 Casas Huerta del Ramo SE
163 Tf 127
21560 Casas Huertos de la Fuente H
161 Se 124
02200 Casas-Ibáñez AB 125 Yd 113
13332 Casa Silverio CR 138 Xa 116

16239 Casasimarro CU 124 Xf 112
46430 Casa Sisentes V 126 Zd 113
35541 Casas La Breña GC
182 Md 173
47452 Casas La Cabaña VA
66 Vb 101
38812 Casas La Cantera TF
184 He 180
13179 Casas La Celadilla CR
121 Wa 115
38677 Casas La Concepción TF
180 Ib 180
06909 Casas la Encomienda BA
148 Tf 120
10195 Casas La Enjarada CC
116 Td 112
13300 Casas La Peana CR
121 Wd 115
03313 Casas Las Alcachofas A
157 Za 121
04888 Casas Las Corinas AL
170 Xd 125
35541 Casas Las Escamas GC
182 Md 173
35350 Casas Las Hoyas GC
184 Kb 180
06228 Casas las Huelgas BA
133 Tf 117
38913 Casas Las Toscas TF
180 Gf 182
02639 Casas las Villas Nuevas AB
123 Xf 114
38758 Casas La Viña TF 181 Ha 176
19361 Casas Los Callejones GU
71 Yc 103
06900 Casas los Codriales BA
133 Ua 119
35613 Casas los Majadas GC
183 Ma 177
30164 Casas Los Martínez MC
157 Za 121
38678 Casas Los Menores TF
180 Ib 180
35611 Casas Los Molinos GC
183 Lf 177
35270 Casas Los Molinos GC
184 Kd 181
10530 Casas Los Secaderos CC
98 Tf 110
16430 Casas Luján CU 104 Xa 109
13412 Casas Martincaro CR
119 Va 115
10181 Casas Mingajila de Ventosa
CC 117 Te 112
35611 Casas Montañeta de Tao GC
183 Lf 178
19119 Casas Monte Chaparral GU
87 Wf 106
16318 Casas Nuevas CU 106 Yd 108
30814 Casas Nuevas MC
156 Yb 121
30177 Casas Nuevas MC
156 Yc 121
30594 Casas Nuevas MC
157 Za 122
47470 Casas Nuevas VA 65 Uf 102
32769 Casasoa OR 24 Sd 94
02124 Casasola AB 140 Xf 117
05140 Casasola AV 84 Vb 104
39527 Casasola CB 17 Ve 88
47170 Casasola VA 47 Vc 99
47110 Casasola de Arión VA
46 Ue 99
37209 Casasola de la Encomienda
SA 64 Te 103
37452 Casasola del Campo SA
82 Ua 104
24166 Casasola de Rueda LE
27 Ue 93
45710 Casas Palomar de Casa Vieja
TO 103 Wc 112
13310 Casas Perzosa CR
121 Wd 115
38916 Casas Pozo de las Calcosas
TF 180 Ha 181
16336 Casas Quemadas CU
106 Ye 109
46140 Casas Quemadas V
106 Yd 108
06290 Casas Quiros BA 133 Tf 118
03570 Casas Salomóns A
143 Ze 117
38580 Casas San Juan TF
180 Id 180
21560 Casas Santa Rosalía H
146 Se 122
41640 Casas Turquillas SE
166 Ue 124
24917 Casasuertes LE 16 Va 90
22590 Casas Vedado HU 74 Ab 100
02328 Casas Viejas AB 124 Ya 115
02640 Casas Viejas AB 125 Ye 115
46310 Casas Viejas V 125 Yd 112
30590 Casas Villa María MC
157 Yf 123
30510 Casas y Chalet de Pascual
García MC 141 Yf 117
46177 Casas y Corrales de Genaro V
106 Yf 110

06500 Casas y Ermita de Mayorga BA 115 Sf 113
06980 Casas y Minas de La Lapa BA 133 Ua 119
10590 Casas y Tinado CC 98 Tf 109
21647 Casa Tabladilla H 148 Td 123
18891 Casa Tarquina GR 154 Xc 123
10520 Casatejada CC 99 Ub 109
16430 Casa Tejar CU 104 Xb 109
10570 Casa Tinado CC 97 Ta 111
02693 Casato de Higinio AB 125 Yc 116
16500 Casa Tomellosa CU 104 Xb 108
06420 Casa Toril BA 118 Ud 115
05146 Casa Torneros de la Hoz AV 84 Uf 104
31493 Casa Torraza NC 33 Yd 94
50800 Casa Torre de Guallar Z 53 Za 98
37799 Casa Torrejón SA 65 Uc 102
37799 Casa Torreperales SA 65 Uc 102
02211 Casa Tranco del Lobo AB 125 Ye 113
21800 Casa Tres Rayas H 161 Tb 126
50170 Casa Trilla Z 74 Ab 100
10189 Casa Trovico CC 117 Ua 112
45612 Casa Trujillano TO 100 Uf 108
22371 Casa Tuartas HU 35 Zf 94
25537 Casau L 37 Ae 92
13194 Casa Valdelagata CR 101 Vf 112
21550 Casa Valdevinas H 160 Sd 123
45165 Casa Valdezarza TO 101 Vc 110
13110 Casa Valle del Rubial CR 119 Vc 112
03578 Casa Vall-llongues A 142 Zd 117
10120 Casa Valverde CC 118 Ud 113
03109 Casa Vanar A 142 Zc 117
10300 Casa Vaqueriza CC 99 Uc 109
34849 Casavegas P 17 Vc 90
44400 Casa Vena TE 107 Zb 107
30528 Casa Venta MC 141 Ye 117
10665 Casa Venta Quemada CC 98 Tf 108
50610 Casa Ventura Z 53 Za 96
03191 Casa Verea A 157 Zb 121
43440 Casa Vidal T 75 Ba 100
46780 Casa Vidal V 127 Zf 115
16150 Casa Vieja CU 89 Ya 107
05450 Casavieja AV 84 Vb 107
39860 Casavieja CB 18 Wd 89
49124 Casa Vieja de Canillos ZA 46 Uc 99
41220 Casa Vieja del Coto SE 148 Ua 123
28976 Casa Vieja del Monte MD 85 Wa 107
47470 Casa Villa Luz VA 65 Uf 102
45780 Casa Villares TO 103 Wd 111
13630 Casa Villena CR 122 Xb 113
43780 Casa Xalamera T 74 Ac 102
32448 Casaxeto OR 24 Sb 94
30176 Casa y Corral del Mariscal MC 156 Yc 121
13391 Casa Yegüeros CR 138 Wf 116
14600 Casa y Molino de los Lorenzos CO 136 Vd 120
46439 Casa Zacarés V 126 Zd 113
10883 Casa Zamarril CC 97 Tc 109
22142 Casbas de Huesca HU 54 Zf 96
40518 Cascajares SG 68 Wd 100
09280 Cascajares de Bureba BU 31 We 92
09640 Cascajares de la Sierra BU 49 Wd 96
38789 Cascajo TF 181 Ha 176
42294 Cascajosa SO 50 Xb 99
03409 Cascante A 142 Zb 116
31520 Cascante NC 52 Yb 96
44191 Cascante del Río TE 90 Yf 107
24630 Cascantes LE 27 Uc 92
36548 Cascaxide PO 23 Re 92
07208 Ca's Concos IB 111 Da 112
31490 Cáseda NC 33 Yd 93
17832 Caselles, Les GI 59 Ce 95
23100 Caserejo J 152 Wc 122
43787 Caseres T 74 Ab 102
04479 Caseria, La AL 169 Xa 127
23700 Casería de Amores J 152 Wb 120
41659 Casería de Jornía SE 166 Uf 125
23220 Casería de la Alcolehuela J 137 Wd 119
23749 Casería de la Corregidora J 137 Wa 120
14940 Casería de la Galiana CO 151 Vd 124
14600 Casería de la Marquesita CO 151 Vd 121

23749 Casería de la Salcedilla J 137 Wa 120
14610 Casería de la Tierna CO 151 Vb 121
23110 Casería del Carratón J 152 Wc 122
14840 Casería de Marcona CO 151 Vd 122
23760 Casería de Mena J 151 Ve 121
11110 Casería de Ossío CA 172 Te 130
41560 Casería de Roga SE 166 Va 125
14857 Casería de San José CO 151 Vd 123
23689 Caserías, Las J 152 Wa 124
25539 Caserilh L 37 Ae 92
40134 Caserío Abad Don Blasco SG 66 Vd 103
13310 Caserío Abertura Consolación CR 122 Wd 115
22348 Caserío Aguilar HU 35 Zf 94
13300 Caserío Alamillo-Campo Santiago CR 138 We 116
10270 Caserío Aldeanueva CC 99 Ua 112
37408 Caserío Aldehuela de Las Flores SA 65 Ue 102
23110 Caserío Alto del Puerto J 152 Wc 122
23392 Caserío Atalayas J 139 Xb 118
37453 Caserío Barcial SA 83 Ub 104
12124 Caserío Benagés CS 107 Zd 107
46811 Caserío Benigüengo V 126 Za 115
10694 Caserío Berzalejo CC 99 Tf 110
07350 Caserío Biniagual IB 111 Cf 110
06010 Caserío Blanco BA
13427 Caserío Boca del Cortijo CR 120 Vf 113
10129 Caserío Brete CC 118 Uc 112
18240 Caserío Búcor GR 168 Wb 125
18568 Caserío Bular Bajo GR 153 Wc 124
29770 Caserío Calaceite MA 168 Wa 128
37766 Caserío Calzadilla de Mendigos SA 83 Ub 104
47680 Caserío Castilleja VA 46 Ue 96
37271 Caserío Centorrillo SA 81 Tc 104
22540 Caserío Centro Agrario HU 55 Ac 98
29787 Caserío Colmenarejo MA 168 Wa 128
46811 Caserío Corrales de Blay V 125 Za 115
18248 Caserío Cortijo Nuevo GR 168 Wb 125
22584 Caserío Cosolla HU 56 Ad 95
11520 Caserío Costa de Rota CA 172 Td 129
10380 Caserío Coto CC 99 Ub 110
10694 Caserío Cuartillo CC 99 Ua 110
10319 Caserío Cuaternos CC 99 Uc 108
31393 Caserío de Abete NC 33 Yc 94
02434 Caserío de Agustín Tomás AB 140 Xf 119
05200 Caserío de Aldehuela de Fuentes AV 66 Vb 102
19390 Caserío de Almallá GU 89 Ya 104
31300 Caserío de Arroyo NC 33 Yb 94
23539 Caserío de Badulla J 153 Wd 121
44147 Caserío de Ballestera TE 91 Za 106
06011 Caserío de Barraquero BA 131 Sf 116
40142 Caserío de Bernúz de Montejo SG 67 Vd 103
09300 Caserío de Bonilla BU 48 Vf 99
31496 Caserío de Canuto NC 33 Yc 94
10210 Caserío de Cañadafría CC 99 Ub 112
34300 Caserío de Cascaje P 47 Vc 95
44162 Caserío de Castil Cabra TE 90 Za 106
13768 Caserío de Curriple CR 137 Wc 118
23240 Caserío de Don Bernardo J 138 Wd 119
06010 Caserío de El Mimbrero BA 132 Ta 116

31300 Caserío de Escobar NC 33 Yb 93
31390 Caserío de Gollena NC 33 Yb 94
31300 Caserío de Gregorio NC 33 Yb 94
06010 Caserío de Guijarra BA 116 Ta 116
19338 Caserío de Guisema GU 71 Yb 103
23479 Caserío Dehesa Alta J 153 Xa 121
34209 Caserío Dehesa de Rebollar P 48 Vd 97
16400 Caserío Dehesilla del Conde CU 103 Wf 109
34248 Caserío de Hoyales P 48 Vf 97
14600 Caserío de Isasa CO 151 Vd 120
10370 Caserío de Juan Collado CC 99 Ub 111
23760 Caserío de la Alamedilla J 151 Vf 121
30410 Caserío de la Bastida MC 140 Xf 119
45662 Caserío de la Berciosa TO 100 Vb 110
06011 Caserío de la Castellana BA 116 Sf 116
05691 Caserío de la Central del Chorro AV 83 Ub 107
02328 Caserío de la Choriza AB 124 Xf 115
41530 Caserío de la Cuerva SE 165 Ud 126
34450 Caserío de la Dehesa P 48 Vd 96
34240 Caserío de la Dehesa de Valverde P 48 Ve 97
06011 Caserío de la Encomienda BA 115 Sf 116
18710 Caserío de la Fábrica GR 168 Wd 127
44193 Caserío de la Fuente del Berro TE 90 Za 106
41350 Caserío de la huerta de las Viñas SE 149 Ub 122
14660 Caserío del Alamillo CO 151 Ve 121
45880 Caserío del Alcalde TO 103 We 110
13248 Caserío del Allonzo CR 122 Xa 115
23770 Caserío de la Marquesa J 151 Ve 120
24218 Caserío de la Mata Moral LE 27 Ue 93
42149 Caserío del Amogable SO 50 Xa 97
06010 Caserío de la Mora BA 116 Ta 116
41670 Caserío de la Morena SE 165 Ue 126
23749 Caserío de la Nava de Andújar J 137 Wa 120
06010 Caserío de la Pluma BA 132 Ta 116
31496 Caserío del Aragonés NC 33 Yc 94
13114 Caserío de las Cabezadas CR 120 Ve 113
40150 Caserío de las Erijuelas SG 85 Vd 104
41450 Caserío de las Mesas del Carril SE 149 Uc 122
02329 Caserío de las Mitras AB 123 Xe 116
30410 Caserío de las Nogueras MC 140 Xf 119
11391 Caserío de las Palomas CA 175 Ub 132
41390 Caserío de la Urbana SE 134 Ub 120
10516 Caserío de la Vega CC 115 Se 112
29314 Caserío de la Vega MA 167 Vd 126
47639 Caserío de la Venta VA 47 Va 98
31370 Caserío del Barón NC 33 Ya 94
45870 Caserío del Batán TO 103 Wd 110
31370 Caserío del Cajo NC 33 Yb 94
06010 Caserío del Campillo BA 132 Ta 116
30413 Caserío del Campillo de Arriba MC 155 Xe 120
41560 Caserío del Cañalveralejo SE 166 Va 125
10638 Caserío del Castillo CC 82 Td 106
29200 Caserío del Cerrón MA 166 Vc 126
10450 Caserío del Chincho CC 99 Uc 108
23760 Caserío del Conde de Hornachuelos J 152 Ve 121

31260 Caserío del Corbo NC 33 Ya 94
22435 Caserío del Embalse de Barasona HU 55 Ab 96
23170 Caserío del Espeso J 152 Wb 122
18430 Caserío del Espolón GR 169 We 127
13110 Caserío del Hornillo CR 119 Vb 113
30178 Caserío del Minglanillo MC 156 Yd 121
31300 Caserío del Monte NC 33 Yb 94
19100 Caserío del Monte Nuevo GU 87 Wf 106
14540 Caserío de los Alamillos CO 150 Vb 123
47283 Caserío de los Cabezos VA 47 Vb 97
30510 Caserío de los Charquillos MC 141 Ye 117
10881 Caserío de los Corrales CC 98 Tb 109
23170 Caserío de los Fontanares J 152 Wb 122
06010 Caserío de los Frailes de Arriba BA 116 Sf 116
06107 Caserío de los Marquinos BA 131 Se 116
34248 Caserío de los Salares P 48 Vf 97
14730 Caserío del Pajarón CO 150 Ue 121
50600 Caserío del Pasiego Z 53 Yf 96
40480 Caserío del Pinar del Conde SG 66 Vd 101
30410 Caserío del Puerto MC 140 Xf 120
30195 Caserío del Puerto Mojante MC 155 Xf 120
30410 Caserío del Rincón MC 140 Ya 119
06195 Caserío del Ronquillo BA 116 Ta 116
30195 Caserío del Tartamudo MC 155 Xf 120
21550 Caserío del Toro H 146 Se 122
23760 Caserío del Valle J 152 Vf 121
31243 Caserío de Mauleón NC 32 Xf 93
50780 Caserío de Menuza Z 73 Zd 101
22560 Caserío de Miporqué HU 55 Ac 98
22520 Caserío de Monreal HU 55 Ac 99
10137 Caserío de Montalbán CC 118 Ue 112
34257 Caserío de Negredo P 48 Ve 96
34248 Caserío de Nieto P 48 Vf 97
50547 Caserío de Orchi Z 52 Yd 99
34305 Caserío de Padilla P 47 Vb 96
30410 Caserío de Pajarejo de Abajo MC 140 Ya 120
34248 Caserío de Pajareros P 48 Vf 97
10181 Caserío de Palacio Barriga CC 117 Tf 112
34191 Caserío de Paradilla del Alcor P 47 Vc 97
40143 Caserío de Párraces SG 66 Vd 103
45567 Caserío de Pela TO 100 Ue 109
19139 Caserío de Piedras Menaras GU 87 We 105
34337 Caserío de Poserna P 47 Vb 96
23100 Caserío de Pozo Blanco J 152 Wc 122
09370 Caserío de Revilla de Gumiel BU 49 Wb 98
44510 Caserío de Romana TE 73 Zd 101
13195 Caserío de Sancho Rey CR 120 Vf 114
34248 Caserío de San Juan de Castellanos P 48 Vf 96
45614 Caserío de Santa Apolonia TO 100 Va 109
23537 Caserío de Santa Inés J 153 Wd 122
23250 Caserío de Santa Rita J 138 We 120
02499 Caserío de Seperos AB 141 Yc 118
30441 Caserío de Somoguil MC 140 Xf 119
02640 Caserío de Sugel AB 125 Yf 115
34249 Caserío de Tablada P 48 Ve 97
44162 Caserío de Tarín TE 90 Yf 106
40135 Caserío de Teldomingo SG 66 Vd 103
19312 Caserío de Terzaguilla GU 89 Ya 104

23009 Caserío de Torrechante J 152 Wb 122
10319 Caserío de Torreseca CC 99 Uc 108
29532 Caserío de Uribe MA 166 Vc 126
31300 Caserío de Valdiferre NC 33 Yb 93
40400 Caserío de Vallestuertos SG 85 Vd 104
33557 Caserío de Ventaniella AS 16 Ue 90
09228 Caserío de Villacista BU 48 Wa 95
47800 Caserío de Villagodio VA 47 Uf 97
23770 Caserío de Villalba J 152 Vf 120
34304 Caserío de Villalinvierno P 47 Va 97
34170 Caserío de Villarramiro P 47 Vb 97
22375 Caserío de Viñes HU 35 Zf 93
30441 Caserío de Vista Alegre MC 140 Xf 119
41599 Caserío de Vistahermosa SE 166 Vb 125
23290 Caserío Don Domingo J 154 Xc 120
10694 Caserío Don Gil CC 99 Ua 110
34210 Caserío El Aguachal P 47 Vc 97
11595 Caserío El Boyal CA 172 Ua 129
13270 Caserío El Campazo CR 121 Wb 115
19323 Caserío El Campo GU 89 Yc 105
18360 Caserío El Carcamo GR 167 Vf 125
11400 Caserío El Casarejo CA 163 Te 128
44477 Caserío El Chopo TE 107 Zb 108
08695 Caserío El Coll de la Abena B 38 Be 95
21210 Caserío El Encinar H 148 Td 121
44480 Caserío El Fuenseca TE 107 Zb 108
16150 Caserío El Hosquillo CU 89 Ya 106
19323 Caserío El Monte GU 89 Yc 105
16161 Caserío El Picazo CU 104 Xc 109
39716 Caserío El Portillo CB 18 Wc 88
14710 Caserío El Puerto CO 150 Va 121
06930 Caserío El Rosal BA 133 Ua 119
16146 Caserío Embid CU 105 Xe 108
13300 Caserío Encomienda-Corral Rubio CR 137 Wd 116
22620 Caserío Fatás HU 35 Zc 94
31311 Caserío Figarol NC 33 Yd 94
02152 Caserío Fraguas AB 125 Yd 114
30195 Caserío Fuente Álamo MC 155 Xf 120
10671 Caserío Fuente-Dueñas CC 98 Te 109
47463 Caserío Fuente la Piedra VA 66 Va 101
16542 Caserío Fuenterruz CU 104 Xe 108
18816 Caserío Fuente Vera GR 154 Xb 123
40241 Caserío Gallegos SG 67 Vd 101
18214 Caserío Gariattaqui GR 168 Wc 125
45700 Caserío Garoces TO 102 Wb 111
39794 Caserío Garzón CB 18 Wc 88
11393 Caserío Gasma CA 172 Ua 132
23650 Caserío Gil Alonso J 152 Vf 122
37120 Caserío Golpejera SA 64 Ub 103
09316 Caserío Haza Nueva BU 48 Wb 99
23539 Caserío Henear J 153 Wc 121
11550 Caserío Hidalogo CA 172 Td 128
30510 Caserío Hoya Muñoz MC 141 Ye 116
18140 Caserío Huenes GR 168 Wc 126
23100 Caserío Huerta de San Rafael J 152 Wc 122
29014 Caserío Humaina MA 167 Vd 128
11392 Caserío Iruelas CA 173 Ub 132

29016 Caserío Jaldarín MA 167 Vd 127
16196 Caserío La Abengózar CU 105 Xe 108
21409 Caserío La Barra H 161 Sd 125
10694 Caserío La Burra CC 99 Tf 110
06010 Caserío La Campana BA 132 Ta 116
06226 Caserío La Canchalosa BA 133 Tf 118
06010 Caserío La Carrona BA 116 Ta 116
13620 Caserío La Cubeta CR 122 Xa 112
26143 Caserío La Dehesa RI 32 Xe 94
23628 Caserío La Hita J 152 Wa 121
02124 Caserío La Jara AB 140 Xf 117
44368 Caserío La Jara TE 90 Yc 105
19314 Caserío La Laguna GU 89 Ya 105
04639 Caserío La Losa AL 171 Ya 126
45700 Caserío La Magdalena TO 121 Wb 112
21760 Caserío La Marismilla H 163 Td 127
12124 Caserío La Masada CS 91 Zc 107
18197 Caserío La Mojaiva GR 168 Wc 125
34191 Caserío La Muela P 47 Vb 97
10129 Caserío La Nava CC 118 Ud 112
02436 Caserío La Nogueruela AB 140 Ya 118
45569 Caserío La Parada TO 100 Ue 108
18290 Caserío La Rata GR 168 Wb 125
18260 Caserío la Rosa GR 168 Wa 125
26586 Caserío Las Bargas RI 51 Xe 95
10694 Caserío Las Corchuelas de Arriba CC 99 Ua 110
22423 Caserío Las Cremadas HU 55 Ab 96
14540 Caserío Las Higueruelas CO 150 Vb 122
30413 Caserío Las Pedrizas MC 155 Xe 120
12124 Caserío Las Umbrías CS 91 Zd 107
44150 Caserío La Tosca TE 91 Zc 104
46392 Caserío La Vallesa V 107 Za 111
39766 Caserío Llueva CB 18 Wc 89
30566 Caserío lo Cortado MC 156 Ye 120
44121 Caserío Los Alemanes TE 90 Ye 107
12126 Caserío Los Almorochos CS 107 Zc 108
10005 Caserío Los Arenales CC 98 Td 112
06106 Caserío Los Arrecifes BA 131 Se 116
18211 Caserío Los Asperones GR 168 Wc 125
44563 Caserío Los Batanes TE 92 Zd 104
02640 Caserío Los Blancos AB 125 Yf 115
30627 Caserío Los Cabañiles MC 141 Ye 119
10521 Caserío Los Calles CC 99 Ub 109
10590 Caserío Los Capillones CC 98 Te 109
44500 Caserío Los Fayos Bajos TE 73 Zd 102
21670 Caserío Los Hermitaños H 147 Tc 122
21800 Caserío Los Llanos H 161 Ta 125
18249 Caserío Los Melerillas GR 168 Wb 124
47209 Caserío Los Milagros VA 47 Vc 98
44125 Caserío Los Molinares TE 90 Yc 107
44420 Caserío Los Morales de Arriba TE 107 Za 108
13710 Caserío Los Navazos CR 122 Xa 115
30178 Caserío Los Ojos MC 156 Yd 121
21540 Caserío Los Pajoso H 146 Se 124
13428 Caserío Los Quiles CR 121 Wa 113
13427 Caserío Los Rebollares CR 120 Vf 113
24325 Caserío Mahudes LE 28 Uf 94
29180 Caserío Majada del Moro MA 167 Ve 127
11550 Caserío Majadales CA 172 Td 128
42145 Caserío Mallumembre SO 50 Xc 98
37120 Caserío Megrillás SA 64 Ub 103
24886 Caserío Mental LE 28 Uf 91
10530 Caserío Mesa CC 98 Tf 110
45114 Caserío Mina La Económica TO 102 Vf 110
14470 Caserío Minas Dificultades CO 135 Va 117
10694 Caserío Moheda CC 99 Ua 110
44169 Caserío Molino TE 91 Za 104
44120 Caserío Molinos de Algarbe TE 90 Yc 107
21668 Caserío Monte Castilla H 148 Tc 122
10710 Caserío Monte del Soto CC 98 Tf 107
19459 Caserío Monte Redondo GU 87 Xb 104
16611 Caserío Monte Viejo CU 123 Xe 113
41410 Caserío Montillas SE 165 Uc 124
29313 Caserío Muriel MA 167 Vd 126
22149 Caserío Nasarre HU 35 Zf 95
39761 Caserío Nates CB 18 Wd 88
13194 Caserío Navalices CR 120 Ve 112
10600 Caserío Navalonguillo de Arriba CC 98 Tf 108
10696 Caserío Navas CC 99 Ua 108
47418 Caserío Ordoño VA 66 Vc 101
10694 Caserío Oreganal CC 99 Tf 110
46198 Caserío Paridera Roya V 126 Zb 113
50694 Caserío Partida Bayo Z 52 Ye 95
10181 Caserío Pedraza del Agua CC 98 Tf 112
16300 Caserío Peñarrubia CU 106 Yc 108
02211 Caserío Peña Rubia AB 125 Yd 114
19390 Caserío Picaza GU 89 Ya 104
16194 Caserío Pinar de los Llanos CU 105 Xe 108
38852 Caserío Playa de Alojera TF 184 Hd 180
38850 Caserío Playa de Vallehermoso TF 184 He 179
34159 Caserío Pombo P 47 Vb 97
37187 Caserío Porqueiros SA 64 Ub 103
22807 Caserío Presa del Gállego HU 53 Zb 95
35625 Caserío Puerto de la Luz GC 182 Lc 180
18413 Caserío Puntal GR 169 Wd 127
47283 Caserío Quintanilla VA 47 Vb 97
46392 Caserío Raidón V 107 Za 111
23657 Caserío Retamillas J 152 Vf 121
18690 Caserío Rioseco Alto GR 168 Wb 128
44510 Caserío Romaneta TE 73 Zd 101
12124 Caserío San Bartolomé CS 107 Zd 107
37120 Caserío San Benito de la Valmuza SA 64 Ub 103
10380 Caserío San Blas de Arriba CC 99 Ua 110
44460 Caserío San Cristóbal TE 107 Za 108
10590 Caserío San Esteban CC 98 Tf 109
31395 Caserío San Lorenzo NC 33 Yc 93
04116 Caserío San Pedro AL 171 Xf 127
34349 Caserío Santa María de Benavides P 47 Va 96
19450 Caserío Santa María de Ovila GU 88 Xc 104
29193 Caserío Santo Pitar MA 167 Ve 128
41640 Caseríos los Veneros SE 166 Ue 125
49177 Caserío Soguino ZA 64 Ua 101
10530 Caserío Taheña CC 98 Tf 110
35415 Caserío Tinocas GC 184 Kd 180
02434 Caserío Tres Puertas AB 139 Xe 119
37183 Caserío Turra SA 83 Ub 103
16760 Caserío Ucero CU 104 Xe 110
10600 Caserío Umbría de Matasanos CC 98 Tf 109
18270 Caserío Valcázar GR 168 Vf 125
45370 Caserío Valdeolivas TO 103 We 109
31390 Caserío Valerio NC 33 Yb 94
10694 Caserío Valero CC 99 Ua 110
45789 Caserío Valle de Algodor TO 102 Wb 111
10420 Caserío Vallejera CC 99 Ua 108
10811 Caserío Vega de la Torrecilla CC 98 Tc 109
37479 Caserío Villar del Rey SA 81 Tc 104
49216 Caserío Villoria ZA 64 Ua 101
10600 Caserío Vinosillas CC 99 Tf 108
37659 Caserito SA 82 Tf 105
03578 Caseriu Covetes A 142 Zd 117
12311 Caseriu del Villar CS 92 Ze 104
03578 Caseriu Figuerete A 143 Ze 117
46870 Caseriu Morera V 126 Zb 116
03578 Caseriu Surcas A 142 Zd 117
22589 Caserras del Castillo HU 55 Ad 96
05230 Caseruelas AV 85 Vd 105
43569 Cases d'Alcanar, Les T 93 Ad 105
03679 Cases d'Alenda, Les A 142 Zb 118
25262 Cases de Barbens, Les L 56 Ba 98
07470 Cases de Cala Murta IB 111 Db 109
03689 Cases de Galiana, Les A 142 Za 119
03649 Cases de Joan Blanco, Les A 141 Za 118
46635 Cases de Jordá, Les V 126 Zb 116
03516 Cases de l'Arc A 143 Ze 117
03130 Cases del Cap, Les A 142 Zc 119
03640 Cases del Coll, Les A 142 Za 118
21570 Cases del Cubujón H 146 Se 122
03658 Cases del Faldar, Les A 141 Yf 118
03460 Cases del Mestre, Les A 142 Zb 116
12511 Cases del Riu, Les CS 92 Ab 105
03640 Cases del Senyor, Les A 141 Za 118
03110 Cases dels Rams, Les A 142 Zc 118
03409 Cases de Menor, Les A 142 Za 117
25286 Cases de Posada, Les L 57 Bd 96
03650 Cases de Sequé, Les A 141 Yf 118
03657 Cases d'Ivanyes, Les A 141 Yf 118
08773 Casesnoves de Cal Pardo, Les B 76 Bd 100
08732 Casesnoves Noia de la Riera, Les B 76 Bd 100
17761 Caseta GI 40 Cf 95
32708 Caseta OR 24 Sc 95
07620 Caseta Blanca IB 110 Ce 111
50160 Caseta de Bolea Z 53 Zc 97
14300 Caseta de Fuente Vieja CO 150 Uf 121
50800 Caseta de la Flamarenca Z 53 Za 97
22213 Caseta de la Sarda HU 54 Ze 98
50461 Caseta de las Reguerillas Z 71 Ye 100
50750 Caseta del Batanero Z 73 Zd 100
22269 Caseta del Guarda HU 54 Zd 97
13740 Caseta del Hoyo CR 138 Wd 117
09199 Caseta del Monte BU 30 Wd 94
44442 Caseta del Sapo TE 90 Za 107
46194 Caseta del Tío Rabalí V 126 Zc 113
22251 Caseta de Majito HU 54 Zd 98
50172 Caseta de Moya Z 53 Zc 99
50770 Caseta de Rodén Z 73 Zc 100
50150 Caseta de Valsamón Z 72 Yf 101
13610 Caseta El Polvorín CR 122 Wf 112
50620 Casetas Z 53 Yf 98
50160 Casetas Alberto Z 53 Zb 97
26529 Casetas de Barnueva RI 52 Ya 96
50162 Casetas de Campoliva Z 53 Zb 98
22375 Casetas de Lomas HU 35 Zf 93
50130 Casetas de los Trujos Z 72 Zc 100
44460 Casetas del Pescatero TE 107 Za 108
08256 Casetes, Les B 57 Be 98
08759 Casetes, Les B 76 Bf 100
12140 Casetes, Les CS 92 Zf 106
03410 Casetes de Gil, Les A 142 Zb 117
08711 Casetes d'En Mussons, Les B 57 Bd 99
08755 Casetes de N'Oliveró, Les B 77 Bf 100
08777 Casetes d'En Raspall, Les B 76 Bd 100
07250 Ca' S'Hostal IB 111 Da 111
02327 Casica del Madroño AB 124 Xf 116
02434 Casicas, Las AB 140 Xe 119
30629 Casicas, Las MC 141 Ye 119
30195 Casicas, Las MC 155 Xf 120
30893 Casicas, Las MC 155 Yb 124
30889 Casicas, Las MC 156 Yc 124
30153 Casicas, Las MC 156 Ye 122
30700 Casicas, Las MC 157 Za 122
23294 Casicas del Río Segura J 139 Xc 119
35629 Casilla Blanca GC 183 Lf 179
02410 Casilla de Altamira AB 140 Ya 117
02249 Casilla de Andresón AB 125 Yd 114
02154 Casilla de Antón AB 125 Yd 114
16235 Casilla de Benigno Tomás CU 105 Yb 112
02240 Casilla de Berrilla AB 124 Yb 113
23214 Casilla de Cascajosa J 137 Wb 118
45620 Casilla de Ganaderos TO 100 Va 108
02154 Casilla de Gaspar AB 125 Yd 114
16660 Casilla de Ginche CU 104 Xc 111
41410 Casilla de la Cascajosa SE 149 Uc 123
23160 Casilla de la Jarica J 152 Wa 122
23688 Casilla de la Moría J 168 Wa 124
23749 Casilla de las Navas de Pedro Bagar J 137 Wa 119
10189 Casilla de las Peñas CC 117 Tf 113
23213 Casilla del Caldo J 137 Wc 118
18890 Casilla del Cocón GR 153 Wf 124
41410 Casilla del Fiscal SE 149 Ub 124
23748 Casilla del Fontanarejo J 137 Vf 119
45918 Casilla del Gotril TO 84 Vc 107
02152 Casilla del Mamporro AB 125 Yd 114
23748 Casilla del Ojuelo J 137 Vf 119
41730 Casilla de los Montecillos SE 163 Ua 127
41600 Casilla del Portillo SE 165 Uc 125
46191 Casilla del Sacristán V 107 Zb 111
23748 Casilla del Villar J 136 Vf 119
02154 Casilla de Martín AB 125 Yc 114
16433 Casilla de Mirabueno CU 104 Xc 110
41410 Casilla de San Antón SE 149 Ua 123
16215 Casilla de Torres, La CU 105 Ya 110
50196 Casilla de Usones Z 53 Yf 99
16510 Casilla Los Altos CU 104 Xb 108
05428 Casillas AV 85 Vc 107
09556 Casillas BU 18 Wc 91
19276 Casillas GU 69 Xa 101
04897 Casillas, Las AL 170 Xc 125
14547 Casillas, Las CO 150 Vb 123
23614 Casillas, Las J 152 Vf 123
29712 Casillas, Las MA 167 Ve 127
37749 Casillas, Las SA 83 Uc 106
23748 Casilla Sadina J 136 Vf 118
41410 Casilla San Germán SE 149 Ub 123
42367 Casillas de Berlanga SO 69 Xb 100
05153 Casillas de Chicapierna AV 83 Ud 105
10818 Casillas de Coria CC 98 Tc 109
37541 Casillas de Flores SA 81 Tb 106
35611 Casillas del Angel GC 183 Ma 178
28752 Casillas del Espaldar MD 68 Wc 103
13109 Casillas del Espinar CR 119 Vb 114
45918 Casillas de los Álamos TO 101 Vc 107
23748 Casillas del Puerto J 137 Vf 119
02694 Casillas de Marín de Abajo AB 125 Ye 115
02694 Casillas de Marín de Arriba AB 125 Yd 115
35638 Casillas de Morales GC 183 Lf 178
16321 Casillas de Ranera CU 106 Ye 110
29313 Casillas de Vacas MA 167 Ve 126
23519 Casillas de Valverde J 152 Wc 121
14600 Casillas de Velasco CO 151 Vd 120
18491 Casimiros, Los GR 169 Wf 127
46171 Casinos V 107 Zb 110
10514 Casiñas, Las CC 115 Se 112
35628 Casitas, Las GC 183 Lf 179
35570 Casitas de Femés, Las GC 182 Mb 175
30890 Casitas Vilerda y Cinco Oliveras, Las MC 155 Yb 123
40590 Casla SG 68 Wc 102
07819 Ca's Mart IB 109 Bb 114
25793 Casó, El L 56 Bb 95
33687 Casomera AS 15 Uc 90
02499 Casón, El AB 141 Yc 118
25552 Casós L 36 Ae 94
50700 Caspe Z 73 Zf 101
07630 Cas Porrerenc IB 111 Da 112
19412 Caspueñas GU 87 Xa 104
17244 Cassà de la Selva GI 59 Cf 97
25572 Cassibròs L 37 Bb 93
04760 Castala AL 169 Xa 127
03420 Castalla A 142 Zb 117
33718 Castanedo AS 13 Tb 88
39150 Castanedo CB 18 Wb 88
22474 Castanesa HU 36 Ad 94
08593 Castanya, La B 58 Cc 98
08553 Castanyera, La B 58 Cb 98
08600 Castanyet, El B 57 Bf 96
17430 Castanyet, El GI 59 Cd 97
45126 Castañar, El TO 102 Ve 111
10340 Castañar de Ibor CC 99 Ud 111
09199 Castañares BU 30 Wc 94
26121 Castañares de las Cuevas RI 32 Xc 95
26240 Castañares de Rioja RI 31 Xa 93
33813 Castañedo AS 14 Tc 90
33829 Castañedo AS 14 Tf 88
27658 Castañedo LU 13 Sf 90
06320 Castaño, El BA 133 Td 119
21280 Castaño, El H 148 Td 120
21290 Castaño del Robledo H 147 Tb 121
04278 Castaños, Los AL 171 Xf 126
06228 Castaños y Trasierra BA 133 Tf 117
21208 Castañuelo H 147 Tc 121
18439 Cástaras GR 169 We 127
22588 Castarlenas HU 55 Ac 96
22487 Castarnés HU 36 Ae 94
16856 Castejón CU 88 Xc 106
31590 Castejón NC 52 Yb 95
50346 Castejón de Alarba Z 71 Yc 101
22121 Castejón de Arbaniés HU 54 Ze 96
19294 Castejón de Henares GU 69 Xb 103
50211 Castejón de las Armas Z 71 Yb 101
42130 Castejón del Campo SO 51 Xf 98
22310 Castejón del Puente HU 55 Aa 97
22222 Castejón de Monegros HU 54 Ze 99
22394 Castejón de Sobrarbe HU 36 Aa 95
22466 Castejón de Sos HU 36 Ac 93
44231 Castejón de Tornos TE 71 Yd 103
50612 Castejón de Valdejasa Z 53 Za 97
44706 Castel de Cabra TE 91 Zb 104
22215 Castelflorite HU 54 Zf 98
12132 Castell, El CS 92 Ze 107
43559 Castell, El T 93 Ac 105
07720 Castell, Es IB 77 Eb 109
08671 Castelladral B 57 Be 97
15317 Castellana C 11 Rf 89
11510 Castellana, La CA 172 Tf 129
17464 Castellana, La GI 59 Cf 96
02600 Castellanos AB 123 Xb 113
24343 Castellanos LE 28 Uf 94

260 | **Caserío Jaldarín**

09593 Castellanos de Bureba BU 30 Wd 92
09227 Castellanos de Castro BU 29 Vf 95
37439 Castellanos de Moriscos SA 65 Uc 102
37797 Castellanos de Villiquera SA 64 Ub 102
05229 Castellanos de Zapardiel AV 66 Va 102
22372 Castellar HU 35 Zf 93
14817 Castellar, El CO 151 Vf 124
44409 Castellar, El TE 91 Zb 106
11349 Castellar de la Frontera CA 173 Ud 131
11350 Castellar de la Frontera CA 173 Ud 131
17858 Castellar de la Mantanya GI 58 Cd 95
19328 Castellar de la Muela GU 89 Yb 104
25289 Castellar de la Ribera L 57 Bc 96
17242 Castellar de la Selva GI 59 Cf 97
08618 Castellar del Riu B 57 Be 96
08211 Castellar del Vallès B 58 Ca 99
08696 Castellar de N'Hug B 38 Bf 95
13750 Castellar de Santiago CR 138 We 117
23260 Castellar de Santisteban J 138 Wf 119
25795 Castellar de Tost L 37 Bc 95
25795 Castellàs L 37 Bb 95
22482 Castellaz HU 36 Ac 94
22149 Castellazo HU 35 Aa 95
08296 Castellbell i el Vialr B 57 Bf 99
08755 Castellbisbal B 77 Bf 100
25712 Castellbó L 37 Bc 94
08183 Castellcir B 58 Ca 98
25710 Castellciutat L 38 Bc 94
25154 Castelldans L 75 Ae 100
17249 Castell d'Aro GI 59 Da 98
12319 Castell de Cabres CS 92 Aa 105
03793 Castell de Castells A 143 Ze 116
08860 Castelldefels B 77 Bf 101
18740 Castell de Ferro GR 169 Wd 128
25632 Castell de la Guàrdia L 56 Af 96
08619 Castell de l'Areny B 58 Bf 95
43517 Castell de Mianes, El T 93 Ad 104
17115 Castell d'Empordà GI 59 Da 97
17773 Castell de Pontós GI 59 Cf 95
08850 Castell d'Eramprunyà B 77 Bf 101
08697 Castell de Saldes B 57 Be 95
25271 Castell de Santa Maria, El L 57 Bc 98
17534 Castell de Segura GI 39 Cb 95
25636 Castellet L 37 Ae 95
08729 Castellet i la Gornal = la Gornal B 76 Bd 101
17856 Castellfollit de la Roca GI 58 Cd 95
08255 Castellfollit del Boix B 57 Be 98
08283 Castellfollit de Riubregós B 57 Bc 98
12159 Castellfort CS 92 Ze 105
08297 Castellgalí B 57 Bf 98
25790 Castell-llebre L 56 Bb 96
25638 Castellnou L 56 Ba 96
25555 Castellnou d'Avellanós L 37 Af 94
08251 Castellnou de Bages B 57 Be 98
25722 Castellnou de Carcolze L 38 Bd 94
25318 Castellnou de Montfalcó L 56 Ba 98
25632 Castellnou de Montsec L 56 Ae 96
25265 Castellnou de Seana L 56 Af 99
25214 Castellnou d'Oluges L 56 Bb 98
12413 Castellnovo CS 107 Zd 109
43891 Castelló T 75 Af 102
25136 Castelló de Farfanya L 55 Ae 98
12002 Castelló de la Plana = Castellón de la Plana CS 108 Zf 109
17486 Castelló d'Empúries GI 40 Da 95
46841 Castelló de Rugat V 126 Zd 115
08719 Castellolí B 57 Be 99
04890 Castellón, El AL 170 Xc 125
12002 Castellón de la Plana = Castelló de la Plana CS 108 Zf 109
04278 Castellones AL 171 Xf 126
04827 Castellones, Los AL 155 Xf 123
46726 Castellonet de la Conquesta V 127 Ze 115
44560 Castellote TE 91 Ze 104
17249 Castell-Platja d'Aro GI 59 Da 98
25795 Castells L 37 Ba 95
25334 Castellserà L 56 Af 98
08183 Castellterçol B 58 Ca 98
43392 Castellvell del Camp T 75 Ba 101
08732 Castellví de la Marca = la Múnia B 76 Bd 101
08769 Castellví de Rosanes B 76 Bf 100
44592 Castelnou TE 73 Zd 101
25289 Castelnou de Bassella L 56 Bb 97
15126 Castelo C 10 Qf 90
15198 Castelo C 11 Rd 89
15687 Castelo C 11 Rd 90
15391 Castelo C 11 Re 90
27559 Castelo LU 24 Sb 92
27185 Castelo LU 24 Sc 91
32768 Casteloais OR 24 Sd 95
27665 Castelo de Doiras LU 25 Ta 92
44630 Castelserás TE 73 Zf 103
44412 Castelvispal TE 91 Zc 107
46141 Castielfabib V 106 Ye 108
22710 Castiello de Jaca HU 35 Zc 93
22587 Castigaleu HU 55 Ad 95
22192 Castilsabás HU 54 Ze 95
05357 Castilblanco AV 84 Va 104
06680 Castilblanco BA 119 Uf 113
19246 Castilblanco de Henares GU 69 Xa 103
41230 Castilblanco de los Arroyos SE 148 Ua 122
46199 Castilblanques V 125 Yf 113
14815 Castil de Campos CO 151 Vf 124
09248 Castil de Carrias BU 30 We 94
09592 Castil de Lences BU 30 Wc 93
09259 Castildelgado BU 31 Wf 94
09258 Castil de Peonos BU 30 Wd 94
42128 Castil de Tierra SO 70 Xe 99
34304 Castil de Vela P 47 Va 97
24206 Castilfalé LE 46 Ud 95
19127 Castilforte GU 88 Xd 105
42180 Castilfrío de la Sierra SO 51 Xe 97
50696 Castiliscar Z 33 Ye 94
02410 Castillarejo AB 140 Xf 117
22313 Castillazuelo HU 55 Aa 96
41907 Castilleja de Guzmán SE 163 Tf 124
41950 Castilleja de la Cuesta SE 164 Tf 124
41810 Castilleja del Campo SE 164 Td 124
41805 Castilleja de Talhara SE 163 Te 125
18818 Castilléjar GR 154 Xc 122
40164 Castillejo SG 68 Wb 102
37552 Castillejo de Azaba SA 81 Tb 106
37488 Castillejo de Dos Casas SA 81 Tb 104
37216 Castillejo de Evans SA 64 Te 103
37493 Castillejo de Huebra SA 82 Tf 104
16250 Castillejo de Iniesta CU 105 Yb 111
16541 Castillejo del Romeral CU 104 Xd 108
37592 Castillejo de Martín Viejo SA 81 Tc 104
40593 Castillejo de Mesleón SG 68 Wc 101
42328 Castillejo de Robledo SO 68 Wd 99
37792 Castillejo de Salvatierra SA 83 Uc 104
42175 Castillejo de San Pedro SO 51 Xe 97
37494 Castillejo de Yeltes SA 82 Td 104
11660 Castillejos CA 165 Uc 128
13110 Castillejos CR 119 Vc 112
11349 Castillejos, Los CA 173 Ud 131
16141 Castillejo-Sierra CU 88 Xf 106
30414 Castillicos, Los MC 155 Xe 120
39192 Castillo CB 18 Wc 88
01194 Castillo VI 31 Xb 92
16143 Castillo, El CU 88 Xf 107
38788 Castillo, El TF 181 Ha 176
16854 Castillo-Albarañez CU 88 Xd 107
11339 Castillo Algibe CA 173 Ud 130
22197 Castillo Bajo de San Juan HU 54 Zd 96
50596 Castillo Barués Z 34 Ye 94
23360 Castillo Bujalamé J 139 Xb 118
49541 Castillo de Alba, El ZA 45 Tf 99
16421 Castillo de Almenara CU 104 Xb 110
18750 Castillo de Baños GR 169 We 128
45641 Castillo de Bayuela TO 101 Vb 108
11500 Castillo de Doña Blanca CA 172 Tf 129
45910 Castillo de Escalona TO 101 Vd 108
37799 Castillo de Fonseca SA 64 Ub 102
29649 Castillo de Fuengirola MA 175 Vc 129
35639 Castillo de Fustes GC 183 Ma 178
16623 Castillo de Garcimuñoz CU 104 Xd 111
22622 Castillo de Guarga HU 35 Ze 94
18770 Castillo de Huarea, El GR 169 Wf 128
33958 Castillo de la Cabeza AS 15 Uc 89
35008 Castillo de la Luz GC 184 Kd 180
41890 Castillo de las Guardas, El SE 148 Te 122
23670 Castillo de Locubín J 152 Wa 123
22589 Castillo del Pla HU 55 Ac 96
22196 Castillo de Pompién HU 54 Zd 96
23530 Castillo de Recena J 153 Wc 121
30591 Castillo de Ros MC 157 Za 122
38715 Castillo de Santa Catalinà TF 181 Hb 176
28590 Castillo de Tajo MD 103 We 108
04648 Castillo de Terreros AL 171 Yc 124
22270 Castillo de Villalpando o Torres Secas HU 54 Zc 96
12123 Castillo de Villamalefa CS 108 Zd 108
50610 Castillo de Villaverde Z 53 Za 95
28679 Castillo de Villaviciosa, El MD 86 Wa 106
10394 Castillo Monroy CC 99 Uc 110
27438 Castillón = San Vicente de Castillón LU 24 Sc 93
22572 Castillonroy HU 55 Ad 97
31454 Castillonuevo NC 34 Yf 92
39699 Castillo Pedroso CB 17 Wa 89
46178 Castillo Pobo V 106 Yf 109
18700 Castillos, Los GR 169 We 128
30592 Castillos, Los MC 157 Za 122
26200 Castillos, Los RI 31 Xa 93
06195 Castillo y Cortijo Casa Colorado BA 116 Ta 115
48142 Castillo y Elejabeitia BI 19 Xa 90
19413 Castilmimbre GU 87 Xb 104
19391 Castilnuevo GU 89 Ya 104
42113 Castilruiz SO 51 Xf 97
26212 Castilseco RI 31 Xa 93
40518 Castiltierra SG 68 Wc 100
15966 Castiñeiras C 22 Ra 93
32779 Castiñeiro OR 24 Sd 94
25635 Castissent L 55 Ae 96
29689 Castor MA 174 Uf 130
44192 Castralvo TE 90 Yf 107
37494 Castraz SA 82 Td 104
34492 Castrecías BU 29 Ve 92
37448 Castrejón SA 64 Ua 103
34850 Castrejón de la Peña P 28 Vc 92
47512 Castrejón de Trabancos VA 65 Ue 101
32610 Castrelo de Abaixo OR 43 Se 97
32610 Castrelo de Cima OR 43 Se 97
32430 Castrelo de Miño OR 23 Rf 95
32625 Castrelo do Val OR 43 Sd 97
49571 Castrelos ZA 44 Ta 96
09510 Castresana BU 18 We 90
09512 Castriciones BU 18 We 91
18816 Castril GR 154 Xb 122
34131 Castrillejo de la Olma P 28 Vc 95
09572 Castrillo de Bezana BU 18 Wb 91
24742 Castrillo de Cabrera LE 26 Tc 94
24711 Castrillo de Cepeda LE 26 Tf 93
34246 Castrillo de Don Juan P 48 Vf 98
47318 Castrillo de Duero VA 48 Ve 99
39418 Castrillo de Haya CB 29 Ve 91
49419 Castrillo de la Guareña ZA 65 Ue 101
09691 Castrillo de la Reina BU 49 We 97
24199 Castrillo de la Ribera LE 27 Uc 93
24721 Castrillo de la Valduerna LE 26 Tf 95
09391 Castrillo de la Vega BU 49 Wb 99
24718 Castrillo de los Polvazares LE 26 Tf 94
09193 Castrillo del Val BU 30 Wc 95
09109 Castrillo de Murcia BU 29 Vf 94
34219 Castrillo de Onielo P 48 Ve 97
24163 Castrillo de Porma LE 27 Ud 93
09108 Castrillo de Riopisuerga BU 29 Ve 93
09141 Castrillo de Rucios BU 30 Wb 93
24356 Castrillo de San Pelayo LE 27 Ua 94
40317 Castrillo de Sepúlveda SG 67 Wb 100
09348 Castrillo de Solarana BU 49 Wc 97
39419 Castrillo de Valdelomar CB 29 Vf 92
24327 Castrillo de Valderaduey LE 28 Va 93
34478 Castrillo de Villavega P 29 Vd 94
09107 Castrillo-Matajudíos BU 29 Ve 95
33727 Castrillón AS 13 Tb 88
33456 Castrillón AS 14 Ua 87
47329 Castrillo-Tejeriego VA 48 Vd 98
15848 Castriz C 10 Rb 90
33841 Castro AS 14 Te 90
15147 Castro C 10 Rb 89
15315 Castro C 11 Sa 89
15822 Castro C 23 Rd 91
39583 Castro CB 17 Vc 89
27373 Castro LU 12 Sb 90
27260 Castro LU 12 Sd 90
27527 Castro LU 24 Sa 93
27530 Castro LU 24 Sb 93
27611 Castro LU 24 Sc 92
32740 Castro OR 24 Sc 94
42315 Castro SO 69 Wf 101
24526 Castro, El LE 25 Sf 92
32560 Castro, O OR 43 Sf 96
36518 Castro, O PO 23 Rf 93
36617 Castro Agudín PO 22 Rb 93
24344 Castroañe LE 28 Uf 93
09514 Castrobarto BU 18 Wd 90
47689 Castrobol VA 46 Ue 96
24760 Castrocalbón LE 45 Ua 95
32760 Castro Caldelas OR 24 Sd 94
09348 Castroceniza BU 49 Wc 96
22485 Castrocit HU 36 Ad 94
24735 Castrocontrigo LE 45 Te 95
49511 Castro de Alcañices ZA 45 Te 99
27577 Castro de Amacante LU 23 Sa 92
24397 Castro de Cepeda LE 26 Tf 93
32706 Castro de Escuadro OR 43 Sc 95
27437 Castro de Ferreira, O LU 24 Sc 93
04212 Castro de Filabres AL 170 Xd 125
40315 Castro de Fuentidueña SG 67 Wa 100
24127 Castro de la Lomba LE 26 Ua 92
14840 Castro del Río CO 151 Vd 122
27774 Castro de Ouro, O LU 12 Sd 87
27250 Castro de Rei LU 12 Sd 89
27611 Castro de Rei LU 24 Sc 92
27213 Castro de Soengas LU 24 Sb 92
32318 Castro de Valdeorras, O OR 25 Ta 94
47192 Castrodeza VA 47 Va 99
37460 Castro Enríquez SA 82 Tf 103
15821 Castrofeito C 23 Rd 91
24222 Castrofuerte LE 46 Uc 95
49660 Castrogonzalo ZA 46 Uc 97
09110 Castrojeriz BU 29 Vf 95
40315 Castrojimeno SG 67 Wa 100
32813 Castrol de Cexo OR 42 Rf 96
32368 Castromao OR 44 Sf 95
47882 Castromembibre VA 46 Ue 98
32548 Castromil OR 44 Ta 96
34305 Castromocho P 47 Vb 96
47641 Castromonte VA 47 Uf 98
09133 Castromorca BU 29 Wa 94
24171 Castromudarra LE 28 Uf 93
49127 Castronuevo ZA 46 Uc 98
47171 Castronuevo de Esgueva VA 47 Vc 98
49660 Castropepe ZA 46 Uc 97
24569 Castropetre LE 25 Ta 93
24314 Castropodame LE 26 Td 93
33760 Castropol AS 13 Sf 87
47664 Castroponce VA 46 Ue 96
24389 Castroquilame LE 25 Tb 94
15339 Castros C 10 Sb 87
40318 Castroserna de Abajo SG 68 Wb 101
40318 Castroserna de Arriba SG 68 Wb 101
40315 Castroserracín SG 67 Wb 100
24290 Castrotierra LE 27 Ue 94
24765 Castrotierra de la Valduerna LE 26 Ua 94
24323 Castrotierra de Valmadrigal LE 27 Ue 94
39709 Castro-Urdiales CB 19 We 88
24323 Castrovega del Valmadrigal LE 27 Ue 95
27120 Castroverde LU 12 Se 90
32901 Castroverde OR 24 Sa 95
37452 Castroverde SA 82 Ua 104
49110 Castroverde de Campos ZA 46 Ue 97
47182 Castroverde de Cerrato VA 48 Ve 98
09613 Castrovido BU 49 We 96
26315 Castroviejo RI 31 Xc 95
06420 Castuera BA 134 Uc 116
02691 Casuto de Don Salvador, El AB 125 Yd 115
46196 Catadau V 126 Zc 113
31396 Cataláin NC 33 Yc 93
29710 Catalán MA 167 Ve 127
12232 Catalanes, Los CS 107 Zc 108
03709 Catamarruc A 126 Ze 116
46470 Catarroja V 126 Zd 112
38208 Catedral El Drago TF 181 Ie 178
12513 Catí = Cati CS 92 Aa 106
43764 Catllar, El T 76 Bb 101
36612 Catoira PO 22 Rb 92
03158 Catral A 142 Zb 120
44396 Caudé TE 90 Ye 106
02660 Caudete AB 141 Za 116
46315 Caudete de las Fuentes V 106 Ye 111
12440 Caudiel CS 107 Zc 109
45519 Caudilla TO 101 Ve 108
33840 Caunedo AS 14 Te 90
30800 Cautivos, Los MC 155 Yb 122
25722 Cava L 38 Bd 95
39720 Cavada, La CB 18 Wb 88
03640 Cavafreda A 142 Za 118
17867 Cavallera GI 39 Cb 95
03658 Cavallusa A 141 Yf 118
39593 Caviedes CB 17 Ve 88
23160 Cávilas, Las J 152 Wb 122
09239 Cayuela BU 30 Wb 95
04827 Cayuelas, Los AL 155 Ya 123
45683 Cazalegas TO 101 Vb 108
23628 Cazalilla J 152 Wa 121
41370 Cazalla de la Sierra SE 149 Ub 121
24796 Cazanuecos LE 46 Ub 95
27824 Cazás LU 12 Sb 89
33557 Cazo AS 16 Ue 89
23470 Cazorla J 153 Xa 121
30810 Cazorla MC 155 Ya 122
18270 Cazuela, La GR 167 Wa 124
18698 Cázulas GR 168 Wb 128
49191 Cazurra ZA 64 Ub 100
24174 Cea LE 28 Uf 94
32130 Cea OR 23 Sa 94
49512 Ceadea ZA 45 Te 98
23486 Ceal J 153 Wf 122
24892 Cebanico LE 28 Uf 92
18816 Cebas GR 154 Xa 122
45680 Cebolla TO 101 Vc 109
09515 Cebolleros BU 30 Wd 91
09348 Cebrecos BU 49 Wc 97
24769 Cebrones del Río LE 45 Ub 95
33582 Ceceda AS 15 Ud 88
Ceceñas CB 18 Wb 88
10870 Ceclavín CC 97 Tb 110
33811 Cecos AS 13 Ta 90
10513 Cedillo CC 96 Sd 111
40550 Cedillo de la Torre SG 68 Wc 100
45214 Cedillo del Condado TO 102 Wa 108
12123 Cedramán CS 91 Zd 108
44147 Cedrillas TE 91 Za 106
38890 Cedro, El TF 184 He 180
15270 Cée C 10 Qe 91
21239 Cefiñas, Las H 147 Ta 121
30329 Cegarras, Los MC 156 Ye 122
06350 Cegón BA 132 Tc 120
24889 Cegoñal LE 28 Va 92
40162 Ceguilla SG 67 Wb 102
30430 Cehegín MC 155 Yb 120
47692 Ceinos de Campos VA 46 Uf 96
30510 Ceja MC 141 Ye 116
16150 Ceja, La CU 89 Ya 107
39232 Cejancas CB 30 Wa 91
04887 Cela AL 170 Xd 124
27163 Cela LU 24 Sd 91
27666 Cela LU 25 Ta 92

32879 Cela OR 42 Rf 97
36938 Cela PO 22 Rb 95
33318 Celada AS 15 Ud 88
24395 Celada LE 26 Tf 94
14979 Celada, La CO 167 Ve 125
09150 Celada, Las BU 30 Wb 94
24326 Celada de Cea LE 28 Va 94
09591 Celada de la Torre BU 30 Wc 94
34846 Celada de Roblecedo P 17 Vd 91
39213 Celada-Marlantes CB 17 Vf 91
44194 Celadas TE 90 Yf 106
24392 Celadilla del Páramo LE 27 Ub 93
34111 Celadilla del Río P 28 Vb 93
09140 Celadilla-Sotobrín BU 30 Wb 94
32800 Celanova OR 42 Sa 96
15199 Celas C 11 Rd 89
30320 Celdranes, Los MC 157 Yf 122
09226 Celeda del Camino BU 29 Wa 95
27863 Celeiro LU 10 Sc 86
32786 Celeiros OR 24 Sd 95
32765 Celeirós OR 24 Sd 94
30520 Celia, La MC 141 Yd 118
31473 Celigueta NC 33 Yd 92
04750 Celín AL 169 Xa 128
39553 Celis CB 17 Vd 89
44370 Cella TE 90 Ye 106
07469 Cella, La IB 111 Cf 109
27143 Cellán de Mosfeiro LU 12 Se 91
17165 Cellera de Ter, La GI 59 Cd 97
25751 Cellers L 57 Bc 98
33519 Celles AS 15 Ub 88
26212 Cellorigo RI 31 Wf 93
33595 Celorio AS 16 Vb 88
17460 Celrà GI 59 Cf 96
27617 Céltigos LU 24 Sd 91
31422 Cemborain NC 33 Yc 92
24231 Cembranos LE 27 Uc 94
34407 Cembrero P 29 Vd 93
06174 Cementerio BA 132 Tb 117
30811 Cementerio, El MC 156 Yb 123
02409 Cenajo AB 140 Yb 118
22870 Cenarbe HU 35 Zc 93
18870 Cenascuras GR 154 Wf 124
19245 Cendajas de en Medio GU 69 Xa 103
27816 Cendán LU 12 Sc 88
19245 Cendejas de la Torre GU 69 Xa 103
19245 Cendejas del Padrastro GU 69 Xa 103
05113 Cendra, La AV 84 Vb 106
25261 Cendrosa, La L 56 Af 98
42342 Cenegro SO 68 Wd 99
18190 Cenes de la Vega GR 168 Wc 126
24218 Cenia, La LE 27 Ud 93
26350 Cenicero RI 31 Xc 94
28650 Cenicientus MD 85 Vd 107
02247 Cenizate AB 124 Yc 113
32454 Cenlle OR 23 Rf 94
32431 Cenlle = Bede OR 23 Rf 95
35450 Cenobia de Valerón GC 184 Kc 180
27390 Centeais LU 25 Se 94
08540 Centelles B 58 Cb 98
33811 Centenales AS 13 Tb 90
37291 Centenares SA 81 Tc 104
23291 Centenaros, Los J 139 Xb 120
19151 Centenera GU 87 Wf 105
22437 Centenera HU 36 Ac 95
42211 Centenera de Andaluz SO 69 Xb 99
42216 Centenera del Campo SO 70 Xc 100
21590 Centenil H 161 Se 125
23214 Centenillo, El J 137 Wb 118
17832 Centenys GI 59 Ce 96
23266 Central, La J 138 We 118
19115 Central de Almoguera GU 87 Xa 107
25515 Central de Cabdella L 37 Af 94
26130 Central del Carmen RI 32 Xd 94
15315 Central do Eume C 11 Rf 88
Central Eléctrica LU 12 Sc 87
22365 Central Eléctrica de Barrosa HU 36 Ab 92
13191 Central Eléctrica de El Martinete CR 120 Ve 115
23540 Central Eléctrica de Fuenmayor J 153 Wc 122
44540 Central Eléctrica de Rivera-Bernad TE 73 Zc 102
15186 Central Termica de Mewama C 11 Rd 90
14220 Central Térmica de Puente Nuevo CO 135 Va 120
35628 Central Termoeléctrica GC 183 Lf 178
45580 Centro Agronómico TO 100 Ud 108
33519 Ceñal AS 15 Uc 88
36817 Cepeda PO 23 Rc 95
37656 Cepeda SA 82 Tf 106
05132 Cepeda la Mora AV 84 Uf 106
32558 Cepedelo OR 44 Sf 96
02651 Cepero, El AB 141 Yd 116
13129 Cepero, El CR 120 Ve 113
41730 Cepija SE 164 Ua 127
02312 Cepillo, El AB 123 Xc 116
36678 Cequeril PO 23 Rc 93
38869 Cerado, El TF 184 He 180
35128 Cerado del Pino GC 184 Kb 181
45290 Cerámica La Paloma TO 102 Vb 108
45290 Cerámica La Sagra TO 102 Wb 108
25588 Cerbi L 37 Ba 93
42181 Cerbón SO 51 Xe 97
25718 Cerc L 38 Bc 94
09514 Cerca, La BU 18 Wd 91
19269 Cercadillo GU 69 Xb 102
02139 Cercado de Catera AB 140 Ya 117
06480 Cercados, Los BA 116 Tc 115
35290 Cercados, Los GC 184 Kc 181
15186 Cerceda C 11 Rd 89
15823 Cerceda C 23 Re 91
28412 Cerceda MD 86 Wa 104
28470 Cercedilla MD 85 Vf 104
08698 Cercs B 57 Bf 96
25747 Cerdanyès, El L 56 Ba 96
32621 Cerdedelo OR 43 Sd 96
36130 Cerdedo PO 23 Rd 93
32537 Cerdeira OR 23 Re 93
32794 Cerdeira OR 24 Se 94
36447 Cerdeira PO 42 Rd 96
32520 Cerdeiroá OR 23 Re 95
15530 Cerdido C 11 Sa 87
39798 Cerdigo CB 19 We 88
33583 Cereceda AS 16 Ue 88
09559 Cereceda BU 30 Wd 92
19128 Cereceda GU 88 Xc 105
37621 Cereceda de la Sierra SA 82 Tf 105
24257 Cerecedo LE 27 Ue 91
49640 Cerecinos de Campos ZA 46 Ud 97
49125 Cerecinos del Carrizal ZA 46 Uc 98
27334 Cereixa LU 24 Sd 93
27695 Cereixal, O LU 25 Se 91
27116 Cereixido LU 13 Sf 90
15147 Cereo C 10 Rb 89
22361 Ceresa HU 36 Ab 93
22623 Ceresola HU 35 Ze 94
22375 Ceresuela HU 35 Aa 93
10627 Cerezal CC 82 Te 106
49164 Cerezal de Aliste ZA 45 Tf 99
24893 Cerezal de la Guzpeña LE 28 Uf 92
37253 Cerezal de Peñahorcada SA 63 Tc 102
37159 Cerezal de Puertas SA 64 Te 102
24150 Cerezales del Condado LE 27 Ud 92
10663 Cerezo CC 82 Te 107
05003 Cerezo, El AV 84 Vb 105
23290 Cerezo, El J 154 Xc 120
37116 Cerezo, El SA 64 Ua 102
40591 Cerezo de Abajo SG 68 Wc 101
40592 Cerezo de Arriba SG 68 Wc 101
19229 Cerezo de Mohernando GU 87 Wf 103
09270 Cerezo de Riotirón BU 31 Wf 93
44422 Cerezos, Los TE 107 Za 108
01192 Cerio VI 31 Xc 91
22449 Cerler HU 36 Ad 93
16150 Cermiñuelo, El CU 89 Xf 106
33859 Cermoño AS 14 Te 88
05196 Cermuño AV 85 Vc 105
32720 Cernada OR 24 Sb 94
49325 Cernadilla ZA 45 Td 96
32785 Cernado OR 43 Se 95
49271 Cernecina ZA 64 Ua 100
32348 Cernego OR 25 Sf 94
09142 Cernégula BU 30 Wc 93
44651 Cerollera, La TE 92 Zf 103
15112 Cerqueda C 10 Rb 89
33314 Cerra AS 15 Uc 87
32813 Cerradela OR 42 Sa 96
23190 Cerradura, La J 152 Wc 122
23670 Cerrajón, El J 152 Wa 123
29569 Cerralba MA 166 Vb 128
37291 Cerralbo SA 63 Tc 103
45682 Cerralbos, Los TO 101 Vc 109
09292 Cerratón de Juarros BU 30 Wd 94
39539 Cerrazo CB 17 Vf 88
33812 Cerredo AS 14 Td 91
04813 Cerricos, Los AL 155 Xe 123
41479 Cerrillares, Los SE 150 Ud 122
13391 Cerrillo de San Antón CR 138 Wf 116
29566 Cerrillos y Chirlita MA 166 Vb 128
44422 Cerrito, El TE 107 Za 109
46351 Cerrito, El V 106 Yf 111
29713 Cerro, El MA 167 Vf 127
37720 Cerro, El SA 82 Ua 107
46175 Cerro-Águila V 106 Yf 110
28210 Cerro Alarcón MD 85 Vf 106
02314 Cerroblanco AB 139 Xd 116
21320 Cerro de Andévalo, El H 147 Ta 122
41389 Cerro del Hierro, El SE 149 Uc 121
14550 Cerro del Humo CO 151 Vb 124
04769 Cerro del Molinero AL 169 Xa 127
06840 Cerro del Moro BA 133 Te 116
04810 Cerrogordo, El AL 171 Xe 124
28490 Cerro Grande MD 85 Wa 104
02511 Cerro Lobo AB 140 Yb 116
14350 Cerro Muriano CO 150 Vb 120
18800 Cerrón, El GR 170 Xb 125
23700 Cerro Pelado J 137 Wb 120
41409 Cerro Perea SE 150 Va 123
24844 Cerulleda LE 15 Ud 90
18690 Cerval, El GR 168 Wb 128
27664 Cervantes = San Román LU 25 Sf 91
15625 Cervás C 11 Re 88
39213 Cervatos CB 17 Vf 91
34309 Cervatos de la Cueza P 28 Vb 95
27833 Cerveira LU 12 Sa 88
27577 Cervela LU 23 Sa 92
27342 Cervela LU 24 Sd 92
08758 Cervelló B 77 Bf 100
25200 Cervera L 56 Bb 98
44422 Cervera, La TE 107 Za 109
28193 Cervera de Buitrago MD 68 Wc 103
50312 Cervera de la Cañada Z 71 Yb 100
16444 Cervera del Llano CU 104 Xd 110
12578 Cervera del Maestre CS 92 Ab 106
45637 Cervera de los Montes TO 100 Vb 108
44720 Cervera del Rincón TE 90 Za 104
26520 Cervera del Río Alham RI 51 Ya 96
34840 Cervera de Pisuerga P 29 Vd 91
50368 Cerveruela Z 72 Ye 101
25460 Cervià de les Garrigues L 75 Af 100
24205 Cervigal, El LE 27 Uc 95
47494 Cervillego de la Cruz VA 66 Va 101
15357 Cervo C 10 Rf 86
27891 Cervo LU 10 Sd 86
25514 Cérvoles L 37 Af 95
36693 Cesantes PO 22 Rc 95
36659 Cesar PO 22 Rc 93
09553 Céspedes BU 18 Wc 91
14749 Céspedes CO 150 Ue 122
37750 Cespedosa SA 83 Uc 105
37510 Cespedosa de Agadones SA 81 Tc 106
15991 Cespón C 22 Ra 92
01138 Cestafe VI 19 Xb 91
15391 Cesuras, Oza- C 11 Re 89
50292 Cetina Z 70 Ya 101
23240 Cetrina J 138 We 120
51001* Ceuta CE 175 Ue 133
30562 Ceutí MC 156 Ye 120
34218 Cevico de la Torre P 48 Vd 97
34247 Cevico Navero P 48 Ve 97
27307 Cezar LU 12 Sa 89
34813 Cezura P 29 Ve 92
30709 Chachimanes, Los MC 157 Za 122
15238 Chacin C 22 Ra 91
14550 Chacón CO 151 Vb 123
30700 Chacón MC 157 Yf 122
50700 Chacón Z 73 Zf 101
04810 Chacones, Los AL 155 Xe 124
37861 Chagarcía Medianero SA 83 Ud 105
32557 Chaguazoso OR 43 Se 95
32548 Chaguazoso OR 43 Sf 97
05309 Chaherrero AV 84 Va 103
15687 Chaián C 11 Rc 91
22233 Chalamera HU 55 Aa 99
26120 Chalet de Íñigo RI 32 Xd 95
20810 Chalet El Oasis SS 20 Xf 89
05141 Chamartín AV 84 Va 104
10120 Chamizas, Las CC 118 Uc 113
27163 Chamoso LU 12 Sd 91
36857 Chan, A PO 23 Rd 94
24723 Chana de Somoza LE 26 Td 94
04890 Chanco, El AL 170 Xd 125
36360 Chandebrito PO 41 Rb 96
27671 Chan de Cena LU 25 Sf 93
32372 Chandoiro OR 25 Sf 95
32786 Chandrexa OR 24 Sd 95
32767 Chandrexa de Queixa OR 24 Sd 95
49573 Chanos ZA 44 Ta 96
27500 Chantada LU 24 Sb 93
23590 Chantre, El J 153 We 122
40216 Chañe SG 66 Vd 100
27835 Chao LU 12 Sb 88
27245 Chao de Pousadoiro, O LU 13 Se 89
42259 Chaorna SO 70 Xe 102
36570 Chapa PO 23 Re 92
06196 Chaparral BA 132 Tb 116
23250 Chaparral J 138 We 119
23485 Chaparral J 154 Xa 122
30439 Chaparral MC 140 Yb 120
11391 Chaparral, El CA 175 Ub 132
18328 Chaparral, El GR 168 Wa 125
18290 Chaparral, El GR 168 Wc 125
21387 Chaparral, El H 132 Tb 120
29150 Chaparral, El MA 167 Vc 127
29649 Chaparral, El MA 175 Vc 129
28729 Chaparral, El MD 86 Wc 104
04887 Chaparral Alto, El AL 154 Xd 124
04877 Chaparral Bajo, El AL 155 Xd 124
18220 Chaparral de Cartuja GR 168 Wc 125
06894 Chaparrales, Los BA 117 Td 114
06228 Chaparral y Chapaya BA 133 Tf 117
14600 Chaparrera, La CO 136 Vd 120
02315 Chaparros AB 139 Xd 117
41728 Chapatales, Los SE 163 Ua 126
36216 Chapela PO 22 Rb 95
28694 Chapinería MD 85 Ve 106
30441 Charán MC 140 Xf 119
30859 Charca, La MC 156 Yc 122
04820 Charche Alto, El AL 155 Xf 123
04827 Charche Bajo, El AL 155 Xf 123
18511 Charches GR 169 Xa 125
35629 Charco, El GC 183 Lf 179
38749 Charco, El TF 181 Ha 177
11580 Charco de los Hurones CA 173 Uc 129
38595 Charco del Pino TF 180 Ic 180
13428 Charco del Tamujo CR 121 Wa 113
11170 Charco Dulce CA 172 Ua 130
41870 Charcofrío SE 148 Td 123
18160 Charcón, El GR 168 Wd 126
18891 Charcón Alto GR 154 Xc 123
18890 Charcones, Los GR 154 Xa 124
30440 Charcos, Los MC 140 Yb 119
30530 Charcos, Los MC 141 Yd 119
23687 Charilla J 152 Wa 124
22336 Charo HU 36 Ab 94
23487 Charrín J 153 Wf 123
40241 Chatún SG 67 Vd 101
18330 Chauchina GR 168 Wb 125
18700 Chaulines, Los GR 169 We 128
32848 Chaus OR 42 Rf 97
42153 Chavaler SO 51 Xd 97
48191 Chavarri BI 19 Wf 89
15214 Chave C 22 Ra 92
40171 Chavida SG 67 Wa 102
27866 Chavín LU 10 Sc 87
19310 Checa GU 89 Yb 105
04897 Checas AL 170 Xc 125
38801 Chejelipes TF 184 He 180
06105 Cheles BA 131 Se 117
46821 Chella V 126 Zc 114
27625 Chelo LU 24 Se 92
46176 Chelva V 107 Za 110
19310 Chequilla GU 89 Yb 105
19353 Chera GU 89 Yb 104
46350 Chera V 107 Za 111
42222 Chércoles SO 70 Xe 100
04859 Chercos AL 170 Xe 125
18494 Cherín GR 169 Wf 127
12360 Chert/Xert CS 92 Aa 105
46380 Cheste V 107 Zb 112
22465 Chía HU 36 Ac 93
22192 Chibluco HU 54 Zd 95
14111 Chica Carlota, La CO 150 Va 122
30648 Chicamo, El MC 141 Za 119
11130 Chiclana de la Frontera CA 172 Tf 130
23264 Chiclana de Segura J 138 Wf 119
16312 Chicoteros, Los CU 106 Yd 110
38688 Chiguergue TF 180 Ib 179
12592 Chilches CS 108 Ze 110
29790 Chilches MA 167 Ve 128
41850 Chilla SE 164 Te 125
16190 Chillarón de Cuenca CU 105 Xe 108
19128 Chillarón del Rey GU 88 Xb 105
13412 Chillón CR 119 Va 116
23479 Chilluévar J 153 Wf 120
19160 Chiloeches GU 87 Wf 105
18329 Chimeneas GR 168 Wb 126
38594 Chimiche TF 180 Ic 180
22194 Chimillas HU 54 Zd 95
15357 Chimparra C 10 Rf 86
06470 China, La BA 117 Tf 115
21291 Chinas, Las H 147 Tb 121
06410 Chinas Blancas BA 117 Tf 115
01207 Chinchetru VI 32 Xd 91
02520 Chinchilla de Monte-Aragón AB 124 Yb 115
28370 Chinchón MD 103 Wd 108
23330 Chincolla J 138 Xa 119
38689 Chío TF 180 Ib 179
11550 Chipiona CA 172 Td 128
50792 Chiprana Z 73 Zf 101
13108 Chiquero, El CR 120 Vd 114
04769 Chirán AL 169 Xa 127
23159 Chircales J 152 Wa 123
38688 Chirche TF 180 Ib 179
04825 Chirivel AL 155 Xe 123
46950 Chirivella V 107 Zd 112
22584 Chiriveta HU 55 Ae 96
13740 Chirivi CR 138 We 117
22587 Chiró HU 55 Ad 95
22365 Chisagüés HU 36 Ab 93
18656 Chite GR 168 Wc 127
46370 Chiva V 107 Zb 112
04271 Chive, El AL 171 Xf 125
50269 Chodes Z 71 Yd 100
30420 Chopillo, El MC 140 Yb 119
46178 Chopo, El V 107 Za 109
23693 Chopos, Los J 152 Wa 123
16150 Chorretas, Las CU 89 Ya 106
02489 Chorretites de Abajo, Los AB 139 Xd 119
04259 Chorrillo, El AL 170 Xd 127
35329 Chorrillo El GC 184 Kc 181
23470 Chorro, El J 154 Wf 121
29552 Chorro, El MA 166 Vb 127
02651 Chortales, Los AB 141 Yd 116
02612 Chospes, Los AB 123 Xd 114
02340 Chospes, Los AB 123 Xd 116
28790 Chotos, Los MD 86 Wb 105
27532 Chouzán LU 24 Sb 93
12499 Chóvar CS 108 Ze 109
21760 Choza del Alamillo H 162 Tc 126
41849 Choza de las Nuevas SE 164 Te 127
04479 Choza del Guarda AL 169 Xa 127
23340 Chozas J 138 Xa 119
18810 Chozas, Las GR 154 Xc 124
18329 Chozas, Las GR 168 Wa 126
24392 Chozas de Abajo LE 27 Ub 93
24392 Chozas de Arriba LE 27 Ub 93
45960 Chozas de Canales TO 102 Vf 108
10815 Chozones, Los CC 98 Td 108
05591 Chozos de la Bardera AV 84 Uf 105
21891 Chucena H 164 Td 124
04410 Chuche, El AL 170 Xd 127
47460 Chucho, El VA 66 Va 101
38595 Chuchurumbache TF 180 Ic 180
45113 Chueca TO 102 Wa 110
46167 Chulilla V 107 Za 111
16216 Chumillas CU 105 Xf 110
15313 Churío C 11 Rf 89
29140 Churriana MA 175 Vc 128
18194 Churriana de la Vega GR 168 Wc 126
31867 Cía NC 33 Yb 91
09228 Ciadoncha BU 48 Wa 96
42210 Ciadueña SO 69 Xc 100
33900 Ciaño AS 15 Ub 89
31799 Ciáurriz NC 33 Yc 91
49230 Cibanal ZA 63 Te 101
33817 Cibea AS 14 Td 90
39580 Cicera CB 17 Vc 89
15845 Cicere C 10 Ra 90
39790 Cicero CB 18 Wd 88
01129 Cicujano VI 32 Xd 92
03610 Cid, El A 142 Zb 118
04760 Cid, El AL 169 Xa 127
15815 Cidadela C 11 Rf 90
26291 Cidamón RI 31 Xa 94
42145 Cidones SO 50 Xc 98
14930 Cid-Toledo CO 151 Vc 124
09588 Ciella BU 19 We 90
28350 Ciempozuelos MD 86 Wc 108
33558 Cien AS 16 Uf 89
33116 Cienfuegos AS 15 Ua 90
11650 Cierva, La CA 165 Ub 127
16340 Cierva, La CU 105 Ya 108
41410 Cierva, La SE 149 Ub 124
36945 Cíes PO 41 Ra 95
30530 Cieza MC 141 Yd 119
19420 Cifuentes GU 88 Xc 104
24166 Cifuentes de Rueda LE 27 Ue 93
47270 Cigales VA 47 Vb 98
42113 Cigudosa SO 51 Xf 97
09556 Cigüenza BU 30 Wc 91
24991 Ciguera LE 15 Uf 91
47191 Cigüñuela VA 47 Va 99

262 | Cela

42126 Cihuela SO 70 Ya 100
26210 Cihuri RI 31 Xa 93
18339 Cijuela GR 168 Wb 125
02215 Cilanco AB 125 Ye 112
31194 Cildoz NC 33 Yb 91
34829 Cillamayor P 29 Ve 91
05149 Cillán AV 84 Va 104
24251 Cillanueva LE 27 Uc 94
26289 Cillarena RI 31 Wf 95
19339 Cillas GU 71 Ya 103
22611 Cillas HU 35 Ze 93
10895 Cilleros CC 97 Tb 108
37621 Cilleros de la Bastida SA 82 Tf 105
37183 Cilleros el Hondo SA 83 Ub 103
02314 Cilleruela AB 139 Xd 116
09349 Cilleruelo de Abajo BU 49 Wb 97
09349 Cilleruelo de Arriba BU 49 Wc 97
09572 Cilleruelo de Bezana BU 18 Wa 91
09572 Cilleruelo de Bricia BU 30 Wa 91
40551 Cilleruelo de San Mamés SG 68 Wc 100
39584 Cillórigo de Liébana CB 17 Vc 89
37874 Cilloruelo SA 65 Ud 103
27226 Cima de Vila, A LU 12 Sb 90
33734 Cimadevilla AS 13 Ta 88
33314 Cimadevilla AS 15 Uc 87
24239 Cimanes de la Vega LE 46 Uc 96
24272 Cimanes del Tejar LE 27 Ub 93
50213 Cimballa Z 71 Yb 102
13720 Cinco Casas CR 122 We 113
32782 Cinco Olivas Z 73 Zd 100
28754 Cinco Villas MD 68 Wc 103
19277 Cincovillas GU 69 Xb 101
40518 Cincovillas SG 68 Wd 100
12318 Cinctorres CS 92 Ze 105
15389 Cines C 11 Re 89
08614 Cint, El B 57 Be 96
04660 Cinta, La AL 171 Xf 124
31592 Cintruénigo NC 52 Yb 96
24660 Ciñera LE 27 Uc 91
49563 Cional ZA 45 Td 97
01450 Ciorraga VI 19 Xa 90
37216 Cipérez SA 64 Te 103
18708 Cipreses, Los GR 169 We 127
36587 Cira PO 23 Rd 92
12231 Cirat CS 107 Zd 108
31131 Ciraugui NC 33 Ya 92
28706 Circuito del Jarama MD 86 Wc 105
43427 Cirera, La T 76 Bb 99
39550 Cires CB 17 Vd 89
22486 Cirés HU 36 Ae 94
42138 Ciria SO 51 Ya 99
33946 Ciriego AS 15 Uc 89
27273 Cirio LU 12 Sd 90
31174 Ciriza NC 33 Yb 92
26258 Cirlñuela RI 31 Xa 94
19266 Cirueches GU 69 Xb 102
42367 Ciruela SO 69 Xb 100
19197 Ciruelas GU 87 Wf 104
40540 Ciruelos SG 68 Wb 100
45314 Ciruelos TO 102 Wc 109
09610 Ciruelos de Cervera BU 49 Wc 97
40496 Ciruelos de Coca SG 66 Vc 101
19281 Ciruelos del Pinar GU 70 Xe 102
26258 Cirueña RI 31 Xa 94
44158 Cirugeda TE 91 Zb 104
24133 Cirujales LE 26 Tf 92
42180 Cirujales del Río SO 51 Xe 97
22589 Ciscar HU 55 Ad 96
05211 Cisla AV 66 Uf 103
34320 Cisneros P 47 Va 95
17741 Cistella GI 40 Cf 95
47193 Cistérniga VA 47 Vb 99
24800 Cistierna LE 28 Uf 92
13129 Citolero, El CR 120 Vf 113
09123 Citores del Páramo BU 29 Wa 94
30720 Ciudad del Aire MC 157 Zb 122
50012 Ciudad Deportiva del Real Zaragoza Z 53 Yf 99
28680 Ciudad de San Ramón MD 85 Vd 106
09574 Ciudad de Valdeporres BU 18 Wb 90
05239 Ciudad Ducal AV 85 Vd 105
04825 Ciudad Granada AL 155 Xe 123
13001*Ciudad Real CR 121 Wa 115
37500 Ciudad-Rodrigo SA 81 Tc 105
50785 Ciudad romana Z 73 Zd 100
29604 Ciudad Sindical MA 175 Vb 130
28707 Ciudalcampo MD 86 Wc 105
07760 Ciutadella de Menorca IB 77 Df 108
08010 Ciutat, La B 77 Ca 100
03699 Ciutat Jardí A 142 Zc 118
19413 Cívica GU 87 Xb 104
36780 Cividáns PO 41 Ra 97
25799 Civís L 38 Bc 94
25213 Civit L 57 Bc 99
31180 Cizur Mayor NC 33 Yb 92
31190 Cizur Menor NC 33 Yb 92
22438 Clamosa HU 36 Ab 95
43839 Clarà T 76 Bc 102
02487 Claras AB 140 Xe 119
22583 Claravalls HU 55 Ae 95
25353 Claravalls L 56 Ba 98
19281 Clares GU 70 Xf 102
50314 Clarés de Ribota Z 71 Ya 99
25749 Claret L 56 Ba 97
25751 Claret de Figuerola L 57 Bc 98
08717 Clariana B 57 Bd 99
08729 Clariana B 76 Bd 101
25290 Clariana de Cardener L 57 Bd 97
41510 Claveles, Los SE 165 Ub 124
25517 Claverol L 56 Af 95
26130 Clavijo RI 32 Xd 94
41510 Clavinque SE 164 Ub 124
04770 Clementes, Los AL 169 Wf 128
06380 Clementes, Los BA 132 Tb 118
17813 Clocalou GI 58 Cc 95
44415 Clochas, Las TE 107 Zc 108
07315 Clot d'Almedrà IB 110 Ce 110
08696 Clot del Moro, El B 58 Bf 95
25632 Clua, La L 56 Ae 96
25737 Clua de Meià, La L 56 Ba 97
07850 Club Cala Llenya IB 109 Bd 114
28680 Club Madrileño MD 85 Vd 106
28680 Club Motonáutico MD 85 Vd 106
08519 Club Nautic Vic-Sau B 58 Cc 97
09454 Clunia Sulpicia BU 49 Wd 98
33829 Coalla AS 14 Tf 88
33795 Coaña AS 13 Tb 87
36612 Coaxe PO 22 Rb 93
33995 Coballes AS 15 Ud 89
30385 Cobaticas MC 157 Zb 123
02420 Cobatillas AB 140 Ya 118
14729 Cobatillas CO 150 Uf 121
14840 Cobatillas CO 151 Vd 122
44157 Cobatillas TE 91 Zb 104
04839 Cobatillas, Las AL 155 Xe 121
11180 Cobatillas, Las CA 173 Ub 130
33538 Cobayas AS 15 Ud 89
04858 Cóbdar AL 171 Xe 125
45291 Cobeja TO 102 Wa 108
39420 Cobejo CB 17 Vf 90
28863 Cobeña MD 86 Wc 105
42212 Cobertelada SO 69 Xc 100
33637 Cobertoria, La AS 15 Ub 90
19443 Cobeta GU 88 Xf 103
45111 Cobisa TO 102 Vf 110
30440 Cobo, El MC 140 Ya 119
25721 Coborriu de Bellver L 38 Be 94
34248 Cobos de Cerrato P 48 Vf 96
40332 Cobos de Fuentidueña SG 67 Wa 100
40144 Cobos de Segovia SG 66 Vd 103
09591 Cobos Junto a la Molina BU 30 Wc 93
39320 Cóbreces CB 17 Ve 88
49396 Cobreros ZA 44 Tb 96
36142 Cobres PO 22 Rc 95
27658 Coca LU 13 Ta 90
40480 Coca SG 66 Vc 101
37830 Coca de Alba SA 83 Ud 103
37609 Coca de Huebra SA 82 Ua 104
03820 Cocentaina A 142 Zd 116
30889 Cocón, El MC 171 Yc 124
04275 Cocón del Peral AL 170 Xe 126
30800 Cocón y Los Clementes, El MC 155 Yb 123
09129 Coculina BU 30 Wa 93
50617 Codera Baja Z 53 Ye 96
19281 Codes GU 70 Xf 102
49594 Codesal ZA 45 Td 97
25340 Codines, Les L 56 Ba 99
50132 Codo Z 72 Zb 100
07818 Codolar, Es IB 109 Bc 115
44558 Codoñera, La TE 72 Zc 103
44640 Codoñera, La TE 73 Zf 103
24342 Codornillos LE 28 Uf 94
40463 Codorniz SG 66 Vc 102
50326 Codos Z 71 Yd 101
06518 Codosera, La BA 115 Se 113
27207 Coence LU 24 Sa 91
15118 Coens C 10 Qf 89
27190 Coeo LU 12 Sd 91
27181 Coeses LU 12 Sc 91
35625 Cofete (Abandonada) GC 182 Ld 180
24857 Cofiñal LE 16 Ue 90
33548 Cofiño AS 16 Ue 88
22417 Cofita HU 55 Ab 97
46625 Cofrentes V 125 Yf 113
47440 Cogeces de Íscar VA 66 Vc 100
47313 Cogeces del Monte VA 67 Ve 99
19490 Cogollor GU 88 Xb 103
09320 Cogollos BU 49 Wb 95
18518 Cogollos de Guadix GR 169 Wf 125
18211 Cogollos Vega GR 168 Wc 125
17173 Cogolls GI 58 Cd 96
19230 Cogolludo GU 69 Wf 103
24712 Cogorderos LE 26 Tf 93
25152 Cogull = Cogul, El L 75 Ae 100
46749 Cogullado V 126 Zd 114
29100 Coín MA 175 Vb 129
32669 Coira OR 42 Sb 95
32137 Coirás OR 23 Sa 93
15258 Coiro C 22 Qf 91
15316 Coirós C 11 Rf 89
18492 Cojáyar GR 169 Wf 127
09620 Cojóbar BU 49 Wb 95
46354 Cojos, Los V 125 Ye 112
37170 Cojos de Rollán SA 64 Ua 103
33873 Coldobrero AS 13 Tc 88
22860 Col du Somport HU 35 Zc 92
17496 Colera GI 40 Da 94
32950 Coles OR 24 Sa 94
18770 Coliches, Los GR 169 Wf 128
05192 Colilla, La AV 84 Vb 105
09514 Colina BU 18 Wd 90
40153 Colina SG 85 Ve 103
29140 Colina, La MA 175 Vc 129
24313 Colinas del Campo de Martín Moro LE 26 Te 92
49623 Colinas de Trasmonte ZA 45 Ub 96
39750 Colindres CB 18 Wd 88
25526 Coll L 37 Ae 94
33874 Collada AS 14 Tc 88
22481 Collada, La HU 55 Ac 95
33527 Colladas AS 15 Uc 89
44493 Colladico, El TE 72 Yf 102
40164 Colladillo SG 68 Wb 102
46140 Colladillo V 106 Ye 108
12123 Colladillo, El CS 108 Zd 108
05580 Collado AV 83 Ud 106
39407 Collado CB 17 Vf 89
10414 Collado CC 99 Ub 108
18492 Collado, El GR 169 Wf 128
26132 Collado, El RI 32 Xd 95
46178 Collado, El V 106 Yf 109
05309 Collado de Contreras AV 66 Va 103
30610 Collado de Gil MC 141 Yd 119
44123 Collado de la Grulla TE 90 Yc 107
30893 Collado de Lirón MC 156 Yb 124
23210 Collado del Lobo J 137 Wc 119
05153 Collado del Mirón AV 83 Ud 105
37520 Collado de Malvarín SA 81 Tc 106
40170 Collado Hermosa SG 67 Wa 102
28450 Collado-Mediano MD 86 Vf 104
44480 Collado Royo y Poviles TE 107 Zb 108
16143 Collados CU 88 Xe 107
44211 Collados TE 72 Yf 103
02449 Collados, Los AB 139 Xd 118
28400 Collado-Villalba MD 85 Wa 105
08253 Coll-Arbós, El B 57 Be 98
34407 Collazos de Boedo P 29 Vd 93
08293 Collbató B 76 Be 99
25717 Colldarnat L 37 Bc 95
43310 Colldejou T 75 Af 102
17251 Coll de la Ganga GI 59 Da 97
08717 Coll de la Panadella B 57 Bc 99
22474 Coll de l'Espina HU 36 Ad 94
25739 Colldelrat L 56 Ba 97
17404 Coll de N'Orri, El GI 58 Cd 98
07007 Coll d'en Rabassa, Es IB 110 Ce 111
07589 Coll de Sant Joan IB 111 Dc 110
25170 Coll de Vinganya, El L 74 Ac 99
24858 Colle LE 28 Ue 91
23488 Collejares J 153 Wf 122
17515 Collfred GI 58 Cc 96
25739 Collfred L 56 Ba 97
33548 Collía AS 16 Ue 88
16194 Cólliga CU 105 Xe 108
16194 Colliguilla CU 105 Xe 108
12316 Coll i Moll CS 92 Zf 105
25632 Collmorter L 56 Af 96
22584 Colls HU 55 Ae 95
08358 Collsacreu B 58 Cd 99
08178 Collsuspina B 58 Cb 98
29170 Colmenar MA 167 Vd 127
02127 Colmenar, El AB 140 Xf 116
18183 Colmenar, El GR 168 Wd 125
29391 Colmenar, El MA 174 Ud 129
13597 Colmenar de Chacaló CR 136 Vf 117
23239 Colmenar de Corral Nuevo J 137 Wd 119
13343 Colmenar de Don Reyes Frías CR 138 Wf 118
13768 Colmenar de la Parilla CR 137 Wb 118
28213 Colmenar del Arroyo MD 85 Ve 106
28190 Colmenar de la Sierra GU 68 Wd 102
37711 Colmenar de Montemayor SA 82 Ua 106
28380 Colmenar de Oreja MD 103 Wd 108
13343 Colmenar de Troyano CR 138 We 118
28270 Colmenarejo MD 85 Wa 105
34483 Colmenares P 29 Vc 92
28770 Colmenar Viejo MD 86 Wb 105
10340 Colmenillas, Las CC 99 Ud 111
06150 Colmenitas, Las BA 132 Tc 117
33590 Colombres AS 17 Vc 88
18564 Colomera GR 168 Wb 124
17144 Colomers GI 59 Cf 96
19411 Colonia GU 87 Xa 104
23620 Colonia J 152 Wb 121
06480 Colonia, La BA 116 Tc 115
18810 Colonia, La GR 154 Xb 123
29520 Colonia Agrícola de los Blancares MA 166 Vb 125
26291 Colonia agrícola de Santa Gertrudis RI 31 Xa 94
41150 Colonia de Alfonso XIII SE 163 Tf 125
29540 Colonia de Ballestero MA 166 Vb 126
13600 Colonia de Caprera CR 122 We 112
22364 Colonia de la Compañía Ibérica HU 36 Ab 93
37480 Colonia de la Estación SA 81 Tb 105
45150 Colonia de la Moraleja TO 101 Vc 110
03409 Colonia de la Sierra de Salinas A 141 Za 117
29631 Colonia de la Verdad MA 175 Vc 129
23711 Colonia del Embalse J 137 Wb 120
28439 Colonia de Mataespesa MD 85 Vf 105
06389 Colonia de Rabalcuzar BA 132 Tb 119
29190 Colonia de Santa Inés MA 167 Vc 128
07640 Colònia de Sant Jordi IB 111 Cf 113
07579 Colònia de Sant Pere IB 111 Db 110
23214 Colonia de Selladores J 137 Wa 118
22282 Colonia de Tormos HU 53 Zb 96
46730 Colonia Ducal V 127 Ze 114
12500 Colonia Europa CS 93 Ac 106
35611 Colonia García Escámez GC 183 Lf 177
45220 Colonia Hispania TO 102 Wb 108
28311 Colonia Iberia MD 102 Wb 109
18813 Colonia Iturraldi GR 154 Xa 123
17860 Colònia Jordana GI 58 Cb 95
09400 Colonia la Enhebrada BU 49 Wc 99
34250 Colonia Militar Infantil General Varela P 48 Ve 96
41140 Colonia Queipo de Llano SE 163 Tf 126
08692 Colònia Riera B 57 Bf 97
08611 Colònia Rosal B 57 Bf 96
08269 Colònia Valls B 57 Be 97
39518 Colsa CB 17 Ve 90
33637 Columbiello AS 15 Ub 90
24490 Columbrianos LE 25 Tc 93
33327 Colunga AS 15 Ue 88
22148 Colungo HU 55 Aa 95
25284 Coma, La L 57 Bd 95
25211 Comabella L 57 Bb 98
25713 Coma de Nabiners, La L 38 Bc 95
17534 Coma de Vaca GI 39 Ca 94
25284 Coma i la Pedra, La L 57 Bd 95
30627 Comala MC 141 Ye 120
07150 Coma Major IB 110 Cc 111
29195 Comares MA 167 Ve 127
43880 Coma-ruga T 76 Bd 101
43776 Comas, Las T 75 Ae 102
07349 Comasema IB 110 Ce 110
36993 Combarro PO 22 Rb 94
24715 Combarros LE 26 Tf 93
08243 Comdals, Els B 57 Be 98
23790 Comendador J 152 Ve 121
29570 Comendador MA 166 Vc 128
50830 Comercio, El Z 53 Zb 98
03710 Cometa, La A 143 Aa 117
39520 Comillas CB 17 Ve 88
30817 Comino, El MC 156 Yc 122
34878 Comoncillo P 28 Vb 92
41130 Compañía, La SE 163 Tf 125
29754 Cómpeta MA 167 Wa 128
Complejo Industrial LU 10 Sd 86
18290 Complejo Polideportivo GR 168 Wb 125
03183 Complejo Turístico Torrejón, El A 157 Zc 121
24414 Compludo LE 26 Td 94
01213 Comunion VI 31 Xa 92
25211 Concabella L 56 Bb 98
25517 Conca de Dalt L 56 Af 95
11630 Concejo, El CA 173 Ub 128
21330 Concepción H 147 Tb 122
42211 Concepción SO 69 Xc 99
14815 Concepción, La CO 151 Vf 124
29660 Concepción, La MA 174 Va 129
19287 Concha GU 70 Ya 102
48891 Concha, La BI 18 Wd 89
39728 Concha, La CB 18 Wb 89
37550 Concha, La SA 81 Tb 105
18659 Cónchar GR 168 Wc 127
33590 Conchas, Las AS 17 Vc 88
22414 Conchel HU 55 Aa 97
22808 Concilio Z 34 Zb 95
46160 Concordia V 107 Zb 110
44397 Concud TE 90 Yf 106
33992 Condado AS 15 Uc 89
09559 Condado BU 30 Wc 92
50172 Condado, El Z 53 Zc 99
17310 Condado de Jaruco GI 59 Ce 98
23280 Conde, El J 138 Xa 119
19275 Condemios de Abajo GU 69 Wf 101
19275 Condemios de Arriba GU 69 Wf 101
03540 Condomina, La A 142 Zd 118
30566 Condomina, La MC 156 Yc 123
33979 Condueño AS 15 Uc 89
42108 Conejares SO 51 Xf 97
37594 Conejera SA 81 Tc 105
45910 Conejeros TO 101 Vd 108
43427 Conesa T 76 Bb 99
24234 Conforcos LE 46 Uc 95
27728 Conforto LU 13 Sf 88
03517 Confrides A 143 Ze 116
36891 Confurco PO 41 Rc 95
49619 Congosta ZA 45 Tf 96
33694 Congostinas AS 15 Ub 90
09124 Congosto BU 29 Vf 93
24398 Congosto LE 26 Tc 93
16771 Congosto, El CU 104 Xc 109
34882 Congosto de Valdavia P 28 Vc 92
19243 Congostrina GU 69 Xa 102
35572 Conil GC 182 Mb 175
11140 Conil de la Frontera CA 172 Tf 131
08282 Conill B 57 Bc 98
25351 Conill L 56 Ba 98
08732 Conilleres, Les B 76 Bd 100
25656 Conques L 56 Ba 96
42230 Conquezuela SO 69 Xc 101
14448 Conquista CO 136 Vd 118
10240 Conquista de la Sierra CC 118 Ub 112
06410 Conquista del Guadiana BA 117 Tf 114
07330 Consell IB 110 Ce 110
15314 Consistorio C 11 Re 89
36430 Consistorio PO 42 Re 96
06350 Consolación BA 132 Tb 120
13310 Consolación CR 122 Wd 115
16270 Consolación CU 124 Yc 112
43120 Constantí T 75 Bb 102
41450 Constantina SE 149 Uc 121
17164 Constantios GI 59 Ce 97
05217 Constanzana AV 66 Va 103
45700 Consuegra TO 121 Wc 112
40389 Consuegra de Murera SG 67 Wb 101
23747 Contadero J 137 Wa 118
04825 Contador, El AL 155 Xd 123
50239 Contamina Z 70 Ya 101
21240 Contienda, La H 147 Ta 120
01117 Contrasta VI 32 Xe 92
09613 Contreras BU 49 Wd 96
16260 Contreras CU 106 Yc 111
27160 Conturiz LU 12 Sc 91
06270 Convento BA 132 Tc 120
36993 Convento, O PO 22 Rb 94
05380 Convento de Duruelo, El AV 84 Uf 104
30813 Conventos, Los MC 156 Yb 123
04647 Convoy, El AL 171 Yb 124
39408 Cóo CB 17 Vf 89

49783 Coomonte ZA 45 Ub 96
30189 Copa, La MC 140 Yc 120
30889 Cope MC 156 Yd 124
19292 Copernal GU 87 Wf 103
08289 Copons B 57 Bd 99
37609 Coquilla de Huebra SA 82 Tf 104
07459 Corall Serra IB 111 Da 110
33556 Corao AS 16 Uf 88
12599 Coratxar CS 92 Aa 104
37450 Corbacera SA 82 Ua 104
44193 Corbalán TE 90 Za 106
44721 Corbatón TE 90 Yf 104
15332 Corbelle C 10 Sb 87
46612 Corbera V 126 Zd 114
08757 Corbera de Baix B 76 Bf 100
43784 Corbera d'Ebre T 74 Ac 102
08757 Corbera de Dalt B 76 Bf 100
24225 Corbillos de los Oteros LE 27 Ud 94
25137 Corbins L 55 Ae 98
23649 Corbunillo J 152 Wa 121
17121 Corçà GI 59 Da 97
25692 Corçà L 55 Ae 96
06131 Corcho, El BA 131 Se 117
45569 Corchuela TO 100 Ue 109
06011 Corchuela, La BA 116 Sf 116
41703 Corchuela, La SE 164 Ua 125
21750 Corchuelo, El H 162 Tb 125
15149 Corcoesto C 10 Ra 89
19127 Córcoles GU 88 Xc 106
46178 Corcolilla V 106 Yf 109
39294 Corconte CB 18 Wa 90
24170 Corcos LE 28 Uf 92
47280 Corcos VA 47 Vb 98
41599 Corcoya SE 166 Vb 125
15130 Corcubión C 10 Qe 91
27737 Cordal LU 12 Sd 88
24915 Cordiñanes de Valdeón LE 16 Va 89
14001*Córdoba CO 150 Vb 121
14820 Cordobilla CO 151 Vc 122
14512 Cordobilla CO 166 Vb 124
06487 Cordobilla de Lácara BA 117 Td 114
02513 Cordovilla AB 140 Yc 117
31191 Cordovilla NC 33 Yc 92
37337 Cordovilla SA 65 Ud 103
34810 Cordovilla de Aguilar P 29 Ve 91
34259 Cordovilla la Real P 48 Ve 96
26311 Cordovín RI 31 Xb 94
19341 Corduente GU 89 Ya 103
31591 Corella NC 52 Yb 96
26144 Corera RI 32 Xe 94
15110 Cores C 10 Ra 89
49530 Coreses ZA 65 Uc 99
27164 Corgo, O LU 12 Sd 91
32348 Córgomo OR 25 Sf 94
10800 Coria CC 98 Tc 109
41100 Coria del Río SE 164 Tf 125
33129 Corias AS 14 Tf 88
33685 Corigos AS 15 Ub 90
41780 Coripe SE 165 Ud 127
15147 Coristanco C 10 Rb 89
12134 Cormana, La CS 92 Ze 107
15114 Corme-Porto C 10 Ra 89
26526 Cornago RI 51 Xf 96
15839 Cornanda C 22 Rb 91
27131 Córneas LU 13 Sf 91
15816 Corneda C 11 Rf 91
15863 Corneira C 10 Rb 91
09568 Cornejo BU 18 Wc 90
08940 Cornella de Llobregat B 77 Ca 100
17844 Cornellà del Terri GI 59 Ce 96
33850 Cornellana AS 14 Tf 88
25717 Cornellana L 38 Bd 95
06444 Cornicabra BA 133 Ua 118
27289 Cornide de Abaixo LU 12 Sd 90
24980 Corniero LE 28 Ue 91
35129 Cornisa GC 184 Kb 182
33887 Cornollo AS 13 Tb 89
34879 Cornón de la Peña P 28 Vb 92
43360 Cornudella de Montsant T 75 Af 101
09246 Cornudilla BU 30 Wd 92
46353 Cornudilla, La V 106 Ye 112
33310 Coro AS 15 Ud 88
08261 Coromina, La B 57 Be 97
08256 Coromines, Les B 57 Bd 98
36620 Corón PO 22 Rb 93
24915 Corona LE 16 Va 89
22336 Corona, La HU 36 Ab 94
22460 Corona, La HU 36 Ac 95
30396 Corona, La MC 157 Yf 123
06469 Coronada, La BA 118 Ub 115
14298 Coronada, La CO 134 Ud 119
33784 Corondeño AS 13 Tb 89
41760 Coronil, El SE 165 Uc 126
28811 Corpa MD 87 We 106
24740 Corporales LE 26 Td 95
26259 Corporales RI 31 Xa 94
37251 Corporario SA 63 Tc 101
33459 Corrada, La AS 14 Tf 87
46117 Corral Caruana V 107 Zd 111
45880 Corral de Almaguer TO 103 Wf 110
40529 Corral de Ayllón SG 68 Wd 100
46822 Corral de Bru V 126 Zb 114
13190 Corral de Calatrava CR 120 Vf 115
50120 Corral de Cazallo Z 53 Yf 98
50619 Corral de Charles Z 34 Za 95
31500 Corral de Curro NC 52 Yd 95
16842 Corral de Domingo Ramos CU 88 Xe 107
40312 Corral de Duratón SG 68 Wb 101
37607 Corral de Garciñigo SA 82 Ua 105
50617 Corral de Gova Z 52 Yd 96
31311 Corral de la Bárbara NC 33 Yd 95
26559 Corral de la Cañada RI 32 Ya 95
50130 Corral de la Domi Z 72 Zb 100
50678 Corral de la Fraila Z 34 Yf 94
26560 Corral de las Romerales RI 51 Xf 96
50268 Corral de la Virgen Z 52 Yc 99
50741 Corral del Calamaquero Z 72 Zc 100
31382 Corral del Cura NC 33 Yc 95
31251 Corral de Linte NC 33 Yb 93
50619 Corral del Judío Z 34 Za 94
50547 Corral de los Vedaos Z 52 Yc 98
31500 Corral del Pachín NC 52 Yd 96
28594 Corral de Manuel Mondéjar MD 87 We 107
50619 Corral de Meleras Z 34 Yf 94
50268 Corral de Minganares Z 52 Yc 98
09127 Corralejo BU 29 Vf 92
Corralejo GC 183 Ma 176
28190 Corralejo GU 68 Wd 102
40530 Corralejo SG 68 Wc 101
21120 Corrales H 162 Ta 125
24521 Corrales LE 25 Ta 93
49700 Corrales ZA 64 Ub 100
18127 Corrales, Los GR 168 Wb 127
41657 Corrales, Los SE 166 Va 126
46313 Corrales, Los V 106 Ye 111
39400 Corrales de Buelna, Los CB 17 Vf 89
45830 Corrales de Concejo TO 103 Wf 111
47317 Corrales de Duero VA 48 Vf 98
35627 Corrales de las Hermosas GC 183 Le 179
35639 Corrales de la Torre, Los GC 183 Ma 178
50793 Corralet, El Z 74 Aa 101
50139 Corralico de Baerta Z 72 Za 99
50130 Corral Petenero Z 72 Zb 100
23450 Corral Rubio J 153 Wc 120
02693 Corral-Rubio AB 125 Yd 115
12194 Corrals, Els CS 108 Zf 108
46759 Corrals, Els V 126 Zd 114
50137 Corral Tejero Z 72 Zb 100
32620 Correchouso OR 43 Sd 96
24849 Correcillas LE 27 Ud 91
23213 Correderas, Las J 137 Wc 118
36856 Corredoira PO 23 Rd 94
15816 Corredoiras, As C 11 Rf 90
33010 Corredoria, La AS 15 Ub 88
25134 Corregó L 56 Ad 98
12130 Correntilla, La CS 108 Zf 108
39518 Correpoco CB 17 Ve 89
32315 Correxais OR 25 Sf 94
25285 Corriu, La L 57 Bd 96
01427 Corro VI 31 We 91
45569 Corrochana TO 100 Uf 109
08520 Corró d'Amunt B 58 Cb 98
08520 Corró d'Avall B 58 Cb 99
25556 Corroncui L 37 Af 94
17734 Corsavell GI 39 Cd 95
30591 Cortados, Los MC 157 Za 122
30710 Cortados, Los MC 157 Za 122
22364 Cortalaviña HU 36 Ab 93
AD200 Cortals, Els ◘ AND 38 Bd 93
17531 Cortals, Els GI 58 Ca 95
27188 Cortapezas LU 24 Sc 92
25721 Cortàs L 38 Be 94
47639 Cortas de Blas VA 47 Vb 98
21230 Corte, La H 147 Tb 121
21359 Corte, La H 147 Tb 121
31210 Cortecampo NC 32 Xe 93
41890 Cortecillas, Las SE 148 Td 122
21209 Corteconcepción H 148 Tc 121
06196 Corte de Peleas BA 132 Tb 116
32213 Cortegada OR 42 Rf 95
32636 Cortegada OR 43 Sc 96
32612 Cortegada OR 43 Sd 96
06800 Cortegana BA 117 Te 115
06209 Cortegana BA 132 Tc 116
21230 Cortegana H 147 Tb 121
32520 Cortegazas OR 23 Re 94
21208 Cortelazor H 147 Tc 121
32411 Cortella OR 42 Re 95
36866 Cortellas, As PO 23 Rc 95
21208 Corterrangel H 147 Tc 121
33116 Cortes AS 15 Ua 90
09193 Cortes BU 30 Wc 95
29679 Cortes MA 174 Uf 130
31530 Cortes NC 52 Yd 97
46312 Cortés V 106 Yf 110
44791 Cortes de Aragón TE 72 Za 103
12127 Cortes de Arenoso CS 107 Zc 107
18814 Cortes de Baza GR 154 Xb 123
29380 Cortes de la Frontera MA 174 Ud 129
46199 Cortes de Pallás V 125 Za 113
19261 Cortes de Tajuña GU 69 Xd 103
29693 Cortesín-La Hedionda MA 174 Ue 130
18196 Cortichuela, La GR 168 Wd 126
09145 Cortiguera BU 30 Wb 92
04638 Cortijada Aljuezar AL 171 Ya 126
18329 Cortijada Arbollar GR 168 Wb 126
18690 Cortijada Barranco y Traba GR 168 Wb 128
18380 Cortijada Barrandillas GR 168 Wa 125
04116 Cortijada Bornos AL 171 Xf 127
04870 Cortijada Campo Bajo AL 170 Xd 124
18690 Cortijada Cantariiján GR 168 Wb 128
35629 Cortijada Cañada de la Mata GC 183 Lf 179
18125 Cortijada Castillejo GR 167 Vf 127
11158 Cortijada de Alquería CA 172 Ua 130
23180 Cortijada de Cañada de Zafra J 152 Wa 121
23649 Cortijada de Capisol J 152 Wa 121
23612 Cortijada de Casasola J 151 Vf 122
04662 Cortijada de Chapí AL 171 Ya 125
23600 Cortijada de Contreras J 152 Wa 122
04212 Cortijada de Febeire AL 170 Xd 125
23529 Cortijada de Gil de Olio J 152 Wc 121
23413 Cortijada de Guadalupe J 153 Wd 120
23460 Cortijada de Guadiana J 153 We 121
18470 Cortijada de Hova Marta GR 169 Wf 126
11392 Cortijada del Aciscar CA 175 Ub 131
23150 Cortijada de La Fresnedilla J 152 Wb 123
11391 Cortijada de La Lapa CA 173 Ub 132
11391 Cortijada de Las Cumbres CA 173 Ub 132
18152 Cortijada de La Sierra GR 168 Wc 126
04887 Cortijada del Chaparral AL 154 Xc 124
04899 Cortijada del Chaparral AL 154 Xc 124
04271 Cortijada del Cura AL 171 Xf 125
04629 Cortijada del Jauro AL 171 Ya 125
14820 Cortijada del Judío Nuevo CO 151 Vb 122
11150 Cortijada de los Atravesados CA 172 Tf 131
18494 Cortijada del Pajarraco GR 169 Wf 127
23649 Cortijada del Peñón J 152 Wa 121
18329 Cortijada de Santa Catalina GR 168 Wb 126
23009 Cortijada de Tarumbillo J 152 Wb 121
35628 Cortijada de Teguereyle GC 183 Lf 179
23650 Cortijada de Torre de Alcázar J 152 Vf 121
23009 Cortijada de Torretoribio J 152 Wb 121
23614 Cortijada de Vado Jaén J 152 Vf 123
18560 Cortijada Doña Marina GR 153 Wd 123
04878 Cortijada El Alamí AL 170 Xd 125
18312 Cortijada El Almendro GR 167 Vf 125
04149 Cortijada El Barranco de García AL 171 Ya 126
04114 Cortijada El Bombón AL 171 Xf 127
04114 Cortijáda El Charco del Lobo AL 171 Xf 127
18380 Cortijada El Nevazo GR 168 Wa 125
18810 Cortijada El Pertiguero GR 154 Xc 124
04271 Cortijada El Pilar AL 171 Xf 125
30170 Cortijada El Rulí MC 141 Yc 120
23006 Cortijada Fuenteleta J 152 Wa 121
04149 Cortijada La Palmerosa AL 171 Ya 127
04711 Cortijada Las Chozas de Redondo AL 170 Xb 128
04647 Cortijada Las Jaulas AL 171 Yb 124
04619 Cortijada las Jaulas AL 171 Yb 125
18564 Cortijada Las Torres GR 168 Wb 125
04140 Cortijada La Torre Vieja AL 171 Ya 127
04277 Cortijada Los Areos AL 171 Xf 126
04271 Cortijada Los Cazaminches AL 171 Xf 125
04149 Cortijada Los Cerrillos AL 171 Ya 127
04270 Cortijada Los Contreras AL 171 Xf 126
04116 Cortijada Los Giménez AL 171 Xf 127
04629 Cortijada Los Gironas de Lisbona AL 171 Xf 125
04114 Cortijada Los Herradas AL 171 Xf 127
04116 Cortijada Los Majanos AL 171 Xf 127
04117 Cortijada Los Matías AL 171 Xf 128
04210 Cortijada Los Morales AL 171 Xe 126
18470 Cortijada Los Retamales GR 169 Wf 126
18181 Cortijada Malajara GR 169 We 125
14700 Cortijada Molino Bajo CO 150 Ue 122
18160 Cortijada Padules GR 169 Wd 125
18600 Cortijada Pataura GR 168 Wc 128
18800 Cortijada Pocopán GR 170 Xb 124
21380 Cortijada Riofrio H 147 Tb 120
23660 Cortijada Ruedo Alto J 152 Vf 123
18494 Cortijada Unquieira GR 169 Wf 127
23180 Cortija de Golosillo J 152 Wa 121
23400 Cortija del Tesorero J 153 We 121
06510 Cortija del Zangallón BA 116 Ta 114
23487 Cortijillos J 153 Wf 122
29711 Cortijillos, Los MA 167 Vf 127
41599 Cortijillos, Los SE 166 Vb 125
18815 Cortijillos de Campocámara GR 154 Xa 122
28669 Cortijo, El MD 86 Wa 106
26007 Cortijo, El RI 32 Xc 94
18562 Cortijo Aguas de los Sauces GR 153 Wd 124
11400 Cortijo Algarve CA 164 Tf 127
11150 Cortijo Altamira CA 172 Tf 131
30440 Cortijo Altarejo MC 140 Ya 120
18569 Cortijo Alto GR 152 Wb 124
23669 Cortijo Alto J 152 Vf 122
29312 Cortijo Alto MA 167 Vd 126
30420 Cortijo Alto MC 140 Yb 119
06430 Cortijo Argallenes BA 134 Ub 117
11630 Cortijo Arrayanosa CA 173 Uc 128
06920 Cortijo Arriba BA 134 Ub 118
18813 Cortijo Azún GR 154 Xa 123
10291 Cortijo Babezuelas CC 99 Ua 111
18700 Cortijo Bajo, El GR 169 We 128
23250 Cortijo Bajo de los Robledos J 138 We 119
18690 Cortijo Bañuelos GR 168 Wb 128
18417 Cortijo Barranco de la Bina GR 169 We 127
06950 Cortijo Barrancos BA 133 Tf 118
04769 Cortijo Barro AL 169 Wf 127
29100 Cortijo Benítez MA 175 Vb 128
14550 Cortijo Blanco CO 151 Vc 123
29602 Cortijo Blanco MA 174 Va 130
04479 Cortijo Brado AL 169 Xa 126
06980 Cortijo Buenavista BA 148 Ua 120
06900 Cortijo Buenvecino BA 133 Tf 119
11400 Cortijo Burujena CA 163 Te 128
10291 Cortijo Cabezuelas CC 99 Ua 111
29230 Cortijo Cadenas MA 167 Vc 127
23760 Cortijo Cansino J 152 Vf 121
06443 Cortijo Canta el Gallo BA 134 Ub 118
23340 Cortijo Cañada Arada J 138 Xa 119
18562 Cortijo Cañada de la Iglesia GR 153 Wd 124
23150 Cortijo Carboneros J 152 Wb 123
06208 Cortijo Carrascal BA 132 Tc 117
41800 Cortijo Carrascalejo SE 163 Te 124
21240 Cortijo Carretero H 147 Sf 121
10291 Cortijo Carrona CC 99 Tf 111
10530 Cortijo Casares de Saliente CC 98 Tf 110
10291 Cortijo Casilla-Grande CC 98 Te 111
11400 Cortijo Castelo CA 164 Te 128
18192 Cortijo Castillejo GR 168 Wd 125
04131 Cortijo Cerro Blanco AL 170 Xe 127
04839 Cortijo Cerro del Muerto AL 155 Xe 122
23487 Cortijo Cerro Miguel J 153 Wf 122
21240 Cortijo Chaparrita H 147 Ta 120
06171 Cortijo Chico de Capela BA 132 Tb 116
23591 Cortijo Chillón J 153 We 122
18810 Cortijo Churrón GR 154 Xb 124
10189 Cortijo Contreras CC 117 Ua 112
06182 Cortijo Cubillo BA 116 Tb 114
04830 Cortijo Cueva Gurillos AL 155 Xf 121
18515 Cortijo Culebra GR 169 We 124
41740 Cortijo de Abajo SE 164 Tf 127
23280 Cortijo de Aceite J 138 Xa 119
13333 Cortijo de Acuña CR 138 Xa 116
35628 Cortijo de Adeje GC 183 Lf 179
02315 Cortijo de Aguamala AB 139 Xc 117
18560 Cortijo de Aguas Morales Alto GR 153 Wd 124
30890 Cortijo de Agüica de Mula MC 155 Ya 122
21240 Cortijo de Aguzaderas Viejas H 147 Ta 120
11370 Cortijo de Ahojiz CA 173 Uc 131
29320 Cortijo de Ahumada MA 166 Va 126
18814 Cortijo de Alacranes GR 154 Xb 122
23790 Cortijo de Albarizas J 151 Ve 121
41640 Cortijo de Albina SE 166 Uf 125
41640 Cortijo de Alcalá SE 166 Uf 125
11179 Cortijo de Alcántara CA 172 Ua 130
11580 Cortijo de Alcornocalejo CA 173 Ub 129
41400 Cortijo de Alcorrín SE 150 Uf 123
14029 Cortijo de Aldea de Don Gil CO 151 Vd 122
41440 Cortijo de Algarín SE 149 Uc 123
18520 Cortijo de Almazara GR 153 We 123
23260 Cortijo de Almorchón J 138 Wf 119
11630 Cortijo de Alperchite CA 165 Ub 128
13597 Cortijo de Antonio Montoya CR 137 Wa 117
29395 Cortijo de Antonio Moreno MA 166 Uf 127
06330 Cortijo de Antón Sánchez BA 132 Tc 119
18500 Cortijo de Apolo GR 169 Wf 125
29230 Cortijo de Arevalillo MA 166 Vc 127
29690 Cortijo de Argüelles MA 174 Ue 130
23320 Cortijo de Armíndez J 153 We 121

264 | Coomonte

02315 Cortijo de la Dehesilla AB 139 Xc 117
11393 Cortijo de la Dehesilla CA 175 Ub 131
41870 Cortijo de la Dehesilla SE 148 Te 124
04210 Cortijo del Administrador AL 170 Xe 126
06477 Cortijo de la Donosa BA 133 Tf 117
41659 Cortijo de la Dueña Alta SE 165 Ue 126
23190 Cortijo de la Encina J 152 Wb 122
29395 Cortijo de la Escalereta MA 166 Uf 127
06106 Cortijo de la Estacada BA 131 Se 117
06475 Cortijo de la Estanquera BA 133 Ua 117
41400 Cortijo de la Estrella SE 150 Uf 123
14540 Cortijo de la Foncubierta CO 150 Vb 123
11630 Cortijo de la Fuensanta CA 165 Uc 128
30195 Cortijo de la Fuenseca MC 140 Xf 120
41479 Cortijo de la Fuente de la Mujer SE 149 Ud 122
13344 Cortijo de la Fuente del Campo CR 138 Wd 117
23660 Cortijo de la Fuente del Espino J 152 Vf 123
18560 Cortijo de la Fuente de los Potros GR 153 Wd 123
21250 Cortijo de la Gama H 146 Se 121
18539 Cortijo de la Girana GR 153 Wf 124
10210 Cortijo de la Gironda CC 99 Ub 111
41540 Cortijo de la Gita SE 165 Ud 126
13332 Cortijo de la Gloria CR 122 Xb 115
18500 Cortijo del Agua GR 169 Wf 125
13343 Cortijo de la Guadineja CR 138 Wf 117
04838 Cortijo del Águila AL 155 Xe 122
04710 Cortijo del Águila AL 170 Xb 128
06477 Cortijo del Águila BA 133 Tf 117
11160 Cortijo del Águila CA 172 Ua 131
23489 Cortijo del Águila J 153 Wf 122
41560 Cortijo de la Habichuela SE 166 Va 125
14029 Cortijo de la Haza de la Caridad CO 150 Va 122
23748 Cortijo de la Herradura J 136 Ve 118
41420 Cortijo de la Herradura SE 149 Ud 124
29520 Cortijo de la Herriza MA 166 Vb 126
41657 Cortijo de la Higuera SE 166 Uf 126
13343 Cortijo de la Higueruela CR 138 Wf 117
23730 Cortijo de la Híncosa J 152 Wa 121
23478 Cortijo de la Hortizuela J 154 Xa 122
02312 Cortijo de la Hoya AB 139 Xc 116
30439 Cortijo de la Hoya MC 140 Yb 120
18830 Cortijo de la Hoya Alta GR 154 Xb 121
02534 Cortijo de la Hoya del Espino de Arriba AB 154 Xd 120
18120 Cortijo de la Huerta de Hoyas GR 168 Vf 127
10164 Cortijo de la Huerta del Zauzar CC 116 Td 113
29530 Cortijo de la Huertezuela MA 166 Vb 125
23320 Cortijo de la Imagen J 153 We 120
30410 Cortijo de Lairón MC 140 Xf 120
04638 Cortijo de la Jara AL 171 Ya 125
13340 Cortijo de la Jara CR 138 Xb 117
41360 Cortijo de la Jarosa SE 149 Ub 122
11390 Cortijo de la Joya CA 173 Uc 132
02486 Cortijo de la Juliana AB 139 Xe 118
30814 Cortijo de la Juncosa MC 156 Yb 122
41440 Cortijo de la Junquilla SE 149 Ud 122

14190 Cortijo de la Jurada CO 151 Vb 122
11649 Cortijo de la Laguna CA 165 Ub 127
23413 Cortijo del Alamillo J 137 Wd 120
11170 Cortijo del Álamo CA 172 Ua 130
23592 Cortijo del Álamo J 153 We 121
29340 Cortijo de la Lapa MA 166 Uf 127
23687 Cortijo de la Lastra Alta J 152 Wa 123
18698 Cortijo del Alcaíde GR 168 Wb 128
41530 Cortijo del Alcornoquillo SE 165 Ue 126
13593 Cortijo del Alhorín CR 136 Vf 117
06182 Cortijo de la Llave BA 116 Tb 114
06800 Cortijo de la Llave BA 116 Td 114
02439 Cortijo de la Lobera AB 140 Ya 118
02410 Cortijo de la Loma AB 140 Ya 118
23298 Cortijo de la Loma J 139 Xd 119
30410 Cortijo de La Loma MC 140 Xf 119
18830 Cortijo de la Losa GR 154 Xc 121
04830 Cortijo del Alto AL 155 Xf 122
04650 Cortijo de la Madroñera AL 171 Xf 125
14820 Cortijo de la Magdalena CO 151 Vc 122
29400 Cortijo de la Majada Vieja MA 174 Uf 128
10199 Cortijo de la Manca CC 116 Td 113
10291 Cortijo de la Mangada Poniente CC 99 Ua 111
41130 Cortijo de la Margazuela SE 164 Tf 126
11150 Cortijo de la Marisma CA 172 Ua 131
41130 Cortijo de la Marmolejo SE 164 Te 125
11179 Cortijo de la Mediana CA 173 Ub 131
18550 Cortijo de la Melera GR 168 Wd 124
18830 Cortijo de la Memoria GR 154 Xc 121
41710 Cortijo de la Mercadeña SE 164 Ub 126
04859 Cortijo de la Merced AL 171 Xe 122
14410 Cortijo del Americano CO 136 Vc 118
11130 Cortijo de la Mesa CA 172 Tf 130
29328 Cortijo de la Mezquita MA 166 Vb 126
06360 Cortijo de la Mimosa BA 133 Td 117
06477 Cortijo de la Mineta BA 133 Tf 117
14549 Cortijo de la Mohedana CO 150 Va 123
18800 Cortijo de la Molinera GR 154 Xa 124
41600 Cortijo de la Montera SE 165 Uc 125
14820 Cortijo de la Moyana CO 151 Vc 122
18550 Cortijo de la Muralla GR 169 Wd 124
23100 Cortijo de la Música J 152 Wc 122
13130 Cortijo de la Nava CR 136 Ve 118
41563 Cortijo de la Nava SE 166 Uf 124
23560 Cortijo de la Nevazuela J 153 Wc 123
41620 Cortijo del Ángel SE 165 Ud 125
18500 Cortijo de la Nogueruela GR 169 Wf 124
23313 Cortijo de la Olivilla Alta J 153 We 120
18270 Cortijo de la Orozca GR 167 Vf 124
04810 Cortijo de la Palma AL 170 Xe 124
11170 Cortijo de la Palmosa CA 172 Ua 130
11180 Cortijo de la Palmosa CA 173 Ub 130
14709 Cortijo de la Palmosa CO 150 Ue 123
13370 Cortijo del Apañado CR 137 Wb 116
18518 Cortijo de la Paridera GR 169 We 125

14749 Cortijo de la Parilla CO 150 Uf 122
23260 Cortijo de la Parilla J 138 Wf 119
41230 Cortijo de la Parrilla SE 149 Ua 122
14440 Cortijo de la Patricia CO 136 Vc 118
06182 Cortijo de la Peralta BA 116 Tb 114
21330 Cortijo de la Perrona H 147 Ta 122
41439 Cortijo de la Picadilla SE 150 Ue 123
06120 Cortijo de la Pila BA 132 Ta 117
06920 Cortijo de la Pipa BA 138 Ub 119
11592 Cortijo de la Plata CA 163 Ua 128
04898 Cortijo de la Polvareda AL 170 Xc 124
11320 Cortijo de la Potrica CA 173 Ud 130
14817 Cortijo de la Presa CO 167 Ve 124
18820 Cortijo de la Presa GR 155 Xd 120
23298 Cortijo de la Puerta J 139 Xc 119
06110 Cortijo de la Quintana BA 131 Sf 119
41530 Cortijo de la Rana SE 165 Ud 125
14820 Cortijo de la Ratosa CO 151 Vb 122
23250 Cortijo del Arcayán J 138 We 119
14620 Cortijo de la Redona CO 151 Vd 121
14029 Cortijo de la Reina CO 150 Va 122
14911 Cortijo de la Reina CO 166 Vc 125
29540 Cortijo de la Rejanada MA 166 Vb 127
41640 Cortijo de la Romera SE 165 Ue 125
06910 Cortijo del Arrendamiento BA 134 Uc 119
06800 Cortijo del Arroyo del Ciervo BA 116 Tc 114
14859 Cortijo del Arroyuelo CO 151 Ve 122
23485 Cortijo de las Acebadillas J 154 Xa 122
30412 Cortijo de las Aguazaderas MC 155 Xf 121
13343 Cortijo de las Águilas CR 138 We 118
41640 Cortijo de las Aguililias SE 166 Uf 125
11310 Cortijo de las Aguzaderas CA 173 Ue 131
14549 Cortijo de la Saladilla CO 150 Va 123
41640 Cortijo de la Saladilla SE 165 Ue 125
29540 Cortijo de las Albinas MA 166 Vb 126
30413 Cortijo de las Almenas MC 155 Xe 121
23479 Cortijo de la Salobreja J 153 Wf 121
18816 Cortijo de la Saludada GR 154 Xb 121
23380 Cortijo de las Anchuricas J 139 Xc 118
18820 Cortijo de las Ánimas GR 155 Xd 121
18120 Cortijo de las Ánimas GR 168 Wa 127
23569 Cortijo de las Ánimas J 153 Wd 123
23291 Cortijo de las Ánimas J 154 Xb 120
11180 Cortijo de las Arenas CA 173 Ub 130
29340 Cortijo de las Arenas MA 166 Uf 127
35613 Cortijo de la Sargenta GC 183 Ma 177
02139 Cortijo de la Sarguilla AB 140 Xf 117
41388 Cortijo de Las Barracas SE 149 Uc 121
41804 Cortijo de las Bartolas SE 148 Tf 124
23311 Cortijo de las Bonas J 154 Xa 121
41380 Cortijo de las Campanillas SE 149 Ub 121
18816 Cortijo de las Canalejas GR 154 Xb 121
13343 Cortijo de las Cañadas CR 138 Wf 118
41450 Cortijo de las Cárdenas SE 149 Uc 121
18891 Cortijo de las Casicas GR 154 Xc 123

23006 Cortijo de las Casillas J 152 Wa 121
18812 Cortijo de las Chirlatas GR 154 Xa 124
13130 Cortijo de las Colladillas CR 136 Ve 118
29395 Cortijo de las Cruces MA 166 Uf 126
06939 Cortijo de las Cruzadas BA 134 Ub 118
30890 Cortijo de las Cuestas MC 155 Ya 123
04838 Cortijo de las Cuevas AL 155 Xe 122
21210 Cortijo de las Dehesillas H 148 Td 122
06443 Cortijo de las Desgracias BA 134 Ua 118
18566 Cortijo de las Encebras GR 152 Wb 124
18570 Cortijo de las Encinillas GR 168 Wc 124
29533 Cortijo de la Serafina MA 166 Vb 125
04768 Cortijo de las Eras AL 169 Wf 127
06106 Cortijo de la Sesera BA 131 Se 117
23540 Cortijo de las Fuentes J 153 Wc 122
11650 Cortijo de las Gateras CA 165 Uc 127
18270 Cortijo de las Grañanas GR 167 Vf 124
11392 Cortijo de las Habas CA 173 Ub 131
18816 Cortijo de las Hazadillas GR 154 Xb 121
23294 Cortijo de las Hoyas J 139 Xc 119
23485 Cortijo de las Hoyas J 154 Xa 122
13326 Cortijo de las Huebras CR 138 Xa 117
14540 Cortijo de la Sierrezuela CO 150 Vb 122
41560 Cortijo de la Sierrezuela SE 164 Va 125
23190 Cortijo de la Sima J 152 Wb 122
29327 Cortijo de la Sima MA 166 Va 127
23313 Cortijo de las Irijuelas J 153 Wf 120
41710 Cortijo de las Jaretas SE 165 Uc 127
23469 Cortijo de las Laderas J 153 Wf 121
06110 Cortijo de las Lapas BA 131 Se 118
10194 Cortijo de las Lapas CC 98 Tf 110
13343 Cortijo de las Loberas CR 138 Xa 117
04694 Cortijo de las Lomas AL 155 Ya 124
29200 Cortijo de las Lomas MA 167 Vd 126
18820 Cortijo de las Lomas de Arriba GR 155 Xe 121
18220 Cortijo de las Mercedes GR 168 Wc 124
10530 Cortijo de las Mesas CC 98 Tf 110
10250 Cortijo de las Mesas CC 99 Uc 111
18451 Cortijo de las Minas GR 169 We 126
06183 Cortijo de las Monjas BA 116 Tb 115
18891 Cortijo de las Monjas GR 154 Xc 124
29540 Cortijo de las Monjas MA 166 Vb 126
41640 Cortijo de las Mozas SE 166 Uf 125
18260 Cortijo de las Navas SE 168 Wa 124
13332 Cortijo de las Nogueras CR 122 Xa 115
18564 Cortijo de las Nogueras GR 168 Wb 124
23150 Cortijo de la Solana J 152 Wa 123
29327 Cortijo de la Soterraña MA 166 Va 127
23650 Cortijo de las Pedruscosas J 152 Wa 122
11648 Cortijo de las Peñas CA 163 Ua 127
18816 Cortijo de las Peñuelas GR 154 Xa 122
41719 Cortijo de las Peñuelas SE 164 Ua 126
29540 Cortijo de las Perdices MA 166 Vc 127
10291 Cortijo de las Pila CC 99 Tf 111
29400 Cortijo de las Pilas MA 166 Uf 128

29570 Cortijo de las Proveedoras MA 166 Vc 128
06443 Cortijo de las Provincias BA 134 Ub 118
10291 Cortijo de las Puertas CC 99 Ua 111
02449 Cortijo de las Ramblas AB 140 Xf 118
02436 Cortijo de las Ramblas AB 140 Ya 118
18820 Cortijo de las Ramblas GR 155 Xd 120
41760 Cortijo de las Reyertas SE 165 Uc 127
18816 Cortijo de las Tabernillas GR 154 Xb 121
11579 Cortijo de la Suara CA 172 Ua 129
41420 Cortijo de la Suerte SE 150 Ue 124
41400 Cortijo de la Suerte SE 150 Uf 123
14549 Cortijo de las Uvadas CO 150 Vb 123
18561 Cortijo de las Vacas GR 153 Wd 123
06182 Cortijo de las Valencianas BA 116 Tb 114
14840 Cortijo de las Vegas CO 151 Vc 123
14440 Cortijo de las Veguillas CO 136 Vc 118
29250 Cortijo de las Ventanas MA 166 Vc 126
14547 Cortijo de las Ventas CO 150 Va 123
06380 Cortijo de las Veranas BA 132 Tb 118
41429 Cortijo de las Yeguas SE 149 Ud 123
23265 Cortijo de la Tablilla J 138 Wf 118
18500 Cortijo de la Tala GR 169 Wf 125
23592 Cortijo del Atanor J 153 Wd 122
18858 Cortijo de la Tejera GR 154 Xd 122
04830 Cortijo de la Tendera AL 155 Xf 122
02536 Cortijo de la Toba AB 139 Xe 119
06380 Cortijo de la Torre BA 132 Tb 119
23760 Cortijo de la Torre J 152 Vf 121
02486 Cortijo de la Torre de Raspilla AB 139 Xd 118
41640 Cortijo de la Turquilla SE 166 Uf 124
23569 Cortijo de la Umbría J 153 We 123
23591 Cortijo de la Urraca J 153 We 122
04769 Cortijo de la Vega AL 169 Wf 127
14540 Cortijo de la Vega CO 150 Vb 123
13343 Cortijo de la Vega CR 138 Xa 117
13341 Cortijo de la Vega CR 138 Xa 117
23230 Cortijo de la Ventilla J 138 Wd 120
29566 Cortijo de la Ventilla MA 166 Va 128
14280 Cortijo de la Ventosa CO 135 Uf 117
10194 Cortijo de la Ventosilla CC 98 Tf 111
14820 Cortijo de la Ventosilla CO 151 Vc 122
41719 Cortijo de la Ventosilla SE 164 Ub 126
18120 Cortijo de la Vera GR 168 Vf 126
14709 Cortijo de la Verduga CO 150 Ud 123
30410 Cortijo de la Vereda MC 155 Ya 120
29420 Cortijo de la Víbora Baja MA 166 Va 128
10200 Cortijo de la Viña CC 117 Ua 112
29100 Cortijo de la Viuda MA 175 Vb 128
41500 Cortijo de la Viuda SE 164 Ub 125
14512 Cortijo de la Yegüeriza CO 166 Vb 124
11400 Cortijo de la Zarpa CA 164 Tf 128
14820 Cortijo de la Zarza CO 151 Vb 122
18820 Cortijo de la Zarza GR 155 Xe 121
11648 Cortijo de la Zorrilla CA 164 Ua 127
11630 Cortijo de la Zorrilla CA 164 Ub 128

02434 Cortijo del Baire AB
140 Xe 119
06195 Cortijo del Barbudo BA
116 Tb 116
18659 Cortijo del Barranco del Agua
GR 168 Wc 127
04480 Cortijo del Barranco de los
Caballos AL 169 Xa 127
10291 Cortijo del Barranquillo CC
99 Ua 111
41530 Cortijo del Barro SE
165 Uc 126
02484 Cortijo del Batán AB
139 Xd 119
18816 Cortijo del Batán GR
154 Xb 122
14413 Cortijo del Berrocal CO
135 Vb 118
41563 Cortijo del Borreguero SE
150 Uf 124
18858 Cortijo del Bosque GR
154 Xd 123
14749 Cortijo del Bramadero Bajo CO
150 Ue 122
21390 Cortijo del Bravo H 147 Ta 120
11170 Cortijo del Brecial CA
172 Ua 130
11400 Cortijo del Bujón CA
163 Tf 128
13592 Cortijo del Burcio CR
137 Wa 117
18567 Cortijo del Burgalés GR
153 Wc 123
06380 Cortijo del Caballero Alto BA
132 Ta 119
06519 Cortijo del Cabila BA
115 Sf 114
14549 Cortijo del Calerón Bajo CO
150 Va 123
02430 Cortijo del Campillo AB
140 Ya 118
04810 Cortijo del Campillo AL
155 Xd 124
23479 Cortijo del Cantalar J
154 Xa 121
29540 Cortijo del Cañaveralejo MA
166 Vb 126
23488 Cortijo del Capellán J
153 We 122
18800 Cortijo del Capricho GR
154 Xb 124
41410 Cortijo del Caracolillo SE
165 Uc 125
18870 Cortijo del Carcajal GR
169 Xa 124
18310 Cortijo del Cárdador GR
167 Vf 126
13594 Cortijo del Cardeal CR
137 Vf 118
10530 Cortijo del Cardoso CC
98 Tf 110
14029 Cortijo del Carmen CO
151 Vd 121
13344 Cortijo del Carraquillo CR
138 We 117
10292 Cortijo del Carrascal CC
99 Ub 111
10161 Cortijo del Castillejo CC
117 Tf 114
23130 Cortijo del Castillo J
152 Wc 123
11180 Cortijo del Cermeño CA
173 Ub 130
41860 Cortijo del Chamorro SE
148 Tf 124
06476 Cortijo del Chaparral BA
133 Tf 116
14940 Cortijo del Chaparral CO
151 Vd 123
41620 Cortijo del Charco SE
165 Ue 125
14940 Cortijo del Charcón CO
151 Vd 123
18128 Cortijo del Chato GR
167 Ve 126
18192 Cortijo del Chato GR
168 Wd 125
04629 Cortijo del Chavo AL
171 Ya 125
41410 Cortijo del Chiste SE
149 Uc 124
18568 Cortijo del Chopo GR
153 Wd 124
29540 Cortijo del Chopo MA
166 Vb 127
14800 Cortijo del Cojo Serrano CO
167 Ve 124
02489 Cortijo del Collado AB
139 Xd 119
30420 Cortijo del Collado MC
140 Yb 118
02436 Cortijo del Collado Alto AB
140 Ya 118
02485 Cortijo del Collado de
Carrasco AB 139 Xd 118
02410 Cortijo del Collado del Rayo
AB 140 Ya 117
18820 Cortijo del Collado Serrano GR
154 Xd 120

11170 Cortijo del Colorado CA
172 Ua 130
18820 Cortijo del Condado GR
154 Xd 121
18515 Cortijo del Conejo GR
153 We 124
18880 Cortijo del Conejo GR
169 Wf 124
14900 Cortijo del Corchado CO
167 Vd 125
41710 Cortijo del Corcovado SE
165 Ub 126
23592 Cortijo del Coronel J
153 We 121
18816 Cortijo del Corralón GR
154 Xb 121
23610 Cortijo del Coto J 152 Wa 122
14270 Cortijo del Cuartanero CO
135 Uf 118
41420 Cortijo del Cuarto de la Casa
SE 149 Ud 123
41400 Cortijo del Cucarón SE
150 Uf 123
04130 Cortijo del Cuco AL
170 Xd 127
21540 Cortijo del Cuco H 161 Se 124
41470 Cortijo del Cuervo SE
149 Ud 122
23240 Cortijo del Culebrón J
138 Wd 119
06196 Cortijo del Cura BA
132 Tc 116
06110 Cortijo del Cura Lechero BA
131 Sf 118
04549 Cortijo del Cura Morales AL
170 Xc 125
18820 Cortijo del Curica GR
154 Xd 121
13331 Cortijo del Curilla CR
122 Xb 116
29754 Cortijo del Daire MA
168 Wa 127
23469 Cortijo del Desillo J
153 We 121
30814 Cortijo del Dorado de Arriba
MC 156 Yb 122
11170 Cortijo del Dorapila CA
172 Ua 130
14840 Cortijo del Duende CO
151 Vc 123
14511 Cortijo del Duque CO
167 Vc 124
18127 Cortijo del Duro GR
168 Wb 127
23750 Cortijo del Empalme J
151 Vf 121
14820 Cortijo del Encineño CO
151 Vc 122
06182 Cortijo de León BA
116 Tb 114
13370 Cortijo de León CR
137 Wc 117
23250 Cortijo de Lero J 138 We 119
18830 Cortijo del Escribano GR
154 Xc 121
23410 Cortijo del Escribano J
138 We 120
18564 Cortijo del Escúzar GR
168 Wb 124
41479 Cortijo del Esparragal SE
149 Ud 122
41500 Cortijo del Estanquero SE
163 Ub 125
18858 Cortijo del Fayo GR
155 Xe 122
18560 Cortijo del Fistel GR
153 Wd 124
29210 Cortijo del Fraile MA
167 Vd 125
14530 Cortijo del Frenil CO
151 Vb 122
18859 Cortijo del Gallinero GR
154 Xd 123
18891 Cortijo del Gatal GR
154 Xc 123
18830 Cortijo del Girón GR
154 Xc 121
11158 Cortijo del Grullo CA
172 Ua 130
41620 Cortijo del Grullo SE
165 Ud 124
06370 Cortijo del Guarda BA
132 Tc 118
11160 Cortijo del Guarda CA
172 Ua 131
21240 Cortijo del Hornito H
147 Ta 120
18814 Cortijo del Horno GR
154 Xb 122
04100 Cortijo del Hualí Nuevo AL
170 Xe 127
04210 Cortijo del Humo AL
171 Xf 127
14920 Cortijo del Improviso CO
151 Vb 123
41640 Cortijo del Inglés SE
166 Uf 125
06007 Cortijo de Liviana BA
116 Ta 115
23569 Cortijo del Jaral J 153 Wd 122

14029 Cortijo del Jarillo CO
151 Vc 121
41019 Cortijo del Judío SE
148 Ua 124
23240 Cortijo del Juncal J
138 We 120
41566 Cortijo del Juncarejo SE
166 Va 125
41740 Cortijo del Labrador SE
164 Tf 127
23489 Cortijo del Lagar J 153 Wf 121
41500 Cortijo de Llamas SE
164 Ub 125
44340 Cortijo de Llano TE 90 Ye 103
30440 Cortijo del Leonés MC
140 Yb 119
04830 Cortijo del Llano AL
155 Xf 121
30890 Cortijo del Llano MC
155 Ya 122
11170 Cortijo del Lobo CA
172 Tf 130
18370 Cortijo del Lobo GR
168 Wa 126
18859 Cortijo del Madroñal GR
154 Xd 123
21239 Cortijo del Majadal H
147 Ta 121
18160 Cortijo del Manantial GR
169 Wd 125
23600 Cortijo del Manchego J
152 Vf 122
23214 Cortijo del Manto J
137 Wb 117
23560 Cortijo del Manzanares J
153 Wd 123
18560 Cortijo del Mármel GR
153 Wd 123
41550 Cortijo del Marqués SE
166 Va 125
23747 Cortijo del Marqués de la
Merced J 152 Vf 120
23006 Cortijo del Marqués de Verdejo
J 152 Wb 122
21500 Cortijo del Matiloso H
147 Sf 124
11178 Cortijo del Médico CA
173 Ua 129
18260 Cortijo del Menchón GR
168 Wa 124
14940 Cortijo del Mingarrón CO
151 Vc 124
41400 Cortijo del Mochalejo SE
150 Ue 123
06840 Cortijo del Mochuelo BA
133 Te 116
30890 Cortijo del Monie MC
155 Xf 122
41400 Cortijo del Montecillo SE
150 Va 123
18811 Cortijo del Moreno GR
154 Xa 122
41620 Cortijo del Morisco SE
165 Ud 125
18816 Cortijo del Moro GR
154 Xb 121
29491 Cortijo del Moro MA
173 Ue 129
14660 Cortijo del Morrón CO
151 Ve 121
18816 Cortijo del Nacimiento GR
154 Xb 121
29520 Cortijo del Navazo MA
166 Vb 126
04825 Cortijo del Nebral AL
155 Xe 123
18860 Cortijo del Negratín GR
153 Xa 123
11650 Cortijo del Novillero CA
165 Uc 127
04650 Cortijo del Olallo AL
171 Xf 125
23294 Cortijo del Olivanco J
139 Xd 119
06195 Cortijo del Olivar BA
116 Tb 116
13248 Cortijo del Olmo CR
122 Wf 115
23569 Cortijo de Lomana J
153 Wd 123
14445 Cortijo del Oreganal CO
136 Ve 118
23265 Cortijo de Lorente J
138 Wf 118
04829 Cortijo de los Adanes AL
155 Xf 122
41710 Cortijo de los Aguaciles Altos
SE 164 Ub 127
30890 Cortijo de los Agustinos MC
155 Ya 123
30410 Cortijo de los Álamos MC
140 Ya 119
04830 Cortijo de los Almagreros AL
155 Xf 121
06182 Cortijo de los Almorchones BA
116 Ta 114
04728 Cortijo de los Amates AL
170 Xb 127
18511 Cortijo de los Andaluces GR
169 Wf 125

04131 Cortijo de los Andújares AL
170 Xe 127
13779 Cortijo de los Aparceros CR
137 Wb 117
29330 Cortijo de los Arcos MA
166 Va 126
23616 Cortijo de los Ares J
152 Wa 123
14511 Cortijo de los Ávalos CO
166 Vc 124
30413 Cortijo de los Ballesteros MC
155 Xe 120
13330 Cortijo de los Baños CR
139 Xb 117
18858 Cortijo de los Barrancos GR
155 Xd 123
13343 Cortijo de los Barrenas CR
138 We 117
11150 Cortijo de los Benitos del Lomo
CA 172 Tf 131
18820 Cortijo de los Bequerones GR
154 Xd 122
18500 Cortijo de los Bernabeles GR
169 Wf 125
04825 Cortijo de los Blancos AL
155 Xe 123
29451 Cortijo de los Blanquizales MA
174 Uf 129
23485 Cortijo de los Blaquillos J
154 Xa 122
30890 Cortijo de los Bonillos MC
155 Ya 123
06477 Cortijo de los Calerizos BA
133 Tf 116
18830 Cortijo de los Cánovas GR
154 Xb 121
13342 Cortijo de los Carboneros CR
138 Xa 117
41370 Cortijo de los Cardales SE
149 Ub 121
14447 Cortijo de los Carreteros CO
136 Vd 119
14911 Cortijo de los Castillas CO
167 Vc 124
04715 Cortijo de los Cerilios AL
169 Xb 128
04830 Cortijo de los Cerricos AL
155 Xe 122
18820 Cortijo de los Cerros de Abajo
GR 155 Xe 121
29530 Cortijo de los Chacones MA
166 Vb 125
11179 Cortijo de los Charcones CA
172 Ua 131
04825 Cortijo de los Chaveses AL
155 Xe 123
23193 Cortijo de los Ciervos J
152 Wc 123
06476 Cortijo de los Codrios BA
133 Te 116
23538 Cortijo de los Cornetales J
153 Wd 122
18550 Cortijo de los Diablos GR
168 Wc 124
23320 Cortijo de los Elementos J
153 We 120
18566 Cortijo de los Espinares GR
152 Wc 124
23592 Cortijo de los Fierrales J
153 We 122
14440 Cortijo de los Frailes CO
136 Vc 119
23590 Cortijo de los Frailes J
153 We 122
23297 Cortijo de los Galdones J
139 Xc 119
41440 Cortijo de los Gallos SE
149 Uc 123
06380 Cortijo de los Galvanes BA
132 Ta 119
18816 Cortijo de los Garandinos GR
154 Xb 122
18270 Cortijo de los Gitanos GR
168 Wa 124
06498 Cortijo de los Granadinos BA
116 Tc 116
02489 Cortijo de los Habares y de
Silvestre AB 139 Xd 119
23479 Cortijo de los Hoyos de Plaza
J 153 Xa 121
13326 Cortijo de los Hoyuelos CR
138 Xa 116
11580 Cortijo de los Isletes CA
172 Ua 129
04830 Cortijo de los Jiménez AL
155 Xf 122
30890 Cortijo de los Jordanes MC
155 Ya 123
14600 Cortijo de los Lázaros CO
136 Vd 119
41130 Cortijo de los Leones SE
163 Tf 126
11648 Cortijo de los Llanos CA
164 Ub 127
14460 Cortijo de los Llanos CO
135 Va 118
14857 Cortijo de los Llanos CO
151 Vd 123
18840 Cortijo de los Llanos GR
154 Xc 122

18120 Cortijo de los Llanos GR
168 Wa 126
02125 Cortijo de los Luisos AB
140 Xf 117
21580 Cortijo de los Madroñuelos H
147 Sf 122
21207 Cortijo de los Majalejos H
147 Tc 122
04813 Cortijo de los Marianes AL
155 Xf 124
18820 Cortijo de los Mirabetes GR
154 Xc 121
14820 Cortijo de los Montecitos CO
151 Vc 121
23529 Cortijo de los Montoros J
153 Wc 121
06840 Cortijo de los Morales BA
133 Te 116
30890 Cortijo de los Morales MC
155 Ya 122
18820 Cortijo de los Morenos GR
155 Xd 121
29230 Cortijo de los Navazos MA
167 Vc 127
41460 Cortijo de los Nogalillos SE
149 Ud 121
06476 Cortijo de los Novillos BA
133 Te 116
18530 Cortijo de los Olivares GR
153 We 123
41150 Cortijo de los Olivillos SE
164 Tf 125
11630 Cortijo de los Olivos CA
163 Ua 127
13248 Cortijo de los Palacios CR
122 Wf 116
11149 Cortijo de los Palominos CA
172 Tf 131
18270 Cortijo de los Palominos GR
168 Wa 124
30420 Cortijo de los Panes MC
140 Yc 119
13411 Cortijo de los Peñoncillos CR
119 Vb 115
04113 Cortijo de los Pescadores AL
171 Xe 127
23369 Cortijo de los Pesebres J
138 Xb 118
11595 Cortijo de los Piletas CA
172 Ua 129
11170 Cortijo de los Portichuelos CA
172 Ua 130
11180 Cortijo de los Poyales CA
173 Ub 130
04825 Cortijo de los Prades AL
155 Xd 123
14600 Cortijo de los Prados CO
151 Vd 121
23120 Cortijo de los Prados J
153 Wc 122
02484 Cortijo de los Prados Altos AB
139 Xd 118
23592 Cortijo de los Propios J
153 We 121
06228 Cortijo de los Puertos BA
133 Ua 117
18860 Cortijo de los Puntales GR
154 Xa 124
10200 Cortijo de los Quintos de San
Pedro CC 117 Ua 112
18820 Cortijo de los Ratones GR
155 Xd 121
18830 Cortijo de los Rayones GR
154 Xc 121
14660 Cortijo de los Rubios CO
151 Ve 121
02512 Cortijo de los Ruices AB
141 Yc 116
41130 Cortijo de los Sartenejales SE
163 Tf 125
14859 Cortijo de los Sercanos CO
151 Vd 122
04830 Cortijo de los Serranos AL
155 Xe 121
02130 Cortijo de los Suancias AB
139 Xe 117
18814 Cortijo de los Términos GR
154 Xb 123
14729 Cortijo de los Trances CO
150 Uf 122
04440 Cortijo de los Trazas AL
170 Xb 126
23320 Cortijo de los Vadillos J
153 We 120
41500 Cortijo de los Valles SE
164 Ub 125
10252 Cortijo de los Vallespedros CC
99 Ub 111
04825 Cortijo de los Venteos AL
155 Xe 123
23649 Cortijo de los Yesos J
152 Wa 122
11691 Cortijo de los Zapateros CA
165 Ue 127
14550 Cortijo de los Zapateros CO
151 Vb 123
30410 Cortijo del Paletón MC
140 Xf 120
29250 Cortijo del Palomar MA
166 Vc 126

23340 Cortijo del Palomo J 138 Xa 118
18539 Cortijo del Parador GR 153 Wf 123
18560 Cortijo del Paulejo GR 153 Wd 123
18314 Cortijo del Pecho de la Mata GR 167 Ve 126
30810 Cortijo del Peñón MC 155 Ya 121
04830 Cortijo del Peral AL 155 Xf 122
18500 Cortijo del Perro GR 169 Wf 125
41560 Cortijo del Perulero SE 166 Va 124
23488 Cortijo del Pilón J 153 We 122
04825 Cortijo del Pinar AL 155 Xe 122
11370 Cortijo del Pino CA 173 Ud 131
14900 Cortijo del Pleito CO 167 Vd 125
04230 Cortijo del Pocico AL 170 Xc 127
23380 Cortijo del Pocino J 139 Xc 118
18192 Cortijo del Polvorista GR 168 Wd 125
18512 Cortijo del Portero GR 169 Wf 125
06195 Cortijo del Portugués BA 116 Tb 116
06427 Cortijo del Postuero BA 134 Ud 117
06209 Cortijo del Potosí BA 132 Tc 116
23479 Cortijo del Poyo J 154 Xa 121
18840 Cortijo del Pozo GR 154 Xc 122
04117 Cortijo del Pozo de Gálvez AL 171 Xe 128
23615 Cortijo del Pozo de la Orden J 152 Ve 122
41400 Cortijo del Prado SE 150 Va 123
41440 Cortijo del Prato SE 149 Ud 123
18810 Cortijo del Puente GR 154 Xb 124
02459 Cortijo del Puerto AB 139 Xd 118
18314 Cortijo del Ranchuelo GR 167 Vf 126
13592 Cortijo del Rasino CR 136 Vf 117
10291 Cortijo del Raso CC 99 Tf 111
29320 Cortijo del Ratero MA 166 Va 126
29250 Cortijo del Realengo MA 167 Vc 125
23478 Cortijo del Recado J 154 Xb 120
18818 Cortijo del Rey GR 154 Xb 122
18511 Cortijo del Rey GR 169 Wf 125
30410 Cortijo del Rey MC 140 Xf 120
06012 Cortijo del Rincón BA 116 Sf 115
06106 Cortijo del Rincón BA 131 Se 117
06193 Cortijo del Rincón de Gila BA 116 Ta 114
41530 Cortijo del Risquillo SE 165 Ud 126
11693 Cortijo del Romeral CA 166 Uf 127
18840 Cortijo del Romo GR 154 Xc 122
23120 Cortijo del Rompedizo J 153 Wc 122
23485 Cortijo del Rubiel J 153 Xa 122
18564 Cortijo del Saladillo GR 152 Wb 124
18820 Cortijo del Saladillo GR 155 Xd 121
23539 Cortijo del Santo J 153 Wd 121
41479 Cortijo del Saucejo SE 149 Ud 121
41400 Cortijo del Segador SE 150 Uf 123
14549 Cortijo del Serrano CO 150 Vb 123
06330 Cortijo del Sesmo BA 133 Td 119
18891 Cortijo del Sillero GR 154 Xc 123
18512 Cortijo del Sobrestante GR 169 Wf 125
10194 Cortijo del Sotillo CC 98 Te 110
14913 Cortijo del Soto CO 167 Vc 125
41620 Cortijo del Soto SE 165 Ud 125
23748 Cortijo del Tagarrillar J 136 Ve 118

23485 Cortijo del Talancar J 154 Xa 122
23213 Cortijo del Tamara J 137 Wc 119
04830 Cortijo del Tambor AL 155 Xf 122
14447 Cortijo del Templado CO 136 Vd 119
06939 Cortijo del Tío Piche BA 133 Ua 118
41410 Cortijo del Toril SE 149 Uc 123
21540 Cortijo del Toril Nuevo H 146 Se 124
41620 Cortijo del Tortolero SE 165 Ud 124
41727 Cortijo del Torviscal SE 164 Ua 126
41450 Cortijo del Travieso SE 149 Uc 122
18515 Cortijo del Tuerto GR 169 We 124
18812 Cortijo del Túnel GR 154 Xa 124
23260 Cortijo de Lucas J 138 Wf 119
14447 Cortijo de Lucas Muraño CO 136 Vd 119
29471 Cortijo de Lucía MA 166 Va 127
14820 Cortijo de Luis Díaz CO 151 Vc 121
23479 Cortijo de Vadillo de Castril J 154 Xa 121
23713 Cortijo del Vado J 137 Wc 120
02485 Cortijo del Vado de Tus AB 139 Xd 118
23569 Cortijo del Val J 153 Wd 123
04830 Cortijo del Valenciano AL 155 Xe 122
11560 Cortijo del Ventu CA 164 Te 127
41400 Cortijo del Villar SE 166 Uf 124
41560 Cortijo del Villar SE 166 Va 125
11170 Cortijo del Vínculo CA 172 Ua 130
41980 Cortijo del Vizcaíno SE 148 Tf 124
23590 Cortijo del Vizco J 153 We 122
11170 Cortijo del Yeso CA 172 Ua 130
30890 Cortijo del Zarzalico MC 155 Ya 123
02434 Cortijo de Macalones AB 140 Xf 118
11180 Cortijo de Macote CA 173 Ub 130
06182 Cortijo de Madroño BA 116 Tb 115
14480 Cortijo de Maestro CO 135 Va 119
41710 Cortijo de Majalquivir SE 165 Ub 126
14820 Cortijo de Malabrigo CO 151 Vb 122
18810 Cortijo de Malagón GR 154 Xb 123
18859 Cortijo de Malagón GR 154 Xd 123
41610 Cortijo de Malajuncia SE 165 Uc 125
18830 Cortijo de Malaño GR 154 Xd 121
41429 Cortijo de Mamé SE 149 Ud 123
14270 Cortijo de Mano Soberbia CO 135 Uf 117
11650 Cortijo de Marcegoso CA 165 Ub 127
18870 Cortijo de Marchales GR 169 Xa 124
41500 Cortijo de Marchamorón SE 165 Ub 125
11207 Cortijo de Marchenilla CA 175 Ud 132
06380 Cortijo de Marianes BA 132 Tb 118
41420 Cortijo de Marifernández SE 150 Ud 123
23400 Cortijo de Marimingo J 153 Wd 121
18564 Cortijo de Marino Vega GR 152 Wc 124
23130 Cortijo de Marisánchez J 152 Wc 123
10370 Cortijo de Marisancho CC 99 Uc 111
23750 Cortijo de Marmolejo J 151 Vf 121
06800 Cortijo de Márquez BA 116 Tc 115
18511 Cortijo de Marraclán GR 169 Xa 125
41600 Cortijo de Martinazo SE 165 Uc 125
18830 Cortijo de Masegosa GR 154 Xc 121
13379 Cortijo de Mata CR 137 Wa 117

41500 Cortijo de Matallana SE 165 Ub 125
18891 Cortijo de Mazarra GR 153 Xc 123
06800 Cortijo de Mazas BA 116 Tc 116
18515 Cortijo de Mecina GR 169 We 124
06380 Cortijo de Media Torre BA 132 Ta 119
41410 Cortijo de Mejía SE 149 Uc 123
14850 Cortijo de Melenas CO 151 Vd 122
41740 Cortijo de Melendo SE 163 Tf 127
18538 Cortijo de Melerillas GR 153 Wf 123
13333 Cortijo de Melgarejo CR 122 Wf 116
23009 Cortijo de Mendo J 152 Wb 122
41740 Cortijo de Micones SE 163 Tf 127
14859 Cortijo de Mirabuenos CO 151 Ve 122
14709 Cortijo de Miravalles CO 150 Ud 123
41440 Cortijo de Mochales SE 149 Uc 123
10199 Cortijo de Moheda CC 116 Tc 113
29314 Cortijo de Mola MA 167 Vd 126
41450 Cortijo de Molgado SE 149 Uc 122
41320 Cortijo de Monge SE 149 Ua 123
23260 Cortijo de Monsálvez J 138 Wf 119
23487 Cortijo de Montalvo J 154 Wf 123
14820 Cortijo de Montefrío Alto CO 151 Vc 122
41410 Cortijo de Montenegro SE 165 Uc 124
41727 Cortijo de Montera SE 163 Ua 126
41400 Cortijo de Montero SE 150 Uf 124
41740 Cortijo de Monterroja SE 163 Tf 127
30613 Cortijo de Mortereta MC 156 Yd 120
23760 Cortijo de Mudapelos J 152 Vf 121
11693 Cortijo de Munición CA 165 Ue 127
13760 Cortijo de Muñoz CR 137 Wd 118
41410 Cortijo de Murillo SE 149 Uc 119
18515 Cortijo de Muros GR 153 Wf 124
29650 Cortijo de Naela MA 175 Vb 129
23313 Cortijo de Narváez J 153 Wf 120
41658 Cortijo de Navacerrada SE 166 Va 126
41530 Cortijo de Nava Grande SE 165 Uc 126
14430 Cortijo de Navajuncosa CO 151 Vc 120
13370 Cortijo de Navalaencina CR 137 Wb 117
21270 Cortijo de Navarredonda H 148 Td 121
02434 Cortijo de Navarro AB 140 Xe 121
29451 Cortijo de Navarro MA 174 Uf 128
23690 Cortijo de Navasequilla J 152 Wb 124
29452 Cortijo de Navazo MA 174 Ue 128
11180 Cortijo de Nobles CA 173 Ub 129
18329 Cortijo de Noniles GR 168 Wb 126
14029 Cortijo de Nora del Cojo CO 151 Vd 121
41410 Cortijo de Nuestra Señora del Socorro SE 149 Ub 124
41540 Cortijo de Obra Pía SE 165 Ue 125
04560 Cortijo de Ochotorena AL 170 Xc 127
41530 Cortijo de Ojuelo SE 165 Uc 125
18817 Cortijo de Onofre GR 154 Xb 123
18515 Cortijo de Onrrubia GR 153 We 124
18891 Cortijo de Orgalla GR 154 Xd 123
23590 Cortijo de Pablo J 153 We 122
14449 Cortijo de Paco El Perito CR 136 Vd 118

18816 Cortijo de Pacos GR 154 Xb 122
23590 Cortijo de Pajares J 153 We 123
29570 Cortijo de Pajares MA 175 Vb 128
11580 Cortijo de Pajarrete CA 173 Ub 129
11180 Cortijo de Palmitoso CA 173 Ub 129
06195 Cortijo de Palomarejo BA 116 Tb 116
23600 Cortijo de Panduro J 152 Vf 122
10194 Cortijo de Parapuños CC 98 Te 111
06110 Cortijo de Paricia BA 131 Se 119
23298 Cortijo de Parralejo J 139 Xc 119
30410 Cortijo de Parriel MC 140 Xf 120
06713 Cortijo de Pasarón BA 118 Uc 114
06960 Cortijo de Pata Caballo BA 133 Ua 119
11179 Cortijo de Pedregosillo CA 173 Ua 130
14447 Cortijo de Pedro Abad CO 136 Vc 119
14870 Cortijo de Pedro Baeza CO 151 Vd 123
29395 Cortijo de Pedro Bueno MA 166 Uf 127
23250 Cortijo de Pedro Manjón J 138 We 119
02139 Cortijo de Pedrosa AB 140 Xe 117
18891 Cortijo de Pedrosa GR 154 Xc 123
23539 Cortijo de Pelotoso J 153 Wc 121
18568 Cortijo de Penate GR 168 Wd 124
41560 Cortijo de Peña SE 166 Vb 125
18564 Cortijo de Peñalver GR 152 Wb 124
04750 Cortijo de Peñas Negras AL 169 Xb 128
29329 Cortijo de Peñuela MA 166 Va 126
23479 Cortijo de Peñuelas J 154 Xa 121
41600 Cortijo de Perafrán SE 165 Uc 125
23006 Cortijo de Perulera J 152 Wb 122
35211 Cortijo de Pichón GC 184 Kd 181
14445 Cortijo de Piedra Empinada CO 136 Ve 119
18800 Cortijo de Piedras Rodadas GR 169 Xa 124
18830 Cortijo de Pinar la Vidriera GR 154 Xc 120
13592 Cortijo de Pinchino CR 137 Wa 118
18127 Cortijo de Pincho GR 168 Wb 127
41730 Cortijo de Pinilla SE 164 Ua 127
18891 Cortijo de Pizarro GR 154 Xd 123
11170 Cortijo de Pocasangre CA 172 Ua 130
23150 Cortijo de Pocopán J 152 Wb 123
23460 Cortijo de Porcel J 153 Wf 121
23392 Cortijo de Portilles J 139 Xb 118
18562 Cortijo de Pozo Alto GR 169 Wd 124
41530 Cortijo de Pozo del Rosal SE 165 Ud 126
14660 Cortijo de Pozodulce CO 151 Vd 122
06290 Cortijo de Pozo Herrera BA 133 Tf 119
14550 Cortijo de Pozotechado CO 151 Vc 123
11180 Cortijo de Pradillo Alto CA 173 Ub 130
02312 Cortijo de Pradogallo AB 139 Xc 117
30812 Cortijo de Prado Jérez MC 155 Ya 121
18830 Cortijo de Prado Puerco GR 154 Xc 120
06475 Cortijo de Prín BA 134 Ua 117
11649 Cortijo de Puertollano CA 165 Ub 127
30413 Cortijo de Pulpite MC 155 Xe 121
41849 Cortijo de Quema SE 164 Te 125
18314 Cortijo de Quijada GR 167 Vf 126

14911 Cortijo de Quirze CO 166 Vc 125
21250 Cortijo de Rabiche H 146 Sf 121
29540 Cortijo de Rábita MA 166 Va 126
41500 Cortijo de Rafael Chacón SE 165 Ub 125
18511 Cortijo de Ramos GR 169 Wf 125
06800 Cortijo de Raposeros de Arriba BA 117 Te 114
18659 Cortijo de Recalde GR 168 Wb 127
11190 Cortijo de Rehuelga CA 173 Ub 129
41400 Cortijo de Reina SE 150 Uf 123
02434 Cortijo de Reolid AB 140 Xf 119
30810 Cortijo de Reverte de Arriba MC 155 Ya 121
29593 Cortijo de Reyes MA 166 Vb 127
23592 Cortijo de Rincón Blanco J 153 We 122
23488 Cortijo de Ríos J 153 Wf 122
11500 Cortijo de Roa La Bota CA 172 Tf 129
23311 Cortijo de Roblado J 153 Xa 120
11630 Cortijo de Robledillo CA 165 Uc 128
29320 Cortijo de Rodahuevos MA 166 Vb 127
02449 Cortijo de Rodríguez AB 140 Xf 117
18181 Cortijo de Romalique GR 169 We 124
11400 Cortijo de Romanito CA 164 Tf 128
14900 Cortijo de Romerico CO 167 Vd 124
06225 Cortijo de Rosita BA 133 Te 117
11580 Cortijo de Rotijón CA 173 Uc 129
41710 Cortijo de Ruchena SE 164 Ub 127
23711 Cortijo de Salcedo J 137 Wb 119
41130 Cortijo de Salgar SE 163 Tf 125
30410 Cortijo de Salinas MC 155 Ya 121
23537 Cortijo de Sàlmerón J 153 Wd 121
41500 Cortijo de Sanabria SE 164 Ub 125
06477 Cortijo de San Antonio BA 133 Tf 117
23009 Cortijo de San Antonio J 152 Wb 122
23380 Cortijo de San Blas J 139 Xc 118
04692 Cortijo de Sánchez AL 171 Ya 124
23700 Cortijo de Sancho J 152 Wb 120
06731 Cortijo de San Isidro BA 118 Uc 114
06445 Cortijo de San José BA 133 Ua 119
18127 Cortijo de San José GR 168 Wb 127
11650 Cortijo de San Lázaro CA 165 Ud 127
41659 Cortijo de San Lucas SE 166 Uf 125
45720 Cortijo de San Nicasio TO 121 Wd 112
18615 Cortijo de San Nicolás GR 168 Wc 127
41410 Cortijo de San Pablo SE 165 Uc 125
06970 Cortijo de San Pedro BA 133 Ua 119
06195 Cortijo de San Román BA 132 Tb 116
18120 Cortijo de Santa Ana GR 167 Ve 126
45124 Cortijo de Santa Catalina TO 102 Vf 110
13414 Cortijo de Santa Clara CR 120 Vc 115
21240 Cortijo de Santa Clara H 147 Sf 121
29395 Cortijo de Santa Cruz MA 166 Uf 127
41640 Cortijo de Santa Cruz SE 166 Uf 125
41620 Cortijo de Santa Eulalia SE 165 Ud 125
06200 Cortijo de Santa María BA 132 Td 116
41410 Cortijo de Santa Marina SE 149 Ub 124
18800 Cortijo de Santaolalla GR 154 Xb 124

41410 Cortijo de Santa Paula SE 165 Uc 124
14840 Cortijo de Santa Sofía CO 151 Vd 122
14449 Cortijo de Santiago CR 136 Vd 118
41410 Cortijo de Santo Domingo SE 165 Uc 124
30890 Cortijo de Santos MC 155 Ya 122
41563 Cortijo de Santo Siervo SE 150 Uf 124
10530 Cortijo de San Valentín CC 98 Tf 110
10194 Cortijo de Saucera CC 98 Tf 111
18816 Cortijo de Sebastián GR 154 Xb 121
30412 Cortijo de Selvalejo MC 155 Xe 121
14447 Cortijo de Serrano CO 136 Vd 118
41860 Cortijo de Serroncillo SE 148 Tf 123
10530 Cortijo de Siete Carrascos CC 98 Tf 110
14447 Cortijo de Siruela CO 136 Vd 119
23649 Cortijo de Soldado J 152 Wa 122
14709 Cortijo de Somonte CO 150 Ud 123
45313 Cortijo de Soria TO 102 Wb 109
18539 Cortijo de Soto Cruz GR 153 Wf 124
23486 Cortijo de Soto Lorenzo J 154 Wf 122
18615 Cortijo de Tajo GR 168 Wb 127
11180 Cortijo de Tamayo CA 173 Ub 129
29420 Cortijo de Tango MA 166 Uf 128
06920 Cortijo de Tarilla BA 134 Ub 119
10194 Cortijo de Téjareo CC 98 Tf 111
23649 Cortijo de Tejerina J 152 Wa 122
41659 Cortijo de Tinoco SE 166 Uf 125
14840 Cortijo de Toril CO 151 Vd 123
18830 Cortijo de Torralba GR 154 Xc 122
23313 Cortijo de Torralba J 153 We 121
41500 Cortijo de Torre Abad SE 165 Ub 125
30420 Cortijo de Torrearenas MC 140 Yb 118
41410 Cortijo de Torrelengua SE 165 Ub 125
41727 Cortijo de Torres SE 163 Ua 126
41410 Cortijo de Torroj SE 165 Uc 124
10270 Cortijo de Torromarcos CC 99 Ua 112
02137 Cortijo de Tortas AB 139 Xd 117
02410 Cortijo de Trifillas AB 140 Ya 117
14820 Cortijo de Trinidades CO 151 Vc 122
41400 Cortijo de Turullote SE 150 Va 123
14859 Cortijo de Vado Fresno CO 151 Ve 122
14840 Cortijo de Vadoseco CO 151 Vc 122
41710 Cortijo de Valcargado SE 165 Ub 126
10198 Cortijo de Valdeaparicio CC 98 Tf 111
06150 Cortijo de Valdelasierpe BA 132 Tc 116
41560 Cortijo de Valderrama SE 166 Va 125
10251 Cortijo de Valderuela CC 99 Uc 111
06192 Cortijo de Valdesquera BA 116 Ta 114
18830 Cortijo de Valentín GR 154 Xc 122
23780 Cortijo de Valenzuela J 151 Ve 121
14412 Cortijo de Valera CO 135 Vb 118
41440 Cortijo de Valero SE 149 Uc 123
14660 Cortijo de Valhondo CO 151 Vd 122
18530 Cortijo de Valle Bajo GR 153 We 123
14820 Cortijo de Valverdejo CO 151 Vd 122
18800 Cortijo de Varea GR 170 Xb 124

41410 Cortijo de Venamalillo SE 165 Ub 125
10695 Cortijo de Ventaquemada CC 99 Tf 109
23380 Cortijo de Ventura J 139 Xc 118
23369 Cortijo de Verjaga J 138 Xa 118
18160 Cortijo de Vicente el Bueno GR 169 We 125
11592 Cortijo de Vico CA 172 Ua 128
04711 Cortijo de Villalobos AL 170 Xb 128
18260 Cortijo de Villaquemado GR 168 Wa 124
14729 Cortijo de Villaseca CO 150 Uf 122
14900 Cortijo de Villegas CO 167 Vd 124
11630 Cortijo de Vista Hermosa CA 165 Ub 128
18830 Cortijo de Zabar GR 154 Xc 121
11690 Cortijo de Zaframagón CA 165 Ud 129
06510 Cortijo de Zajanón Bajo BA 116 Tb 113
06129 Cortijo de Zamorejas BA 132 Sf 118
14650 Cortijo de Zaragoza CO 151 Vd 121
41710 Cortijo de Zarracatín SE 164 Ub 126
04210 Cortijo Don Pepe AL 171 Xe 126
41410 Cortijo El Acebuchal SE 149 Ub 124
23340 Cortijo El Álamo J 138 Xa 119
04810 Cortijo El Blanco AL 155 Xe 124
29710 Cortijo El Blanco MA 167 Ve 127
04460 Cortijo El Boliche AL 170 Xa 127
10291 Cortijo El Borril CC 99 Ua 111
06260 Cortijo El Bóvedo BA 148 Tf 120
06980 Cortijo El Campillo BA 133 Ua 120
23649 Cortijo El Castil J 152 Wa 122
21260 Cortijo El Concho H 148 Te 121
41703 Cortijo El Copero SE 164 Tf 125
04100 Cortijo El Corral AL 170 Xe 127
14412 Cortijo El Coto CO 135 Vb 118
11349 Cortijo El Espadañal CA 173 Ud 131
41210 Cortijo El Gergal SE 148 Tf 123
21291 Cortijo El Helechoso H 147 Tb 121
04116 Cortijo El Hornillo AL 171 Xf 127
18812 Cortijo El Manes GR 154 Xa 124
11339 Cortijo El Marqués CA 174 Ud 130
21260 Cortijo El Martajal H 148 Te 121
10194 Cortijo El Matón CC 98 Te 110
06200 Cortijo El Mazo BA 133 Td 116
18810 Cortijo El Olivarillo GR 154 Xb 123
06260 Cortijo El Palancar BA 148 Tf 120
11510 Cortijo El Pedroso CA 172 Tf 129
18820 Cortijo El Peral GR 154 Xd 121
04149 Cortijo El Plomo AL 171 Ya 127
02530 Cortijo El Pocico AB 139 Xe 120
23686 Cortijo El Quejigar J 168 Wa 124
06227 Cortijo El Recorvo BA 133 Tf 118
18329 Cortijo El Romeral GR 168 Wa 126
29200 Cortijo El Romeral MA 167 Vc 126
11339 Cortijo El Sancho CA 174 Ud 130
23180 Cortijo El Tiro J 152 Wa 121
10251 Cortijo El Toledillo CC 99 Uc 112
18891 Cortijo El Toril GR 154 Xc 123
06909 Cortijo El Viar BA 133 Tf 120
18569 Cortijo Elvira GR 152 Wb 124
18567 Cortijo El Zegrí GR 152 Wc 124
06293 Cortijo Encina Colorado BA
29230 Cortijo Enebro MA 167 Vd 127
18249 Cortijo Esquiladero GR 168 Wb 124
18830 Cortijo Ferrer GR 154 Xc 122

18561 Cortijo Fresneda GR 153 Wd 123
18260 Cortijo Fuente de Madrid GR 168 Wa 125
23611 Cortijo Fuente Palacios J 152 Ve 122
29250 Cortijo Gaén Grande MA 166 Vc 125
10291 Cortijo Galocha CC 99 Tf 111
04400 Cortijo Gatuna AL 170 Xc 127
23614 Cortijo Grande J 152 Wa 123
29718 Cortijo Grande MA 167 Ve 127
04639 Cortijo Grande, El AL 171 Ya 126
10697 Cortijo Guijo de los Frailes CC 99 Tf 109
41410 Cortijo Harinera SE 149 Uc 123
41710 Cortijo Higueralejo SE 165 Ub 127
29610 Cortijo Holgado MA 175 Va 129
10194 Cortijo Hondo del Cura CC 98 Tf 110
10291 Cortijo Jarrín Grande CC 99 Ua 111
41540 Cortijo La Adelfa SE 165 Ue 125
11659 Cortijo La Alcabala Alta CA 165 Ud 126
29230 Cortijo La Alcobilla MA 166 Vc 127
13370 Cortijo La Berenjena CR 137 Wb 117
11592 Cortijo La Blanquita CA 163 Ua 128
06174 Cortijo La Caballera Nueva BA 132 Tb 118
04288 Cortijo La Carabinera AL 171 Ya 126
11400 Cortijo La Compañía CA 163 Tf 128
10291 Cortijo La Covacha CC 99 Ua 111
06280 Cortijo La Dehesa de la Higuera BA 148 Tc 120
18620 Cortijo La Escribana GR 168 Wb 126
06444 Cortijo La Gavilana BA 133 Ua 118
18540 Cortijo La Goleta GR 153 Wd 124
11179 Cortijo La Maestranza CA 173 Ub 130
06920 Cortijo La Merchana BA 134 Ub 118
04619 Cortijo La Morcilla AL 171 Yb 125
06980 Cortijo La Nava BA 148 Ua 120
41410 Cortijo La Nava SE 149 Ub 123
41410 Cortijo La Navarra SE 149 Uc 123
18562 Cortijo La Ñora GR 153 Wd 124
21240 Cortijo La Parrita H 147 Sf 121
21250 Cortijo La Pasada del Abad de Arriba H 146 Sf 121
11330 Cortijo La Sangre CA 173 Uc 130
06443 Cortijo Las Arcas BA 134 Ua 117
06909 Cortijo Las Calderonas BA 133 Ua 120
10591 Cortijo Las Cansinas CC 99 Ua 109
10291 Cortijo Las Canteras CC 99 Ua 111
23691 Cortijo Las Carrillas J 152 Wb 124
04149 Cortijo Las Contraviesas AL 171 Xf 127
10694 Cortijo Las Corchuelas del Saliente CC 99 Ua 110
06380 Cortijo Las Monjas BA 132 Ta 118
06430 Cortijo La Solana BA 134 Uc 117
04114 Cortijo Las Paulinas AL 171 Xf 127
29320 Cortijo Las Pilillas MA 166 Vb 126
10198 Cortijo Las Suertes CC 98 Tf 111
06290 Cortijo Las Torrecillas BA 133 Tf 118
41530 Cortijo La Sucilla Alta SE 165 Uc 126
11560 Cortijo Las Vetas CA 163 Te 127
18329 Cortijo Las Villas GR 168 Wa 126
23280 Cortijo La Teja J 138 Xa 119
21610 Cortijo La Torre H 162 Ta 124
18858 Cortijo La Venta GR 154 Xd 123
41530 Cortijo La Victoria SE 165 Ud 126

18568 Cortijo La Zorrera GR 153 Wd 124
04639 Cortijo Limerica AL 171 Ya 126
18260 Cortijo Los Alcachofares GR 168 Wa 125
41400 Cortijo Los Algarbes SE 150 Uf 124
23260 Cortijo los Barrancos J 138 Wf 119
06380 Cortijo Los Buenos BA 132 Tb 118
04149 Cortijo Los Cerrillos AL 171 Xf 127
18260 Cortijo Los Cierzos GR 168 Wa 124
41410 Cortijo Los Corrales SE 165 Uc 124
14820 Cortijo Los Fontalbas CO 151 Vc 122
13248 Cortijo Los Llanillos CR 122 Xa 114
06442 Cortijo Los Llanos BA 134 Ua 117
04212 Cortijo Los Llanos de Lucas AL 170 Xd 126
18800 Cortijo Los Mellizos GR 169 Xb 125
04479 Cortijo Los Murillos AL 169 Xa 126
29230 Cortijo Los Nogales MA 166 Vc 127
04691 Cortijo Los Ortegas AL 155 Ya 124
11560 Cortijo Los Prados CA 164 Tf 127
06227 Cortijo Los Riscos BA 133 Tf 118
30890 Cortijo Los Valera MC 155 Ya 122
04212 Cortijo Luis Espinar AL 170 Xd 126
21239 Cortijo Maladua H 147 Ta 121
10291 Cortijo Mamparilla CC 99 Tf 111
21260 Cortijo Mancha Llana Alta H 148 Te 121
41600 Cortijo María Sala SE 165 Ud 125
11540 Cortijo Marisma del Guadalquivir CA 163 Te 127
06010 Cortijo Matacebada BA 132 Ta 117
06800 Cortijo Matarratas BA 117 Td 114
11349 Cortijo Matillas CA 173 Ud 130
41740 Cortijo Merlina SE 163 Tf 127
10291 Cortijo Millaróncillo CC 99 Tf 111
10198 Cortijo Mohedas CC 98 Tf 111
04694 Cortijo Molina AL 155 Ya 124
18830 Cortijo Molina GR 154 Xc 121
30890 Cortijo Monja de Abajo MC 155 Ya 122
41540 Cortijo Morcillo SE 165 Ud 126
18120 Cortijo Moreno GR 168 Vf 126
14749 Cortijo Mosquera CO 150 Ud 121
02312 Cortijo Nuevo AB 139 Xc 117
06800 Cortijo Nuevo BA 116 Tc 114
13331 Cortijo Nuevo CR 122 Xb 116
13326 Cortijo Nuevo CR 139 Xc 117
18561 Cortijo Nuevo GR 153 Wd 123
18530 Cortijo Nuevo GR 153 We 123
Cortijo Nuevo GR 154 Xc 123
Cortijo Nuevo GR 169 Xb 124
23300 Cortijo Nuevo J 138 Wf 120
23486 Cortijo Nuevo J 154 Wf 123
29250 Cortijo Nuevo MA 166 Vc 126
29690 Cortijo Nuevo MA 173 Ue 130
41429 Cortijo Nuevo SE 149 Ud 123
41727 Cortijo Nuevo SE 154 Xc 123
41540 Cortijo Nuevo SE 165 Ue 125
23250 Cortijo Nuevo de Hierracaballos J 138 We 119
23350 Cortijo Nuevos J 138 Xb 118
14850 Cortijo Ovejero CO 151 Vd 123
29150 Cortijo Pacheco MA 167 Vc 127
10291 Cortijo Palanco CC 99 Ua 111
10280 Cortijo Palazuelo de Marqués CC 117 Ua 112
29310 Cortijo Pantoja MA 167 Vd 125
41710 Cortijo Pardales SE 165 Ub 126
18560 Cortijo Pastelero GR 153 Wd 123
02534 Cortijo Pedro Andrés AB 139 Xd 120
21240 Cortijo Peña Sierpes H 147 Sf 121
06227 Cortijo Peña Traviesa BA 133 Tf 118
41620 Cortijo Peñón de la Batata SE 165 Ue 124

10590 Cortijo Perdiguerilla CC 98 Te 109
06940 Cortijo Piedras Gordas BA 133 Ua 119
10004 Cortijo Pie Moro CC 98 Tf 111
18530 Cortijo Pierre GR 153 We 123
18370 Cortijo Piñonero GR 168 Wa 126
02313 Cortijo Portelano AB 139 Xd 117
06444 Cortijo Potrico BA 133 Tf 118
04839 Cortijo Pozo Gallardo AL 155 Xe 122
18183 Cortijo Pozuelo GR 168 Wd 125
10671 Cortijo Pradochano CC 98 Te 109
18413 Cortijo Prado Hondo GR 169 Wd 126
18659 Cortijo Prados de Lopera GR 168 Wb 127
41400 Cortijo Prensa Vega SE 150 Uf 123
18550 Cortijo Prinque GR 168 Wc 124
04711 Cortijo Puesto de la Muela AL 170 Xb 128
04711 Cortijo Puesto de los Pérez AL 170 Xb 128
06182 Cortijo Quintana BA 116 Tb 115
23150 Cortijo Ranera J 152 Wb 123
18120 Cortijo Rincón GR 167 Vf 126
10530 Cortijo Rodesnera del Poniente CC 98 Te 110
04160 Cortijo Rodríguez AL 170 Xe 127
10291 Cortijo Ronjilón CC 99 Ua 111
18518 Cortijo Rosca GR 169 We 126
18120 Cortijo Rozuela GR 167 Vf 126
41130 Cortijo Rubiales SE 163 Tf 125
10550 Cortijo Rufino Liebre CC 116 Tb 113
16318 Cortijos, Los CU 89 Yd 108
18816 Cortijos, Los GR 154 Xb 122
28609 Cortijos, Los MD 85 Vf 106
23486 Cortijo Salinas de Don Marcos J 154 Xa 123
41410 Cortijo Salinera SE 149 Uc 123
23488 Cortijo Salón J 153 Wf 122
11339 Cortijo Sambana CA 174 Ud 130
29250 Cortijo San Juan MA 167 Vc 126
41410 Cortijo Santa Catalina SE 149 Ub 123
06443 Cortijo Santa María BA 134 Ub 117
14709 Cortijo Santa Rosa CO 149 Ud 123
10694 Cortijo Santo Tomás CC 99 Ua 110
23628 Cortijos Barranco J 152 Wa 121
18891 Cortijos Bautista GR 154 Xc 123
18830 Cortijos Cayetana GR 154 Xc 121
13427 Cortijos de Abajo CR 120 Vf 113
13427 Cortijos de Arriba CR 120 Vf 113
04830 Cortijos de Benavente AL 155 Xf 122
14600 Cortijos de Fimía CO 136 Ve 119
18816 Cortijos de Fuentesnuevas GR 154 Xa 122
18859 Cortijos de La Bermeja GR 154 Xd 123
18820 Cortijos de La Laguna GR 154 Xc 121
06196 Cortijos de La Pijotilla BA 132 Tb 116
30439 Cortijos de La Pilara MC 140 Yb 120
18859 Cortijos de La Pililla GR 154 Xd 123
18160 Cortijos de La Remonta GR 169 We 125
13740 Cortijos de las Muñozas CR 138 We 117
04830 Cortijos de Las Piedras Bermejas AL 155 Xf 122
23430 Cortijos de La Torre del Obispo J 137 Wd 120
04500 Cortijos del Capitán AL 169 Xa 126
02459 Cortijos del Cura AB 139 Xd 117
04160 Cortijos del Maltés AL 170 Xe 127
04130 Cortijos del Marchal de Fuentes AL 170 Xd 127
04691 Cortijos de Los Benitos AL 155 Ya 124

04259 Cortijos de Los Cecilios AL 170 Xd 127
30890 Cortijos de Los Escribanos MC 155 Ya 122
04870 Cortijos de Los Navarros AL 155 Xd 124
02460 Cortijos de Los Tribaldos AB 139 Xd 118
23295 Cortijos del Prado Espinosilla J 139 Xc 119
18830 Cortijos del Rincón GR 154 Xc 121
18814 Cortijos del Río GR 154 Xb 122
02350 Cortijos del Río de Casa AB 139 Xc 117
18690 Cortijos del Saucillo GR 168 Wb 128
04741 Cortijos de Marín AL 170 Xc 128
23615 Cortijos de Mingoyustre J 151 Vf 122
23150 Cortijos de Riguelos J 152 Wb 123
30890 Cortijos de Talancón MC 155 Ya 123
18813 Cortijo Seco GR 154 Xa 123
23537 Cortijos El Valle J 153 Wd 122
10004 Cortijo Serrezuelo CC 98 Te 111
23479 Cortijo Sierra J 154 Xa 121
06900 Cortijo Sierra de Enmedio BA 133 Tf 119
41410 Cortijos La Nava SE 149 Ub 124
18564 Cortijos las Provincias GR 152 Wb 124
18820 Cortijos Mesías GR 154 Xd 122
23293 Cortijos Nuevos J 139 Xb 119
Cortijos Nuevos de la Sierra GR 154 Xc 121
Cortijos Nuevos de la Sierra GR 155 Xe 121
18820 Cortijos Nuevos del Campo GR 155 Xd 121
10291 Cortijo Solanilla de Los Lobos CC 98 Tf 111
23150 Cortijos Saltadero Bajo J 152 Wb 123
23746 Cortijos Silvente J 152 Wa 121
41400 Cortijo Suerte Alta del Montecillo SE 150 Uf 123
35570 Cortijos Viejos GC 182 Mb 175
04710 Cortijo Tajillo Blanco AL 170 Xb 128
21240 Cortijo Tapia H 147 Ta 121
41410 Cortijo Torre del Viejo SE 149 Uc 124
18830 Cortijo Tovilla GR 154 Xc 120
18814 Cortijo Trillo GR 154 Xa 122
10291 Cortijo Umbría CC 98 Tf 111
14820 Cortijo Valcalentejo CO 151 Vc 122
10291 Cortijo Valdecebuches CC 98 Tf 111
21500 Cortijo Valdepalina H 162 Ta 124
18812 Cortijo Valenciano GR 154 Xa 124
14600 Cortijo Valle Bajo CO 151 Vd 121
21570 Cortijo Vegalajetas H 146 Se 121
29200 Cortijo Ventilla MA 167 Vc 127
14248 Cortijo Viejo CO 134 Ue 119
06200 Cortijo Villa Catalina BA 132 Td 116
10189 Cortijo Villarejo CC 117 Ua 112
41410 Cortijo y Molino de Las Albaidas SE 165 Uc 124
23569 Cortijo Zamarrón J 153 Wd 123
23478 Cortijo Zarzalar J 154 Xa 120
14913 Cortijo Zurreón CO 167 Vc 125
23120 Cortijuelo J 152 Wc 122
04889 Cortijuelo, El AL 170 Xd 125
23488 Cortijuelo, El J 153 We 122
14700 Cortijuelo del Remolino CO 150 Ue 122
29712 Cortijuelos, Los MA 167 Vf 127
22611 Cortillas HU 35 Ze 93
33783 Cortina AS 14 Td 87
33628 Cortina, La AS 15 Ub 90
15319 Cortiñán C 11 Re 89
25790 Cortiuda L 56 Bb 96
05289 Cortos AV 85 Vc 104
42180 Cortos SO 51 Xe 98
40312 Cortos, Los SG 68 Wc 101
37452 Cortos de la Sierra SA 82 Ua 104
17844 Corts GI 59 Ce 96
38399 Corujera, La TF 180 Id 178
24514 Corullón LE 25 Tb 93
29753 Corumbela MA 168 Vf 128
35350 Coruña GC 184 Kc 180
15001* Coruña = A Coruña, La C 11 Rd 88
09410 Coruña del Conde BU 49 Wd 98
47816 Coruñeses VA 47 Va 98
33428 Coruño AS 15 Ua 88
36191 Coruto PO 22 Rc 93
36330 Coruxo PO 41 Rb 95
27843 Corvelle LU 12 Sc 88
27286 Corvelle LU 12 Sd 89
27614 Corvelle LU 24 Sd 92
32849 Corvelle OR 42 Rf 96
39697 Corvera CB 17 Wa 89
30153 Corvera MC 157 Yf 122
30329 Corverica MC 157 Ye 122
42248 Corvesún SO 70 Xd 101
32839 Corvillón OR 42 Sa 95
30835 Corvillones MC 156 Yd 123
24195 Corvillos de la Sobarriba LE 27 Uc 93
34810 Corvio P 29 Ve 92
36457 Corzáns PO 41 Rd 96
32369 Corzos OR 44 Sf 95
15318 Cos C 11 Re 89
39592 Cos CB 17 Ve 89
39573 Cos, Los CB 17 Vc 90
44358 Cosa TE 90 Yf 103
25749 Coscó L 56 Ba 98
50374 Coscojar Z 71 Yc 103
22312 Coscojuela de Fantova HU 55 Ab 96
22395 Coscojuela de Sobrarbe HU 36 Aa 94
12004 Coscollosa-Zafra CS 108 Zf 108
22141 Coscullano HU 54 Ze 95
42216 Coscurita SO 69 Xd 100
39582 Cosgaya CB 16 Vb 90
41450 Cosilla del Romero SE 149 Uc 121
39554 Cosio CB 17 Vd 89
28821 Coslada MD 86 Wc 106
24143 Cospedal LE 14 Tf 91
15110 Cospindo C 10 Ra 89
32514 Costa OR 23 Re 94
27816 Costa, A LU 12 Sc 88
11380 Costa, La CA 173 Uc 132
35560 Costa, La GC 182 Mc 174
35018 Costa, La GC 184 Kd 180
38770 Costa, La TF 181 Ha 177
29604 Costa Bella MA 175 Vb 129
04120 Costacabana AL 170 Xd 127
07589 Costa de Canyamel IB 111 Dc 111
07108 Costa de la Talaia IB 110 Ce 110
38630 Costa del Silencio TF 180 Ic 180
28680 Costa de Madrid MD 85 Vd 106
07181 Costa d'en Blanes IB 110 Cd 111
07180 Costa de Sa Calma IB 110 Cc 111
11550 Costa de Sanlúcar CA 162 Td 128
07559 Costa des Pinos IB 111 Dc 111
39292 Costana, La CB 17 Vf 90
03738 Costa Nova A 143 Ab 116
35539 Costa Teguise GC 182 Md 175
22312 Costeán HU 55 Ab 96
17752 Costes, Les GI 40 Cf 94
07144 Costitx IB 111 Cf 111
43512 Costunà T 74 Ad 103
12119 Costur CS 108 Ze 108
50409 Cosuenda Z 71 Ye 100
27299 Cotá LU 12 Sb 90
07730 Cotaina des Pou IB 77 Ea 109
49639 Cotanes ZA 46 Ue 98
09192 Cotar BU 30 Wc 94
32135 Cotelas OR 23 Sa 94
39639 Coterillo CB 18 Wb 89
02461 Cotillas AB 139 Xc 118
14850 Cotillas CO 151 Ve 123
39451 Cotillo CB 17 Vf 89
35650 Cotillo GC 183 Lf 176
13191 Coto CR 120 Vf 115
36419 Coto PO 41 Rb 95
06910 Coto, El BA 134 Uc 118
36800 Coto, O PO 22 Rc 95
36857 Cotobade PO 23 Rd 94
06891 Coto Capitán BA 117 Te 114
11649 Coto de Bornos CA 165 Ub 127
33840 Coto de Buenamadre AS 14 Te 90
02154 Coto de la Milagrosa AB 125 Yd 114
09360 Coto de Pinilla BU 49 Wb 97
06392 Coto Murillo BA 133 Te 118
10600 Coto Navacebrera CC 99 Tf 108
33929 Cotorraso AS 15 Ub 89
28976 Cotorredondo MD 86 Wa 107
37405 Cotorrillo SA 65 Ue 102
28729 Cotos de Monterrey MD 86 Wc 104
09410 Coto Valverde BU 49 Wd 98
23760 Cotrufe J 152 Vf 121
15125 Coucieiro C 10 Qe 90
32536 Couciero OR 23 Rf 94
15148 Couso C 10 Rb 90
32520 Couso OR 23 Re 94
36682 Couso PO 23 Rc 92
36511 Couso PO 24 Sa 93
36892 Couso PO 41 Rc 96
36119 Couso, O PO 23 Rc 93
32880 Couso de Salas OR 42 Sa 97
15846 Couto C 10 Rb 90
36154 Couto PO 23 Rc 94
36886 Couto PO 42 Re 95
15846 Couto, O C 10 Rb 90
36639 Couto de Abaixo PO 22 Rb 94
15339 Couzadoiro C 10 Sb 87
33535 Cova AS 15 Ud 88
27532 Cova LU 24 Sb 94
32786 Cova OR 24 Se 95
40531 Covachuelas SG 68 Wb 101
46728 Cova del Parpalló V 127 Ze 115
03738 Cova dels Orguens A 143 Ab 116
42157 Covaleda SO 50 Xa 97
09143 Covanera BU 30 Wb 92
09346 Covarrubias BU 49 Wc 96
42212 Covarrubias SO 69 Xc 100
27861 Covas LU 10 Sc 86
27686 Covas LU 24 Se 91
32141 Covas OR 23 Sa 94
32311 Covas OR 25 Ta 94
32634 Covas OR 42 Sb 97
30420 Covatillas, Las MC 140 Ya 119
27714 Covelas LU 13 Sf 88
32611 Covelas OR 43 Se 97
32412 Covelo OR 23 Re 95
03669 Coves, Les A 142 Za 118
12185 Coves de Vinromà, les = Cuevas de Vinromà, les CS 92 Aa 107
25653 Covet L 56 Ba 96
03560 Coveta Fumada, La A 143 Zd 118
28523 Covíbar MD 86 Wc 106
27688 Covo LU 25 Se 91
03350 Cox A 142 Za 120
30812 Coy MC 155 Yb 121
33680 Coyanzo AS 15 Uc 90
13345 Cózar CR 138 Wf 117
18708 Cózares, Los GR 169 We 127
18291 Cozcojar GR 168 Wb 125
49214 Cozcurrita ZA 63 Te 100
10811 Cozuelo CC 98 Td 109
40354 Cozuelos de Fuentidueña SG 67 Vf 100
34486 Cozuelos de Ojeda P 29 Vd 92
18650 Cozvíjar GR 168 Wc 126
27246 Crecente LU 12 Se 89
36420 Crecente PO 42 Re 96
07198 Cred Vermella IB 110 Ce 111
22315 Cregenzán HU 55 Aa 96
17770 Creixell GI 59 Cf 95
43839 Creixell T 76 Bc 101
24980 Crémenes LE 28 Uf 91
17832 Crespià GI 59 Ce 95
09572 Crespo BU 30 Wb 91
44562 Crespol TE 91 Zd 104
05300 Crespos AV 84 Va 103
07420 Crestaix IB 111 Cf 110
44623 Cretas TE 74 Ab 103
17310 Creu de Lloret, La GI 59 Ce 98
12131 Crevadas, Les CS 92 Zf 107
03330 Crevillent A 142 Zb 119
09512 Criales BU 30 We 91
07769 Crio Son Morell IB 77 Df 108
01308 Cripan VI 32 Xc 93
01195 Crispijana VI 31 Xb 91
36749 Cristelos PO 41 Rb 96
38650 Cristianos, Los TF 180 Ib 180
36519 Cristimil PO 23 Re 92
06479 Cristina BA 117 Tf 115
36863 Cristiñade PO 41 Rc 96
37684 Cristóbal SA 82 Ua 106
37639 Cristo de la Laguna SA 82 Te 104
13429 Cristo del Espíritu Santo CR 120 Vf 113
32765 Cristosende OR 24 Sd 94
44557 Crivillén TE 91 Zc 103
17869 Cros GI 39 Cb 95
17249 Crota GI 59 Da 98
35110 Cruce de Sardina GC 184 Kd 181
05278 Cruceras, Las AV 85 Vc 106
06400 Cruces BA 117 Ua 115
15815 Cruces, As C 11 Rf 90
33785 Cruces, Las AS 15 Ub 88
23392 Crucetas J 139 Xb 118
30889 Cruceticas, Las MC 156 Yb 124
36687 Cruxa, A PO 23 Rd 92
33957 Cruz, La AS 15 Uc 89
48960 Cruz, La BI 19 Xa 89
14650 Cruz, La CO 151 Vd 121
23700 Cruz, La J 137 Wc 120
46980 Cruz de Gracia V 107 Zd 111
27346 Cruz de Incio LU 24 Sd 93
37542 Cruz del Rayo SA 81 Ta 107
13680 Cruz de Piedra CR 121 Wa 113
35414 Cruz de Pineda GC 184 Kc 180
38460 Cruz Grande TF 180 Ib 178
38411 Cruz Santa TF 180 Ic 178
10430 Cuacos de Yuste CC 99 Ub 108
08773 Cuadra d'Agulladets, La B 76 Bd 100
14840 Cuadradillo CO 151 Vd 122
30876 Cuadras, Las MC 156 Yd 123
37149 Cuadrilleros SA 64 Ua 102
37149 Cuadrilleros de Gusanos SA 64 Tf 102
33456 Cuadro, El AS 14 Ua 87
28749 Cuadrón, El MD 68 Wc 103
24620 Cuadros LE 27 Uc 92
33548 Cuadroveña AS 16 Ue 88
32689 Cualedro OR 43 Sc 97
46980 Cuart de Poblet = Quart de Poblet V 126 Zd 111
22197 Cuarte HU 54 Zd 96
06475 Cuarteles de la Osa y las Navas BA 133 Ua 117
02162 Cuartico, El AB 124 Xf 115
10895 Cuarto, El CC 97 Ta 108
13720 Cuarto Alto, El CR 122 We 114
37494 Cuarto de Doña María Luisa SA 82 Te 104
06160 Cuarto de Enmedio BA 132 Ta 117
02639 Cuarto del Bolo AB 123 Xf 114
02328 Cuarto del Moral AB 124 Xf 114
02160 Cuarto de Maribáñez AB 123 Xd 114
11380 Cuartón, El CA 173 Uc 132
05580 Cuartos, Los AV 83 Ud 106
18820 Cuartos Nuevos de Abajo GR 155 Xd 121
46837 Cuatretonda = Quatretonda V 126 Zd 115
37891 Cuatro Calzadas SA 83 Uc 104
22569 Cuatrocorz HU 55 Ac 97
28024 Cuatro Vientos MD 86 Wb 106
44141 Cuba TE 91 Ze 105
50133 Cuba, La Z 72 Zb 101
38852 Cubaba TF 184 Hd 179
02249 Cubas AB 124 Yc 114
39793 Cubas CB 18 Wb 88
14840 Cubas CO 151 Vc 122
28978 Cubas de la Sagra MD 102 Wa 107
50376 Cubel Z 71 Yc 102
08880 Cubelles B 76 Be 101
25737 Cubells L 56 Af 97
07839 Cubells, Es IB 109 Bb 115
09211 Cubilla BU 31 We 92
42148 Cubilla SO 50 Xa 98
06800 Cubillana BA 116 Td 115
42148 Cubillas SO 50 Xa 98
47520 Cubillas VA 65 Ue 100
24688 Cubillas de Arbás LE 27 Ub 91
34219 Cubillas de Cerrato P 47 Vd 98
24224 Cubillas de los Oteros LE 27 Uc 94
19263 Cubillas del Pinar GU 69 Xc 102
24940 Cubillas de Rueda LE 28 Ue 93
47290 Cubillas de Santa Marta VA 47 Vc 97
27278 Cubilledo LU 13 Se 90
09642 Cubillejo BU 49 Wc 96
19362 Cubillejo de la Sierra GU 71 Yb 103
19363 Cubillejo del Sitio GU 71 Yb 103
40185 Cubillo SG 67 Wa 102
02340 Cubillo, El AB 123 Xd 116
16315 Cubillo, El CU 106 Yd 108
34859 Cubillo de Castrejón P 29 Vc 92
09551 Cubillo del Butrón BU 30 Wb 92
09352 Cubillo del Campo BU 49 Wc 95
09352 Cubillo del César BU 49 Wc 96
34486 Cubillo de Ojeda P 29 Vd 92
19186 Cubillo de Uceda, El GU 86 Wd 104
49730 Cubillos ZA 46 Ub 99
09514 Cubillos de Losa BU 18 Wd 90
09572 Cubillos del Rojo BU 18 Wb 91
24492 Cubillos de Sil LE 26 Tc 93
44191 Cubla TE 90 Yf 107
49327 Cubo de Benavente ZA 45 Tf 96
09280 Cubo de Bureba BU 31 We 93
37281 Cubo de Don Sancho, El SA 63 Te 103
42134 Cubo de Hogueras SO 51 Xd 98
06390 Cubo de la Canal BA 132 Tc 117
42167 Cubo de la Sierra SO 51 Xd 97
42191 Cubo de la Solana SO 51 Xd 99
49710 Cubo de Tierra del Vino, El ZA 64 Ub 101
44491 Cucalón TE 72 Ye 102
11179 Cucarrete CA 172 Ua 131
39575 Cucayo CB 16 Vc 90
02329 Cucharal AB 139 Xe 116
39318 Cuchia CB 17 Vf 88
35560 Cuchillo, El GC 182 Mc 174
09215 Cucho BU 31 Xb 92
33150 Cudillero AS 14 Tf 87
39318 Cudón CB 17 Vf 88
33509 Cué AS 16 Vb 88
49717 Cuelgamures ZA 65 Uc 101
37497 Cuéllar SA 81 Tc 105
40200 Cuéllar SG 67 Ve 100
42172 Cuéllar de la Sierra SO 51 Xd 97
22375 Cuello Arenas HU 35 Zf 93
23211 Cuellos, Los J 137 Wb 119
39418 Cuena CB 29 Ve 91
24917 Cuénabres LE 16 Va 90
14297 Cuenca CO 134 Uc 119
16001* Cuenca CU 105 Xf 108
23486 Cuenca J 153 Xa 122
42192 Cuenca, La SO 50 Xb 98
44495 Cuencabuena TE 71 Ye 102
47650 Cuenca de Campos VA 47 Uf 96
33529 Cuenya AS 15 Ud 88
50373 Cuerlas, Las Z 71 Yc 103
33829 Cuero AS 14 Tf 88
45126 Cuerva TO 101 Ve 111
41749 Cuervo, El SE 164 Tf 127
44134 Cuervo, El TE 106 Ye 108
24740 Cuesta, La LE 26 Td 95
40181 Cuesta, La SG 67 Wa 102
42173 Cuesta, La SO 51 Xe 96
38915 Cuesta, La TF 180 Ha 182
38710 Cuesta, La TF 181 Hb 176
38726 Cuesta, La TF 181 Hb 176
30558 Cuesta Alta MC 141 Yd 119
14812 Cuesta Blanca CO 152 Vf 124
30396 Cuesta Blanca MC 157 Yf 123
30335 Cuesta de la Pinilla MC 156 Ye 122
04008 Cuesta del Gato, La AL 170 Xd 127
18492 Cuesta del Largo GR 169 We 127
30890 Cuesta del Mellado MC 155 Yb 123
46141 Cuesta del Rato V 106 Ye 108
09567 Cuestaedo BU 18 Wc 90
18492 Cuesta Vieja GR 169 Wf 128
24141 Cueta, La LE 14 Te 90
39011 Cueto CB 18 Wb 88
09568 Cueva BU 18 Wc 90
16150 Cueva CU 89 Ya 106
02510 Cueva, La AB 124 Yb 116
02650 Cueva, La AB 125 Ye 116
38180 Cueva Bermeja TF 181 Ie 177
04700 Cueva Blanca, La AL 169 Xb 128
09258 Cueva-Cardiel BU 30 Wd 94
46178 Cuevacruz Alta V 107 Za 109
23487 Cueva Cuarta J 153 Wf 122
42107 Cueva de Ágreda SO 52 Ya 98
04830 Cueva de Ambrosio, La AL 155 Xf 122
09198 Cueva de Atapuerca BU 30 Wc 95
18858 Cueva de Chalá GR 154 Xd 122
09198 Cueva de Juarros BU 30 Wc 95
04778 Cueva de la Juana, La AL 169 Wf 128
21330 Cueva de la Mora H 147 Tb 122
16879 Cueva del Hierro CU 89 Xf 105
33594 Cueva de Lledías AS 16 Va 88
18858 Cueva de los Atochares GR 154 Xd 122
18817 Cueva de los Granadinos GR 154 Xb 122
04149 Cueva del Pájaro, La AL 171 Ya 126
18880 Cueva del Pepín GR 153 Wf 124
30335 Cueva de Pagán MC 156 Ye 122
16410 Cueva de Plaza CU 103 Wf 109
09315 Cueva de Roa, La BU 48 Wa 98
45370 Cueva de Rompelaire TO 103 Wf 109

270 | Cortijos de Los Cecilios

D

E

25152 el Cogull = Cogul L 75 Ae 100
El Cuervo, Apt. CA 163 Tf 127
03600 Elda A 142 Zb 118
20493 Eldua SS 20 Xf 90
20493 Elduain SS 20 Ya 90
48289 Eleizalde BI 20 Xc 89
48650 Elejade BI 19 Xa 88
48312 Elejalde BI 20 Xc 89
48940 Elexalde BI 19 Xa 89
48390 Elexalde BI 19 Xb 89
48630 Elexalde Auzoa BI 19 Xa 88
48313 Elexalde-Zeeta (Ereño) BI 20 Xc 88
20690 Elgeta SS 20 Xd 90
20870 Elgoibar SS 20 Xd 89
01206 Elguea VI 32 Xc 91
31699 Elía NC 33 Yc 91
46190 Eliana, L' V 107 Zc 111
48111 Elizalde BI 19 Xa 88
20180 Elizalde = Oiartzun SS 21 Ya 89
31700 Elizondo NC 21 Yc 90
10891 Eljas CC 81 Ta 107
20800 Elkano SS 20 Xe 89
25721 Éller L 38 Be 94
48330 Elorriaga BI 19 Xb 89
48230 Elorrio BI 20 Xc 90
31470 Elorz NC 33 Yc 92
01170 Elosu VI 19 Xb 91
20570 Elosua SS 20 Xd 90
48180 Elotxelerri BI 19 Xa 89
25746 el Tosal = Tossal L 56 Ba 97
31799 Eltso NC 21 Yb 91
01340 Eltziego = Elciego VI 31 Xc 93
01309 Elvillar = Bilar VI 32 Xc 93
29604 Elviria MA 175 Vb 129
03200* Elx = Elche A 142 Zb 119
31797 Elzaburu NC 21 Yb 90
41200 Embalse de Alcalá del Río SE 148 Ua 123
22662 Embalse de Búbal HU 35 Ze 92
15258 Embalse de Castrelo C 10 Qf 91
09213 Embalse de Cillaperlata BU 30 Wd 92
23430 Embalse de Giribaile J 137 Wd 120
02500 Embalse de los Charcos AB 140 Yb 117
28470 Embalse de Navalmedio MD 85 Vf 104
28749 Embalse de Riosequillo MD 68 Wc 103
41710 Embalse Torre del Águila SE 164 Ub 126
38911 Embarcadero de Punta Grande TF 180 Ha 182
19339 Embid GU 71 Yb 103
50239 Embid de Ariza Z 70 Ya 100
50299 Embid de la Ribera Z 71 Yc 100
22740 Embún HU 34 Zb 93
48120 Emerando BI 19 Xb 88
21420 Empalme, El H 161 Se 125
14730 Emparedada CO 150 Uf 122
46136 Emperador V 108 Zd 111
45450 Emperador, El TO 121 Wa 113
17487 Empuriabrava GI 59 Da 95
17130 Empúries GI 59 Da 96
22830 Ena HU 34 Zb 94
22312 Enate HU 55 Ab 96
04211 Encalmados, Los AL 170 Xe 126
AD200 Encamp ◘ AND 38 Bd 93
41530 Encarnaciones, Las SE 165 Ue 126
33946 Encarnada, La AS 15 Uc 89
30529 Encebras, Las MC 141 Ye 118
03658 Encebres, Les A 141 Za 118
02137 Encebrico, El AB 139 Xd 117
15566 Enchousas, As C 12 Sa 87
25283 Encies L 57 Bd 96
17172 Encies, Les GI 58 Cd 96
09588 Encima Angulo BU 19 We 90
28870 Encín, El MD 87 We 105
03408 Encina, L' A 141 Za 116
37515 Encina, La SA 81 Tc 106
13117 Encinacaída CR 100 Vb 112
50470 Encinacorba Z 71 Ye 101
06906 Encinar BA 133 Tf 120
41380 Encinar, El SE 149 Uc 120
28630 Encinar de Alberche MD 85 Vd 107
28109 Encinar de los Reyes, El MD 86 Wc 105
23747 Encinarejo, El J 137 Vf 120
05696 Encinares AV 83 Ud 106
06290 Encinares BA 133 Tf 118
23610 Encinares, Los J 152 Wa 123
28260 Encinar y San Alberto, El MD 86 Vf 105
40531 Encinas SG 68 Wb 100
41500 Encinas, Las SE 164 Ub 124
37114 Encina San Silvestre SA 64 Tf 102
37893 Encinas de Abajo SA 65 Ud 103
37892 Encinas de Arriba SA 83 Uc 104
47186 Encinas de Esgueva VA 48 Vf 98
21390 Encinasola H 132 Ta 120
37256 Encinasola de los Comendadores SA 63 Tc 102
14913 Encinas Reales CO 167 Vd 125
24745 Encinedo LE 25 Tc 95
09330 Encinilla BU 49 Wb 96
41710 Encinilla, La SE 165 Ub 127
40391 Encinillas SG 67 Vf 102
09219 Encío BU 31 Wf 92
26586 Enciso RI 51 Xe 96
13739 Encomienda de Mudela CR 137 Wc 117
15187 Encrobas, As C 11 Rd 89
31789 Endarlatsa NC 21 Yb 89
31799 Endériz NC 33 Yc 91
20740 Endoia SS 20 Xe 89
37766 Endrinal SA 83 Ub 105
28793 Endrinales, Los MD 86 Wb 104
42133 Enebral, El SO 69 Wf 99
31153 Enériz NC 33 Yb 92
08281 Enfesta L 57 Bc 98
33677 Enfistiella AS 15 Ub 90
46810 Enguera V 126 Zb 115
16372 Enguídanos CU 106 Yc 110
49172 Enillas, Las ZA 64 Ua 100
04729 Enix AL 170 Xc 127
39200 Enmedio CB 17 Vf 91
46669 Énova, l' V 126 Zd 114
25592 Enseu L 37 Ba 95
36471 Entenza PO 41 Rc 96
39582 Enterría CB 16 Vb 90
39577 Enterrías CB 16 Vb 90
04711 Entinas, Las AL 170 Xb 128
15237 Entíns C 22 Ra 91
32336 Éntoma OR 25 Ta 94
33111 Entrago AS 14 Tf 89
49721 Entrala ZA 64 Ub 100
39715 Entrambasaguas CB 18 Wb 88
09585 Entrambasaguas Caniego BU 19 We 90
27234 Entrambasaugas LU 24 Sb 91
39682 Entrambasmestas CB 18 Wa 89
09568 Entrambosríos BU 18 Wb 90
41410 Entrearroyos SE 149 Ub 124
32552 Entrecinsa OR 43 Se 96
15109 Entrecruces C 10 Rb 90
02449 Entredicho, El AB 140 Xe 118
14249 Entredicho, El CO 135 Ue 119
30414 Entredicho, El MC 155 Xe 121
33940 Entrego, El AS 15 Uc 89
26375 Entrena RI 32 Xc 94
33686 Entrepeñas AS 15 Uc 90
49325 Entrepeñas ZA 44 Td 96
06710 Entrerríos BA 118 Ub 115
33401 Entreviñas AS 15 Ua 88
32860 Entrimo A = Terrachá OR 42 Rf 97
06197 Entrín Alto BA 132 Tb 116
06197 Entrín Bajo BA 132 Tb 116
25513 Envall L 37 Af 94
27652 Envernallas LU 13 Ta 91
16856 Envía, La CU 83 Xc 106
25568 Enviny L 37 Ba 94
31448 Epároz NC 34 Ye 92
20128 Epele SS 21 Ya 89
50290 Épila Z 52 Ye 99
38849 Epina TF 184 He 179
30168 Era Alta MC 157 Yf 121
25551 Era Bordeta L 36 Ad 92
11687 Era de la Viña CA 165 Ud 127
48950 Erandio BI 19 Xa 89
31486 Eransus NC 33 Yc 92
25598 Era Peira Roja L 37 Af 92
25598 Era Restanca L 37 Ae 93
02214 Eras, Las AB 125 Yd 113
46178 Eras, Las V 106 Yf 109
31869 Eraso NC 21 Yb 91
31748 Eratsun NC 21 Yb 90
31290 Eraul NC 32 Xf 92
15147 Erbecedo C 10 Rb 90
27515 Erbedeiro LU 24 Sb 93
48450 Erbera o San Andres BI 19 Xa 89
48277 Erbera o San Andres BI 20 Xd 89
01477 Erbi VI 19 Wf 90
36412 Erbille PO 41 Rc 96
31866 Erbiti NC 21 Yb 91
22437 Erdao HU 36 Ac 95
31481 Erdozáin NC 33 Yd 92
01193 Erenchum VI 32 Xc 92
48313 Ereño BI 20 Xc 88
20128 Ereñozu SS 21 Ya 89
22807 Erés HU 53 Zb 95
25712 Eres, Les L 56 Af 95
38916 Erese TF 180 Ha 182
22467 Eresué HU 36 Ac 93
48112 Ergoien BI 19 Xa 88
48113 Ergoien BI 19 Xb 89
20180 Ergoien SS 21 Ya 89
20268 Ergoiena SS 20 Xf 91
33449 Ería, La AS 15 Ua 87
10638 Erías CC 82 Td 106
31867 Erice NC 21 Yb 91
31892 Erice NC 33 Yb 91
31174 Eriete NC 33 Yb 92
14900 Erillas CO 167 Vd 124
25516 Erinyà L 37 Af 95
31396 Eristáin NC 33 Yc 93
22469 Eriste HU 36 Ac 93
38435 Erjos TF 180 Ib 179
50611 Erla Z 53 Za 96
17253 Ermedàs GI 59 Da 97
15282 Ermedelo C 22 Rb 92
15338 Ermida C 12 Sa 87
27744 Ermida LU 13 Se 89
15860 Ermida de San Bartolomé C 10 Ra 90
15149 Ermida de Santa Margarita C 10 Ra 89
03570 Ermita, L' A 143 Ze 117
Ermita, La AL 155 Xd 124
Ermita, La AL 155 Xe 124
Ermita, La AL 155 Xe 124
18815 Ermita, La GR 154 Xa 122
18183 Ermita, La GR 168 Wd 125
21590 Ermita, La H 160 Sd 125
06310 Ermita Belén BA 133 Td 118
06194 Ermita de Bótoa y Colonia Escolar BA 116 Ta 114
03699 Ermita de Don Jaume A 142 Zc 118
13310 Ermita de la Consolación CR 122 Wd 115
28818 Ermita de la Virgen de La Soledad MD 87 We 106
47008 Ermita del Humilladero VA 47 Vb 99
30876 Ermita del Ramonete MC 156 Yd 123
44195 Ermita de San Blas TE 90 Ye 106
42313 Ermita de San Julián SO 69 Wf 99
48120 Ermita de San Martín BI 19 Xb 88
09239 Ermita de San Pedro BU 49 Wb 95
01128 Ermita de San Román VI 32 Xd 92
26131 Ermita de Santa Bárbara RI 32 Xe 94
03292 Ermita de Sant Andreu A 142 Zc 119
26130 Ermita de Santiago RI 32 Xd 94
48120 Ermita de Santillandi BI 19 Xb 88
03599 Ermita de Sant Llorenç A 143 Zf 117
25795 Ermita de Sant Martí L 37 Bb 95
25655 Ermita de Sant Pere L 56 Ba 96
03503 Ermita de Sanz A 143 Zf 117
30410 Ermita de Singla MC 155 Ya 120
23686 Ermita Nueva J 168 Wa 124
32375 Ermitas, As OR 25 Sf 95
45880 Ermita Virgen de la Muela TO 103 We 110
14940 Ermita Virgen de la Sierra CO 151 Vd 124
23537 Ermita y Torreón de Cuadros J 153 Wd 122
14850 Ermiticas, Las CO 151 Vd 122
15338 Ermo C 10 Sa 87
48260 Ermua BI 20 Xd 89
27113 Ernes LU 13 Ta 90
25635 Eroles L 56 Ae 95
32546 Erosa OR 43 Se 96
38869 Erque TF 184 He 180
31714 Erratzu NC 21 Yd 89
31891 Errazkin NC 20 Ya 90
31698 Errea NC 33 Yd 91
31448 Erremendia NC 34 Ye 91
20100 Errenteria SS 21 Ya 89
20737 Errezil SS 20 Xe 90
01213 Erribeira Beitia = Ribera Baja VI 31 Xa 92
48309 Errigoiti BI 19 Xb 89
25528 Erril-la-vall L 37 Ae 93
31697 Erro NC 21 Yd 91
31868 Errotz NC 33 Yb 91
25555 Erta L 37 Af 94
AD400 Erts ◘ AND 38 Bc 93
45540 Erustes TO 101 Vd 109
39584 Esanos CB 17 Vc 89
43816 Esblada T 76 Bc 100
21870 Escacena del Campo H 163 Td 124
27540 Escairón = O Saviñao LU 24 Sc 93
17130 Escala, l' GI 59 Da 96
09145 Escalada BU 30 Wb 92
09145 Escalada BU 30 Wb 92
21342 Escalada H 147 Tb 121
39795 Escalante CB 18 Wc 88
25588 Escalarre L 37 Ba 93
19390 Escalera GU 89 Xf 104
44424 Escaleruela, La TE 107 Zb 108
25596 Escaló L 37 Ba 93
22363 Escalona HU 36 Aa 94
38614 Escalona TF 180 Ic 180
45910 Escalona TO 101 Vd 107
40350 Escalona del Prado SG 67 Vf 101
14749 Escalonias, Las CO 150 Ue 122
05190 Escalonilla AV 84 Vb 105
05289 Escalonilla AV 84 Vc 104
45517 Escalonilla TO 101 Vd 109
19127 Escamilla GU 88 Xc 105
33191 Escamplero AS 15 Ua 88
03698 Escanelia A 142 Zc 118
22393 Escanilla HU 36 Ab 95
01211 Escanzana VI 31 Xa 92
09557 Escaño BU 18 Wc 91
23657 Escañuela J 152 Vf 121
22394 Escapa, La HU 36 Aa 95
40291 Escarabajosa de Cabezas SG 67 Ve 102
40210 Escarabajosa de Cuéllar SG 67 Ve 100
15992 Escarabote C 22 Ra 93
47470 Escargamaría VA 65 Uf 102
19119 Escariche GU 87 Wf 106
30893 Escarihuela, La MC 156 Yb 124
25637 Escarlà L 56 Ae 95
31690 Escároz = Eskaroze NC 34 Yf 91
22660 Escarrilla HU 35 Ze 92
25596 Escart L 37 Ba 93
22372 Escartín HU 35 Ze 93
50790 Escatrón Z 73 Ze 101
17723 Escaules, Les GI 40 Cf 95
17213 Esclanyà GI 59 Db 97
17244 Esclet GI 59 Cf 97
50682 Escó Z 34 Yf 93
09559 Escóbados de Abajo BU 30 Wc 92
09559 Escóbados de Arriba BU 30 Wc 92
33555 Escobal AS 16 Va 88
23749 Escobar J 152 Wa 120
30439 Escobar MC 140 Yb 120
30333 Escobar MC 156 Ye 122
40154 Escobar SG 67 Ve 103
24341 Escobar de Campos LE 28 Va 95
40393 Escobar de Polendos SG 67 Vf 102
39108 Escobedo CB 18 Wa 88
39638 Escobedo CB 18 Wa 89
49540 Escober ZA 45 Ua 98
42223 Escobosa de Almazán SO 70 Xd 100
42193 Escobosa de Calatañazor SO 50 Xa 99
27868 Escola LU 10 Sb 87
30350 Escombreras MC 157 Za 123
02359 Escondite AB 139 Xd 117
19119 Escopete GU 87 Wf 106
07315 Escorca IB 110 Cf 110
02315 Escorial AB 139 Xd 117
28280 Escorial, El MD 85 Vf 105
23747 Escoriales, Los J 137 Wa 119
44161 Escorihuela TE 90 Za 105
32696 Escornabois OR 43 Sc 96
01428 Escota VI 31 Xa 91
18293 Escóznar GR 168 Wa 125
15980 Escravitude, A C 22 Rc 92
36547 Escuadro PO 23 Re 92
49177 Escuadro ZA 64 Tf 101
22362 Escuaín HU 36 Aa 93
44770 Escucha TE 91 Zb 104
46640 Escudero V 126 Za 115
09127 Escuderos BU 29 Vf 92
09342 Escuderos BU 48 Wa 96
23539 Escuelas, Las J 153 Wc 121
22636 Escuer HU 35 Zd 93
37216 Escuernavacas SA 63 Td 103
04532 Escúllar AL 170 Xb 125
04118 Escullos, Los AL 171 Xf 128
32549 Esculqueira OR 43 Sf 97
24397 Escuredo LE 26 Ua 92
49323 Escuredo ZA 44 Tc 95
10133 Escurial CC 117 Ua 114
37762 Escurial de la Sierra SA 82 Ua 105
26586 Escurquilla, Las RI 51 Xe 96
36993 Escusa PO 22 Rb 94
18130 Escúzar GR 168 Wb 126
22482 Esdolomada HU 36 Ac 95
36470 Esfarrapada = Salceda de Caselas PO 41 Rc 96
18511 Esfiliana GR 169 Wf 125
25555 Esglésies, Les L 37 Af 94
32720 Esgos OR 24 Sb 95
47176 Esguevillas de Esgueva VA 48 Vd 98
31690 Eskaroze = Escároz NC 34 Yf 91
20540 Eskoriatza SS 20 Xc 90
31494 Eslava NC 33 Yd 93
39694 Esles CB 18 Wb 89
12528 Eslida CS 108 Ze 109
15594 Esmelle C 11 Re 87
35627 Esmeralda Jandía GC 183 Le 180
15846 Esmorode C 10 Rb 90
31697 Esnotz NC 21 Yd 91
08697 Espà, L' B 57 Be 95
30627 Espada MC 141 Ye 120
37148 Espadaña SA 63 Te 102
10300 Espadañal CC 99 Uc 109
49342 Espadañedo ZA 45 Td 96
12230 Espadilla CS 108 Zd 108
25795 Espaén L 37 Bb 95
14600 Españares CO 136 Ve 119
17421 Esparra, L' GI 59 Cd 98
30891 Esparragal MC 156 Yb 123
30163 Esparragal MC 157 Yf 120
11180 Esparragal, El CA 173 Ub 129
14816 Esparragal, El CO 151 Ve 123
41860 Esparragal, El SE 148 Tf 123
06860 Esparragalejo BA 117 Td 115
30891 Esparragalico MC 156 Yb 123
06620 Esparragosa de Lares BA 118 Ue 115
06439 Esparragosa de la Serena BA 134 Uc 117
08292 Esparreguera B 76 Bf 99
03100 Espartal A 142 Zd 117
28722 Espartal, El MD 86 Wc 104
06172 Espartales BA 132 Tb 117
30890 Espartal y Mirones MC 155 Yb 123
41807 Espartinas SE 164 Tf 124
31191 Esparza NC 33 Yb 92
31453 Esparza NC 34 Yf 91
15339 Espasante C 10 Sb 86
37114 Espayos SA 64 Tf 102
37497 Espeja SA 81 Tb 105
42142 Espeja de San Marcelino SO 49 We 98
03679 Espejeras A 142 Zc 118
14830 Espejo CO 151 Vc 122
01423 Espejo VI 31 Wf 92
45910 Espejo, El TO 85 Vd 108
42164 Espejo de Tera SO 51 Xd 97
42142 Espejón SO 49 We 98
24913 Espejos de la Reina, Los LE 16 Va 91
04200 Espeliz AL 170 Xd 126
08711 Espelt, L' B 57 Bd 99
23628 Espelúy J 152 Wa 120
11648 Espera CA 164 Ub 127
27559 Esperante LU 24 Sb 92
10828 Esperanza, La CC 98 Td 110
18300 Esperanza, La GR 167 Vf 125
38290 Esperanza, La TF 181 Id 178
47639 Esperanza, La VA 47 Va 97
22472 Espés Alto HU 36 Ad 94
14220 Espiel CO 135 Uf 119
22351 Espierba HU 36 Aa 93
22348 Espierlo HU 35 Aa 94
22637 Espierre HU 35 Ze 93
22584 Espills L 56 Ae 95
33779 Espina AS 13 Sf 88
33891 Espina, La AS 14 Te 88
24889 Espina, La LE 28 Va 92
08618 Espinabet B 57 Be 96
24376 Espina de Tremor LE 26 Tf 92
39588 Espinama CB 16 Vb 90
19223 Espinar GU 68 We 102
30510 Espinar MC 141 Yf 117
30320 Espinar, El MC 157 Yf 122
40400 Espinar, El SG 85 Ve 104
45490 Espinar, El TO 102 Wa 109
18614 Espinar Alto GR 169 Wd 128
30100 Espinardo MC 157 Yf 120
24433 Espinaredo de Ancares LE 25 Tb 92
17869 Espinauga GI 39 Cb 95
17868 Espinavell GI 39 Cc 94
17747 Espinavessa GI 59 Cf 95
33629 Espinedo AS 15 Ua 90
17405 Espinelves GI 58 Cc 97
02459 Espineras del León, Las AB 139 Xd 117
39210 Espinilla CB 17 Ve 90
02611 Espinillo, El AB 123 Xb 115
35329 Espinillo, El GC 184 Kc 181
28804 Espinillos MD 86 Wd 106
29711 Espino MA 167 Vf 127
02640 Espino, El AB 125 Yf 115
42189 Espino, El SO 51 Xe 97
37429 Espino-Arcillo SA 65 Uc 102
37419 Espino de la Orbada SA 65 Ud 102
37170 Espino de los Doctores SA 64 Ua 102
24888 Espinosa de Almanza LE 28 Uf 92
39232 Espinosa de Bricia CB 30 Wa 91
34248 Espinosa de Cerrato P 48 Wa 97
09610 Espinosa de Cervera BU 49 Wd 97
19292 Espinosa de Henares GU 69 Wf 103
09198 Espinosa de Juarros BU 30 Wc 95
24274 Espinosa de la Ribera LE 27 Ub 92
09258 Espinosa del Camino BU 30 We 94
09268 Espinosa del Monte BU 31 Wf 94

272 | el Cogull

43364 Febró, La T 75 Ba 101
Feces de Abaixo OR 43 Sd 98
Feces de Cima OR 43 Sd 97
09566 Fefugio del C.D. de Bilbao BU 18 Wc 90
27375 Feira do Monte LU 12 Sc 89
15111 Feira Nova C 10 Rb 89
32847 Feira Nova, A OR 42 Sa 96
07200 Felanitx IB 111 Da 112
24734 Felechares de la Valdería LE 45 Tf 95
24858 Felechas LE 28 Ue 91
33687 Felechesa AS 15 Uc 90
15569 Felgosas C 11 Sa 87
33160 Felguera AS 15 Ua 89
33189 Felguera, La AS 15 Ub 88
33610 Felguera, La AS 15 Ub 89
33694 Felgueras AS 15 Ub 90
33995 Felguerina, La AS 15 Ud 90
30813 Feli MC 156 Yc 123
02156 Felipa, La AB 124 Yb 114
04728 Felix AL 170 Xc 127
24837 Felmín LE 27 Uc 91
35570 Femés GC 182 Mb 175
17310 Fenals GI 59 Ce 98
30627 Fenazar MC 141 Ye 120
15500 Fene C 11 Rf 88
22623 Fenillosa HU 35 Ze 94
32520 Fenteira OR 23 Re 94
36839 Fentosa PO 23 Rd 94
32315 Ferberza OR 25 Sf 94
02436 Férez AB 140 Xf 118
06390 Feria BA 132 Tc 117
50012 Feria Z 53 Za 99
49220 Fermoselle ZA 63 Td 101
13140 Fernancaballero CR 121 Wa 114
04827 Fernández, Los AL 155 Xf 123
23214 Fernandina J 137 Wc 119
14520 Fernán-Núñez CO 151 Vb 122
04116 Fernán Pérez AL 171 Xf 127
24415 Ferradillo LE 25 Tc 94
24010 Ferral del Bernesga LE 27 Uc 93
27328 Ferramubín LU 25 Sf 93
25216 Ferran L 57 Bc 98
15560 Ferreira C 11 Rf 87
18513 Ferreira GR 169 Wf 125
27830 Ferreira LU 12 Sb 88
27206 Ferreira LU 12 Sb 91
27770 Ferreira LU 12 Sd 87
27675 Ferreiras LU 25 Sf 92
27744 Ferreiravella LU 13 Se 89
18414 Ferreirola GR 169 We 127
27619 Ferreiros LU 24 Sd 92
27336 Ferreiros LU 24 Sd 93
27680 Ferreiros LU 24 Se 91
36599 Ferreirós PO 23 Re 92
27325 Ferreiros de Arriba LU 25 Se 93
32448 Ferreirúa OR 24 Sb 94
33969 Ferrera AS 15 Uc 89
24397 Ferreras LE 26 Ua 93
49335 Ferreras de Abajo ZA 45 Tf 97
49335 Ferreras de Arriba ZA 45 Te 97
24886 Ferreras del Puerto LE 28 Uf 91
17463 Ferreres GI 59 Cf 96
08611 Ferreres, Les B 57 Bf 96
27347 Ferrería LU 24 Se 93
07750 Ferreries IB 77 Ea 109
49321 Ferreros ZA 44 Tc 96
44490 Ferreruela de Huerva TE 72 Ye 102
49550 Ferreruela de Távara ZA 45 Tf 98
29690 Ferrete MA 173 Ue 130
27305 Ferrieros LU 12 Sb 89
27181 Ferroi LU 24 Sc 91
15403 Ferrol C 11 Re 88
27191 Fervedoira LU 12 Sc 90
15317 Fervenzas C 11 Rf 89
36875 Festín PO 23 Rd 95
22585 Fet HU 55 Ad 96
27329 Fiais LU 25 Sf 94
36990 Fianteira PO 22 Ra 94
33708 Figal, La AS 14 Tc 87
33683 Figaredo AS 15 Ub 89
33867 Figares AS 14 Te 88
31311 Figarol NC 33 Yd 94
25634 Fígols de la Conca = Fígols de Tremp L 56 Ae 96
08698 Fígols de les Mines B 57 Bf 95
25634 Fígols de Tremp L 56 Ae 96
25794 Fígols i Alinyà L 57 Bc 95
15809 Figueiras C 11 Rf 91
15896 Figueiras C 23 Rc 91
27749 Figueiras LU 12 Sd 88
15819 Figueiroa C 23 Rf 91
25130 Figuera, La L 56 Ad 97
43736 Figuera, La T 75 Ae 101
03410 Figueral A 142 Zb 117
07850 Figueral, Es IB 109 Bd 114
33794 Figueras AS 13 Sf 87
17600 Figueres GI 40 Cf 95
33887 Figuerina, La AS 13 Tb 89
15365 Figueroa C 10 Sa 86
43811 Figuerola del Camp T 75 Bb 100
25615 Figuerola de Meià L 56 Af 97
25655 Figuerola d'Orcau L 56 Af 96
12122 Figueroles CS 108 Ze 108
25351 Figuerosa, La L 56 Ba 98
49520 Figueruela de Abajo ZA 44 Td 97
49520 Figueruela de Arriba ZA 44 Td 97
49177 Figueruela de Sayago ZA 64 Ua 101
50639 Figueruelas Z 53 Ye 98
48113 Fika BI 19 Xb 89
15112 Filgueira C 10 Rb 89
27205 Filgueira LU 24 Sa 91
36490 Filgueira PO 42 Re 95
15390 Filgueira de Barranca C 11 Rf 90
15391 Filgueira de Traba C 11 Re 90
15613 Filgueiras C 11 Rf 88
27727 Filgueirua LU 13 Sf 88
24723 Filiel LE 26 Td 94
08712 Fillol B 76 Bc 99
16878 Finca de Belvalle CU 89 Ya 105
12598 Finca del Moro CS 93 Ac 106
35639 Finca del Vicario GC 183 Ma 178
04869 Fines AL 170 Xe 124
22585 Finestras HU 55 Ad 96
03509 Finestrat A 143 Ze 117
24492 Finolledo LE 26 Tc 93
04500 Fiñana AL 170 Xa 125
27418 Fiolleda LU 24 Sc 93
36457 Fiolledo PO 41 Rd 96
27548 Fión LU 24 Sc 93
15864 Fiopáns C 22 Rb 91
32748 Fiós OR 24 Sc 94
23489 Fique J 153 Wf 122
35430 Firgas GC 184 Kc 180
22373 Fiscal HU 35 Zf 94
15155 Fisterra C 22 Qe 91
15379 Fisteus C 11 Rf 90
31593 Fitero NC 52 Ya 96
32767 Fitoiro OR 24 Sd 95
36913 Fixón PO 22 Rb 94
17463 Flaçà GI 59 Cf 96
28312 Flamenca, La MD 102 Wc 108
32618 Flariz OR 43 Sc 97
47195 Flecha, La VA 47 Vb 99
03791 Fleix A 127 Zf 116
08712 Flix B 76 Bd 99
25617 Flix L 56 Af 98
43750 Flix T 74 Ad 101
33693 Flor de Acebos AS 15 Ub 90
25211 Florejacs L 56 Bb 98
48115 Flores BI 19 Xb 89
21390 Flores H 132 Ta 120
49559 Flores ZA 45 Te 98
05370 Flores de Ávila AV 65 Va 103
08173 Floresta, La B 77 Ca 100
25413 Floresta, La L 75 Af 99
41390 Florida SE 134 Ua 120
03150 Florida, La A 142 Zb 120
02140 Florida, La AB 124 Ya 115
33879 Florida, La AS 14 Td 89
11149 Florida, La CA 172 Tf 131
39593 Florida, La CB 17 Vd 89
35119 Florida, La GC 184 Kd 182
28048 Florida, La MD 86 Wb 106
37129 Florida de Liébana SA 64 Ub 102
30848 Flotas de Butrón, Las MC 156 Yd 122
33111 Focella AS 14 Tf 90
36873 Fofe PO 23 Rd 95
08495 Fogars de la Selva B 59 Ce 98
08470 Fogars de Montclús B 58 Cc 98
17861 Fogonells GI 39 Cb 95
17401 Fogueres del Pla GI 58 Cc 98
03294 Foia, La A 142 Zb 119
03503 Foiamanera, La A 143 Zf 117
12160 Foies, Les CS 92 Zf 106
27611 Foilebar LU 24 Sc 92
27346 Foilebar LU 24 Se 92
46134 Foios V 108 Zd 111
17132 Foixà GI 59 Cf 96
24392 Fojedo LE 27 Ub 93
17539 Folch GI 38 Bf 94
34810 Foldada P 29 Vd 92
27145 Folgosa LU 12 Sd 91
33810 Folgoso AS 13 Ta 90
27325 Folgoso LU 25 Se 93
36558 Folgoso PO 23 Rd 93
49594 Folgoso de la Carballeda ZA 44 Td 97
24311 Folgoso de la Ribera LE 26 Te 93
24413 Folgoso del Monte LE 26 Td 93
27325 Folgoso do Courel LU 25 Se 93
27777 Folgueiras LU 12 Sc 88
27659 Folgueiras LU 25 Ta 91
27861 Folgueiro LU 10 Sc 86
25738 Folguer L 56 Ba 96
33194 Folgueras AS 15 Ua 88
08519 Folgueroles B 58 Cb 97
24608 Folledo LE 27 Ub 91
33779 Folqueiras AS 13 Sf 88
39213 Fombellida CB 17 Vf 91
47184 Fombellida VA 48 Ve 98
50491 Fombuena Z 72 Ye 102
47311 Fompedraza VA 67 Vf 99
47492 Foncastín VA 66 Uf 100
26211 Foncea RI 31 Wf 93
24722 Foncebadón LE 26 Td 94
22474 Fonchanina HU 36 Ad 93
05198 Fonda de Santa Teresa AV 84 Uf 106
25244 Fondarella L 56 Af 99
38570 Fondeadero de Fasnia TF 181 Id 179
03640 Fondó de Monòver, El A 142 Za 118
04460 Fondón AL 170 Xa 127
33812 Fondos de Vegas AS 13 Tc 91
18515 Fonelas GR 153 We 124
27665 Fonfría LU 25 Sf 92
33314 Fonfría AS 15 Uc 88
24378 Fonfría LE 26 Te 93
27113 Fonfría LU 13 Sf 90
44492 Fonfría TE 72 Yf 103
49510 Fonfría ZA 45 Tf 99
43425 Fonoll T 75 Bb 99
25218 Fonolleres L 56 Bb 99
08259 Fonollosa B 57 Be 98
27113 Fonsagrada, A LU 13 Sf 90
37497 Fonseca SA 81 Tc 105
15009 Fontaiña C 11 Rd 89
03430 Fontanar A 142 Zb 117
19290 Fontanar GU 87 We 104
23486 Fontanar J 153 Xa 122
14547 Fontanar, El CO 150 Vb 123
02127 Fontanar de Alarcón, El AB 140 Xf 116
02129 Fontanar de las Viñas AB 140 Xf 116
13193 Fontanarejo CR 120 Vc 113
30811 Fontanares MC 155 Ya 122
46635 Fontanars dels Alforins V 126 Zb 116
AD600 Fontaneda ◘ AND 38 Bc 94
27133 Fontaneira, A LU 13 Se 90
03410 Fontanelíes, Les A 142 Zb 117
24291 Fontanil de los Oteros LE 27 Ud 94
49743 Fontanillas de Castro ZA 45 Ub 98
17257 Fontanilles GI 59 Da 96
13473 Fontanosas CR 136 Vc 116
24891 Fontanos de Torío LE 27 Uc 92
27210 Fontao LU 24 Sc 91
27610 Fontao LU 24 Sd 92
36583 Fontao PO 23 Re 92
03113 Font Calent A 142 Zc 118
17256 Fontclara GI 59 Da 97
17833 Fontcoberta GI 59 Ce 96
03578 Font de la Figuera A 142 Zd 117
46630 Font de la Figuera, La V 126 Za 116
46717 Font d'En Carròs, La V 127 Ze 115
12160 Font d'En Segures, La CS 92 Zf 106
25611 Fontdepou L 56 Ae 97
43897 Font de Quinto, La T 93 Ad 104
04271 Fonte, El AL 171 Xf 126
33828 Fontebona AS 14 Tf 88
15837 Fontecada C 10 Ra 91
24250 Fontecha LE 27 Ub 94
34878 Fontecha P 28 Vb 92
01423 Fontecha VI 31 Wf 92
32750 Fontedoso OR 24 Sd 95
22809 Fontellas HU 53 Zb 95
31512 Fontellas NC 52 Yc 96
25796 Fontelles L 38 Bc 95
28400 Fontenebro MD 85 Wa 105
10516 Fonteñera, La CC 115 Se 112
27278 Fonteo LU 13 Se 90
27866 Fonterova LU 10 Sc 87
17110 Fonteta GI 59 Da 97
39212 Fontibre CB 17 Ve 90
47609 Fontihoyuelo VA 47 Uf 96
03791 Fontilles A 127 Zf 116
09349 Fontioso BU 49 Wb 97
05310 Fontiveros AV 66 Va 103
25615 Fontllonga L 56 Af 97
43528 Font Nova T 74 Ac 103
24434 Fontoria LE 25 Tc 92
24711 Fontoria de Cepeda LE 26 Tf 93
17170 Font Picant, La GI 58 Cd 96
17834 Font Pudosa, La GI 59 Ce 96
08736 Fontrubí B 76 Bd 100
08194 Fonts, Les B 77 Ca 99
25639 Fontsagrada L 56 Af 96
43811 Fontscaldetes T 76 Bb 100
22422 Fonz HU 55 Ab 96
26211 Fonzaleche RI 31 Wf 93
25737 Foradada L 56 Ba 97
22452 Foradada del Toscar HU 36 Ac 94
17111 Forallac GI 59 Da 97
32786 Forcadas OR 43 Sd 95
25746 Força d'Estany, La L 56 Ba 97
27546 Forcados LU 24 Sc 92
12310 Forcall CS 92 Ze 105
36550 Forcarei PO 23 Rd 93
32748 Forcas OR 24 Sc 94
22487 Forcat HU 36 Ae 93
43425 Forès T 75 Bb 100
37799 Forfoleda SA 64 Ub 102
32643 Forja OR 42 Sa 96
15705 Formaris C 23 Rd 91
49230 Formariz ZA 63 Te 100
03179 Formentera del Segura A 157 Zb 120
07470 Formentor IB 111 Da 109
07712 Formet IB 77 Eb 109
44440 Formiche Alto TE 91 Za 107
44441 Formiche Bajo TE 91 Za 107
22640 Formigal, El HU 35 Zd 92
22336 Formigales HU 36 Ab 95
24124 Formigones LE 27 Ua 92
25794 Forn L 57 Bc 95
03786 Forna A 127 Ze 115
24746 Forna LE 25 Tc 95
07109 Fornalutx IB 110 Ce 110
07712 Fornàs de Torrelo IB 77 Eb 109
46600 Forn de Carrascosa, El V 126 Zd 113
27768 Fórnea, A LU 13 Se 88
27334 Fornelas LU 24 Sd 93
17255 Fornells GI 59 Db 97
07748 Fornells IB 77 Ea 108
07160 Fornells IB 110 Cc 111
17536 Fornells de la Muntanya GI 38 Ca 95
17458 Fornells de la Selva GI 59 Ce 97
15150 Fornelos C 10 Ra 89
32373 Fornelos OR 25 Sf 95
36770 Fornelos PO 41 Ra 97
36770 Fornelos PO 41 Rb 97
36455 Fornelos PO 41 Rd 96
32562 Fornelos de Filloas OR 43 Se 96
36847 Fornelos de Montes PO 23 Rd 95
18127 Fornes GR 168 Wa 127
22415 Fornillos HU 55 Aa 97
49513 Fornillos de Aliste ZA 45 Te 99
22006 Fornillos de Apiés HU 54 Zd 95
49232 Fornillos de Fermoselle ZA 63 Te 100
44650 Fórnoles TE 73 Zf 103
25717 Fórnols L 38 Bd 95
33986 Fornos AS 15 Uc 89
15807 Foro C 11 Rf 90
46418 Fortaleny V 126 Ze 113
44143 Fortanete TE 91 Zc 105
08281 Fortesa, La B 57 Bd 98
08784 Fortesa, La B 76 Be 100
17469 Fortià GI 59 Da 95
30620 Fortuna MC 141 Yf 119
28917 Fortuna, La MD 86 Wb 106
32456 Forxa, A OR 23 Rf 94
36853 Forzáns PO 23 Rd 94
22452 Fosado HU 36 Ab 94
17230 Fosot, La GI 59 Da 97
30441 Fotuya MC 140 Xf 119
15310 Foxados C 11 Rf 90
15142 Foxo C 11 Rc 89
36686 Foxo PO 23 Rd 92
33873 Foyedo AS 14 Tc 88
33785 Foyedo AS 14 Te 87
27780 Foz LU 13 Se 87
33161 Foz, La AS 15 Ua 89
33996 Foz, La AS 15 Ue 90
36866 Fozara PO 41 Rc 95
44579 Foz-Calanda TE 73 Ze 103
49519 Fradellos ZA 45 Te 98
32557 Fradelo OR 43 Sf 95
37766 Frades de la Sierra SA 83 Ub 105
37115 Frades Viejo SA 64 Ua 102
22268 Fraella HU 54 Ze 97
22520 Fraga HU 74 Ac 99
36955 Fraga PO 22 Rb 95
32858 Fraga, A OR 42 Rf 96
22377 Fragén HU 35 Zf 93
50610 Frago, El Z 34 Za 95
10627 Fragosa CC 82 Te 106
36330 Fragoselo PO 41 Rb 95
19239 Fraguas GU 68 Wf 102
36856 Fraguas PO 23 Rd 94
37120 Fraguas SA 64 Ub 103
39450 Fraguas, Las CB 17 Vf 89
42192 Fraguas, Las SO 50 Xb 98
18567 Frague, El GR 168 Wc 124
23690 Frailes J 152 Wa 124
27124 Frairia, A LU 13 Se 90
11180 Fraja CA 173 Ub 129
39574 Frama CB 17 Vc 90
27569 Frameán LU 24 Sb 92
33590 Franca, La AS 17 Vc 88
43880 Francàs, El T 76 Bc 101
18810 Francés, El GR 154 Xb 124
38728 Franceses TF 181 Ha 176
17456 Franciac GI 59 Ce 97
09215 Franco BU 31 Xb 92
33746 Franco, El AS 13 Ta 87
39788 Francos CB 18 We 88
37893 Francos SA 65 Ud 103
40514 Francos SG 68 Wd 100
09230 Frandovínez BU 30 Wa 95
36889 Franqueira, A PO 42 Rd 95
08521 Franqueses del Vallès, Les B 58 Cb 99
50320 Frasno, El Z 71 Yd 100
22714 Frauca HU 35 Zd 93
27547 Freán LU 24 Sb 93
32631 Freande OR 43 Sc 96
32135 Freás OR 23 Sa 94
32226 Freás OR 42 Rf 96
34306 Frechilla P 47 Va 96
42216 Frechilla de Almazán SO 70 Xc 100
12599 Fredes CS 92 Ab 104
06340 Fregenal de la Sierra BA 132 Tc 120
37220 Fregeneda SA 63 Ta 103
18710 Fregenite GR 169 Wd 128
43558 Freginals T 93 Ad 104
33775 Freije AS 13 Sf 88
18812 Freila GR 154 Xa 123
15338 Freires C 10 Sa 87
25713 Freita, La L 38 Bc 95
25566 Freixe L 37 Bb 94
15846 Freixeiro C 10 Rb 90
36544 Freixeiro PO 23 Re 93
17867 Freixenet GI 39 Cc 95
25270 Freixenet de Segarra L 57 Bc 99
32358 Freixido OR 25 Sf 94
15326 Freixo C 12 Sb 87
27624 Freixo LU 24 Se 92
32825 Freixo OR 42 Sa 95
50562 Fréscano Z 52 Yd 97
23380 Fresnadilla, La J 139 Xc 118
49255 Fresnadillo ZA 64 Tf 100
05196 Fresneda AV 84 Vb 105
39518 Fresneda CB 17 Ve 89
33429 Fresneda, La AS 15 Ub 88
44596 Fresneda, La TE 74 Aa 103
45651 Fresneda, La TO 100 Va 110
16781 Fresneda de Altarejos CU 104 Xe 109
40217 Fresneda de Cuéllar SG 66 Vd 101
16141 Fresneda de la Sierra CU 88 Xf 106
09267 Fresneda de la Sierra Tirón BU 31 Wf 95
40311 Fresneda de Sepúlveda SG 68 Wb 101
05427 Fresnedilla AV 84 Vc 107
23300 Fresnedilla, La J 154 Xa 120
28214 Fresnedillas MD 85 Ve 106
33111 Fresnedo AS 14 Tf 90
33116 Fresnedo AS 15 Ua 90
33529 Fresnedo AS 15 Ud 88
09553 Fresnedo BU 18 Wc 91
39738 Fresnedo CB 18 Wc 88
39806 Fresnedo CB 18 Wd 89
24492 Fresnedo LE 25 Tc 92
24878 Fresnedo de Valdellorma LE 28 Ue 92
37775 Fresnedoso SA 83 Ub 106
10328 Fresnedoso de Ibor CC 99 Uc 110
24232 Fresnellino del Monte LE 27 Uc 94
09259 Fresneña BU 31 Wf 94
33585 Fresnidiello AS 16 Ue 89
09471 Fresnillo de las Dueñas Fuentespina BU 49 Wb 99
05197 Fresno, El AV 84 Vb 105
10849 Fresno, El CC 98 Tc 108
19182 Fresno, El GU 87 We 104
37789 Fresno-Alhándiga SA 83 Uc 104
40516 Fresno de Cantespino SG 68 Wd 100
42311 Fresno de Caracena SO 69 Wf 100
49318 Fresno de la Carballeda ZA 45 Td 97
40540 Fresno de la Fuente SG 68 Wc 100
49693 Fresno de la Polvorosa ZA 45 Ub 96
49590 Fresno de la Ribera ZA 65 Uc 99
24765 Fresno de la Valduerna LE 26 Tf 94
24223 Fresno de la Vega LE 27 Uc 94
24391 Fresno del Camino LE 27 Uc 93
09511 Fresno de Losa BU 19 Wf 91
39212 Fresno del Río CB 17 Vf 90
34889 Fresno del Río P 28 Vb 92
09272 Fresno de Riotirón BU 31 We 94
09290 Fresno de Rodilla BU 30 Wd 94
49216 Fresno de Sayago ZA 64 Ua 101

274 | Febró, La

34116 Gañinas de la Vega P 28 Vb 94
30849 Gañuelas MC 156 Yd 122
30877 Gañuelas MC 156 Yd 123
16312 Garaballa CU 106 Yd 110
24768 Garaballes LE 27 Ua 94
15686 Garabanxa C 11 Re 90
38849 Garabato TF 184 He 180
14100 Garabato, El CO 150 Va 122
38450 Garachico TF 180 Ib 178
20569 Garagaltza SS 20 Xd 90
48110 Garai BI 19 Xa 88
48200 Garai BI 19 Xc 89
31692 Garaioa NC 20 Ye 91
48196 Garaiolza BI 19 Xb 89
24374 Garanja de San Vicente, La LE 26 Te 93
33591 Garaña AS 16 Va 88
24120 Garaño LE 27 Ub 92
30629 Garapacha, La MC 141 Ye 119
48190 Garape BI 19 Wf 89
20500 Garartza SS 20 Xc 90
27861 Garavide LU 10 Sb 86
48200 Garay BI 19 Xb 89
19283 Garbajosa GU 70 Xd 102
06690 Garbayuela BA 119 Va 114
17496 Garbet GI 40 Da 94
43749 Garcia T 74 Ad 102
04600 García AL 155 Ya 124
44480 García, La TE 107 Zc 108
30153 Garcías, Los MC 157 Ye 121
30590 Garcías, Los MC 157 Za 121
10250 Garciaz CC 118 Uc 112
37658 Garcibuey SA 82 Ua 105
23649 Garcíez J 152 Wa 121
23537 Garcíez J 153 Wd 121
23529 Garcíez-Jimena J 153 Wd 121
37452 Garcigalindo SA 82 Ua 104
37447 Garcigrande SA 64 Ua 103
37312 Garcigrande SA 83 Ud 104
40120 Garcillán SG 67 Ve 103
16510 Garcinarro CU 87 Xb 107
37607 Garciñigo SA 82 Ua 105
45643 Garciotún TO 101 Vc 108
31193 Garciriáin NC 33 Yb 91
37460 Garcirrey SA 64 Tf 103
11580 Garcisobaco CA 173 Uc 129
31491 Gardaláin NC 33 Yd 93
31414 Garde NC 34 Za 92
01400 Gardea VI 19 Xa 90
24160 Garfín LE 28 Ue 92
06711 Gargáligas BA 118 Uc 114
08612 Gargallà B 57 Be 97
44558 Gargallo TE 91 Zc 104
06350 Gargallón BA 132 Tb 120
36118 Gargallóns PO 23 Rc 94
09268 Garganchón BU 31 We 95
33776 Garganta, La AS 13 Sf 88
10759 Garganta, La CC 83 Ub 107
14449 Garganta, La CR 136 Vd 118
23293 Garganta, La J 139 Xc 119
33939 Gargantada AS 15 Uc 88
05571 Garganta de los Hornos AV 84 Ue 106
28743 Garganta de los Montes MD 68 Wb 103
05134 Garganta del Villar AV 84 Uf 106
10412 Garganta la Olla CC 99 Ub 108
13414 Gargantiel CR 119 Vb 116
10749 Gargantilla CC 82 Ua 107
45671 Gargantilla TO 100 Va 111
28739 Gargantilla del Lozoya MD 68 Wb 103
28739 Gargantilla del Lozoya y Pinilla del Buitrago MD 68 Wb 103
13100 Gargantón, El CR 120 Ve 114
19459 Gárgoles de Abajo GU 88 Xc 104
19459 Gárgoles de Arriba GU 88 Xc 104
10696 Gargüera CC 99 Ua 108
20569 Garibai SS 20 Xd 90
43153 Garidells, La T 75 Bb 101
20218 Garin SS 20 Xe 90
31395 Garínoain NC 33 Yc 93
31291 Garísoain NC 33 Ya 92
35214 Garita, La GC 184 Kd 180
06656 Garlitos BA 119 Uf 115
18614 Garnatilla, La GR 168 Wd 128
08872 Garraf B 76 Bf 101
24891 Garrafe de Torío LE 27 Uc 92
31693 Garralda NC 21 Ye 91
43739 Garranxa, La T 75 Af 101
26586 Garranzo RI 51 Xe 96
50190 Garrapinillos Z 53 Yf 98
06291 Garrapito BA 133 Te 120
42162 Garray SO 51 Xd 98
30158 Garres, Los MC 157 Yf 121
36314 Garrida PO 41 Rb 95
08698 Garriga, La B 57 Bf 96
08530 Garriga, La B 58 Cb 98
17476 Garrigàs GI 59 Cf 95
17466 Garrigoles GI 59 Da 96
17780 Garriguella GI 40 Da 94
30889 Garrobillo MC 156 Yd 124
41888 Garrobo, El SE 148 Te 123
06870 Garrovilla, La BA 116 Td 115
10940 Garrovillas CC 98 Tc 110
04630 Garrucha AL 171 Yb 125
21740 Garruchena H 163 Td 124
31866 Gartzaron NC 21 Yb 91
24132 Garueña LE 26 Tf 92
10333 Garvín CC 100 Ud 110
06475 Garza, La BA 133 Tf 116
25736 Gàrzola L 56 Ba 97
41650 Garzón SE 166 Uf 126
29150 Gascar MA 166 Vc 128
10627 Gasco, El CC 82 Te 106
28737 Gascones MD 68 Wc 102
31867 Gascue NC 21 Yc 91
16532 Gascueña CU 88 Xc 107
19243 Gascueña de Bornova GU 69 Wf 102
02430 Gaspares AB 140 Ya 118
31283 Gastiáin NC 32 Xe 92
11687 Gastor, El CA 165 Ue 127
10860 Gata CC 81 Tc 107
03740 Gata de Gorgos A 127 Aa 116
36839 Gateira PO 23 Rd 94
48110 Gatika BI 19 Xa 88
47606 Gatón de Campos VA 47 Va 96
04826 Gatos, Los AL 155 Xf 123
46169 Gátova V 107 Zc 110
29480 Gaucín MA 173 Ue 129
01193 Gauna VI 32 Xd 92
17466 Gaüses GI 59 Cf 96
48314 Gautegiz Arteaga BI 19 Xc 88
48314 Gautegiz Arteaga/Zelaieta BI 19 Xc 88
08850 Gavà B 77 Ca 101
43891 Gavadà T 75 Ae 103
46267 Gavarda V 126 Zc 114
25793 Gavarra L 56 Bb 96
08694 Gavarrós B 38 Bf 95
25588 Gavàs L 37 Ba 93
25214 Gàver L 57 Bc 98
25639 Gavet de la Conca L 56 Af 96
37593 Gavilán SA 82 Td 105
05460 Gavilanes AV 84 Va 107
24285 Gavilanes LE 27 Ua 93
22639 Gavín HU 35 Ze 93
07440 Gaviotas, Las IB 111 Da 110
09569 Gayangos BU 18 Wc 90
01206 Gazeo VI 32 Xd 91
31190 Gazólaz NC 33 Yb 92
04830 Gázquez, Los AL 155 Xf 122
04827 Gázquez, Los AL 155 Ya 123
04827 Gázquez de Arriba, Los AL 155 Ya 123
20491 Gaztelu SS 20 Xf 90
31454 Gazteluberri = Castillonuevo NC 34 Yf 92
44110 Gea de Albarracín TE 90 Yd 106
30848 Gebas MC 156 Yd 121
04568 Gebera AL 170 Xc 126
33811 Gedrez AS 14 Tc 90
37453 Gejo SA 82 Ua 103
37130 Gejo de Diego Gómez SA 64 Tf 103
37150 Gejo de los Reyes SA 64 Te 102
37159 Gejuelito del Monte SA 63 Te 102
37114 Gejuelo del Barro SA 64 Tf 102
12412 Geldo CS 107 Zd 109
18690 Gelibra, La GR 168 Wb 128
08790 Gelida B 76 Bf 100
41805 Gelo SE 164 Te 125
41120 Gelves SE 164 Tf 124
37219 Gema SA 63 Tc 103
49151 Gema ZA 65 Uc 100
05197 Gemuño AV 84 Vb 105
29492 Genalguacil MA 174 Ue 129
23392 Génave J 139 Xb 118
24792 Genestacio de la Vega LE 45 Ua 95
33876 Genestaza AS 14 Td 89
24144 Genestosa LE 14 Tf 90
33817 Genestoso AS 14 Td 90
31227 Genevilla NC 32 Xd 93
24837 Genicera LE 15 Ud 91
14816 Genilla CO 151 Ve 124
07015 Génova IB 110 Cd 111
46894 Genovés V 126 Zd 115
17539 Ger GI 38 Bf 94
33875 Gera AS 14 Td 89
20215 Geralekua Apeadero SS 20 Xe 91
24608 Geras LE 27 Ub 91
25614 Gerb L 56 Ae 98
22339 Gerbe HU 36 Ab 94
22372 Geré HU 35 Zf 93
48269 Gerena BI 20 Xc 89
41860 Gerena SE 148 Tf 123
44313 Gerenica, La TE 90 Yc 104
01207 Gereñu VI 32 Xd 92
04550 Gérgal AL 171 Xc 126
47131 Geria VA 47 Va 99
45518 Gerindote TO 101 Ve 109
04660 Germán AL 171 Xf 126
48300 Gernika-Lumo BI 19 Xb 89
25590 Gerri de la Sal L 37 Ba 95
25717 Ges, El L 38 Bc 95
20500 Gesalibar SS 20 Xc 90
22622 Gésera HU 35 Ze 94
25598 Gessa L 37 Af 92
46166 Gestalgar V 107 Za 111
24568 Gestoso LE 25 Sf 93
28901 Getafe MD 86 Wb 107
20808 Getaria SS 20 Xe 89
09612 Gete BU 49 We 97
24837 Gete LE 27 Uc 91
24837 Getino LE 15 Uc 91
13670 Getór CR 121 Wb 113
06180 Gévora del Caudillo BA 116 Ta 115
48499 Gezala BI 19 Xa 90
11592 Gibalbín CA 163 Ua 128
21500 Gibraleón H 162 Ta 124
29569 Gibralgalia MA 166 Vb 128
GI Gibraltar □ GBZ 174 Ud 132
30890 Gigante, El MC 155 Ya 122
24224 Gigosos de los Oteros LE 27 Uc 94
09585 Gijano BU 19 We 89
33206 Gijón = Xixón AS 15 Uc 87
33187 Gijún AS 15 Ub 88
02211 Gila, La AB 125 Yd 113
05619 Gilbuena AV 83 Uc 106
41565 Gilena SE 166 Va 125
41640 Gilenilla SE 166 Uf 125
04289 Giles, Los AL 171 Xf 126
44478 Giles, Los TE 107 Zc 108
46149 Gilet V 108 Ze 110
05693 Gil García AV 83 Uc 107
30439 Gilico MC 140 Yc 120
22623 Gillué HU 35 Ze 94
04549 Gilma AL 170 Xb 125
21342 Gil Márquez H 147 Tb 121
25112 Gimenells L 55 Ac 99
25180 Gimenells i el Pla de la Font L 55 Ac 99
02612 Gimeno AB 123 Xc 114
05380 Gimialcón AV 84 Uf 103
26221 Gimileo RI 31 Xb 93
44643 Ginebrosa, La TE 92 Zf 103
41960 Gines SE 163 Tf 124
43748 Ginestar T 74 Ad 102
31540 Ginestar, El NC 52 Yd 97
25571 Ginestarre L 37 Bb 93
02110 Gineta, La AB 124 Ya 114
30530 Ginete MC 141 Yd 119
02410 Ginete, El AB 140 Ya 117
35629 Giniginamar GC 183 Lf 179
22372 Ginuábel HU 35 Zf 94
33732 Gío AS 13 Ta 88
12123 Giraba de Arriba CS 107 Zd 108
22372 Giral HU 35 Zf 93
17002 Girona GI 59 Ce 97
41600 Gironda, La SE 165 Uc 126
08680 Gironella B 57 Bf 96
08695 Gisclareny B 57 Be 95
22367 Gistaín HU 36 Ab 93
17320 Giverola GI 59 Cf 98
48289 Gizaburuaga BI 20 Xc 88
03408 Gloria, La A 142 Za 116
37700 Gloria, La SA 83 Ub 106
43425 Glorieta T 75 Bb 99
01468 Goba Aundi VI 19 Wf 91
09512 Gobantes BU 18 Wd 91
29553 Gobantes MA 166 Vb 127
01191 Gobeo VI 31 Xb 91
18563 Gobernador GR 153 We 124
27259 Goberno LU 12 Sd 89
33342 Gobiendes AS 16 Ue 88
04279 Gochar AL 171 Xf 126
43516 Godall T 93 Ac 105
33869 Godán AS 14 Te 88
33758 Godella AS 13 Tb 87
46110 Godella V 126 Zd 111
46388 Godelleta V 126 Zb 112
50238 Godojos Z 70 Ya 101
36873 Godóns PO 23 Re 95
44221 Godos TE 72 Yf 103
15325 Goente C 11 Sa 88
Goi LU 12 Sd 91
20215 Goialdea SS 20 Xe 91
27614 Goián LU 24 Sd 92
36750 Goián PO 41 Rb 97
15999 Goiáns C 22 Ra 92
36510 Goiás PO 23 Rf 92
48650 Goierri BI 19 Xa 88
27840 Goiriz LU 12 Sc 89
48269 Goitana BI 20 Xc 89
48196 Goitiolza BI 19 Xb 89
31754 Goizueta NC 21 Ya 89
18150 Gójar GR 168 Wc 126
07470 Gola, La IB 111 Da 109
15819 Golán C 11 Rf 91
18450 Golco GR 169 Wf 127
31869 Goldáraz NC 21 Ya 91
23291 Goldines, Los J 139 Xb 120
09215 Golerinio BU 31 Xb 94
46409 Goleta, La V 127 Ze 114
31272 Gollano NC 32 Xf 92
02459 Gollizo, El AB 139 Xd 117
15357 Golmar C 10 Rf 86
15145 Golmar C 11 Rc 89
42190 Golmayo SO 51 Xc 98
25241 Golmés L 56 Af 99
10181 Golondrinas, Las CC 117 Tf 112
02253 Golosalvo AB 124 Yc 113
28760 Goloso, El MD 86 Wb 105
24689 Golpejar de la Tercia LE 15 Uc 91
37170 Golpejas SA 64 Ua 102
27191 Golpilleiras LU 12 Sd 90
36635 Gomara PO 22 Rb 93
42120 Gómara SO 51 Xe 99
32429 Gomariz OR 23 Rf 94
17531 Gombrèn GI 58 Ca 95
27164 Gomeán LU 24 Sd 91
37420 Gomecello SA 65 Uc 102
01195 Gomecha VI 31 Xb 92
37216 Gomeciego SA 63 Te 102
32212 Gomesende OR 42 Rf 95
32212 Gomesende OR 42 Rf 96
47493 Gomeznarro VA 66 Va 101
40516 Gómeznarro SG 68 Wd 101
40240 Gomezserracín SG 67 Ve 101
37882 Gómez Velasco SA 83 Ud 104
27293 Gondar LU 12 Sd 90
36990 Gondar PO 22 Rb 94
36380 Gondomar PO 41 Rb 96
27363 Gondrame LU 24 Sc 92
32626 Gondulfes OR 43 Sd 97
31192 Góngora NC 33 Yc 92
04200 Góngoras, Los AL 170 Xd 127
27738 Gontán LU 12 Sd 88
32813 Gontán OR 42 Sa 96
02489 Gontar AB 139 Xd 119
15839 Gonte C 22 Rb 91
15887 Gonzar C 11 Re 91
27188 Gonzar LU 24 Sb 92
04691 Goñar MC 155 Ya 124
31172 Goñi NC 33 Ya 92
01138 Gopegui VI 19 Xb 91
18870 Gor GR 169 Xa 124
18890 Gorafe GR 153 Wf 124
07850 Gorch, Es IB 109 Bd 114
47608 Gordaliza de la Loma VA 46 Uf 96
24325 Gordaliza del Pino LE 28 Uf 94
01478 Gordeliz VI 19 Wf 90
48192 Gordexola = Sandamendi BI 19 Wf 89
10392 Gordo, El CC 100 Ud 109
01208 Gordoa VI 32 Xd 91
37488 Gordón, El SA 81 Tb 104
24294 Gordoncillo LE 46 Ud 96
50685 Gordues Z 34 Ye 93
50686 Gordún Z 34 Yf 94
03811 Gorga A 143 Zd 116
15838 Gorgal C 22 Ra 91
23298 Gorgollitas, Las J 139 Xc 119
18616 Gorgoracha, La GR 168 Wc 128
36843 Gorgoreiro PO 23 Rc 95
15684 Gorgullos C 11 Rd 90
22375 Goriz HU 35 Aa 92
42313 Gormaz SO 69 Wf 100
08729 Gornal, La B 76 Bd 101
35215 Goro, El GC 184 Kd 181
48392 Gorocica Elixaldea BI 19 Xb 89
20550 Goroeta SS 20 Xd 90
31714 Gorostapolo de Errazu NC 21 Yd 90
01322 Gorrebusto VI 32 Xd 93
31877 Gorriti NC 20 Ya 90
31481 Gorriz NC 33 Yd 92
31799 Gorronz-Olano NC 21 Yb 91
25749 Gos, El L 56 Ba 97
15685 Gosende C 11 Re 90
25716 Gósol L 57 Bd 95
27375 Gospeito LU 12 Sc 89
25216 Gospí L 57 Bc 98
05163 Gotarrendura AV 84 Vb 104
50257 Gotor Z 71 Yc 99
33440 Gozón AS 15 Ua 87
34128 Gozón de Ucieza P 28 Vc 94
28339 Gózquez de Abajo MD 86 Wc 107
28339 Gózquez de Arriba MD 86 Wc 107
36548 Graba PO 23 Re 92
12550 Gràcia CS 108 Zf 109
22714 Gracionépel HU 35 Zd 93
24160 Gradefes LE 28 Ue 93
33820 Grado AS 14 Tf 88
22349 Grado, El HU 36 Aa 94
22390 Grado, El HU 55 Ab 96
40512 Grado del Pico SG 68 We 101
18517 Graena GR 169 We 125
32151 Graíces OR 24 Sb 94
14730 Graja, La CO 150 Ue 122
16339 Graja de Campalbo CU 106 Ye 109
16251 Graja de Iniesta CU 105 Yb 111
24340 Grajal de Campos LE 28 Uf 95
24796 Grajal de Ribera LE 46 Ub 95
24339 Grajalejo de las Matas LE 27 Ud 94
40569 Grajera SG 68 Wc 100
02110 Grajuela, La AB 124 Ya 114
41670 Gramadales, Los SE 166 Ue 126
33310 Gramedo AS 15 Ud 88
34846 Gramedo P 29 Vd 91
25512 Gramenet L 37 Af 94
25796 Gramós L 37 Bb 95
25217 Gramuntell L 56 Bb 99
18001*Granada GR 168 Wc 125
08792 Granada, La B 76 Be 100
21668 Granada de Riotinto, La H 148 Tc 122
03738 Granadella, La A 143 Ab 116
25177 Granadella, La L 74 Ae 100
30440 Granadicos, Los MC 140 Ya 119
10710 Granadilla CC 82 Tf 107
14950 Granadilla CO 167 Vd 124
38616 Granadilla de Abona TF 180 Ic 180
21594 Granado, El H 160 Sd 123
13360 Granátula de Calatrava CR 121 Wb 116
33418 Granda AS 15 Ua 87
33199 Granda AS 15 Ub 88
33390 Granda de Arriba AS 15 Uc 87
15616 Grandal C 11 Rf 88
33730 Grandas AS 13 Ta 89
05357 Grandes AV 84 Va 104
37468 Grandes SA 64 Te 103
05141 Grandes y San Martín AV 84 Va 104
33161 Grandiella AS 15 Ua 89
33986 Grandiella AS 15 Uc 89
27122 Grandón LU 12 Se 90
24858 Grandoso LE 27 Ue 91
38714 Granel, El TF 181 Hb 176
08183 Granera B 58 Ca 98
04814 Graneros de Abajo, Los AL 155 Xf 124
45280 Granja TO 102 Wa 109
10711 Granja, La CC 82 Ua 107
30420 Granja, La MC 140 Yb 119
31487 Granja, La NC 34 Ye 93
37810 Granja, La SA 65 Ud 103
47641 Granja, La VA 47 Uf 98
45860 Granja de Borregas TO 103 Wd 111
09239 Granja de la Cogalla BU 49 Wb 95
46816 Granja de la Costera, La V 126 Zc 115
34239 Granja de la Encomienda P 48 Vd 97
10291 Granja del Campazo CC 99 Ua 111
09316 Granja del Carrascal BU 48 Wa 98
09240 Granja del Hojalatero BU 30 Wd 93
50213 Granja de Llunes Z 71 Yb 102
09246 Granja del Moscadero BU 30 Wd 93
44780 Granja de los Juaneses TE 72 Zb 102
49740 Granja de Moreruela ZA 46 Ub 98
34257 Granja de Olmos de Cerrato P 48 Vf 96
45664 Granja de Pompajuela TO 100 Va 109
03348 Granja de Rocamora A 142 Za 120
24224 Granja de San Antolín LE 27 Uc 94
24325 Granja de San Esteban LE 28 Uf 94
22559 Granja de San José HU 55 Ac 98
40237 Granja de San Juan SG 67 Wa 100
47314 Granja de San Mamés VA 67 Ve 99
42269 Granja de San Pedro Z 70 Xf 101
50693 Granja de Santa Inés Z 53 Yf 98
09128 Granja de Santibáñez BU 29 Vf 94
25185 Granja d'Escarp, La L 74 Ac 100
06910 Granja de Torrehermosa BA 134 Uc 119
09240 Granja de Valdelaencina BU 30 We 93
09240 Granja de Valdevín BU 31 We 93
50341 Granja de Zaragocilla Z 71 Yb 101
31320 Granjafrío NC 52 Yb 95
42134 Granja la Salma SO 51 Xd 98
09191 Granja Las Mijarades BU 30 Wc 94
44370 Granjas, Las TE 90 Ye 105
43786 Granja Venta de Sant Joan T 74 Ab 102
14207 Granjuela, La CO 134 Ud 118
08400 Granollers B 58 Cb 99
25212 Granollers de Segarra L 56 Bb 97
35620 Gran Tarajal GC 183 Lf 179
49621 Granucillo ZA 45 Ua 96
36307 Granxa PO 41 Rb 96
25218 Granyadella L 56 Bb 99
25218 Granyanella L 56 Bb 99

276 | Gañinas de la Vega

25160 Granyena de les Garrigues L 74 Ad 100
25217 Granyena de Segarra L 56 Bb 99
15635 Graña C 11 Rf 89
15590 Graña, A C 11 Re 88
32678 Graña, A OR 42 Sb 96
36873 Graña, A PO 23 Re 95
15339 Grañas C 12 Sb 87
22260 Grañén HU 54 Zd 97
23009 Grañena J 152 Wb 121
24343 Grañeras LE 28 Ue 94
02420 Grao, El AB 140 Yb 118
22622 Grasa HU 35 Ze 94
33313 Grases AS 15 Ud 88
43737 Gratallops T 75 Ae 101
07712 Grau, Es IB 77 Eb 109
12530 Grau de Borriana, El CS 108 Zf 109
46730 Grau de Gandía, El V 127 Zf 115
12593 Grau de Moncófa, El CS 108 Zf 110
08610 Graugés B 57 Bf 96
22430 Graus HU 55 Ac 95
26587 Grávalos RI 51 Ya 96
02489 Graya AB 139 Xd 119
11610 Grazalema CA 165 Ud 128
09142 Gredilla de Sedano BU 30 Wb 92
09141 Gredilla la Polera BU 30 Wb 93
08695 Gréixer B 38 Bf 95
15116 Grelas C 10 Ra 89
36587 Gres PO 23 Rd 92
36519 Gresande PO 23 Re 93
08255 Grevalosa B 57 Bd 98
31480 Grez NC 33 Yd 92
22339 Griebal HU 36 Ab 94
02139 Griego, El AB 140 Xf 117
44114 Griegos TE 89 Yb 106
17258 Griells, Les GI 59 Db 96
09128 Grijalba BU 29 Vf 94
49621 Grijalba de Vidriales ZA 45 Ua 96
34810 Grijera P 29 Ve 92
34192 Grijota P 47 Vc 96
30396 Grillas, Las MC 157 Yf 123
16191 Grillera, La CU 105 Xf 108
04619 Grima AL 171 Yb 125
10829 Grimaldo CC 98 Td 109
28971 Griñón MD 86 Wa 107
09245 Grisaleña BU 30 We 93
50513 Grisel Z 52 Yb 97
50297 Grisén Z 53 Yf 98
49519 Grisuela ZA 45 Te 98
24357 Grisuela del Páramo LE 27 Ub 94
15845 Grixoa C 10 Ra 90
32557 Grixoa OR 43 Sf 95
31292 Grocin NC 32 Ya 92
27183 Grolos LU 24 Sc 91
37159 Groo, El SA 64 Te 102
08275 Grossa, La B 58 Ca 98
36980 Grove, O PO 22 Ra 94
33829 Grullas AS 14 Tf 88
24994 Grullas LE 16 Uf 90
24346 Grulleros LE 27 Uc 93
22438 Grustán HU 55 Ab 95
23293 Guadabraz J 139 Xb 119
11379 Guadacorte CA 175 Ud 131
23280 Guadahornillos J 138 Xa 119
18560 Guadahortuna GR 153 Wd 123
06187 Guadajira BA 116 Tb 115
41339 Guadajoz SE 149 Ub 123
19003 Guadalajara GU 87 Wf 105
44115 Guadalaviar TE 89 Yb 106
41390 Guadalcanal SE 134 Ub 120
14130 Guadalcázar CO 150 Va 122
41719 Guadalema de los Quinteros SE 164 Ua 126
23713 Guadalén J 137 Wc 120
03517 Guadalest A 143 Ze 116
28794 Guadalix de la Sierra MD 86 Wb 104
29689 Guadalmansa MA 174 Uf 130
29011 Guadalmedina MA 167 Vd 128
29678 Guadalmina MA 174 Uf 130
29693 Guadalobón MA 174 Ue 130
10392 Guadalperal CC 99 Ud 110
06713 Guadalperales, Los BA 118 Ub 114
10140 Guadalupe CC 118 Ue 112
11690 Guadamanil CA 165 Ud 127
28691 Guadamonte MD 85 Wa 106
45160 Guadamur TO 101 Vf 110
37590 Guadapero SA 82 Td 105
28440 Guadarrama MD 85 Vf 104
11369 Guadarranque CA 173 Ud 131
46839 Guadasequies V 126 Zd 115
46610 Guadassuar V 126 Zd 113
11339 Guadiana CA 174 Ud 130
06186 Guadiana del Caudillo BA 116 Tb 115
11311 Guadiaro CA 174 Ud 131
09135 Guadilla de Villamar BU 29 Ve 93
10137 Guadisa CC 119 Uf 112
18500 Guadix GR 169 Wf 125
37219 Guadramiro SA 63 Td 102
04778 Guainos Altos AL 169 Wf 128
04778 Guainos Bajos AL 169 Wf 128
18615 Guájar Alto GR 168 Wc 127
10817 Guajardo y Malhincada CC 98 Tc 108
18615 Guájares, Los GR 168 Wc 127
18615 Guajar-Faragüit GR 168 Wc 127
18615 Guájar-Fondón GR 168 Wc 127
08474 Gualba de Dalt B 58 Cc 98
18614 Gualchos GR 169 Wd 128
17257 Gualda GI 59 Da 96
19459 Gualda GU 88 Xb 104
13490 Gualdálmez CR 135 Va 116
38330 Guamasa TF 181 Id 178
38440 Guancha, La TF 180 Ic 178
38916 Guarazoca TF 180 Ha 182
36780 Guarda, A = La Guardia PO 41 Ra 97
06459 Guarda, La BA 118 Ub 116
36780 Guarda = La Guardia, A PO 41 Ra 97
03140 Guardamar del Segura A 157 Zc 120
22312 Guardia HU 55 Aa 96
45760 Guardia, La TO 103 Wd 110
36780 Guardia, La = A Guarda PO 41 Ra 97
25795 Guàrdia d'Ares, La L 37 Bb 95
23170 Guardia de Jaén, La J 152 Wb 122
17731 Guàrdia de la Muga, La GI 40 Cf 95
43410 Guàrdia dels Prats, La T 75 Bb 100
08517 Guàrdia de Sagàs, La B 57 Bf 96
25632 Guàrdia de Tremp L 56 Ae 96
25331 Guàrdia d'Urgell, La L 56 Ba 98
25217 Guardia Lada, La L 56 Bb 99
08280 Guàrdia Pilosa, La B 57 Bc 98
04715 Guardias Viejas AL 170 Xa 128
04210 Guardines, Los AL 171 Xf 126
08694 Guardiola de Berguedà B 57 Bf 95
08736 Guardiola de Font-rubí B 76 Bd 100
25792 Guardiola de Segre L 56 Bb 97
34880 Guardo P 28 Va 92
05540 Guareña AV 84 Va 105
06470 Guareña BA 117 Tf 115
47513 Guareña, La VA 65 Ue 101
06220 Guarida BA 133 Te 117
29108 Guaro MA 175 Vb 129
49156 Guarrate ZA 65 Ud 101
23210 Guarromán J 137 Wb 119
04479 Guarros AL 169 Xa 126
22714 Guasa HU 35 Zc 93
22713 Guasillo HU 35 Zc 93
22349 Guaso HU 36 Aa 94
35544 Guatiza GC 182 Md 174
38358 Guayonje TF 181 Id 178
38413 Guaza TF 180 Ib 180
34306 Guaza de Campos P 47 Va 96
44433 Gúdar TE 91 Zb 106
40419 Gudillos SG 85 Ve 104
32540 Gudiña, A OR 43 Sf 96
20218 Gudugarreta SS 20 Xe 90
44001 Guea, La TE 90 Yf 106
32704 Guede OR 24 Sb 95
18160 Güéjar-Sierra GR 168 Wd 126
22437 Güel HU 55 Ac 95
31799 Guelbenzu NC 21 Yc 91
31176 Guembe NC 33 Ya 92
39191 Güemes CB 18 Wc 88
31190 Guenduláin NC 33 Yb 92
31799 Guenduláin NC 33 Yc 91
48840 Güeñes BI 19 Wf 89
32152 Gueral OR 24 Sa 94
31119 Guerendiáin NC 33 Yc 92
31421 Guerguitiáin NC 33 Yd 92
30333 Guerreros, Los MC 156 Ye 122
31452 Güesa = Gotza NC 34 Yf 92
18212 Güevéjar GR 168 Wc 125
30391 Guía, La MC 157 Yf 123
38680 Guía de Isora TF 180 Ib 179
43429 Guialmons T 76 Bc 99
43777 Guiamets, Els T 75 Ae 102
33779 Guiar AS 13 Sf 88
40185 Guijar, El SG 67 Wa 102
14547 Guijarrosa, La CO 150 Va 123
40423 Guijasalbas SG 85 Ve 104
21840 Guijillo, El H 147 Tb 124
11620 Guijo, El CA 164 Ua 128
14413 Guijo, El CO 135 Vb 118
21840 Guijo, El H 147 Tc 124
37774 Guijo de Ávila SA 83 Uc 105
10815 Guijo de Coria CC 98 Td 108
10816 Guijo de Galisteo CC 98 Td 108
10665 Guijo de Granadilla CC 98 Tf 107
10459 Guijo de Santa Bárbara CC 99 Uc 108
19263 Guijosa GU 69 Xc 102
42141 Guijosa SO 49 We 98
02610 Guijoso, El AB 123 Xb 115
37770 Guijuelo SA 83 Ub 105
05690 Guijuelos, Los AV 83 Ud 107
36538 Guillar PO 23 Sa 92
36720 Guillarei PO 41 Rc 96
01439 Guillarte VI 31 Xa 91
41210 Guillena SE 148 Tf 123
25714 Guils = Guils del Contó L 37 Bb 94
17528 Guils de Cerdanya GI 38 Bf 94
17528 Guils i Fontanera GI 38 Be 94
35559 Güima GC 182 Mc 175
38500 Güímar TF 181 Id 179
24429 Guímara LE 25 Tb 91
09349 Guímara BU 49 Wb 97
32539 Guimarás OR 23 Rf 94
49025 Guimaré ZA 64 Ub 99
27235 Guimarei LU 12 Sb 91
27680 Guimarei LU 24 Se 91
36681 Guimarel PO 23 Rd 92
25341 Guimerà L 75 Bb 99
05003 Guimorcondo AV 84 Vc 105
35541 Guinate GC 182 Md 173
38639 Guincho, El TF 180 Ic 180
47151 Guindaleras, Las VA 66 Vb 99
31448 Guíndano NC 34 Ye 92
01428 Guinea VI 31 Wf 91
25597 Guingueta d'Anen, La L 37 Ba 93
09219 Guinicio BU 31 Wf 92
04826 Guiraos, Los AL 155 Xf 123
04647 Guiraos, Los AL 171 Yb 124
31291 Guirguillano NC 33 Ya 92
25511 Guiró L 37 Af 94
15640 Guísamo C 11 Re 89
05417 Guisando AV 84 Uf 107
24131 Guisatecha LE 26 Tf 92
35612 Guisgey GC 183 Ma 177
25210 Guissona L 56 Bb 98
04500 Güitamarín AL 169 Xb 125
27300 Guitiriz LU 12 Sa 89
08272 Guix, El B 57 Bf 98
25285 Guixers = Valls (Guixers) L 57 Bd 96
01449 Gujuli VI 19 Xa 91
31867 Gulina NC 33 Yb 91
09491 Gumá BU 49 Wc 99
09370 Gumiel de Hizán BU 49 Wb 98
09443 Gumiel de Mercado BU 49 Wb 98
27469 Gundivós LU 24 Sc 94
32635 Guntimil OR 42 Sb 96
27211 Guntín LU 24 Sb 91
27416 Guntín LU 24 Sc 94
08793 Gunyoles, Les B 76 Be 100
43154 Gunyoles, Les T 75 Bb 101
08503 Gurb B 58 Cb 97
01427 Gurendes VI 31 Wf 91
38879 Guro, El TF 184 He 180
25636 Gurp L 56 Af 95
31438 Gurpegui NC 33 Yd 91
22280 Gurrea Gállego HU 53 Zb 96
39686 Gurueba, La CB 18 Wa 89
33825 Gurullés AS 14 Tf 88
24209 Gusendos de los Oteros LE 27 Ud 94
32100 Gustei OR 24 Sa 94
23339 Gutar J 138 Xa 119
05197 Guterreño AV 84 Vb 105
05296 Gutierre-Muñoz AV 66 Vc 103
48480 Gutiolo BI 19 Xa 89
26530 Gutur RI 51 Ya 97
32868 Guxinde OR 42 Rf 97
09314 Guzmán BU 48 Wa 98

H

06714 Haba, La BA 118 Ub 115
13700 Habana, La CR 122 Wf 113
18520 Hacho, El GR 153 We 123
41410 Hacienda Alabarra SE 149 Ua 123
41703 Hacienda de Bujalmoro SE 163 Ua 125
18132 Hacienda de Don Juan GR 168 Wa 126
21891 Hacienda de Genís H 164 Td 124
41530 Hacienda de la Alcoba SE 165 Uc 126
41720 Hacienda de la Capitana SE 164 Ua 125
41410 Hacienda de la Florida SE 149 Ub 124
21800 Hacienda de la Luz H 161 Tb 125
41600 Hacienda de la Mata SE 165 Uc 125
41710 Hacienda del Ángel SE 165 Ub 126
41500 Hacienda de las Andradas SE 163 Ua 125
41770 Hacienda de las Cañas SE 165 Uc 126
41410 Hacienda de la Sillera SE 149 Ub 124
41500 Hacienda de la Soledad SE 164 Ua 124
41300 Hacienda del Bodegón de las Cañas SE 149 Ua 123
41410 Hacienda del Córdoba SE 149 Ub 124
41410 Hacienda del Corzo SE 149 Ua 124
41730 Hacienda del Mosquito SE 164 Ua 127
41600 Hacienda de los Locos SE 165 Ud 125
14979 Hacienda de los López CO 167 Ve 125
41230 Hacienda de los Melonares SE 149 Ua 122
30368 Hacienda del Pino MC 157 Za 122
41410 Hacienda del Rosal SE 149 Ub 124
41500 Hacienda de Maestre SE 163 Ua 125
41770 Hacienda de Morejón SE 165 Uc 127
41710 Hacienda de Orán SE 164 Ua 125
41710 Hacienda de Pajarero SE 165 Ub 125
30380 Hacienda Dos Mares MC 157 Zb 122
41410 Hacienda El Oidor SE 149 Ub 123
41410 Hacienda El Pino SE 149 Ub 123
38300 Hacienda Perdida, La TF 180 Ic 178
41210 Hacienda y Cortijo de la Lapa SE 148 Tf 123
09611 Hacinas BU 49 We 97
09268 Haedillo BU 30 We 94
09613 Haedo BU 49 Wd 97
09573 Haedo de las Pueblas BU 18 Wb 90
09557 Haedo de Linares BU 18 Wc 90
01117 Harana VI 32 Xd 92
35520 Haría GC 182 Md 174
41730 Harinosa, La SE 163 Ua 127
26200 Haro RI 31 Xa 93
39418 Haya, El CB 29 Vf 91
38892 Hayas, Las TF 184 He 180
09463 Haza BU 48 Wb 99
23340 Haza Alta J 138 Xa 118
10697 Haza de la Concepción CC 99 Ua 109
18710 Haza del Lino GR 169 We 128
04532 Haza del Riego, El AL 170 Xb 125
23610 Haza Mora J 152 Wa 123
18760 Haza Mora, La GR 169 We 128
39806 Hazas CB 18 Wc 89
39776 Hazas CB 18 Wd 88
39738 Hazas de Cesto CB 18 Wc 88
22720 Hecho HU 34 Zb 92
09212 Hedeso BU 30 We 92
49573 Hedradas, Las ZA 44 Ta 96
32366 Hedreira OR 25 Ta 95
06613 Helechal BA 134 Ud 116
06692 Helechosa de los Montes BA 119 Va 113
39709 Helguera CB 19 We 88
39569 Helgueras CB 17 Vc 88
39809 Helguero CB 18 Wd 89
02400 Hellín AB 140 Yb 117
40299 Henar, El SG 67 Vd 100
16312 Henarejos CU 106 Yd 109
30890 Henares MC 155 Ya 123
19491 Henche GU 88 Xb 104
39805 Herada CB 18 Wd 89
39792 Heras CB 18 Wb 88
19197 Heras GU 87 Wf 104
34879 Heras de la Peña, Las P 28 Vb 92
25518 Herba-savina L 56 Ba 95
15183 Herbes C 11 Rd 89
12317 Herbés CS 92 Zf 104
12319 Herbeset CS 92 Zf 105
48870 Herbosa BI 19 We 89
09571 Herbosa BU 18 Wa 91
48890 Herboso BI 18 Wd 89
26584 Herce RI 51 Xe 95
04500 Heredad, La AL 169 Xa 126
16520 Heredad de Bardaji CU 104 Xc 108
23489 Heredamiento J 153 Wf 121
01206 Heredia VI 32 Xd 91
13640 Herencia CR 122 Wd 112
45664 Herencias, Las TO 100 Va 109
01420 Hereña VI 31 Xa 92
33448 Heres AS 15 Ub 87
10230 Herguijuela CC 118 Ub 112
05631 Herguijuela, La AV 83 Ue 106
10591 Herguijuela, La CC 99 Ua 109
37619 Herguijuela de la Sierra SA 82 Tf 106
37762 Herguijuela del Campo SA 82 Ua 105
37516 Herguijuelo de Ciudad-Rodrigo SA 81 Tc 106
33717 Herías AS 13 Tb 88
02440 Hermanas, Las AB 139 Xe 118
34247 Hérmedes de Cerrato P 48 Ve 98
39580 Hermida, La CB 17 Vc 89
38890 Hermigua TF 184 He 180
49572 Hermisende ZA 44 Ta 97
Hermosa CB 18 Wb 88
09246 Hermosilla BU 30 Wd 93
05690 Hermosillo AV 83 Ud 106
13720 Hermosura CR 122 We 114
01208 Hermua VI 32 Xd 91
06620 Hernán Cabrera BA 118 Ud 115
06412 Hernán Cortés BA 117 Ua 114
04890 Hernández, Los AL 170 Xc 124
20120 Hernani SS 20 Ya 89
10868 Hernán-Pérez CC 81 Td 107
05164 Hernansancho AV 84 Vb 103
18880 Hernán Valle GR 169 Wf 124
20494 Hernialde SS 20 Xf 90
30510 Herrada del Manco MC 141 Yf 117
46320 Herradas V 106 Ye 110
02154 Herradilla, La AB 125 Yd 114
05268 Herradón, El AV 85 Vc 105
04277 Herradura AL 171 Xf 126
18697 Herradura, La GR 168 Wb 128
50709 Herradura, La Z 74 Aa 101
26213 Herramélluri RI 31 Wf 93
30170 Herreña MC 156 Yc 121
39608 Herrera CB 18 Wa 88
41567 Herrera SE 166 Va 124
02162 Herrera, La AB 123 Xf 115
48869 Herrera, La BI 19 We 89
10512 Herrera de Alcántara CC 96 Sd 111
47161 Herrera de Duero VA 66 Vc 99
39509 Herrera de Ibio CB 17 Ve 89
06670 Herrera del Duque BA 119 Uf 113
50150 Herrera de los Navarros Z 72 Yf 101
34400 Herrera de Pisuerga P 29 Ve 93
42148 Herrera de Soria SO 50 Wf 98
34259 Herrera de Valdecañas P 48 Ve 96
09593 Herrera de Valdivielso BU 30 Wd 92
23315 Herrera-Puente del Condado J 138 We 120
28296 Herreras, Las MD 85 Ve 105
19342 Herrería GU 70 Ya 103
02124 Herrería, La AB 140 Xf 117
04289 Herrería, La AL 171 Xf 126
06174 Herrería, La BA 132 Tb 117
14129 Herrería, La CO 150 Uf 122
41800 Herrería, La SE 163 Te 124
16152 Herrería de los Chorros CU 89 Yb 107
16879 Herrería de Santa Cristina CU 88 Xe 105
39550 Herrerías CB 17 Vd 89
04618 Herrerías, Las AL 171 Yb 125
21559 Herrerías, Las H 146 Se 123
19392 Herrería Vieja GU 89 Xf 104
37609 Herreros SA 82 Ua 104
42145 Herreros SO 50 Xb 98
47116 Herreros VA 65 Uf 100
04770 Herreros, Los AL 169 Wf 128
46199 Herreros, Los V 125 Za 113
24767 Herreros de Jamuz LE 26 Ua 95
24161 Herreros de Rueda LE 28 Ue 93
05146 Herreros de Suso AV 84 Uf 104
10560 Herreruela CC 116 Ta 112
34846 Herreruela de Castillería P 29 Vd 91
45588 Herreruela de Oropesa TO 100 Ue 109
37864 Herrezuelo SA 83 Ud 104
47607 Herrín de Campos VA 47 Va 96
16290 Herrumblar, El CU 124 Yc 112
02410 Heruela AB 140 Ya 117
10700 Hervás CC 82 Ua 107
24410 Hervededo LE 25 Tc 93
26257 Hervías RI 31 Xa 94
46625 Hervideros, Los V 125 Yf 113
08619 Heures, Les B 57 Ca 96
33187 Hevia AS 15 Ub 88
19242 Hiendelaencina GU 69 Wf 102
09515 Hierra BU 30 Wd 91
45270 Higares TO 102 Wa 109
09571 Higón BU 18 Wa 91
10359 Higuera CC 99 Ub 110
05491 Higuera, La AV 100 Va 107
29310 Higuera, La MA 167 Vd 126
40191 Higuera, La SG 67 Vf 102
44421 Higuera, La TE 106 Yf 108

Higuera, La | 277 E

23746 Higuera de Arjona J 152 Wa 121
23611 Higuera de Calatrava J 151 Vf 122
05427 Higuera de las Dueñas AV 85 Vc 107
06441 Higuera de la Serena BA 134 Ub 117
21220 Higuera de la Sierra H 148 Td 121
06445 Higuera de Llerena BA 133 Ua 118
06132 Higuera de Vargas BA 132 Ta 118
04887 Higueral AL 170 Xd 124
23488 Higueral J 153 Wf 122
14979 Higueral, El CO 167 Ve 125
44559 Higueral, El TE 91 Zc 104
06350 Higuera la Real BA 132 Tb 120
04660 Higuerales, Los AL 171 Xf 124
12449 Higueras CS 107 Zc 109
14816 Higueras, Las CO 151 Vf 124
23160 Higueras, Las J 152 Wa 122
35329 Higuerilla, La GC 184 Kb 181
38320 Higuerita, La TF 181 Ie 178
14193 Higuerón, El CO 150 Va 121
02694 Higueruela AB 125 Yd 115
46162 Higueruelas V 107 Za 110
05131 Hija de Dios, La AV 84 Va 105
02410 Híjar AB 140 Xf 117
44530 Híjar TE 73 Zd 101
39670 Hijas CB 17 Wa 89
04898 Hijate, El AL 170 Xc 124
19276 Hijes GU 69 Xa 101
01193 Hijona VI 32 Xc 92
34405 Hijosa de Boedo P 29 Ve 94
37497 Hincapié SA 81 Tc 105
09119 Hinestrosa BU 29 Vf 95
49192 Hiniesta, La ZA 64 Ub 99
09199 Hiniestra BU 30 Wd 94
10192 Hinojal CC 98 Td 110
09108 Hinojal de Riopisuerga BU 29 Ve 93
21388 Hinojales H 147 Tc 120
30816 Hinojar MC 156 Yc 122
09610 Hinojar de Cervera BU 49 Wd 97
09454 Hinojar del Rey BU 49 We 98
23486 Hinojares J 153 Xa 122
39350 Hinojedo CB 17 Vf 88
21740 Hinojos H 164 Td 125
19334 Hinojosa GU 70 Ya 102
16435 Hinojosa, La CU 104 Xd 110
42142 Hinojosa, La SO 49 We 98
44157 Hinojosa de Jarque TE 91 Zb 104
42153 Hinojosa de la Sierra SO 50 Xc 97
42112 Hinojosa del Campo SO 51 Xf 98
37230 Hinojosa del Duero SA 63 Tb 103
14270 Hinojosa del Duque CO 135 Uf 118
06226 Hinojosa del Valle BA 133 Te 118
45645 Hinojosa de San Vicente TO 101 Vb 108
13590 Hinojosas de Calatrava CR 136 Vf 117
40317 Hinojosas del Cerro SG 67 Wa 100
16417 Hinojosos, Los CU 104 Xb 111
10164 Hirguijuelas de Abajo CC 117 Te 112
31671 Hiriberri/Villanueva de Aezkoa NC 20 Ye 91
04769 Hirmes AL 169 Xa 127
28191 Hiruela, La MD 68 Wd 102
19248 Hita GU 87 Wf 104
16441 Hito, El CU 104 Xb 109
09558 Hocina BU 30 Wc 91
04850 Hojilla, La AL 171 Xe 124
10829 Holguera CC 98 Td 109
19328 Hombrados GU 89 Yb 104
47219 Honcalada VA 66 Va 102
20280 Hondarribia SS 21 Yb 88
03409 Hondo de Carboneras, El A 142 Za 117
11612 Hondón CA 174 Ud 128
16317 Hondonada, La CU 106 Yc 107
16318 Hondonadas, Las CU 106 Yd 108
03688 Hondón de las Nieves A 142 Za 119
03689 Hondón de los Frailes A 142 Za 119
37607 Hondura SA 82 Ua 105
47219 Honquilana VA 66 Vb 102
06498 Honrada, La BA 116 Tc 116
16730 Honrubia CU 104 Xe 111
40541 Honrubia de la Cuesta SG 68 Wb 99
40353 Hontalbilla SG 67 Vf 100
45159 Hontanar TO 101 Vc 111
46140 Hontanar V 106 Yd 108
46178 Hontanar, El V 106 Yf 109
23748 Hontanar de Flores J 136 Vf 118
05418 Hontanares AV 100 Va 108
19413 Hontanares GU 87 Xb 103
40490 Hontanares de Eresma SG 67 Ve 103
09227 Hontanas BU 29 Vf 95
16421 Hontanaya CU 104 Xa 110
09462 Hontangas BU 49 Wb 99
19129 Hontanillas GU 88 Xc 105
16118 Hontecillas CU 105 Xe 110
19119 Hontoba GU 87 Wf 106
09141 Hontomín BU 30 Wc 93
33593 Hontoria AS 16 Va 88
40195 Hontoria SG 67 Vf 103
34209 Hontoria de Cerrato P 48 Vd 97
09351 Hontoria de la Cantera BU 49 Wc 95
09660 Hontoria del Pinar BU 49 Wf 97
09345 Hontoria de Ríofranco BU 48 Vf 96
09450 Hontoria de Valdearados BU 49 Wc 98
02499 Horca, La AB 140 Yc 118
24918 Horcadas LE 16 Uf 91
05695 Horcajada, La AV 83 Ud 106
16162 Horcajada de la Torre CU 104 Xc 108
10638 Horcajo CC 82 Td 106
02314 Horcajo, El AB 139 Xd 116
26126 Horcajo, El RI 50 Xc 96
41740 Horcajo, El SE 163 Tf 127
05630 Horcajo de la Ribera AV 83 Ud 106
28755 Horcajo de la Sierra MD 68 Wc 102
05210 Horcajo de las Torres AV 65 Uf 102
13110 Horcajo de los Montes CR 119 Vc 113
37712 Horcajo de Montemayor SA 82 Ua 106
16410 Horcajo de Santiago CU 103 Wf 109
37860 Horcajo Medianero SA 83 Ud 105
05357 Horcajuelo AV 84 Va 104
28191 Horcajuelo de la Sierra MD 68 Wc 102
19140 Horche GU 87 Wf 105
09230 Hormaza BU 29 Wa 95
09133 Hormazas, Las BU 30 Wa 93
09129 Hormazuela BU 30 Wa 93
09124 Hormicedo BU 29 Vf 93
41566 Hormigo SE 166 Va 125
45919 Hormigos TO 101 Vd 108
39419 Hormiguera CB 29 Vf 91
26323 Hormilla RI 31 Xb 94
02691 Horna AB 124 Yc 115
19264 Horna GU 69 Xc 102
03660 Horna Alta A 142 Zb 118
03660 Horna Baja A 142 Zb 118
06228 Hornachos BA 133 Tf 117
14740 Hornachuelos CO 150 Ue 122
39213 Horna de Ebro CB 17 Vf 91
39686 Hornedillo CB 18 Wb 90
39716 Hornedo CB 18 Wc 88
30627 Hornera MC 141 Ye 120
14850 Hornerico CO 151 Vd 123
09587 Hornes BU 18 We 90
13100 Hornillas Bajas CR 120 Ve 114
30413 Hornico MC 155 Xe 120
09568 Hornillalastra BU 18 Wc 90
09568 Hornillayuso BU 18 Wc 90
47451 Hornillejos de Cotes VA 66 Vb 101
04117 Hornillo AL 171 Xe 127
38879 Hornillo TF 184 He 180
05415 Hornillo, El AV 84 Uf 107
35489 Hornillo, El GC 184 Kc 180
47238 Hornillos VA 66 Vb 100
26133 Hornillos de Cameros RI 51 Xd 95
34249 Hornillos de Cerrato P 48 Ve 97
09230 Hornillos del Camino BU 29 Wa 94
10110 Horno CC 118 Uc 114
30530 Horno MC 141 Yc 119
02486 Horno-Ciego AB 140 Xe 118
46177 Horno de Cal V 106 Yf 110
23568 Horno del Vidrio J 153 Wd 122
05113 Horno Robledo AV 84 Vb 106
23293 Hornos J 139 Xb 119
23468 Hornos J 153 We 121
06880 Hornos, Los BA 116 Tc 115
26372 Hornos de Moncalvillo RI 32 Xc 94
23293 Hornos el Viejo J 139 Xb 119
37591 Horquera, La SA 82 Td 106
09311 Horra, La BU 48 Wa 98
08279 Horta d'Avinyó B 58 Bf 98
43596 Horta de Sant Joan T 74 Ab 103
11670 Hortales CA 173 Uc 128
28050 Hortaleza MD 86 Wc 106
15819 Hortas C 23 Re 91
27466 Hortás LU 24 Sc 94
07730 Hort de Alcaidus IB 77 Ea 109
07310 Hort de Biniatro IB 111 Cf 110
07520 Hort d'En Mosson IB 111 Da 111
42366 Hortezuela SO 69 Xa 100
19445 Hortezuela de Océn, La GU 70 Xd 103
09610 Hortezuelos BU 49 Wd 97
23689 Hortichuela J 152 Wa 124
30629 Hortichuela, La MC 141 Ye 119
04116 Hortichuelas AL 171 Xf 127
04720 Hortichuelas, Las AL 170 Xc 128
39549 Hortigal CB 17 Vd 88
09640 Hortigüela BU 49 Wd 96
16141 Hortizuela CU 89 Xf 106
16196 Hortizuela CU 104 Xe 108
25286 Hortoneda L 57 Bd 97
25517 Hortoneda de la Conca L 56 Ba 95
08490 Hortsavinyà B 58 Cd 99
46357 Hortunas de Abajo V 125 Yf 112
46357 Hortunas de Arriba V 125 Yf 112
22362 Hospital HU 36 Aa 93
27347 Hospital LU 24 Sd 93
27671 Hospital LU 25 Sf 92
08795 Hospital de Cervelló B 76 Bf 100
22367 Hospital de Gistaín HU 36 Ac 93
26329 Hospital del Duque RI 50 Xa 95
24286 Hospital de Órbigo LE 27 Ua 94
22365 Hospital de Parzán HU 36 Aa 92
22148 Hospitaled HU 36 Aa 95
43890 Hospitalet de l'Infant, L' T 75 Af 103
08900* Hospitalet de Llobregat, l' B 77 Ca 100
02328 Hospital Provincial Virgen de la Purificación AB 124 Xf 114
25211 Hostafrancs L 56 Bb 98
22621 Hostal de Ipiés HU 35 Zd 94
43896 Hostal dels Alls, L' T 93 Ad 104
07300 Hostal des Bovo IB 111 Cf 110
31272 Hostal de Urbasa NC 32 Xf 92
12513 Hostal de Villar de Canes, L' CS 92 Zf 106
12450 Hostalejo, El CS 107 Zc 109
50176 Hostal El Ciervo Z 73 Ze 100
25213 Hostalets de Cervera, Els L 57 Bc 99
17177 Hostalets d'en Bas, Els GI 58 Cc 96
25795 Hostalets de Tost, Els L 37 Bc 95
25281 Hostal Nou, L' L 57 Bc 97
17813 Hostalnou de Bianya, L' GI 58 Cc 95
43713 Hostal Nou la Torregassa, L' T 76 Bd 101
17450 Hostalric GI 59 Cd 98
28412 Hotel de Torrelaguna MD 86 Wa 104
07470 Hotel Formentor IB 111 Da 109
22378 Hotel Ordesa HU 35 Zf 92
17534 Hotel Puigmal GI 39 Ca 94
23250 Hoya J 138 We 119
04693 Hoya, La AL 155 Xf 124
04850 Hoya, La AL 170 Xe 124
23391 Hoya, La J 139 Xb 118
30816 Hoya, La MC 156 Yc 122
28297 Hoya, La MD 85 Ve 105
37716 Hoya, La SA 83 Ub 106
30410 Hoya Alazor MC 140 Xe 120
46175 Hoya de Antaño V 107 Za 110
44421 Hoya de la Carrasca TE 106 Yf 109
02486 Hoya de la Parrilla AB 139 Xd 118
23293 Hoya del Cambrón, La J 139 Xb 119
30559 Hoya del Campo MC 141 Yd 119
02312 Hoya del Conejo, La AB 139 Xc 116
18830 Hoya del Espino, La GR 154 Xc 120
30510 Hoya del Mollidar MC 141 Yf 118
16318 Hoya del Peral CU 106 Yd 108
30510 Hoya del Pozo MC 141 Yf 117
40142 Hoya del Pozo, La SG 85 Vd 103
23140 Hoya del Salobral J 152 Wb 124
38438 Hoya de Redonda TF 180 Ib 178
30540 Hoya de San Roque MC 141 Ye 119
02512 Hoya de Santa Ana AB 141 Yc 116
38296 Hoya Fria TF 181 Ie 178
02696 Hoya-Gonzalo AB 124 Yc 115
38788 Hoya Grande TF 181 Ha 176
30629 Hoyahermosa MC 141 Yf 119
03409 Hoya Hermosa, La A 141 Za 117
09316 Hoyales de Roa BU 48 Vf 99
46811 Hoya Redonda V 125 Za 115
02449 Hoyas, Las AB 139 Xe 118
23687 Hoyas, Las J 152 Wa 123
02137 Hoyas del Pino, Las AB 139 Xd 117
35217 Hoyas de San Gregorio GC 184 Kd 181
30510 Hoyo MC 141 Yf 117
05696 Hoyo, El AV 83 Ud 106
14209 Hoyo, El CO 134 Ue 119
13594 Hoyo, El CR 137 Wa 118
05123 Hoyocasero AV 84 Va 106
38916 Hoyo del Barrio TF 180 Ha 182
28240 Hoyo de Manzanares MD 86 Wa 105
05250 Hoyo de Pinares, El AV 85 Vd 106
05516 Hoyorredondo AV 83 Ud 106
10850 Hoyos CC 97 Tb 107
11330 Hoyos de Guadarranque o Buenas Noches CA 173 Uc 130
05634 Hoyos del Collado AV 84 Ue 106
05634 Hoyos del Espino AV 84 Ue 106
09126 Hoyos del Tozo BU 29 Wa 92
05132 Hoyos de Miguel Muñoz AV 84 Uf 106
41880 Hoyuelo, El SE 148 Te 122
40136 Hoyuelos SG 66 Vd 102
09615 Hoyuelos de la Sierra BU 49 We 96
02314 Hoz, La AB 139 Xd 116
14960 Hoz, La CO 167 Vd 125
46621 Hoz, La V 125 Yf 114
09593 Hozabejas BU 30 Wc 92
09511 Hozalla BU 31 Wf 91
42311 Hoz de Abajo SO 68 Wf 100
39793 Hoz de Anero CB 18 Wc 88
09572 Hoz de Arreba BU 30 Wb 91
42311 Hoz de Arriba SO 68 Wf 100
22312 Hoz de Barbastro HU 55 Aa 96
22662 Hoz de Jaca HU 35 Ze 92
44791 Hoz de la Vieja, La TE 72 Za 103
09559 Hoz de Valdivielso BU 30 Wd 92
39716 Hoznayo CB 18 Wb 88
22312 Hoz y Costeán HU 55 Aa 96
31794 Huarte NC 21 Yc 90
31620 Huarte NC 33 Yc 92
04119 Huebro AL 171 Xe 127
45511 Huecas TO 101 Ve 108
50570 Huechaseca Z 52 Yc 98
04409 Huécija AL 170 Xc 127
23410 Hueco del Píco J 153 We 120
10849 Huélaga CC 98 Tc 108
16152 Huélamo CU 89 Yb 107
24991 Huelde LE 16 Uf 91
04289 Huelga, La AL 171 Xf 126
14620 Huelga, La CO 151 Vd 121
23560 Huelma J 153 Wd 123
37216 Huelmo SA 64 Te 103
37798 Huelmos de Cañedo SA 64 Ub 102
37798 Huelmos de San Joaquín SA 64 Ub 102
37451 Huelmos y Casasolilla SA 82 Ua 104
21001* Huelva H 162 Ta 125
11170 Huelvacar CA 172 Ua 129
21208 Huelvas, Las H 147 Tc 121
16465 Huelves CU 104 Xa 108
18512 Huéneja GR 169 Xa 125
04230 Huércal de Almería AL 170 Xd 127
04600 Huércal-Overa AL 171 Ya 124
26314 Huércanos RI 31 Xb 94
19238 Huerce, La GU 68 We 102
16373 Huércemes CU 105 Yb 110
33350 Huerces AS 15 Ub 88
37114 Huérfana, La SA 64 Tf 102
24356 Huerga de Frailes LE 27 Ua 94
24143 Huergas de Babia LE 14 Tf 91
24609 Huergas de Gordón LE 27 Uc 91
16311 Huérguina CU 106 Yc 108
09150 Huérmeces BU 30 Wb 93
19295 Huérmeces del Cerro GU 69 Xb 102
50300 Huérmeda Z 71 Yc 100
28810 Hueros, Los MD 87 Wd 106
22194 Huerrios HU 54 Zd 96
10629 Huerta CC 82 Te 106
37338 Huerta SA 65 Ud 103
40164 Huerta SG 68 Wb 102
04810 Huerta, La AL 155 Xe 123
04629 Huerta, La AL 171 Ya 125
30648 Huerta, La MC 141 Yf 119
50650 Huerta Alta Z 52 Ye 97
06360 Huerta Cruz BA 133 Td 117
09614 Huerta de Abajo BU 49 Wf 96
09614 Huerta de Arriba BU 50 Wf 96
10672 Huerta de Gorronoso CC 98 Te 108
06413 Huerta de Granda BA 117 Ua 115
30889 Huerta del Abad MC 156 Yc 124
29392 Huerta del Americano MA 173 Ue 129
16195 Huerta de la Obispalía CU 104 Xd 109
21580 Huerta de la Pila H 147 Sf 122
41550 Huerta del Colegio SE 166 Uf 125
06906 Huerta del Coto BA 148 Tf 120
23290 Huerta del Manco J 139 Xc 120
16316 Huerta del Marquesado CU 105 Yb 108
35412 Huerta del Palmar GC 184 Kc 180
09430 Huerta del Rey BU 49 Wd 97
13690 Huerta de Peñalva CR 122 Wf 113
06340 Huerta de San Benito BA 132 Tb 119
05003 Huerta de Tohús AV 84 Vb 105
45750 Huerta de Valdecarábanos TO 102 Wc 109
22313 Huerta de Vero HU 54 Aa 96
21530 Huerta Grande H 146 Sf 123
19441 Huertahernando GU 88 Xe 104
06360 Huerta Julián BA 133 Td 118
41899 Huerta Medialegua SE 148 Te 122
35149 Huerta Nueva, La GC 184 Kb 181
29360 Huerta Nueva-Sancho Jaén MA 165 Ue 128
19495 Huertapelayo GU 88 Xe 104
14530 Huertas, Las CO 151 Vb 123
18310 Huertas, Las GR 167 Vf 126
06393 Huertas Concejo BA 132 Td 118
10291 Huertas de la Magdalena CC 99 Ua 112
14549 Huertas del Ingeniero CO 150 Va 124
29314 Huertas del Río MA 167 Vd 126
13118 Huertas del Sauceral, Las CR 119 Vb 112
16260 Huertas de Mateo CU 106 Yc 112
06240 Huerta Sevilla BA 133 Td 119
14512 Huertas Nuevas CO 150 Vb 124
29566 Huertas y Lomas MA 166 Vb 128
29327 Huertas y Montes MA 166 Va 127
38355 Huerta Vicho TF 181 Id 178
04859 Huertecicas Altas, Las AL 170 Xe 125
42174 Huérteles SO 51 Xe 96
13779 Huertezuelas CR 137 Wb 117
22210 Huerto HU 54 Ze 97
02155 Huerto del Rincón AB 124 Yb 114
37500 Huerto de Pedrotello SA 81 Tc 105
46230 Huerto Isaura V 126 Zd 113
40490 Huertos, Los SG 67 Ve 102
23487 Huesa J 153 Wf 122
44213 Huesa del Común TE 72 Za 102
22001* Huesca HU 54 Zd 96
18830 Huéscar GR 154 Xc 122
09593 Huéspeda BU 30 Wc 92
23499 Hueta, La J 139 Xc 118
16500 Huete CU 104 Xb 108
01191 Hueto Arriba VI 31 Xb 91
18183 Huétor-Santillán GR 168 Wc 125
18360 Huétor-Tájar GR 167 Vf 125
18198 Huétor-Vega GR 168 Wc 126
19429 Huetos GU 88 Xc 104
10628 Huetre CC 82 Te 106
19119 Hueva GU 87 Xa 106
41830 Huévar del Aljarafe SE 164 Te 124
09559 Huidobro BU 30 Wb 92
29793 Huit MA 167 Wa 128
09124 Humada BU 29 Vf 92
19220 Humanes GU 87 Wf 104
28970 Humanes de Madrid MD 86 Wb 107
48191 Humarán BI 19 Wf 89
30876 Humbrías MC 156 Yd 123
28223 Humera MD 86 Wb 106
09620 Humienta BU 49 Wb 95
13429 Humilladero CR 121 Wa 113

278 | Higuera de Arjona

11300 Línea de la Concepción, La CA 175 Ud 131
37450 Linejo SA 82 Ua 104
39728 Linto CB 18 Wb 89
25240 Linyola L 56 Af 98
31696 Linzoain NC 21 Yd 91
27413 Liñarán LU 24 Sd 94
27413 Liñares LU 13 Sf 90
32520 Liñares OR 23 Re 94
32172 Liñares OR 23 Sa 94
36449 Liñares PO 41 Rd 96
15292 Lira C 22 Qf 92
36459 Lira PO 41 Rd 96
15138 Lires C 10 Qe 91
22466 Liri HU 36 Ad 93
36687 Liripio PO 23 Rd 93
32574 Listanco OR 23 Rf 94
50582 Litago Z 52 Yb 98
22585 Litera HU 55 Ad 96
49334 Litos ZA 45 Tf 97
50581 Lituénigo Z 52 Yb 97
45479 Lituero TO 102 Wa 111
02160 Lituero, El AB 123 Xd 114
31200 Lizarra = Estella NC 32 Xf 92
31829 Lizarraga NC 32 Xf 91
31421 Lizarraga NC 33 Yc 92
31820 Lizarragabengoa NC 32 Xf 91
20490 Lizartza SS 20 Xf 90
31799 Lizaso NC 21 Yb 91
31171 Lizasoáin NC 33 Yb 92
31482 Lizoáin NC 33 Yd 92
43320 Llaberia T 75 Af 102
17257 Llabià GI 59 Da 96
12316 Llacova, La CS 92 Zf 106
08779 Llacuna, La B 76 Bd 100
03818 Llacunes A 142 Zc 116
25566 Llacunes, Les L 37 Bb 94
17745 Lladó GI 40 Ce 95
25576 Lladorre L 37 Bb 93
25283 Lladurs L 57 Bd 96
17211 Llafranc GI 59 Db 97
08120 Llagosta, La B 77 Cb 99
17240 Llagostera GI 59 Cf 98
39880 Llaguno CB 19 We 89
24893 Llama de la Guzpeña LE 28 Uf 92
33687 Llamas AS 15 Uc 90
24388 Llamas de Cabrera LE 25 Tc 94
24271 Llamas de la Ribera LE 27 Ub 93
33816 Llamas del Mouro AS 14 Td 89
24161 Llamas de Rueda LE 28 Uf 93
24843 Llamazares LE 15 Ud 91
17243 Llambilles GI 59 Cf 97
24869 Llamera LE 27 Ud 91
33127 Llamera, La AS 14 Tf 88
33829 Llamero AS 14 Tf 88
33591 Llames AS 16 Uf 88
33839 Llamoso AS 14 Te 89
42291 Llamosos, Los SO 50 Xc 99
07150 Llamp, Es IB 110 Cc 111
17465 Llampaies GI 59 Cf 96
33687 Llananzanes AS 15 Uc 90
17869 Llanars GI 39 Cc 95
33116 Llanas, Las AS 15 Ua 90
24912 Llánaves de la Reina LE 16 Vb 90
17490 Llançà GI 40 Da 94
33879 Llaneces de la Barca AS 14 Td 89
33425 Llanera AS 15 Ua 88
25751 Llanera de Solsonès L 57 Bc 97
33500 Llanes AS 16 Vb 88
04430 Llanetes, Los AL 170 Xc 127
33930 Llangréu AS 15 Ub 89
09127 Llanillo BU 29 Vf 92
38913 Llanillos, Los TF 180 Gf 182
38713 Llanito, El TF 181 Hb 177
39213 Llano CB 17 Wa 91
33774 Llano, El AS 13 Sf 88
33547 Llano, El AS 16 Uf 88
30381 Llano de Beal MC 157 Za 123
30161 Llano de Brujas MC 157 Yf 120
09246 Llano de Bureba BU 30 Wd 93
38820 Llano de Campos TF 184 He 179
33556 Llano de Con AS 16 Uf 89
04149 Llano de Don Antonio, El AL 171 Ya 126
18859 Llano del Abad GR 154 Xc 123
23260 Llano de la Mata J 138 Wf 119
02486 Llano de la Torre AB 139 Xe 118
03530 Llano del Castillo A 143 Zf 117
04812 Llano del Espino AL 155 Xe 124
04812 Llano de los Olleres AL 155 Xf 124
47418 Llano de Olmedo VA 66 Vc 101
38788 Llano Negro TF 181 Ha 176
33416 Llanos AS 15 Ua 87
33687 Llanos AS 15 Uc 90
39627 Llanos CB 18 Wb 89
02049 Llanos, Los AB 124 Ya 115
04692 Llanos, Los AL 155 Xf 124
04661 Llanos, Los AL 171 Xf 124
06150 Llanos, Los BA 132 Tc 117
06477 Llanos, Los BA 133 Ua 117
35468 Llanos, Los GC 184 Kb 180
18310 Llanos, Los GR 168 Vf 126
18416 Llanos, Los GR 169 We 127
29510 Llanos, Los MA 166 Vb 128
38915 Llanos, Los TF 180 Ha 182
46780 Llanos, Los V 127 Zf 115
24649 Llanos de Alba LE 27 Uc 92
29250 Llanos de Antequera, Los MA 167 Vc 126
38760 Llanos de Aridane, Los TF 181 Ha 177
23360 Llanos de Arriba J 139 Xb 118
18120 Llanos de Buenavista GR 168 Vf 126
14950 Llanos de Don Juan CO 167 Vd 124
35611 Llanos de la Concepción GC 183 Lf 178
23150 Llanos del Ángel J 152 Wb 123
47100 Llanos de la Peña, Los VA 66 Va 100
13220 Llanos del Caudillo CR 122 Wd 114
22440 Llanos del Hospital HU 36 Ad 92
04628 Llanos del Mayor, Los AL 171 Ya 125
33693 Llanos de Somerón AS 15 Ub 90
05690 Llanos de Tormes, Los AV 83 Ud 107
17515 Llanses, Les GI 58 Cb 96
01478 Llanteno VI 19 Wf 90
33117 Llanuces AS 15 Ua 90
25186 Llardecans L 74 Ad 100
33534 Llares AS 15 Ud 88
39450 Llares, Los CB 17 Vf 89
25568 Llarvén L 37 Ba 94
25636 Llastarri L 37 Ae 95
46613 Llaurí V 126 Ze 114
17745 Llavanera GI 40 Ce 95
17832 Llavanera GI 59 Ce 95
25595 Llavorsí L 37 Bb 94
34849 Llazos, Los P 17 Vd 91
17869 Llebro GI 39 Cb 94
44624 Lledó TE 74 Ab 103
25001*Lleidda L 55 Ad 99
37450 Llen SA 82 Ua 104
33556 Llenín AS 16 Uf 88
06227 Llera BA 133 Tf 118
39639 Llerana CB 18 Wb 89
33546 Llerandi AS 16 Ue 89
06900 Llerena BA 133 Tf 119
33557 Llerices AS 16 Uf 89
08520 Llerona B 58 Cb 99
17730 Llers GI 40 Cf 95
22451 Llert (Valle de Bardají) HU 36 Ac 94
25726 Lles de Cerdanya L 38 Be 94
25526 Llesp L 37 Ae 94
25567 Llessui L 37 Ba 94
25718 Lletó L 38 Bd 95
03729 Llíber A 143 Aa 116
08186 Lliçà d'Amunt B 58 Cb 99
08185 Lliçà de Vall B 58 Cb 99
43894 Lligallo del Gàguil, El T 93 Ad 104
25639 Llimiana L 56 Af 96
08618 Llinars B 57 Be 96
25283 Llinars L 57 Bc 96
08450 Llinars del Vallès B 58 Cc 99
07840 Llinigol, Es IB 109 Bc 115
46160 Llíria V 107 Zc 111
08186 Llissa de Munt = Lliçà d'Amunt B 58 Cb 99
17527 Llívia GI 38 Bf 94
25195 Llívia L 55 Ad 99
12316 Llivis, Els CS 92 Zf 105
43737 Lloar, El T 75 Ae 101
25281 Llobera L 57 Bc 97
25794 Llobera les Sorts L 57 Bc 95
25753 Lloberola L 57 Bc 97
07609 Llobets, Es IB 111 Cf 112
03159 Llobregales A 142 Zb 120
08660 Llobregat, El B 57 Bf 97
07730 Lloc Nou de Mestres IB 77 Ea 109
46668 Llocnou d'En Fenollet V 126 Zd 114
46726 Llocnou de Sant Jeroni V 127 Ze 115
01400 Llodio VI 19 Xa 90
17124 Llofriu GI 59 Da 97
46191 Llomaina, La V 107 Zb 111
46197 Llombai V 126 Zc 113
08737 Llombardes, Les B 76 Bd 100
07690 Llombards, Es IB 111 Da 112
24609 Llombera LE 27 Uc 91
33578 Llonín AS 16 Vc 88
25211 Llor, El L 56 Bb 98
17152 Llorà GI 59 Ce 96
43427 Llorac T 76 Bb 99
25657 Llordà L 56 Ba 96
33418 Lloreda AS 15 Ua 87
39694 Lloreda CB 18 Wb 89
25613 Llorenç de Montgai L 56 Af 97
25267 Llorenç de Vallbona L 75 Ba 99
09511 Llorengoz BU 19 Wf 91
43812 Lloret, El T 75 Bc 101
17310 Lloret Blau GI 59 Ce 98
17310 Lloret de Mar GI 59 Cf 98
07518 Lloret de Vistalegre IB 111 Cf 111
AD300 Llorts ◘ AND 38 Bd 93
12591 Llosa, La CS 108 Ze 110
03723 Llosa de Camatxo, La A 127 Zf 116
46815 Llosa de Ranes V 126 Zc 114
12150 Llosar, El CS 91 Ze 106
07360 Lloseta IB 110 Cf 110
33795 Llosoiro AS 13 Tb 88
17512 Llosses, Les GI 58 Ca 96
33569 Llovio AS 16 Uf 88
33440 Lluanco = Luanco AS 15 Ub 87
07430 Llubí IB 111 Da 110
08514 Lluçà B 58 Ca 96
25514 Lluçà L 37 Af 95
07179 Llucalcari IB 110 Cd 110
25736 Lluçars L 56 Ba 97
07730 Llucasaldent IB 77 Ea 109
07712 Llucmaçanes IB 77 Eb 109
07620 Llucmajor IB 111 Cf 112
25213 Lluides L 56 Bb 99
07730 Llumena Nou IB 77 Ea 109
50213 Llunes Z 71 Yb 102
07748 Lluriach Nou IB 77 Ea 108
46838 Llutxent V 126 Zd 115
22809 Loarre HU 34 Zc 95
33459 Loba, La AS 14 Tf 87
39400 Lobado CB 17 Vf 89
32539 Lobagueira OR 23 Re 93
32510 Lobás OR 23 Rf 94
32850 Lobeira OR 42 Rf 97
27865 Lobeiras LU 12 Sc 87
49512 Lober ZA 45 Te 98
05100 Lobera, La AV 84 Vc 106
41200 Lobera, La SE 148 Ua 123
34116 Lobera de la Vega P 28 Vb 94
50687 Lobera de Onsella Z 34 Yf 94
04277 Loberos, Los AL 171 Ya 126
30876 Loberos, Los MC 156 Yd 123
46339 Loberuela, La V 106 Yd 110
49392 Lobeznos ZA 44 Tc 96
13710 Lobillo, El CR 122 Wf 115
32643 Lobios OR 42 Rf 97
06498 Lobón BA 116 Tc 115
40490 Lobones SG 67 Ve 103
04619 Lobos, Los AL 171 Yb 125
30331 Lobosillo MC 157 Yf 122
18449 Lobras GR 169 We 127
18820 Lóbrega GR 154 Xd 121
18610 Lobres GR 168 Wc 128
04812 Locaiba AL 171 Xf 124
42248 Lodares SO 70 Xd 101
42212 Lodares del Monte SO 69 Xc 100
42313 Lodares de Osma SO 69 Wf 99
33535 Lodeña AS 15 Ud 88
38738 Lodero TF 181 Hb 177
31580 Lodosa NC 32 Xf 94
32696 Lodoselo OR 43 Sc 96
09131 Lodoso BU 30 Wb 94
28890 Loeches MD 86 Wd 106
27266 Loentia LU 12 Sd 90
30709 Lo Ferro MC 157 Za 122
27112 Logares LU 13 Sf 89
30590 Lo Gea MC 157 Yf 121
26005 Logroño RI 32 Xd 94
10120 Logrosán CC 118 Ud 112
15339 Loiba C 10 Sb 86
48383 Loiola BI 19 Xc 89
15239 Loios C 22 Ra 91
36913 Loira PO 22 Rb 94
32890 Loiro OR 24 Sa 95
24991 Lois LE 16 Uf 91
36635 Lois PO 22 Rb 93
48180 Loiu BI 19 Xa 89
31697 Loizu NC 33 Yd 91
18312 Loja GR 167 Vf 125
18270 Lojilla GR 168 Vf 124
30154 Lo León MC 157 Ye 122
09142 Loma BU 30 Wb 92
19441 Loma, La GU 88 Xe 103
04890 Loma Alta, La AL 170 Xc 125
04770 Loma Colorada, La AL 169 Wf 128
38788 Lomada Grande TF 181 Ha 176
34859 Loma de Castrejón P 29 Vc 92
23486 Loma de la Mesa J 153 Xa 122
10319 Loma del Saliente CC 99 Uc 108
04716 Loma del Viento, La AL 170 Xb 128
09569 Loma de Montija BU 18 Wd 90
18381 Loma de Tabora GR 168 Wa 125
34127 Loma de Ucieza P 29 Vc 94
32366 Loma Longa OR 25 Ta 95
09213 Lomana BU 30 We 92
34449 Lomas P 29 Vc 95
11660 Lomas, Las CA 165 Uc 128
11158 Lomas, Las CA 172 Ua 131
18820 Lomas, Las GR 155 Xd 122
29602 Lomas, Las MA 174 Va 129
30330 Lomas, Las MC 157 Yf 122
28669 Lomas, Las MD 86 Wa 106
30812 Lomas de Lastón, Las MC 155 Yb 121
50800 Lomas del Gállego, Las Z 53 Zb 98
03188 Lomas del Mar A 157 Zc 120
10319 Lomas del Medio CC 99 Uc 108
10319 Lomas del Poniente CC 99 Uc 108
18270 Lomas de Marcos GR 167 Vf 124
39419 Loma Somera CB 29 Vf 91
24388 Lomba LE 25 Tb 94
39210 Lomba, La CB 17 Ve 90
39860 Lombera CB 18 Wd 89
39557 Lombraña CB 17 Vd 90
42257 Lomeda SO 70 Xd 102
30155 Lo Mendigo MC 157 Yf 121
39572 Lomeña-Baseda CB 17 Vc 90
21320 Lomero H 147 Ta 122
34815 Lomilla P 29 Ve 92
45212 Lominchar TO 102 Wa 108
35430 Lomitos, Los GC 184 Kc 180
38129 Lomo Bermejo TF 181 If 177
38589 Lomo de Arico TF 180 Id 180
35290 Lomo de la Palma GC 184 Kc 181
38129 Lomo de las Bodegas TF 181 If 177
38879 Lomo del Balo TF 184 He 180
06410 Lomo de Liebre BA 117 Ua 114
38715 Lomo de los Gomeros TF 181 Hb 176
38590 Lomo de Mena TF 181 Id 179
35211 Lomo Magullo, El GC 184 Kd 181
38589 Lomo Oliva TF 180 Id 179
11593 Lomopardo CA 172 Tf 128
38390 Lomo Román TF 180 Id 178
47494 Lomoviejo VA 66 Va 102
30700 Lo Navarro MC 157 Yf 122
30709 Lo Navarro MC 157 Yf 122
50460 Longares Z 72 Ye 100
50688 Longás Z 34 Za 94
31481 Longida NC 33 Yd 92
31481 Lónguida = Longida NC 33 Yd 92
36599 Loño PO 23 Rf 91
14820 Lope Amargo CO 151 Vc 122
18517 Lopera GR 169 We 125
23780 Lopera J 151 Ve 121
04770 López, Los AL 169 Wf 128
30877 López, Los MC 156 Yd 122
30739 López, Los MC 157 Za 121
22192 Loporzano HU 54 Ze 96
11690 Lora CA 165 Uf 127
41564 Lora de Estepa SE 166 Vb 125
41440 Lora del Río SE 149 Uc 123
28942 Loranca MD 86 Wa 107
16550 Loranca del Campo CU 104 Xb 108
19141 Loranca de Tajuña GU 87 Wf 106
09272 Loranquillo BU 31 We 94
15177 Lorbé C 11 Re 88
50684 Lorbés Z 34 Za 92
30800 Lorca MC 156 Yb 122
31292 Lorca NC 32 Ya 92
30740 Lorcas, Los MC 157 Zb 122
03860 Lorcha = l'Orxa A 126 Ze 115
32236 Lordelo OR 42 Re 96
24239 Lordemanos LE 46 Uc 96
39160 Loredo CB 18 Wb 88
30868 Lorentes, Los MC 156 Ye 123
24122 Lorenzana LE 27 Uc 92
34848 Lores P 17 Vc 91
18370 Loreto GR 168 Wa 125
33191 Loriana AS 15 Ua 88
30441 Lorigas MC 140 Xf 119
46168 Loriguilla V 107 Za 110
46393 Loriguilla V 107 Zc 112
09144 Lorilla BU 29 Wa 92
14979 Lorite CO 167 Ve 125
15856 Loroño C 10 Ra 90
38849 Loros, Los TF 184 He 180
30564 Lorquí MC 156 Ye 120
16707 Losa, La CU 124 Xf 112
40420 Losa, La SG 85 Vf 103
49541 Losacino ZA 45 Tf 98
49540 Losacio ZA 45 Tf 98
24318 Losada LE 26 Td 93
46168 Losa del Obispo V 107 Za 110
24746 Losadilla LE 25 Tc 95
42315 Losana SO 69 Wf 101
40192 Losana de Pirón SG 67 Vf 102
22807 Losanglis HU 53 Zb 95
05692 Losar, El AV 83 Uc 106
10460 Losar de la Vera CC 99 Uc 108
05692 Losar del Campo, El AV 83 Uc 106
22141 Loscertales HU 54 Ze 95
22809 Loscorrales, Los HU 34 Zc 95
44493 Loscos TE 72 Yf 102
39571 Losiezo CB 17 Vc 90
46179 Losilla V 106 Yf 109
49161 Losilla ZA 45 Ua 98
02691 Losilla, La AB 124 Yb 115
42181 Losilla, La SO 51 Xe 97
24860 Losilla y San Adrián, La LE 27 Ue 91
36876 Lougares PO 41 Rd 95
15881 Loureda C 23 Rd 91
36415 Louredo PO 41 Rc 95
27865 Loureiro LU 12 Sc 87
36855 Loureiro PO 23 Rd 94
32163 Loureiros OR 24 Sc 94
36455 Lourido PO 41 Rd 96
36003 Lourizán PO 22 Rc 94
15291 Louro C 22 Qf 92
15317 Lousa C 11 Sa 89
27835 Lousada LU 12 Sb 88
27628 Lousada LU 24 Se 92
15214 Lousame C 22 Ra 92
27241 Louseira LU 13 Se 89
27672 Louzarela LU 25 Sf 92
40231 Lovingos SG 67 Ve 100
15823 Loxo C 23 Re 91
31491 Loya NC 33 Yd 93
20730 Loyola = Loiola SS 20 Xe 89
33719 Loza AS 13 Tb 87
31195 Loza NC 33 Yb 91
01212 Loza VI 31 Xb 93
33537 Lozana AS 15 Ud 89
04814 Lozanos, Los AL 155 Xf 124
28752 Lozoyela MD 68 Wc 103
28752 Lozoyela-Navas-Sieteiglesias MD 68 Wc 103
27247 Lúa LU 13 Se 90
27270 Luaces LU 12 Sd 90
33440 Luanco = Lluanco AS 15 Ub 87
33700 Luarca AS 14 Tc 87
42290 Lubia SO 51 Xc 99
49570 Lubián ZA 44 Ta 96
01192 Lubiano VI 32 Xc 91
04271 Lubrín AL 171 Xf 125
04768 Lucainena AL 169 Wf 127
04210 Lucainena de las Torres AL 171 Xe 126
04887 Lúcar AL 170 Xd 124
14900 Lucena CO 151 Vd 124
50294 Lucena de Jalón Z 71 Ye 99
12120 Lucena del Cid CS 108 Ze 108
21820 Lucena del Puerto H 162 Tb 125
50640 Luceni Z 53 Ye 98
32688 Lucenza OR 43 Sc 97
33328 Luces AS 15 Ue 87
30810 Luchena MC 155 Ya 122
21291 Lucía H 147 Tb 121
13108 Luciana CR 120 Ve 115
24723 Lucillo LE 26 Te 94
24723 Lucillo de Somoza LE 26 Te 94
44563 Luco de Bordón TE 91 Ze 104
44391 Luco de Jiloca TE 71 Ye 103
12123 Ludiente CS 108 Zd 108
33340 Lue AS 15 Ue 88
49215 Luelmo ZA 64 Tf 100
24339 Luengos LE 27 Ud 94
33129 Luerces AS 14 Tf 88
50619 Luesia Z 34 Yf 94
50151 Luesma Z 72 Yf 102
22337 Lueza, La HU 36 Ab 94
26132 Luezas RI 32 Xd 95
24152 Lugán LE 27 Ue 92
50195 Lugarico Cerdán Z 53 Zb 99
41703 Lugar Nuevo SE 163 Ua 125
50213 Lugar Nuevo Z 71 Yb 101
02459 Lugar Nuevo, El AB 139 Xd 118
33311 Lugás AS 15 Ud 88
27004 Lugo LU 12 Sc 90
33420 Lugones AS 15 Ub 88
18516 Lugros GR 169 We 125
24843 Lugueros LE 15 Ud 91
01408 Luiaondo VI 19 Wf 90
32160 Luintra OR 24 Sb 94
16612 Luises, Los CU 123 Xd 113
41430 Luisiana, La SE 150 Ue 123
31660 Luizalde/Valcarlos NC 21 Ye 90
22336 Luján HU 36 Ab 94
18614 Lújar GR 169 Wd 128
33155 Luma AS 14 Te 87
24140 Lumajo LE 14 Te 91
31440 Lumbier NC 33 Ye 93
37240 Lumbrales SA 63 Tb 103
26126 Lumbreras RI 50 Xc 96
24433 Lumeras LE 25 Tb 92
42368 Lumías SO 69 Xa 100
50295 Lumpiaque Z 52 Ye 99
02639 Luna AB 123 Xe 114
01439 Luna VI 31 Xa 91
50610 Luna Z 53 Za 96
36887 Luneda PO 42 Re 96
15883 Luou C 23 Rc 92

44430 Masía de la Rinconada TE 107 Za 107
22232 Masía de la Sardera HU 54 Aa 99
44460 Masía de las Cuestas TE 107 Za 108
44159 Masía de la Serna TE 91 Zb 105
43786 Masia de la Serra T 74 Ac 102
44400 Masía de las Incosas TE 91 Zb 107
44157 Masía de la Solana TE 91 Zb 105
44145 Masía de la Sonana TE 91 Zb 106
44145 Masía de las Pupilas TE 91 Zb 105
12513 Masia de la Torreta CS 92 Aa 106
44100 Masía de la Toyuela TE 90 Yd 106
12429 Masía del Bolado CS 107 Zb 108
44367 Masía del Borrocal TE 90 Yc 106
22232 Masía del Campo HU 54 Aa 99
44440 Masía del Campo TE 90 Za 107
46169 Masía del Capella V 107 Zc 110
44409 Masía del Carbonero TE 90 Za 106
44431 Masía del Carrascalejo TE 91 Zb 106
44100 Masía del Cebrero TE 89 Yc 106
44530 Masía del Ceperuelo TE 73 Zd 102
12430 Masía del Collado CS 107 Zb 109
44155 Masía del Collado TE 91 Za 105
44300 Masía del Colorado TE 90 Yd 104
12599 Masia del Esparavé CS 92 Aa 105
12135 Masia de les Pomeres CS 91 Ze 107
12315 Masia de les Pruneres CS 92 Aa 105
12513 Masia del Gatellá CS 92 Zf 106
44400 Masía del Hocico TE 91 Zb 107
44167 Masía del Hoyo TE 90 Ye 105
46171 Masía del Juez V 107 Zb 110
44330 Masía del Mas TE 71 Yd 103
03516 Masia del Oficial A 143 Ze 117
12370 Masia de l'Om CS 92 Aa 105
44100 Masía de los Gatos TE 90 Yd 106
12430 Masía de los Pérez CS 107 Zb 109
44143 Masía del Padre Santo TE 91 Zc 105
44100 Masía del Palomo TE 90 Yd 106
44146 Masía del Portero TE 91 Zb 106
44161 Masía del Pozuelo TE 90 Za 105
44433 Masía del Prado TE 91 Zb 106
12125 Masía del Rebollo CS 107 Zd 108
44164 Masía del Recuenco TE 90 Yf 104
44440 Masía del Río TE 91 Za 107
12125 Masia del Rull CS 107 Zd 108
12162 Masia del Senyor CS 92 Zf 106
44191 Masía del Villarejo TE 90 Ye 108
12135 Masia de Manzanares CS 91 Ze 107
44145 Masía de Marta TE 91 Zc 106
44155 Masía de Millán TE 91 Zb 105
44100 Masía de Monteagudo TE 89 Yc 106
44394 Masía de Morata TE 90 Yd 104
44431 Masía de Ontejas Altas TE 91 Zb 106
44161 Masía de Portachuelo TE 90 Za 106
44563 Masía de Ricoll TE 91 Ze 104
12410 Masía de Rivas CS 107 Zc 109
44100 Masía de Roclos TE 90 Yd 106
12162 Masia de Romeo CS 92 Zf 106
44300 Masía de Ruecas TE 90 Ye 104
44394 Masía de Saletas TE 90 Yd 104
12135 Masia de Salvador CS 91 Ze 107
12400 Masía de San Juan CS 107 Zd 110
44123 Masía de San Pedro TE 90 Yc 107
44155 Masía de Santa Ana TE 91 Za 105
50170 Masía de Satué Z 74 Ab 101
12513 Masia de Segarra de Arriba CS 92 Zf 106
12319 Masia de Segures CS 92 Aa 104
43749 Masia de Senier T 74 Ad 102
43790 Masía d'Estrada T 74 Ac 101
12135 Masia de Toni CS 91 Zd 107
12313 Masia de Torre Miró CS 92 Zf 104
12410 Masía de Uñoz CS 107 Zc 110
44393 Masía de Val TE 90 Yd 104
44556 Masía de Valdecascallo TE 91 Zd 104
44162 Masía de Valdomingo TE 90 Yf 106
44300 Masía de Villarrubio TE 90 Yd 104
43896 Masia de Vinaixarop T 93 Ad 104
44143 Masía de Zoticos TE 91 Zc 106
12127 Masía el Camino CS 91 Zc 108
44144 Masía El Cañamillo TE 91 Zb 105
12513 Masia Enramon CS 92 Zf 106
12513 Masia Font Nova CS 92 Zf 105
44440 Masía La Cañada TE 91 Za 106
25180 Masía la Vaqueria L 55 Ac 99
44586 Masía Nova TE 92 Aa 104
44195 Masía Nueva del Cerrito TE 90 Ye 107
12578 Masia Pallaresa CS 92 Ab 106
12450 Masía Paredes CS 107 Zc 109
12140 Masia Pati CS 92 Zf 107
12570 Masia Piedra Seca CS 92 Ab 106
46610 Masia Quitorras V 126 Zc 114
08275 Masia Rubi B 58 Ca 98
12469 Masías Blancas CS 107 Zc 109
12469 Masías del Cristo CS 107 Zc 109
44530 Masías de los Albadales TE 73 Zd 102
12460 Masías del Río CS 107 Zc 109
12469 Masías de Parrela CS 107 Zc 109
44360 Masías El Bao TE 90 Ye 105
12122 Masia Traguanta CS 108 Ze 108
12448 Masía Valdesánchez CS 107 Zc 108
44410 Masico de Albardero TE 91 Zd 106
44410 Masico de Bertoldo TE 91 Zc 106
44410 Masico de la Bireta TE 91 Zc 106
27619 Maside LU 24 Sd 92
32570 Maside OR 23 Rf 94
43440 Masies, Les T 75 Ba 100
43718 Masies del Torrent, Les T 76 Bd 101
08510 Masies de Roda, Les B 58 Cb 97
08509 Masies de Voltregà, Les B 58 Cb 96
44450 Masío de los Enebrales TE 90 Za 107
17244 Mas la Caseta GI 59 Cf 97
43718 Masllorenç T 76 Bc 101
43813 Masmolets T 75 Bb 101
17464 Mas Nicolau GI 59 Cf 96
17249 Mas Nou GI 59 Da 97
08328 Masnou, El B 77 Cb 100
43786 Masnou, El T 74 Ab 102
43143 Masó, La T 75 Bb 101
17256 Masos de Pals, Els GI 59 Db 97
25653 Masos de Sant Martí L 56 Ba 96
25692 Masos de Sant Romà, Els L 55 Ae 97
25636 Masos de Tamúrcia, Els L 37 Ae 95
43763 Masos de Vespella, Els T 75 Bb 101
35100 Maspalomas GC 184 Kc 182
43549 Mas Pin T 93 Ad 104
17257 Mas Pinel GI 59 Db 96
43558 Mas Pinyol T 93 Ac 104
43382 Masprujols T 75 Ba 101
08783 Masquefa B 76 Be 99
12124 Mas Quemado CS 91 Zd 107
25160 Mas Quintana L 74 Ad 100
43891 Masriudoms T 75 Af 102
43736 Masroig, El T 75 Ae 102
46560 Massalfassar V 108 Ze 111
46130 Massamagrell V 108 Ze 111
AD400 Massana, La □ AND 38 Bd 93
46470 Massanassa V 126 Zd 112
17452 Massanes GI 59 Cd 98
17720 Massanet de Cabrenys = Maçanet de Cabrenys GI 40 Ce 94
46112 Massarrojos V 107 Zd 111
25529 Massivert L 37 Ae 94
25211 Massoteres L 56 Bb 98
37251 Masueco SA 63 Tc 101
08729 Masuques, Les B 76 Bd 101
44150 Mas Valenciano TE 91 Zc 105
17406 Mas Vidal GI 58 Cc 97
09141 Mata BU 30 Wb 93
39409 Mata CB 17 Vf 89
17846 Mata GI 59 Ce 96
03430 Mata, La A 142 Zb 117
03130 Mata, La A 142 Zc 119
33825 Mata, La AS 14 Tf 88
08278 Mata, La B 58 Bf 99
11520 Mata, La CA 172 Te 129
10895 Mata, La CC 97 Tb 108
17464 Mata, La GI 59 Cf 96
40170 Mata, La SG 67 Wa 102
45534 Mata, La TO 101 Vd 109
40446 Mata Alegre SG 66 Vc 102
23120 Mata Bejid J 153 Wc 122
40163 Matabuena SG 67 Wb 102
23620 Matacas J 152 Wa 121
10970 Mata de Alcántara CC 97 Tb 110
37798 Mata de Armuña, La SA 65 Uc 102
37765 Mata de Arriba SA 82 Ua 105
04828 Mata de Bolaimí, La AL 155 Xf 123
40214 Mata de Cuéllar SG 66 Vd 100
24848 Mata de Curueño, La LE 27 Ud 92
39418 Mata de Hoz CB 17 Ve 91
24852 Mata de la Riba, La LE 27 Ud 91
37130 Mata de Ledesma, La SA 64 Ua 102
44557 Mata de los Olmos, La TE 91 Zc 103
24252 Mata del Páramo, La LE 27 Ub 94
24887 Mata de Monteagudo, La LE 28 Uf 91
12312 Mata de Morella, La CS 91 Ze 105
24291 Matadeón de los Oteros LE 27 Ud 94
08230 Matadepera B 58 Ca 99
25125 Mata de Pinyana, La L 55 Ad 98
40392 Mata de Quintanar SG 67 Vf 102
06800 Matadero Provincial BA 117 Td 115
40185 Mata de Rosueros SG 67 Wa 102
28492 Mataelpino MD 85 Wa 104
04715 Matagorda AL 170 Xa 128
11519 Matagorda CA 172 Te 129
21760 Matalascañas H 162 Tc 127
42132 Matalasilla SO 51 Xf 98
34810 Matalbaniega P 29 Ve 91
42113 Matalebreras SO 51 Xf 97
30889 Matalentisco MC 171 Yc 124
09198 Matalindo BU 49 Wd 95
16250 Mata Llana CU 105 Yb 111
19223 Matallana GU 68 Wd 102
24836 Matallana de Torío LE 27 Uc 91
24290 Matallana de Valmadrigal LE 27 Ue 94
36689 Matalobos PO 23 Rc 92
24357 Matalobos del Páramo LE 27 Ub 94
36210 Matamá PO 41 Rb 95
37891 Matamala SA 83 Uc 104
40163 Matamala SG 68 Wb 102
42211 Matamala de Almazán SO 69 Xc 99
40153 Matamanzano SG 85 We 103
25287 Matamargó L 57 Bd 97
34810 Matamorisca P 29 Ve 91
39200 Matamorosa CB 17 Ve 91
47410 Matamozos VA 66 Vb 101
40165 Matandrino SG 68 Wb 102
06392 Matanegra BA 133 Te 118
24793 Matanza LE 26 Tf 94
03316 Matanza, La A 141 Yf 120
02410 Matanza, La AB 140 Ya 118
39880 Matanza, La CB 19 We 89
35220 Matanza, La GC 184 Kd 180
38370 Matanza de Acentejo, La TF 181 Id 178
24207 Matanza de los Oteros LE 46 Ud 95
42351 Matanza de Soria SO 50 We 99
04100 Matanzas, Las AL 170 Xe 127
14900 Mataosos CO 151 Vd 124
39410 Mataporquera CB 29 Vf 91
47230 Matapozuelos VA 66 Vb 100
43540 Mata-redona T 93 Ad 105
08302 Mataró B 77 Cc 99
41569 Matarredonda SE 166 Va 124
39418 Matarrepudio CB 29 Vf 91
19227 Matarrubia GU 87 We 103
19265 Matas GU 69 Xb 102
06430 Matas, Las BA 134 Ub 116
28290 Matas, Las MD 86 Wa 105
41530 Matas, Las SE 165 Ud 125
42175 Matasejún SO 51 Xe 97
25638 Mata-solana L 56 Af 96
01192 Matauco VI 32 Xc 91
24378 Matavenero y Poibueno LE 26 Td 93
08230 Mata-xica B 58 Ca 99
23290 Matea, La J 154 Xc 120
49519 Matellanes ZA 45 Te 98
03316 Mateos, Los A 141 Yf 120
12415 Matet CS 107 Zd 109
18859 Matián GR 154 Xd 123
22311 Matidero HU 35 Zf 94
39812 Matienzo CB 18 Wc 89
35613 Matilla, La GC 183 Ma 177
21760 Matilla, La H 162 Tb 125
40175 Matilla, La SG 67 Wb 101
49692 Matilla de Arzón ZA 46 Uc 96
24359 Matilla de la Vega LE 27 Ua 94
47114 Matilla de los Caños VA 66 Va 99
37450 Matilla de los Caños del Río SA 82 Ua 104
49590 Matilla la Seca ZA 46 Uc 99
27375 Mato LU 12 Sc 89
27555 Mato LU 24 Sa 92
27637 Mato LU 24 Sd 92
03296 Matola A 142 Zb 119
35610 Matorral, El GC 183 Ma 178
06290 Matorrales BA 133 Tf 118
04271 Matreros, Los AL 171 Ya 125
24820 Matueca de Torío LE 27 Uc 92
01206 Maturana VI 32 Xc 91
46391 Matutano, El V 107 Za 112
26321 Matute RI 31 Xb 95
42211 Matute de Almazán SO 69 Xc 100
42167 Matute de la Sierra SO 51 Xd 97
20738 Matxinbenta SS 20 Xe 90
10591 Maulique CC 99 Ua 109
18710 Maurel, El GR 169 We 128
32705 Maus, As OR 43 Sc 95
32880 Maus de Salas OR 42 Sa 97
34492 Mave P 29 Ve 92
31715 Maya, Amaiur/ NC 21 Yd 89
37780 Maya, La SA 83 Uc 104
49718 Mayalde ZA 64 Ub 101
03680 Mayorazogo A 142 Zb 119
04279 Mayordomo, El AL 171 Xf 126
30334 Mayordomos, Los MC 157 Yf 122
47680 Mayorga VA 46 Ue 96
37882 Maza de Alba, La SA 83 Uc 103
37451 Maza de San Pedro SA 82 Tf 104
40556 Mazagatos SG 68 Wd 100
21800 Mazagón H 162 Tb 126
44621 Mazaleón TE 74 Aa 102
05691 Mazalinos AV 83 Uc 106
42130 Mazalvete SO 51 Xe 98
37149 Mazán SA 64 Tf 102
22481 Mazana, La HU 55 Ad 95
39210 Mazandrero CB 17 Ve 90
45593 Mazarabeas Altas TO 102 Vf 109
45593 Mazarabeas Bajas TO 101 Ve 109
45114 Mazarambroz TO 102 Vf 110
19286 Mazarete GU 70 Xf 102
09346 Mazariegos BU 49 Wc 96
34170 Mazariegos P 47 Vb 96
04131 Mazarulleque AL 170 Xe 128
16510 Mazarulleque CU 104 Xb 107
42126 Mazaterón SO 70 Xf 99
39509 Mazcuerras CB 17 Ve 89
27677 Mazo LU 25 Sf 92
27667 Mazo LU 25 Ta 91
33579 Mazo, El AS 17 Vc 89
45138 Mazo, El TO 101 Vb 111
45138 Mazo, El TO 101 Vb 111
38739 Mazo = Villa de Mazo TF 181 Hb 177
37406 Mazores Nuevo SA 65 Ue 102
37406 Mazores Viejo SA 65 Ue 102
33507 Mazuco, El AS 16 Va 88
09646 Mazueco BU 49 Wd 95
41440 Mazueco SE 152 Ud 122
19114 Mazuecos GU 87 Wf 107
34306 Mazuecos de Valdeginate P 47 Va 95
09228 Mazuela BU 48 Wa 95
34473 Mazuelas P 28 Vc 93
09239 Mazuelo de Muñó BU 48 Wa 95
30442 Mazuza MC 140 Xf 119
30870 Mazzarón MC 156 Ye 123
48115 Meaca BI 19 Xb 89
48115 Meaka BI 19 Xb 89
12133 Meanes CS 92 Zf 107
31227 Meano VI 32 Xd 93
15857 Meáns C 10 Ra 90
36968 Meaño PO 22 Rb 94
20500 Meatzerreka Beneras SS 20 Xd 90
32633 Meaus OR 42 Sb 97
36557 Meavía PO 23 Rd 93
09346 Mecerreyes BU 49 Wc 96
18470 Mecina Alfahar GR 169 Wf 127
18450 Mecina Bombarrón GR 169 We 127
18414 Mecina Fondales GR 169 Wd 127
18490 Mecina-Tedel GR 169 Wf 127
28880 Meco MD 87 We 105
27293 Meda LU 12 Sd 90
32368 Meda OR 25 Sf 95
38610 Médano, El TF 180 Ic 180
32618 Medeiros OR 43 Sc 97
06411 Medellín BA 117 Ua 115
39419 Mediadoro CB 29 Vf 91
13720 Media Luna, La CR 122 We 114
50135 Mediana de Aragón Z 72 Zb 100
05194 Mediana de Voltoya AV 85 Vc 104
09588 Medianas BU 19 We 90
03570 Mediases A 143 Ze 117
33508 Mediavilla AS 16 Va 88
38590 Medida, La TF 181 Id 179
15821 Medín C 11 Re 91
42240 Medinaceli SO 70 Xd 101
06320 Medina de las Torres BA 133 Td 118
47400 Medina del Campo VA 66 Va 101
09500 Medina de Pomar BU 30 Wd 91
47800 Medina de Ríoseco VA 47 Uf 97
04276 Medinas, Los AL 171 Xe 125
11170 Medina-Sidonia CA 172 Ua 130
05619 Medinilla AV 83 Uc 106
09230 Medinilla de la Dehesa BU 30 Wa 95
17482 Medinyà GI 59 Cf 96
39724 Medio Cuyedo CB 18 Wb 88
11610 Mediodía CA 165 Ud 128
32779 Medos OR 24 Sd 94
19246 Medranda GU 69 Xa 103
26374 Medrano RI 32 Xc 94
24442 Medulas, Las LE 25 Tb 94
47440 Megeces VA 66 Vc 100
19315 Megina GU 89 Ya 105
27296 Meilán LU 12 Sc 90
27240 Meira LU 13 Se 89
15188 Meirama C 11 Rd 89
27324 Meiraos LU 25 Se 93
15168 Meirás C 11 Re 88
15806 Meire, O C 23 Sa 91
36877 Meirol PO 41 Rd 95
36637 Meis PO 22 Rb 93
27211 Meixaboi LU 24 Sb 91
32366 Meixide OR 25 Ta 95
15109 Meixonfrío C 10 Rc 90
27558 Meixonfrío LU 24 Sb 92
24250 Méizara LE 27 Ub 94
45622 Mejorada TO 100 Va 108
45593 Mejorada TO 102 Vf 109
28840 Mejorada del Campo MD 86 Wd 106
37478 Mejorito, El SA 82 Td 104
20570 Mekolalde SS 20 Xd 90
48210 Mekoleta BI 19 Xb 90
04271 Mela, La AL 171 Xf 126
18658 Melegís GR 168 Wc 127
02049 Melegriz AB 124 Ya 115
35214 Melenara GC 184 Kd 181
30889 Melenchones, Los MC 156 Yc 124
33691 Melendrera AS 15 Ub 87
33536 Melendreras AS 15 Ud 89
33528 Melendreros AS 15 Uc 89
24515 Melezna y Mazos LE 25 Ta 93
47687 Melgar de Abajo VA 46 Uf 95
47686 Melgar de Arriba VA 28 Uf 95
09100 Melgar de Fernamental BU 29 Ve 94
49626 Melgar de Tera ZA 45 Tf 97
34467 Melgar de Yuso P 29 Ve 95
09591 Melgosa BU 30 Wc 93
16193 Melgosa, La CU 105 Xf 108
09129 Melgosa de Villadiego BU 29 Wa 93
46133 Meliana V 108 Zd 111
32711 Melias OR 24 Sb 94
18713 Melicena GR 169 We 128
31382 Mélida NC 33 Yc 94
47318 Mélida VA 48 Ve 99
15800 Melide C 23 Rf 91
52001* Melilla ML 174 Xa 136
37520 Melimbrazos SA 81 Tc 105
10696 Melinchón, El CC 99 Ua 108
49512 Mellanes ZA 45 Te 98
24165 Mellanzos LE 27 Ue 93

284 | **Masía de la Rinconada**

01213 Melledes VI 31 Xa 92
29593 Mellizas, Las MA 166 Vb 127
32411 Melón OR 23 Re 95
40444 Melque SG 66 Vd 102
45165 Melque TO 101 Vd 110
22549 Melusa, La HU 55 Ac 98
40234 Membibre de la Hoz SG 67 Vf 100
37766 Membibre de la Sierra SA 83 Ub 104
13230 Membrilla CR 122 Wd 115
34115 Membrillar P 28 Vb 93
19247 Membrillera GU 69 Xa 103
45663 Membrillo, El TO 100 Vb 109
21647 Membrillo Alto H 147 Tc 123
21647 Membrillo Bajo H 147 Tc 123
10580 Membrío CC 97 Sf 111
01477 Menagaray VI 19 Wf 90
09585 Menamayor BU 19 We 90
25139 Menàrguens L 56 Ae 98
04890 Menas, Las AL 170 Xc 125
04662 Menas, Los AL 171 Ya 124
45128 Menasalbas TO 101 Ve 111
34810 Menaza P 29 Ve 92
04650 Menchores, Los AL 171 Xf 124
25593 Mencui L 37 Ba 94
01510 Mendarozqueta VI 31 Xb 91
48382 Mendata BI 19 Xc 89
31587 Mendavia NC 32 Xe 94
31282 Mendaza NC 32 Xe 93
48460 Mendeica BI 19 Wf 90
48289 Mendexa BI 20 Xd 88
02420 Méndez AB 140 Yb 118
48383 Mendieta BI 19 Xc 89
31150 Mendigorría NC 33 Ya 93
01196 Mendiguren VI 31 Xb 91
01206 Mendijur VI 32 Xc 91
31280 Mendilibarri NC 32 Xe 93
48220 Mendiola BI 19 Xc 90
20550 Mendiola SS 20 Xd 90
01194 Mendiola VI 31 Xc 92
31485 Mendióroz NC 33 Yd 92
01520 Mendívil VI 31 Xc 91
01191 Mendoza VI 31 Xb 91
48230 Mendraka BI 20 Xc 90
36946 Menduiña PO 22 Rb 95
34305 Meneses de Campos P 47 Va 97
06413 Mengabril BA 117 Ua 115
05131 Mengamuñoz AV 84 Uf 106
14620 Mengemor CO 151 Vc 121
23620 Mengíbar J 152 Wb 121
01477 Menoyo VI 19 Wf 90
15113 Mens C 10 Ra 89
39812 Mentera-Barruelo CB 18 Wc 89
45930 Méntrida TO 85 Ve 107
25513 Mentui L 37 Af 94
33707 Menudero AS 14 Tc 88
50780 Menuza Z 73 Zd 101
48120 Meñaka BI 19 Xb 88
50170 Mequinenza Z 74 Ab 100
15349 Mera C 10 Sa 87
17539 Meranges GI 38 Be 94
33785 Merás AS 14 Td 88
25749 Meravella L 56 Ba 97
32830 Merca, A OR 42 Sa 95
39311 Mercadal CB 17 Vf 89
07740 Mercadal, Es IB 77 Ea 109
42193 Mercadera, La SO 50 Xa 99
12163 Mercades de Baix CS 92 Ze 107
05154 Mercadillo AV 83 Ud 105
37493 Mercadillo SA 82 Te 104
39722 Mercadillo, El CB 18 Wb 88
02510 Mercadillos AB 124 Yb 116
28051 Mercamadrid MD 86 Wc 106
30890 Merced, La MC 155 Ya 122
32680 Mercedes OR 43 Sc 96
34828 Mercedes P 29 Ve 91
28620 Mercedes, Las MD 85 Ve 107
33507 Meré AS 16 Va 88
25638 Merea L 56 Ba 96
48710 Mereludi BI 20 Xd 89
32213 Meréns OR 42 Rf 95
15126 Merexo C 10 Qe 90
06800 Mérida BA 117 Td 115
39728 Merilla CB 18 Wb 89
27866 Merille LU 12 Sc 87
33876 Merillés AS 14 Td 89
09515 Merindad de Cuesta-Urria BU 30 Wd 92
09568 Merindad de Sotoscueva BU 18 Wc 90
09574 Merindad de Valdeporres BU 18 Wb 90
09559 Merindad de Valdivielso BU 30 Wc 92
05197 Merino, El AV 84 Vb 105
22482 Merli HU 36 Ac 94
33579 Merodio AS 17 Vc 89
30708 Meroñes, Los MC 157 Za 122
36580 Merza PO 23 Re 92
11339 Mesa, La CA 174 Ud 130
23211 Mesa, La J 137 Wc 119
45760 Mesa, La TO 102 Wc 110
38358 Mesa del Mar TF 181 Id 177
09216 Mesanza BU 31 Xc 92
04149 Mesa Roldán, La AL 171 Ya 127
16650 Mesas, Las CU 122 Xb 112
18810 Mesas, Los GR 154 Xb 124
14729 Mesas Altas CO 150 Uf 121
11590 Mesas de Asta CA 163 Te 128
21620 Mesas de en Medio H 147 Ta 124
14709 Mesas de Guadalora CO 150 Ue 122
10329 Mesas de Ibor CC 99 Uc 110
11592 Mesas de Santiago CA 164 Ua 128
10638 Mesegal CC 82 Te 107
05514 Mesegar de Corneja AV 83 Ue 105
45541 Mesegar de Tajo TO 101 Vc 109
32516 Mesego OR 23 Rf 94
24394 Meseta, La LE 26 Ua 94
15685 Mesía C 11 Re 90
30835 Mesillo MC 156 Yc 123
49660 Mesón de las Palomas ZA 46 Uc 97
15689 Mesón do Vento C 11 Rd 90
02449 Mesones AB 139 Xd 118
19185 Mesones GU 86 Wd 104
50267 Mesones de Isuela Z 71 Yc 99
02359 Mesta, La AB 139 Xd 117
13592 Mestanza CR 136 Vf 117
33507 Mestas AS 16 Va 88
10624 Mestas, Las CC 82 Tf 106
33556 Mestas de Con AS 16 Uf 88
07871 Mestre IB 109 Bc 116
31241 Metauten NC 32 Xf 92
48309 Metxika BI 19 Xb 88
25632 Meüll, El L 56 Ae 96
50152 Mezalocha Z 72 Yf 100
31695 Mezkiritz NC 21 Yd 91
42213 Mezquetillas SO 69 Xc 101
35628 Mézquez GC 183 Lf 178
01207 Mezquia VI 32 Xd 91
32549 Mezquita, A OR 44 Sf 96
44708 Mezquita, La TE 91 Zb 104
44169 Mezquita de Jarque TE 91 Za 104
44493 Mezquita de Loscos TE 72 Yf 102
41659 Mezquitilla, La SE 166 Uf 126
10100 Miajadas CC 117 Ua 114
32701 Miamán OR 43 Sc 95
17850 Miana, La GI 58 Cd 95
50683 Mianos Z 34 Za 93
37660 Miaranda del Castañar SA 82 Ua 106
49624 Micereces de Tera ZA 45 Ua 97
34485 Micieces de Ojeda P 29 Vd 92
50330 Miedes de Aragón Z 71 Yd 101
19276 Miedes de Atienza GU 69 Xa 101
33816 Mieldes AS 14 Td 89
39310 Miengo CB 17 Vf 88
39723 Miera CB 18 Wb 89
33199 Mieres AS 15 Ub 88
33611 Mieres AS 15 Ub 89
17830 Mieres GI 59 Cd 96
19225 Mierla, La GU 68 We 103
39586 Mieses CB 16 Vc 90
37254 Mieza SA 63 Tb 102
30593 Migaznares MC 157 Za 122
07749 Migjorn Gran S. Cristóbal, Es IB 77 Ea 109
40441 Migueláñez SG 67 Vd 102
45830 Miguel Esteban TO 103 Wf 111
40494 Miguel-Ibáñez SG 67 Vd 102
37788 Miguel Muñoz SA 83 Ub 104
13170 Miguelturra CR 121 Wa 115
09511 Mijala BU 19 Wf 91
09515 Mijangos BU 30 Wd 91
09212 Mijaraluenga BU 31 We 92
05461 Mijares AV 84 Va 107
16330 Mijares CU 106 Yd 109
46360 Mijares V 125 Za 112
29650 Mijas MA 175 Vc 129
29649 Mijas Costa MA 175 Vb 129
43143 Milà, El T 75 Bb 101
31320 Milagro NC 52 Yb 95
09460 Milagros BU 68 Wb 99
42218 Milana, La SO 69 Xd 100
37256 Milano SA 63 Tc 102
18128 Milanos GR 167 Ve 126
18312 Milanos GR 167 Vf 125
30333 Milanos, Los MC 156 Ye 122
43559 Miliana, La T 93 Ac 105
30420 Milicianos, Los MC 140 Yb 119
25692 Milla L 55 Ae 96
24393 Milla del Páramo, La LE 27 Ub 94
24283 Milla del Río, La LE 27 Ua 93
49330 Milla de Tera ZA 45 Te 96
19127 Millana GU 88 Xc 105
29109 Millanas, Las MA 174 Va 128
10394 Millanes CC 99 Uc 109
36556 Millarada PO 23 Rd 93
46198 Millares V 126 Zb 113
04560 Millares, Los AL 170 Xc 127
10391 Millares, Los CC 99 Ud 109
32314 Millarouso OR 25 Ta 94
17462 Millars GI 59 Cf 97
27275 Milleirós LU 13 Se 90
03812 Millena A 142 Zd 116
23296 Miller J 139 Xd 119
49699 Milles de la Polvorosa ZA 46 Ub 97
32815 Milmanda OR 42 Rf 96
19287 Milmarcos GU 70 Ya 102
11580 Mimbral, El CA 173 Ub 129
37497 Mimbre, La SA 81 Tb 105
10280 Mimbrera CC 117 Ua 113
48860 Mimetiz BI 19 Wf 89
21660 Mina H 147 Tc 122
42138 Mina SO 52 Ya 98
14512 Mina, La CO 166 Vb 124
22790 Mina, La HU 34 Zb 91
41870 Mina Caridad SE 148 Te 123
21270 Mina de Cala H 148 Td 121
13593 Mina de Diógenes CR 136 Vf 117
21647 Mina de Guadiana H 147 Tb 123
21594 Mina de Santa Catalina H 160 Sd 123
06389 Mina de Santa Justa BA 132 Tc 119
30876 Mina La Positiva MC 156 Yc 123
02499 Minas, Las AB 140 Yb 119
04560 Minas, Las AL 170 Xc 127
16312 Minas, Las CU 106 Yd 110
50269 Minas, Las Z 52 Yc 99
14449 Minas de Horcajo CR 136 Vd 117
41898 Minas del Castillo de las Guardas SE 148 Td 122
18518 Minas del Marquesado GR 169 Wf 125
21660 Minas de Riotinto H 147 Tc 122
15215 Minas de San Fix C 22 Ra 92
18518 Minas de Santa Constanza GR 169 We 125
45672 Minas de Santa Quiteria TO 119 Va 112
02499 Minateda AB 140 Yc 118
13189 Mina Victoria CR 120 Vd 116
02620 Minaya AB 123 Xe 113
07620 Miner IB 111 Cf 111
16260 Minglanilla CU 106 Yc 111
02409 Mingogil AB 140 Yb 118
05280 Mingorría AV 84 Vc 104
02610 Mingote, El AB 123 Xd 115
30335 Mingrano, El MC 156 Ye 123
10895 Minguillana CC 97 Ta 108
23330 Minillas J 138 Wf 119
33798 Miñagón AS 13 Tb 88
24765 Miñambres LE 26 Ua 95
36914 Miñán PO 22 Rb 94
42126 Miñana SO 70 Xf 99
34127 Miñanes P 29 Vc 94
01510 Miñano Menor VI 31 Xb 91
15630 Miño C 11 Re 88
42230 Miño de Medinaceli SO 70 Xc 101
42328 Miño de San Esteban SO 68 Wd 99
09553 Miñón BU 18 Wc 91
09150 Miñón BU 30 Wb 94
15999 Miñortos C 22 Ra 92
19278 Miñosa, La GU 69 Xa 101
42216 Miñosa, La SO 70 Xc 100
27744 Miñotelo LU 12 Se 89
27865 Miñotos LU 12 Sc 87
01427 Mioma VI 31 Wf 91
39709 Mioño CB 19 We 88
22393 Mipanas HU 55 Ab 95
16393 Mira CU 106 Yd 110
50669 Mira Z 53 Ye 97
10540 Mirabel CC 98 Te 109
19268 Mirabueno GU 69 Xb 103
25287 Miracle, El L 57 Bd 97
30739 Mirador, El MC 157 Za 121
28210 Mirador del Romero MD 85 Vf 106
23713 Miraelrío J 137 Wc 120
03779 Miraflor A 127 Aa 115
11369 Miraflores CA 164 Td 128
28792 Miraflores de la Sierra MD 86 Wb 104
31219 Mirafuentes NC 32 Xe 93
25242 Miralcamp L 56 Af 99
02155 Miralcampo AB 124 Yb 114
19246 Miralrío GU 69 Xa 103
28598 Miralrío MD 103 We 108
22529 Miralsot de Abajo HU 74 Ab 99
22528 Miralsot de Arriba HU 74 Ab 99
46711 Miramar V 127 Zf 115
44141 Mirambel TE 91 Zd 105
25792 Mirambell L 56 Bb 97
33410 Miranda AS 15 Ua 87
27144 Miranda LU 12 Se 91
30319 Miranda MC 157 Yf 122
38715 Miranda TF 181 Hb 176
31253 Miranda de Arga NC 33 Yb 94
37187 Miranda de Azán SA 64 Ub 103
42191 Miranda de Duero SO 51 Xd 99
09200 Miranda de Ebro BU 31 Xa 92
23213 Miranda del Rey J 137 Wc 118
37449 Miranda de Pericalvo SA 64 Ua 103
06891 Mirandilla BA 117 Te 114
24147 Mirantes de Luna LE 27 Ua 91
28035 Mirasierra MD 86 Wb 106
14140 Mirasivienes CO 150 Va 122
25795 Miravall L 37 Bb 95
25430 Miravall L 75 Ae 99
09280 Miraveche BU 31 We 92
43747 Miravet T 74 Ad 102
44159 Miravete de la Sierra TE 91 Zb 105
27229 Miraz LU 12 Sa 90
32136 Mirela OR 23 Sa 93
05154 Mirón, El AV 83 Ud 105
05191 Mironcillo AV 84 Vb 105
13739 Mirones, Los CR 137 Wb 117
05146 Mirueña de los Infanzones AV 84 Uf 104
46920 Mislata V 107 Zd 112
18570 Mitagalán GR 168 Wc 124
01211 Mixancas = Mijancas VI 31 Xb 92
33583 Miyares AS 15 Ue 88
22311 Miz HU 35 Zf 94
04277 Mizala AL 171 Xf 126
02510 Mizquitillas AB 140 Yc 116
36950 Moaña PO 22 Rb 95
15686 Moar C 11 Re 90
34486 Moarves de Ojeda P 29 Vd 92
38916 Mocanal TF 180 Ha 182
38911 Mocanes Casas, Los TF 180 Gf 182
46230 Mocarrá-Bobalar V 126 Zd 113
45270 Mocejón TO 102 Wa 109
19332 Mochales GU 70 Xf 102
14729 Mochos, Los CO 150 Va 122
23268 Mochuelos, Los J 138 Wf 118
32813 Mociños OR 42 Rf 96
18247 Moclín GR 168 Wb 124
29738 Moclinejo MA 167 Ve 128
42315 Modamio SO 69 Wf 100
24815 Modino LE 28 Uf 92
09194 Modúbar de la Cuesta BU 30 Wc 95
09620 Modúbar de la Emparedada BU 30 Wc 95
09194 Modúbar de San Cibrián BU 49 Wc 95
15563 Moeche C 11 Rf 87
35140 Mogán GC 184 Kb 181
37610 Mogarraz SA 82 Tf 106
49174 Mogátar ZA 64 Ua 100
46640 Mogente = Moixent V 126 Zb 115
23250 Mogino J 138 Wf 119
23310 Mogón J 153 Wf 120
36911 Mogor PO 22 Rb 94
33318 Mogovio AS 15 Ud 88
39310 Mogro CB 17 Wa 88
21800 Moguer H 161 Ta 125
30420 Moharque MC 140 Yb 118
02600 Moharras AB 123 Xd 113
29160 Moheda MA 167 Vd 127
10849 Moheda, La CC 98 Tc 108
02139 Mohedas, Las AB 139 Xe 117
10664 Mohedas de Granadilla CC 82 Te 107
45576 Mohedas de la Jara TO 100 Uf 111
19226 Mohernando GU 87 We 104
16193 Mohorte CU 105 Xf 108
27655 Moia LU 25 Ta 91
08180 Moià B 58 Ca 98
32617 Moialde OR 43 Se 97
15937 Moimenta C 22 Ra 92
46640 Moixent = Mogente V 126 Zb 115
08734 Moja B 76 Be 101
04638 Mojácar AL 171 Ya 126
04638 Mojácar Playa AL 171 Yb 126
47250 Mojados VA 66 Vc 100
19264 Mojares GU 69 Xc 102
35530 Mojón, El GC 182 Mc 174
30130 Mojón, El MC 157 Za 120
04825 Mojonar, El AL 155 Xe 123
04270 Mojonera AL 171 Xe 126
04745 Mojonera, La AL 170 Xb 128
04889 Mojonera, La AL 170 Xd 125
03660 Mola A 142 Zb 118
43736 Molá, El = Molar T 75 Ae 102
07209 Mola, La IB 111 Da 112
43736 Molá = Molar, El T 75 Ae 102
49120 Molacillos ZA 46 Uc 99
23469 Molar, El J 153 Wf 121
28710 Molar, El MD 86 Wc 104
02251 Molar de Arriba AB 124 Yc 113
21342 Molares H 147 Tb 121
30868 Molares, Los MC 156 Ye 123
41750 Molares, Los SE 165 Ub 126
12448 Molarico, El CS 107 Zc 108
02129 Molata, La AB 140 Xf 116
30849 Molata, La MC 156 Yd 122
15809 Moldes C 23 Rf 91
24521 Moldes LE 25 Ta 93
49521 Moldones ZA 44 Td 97
27244 Moleiras LU 13 Se 89
08697 Molers B 57 Be 95
08788 Moletons, Els B 76 Bd 99
49327 Molezuelas de la Carballeda ZA 45 Te 96
12135 Molí Azor CS 91 Zd 107
07750 Molí de Dalt, Es IB 77 Df 109
25331 Molí d'Espígol L 56 Ba 98
08513 Molí Galobardes B 58 Ca 97
33555 Molina, La AS 16 Va 89
08517 Molina, La B 57 Bf 97
17537 Molina, La GI 38 Bf 94
19300 Molina de Aragón GU 89 Ya 103
09593 Molina del Portillo de Busto, La BU 31 We 92
30500 Molina de Segura MC 156 Ye 120
09591 Molina de Ubierna, La BU 30 Wc 93
24724 Molinaferrera LE 26 Td 94
48890 Molinar BI 18 Wd 89
02129 Molinar, El AB 140 Xf 116
12429 Molinar, El CS 107 Zb 109
07006 Molinar, El IB 110 Ce 111
17496 Molinàs GI 40 Da 94
24413 Molinaseca LE 26 Tc 93
03779 Molinell A 127 Zf 115
18810 Molineras, Las GR 154 Xb 124
02440 Molinicos AB 139 Xe 118
01213 Molinilla VI 31 Xa 92
37683 Molinillo SA 82 Ua 106
13194 Molinillo, El CR 101 Ve 112
18183 Molinillo, El GR 168 Wd 125
38800 Molinito, El TF 184 Hf 180
02100 Molino AB 124 Xf 113
16649 Molino CU 104 Xc 111
04640 Molino, El AL 156 Yb 124
16150 Molino, El CU 89 Ya 106
16360 Molino, El CU 105 Ya 110
11510 Molino aceitero de Guerra CA 172 Tf 129
50135 Molino Alto Z 72 Zb 100
40441 Molino Berral SG 66 Vd 102
11180 Molino Castro CA 173 Uc 130
40340 Molino Cega SG 67 Vf 101
02312 Molino de Abajo AB 139 Xb 117
16370 Molino de Abajo CU 106 Yc 109
19442 Molino de Abajo GU 70 Xe 103
45860 Molino de Abajo TO 103 We 111
13195 Molino de Alarcos CR 120 Vf 115
11139 Molino de Almaza CA 172 Te 130
23600 Molino de Aramundo J 152 Wa 122
41660 Molino de Arjona SE 166 Uf 126
19275 Molino de Arriba GU 68 We 101
19320 Molino de Arriba GU 89 Yb 105
13770 Molino de Bartolo CR 137 Wc 117
29770 Molino de Blas MA 168 Wa 128
19314 Molino de Cabrillas GU 89 Ya 104
19432 Molino de Canales del Ducado GU 88 Xd 104
13597 Molino de Delio CR 137 Wa 117
02214 Molino de Don Benito AB 125 Yd 113
45840 Molino de Doña Sol TO 103 We 111
19442 Molino de En Medio GU 70 Xe 103
10570 Molino de Enmedio CC 97 Sf 112
29491 Molino de Enmedio MA 174 Ue 129
10004 Molino de Gabriel CC 98 Td 111
30413 Molino de Javana MC 139 Xe 120
18840 Molino de la Alquería GR 154 Xc 122
14549 Molino de la Cañada CO 150 Vb 123
03312 Molino de la Ciudad, El A 141 Za 120
39518 Molino de la Mina de Lápiz CB 17 Ve 90
18817 Molino de Lanas GR 154 Xb 123
30440 Molino de las Ánimas MC 140 Ya 119
30708 Molino de las Ánimas MC 157 Za 122

A B C D E F G H I J K L M N Ñ O P Q R S T U V W X Y Z

Molino de las Ánimas | 285

41400 Molino de la Sargenta SE 150 Ue 124
02489 Molino de las Bojas AB 139 Xd 119
49153 Molino de la Sierra ZA 65 Uc 100
06444 Molino de las Monjas BA 133 Tf 118
16147 Molino de la Torre CU 89 Xf 108
40217 Molino del Barado SG 66 Vd 101
16649 Molino del Blanco CU 104 Xc 111
13247 Molino del Blanquillo CR 122 We 115
13230 Molino del Comendador CR 122 We 115
41400 Molino del Cordobés SE 150 Uf 123
41400 Molino del Corregidor SE 150 Uf 123
23669 Molino del Despeñadero J 152 Vf 123
23749 Molino de Lemos J 152 Wa 120
02637 Molino del Francés AB 124 Xf 113
16220 Molino del Francés CU 124 Ya 112
41370 Molino del Monte SE 149 Ub 121
41400 Molino del Notario SE 150 Uf 122
41370 Molino de los Agustinos SE 149 Ub 121
13240 Molino de los Álamos CR 122 We 115
13779 Molino de los Frailes CR 137 Wa 117
41429 Molino de los Frailes SE 149 Ud 123
13240 Molino de los Moros CR 122 We 115
10513 Molino de los Muertos CC 96 Sd 111
06518 Molino de los Piernos BA 115 Se 113
23294 Molino del Prado de la Porca J 139 Xc 119
41410 Molino del Puente SE 149 Uc 124
41740 Molino del Salado SE 163 Ua 127
13326 Molino de Macayo CR 138 Xa 118
41460 Molino de Manuel García SE 149 Ud 121
13230 Molino de María CR 122 Wd 115
02155 Molino de Marmota AB 124 Ya 113
11380 Molino de Mastral CA 173 Uc 132
06110 Molino de Medrana BA 131 Sf 118
19275 Molino de Mochinga GU 69 Wf 101
06510 Molino de Morro BA 115 Sf 113
41560 Molino de Osorio SE 166 Va 125
23220 Molino de Panzacola J 137 Wc 119
41400 Molino de Pareja SE 150 Uf 122
41400 Molino de Pavía SE 150 Ue 124
18615 Molino de Pepe GR 168 Wc 128
13230 Molino de Piña CR 122 Wd 115
13326 Molino de Rajamantas CR 138 Xb 117
41630 Molino de Recacha SE 165 Ue 124
28370 Molino de Ruas MD 103 Wd 107
11391 Molino de Saladavieja CA 175 Uc 132
11650 Molino de Serracín CA 165 Uc 127
23569 Molino de Solera J 153 Wd 122
40270 Molino de Temeroso SG 67 Ve 101
41400 Molino de Valdecañas SE 150 Ue 124
14549 Molino de Valderrama CO 150 Va 123
14547 Molino Dos Vigas CO 150 Va 123
16707 Molino el Batanejo CU 124 Xf 112
40270 Molino El Paredón SG 67 Ve 102
30740 Molino La Calcetera MC 157 Zb 122
18519 Molino Las Vallicas GR 169 We 124
06228 Molino la Zalía BA 133 Tf 117
45121 Molino los Tejos TO 101 Vd 111
40241 Molino Maluca SG 67 Vd 101
18812 Molino Rasma GR 154 Xa 123
41670 Molino Raya SE 166 Ue 126
11380 Molinos CA 175 Uc 132
12592 Molinos CS 108 Ze 110
18270 Molinos GR 167 Wa 125
25512 Molinos L 37 Af 94
44556 Molinos TE 91 Zd 104
04858 Molinos, Los AL 171 Xf 125
04277 Molinos, Los AL 171 Xf 126
05593 Molinos, Los AV 83 Ud 106
06900 Molinos, Los BA 133 Tf 119
35541 Molinos, Los GC 182 Md 173
35470 Molinos, Los GC 184 Kb 181
22338 Molinos, Los HU 36 Ab 94
28460 Molinos, Los MD 85 Vf 104
44195 Molinos, Los TE 90 Ye 106
42156 Molinos de Duero SO 50 Xb 97
18630 Molinos de la Torrecilla GR 168 Wc 126
16192 Molinos del Papel CU 105 Xf 108
26145 Molinos de Ocón, Los RI 32 Xe 95
42165 Molinos de Razón SO 50 Xc 97
37540 Molino Sobrao SA 81 Tb 106
29400 Molinos-Sijuela, Los MA 166 Ue 128
18512 Molinos y Sierra GR 169 Xa 125
29500 Molino Tallista MA 166 Vb 127
03322 Molins A 157 Za 120
03640 Molins, Els A 142 Za 118
44143 Moljno Harinero TE 91 Zc 105
39560 Molleda CB 17 Vc 88
33937 Molledo AS 15 Ub 88
39430 Molledo CB 17 Vf 90
38690 Molledo, El TF 180 Ib 179
25230 Mollerussa L 56 Af 99
08100 Mollet del Vallès B 77 Cb 99
17752 Mollet de Peralada GI 40 Da 94
29532 Mollina MA 166 Vc 126
17868 Molló GI 39 Cc 94
47313 Molpeceres VA 67 Vf 99
08281 Molsosa, La L 57 Bd 98
18611 Molvízar GR 168 Wc 128
27378 Momán LU 12 Sc 89
05410 Mombeltrán AV 84 Uf 107
42225 Momblona SO 70 Xd 100
49310 Mombuey ZA 45 Te 96
09512 Momediano BU 18 Wd 91
22460 Mon, El HU 36 Ab 95
18193 Monachil GR 168 Wc 126
19239 Monasterio GU 69 Wf 103
42291 Monasterio SO 50 Xb 99
33811 Monasterio de Hermo AS 14 Tc 91
09613 Monasterio de la Sierra BU 50 We 96
33814 Monasterio del Coto AS 13 Tb 90
09292 Monasterio de Rodilla BU 30 Wd 94
24166 Monasterio de San Miguel de Escalada LE 27 Ue 93
34126 Monasterio de Santa María de la Vega P 28 Vb 94
47688 Monasterio de Vega VA 46 Ue 95
01194 Monasterioguren VI 31 Xc 92
46500 Monasterios, Los V 108 Zd 111
46113 Moncada V 108 Zd 111
39791 Moncalián CB 18 Wc 88
09691 Moncalvillo BU 50 We 97
16520 Moncalvillo del Huete CU 88 Xb 107
06110 Moncar BA 131 Sf 118
46174 Moncatí V 107 Zc 111
18830 Moncayo GR 154 Xc 121
03149 Moncayo, El A 157 Zc 120
41420 Monclava, La SE 149 Ue 123
33811 Moncó AS 13 Tc 90
12593 Moncofa CS 108 Zf 110
25212 Moncortès de Segarra L 56 Bb 98
29110 Monda MA 175 Vb 129
36870 Mondariz PO 41 Rd 95
36890 Mondariz-Balneario PO 41 Rd 95
19110 Mondéjar GU 87 Wf 107
27740 Mondoñedo LU 12 Sd 88
27787 Mondoñedo LU 12 Se 87
22394 Mondot HU 36 Aa 95
24892 Mondreganes LE 28 Uf 92
27271 Mondriz LU 12 Sd 90
29710 Mondrón MA 167 Ve 127
18656 Mondújar GR 168 Wc 127
50164 Monegrillo Z 54 Zd 99
39292 Monegro CB 17 Vf 90
17121 Monells GI 59 Cf 97
17117 Monells i Sant Sadurní de l'Heura Cruïlles GI 59 Cf 97
09515 Moneo BU 30 Wd 91
33785 Mones AS 14 Te 87
33584 Mones AS 15 Ue 88
32357 Mones OR 25 Sf 94
22415 Monesma HU 55 Aa 97
22587 Monesma y Cajigar HU 55 Ad 95
06260 Monesterio BA 148 Te 120
08293 Monestir de Montserrat B 57 Bf 99
25341 Monestir de Vallsanta L 75 Ba 99
50144 Moneva Z 72 Zb 102
22585 Monfalcó HU 55 Ad 96
49121 Monfarracinos ZA 64 Ub 99
15315 Monfero C 11 Rf 89
37607 Monflorido SA 82 Tf 105
22005 Monflorite-Lascasas HU 54 Zd 96
37618 Monforte de la Sierra SA 82 Tf 106
03670 Monforte del Cid A 142 Zb 118
27400 Monforte de Lemos LU 24 Sc 93
44493 Monforte de Moyuela TE 72 Yf 102
22585 Mongay HU 55 Ae 96
33449 Moniello AS 15 Ub 87
08691 Monistrol = Monistrol de Montserrat B 57 Bf 99
08770 Monistrol d'Anoia B 76 Be 100
08275 Monistrol de Calders B 58 Ca 98
08691 Monistrol de Montserrat B 57 Bf 99
02340 Monja, La AB 123 Xd 116
13210 Monjas CR 121 Wd 113
41600 Monjas, Las SE 165 Uc 125
41659 Monjas, Las SE 165 Uf 126
46310 Monjas, Las V 106 Ye 112
47100 Monjas, Las VA 66 Va 100
26586 Monjía, La RI 51 Xd 95
04533 Monjos, Los AL 169 Xb 126
37765 Monleón SA 82 Ua 105
37171 Monleras SA 64 Te 101
12163 Monllat CS 92 Zf 107
07109 Monnàber IB 110 Ce 110
43007 Monnars T 76 Bb 102
03640 Monóvar = Monòver A 142 Za 118
03640 Monòver = Monóvar A 142 Za 118
06620 Monreal BA 118 Ud 115
31471 Monreal NC 33 Yc 92
50291 Monreal de Ariza Z 70 Xf 101
44300 Monreal del Campo TE 90 Yd 104
16649 Monreal del Llano CU 104 Xb 111
10194 Monroy CC 98 Te 111
44652 Monroyo TE 92 Zf 104
37500 Monsagreño SA 81 Tc 104
37532 Monsagro SA 82 Te 105
06340 Monsalbe BA 132 Tc 120
05163 Monsalupe AV 84 Vb 104
46192 Monserrat V 126 Zc 112
39420 Montabliz CB 17 Vf 90
03660 Montagut A 142 Zb 118
17855 Montagut GI 58 Cd 95
25180 Montagut L 55 Ad 99
44700 Montalbán TE 91 Zb 104
14548 Montalbán de Córdoba CO 151 Vb 123
16434 Montalbanejo CU 104 Xd 110
18567 Montalbanes GR 153 Wc 124
16440 Montalbo CU 104 Xb 109
26133 Montalbo en Cameros RI 32 Xd 95
25331 Montalé L 56 Ba 98
08391 Montalegre B 77 Cb 100
43421 Montalegre T 76 Bc 100
04830 Montalviche AL 155 Xf 122
23291 Montalvo J 139 Xb 120
02638 Montalvos AB 124 Xf 114
49149 Montamarta ZA 45 Ub 99
12447 Montán CS 107 Zc 108
10170 Montánchez CC 117 Tf 113
13360 Montanchuelos CR 137 Wc 116
25795 Montan de Tost = Montau L 57 Bc 95
12448 Montanejos CS 107 Zc 108
25794 Montanissell L 56 Bb 95
22487 Montanuy HU 36 Ae 94
07315 Montanya IB 111 Cf 109
33734 Montaña, La AS 13 Tc 88
39300 Montaña, La CB 17 Vf 89
35558 Montaña Blanca GC 182 Mc 175
35100 Montaña Blanca GC 184 Kc 182
35627 Montaña Hendida GC 183 Lf 179
35106 Montaña La Data GC 184 Kc 182
09219 Montañana BU 31 Wf 92
22584 Montañana HU 55 Ae 96
50059 Montañana Z 53 Zb 98
11650 Montañas, Las CA 165 Uc 128
02440 Montañés, El AB 139 Xe 118
38459 Montañeta, La TF 180 Ib 178
38916 Montañetas, Las TF 180 Ha 182
02536 Montáñez AB 139 Xd 120
15689 Montaos C 11 Rd 90
25568 Montardit L 37 Ba 94
25738 Montargull L 56 Ba 97
43427 Montargull T 76 Bc 99
19229 Montarrón GU 69 Wf 103
22320 Montaruedo HU 55 Ab 95
03590 Montaud A 143 Zf 117
46892 Montaverner V 126 Zd 115
42174 Montaves SO 51 Xe 96
43400 Montblanc T 75 Ba 100
07519 Montblanch IB 111 Da 110
25268 Montblanquet L 75 Ba 100
43425 Montbrió de la Marca T 76 Bb 100
43340 Montbrió de Tarragona = Montbrió del Camp T 75 Ba 102
08105 Montcada i Reixax B 77 Cb 100
17199 Montcal GI 59 Ce 96
08614 Montclar B 57 Be 96
25317 Montclar d'Urgell L 56 Ba 97
25591 Montcortès L 37 Ba 95
22482 Mont de Roda HU 55 Ad 95
33350 Monte AS 15 Ud 88
15563 Monte C 11 Rf 87
39720 Monte CB 18 Wc 89
27143 Monte LU 12 Sd 90
27511 Monte LU 24 Sa 92
27415 Monte LU 24 Sd 93
36350 Monte PO 41 Rb 96
47462 Monte, El VA 66 Uf 102
27879 Monte, O LU 10 Sd 87
37451 Monte Abajo SA 82 Tf 104
37183 Monte Abajo SA 83 Ub 104
28514 Monte Acebedo MD 87 We 106
16360 Monteagudo de las Salinas CU 105 Ya 110
42220 Monteagudo de las Vicarías SO 70 Xe 100
44146 Monteagudo del Castillo TE 91 Zb 106
46190 Monte Alcedo V 107 Zc 111
11406 Montealegre CA 172 Tf 128
47816 Montealegre de Campos VA 47 Va 97
02650 Montealegre del Castillo AB 125 Ye 116
Monte Alto CO 150 Va 122
14100 Monte Alto CO 150 Va 123
47359 Monte Alto VA 48 Ve 98
14749 Montealto CO 150 Ue 122
33691 Monteana AS 15 Ub 87
45685 Montearagón TO 101 Vc 109
19170 Monte Calderón GU 86 Wd 104
27286 Montecelo LU 12 Sd 89
27215 Montecelo LU 24 Sb 91
39250 Montecillo CB 29 Wa 92
47320 Montecillo VA 66 Vd 99
28223 Monte Claro MD 86 Wa 106
35310 Monte Coello GC 184 Kd 180
29430 Montecorto MA 165 Ue 128
11159 Montecote CA 172 Tf 131
27128 Montecubeiro LU 12 Se 90
38739 Monte de Breña TF 181 Hb 177
28669 Monte de las Encinas MD 86 Wa 106
34159 Monte de La Torre P 47 Vb 97
38738 Monte de Luna TF 181 Hb 177
47639 Monte de Matallana VA 47 Va 97
27210 Monte de Meda LU 12 Sc 91
28570 Monte de Orusco, El MD 87 We 107
47640 Monte de Peñaflor VA 47 Va 98
32750 Montederramo OR 24 Sc 95
47129 Monte de San Lorenzo VA 47 Uf 98
15550 Montefaro C 11 Re 87
18270 Montefrío GR 168 Vf 125
27390 Montefurado LU 25 Se 94
41530 Montegil SE 165 Uc 126
24222 Monte Grande LE 46 Ud 95
47680 Monte Grande y San Martín VA 46 Ud 95
10810 Montehermoso CC 98 Td 108
29360 Montejaque MA 174 Ue 128
18561 Montejícar GR 153 Wc 123
37795 Montejo SA 83 Uc 105
40468 Montejo de Arévalo SG 66 Vc 102
09571 Montejo de Bricia BU 18 Wa 91
09211 Montejo de Cebas BU 30 We 92
28190 Montejo de la Sierra MD 68 Wc 102
40542 Montejo de la Vega de la Serrezuela SG 68 Wc 99
09211 Montejo de San Miguel BU 30 We 92
42341 Montejo de Tiermes SO 68 We 100
24282 Montejos del Camino LE 27 Ub 93
49881 Monte la Reina ZA 65 Ud 99
25725 Montellà de Cadi L 38 Be 94
25726 Montellà i Martinet = Martinet L 38 Be 94
41770 Montellano SE 165 Uc 127
06106 Montelongo BA 131 Sf 117
15315 Montelongo C 11 Rf 88
23615 Monte Lope-Álvarez J 152 Vf 122
32539 Monte Madalena OR 23 Rf 94
15145 Montemaior C 11 Rc 89
29620 Montemar MA 175 Vc 129
02329 Montemayor AB 139 Xe 116
14530 Montemayor CO 151 Vb 123
Montemayor, Apt. CO 151 Vb 123
37727 Montemayor del Río SA 82 Ua 106
47320 Montemayor de Pililla VA 66 Vd 99
06291 Montemolín BA 133 Te 120
41620 Montemolín SE 165 Ud 125
25595 Montenartró L 37 Bb 94
11349 Montenegral Alto CA 174 Ud 131
42113 Montenegro de Ágreda SO 51 Xf 97
26127 Montenegro de Cameros SO 50 Xb 96
16612 Monte Orenes CU 123 Xd 113
24200 Monte Pequeño LE 27 Uc 95
46500 Monte Picayo V 108 Ze 111
50430 Monte Pinar Z 72 Za 100
28668 Monte Príncipe MD 86 Wa 106
50213 Monterde Z 71 Yb 101
44368 Monterde de Albarracín TE 89 Yd 106
32228 Monte Redondo OR 42 Rf 96
28596 Monte Robledal MD 87 Wf 107
29603 Monteros, Los MA 175 Vb 129
32618 Monterrei OR 43 Sd 97
06160 Monterroso BA 132 Ta 117
27560 Monterroso LU 24 Sa 92
40142 Monterrubio SG 85 Vd 103
49324 Monterrubio ZA 44 Td 96
37798 Monterrubio de Armuña SA 65 Uc 102
09615 Monterrubio de Demanda BU 50 Wf 96
06427 Monterrubio de la Serena BA 134 Ud 117
37788 Monterrubio de la Sierra SA 83 Ub 104
06370 Montes BA 132 Tc 118
32689 Montes OR 43 Sc 97
06443 Montes, Los BA 134 Ua 118
46692 Montesa V 126 Zc 115
15317 Monte Salgueiro C 11 Rf 89
21200 Monte San Miguel H 148 Tc 121
25595 Montesclado L 37 Bb 93
45620 Montesclaros TO 100 Va 108
39417 Montes-Claros CB 29 Vf 91
14978 Montes-Claros CO 167 Vd 125
45470 Montes de Mora TO 120 Vf 112
47840 Montes de Quijada VA 46 Uf 98
21580 Montes de San Benito H 147 Sf 122
24415 Montes de Valdueza LE 26 Tc 94
27113 Monteseiro LU 13 Ta 90
03187 Montesinos A 157 Zb 120
22212 Montesodeto HU 54 Ze 97
21647 Monte Sorromero H 147 Tc 122
08585 Montesquiu B 58 Cb 96
25655 Montesquiu L 56 Af 95
25268 Montesquiu L 75 Ba 99
22269 Montesusín HU 54 Zd 97
47640 Monte Torozos VA 47 Va 98
46901 Monte Vedat V 126 Zd 112
32611 Monteveloso OR 43 Sd 96
25318 Montfalcó d'Agramunt L 56 Ba 98
25271 Montfalcó el Gros B 57 Bc 99
25214 Montfalcó Murallat L 57 Bc 98
25213 Montfar L 57 Bc 99
25711 Montferrer L 38 Bc 94
25712 Montferrer i Castellbó L 38 Bc 94
43812 Montferri T 76 Bc 101
25616 Montgai L 56 Af 98
08390 Montgat B 77 Cb 100
09588 Montiano BU 19 We 90
46842 Montichelvo V 126 Zd 115
33438 Montico, El AS 15 Ub 87
13326 Montiel CR 138 Xa 116
14549 Montiela, La CO 150 Va 123
06480 Montijo BA 116 Tc 115
14550 Montilla CO 151 Vc 123
18569 Montillana GR 152 Wb 123

286 | Molino de la Sargenta

36684 Montillón de Arriba PO 23 Rd 93
17472 Montiró GI 59 Da 96
23266 Montizón J 138 Wf 118
17480 Montjoi GI 40 Db 95
12150 Montllats, Els CS 91 Ze 106
25738 Montmagastre L 56 Ba 97
08612 Montmajor B 57 Be 96
08717 Montmaneu B 57 Bc 99
08590 Montmany B 58 Cb 98
43718 Montmell, El T 76 Bc 101
08160 Montmeló B 77 Cb 99
22811 Montmesa HU 53 Zc 96
03115 Montnegre A 142 Zc 118
17242 Montnegre GI 59 Cf 97
03100 Montnegre de Dalt A 142 Zc 118
25172 Montoliu de Lérida = Montoliu de Lleida L 74 Ad 99
25217 Montoliu de Segarra L 56 Bb 99
50391 Montón Z 71 Yc 101
17130 Montoó GI 59 Db 96
01212 Montoria VI 31 Xb 93
09125 Montorio BU 30 Wb 93
08170 Montornés del Vallès B 77 Cb 99
25217 Montornès de Segarra L 56 Bb 99
14600 Montoro CO 151 Vd 120
44559 Montoro de Mezquita TE 91 Zc 104
18495 Montoros, Los GR 169 Wf 127
46250 Montortal V 126 Zc 113
34486 Montoto de Ojeda P 29 Vd 92
15318 Montouto C 11 Rd 89
27737 Montouto LU 12 Sc 88
15359 Montoxo C 10 Sa 87
02600 Montoyas, Los AB 123 Xd 113
25271 Montpalau L 57 Bc 99
25250 Montperler L 56 Ba 99
25288 Montpolt L 57 Bc 96
17253 Mont-ras GI 59 Da 97
43364 Montreal = Mont-ral T 75 Ba 101
07100 Mont Reals IB 110 Ce 110
43300 Mont-roig del Camp T 75 Af 102
25512 Mont-ros L 37 Af 94
08460 Montseny B 58 Cc 98
25513 Montsor L 37 Af 95
09390 Montuenga BU 49 Wb 96
40464 Montuenga SG 66 Vc 102
42259 Montuenga de Soria SO 70 Xe 101
24846 Montuerto LE 27 Ud 91
07230 Montuïri IB 111 Cf 111
14930 Monturque CO 151 Vc 124
49215 Monumenta ZA 64 Tf 100
50120 Monzalbarba Z 53 Za 98
15686 Monzo C 11 Rc 90
22400 Monzón HU 55 Ab 97
09258 Monzoncillo de Oca BU 30 We 94
34410 Monzón de Campos P 47 Vd 96
33937 Moñeca AS 15 Ub 88
40145 Moñibas SG 66 Vc 103
42218 Moñux SO 70 Xd 99
29566 Mopagán, El MA 166 Vb 128
45400 Mora TO 102 Wb 110
22513 Mora, La HU 55 Ac 97
22586 Mora, La HU 55 Ad 95
17464 Móra, La GI 59 Cf 96
25218 Móra, La L 56 Bb 99
02694 Morabios, Los AB 125 Yd 114
25283 Móra Comdal, La L 57 Bc 96
27416 Morade LU 24 Sd 94
43740 Móra d'Ebre T 74 Ad 102
24149 Mora de Luna LE 27 Ua 92
22584 Mora de Montañana, La HU 56 Ad 95
44400 Mora de Rubielos TE 91 Zb 107
02513 Mora de Santa Quiteria AB 140 Yc 117
09143 Moradillo del Castillo BU 30 Wa 92
09462 Moradillo de Roa BU 67 Wb 99
09142 Moradillo de Sedano BU 30 Wb 92
15125 Moraime C 10 Qe 90
30848 Moraina MC 156 Yd 121
03724 Moraira A 143 Aa 116
06225 Moral, El BA 133 Te 118
30413 Moral, El MC 155 Xe 120
06443 Morala, La BA 134 Ua 117
43770 Móra la Nova T 74 Ad 102
13350 Moral de Calatrava CR 121 Wc 116
37460 Moral de Castro SA 82 Tf 103
40542 Moral de Hornúez SG 68 Wc 100
47691 Moral de la Reina VA 47 Uf 97
24155 Moral del Condado LE 27 Ud 93
24287 Moral de Órbigo LE 26 Ua 94
49254 Moral de Sayago ZA 64 Tf 100
18370 Moraleda de Zafayona GR 167 Wa 125
10840 Moraleja CC 97 Tc 108
16147 Moraleja, La CU 89 Xf 107
28109 Moraleja, La MD 86 Wc 105
40461 Moraleja de Coca SG 66 Vc 102
40233 Moraleja de Cuéllar SG 67 Ve 100
28950 Moraleja de Enmedio MD 86 Wa 107
37607 Moraleja de Huebra SA 82 Ua 104
47454 Moraleja de las Panaderas VA 66 Vb 101
49150 Moraleja del Vino ZA 65 Uc 100
05299 Moraleja de Matacabras AV 66 Va 102
49177 Moraleja de Sayago ZA 64 Tf 101
30412 Moralejo MC 155 Xf 121
16512 Moralejo, El CU 88 Xb 107
18562 Moralejo, El GR 153 Wd 124
26259 Morales RI 31 Wf 94
42366 Morales SO 69 Xa 100
02639 Morales, Los AB 123 Xf 114
18120 Morales, Los GR 168 Wa 127
18711 Morales, Los GR 169 Wd 128
24731 Morales de Arcediano LE 26 Tf 94
47811 Morales de Campos VA 46 Ue 97
49190 Morales del Vino ZA 64 Ub 100
49693 Morales de Rey ZA 45 Ub 96
49810 Morales de Toro ZA 65 Ue 99
49697 Morales de Valverde ZA 45 Ua 97
29400 Morales-Santa María MA 166 Uf 128
29400 Morales-Santa María, Los MA 166 Ue 128
03699 Moralet A 142 Zc 118
23393 Moralico, El J 139 Xb 118
49253 Moralina ZA 64 Tf 100
37216 Moralita, La SA 64 Te 103
28411 Moralzarzal MD 85 Wa 104
22806 Morán Z 34 Zb 95
25211 Morana, La L 56 Bb 98
15138 Morancelle C 10 Qe 91
19491 Moranchel GU 88 Xb 104
06190 Morante BA 116 Tb 114
36668 Moraña PO 23 Rc 93
05350 Morañuela AV 84 Va 104
04279 Moras AL 171 Xf 126
27876 Morás LU 10 Sd 86
37590 Morasverdes SA 82 Te 105
50260 Morata de Jalón Z 71 Yd 100
50344 Morata de Jiloca Z 71 Yc 101
28530 Morata de Tajuña MD 86 Wd 107
28030 Moratalaz MD 86 Wc 106
14749 Moratalla CO 150 Ue 122
30440 Moratalla MC 140 Ya 119
19267 Moratilla de Henares GU 69 Xb 102
19144 Moratilla de los Meleros GU 87 Xa 105
34349 Moratinos P 28 Va 94
49622 Moratones ZA 45 Ua 96
03660 Moraxel A 142 Zb 118
01211 Moraza BU 31 Xb 92
22348 Morcat HU 35 Aa 94
29793 Morche MA 167 Wa 128
02440 Morcillar, El AB 139 Xe 118
10811 Morcillo CC 98 Td 108
02612 Morcillos, Los AB 123 Xd 114
14270 Morconcillo, El CO 134 Ue 118
42340 Morcuera SO 68 We 100
33678 Moreda AS 15 Ub 90
18540 Moreda GR 153 We 124
24436 Moreda LE 25 Tb 92
27324 Moreda LU 25 Sf 93
01322 Moreda de Álava VI 32 Xd 93
27205 Moredo LU 24 Sa 91
27142 Moreira LU 24 Sa 91
36688 Moreira PO 23 Rd 92
32920 Moreiras OR 23 Sa 95
32635 Moreiras OR 43 Sb 96
43760 Morell, El T 75 Bb 101
12300 Morella CS 92 Zf 105
14880 Morellana CO 151 Ve 123
07712 Morella Vell IB 77 Eb 109
19328 Morenilla GU 89 Yb 104
02534 Morenos, Los AB 139 Xd 119
14299 Morenos, Los CO 134 Ud 120
30333 Morenos, Los MC 156 Ye 122
22485 Moréns HU 36 Ad 94
14659 Morente CO 151 Vd 121
31264 Morentin NC 32 Xf 93
30591 Moreños de Camachos, Los MC 157 Za 122
06176 Morera, La BA 132 Tc 117
43361 Morera de Montsant, La T 75 Af 101
10880 Moreras CC 97 Ta 109
37111 Moreras SA 64 Ua 102
03184 Moreras, Las A 157 Zb 120
30877 Moreras, Las MC 156 Ye 123
07609 Moreria, La IB 110 Ce 112
49731 Moreruela de los Infanzones ZA 46 Ub 99
49148 Moreruela de Tábara ZA 45 Ua 98
50240 Morés Z 71 Yc 100
17514 Moreta, La GI 58 Ca 95
48115 Morga BI 19 Xb 89
27546 Morgade LU 24 Sc 93
32636 Morgade OR 43 Sb 96
24884 Morgovejo LE 28 Va 91
09219 Moriana BU 31 Wf 92
14510 Moriles CO 151 Vc 124
22415 Morilla HU 54 Aa 97
24223 Morilla de los Oteros LE 27 Ud 94
36119 Morillas PO 23 Rc 93
01428 Morillas VI 31 Xa 92
04889 Morillas de Albánchez, Los AL 170 Xc 125
37183 Morille SA 83 Ub 104
19492 Morillejo GU 88 Xd 104
22462 Morillo de Liena HU 36 Ac 94
22336 Morillo de Monclús HU 36 Ab 94
22347 Morillo de San Pietro HU 36 Aa 94
22395 Morillo de Tou HU 36 Aa 94
37337 Moriñigo SA 65 Ud 103
31491 Moriones NC 33 Yd 93
25716 Moripol L 57 Bd 95
29170 Moriscos MA 167 Vd 127
37430 Moriscos SA 65 Uc 102
02139 Moriscote AB 140 Xf 117
24736 Morla de la Valdería LE 45 Te 95
33776 Morlongo AS 13 Ta 88
32551 Mormontelos OR 43 Se 95
42223 Morón de Almazán SO 70 Xd 100
41530 Morón de la Frontera SE 165 Ud 126
18449 Morones, Los GR 169 We 127
37258 Moronta SA 63 Td 103
02485 Moropeche AB 139 Xd 118
25632 Moror L 56 Af 96
50215 Moros Z 71 Yb 100
15125 Morpeguite C 10 Qe 90
37406 Morquera SA 65 Ue 102
46842 Morquí V 126 Ze 115
22141 Morrano HU 54 Zf 95
24740 Morredero LE 26 Td 94
24397 Morriondo LE 26 Ua 93
28695 Morro, El MD 85 Ve 106
35625 Morro Jable GC 182 Ld 180
39120 Mortera CB 18 Wa 88
33785 Mortera, La AS 14 Tc 89
02650 Morteruelo, El AB 141 Ye 116
39723 Mortesante CB 18 Wb 89
07769 Morvedre Nou IB 77 Df 109
27268 Mos LU 12 Sc 90
36415 Mos PO 41 Rc 95
42315 Mosarejos SO 69 Wf 100
44124 Moscardón TE 90 Yc 107
07314 Moscari IB 111 Cf 110
24791 Moscas del Páramo LE 45 Ub 95
04560 Moscolux AL 170 Xd 127
37149 Moscosa y Gusende SA 64 Tf 102
27861 Mosende LU 10 Sc 86
32554 Mosexos OR 43 Sf 96
34126 Moslares de la Vega P 28 Vb 94
12182 Mosqueres, Les CS 92 Zf 107
08470 Mosqueroles B 58 Cc 98
44410 Mosqueruela TE 91 Zd 106
15992 Mosquete C 22 Ra 93
03430 Mossén Joan A 142 Zb 117
27153 Mosteiro LU 12 Sc 90
27279 Mosteiro LU 12 Sd 90
27279 Mosteiro LU 12 Se 90
27658 Mosteiro LU 13 Ta 90
32810 Mosteiro OR 42 Rf 95
36637 Mosteiro PO 22 Rb 93
36842 Mosteiro PO 23 Rc 95
32136 Mosteirón OR 23 Sa 93
24521 Mosteiros LE 25 Ta 93
28931 Móstoles MD 86 Wa 107
17843 Mota, La GI 59 Ce 96
16780 Mota de Altarejos CU 104 Xe 109
16630 Mota del Cuervo CU 104 Xa 111
47120 Mota del Marqués VA 46 Ue 99
20211 Motasoro SS 20 Xe 91
50012 Motel del Cisne Z 53 Yf 99
16200 Motilla del Palancar CU 105 Ya 111
02220 Motilleja AB 124 Yb 113
19320 Motos GU 89 Yc 105
18600 Motril GR 168 Wc 128
15100 Moucho C 10 Rc 89
27779 Moucide LU 12 Sd 87
27185 Mougán LU 24 Sc 91
36309 Mougás PO 41 Ra 96
32697 Mourazos OR 43 Sd 97
15860 Mourelle C 10 Rb 90
27548 Mourelos LU 24 Sb 93
36990 Mourelos PO 22 Ra 94
36437 Mourentán PO 42 Re 96
36868 Mourigade PO 41 Rd 95
32556 Mourisca OR 43 Sf 95
36877 Mouriscados PO 41 Rd 95
27217 Mouromorto LU 24 Sb 91
49514 Moveros ZA 45 Te 99
09246 Movilla BU 30 Wd 93
16337 Moya CU 106 Yd 109
35420 Moya GC 184 Kc 180
21450 Moyaga, La H 161 Sf 125
50143 Moyuela Z 72 Za 102
35561 Mozago GC 182 Mc 174
46176 Mozaira, La V 106 Yf 110
49698 Mozar ZA 45 Ub 97
37796 Mozárbez SA 83 Uc 103
09555 Mozares BU 18 Wc 91
37140 Mozodiel SA 64 Tf 102
37798 Mozodiel del Camino SA 65 Uc 102
37797 Mozodiel de Sachíñigo SA 64 Ub 102
40250 Mozoncillo SG 67 Ve 102
09198 Mozoncillo de Juarros BU 30 Wc 95
24250 Mozóndiga LE 27 Ub 94
24172 Mozos de Cea LE 28 Uf 93
50440 Mozota Z 72 Yf 100
09142 Mozuelos BU 30 Wb 92
37116 Muchachos SA 64 Ua 102
47194 Mucientes VA 47 Vb 98
41220 Mudapelos SE 149 Ua 123
47630 Mudarra, La VA 47 Va 98
46143 Mudos, Los V 106 Ye 108
40295 Mudrián SG 67 Ve 101
19196 Muduex GU 87 Xa 104
50450 Muel Z 72 Yf 100
10638 Muela CC 82 Te 107
11689 Muela, La CA 165 Ud 127
11150 Muela, La CA 172 Ua 131
23296 Muela, La J 139 Xd 119
42294 Muela, La SO 50 Xb 99
46825 Muela, La V 126 Za 114
50196 Muela, La Z 53 Yf 99
49341 Muelas de los Caballeros ZA 45 Td 96
49167 Muelas del Pan ZA 64 Ua 99
09215 Muergas BU 31 Xb 92
31219 Mués NC 32 Xe 93
31176 Muez NC 32 Ya 92
17486 Muga, La GI 40 Da 95
49543 Muga de Alba ZA 45 Tf 98
49212 Muga de Sayago ZA 64 Te 100
15620 Mugardos C 11 Re 88
32930 Mugares OR 23 Sa 95
31879 Mugiro NC 21 Ya 91
31481 Mugueta NC 33 Ye 92
31473 Muguetajarra NC 33 Yd 92
27377 Muimenta LU 12 Sd 89
32616 Muimenta OR 43 Sd 97
36119 Muimenta PO 23 Rc 93
36514 Muimenta PO 23 Rf 92
27277 Muiña LU 13 Se 90
15125 Muiños C 10 Qe 90
32880 Muíños OR 42 Sa 97
08670 Mujal, El B 57 Bf 97
04716 Mujer, La AL 170 Xb 128
30170 Mula MC 156 Yd 120
19139 Mula Hermosa GU 87 Wf 105
11600 Mulera Bujeos CA 173 Ud 129
14400 Muleras, Las CO 135 Vb 119
04618 Mulería, La AL 171 Yb 125
25212 Muller L 56 Bb 98
02142 Mullidar AB 140 Ya 117
01207 Munain VI 32 Xd 91
33519 Muncó AS 15 Uc 88
09127 Mundilla BU 29 Vf 92
32577 Mundín OR 23 Rf 94
04692 Mundos, Los AL 155 Xf 124
09558 Mundóval BU 30 Wb 91
50219 Munébrega Z 71 Yb 101
02600 Munera AB 123 Xb 114
02612 Munera AB 123 Xd 114
31290 Muneta NC 32 Xf 92
48100 Mungia BI 19 Xa 88
08732 Múnia, La B 76 Bd 101
31175 Muniáin NC 33 Ya 92
31264 Muniain de la Solana NC 32 Xf 93
20759 Muniasoro SS 20 Xe 89
02691 Munibáñez AB 124 Yc 115
44780 Muniesa TE 72 Zb 102
15317 Muniferral C 11 Rf 89
09572 Munilla BU 30 Wb 91
26586 Munilla RI 51 Xe 95
48381 Munitibar BI 20 Xc 89
48381 Munitibar-Arbatzegi-Gerrikaitz BI 20 Xc 89
46260 Muntanyeta, La V 126 Zc 114
46419 Muntanyeta dels Sants V 126 Ze 113
08505 Muntanyola B 58 Cb 97
08551 Múntel B 58 Cb 97
43879 Muntells, Els T 93 Ae 104
23649 Muña, La J 152 Wa 122
05540 Muñana AV 84 Uf 105
33783 Muñás AS 14 Td 88
34879 Muñeca P 28 Vb 92
42142 Muñecas SO 50 We 98
24886 Muñecas, Las LE 28 Uf 91
33991 Muñera AS 15 Uc 89
05540 Muñez AV 84 Va 105
05145 Muñico AV 84 Uf 104
35558 Muñique GC 182 Mc 174
27652 Muñis LU 13 Ta 91
33519 Muñó AS 15 Uc 88
30849 Muñoces, Los MC 156 Ye 122
05520 Muñochas AV 84 Va 105
05530 Muñogalindo AV 84 Va 105
05309 Muñogrande AV 84 Va 104
05358 Muñomer del Peco AV 84 Va 103
33639 Muñón Cimero AS 15 Ua 89
40145 Muñopedro SG 66 Vd 103
05192 Muñopepe AV 84 Vb 105
39594 Muñorrodero CB 17 Vd 88
05301 Muñosancho AV 66 Uf 103
05560 Muñotello AV 84 Uf 105
40183 Muñoveros SG 67 Wa 101
05357 Muñoyerro AV 84 Va 104
37493 Muñoz SA 82 Te 104
32880 Muqueimes OR 42 Sa 97
08278 Mura B 58 Bf 98
03315 Murada, La A 141 Za 119
27510 Muradelle LU 24 Sa 93
Muralles IB 77 Eb 109
27836 Muras LU 12 Sb 88
36557 Murás PO 23 Rd 93
31521 Murchante NC 52 Yc 96
18656 Murchas GR 168 Wc 127
30001*Murcia MC 157 Yf 121
50366 Murero Z 71 Yd 102
23686 Mures J 152 Wb 124
01479 Murga VI 19 Wf 90
01139 Murguia VI 19 Xb 91
22470 Muria, La HU 36 Ad 94
33829 Murias AS 14 Tf 88
33114 Murias AS 14 Tf 89
33117 Murias AS 15 Ua 90
33676 Murias AS 15 Ub 90
27655 Murias LU 25 Ta 91
49359 Murias ZA 44 Tb 96
33785 Murias, Las AS 14 Tf 89
24130 Murias de Paredes LE 26 Te 91
24720 Murias de Pedredo LE 26 Te 94
24127 Murias de Ponjos LE 26 Tf 92
39600 Muriedas CB 18 Wa 88
19225 Muriel GU 68 We 103
42193 Muriel de la Fuente SO 50 Xa 98
47219 Muriel de Zapardiel VA 66 Va 102
33117 Muriellos AS 15 Ua 90
42148 Muriel Viejo SO 50 Xa 98
31280 Murieta NC 32 Xf 93
31292 Murillo NC 32 Ya 92
31454 Murillo-Berroya NC 33 Ye 92
26500 Murillo de Calahorra RI 32 Ya 94
22808 Murillo de Gállego Z 34 Zb 94
31500 Murillo de las Limas NC 52 Yc 96
31481 Murillo de Lónguida NC 33 Yd 92
26143 Murillo de Río Leza RI 32 Xe 94
31391 Murillo El Cuende NC 33 Yc 94
31313 Murillo el Fruto NC 33 Yd 94
09511 Múrita BU 31 Wf 91
03792 Murla A 143 Zf 116
22372 Muro HU 35 Zf 94
22363 Muro HU 36 Aa 94
07440 Muro IB 111 Da 110
03839 Muro = Muro de Alcoy A 126 Zd 116
42108 Muro de Ágreda SO 51 Ya 98
26587 Muro de Aguas RI 51 Xf 96
03839 Muro del Alcoy A 126 Zd 116
26134 Muro en Cameros RI 51 Xc 95
15250 Muros C 22 Qf 92
33138 Muros de Nalón = Muros AS 14 Tf 87
30153 Murta, La MC 156 Ye 122
21280 Murtales, Los H 148 Td 120
18490 Murtas GR 169 Wf 127
30420 Murtas, Las MC 140 Ya 119
07400 Murtera, Es IB 111 Da 110
01138 Murua VI 19 Xb 91
31398 Muruarte de Reta NC 33 Yb 93
31190 Muru-Astráin NC 33 Yb 92
48410 Murueta BI 19 Xa 90
48394 Murueta BI 19 Xb 88
31292 Murugarren NC 32 Xf 92
31152 Muruzábal NC 33 Yb 92
31150 Muruzábal de Andión NC 33 Ya 93
46136 Museros V 108 Zd 111
03580 Mushara A 143 Zf 117
01129 Musitu VI 32 Xd 92
48550 Muskiz BI 19 Wf 89
43380 Mussara, La T 75 Ba 101
25726 Musser L 38 Bd 94
21240 Mustio, El H 147 Sf 121

Mustio, El | 287

E

03860 Orxa, l' = Lorcha A 126 Ze 115
15819 Orxal C 11 Re 91
03579 Orxeta A 143 Ze 117
39292 Orzales CB 17 Vf 90
35541 Orzola GC 182 Md 173
24839 Orzónaga LE 27 Uc 91
31799 Osacáin NC 33 Yc 91
31193 Osácar NC 33 Yb 91
16423 Osa de la Vega CU 104 Xb 111
27775 Os Agros LU 12 Sd 88
22611 Osán HU 35 Ze 94
15865 Os Ánxeles C 22 Rb 91
27540 O Saviñao = Escairón LU 24 Sc 93
32634 Os Blancos OR 42 Sb 97
15310 Os Couceiros C 11 Rf 90
25610 Os de Balaguer L 55 Ae 97
15911 Os Dices C 22 Rb 92
32136 Oseira OR 23 Sa 93
15141 Oseiro C 11 Rd 89
50258 Oseja Z 52 Yb 99
24916 Oseja de Sajambre LE 16 Uf 90
50175 Osera de Ebro Z 73 Zc 99
46162 Oset V 107 Zb 110
22830 Osia HU 34 Zc 94
20580 Osintxu SS 20 Xd 90
31869 Oskotz NC 21 Yb 91
48269 Osma BI 20 Xc 89
42318 Osma SO 50 Wf 99
01426 Osma VI 31 Wf 91
05164 Oso, El AV 84 Vb 103
42294 Osona SO 50 Xb 99
42291 Osonilla SO 50 Xb 99
17161 Osor GI 58 Cd 97
34468 Osornillo P 29 Ve 94
34460 Osorno P 29 Vd 94
36491 Os Padrosos = Padrosos PO 42 Re 95
02611 Ossa de Montiel AB 123 Xb 115
25717 Ossera L 57 Bc 95
02611 Ossero, El AB 122 Xb 115
22532 Osso de Cinca HU 55 Ab 99
25318 Ossó de Sió L 56 Ba 98
31799 Ostiz NC 33 Yc 91
41659 Osuna SE 166 Uf 125
27111 Os Vaos LU 13 Sf 89
22372 Otal HU 35 Ze 93
31470 Otano NC 33 Yc 92
39707 Otañes CB 19 We 89
01194 Otazu VI 31 Xc 92
32417 Oteiro-Cruz OR 23 Rf 95
31740 Oteitza NC 21 Yc 90
31250 Oteiza NC 32 Ya 93
31195 Oteiza NC 33 Yb 91
09512 Oteo BU 18 We 91
01117 Oteo VI 32 Xd 92
19431 Oter GU 88 Xd 104
24126 Oterico LE 26 Ua 92
33791 Otero AS 15 Ud 89
37766 Otero SA 82 Ua 104
45543 Otero TO 101 Vc 108
49336 Otero de Bodas ZA 45 Tf 97
24719 Otero de Escarpizo LE 26 Tf 93
34888 Otero de Guardo P 28 Vb 91
40422 Otero de Herreros SG 85 Ve 104
24123 Otero de las Dueñas LE 27 Ub 92
49319 Otero de los Centenos ZA 45 Te 96
37191 Otero de María Asensio SA 65 Uc 103
49320 Otero de Sanabria ZA 44 Tc 96
49137 Otero de Sariegos ZA 46 Uc 98
24887 Otero de Valdetuéjar, El LE 27 Uf 92
16340 Oteros, Los CU 105 Ya 109
34406 Oteros de Boedo P 29 Vd 93
37186 Otero Vaciadores SA 83 Ub 103
26145 Oteruelo RI 32 Xe 95
24009 Oteruelo de la Valdoncina LE 27 Uc 93
28749 Oteruelo del Valle MD 67 Wa 103
42190 Oteruelos SO 50 Xc 97
19356 Otilla GU 89 Yb 104
22149 Otín HU 35 Zf 95
31219 Otiñano NC 32 Xe 93
23196 Otíñar o Santa Cristina J 152 Wb 122
20140 Otita Leitzaran SS 20 Xf 89
18698 Otívar GR 168 Wb 128
22370 Oto HU 35 Zf 93
01191 Oto Barren = Hueto Abajo VI 31 Xb 91
46199 Otonel V 126 Za 113
40394 Otones de Benjumea SG 67 Vf 102
30442 Otos MC 140 Xf 119
46844 Otos V 126 Zd 115
20215 Otsaurte SS 20 Xe 91
20128 Otsaregi SS 20 Ya 89
33792 Otur AS 13 Tc 87
18630 Otura GR 168 Wc 126
48210 Otxandio BI 19 Xc 90
15167 Ouces C 11 Re 88
32312 Oulego OR 25 Ta 93
27392 Oural LU 24 Sd 92
32003 Ourense OR 24 Sa 94
33775 Ouría AS 13 Sf 88
15984 Ourille C 22 Rb 92
32813 Ourille OR 42 Sa 96
27865 Ourol LU 12 Sc 87
27156 Ousá LU 12 Sb 90
27546 Ousende LU 24 Sc 93
27647 Ousón LU 25 Sf 91
27244 Outariz LU 13 Se 90
27256 Outeiro LU 12 Sd 89
27328 Outeiro LU 25 Sf 93
27518 Outeiro, O LU 24 Sb 93
15314 Outeiro de Cela C 11 Rf 89
27150 Outeiro de Rei LU 12 Sc 90
15230 Outes C 22 Ra 91
32824 Outomuro = Cartelle OR 42 Rf 95
27113 Ouviaño LU 13 Ta 90
36681 Ouzande PO 23 Rd 92
33536 Ovana AS 15 Ud 89
10639 Ovejuela CC 81 Td 107
47009 Overuela, La VA 47 Vb 98
33001 Oviedo AS 15 Ua 88
24853 Oville LE 27 Ud 91
33846 Oviñana AS 14 Te 88
01449 Oyardo VI 19 Xa 91
01320 Oyón-Oion VI 32 Xd 93
15107 Oza C 10 Rb 89
15388 Oza-Cezuras C 11 Re 89
01206 Ozaeta VI 32 Xd 91
09217 Ozana BU 31 Xb 92
31483 Ozcáriz NC 33 Yd 92
31448 Ozcoidi NC 33 Ye 92

P

28523 Pablo Iglesias MD 86 Wc 106
30812 Paca, La MC 156 Ya 121
13710 Pachecas, Las CR 122 Wf 114
32789 Pacio OR 25 Se 95
27372 Pacios LU 12 Sb 89
27256 Pacios LU 12 Sd 89
27136 Pacios LU 13 Sf 90
27611 Pacios LU 24 Sc 92
27346 Pacios LU 24 Sd 92
27748 Pacios de Arriba LU 12 Sd 88
27328 Paciros da Serra LU 25 Sf 93
08796 Pacs del Penedès B 76 Be 100
22451 Padarníu HU 36 Ac 94
15314 Paderne C 11 Re 89
15391 Paderne C 11 Re 89
32112 Paderne de Allariz OR 24 Sb 95
05520 Padiernos AV 84 Va 105
09109 Padilla de Abajo BU 29 Ve 94
09108 Padilla de Arriba BU 29 Ve 94
47314 Padilla de Duero VA 48 Ve 99
19246 Padilla de Hita GU 87 Xa 103
19445 Padilla del Ducado GU 70 Xd 103
36119 Padin PO 23 Rc 93
49574 Padornelo ZA 44 Ta 96
33737 Padraira AS 13 Ta 89
36638 Padrenda PO 22 Rb 94
25717 Padrinàs L 57 Bc 95
15900 Padrón C 22 Rc 92
27116 Padrón, O LU 13 Sf 90
09593 Padrones de Bureba BU 30 Wc 92
36866 Padróns PO 41 Rc 95
32631 Padroso OR 43 Sc 96
36491 Padrosos PO 42 Re 95
18640 Padul GR 168 Wc 126
04458 Padules AL 170 Xb 127
35422 Pagador, El GC 184 Kc 180
30333 Paganes, Los MC 156 Ye 122
01309 Páganos VI 31 Xc 93
20128 Pagoaga SS 21 Ya 89
04212 Pago Aguilar Bajo AL 170 Xd 126
04533 Pago de Escuchagranos AL 169 Xb 126
11130 Pago del Humo CA 172 Tf 130
41740 Pago Dulce SE 164 Tf 127
07260 Pagos, Es IB 111 Da 111
18400 Pago y Benisalte GR 168 Wd 127
07839 Pahisa d'en Font IB 109 Bb 115
46370 Pa i Capellades V 126 Zc 112
15144 Paiosaco C 11 Rc 89
46200 Paiporta V 126 Zd 112
41219 Pajanosas, Las SE 148 Tf 123
35628 Pájara GC 183 Lf 178
38560 Pajara TF 181 Id 179
45640 Pajar de Celedonio Morales TO 84 Vb 108
05571 Pajarejos AV 84 Ue 105
40567 Pajarejos SG 68 Wc 100
33693 Pajares AS 15 Ub 90
09212 Pajares BU 31 We 92
16145 Pajares CU 88 Xe 107
19413 Pajares GU 87 Xb 104
26126 Pajares RI 50 Xc 96
37671 Pajares, Los SA 82 Ua 105
46143 Pajares, Los V 106 Ye 108
05214 Pajares de Adaja AV 66 Vc 103
50238 Pajares de Calmarza Z 70 Ya 101
40518 Pajares de Fresno SG 68 Wd 100
37428 Pajares de la Laguna SA 65 Uc 102
49142 Pajares de la Lampreana ZA 46 Ub 98
10829 Pajares de la Rivera CC 98 Td 109
05440 Pajares de los Marañones AV 84 Vb 107
24209 Pajares de los Oteros LE 27 Ud 95
40184 Pajares de Pedraza SG 67 Wa 101
10600 Pajares de San Pedrillo el Raso, Los CC 98 Te 108
14920 Pajarito CO 151 Vb 124
16390 Pajarón CU 105 Yb 109
16390 Pajaroncillo CU 105 Yb 109
44750 Pajazo, El TE 90 Za 104
21580 Pajeros, Los H 147 Sf 122
06488 Pajonal Abajo BA 117 Td 114
37453 Pajuelas SA 82 Ua 104
AD400 Pal ◘ AND 38 Bc 93
04661 Palacés, El AL 171 Xf 124
37111 Palacinos SA 64 Ua 102
05198 Palacio AV 84 Va 105
05309 Palacio de Castronuevo AV 66 Uf 103
21760 Palacio de Doñana H 162 Td 127
10520 Palacio de las Cabezas CC 99 Ub 109
21740 Palacio del Rey H 164 Td 126
28609 Palacio de Milla MD 85 Vf 106
05148 Palacio de Revilla AV 84 Ue 105
24890 Palacio de Torío LE 27 Uc 92
24878 Palacio de Valdellorma LE 28 Ue 92
10697 Palacio Nuevo de Fresnedoso CC 99 Ua 109
06840 Palacio Quemado BA 133 Te 116
37497 Palacios SA 81 Tc 105
30892 Palacios, Los MC 156 Yd 121
05694 Palacios de Becedas AV 83 Uc 106
09654 Palacios de Benaver BU 30 Wa 94
47816 Palacios de Campos VA 47 Va 97
24414 Palacios de Compludo LE 26 Td 94
05516 Palacios de Corneja AV 83 Ud 106
05516 Palacios de Corneja AV 83 Ud 106
24250 Palacios de Fontecha LE 27 Uc 94
05215 Palacios de Goda AV 66 Vb 102
24767 Palacios de Jamuz LE 45 Tf 95
34490 Palacios del Alcor P 48 Vd 95
37111 Palacios del Arzobispo SA 64 Ua 102
09680 Palacios de la Sierra BU 50 Wf 97
24764 Palacios de la Valduerna LE 26 Ua 95
49162 Palacios del Pan ZA 45 Ua 99
24495 Palacios del Sil LE 26 Td 91
09107 Palacios de Riopisuerga BU 29 Ve 94
24940 Palacios de Rueda LE 28 Uf 92
37795 Palacios de Salvatierra SA 83 Ub 105
49322 Palacios de Sanabria ZA 44 Tc 96
24397 Palaciosmil LE 26 Tf 92
05216 Palacios Rubios AV 66 Vb 102
37406 Palaciosrubios SA 65 Ue 102
41720 Palacios y Villafranca, Los SE 163 Ua 126
39880 Palacio Villanuevo CB 19 We 89
08269 Palà de Torroella, El B 57 Be 97
24127 Paladín LE 27 Ua 92
08389 Palafolls B 59 Ce 98
17200 Palafrugell GI 59 Da 97
17462 Palagret GI 59 Cf 96
17230 Palamós GI 59 Da 97
18295 Palancar GR 167 Ve 125
41760 Palancar SE 165 Uc 127
19225 Palancares GU 68 We 102
21647 Palanco H 147 Ta 123
12311 Palanques CS 92 Ze 104
24225 Palanquinos LE 27 Uc 94
30334 Palas MC 157 Ye 123
27200 Palas de Rei LU 24 Sa 91
25243 Palau d'Anglesola, El L 56 Af 99
08140 Palaudàries B 58 Cb 99
43890 Palau del Duc de Medinacelli T 75 Af 103
25633 Palau de Noguera L 56 Af 96
08184 Palau de Plegamans B 58 Cb 99
25747 Palau de Rialb L 56 Bb 96
17476 Palau de Santa Eulàlia GI 59 Cf 95
17003 Palau-sacosta GI 59 Ce 97
17256 Palau-sator GI 59 Da 97
17495 Palausaverdera GI 40 Da 95
06717 Palazuelo BA 118 Ub 114
24839 Palazuelo LE 27 Ud 91
24869 Palazuelo de Boñar LE 27 Ud 91
24163 Palazuelo de Eslonza LE 27 Ud 93
49592 Palazuelo de las Cuevas ZA 45 Te 98
49213 Palazuelo de Sayago ZA 63 Te 100
24890 Palazuelo de Torío LE 27 Uc 92
47812 Palazuelo de Vedija VA 46 Uf 97
10590 Palazuelo-Empalme CC 98 Tf 109
09213 Palazuelos de Cuesta Urria BU 30 Wd 92
40194 Palazuelos de Eresma SG 67 Vf 103
09649 Palazuelos de la Sierra BU 49 Wd 95
09220 Palazuelos de Muñó BU 48 Wa 95
09124 Palazuelos de Villadiego BU 29 Vf 93
27837 Paleira LU 12 Sb 88
34005 Palencia P 47 Vc 96
37799 Palencia de Negrilla SA 65 Uc 102
05003 Palenciana AV 84 Vc 105
14914 Palenciana CO 167 Vc 125
34257 Palenzuela P 48 Vf 96
15175 Paleo C 11 Rd 89
36596 Palio PO 23 Rf 92
27418 Pallares LU 24 Sc 93
06907 Pallarés BA 133 Tf 120
30890 Pallareses, Los MC 155 Yb 123
43151 Pallaresos, Els T 75 Bb 101
25212 Pallargues, Les L 56 Bb 98
22221 Pallaruelo de Monegros HU 54 Ze 98
32785 Palleiros OR 43 Se 95
08780 Pallejà B 77 Bf 100
25747 Pallerols L 56 Bb 96
25714 Pallerols del Cantó L 37 Bb 94
24856 Pallide LE 16 Ue 91
30593 Palma, La MC 157 Za 122
19245 Pálmaces de Jadraque GU 69 Xa 102
43370 Palma d'Ebre, La T 74 Ad 101
08756 Palma de Cervelló, La B 77 Bf 100
46724 Palma de Gandía V 127 Ze 115
21700 Palma del Condado, La H 162 Tc 124
14700 Palma del Río CO 150 Ue 122
07012 Palma de Mallorca IB 110 Cd 111
07181 Palma Nova IB 110 Cd 111
07110 Palmanyola IB 110 Cd 111
11159 Palmar, El CA 172 Tf 131
30120 Palmar, El MC 157 Yf 121
38489 Palmar, El TF 180 Ia 178
38728 Palmar, El TF 181 Ha 175
46012 Palmar, El V 126 Ze 113
41719 Palmar de Troya, El SE 164 Ub 126
41620 Palmares, Los SE 165 Ue 124
36957 Palmás PO 22 Rb 95
38129 Palmas, Las TF 181 If 177
35010 Palmas de Gran Canaria, Las GC 184 Kd 180
15950 Palmeira C 22 Ra 93
04858 Palmera, La AL 171 Xe 125
03560 Palmeral, El A 142 Zd 118
30833 Palmeral, El MC 156 Ye 121
46419 Palmeres, Les V 127 Ze 113
17514 Palmerola GI 58 Ca 96
32981 Palmés OR 23 Sa 94
38890 Palmita, La TF 184 He 179
35457 Palmital, El GC 184 Kc 179
38632 Palm-Mar, El TF 180 Ib 180
11379 Palmones CA 175 Ud 131
22337 Palo HU 36 Ab 95
29018 Palo, El MA 175 Vd 128
17843 Palol de Revardit GI 59 Ce 96
30120 Paloma, La MC 157 Ye 121
33172 Palomar AS 15 Ua 89
11500 Palomar CA 172 Te 129
Palomar CO 151 Ve 122
14512 Palomar CO 166 Vb 124
23479 Palomar, El J 153 Xa 121
41410 Palomar, El SE 165 Uc 124
38280 Palomar, El TF 181 Id 177
46891 Palomar, El V 126 Zc 115
44708 Palomar de Arroyos TE 91 Zb 104
04617 Palomares AL 171 Yb 125
23130 Palomares J 152 Wb 123
37700 Palomares SA 83 Ub 106
37893 Palomares de Alba SA 83 Uc 103
16160 Palomares del Campo CU 104 Xc 109
41928 Palomares del Río SE 164 Tf 125
03610 Palomaret A 142 Zb 118
06300 Palomar Navas BA 133 Td 118
06476 Palomas BA 133 Tf 116
38600 Palomas, Las TF 180 Ic 180
45213 Palomeque TO 102 Wa 108
14811 Palomeques CO 151 Ve 124
16192 Palomera CU 105 Xf 108
10660 Palomero CC 82 Te 107
21810 Palos de la Frontera H 161 Ta 125
08401 Palou B 58 Cb 99
25212 Palou de Sanaüja L 56 Bb 98
25212 Palou de Torà L 57 Bc 98
17256 Pals GI 59 Da 97
39718 Pámanes CB 18 Wb 88
18411 Pamapaneira GR 169 Wd 127
04715 Pampanico AL 169 Xb 128
25289 Pampe L 57 Bc 96
09220 Pampliega BU 48 Wa 95
31013 Pamplona = Iruña NC 33 Yc 92
22336 Pamporciello, El HU 36 Ab 94
08717 Panadella, La B 57 Bc 99
33509 Pancar AS 16 Vb 88
36770 Pancenteo PO 41 Ra 97
15295 Panchés C 22 Qf 91
14249 Pánchez, Los CO 134 Ue 119
09280 Pancorbo BU 31 Wf 93
44720 Pancrudo TE 90 Yf 104
33529 Pandenes AS 15 Ud 88
33829 Pandiellos AS 14 Tf 88
39685 Pandillo CB 18 Wb 90
33930 Pando AS 15 Ub 89
48891 Pando BI 18 We 89
39691 Pando CB 18 Wa 89
39687 Pandos, Los CB 18 Wa 90
48800 Pandozales BI 19 We 89
33570 Panes AS 17 Vc 89
09294 Pangua BU 31 Xb 92
09212 Pangusión BU 31 We 92
22438 Panillo HU 55 Ab 95
50480 Paniza Z 72 Ye 101
33829 Panizal AS 14 Tf 88
09559 Panizares BU 30 Wd 92
22438 Pano HU 36 Ab 95
03581 Panorama A 143 Zf 117
25611 Panta de Canelles L 55 Ad 97
25282 Pantà de la Llosa del Covall L 57 Bd 96
25182 Pantà d' Utxesa L 74 Ad 100
30335 Pantaleón MC 156 Ye 122
21720 Pantanar H 162 Tc 125
16512 Pantano de Buendía CU 87 Xb 106
10137 Pantano de Cíjara CC 119 Uf 112
19225 Pantano de El Vado GU 68 We 103
10712 Pantano de Gabriel y Galán CC 82 Tf 107
31670 Pantano de Irabia NC 20 Yf 91
41710 Pantano de la Torre del Águila SE 165 Ub 126
29550 Pantano del Chorro MA 166 Vb 127
46312 Pantano del Generalísimo V 106 Yf 110
23713 Pantano del Guadalén J 137 Wd 120
18127 Pantano de los Bermejales GR 168 Wa 126
50140 Pantano de Moneva Z 72 Za 101
10697 Pantano de Navabuena CC 99 Ua 109
30800 Pantano de Puentes MC 155 Yb 122
37795 Pantano de Santa Teresa SA 83 Uc 104
06620 Pantano de Zújar BA 118 Ud 115
22650 Panticosa HU 35 Ze 92
15553 Pantín C 11 Rf 87
15819 Pantiñobre C 23 Re 91
45290 Pantoja TO 102 Wb 108
03409 Pantojo, El A 141 Za 117
27439 Pantón LU 24 Sb 93
36340 Panxón PO 41 Rb 96
22141 Panzano HU 54 Zf 95
26121 Panzares RI 32 Xc 95
33189 Pañeda Nueva AS 15 Ub 88

290 I Orxa, l'

42368 Paones SO 69 Xa 100
05358 Papatrigo AV 84 Va 103
23150 Papel, El J 152 Wa 123
08754 Papiol, El B 77 Ca 100
43713 Papiolet, El T 76 Bd 101
29690 Papudo-Acebuchal-Soto Colorado MA 173 Ue 130
13720 Paquines, Las CR 122 We 113
33579 Para AS 16 Vc 89
39212 Paracuelles CB 17 Ve 90
16373 Paracuellos CU 105 Yb 110
28860 Paracuellos de Jarama MD 86 Wc 105
50342 Paracuellos de Jiloca Z 71 Yc 101
50299 Paracuellos de la Ribera Z 71 Yc 100
15689 Parada C 11 Rd 90
15316 Parada C 11 Rf 89
27155 Parada LU 12 Sc 90
27626 Parada LU 24 Se 93
27325 Parada LU 25 Sf 93
32740 Parada OR 24 Sc 94
36117 Parada PO 23 Rd 93
32930 Parada, A OR 24 Sa 95
32546 Parada da Serra OR 43 Se 96
36888 Parada de Achas PO 42 Re 95
37129 Parada de Arriba SA 64 Ub 103
32635 Parada de Ribeira OR 42 Sb 96
37419 Parada de Rubiales SA 65 Ud 102
32896 Parada de Ventosa OR 42 Rf 97
27339 Parada dos Montes LU 24 Se 93
27329 Paradapiñol LU 25 Se 94
41610 Paradas SE 165 Ud 125
32787 Parada Seca OR 24 Sd 95
24398 Paradasolana LE 26 Td 93
27135 Paradavella LU 13 Se 90
15108 Paradela C 11 Rc 89
15145 Paradela C 11 Rd 89
15310 Paradela C 11 Sa 90
15806 Paradela C 11 Sa 91
27659 Paradela LU 13 Sf 91
27613 Paradela LU 24 Sc 92
32981 Paradela OR 24 Sa 94
32765 Paradela OR 24 Sd 94
32782 Paradela OR 25 Se 95
32646 Paradela OR 42 Sa 97
36685 Paradela PO 23 Rd 92
32748 Paradellas OR 24 Sc 94
24510 Paradeseca LE 25 Tb 92
24608 Paradilla de Gordón LE 27 Ub 91
24228 Paradilla de la Sobarriba LE 27 Ud 93
37479 Paradinas SA 81 Tc 104
40123 Paradinas SG 67 Vd 102
37318 Paradinas de San Juan SA 65 Va 103
30893 Parador MC 156 Yb 124
21593 Parador, El H 146 Sd 123
04720 Parador de las Hortichuelas, El AL 170 Xc 128
45009 Parador Nacional Conde de Orgaz TO 102 Vf 109
39588 Parador Nacional de Fuente Dé CB 16 Vb 90
04638 Parador Nacional de los Reyes Católicos AL 171 Yb 126
33529 Paraes AS 15 Uc 88
32780 Paraisás OR 24 Se 94
28210 Paraíso, El MD 85 Vf 105
44422 Paraíso Alto TE 107 Za 108
44422 Paraíso Bajo TE 107 Za 108
33890 Parajas AS 14 Tc 89
24525 Parajis LE 25 Ta 92
09515 Paralacuesta BU 30 Wd 91
02489 Paralis las Juntas AB 139 Xd 119
33111 Páramo AS 14 Tf 90
34407 Páramo de Boedo P 29 Vd 93
09131 Páramo del Arroyo BU 30 Wb 94
24470 Páramo del Sil LE 26 Td 92
15871 Páramos C 10 Rb 91
36729 Páramos PO 41 Rc 96
33694 Parana AS 15 Ub 90
36872 Paraños PO 42 Rd 95
04692 Parata, La AL 155 Ya 124
03720 Paratella A 143 Aa 116
29451 Parauta MA 174 Uf 129
27246 Paraxes LU 12 Sd 89
33687 Paraya, La AS 15 Uc 90
39612 Parbayón CB 18 Wa 88
41120 Parcelas de Porsiver SE 164 Tf 125
03792 Parcent A 143 Zf 116
29394 Parchite MA 166 Uf 128
02449 Pardal, El AB 139 Xe 118
46162 Pardanchinos V 107 Zb 110
24820 Pardavé LE 27 Uc 92
32730 Pardeconde OR 24 Sc 94
27235 Pardellas, As LU 12 Sb 90
36686 Pardemarín PO 23 Rd 92
32830 Parderrubias OR 42 Sa 95
24848 Pardesivil LE 27 Ud 92
09462 Pardilla BU 68 Wb 99
35213 Pardilla, La GC 184 Kd 180
09572 Pardilla de Hoz de Arreba BU 30 Wb 91
22394 Pardina, La HU 36 Aa 95
22339 Pardina, La HU 36 Ab 94
22760 Pardina de Lardiés HU 34 Zb 93
22622 Pardina de Orlato HU 35 Ze 95
22150 Pardina de Ubieto HU 35 Ze 94
22760 Pardina Pueyo HU 34 Zb 93
22484 Pardinella HU 36 Ad 94
17534 Pardines GI 39 Cb 95
15126 Pardiñas C 10 Qf 90
04779 Pardo, El AL 169 Xa 128
30812 Pardo, El MC 155 Yb 121
28048 Pardo, El MD 86 Wb 105
19336 Pardos GU 70 Ya 103
50375 Pardos Z 71 Yc 102
04692 Pardos, Los AL 155 Xf 123
02213 Pared, La AB 125 Ye 113
39805 Pared, La CB 18 Wd 89
35627 Pared, La GC 183 Le 179
02639 Paredazos, Los AB 123 Xe 114
33785 Paredes AS 14 Tc 88
16465 Paredes CU 104 Xa 108
32750 Paredes OR 24 Sd 95
28196 Paredes de Buitrago MD 68 Wc 102
45908 Paredes de Escalona TO 85 Vd 107
34191 Paredes de Monte P 47 Vc 97
34300 Paredes de Nava P 47 Vb 96
19277 Paredes de Sigüenza GU 69 Xb 101
42132 Paredesroyas SO 51 Xe 99
03657 Paredó, El A 141 Yf 118
19129 Pareja GU 88 Xc 105
07769 Parella Nou IB 77 Df 109
09512 Paresotas BU 18 We 91
30858 Paretón, El MC 156 Yd 122
17468 Parets d'Empordà GI 59 Cf 96
27305 Parga LU 12 Sb 89
50741 Paridera Abejar Alto Z 72 Zc 100
50461 Paridera Amplanes Z 71 Ye 100
50461 Paridera Carraquilla Z 71 Ye 100
50193 Paridera Corral de la Blanca Z 53 Zb 98
50161 Paridera de Cabezones Z 53 Zc 98
22215 Paridera de Carlos HU 54 Zf 97
50160 Paridera de Escartín Z 53 Zc 97
50139 Paridera de Estrén Z 72 Za 99
50750 Paridera de la Rabosa Z 73 Zd 99
50290 Paridera de la Rioja Z 53 Ye 99
50612 Paridera del Castillo Z 53 Yf 96
46450 Paridera del Hondo V 126 Zd 113
22216 Paridera del Médico HU 54 Zd 97
50750 Paridera de los Caños Z 73 Zc 99
50161 Paridera de los Quemados Z 53 Zc 98
50741 Paridera del Pastejón Z 72 Zc 100
50741 Paridera del Rojo Z 72 Zc 100
50020 Paridera del Santísimo Z 53 Za 98
22280 Paridera de Rivas HU 53 Zb 96
50139 Paridera de Santa Engracia Z 72 Zb 99
50741 Paridera de Sopapos Z 72 Zc 100
50547 Paridera Huerta del Sastre Z 52 Yc 98
50135 Paridera La Viuda Z 72 Zb 100
50461 Paridera Lomeros Z 71 Ye 100
50770 Paridera Los Cuervos Z 73 Zc 100
02315 Parideras, Las AB 139 Xc 117
50546 Parideras Cerro Pellar Z 52 Yc 98
50141 Paridera Tía Dionisia Z 72 Yf 100
50137 Paridero Lamarca Z 72 Zb 100
50137 Paridero Tío Paco Z 72 Zb 100
21291 Parilla, La H 147 Tb 121
09216 Páriza BU 31 Xc 92
28981 Parla MD 86 Wb 107
17133 Parlavà GI 59 Da 96
33717 Parlero AS 13 Tc 88
41020 Parque Alcosa SE 163 Ua 124
28935 Parque Coimbra MD 86 Wa 107
19174 Parque de Las Castillas GU 86 Wd 104
13250 Parque Nacional Tablas de Daimiel CR 121 Wb 114
04828 Parra, La AL 155 Xf 123
04770 Parra, La AL 169 We 128
05400 Parra, La AV 84 Uf 107
06176 Parra, La BA 132 Tc 117
11591 Parra, La CA 164 Tf 128
16113 Parra de las Vegas, La CU 105 Xe 109
13690 Párraga CR 122 Wf 113
10859 Parra Grande CC 98 Tc 108
05146 Parral, El AV 84 Va 104
40393 Parral de Villovela SG 67 Vf 102
11150 Parralejo, El CA 172 Ua 131
23268 Parralejo, El J 138 Xa 118
35280 Parral Grande GC 184 Kc 181
44566 Parras de Castellote, Las TE 92 Ze 104
44769 Parras de Martín, Las TE 90 Za 104
33509 Parres AS 16 Vb 88
12232 Parreta Grande, La CS 107 Zd 108
11580 Parrilla, La CA 173 Ua 129
14290 Parrilla, La CO 134 Ue 119
23392 Parrilla, La J 139 Xb 118
29311 Parrilla, La MA 167 Vd 125
47328 Parrilla, La VA 66 Vc 99
45611 Parrillas TO 100 Uf 108
23380 Parrizón AB 139 Xc 118
23196 Parrizoso, El J 152 Wb 123
25796 Parròqia d'Hortó, La V 37 Bc 94
04810 Partaloa AL 171 Xe 124
09133 Parte, La BU 29 Wa 93
09587 Partearroyo BU 19 We 90
09249 Parte de Bureba, La BU 30 Wd 92
27329 Parteme LU 24 Se 94
50695 Partida Casilla Z 52 Ye 95
09211 Partido de la Sierra en Tobalina BU 31 We 92
41849 Partido de Resina SE 164 Te 125
30648 Partidor, El MC 141 Yf 119
02320 Partidores, Los AB 124 Xf 115
28523 Partija, La MD 86 Wc 106
32515 Partovia OR 23 Rf 94
22365 Parzán HU 36 Ab 93
22533 Pas, El HU 55 Ab 98
43559 Pas, El T 93 Ac 105
21450 Pasada de los Bayos H 161 Sf 125
21450 Pasada del Palo H 161 Sf 124
35259 Pasadilla GC 184 Kd 181
43425 Pasanant = Passanant T 75 Bb 99
15129 Pasarela C 10 Qf 90
49240 Pasariegos ZA 64 Tf 100
05143 Pasarilla del Rebollar AV 84 Uf 104
10411 Pasarón de la Vera CC 99 Ub 108
37520 Pascualarina SA 81 Tc 105
05150 Pascualcobo AV 83 Ue 105
05164 Pascualcobo AV 84 Vb 103
40122 Pascuales SG 67 Vd 102
23369 Pascuales, Los J 138 Xb 118
05309 Pascualgrande AV 66 Va 103
05560 Pascual Muñoz AV 84 Uf 105
30811 Pasico MC 156 Yb 123
35106 Pasito Blanco GC 184 Kc 182
38758 Paso, El TF 181 Ha 177
07609 Passessió des Cap Blanc IB 110 Ce 112
15821 Pastor C 11 Re 90
37510 Pastores SA 81 Tc 105
11206 Pastores, Los CA 173 Ud 132
44480 Pastores, Los TE 107 Zc 108
27287 Pastoriza, A LU 12 Sd 89
11540 Pastrana CA 164 Te 128
19100 Pastrana GU 87 Xa 106
30876 Pastrana MC 156 Yd 123
50195 Pastriz Z 53 Zb 99
14512 Pata de Mulo CO 150 Vb 124
35130 Patalavaca GC 184 Kb 182
14730 Paterna CO 150 Ue 122
46980 Paterna V 126 Zd 111
21880 Paterna del Campo H 163 Td 124
02136 Paterna del Madera AB 139 Xd 117
04479 Paterna del Río AL 169 Xa 126
11178 Paterna de Rivera CA 172 Ua 129
31190 Paternáin NC 33 Yb 92
22760 Paternoy HU 34 Zb 94
28189 Patones MD 86 Wd 103
28189 Patones de Abajo MD 86 Wd 103
21330 Patrás H 147 Tb 122
11150 Patria CA 172 Tf 131
11180 Patrite CA 173 Uc 130
23290 Patronato, El J 154 Xc 120
41580 Patronato, El SE 166 Vb 125
30610 Patruena MC 141 Yd 120
17494 Pau GI 40 Da 95
22393 Paúl HU 55 Ab 95
01420 Paúl VI 31 Xa 92
44422 Paúl, El TE 107 Zb 108
22281 Paúl, La HU 53 Zb 97
18519 Paulenca GR 169 We 125
48890 Paules BI 18 We 89
02489 Paúles AB 139 Xd 119
50610 Paúles Z 53 Za 96
09345 Paúles del Agua BU 48 Wa 96
09640 Paúles de Lara BU 49 Wd 96
22149 Paúles de Vero HU 35 Aa 95
25512 Pauls L 37 Af 94
43593 Paüls T 74 Ac 103
30410 Pava, La MC 140 Ya 119
25213 Pavia L 57 Bc 99
40182 Pavía SG 67 Wa 102
12449 Pavías CS 107 Zd 109
38869 Pavón TF 184 He 180
30848 Pavos, Los MC 156 Yd 121
23293 Payer J 139 Xb 119
21560 Paymogo H 146 Sd 122
37524 Payo, El SA 81 Tb 107
34485 Payo de Ojeda P 29 Vd 92
01211 Payueta VI 31 Xb 93
14100 Paz, La CO 150 Va 123
15817 Pazo C 11 Re 90
15913 Pazo C 22 Rb 92
15985 Pazo C 22 Rb 93
27889 Pazo LU 10 Sd 87
27835 Pazo LU 12 Sb 88
15110 Pazos C 10 Rb 89
15881 Pazos C 23 Rd 92
32915 Pazos OR 24 Sb 95
32636 Pazos OR 43 Sc 96
36841 Pazos de Borbén PO 23 Rc 95
15313 Pazos de Irixoa C 11 Rf 89
36715 Pazos de Reis PO 41 Rc 96
26261 Pazuengos RI 31 Xa 95
46191 Pea, La V 107 Zc 111
23460 Peal de Becerro J 153 Wf 121
46630 Pebrades, Les V 126 Za 116
43718 Peces, Les T 76 Bd 101
40238 Pecharromán SG 67 Wa 100
04897 Pechina AL 170 Xc 124
04250 Pechina AL 170 Xd 127
04500 Pecho, El AL 170 Xa 126
39594 Pechón CB 17 Vd 88
26339 Peciña RI 31 Xb 93
37148 Pedernal SA 64 Te 102
16638 Pedernoso, El CU 104 Xb 112
36309 Pedornes PO 41 Ra 96
15365 Pedra C 10 Sa 86
25284 Pedra, La L 57 Bd 96
15293 Pedrafigueira C 22 Qf 92
27389 Pedrafita LU 12 Sb 90
27595 Pedrafita LU 24 Sb 93
27325 Pedrafita LU 25 Se 93
27695 Pedrafita de Camporredondo LU 13 Se 91
27670 Pedrafita do Cebreiro LU 25 Sf 92
47196 Pedraja de Portillo, La VA 66 Vc 100
42391 Pedraja de San Esteban SO 68 Wf 99
42190 Pedrajas SO 50 Xc 98
47430 Pedrajas de San Esteban VA 66 Vc 100
46164 Pedralba V 107 Zb 111
49392 Pedralba de la Pradería ZA 44 Tb 96
03720 Pedramala A 143 Aa 116
10748 Pedrarías CC 82 Tf 107
18820 Pedrarías GR 155 Xe 121
27569 Pedraza LU 24 Sa 92
40172 Pedraza SG 67 Wb 102
42162 Pedraza SO 51 Xd 97
37882 Pedraza de Alba SA 83 Ud 104
34170 Pedraza de Campos P 47 Vb 97
37494 Pedraza de Yeltes SA 82 Td 104
32702 Pedreda OR 43 Sc 95
39450 Pedredo CB 17 Vf 89
24273 Pedregal LE 27 Ua 92
45215 Pedregal TO 102 Vf 108
33877 Pedregal, El AS 14 Td 88
19327 Pedregal, El GU 89 Yc 104
03750 Pedreguer A 127 Aa 116
15595 Pedreira, A C 11 Re 87
39130 Pedreña CB 18 Wb 88
41566 Pedrera SE 166 Va 125
33194 Pedrera, La AS 15 Ua 88
33390 Pedrera, La AS 15 Ub 88
30700 Pedrera, La MC 157 Yf 122
03610 Pedreras A 142 Zb 117
30877 Pedreras, Las MC 156 Yd 123
17493 Pedret GI 40 Da 95
28723 Pedrezuela MD 86 Wc 104
46310 Pedriches V 106 Ye 111
25337 Pedrís L 56 Af 98
23688 Pedriza, La J 152 Wa 124
10840 Pedrizas CC 98 Tb 108
42344 Pedro SO 68 We 101
14630 Pedro Abad CO 151 Vd 121
38292 Pedro Álvarez TF 181 Ie 177
37267 Pedro Álvaro SA 63 Td 103
35540 Pedro Barba GC 182 Md 173
05470 Pedro Bernardo AV 84 Va 107
14412 Pedroche CO 135 Vb 118
14029 Pedroches CO 151 Vb 121
14709 Pedro Díaz CO 150 Ue 122
37755 Pedro Fuertes SA 83 Ud 105
16337 Pedro Izquierdo CU 106 Yd 109
50690 Pedrola Z 53 Ye 98
37455 Pedro Llen SA 83 Ub 104
06131 Pedro Martín BA 132 Sf 118
37451 Pedro Martín SA 82 Ua 104
37892 Pedro Martín SA 83 Uc 104
18530 Pedro Martínez GR 153 We 123
06340 Pedro Moreno BA 133 Td 119
10630 Pedro Muñoz CC 82 Td 107
13620 Pedro Muñoz CR 122 Xa 112
46355 Pedrones de Abajo V 125 Yf 112
46355 Pedrones de Arriba V 125 Yf 112
16660 Pedroñeras, Las CU 123 Xb 112
05165 Pedro Rodríguez AV 66 Vb 103
09574 Pedrosa BU 18 Wb 90
32688 Pedrosa OR 43 Sc 97
32612 Pedrosa OR 43 Se 96
09314 Pedrosa de Duero BU 48 Wa 98
34116 Pedrosa de la Vega P 28 Vb 94
09139 Pedrosa del Páramo BU 29 Wa 94
09119 Pedrosa del Príncipe BU 48 Ve 95
24918 Pedrosa del Rey LE 16 Va 91
47112 Pedrosa del Rey VA 65 Ue 99
09239 Pedrosa de Muñó BU 49 Wb 95
09131 Pedrosa de Río-Urbel BU 30 Wb 94
09549 Pedrosa de Tobalina BU 30 Wd 91
09127 Pedrosa de Valdelucio BU 29 Vf 92
50612 Pedrosas, Las Z 53 Za 96
06900 Pedrosillo, El BA 133 Ua 119
41890 Pedrosillo, El SE 148 Td 123
37871 Pedrosillo de Alba SA 83 Ud 104
37788 Pedrosillo de los Aires SA 83 Ub 104
37427 Pedrosillo el Ralo SA 65 Uc 102
33556 Pedroso AS 16 Va 88
39649 Pedroso CB 18 Wa 89
39180 Pedroso CB 18 Wc 88
26321 Pedroso RI 31 Xb 95
41360 Pedroso, El SE 149 Ub 121
10829 Pedroso de Acim CC 98 Td 110
47132 Pedroso de la Abadesa VA 66 Va 99
37410 Pedroso de la Armuña, El SA 65 Ud 102
49594 Pedroso de la Carballeda ZA 44 Td 97
37590 Pedrotoro SA 81 Td 105
15821 Pedrouzo C 23 Rd 91
15865 Pedrouzos C 22 Rb 91
11380 Pedro Valiente CA 173 Uc 132
33115 Pedroveya AS 14 Ua 89
22149 Pedruel HU 35 Zf 95
24820 Pedrún de Torío LE 27 Ud 92
23110 Pegalajar J 152 Wc 122
03780 Pego A 127 Zf 115
49154 Pego, El ZA 65 Ud 100
08698 Peguera B 57 Be 95
07160 Peguera IB 110 Cc 111
23298 Peguera del Madroño J 139 Xc 119
21610 Peguerillas H 162 Ta 124
05239 Peguerinos AV 85 Ve 105
27579 Peibás LU 24 Sa 92
44480 Peirós, Los TE 107 Zc 108
27318 Peites LU 25 Se 94
07518 Peixeri IB 111 Cf 111
31669 Pekotxeta NC 21 Ye 90
37181 Pelabravo SA 65 Uc 103
40195 Peladera, La SG 67 Vf 103
29312 Peláez, Los MA 167 Vd 126
25212 Pelagalls L 56 Bb 98
37188 Pelagarcía SA 65 Uc 103
45918 Pelahustán TO 101 Vc 107
37209 Pelarrodríguez SA 64 Te 103
11390 Pelayo, El CA 175 Ud 132
37787 Pelayos SA 83 Uc 105
28696 Pelayos de la Presa MD 85 Vd 106
40170 Pelayos del Arroyo SG 67 Wa 102
49880 Peleagonzalo ZA 65 Ud 100
49191 Peleas de Abajo ZA 64 Ub 100
49706 Peleas de Arriba ZA 64 Ub 101

Peleas de Arriba | 291 E

19268 Pelegrina GU 69 Xc 102
18492 Pelegrinas GR 169 Wf 127
12193 Pelejaneta CS 92 Zf 107
27655 Peliceira LU 13 Ta 91
18210 Peligros GR 168 Wc 125
30813 Pelile y El Jurado MC 156 Yb 123
37116 Pelilla SA 64 Tf 101
06679 Peloche BA 119 Uf 113
33735 Pelorde AS 13 Ta 89
33686 Pelúgano AS 15 Uc 90
29540 Pelusa, La MA 166 Vb 126
39582 Pembes CB 16 Vb 90
33558 Pen AS 16 Uf 89
33783 Pena AS 14 Td 88
15552 Pena C 11 Rf 87
27129 Pena LU 12 Sd 90
27418 Pena LU 24 Sc 93
15838 Pena, A C 22 Rb 91
32636 Pena, A OR 43 Sb 96
27865 Penabad LU 12 Sc 87
27243 Pena de Cabras LU 13 Se 89
15582 Penadeiriz C 11 Sa 88
32788 Pena Folenche OR 24 Se 94
39627 Penagos CB 18 Wb 88
03815 Penàguila A 142 Zd 116
32634 Penalonga OR 42 Sb 97
27283 Penamazada LU 13 Se 89
27659 Penamil LU 13 Sf 91
15338 Penamoura C 12 Sb 87
32789 Pena Petade OR 24 Se 95
27568 Penas LU 24 Sb 92
27328 Penasrubias LU 25 Se 93
15576 Penavidreira C 11 Rf 87
09593 Penches BU 30 Wd 92
24699 Pendilla de Arbás LE 15 Ub 90
33997 Pendones AS 16 Ue 90
17240 Penedès GI 59 Cf 97
15684 Penela C 11 Rc 90
27414 Penela LU 24 Sd 94
32654 Penelas OR 42 Sa 96
03870 Penella A 142 Zd 116
25335 Penelles L 56 Af 98
27112 Penide LU 13 Sf 89
39626 Penilla, La CB 18 Wa 89
24437 Penoselo LE 25 Tc 92
32558 Penouta OR 44 Sf 95
32547 Pentes OR 43 Se 96
17731 Penya, La GI 40 Ce 95
03296 Penya de las Àguiles, La A 142 Zb 119
33778 Penzol AS 13 Ta 88
31409 Peña NC 33 Ye 94
33891 Peña, La AS 14 Te 88
30708 Peña, La MC 157 Za 122
37214 Peña, La SA 63 Tc 101
37727 Peñacaballera SA 82 Ua 106
39110 Peña-Castillo CB 18 Wa 88
01212 Peñacerrada = Urizaharra VI 31 Xb 93
09610 Peñacoba BU 49 Wd 97
37609 Peña de Cabra SA 82 Ua 104
37532 Peña de Francia SA 82 Te 105
11520 Peña del Águila CA 172 Uc 128
30629 Peña de la Zafra MC 141 Yf 119
33192 Peñaferruz AS 15 Ub 88
47300 Peñafiel VA 48 Ve 99
33829 Peñaflor AS 14 Tf 88
50192 Peñaflor Z 53 Zb 98
47640 Peñaflor de Hornija VA 47 Va 98
33739 Peñafuente AS 13 Ta 90
09591 Peñahorada BU 30 Wc 94
14240 Peñaladrones CO 135 Uf 119
19128 Peñalagos GU 88 Xb 105
13738 Peñalajo CR 137 Wd 117
12414 Peñalba CS 107 Zd 109
22592 Peñalba HU 73 Zf 100
05163 Peñalba de Ávila AV 84 Vb 104
09454 Peñalba de Castro BU 49 Wd 98
24142 Peñalba de Cilleros LE 26 Tf 91
47329 Peñalba de Duero VA 47 Vd 99
28190 Peñalba de la Sierra GU 68 Wd 102
09558 Peñalba de Manzanedo BU 30 Wb 91
42345 Peñalba de San Esteban SO 68 We 99
24415 Peñalba de Santiago LE 26 Tc 94
37148 Peñalbo SA 64 Tf 102
42126 Peñalcázar SO 70 Xf 99
19462 Peñalén GU 89 Xf 105
14129 Peñalosa CO 150 Uf 122
21870 Peñalosa H 148 Td 124
26124 Peñaloscintos RI 50 Xb 95
06610 Peñalsordo BA 119 Uf 116
19134 Peñalver GU 87 Xa 105
22250 Peñalveta HU 54 Zd 98
30810 Peña María y Fuente Atocha MC 155 Ya 121
37130 Peñamecer SA 64 Ua 102
37523 Peñaparda SA 81 Tb 107
37300 Peñaranda de Bracamonte SA 65 Ue 103
09410 Peñaranda de Duero BU 49 Wd 98
37820 Peñarandilla SA 83 Ud 103
22536 Peña-Roa HU 55 Ab 98
04769 Peñarrodada, La AL 169 Xa 127
44586 Peñarroya de Tastavíns TE 92 Aa 104
14200 Peñarroya-Pueblonuevo CO 134 Ue 119
44709 Peñarroyas TE 91 Zd 102
02314 Peñarrubia AB 139 Xe 116
02486 Peñarrubia AB 140 Xe 118
39580 Peñarrubia CB 17 Vc 89
23295 Peña Rubia J 139 Xc 119
30400 Peña-Rubia MC 140 Ya 120
03639 Peña Rubia, La A 142 Zb 117
30629 Peñas, Las MC 141 Yf 119
14210 Peñas Blancas CO 135 Va 120
28250 Peñascales, Los MD 86 Wa 105
02313 Peñascosa AB 139 Xd 116
22808 Peñas de Riglos, Las HU 34 Zb 94
02120 Peñas de San Pedro AB 140 Xf 116
04277 Peñas Negras AL 171 Xf 126
40393 Peñasrubias de Pirón SG 67 Vf 102
49178 Peñausende ZA 64 Ua 101
42174 Peñazcurna SO 51 Xe 96
14880 Peñillas CO 151 Ve 123
12598 Peñíscola CS 93 Ac 106
23359 Peñolite J 139 Xb 119
02536 Peñón, El AB 139 Xe 119
18520 Peñón, El GR 153 We 123
04810 Peñón Alto, El AL 155 Xe 124
35149 Peñones, Los GC 184 Kb 181
48800 Peñueco BI 19 We 89
13650 Peñuela, La CR 121 Wd 113
21840 Peñuela, La H 162 Tb 124
18328 Peñuelas GR 168 Wa 125
33314 Peón AS 15 Uc 88
09136 Peones BU 29 Vf 93
15689 Pepín C 11 Rd 90
45638 Pepino TO 100 Vb 108
49318 Peque ZA 45 Te 96
18130 Pera, La GR 168 Wb 126
25513 Peracalç L 37 Ba 95
44369 Peracense TE 90 Yd 105
08589 Perafita B 58 Ca 96
43152 Perafort T 75 Bb 101
29570 Peral MA 166 Vc 128
16240 Peral, El CU 105 Ya 112
33411 Peral, La AS 14 Ua 88
17491 Peralada GI 40 Da 95
09342 Peral de Arlanza BU 48 Vf 96
10335 Peraleda de la Mata CC 99 Ud 109
10334 Peraleda de San Román CC 100 Ud 110
06919 Peraleda de Zaucejo BA 134 Uc 118
16532 Peraleja, La CU 88 Xc 107
16235 Peraleja, La CU 105 Ya 111
28211 Peralejo MD 85 Vf 105
02136 Peralejo, El AB 139 Xd 117
41898 Peralejo, El SE 148 Td 122
42315 Peralejo de los Escuderos SO 69 Wf 101
44162 Peralejos TE 90 Yf 106
23470 Peralejos, Los J 153 Wf 121
37216 Peralejos de Abajo SA 63 Td 102
37216 Peralejos de Arriba SA 64 Td 102
19313 Peralejos de las Truchas GU 89 Ya 105
37609 Peralejos de Solís SA 82 Ua 104
34429 Perales P 47 Vc 95
16150 Perales, Los CU 89 Ya 106
37882 Perales, Los SA 83 Uc 103
38356 Perales, Los TF 181 Id 177
44163 Perales del Alfambra TE 90 Yf 105
10896 Perales del Puerto CC 98 Tb 108
28909 Perales del Río MD 86 Wc 107
28693 Perales de Milla MD 85 Vf 106
28540 Perales de Tajuña MD 87 Wd 107
13429 Peralosas, Las CR 120 Vf 114
02486 Peralta AB 140 Xe 118
31350 Peralta NC 33 Yb 96
22210 Peralta de Alcofea HU 54 Zf 97
22513 Peralta de la Sal HU 55 Ac 97
22311 Peraltilla HU 54 Zf 96
19493 Peralveche GU 88 Xd 105
13140 Peralvillo Alto CR 121 Wa 114
13140 Peralvillo Bajo CR 121 Wa 114
50297 Peramán Z 53 Yf 98
37493 Peramato SA 82 Te 103
25591 Peramea L 37 Ba 95
25790 Peramola L 56 Bb 96
24516 Perandones LE 25 Tb 93
24429 Peranzanes LE 25 Tc 91
34839 Perapertú P 29 Vd 91
17530 Perarnau GI 39 Ca 95
22460 Perarrúa HU 36 Ac 95
17113 Peratallada GI 59 Da 97
34486 Perazancas P 29 Vd 92
15608 Perbes C 11 Re 88
37497 Perchas, Las SA 81 Tb 106
16150 Perchel, El CU 89 Ya 106
12118 Perchet CS 92 Zf 108
50709 Percuñan Z 73 Aa 101
42218 Perdices SO 69 Xd 100
49720 Perdigón, El ZA 64 Ub 100
50161 Perdiguera Z 53 Zc 98
13720 Perdigueras, Las CR 122 We 113
30893 Perdiz MC 156 Yb 123
38312 Perdoma, La TF 180 Ic 178
23488 Perea J 153 Wf 121
33827 Pereda AS 14 Tf 88
09568 Pereda BU 18 Wc 90
33509 Pereda, La AS 16 Vb 88
24433 Pereda de Ancares LE 25 Tb 92
24609 Peredilla LE 27 Uc 92
06220 Peregrina y Bodegas BA 133 Td 117
27533 Pereira LU 24 Sb 93
27416 Pereira LU 24 Sd 94
32868 Pereira OR 42 Rf 97
36557 Pereira PO 23 Re 93
15837 Pereira, A C 10 Ra 91
32830 Pereira de Montes OR 42 Sa 95
15563 Pereiro C 11 Rf 87
32549 Pereiro OR 43 Sf 96
32793 Pereiro de Aguiar OR 24 Sb 94
24523 Pereje LE 25 Ta 93
43519 Perelló, El T 93 Ae 103
46420 Perelló, El V 127 Ze 113
41599 Perenos, Los SE 166 Vb 125
37175 Pereña SA 63 Tc 101
42315 Perera, La SO 69 Wf 100
49280 Pererueла ZA 64 Ua 100
25281 Peret L 57 Bc 97
09512 Pérex BU 18 We 91
03187 Pérez, Los A 157 Zb 120
04770 Pérez, Los AL 169 Wf 128
04890 Pérez, Los AL 170 Xc 124
30396 Pérez, Los MC 157 Yf 123
41599 Pérez, Los SE 166 Vb 125
29710 Periana MA 167 Ve 127
37449 Pericalvo SA 64 Ub 103
49145 Perilla de Castro ZA 45 Ua 98
10291 Perillas, Las CC 98 Tf 111
15172 Perillo C 11 Rd 88
30396 Perín MC 157 Yf 123
40230 Perla, La SG 67 Ve 100
47800 Perla Sofía VA 47 Uf 97
03295 Perleta A 142 Zc 119
33491 Perlora AS 15 Ub 87
37260 Permalona, La SA 81 Td 103
22415 Permisán HU 55 Aa 97
14850 Pernea CO 151 Ve 123
41400 Pernía SE 150 Uf 123
34847 Pernia, La P 17 Vc 91
33327 Pernús AS 15 Ue 88
41890 Peroamigo SE 148 Td 122
26586 Peroblasco RI 51 Xe 95
40141 Perocojo SG 67 Ve 103
40154 Perogordo SG 67 Vf 103
25638 Perolet L 56 Ba 96
37791 Peromingo SA 83 Ub 106
16600 Perona CU 104 Xe 112
42130 Peroniel del Campo SO 51 Xe 98
40310 Perorrubio SG 68 Wb 101
40354 Perosillo SG 67 Vf 100
32151 Peroxa, A OR 24 Sb 94
39571 Perrozo CB 17 Vc 90
21310 Perrunal, El H 147 Ta 122
22132 Pertusa HU 54 Zf 96
04692 Perulera, La AL 155 Xf 124
33547 Peruyes AS 16 Uf 88
33557 Pervis AS 16 Uf 89
09559 Pesadas de Burgos BU 30 Wc 92
15838 Pesadoira C 10 Ra 91
39572 Pesaguero-Laparte CB 17 Vc 90
36538 Pescoso PO 23 Sa 92
10882 Pescueza CC 98 Tc 109
02314 Pesebre AB 139 Xd 116
10649 Pesga, La CC 82 Te 107
33735 Pesoz AS 13 Ta 89
15939 Pesqueira C 22 Ra 93
36456 Pesqueiras PO 41 Rd 96
39491 Pesquera CB 17 Vf 90
24815 Pesquera LE 28 Uf 92
16269 Pesquera, La CU 106 Yc 111
47315 Pesquera de Duero VA 48 Ve 99
09146 Pesquera de Ebro BU 30 Wb 92
33583 Pesquerín AS 15 Ue 88
47130 Pesqueruela VA 66 Va 99
25518 Pessonada L 56 Ba 95
39548 Pesues CB 17 Vd 88
36419 Petelos PO 41 Rc 95
50686 Petilla de Aragón NC 34 Yf 94
32356 Petín OR 25 Sf 94
07520 Petra IB 111 Da 111
03610 Petrer A 142 Zb 118
46501 Petrés V 108 Ze 110
02692 Pétrola AB 124 Yc 116
18517 Peza, La GR 169 We 125
15808 Pezobres C 23 Rf 91
28812 Pezuela de las Torres MD 87 We 106
25721 Pi L 38 Be 94
33778 Piantón AS 13 Sf 88
04829 Piar de Abajo, El AL 155 Xf 122
36760 Pías PO 41 Ra 97
49580 Pías ZA 44 Ta 96
39573 Piasca CB 17 Vc 90
35541 Picachos Punta de Mujeres, Los GC 182 Md 174
28680 Picadas, Las MD 85 Ve 107
43491 Picamoixons T 75 Bb 101
46210 Picanya = Picaña V 126 Zd 112
46210 Picaña = Picanya V 126 Zd 112
15980 Picaraña de Arriba C 22 Rc 92
02449 Picarzos AB 140 Xf 118
46225 Picassent V 126 Zd 112
19459 Picazo GU 88 Xb 104
16211 Picazo, El CU 124 Xf 112
04211 Pichiriches, Los AL 170 Xe 126
33584 Pico, El AS 16 Ue 89
35468 Pico del Viento GC 184 Kc 180
15339 Picón C 10 Sb 86
13196 Picón CR 120 Vf 114
14298 Piconcillo CO 134 Ud 119
37256 Picones SA 63 Tc 102
36470 Picoña PO 41 Rc 96
23487 Picos del Guadiana J 153 Wf 122
15256 Picota, A C 10 Ra 91
32810 Picouto, O OR 42 Rf 95
30180 Pidal MC 156 Yb 120
25280 Pi de Sant Just, El L 57 Bd 97
39588 Pido CB 16 Vb 90
27207 Pidro LU 23 Sa 92
33439 Piedeloro AS 15 Ub 87
28510 Piedra MD 87 Wd 107
09125 Piedra, La BU 30 Wa 93
13100 Piedrabuena CR 120 Ve 114
33638 Piedraceda AS 15 Ua 90
41440 Piedra de la Sal SE 149 Uc 123
06460 Piedraescrita BA 118 Uc 115
45678 Piedraescrita TO 101 Vb 111
24838 Piedrafita LE 15 Uc 90
24141 Piedrafita de Babia LE 14 Te 91
22665 Piedrafita de Jaca HU 35 Ze 92
05500 Piedrahíta AV 83 Ue 106
44212 Piedrahíta TE 72 Yf 102
49143 Piedrahita de Castro ZA 46 Ub 98
09292 Piedrahita de Juarros BU 30 Wd 94
09613 Piedrahita de Muñó BU 49 We 96
13428 Piedralá CR 120 Vf 113
05440 Piedralaves AV 84 Vb 107
31219 Piedramillera NC 32 Xe 93
22807 Piedramorrera HU 53 Zb 95
33193 Piedramuelle AS 15 Ua 88
14950 Piedras, Las CO 167 Ve 124
10991 Piedras Albas CC 97 Ta 110
33450 Piedras Blancas AS 14 Ua 87
24123 Piedrasecha LE 27 Ub 92
34849 Piedrasluengas P 17 Vd 90
50616 Piedratajada Z 53 Zb 96
45700 Piedrola-Acebrón TO 121 Wb 112
14511 Piedros, Los CO 166 Vc 124
15593 Pieiro C 11 Re 88
32136 Pielas OR 23 Sa 93
08784 Piera B 76 Be 99
09246 Piérnigas BU 30 Wd 93
08781 Pierola B 76 Be 99
24547 Pieros LE 25 Tb 93
50320 Pietas Z 71 Yd 100
33900 Piezas, Las AS 15 Ub 89
36836 Pigarzos PO 23 Rd 94
33842 Pigüeña AS 14 Te 90
29210 Pilar, El MA 167 Vd 125
04648 Pilar de Jaravia AL 171 Yb 124
03190 Pilar de la Horadada A 157 Zb 121
07872 Pilar de la Mola, El IB 109 Bd 116
41770 Pilares SE 165 Uc 126
47300 Pilar y Fuensanta, La VA 48 Ve 99
39808 Pilas CB 18 Wd 89
41840 Pilas SE 163 Te 125
39793 Pilas, Las CB 18 Wc 88
18120 Pilas Dedil GR 167 Vf 126
43428 Piles, Les T 75 Bc 99
18512 Piletas, Las GR 169 Xa 125
04540 Piletas, Los AL 170 Xb 126
14950 Pililla, La CO 167 Vd 124
21450 Pilitas, Las H 161 Sf 124
33530 Piloña = Infiesto (Piloña) AS 15 Ud 88
17754 Pils, El GI 40 Da 94
22589 Pilzán HU 55 Ac 96
33590 Pimiango AS 17 Vc 88
28296 Pimpollar, El MD 85 Ve 105
07511 Pina IB 111 Cf 111
50750 Pina de Ebro Z 73 Zc 100
12429 Pina de Montalgrao CS 107 Zc 108
18658 Pinar, El GR 168 Wc 127
29620 Pinar, El MA 175 Vc 129
38914 Pinar, El TF 180 Ha 182
38780 Pinar, El TF 181 Ha 176
47153 Pinar, El VA 47 Vb 99
45900 Pinar de Almorox, El TO 85 Vd 107
03191 Pinar de Campoverde, El A 157 Zb 121
47152 Pinar del Esparragal VA 66 Vb 99
11130 Pinar de los Franceses CA 172 Tf 130
05291 Pinar de Puenteviejo AV 85 Vc 103
47130 Pinar de Simancas VA 47 Vb 99
16622 Pinarejo CU 104 Xd 111
40296 Pinarejos SG 67 Ve 101
04647 Pinares, Los AL 155 Yb 124
28935 Pinares Llanos MD 86 Wa 106
30170 Pinar Hermoso MC 156 Yc 121
40294 Pinarnegrillo SG 67 Ve 101
15296 Pindo, O C 22 Qf 91
43481 Pineda, La T 75 Bb 102
16541 Pineda de Gigüela CU 104 Xc 108
09199 Pineda de la Sierra BU 49 We 95
08397 Pineda de Mar B 59 Ce 99
37712 Pinedas SA 82 Ua 106
14111 Pinedas, Las CO 150 Va 122
09349 Pineda-Trasmonte BU 49 Wb 97
09345 Pinedillo BU 48 Wa 96
01427 Pinedo VI 31 Wf 91
43594 Pinell de Brai, El T 74 Ad 102
25286 Pinell de Solsonès L 57 Bc 97
18858 Pinelo GR 155 Xd 122
46838 Pinet V 126 Zd 115
03194 Pinet, El A 142 Zc 120
43459 Pinetell, El T 75 Ba 101
02310 Pinilla AB 123 Xc 116
02448 Pinilla AB 139 Xe 118
02512 Pinilla AB 141 Yc 116
30410 Pinilla MC 155 Ya 120
30335 Pinilla, La MC 156 Ye 122
40592 Pinilla, La SG 68 Wc 101
40122 Pinilla Ambroz SG 67 Vd 102
09342 Pinilla de Arlanza BU 48 Vf 96
28739 Pinilla de Buitrago MD 68 Wb 103
42162 Pinilla de Caradueña SO 51 Xd 97
49231 Pinilla de Fermoselle ZA 63 Td 100
19246 Pinilla de Jadraque GU 69 Xa 102
42112 Pinilla del Campo SO 51 Xf 98
42214 Pinilla del Olmo SO 69 Xc 101
09612 Pinilla de los Barruecos BU 49 We 97
09613 Pinilla de los Moros BU 49 We 96
28749 Pinilla del Valle MD 67 Wb 103
19312 Pinilla de Molina GU 89 Ya 104
49850 Pinilla de Toro ZA 46 Ud 99
09360 Pinilla-Trasmonte BU 49 Wc 97
30510 Pinillos MC 141 Yf 117
26111 Pinillos RI 50 Xc 95
09440 Pinillos de Esgueva BU 48 Wa 98
40397 Pinillos de Polendos SG 67 Vf 102
06228 Pino BA 133 Tf 117
27375 Pino LU 12 Sc 89
49514 Pino ZA 45 Tf 99
33687 Pino, El AS 15 Uc 90
10514 Pino, El CC 115 Se 113
15821 Pino, O C 11 Rd 91
28210 Pino Alto MD 85 Vf 105
09246 Pino de Bureba BU 30 Wd 92
34110 Pino del Río P 28 Vb 93
37170 Pino de Tormes, El SA 64 Ub 102
15238 Pino de Val C 22 Ra 91
34879 Pino de Viduerna P 28 Vb 92
10630 Pinofranqueado CC 82 Td 107
03720 Pinos A 143 Zf 116
24144 Pinos LE 14 Ua 91
25287 Pinós L 57 Bd 98

292 | Pelegrina

04288 Pinos, Los AL 171 Ya 125
10610 Pinos, Los CC 83 Ub 107
18810 Pinos, Los GR 154 Xb 124
21609 Pinos, Los H 161 Tb 123
30739 Pinos, Los MC 157 Za 121
35328 Pino Santo GC 184 Kc 180
18658 Pinos del Valle GR 168 Wc 127
18191 Pinos-Genil GR 168 Wc 126
03650 Pinoso A 141 Yf 118
28212 Pinosol MD 85 Vf 105
18240 Pinos-Puente GR 168 Wb 125
17466 Pins GI 59 Cf 96
43892 Pins de Miramar, El T 75 Af 102
50298 Pinseque Z 53 Yf 98
50694 Pinsoro Z 52 Yd 95
41370 Pintado, El SE 148 Ua 121
50685 Pintano Z 34 Yf 93
50685 Pintanos, Los Z 34 Yf 93
46249 Pintarrafes V 126 Zc 113
32648 Pintás OR 42 Sa 97
27619 Pintín LU 24 Sd 92
28320 Pinto MD 86 Wb 107
32720 Pinto, O OR 24 Sb 95
17179 Pinya, La GI 58 Cc 95
43786 Pinyeres T 74 Ab 102
32554 Pinza OR 43 Sf 96
36749 Pinzás PO 41 Rb 96
41728 Pinzón SE 164 Tf 126
15108 Piña, A C 11 Rc 89
34430 Piña de Campos P 48 Vd 95
47175 Piña de Esgueva VA 48 Vd 98
18568 Piñar GR 153 Wd 124
11391 Piñas, Las CA 173 Ub 132
27135 Piñeira LU 13 Se 90
27797 Piñeira LU 13 Sf 87
27559 Piñeira LU 24 Sb 92
27420 Piñeira LU 24 Sc 93
27680 Piñeira LU 25 Se 91
27318 Piñeira LU 25 Se 94
32693 Piñeira de Arcos OR 42 Sb 96
27833 Piñeiro LU 12 Sa 88
27547 Piñeiro LU 24 Sc 93
32453 Piñeiro OR 23 Rf 94
36193 Piñeiro PO 22 Rb 93
36913 Piñeiro PO 22 Rb 94
36677 Piñeiro PO 23 Rc 93
36739 Piñeiro PO 41 Rb 96
15128 Piñeiros C 10 Qf 90
15819 Piñeiros C 11 Rf 91
47316 Piñel de Abajo VA 48 Vf 98
47316 Piñel de Arriba VA 48 Vf 98
33719 Piñera AS 13 Tb 87
33392 Piñera AS 15 Ub 88
33528 Piñera AS 15 Uc 89
33161 Piñera, La AS 15 Ua 89
33629 Piñera de Abajo AS 15 Ua 90
33679 Piñeres AS 15 Ub 89
39580 Piñeres CB 17 Vc 89
49715 Piñero, El ZA 65 Uc 100
32137 Piñor OR 23 Rf 93
28737 Piñuécar-Gandullas MD 68 Wc 102
49216 Piñuel ZA 64 Tf 100
24916 Pío de Sajambre LE 16 Uf 90
24838 Piornedo LE 15 Uc 90
19162 Pioz GU 87 We 106
01118 Pipaón VI 31 Xc 93
26147 Pipaona RI 32 Xe 95
23268 Pipe, El J 138 Xa 118
42342 Piquera de San Esteban SO 68 We 99
19325 Piqueras GU 89 Yb 105
16118 Piqueras del Castillo CU 105 Xf 110
27245 Piquín LU 13 Se 89
43423 Pira T 75 Bb 100
22268 Piracés HU 54 Ze 96
34858 Pisón de Castrejón P 28 Vc 92
34485 Pisón de Ojeda P 29 Vd 92
39696 Pisueña CB 18 Wb 89
37490 Pitiegua SA 65 Ud 102
31392 Pitillas NC 33 Yc 94
18414 Pitres GR 169 Wd 127
27470 Piuca LU 24 Sb 94
32708 Piúca ou Araúxo OR 24 Sb 95
28521 Piul, El MD 86 Wd 106
33326 Pivierda AS 15 Ud 88
29560 Pizarra MA 166 Vb 128
06240 Pizarral BA 133 Te 119
37795 Pizarral SA 83 Uc 105
28210 Pizarrera, La MD 85 Vf 105
10134 Pizarro CC 118 Ub 114
13344 Pizorro del Cañete CR 138 Wf 117
29314 Plácidos, Los MA 167 Ve 126
32785 Placín OR 25 Se 95
25114 Pla de la Font, El L 55 Ac 98
03690 Pla de l'Olivera Alta A 142 Zc 118
08733 Pla del Penedès, El B 76 Be 100
08458 Pla del Remei, El B 58 Cc 98
17869 Pla dels Hospitalets GI 39 Cb 94
43815 Pla de Manelleu, El T 76 Bd 100
07009 Pla de Na Tosa IB 110 Ce 111
25570 Pla de Negua L 37 Bb 93
08719 Plá de Rubió, El B 57 Bd 99
12163 Pla de Sabater CS 92 Zf 107
43810 Pla de Santa Maria, El T 76 Bb 100
25796 Pla de Sant Tirs, El L 37 Bc 95
07579 Plà d'es Caló, Es IB 111 Db 110
09212 Plágaro BU 31 We 92
22367 Plan HU 36 Ab 93
08610 Plana, La B 57 Bf 96
17179 Plana, La GI 58 Cc 95
44563 Planas, Las TE 91 Ze 104
25748 Plandogau L 56 Bb 97
03828 Planes A 143 Zd 116
08017 Planes, Les B 77 Ca 100
43739 Planes, Les T 75 Ae 101
17172 Planes d'Hostoles, Les GI 58 Cd 96
50785 Planico, El Z 73 Zd 100
22371 Planillo HU 35 Zf 94
22338 Plano, El HU 36 Ab 94
12232 Plano de Arriba, El CS 107 Zd 108
12125 Plano de Herrera, El CS 107 Zd 108
17535 Planoles GI 39 Ca 95
AD100 Plans, Els ◘ AND 38 Bd 94
25212 Plans de Sió, Els L 56 Bb 98
47350 Planta, La VA 48 Vc 99
46520 Planta Siderúrgica V 108 Ze 111
28221 Plantío, El MD 86 Wa 106
18439 Plantonada, La GR 169 We 127
10600 Plasencia CC 98 Tf 108
50296 Plasencia de Jalón Z 53 Ye 98
22810 Plasencia del Monte HU 54 Zc 95
10271 Plasenzuela CC 117 Tf 112
35290 Plata, La GC 184 Kc 181
30890 Plata y Los Palanquines MC 156 Yb 123
23293 Platera, La J 139 Xb 119
12592 Platja, la CS 108 Zf 110
07400 Platja d'Alcúdia IB 111 Da 110
43820 Platja de Calafell, La T 76 Bd 101
17490 Platja de Grifeu GI 40 Da 94
46139 Platja de la Pobla de Farnals V 108 Ze 111
46712 Platja de la Torre de Piles, La V 127 Zf 115
12594 Platja de les Amplàries CS 108 Aa 108
12579 Platja de les Fonts CS 92 Ab 107
03710 Platja del Port A 143 Aa 117
46012 Platja del Recatí V 127 Ze 113
43892 Platja de Miami, La T 75 Af 102
12520 Platja de Nules CS 108 Zf 110
46530 Platja de Puçol, La V 108 Ze 111
03540 Platja de Sant Joan, La A 142 Zd 118
46770 Platja de Xeraco V 127 Ze 114
46780 Platja d'Oliva V 127 Zf 115
07819 Platja Talamanca IB 109 Bc 115
07440 Platjes de Mallorca IB 111 Da 110
41400 Platosa SE 150 Ue 123
41620 Platosa, La SE 165 Ue 124
35580 Playa Blanca GC 182 Mb 175
04149 Playa de Agua Amarga AL 171 Ya 127
35128 Playa de Arguineguín, La GC 184 Kb 182
48993 Playa de Azkorri BI 19 Wf 88
45910 Playa de Escalona TO 101 Vd 108
21409 Playa de Isla Canela H 160 Sd 125
04002 Playa de La Garrofa AL 170 Xc 128
48360 Playa de Laida BI 19 Xb 88
Playa de la Pinada A 142 Zc 120
38650 Playa de las Américas TF 180 Ib 180
04116 Playa de Las Negras AL 171 Xf 127
35214 Playa del Hombre GC 184 Kd 181
21410 Playa del Hoyo H 161 Se 125
35100 Playa del Inglés GC 184 Kc 182
30366 Playa de los Nietos MC 157 Zb 122
30380 Playa del Pedrucho MC 157 Zb 122
39547 Playa de Merón CB 17 Vd 88
35138 Playa de Mogan, La GC 184 Kb 182
39780 Playa de Oriñón CB 18 We 88
33716 Playa de Ortiguera AS 13 Tb 87
33598 Playa de Pendueles AS 16 Vc 88
33405 Playa de Salinas AS 15 Ua 87
38813 Playa de Santiago TF 184 He 180
35138 Playa de Tauro, La GC 184 Kb 182
04149 Playa de Torre Vieja AL 171 Ya 127
33345 Playa de Vega AS 16 Uf 88
35138 Playa de Veneguera, La GC 184 Kb 181
33418 Playa de Xago AS 15 Ua 87
18613 Playa Granada GR 168 Wc 128
30385 Playa Honda MC 157 Zb 123
38779 Playa Nueva TF 181 Ha 177
35570 Playa Quemada GC 182 Mb 175
35629 Playas, Las GC 183 Ma 179
03189 Playas de Orihuela A 157 Zb 121
04740 Playa Serena AL 170 Xc 128
33111 Plaza, La AS 14 Tf 90
48276 Plazakola BI 20 Xd 89
50297 Pleitas Z 53 Ye 98
50143 Plenas Z 72 Za 102
48620 Plentzia BI 19 Xa 88
30176 Pliego MC 156 Yc 121
23749 Plomeros J 137 Wa 120
44213 Plou TE 72 Za 103
09452 Plumarejos BU 49 Wd 97
33691 Poago AS 15 Ub 87
08243 Poal, El B 57 Be 98
25143 Poal, El L 56 Af 98
32136 Pobadura OR 23 Sa 93
42181 Pobar SO 51 Xe 97
25512 Pobella L 37 Af 94
48550 Pobeña BI 19 Wf 88
01420 Pobes VI 31 Xa 92
25177 Pobla, La L 75 Ae 100
13195 Poblachuela, La CR 121 Wa 115
39294 Población, La CB 17 Wa 90
39230 Población de Abajo CB 29 Wa 91
39230 Población de Arriba CB 29 Wa 91
34347 Población de Arroyo P 28 Va 94
34449 Población de Campos P 29 Vd 95
34219 Población de Cerrato P 48 Vd 98
34128 Población de Soto P 28 Vc 94
12313 Pobla d'Alcolea, La CS 92 Zf 104
12599 Pobla de Benifassà, La CS 92 Aa 105
43429 Pobla de Carivenys, La T 76 Bc 99
25471 Pobla de Cérvoles, La L 75 Af 100
08787 Pobla de Claramunt, La B 76 Be 99
46137 Pobla de Farnals, La V 108 Ze 111
43425 Pobla de Ferran, La T 75 Bb 99
12150 Pobla del Bellestar, La CS 91 Ze 106
08696 Pobla de Lillet, La B 58 Bf 95
43140 Pobla de Mafumet, La T 75 Bb 101
43783 Pobla de Massaluca, La T 74 Ac 101
43761 Pobla de Montornès, La T 76 Bc 101
27360 Pobla de San Xulián LU 24 Sd 91
25500 Pobla de Segur, La L 56 Af 95
46185 Pobla de Vallbona, La V 107 Zc 111
10591 Poblado de Embalse CC 99 Ua 109
46317 Poblado del Embalse V 106 Yd 111
28339 Poblado Nuevo MD 86 Wc 107
49522 Pobladura de Aliste ZA 45 Te 97
24121 Pobladura de Bernesga LE 27 Uc 93
24250 Pobladura de Fontecha LE 27 Uc 94
24375 Pobladura de la Reguera LE 26 Te 92
24724 Pobladura de la Sierra LE 26 Td 94
24223 Pobladura de los Oteros LE 27 Ud 94
49780 Pobladura del Valle ZA 46 Ub 96
24249 Pobladura de Pelayo García LE 27 Ub 95
24512 Pobladura de Somoza LE 25 Tb 93
47881 Pobladura de Sotiedra VA 46 Ue 99
49127 Pobladura de Valderaduey ZA 46 Uc 98
46670 Pobla Llarga, la = Puebla Larga, la V 126 Zd 114
12191 Pobla Tornesa, La CS 108 Zf 108
03726 Poble Nou de Benitatxell, el = Benitachell A 143 Aa 116
43549 Poblenou del Delta, El T 93 Ae 105
03818 Poble Nou de Sant Rafael, El A 142 Zd 116
43815 Pobles, Les T 76 Bc 100
46162 Pobleta de Andilla, La V 107 Zb 109
25513 Pobleta de Bellveí, La L 37 Af 94
13195 Poblete CR 121 Wa 115
03779 Poblets, El A 127 Aa 115
46880 Poblets dels Ferrers, Els V 142 Zc 116
44155 Pobo, El TE 91 Za 105
19326 Pobo de Dueñas, El GU 89 Yc 104
43376 Poboleda T 75 Af 101
32780 Pobra de Trives, A OR 25 Se 94
27330 Pobra do Brollón = Puebla de Brollón LU 24 Sd 93
15940 Pobra do Caramiñal, A C 22 Ra 93
06130 Pocacivera BA 132 Sf 116
08471 Pocafarina B 58 Cd 99
17178 Pocafarina GI 58 Cc 96
04813 Pocicas, Las AL 155 Xf 124
30890 Pocicas, Las MC 156 Yb 123
04279 Pocico, El AL 171 Xe 126
04271 Pocico, El AL 171 Xf 125
18512 Pocico, El GR 169 Xa 125
02129 Pocicos, Los AB 140 Ya 116
22337 Pocino, El HU 36 Ab 94
21540 Pocitos, Los H 146 Sf 124
33718 Pojos AS 13 Tb 88
15338 Pol C 10 Sa 87
27279 Pol LU 12 Sd 90
27686 Pol LU 24 Se 91
32766 Pola OR 24 Sd 94
33993 Pola, La AS 15 Ud 89
39557 Polaciones CB 17 Vd 90
33880 Pola de Allande AS 13 Tc 89
24600 Pola de Gordón, La LE 27 Ub 91
33980 Pola de Laviana AS 15 Uc 89
33630 Pola de Lena AS 15 Ub 90
33510 Pola de Siero AS 15 Uc 88
33840 Pola de Somiedo AS 14 Te 90
45161 Polán TO 101 Vf 110
34846 Polentinos P 17 Vc 91
22216 Poleñino HU 54 Ze 97
18516 Policar GR 169 We 125
33456 Polide AS 14 Tf 87
39250 Polientes BU 29 Wa 92
25747 Polig L 56 Bb 97
45007 Polígono de Santa María de Benquerencia TO 102 Wa 109
08213 Polinyà B 77 Ca 99
46688 Polinyà de Xúquer V 126 Zd 113
22665 Polituara HU 35 Ze 92
07469 Pollença IB 111 Da 109
47116 Pollos VA 65 Uf 100
07210 Polo IB 111 Cf 111
03520 Polop A 143 Zf 117
02500 Polope AB 140 Yb 117
04114 Polopos AL 171 Xf 126
18710 Polopos GR 169 We 128
23293 Polvillar J 139 Xb 119
24995 Polvoredo LE 16 Uf 90
11370 Polvorilla, La CA 173 Uc 131
11320 Polvorín, El CA 173 Ud 130
34473 Polvorosa de Valdavia P 28 Vc 93
39660 Pomaluengo CB 18 Wa 89
09513 Pomar BU 18 Wd 91
22413 Pomar de Cinca HU 55 Aa 97
34813 Pomar de Valdivia P 29 Ve 92
03669 Pomares A 142 Za 118
27470 Pombeiro LU 24 Sb 94
24389 Pombriego LE 25 Tb 94
50259 Pomer Z 52 Ya 99
22196 Pompenillo HU 54 Zd 96
17746 Pompià GI 59 Ce 95
18770 Pómpolos, Los GR 169 Wf 128
43860 Ponç T 75 Ae 103
28492 Ponderosa, La MD 85 Wa 104
39809 Pondra CB 18 Wd 89
24400 Ponferrada LE 25 Tc 93
33557 Ponga AS 16 Uf 89
24127 Ponjos LE 26 Tf 92
07500 Pon Nou, Es IB 111 Da 111
07209 Pon Nou des Frares IB 111 Da 112
25740 Pons = Ponts L 56 Bb 97
25739 Pont D'Alentorn, El L 56 Ba 97
43817 Pont d'Armentera, El T 76 Bc 100
25517 Pont de Claverol, El L 56 Af 95
17706 Pont de Molins GI 40 Cf 95
25520 Pont de Suert, El L 37 Ae 94
08254 Pont de Vilomara, El B 57 Bf 98
08254 Pont de Vilomara i Rocafort, El B 57 Bf 98
36853 Ponte PO 23 Rd 94
32365 Ponte, A OR 44 Ta 95
15317 Ponte Aranga C 11 Sa 89
36860 Ponteareas PO 41 Rc 95
32229 Ponte Barxas OR 42 Re 96
36820 Pontecaldelas PO 23 Rc 94
15688 Ponte Carreira C 11 Rd 90
32430 Ponte Castrelo OR 23 Rf 95
15110 Ponteceso C 10 Ra 89
36649 Pontecesures PO 22 Rc 92
15600 Pontedeume C 11 Re 88
32235 Pontedeva OR 42 Rf 96
15510 Ponte de Xubia C 11 Rf 87
24838 Pontedo LE 15 Uc 91
15121 Ponte do Porto C 10 Qf 90
49191 Pontejos ZA 64 Ub 100
36412 Pontellas PO 41 Rc 96
15864 Ponte Maceira C 22 Rb 91
15340 Ponte Mera C 10 Sa 86
15211 Ponte Nafonso C 22 Ra 92
27720 Pontenova, A LU 13 Se 88
15683 Pontepedra C 11 Rc 90
36690 Ponte Sampaio PO 22 Rc 94
15320 Pontes de García Rodríguez, As C 12 Sa 88
15880 Ponte-Ulla C 23 Rd 92
15883 Pontevea C 23 Rc 92
36001 Pontevedra PO 22 Rc 94
45002 Pontezuelas, Las TO 102 Vf 109
43421 Pontils T 76 Bc 100
48192 Ponton, El BI 19 Wf 89
46357 Pontón, El V 106 Yf 112
23291 Pontón Alto J 139 Xb 120
39793 Pontones CB 18 Wb 88
23291 Pontones J 139 Xb 120
08738 Pontons B 76 Bd 100
33509 Póo AS 16 Vb 88
24511 Porcarizas LE 25 Tb 92
33392 Porceyo AS 15 Ub 87
33878 Porciles AS 14 Tc 89
18820 Porcuna GR 154 Xd 121
23790 Porcuna J 152 Ve 121
38588 Porís de Abona TF 181 Id 180
33819 Porley AS 14 Td 89
32643 Porqueira OR 42 Sa 96
37216 Porquera, La SA 64 Te 103
09551 Porquera del Butrón BU 30 Wb 92
34813 Porquera de los Infantes P 29 Ve 92
17834 Porqueres GI 59 Ce 96
37130 Porqueriza SA 64 Ua 103
11180 Porquerizas CA 173 Ub 130
39727 Porquerizas, Las CB 18 Wb 89
24397 Porqueros LE 26 Tf 93
07181 Porrasa, La IB 110 Cd 112
43739 Porrera T 75 Af 101
07260 Porreres IB 111 Da 111
14549 Porretal, El CO 150 Va 123
36400 Porriño, O PO 41 Rc 96
07839 Porroig IB 109 Bb 115
23239 Porrosillo J 137 Wd 119
33509 Porrúa AS 16 Vb 88
07815 Port, Es IB 109 Bc 114
07811 Port, Es IB 109 Bd 114
07690 Port, Es IB 110 Cf 114
46012 Porta del Sol V 127 Ze 113
25594 Port Ainé L 37 Bb 94
10883 Portaje CC 98 Tc 109
11408 Portal, El CA 172 Tf 129
29160 Portales MA 167 Vd 127
44730 Portalrubio TE 90 Yf 104
16522 Portalrubio de Guadamajud CU 88 Xc 107
07181 Portals Nous IB 110 Cd 111
07181 Portals Vells IB 110 Cd 112
32101 Portamieiro OR 24 Sa 94
36658 Portas PO 22 Rc 93
50810 Portazgo Z 53 Zb 97
49660 Portazgo, El ZA 46 Uc 97
06230 Portazgo o San Antonio BA 133 Td 118
12598 Port Blau, El CS 93 Ac 106
17497 Port-Bou = Portbou GI 40 Da 94
07740 Port d'Addaia IB 77 Eb 108
07400 Port d'Alcúdia IB 111 Da 110
07157 Port d'Andratx IB 110 Cc 111
12530 Port de Borriana, El CS 108 Zf 109
07191 Port de Canonge IB 110 Cd 110
43569 Port de Cementos del Mar, El T 93 Ad 105
17489 Port de la Selva, El GI 40 Db 94
08392 Port del Balís, El B 77 Cd 99
25283 Port del Comte L 57 Bd 96
17490 Port de Llançà, El GI 40 Da 94
AD200 Port d'Envalira ◘ AND 38 Be 93

Port d'Envalira | 293

07470 Port de Pollença IB 111 Da 109
46520 Port de Sagunt, El V 108 Ze 111
07108 Port de Sóller IB 110 Ce 110
07829 Port d'es Torrent IB 109 Bb 115
07170 Port de Valldemossa IB 110 Cd 110
36677 Portela PO 23 Rc 92
15819 Portela, A C 23 Rf 91
36939 Portela, A PO 22 Rb 95
24524 Portela, La LE 25 Ta 92
32549 Portela da Canda OR 44 Ta 96
24569 Portela de Aguiar LE 25 Ta 93
36568 Portela de Lamas PO 23 Re 93
32337 Portela do Trigal OR 25 Ta 94
42167 Portelárbol SO 51 Xd 97
25216 Portell L 57 Bc 98
25134 Portella, La L 55 Ad 98
44589 Portellada, La TE 92 Aa 103
12318 Portell de Morella CS 92 Ze 105
24525 Portelo, El LE 25 Ta 92
42162 Portelrubio SO 51 Xd 97
46357 Portera, La V 125 Yf 112
06175 Portero, El BA 132 Tc 118
37170 Porteros SA 64 Ua 103
37530 Porteros SA 82 Td 106
04887 Porteros, Los AL 170 Xd 124
10828 Portezuelo CC 98 Td 110
16141 Portilla CU 89 Xf 107
01212 Portilla VI 31 Xa 92
04619 Portilla, La AL 171 Ya 125
24913 Portilla de la Reina LE 16 Va 90
24149 Portilla de Luna LE 27 Ub 92
34114 Portillejo P 28 Vc 94
37891 Portillo SA 83 Uc 104
47160 Portillo VA 66 Vc 100
42138 Portillo de Soria SO 51 Xf 99
45512 Portillo de Toledo TO 101 Ve 108
07820 Portinatx IB 109 Bd 114
30510 Portishuelo MC 141 Yf 117
30364 Portman MC 157 Za 123
36685 Porto PO 23 Rd 92
36458 Porto PO 41 Rc 96
49583 Porto ZA 44 Ta 95
32357 Porto, O OR 25 Ta 94
15214 Portobravo C 22 Ra 92
32626 Portocamba OR 43 Sd 96
04550 Portocarrero AL 170 Xc 125
15684 Portociños C 11 Rc 90
07670 Portocolom IB 111 Db 112
15969 Porto-Corrubedo C 22 Qf 93
07680 Portocristo IB 111 Dc 111
07680 Portocristo Novo IB 111 Db 111
27712 Porto de Abaixo LU 13 Sf 88
15337 Porto de Bares LU 10 Sb 86
15339 Porto de Espasante C 10 Sb 86
36599 Portodemouros PO 23 Re 91
15970 Porto do Son C 22 Qf 92
07141 Portòl IB 110 Ce 111
27188 Portomarín LU 24 Sc 92
15871 Portomeiro C 11 Rc 91
32371 Portomourisco OR 25 Sf 94
15871 Portomouro C 10 Rc 91
36970 Portonovo PO 22 Ra 94
07691 Portopetro IB 111 Db 112
15999 Portosín C 22 Ra 92
29712 Portugalejo MA 167 Vf 127
48920 Portugalete BI 19 Wf 89
18415 Pórtugos GR 169 We 127
30393 Portús MC 157 Yf 123
45161 Portusa TO 101 Ve 109
14209 Porvenir de la Industria CO 134 Ue 119
33778 Porzún AS 13 Sf 88
13120 Porzuna CR 120 Vf 114
33424 Posada AS 15 Ua 88
33594 Posada AS 16 Va 88
14900 Posada de Flores CO 167 Vd 124
46780 Posada de Sant Jaume, La V 127 Zf 115
24915 Posada de Valdeón LE 16 Va 90
14730 Posadas CO 150 Uf 122
26289 Posadas RI 50 Wf 95
23520 Posadas Ricas J 152 Wc 121
24766 Posada y Torre LE 26 Tf 95
14248 Posadilla CO 134 Ue 119
24795 Posadilla de la Vega LE 26 Ua 94
41659 Postero SE 166 Uf 126
35149 Postreragua de Veneguera, La GC 184 Kb 181
39570 Potes CB 17 Vc 90
02139 Potiche AB 140 Xe 117
46721 Potríes V 127 Ze 115
03698 Poublanc A 142 Zb 118
46870 Pou Clar V 126 Zc 116
07530 Pou Colomer Vell IB 111 Db 110
12118 Pou d'En Calbo, El CS 108 Zf 108
32212 Poulo OR 42 Rf 95
27332 Pousa LU 24 Sd 93
27246 Pousada LU 12 Sd 89
27680 Pousada LU 24 Se 91
32611 Pousada OR 43 Se 97
15996 Pouscarro C 22 Ra 92
27233 Poutomillos LU 12 Sc 91
05560 Poveda AV 84 Uf 105
28630 Poveda, La MD 85 Ve 107
28500 Poveda, La MD 86 Wd 107
16195 Poveda de la Obispalía CU 104 Xd 109
37406 Poveda de las Cintas SA 65 Ue 102
19463 Poveda de la Sierra GU 89 Xf 105
42169 Póveda de Soria, La SO 51 Xc 96
02311 Povedilla AB 139 Xc 116
13428 Povedillas, Las CR 120 Vf 113
32172 Povoanza OR 23 Sa 94
05592 Poyal, El AV 83 Ud 106
26586 Poyales RI 51 Xe 96
05492 Poyales del Hoyo AV 100 Uf 107
14817 Poyata, La CO 167 Ve 124
38829 Poyatas, Las TF 184 He 180
23250 Poyato J 138 We 119
16878 Poyatos CU 89 Xf 106
49524 Poyo, El ZA 45 Td 98
44392 Poyo del Cid, El TE 71 Ye 103
02534 Poyos, Los AB 139 Xd 120
23296 Poyos, Los J 139 Xc 119
23160 Poyos, Los J 152 Wa 122
23291 Poyotello J 139 Xc 120
09246 Poza de la Sal BU 30 Wd 93
34111 Poza de la Vega P 28 Vb 93
47450 Pozal de Gallinas VA 66 Va 101
47220 Pozaldes VA 66 Va 100
42112 Pozalmuro SO 51 Xf 98
05292 Pozanco AV 84 Vb 104
19265 Pozancos GU 69 Xb 102
34492 Pozancos P 29 Ve 92
22313 Pozán de Vero HU 54 Aa 96
35630 Pozetas, Las GC 183 Lf 178
23485 Pozo Alcón J 154 Xa 122
30739 Pozo Aledo MC 157 Za 122
16708 Pozoamargo CU 123 Xe 112
49835 Pozoantiguo ZA 46 Ud 99
14400 Pozoblanco CO 135 Va 118
02510 Pozo Bueno AB 124 Yb 116
06120 Pozo Campo BA 132 Sf 119
02510 Pozo-Cañada AB 124 Yb 116
06192 Pozo Cortijo BA 116 Tb 114
02460 Pozo de Abajo AB 139 Xc 118
19112 Pozo de Almoguera GU 87 Wf 106
19161 Pozo de Guadalajara GU 87 We 106
02650 Pozo de la Higuera AB 125 Ye 116
04647 Pozo de la Higuera AL 156 Yb 124
02520 Pozo de la Peña AB 124 Yb 115
18858 Pozo de la Rueda GR 155 Xe 122
38912 Pozo de la Salud TF 180 Gf 182
13390 Pozo de la Serna CR 122 We 116
21420 Pozo del Camino H 161 Se 125
04117 Pozo del Captián, El AL 171 Xf 127
04648 Pozo del Esparto AL 171 Yb 124
04887 Pozo del Lobo AL 154 Xc 124
04118 Pozo de los Frailes, El AL 171 Xf 128
30391 Pozo de los Palos MC 157 Yf 123
34347 Pozo de Urama P 47 Va 95
30594 Pozo Estrecho MC 157 Za 122
02141 Pozohondo AB 140 Ya 116
18891 Pozo Iglesias GR 154 Xc 124
02154 Pozo-Lorente AB 125 Yc 114
44480 Pozo Muela y Puntalico TE 107 Zb 108
33875 Pozón AS 14 Td 89
44368 Pozondón TE 90 Yd 105
47800 Pozo Pedro VA 47 Uf 97
16212 Pozorrubielos de la Mancha CU 124 Xf 112
16414 Pozorrubio de Santiago CU 103 Xa 110
24738 Pozos LE 26 Te 95
23591 Pozos, Los J 153 We 122
37216 Pozos de Hinojo SA 63 Td 103
06442 Pozos de la Fuente Santa BA 133 Ua 117
37170 Pozos de Mondar SA 64 Ua 103
16212 Pozoseco CU 105 Ya 112
04149 Pozo Usero, El AL 171 Xf 127
42220 Pozuel de Ariza Z 70 Xf 100
44315 Pozuel del Campo TE 90 Yc 104
02327 Pozuelo AB 124 Xf 116
02125 Pozuelo AB 140 Xf 117
30510 Pozuelo MC 141 Ye 117
31395 Pozuelo NC 33 Yc 93
42311 Pozuelo SO 69 Wf 100
16812 Pozuelo, El CU 88 Xe 105
18770 Pozuelo, El GR 169 Wf 128
21647 Pozuelo, El H 147 Tb 123
28223 Pozuelo de Alarcón MD 86 Wb 106
50529 Pozuelo de Aragón Z 52 Yd 98
13179 Pozuelo de Calatrava CR 121 Wa 115
47831 Pozuelo de la Orden VA 46 Ue 98
24796 Pozuelo del Páramo LE 45 Ub 95
28813 Pozuelo del Rey MD 87 We 106
49148 Pozuelo de Tábara ZA 45 Ua 98
49621 Pozuelo de Vidriales ZA 45 Ua 96
10813 Pozuelo de Zarzón CC 98 Td 108
02640 Pozuelos, Los AB 125 Ye 116
13191 Pozuelos de Calatrava, Los CR 120 Ve 115
34349 Pozuelos del Rey P 28 Va 95
33889 Prada AS 13 Tc 89
32368 Prada OR 25 Sf 95
32782 Prada OR 43 Se 95
09212 Prada, La BU 30 We 91
24722 Prada de la Sierra LE 26 Td 94
24915 Prada de Valdeón LE 16 Va 90
27277 Pradairo LU 13 Se 90
40540 Pradales SG 68 Wb 100
09248 Prádanos de Bureba BU 30 Wd 93
09126 Prádanos del Tozo BU 29 Wa 92
34486 Prádanos de Ojeda P 29 Vd 92
27210 Pradeda LU 24 Sc 91
26510 Pradejón RI 32 Xf 95
24523 Pradela LE 25 Ta 93
43774 Pradell T 75 Af 102
43774 Pradell de la Teixeta T 75 Af 102
25316 Pradell de Sió L 56 Ba 98
40165 Prádena SG 68 Wb 102
19243 Prádena de Atienza GU 69 Wf 101
28191 Prádena del Rincón MD 68 Wc 102
40165 Pradenilla SG 68 Wb 102
40100 Pradera de Navalhorno SG 86 Vf 103
43364 Prades T 75 Af 101
08281 Prades de la Molosa L 57 Bd 98
17844 Prades del Terri GI 59 Ce 96
19391 Pradilla GU 89 Yb 104
09267 Pradilla de Belorado BU 31 Wf 95
50668 Pradilla de Ebro Z 52 Ye 97
26122 Pradillo RI 50 Xc 95
16150 Pradillos, Los CU 89 Ya 105
33344 Prado AS 16 Ue 88
27235 Prado LU 12 Sb 90
32890 Prado OR 24 Sa 95
32898 Prado OR 42 Sa 97
32702 Prado OR 43 Sc 96
36512 Prado PO 23 Re 92
36873 Prado PO 23 Re 95
36895 Prado PO 41 Rc 95
49638 Prado ZA 46 Ud 97
04500 Prado, El AL 169 Xb 125
04860 Prado, El AL 170 Xe 124
30180 Prado, El MC 156 Yc 120
32552 Pradoalvar OR 43 Se 95
32560 Pradocabalos OR 43 Sf 96
10671 Pradochano CC 98 Te 108
24893 Prado de la Guzpeña LE 28 Uf 92
02534 Prado de las Yeguas AB 139 Xd 120
02139 Prado del Caño, El AB 139 Xe 117
11660 Prado del Rey CA 165 Uc 128
24512 Prado de Paradiña LE 25 Tb 92
28223 Prado de Somosaguas MD 86 Wb 106
06980 Prado Gil BA 148 Ua 120
09515 Pradolamata BU 30 Wd 91
28223 Prado Largo MD 86 Wa 106
32368 Pradolongo OR 43 Sf 95
09260 Pradoluengo BU 31 We 95
18183 Prado Negro GR 168 Wd 125
02536 Prado Redondo AB 139 Xd 119
32558 Pradorramisquedo OR 44 Ta 96
02161 Pradorredondo AB 123 Xe 115
24714 Pradorrey LE 26 Tf 94
40400 Prados SG 85 Ve 104
14800 Prados, Los CO 152 Ve 124
23391 Prados, Los J 139 Xb 118
30413 Prados, Los MC 139 Xe 120
30410 Prados, Los MC 155 Ya 120
23289 Prados de Armijo J 138 Xa 119
02534 Prados de Arriba, Los AB 139 Xd 120
05560 Pradosegar AV 84 Uf 105
19352 Prados Redondos GU 89 Yb 104
14820 Prágdena CO 151 Vd 122
36390 Praia de Canido PO 41 Rb 95
39697 Prases CB 17 Wa 89
43595 Prat de Comte T 74 Ac 103
08140 Prat de Dalt, El B 58 Ca 99
08820 Prat de Llobregat, El B 77 Ca 101
43320 Pratdip T 75 Af 102
25721 Prats L 38 Bf 94
25793 Prats L 56 Bb 95
08513 Prats de Lluçanès B 58 Ca 96
08281 Prats de Rei, Els B 57 Bd 98
25721 Prats i Sansor L 38 Be 94
39730 Praves CB 18 Wc 88
33120 Pravia AS 14 Tf 88
25263 Preixana L 56 Ba 99
25316 Preixens L 56 Ba 98
26589 Préjano RI 51 Xe 95
33728 Prelo AS 13 Tc 88
08330 Premià de Mar B 77 Cc 100
33190 Premoño AS 14 Ua 88
43400 Prenafeta T 75 Bb 100
25214 Prenyanosa, La L 56 Bb 98
48891 Presa BI 18 Wd 89
21359 Presa, La H 147 Tb 121
37176 Presa de Almendra SA 63 Te 101
28754 Presa del Villar MD 68 Wc 103
28754 Presa de Puentes Viejas MD 68 Wc 103
15807 Présaras C 11 Rf 90
10191 Prescribanillos CC 98 Td 111
15318 Presedo C 11 Re 89
09228 Presencio BU 48 Wa 95
17178 Preses, Les GI 58 Cc 96
09585 Presilla, La BU 19 We 90
09233 Presillas BU 30 Wa 91
39679 Presillas, Las CB 17 Wa 89
04118 Presillas Bajas, Las AL 171 Xf 128
03569 Preventorio A 142 Zd 117
32418 Prexigueiro OR 23 Re 95
32793 Prexiguieros OR 24 Sb 94
24721 Priaranza de la Valduerna LE 26 Te 94
24448 Priaranza del Bierzo LE 25 Tb 93
33584 Priede AS 16 Ue 88
16800 Priego CU 88 Xe 106
14815 Priego de Córdoba CO 152 Ve 124
36350 Priegue PO 41 Rb 96
33867 Priero AS 14 Te 88
33317 Priesca AS 15 Ud 88
33557 Priesca AS 16 Ue 89
33196 Prietos, Los AS 15 Ub 88
24856 Primajas LE 28 Ue 91
45910 Prime TO 101 Vd 108
24457 Primout LE 26 Td 92
51002 Príncipe Alfonso CE 175 Ud 133
06280 Prior BA 147 Tc 120
41440 Priorato, El SE 149 Ud 122
33193 Priorio AS 15 Ua 88
24885 Prioro LE 28 Va 91
14540 Privilegio, El CO 150 Vb 123
15146 Proame C 10 Rc 89
39210 Proaño CB 17 Ve 90
33114 Proaza AS 14 Tf 89
27113 Proba de Burón, A LU 13 Sf 90
27460 Proendos LU 24 Sc 94
32611 Progo OR 43 Se 97
16670 Provencio, El CU 123 Xc 112
46117 Providència, La V 107 Zd 111
30811 Provincias y La Jarosa, Las MC 155 Yb 123
08569 Pruit B 58 Cc 96
25727 Prullans L 38 Be 94
41670 Pruna SE 165 Ue 127
33423 Pruvia AS 15 Ub 88
17120 Púbol GI 59 Cf 96
46530 Puçol V 108 Ze 111
13195 Puebla CR 121 Wa 115
27658 Puebla LU 13 Sf 91
30395 Puebla, La MC 157 Za 122
50137 Puebla de Albortón Z 72 Za 100
06630 Puebla de Alcocer BA 118 Ue 115
06717 Puebla de Alcollarín BA 118 Ub 114
50171 Puebla de Alfindén Z 53 Zb 99
45840 Puebla de Almoradiel, La TO 103 Wf 111
12428 Puebla de Arenoso CS 107 Zc 108
09294 Puebla de Arganzón, La BU 31 Xa 92
10811 Puebla de Argeme CC 98 Td 109
37553 Puebla de Azaba SA 81 Tb 106
19229 Puebla de Beleña GU 68 We 103
22435 Puebla de Castro, La HU 55 Ab 96
41540 Puebla de Cazalla, La SE 165 Ue 125
18820 Puebla de Don Fadrique GR 154 Xd 121
13109 Puebla de Don Rodrigo CR 119 Vc 114
42222 Puebla de Eca SO 70 Xd 100
22437 Puebla de Fantova, La HU 36 Ac 95
21550 Puebla de Guzmán H 146 Se 123
44510 Puebla de Híjar, La TE 73 Zd 101
06490 Puebla de la Calzada BA 116 Tc 115
06477 Puebla de la Reina BA 133 Tf 116
28190 Puebla de la Sierra MD 68 Wd 102
24855 Puebla de Lillo LE 16 Ue 90
06906 Puebla del Maestre BA 148 Tf 120
22588 Puebla del Mon, La HU 55 Ac 96
41479 Puebla de los Infantes, La SE 149 Ud 122
13342 Puebla del Príncipe CR 138 Xa 117
06229 Puebla del Prior BA 133 Te 117
41130 Puebla del Río, La SE 163 Tf 125
16269 Puebla del Salvador CU 105 Yb 111
45516 Puebla de Montalbán, La TO 101 Vd 109
30193 Puebla de Mula, La MC 156 Yd 120
10392 Puebla de Naciados CC 100 Ue 109
06191 Puebla de Obando BA 116 Tc 113
27388 Puebla de Parga LU 12 Sa 90
40184 Puebla de Pedraza SG 67 Wa 101
03159 Puebla de Rocamora A 142 Zb 120
22482 Puebla de Roda, La HU 36 Ad 95
49300 Puebla de Sanabria ZA 44 Tc 96
06310 Puebla de Sancho Pérez BA 133 Td 118
37791 Puebla de San Medel SA 83 Ub 105
46140 Puebla de San Miguel V 106 Yf 108
34487 Puebla de San Vicente P 29 Ve 92
30152 Puebla de Soto MC 157 Ye 121
34470 Puebla de Valdavia, La P 28 Vc 92
19225 Puebla de Vallés GU 68 We 103
44450 Puebla de Valverde, La TE 90 Za 107
04738 Puebla de Vícar AL 170 Xc 128
37606 Puebla de Yeltes SA 82 Te 105
46670 Puebla Larga, la = Pobla Llarga, la V 126 Zd 114
45690 Pueblanueva, La TO 101 Vb 109
22535 Pueblas, Las HU 55 Ab 98
49171 Pueblica de Campeán ZA 64 Ub 100
49697 Pueblica de Valverde ZA 45 Ua 97
38739 Pueblo, El TF 181 Hb 177
21760 Pueblo Andaluz H 162 Tc 127
04117 Puebloblanco AL 171 Xf 127
11350 Pueblo Nuevo CA 173 Ud 131
21530 Pueblo Nuevo H 146 Sf 123
13194 Pueblonuevo del Bullaque CR 120 Ve 113
06184 Pueblonuevo del Guadiana BA 116 Tb 115
10318 Pueblonuevo de Miramontes CC 100 Ud 108
22822 Pueblo Nuevo de Salinas HU 34 Zb 94
33312 Puelles AS 15 Uc 88
25318 Puelles, Les L 56 Ba 98
50614 Puendeluna Z 53 Zb 96
39788 Puente, El CB 18 We 88
21500 Puente, El H 162 Ta 124

294 | Port de Pollença

49395 Puente, El ZA 44 Tc 96
39687 Puente, La CB 18 Wa 90
39719 Puente-Agüero CB 18 Wb 88
24880 Puente Almuhey LE 28 Va 92
39478 Puente Arce = Arce CB 17 Wa 88
09559 Puente-Arenas BU 30 Wc 91
39350 Puente-Avíos CB 17 Vf 88
47420 Puente Blanca VA 66 Vd 100
24649 Puente de Alba LE 27 Uc 92
24380 Puente de Domingo Flórez LE 25 Tb 94
23350 Puente de Génave J 138 Xb 118
10895 Puente de la Merced CC 97 Tb 108
45570 Puente del Arzobispo, El TO 100 Ue 110
23479 Puente de las Herrerías J 154 Xa 121
23196 Puente de la Sierra J 152 Wb 122
24005 Puente del Castro LE 27 Uc 93
37748 Puente del Congosto SA 83 Uc 106
37521 Puente del Granadero SA 81 Tc 106
05122 Puente del Moriaco AV 84 Va 106
23529 Puente del Obispo J 153 Wc 121
33693 Puente de los Fierros AS 15 Ub 90
04779 Puente del Río, El AL 169 Xa 128
23659 Puente del Villar J 152 Wa 122
22584 Puente de Montañana HU 55 Ae 96
24513 Puente de Rey LE 25 Tb 93
22609 Puente de Sabiñánigo HU 35 Zd 94
29713 Puente de Salia MA 167 Vf 127
02150 Puente de Torres AB 124 Yc 114
16892 Puente de Vadillos CU 88 Xf 105
39250 Puente de Valle CB 29 Wa 92
28038 Puente de Vallecas MD 86 Wb 106
09557 Puentedey BU 18 Wb 91
18830 Puente Duda GR 154 Xb 122
47152 Puente Duero-Esparragal VA 66 Vb 99
09347 Puentedura BU 49 Wc 96
44562 Puente Fonseca TE 91 Zd 104
14500 Puente-Genil CO 166 Vb 124
14817 Puente Grande CO 167 Vf 124
39584 Puente Hojedo CB 17 Vc 90
23390 Puente Honda J 139 Xc 118
31100 Puente La Reina NC 33 Yb 92
22753 Puente la Reina de Jaca HU 34 Zb 93
09214 Puentelarrá BU 31 Wf 92
28210 Puente la Sierra MD 85 Vf 106
11369 Puente Mayorga CA 175 Ud 131
39554 Puentenansa CB 17 Vd 89
23009 Puente Nuevo J 152 Wb 122
39556 Puente-Pumar CB 17 Vd 90
33692 Puentes, Las AS 15 Ub 90
09136 Puentes de Amaya BU 29 Ve 93
28754 Puentes Viejas MD 68 Wc 103
34813 Puentetoma P 29 Ve 92
05291 Puenteviejo AV 85 Vc 103
39670 Puente Viesgo CB 17 Wa 89
37497 Puenticilla SA 81 Tb 105
49559 Puercas ZA 45 Tf 98
19492 Puerta, La GU 88 Xc 105
23360 Puerta de Segura, La J 139 Xb 118
33555 Puertas AS 16 Va 89
33597 Puertas AS 16 Vb 88
37159 Puertas SA 63 Te 102
14670 Puertas, Las CO 151 Ve 122
04693 Puertecico, El AL 155 Ya 123
33174 Puerto AS 15 Ua 89
38789 Puerto TF 181 Ha 177
02137 Puerto, El AB 139 Xd 117
02329 Puerto, El AB 140 Xf 116
33840 Puerto, El AS 14 Te 90
33457 Puerto, El AS 14 Ua 87
21239 Puerto, El H 147 Ta 121
49193 Puerto, El ZA 64 Ua 99
14512 Puerto Alegre CO 150 Vb 124
23196 Puerto Alto J 152 Wb 122
29602 Puerto Banús MA 174 Va 130
18564 Puerto Blanco GR 168 Wb 124
21595 Puerto Carbón H 160 Sd 124
05621 Puerto Castilla AV 83 Uc 107
37720 Puerto de Béjar SA 83 Ub 106
38508 Puerto de Güimar TF 181 Id 179
35479 Puerto de la Aldea GC 184 Ka 180
37129 Puerto de la Anunciación SA 64 Ub 102
38400 Puerto de la Cruz TF 180 Ic 178
41640 Puerto de la Encina SE 166 Ue 126
38910 Puerto de la Estaca TF 180 Ha 182
03409 Puerto de la Harina, El A 141 Za 117
21594 Puerto de la Laja H 160 Sd 123
29391 Puerto del Algarrobo MA 173 Uc 129
35006 Puerto de la Luz GC 184 Kd 180
38356 Puerto de la Madera TF 181 Id 177
35489 Puerto de la Nieves GC 184 Kb 180
35628 Puerto de la Peña GC 183 Lf 178
29490 Puerto de las Eras MA 173 Ue 129
48190 Puerto de Las Muñecas BI 19 Wf 89
29190 Puerto de la Torre MA 167 Vd 128
35510 Puerto del Carmen GC 182 Mc 175
11370 Puerto del Castaño CA 173 Uc 131
38678 Puerto de los Mozos TF 180 Ib 180
02449 Puerto del Pino AB 140 Xe 118
10615 Puerto del Piornal CC 99 Ua 108
04621 Puerto del Rey AL 171 Yb 125
35600 Puerto del Rosario GC 183 Ma 177
44158 Puerto de Majalinos TE 91 Zc 104
30860 Puerto de Mazarrón MC 156 Ye 123
10261 Puerto de Santa Cruz CC 118 Ua 113
11500 Puerto de Santa María, El CA 172 Te 129
45577 Puerto de San Vicente TO 100 Uf 111
37717 Puerto de Vallejera SA 83 Ub 106
33790 Puerto de Vega AS 13 Tc 87
44559 Puerto de Villarluengo TE 91 Zc 104
29692 Puerto Duquesa MA 174 Ue 130
33776 Puerto Garganta AS 13 Sf 88
21209 Puerto Gil H 147 Tc 121
30414 Puerto Hondo MC 139 Xe 120
06428 Puerto Hurraco BA 134 Uc 117
35612 Puerto Lajas GC 183 Ma 177
13650 Puerto Lápice CR 121 Wd 113
22362 Puértolas HU 36 Aa 93
13500 Puertollano CR 136 Vf 116
06260 Puerto Lobo y Endrinales BA 148 Te 121
18249 Puerto-López GR 168 Wb 124
30890 Puerto Lumbreras MC 155 Yb 123
44411 Puertomingalvo TE 91 Zd 107
21209 Puerto-Moral H 148 Td 121
38769 Puerto Naos TF 181 Ha 177
35627 Puerto Nuevo GC 183 Le 179
11510 Puerto Real CA 172 Te 129
45672 Puerto Rey TO 119 Uf 112
35139 Puerto Rico GC 184 Kb 182
02512 Puertos, Los AB 140 Yc 117
37488 Puerto Seguro SA 81 Tb 104
11659 Puerto Serrano CA 165 Uc 127
22451 Pueyo HU 36 Ad 94
31394 Pueyo NC 33 Yc 93
22311 Pueyo, El HU 35 Aa 94
22437 Pueyo, El HU 55 Ac 95
22338 Pueyo de Aragüás, El HU 36 Aa 94
22135 Pueyo de Fañanás HU 54 Ze 96
22662 Pueyo de Jaca, El HU 35 Ze 92
22588 Pueyo de Marguillén HU 55 Ac 96
22416 Pueyo de Santa Cruz HU 55 Aa 97
22161 Puiboela HU 35 Zc 95
46540 Puig V 108 Ze 111
17492 Puig, El GI 40 Da 95
07816 Puig, Es IB 109 Bc 115
17214 Puigcalent GI 59 Db 97
25633 Puigcercós L 56 Af 96
17520 Puigcerdà GI 38 Bf 94
25514 Puigcerver L 37 Af 95
08733 Puigdàlber B 76 Be 100
07800 Puig de Can Damiá IB 109 Bc 115
25747 Puig de Rialb, El L 56 Bb 96
07609 Puig de Ros de Dalt IB 110 Ce 112
07816 Puig d'es Furnat IB 109 Bb 115
17844 Puigemma GI 59 Ce 96
22583 Puigfell HU 55 Ae 95
25420 Puiggròs L 75 Af 99
46758 Puigmola, La V 126 Ze 114
44660 Puig Moreno TE 73 Ze 102
17178 Puigpardines GI 58 Cc 96
43812 Puigpelat T 76 Bb 101
07194 Puigpunyent IB 110 Cd 111
25751 Puig-redon L 57 Bc 97
08692 Puig-Reig B 57 Bf 97
08692 Puigreig = Puig-Reig B 57 Bf 97
08660 Puigventós B 57 Be 97
25318 Puigverd d'Agramunt L 56 Ba 98
25153 Puigverd de Lleida L 75 Ae 99
25318 Puigvert d'Agramunt = Puigverd d'Agramunt L 56 Ba 98
50810 Puilatos Z 53 Zb 97
22583 Puimolar HU 36 Ad 95
22282 Puipullín HU 53 Zb 96
25794 Pujal, El L 56 Bb 95
17844 Pujals dels Cavallers GI 59 Ce 96
17844 Pujals dels Pagesos GI 59 Ce 96
08282 Pujalt B 57 Bc 98
17834 Pujarnol GI 59 Ce 96
39420 Pujayo CB 17 Vf 90
29450 Pujerra MA 174 Uf 129
17745 Pujol GI 40 Ce 95
25591 Pujol L 37 Ba 95
25736 Pujol L 56 Ba 96
17493 Pujolà GI 40 Da 94
17406 Pujol de la Muntanya GI 58 Cc 97
08612 Pujol de Planès, El B 57 Be 97
07871 Pujols, Es IB 109 Bc 116
45125 Pulgar TO 101 Vf 110
02049 Pulgosa, La AB 124 Ya 115
18197 Pulianas GR 168 Wc 125
18197 Pulianillas GR 168 Wc 125
30561 Pullas, Las MC 156 Ye 120
04640 Pulpí AL 156 Yb 124
30510 Pulpillo, El MC 141 Ye 116
18859 Pulpite GR 154 Xc 123
39507 Pumalverde CB 17 Ve 88
33936 Pumarabule AS 15 Uc 88
27143 Pumarega, A LU 12 Se 91
49626 Pumarejo de Tera ZA 45 Tf 97
39584 Pumareña CB 17 Vc 89
32338 Pumares OR 25 Ta 94
38789 Punta, La TF 181 Ha 176
46013 Punta, La V 126 Zd 112
30368 Punta Brava MC 157 Za 122
38312 Punta Brava TF 180 Ic 178
43860 Punta de Cala Mosques T 75 Ae 103
41130 Punta de la Margazuela SE 163 Tf 126
21410 Punta del Caimán H 161 Se 125
38240 Punta del Hidalgo TF 181 Ie 177
29692 Punta Europa MA 174 Ue 131
07820 Punta Galeria IB 109 Bb 114
38789 Puntagorda TF 181 Ha 176
03630 Puntal, El A 142 Zb 117
02360 Puntal, El AB 139 Xc 117
04810 Puntal, El AL 155 Xd 124
04271 Puntal, El AL 171 Xf 125
04210 Puntal, El AL 171 Xf 126
33315 Puntal, El AS 15 Ud 87
30110 Puntal, El MC 157 Yf 120
46811 Puntal, El V 126 Za 115
38715 Puntallana TF 181 Hb 176
18720 Puntalón GR 168 Wd 128
03185 Punta Prima A 157 Zb 121
07712 Puntarró, Es IB 77 Eb 109
30835 Puntarrón MC 156 Yd 123
38911 Puntas, Las TF 180 Ha 182
30876 Puntas de Calnegre MC 156 Yd 123
21100 Punta Umbría H 161 Ta 125
07199 Puntiro IB 110 Ce 111
32457 Punxín OR 23 Rf 94
03339 Puol A 142 Zb 119
47419 Puras VA 66 Vc 101
09258 Puras de Villafranca BU 31 We 94
04870 Purchena AL 170 Xd 124
18102 Purchil GR 168 Wb 125
30850 Purgatorio, El MC 156 Yc 121
30813 Purias MC 156 Yc 123
33596 Purón AS 16 Vb 88
50240 Purroy Z 71 Yc 100
22589 Purroy de la Solana HU 55 Ac 96
50268 Purujosa Z 52 Yb 98
18519 Purullena GR 169 We 125
03610 Pusa A 142 Zb 118
32336 Pusmazán OR 25 Ta 94
07816 Putxet d'En Puig IB 109 Bc 115
27206 Puxeda LU 24 Sa 91
32879 Puxedo OR 42 Rf 97
22363 Puyarruego HU 36 Aa 93
22439 Puy de Cinca HU 55 Ab 95
22372 Puyuelo HU 35 Zf 94

Q

08619 Quar B 58 Bf 96
17242 Quart GI 59 Cf 97
43205 Quart T 75 Ba 102
46515 Quart de les Valls V 108 Ze 110
46980 Quart de Poblet = Cuart de Poblet V 126 Zd 111
46510 Quartell V 108 Ze 110
12181 Quartico, El CS 108 Aa 107
46837 Quatretonda = Cuatretonda V 126 Zd 115
03811 Quatretondeta A 143 Ze 116
02486 Quebradas AB 139 Xd 118
02536 Quebradas, Las AB 139 Xe 119
09559 Quecedo BU 30 Wc 91
32868 Queguas OR 42 Rf 97
15386 Queimada, A C 11 Rf 89
32768 Queixa OR 43 Sd 95
17538 Queixans GI 38 Bf 94
15186 Queixas C 11 Rd 90
17746 Queixas GI 59 Ce 95
27162 Queizán LU 12 Sd 91
27651 Queizán LU 13 Sf 90
02448 Quejigal AB 139 Xe 118
29460 Quejigal, El MA 174 Ue 128
21290 Quejigo, El H 147 Tb 121
39193 Quejo CB 18 Wc 88
01426 Quejo VI 31 Wf 92
26570 Quel RI 51 Xf 95
09454 Quemada BU 49 Wc 98
14014 Quemadas, Las CO 151 Vb 121
38749 Quemados, Los TF 181 Ha 178
15183 Quembre C 11 Rd 89
32940 Quenlle OR 23 Sa 94
18192 Quéntar GR 168 Wd 125
19209 Quer GU 87 We 105
17534 Queralbs GI 39 Ca 94
19269 Querencia GU 69 Xb 101
32320 Quereño OR 25 Ta 94
25723 Querforadat, El L 38 Bd 95
45790 Quero TO 103 We 111
43816 Querol T 76 Bc 100
46824 Quesa V 126 Zb 114
23480 Quesada J 153 Wf 121
05260 Quexigal, El AV 85 Vd 106
22191 Quicena HU 54 Zd 96
39477 Quijano CB 17 Wa 88
39590 Quijas CB 17 Vf 88
28693 Quijorna MD 85 Vf 106
15295 Quilmas C 22 Qf 91
24548 Quilós LE 25 Tb 93
39550 Quinatanilla CB 17 Vd 89
09510 Quincoces de Yuso BU 19 We 91
27662 Quindóus LU 25 Ta 91
46367 Quinete V 126 Za 112
11500 Quinientas, Las CA 172 Tf 129
27132 Quinta, A LU 13 Se 91
28049 Quinta, La MD 86 Wb 106
45470 Quinta de Lora TO 121 Wb 112
41400 Quinta de Nuestra Señora de las Mercedes SE 150 Uf 123
41640 Quinta de Vista Hermosa SE 166 Uf 124
33836 Quintana AS 14 Te 89
33391 Quintana AS 15 Uc 88
39806 Quintana CB 18 Wc 89
26259 Quintana RI 31 Wf 94
01128 Quintana VI 32 Xd 93
39418 Quintana, La CB 29 Ve 91
09574 Quintanabaldo BU 18 Wb 91
09246 Quintanabureba BU 30 Wd 93
24712 Quintana de Fon LE 26 Tf 93
24319 Quintana de Fuseros LE 26 Te 92
06450 Quintana de la Serena BA 134 Ub 116
24397 Quintana del Castillo LE 26 Tf 93
24762 Quintana del Marco LE 45 Ua 95
24930 Quintana del Monte LE 28 Uf 93
09569 Quintana de los Prados BU 18 Wc 90
09370 Quintana del Pidio BU 49 Wb 98
09125 Quintana del Pino BU 30 Wb 93
34250 Quintana del Puente P 48 Ve 96
24391 Quintana de Raneros LE 27 Uc 93
24930 Quintana de Rueda LE 27 Ue 93
09555 Quintana de Rueda, La BU 18 Wc 91
39699 Quintana de Toranzo CB 17 Wa 89
34113 Quintanadiez de la Vega P 28 Vb 94
09190 Quintanadueñas BU 30 Wb 94
09244 Quintanaélez BU 30 We 92
09572 Quintanaentello BU 18 Wb 91
09549 Quintana-Entrepeñas BU 30 We 91
09142 Quintanajuar BU 30 Wc 93
09515 Quintanalacuesta BU 30 Wd 91
09647 Quintanalara BU 49 Wc 95
09142 Quintanaloma BU 30 Wb 92
09248 Quintanaloranco BU 31 We 94
34839 Quintanaluengos P 29 Vd 91
09314 Quintanamanvirgo BU 48 Wa 98
09213 Quintana-María BU 30 We 92
09210 Quintana Martín Galíndez BU 30 We 92
09593 Quintanaopio BU 30 Wd 92
09140 Quintanaortuño BU 30 Wb 94
09290 Quintanapalla BU 30 Wc 94
23311 Quintanar, El J 153 Wf 120
45800 Quintanar de la Orden TO 103 Wf 111
09670 Quintanar de la Sierra BU 50 Wf 97
16220 Quintanar del Rey CU 124 Ya 112
26259 Quintanar de Rioja RI 31 Wf 94
42291 Quintana Redonda SO 50 Xc 99
42150 Quintanar o El Quintanarejo SO 50 Xb 97
09454 Quintanarraya BU 49 Wd 98
09141 Quintanarruz BU 30 Wb 93
09141 Quintanarruz BU 30 Wc 93
42313 Quintanas de Gormaz SO 69 Xa 99
34811 Quintanas de Hormiguera P 29 Vf 91
09127 Quintanas de Valdelucio BU 29 Vf 92
39220 Quintanas-Olmo CB 29 Wa 92
42345 Quintanas Rubias de Abajo SO 68 Wf 100
42345 Quintanas Rubias de Arriba SO 68 Wf 100
34485 Quintanatello de Ojeda P 29 Vd 92
09592 Quintana-Urría BU 30 Wd 93
09292 Quintanavides BU 30 Wd 94
24767 Quintana y Congosto LE 26 Tf 95
24124 Quintanilla LE 27 Ua 92
01427 Quintanilla VI 31 We 91
49340 Quintanilla ZA 45 Te 96
02639 Quintanilla, La AB 123 Xf 114
09249 Quintanillabón BU 30 We 93
09246 Quintanilla Cabe Rojas BU 30 Wd 93
09640 Quintanilla-Cabrera BU 49 Wd 95
09146 Quintanilla-Colina BU 30 Wb 91
24743 Quintanilla da Losada LE 26 Tc 95
47360 Quintanilla de Arriba VA 48 Vd 99
24141 Quintanilla de Babia LE 14 Te 91
24715 Quintanilla de Combarros LE 26 Tf 93
24733 Quintanilla de Flórez LE 26 Tf 95
34309 Quintanilla de la Cueza P 28 Vb 95
09347 Quintanilla del Agua BU 49 Wc 96
09349 Quintanilla de la Mata BU 49 Wb 97
09129 Quintanilla de la Presa BU 29 Wa 93
09230 Quintanilla de las Carretas BU 30 Wb 95
34811 Quintanilla de las Torres P 29 Ve 92
09642 Quintanilla de las Viñas BU 49 Wd 96
09348 Quintanilla del Coco BU 49 Wc 97
47673 Quintanilla del Molar VA 46 Ud 97
09270 Quintanilla del Monte BU 31 Wf 94
24285 Quintanilla del Monte LE 26 Ua 93
49639 Quintanilla del Monte ZA 46 Ud 97
09292 Quintanilla del Monte en Juarros BU 30 Wd 94

A B C D E F G H I J K L M N Ñ O P Q R S T U V W X Y Z

Quintanilla del Monte en Juarros | 295
E

49638 Quintanilla del Olmo ZA 46 Ud 97
09513 Quintanilla de los Adrianos BU 18 Wc 91
24208 Quintanilla de los Oteros LE 27 Ud 95
09568 Quintanilla del Rebollar BU 18 Wc 90
24281 Quintanilla del Valle LE 26 Ua 93
42141 Quintanilla de Nuño Pedro SO 49 We 98
09512 Quintanilla de Ojada BU 30 We 91
47350 Quintanilla de Onésimo VA 48 Vc 99
34114 Quintanilla de Onsoña P 28 Vc 94
09492 Quintanilla de Ricuerda BU 49 Wc 98
09135 Quintanilla de Riofresno BU 29 Ve 93
24940 Quintanilla de Rueda LE 28 Ue 92
09571 Quintanilla de San Román BU 18 Wa 91
24271 Quintanilla de Sollamas LE 27 Ub 93
24717 Quintanilla de Somoza LE 26 Te 94
42351 Quintanilla de Tres Barrios SO 50 We 99
47283 Quintanilla de Trigueros VA 47 Vc 97
09614 Quintanilla de Urrilla BU 50 We 96
49622 Quintanilla de Urz ZA 45 Ua 96
24738 Quintanilla de Yuso LE 45 Td 95
09549 Quintanilla-Montecabezas BU 30 We 91
09125 Quintanilla-Pedro Abarca BU 30 Wb 93
09131 Quintanillas, Las BU 30 Wa 94
09271 Quintanilla San-García BU 31 We 93
09141 Quintanilla-Sobresierra BU 30 Wb 93
09239 Quintanilla-Somuñó BU 48 Wa 95
09557 Quintanilla-Valdebodres BU 18 Wb 91
09140 Quintanilla-Vivar o Quintanilla Morocisla BU 30 Wb 94
09196 Quintanilleja BU 49 Wb 95
15126 Quintáns C 10 Qe 90
36875 Quintáns PO 41 Rd 95
15822 Quintás C 23 Rd 91
24525 Quintela LE 25 Ta 92
27258 Quintela LU 12 Sd 89
32860 Quintela OR 42 Rf 97
36428 Quintela PO 42 Re 96
32558 Quintela de Humoso OR 44 Sf 96
32212 Quintela do Leirado OR 42 Rf 96
32558 Quintela Hedroso OR 44 Sf 95
13360 Quintería, La CR 137 Wb 116
23749 Quintería, La J 152 Wa 120
13679 Quintería de Mateo CR 121 Wd 114
41089 Quinto SE 163 Ua 125
50770 Quinto Z 73 Zc 100
33129 Quinzanas AS 15 Uc 89
22810 Quinzano HU 53 Zc 95
42126 Quiñonería, La SO 70 Xf 99
47209 Quiñones VA 47 Vc 98
30510 Quiñones, Los MC 141 Yf 117
15824 Quión C 23 Re 91
36117 Quireza PO 23 Rd 93
27320 Quiroga LU 24 Se 94
32627 Quiroganes OR 43 Sd 97
33117 Quirós AS 14 Ua 90
49622 Quiruelas de Vidriales ZA 45 Ub 96
38812 Quise TF 184 He 180
09568 Quisicedo BU 18 Wc 90
45514 Quismondo TO 101 Ve 108
30510 Quitapellejos MC 141 Yf 118
40193 Quitapesares SG 67 Vf 103

R

27370 Rábade LU 12 Sc 90
32696 Rabal OR 43 Sc 96
32698 Rabal OR 43 Sd 97
30332 Rabales, Los MC 157 Yf 122
14500 Rabanal, El CO 150 Vb 124
24648 Rabanal de Fenar LE 27 Uc 92
24722 Rabanal del Camino LE 26 Te 94
34846 Rabanal de los Caballeros P 29 Vd 91
49519 Rabanales ZA 45 Te 98
26133 Rabanera RI 51 Xd 95
42191 Rabanera del Campo SO 51 Xd 99
09660 Rabanera del Pinar BU 50 We 97
47319 Rábano VA 67 Vf 99
49515 Rábano de Aliste ZA 44 Td 98
49358 Rábano de Sanabria ZA 44 Tc 96
09268 Rábanos BU 30 We 95
42191 Rábanos, Los SO 51 Xd 98
25271 Rabassa, La L 38 Bd 94
25271 Rabassa, La L 57 Bc 99
09130 Rabé de las Calzadas BU 30 Wa 94
09349 Rabé de los Escuderos BU 49 Wb 97
08660 Rabeia, La B 57 Bf 97
21819 Rábida, La H 161 Ta 125
06320 Rabilero, El BA 133 Td 119
13129 Rabinadas, Las CR 120 Vf 113
18760 Rábita, La GR 169 We 128
23685 Rábita, La J 152 Vf 123
21840 Raboconejo H 147 Tb 124
17754 Rabós GI 40 Da 94
30510 Rabosera MC 141 Yf 117
44146 Rabosero, El TE 91 Zb 106
03503 Racó de l'Oix, El A 143 Zf 117
46880 Racó dels Cirers, El V 142 Zc 116
37449 R. A. D., La SA 64 Ub 103
09126 Rad, La BU 30 Wa 92
31383 Rada NC 33 Yc 95
02436 Rada, La AB 140 Ya 118
16649 Rada de Haro CU 104 Xc 111
40590 Rades, La SG 68 Wc 101
40172 Rades de Abajo SG 67 Wb 102
40172 Rades de Arriba SG 67 Wb 102
22145 Radiquero HU 54 Zf 95
42213 Radona SO 70 Xd 101
30648 Rafaeles, Los MC 141 Yf 119
07509 Rafael Pudent, Es IB 111 Db 111
03369 Rafal A 142 Za 120
07469 Rafal, El IB 111 Cf 109
07469 Rafal d' Ariant IB 111 Cf 109
07469 Rafal de Casellas IB 111 Cf 110
07690 Rafal des Porcs, Es IB 111 Da 113
22535 Ráfales HU 55 Ab 98
44589 Ráfales TE 92 Aa 103
07316 Rafalet, El IB 111 Cf 109
07559 Rafalet, Es IB 111 Dc 111
07500 Rafalet Drac, Es IB 111 Db 111
07730 Rafal Fort IB 77 Ea 109
07500 Rafalot, Es IB 111 Da 111
07730 Rafal Rubi IB 77 Eb 109
07712 Rafal Vell IB 77 Eb 109
46138 Rafelbunyol = Rafelbuñol V 108 Ze 111
46138 Rafelbuñol = Rafelbunyol V 108 Zc 111
46716 Rafelcofer V 127 Ze 115
46666 Rafelguaraf V 126 Zd 114
03769 Ráfol de Almunia A 127 Zf 116
46843 Ráfol de Salem V 126 Zd 115
37318 Rágama SA 65 Va 103
04440 Rágol AL 170 Xb 127
32785 Raigada OR 25 Se 95
30850 Raiguero MC 156 Yd 122
30850 Raiguero Bajo MC 156 Yd 122
25111 Raïmat L 55 Ac 98
32652 Rairiz de Veiga OR 42 Sb 96
32971 Rairo OR 24 Sa 95
07110 Raixa IB 110 Cd 110
30529 Raja, La MC 141 Ye 118
03659 Raja, La MC 141 Yf 118
08256 Rajadell B 57 Be 98
38869 Rajita, La TF 184 He 180
02486 Rala AB 139 Xe 118
46199 Ral de Abajo V 125 Yf 113
33594 Rales AS 16 Va 88
22484 Raluy HU 36 Ad 94
17500 Rama GI 58 Cb 95
05418 Ramacastañas AV 100 Uf 107
39800 Ramales de la Victoria CB 18 Wd 89
15883 Ramallosa, A C 23 Rc 92
36379 Ramallosa, A PO 41 Rb 96
22466 Ramastué HU 36 Ac 93
22267 Rambla HU 54 Ze 97
02127 Rambla, La AB 140 Xf 116
14540 Rambla, La CO 151 Vb 123
30700 Rambla, La MC 157 Za 122
41440 Rambla, La SE 149 Ud 123
38416 Rambla, La TF 180 Ic 178
18480 Rambla Carlonca GR 169 Wf 127
18890 Rambla de Balata GR 153 Xa 124
18517 Rambla de Cauzón GR 169 We 125
12232 Rambla de David CS 107 Zd 108
04567 Rambla de Gérgal AL 170 Xc 126
23590 Rambla de Juan Manchego J 153 We 123
18711 Rambla del Agua GR 169 We 128
18511 Rambla del Agua GR 169 Xa 125
18890 Rambla de la Matanza GR 154 Wf 123
23488 Rambla de la Teja J 153 Wf 122
18440 Rambla del Banco, La GR 169 We 127
04275 Rambla del Marqués AL 170 Xe 125
18520 Rambla de los Lobos GR 153 We 123
04540 Rambla Encira, La AL 170 Xc 126
04692 Rambla Grande, La AL 155 Ya 124
04210 Rambla Honda, La AL 171 Xe 126
04450 Ramblas, Las AL 170 Xb 126
30628 Rambla Salada MC 141 Yf 120
46199 Rambla Seca V 126 Za 113
46360 Rambla y Condesa, La V 126 Za 112
12194 Ramblelles, Les CS 92 Zf 107
27554 Ramil LU 24 Sb 92
36527 Ramil PO 23 Sa 91
32558 Ramilo OR 44 Ta 95
32810 Ramirás OR 42 Rf 95
47453 Ramiro VA 66 Vb 101
45700 Ramón TO 102 Wb 111
23191 Ramona, La J 152 Wc 123
30589 Ramos, Los MC 157 Yf 121
44750 Rampla de Martin, La TE 90 Za 104
28791 Rancajales, Los MD 86 Wb 104
41620 Rancho Cazolita SE 165 Ud 125
41659 Rancho de Aparicio SE 166 Uf 125
11370 Rancho de Carbones CA 175 Uc 131
41530 Rancho de Coto Ruiz SE 165 Ud 126
41640 Rancho de Don Manuel Romero SE 166 Uf 125
11580 Rancho de Frontán CA 172 Ua 129
41640 Rancho de Gamarra SE 166 Ue 125
11648 Rancho de Ibáñez CA 163 Ua 127
41710 Rancho de la Asomadilla SE 163 Ua 126
11170 Rancho de la Atalaya CA 172 Ua 130
41770 Rancho de la Ballestera SE 165 Uc 126
29391 Rancho de la Casilla MA 173 Ud 129
41530 Rancho de la Reina SE 165 Ud 126
41727 Rancho de la Romana SE 163 Ua 126
41760 Rancho de las Mulas SE 165 Uc 126
41540 Rancho de las Salinas SE 165 Ue 126
41740 Rancho de Lila SE 163 Tf 126
41670 Rancho del Navazo SE 166 Ue 127
41740 Rancho de los Rasillos SE 164 Tf 127
11178 Rancho del Pino CA 173 Ua 129
11580 Rancho del Puerto de Picao CA 173 Ub 129
41530 Rancho de Malagón SE 165 Ud 126
41510 Rancho de Manuel Girardo SE 165 Ub 125
11180 Rancho de Montaño CA 173 Uc 130
41659 Rancho de Pozo Santo SE 165 Ue 126
41530 Rancho de Roceros SE 165 Ud 126
41659 Rancho de San Antonio SE 166 Ue 125
41640 Rancho de Sarría SE 166 Uf 124
41659 Rancho de Sol SE 166 Uf 126
11692 Rancho de Tenorio CA 166 Uf 127
41659 Rancho de Terrones SE 166 Ue 126
41620 Rancho de Vargas SE 165 Ud 125
41670 Rancho la Rosa Alta SE 165 Ue 126
28260 Ranchos, Los MD 85 Wa 105
21250 Ranchos del Romeral H 146 Se 121
07629 Randa IB 111 Cf 111
36812 Rande PO 22 Rc 95
32646 Randín OR 42 Sa 97
36713 Randufe PO 41 Rc 96
09212 Ranedo BU 31 We 92
09593 Ranera BU 30 We 92
48890 Ranero BI 18 Wd 89
AD100 Ransol ◘ AND 38 Bd 93
32910 Rante OR 24 Sa 95
22337 Rañín HU 36 Ab 94
15928 Raño C 22 Rb 93
27652 Rao LU 13 Ta 91
40466 Rapariegos SG 66 Vc 102
08730 Ràpita, La B 76 Bd 101
25680 Ràpita, La L 56 Af 98
06392 Raposo, El BA 133 Te 118
18511 Raposo, El GR 169 Xa 125
22621 Rapún HU 35 Zd 94
22821 Rasal HU 35 Zc 94
28740 Rascafría MD 67 Wa 103
39849 Rascón CB 18 Wd 88
06390 Rascón, El BA 132 Tc 117
17464 Raset GI 59 Cf 96
39419 Rasgada CB 29 Vf 91
39638 Rasillo CB 18 Wa 89
30510 Rasillo MC 141 Yf 117
26124 Rasillo de Cameros, El RI 50 Xb 95
39860 Rasines CB 18 Wd 89
02500 Raso AB 140 Yb 117
05489 Raso, El AV 100 Ud 107
31350 Raso Jaurrieta NC 33 Ya 94
14600 Rasos CO 136 Ve 120
30814 Raspajos, Los MC 156 Yb 122
03657 Raspay MC 141 Yf 118
02486 Raspilla AB 139 Xd 118
43513 Rasquera T 74 Ad 102
05298 Rasueros AV 65 Uf 102
41659 Ratera Nueva SE 165 Uf 126
41659 Ratera Vieja SE 166 Uf 126
43427 Rauric T 76 Bc 99
43529 Raval de Crist, El T 93 Ac 104
43590 Raval de Jesús, El T 93 Ad 103
08711 Raval de l'Aguilera, El B 57 Bd 99
36966 Raxó PO 22 Rb 94
36646 Raxoi PO 22 Rc 92
15595 Raxón C 11 Re 87
34159 Rayaces P 47 Vb 97
18870 Rayo del Serval GR 169 Xa 124
19229 Razbona GU 87 We 103
15107 Razo da Costa C 10 Rb 89
04628 Real, El AL 171 Ya 125
30130 Real, El MC 157 Yf 120
27276 Real, O LU 13 Se 90
28300 Real Cortijo de San Isidro MD 102 Wc 108
41250 Real de la Jara, El SE 148 Tf 121
46194 Real de Montroi V 126 Zc 112
45640 Real de San Vicente, El TO 101 Vb 108
38412 Realejo Alto TF 180 Ic 178
38419 Realejos, Los TF 180 Ic 178
46666 Realenc, El V 126 Zd 114
30397 Realenco, El MC 157 Yf 122
07200 Realeng, Es IB 111 Db 112
29531 Realenga, La MA 166 Vb 126
03339 Realengo, El A 142 Zb 119
09140 Real Monasterio de las Huelgas BU 30 Wb 94
27362 Reascos LU 24 Sc 91
46350 Reatillo, El V 107 Za 111
03689 Rebalse, El A 142 Za 119
34844 Rebanal de las Llantas P 28 Vc 91
03313 Rebate A 157 Za 121
08630 Rebato, El B 76 Bf 99
27307 Reboira LU 12 Sa 89
27346 Reboiro LU 24 Sd 92
33438 Rebollada AS 15 Ub 87
33989 Rebollada AS 15 Uc 89
33842 Rebollada, La AS 14 Td 90
33619 Rebollada, La AS 15 Ub 89
10617 Rebollar CC 99 Ua 108
40389 Rebollar SG 67 Wa 101
42165 Rebollar SO 51 Xc 97
28791 Rebollar, El MD 86 Wb 104
46391 Rebollar, El V 106 Yf 112
24225 Rebollar de los Oteros LE 27 Ud 94
34492 Rebolleda, La P 29 Ve 92
09150 Rebolledas, Las BU 30 Wb 94
09136 Rebolledillo de la Orden BU 29 Ve 93
03113 Rebolledo A 142 Zc 118
34813 Rebolledo de la Inera P 29 Ve 92
34492 Rebolledo de la Torre BU 29 Ve 92
09124 Rebolledo de Traspeña BU 29 Vf 92
40184 Rebollo SG 67 Wa 101
33888 Rebollo, El AS 13 Tb 89
42210 Rebollo de Duero SO 69 Xb 100
37617 Rebollosa SA 82 Tf 106
19197 Rebollosa de Hita GU 87 Wf 104
19245 Rebollosa de Jadraque GU 69 Xa 102
42344 Rebollosa de los Escuderos SO 69 Wf 101
42344 Rebollosa de Pedro SO 68 We 101
36669 Rebón PO 22 Rc 93
27813 Rebordaos LU 12 Sb 89
36491 Rebordechán PO 23 Re 95
32702 Rebordechao OR 43 Sd 95
15619 Rebordelo C 11 Rf 88
15938 Rebordelo C 22 Ra 93
36826 Rebordelo PO 23 Rd 94
15890 Reboredo C 23 Rd 91
27811 Reboredo LU 12 Sc 89
27577 Reboredo LU 23 Sa 92
15897 Reborido C 22 Rc 91
45211 Recas TO 102 Wa 108
27726 Rececende LU 13 Se 88
15568 Recemel C 12 Sa 88
37795 Recios, Los SA 83 Ub 105
02249 Recueja, La AB 125 Yd 113
19492 Recuenco, El GU 88 Xd 105
42313 Recuerda SO 69 Xa 100
34858 Recueva de la Peña P 28 Vc 92
23250 Réculo J 138 We 119
26146 Redal, El RI 32 Xe 94
32814 Redemuíños OR 42 Rf 96
15623 Redes C 11 Re 88
09270 Redicilla del Campo BU 31 Wf 94
24843 Redilluera LE 15 Ud 91
24855 Redipollos LE 16 Ue 90
24844 Redipuertas LE 15 Ud 90
16317 Redoba, La CU 89 Yc 107
37247 Redonda, La SA 63 Tb 103
40132 Redonda el Nuevo SG 67 Vd 103
40132 Redonda El Viejo SG 67 Vd 103
21430 Redondela, La H 161 Se 125
14130 Redondo Bajo CO 150 Va 122
17869 Redonella, La GI 39 Cb 94
30893 Redón y Venta de Ceferino MC 156 Yb 123
03370 Redován A 142 Za 120
28721 Redueña MD 86 Wc 104
Refinería H 161 Ta 125
36542 Refoxos PO 23 Re 93
36779 Refoxos PO 41 Rb 97
03818 Refugi de la Sarga A 142 Zd 117
08697 Refugi d' Estasen B 57 Be 95
08697 Refugi D. Ubeda B 57 Be 95
33628 Refugio Casa de Mieres AS 15 Ua 90
39210 Refugio C. A. Tresmares CB 17 Ve 90
22790 Refugio Choza Fumia HU 34 Zb 92
22640 Refugio de Alfonso XIII HU 35 Ze 92
39582 Refugio de Aliva CB 16 Vb 90
24915 Refugio de Collado Jermoso LE 16 Va 89
18413 Refugio de Félix Méndez GR 169 Wd 126
39210 Refugio de la Hoz de Abiada CB 17 Ve 90
18650 Refugio de Lanjarón GR 168 Wd 126
05633 Refugio del Club Alpino AV 83 Ue 107
05633 Refugio del Rey AV 83 Ue 107
18650 Refugio de Peñón Colorado GR 168 Wd 126
24915 Refugio de Vega Huerta LE 16 Va 89
33554 Refugio de Vega Urriello AS 16 Vb 89
18420 Refugio de Ventura GR 168 Wd 127
33556 Refugio Vega Redonda AS 16 Uf 89
22365 Refugio de Trigoniero HU 36 Ab 92
03818 Regadiu, El A 142 Zd 116
02640 Regajo, El AB 125 Yf 116
46680 Regal V 126 Zd 113
37183 Regañada, La SA 83 Ub 104
45700 Regates TO 102 Wb 111
17214 Regencós GI 59 Db 97
33814 Regla de Perandones, La AS 14 Tc 90
27721 Rego de Bidueiro LU 13 Sf 89
15151 Regoelle C 10 Qf 90
25692 Règola, La L 56 Ae 97
48879 Regomedo BI 19 We 89
27305 Rego Pequeno LU 12 Sb 89
25514 Reguard L 37 Af 95
49394 Reguejo ZA 44 Tb 96
23616 Regüelo J 152 Wa 123
36415 Reguengo PO 41 Rc 95
33190 Regueras, Las AS 14 Ua 88
24763 Regueras de Arriba LE 27 Ua 95
43527 Reguers, Els T 93 Ac 103
09693 Regumiel de la Sierra BU 50 Xa 97

296 | Quintanilla del Olmo

27259 Reguntille LU 12 Sd 89
21720 Rehoya H 162 Tc 124
39808 Rehoyos CB 18 Wd 89
44600 Rehuerta, La TE 73 Zf 102
27333 Rei LU 24 Sd 93
46680 Reig V 126 Zd 113
33888 Reigada, La AS 13 Tc 89
27286 Reigosa LU 12 Sd 89
36827 Reigosa, A PO 23 Rc 94
16390 Reíllo CU 105 Ya 109
06970 Reina BA 133 Ua 119
41140 Reina Victoria SE 164 Tf 126
46880 Reiner V 142 Zc 116
48520 Reineta, La BI 19 Wf 89
14130 Reinilla y Ladrillos CO 150 Uf 122
39200 Reinosa CB 17 Vf 91
39418 Reinosilla CB 29 Ve 91
09248 Reinoso BU 30 Wd 93
34208 Reinoso de Cerrato P 48 Vd 97
15686 Reiris C 11 Re 90
36151 Reiris PO 22 Rc 94
18810 Rejano GR 170 Xb 124
41658 Rejano SE 166 Va 126
42320 Rejas de San Esteban SO 49 We 99
42141 Rejas de Ucero SO 50 Wf 98
20009 Rekalde SS 20 Xf 89
34115 Relea P 28 Vb 93
24339 Reliegos LE 27 Ud 94
33873 Rellanos AS 13 Tc 88
36547 Rellas PO 23 Re 92
04533 Relleno AL 170 Xa 126
03578 Relleu A 143 Ze 117
08299 Rellinars B 57 Bf 99
42368 Rello SO 69 Xb 101
09510 Relloso BU 19 We 90
06340 Remedios, Los BA 132 Tc 119
43460 Remei d'Alcover, El T 75 Ba 101
49321 Remesal ZA 44 Tc 96
24990 Remolina LE 28 Uf 91
14512 Remolino, El CO 150 Vb 124
50637 Remolinos Z 53 Ye 97
40216 Remondo SG 66 Vd 100
43891 Remullà T 75 Ae 102
33449 Ren, La AS 15 Ub 87
06715 Rena BA 117 Ub 114
19432 Renales GU 70 Xc 103
22470 Renanué HU 36 Ad 94
43886 Renau T 76 Bb 101
27627 Renche LU 24 Se 92
22440 Renclusa, La HU 36 Ad 93
27346 Rendar LU 24 Sd 92
36800 Rendondela PO 22 Rb 95
39511 Renedo CB 17 Ve 89
39213 Renedo CB 17 Vf 91
47170 Renedo VA 47 Vc 99
24847 Renedo de Curueño LE 27 Ud 91
09127 Renedo de la Escalera BU 29 Vf 92
34126 Renedo de la Vega P 28 Vb 94
34115 Renedo del Monte P 28 Vb 93
39470 Renedo de Piélagos CB 17 Wa 88
34473 Renedo de Valdavia P 28 Vc 93
24327 Renedo de Valderaduey LE 28 Va 93
24880 Renedo de Valdetuéjar LE 28 Va 92
34830 Renedo de Zalima P 29 Vd 92
19145 Renera GU 87 Wf 106
42189 Renieblas SO 51 Xd 98
48710 Rentería BI 20 Xd 89
16318 Rento Artigas CU 89 Yc 108
16338 Rento Callejones CU 106 Yd 108
16300 Rento de Fuente de la Sierra CU 105 Yb 108
09195 Renuncio BU 30 Wb 95
13248 Renúñez Grande CR 122 Wf 115
39311 Reocín CB 17 Vf 89
39419 Reocín de los Molinos CB 29 Vf 91
02316 Reolid AB 139 Xc 117
22483 Reperós HU 36 Ac 94
21360 Repilado, El H 147 Tb 121
30420 Reposaderas, Las MC 140 Yb 119
10810 Represa CC 98 Te 108
24155 Represa del Condado LE 27 Ud 93
27306 Requeixo LU 12 Sa 89
27513 Requeixo LU 24 Sa 93
32161 Requeixo OR 24 Sb 94
32785 Requeixo OR 25 Se 95
32895 Requeixo OR 42 Rf 97
32786 Requeixo OR 43 Sd 95
32369 Requeixo OR 44 Ta 95
39312 Requejada CB 17 Vf 88
24567 Requejo LE 25 Tb 93
46340 Requena V 106 Yf 112
34469 Requena de Campos P 29 Vd 95
32898 Requiás OR 42 Sa 97
40173 Requijada SG 67 Wa 102
42200 Requijada SO 70 Xc 99
18690 Rescate, El GR 168 Wb 128
39681 Resconorio CB 18 Wa 90
34005 Residencia Virgen de la Calle P 47 Vc 97
16312 Resinera CU 106 Yd 110
18127 Resinera, La GR 168 Wa 127
34844 Resoba P 29 Vc 91
01476 Respaldiza VI 19 Wf 90
34813 Respenda de Aguilar P 29 Vf 92
34870 Respenda de la Peña P 28 Vb 92
18658 Restábal GR 168 Wc 127
15686 Restande C 11 Rc 90
33826 Restiello AS 14 Te 89
38917 Restinga, La TF 180 Ha 183
31421 Reta NC 33 Yd 92
04211 Retacos, Los AL 170 Xe 126
06209 Retamal BA 132 Tc 116
06442 Retamal de Llerena BA 134 Ua 117
30412 Retamalejo MC 155 Xf 121
18127 Retamales o La Colonia GR 168 Wa 127
04131 Retamar AL 170 Xe 127
13598 Retamar CR 136 Ve 116
28110 Retamar MD 86 Wd 105
38684 Retamar, El TF 180 Ib 179
10372 Retamosa CC 99 Uc 111
45652 Retamoso TO 101 Vb 110
50367 Retascón Z 71 Yd 102
01477 Retes Llanteno VI 19 Wf 90
19225 Retiendas GU 68 We 103
28009 Retiro, El MD 86 Wb 106
39213 Retorillo CB 17 Vf 91
15564 Retorno C 11 Sa 87
46310 Retorno, El AB 125 Yd 112
32621 Retorta OR 43 Sd 96
27233 Retorta, A LU 12 Sb 91
09345 Retortillo BU 48 Vf 96
37495 Retortillo SA 82 Td 104
42315 Retortillo de Soria SO 69 Xa 101
05693 Retuerta AV 83 Uc 107
09347 Retuerta BU 49 Wc 96
47340 Retuerta VA 48 Vc 99
13194 Retuerta del Bullaque CR 120 Vd 112
24917 Retuerto LE 16 Uf 90
04867 Reul Alto, El AL 170 Xd 125
04867 Reul Bajo y Marchalico, El AL 170 Xd 125
43201 Reus T 75 Ba 102
37756 Revallos SA 83 Ud 105
49135 Revellinos ZA 46 Uc 97
09228 Revenga BU 48 Wa 96
40195 Revenga SG 85 Vf 103
34447 Revenga de Campos P 29 Vd 95
06444 Reventón BA 133 Tf 118
39609 Revilla CB 18 Wa 88
22364 Revilla HU 36 Aa 93
37891 Revilla SA 83 Uc 104
37882 Revilla SA 83 Ud 104
40176 Revilla SG 67 Wb 102
09613 Revilla, La BU 49 Wd 96
39547 Revilla, La CB 17 Vd 88
39808 Revilla, La CB 18 Wd 89
09348 Revilla-Cabriada BU 49 Wb 96
42291 Revilla de Calatañazor, La SO 50 Xb 99
34170 Revilla de Campos P 47 Vb 96
34407 Revilla de Collazos P 29 Vc 93
09212 Revilla de Herrán, La BU 31 We 92
09194 Revilla del Campo BU 49 Wc 95
09514 Revilla de Pienza BU 18 Wd 90
34828 Revilla de Santullán P 29 Ve 91
09292 Revillagodos BU 30 Wd 94
09247 Revillalcón BU 30 Wd 93
09620 Revillarruz BU 49 Wc 95
09613 Revilla Vallejera BU 48 Vf 96
24856 Reyero LE 16 Ue 91
32981 Reza OR 24 Sa 94
32417 Reza, A OR 23 Rf 95
09108 Rezmondo BU 29 Ve 93
42126 Reznos SO 51 Xf 99
32102 Ría, A OR 24 Sa 94
27766 Ría de Abres AS 13 Sf 88
15350 Ría de Cedeira C 10 Rf 87
15337 Ría do Barqueiro LU 10 Sb 86
40529 Riaguas de San Bartolomé SG 68 Wd 100
40518 Riahuelas SG 68 Wc 100
15874 Rial C 10 Rb 90
27579 Rial LU 24 Sa 92
17534 Rialb GI 39 Cb 95
25594 Rialb de Noguera = Rialp L 37 Ba 94
22336 Riana, La HU 36 Ab 94
15920 Rianxo C 22 Rb 93
33929 Riaño AS 15 Ub 89
09572 Riaño BU 18 Wb 91
39716 Riaño CB 18 Wc 88
05198 Riatas AV 84 Va 105
40500 Riaza SG 68 Wd 101
27515 Riba LU 24 Sb 93
08519 Riba, La B 58 Cc 97
09514 Riba, La BU 18 Wd 91
24892 Riba, La LE 28 Uf 92
43450 Riba, La T 75 Ba 101
26100 Ribabellosa RI 50 Xc 95
32400 Ribadavia OR 23 Rf 95
33590 Ribadedeba AS 17 Vc 88
42368 Riba de Escalote, La SO 69 Xb 100
49362 Ribadelago de Franco ZA 44 Tb 96
27686 Riba de Neira LU 24 Se 91
27700 Ribadeo LU 13 Sf 87
19441 Riba de Saelices GU 70 Xe 103
19269 Riba de Santiuste GU 69 Xb 101
33560 Ribadesella AS 16 Uf 88
36866 Ribadetea PO 41 Rc 95
15329 Ribadeume C 12 Sa 88
15880 Ribadulla C 23 Rd 92
36636 Ribadumia PO 22 Rb 93
26130 Ribafrecha RI 32 Xd 94
16144 Ribagorda CU 88 Xe 106
26586 Ribalmaguillo RI 51 Xd 95
39794 Ribamontán al Monte CB 18 Wc 88
46190 Riba-roja del Túria = Ribarroja de Turia V 107 Zc 111
46190 Riba-roja de Túria = Ribarroja del Turia V 107 Zc 111
19441 Ribarredonda GU 88 Xe 103
43790 Ribarroja de Ebro = Riba-roja d'Ebre T 74 Ac 101
46190 Ribarroja del Turia = Riba-roja de Túria V 107 Zc 111
42134 Ribarroya SO 51 Xd 99
49515 Ribas ZA 45 Td 98
32849 Ribas, As OR 42 Rf 96
27590 Ribasaltas LU 24 Sd 93
34411 Ribas de Campos P 47 Vc 96
27545 Ribas de Miño LU 24 Sb 92
27363 Ribas de Miño LU 24 Sc 92
27310 Ribas de Sil LU 24 Se 94
26339 Ribas de Tereso RI 31 Xb 93
16145 Ribatajada CU 88 Xe 106
16145 Ribatajadilla CU 88 Xf 107
28815 Ribatejada MD 86 Wd 104
30439 Ribazo MC 140 Yb 120
15960 Ribeira C 22 Ra 93
27654 Ribeira LU 13 Ta 90
27661 Ribeira, A LU 25 Sf 91
27260 Ribeirás de Lea LU 12 Sc 90
15337 Ribeiras do Sor C 10 Sb 86
32847 Ribeiro, O OR 42 Sa 96
32950 Ribela OR 24 Sb 94
36687 Ribela PO 23 Rd 93
25211 Riber L 56 Bb 98
01427 Ribera VI 31 We 91
48710 Ribera = Berritua BI 20 Xd 89
22587 Ribera, La HU 55 Ac 95
14512 Ribera Alta CO 166 Vb 124
23691 Ribera Alta J 152 Wa 124
01420 Ribera Alta VI 31 Xa 92
14512 Ribera Baja CO 150 Vb 124
23691 Ribera Baja J 152 Wa 124
01213 Ribera Baja/Erribeira Beitia = Ribabellosa VI 31 Xa 92
24796 Ribera de Grajal o de la Polvorosa LE 46 Uc 95
04720 Ribera de la Algaida, La AL 170 Xc 128
11150 Ribera de la Oliva, La CA 172 Ua 131
06225 Ribera del Fresno BA 133 Te 117
16211 Ribera de San Benito CU 124 Xf 112
22583 Ribera de Vall HU 36 Ae 95
25213 Ribera d'Ondara L 56 Bb 99
25796 Ribera d'Urgellet L 37 Bc 95
33127 Riberas AS 14 Tf 87
09514 Ribero, El BU 18 Wd 90
34309 Riberos de la Cueza P 28 Vb 95
12210 Ribesalbes CS 108 Ze 108
17534 Ribes de Freser GI 39 Cb 95
40513 Ribota SG 68 Wd 100
50300 Ribota Z 71 Yc 100
24916 Ribota de Sajambre LE 16 Uf 90
33116 Ricabo AS 14 Ua 90
50270 Ricla Z 71 Yd 99
49165 Ricobayo ZA 64 Ua 99
30610 Ricote MC 141 Yd 120
13516 Riegoabajo AS 14 Te 87
24413 Riego de Ambrós LE 26 Td 93
24794 Riego de la Vega LE 26 Ua 94
49742 Riego del Camino ZA 45 Ub 98
24225 Riego del Monte LE 27 Ud 94
24127 Riello LE 26 Ua 92
17130 Riells de Dalt GI 59 Da 96
08416 Riells del Fai B 58 Cb 98
17404 Riells de Montseny GI 58 Cd 98
17404 Riells i Viabrea GI 58 Cd 98
45524 Rielves TO 101 Vc 109
19269 Rienda GU 69 Xb 101
33592 Riensena AS 16 Uf 88
33841 Riera, La AS 14 Te 90
33324 Riera, La AS 15 Ue 88
33556 Riera, La AS 16 Uf 89
43762 Riera de Gaià, la T 76 Bc 102
23100 Ríez J 152 Wc 121
31176 Riezu NC 32 Ya 92
48550 Rigada, La BI 19 Wf 88
22808 Riglos HU 34 Zb 94
22482 Riguala HU 36 Ad 95
27879 Rigueira, A LU 10 Sd 87
41580 Rigüelo SE 166 Vb 125
44710 Rillo TE 90 Za 104
19340 Rillo de Gallo GU 89 Ya 103
33518 Rimada, La AS 15 Uc 88
24448 Rimor LE 25 Tc 93
06280 Rincón BA 147 Td 120
23311 Rincón J 153 Xa 120
03700 Rincón, El A 127 Aa 115
02520 Rincón, El AB 124 Yc 115
04647 Rincón, El AL 171 Yb 124
22437 Rincón, El HU 55 Ac 95
30810 Rincón, El MC 155 Ya 121
30893 Rincón, El MC 155 Yb 124
28620 Rincón, El MD 85 Ve 107
05145 Rinconada AV 84 Uf 104
47520 Rinconada VA 65 Ue 100
05278 Rinconada, La AV 85 Vc 106
41309 Rinconada, La SE 148 Ua 124
45516 Rinconada, La TO 101 Vd 109
37607 Rinconada de la Sierra, La SA 82 Tf 105
11205 Rinconcillo, El CA 174 Ud 132
14100 Rinconcillo, El CO 150 Va 122
30889 Rincón de la Casa Grande MC 156 Yc 124
29730 Rincón de la Victoria MA 175 Ve 128
02400 Rincón del Moro AB 140 Yb 117
03409 Rincón del Moro, El A 142 Za 117
10811 Rincón del Obispo CC 98 Td 109
16142 Rincón de los Olmos CU 89 Xf 106
41740 Rincón del Prado SE 163 Tf 126
04117 Rincón de Martos, El AL 171 Xe 128
26527 Rincón de Olivedo o Las Casas RI 51 Ya 96
26550 Rincón de Soto RI 52 Ya 95
30398 Rincón de Tallante MC 157 Yf 123
18270 Rincón de Turca GR 167 Vf 124
23487 Rincones J 153 Wf 122
30870 Rincones, Los MC 156 Ye 123
30893 Rincón y Las Ramblicas MC 155 Yb 124
25290 Riner L 57 Bd 97
27715 Rinlo LU 13 Sf 87
27134 Río LU 13 Sf 90
27691 Río LU 24 Se 92
29195 Río MA 167 Ve 127
13120 Río, El CR 120 Ve 114
26326 Río, El RI 31 Xa 95
38589 Río, El TF 180 Ic 180
32101 Río, O OR 24 Sa 94
19277 Río Alcolea GU 69 Xb 101
33687 Río-Aller AS 15 Uc 90
27812 Rioaveso LU 12 Sc 89
27868 Río Barba LU 10 Sb 86
22610 Río Basa HU 35 Ze 94
29712 Río Bermuza MA 167 Vf 127
15149 Riobó C 10 Ra 89
32702 Riobó OR 43 Sc 96
36685 Riobó PO 23 Rd 92
02130 Río Bogarra AB 140 Xe 117
05164 Riocabado AV 84 Vb 104
48891 Río Calera BI 18 Wd 90
24608 Río Casares LE 27 Ub 91
46623 Río Cautabán V 125 Yf 114
09615 Riocavado de la Sierra BU 50 We 96
09591 Riocerezo BU 30 Wc 94
04769 Río Chico, El AL 169 Xa 128
28294 Río Cofio MD 85 Ve 105
28294 Río Cofío MD 85 Ve 105
39460 Riocorvo CB 17 Vf 89
04277 Río de Aguas, El AL 171 Xf 126
29718 Río de Almáchar MA 167 Ve 128
29719 Río de Iznate MA 167 Vf 128
09566 Río de la Sía BU 18 Wc 90
13194 Río de las Navas CR 120 Ve 112
09512 Río de Losa BU 19 We 91
09566 Río de Lunada BU 18 Wb 89
04826 Río de Mula, El AL 155 Xf 123
09566 Río de Rioseco BU 18 Wc 90
06475 Río de San Juan BA 133 Tf 116
09566 Río de Trueba BU 18 Wc 90
27124 Río de Uría LU 13 Se 91
44133 Riodeva TE 106 Yf 108
32336 Riodolas OR 25 Ta 94
19294 Río Dulce GU 69 Xb 103
33785 Río Esva AS 14 Td 88
33537 Riofabar AS 15 Ud 89
05191 Riofortes AV 84 Vb 105
05696 Riofraguas AV 83 Ud 106
09344 Río Franco BU 48 Vf 97
13109 Río Frío CR 120 Vd 114
05190 Riofrío AV 84 Vb 105
14940 Riofrío CO 151 Vc 123
18313 Riofrío GR 167 Ve 126
24285 Riofrío LE 26 Ua 93
49591 Riofrío de Aliste ZA 45 Te 98
19269 Riofrío del Llano GU 69 Xb 102
40515 Riofrío de Riaza SG 68 Wd 101
29180 Riogordo MA 167 Ve 127
18127 Río Granada GR 168 Wb 127
04769 Río Grande, El AL 169 Wf 128
50590 Río Huecha Z 52 Yb 98
01479 Río Izoría VI 19 Wf 90
04260 Rioja AL 170 Xd 127
46417 Riola V 126 Zd 113
24143 Riolago LE 14 Tf 91
39764 Riolastras CB 18 Wc 88
10693 Riolobos CC 98 Te 109
02137 Río Madera AB 139 Xe 117
23293 Río Madera J 139 Xc 119
10624 Riomalo de Abajo CC 82 Tf 106
10625 Riomalo de Arriba CC 82 Te 106
33681 Río-Mañón AS 15 Uc 90
32368 Riomao OR 25 Sf 94
02137 Río Mencal AB 139 Xe 117
27124 Riomol LU 12 Se 91
49521 Riomonzanas ZA 44 Tc 97
39554 Rionansa CB 17 Vd 89
49326 Rionegro del Puente ZA 45 Te 96
27367 Río Neira LU 24 Sd 91
24273 Río Omañas LE 27 Ua 92
39232 Riopanero CB 30 Wa 91
02459 Riópar AB 139 Xd 117
09124 Rioparaíso BU 29 Vf 93
42141 Río Pilde SO 49 We 98
29603 Río Real MA 175 Va 129
31153 Río Robo NC 33 Yb 92
42191 Riorruerto SO 51 Xd 99
32611 Ríos OR 43 Se 97
06280 Ríos BA 132 Tc 120
23210 Ríos, Los J 137 Wb 119
39612 Riosapero CB 18 Wa 88
24139 Rioscuro LE 14 Te 91
12469 Ríos de Abajo, Los CS 107 Zb 109
12430 Ríos de Arriba, Los CS 107 Zb 109
33993 Rioseco AS 15 Ud 89
33508 Rioseco AS 16 Va 88
48890 Rioseco BI 18 Wd 89
39490 Rioseco CB 17 Vf 90
39788 Rioseco CB 18 We 88
27836 Rioseco LU 12 Sb 87
33160 Rioseco AS 15 Ua 89
09558 Rioseco BU 30 Wc 91
42193 Rioseco de Soria SO 50 Xa 99
24275 Rioseco de Tapia LE 27 Ub 92
24326 Riosequillo LE 28 Va 94
24890 Riosequino de Torío LE 27 Uc 92
09591 Rioseras BU 30 Wc 94
33190 Río Soto AS 14 Ua 88
27744 Riotorto LU 13 Se 88
19269 Riotoví del Valle GU 69 Xb 102
23468 Río Toya J 153 Wf 121
39720 Riotuerto CB 18 Wb 88
39528 Rioturbio CB 17 Ve 88
33614 Rioturbio AS 15 Ub 89
20749 Río Urola SS 20 Xe 89
34878 Río Valdavia P 28 Vb 92
34475 Río Valdavia P 29 Vc 93
01191 Río Zadorra VI 31 Xb 91
09693 Río Zumel BU 50 Xa 97
31799 Ripa NC 21 Yc 91
31480 Ripodas NC 33 Ye 92
17500 Ripoll GI 58 Cb 95
08291 Ripollet B 77 Ca 100
06195 Risca, La BA 116 Tb 116
30441 Risca, La MC 140 Xf 119
06657 Risco BA 119 Uf 115
35489 Risco, El GC 184 Kb 180
37555 Risco, El SA 81 Tb 106
17462 Rissec GI 59 Cf 96
43430 Riudabella T 75 Ba 100
17421 Riudarenes GI 59 Ce 98
17179 Riudaura GI 58 Cc 95
43771 Riudecanyes T 75 Af 102
25721 Riu de Cerdanya L 38 Be 94
43390 Riudecols T 75 Af 101
25721 Riu de Santa Maria L 38 Be 94
25796 Riu de Tost L 38 Bc 95

Riu de Tost | 297

43330 Riudoms T 75 Ba 102
25352 Riudovelles L 56 Bb 98
43580 Riumar T 93 Af 104
17469 Riumors GI 59 Da 95
46666 Riu-rau V 126 Zd 114
39815 Riva CB 18 Wc 89
39294 Riva, La CB 17 Wa 90
50619 Rivas Z 53 Yf 95
18770 Rivas, Los GR 169 We 128
28529 Rivas de Jarama MD 86 Wc 106
28521* Rivas-Vaciamadrid MD 86 Wc 106
37120 Rivera de la Valmuza SA 64 Ub 103
40421 Rivera de Los Molinos SG 85 Ve 103
10649 Rivera-Oveja CC 82 Te 107
39409 Rivero CB 17 Vf 89
14739 Rivero de Posadas CO 150 Uf 122
25516 Rivert L 56 Af 95
30508 Riviera MC 156 Ye 120
29649 Riviera del Sol MA 175 Vb 130
05309 Rivilla de Barajas AV 66 Va 103
27274 Rixoán LU 13 Se 90
30367 Rizos, Los MC 157 Za 123
09300 Roa BU 48 Wa 98
15815 Roade C 11 Sa 90
49192 Roales ZA 64 Ub 99
47673 Roales de Campos VA 46 Ud 96
33556 Robellada AS 16 Va 88
26131 Roberes del Castillo RI 32 Xe 95
24640 Robla, La LE 27 Uc 92
47131 Robladillo VA 47 Va 99
34127 Robladillo de Ucieza P 29 Vc 94
02127 Roble, El AB 140 Xf 116
37521 Robleda SA 81 Tc 106
49321 Robleda ZA 44 Tc 96
49321 Robleda-Cervantes ZA 44 Tc 96
05130 Robledillo AV 84 Va 105
45676 Robledillo TO 100 Vb 111
45140 Robledillo TO 101 Vc 110
10867 Robledillo de Gata CC 81 Td 107
28194 Robledillo de la Jara MD 68 Wc 103
10493 Robledillo de la Vera CC 99 Uc 108
19227 Robledillo de Mohernando GU 87 We 103
10269 Robledillo de Trujillo CC 117 Ua 113
24730 Robledino LE 26 Tf 95
02340 Robledo AB 139 Xd 116
33480 Robledo AS 15 Ub 88
33583 Robledo AS 16 Ue 88
10638 Robledo CC 82 Td 107
49393 Robledo ZA 44 Tc 96
10460 Robledo, El CC 99 Uc 108
13114 Robledo, El CR 120 Ve 113
24146 Robledo de Caldas LE 15 Ua 91
28294 Robledo de Chavela MD 85 Ve 106
19243 Robledo de Corpes GU 69 Xa 102
24648 Robledo de Fenar LE 27 Uc 92
32312 Robledo de Lastra, O OR 25 Ta 94
24391 Robledo de la Valdoncina LE 27 Ub 93
24730 Robledo de la Valduerna LE 26 Tf 95
45138 Robledo del Buey TO 101 Vb 111
45674 Robledo del Mazo TO 100 Va 111
37217 Robledo Hermoso SA 63 Td 102
10371 Robledollano CC 99 Uc 111
28297 Robledondo MD 85 Ve 105
19223 Roblelacasa GU 68 We 102
19223 Robleluengo GU 68 We 102
24839 Robles de la Valcueva LE 27 Uc 91
32357 Roblido OR 25 Sf 94
37515 Robliza SA 81 Tc 105
37130 Robliza de Cojos SA 82 Ua 103
37130 Robliza de Cojos SA 82 Ua 103
27154 Robra LU 12 Sc 90
19237 Robredarcas GU 69 Wf 102
09512 Robredo de Losa BU 19 We 91
09141 Robredo-Sobresierra BU 30 Wb 93
09591 Robredo-Temiño BU 30 Wc 94
28755 Robregordo MD 68 Wc 102
22252 Robres HU 54 Zd 97
08505 Roca, La B 58 Cb 97
08731 Roca, La B 76 Bd 100
12161 Roca, La CS 92 Zf 107
17867 Rocabruna GI 39 Cc 94
08880 Rocacrespa B 76 Bd 101
06190 Roca de la Sierra, La BA 116 Tb 114
08430 Roca del Vallès, La B 58 Cb 99
08254 Rocafort B 57 Bf 98
22560 Rocafort HU 55 Ac 97
46111 Rocafort V 107 Zd 111
43426 Rocafort de Queralt T 76 Bb 100
25344 Rocafort de Vallbona L 75 Ba 99
31409 Rocaforte NC 33 Ye 93
17310 Roca Grossa GI 59 Cf 98
25269 Rocallaura L 75 Ba 99
21390 Rocamador H 132 Ta 120
08717 Rocamora B 57 Bc 99
03316 Rocamoras de Matanza, Los A 141 Yf 120
39250 Rocamundo CB 29 Wa 92
07850 Rocas IB 109 Bd 114
30700 Rocas, Los MC 157 Yf 122
30739 Rocas, Los MC 157 Za 121
30700 Rocas Viejos, Los MC 157 Yf 122
33211 Roces AS 15 Ub 87
36408 Rocha, A PO 41 Rc 96
11149 Roche CA 172 Tf 131
30369 Roche Bajo MC 157 Za 123
21720 Rociana del Condado H 162 Tc 125
24134 Rocidol LE 26 Tf 91
39860 Rocillo CB 18 Wd 89
21750 Rocío, El H 162 Td 126
30739 Roda MC 157 Za 122
02630 Roda, La AB 123 Xf 113
33747 Roda, La AS 13 Ta 87
41590 Roda de Andalucía, La SE 166 Vb 125
43883 Roda de Berà T 76 Bc 101
40290 Roda de Eresma SG 67 Ve 102
22482 Roda de Isábena HU 36 Ad 95
08510 Roda de Ter B 58 Cb 97
04115 Rodalquilar AL 171 Xf 127
50290 Rodanas Z 52 Yd 99
24318 Rodanillo LE 26 Td 93
37460 Rodasviejas SA 82 Tf 103
15386 Rodeiro C 11 Rf 89
15816 Rodeiros C 11 Rf 91
22144 Rodellar HU 35 Zf 95
50741 Rodén Z 72 Zc 100
44310 Ródenas TE 90 Yc 105
26222 Rodenzo RI 31 Xa 93
11207 Rodeo, El CA 174 Ud 132
30192 Rodeo de Enmedio MC 156 Ye 120
30192 Rodeo de los Tenderos MC 156 Ye 120
24226 Roderos LE 27 Ud 94
25594 Rodés L 37 Ba 94
33879 Rodical AS 14 Td 89
36530 Rodiero PO 23 Sa 93
24687 Rodiezmo de la Tercia LE 15 Ub 91
47492 Rodilana VA 66 Va 100
45519 Rodillas TO 101 Ve 108
24837 Rodillazo LE 27 Uc 91
37449 Rodillo SA 64 Ub 103
15185 Rodis C 11 Rc 90
36517 Rodís PO 23 Rf 92
27646 Rodís LU 25 Se 92
43812 Rodonyà T 76 Bc 101
27743 Rodrigás, As LU 13 Se 88
24715 Rodrigatos de la Obispalía LE 26 Te 93
33579 Rodriguero AS 17 Vc 89
04813 Rodríguez, Los AL 155 Xe 124
03658 Rodriguillo, El A 141 Yf 118
49211 Roelos ZA 64 Te 101
08779 Rofes B 76 Bd 100
03698 Roget A 142 Zc 118
27229 Roimil LU 12 Sa 90
15911 Rois C 22 Rb 92
01129 Roitegui VI 32 Xd 92
39593 Roiz CB 17 Vd 88
03170 Rojales A 157 Zb 120
43415 Rojalons T 75 Ba 100
43415 Rojals T 75 Ba 100
09246 Rojas BU 30 Wd 93
04549 Rojas, Los AL 170 Xb 125
30709 Roldán MC 157 Yf 122
42165 Rollamienta SO 51 Xc 97
37447 Rollán SA 64 Ua 103
46390 Roma V 106 Yf 111
25595 Romadriu, El L 37 Bb 94
27841 Román LU 12 Sc 89
03669 Romana, La A 142 Za 118
14400 Romana, La CO 135 Vb 118
03640 Romana Alta, La A 142 Za 118
19411 Romancos GU 87 Xa 104
29713 Romanes, Los MA 167 Ve 127
10359 Romangordo CC 99 Ub 110
08731 Romaní B 76 Bd 100
19276 Romanillos de Atienza GU 69 Xa 101
42213 Romanillos de Medinaceli SO 69 Xc 101
11592 Romanina Alta CA 163 Tf 128
19143 Romanones GU 87 Xa 105
50491 Romanos Z 71 Ye 102
38418 Romántica, La TF 180 Ic 178
17240 Romanyà de la Selva GI 59 Cf 97
31454 Romanzado NC 34 Ye 92
27737 Romariz LU 12 Sd 88
10199 Romas, Las CC 117 Td 113
27146 Romeán LU 12 Sd 90
27162 Romeán LU 12 Sd 91
27324 Romeor LU 25 Sf 93
04520 Romera AL 169 Xb 126
41770 Romera, La SE 165 Uc 127
29130 Romeral MA 175 Vc 128
04118 Romeral, El AL 171 Xf 128
45770 Romeral, El TO 103 Wd 110
30414 Romeralejo, El MC 155 Xe 120
Romerano, El H 160 Sd 124
11400 Romero, El CA 173 Ub 129
30858 Romero, El MC 156 Yd 122
03191 Romeros, Los A 157 Za 121
21290 Romeros, Los H 147 Tb 121
02155 Romica AB 124 Yb 114
18339 Romilla GR 168 Wb 125
21459 Rompido, El H 161 Sf 125
31415 Roncal NC 34 Za 92
29400 Ronda MA 165 Uf 128
29691 Rondana, La MA 173 Ue 130
33424 Rondiella AS 15 Ua 88
25594 Roní L 37 Bb 94
41880 Ronquillo, El SE 148 Te 122
15212 Roo C 22 Ra 92
23747 Ropera, La J 152 Vf 120
24791 Roperuelos del Páramo LE 45 Ub 95
35650 Roque GC 183 Lf 176
38620 Roque, El TF 180 Ic 180
38728 Roque del Faro TF 181 Ha 176
38294 Roque Negro TF 181 Ie 177
43519 Roquer T 74 Ad 103
08717 Roques d'Aguiló, Les B 57 Bc 99
43860 Roques Daurades, Les T 93 Ae 103
12163 Roques de Lleó, Les CS 92 Ze 107
04740 Roquetas de Mar AL 170 Xc 128
43520 Roquetes T 93 Ad 104
04825 Róquez AL 155 Xe 123
09150 Ros BU 30 Wb 94
38738 Rosa, La TF 181 Hb 177
35629 Rosa de Catalina García GC 183 Lf 179
35627 Rosa de los James GC 183 Lf 179
04500 Rosal, El AL 169 Xa 126
14029 Rosal, El CO 150 Vb 121
32613 Rosal, O OR 43 Sd 97
36770 Rosal, O PO 41 Ra 97
21250 Rosal de La Frontera H 146 Se 121
10391 Rosalejo CC 99 Ud 109
13117 Rosalejo CR 119 Va 112
29400 Rosalejo MA 165 Uf 128
14230 Rosalejo, El CO 135 Ue 119
09514 Rosales BU 18 Wd 91
24127 Rosales LE 26 Tf 92
23690 Rosales, Los J 152 Wb 123
23488 Rosales, Los J 153 Wf 122
28691 Rosales, Los MD 85 Wa 106
41330 Rosales, Los SE 149 Ub 123
41927 Rosales, Los SE 164 Tf 124
17246 Rosamar GI 59 Cf 98
38290 Rosario, El TF 181 Id 178
35269 Rosas, Las GC 184 Kd 181
41530 Rosas, Las SE 165 Ue 126
38915 Rosas, Las TF 180 Ha 182
38760 Rosas, Las TF 181 Ha 177
38290 Rosas, Las TF 181 Id 178
38890 Rosas, Las TF 184 He 179
34858 Roscales de la Peña P 28 Vc 92
12511 Rosell = Rossell CS 92 Ab 105
07208 Rosells, Es IB 111 Da 112
27229 Rosende LU 12 Sa 90
17480 Roses GI 40 Da 95
30394 Roses, Los MC 157 Yf 123
22320 Rosico HU 55 Ab 95
49322 Rosinos de la Requejada ZA 44 Tc 96
49618 Rosinos de Vidriales ZA 45 Ua 96
09514 Rosío BU 18 Wd 91
12511 Rossell = Rosell CS 92 Ab 105
25124 Rosselló L 55 Ad 98
40590 Rosuero SG 68 Wc 101
11520 Rota CA 172 Td 129
03700 Rotes, Les A 127 Aa 116
46816 Rotglá y Corberá V 126 Zc 114
46725 Rótova V 127 Ze 115
10373 Roturas CC 99 Ud 111
47316 Roturas VA 48 Vf 98
27835 Roupar LU 12 Sb 88
43142 Rourell, El T 75 Bb 101
08796 Rovellats B 76 Bd 100
08731 Rovira Roja, La B 76 Bd 100
15896 Roxos C 22 Rc 91
02694 Royo, El AB 125 Yd 115
02129 Royo, El AB 140 Xf 116
42153 Royo, El SO 50 Xc 97
02125 Royo-Odrea AB 140 Xf 117
30412 Royos MC 155 Xf 121
44125 Royuela TE 90 Yc 106
09344 Royuela de Río-Franco BU 48 Wa 97
33580 Roza, La AS 15 Uc 88
39813 Roza, La CB 18 Wc 89
10840 Rozacorderos CC 98 Tb 108
33729 Rozadas AS 13 Ta 88
33313 Rozadas AS 15 Uc 88
39559 Rozadío CB 17 Vd 89
16452 Rozalén del Monte CU 104 Xb 109
33537 Rozapanera AS 15 Ue 89
09574 Rozas BU 18 Wb 90
39808 Rozas CB 18 Wd 89
49357 Rozas ZA 44 Tc 96
28649 Rozas de Puerto Real MD 85 Vd 107
39213 Rozas de Valdearroyo, Las CB 17 Vf 91
28250 Rozuelas, Las MD 86 Wa 105
27889 Rúa LU 10 Sd 87
36875 Rúa PO 23 Rd 95
15821 Rúa, A C 23 Rd 91
32350 Rúa, A OR 25 Sf 94
25651 Rua, La L 56 Ba 96
32357 Rúa de Valdeorras, A OR 25 Sf 94
39232 Ruanales CB 30 Wa 91
10272 Ruanes CC 117 Tf 113
15884 Ruatraviesa C 11 Rd 91
39727 Rubalcaba CB 18 Wb 89
39719 Rubayo CB 18 Wb 88
09199 Rubena BU 30 Wc 94
07511 Ruberts IB 111 Cf 111
08191 Rubí B 77 Ca 100
32318 Rubiá OR 25 Ta 94
18711 Rubia, La GR 169 Wd 128
42162 Rubia, La SO 51 Xd 97
10629 Rubiaco CC 82 Te 106
32160 Rubiacós OR 24 Sb 94
32558 Rubiais OR 44 Sf 96
36447 Rubial PO 41 Rd 96
06445 Rubiales BA 133 Ua 118
44121 Rubiales TE 90 Ye 107
27191 Rubiás LU 12 Sc 90
32849 Rubiás OR 42 Sa 96
33891 Rubias, Las AS 14 Td 88
32646 Rubiás dos Mistos OR 42 Sb 97
47494 Rubí de Bracamonte VA 66 Va 101
44100 Rubielos TE 90 Yd 105
16212 Rubielos Altos CU 105 Xf 112
44166 Rubielos de la Cérida TE 90 Ye 104
44470 Rubielos de Mora TE 107 Zc 107
25736 Rúbies L 56 Af 96
32520 Rubillón OR 23 Re 94
36686 Rubín PO 23 Rd 92
25213 Rubinat L 56 Bb 99
10817 Rubiño CC 98 Tc 108
08719 Rubió B 57 Bd 99
25566 Rubió L 37 Bb 94
41710 Rubio, El SE 165 Ub 127
41568 Rubio, El SE 166 Va 124
25737 Rubió d'Agramunt L 56 Af 97
36449 Rubiós PO 41 Rd 96
06929 Rubios, Los BA 134 Uc 119
25575 Rubiru L 37 Bc 93
18711 Rubite GR 169 Wd 128
29719 Rubite MA 167 Vf 127
09592 Rublacedo de Abajo BU 30 Wc 93
09592 Rublacedo de Arriba BU 30 Wc 93
09593 Rucandio BU 30 Wc 92
24854 Rucayo LE 15 Ue 91
39539 Rudaguera CB 17 Vf 88
44212 Rudilla TE 72 Yf 102
04151 Ruecas AL 171 Xe 128
06412 Ruecas BA 117 Ua 114
47490 Rueda VA 66 Va 100
50295 Rueda de Jalón Z 52 Ye 99
19339 Rueda de la Sierra GU 71 Ya 103
34839 Rueda de Pisuerga P 29 Vd 91
26586 Ruedas de Enciso, Las RI 51 Xe 96
26145 Ruedas de Ocón, Las RI 32 Xe 95
33576 Ruenes AS 16 Vb 89
39513 Ruente CB 17 Ve 89
39232 Ruerrero CB 30 Wa 91
50331 Ruesca Z 71 Yd 101
34844 Ruesga P 29 Vc 91
50685 Ruesta Z 34 Yf 93
46842 Rugat V 126 Zd 115
19429 Rugilla GU 88 Xc 104
30334 Ruices, Los MC 157 Ye 123
46353 Ruices, Los V 106 Ye 112
30877 Ruíces, Los MC 156 Yd 122
30156 Ruíces, Los MC 157 Yf 122
13249 Ruidera CR 122 Xa 115
24891 Ruiforco de Torío LE 27 Uc 92
38435 Ruigómez TF 180 Ib 178
39230 Ruijas CB 30 Wa 92
39527 Ruiloba CB 17 Ve 88
04560 Ruiní, El AL 170 Xd 127
39528 Ruiseñada CB 17 Ve 88
24520 Ruitelán LE 25 Ta 92
02140 Ruiza, La AB 124 Ya 115
23560 Ruiz Cerezo J 153 Wd 123
13720 Ruizgarcía CR 122 We 113
02410 Ruiz Sánchez AB 140 Ya 117
39312 Rumoroso CB 17 Wa 88
22465 Run, El HU 36 Ac 93
09640 Rupelo BU 49 Wd 96
17131 Rupià GI 59 Da 96
08569 Rupit B 58 Cc 96
08569 Rupit i Pruit B 58 Cc 96
08696 Rus B 58 Bf 95
15109 Rus C 10 Rb 90
23430 Rus J 153 Wd 120
16600 Rus, El CU 104 Xd 112
14960 Rute CO 167 Vd 125
09341 Ruyales del Agua BU 49 Wb 96
09125 Ruyales del Páramo BU 30 Wb 93

S

36312 Sá PO 41 Rb 95
27188 Saa LU 12 Sc 91
27693 Saá LU 24 Se 92
08201 Sabadell B 77 Ca 99
27517 Sabadella LU 24 Sb 93
27178 Sabadelle LU 24 Sc 92
32711 Sabadelle OR 24 Sb 94
31491 Sabaiza NC 33 Yd 93
01129 Sabando VI 32 Xd 92
23685 Sabariego J 152 Vf 123
36938 Sabarigo PO 22 Rb 94
07400 Sa Bassa Blanca IB 111 Da 109
22193 Sabayés HU 54 Zd 95
24810 Sabero LE 28 Uf 91
29500 Sabinal MA 166 Vb 127
03690 Sabinar, El A 142 Zc 118
02534 Sabinar, El AB 139 Xd 120
30441 Sabinar, El MC 140 Xf 119
50617 Sabinar, El Z 53 Ye 96
02611 Sabinares AB 122 Xb 115
38649 Sabinita TF 180 Ib 180
38589 Sabinita, La TF 180 Ic 179
38912 Sabinosa TF 180 Gf 182
50299 Sabiñán Z 71 Yc 100
22600 Sabiñánigo HU 35 Zd 93
23410 Sabiote J 153 We 120
36519 Saborida PO 23 Re 93
36581 Sabrexo PO 23 Re 92
32643 Sabucedo OR 42 Sb 96
36684 Sabucedo PO 23 Rd 93
32821 Sabucedo de Montes OR 23 Sa 95
15815 Sabugueira C 11 Sa 90
07141 Sa Cabaneta IB 110 Ce 111
07529 Sa Cabaneta IB 111 Da 110
07839 Sa Caleta IB 109 Bc 115
07315 Sa Calobra IB 110 Ce 109
07818 Sa Canal IB 109 Bc 115
07579 Sa Canova de Morell IB 111 Db 110
12469 Sacañet CS 107 Zb 109
07198 Sa Casa Blanca IB 110 Ce 111
07609 Sa Casa de Guarda IB 110 Ce 112
19432 Sacecorbo GU 88 Xd 104
24744 Saceda LE 26 Tc 95
16520 Saceda del Río CU 88 Xc 107
16463 Saceda-Trasierra CU 87 Xa 108
23267 Sacedillas, Las J 138 We 118
19120 Sacedón GU 88 Xb 106
16191 Sacedoncillo CU 88 Xe 107
19222 Sacedoncillo GU 68 We 103
13414 Saceruela CR 119 Vc 115
07430 Sa Cleda IB 111 Da 110
36121 Sacos PO 23 Rd 93
07579 Sa Cova IB 111 Dc 110
40237 Sacramenia SG 67 Wa 100
41730 Sacramento SE 164 Ua 126
18818 Sacristía, La GR 154 Xc 122
07700 Sa Cudia Vella IB 77 Eb 109
15160 Sada C 11 Re 88
31491 Sada NC 33 Yd 93
50670 Sádaba Z 33 Ye 95
17855 Sadernes GI 39 Cd 95
07579 Sa Devesa IB 111 Db 110
32415 Sadurnín OR 23 Rf 95
16430 Saelices CU 104 Xb 109

298 | Riudoms

09124 Sandoval de la Reina BU 29 Vf 93
24144 San Emiliano LE 14 Tf 91
11312 San Enrique CA 173 Ue 131
33734 San Esteban AS 13 Ta 89
33843 San Esteban AS 14 Te 89
33579 San Esteban AS 16 Vc 89
09119 San Esteban BU 48 Vf 95
39590 San Esteban CB 17 Vf 88
48191 San Esteban de Galdames BI 19 Wf 89
42330 San Esteban de Gormaz SO 50 We 99
37671 San Esteban de la Sierra SA 82 Ua 105
22512 San Esteban de Litera HU 55 Ab 97
22482 San Esteban del Mall HU 36 Ad 95
49650 San Esteban del Molar ZA 46 Uc 97
05289 San Esteban de los Patos AV 84 Vc 104
05412 San Esteban del Valle AV 84 Va 107
24760 San Esteban de Nogales LE 45 Ua 96
33130 San Esteban de Pravia AS 14 Tf 87
24415 San Esteban de Valdueza LE 26 Tc 93
24234 San Esteban de Villacalbiel LE 27 Uc 94
05229 San Esteban de Zapardiel AV 66 Va 102
03769 Sanet y Negrals A 127 Zf 116
24378 San Facundo LE 26 Td 93
32139 San Fagundo OR 23 Rf 94
22808 San Felices HU 34 Zb 94
26292 San Felices RI 31 Xa 93
42113 San Felices SO 51 Xf 97
34846 San Felices de Castillería P 29 Vd 91
37270 San Felices de los Gallegos SA 81 Tb 103
22372 Sanfelices de Solana HU 35 Zf 94
35450 San Felipe GC 184 Kc 180
24228 Sanfelismo LE 27 Ud 93
22470 San Feliú de Veri HU 36 Ad 94
24760 San Félix de la Valdería LE 45 Tf 95
33785 San Feliz AS 14 Td 88
33326 San Feliz AS 15 Ud 88
24397 San Feliz de las Lavanderas LE 26 Ua 92
24287 San Feliz de Órbigo LE 27 Ua 94
24890 San Feliz de Torío LE 27 Uc 92
11100 San Fernando CA 172 Te 130
35457 San Fernando GC 184 Kc 180
37492 San Fernando SA 82 Ua 103
28830 San Fernando de Henares MD 86 Wc 106
15337 San Fiz C 10 Sb 86
32368 San Fiz OR 25 Sf 94
27516 San Fiz de Asma LU 24 Sb 93
04500 San Francisco AL 155 Ya 124
33610 San Francisco AS 15 Ub 89
06109 San Francisco de Olivenza BA 131 Sf 116
03177 San Fulgencio A 142 Zb 120
40134 Sangarcía SG 66 Vd 103
05146 San García de Ingelmos AV 84 Uf 104
22100 Sangarrén HU 54 Zd 96
10690 San Gil CC 98 Te 109
23747 San Ginés J 136 Vf 120
30382 San Ginés de la Jara MC 157 Zb 123
30834 Sangonera la Seca MC 156 Ye 121
30833 Sangonera La Verde MC 157 Ye 121
20211 San Gregorio SS 20 Xe 91
31400 Sangüesa = Zangoza NC 33 Ye 93
29400 Sanguijuela MA 166 Ue 128
36518 Sanguiñedo PO 23 Rf 93
32626 Sanguñedo OR 43 Se 96
11500 San Ignacio CA 172 Te 129
28420 San Ignacio MD 85 Vf 105
41209 San Ignacio del Viar SE 148 Ua 123
40100 San Ildefonso o La Granja SG 67 Vf 103
32415 Sanín OR 23 Rf 95
06220 San Isidro BA 133 Td 117
30397 San Isidro MC 157 Yf 123
38611 San Isidro TF 180 Ic 180
03349 San Isidro de Albatera A 142 Za 119
34208 San Isidro de Dueñas P 47 Vc 97
11594 San Isidro de Guadalete CA 172 Ua 129
31312 San Isidro del Pinar NC 33 Yd 94
04117 San Isidro de Níjar AL 171 Xe 127
30730 San Javier MC 157 Za 122
21200 San Jerónimo H 147 Tc 121
41092 San Jerónimo SE 148 Tf 124
34406 San Jorde P 29 Vd 93
12320 San Jorge CS 93 Ab 105
22283 San Jorge HU 53 Zc 97
06108 San Jorge de Alor BA 132 Sf 117
04118 San José AL 171 Xf 128
35307 San José GC 184 Kd 180
38712 San José TF 181 Hb 177
23684 San José de la Rábita J 152 Vf 124
41300 Sanjosé de la Rinconada SE 148 Ua 124
11580 San José del Valle CA 173 Ub 129
30540 San Joy MC 141 Ye 119
03400 San Juan A 142 Za 117
06176 San Juan BA 132 Tc 117
48145 San Juan BI 19 Xb 90
09194 San Juan BU 49 Wc 95
39808 San Juan CB 18 Wd 89
10859 San Juan CC 81 Tc 107
22452 San Juan HU 36 Ab 94
28680 San Juan MD 85 Ve 106
38686 San Juan TF 180 Ib 179
38729 San Juan TF 181 Hb 176
38270 San Juan TF 181 Id 177
46390 San Juan V 106 Ye 111
33312 San Juan de Amandi AS 15 Ud 88
41920 San Juan de Aznalfarache SE 164 Tf 124
48192 San Juan de Berbikiz BI 19 Wf 89
46669 San Juan de Énova V 126 Zd 114
05358 San Juan de la Encinilla AV 84 Va 104
47114 San Juan de la Guarda VA 65 Uf 100
24545 San Juan de la Mata LE 25 Tc 93
05111 San Juan de la Nava AV 84 Vb 106
San Juan de la Rambla TF 180 Ic 178
22213 San Juan del Flumen HU 54 Ze 98
05120 San Juan del Molinillo AV 84 Vb 106
09490 San Juan del Monte BU 49 Wc 98
05145 San Juan del Olmo AV 84 Uf 105
21610 San Juan del Puerto H 162 Ta 125
49525 San Juan del Rebollar ZA 45 Td 98
38450 San Juan del Reparo TF 180 Ib 178
50820 San Juan de Mozarrifar Z 53 Za 98
48550 San Juan de Muskiz BI 19 Wf 89
33417 San Juan de Nieva AS 15 Ua 87
09199 San Juan de Ortega BU 30 Wd 94
22367 San Juan de Plan HU 36 Ac 93
39450 San Juan de Raicedo CB 17 Vf 89
24769 San Juan de Torres LE 27 Ua 95
37500 Sanjuanejo SA 81 Td 105
49627 San Juanico el Nuevo ZA 45 Tf 96
23770 San Julián J 152 Ve 120
29140 San Julián MA 175 Vd 128
30817 San Julián MC 156 Yc 122
22192 San Julián de Banzo HU 54 Zd 95
22611 San Julián de Basa HU 35 Ze 94
49358 San Justo ZA 44 Tc 96
24226 San Justo de las Regueras LE 27 Ud 93
24710 San Justo de la Vega LE 26 Tf 94
24225 San Justo de los Oteros LE 27 Ud 94
41730 San Leandro SE 164 Ua 126
42140 San Leonardo de Yagüe SO 50 Wf 98
09512 San Llorente BU 19 We 91
47317 San Llorente VA 48 Vf 98
34405 San Llorente de la Vega BU 29 Ve 94
34113 San Llorente del Páramo P 28 Vb 94
33394 San Lorenzo AS 15 Uc 87
35018 San Lorenzo GC 184 Kd 180
22585 San Lorenzo HU 55 Ad 95
24415 San Lorenzo LE 25 Tc 93
49140 San Lorenzo ZA 45 Ua 98
13779 San Lorenzo de Calatrava CR 137 Wb 118
28200 San Lorenzo de El Escorial MD 85 Vf 105
16770 San Lorenzo de la Parrilla CU 104 Xd 109
22212 San Lorenzo del Flumen HU 54 Ze 97
48120 San Lorenzo de Mesterica BI 19 Xb 88
32545 San Lorenzo de Pentes OR 43 Se 96
05696 San Lorenzo de Tormes AV 83 Ud 106
22338 San Lorién HU 36 Ab 94
32366 San Lourenzo OR 44 Sf 95
11540 Sanlúcar de Barrameda CA 164 Td 128
21595 Sanlúcar de Guadiana H 146 Sd 124
41800 Sanlúcar La Mayor SE 164 Te 124
29693 San Luis de Sabinillas MA 174 Ue 130
15885 San Mamede C 23 Rd 92
27530 San Mamede LU 24 Sb 93
32552 San Mamede de Edrada OR 43 Se 96
15824 San Mamede de Ferreiros C 23 Re 91
48160 San Mames BI 19 Xa 89
39557 San Mamés CB 17 Vd 90
22367 San Mamés HU 36 Ac 93
24764 San Mamés LE 27 Ua 95
28739 San Mamés MD 68 Wb 103
15320 San Mames das Pontes de García Rodríguez C 12 Sa 88
09126 San Mamés de Abar BU 29 Vf 92
09230 San Mamés de Burgos BU 30 Wb 94
34127 San Mamés de Campos P 29 Vc 94
39192 San Mamés de Meruelo CB 18 Wc 88
49722 San Marcial ZA 64 Ub 100
48215 San Marcos BI 19 Xc 89
15509 San Marcos C 11 Rf 88
15890 San Marcos C 23 Rd 91
10318 San Marcos CC 99 Ud 109
22300 San Marcos HU 55 Aa 96
38430 San Marcos TF 180 Ib 178
20211 San Martin SS 20 Xe 90
33111 San Martín AS 14 Tf 90
48410 San Martín BI 19 Xa 90
39638 San Martín CB 18 Wa 89
39698 San Martín CB 18 Wa 89
39806 San Martín CB 18 Wc 89
22470 San Martín HU 36 Ad 94
23479 San Martín J 153 Xa 121
27556 San Martín LU 24 Sb 92
31272 San Martín NC 32 Xe 92
26131 San Martín RI 32 Xe 95
37220 San Martín SA 63 Ta 102
40295 San Martín SG 67 Ve 101
27390 San Martín de Albaredos LU 25 Se 94
16370 San Martín de Boniches CU 106 Yc 109
48190 San Martín de Carral BI 19 Wf 89
49361 San Martín de Castañeda ZA 44 Tb 96
09212 San Martín de Don BU 31 We 92
39232 San Martín de Elines CB 30 Wa 92
09217 San Martín de Galvarín BU 31 Xb 92
39418 San Martín de Hoyos CB 29 Vf 91
09126 San Martín de Humada BU 29 Vf 93
24326 San Martín de la Cueza LE 28 Va 94
24273 San Martín de la Falamosa LE 27 Ua 92
34349 San Martín de la Fuente P 28 Va 94
24720 San Martín del Agostedo LE 26 Te 94
05357 San Martín de las Cabezas AV 84 Va 104
09574 San Martín de las Ollas BU 18 Wb 91
24688 San Martín de la Tercia LE 15 Ub 91
28330 San Martín de la Vega MD 86 Wc 107
05133 San Martín de la Vega del Alberche AV 84 Uf 106
50584 San Martín de la Virgen de Moncayo Z 52 Yb 97
24393 San Martín del Camino LE 27 Ub 94
37659 San Martín del Castañar SA 82 Tf 105
34407 San Martín del Monte P 29 Vd 93
34111 San Martín del Obispo P 28 Vb 93
09511 San Martín de Losa BU 19 We 91
34844 San Martín de los Herreros P 28 Vc 91
49516 San Martín del Pedroso ZA 44 Tc 98
05132 San Martín del Pimpollar AV 84 Uf 106
33957 San Martín del Rey Aurelio = Sotondrio (San Martín del Rey Aurelio) AS 15 Uc 89
44390 San Martín del Río TE 71 Yd 102
09558 San Martín del Rojo BU 30 Wc 91
34116 San Martín del Valle P 28 Vb 94
09512 San Martín de Mancobo BU 30 Wd 91
45165 San Martín de Montalbán TO 101 Vd 110
24436 San Martín de Moreda LE 25 Tb 92
33777 San Martín de Oscos AS 13 Ta 89
45170 San Martín de Pusa TO 101 Vc 110
09317 San Martín de Rubiales BU 48 Vf 99
49540 San Martín de Tábara ZA 45 Ua 98
24763 San Martín de Torres LE 27 Ua 95
10892 San Martín de Trevejo CC 81 Tb 107
09141 San Martín de Ubierna BU 30 Wb 93
31495 San Martín de Unx NC 33 Yc 93
28680 San Martín de Valdeiglesias MD 85 Vd 106
39419 San Martín de Valdelomar CB 29 Vf 92
49129 San Martín de Valderaduey ZA 46 Ud 98
47209 San Martín de Valvení VA 47 Vc 98
09217 San Martín de Zar BU 31 Xb 92
11340 San Martín o el Tesorillo CA 173 Ue 130
32767 San Martiño OR 24 Sd 94
32372 San Martiño OR 25 Sf 95
32689 San Martiño OR 43 Sc 97
27816 San Martiño de Lanzós LU 12 Sc 88
36637 San Martiño de Meis PO 22 Rb 94
27235 San Martiño dos Condes LU 12 Sb 91
39400 San Mateo CB 17 Vf 89
50840 San Mateo de Gállego Z 53 Zb 98
09199 San Medel BU 30 Wc 95
37791 San Medel SA 83 Ub 106
33679 San Miguel AS 15 Ub 90
06510 San Miguel BA 116 Sf 114
48370 San Miguel BI 19 Xb 88
48290 San Miguel BI 19 Xb 89
39300 San Miguel CB 17 Vf 88
39311 San Miguel CB 17 Vf 89
21330 San Miguel H 147 Tb 122
22549 San Miguel HU 55 Ab 98
23469 San Miguel J 153 We 121
27178 San Miguel LU 24 Sc 92
28380 San Miguel MD 102 Wc 108
32785 San Miguel OR 25 Se 95
34839 San Miguel P 29 Vd 91
38620 San Miguel TF 180 Ic 180
39491 San Miguel de Aguayo CB 17 Vf 90
39766 San Miguel de Aras CB 18 Wc 89
37607 San Miguel de Asperones SA 82 Tf 105
40332 San Miguel de Bernúy SG 67 Wa 100
22413 San Miguel de Cinca HU 55 Aa 97
05514 San Miguel de Corneja AV 83 Ue 106
09572 San Miguel de Cornezuelo BU 30 Wb 91
49717 San Miguel de la Ribera ZA 65 Uc 100
47164 San Miguel del Arroyo VA 66 Vd 100
24398 San Miguel de las Dueñas LE 26 Tc 93
24391 San Miguel del Camino LE 27 Ub 93
49691 San Miguel del Esla ZA 46 Uc 96
48879 San Miguel de Linares BI 19 We 89
49396 San Miguel de Lomba ZA 44 Tb 96
47132 San Miguel del Pino VA 66 Va 99
39687 San Miguel de Luena CB 18 Wa 90
49680 San Miguel del Valle ZA 46 Ud 96
39192 San Miguel de Meruelo CB 18 Wc 88
24324 San Miguel de Montañán LE 28 Ue 95
40380 San Miguel de Neguera SG 67 Wa 101
09258 San Miguel de Pedroso BU 31 We 94
27792 San Miguel de Reinante LU 13 Se 87
03193 San Miguel de Salinas A 157 Zb 121
05150 San Miguel de Serrezuela AV 83 Ue 104
37763 San Miguel de Valero SA 82 Ua 105
27423 Sanmil LU 24 Sc 94
01208 San Millán/Donemiliaga VI 32 Xd 91
09198 San Millán de Juarros BU 30 Wc 95
26326 San Millán de la Cogolla RI 31 Xa 95
09640 San Millán de Lara BU 49 Wd 96
24237 San Millán de los Caballeros LE 27 Uc 95
01427 San Millán de San Zardonil BU 31 Wf 91
26216 San Millán de Yécora RI 31 Wf 93
32688 San Millao OR 43 Sc 97
37340 San Morales SA 65 Uc 103
37208 San Muñoz SA 82 Tf 104
18800 San Nicolás del Moro GR 170 Xb 125
41388 San Nicolás del Puerto SE 149 Uc 121
34349 San Nicolás del Real Camino P 28 Va 94
12140 San Pablo CS 92 Zf 106
41020 San Pablo SE 163 Ua 124
47219 San Pablo de la Moraleja VA 66 Vb 102
45120 San Pablo de los Montes TO 101 Ve 111
11320 San Pablo o Buceite CA 174 Ud 130
32633 San Paio OR 42 Sb 97
36817 San Paio PO 23 Rc 95
23790 San Pantaleón J 151 Ve 121
39764 San Pantaleón de Aras CB 18 Wd 88
09512 San Pantaleón de Losa BU 30 We 91
09125 San Pantaleón del Páramo BU 30 Wb 93
05164 San Pascual AV 84 Vb 103
07819 San Patricio IB 109 Bb 114
15145 San Payo C 11 Rc 89
10600 San Pedrillo de Abajo CC 98 Te 108
02326 San Pedro AB 123 Xe 116
04500 San Pedro AL 169 Xb 125
33347 San Pedro AS 16 Uf 88
06176 San Pedro BA 132 Tc 117
48191 San Pedro BI 19 Wf 89
15116 San Pedro C 10 Ra 89
39806 San Pedro CB 18 Wc 89
10516 San Pedro CC 115 Se 112
35489 San Pedro GC 184 Kb 180
23790 San Pedro J 151 Ve 122
23590 San Pedro J 153 We 122
24141 San Pedro LE 14 Te 90
27111 San Pedro LU 13 Sf 90
40493 San Pedro SG 67 Ve 102
36448 San Pedro = Batalláns PO 41 Rd 96
24252 San Pedro Bercianos LE 27 Ub 94
34889 San Pedro Cansoles P 28 Va 92
24316 San Pedro Castañero LE 26 Td 93
48540 San Pedro de Abanto BI 19 Wf 89
29670 San Pedro de Alcántara MA 174 Va 130
09640 San Pedro de Arlanza BU 49 Wd 96
38713 San Pedro de Breña Alta TF 180 Hb 176
49628 San Pedro de Ceque ZA 45 Tf 96
24879 San Pedro de Foncollada LE 28 Ue 92
09247 San Pedro de la Hoz BU 30 Wd 93
49183 San Pedro de la Nave-Almendra ZA 45 Tf 99
49145 San Pedro de las Cuevas ZA 45 Ua 98
24248 San Pedro de las Dueñas LE 27 Ub 95

300 | Sandoval de la Reina

35450 Santa María de Guía de Gran Canaria GC 184 Kc 180
42260 Santa María de Huerta SO 70 Xe 101
28296 Santa María de la Alameda MD 85 Ve 105
04710 Santa María del Águila AL 170 Xb 128
24795 Santa María de la Isla LE 26 Ua 94
22148 Santa María de la Nuez HU 35 Aa 95
05530 Santa María del Arroyo AV 84 Va 105
42141 Santa María de las Hoyas SO 50 Wf 98
10318 Santa María de las Lomas CC 99 Uc 108
49696 Santa María de la Vega ZA 45 Ub 96
34126 Santa María de la Vega P 28 Vb 94
05510 Santa María del Berrocal AV 83 Ud 105
07320 Santa Maria del Camí IB 110 Ce 111
08717 Santa Maria del Camí B 57 Bc 99
09342 Santa María del Campo BU 48 Wa 96
16621 Santa María del Campo Rus CU 104 Xd 111
40310 Santa María del Cerro SG 68 Wb 101
05193 Santa María del Cubillo AV 85 Vd 104
39583 Santa María de Lebeña CB 17 Vc 89
19445 Santa María del Espino GU 70 Xe 103
09292 Santa María del Invierno BU 30 Wd 94
09588 Santa María de Llano de Tudela BU 19 We 90
17320 Santa Maria de Llorell GI 59 Cf 98
38111 Santa María del Mar TF 181 Ie 178
24343 Santa María del Monte de Cea LE 28 Uf 94
24153 Santa María del Monte del Condado LE 27 Ud 92
05580 Santa María de los Caballeros AV 83 Uc 106
16639 Santa María de los Llanos CU 104 Xb 112
37682 Santa María de los Llanos SA 82 Ua 106
24291 Santa María de los Oteros LE 27 Ud 94
24240 Santa María del Páramo LE 27 Ub 94
42211 Santa María del Prado SO 69 Xc 100
24344 Santa María del Río LE 28 Uf 93
05429 Santa María del Tiétar AV 85 Vc 107
16878 Santa María del Val CU 89 Xf 105
08106 Santa Maria de Martor. B 77 Cb 99
17512 Santa Maria de Matamala GI 58 Ca 96
34492 Santa María de Mave P 29 Ve 92
09353 Santa María de Mercadillo BU 49 Wc 97
08517 Santa Maria de Merlès B 58 Bf 96
08787 Santa Maria de Miralles B 76 Bd 99
08110 Santa Maria de Montcada B 77 Cb 100
25354 Santa Maria de Montma-gastrell L 56 Ba 98
34828 Santa María de Nava P 29 Ve 91
06908 Santa María de Nava la Zapatera u Hoya de Santa María BA 148 Tf 120
04693 Santa María de Nieva AL 155 Ya 124
24276 Santa María de Ordás LE 27 Ub 92
08460 Santa Maria de Palautordera B 58 Cc 98
34849 Santa María de Redondo P 17 Vd 91
40594 Santa María de Riaza SG 68 Wd 100
37468 Santa María de Sando SA 64 Tf 103
14710 Santa María de Trasierra CO 150 Va 121
49333 Santa María de Valverde ZA 45 Ua 97
08455 Santa Maria de Vilalba B 58 Cc 99
26133 Santa María en Cameros RI 51 Xc 95
22131 Santa María la Blanca HU 54 Aa 97
40440 Santa María la Real de Nieva SG 66 Vd 102
07712 Santa Mariana IB 77 Eb 109
09219 Santa María Ribarredonda BU 31 We 93
09131 Santa María Tajadura BU 30 Wb 94
33117 Santa Marina AS 14 Ua 90
09292 Santa Marina BU 30 Wd 94
13195 Santa Marina CR 121 Wa 115
21207 Santa Marina H 148 Td 121
23338 Santa Marina J 138 Wf 119
26132 Santa Marina RI 51 Xd 95
37116 Santa Marina SA 64 Tf 102
20495 Santa Marina SS 20 Xe 90
24393 Santa Marina del Rey LE 27 Ua 93
24493 Santa Marina del Sil LE 26 Tc 93
24722 Santa Marina de Somoza LE 26 Te 94
24378 Santa Marina de Torre LE 26 Td 93
24915 Santa Marina de Valdeón LE 16 Va 90
24763 Santa Marinica LE 27 Ua 94
15122 Santa Mariña C 10 Qf 89
27439 Santa Mariña LU 24 Sb 93
32557 Santa Mariña da Ponte OR 43 Sf 95
32669 Santa Mariña de Augasantas OR 42 Sb 95
27309 Santa Mariña de Lagostelle LU 11 Sa 89
36569 Santa Mariña de Presqueiras PO 23 Rd 93
15561 Santa Mariña do Monte C 11 Rf 87
02630 Santa Marta AB 123 Xe 113
02639 Santa Marta AB 123 Xe 114
06150 Santa Marta BA 132 Tc 117
10198 Santa Marta CC 98 Tf 111
27299 Santa Marta LU 12 Sb 90
10198 Santa Marta de Magasca CC 98 Tf 111
27745 Santa Marta de Meilán LU 12 Se 88
49626 Santa Marta de Tera ZA 45 Ua 97
37900 Santa Marta de Tormes SA 65 Uc 103
22451 Santa Maura HU 36 Ac 94
19269 Santamera GU 69 Xb 102
34878 Santana P 28 Vc 92
39001*Santander CB 18 Wb 88
08397 Sant Andreu B 59 Cd 99
08740 Sant Andreu de la Barca B 77 Bf 100
17800 Sant Andreu del Coll GI 58 Cc 95
08318 Sant Andreu del Far B 58 Cc 99
08392 Sant Andreu de Llavaneres B 58 Cc 99
17845 Sant Andreu del Terri GI 59 Cf 96
17455 Sant Andreu Salou GI 59 Ce 97
07769 Santandria IB 77 Df 109
17154 Sant Aniol de Finestres GI 58 Cd 96
25213 Sant Antolí i Vilanova L 57 Bc 99
03570 Sant Antoni A 143 Ze 117
Sant Antoni IB 109 Bb 115
46195 Sant Antoni de Llombai V 126 Zc 113
07820 Sant Antoni de Portmany IB 109 Bb 115
08459 Sant Antoni de Vilamajor B 58 Cc 98
07650 Santanyí IB 111 Da 112
09588 Santa Olaja BU 19 We 90
24164 Santa Olaja de Eslonza LE 27 Ud 93
24892 Santa Olaja de la Acción LE 28 Uf 92
24199 Santa Olaja de la Ribera LE 27 Uc 93
24813 Santa Olaja de la Varga LE 28 Uf 91
34112 Santa Olaja de la Vega P 28 Vb 93
24156 Santa Olaja de Porma LE 27 Uf 93
39418 Santa Olalla CB 29 Ve 91
18800 Santa Olalla GR 170 Xa 125
45530 Santa Olalla TO 101 Vd 108
39491 Santa Olalla de Aguayo CB 17 Vf 90
09292 Santa Olalla de Bureba BU 30 Wd 94
21260 Santa Olalla del Cala H 148 Te 121
09268 Santa Olalla del Valle BU 31 We 94
09559 Santa Olalla de Valdivielso BU 30 Wc 92
37690 Santa Olalla de Yeltes SA 82 Te 104
43710 Santa Oliva T 76 Bd 101
17811 Santa Pau GI 58 Cd 96
17244 Santa Pellaia GI 59 Cf 97
43421 Santa Perpètua de Gaià T 76 Bc 100
08130 Santa Perpètua de Mogoda B 77 Cb 99
03130 Santa Pola A 142 Zc 119
03114 Santa Pola de l'Est A 142 Zc 119
07750 Santa Ponça IB 77 Df 109
07180 Santa Ponça IB 110 Cc 111
07509 Santa Ponça IB 111 Db 111
13115 Santa Quiteria CR 120 Vd 113
44165 Santa Quiteria TE 90 Ye 104
15818 Santarandel C 11 Rf 90
49177 Santarén de los Peces ZA 64 Ua 102
07712 Santa Rito IB 77 Eb 109
33614 Santa Rosa AS 15 Ub 89
14029 Santa Rosa CO 150 Va 122
34260 Santa Rosalía BU 48 Vf 95
29591 Santa Rosalía MA 175 Vc 128
36457 Santas PO 41 Rd 96
15860 Santa Sabiña C 10 Ra 90
17240 Santa Sedina GI 59 Cf 98
15859 Santa Sía de Roma C 10 Ra 90
07500 Santa Sirga IB 111 Db 111
24330 Santas Martas LE 27 Ud 94
08398 Santa Susanna B 59 Ce 99
25290 Santa Susanna L 57 Bd 97
17110 Santa Susanna de Peralta GI 59 Da 97
37891 Santa Teresa SA 83 Uc 104
38390 Santa Ursula TF 180 Id 178
15960 Santa Uxía de Ribeira C 22 Ra 93
08519 Sant Bartomeu del Grau B 58 Cb 97
08511 Sant Bartomeu Sesgorgues B 58 Cc 96
03818 Sant Benet A 142 Zd 116
17863 Sant Bernabé de les Tenes GI 58 Cb 95
07712 Sant Bernat IB 77 Eb 109
08200 Sant Boi de Llobregat B 77 Ca 100
08589 Sant Boi de Lluçanès B 58 Ca 96
43540 Sant Carles de la Ràpita T 93 Ad 105
07850 Sant Carles de Peralta IB 109 Bd 114
17244 Sant Cebrià de Lledó GI 59 Cf 97
08396 Sant Cebrià de Vallalta B 58 Cd 99
42173 Sant Cecilia SO 51 Xd 96
08470 Sant Celoni B 58 Cc 98
25286 Sant Climenç L 57 Bc 97
07712 Sant Climent IB 77 Eb 109
25793 Sant Climent L 56 Bb 95
17170 Sant Climent d'Amer GI 59 Cd 96
08849 Sant Climent de Llobregat B 77 Bf 100
17110 Sant Climent de Peralta GI 59 Da 97
17751 Sant Climent Sescebes GI 40 Cf 94
08698 Sant Corneli B 57 Bf 95
17246 Sant Cristina d'Aro GI 59 Da 98
08296 Sant Cristòfol de Castellbell B 57 Be 99
25747 Sant Cristòfol de la Donzell L 56 Ba 96
08172 Sant Cugat del Vallès B 77 Ca 100
08798 Sant Cugat de Sesgarrigues B 76 Be 100
17183 Sant Dalmai GI 59 Ce 97
33719 Sante AS 13 Tb 87
48890 Santecilla BI 18 Wd 89
50373 Santed Z 71 Yc 102
36689 Santeles C 23 Rd 92
36689 Santeles PO 23 Rc 92
09574 Santelices BU 18 Wb 90
07159 Sant Elm IB 110 Cc 111
21330 San Telmo H 147 Ta 122
07730 Sant Eloi IB 77 Ea 109
47609 Santervás de Campos VA 46 Uf 95
42153 Santervás de la Sierra SO 50 Xc 97
34112 Santervás de la Vega P 28 Vb 93
42141 Santervás del Burgo SO 49 Wf 98
43815 Santes Creus (Aiguamúrcia) T 76 Bc 100
31740 Santesteban NC 21 Yb 90
08660 Sant Esteve B 57 Bf 97
25651 Sant Esteve L 56 Ba 96
17468 Sant Esteve de Guialbes GI 59 Cf 96
17512 Sant Esteve de la Riba GI 58 Ca 95
25632 Sant Esteve de la Sarga L 56 Ae 96
17154 Sant Esteve de Llémena GI 59 Cd 96
08461 Sant Esteve de Palautordera B 58 Cc 98
17512 Sant Esteve de Vallespiráns GI 58 Ca 95
08635 Sant Esteve Sesrovires B 76 Bf 100
08211 Sant Feliçu del Racò B 58 Ca 99
07769 Sant Felip IB 77 Df 108
03158 Sant Felip Neri A 142 Zb 119
17256 Sant Feliu de Boada GI 59 Da 97
17451 Sant Feliu de Buixalleu GI 58 Cd 98
08182 Sant Feliu de Codines B 58 Ca 98
17220 Sant Feliu de Guixols GI 59 Da 98
08690 Sant Feliu de Llobregat B 77 Ca 100
17174 Sant Feliu de Pallerols GI 58 Cd 96
08274 Sant Feliu Sasserra B 58 Ca 97
17850 Sant Ferriol GI 59 Ce 95
08105 Sant Fost de Campsentelles B 77 Cb 99
07860 Sant Francesc de Formentera IB 109 Bc 116
07818 Sant Francesc de ses Salines IB 109 Bc 115
08272 Sant Fruitós de Bages B 57 Bf 98
43429 Sant Gallard T 76 Bc 99
08719 Sant Genís B 57 Bd 99
08389 Sant Genís de Palafolls B 59 Ce 99
17170 Sant Genís Sacosta GI 58 Cd 96
08339 Sant Ginés de Vilassar = Vilassar de Dalt B 77 Cc 99
17150 Sant Gregori GI 59 Ce 97
08670 Sant Gugat B 57 Be 97
25270 Sant Guim de Freixenet B 57 Bc 98
25211 Sant Guim de la Plana L 56 Bb 98
17403 Sant Hilari Sacalm GI 58 Cd 97
08512 Sant Hipòlit de Voltregà B 58 Cb 96
48291 Santiago BI 20 Xc 90
23760 Santiago J 151 Vf 121
20690 Santiago SS 20 Xd 90
45910 Santiago Apóstol TO 101 Vd 107
10510 Santiago de Alcántara CC 97 Se 111
05621 Santiago de Aravalle AV 83 Uc 107
23612 Santiago de Calatrava J 152 Ve 122
15705 Santiago de Compostela C 23 Rc 91
23290 Santiago de la Espada J 139 Xc 120
37311 Santiago de la Puebla SA 83 Ue 104
49323 Santiago de la Requejada ZA 44 Tc 96
30720 Santiago de la Ribera MC 157 Zb 122
47164 Santiago del Arroyo VA 66 Vc 100
16670 Santiago de la Torre CU 123 Xc 112
24766 Santiago de la Valduerna LE 26 Ua 95
10191 Santiago del Campo CC 98 Td 111
05592 Santiago del Collado AV 83 Ud 106
05630 Santiago del Collado AV 83 Ud 107
24273 Santiago del Molinillo LE 27 Ua 93
38690 Santiago del Teide TF 180 Ib 179
34490 Santiago del Val P 48 Vd 95
02513 Santiago de Mora AB 140 Yc 117
09588 Santiago de Tudela BU 19 We 90
36872 Santiago do Covelo = O Covelo PO 42 Rd 95
24732 Santiago Millas LE 26 Tf 94
23290 Santiago Pontones J 139 Xc 120
27350 Santiago Rubián LU 24 Sd 93
33826 Santianes AS 14 Te 89
33660 Santianes AS 15 Ub 89
33569 Santianes AS 16 Uf 88
39500 Santibáñez CB 17 Ve 89
40512 Santibáñez de Ayllón SG 68 We 100
37740 Santibáñez de Béjar SA 83 Uc 106
34486 Santibáñez de Ecla P 29 Vd 92
09350 Santibáñez de Esgueva BU 49 Wb 98
24795 Santibáñez de la Isla LE 26 Ua 94
34870 Santibáñez de la Peña P 28 Vb 92
37670 Santibáñez de la Sierra SA 82 Ua 106
37799 Santibáñez del Cañedo SA 64 Ub 102
37120 Santibáñez del Río SA 64 Ub 103
24315 Santibañez del Toral LE 26 Td 93
09617 Santibáñez del Val BU 49 Wd 97
24379 Santibañez de Montes LE 26 Te 93
33676 Santibáñez de Murias AS 15 Uc 90
24228 Santibáñez de Porma LE 27 Ud 93
34844 Santibáñez de Resoba P 28 Vc 91
24815 Santibáñez de Rueda LE 28 Ue 92
49625 Santibáñez de Tera ZA 45 Ua 97
47331 Santibáñez de Valcorba VA 66 Vd 99
24288 Santibáñez de Valdeiglesias LE 26 Ua 94
49610 Santibáñez de Vidriales ZA 45 Tf 96
10859 Santibáñez el Alto CC 98 Tc 107
10666 Santibáñez el Bajo CC 98 Te 107
09150 Santibáñez-Zarzaguda BU 30 Wb 94
35411 Santidad GC 184 Kc 180
46811 Santig V 125 Za 115
32314 Santigoso OR 25 Ta 94
33557 Santillan AS 16 Ue 89
09340 Santillán BU 49 Wb 96
39540 Santillán CB 17 Vd 88
04532 Santillana AL 170 Xb 126
39330 Santillana CB 17 Vf 88
40109 Santillana SG 85 Vf 103
34469 Santillana de Campos P 29 Vd 94
34126 Santillán de la Vega P 28 Vb 94
27422 Santiorxo LU 24 Sc 94
41970 Santiponce SE 148 Tf 124
33189 San Tirso AS 15 Ub 88
33619 San Tirso AS 15 Ub 89
11630 Santiscal, El CA 165 Ub 128
08272 Sant Iscle B 57 Bf 98
17133 Sant Iscle GI 59 Da 96
08359 Sant Iscle de Vallalta B 58 Cd 99
06320 Santísimo Cristo del Humilladero BA 133 Td 118
15808 Santiso = Agro do Chao (Santiso) C 23 Rf 91
15113 Santiso de Vilanova C 10 Rb 89
23250 Santisteban del Puerto J 138 We 119
39698 Santiude de Toranzo CB 17 Wa 89
39490 Santiurde de Reinosa CB 17 Vf 90
09226 Santiuste BU 48 Wa 95
19245 Santiuste GU 69 Xb 102
42193 Santiuste SO 50 Xa 99
40460 Santiuste de San Juan Bautista SG 66 Vc 102
37110 Santiz SA 64 Ua 101
08458 Sant Jaume de Fifà B 58 Cc 98
08619 Sant Jaume de Frontanyà B 58 Ca 95
17854 Sant Jaume de Llierca GI 58 Cd 95
43877 Sant Jaume d'Enveja T 93 Ae 104
07730 Sant Jaume Mediterrani IB 77 Ea 109
08784 Sant Jaume Sesoliveres B 76 Be 100
17230 Sant Joan GI 59 Da 97
07240 Sant Joan IB 111 Da 111
03550 Sant Joan d'Alacant A 142 Zd 118
08569 Sant Joan de Fàbregues B 58 Cc 96
07810 Sant Joan de Labritja IB 109 Bd 114
17860 Sant Joan de les Abadesses GI 58 Cb 95

302 | Santa María de Guía de Gran Canaria

31395 Solchaga NC 33 Yc 93
12182 Sol de la Foia, El CS 92 Zf 107
03698 Sol del Camp A 142 Zc 118
07181 Sol de Mallorca IB 110 Cd 112
AD100 Soldeu ◘ AND 38 Be 93
27328 Soldón LU 25 Sf 93
09249 Solduengo BU 30 Wd 93
19283 Soledad, La GU 70 Xd 102
21610 Soledad, La H 161 Ta 125
22480 Soler, El HU 55 Ac 95
23569 Solera J 153 Wd 122
16216 Solera del Gabaldón CU 105 Ya 110
25163 Soleràs, El L 75 Ae 100
04647 Soleres, Los AL 155 Yb 124
11400 Solete Alto, El CA 172 Tf 129
42223 Soliedra SO 70 Xd 100
12560 Sol i Mar CS 108 Aa 108
17246 Solius GI 59 Cf 98
22584 Soliva HU 56 Ad 95
43412 Solivella T 75 Bb 100
07816 S'Olivera IB 109 Bc 115
22587 Soliveta HU 55 Ae 95
46430 Sollana V 126 Zd 113
48860 Sollano-Llantada BI 19 Wf 89
44145 Sollavientos TE 91 Zc 106
24857 Solle LE 16 Ue 91
15240 Solleiros C 22 Ra 92
07100 Sóller IB 110 Ce 110
07340 Solleric IB 110 Ce 110
39738 Solórzano CB 18 Wc 88
05130 Solosancho AV 84 Va 105
25280 Solsona L 57 Bd 97
18196 Solynieve GR 169 Wd 126
42257 Somaén SO 70 Xe 101
39400 Somahoz CB 17 Vf 89
26313 Somalo RI 31 Xb 94
22752 Somanés HU 34 Zb 93
01307 Somaniego VI 31 Xb 93
39490 Somballe CB 17 Vf 90
38589 Sombrera TF 180 Id 179
07620 Som de Baix IB 110 Ce 111
33840 Somiedo AS 14 Te 90
33203 Somio AS 15 Uc 87
39140 Somo CB 18 Wb 88
19275 Somolinos GU 69 Wf 101
04877 Somontín AL 170 Xd 124
28223 Somosaguas MD 86 Wb 106
28756 Somosierra MD 68 Wc 102
27578 Somoza LU 24 Sa 92
27653 Son LU 25 Sf 91
07750 So N' Abalzer IB 77 Df 108
39780 Sonabia CB 18 We 88
07629 Son Agusti IB 110 Cf 111
07690 So N'Alegre IB 111 Da 112
07509 So N'Amer IB 111 Da 111
07748 So N'Ametler IB 77 Df 108
07509 Son Amoixa IB 111 Db 111
07769 So N' Angel IB 77 Df 108
07190 Son Antich IB 110 Cd 110
07769 So Na Parets Nou IB 77 Df 109
07750 Son Arro Gran IB 77 Ea 109
07194 Son Balagner IB 110 Cc 111
07190 Son Bauza IB 110 Cd 111
07590 Son Besso IB 111 Dc 110
07639 Son Bielo IB 111 Cf 112
07519 Son Bisbal IB 111 Da 110
07150 Son Bosc IB 110 Cc 111
07609 Son Boscana IB 111 Cf 112
07730 Son Bou de Baix IB 77 Ea 109
07469 Son Bruy IB 111 Da 109
07639 Son Busqueret IB 111 Cf 112
07240 Son Calderer IB 111 Da 111
07500 Son Campanario IB 111 Db 111
07749 Son Carabata IB 77 Ea 109
07540 Son Carrio IB 111 Db 111
07609 Son Catany IB 110 Cf 112
07511 Son Cervera IB 111 Cf 111
09572 Soncillo BU 18 Wb 91
07210 Son Coll Vell IB 111 Cf 111
07659 Son Corne Pons IB 111 Da 112
07730 Son Costas IB 77 Ea 109
07690 Son Danuset IB 111 Da 112
07609 Son Delebau Nou IB 110 Ce 112
44712 Son del Puerto TE 90 Za 104
25589 Son de Pino = Son L 37 Ba 93
07260 Son Doctor IB 111 Da 111
12480 Soneja CS 107 Zd 110
07769 Son Escudero IB 77 Df 108
07170 Son Ferrandell IB 110 Cd 110
07007 Son Ferriol IB 110 Ce 111
07750 Son Fonoll IB 77 Df 109
07509 Son Gall Vell IB 111 Db 111
07609 Son Garauet IB 111 Cf 112
07620 Son Garcies de S'Aljub IB 110 Ce 111
07260 Son Gornals IB 111 Da 111
07340 Son Grau IB 110 Ce 110
07199 Son Gual IB 110 Ce 111
07529 Son Guillot IB 111 Da 111
07144 So N'Horrac IB 111 Cf 110
07509 Son Joan Jaume IB 111 Da 111
07220 Son Llubi IB 111 Cf 111
07509 Son Macià IB 111 Db 111
07769 Son March IB 77 Df 109
07459 Son Mari IB 111 Db 110
07609 Son Marranet IB 111 Cf 112
07750 Son Martorellet IB 77 Ea 109
07579 Son Mascaro IB 111 Db 110
07142 Son Matzina IB 110 Ce 111
07210 Son Mesquida IB 111 Cf 111
07609 Son Mesquida IB 111 Cf 112
07209 Son Mesquida IB 111 Da 112
07500 Son Mesquida Vell IB 111 Db 111
07579 Son Morei Vell IB 111 Dc 110
07639 Son Moro IB 110 Cf 112
07208 Son Moro IB 111 Da 112
07560 Son Moro IB 111 Dc 111
07170 Son Morp IB 110 Cd 110
07769 Son Morro IB 77 De 109
07450 Son Morro IB 111 Da 110
07100 Son Muleta IB 110 Cd 110
07110 Son Muntaner IB 110 Ce 111
07208 Son Negre IB 111 Da 112
07540 Son Negre IB 111 Db 111
07638 Son N'Elegant IB 111 Da 112
07630 Son Nicolan IB 111 Da 112
07194 Son Noguera IB 110 Cd 111
07369 So N'Odre IB 110 Cf 110
07760 Son Oleo IB 77 De 109
07170 Son Oleza IB 110 Cd 110
07320 Son Oliver IB 110 Ce 110
07199 So N'Oliveret IB 110 Ce 111
07220 Son Palou Nou IB 111 Cf 111
07740 Son Parc IB 77 Ea 108
07440 Son Parera IB 111 Da 110
07639 Son Pau IB 111 Cf 112
07620 Son Perdiuet IB 110 Ce 112
07110 Son Perot IB 110 Ce 110
07184 Son Pieras IB 110 Cd 111
07769 Son Planas IB 77 Df 108
07769 Son Pomar IB 77 Df 108
07250 Son Pou Nou IB 111 Da 111
07730 Son Puig Gran IB 77 Ea 109
07170 Son Puing IB 110 Cd 110
07208 Son Ramonet IB 111 Da 112
07529 Son Ribot IB 111 Da 111
07010 Son Roca IB 110 Cd 111
07510 Son Rossinyol IB 111 Da 111
07769 Son Salomón IB 77 De 108
07620 Son Sampoli IB 111 Cf 111
07440 Son San Marti IB 111 Da 110
07520 Son Santandreu IB 111 Da 111
07120 Son Sardina IB 110 Cd 111
07609 Son Sart IB 111 Cf 112
07260 Son Sastre IB 111 Cf 111
07210 Son Sastre Vell IB 111 Cf 111
07184 Son Satre IB 110 Cd 111
07740 Son Saura IB 77 Ea 108
45100 Sonseca TO 102 Wa 110
07579 Son Serra de Marina IB 111 Db 110
07193 Son Serralta IB 110 Cd 111
07459 Son Serra Nou IB 111 Db 110
07550 Son Servera IB 111 Dc 111
07691 Son Sestri IB 111 Da 112
40194 Sonsoto SG 67 Vf 103
07430 Son Suan IB 111 Da 110
07740 Son Tema IB 77 Eb 109
07609 Son Texiquet IB 110 Ce 112
07638 Son Toni Amer IB 111 Da 112
07769 Son Toni Marti IB 77 Df 108
07260 Son Valent IB 111 Da 111
07209 Son Valls de Pac IB 111 Da 111
07230 Son Valls de Satre IB 111 Cf 111
07769 Son Ve Ce Te IB 77 Df 109
07630 Son Virgili IB 111 Cf 112
07750 Son Vives IB 77 Ea 108
07630 Son Xorc IB 111 Da 112
07220 Son Xotano IB 111 Cf 111
15168 Soñeiro C 11 Re 89
35558 Sóo GC 182 Mc 174
04638 Sopalmo AL 171 Ya 126
22583 Sopeira HU 37 Ae 95
48600 Sopelana BI 19 Xa 88
39409 Sopenilla CB 17 Vf 89
39510 Sopeña CB 17 Ve 89
39213 Sopeña CB 17 Vf 91
24719 Sopeña de Carneros LE 26 Tf 94
09589 Sopeñano BU 18 Wd 90
22583 Soperún HU 36 Ad 95
18410 Soportújar GR 169 Wd 127
14512 Soprán CO 151 Vb 124
48190 Sopuerta BI 19 Wf 89
08588 Sora B 58 Ca 96
20140 Sorabilla SS 20 Xf 89
20590 Soraluce-Placencia de las Armas SS 20 Xd 89
31194 Sorauren NC 33 Yc 91
08612 Sorba B 57 Be 97
04270 Sorbas AL 171 Xf 126
24478 Sorbeda del Sil LE 26 Tc 92
09128 Sordillos BU 29 Vf 94
32847 Sordos OR 42 Sa 96
35128 Soria GC 184 Kb 181
42003 Soria SO 51 Xd 98
22589 Soriana HU 55 Ad 96
37777 Sorihuela SA 83 Ub 106
23270 Sorihuela de Guadalimar J 138 Wf 119
31219 Sorlada NC 32 Xe 93
AD300 Sornàs ◘ AND 38 Bd 93
31800 Sorozarreta NC 32 Xe 91
25587 Sorpe L 37 Ba 93
25567 Sorre L 37 Ba 94
24815 Sorriba LE 28 Uf 92
33584 Sorribas AS 16 Ue 88
25717 Sorribes L 57 Bc 95
25716 Sorribos L 57 Be 95
24649 Sorribos de Alba LE 27 Ub 92
22666 Sorripas HU 35 Zd 93
25560 Sort L 37 Ba 94
25794 Sorts, Les L 57 Bc 95
18713 Sorvilán GR 169 We 128
26191 Sorzano RI 32 Xc 94
22467 Sos HU 36 Ac 93
24139 Sosas de Laciana LE 14 Te 91
24132 Sosas del Cumbral LE 26 Tf 91
07630 So's Besons IB 111 Da 112
48891 Soscaño BI 18 Wd 89
50680 Sos del Rey Católico Z 34 Ye 94
25181 Soses L 74 Ac 99
25517 Sossís L 37 Af 95
33317 Sota, La AS 15 Ua 88
05198 Sotalvo AV 84 Va 105
46168 Sot de Chera V 107 Za 111
12489 Sot de Ferrer CS 107 Zd 110
24523 Sotelo LE 25 Ta 92
26371 Sotés RI 31 Xc 94
21309 Sotiel Coronada H 147 Ta 123
33392 Sotiello AS 15 Ub 88
40311 Sotillo SG 68 Wc 101
50295 Sotillo Z 52 Yd 99
13429 Sotillo, El CR 120 Vf 114
13710 Sotillo, El CR 122 Xa 114
19491 Sotillo, El GU 88 Xc 103
34407 Sotillo de Boedo P 29 Vd 93
24389 Sotillo de Cabrera LE 25 Tb 94
24328 Sotillo de Cea LE 28 Va 94
05420 Sotillo de la Adrada AV 85 Vc 107
09441 Sotillo de la Ribera BU 49 Wb 98
45635 Sotillo de las Palomas TO 100 Vb 108
42165 Sotillo del Rincón SO 50 Xc 97
09259 Sotillo de Rioja BU 31 Wf 94
49395 Sotillo de Sanabria ZA 44 Tb 96
42344 Sotillos de Caracena SO 68 Wf 101
24814 Sotillos de Sabero LE 28 Ue 91
33100 Soto AS 14 Ua 88
33685 Soto AS 15 Uc 90
33993 Soto AS 15 Ud 89
33996 Soto AS 15 Ue 90
39649 Soto CB 18 Wa 89
22338 Soto HU 36 Ab 94
04859 Soto, El AL 170 Xe 125
05515 Soto, El AV 83 Ue 106
11150 Soto, El CA 172 Ua 131
10891 Soto, El CC 81 Tb 107
28109 Soto, El MD 86 Wc 105
31340 Soto, El NC 33 Yb 95
39210 Soto (Hermandad de Campoo de Suso) CB 17 Ve 90
34407 Sotobañado y Priorato P 29 Vd 93
16190 Sotoca CU 104 Xd 107
19429 Sotoca de Tajo GU 88 Xc 104
50693 Soto Candespina Z 53 Yf 98
28830 Soto de Aldovea MD 86 Wd 106
34209 Soto de Cerrato P 48 Vd 97
39110 Soto de la Marina CB 18 Wa 88
24768 Soto de la Vega LE 27 Ua 95
33126 Soto del Barco AS 14 Tf 87
28311 Soto del Lugar MD 102 Wb 109
33991 Soto de Lorío AS 15 Uc 89
33869 Soto de los Infantes AS 14 Te 88
28791 Soto del Real MD 86 Wb 104
33156 Soto de Luiña AS 14 Te 87
28529 Soto de Pajares MD 86 Wc 107
33172 Soto de Ribera AS 15 Ua 89
24916 Soto de Sajambre LE 16 Uf 89
42345 Soto de San Esteban SO 49 We 99
24914 Soto de Valdeón LE 16 Va 90
24882 Soto de Valderrueda LE 28 Va 92
28760 Soto de Viñuelas MD 86 Wb 105
19445 Sotodosos GU 70 Xd 103
26132 Soto en Cameros RI 32 Xd 95
14512 Sotogordo CO 166 Vb 124
11310 Sotogrande del Guadiaro CA 173 Ue 131
28119 Soto Mozaraque MD 86 Wc 105
09591 Sotopalacios BU 30 Wb 94
24523 Sotoparada LE 25 Ta 93
16143 Sotorribas CU 88 Xf 107
39232 Soto-Rucandio CB 30 Wa 91
16143 Sotos CU 88 Xf 107
40170 Sotosalbos SG 67 Wa 102
42318 Sotos del Burgo SO 50 Wf 99
40593 Sotos de Sepúlveda SG 68 Wc 101
37657 Sotoserrano SA 82 Tf 106
30708 Sotos Nuevos MC 157 Za 122
09135 Sotovellanos BU 29 Ve 93
24125 Soto y Amío LE 27 Ua 92
09197 Sotragero BU 30 Wb 94
33554 Sotres AS 16 Vb 89
09135 Sotresgudo BU 29 Ve 93
37850 Sotrobal SA 83 Ue 103
33957 Sotrondio AS 15 Uc 89
02600 Sotuélamos AB 123 Xc 114
17734 Sous GI 39 Ce 95
32336 Soutadoiro OR 25 Ta 95
32552 Soutelo OR 43 Se 96
36560 Soutelo PO 23 Re 93
36460 Soutelo PO 41 Rc 96
32622 Soutelo Verde OR 43 Sd 96
15806 Souto C 11 Sa 91
27359 Souto LU 24 Sc 93
36682 Souto PO 23 Rc 92
36684 Souto PO 23 Rd 93
36863 Souto PO 41 Rc 96
32617 Soutochao OR 43 Se 97
32616 Soutocobo OR 43 Se 97
36519 Soutolongo PO 23 Rf 93
36691 Soutomaior = O Rial PO 23 Rc 94
32910 Soutopenedo OR 24 Sa 95
15145 Soutullo C 11 Rc 89
33611 Sovilla AS 15 Ub 89
15118 Srantes C 10 Qf 89
08295 St. Vicenç de Castellet B 57 Bf 98
25287 Su L 57 Bd 97
39340 Suances CB 17 Vf 88
39213 Suano CB 17 Ve 91
31797 Suarbe NC 21 Yb 91
24433 Suarbol LE 25 Ta 91
33528 Suares AS 15 Uc 88
33579 Suarias AS 17 Vc 89
27113 Suarna LU 13 Sf 90
01428 Subijana-Morillas VI 31 Xa 92
01195 Subilana Gasteiz = Subijana de Álava VI 31 Xb 92
08739 Subirats B 76 Be 100
08739 Subirats B 76 Be 100
31191 Subiza NC 33 Yb 92
27619 Sucarral LU 24 Sd 92
27569 Sucastro LU 24 Sb 92
30590 Sucina MC 157 Za 121
25113 Sucs L 55 Ac 98
25173 Sudanell L 74 Ad 99
46410 Sueca V 126 Ze 113
27279 Suegos LU 12 Sd 90
33759 Sueiro AS 13 Ta 87
42189 Suellacabras SO 51 Xe 97
22320 Suelves HU 55 Aa 95
12223 Suera CS 108 Zd 109
24713 Sueros de Cepeda LE 26 Tf 93
22583 Suerri HU 56 Ad 95
30334 Suertes, Los MC 157 Ye 122
28420 Suertes de Villalba, Las MD 86 Vf 105
39140 Suesa CB 18 Wb 88
15142 Suevos C 11 Rd 88
04878 Suflí AL 170 Xd 124
29150 Suizo MA 167 Vc 128
02487 Sujayal AB 139 Xe 119
48395 Sukarrieta BI 19 Xb 88
50139 Sulfúrica, La Z 72 Zb 99
46295 Sumacàrcer V 126 Zc 114
31791 Sumbilla NC 21 Yc 90
15183 Sumio C 11 Rd 89
25174 Sunyer L 74 Ad 99
17537 Super Molina GI 38 Bf 94
25113 Suquets L 55 Ac 98
08260 Súria B 57 Be 98
25594 Surp L 37 Ba 94
17861 Surroca de Baix GI 39 Cb 95
15893 Susana, A C 23 Rd 92
24489 Susañe del Sil LE 26 Td 91
39250 Susilla CB 29 Vf 92
09133 Susinos del Páramo BU 29 Wa 94
18630 Suspiro del Moro GR 168 Wc 126
17166 Susqueda GI 58 Cd 96
25654 Suterranya L 56 Af 96
15126 Suxo C 10 Qf 90
09219 Suzana BU 31 Xa 92

T

36760 Tabagón PO 41 Rb 97
38109 Tabaiba TF 181 Ie 178
11400 Tabajete CA 164 Te 128
34257 Tabanera de Cerrato P 48 Vf 96
40194 Tabanera del Monte SG 67 Vf 103
34473 Tabanera de Valdavia P 28 Vb 93
40291 Tabanera la Luenga SG 67 Ve 102
02270 Tabaqueros AB 125 Yd 112
31480 Tabar NC 33 Yd 92
49140 Tábara ZA 45 Ua 98
35542 Tabayesco GC 182 Md 174
33469 Tabaza AS 15 Ub 87
32558 Tabazoa de Humoso OR 44 Sf 96
32558 Tabazoa de Umoso OR 44 Sf 95
15182 Tabeaio C 11 Rd 89
36684 Tabeirós PO 23 Rd 93
37130 Tabera de Abajo SA 64 Tf 103
04200 Tabernas AL 170 Xd 126
22196 Tabernas de Isuela HU 54 Zd 96
46760 Tabernes de Valldigna = Tavernes de la Valldigna V 127 Ze 114
04692 Taberno AL 155 Xf 124
37491 Taberuela SA 64 Tf 103
49741 Tabla, La ZA 46 Ub 97
28480 Tablada MD 85 Vf 104
09143 Tablada del Rudrón BU 30 Wa 92
09125 Tablada de Villadiego BU 29 Vf 93
05193 Tabladillo AV 85 Vc 104
39813 Tabladillo CB 18 Wc 89
19129 Tabladillo GU 88 Xb 105
24722 Tabladillo LE 26 Te 94
40122 Tabladillo SG 67 Vd 102
33638 Tablado AS 15 Ua 90
38728 Tablado, El TF 181 Ha 176
38591 Tablado, El TF 181 Id 179
41800 Tablante SE 148 Te 124
18800 Tablas GR 170 Xb 125
04559 Tablas, Las AL 170 Xc 126
33536 Tablas, Las AS 15 Ud 89
18660 Tablate GR 168 Wc 127
35106 Tablero, El GC 184 Kc 182
38111 Tablero, El TF 181 Id 178
09514 Tabliega BU 18 Wd 90
13114 Tablillas, Las CR 120 Vd 113
18614 Tablones, Los GR 168 Wd 128
18418 Tablones, Los GR 169 Wd 127
15617 Taboada C 11 Rf 88
27559 Taboada LU 24 Sb 92
32690 Taboadela OR 42 Sb 95
36827 Taboadelo PO 23 Rc 94
32768 Taboazas OR 43 Sd 95
36448 Taboexa PO 41 Rd 96
38294 Taborno TF 181 Ie 177
50547 Tabuenca Z 52 Yc 98
24721 Tabuyo del Monte LE 26 Te 95
24767 Tabuyuelo de Jamuz LE 26 Ua 95
38296 Taco TF 181 Ie 178
38357 Tacoronte TF 181 Id 178
31300 Tafalla NC 33 Yb 93
35018 Tafira GC 184 Kd 180
35017 Tafira Baja GC 184 Kd 180
08593 Tagamanent B 58 Cb 98
38139 Taganana TF 181 Ie 177
49836 Tagarabuena ZA 65 Ud 99
09108 Tagarrosa BU 29 Ve 94
39360 Tagle CB 17 Vf 88
38852 Taguluche TF 184 Hd 180
18414 Tahá, La GR 169 We 127
04275 Tahal AL 170 Xe 125
35507 Tahiche GC 182 Mc 174
11392 Tahivilla CA 175 Ub 131
25795 Tahús = Taús L 37 Bb 95
17150 Taialà GI 59 Ce 97
16200 Taina de Vega CU 105 Ya 111
33111 Taja AS 14 Te 89
38915 Tajace de Abajo TF 180 Ha 182
42112 Tajahuerce SO 51 Xf 98
18329 Tajarja GR 168 Wa 126
31192 Tajonar NC 33 Yc 92
42366 Tajueco SO 69 Xa 99
40153 Tajuña SG 85 Ve 103
38769 Tajuya TF 181 Ha 177
04825 Tala, La AL 155 Xd 123
23391 Tala, La J 139 Xb 118
37752 Tala, La SA 83 Uc 105
12598 Talaies, Les CS 93 Ac 106
50710 Talaies, Les Z 73 Zf 102
17856 Talaixa GI 39 Cd 95
08278 Talamanca B 58 Bf 98
28160 Talamanca de Jarama MD 86 Wc 104
50546 Talamantes Z 52 Yb 98
09126 Talamillo del Tozo BU 29 Wa 93
18656 Talara GR 168 Wc 127
25630 Talarn L 56 Af 95
06640 Talarrubias BA 118 Ue 114
Talatí de Dalt IB 77 Eb 109
10193 Talaván CC 98 Te 110

Talaván | 305 E

02410 Talave AB 140 Ya 117
25213 Talavera L 57 Bc 99
45600 Talavera de la Reina TO 100 Vb 109
45694 Talavera la Nueva TO 100 Va 109
06140 Talavera la Real BA 116 Tb 115
10492 Talaveruela de la Vera CC 99 Uc 108
10310 Talayuela CC 99 Uc 109
16320 Talayuelas CU 106 Ye 109
15290 Tal de Arriba C 22 Qf 92
06106 Talegón BA 131 Sf 117
12221 Tales CS 108 Ze 109
06133 Táliga BA 132 Sf 117
25271 Tallada, La L 57 Bc 99
17134 Tallada d'Empordà, La GI 59 Da 96
25360 Talladell, El L 56 Ba 99
15216 Tállara C 22 Ra 92
39707 Talledo CB 19 We 89
04212 Tallón Alto, El AL 170 Xc 125
04212 Tallón Bajo, El AL 170 Xc 125
15981 Tallós C 22 Rb 92
25721 Talltendre L 38 Be 94
15124 Talon C 10 Qe 90
25212 Talteüll L 57 Bb 98
42148 Talveila SO 50 Xa 98
39584 Tama CB 17 Vc 89
38910 Tamaduste TF 180 Ha 182
32697 Tamagos OR 43 Sd 97
32697 Tamaguelos OR 43 Sd 97
38684 Tamaimo TF 180 Ib 179
19222 Tamajón GU 68 We 102
32102 Tamallancos OR 24 Sa 94
49176 Tamame ZA 64 Ua 101
37600 Tamames SA 82 Tf 105
35018 Tamaraceite GC 184 Kd 180
34439 Támara de Campos P 48 Vd 95
23350 Tamaral, El J 138 Xb 118
38891 Tamargada TF 184 He 179
07769 Tamarinda IB 77 De 109
43008 Tamarit T 76 Bc 102
22550 Tamarite de Litera HU 55 Ac 97
17212 Tamariu GI 59 Db 97
47815 Tamariz de Campos VA 47 Uf 97
09227 Tamarón BU 29 Wa 95
02270 Tamayo AB 125 Yd 112
09593 Tamayo BU 30 Wd 92
36416 Tameiga PO 41 Rb 95
32548 Tameirón OR 43 Sf 96
18538 Tamojares GR 154 Wf 123
06458 Tamujoso BA 134 Ub 116
Tamujoso (apeadero), El H 147 Ta 122
06658 Tamurejo BA 119 Va 115
40312 Tanarro SG 68 Wb 101
12180 Tancal, El CS 108 Aa 108
33994 Tanes AS 15 Ud 89
03112 Tangel A 142 Zd 118
42174 Taniñe SO 51 Xe 96
39300 Tanos CB 17 Vf 88
38460 Tanque TF 180 Ib 178
09640 Tañabueyes BU 49 Wd 96
35561 Tao GC 182 Mc 174
09124 Tapia BU 29 Vf 93
15864 Tapia C 22 Rc 91
33740 Tapia de Casariego AS 13 Ta 87
24275 Tapia de la Ribera LE 27 Ub 92
42128 Tapiela SO 51 Xe 99
17721 Tàpies GI 39 Ce 94
49639 Tapioles ZA 46 Ud 97
19193 Taracena GU 87 Wf 105
08552 Taradell B 58 Cb 97
15985 Taragoña C 22 Rb 92
37429 Taraguda SA 65 Uc 101
19227 Taragudo GU 87 Wf 104
11369 Taraguilla CA 173 Ud 131
23488 Tarahal J 153 Wf 123
30566 Taraíz, El MC 156 Ye 120
14814 Tarajal, El CO 152 Ve 124
35627 Tarajalejo GC 183 Lf 179
04715 Tarambana AL 170 Xa 128
33775 Taramundi AS 13 Sf 88
09587 Taranco BU 18 We 90
16400 Tarancón CU 103 Wf 108
42315 Tarancueña SO 69 Wf 100
33557 Taranes AS 16 Ue 89
24887 Taranilla LE 28 Va 92
25310 Tarassó L 56 Ba 98
17741 Taravaus GI 59 Cf 95
19314 Taravilla GU 89 Ya 104
44555 Tarayuelas, Las TE 91 Zc 105
15550 Taraza C 11 Re 87
41300 Tarazona SE 163 Ub 124
50500 Tarazona Z 52 Yb 97
37409 Tarazona de Guareña SA 65 Ue 101
02100 Tarazona de la Mancha AB 124 Ya 113
03518 Tárbena A 143 Zf 116
27823 Tardade LU 12 Sb 89
37429 Tardáguila SA 65 Uc 102
09130 Tardajos BU 30 Wb 94
42191 Tardajos de Duero SO 51 Xd 98
42294 Tardelcuende SO 50 Xc 99
49618 Tardemézar ZA 45 Ua 96
42162 Tardesillas SO 51 Xd 98
22240 Tardienta HU 54 Zc 97
49170 Tardobispo ZA 64 Ub 100
38813 Targa TF 184 He 180
34209 Tariego de Cerrato P 47 Vd 97
11380 Tarifa CA 173 Uc 132
18859 Tarifa GR 154 Xd 123
34869 Tarilonte de la Peña P 28 Vc 92
44480 Tarín TE 107 Zb 108
21540 Tariquejos H 146 Sf 124
50135 Tarja, La Z 72 Zb 100
33997 Tarna AS 16 Ue 90
42216 Taroda SO 70 Xd 100
43003 Tarragona T 75 Bb 102
30412 Tarragoya MC 155 Xf 121
03739 Tarraula A 143 Aa 116
25300 Tàrrega L 56 Ba 99
25480 Tarrés L 75 Ba 100
39409 Tarriba CB 17 Vf 89
15998 Tarrío C 22 Qf 92
27560 Tarrío LU 24 Sb 91
36612 Tarrío PO 22 Rb 92
15821 Tarroeira C 11 Rd 91
25211 Tarroja de Segarra L 56 Bb 98
09540 Tartalés de Cilla BU 30 Wd 92
09559 Tartalés de los Montes BU 30 Wd 92
19333 Tartanedo GU 70 Ya 103
25611 Tartareu L 55 Ae 97
35478 Tasarte GC 184 Kb 181
38677 Taucho TF 180 Ib 180
Taula IB 77 Eb 109
Taula Talaiot IB 77 Eb 109
25528 Taüll L 37 Af 93
35138 Tauro GC 184 Kb 182
50660 Tauste Z 52 Ye 97
25577 Tavascan L 37 Bb 93
46760 Tavernes de la Valldigna = Tabernes de Valldigna V 127 Ze 114
08519 Tavèrnoles B 58 Cb 97
08511 Tavertet B 58 Cc 97
11612 Tavizna CA 173 Ud 128
38779 Tazacorte TF 181 Ha 177
38852 Tazo TF 184 He 179
02437 Tazona AB 140 Ya 119
33315 Tazones AS 15 Ud 87
23313 Teatinos, Los J 153 Wf 120
23290 Teatinos, Los J 154 Xc 120
29327 Teba MA 166 Va 127
16710 Tébar CU 105 Xf 112
30889 Tébar MC 156 Yc 123
37460 Tebera de Arriba SA 64 Tf 103
33816 Tebongo AS 14 Tc 89
36747 Tebra PO 41 Rb 96
36746 Tebra PO 41 Rb 96
38869 Tecomodá TF 184 He 180
35611 Tefía GC 183 Ma 177
38280 Tegueste TF 181 Id 177
35530 Teguise GC 182 Mc 174
35629 Teguital GC 183 Ma 179
27546 Teibel LU 24 Sc 92
15969 Teira C 22 Qf 93
27638 Teivilide LU 24 Sd 92
03108 Teix, El A 143 Zd 117
27722 Teixedáis LU 13 Sf 89
32765 Teixeira, A OR 24 Sd 94
15310 Teixeiro C 11 Rf 90
27289 Teixeiro LU 12 Sd 90
18814 Teja GR 154 Xb 122
08329 Tejà B 77 Cb 99
09616 Tejada BU 49 Wc 97
37520 Tejadillo SA 81 Tc 105
37460 Tejadillo SA 82 Tf 104
16317 Tejadillos CU 105 Yc 108
24732 Tejadinos LE 26 Tf 94
42128 Tejado SO 51 Xe 99
37448 Tejado, El SA 82 Ua 103
37749 Tejado, El SA 83 Uc 106
24732 Tejados LE 26 Tf 94
05146 Tejar, El AV 84 Uf 104
14915 Tejar, El CO 167 Vc 125
28220 Tejar, El MD 86 Wa 106
07250 Tejar de sa Moleta IB 111 Da 111
06630 Tejares BA 118 Ue 114
40314 Tejares SG 67 Wa 100
50690 Tejares, Los Z 53 Ye 98
35360 Tejeda GC 184 Kc 181
10420 Tejeda de Tiétar CC 99 Ua 108
37607 Tejeda y Segoyuela SA 82 Tf 105
24497 Tejedo del Sil LE 26 Td 91
24511 Tejeira LE 25 Ta 92
49572 Tejera, La ZA 44 Ta 97
44134 Tejería, La TE 106 Yd 107
24885 Tejerina LE 28 Uf 91
42211 Tejerizas SO 69 Xc 99
38688 Tejina TF 180 Ib 179
38260 Tejina TF 181 Id 177
35200 Telde GC 184 Kd 180
11560 Teléfono, El CA 163 Te 127
33556 Teleña AS 16 Uf 89
15110 Tella C 10 Ra 89
22364 Tella HU 36 Ab 93
22364 Tella-Sin HU 36 Ab 93
33628 Telledo AS 15 Ua 90
20220 Telleriarte SS 20 Xd 90
37491 Tellosancho SA 64 Tf 103
27335 Telo LU 24 Sd 93
45780 Tembleque TO 103 Wc 110
09591 Temiño BU 30 Wc 94
35270 Temisas GC 184 Kc 181
14729 Temple, El CO 150 Va 122
22281 Temple, El HU 53 Zb 97
09615 Tenada Becedo BU 50 We 95
09194 Tenada de Fresnada BU 49 Wc 95
09199 Tenada de la Cabezada BU 49 Wd 95
09194 Tenada de la Tejera BU 49 Wc 95
09614 Tenada de Peñalengua BU 49 We 96
09199 Tenada Quiñones BU 49 Wd 95
09257 Tenadas de Abajo BU 30 We 94
09339 Tenadas de la Pasadera BU 49 Wb 96
09199 Tenadas de la Portilla BU 30 Wd 95
09347 Tenadas de la Rasa BU 49 Wc 96
09347 Tenadas de la Renovilla BU 49 Wb 96
09641 Tenadas del Monte BU 49 Wc 96
09640 Tenadas del Monte BU 49 Wd 96
38715 Tenagua TF 181 Hb 176
19134 Tendilla GU 87 Xa 105
25637 Tendrui L 56 Ae 95
37590 Tenebrón SA 82 Td 105
36120 Tenorio PO 23 Rc 94
35018 Tenoya GC 184 Kd 180
25286 Tentellatge L 57 Be 96
35216 Tentiniguada GC 184 Kc 181
40180 Tenzuela SG 67 Wa 102
15886 Teo C 23 Rc 92
04814 Teones, Los AL 155 Xf 124
42164 Tera SO 51 Xd 97
39510 Terán CB 17 Ve 89
30442 Tercia, La MC 140 Ya 119
15314 Tercio C 11 Re 89
22584 Tercui L 55 Ae 95
33347 Tereñes AS 16 Uf 88
12469 Teresa CS 107 Zc 109
46622 Teresa de Cofrentes V 125 Yf 114
50292 Termas Pallarés Z 70 Ya 101
25670 Térmens L 56 Ae 98
41400 Término, El SE 165 Uf 124
30528 Término de Arriba MC 141 Yd 117
09593 Terminón BU 30 Wd 92
26212 Ternero BU 31 Xa 93
19390 Teroleja GU 89 Ya 104
35330 Teror GC 184 Kc 180
04569 Terque AL 170 Xc 127
32860 Terrachá = Entrimo, A OR 42 Rf 97
17468 Terradelles GI 59 Cf 96
17731 Terrades GI 40 Cf 95
37882 Terradillos SA 83 Uc 103
09440 Terradillos de Esgueva BU 48 Wa 98
34349 Terradillos de los Templarios P 28 Va 94
09142 Terradillos de Sedano BU 30 Wb 93
37789 Terrados SA 83 Uc 104
07750 Terra Rotja IB 77 Ea 109
08221 Terrassa B 77 Ca 99
46842 Terrateig V 126 Ze 115
19392 Terraza GU 89 Ya 104
09613 Terrazas BU 49 We 96
09249 Terrazos BU 30 Wd 93
11500 Terrcios, Los CA 172 Te 129
18567 Terre GR 153 Wc 124
07015 Terreno, El IB 110 Cd 111
50293 Terrer Z 71 Yb 101
30812 Terreras, Las MC 155 Yb 121
44120 Terriente TE 90 Yc 107
13341 Terrinches CR 138 Xa 117
06620 Terrines BA 118 Ud 115
23220 Terriza de la Virgen J 137 Wd 119
26132 Terroba RI 32 Xd 95
37609 Terrones SA 82 Ua 104
32616 Terroso OR 43 Se 97
49394 Terroso ZA 44 Tb 96
44003 Teruel TE 90 Yf 106
19312 Terzaga GU 89 Ya 104
38916 Tesbabo TF 180 Ha 182
35627 Tesejerague GC 183 Lf 179
35613 Tesjuates GC 183 Ma 178
10895 Teso Moreno CC 97 Ta 108
37185 Tesonera SA 64 Ub 102
04277 Tesoro, El AL 171 Xf 126
37479 Tesos Miradores SA 81 Td 104
35613 Tetír GC 183 Ma 177
28039 Tetuán MD 86 Wb 106
03725 Teulada A 143 Aa 116
33111 Teverga AS 14 Tf 90
09511 Teza de Lodosa BU 19 We 91
39649 Tezanos CB 18 Wa 89
21530 Tharsis H 161 Sf 123
35558 Tiagua GC 182 Mc 174
35572 Tías GC 182 Mc 175
03109 Tibi A 142 Zc 117
08017 Tibidabo B 77 Ca 100
04459 Tices AL 170 Xb 126
31398 Tiebas NC 33 Yc 92
31398 Tiebas-Muruarte de Reta NC 33 Yc 92
47870 Tiedra VA 46 Ue 99
28550 Tielmes MD 87 We 107
33554 Tielve AS 16 Vb 89
05270 Tiemblo, El AV 85 Vc 106
30814 Tiemblos y Las Cañadas, Los MC 156 Yb 122
18248 Tiena la Baja GR 168 Wb 125
06800 Tiendas, Las BA 116 Td 114
50269 Tierga Z 52 Yc 99
50682 Tiermas Z 34 Yf 93
38441 Tierra de Costa TF 180 Ib 178
22336 Tierrantona HU 36 Ab 94
22192 Tierz HU 54 Zd 96
19390 Tierzo GU 89 Ya 104
21647 Tiesa, La H 148 Tc 123
02328 Tiesas, Las AB 124 Xf 114
10319 Tiétar del Caudillo CC 99 Ud 108
38911 Tigaday TF 180 Gf 182
38738 Tigalate TF 181 Hb 177
38738 Tiguerorte TF 181 Hb 177
38789 Tijarafe TF 181 Ha 176
38677 Tijoce de Arriba TF 180 Ib 179
38677 Tijoco Bajo TF 180 Ib 180
04880 Tíjola AL 170 Xd 124
35368 Timagada GC 184 Kc 181
18449 Timar GR 169 We 127
35613 Time, El GC 183 Ma 177
25288 Timoneda L 57 Bc 96
16330 Tinada, La CU 106 Yd 109
16316 Tinada de las Casillas CU 105 Ya 108
16316 Tinada del Vallejo del Cerezo CU 105 Ya 108
04200 Tinadas AL 170 Xe 126
16142 Tinadas de Chiriveche CU 89 Xf 107
16141 Tinadas de la Fuente del Soto CU 88 Xf 106
16890 Tinadas del Collado CU 88 Xe 106
16522 Tinajas CU 88 Xc 107
02155 Tinajeros AB 124 Yb 114
35560 Tinajo GC 182 Mb 174
02480 Tindavar AB 139 Xe 118
35649 Tindaya GC 183 Ma 177
33870 Tineo AS 14 Td 88
15126 Tines C 10 Ra 90
33870 Tinéu = Tineo AS 14 Td 88
09649 Tinieblas de la Sierra BU 49 Wd 95
13720 Tintoreros, Los CR 122 We 113
33199 Tiñana AS 15 Ub 88
38915 Tiñor TF 180 Ha 182
30570 Tiñosa Alta MC 157 Yf 121
13128 Tiñosillas, Las CR 120 Ve 114
05165 Tiñosillos AV 66 Vb 103
32707 Tioira OR 24 Sc 95
16150 Tío Miguelete, El CU 89 Ya 106
11370 Tiradero, El CA 175 Uc 132
37170 Tirados de la Vega SA 64 Ua 102
33979 Tiraña AS 15 Uc 89
31154 Tirapu NC 33 Yb 93
26211 Tirgo RI 31 Xa 93
02161 Tiriez AB 123 Xe 115
30890 Tirieza Alta MC 155 Ya 122
30890 Tirieza Baja MC 155 Ya 122
12179 Tírig CS 92 Aa 106
27298 Tirimol LU 12 Sc 90
12004 Tiro de Pichón CS 108 Aa 108
13192 Tirteafuera CR 120 Ve 116
25595 Tírvia L 37 Bb 93
35628 Tiscamanita GC 183 Lf 178
14512 Tiscar CO 150 Vb 124
23489 Tiscar-Don Pedro J 154 Wf 122
46178 Titaguas V 106 Yf 109
28359 Titulcia MD 102 Wc 108
43511 Tivenys T 74 Ad 103
43746 Tivisa = Tivissa T 75 Ae 102
40191 Tizneros SG 67 Vf 103
16152 Toba, La CU 89 Ya 107
16373 Toba, La CU 105 Yb 109
19243 Toba, La GU 69 Xa 102
23297 Toba, La J 139 Xc 119
09212 Tobalinilla BU 31 Wf 92
09133 Tobar BU 29 Wa 94
47493 Tobar VA 66 Va 101
16879 Tobar, El CU 89 Xf 105
30510 Tobarilla MC 141 Ye 116
02500 Tobarra AB 140 Yb 117
23700 Tobaruela J 152 Wb 120
23685 Tobazo J 152 Vf 123
50325 Tobed Z 71 Yd 100
09211 Tobera BU 30 We 92
01211 Tobera VI 31 Xb 92
09591 Tobes BU 30 Wc 93
19269 Tobes GU 69 Xc 101
26321 Tobía RI 31 Xb 95
02486 Tobillas AB 140 Xf 118
01427 Tobillas VI 31 We 91
19286 Tobillos GU 70 Xf 103
23294 Tobos J 139 Xd 120
41340 Tocina SE 149 Ub 123
06340 Tocinillos, Los BA 132 Tc 119
35478 Tocodomán GC 184 Kb 181
18380 Tocón GR 168 Wa 125
18192 Tocón GR 169 Wd 125
12312 Todolella CS 92 Ze 105
14815 Todosaires CO 152 Vf 123
36689 Toedo PO 23 Rd 92
32930 Toén OR 23 Sa 95
12230 Toga CS 108 Zd 108
27366 Toirán LU 24 Sd 91
27593 Toiriz LU 24 Sc 93
36597 Toiriz PO 23 Rf 92
39517 Tojo, El CB 17 Ve 90
39518 Tojos, Los CB 17 Ve 90
33794 Tol AS 13 Ta 87
49525 Tola ZA 45 Td 98
05289 Tolbaños AV 85 Vc 104
09614 Tolbaños de Abajo BU 50 Wf 96
09614 Tolbaños de Arriba BU 50 Wf 96
24226 Toldanos LE 27 Ud 93
27639 Toldaos LU 25 Se 92
32120 Toldavia OR 24 Sa 94
42190 Toledillo SO 50 Xc 98
45001 Toledo TO 102 Vf 109
24845 Tolibia de Abajo LE 15 Ud 91
24845 Tolibia de Arriba LE 15 Ud 91
49512 Tolilla ZA 45 Te 98
33826 Tolinas AS 14 Te 89
33986 Tolivia AS 15 Uc 89
33557 Tolivia AS 16 Uf 90
30648 Tollé, El MC 141 Yf 119
03813 Tollos A 143 Ze 116
40467 Tolocirio SG 66 Vc 102
03680 Tolomón A 142 Zb 119
25723 Toloriu L 38 Bd 94
02211 Tolosa AB 125 Yd 113
20400 Tolosa SS 20 Xf 90
29109 Tolox MA 174 Va 128
22585 Tolva HU 55 Ad 96
36379 Tomadas PO 41 Rb 96
41940 Tomares SE 164 Tf 124
30591 Tomases, Los MC 157 Yf 122
24438 Tombrio de Abajo LE 26 Tc 92
19411 Tomellosa GU 87 Xa 105
13700 Tomelloso CR 122 Wf 114
36158 Tomeza PO 22 Rc 94
04618 Tomillar, El AL 171 Yb 125
28490 Tomillar, El MD 86 Wc 104
50316 Tomillares Z 51 Ya 99
36740 Tomiño PO 41 Rb 97
36116 Tomonde PO 23 Rd 93
08551 Tona B 58 Cb 97
26270 Tondeluna RI 31 Wf 94
16191 Tondos CU 88 Xe 108
24699 Tonín de Arbás LE 15 Ub 90
04827 Tonosas, Los AL 155 Xf 123
17476 Tonyà GI 59 Cf 95
39329 Toñanes CB 17 Ve 88
04839 Topares AL 155 Xe 121
37799 Topas SA 65 Uc 102
15806 Toques C 11 Sa 91
25574 Tor L 37 Bc 93
27591 Tor LU 24 Sc 93
25750 Torà L 57 Bc 98
24794 Toral de Fondo LE 26 Ua 94
24237 Toral de los Guzmanes LE 46 Uc 95
24560 Toral de los Vados LE 25 Tb 93
24448 Toral de Merayo LE 25 Tc 93
24794 Toralino LE 26 Ua 94
25516 Toralla L 37 Af 95
25516 Torallola L 56 Af 95
12431 Torás CS 107 Zb 109
33535 Torazo AS 15 Ud 88
27317 Torbeo LU 24 Sd 94
47830 Tordehumos VA 46 Uf 98
37453 Tordelalosa-Milanera SA 83 Ub 103
19325 Tordellego GU 89 Yb 104
19276 Tordelloso GU 69 Xa 101
19351 Tordelpalo GU 89 Yb 104
19277 Tordelrábano GU 69 Xb 101
08490 Tordera B 59 Ce 98
25218 Tordera L 56 Bb 98
42138 Tordesalas SO 51 Xf 99
47100 Tordesillas VA 65 Va 99
19323 Tordesilos GU 89 Yc 104
37840 Tordillos SA 83 Ud 103
15683 Tordoia C 11 Rc 90
09341 Tordómar BU 48 Wa 96
09347 Tordueles BU 49 Wc 96
15290 Torea C 22 Qf 91
48890 Toreachas, Las BI 18 We 89
46814 Torella V 126 Zc 115
08729 Torelletes B 76 Bd 101
08570 Torelló B 58 Cb 96
24450 Toreno LE 26 Tc 92

306 | Talave

21309 Torerera, La H 147 Ta 123
19392 Torete GU 89 Xf 104
39571 Torices CB 17 Vc 90
35639 Toricosquey GC 183 Ma 179
33568 Toriello AS 16 Uf 88
24316 Torienzo Castañero LE 26 Td 93
19190 Torija GU 87 Wf 104
10521 Toril CC 99 Ub 109
44123 Toril TE 89 Yd 107
02487 Toril, El AB 139 Xe 118
14547 Toril, El CO 150 Vb 123
14730 Torilejo Bajo CO 150 Uf 121
46389 Torís V 126 Zb 112
22376 Torla HU 35 Zf 93
42220 Torlengua SO 70 Xf 100
33812 Tormaleo AS 13 Tb 91
26213 Tormantos RI 31 Wf 94
09555 Torme BU 18 Wc 91
05697 Tormellas AV 83 Uc 107
22215 Tormillo, El HU 54 Zf 97
22215 Tormillo-Lastanosa HU 54 Zf 97
12232 Tormo, El CS 107 Zd 108
44134 Tormón TE 90 Yd 107
03795 Tormos A 127 Zf 116
25164 Torms, Els L 75 Ae 100
17830 Torn, El GI 59 Cd 96
25331 Tornabous L 56 Ba 98
09320 Tornadijo BU 49 Wc 96
37765 Tornadizo, El SA 82 Ua 105
37453 Tornadizos SA 83 Ub 104
05215 Tornadizos de Arévalo AV 66 Vb 102
05196 Tornadizos de Ávila AV 84 Vc 105
25569 Tornafort L 37 Ba 94
10611 Tornavacas CC 83 Ub 107
27280 Torneiros LU 12 Sd 89
32870 Torneiros OR 42 Rf 97
24733 Torneros de Jamuz LE 26 Tf 95
24736 Torneros de la Valdería LE 45 Te 95
24231 Torneros del Bernesga LE 27 Uc 93
28739 Tornillar, El MD 68 Wb 103
33559 Tornín AS 16 Uf 89
32892 Torno OR 42 Rf 97
11594 Torno, El CA 172 Ua 129
10617 Torno, El CC 99 Ua 108
13194 Torno, El CR 120 Ve 113
44230 Tornos TE 71 Yd 103
32621 Toro OR 43 Sd 96
12429 Toro, El CS 107 Zb 109
07180 Toro, El IB 110 Cc 112
13150 Toronjil CA 164 Ub 128
14208 Torozo, El CO 134 Ud 118
47640 Torozos VA 47 Va 98
34230 Torquemada P 48 Ve 96
16842 Torralba CU 88 Xe 107
30814 Torralba MC 156 Yb 122
22254 Torralba de Aragón HU 54 Zc 97
42132 Torralba de Arciel SO 51 Xe 99
13160 Torralba de Calatrava CR 121 Wb 114
42193 Torralba del Burgo SO 50 Xa 99
42230 Torralba del Moral SO 69 Xd 102
50374 Torralba de los Frailes Z 71 Yc 102
44359 Torralba de los Sisones TE 71 Yd 103
12225 Torralba del Pinar CS 107 Zd 109
31228 Torralba del Río NC 32 Xe 93
45569 Torralba de Oropesa TO 100 Uf 109
50311 Torralba de Ribota Z 71 Yb 100
07769 Torralbet IB 77 Df 109
50368 Torralbilla Z 71 Yd 101
31829 Torrano NC 32 Xf 91
42342 Torraño SO 68 We 100
36389 Torre PO 41 Rb 96
03530 Torre, La A 142 Zb 117
05540 Torre, La AV 84 Va 105
23370 Torre, La J 139 Xb 119
23689 Torre, La J 152 Wa 124
25566 Torre, La L 37 Bb 94
30530 Torre, La MC 141 Yc 119
31350 Torre, La NC 33 Yb 94
38915 Torre, La TF 180 Ha 182
46321 Torre, La V 106 Ye 110
46178 Torre, La V 106 Yf 109
40313 Torreadrada SG 67 Wa 100
18312 Torre Agicampe GR 167 Vf 125
18312 Torre Agricampo GR 167 Ve 125
30579 Torreagüera MC 157 Yf 121
11691 Torre-Alháquime CA 165 Ue 127
46144 Torre Alta V 106 Ye 108
30506 Torrealta MC 156 Ye 120
30814 Torrealvilla MC 156 Yb 122
42294 Torreandaluz SO 50 Xb 99
42161 Torrearévalo SO 51 Xd 97
20568 Torreauso SS 20 Xd 90
46143 Torrebaja V 106 Ye 108
24144 Torrebarrio LE 14 Ua 90
19229 Torrebeleña GU 68 Wf 103
25176 Torrebesses L 74 Ad 100
42193 Torreblacos SO 50 Xa 98
08233 Torreblanca B 57 Bf 99
12596 Torreblanca CS 92 Ab 107
25746 Torreblanca L 56 Ba 97
41020 Torreblanca de los Caños SE 163 Ua 124
29640 Torreblanca del Sol MA 175 Vc 129
23510 Torreblascopedro J 152 Wc 121
16161 Torrebuceit CU 104 Xc 109
08779 Torrebusqueta B 76 Bd 100
30331 Torre-Calín MC 157 Yf 122
14410 Torrecampo CO 135 Vb 118
11310 Torre Carbonera CA 173 Ue 131
18563 Torre-Cardela GR 153 Wd 123
11595 Torrecera CA 172 Ua 129
12232 Torrechiva CS 107 Zd 108
02155 Torrecica, La AB 124 Yb 114
14600 Torrecilla CO 136 Vd 120
13195 Torrecilla CR 120 Vf 115
16145 Torrecilla CU 88 Xe 107
40318 Torrecilla SG 68 Wb 101
44640 Torrecilla de Alcañiz TE 73 Zf 103
47114 Torrecilla de la Abadesa VA 65 Uf 100
45651 Torrecilla de la Jara TO 101 Vb 110
47513 Torrecilla de la Orden VA 65 Ue 101
47129 Torrecilla de la Torre VA 47 Uf 99
19269 Torrecilla del Ducado GU 69 Xc 101
09390 Torrecilla del Monte BU 49 Wb 96
10869 Torrecilla de los Angeles CC 82 Td 107
19392 Torrecilla del Pinar GU 89 Xf 104
40359 Torrecilla del Pinar SG 67 Vf 100
44222 Torrecilla del Rebollar TE 72 Yf 103
37170 Torrecilla del Río SA 64 Ua 102
47509 Torrecilla del Valle VA 66 Uf 100
37170 Torrecilla de Miranda SA 64 Ua 103
50139 Torrecilla de Valmadrid Z 72 Za 99
26100 Torrecilla en Cameros RI 31 Xc 95
14920 Torrecillas CO 151 Vb 124
04510 Torrecillas, Las AL 170 Xb 126
10252 Torrecillas de la Tiesa CC 99 Ub 111
26224 Torrecilla sobre Alesanco RI 31 Xa 94
09345 Torrecitores BU 48 Wa 97
25222 Torre Concordio L 56 Ae 99
19491 Torrecuadrada de los Valles GU 69 Xc 103
19355 Torrecuadrada de Molina GU 89 Yb 104
19431 Torrecuadradilla GU 88 Xc 103
21740 Torrecuadros H 164 Td 125
12550 Torre d'Almassora, La CS 108 Zf 109
25632 Torre d'Amargós, La L 56 Ae 96
09572 Torre de Abajo BU 18 Wb 91
44422 Torre de Alcotas TE 107 Zb 109
50190 Torre de Alejandro Martínez Z 53 Yf 98
44653 Torre de Arcas TE 92 Zf 104
24141 Torre de Babia LE 14 Tf 91
22584 Torre de Baró HU 56 Ad 96
29730 Torre de Benagalbón MA 175 Ve 128
22486 Torre de Buira HU 36 Ae 94
08789 Torre de Claramunt, La B 76 Bd 99
22400 Torre de Corvinos HU 55 Ab 97
14140 Torre de Don Lucas CO 150 Va 122
10864 Torre de Don Miguel CC 81 Tc 107
22436 Torre de Ésera HU 55 Ac 95
47183 Torre de Esgueva VA 48 Ve 98
45920 Torre de Esteban Hambrán, La TO 85 Ve 108
25737 Torre de Fluvià, La L 56 Af 97
43774 Torre de Fontaubella, La T 75 Af 102
22310 Torre de Gardiel HU 55 Aa 97
11391 Torre de Gracia CA 172 Ua 132
43792 Torre de l'Espanyol, La T 74 Ad 101
13344 Torre de Juan Abad CR 138 Wf 117
44593 Torre de la Campana TE 73 Zd 101
22415 Torre de Laguna HU 54 Aa 97
21760 Torre de la Higuera H 162 Tc 126
03191 Torre de la Horadada, La A 157 Zb 121
22400 Torre de la Menudilla HU 55 Ab 97
30334 Torre del Ángel MC 157 Ye 122
41218 Torre de la Reina SE 148 Tf 123
29693 Torre de la Sal MA 174 Ue 130
44709 Torre de las Arcas TE 91 Zb 103
22415 Torre de la Venau HU 55 Aa 97
24370 Torre del Bierzo LE 26 Te 93
19197 Torre del Burgo GU 87 Wf 104
22415 Torre del Calvo HU 54 Aa 97
23640 Torre del Campo J 152 Wa 122
46408 Torre del Cap, La V 127 Ze 113
22513 Torre del Chiribas HU 55 Ab 97
44597 Torre del Compte TE 74 Aa 103
38800 Torre del Conde (Museo) TF 184 Hf 180
31500 Torre de Leoz NC 52 Yd 97
25139 Torre de les Comas L 55 Ae 98
03108 Torre de les Maçanes, La A 142 Zd 117
43792 Torre del Espagñol = la Torre de l'Espanyol T 74 Ad 101
29740 Torre del Mar MA 167 Vf 128
34131 Torre de los Molinos P 28 Vc 95
04638 Torre del Peñón AL 171 Ya 126
14857 Torre del Puerto CO 151 Vc 123
30710 Torre del Rame MC 157 Za 122
30528 Torre del Rico MC 141 Yd 117
03659 Torre del Rico MC 141 Yf 118
03659 Torre del Rico MC 141 Yf 118
12165 Torre dels Beltrans, La CS 92 Zf 106
37449 Torre de Martín Pascual SA 64 Ub 103
12163 Torre de Matella, La CS 92 Zf 107
43830 Torredembarra T 76 Bc 102
06172 Torre de Miguel Sesmero BA 132 Tb 117
25139 Torre de Miranda L 55 Ae 98
37405 Torre de Moncantar SA 65 Ud 102
12161 Torre d'En Besora, La CS 92 Zf 107
25281 Torredenegó L 57 Bc 97
46800 Torre d'En Lloris V 126 Zd 114
44540 Torre de Norna TE 73 Zc 102
07769 Torre d'en Quart IB 77 Df 108
07850 Torre d'en Valls IB 109 Bd 114
22438 Torre de Obato HU 55 Ac 95
47319 Torre de Peñafiel VA 67 Vf 99
50709 Torre de Poblador Z 73 Aa 101
46540 Torre de Puig, La V 108 Ze 111
07690 Torre de s'Almonia IB 111 Da 113
27235 Torre de Sampaio LU 12 Sb 90
10186 Torre de Santa María CC 117 Tf 113
12560 Torre de Sant Vicent CS 108 Aa 108
07160 Torre de Son Boisa IB 110 Cc 111
25636 Torre de Tamúrcia, La L 37 Ae 95
19269 Torre de Valdealmendras GU 69 Xc 102
37609 Torre de Velajos SA 82 Tf 104
08731 Torre de Vernet, La B 76 Bd 100
40154 Torredondo SG 67 Ve 103
23650 Torredonjimeno J 152 Wa 122
08518 Torre d'Oristà, La B 58 Ca 97
47520 Torre Duero o Ribera del Cebo VA 65 Uf 100
26134 Torre en Cameros RI 51 Xc 95
12184 Torre Endoménech CS 92 Aa 107
25123 Torrefarrera L 55 Ad 98
25211 Torrefeta L 56 Bb 98
25212 Torrefeta i Florejacs L 56 Bb 98
46635 Torrefiel V 126 Zb 116
43006 Torreforta T 75 Bb 102
49216 Torrefrades ZA 64 Tf 100
06410 Torrefresneda BA 117 Tf 115
23650 Torrefuencubierta J 152 Vf 122
09493 Torregalindo BU 49 Wb 99
49252 Torregamones ZA 64 Te 100
25286 Torregassa L 57 Bc 97
Torre Gavina IB 109 Bc 116
11011 Torre Gorda CA 172 Te 130
22535 Torregrosa HU 55 Ac 98
25141 Torregrosa = Torregrossa L 56 Ae 99
11312 Torreguadiaro CA 173 Ue 131
30834 Torre Guil MC 156 Ye 121
40211 Torregutiérrez SG 67 Vd 100
42269 Torrehermosa Z 70 Xf 101
40192 Torreiglesias SG 67 Vf 102
10830 Torrejancillo CC 98 Td 109
46310 Torrejón AB 125 Yd 112
16161 Torrejoncillo del Rey CU 104 Xc 108
28850 Torrejón de Ardoz MD 86 Wd 106
28991 Torrejón de la Calzada MD 86 Wb 107
19174 Torrejón del Rey GU 87 Wd 105
28990 Torrejón de Velasco MD 102 Wb 107
10694 Torrejón el Rubio CC 99 Tf 110
14820 Torre Juan Gil Alto CO 151 Vc 122
22480 Torrelabad HU 55 Ac 95
44382 Torrelacárcel TE 90 Ye 105
25138 Torrelameu L 55 Ae 98
50316 Torrelapaja Z 51 Ya 99
09645 Torrelara BU 49 Wc 96
22483 Torre la Ribera HU 36 Ad 94
12595 Torre La Sal CS 108 Aa 108
15316 Torrelavandeira C 11 Rf 89
39300 Torrelavega CB 17 Vf 88
08775 Torrelavit B 76 Be 100
16414 Torrelengua CU 104 Xa 110
22338 Torrelisa HU 36 Ab 94
03320 Torrellano Alto A 142 Zc 119
03320 Torrellano Bajo A 142 Zc 119
50512 Torrellas Z 52 Yb 97
08737 Torrelles de Foix B 76 Bd 100
08629 Torrelles de Llobregat B 77 Bf 100
08629 Torrelletes B 77 Bf 100
07730 Torrellissa Vell IB 77 Ea 109
28250 Torrelodones MD 85 Wa 105
44358 Torre los Negros TE 90 Yf 103
30395 Torre Los Siles MC 157 Za 122
23628 Torre María Martín, La J 152 Wa 121
02511 Torremarín AB 124 Yb 116
06880 Torremayor BA 116 Tc 115
42216 Torremediana SO 70 Xc 100
06210 Torremejía BA 117 Td 116
03313 Torremendo A 157 Za 121
10413 Torremenga CC 99 Ub 108
10184 Torremocha CC 117 Te 112
42342 Torremocha de Ayllón SO 68 We 100
19245 Torremocha de Jadraque GU 69 Xa 102
28189 Torremocha de Jarama MD 86 Wd 103
44381 Torremocha de Jiloca TE 90 Ye 105
19268 Torremocha del Campo GU 69 Xc 103
19345 Torremocha del Pinar GU 70 Xf 103
19391 Torremochuela GU 89 Ya 104
30153 Torre Mochuelo MC 157 Yf 122
29620 Torremolinos MA 175 Vd 129
26359 Torremontalbo RI 31 Xb 93
34305 Torremormojón P 47 Vb 97
29790 Torre Moya MA 167 Ve 128
29631 Torremuelle MA 175 Vc 129
26133 Torremuña RI 51 Xd 95
25335 Torreneral L 56 Af 98
12596 Torrenostra CS 92 Ab 107
07769 Torre Nova IB 77 Df 108
46900 Torrent V 126 Zd 112
30420 Torrentas, Las MC 140 Yb 119
08358 Torrentbò B 58 Cd 99
17123 Torrent d'Emporda = Torrent GI 59 Da 97
46900 Torrente = Torrent V 126 Zd 112
22590 Torrente de Cinca HU 74 Ac 100
04827 Torrentes, Los AL 155 Ya 123
11310 Torre Nueva CA 174 Ud 131
13740 Torrenueva CR 138 Wd 117
18720 Torrenueva GR 168 Wd 128
29649 Torrenueva MA 175 Vb 130
30739 Torre-Octavio MC 157 Za 122
12598 Torreó de Badún CS 93 Ac 107
23539 Torreón de Fique J 153 Wd 121
10182 Torreorgaz CC 117 Te 112
30700 Torre-Pacheco MC 157 Za 122
09226 Torrepadierne BU 48 Wa 95
09345 Torrepadre BU 48 Wa 96
02449 Torre-Pedro AB 139 Xe 118
44420 Torre-Peones TE 107 Zb 108
23320 Torreperogil J 153 We 120
29630 Torrequebrada MA 175 Vc 129
23638 Torrequebradilla J 152 Wc 121
10183 Torrequemada CC 117 Te 112
29601 Torre Real MA 174 Va 129
25001 Torre Ribera L 55 Ae 99
03570 Torres A 143 Ze 117
09512 Torres BU 18 Wd 91
23540 Torres J 153 Wc 122
50335 Torres Z 71 Yc 100
16612 Torres, Las CU 123 Xd 112
35018 Torres, Las GC 184 Kd 180
37796 Torres, Las SA 65 Uc 103
09310 Torresandino BU 48 Wa 98
19268 Torresaviñán, La GU 69 Xc 103
14820 Torres Cabrera CO 151 Vb 122
39300 Torres Campuzano CB 17 Vf 88
47313 Torrescarcela VA 67 Ve 100
23391 Torres de Albánchez J 139 Xb 118
44111 Torres de Albarracín TE 90 Yc 106
22132 Torres de Alcanadre HU 54 Zf 97
49522 Torres de Aliste, Las ZA 45 Te 97
09572 Torres de Arriba BU 18 Wb 91
22255 Torres de Barbués HU 54 Zd 97
50693 Torres de Berrellén Z 53 Yf 98
30565 Torres de Cotillas, Las MC 156 Ye 120
28813 Torres de la Alameda MD 87 Wd 106
25617 Torres de la Plana L 56 Ae 98
49122 Torres del Carrizal ZA 46 Ub 99
22588 Torres del Obispo HU 55 Ac 96
31229 Torres del Río NC 32 Xe 93
22134 Torres de Montes HU 54 Ze 96
25192 Torres de Sanui, Les L 55 Ad 99
25170 Torres de Segre L 74 Ad 99
25131 Torre-serona L 55 Ad 98
37110 Torresmenudas SA 64 Ub 102
18120 Torresolana GR 168 Vf 126
24144 Torrestío LE 14 Tf 90
46595 Torres-Torres V 108 Zd 110
42344 Torresuso SO 68 We 100
07711 Torret IB 77 Eb 109
04814 Torreta, La AL 171 Xf 124
46630 Torretallada V 126 Za 115
42181 Torretarrancho SO 51 Xe 97
42180 Torretartajo SO 51 Xe 98
07769 Torreta Saura IB 77 Df 109
25335 Torretosquella L 56 Af 98
08211 Torre Turull B 58 Ca 99
40171 Torre Val de San Pedro SG 67 Wa 102
17252 Torre Valentina GI 59 Da 98
44641 Torrevelilla TE 73 Zf 103
07769 Torre Vella IB 77 De 108
07711 Torre Vella IB 77 Eb 109
46635 Torrevellisca V 126 Zb 116
42315 Torrevicente SO 69 Xa 100
03181 Torrevieja A 157 Zb 121
30815 Torre y El Charco, La MC 156 Yc 123
37788 Torre Zapata SA 83 Ub 104
46670 Torrica V 126 Zd 114
45572 Torrico TO 100 Ue 110
44421 Torrijas TE 107 Za 108
50217 Torrijo de la Cañada Z 70 Ya 100
44393 Torrijo del Campo TE 90 Yd 104
45500 Torrijos TO 101 Ve 109
28380 Torrique MD 103 Wd 108
17110 Torroella GI 59 Da 97
17474 Torroella de Fluvià GI 59 Da 95
17257 Torroella de Montgrí GI 59 Da 96
17495 Torroelles, Les GI 40 Da 95
43737 Torroja = Torroja del Priorat T 75 Ae 101
27470 Torrón LU 24 Sb 94
19127 Torronteras GU 88 Xc 105
36309 Torroña PO 41 Rb 96
03109 Torrosella A 142 Zc 117
29770 Torrox MA 168 Wa 128
29793 Torrox-Costa MA 168 Wa 128

Torrox-Costa | 307 E

14447 Torrubia CO 136 Vd 118
19337 Torrubia GU 70 Ya 103
23700 Torrubia J 152 Wc 120
16413 Torrubia del Campo CU 103 Xa 109
16739 Torrubia del Castillo CU 104 Xe 111
42138 Torrubia de Soria SO 51 Xf 99
22437 Torruella de Aragón HU 36 Ac 95
22311 Torruéllola de la Plana HU 35 Zf 94
44162 Tortajada TE 90 Yf 106
17853 Tortellà GI 59 Cd 95
23700 Tortilla, La J 152 Wc 120
16122 Tórtola CU 105 Xf 109
19198 Tórtola de Henares GU 87 Wf 104
05514 Tórtoles AV 83 Ue 105
50514 Tórtoles Z 52 Yb 97
09312 Tórtoles de Esgueva BU 48 Vf 98
19261 Tortonda GU 70 Xc 103
43500 Tortosa T 93 Ad 104
18859 Tortosa, La GR 154 Xd 123
19338 Tortuera GU 71 Yb 103
19225 Tortuero GU 68 Wd 103
01439 Tortura VI 31 Xa 91
06719 Torviscal, El BA 118 Ub 114
10335 Torviscoso CC 99 Ud 109
18430 Torvizcón GR 169 We 127
25746 Tosal = Tossal, El L 56 Ba 97
09258 Tosantos BU 31 We 94
18820 Toscana Nueva GR 155 Xd 121
38715 Toscas, Las TF 181 Hb 176
38813 Toscas, Los TF 184 He 180
35018 Toscón, El GC 184 Kc 180
35368 Toscón, El GC 184 Kc 181
32633 Tosende OR 42 Sb 97
17536 Toses GI 38 Ca 95
50154 Tosos Z 72 Yf 101
33546 Tospe AS 16 Ue 89
29312 Tosquilla, La MA 167 Vd 126
25124 Tossa, La L 55 Ad 98
17320 Tossa de Mar GI 59 Cf 98
29197 Totalán MA 167 Ve 128
30850 Totana MC 156 Yc 122
45163 Totanés TO 101 Ve 110
35628 Toto GC 183 Lf 178
36141 Toural, O PO 22 Rc 94
15124 Touriñán C 10 Qe 90
15822 Touro C 23 Re 91
36828 Tourón PO 23 Rc 94
46269 Tous V 126 Zc 114
27835 Touza LU 12 Sb 88
36883 Touzosas, As PO 42 Re 96
23293 Tovar, El J 139 Xb 119
46140 Tóveda Alta V 106 Yd 108
46140 Tóvedas Tóveda Baja V 106 Yd 108
23293 Tovilla J 139 Xc 119
32641 Toxal, O OR 42 Sb 96
15214 Toxosoutos C 22 Rb 92
42112 Tozalmoro SO 51 Xe 98
18249 Tózar GR 168 Wb 124
15118 Traba C 10 Qf 89
33718 Trabada AS 13 Tb 88
27765 Trabada LU 13 Se 88
37149 Trabadillo SA 64 Tf 102
24523 Trabaledo LE 25 Ta 93
37173 Trabanca SA 63 Td 101
27164 Trabazas LU 25 Sf 93
24745 Trabazos LE 25 Tc 95
32785 Trabazos OR 25 Se 95
49516 Trabazos ZA 44 Td 98
32617 Trabe, A OR 43 Se 97
32235 Trado OR 42 Rf 95
16150 Tragacete CU 89 Ya 106
25790 Tragó L 56 Bb 96
25611 Tragò de Noguera L 55 Ad 97
37216 Traguntía SA 63 Td 103
31315 Traibuenas NC 33 Yc 94
19312 Traid GU 89 Yb 104
12330 Traiguera CS 92 Ab 105
41727 Trajano SE 163 Ua 126
12118 Trallanta, La CS 108 Ze 108
44133 Tramacastiel TE 106 Ye 107
44112 Tramacastilla TE 89 Yc 106
22663 Tramacastilla de Tena HU 35 Ze 92
22268 Tramaced HU 54 Ze 97
23293 Tranco J 139 Xb 119
32636 Trandeiras OR 43 Sc 96
46811 Transformador, El V 126 Zb 115
27112 Trapa, A AS 13 Sf 89
33934 Trapa, La AS 15 Ub 89
50710 Trapa, La Z 74 Aa 102
48510 Trapagaran BI 19 Wf 89
14280 Trapero CO 135 Uf 117
35431 Trapiche GC 184 Kc 180
29719 Trapiche MA 167 Vf 128
10661 Trapilabado CC 98 Td 107
32172 Trasalba OR 23 Sa 94
15540 Trasancos C 11 Re 87
15540 Trasancos C 11 Re 87
15390 Trasanquelos C 11 Re 89
33818 Trascastro AS 14 Td 90
24429 Trascastro LE 25 Tc 91
24127 Trascastro de Luna LE 26 Ua 92
06176 Trasierra BA 132 Tc 118
06909 Trasierra BA 133 Ua 119
39527 Trasierra CB 17 Ve 88
21650 Traslasierra H 147 Tc 122
48879 Traslaviña BI 19 We 89
32695 Trasmirás OR 43 Sc 96
33190 Trasmonte AS 14 Ua 88
15688 Trasmonte C 11 Rd 90
27229 Trasmonte LU 12 Sb 90
27786 Trasmonte LU 12 Sd 87
36685 Trasmonte PO 23 Rd 92
50583 Trasmoz Z 52 Yb 98
18328 Trasmulas GR 168 Wa 125
50268 Trasobares Z 52 Yc 99
33518 Traspando AS 15 Uc 88
27305 Trasparga LU 12 Sa 89
34858 Traspeña de la Peña P 28 Vc 92
47330 Traspinedo VA 47 Vd 99
36537 Trasulfe PO 24 Sa 93
39520 Trasvía CB 17 Ve 88
08719 Traver B 57 Bd 99
15184 Travesas, As C 11 Rd 89
15687 Trazo C 11 Rc 90
42113 Trébago SO 51 Xf 97
07720 Trebaluger IB 77 Eb 109
32573 Treboedo OR 23 Rf 94
27363 Trebolle LU 24 Sc 92
39788 Trebuesto CB 18 We 89
39528 Treceño CB 17 Ve 88
39592 Treceño CB 17 Ve 89
25598 Tredòs L 37 Af 92
49359 Trefacio ZA 44 Tc 96
39180 Tregandín CB 18 Wc 88
26132 Treguajantes RI 51 Xd 95
17869 Treguà de Dalt GI 39 Cb 94
04826 Treinta, Los AL 155 Xf 123
25795 Trejuvell L 37 Bb 95
32920 Trelle OR 23 Sa 95
32920 Trellerma OR 23 Sa 95
33718 Trelles AS 13 Tb 88
33211 Tremañes AS 15 Ub 87
34847 Tremaya P 17 Vd 91
05691 Tremedal AV 83 Uc 106
37148 Tremedal de Tormes SA 64 Te 102
09150 Tremellos, Los BU 30 Wa 93
24374 Tremor de Abajo LE 26 Te 93
24377 Tremor de Arriba LE 26 Te 92
25620 Tremp L 56 Af 95
39557 Tresabuela CB 17 Vd 90
33529 Tresali AS 15 Ud 88
33589 Tresano AS 16 Uf 88
28760 Tres Cantos MD 86 Wb 105
33576 Trescares AS 16 Vb 89
40194 Trescasas SG 67 Vf 103
46540 Tres Colinas V 108 Ze 111
35530 Treseguite GC 182 Mc 174
22583 Treserra HU 56 Ad 95
03658 Tresfonts A 141 Za 118
33590 Tresgrandas AS 17 Vc 88
47155 Tres Hermanos VA 47 Vb 98
16422 Tresjuncos CU 104 Xb 110
33586 Tresmonte AS 16 Uf 88
04897 Tres Morales AL 170 Xc 125
09540 Trespaderne BU 30 Wd 92
39553 Trespeñas CB 17 Vd 89
01191 Trespuentes VI 31 Xb 91
08261 Tresserres B 57 Be 97
04530 Tres Villas, Las AL 170 Xb 126
33554 Tresviso CB 16 Vb 89
48891 Treto BI 18 Wd 89
39760 Treto CB 18 Wd 88
10894 Trevejo CC 97 Tb 107
18417 Trevélez GR 169 We 126
26215 Treviana RI 31 Xa 93
26132 Trevijano RI 32 Xd 95
09215 Treviño BU 31 Xb 92
32621 Trez OR 43 Sd 96
27631 Triacastela LU 25 Se 92
23670 Triana J 152 Wa 123
29718 Triana MA 167 Ve 128
24175 Trianos LE 28 Uf 94
16452 Tribaldos CU 104 Xa 109
22372 Tricás HU 35 Zf 94
38788 Tricias, La TF 181 Ha 176
26312 Tricio RI 31 Xb 94
32510 Trigás OR 23 Rf 94
36519 Trigueira, A PO 23 Re 93
21620 Trigueros H 162 Ta 124
47282 Trigueros del Valle VA 47 Vc 98
05196 Triguezuelos AV 85 Vc 105
19192 Trijueque GU 87 Xa 104
19450 Trillo GU 88 Xc 104
22438 Trillo HU 36 Ab 95
13129 Trincheto, El CR 120 Ve 113
41600 Trinidad, La SE 165 Uc 125
34887 Triollo P 28 Vb 91
35639 Triquivijate GC 183 Ma 178
04114 Tristanes AL 171 Xf 127
22820 Triste HU 34 Zb 94
49320 Triufé ZA 44 Tc 96
24009 Trobajo del Camino LE 27 Uc 93
24005 Trobajo del Cerecedo LE 27 Uc 93
41727 Trobal, El SE 164 Ua 126
27375 Trobo LU 12 Sc 89
27112 Trobo, O LU 13 Sf 89
11519 Trocadero, El CA 172 Te 129
01193 Troconiz VI 32 Xc 92
15839 Troitosende C 10 Rc 91
15819 Tronceda C 23 Re 91
32766 Tronceda OR 24 Sd 94
22438 Troncedo HU 36 Ab 95
44141 Tronchón TE 91 Zd 105
33100 Trubia AS 14 Ua 88
27660 Trucende LU 13 Sf 91
24740 Truchas LE 26 Td 95
24740 Truchillas LE 44 Td 95
48880 Trucios-Turtzioz BI 19 We 89
24144 Truébano LE 14 Tf 91
06892 Trujillanos BA 117 Te 115
29150 Trujillas, Las MA 167 Vc 127
10200 Trujillo CC 117 Ua 112
41500 Trujillo SE 164 Ub 125
18564 Trujillos GR 152 Wb 124
09557 Tubilla BU 18 Wc 91
09143 Tubilla del Agua BU 30 Wb 92
09453 Tubilla del Lago BU 49 Wc 98
09146 Tubilleja BU 30 Wb 91
49173 Tuda, La ZA 64 Ua 100
09146 Tudanca BU 30 Wb 91
39555 Tudanca CB 17 Vd 90
31500 Tudela NC 52 Yc 96
33669 Tudela de Agüeria AS 15 Ub 89
47320 Tudela de Duero VA 47 Vc 99
25739 Tudela de Segre L 56 Ba 97
33669 Tudela-Veguín AS 15 Ub 89
26512 Tudelilla RI 32 Xf 95
49214 Tudera ZA 64 Te 100
39575 Tudes CB 17 Vc 90
46177 Tuéjar V 106 Yf 110
30858 Tuelas, Los MC 156 Yd 122
01423 Tuesta VI 31 Wf 92
15121 Tufiones C 10 Qf 90
36700 Tui PO 41 Rc 96
33935 Tuilla AS 15 Uc 89
27343 Tuimil LU 24 Sd 93
35628 Tuineje GC 183 Lf 179
25717 Tuixén L 57 Bd 95
25717 Tuixén-la Vansa L 57 Bd 95
33628 Tuiza de Abajo AS 15 Ua 90
33628 Tuiza de Arriba AS 15 Ua 90
21880 Tujena H 148 Td 124
31522 Tulebras NC 52 Yb 97
21840 Tumbalejo, El H 147 Tc 124
33876 Tuña AS 14 Td 89
03839 Turballos A 126 Zd 116
33313 Turbeño AS 15 Uc 88
30813 Turbinto MC 156 Yb 123
24285 Turcia LE 27 Ua 93
40370 Turégano SG 67 Vf 102
39586 Turieno CB 16 Vc 90
01213 Turiso VI 31 Xa 93
45789 Turleque TO 102 Wc 111
07730 Turmadén IB 77 Ea 109
19287 Turmiel GU 70 Xf 102
18491 Turón GR 169 Wf 127
46390 Turquía V 106 Yf 111
37871 Turra de Alba SA 83 Ud 104
04639 Turre AL 171 Ya 126
09292 Turrientes BU 30 Wd 94
02536 Turrilla AB 139 Xe 119
04211 Turrillas AL 170 Xe 126
31421 Turrillas NC 33 Yd 92
18129 Turro, El GR 168 Wa 126
40560 Turrubuelo SG 68 Wc 101
26587 Turruncún RI 51 Xf 96
26289 Turza RI 31 Xa 95
02485 Tus AB 139 Xd 118
36700 Tuy = Tui PO 41 Rc 96
01428 Tuyo VI 31 Xa 92
20170 Txikierdi = Chiquierdi SS 20 Xf 89

U

31219 Ubago NC 32 Xe 93
31174 Ubani NC 33 Yb 92
03658 Úbeda A 141 Yf 118
23400 Úbeda J 153 Wd 120
20809 Ubegun SS 20 Xf 89
20579 Ubera SS 20 Xd 90
39360 Ubiarco CB 17 Vf 88
48145 Ubide VI 19 Xb 90
22439 Ubiergo HU 55 Ab 96
09141 Ubierna BU 30 Wb 94
48276 Ubilla-Urberuaga BI 20 Xd 89
11600 Ubrique CA 173 Ud 128
31154 Úcar NC 33 Yb 92
19187 Uceda GU 86 Wd 103
24369 Ucedo LE 26 Te 93
15320 Uceira C 12 Sb 87
30180 Ucenda MC 156 Yb 120
42317 Ucero SO 50 Wf 98
37217 Uces, Las SA 63 Td 102
02409 Uchea AB 140 Yc 117
39513 Ucieda CB 17 Ve 89
33569 Ucio AS 16 Uf 88
16452 Uclés CU 104 Xa 109
31869 Udabe NC 21 Yb 91
20500 Udala SS 20 Xc 90
39850 Udalla CB 18 Wd 89
33193 Udrión AS 15 Ua 88
49519 Ufones ZA 45 Te 98
35570 Uga GC 182 Mb 175
20180 Ugaldecho = Ugaldetxo SS 21 Ya 89
20180 Ugaldetxo SS 21 Ya 89
48490 Ugao-Miraballes BI 19 Xa 89
31177 Úgar NC 32 Ya 92
48141 Ugarana BI 19 Xb 90
48392 Ugarte BI 19 Xb 89
20268 Ugarte = Nuestra Señora del Rosario SS 20 Xf 90
20829 Ugarte Berri SS 20 Xd 89
45217 Ugena TO 86 Wa 108
18480 Ugíjar GR 169 Wf 127
31840 Uharte-Arakil NC 32 Ya 91
31877 Uitzi NC 21 Ya 90
19276 Ujados GU 69 Wf 101
33640 Ujo AS 15 Ub 89
31496 Ujué NC 33 Yd 93
30612 Ulea MC 141 Ye 120
04279 Uleila del Campo AL 171 Xe 125
31283 Ulibarri NC 32 Xe 92
26270 Uliuzarna RI 31 Xa 94
17140 Ullà GI 59 Da 96
08231 Ullastrell B 77 Bf 99
17114 Ullastret GI 59 Da 97
43363 Ulldemolins T 75 Af 101
01117 Ullíbarri-Arana VI 32 Xe 92
01520 Ullíbarri Arrazua VI 31 Xc 91
01194 Ullíbarri de los Olleros VI 31 Xc 92
01520 Ullíbarri Gamboa VI 19 Xc 91
01196 Ullíbarri-Viña VI 31 Xb 91
01439 Ullivarri Cuartango VI 31 Xa 91
27205 Ulloa LU 24 Sa 91
17133 Ultramort GI 59 Da 96
31172 Ulzurrun NC 33 Ya 92
19238 Umbralejo GU 68 We 102
41806 Umbrete SE 164 Tf 124
44140 Umbría TE 91 Zd 105
14811 Umbría CO 151 Ve 124
12118 Umbría, L' CS 108 Zf 108
21207 Umbría, La H 148 Td 121
23140 Umbría, La J 153 Wc 123
04811 Umbría de Arriba, La AL 155 Xe 123
13770 Umbría de Fresnedas CR 137 Wc 117
30510 Umbría del Factor MC 141 Ye 117
05693 Umbrías AV 83 Uc 107
12125 Umbrías, Las CS 107 Zd 108
29712 Umbrías, Las MA 167 Vf 127
31790 Unanua NC 32 Xf 91
25588 Unarre L 37 Ba 93
48111 Unbe BI 19 Xa 88
50678 Uncastillo Z 34 Yf 94
31422 Unciti NC 33 Yc 92
46620 Unde, La V 125 Ye 114
31190 Undiano NC 33 Yb 92
50689 Undués de Lerda Z 34 Ye 93
48144 Undurraga BI 19 Xb 90
49393 Ungilde ZA 44 Tc 96
33590 Unguera AS 17 Vc 88
30360 Unión, La MC 157 Za 123
47670 Unión de Campos, La VA 46 Ue 96
26130 Unión de los Tres Ejércitos, La RI 32 Xd 94
28760 Universidad Autónoma de Madrid MD 86 Wb 105
01449 Unza VI 19 Xa 91
31396 Unzué NC 33 Yc 93
16152 Uña CU 89 Ya 107
24996 Uña, La LE 16 Uf 90
49327 Uña de Quintana ZA 45 Tf 96
05268 Uposa AV 85 Vc 105
09347 Ura BU 49 Wc 96
48960 Uransolo BI 19 Xb 89
01216 Urarte VI 31 Xc 92
07157 Urbanització Bihiorella IB 110 Cc 111
43850 Urbanització Cambrils Mediterrània T 75 Ba 102
35580 Urbanización Atlante del Sol GC 182 Ma 175
35627 Urbanización Calma Bahia GC 183 Le 180
35627 Urbanización Costa Calma GC 183 Le 180
38639 Urbanización El Guincho TF 180 Ic 180
43850 Urbanización el Tarraco T 75 Ba 102
35539 Urbanización Famara GC 182 Mc 174
35507 Urbanización Las Cabreras GC 182 Mc 174
35610 Urbanización Llano del Sol GC 183 Ma 178
35544 Urbanización Los Cocoteros GC 182 Mc 174
35650 Urbanización Los Lagos GC 183 Lf 176
35519 Urbanización Los Pocillos GC 182 Mc 175
35613 Urbanización Los Pozos GC 183 Ma 178
35626 Urbanización Marabul GC 183 Le 180
35580 Urbanización Montaña Baja GC 182 Ma 175
46191 Urbanización Monte Orquera V 107 Zc 111
04711 Urbanización Oasis de Costa del Sol AL 170 Xb 128
35530 Urbanización Oasis de Nazaret GC 182 Mc 174
35559 Urbanización Playa Honda GC 182 Mc 175
50700 Urbanización Playas de Chacón Z 73 Zf 101
04740 Urbanización Roquetas de Mar AL 170 Xc 128
35613 Urbanización Rosa de la Monja GC 183 Ma 177
35519 Urbanización San Antonio GC 182 Mc 175
35558 Urbanización Vista Graciosa GC 182 Mc 174
03195 Urbanova A 142 Zc 119
09125 Urbel del Castillo BU 30 Wa 93
31421 Urbicáin NC 33 Yd 92
33613 Urbiés AS 15 Ub 89
01510 Urbina VI 19 Xc 91
02600 Urbina, La AB 122 Xb 113
31243 Urbiola NC 32 Xf 93
04691 Úrcal AL 155 Ya 124
50196 Urcamusa Z 72 Yf 99
45480 Urda TO 121 Wb 112
31810 Urdain NC 32 Xf 91
20800 Urdaneta SS 20 Xe 89
31698 Urdániz NC 33 Yc 91
31172 Urdánoz NC 33 Ya 92
26289 Urdanta RI 31 Xa 95
31711 Urdax = Urdazubi NC 21 Yc 89
31711 Urdazubi = Urdax NC 21 Yc 89
24313 Urdiales de Colinas LE 26 Td 92
24248 Urdiales del Páramo LE 27 Ub 94
15281 Urdilde C 22 Rb 92
10697 Urdimalas CC 99 Ua 109
31438 Urdíroz NC 33 Yd 91
22732 Urdués HU 34 Zb 92
48610 Urduliz BI 19 Xa 88
19265 Ures GU 69 Xb 102
42240 Ures de Medina SO 70 Xe 102
20800 Ureta SS 20 Xe 89
36307 Urgal PO 41 Rb 96
20568 Uribarri SS 20 Xd 90
01169 Uribarri VI 20 Xc 90
01194 Uribarri-Nagusi = Ullívarri-Olleros VI 31 Xc 92
48144 Uribe BI 19 Xb 90
48419 Urigoiti BI 19 Xa 90
27157 Uriz LU 12 Sc 90
31438 Uriz NC 33 Yd 91
48620 Urizar BI 19 Xa 88
01440 Urkabustaiz VI 19 Xa 91
48277 Urkaregi BI 20 Xd 89
20400 Urkizu SS 20 Xf 90
20600 Urko SS 20 Xd 89
22466 Urmella HU 36 Ad 93
20130 Urnieta SS 20 Ya 89
47671 Urones de Castroponce VA 46 Ue 96
31485 Uroz NC 33 Yd 92
20400 Urquizu = Urkizu SS 20 Xf 90
04879 Urrácal AL 155 Xd 124
05195 Urraca-Miguel AV 85 Vc 104
31448 Urraul Alto NC 33 Ye 92
31480 Urraul Bajo NC 33 Yd 92
44593 Urrea de Gaén TE 73 Zd 102
50296 Urrea de Jalón Z 53 Ye 98
30331 Urreas, Los MC 157 Yf 122
20738 Urrestilla SS 20 Xe 90
20568 Urrexola = Urrejola SS 20 Xd 90
09199 Urrez BU 30 Wd 95
09515 Urría BU 30 Wd 91
22330 Urriales HU 35 Aa 94
31484 Urricelqui NC 33 Yd 91
50685 Urriés Z 34 Yf 93
31868 Urrizola NC 33 Ya 91
31799 Urrizola-Galáin NC 21 Yc 91
32664 Urros OR 42 Sa 95
31752 Urrotz NC 21 Yb 90
31420 Urroz NC 33 Yd 92
01170 Urrunaga VI 19 Xc 91
30368 Urrutias, Los MC 157 Zb 122
31753 Urrutiña NC 21 Yb 90
48391 Urrutxua BI 19 Xc 89
20213 Ursuaran SS 20 Xe 91
31639 Urtasun NC 21 Yc 91
01118 Urturi VI 32 Xc 93
47862 Urueña VA 46 Ue 98
40317 Urueñas SG 67 Wb 100
26313 Uruñuela RI 31 Xb 94
17538 Urús GI 38 Bf 94
24127 Urz, La LE 26 Ua 92
31416 Urzainqui NC 34 Za 92
31521 Urzante NC 52 Yc 96

308 | Torrubia

06290 Usagre BA 133 Tf 118
22339 Usana HU 36 Aa 94
19182 Usanos GU 87 We 104
31451 Uscarrés NC 34 Yf 92
22622 Used HU 35 Ze 95
50374 Used Z 71 Yc 102
12118 Useras = les Useres CS 92 Zf 108
12118 Useres, les = Useras CS 92 Zf 108
25592 Useu L 37 Ba 95
31193 Usi NC 33 Yb 91
22210 Usón HU 54 Ze 97
31486 Ustárroz NC 33 Yc 92
31450 Ustés NC 34 Yf 92
31491 Usumbeiz NC 33 Yd 93
31454 Usún NC 34 Ye 93
20170 Usurbil SS 20 Xf 89
20170 Usúrbil = Usurbil SS 20 Xf 89
19196 Utande GU 87 Xa 103
50180 Utebo Z 53 Za 98
31133 Uterga NC 33 Yb 92
46300 Utiel V 106 Ye 111
41710 Utrera SE 164 Ub 125
04858 Utreras, Los AL 171 Xf 125
42258 Utrilla SO 70 Xe 101
44760 Utrillas TE 91 Za 104
25245 Utxafava L 56 Af 99
15690 Uxes C 11 Rd 89
26270 Uyarra RI 31 Xa 94
39556 Uznayo CB 17 Vd 90
09217 Uzquiano BU 31 Xb 92
01449 Uzquiano VI 19 Xa 91
31395 Uzquita NC 33 Yc 93
09199 Uzquiza BU 30 Wd 95
31418 Uztárroz = Uztarroze NC 34 Za 91
31418 Uztarroze = Uztárroz NC 34 Za 91
31891 Uztegi NC 20 Xf 90

V

36418 Vacaria PO 41 Rc 96
08233 Vacarisses B 57 Bf 99
23260 Vacarizo J 138 We 118
28529 Vaciamadrid MD 86 Wc 107
39577 Vada CB 16 Vb 90
16813 Vadeolivas CU 88 Xd 105
37495 Vadera-Baldía SA 82 Td 104
42148 Vadillo SO 50 Wf 98
14960 Vadillo, El CO 167 Ve 125
49420 Vadillo de la Guareña ZA 65 Ud 101
05560 Vadillo de la Sierra AV 84 Uf 105
26133 Vadillos RI 51 Xd 95
37116 Vadima, La SA 64 Tf 102
09513 Vado, El BU 30 Wc 91
09491 Vadocondes BU 49 Wc 99
29500 Vado del Álamo MA 166 Vb 127
10600 Vado de las Palomas CC 98 Tf 108
45919 Vado de los Morales TO 101 Vd 108
14912 Vadofresno CO 167 Vd 125
18003 Vados, Los GR 168 Wb 125
29719 Vados, Los MA 167 Vf 128
23529 Vados de Torralba J 152 Wc 121
30811 Vainazo, El MC 156 Yb 123
17707 Vajol, La GI 40 Ce 94
36526 Val PO 23 Rf 92
15541 Val, O C 11 Re 87
44191 Valacloche TE 106 Yf 107
15239 Valadares C 22 Ra 91
36314 Valadares PO 41 Rb 95
27770 Valadouro, O LU 12 Sd 87
50617 Valareña Z 52 Ye 96
34829 Valberzoso P 29 Ve 91
36685 Valboa PO 23 Rd 92
44430 Valbona TE 91 Zb 107
09119 Valbonilla BU 48 Ve 95
37718 Valbuena SA 82 Ua 106
47359 Valbuena de Duero VA 48 Vd 99
34465 Valbuena de Pisuerga P 48 Ve 96
32375 Valbuxán OR 25 Sf 95
39806 Valcaba CB 18 Wc 89
34117 Valcabadillo P 28 Vb 93
49192 Valcabado ZA 64 Ub 99
24790 Valcabado del Páramo LE 45 Ub 95
22511 Valcarca HU 55 Ab 97
09125 Valcárceres, Los BU 29 Wa 93
23780 Valcargado J 151 Ve 121
31660 Valcarlos, Luizalde/ NC 21 Ye 90
27866 Valcarria LU 10 Sc 87
45909 Valcarrillo de Alberche TO 85 Vd 107
09317 Valcavado de Roa BU 48 Wa 98
14029 Valchillón CO 150 Va 122
34886 Valcobero P 28 Vb 91
21230 Valconejo H 147 Ta 121
24889 Valcuende LE 28 Va 92
24839 Valcueva, La LE 27 Ud 91
37116 Valcuevo SA 64 Ub 102
45360 Valdajos TO 103 Wd 108
39593 Valdáliga CB 17 Vd 89
42328 Valdanzo SO 68 Wd 99
42328 Valdanzuelo SO 68 Wd 99
28594 Valdaracete MD 87 We 107
19141 Valdarachas GU 87 Wf 105
10614 Valdastillas CC 99 Ua 108
24171 Valdavida LE 28 Uf 93
24740 Valdavido LE 44 Td 95
09248 Valdazo BU 30 Wd 93
10990 Valdeaicalde de Arriba CC 97 Ta 109
09145 Valdeajos BU 30 Wa 92
42141 Valdealbín SO 50 Wf 98
24160 Valdealcón LE 27 Ue 93
44594 Valdealgorfa TE 73 Zf 103
24165 Valdealiso LE 27 Ue 93
19269 Valdealmendras GU 69 Xc 102
42193 Valdealvillo SO 50 Xa 99
19292 Valdeancheta GU 87 Wf 103
09453 Valdeande BU 49 Wc 98
24330 Valdearcos LE 27 Ud 94
47317 Valdearcos de la Vega VA 48 Ve 99
06470 Valdearenales BA 117 Tf 116
19196 Valdearenas GU 87 Xa 104
09592 Valdearnedo BU 30 Wc 93
39813 Val de Asón CB 18 Wc 89
19142 Valdeavellano GU 87 Xa 105
42165 Valdeavellano de Tera SO 50 Xc 97
42317 Valdeavellano de Ucero SO 50 Wf 98
28816 Valdeavero MD 87 Wd 105
19174 Valdeaveruelo GU 87 We 105
13470 Valdeazogues CR 136 Vd 116
45139 Valdeazores TO 119 Vb 112
06194 Valdebótoa BA 116 Ta 115
34159 Valdebusto P 47 Vb 97
06689 Valdecaballeros BA 119 Ue 113
28669 Valdecabañas MD 86 Wa 106
16146 Valdecabras CU 89 Xf 108
44126 Val de Cabriel TE 89 Yc 107
16542 Valdecabrillas CU 104 Xd 108
24415 Valdecañada LE 25 Tc 94
14810 Valdecañas CO 151 Vd 124
16843 Valdecañas CU 88 Xd 107
34249 Valdecañas de Cerrato P 48 Ve 97
10329 Valdecañas de Tajo CC 99 Uc 110
37593 Valdecarpinteros SA 81 Td 105
37500 Valdecarros SA 81 Tc 105
37881 Valdecarros SA 83 Ud 104
05143 Valdecasa AV 84 Uf 105
24853 Valdecastillo LE 27 Ud 91
23469 Valdecazorla J 153 Wf 121
44193 Valdecebro TE 90 Yf 106
05196 Valdeciervos AV 84 Vc 105
39724 Valdecilla CB 18 Wb 88
16541 Valdecolmenas, Los CU 104 Xc 108
16541 Valdecolmenas de Abajo CU 104 Xd 108
16541 Valdecolmenas de Arriba CU 104 Xd 108
19132 Valdeconcha GU 87 Xa 106
44779 Valdeconejos TE 91 Za 104
44122 Valdecuenca TE 90 Yd 107
33615 Valdecuna AS 15 Ub 89
33810 Valdeferreiro AS 13 Ta 90
49882 Valdefinjas ZA 65 Ud 100
41899 Valdeflores SE 148 Td 122
24228 Valdefresno LE 27 Ud 93
10180 Valdefuentes CC 117 Tf 113
24220 Valdefuentes LE 46 Ud 96
28939 Valdefuentes MD 86 Wa 107
24253 Valdefuentes del Páramo LE 27 Ub 95
37680 Valdefuentes de Sangusín SA 83 Ub 106
47861 Valdefuentes o Griegos VA 46 Ue 98
34492 Valdegama P 29 Ve 92
02150 Valdeganga AB 124 Yb 114
16122 Valdeganga de Cuenca CU 105 Xe 109
01427 Valdegovía = Villanuova de Valdegovía VI 31 Wf 91
14813 Valdegranada CO 168 Vf 124
19412 Valdegrudas GU 87 Wf 104
42350 Valdegrulla SO 50 Wf 99
26529 Valdegutur RI 51 Ya 97
37799 Valdehermoso SA 65 Uc 101
06190 Valdeherreros BA 116 Tc 114
06173 Valdehierro BA 132 Tb 117
13428 Valdehierro CR 120 Vf 113
37713 Valdehijaderos SA 82 Ua 106
50371 Valdehorna Z 71 Yd 102
06410 Valdehornillo BA 117 Ua 114
24854 Valdehuesa LE 15 Ue 91
10393 Valdehúncar CC 99 Uc 109
14749 Valdeinfierno CO 134 Uc 120
10420 Valdeíñigos CC 99 Ua 109
42112 Valdejeña SO 51 Xe 98
06185 Valdelacalzada BA 116 Tb 115
21230 Valdelacanal H 147 Tb 121
37791 Valdelacasa SA 83 Ub 105
10332 Valdelacasa de Tajo CC 100 Ue 110
09515 Valdelacuesta BU 30 Wd 91
24227 Valdelafuente LE 27 Uc 93
37724 Valdelageve SA 82 Ua 106
11500 Valdelagrana CA 172 Te 129
19459 Valdelagua GU 88 Xb 104
28750 Valdelagua MD 86 Wc 105
42113 Valdelagua del Cerro SO 51 Xf 97
28810 Valdeláguila MD 87 We 106
05592 Valdelaguna AV 83 Ud 106
24342 Valdelaguna LE 28 Uf 94
28391 Valdelaguna MD 86 Wd 108
24459 Valdelaloba LE 26 Tc 92
49193 Valdelaloba ZA 64 Ub 99
21330 Valdelamusa H 147 Ta 122
21291 Valdelarco H 147 Tb 121
46140 Val de la Sabina, El V 106 Ye 108
28760 Valdelatas MD 86 Wb 105
09145 Valdelateja BU 30 Wb 92
05196 Valdelavia AV 85 Vc 105
42175 Valdelavilla SO 51 Xe 97
19269 Valdelcubo GU 69 Xb 101
42318 Valdelinares SO 50 Wf 98
44413 Valdelinares TE 91 Zc 106
23747 Valdelipe J 136 Vf 120
24342 Valdelocajos LE 28 Uf 94
37799 Valdelosa SA 64 Ub 101
44620 Valdeltormo TE 74 Aa 103
42318 Valdelubiel SO 50 Wf 99
26532 Valdemadera RI 51 Xf 97
42318 Valdemaluque SO 50 Wf 98
28729 Valdemanco MD 86 Wc 103
13411 Valdemanco del Esteras CR 119 Vb 115
18538 Valdemanzanos GR 154 Wf 123
28295 Valdemaqueda MD 85 Ve 105
17412 Valdemaria GI 59 Ce 98
45165 Valdemarías TO 101 Vd 110
23370 Valdemarín J 139 Xb 119
28701 Valdemasa MD 86 Wb 105
16152 Valdemeca CU 89 Yb 107
37891 Valdemierque SA 83 Uc 104
49152 Valdemimbre ZA 65 Uc 100
05154 Valdemolinos AV 83 Ud 105
24206 Valdemora LE 46 Ud 95
10131 Valdemorales CC 117 Tf 113
24293 Valdemorilla LE 46 Ue 95
28210 Valdemorillo MD 85 Vf 105
16340 Valdemorillo de la Sierra CU 105 Yb 108
28343 Valdemoro MD 102 Wb 107
16521 Valdemoro del Rey CU 88 Xc 107
16316 Valdemoro-Sierra CU 105 Yb 108
42193 Valdenarros SO 50 Xa 99
10839 Valdencin CC 98 Td 109
42313 Valdenebro SO 50 Xa 99
47816 Valdenebro de los Valles VA 47 Va 97
42175 Valdenegrillos SO 51 Xf 97
09559 Valdenoceda BU 30 Wc 91
19197 Valdenoches GU 87 Wf 104
37220 Valdenoguera SA 63 Ta 103
19185 Valdenuño-Fernández GU 86 Wd 104
10672 Valdeobispo CC 98 Te 108
34239 Valdeolmillos P 48 Vd 96
28130 Valdeolmos MD 86 Wd 105
26133 Valdeosera RI 51 Xd 95
28590 Valdepardillo MD 103 We 108
13300 Valdepeñas CR 138 Wd 116
23150 Valdepeñas de Jaén J 152 Wb 123
19184 Valdepeñas de la Sierra GU 68 Wd 103
28540 Valdeperales MD 87 Wd 107
49182 Valdeperdices ZA 45 Ua 99
26527 Valdeperillo RI 51 Xf 96
24847 Valdepiélago LE 27 Ud 91
28170 Valdepiélagos MD 86 Wd 104
50430 Valdepinar Z 72 Za 100
19238 Valdepinillos GU 68 We 101
37500 Valdepiñuela SA 81 Td 104
24930 Valdepolo LE 28 Ue 93
39574 Valdeprado CB 17 Vd 90
24488 Valdeprado LE 25 Tc 91
42181 Valdeprado SO 51 Xf 97
39419 Valdeprado del Río CB 29 Vf 91
05197 Valdeprados AV 84 Vb 105
40423 Valdeprados SG 85 Ve 104
10250 Valdepuertas CC 118 Uc 112
15215 Val de Quintáns C 22 Rb 92
24220 Valderas LE 46 Ud 96
30156 Valderas MC 157 Yf 122
39232 Valderias BU 30 Wa 91
34473 Valderrábano P 28 Vc 93
09211 Valderrama BU 31 We 92
46352 Valderrama V 125 Ye 112
10670 Valderraosas CC 98 Te 108
19490 Valderrebollo GU 88 Xb 104
24793 Valderrey LE 26 Tf 94
49024 Valderrey ZA 64 Ub 99
44580 Valderrobres TE 92 Aa 103
42294 Valderrodilla SO 69 Xb 99
37256 Valderrodrigo SA 63 Tc 102
42344 Valderromán SO 69 Wf 100
05196 Valderrosas AV 84 Vc 105
18250 Valderrubio GR 168 Wb 125
24882 Valderrueda LE 28 Va 92
42294 Valderrueda SO 69 Xb 99
29738 Valdés MA 167 Ve 128
10164 Valdesalor CC 117 Td 112
24127 Valdesamario LE 26 Ua 92
24763 Valdesandinas LE 27 Ua 94
19429 Val de San García GU 88 Xc 104
37777 Valdesangil SA 83 Ub 106
24717 Val de San Lorenzo LE 26 Tf 94
50372 Val de San Martín Z 71 Yd 102
24717 Val de San Román LE 26 Tf 94
49337 Val de Santa María ZA 45 Te 97
39548 Val de San Vicente CB 17 Vd 88
19412 Valdesaz GU 87 Xa 104
40318 Valdesaz SG 67 Wb 101
24208 Valdesaz de los Oteros LE 27 Ud 95
24172 Valdescapa LE 28 Va 93
49680 Valdescorriel ZA 46 Uc 96
40389 Valdesimonte SG 67 Wa 101
24226 Valdesogo de Abajo LE 27 Uc 93
33938 Valdesoto AS 15 Uc 88
19225 Valdesotos GU 68 We 103
34419 Valdespina P 48 Vd 96
42191 Valdespina SO 51 Xd 99
37515 Valdespino SA 81 Tc 105
49357 Valdespino ZA 44 Tc 96
24207 Valdespino Cerón LE 27 Ud 95
24717 Valdespino de Somoza LE 26 Tf 94
24324 Valdespino de Vaca LE 28 Uf 95
47240 Valdestillas VA 66 Vb 100
24837 Valdeteja LE 27 Ud 91
06474 Valdetorres BA 117 Tf 115
28150 Valdetorres de Jarama MD 86 Wc 104
16122 Valdetórtola CU 105 Xe 109
34127 Valde-Ucieza P 29 Vc 94
40185 Valdevacas SG 67 Wb 102
40185 Valdevacas de Montejo SG 68 Wc 99
40553 Valdevarnés SG 68 Wc 100
45572 Valdeverdeja TO 100 Ue 110
26586 Valdevigas RI 51 Xe 95
24230 Valdevimbre LE 27 Uc 94
06487 Valdezaque BA 117 Td 114
09318 Valdezate BU 48 Vf 99
26289 Valdezcaray RI 31 Xa 95
41019 Valdezorras SE 163 Ua 124
21207 Valdezufre H 147 Td 121
37799 Valdibáñez SA 65 Uc 101
39728 Valdicio CB 18 Wb 89
28511 Valdilecha MD 87 We 107
32369 Valdín OR 44 Ta 95
37799 Valdío SA 65 Uc 101
37523 Valdio de Robleda SA 81 Tc 107
06720 Valdivia BA 118 Ub 114
15873 Val do Dubra C 10 Rb 90
24970 Valdoré LE 28 Ue 91
09320 Valdorros BU 49 Wb 95
15552 Valdoviño C 11 Rf 87
42173 Valduérteles SO 51 Xd 96
37798 Valdunciel SA 64 Ub 102
47672 Valdunquillo VA 46 Ue 96
24165 Valduvieco LE 27 Ue 93
36883 Valeixe PO 42 Re 95
37724 Valematanza SA 82 Ua 107
46000* València V 108 Zd 112
24200 Valencia de Don Juan LE 27 Uc 95
37799 Valencia de la Encomienda SA 64 Ub 102
06444 Valencia de las Torres BA 133 Tf 118
06134 Valencia del Mombuey BA 131 Sf 119
06330 Valencia del Ventoso BA 132 Td 119
08790 Valenciana, La B 76 Bf 100
41907 Valencina de la Concepción SE 163 Tf 124
10500 Valencja de Alcántara CC 115 Se 112
34115 Valenoso P 28 Vc 93
30420 Valentín MC 140 Yb 119
04770 Valentines, Los AL 169 Wf 128
43559 Valentins, Els T 93 Ac 105
23490 Valenzuela J 152 Wc 120
13279 Valenzuela de Calatrava CR 121 Wb 115
49559 Valer ZA 45 Te 98
16120 Valera de Abajo CU 105 Xf 110
16216 Valeria CU 105 Xf 110
29689 Valerín, El MA 174 Uf 130
37764 Valero SA 82 Ua 105
02129 Valero, El AB 140 Xf 116
37874 Valeros SA 83 Ud 104
32136 Vales OR 24 Sa 93
22223 Valfarta HU 73 Zf 99
19196 Valfermoso de las Monjas GU 87 Xa 103
19411 Valfermoso de Tajuña GU 87 Xa 105
22255 Valfonda de Barbués HU 54 Zd 97
36645 Valga PO 22 Rc 92
26288 Valgañón RI 31 Wf 95
09559 Valhermosa BU 30 Wc 92
19390 Valhermoso GU 89 Ya 104
16214 Valhermoso de la Fuente CU 105 Xf 111
37500 Valhondo y Brocheros SA 81 Tc 105
30627 Valientes, Los MC 141 Yf 120
44595 Valjunquera TE 73 Aa 103
17706 Vall, La GI 40 Cf 95
46691 Vallada V 126 Zb 115
42248 Valladares SO 70 Xd 101
33818 Vallado AS 14 Td 90
47001 Valladolid VA 47 Vb 99
30154 Valladolises MC 157 Yf 122
46145 Vallanca V 106 Yd 108
09245 Vallarta de Bureba BU 31 We 93
12230 Vallat CS 108 Zd 108
08785 Vallbona d'Anoia B 76 Be 99
25268 Vallbona de les Monges L 75 Ba 99
17410 Vallcanera GI 59 Ce 97
08872 Vallcarca B 76 Bf 101
25187 Vallcarca L 74 Ac 100
08699 Vallcebre B 57 Be 95
43439 Vallclara T 75 Af 100
12194 Vall d'Alba CS 108 Zf 107
03786 Vall d'Alcalà, La A 127 Ze 116
25283 Valldan L 57 Bc 96
08617 Valldan, La B 57 Be 96
25737 Vall d'Ariet, La L 56 Af 97
25793 Valldarques L 56 Bb 96
12414 Vall de Almonacid CS 107 Zd 109
17813 Vall de Bac GI 39 Cc 95
25527 Vall de Boí, La L 37 Ae 93
25570 Vall de Cardós L 37 Bb 93
03789 Vall de Ebo A 127 Zf 116
03787 Vall de Gallinera A 127 Ze 116
25737 Valldeixils L 56 Ba 98
07170 Valldemossa IB 110 Cd 110
17176 Vall d'en Bas, La GI 58 Cc 96
43421 Valldeperes T 76 Bc 100
03730 Vall-de-Ros A 127 Aa 116
08173 Valldoreix B 77 Ca 100
43816 Valldossera T 76 Bc 100
12600 Vall d'Uixo, La CS 108 Ze 110
07013 Vall Durgent IB 110 Cd 111
33829 Valle AS 14 Tf 88
33629 Valle AS 15 Ua 90
33438 Valle AS 15 Ub 87
33539 Valle AS 15 Ue 88
39812 Valle CB 18 Wc 89
04897 Valle, El AL 170 Xc 125
33890 Valle, El AS 13 Tc 89
18658 Valle, El GR 168 Wc 127
23479 Valle, El J 154 Xa 121
24315 Valle, El LE 26 Td 93
22348 Valle, La HU 35 Aa 94
35649 Vallebrón GC 183 Ma 177
24324 Vallecillo LE 28 Ue 94
44123 Vallecillo, El TE 89 Yc 107
26120 Vallecosa, La RI 32 Xc 94
38150 Valle Crispin TF 181 Ie 177
29240 Valle de Abdalajís MA 166 Vb 127
01117 Valle de Arana VI 32 Xd 92
39510 Valle de Cabuérniga CB 17 Ve 89
34209 Valle de Cerrato P 48 Vd 97
24848 Valle de Curueño LE 27 Ud 92
30350 Valle de Escombreras MC 157 Za 123
24435 Valle de Finolledo LE 25 Tb 92
38270 Valle de Guerra TF 181 Id 177
24412 Valle del Agua LE 25 Tc 93
09270 Valle de la Paúl BU 31 Wf 94
05190 Valle de la Pavona AV 84 Vb 105
24892 Valle de las Casas LE 28 Uf 92
06458 Valle de la Serena BA 134 Ub 116
09591 Valle de las Navas BU 30 Wc 94
22451 Valle de Lierp HU 36 Ac 94
31439 Valle del Irati NC 33 Ye 91
33557 Valle del Moro AS 16 Ue 89
09511 Valle de Losa BU 19 We 91
34307 Valle del Retortillo P 47 Va 95

Valle del Retortillo | 309 E

45120 Valle del Robledillo TO 101 Vd 111
09199 Valle del Sol BU 49 We 95
18511 Valle del Zalabí GR 169 Wf 125
24219 Valle de Mansilla LE 27 Ud 93
09558 Valle de Manzanedo BU 30 Wb 91
06177 Valle de Matamoros BA 132 Tb 118
09580 Valle de Mena BU 19 We 90
38649 Valle de San Lorenzo TF 180 Ic 180
40171 Valle de San Pedro SG 67 Wa 102
35210 Valle de San Roque GC 184 Kd 180
06178 Valle de Santa Ana BA 132 Tb 118
35637 Valle de Santa Inés GC 183 Lf 178
34828 Valle de Santullán P 29 Vd 91
09142 Valle de Sedano = Sedano BU 30 Wb 92
40331 Valle de Tabladillo SG 67 Wa 100
48510 Valle de Trápaga BI 19 Wf 89
09572 Valle de Valdebezana BU 18 Wb 91
09614 Valle de Valdelaguna BU 50 We 96
09127 Valle de Valdelucio = Llanillo BU 29 Vf 92
10890 Valle de Venta CC 81 Ta 108
22367 Valle de Xistau HU 36 Ab 93
34260 Vallegera BU 48 Vf 95
38879 Valle Gran Rey TF 184 Hd 180
38840 Vallehermoso TF 184 He 179
11690 Valle Hermoso Alto CA 166 Ue 127
11690 Valle Hermoso Bajo CA 166 Ue 127
05696 Vallehondo AV 83 Uc 106
11630 Vallejas CA 173 Ub 128
37717 Vallejera de Riofrío SA 83 Ub 106
09614 Vallejimeno BU 50 We 96
29791 Vallejo MA 167 Ve 128
42175 Vallejo, El SO 51 Xe 97
09589 Vallejo de Mena BU 18 We 90
34829 Vallejo de Orbó P 29 Ve 91
40213 Vallelado SG 66 Vd 100
49326 Valleluengo ZA 45 Te 96
40174 Valleruela de Pedraza SG 67 Wb 101
40176 Valleruela de Sepúlveda SG 67 Wb 101
33583 Valles AS 15 Ue 88
39809 Valles, Los CB 18 Wd 89
35539 Valles, Los GC 182 Mc 174
49450 Vallesa ZA 65 Ud 102
49450 Vallesa de la Guareña ZA 65 Ue 102
21386 Valles de Carrasco H 147 Tb 120
40357 Valles de Fuentidueñas SG 67 Wa 100
35638 Valles de Ortega GC 183 Lf 178
09338 Valles de Palenzuela BU 48 Vf 96
34115 Valles de Valdavia P 28 Vc 93
35340 Valleseco GC 184 Kc 180
38150 Valleseco TF 181 Ie 178
43428 Vallespinosa T 76 Bc 100
34810 Vallespinoso de Aguilar P 29 Vd 92
34839 Vallespinoso de Cervera P 29 Vd 91
25751 Vallferosa L 57 Bc 97
25575 Vall Ferrera L 37 Bc 93
25680 Vallfogona de Balaguer L 56 Ae 98
17862 Vallfogona de Ripollès GI 58 Cb 95
43427 Vallfogona de Riucorb T 75 Bb 99
08471 Vallgorguina B 58 Cd 99
07639 Vallgornera IB 111 Cf 112
12315 Vallibona CS 92 Aa 105
33791 Vallín AS 14 Tc 87
33314 Vallina AS 15 Ud 87
08759 Vallirana B 76 Bf 100
12513 Vallivana, La CS 92 Aa 105
25738 Vall-llebrera L 56 Ba 97
17253 Vall-llobrega GI 59 Da 97
03291 Vall-llongues, Les A 142 Zb 119
03113 Vall-longa A 142 Zc 118
08490 Vallmanya B 59 Ce 98
25284 Vallmanya L 55 Ac 99
25287 Vallmanya L 57 Bd 98
43144 Vallmoll T 75 Bb 101
27659 Vallo LU 25 Ta 91
33583 Vallobal AS 15 Ue 88
33559 Vallobil AS 16 Ue 88
42173 Valloria SO 51 Xd 97
08188 Vallromanes B 77 Cb 99
25285 Valls (Guixers) L 57 Bd 96
25795 Valls d'Aguilar, Les L 37 Bc 95
25798 Valls de Valira, Les L 38 Bc 94
17869 Vallter 2000 GI 39 Cb 94
01427 Valluerca VI 31 Wf 91
09219 Valluércanes BU 31 Wf 93
09119 Vallunquera BU 48 Vf 95
17475 Vallveralla GI 59 Da 96
25261 Vallverd L 56 Af 98
03139 Vallverda A 142 Zc 119
43425 Vallverd de Queralt T 76 Bb 100
50138 Valmadrid Z 72 Za 100
09268 Valmala BU 31 We 95
24816 Valmartino LE 28 Uf 92
09594 Valmayor de Cuesta Urría BU 30 Wd 91
06171 Valmojado BA 132 Ta 117
45940 Valmojado TO 85 Vf 107
37453 Valmucina SA 83 Ub 103
48895 Valnera BI 18 Wd 89
15591 Valón C 11 Re 88
22533 Valonga HU 55 Ab 98
32213 Valongo OR 42 Rf 95
36854 Valongo PO 23 Rd 94
18470 Válor GR 169 Wf 127
34815 Valoria de Aguilar P 29 Ve 92
34191 Valoria del Alcor P 47 Vb 97
47200 Valoria la Buena VA 47 Vc 98
50615 Valpalmas Z 53 Za 96
49318 Valparaíso ZA 45 Te 97
16550 Valparaíso de Abajo CU 104 Xc 108
16550 Valparaíso de Arriba CU 104 Xc 108
24878 Valporquero de Rueda LE 28 Ue 92
24836 Valporquero de Torío LE 27 Uc 91
01427 Valpuesta BU 31 Wf 91
37520 Valquemada SA 81 Tc 106
10816 Valrío CC 98 Td 108
34846 Valsadornín P 29 Vd 91
40109 Valsaín SG 86 Vf 103
37214 Valsalabroso SA 63 Tc 102
22283 Valsalada HU 53 Zc 96
16879 Valsalobre CU 89 Xf 105
16142 Valsalobre CU 89 Ya 107
19390 Valsalobre GU 89 Ya 104
40390 Valseca SG 67 Ve 103
24495 Valseco LE 26 Td 91
24620 Valsemana LE 27 Ub 92
35340 Valsendero GC 184 Kc 180
14206 Valsequillo CO 134 Ud 118
35217 Valsequillo de Gran Canaria GC 184 Kc 181
34886 Valsurbio P 28 Vb 91
16879 Valtablado de Beteta CU 89 Xf 105
19492 Valtablado del Río GU 88 Xd 104
40314 Valtiendas SG 67 Wa 100
31514 Valtierra NC 52 Yc 95
34492 Valtierra de Albacastro BU 29 Vf 92
09108 Valtierra de Riópisuerga BU 29 Ve 94
42181 Valtojeros SO 51 Xe 97
50219 Valtorres Z 71 Yb 101
10667 Valtravieso CC 98 Te 108
26131 Valtrujal RI 32 Xe 95
42220 Valtueña SO 70 Xe 100
06389 Valuengo BA 132 Tb 119
09549 Valujera BU 30 Wd 91
33810 Valvaler AS 13 Tb 90
26528 Valvarde RI 52 Ya 97
42315 Valvenedizo SO 69 Wf 101
03139 Valverda Baixa, La A 142 Zc 119
13195 Valverde CR 120 Vf 115
32667 Valverde OR 42 Sb 95
42108 Valverde SO 52 Ya 97
44211 Valverde TE 72 Ye 103
38900 Valverde TF 180 Ha 182
29715 Valverde, Los MA 167 Vf 127
28812 Valverde de Alcalá MD 87 We 106
06378 Valverde de Burguillos BA 132 Tc 119
47690 Valverde de Campos VA 47 Uf 97
24837 Valverde de Curueño LE 15 Ud 91
37862 Valverde de Gonzaliáñez SA 83 Ud 104
16100 Valverde de Júcar CU 105 Xe 110
24911 Valverde de la Sierra LE 28 Va 91
10490 Valverde de la Vera CC 99 Ud 108
24391 Valverde de la Virgen LE 27 Ub 93
21600 Valverde del Camino H 147 Tb 123
06130 Valverde de Leganés BA 132 Ta 116
10890 Valverde del Fresno CC 81 Ta 107
06927 Valverde de Llerena BA 134 Ub 119
40140 Valverde del Majano SG 67 Ve 103
42366 Valverde de los Ajos SO 69 Xa 99
19224 Valverde de los Arroyos GU 68 We 102
06890 Valverde de Mérida BA 117 Te 115
09293 Valverde de Miranda BU 31 Xa 93
37791 Valverde de Valdelacasa SA 83 Ub 106
24292 Valverde Enrique LE 27 Ue 95
10667 Valverdejo CC 98 Tf 108
16214 Valverdejo CU 105 Xf 111
24838 Valverdín LE 15 Uc 91
37115 Valverdón SA 64 Ub 102
47410 Valviadero VA 66 Vc 100
40514 Valvieja SG 68 Wd 100
46160 Vanacloig V 107 Zb 110
02161 Vandelaras de Abajo AB 123 Xe 115
02161 Vandelaras de Arriba AB 123 Xe 115
43891 Vandellòs T 75 Ae 102
43891 Vandellòs i l'Hospitalet de l'Infant T 75 Ae 102
24396 Vanidodes LE 26 Tf 93
34846 Vañes P 29 Vc 91
25598 Vaquèira = Baqueira L 37 Af 92
16709 Vara de Rey CU 123 Xe 112
18613 Varadero, El GR 168 Wc 128
15809 Varelas C 23 Rf 91
39679 Vargas CB 17 Wa 89
18708 Vargas, Los GR 169 We 127
04769 Vázquez, Los AL 169 Xa 128
36682 Vea PO 23 Rc 92
42174 Vea SO 51 Xe 96
30193 Véchar MC 156 Yd 120
25271 Veciana B 57 Bc 99
24840 Vecilla de Curueño, La LE 27 Ud 91
49693 Vecilla de la Polvorosa ZA 46 Ub 96
49623 Vecilla de Trasmonte ZA 45 Ub 97
35110 Vecindario GC 184 Kd 181
37440 Vecino, El SA 82 Ua 103
37450 Vecinos SA 82 Ua 104
15885 Vedra C 23 Rc 92
39630 Vega CB 18 Wa 89
04211 Vega, La AL 170 Xe 126
33836 Vega, La AS 14 Te 89
33160 Vega, La AS 15 Ua 89
33638 Vega, La AS 15 Ub 89
33317 Vega, La AS 15 Ud 88
39577 Vega, La CB 16 Vc 90
39723 Vega, La CB 18 Wb 89
41100 Vega, La SE 163 Tf 125
42172 Vega, La SO 51 Xe 96
44550 Vega, La TE 73 Zd 103
38430 Vega, La TF 180 Ib 178
46620 Vega, La V 125 Yf 114
33518 Vega, la (Sariego) AS 15 Uc 88
24836 Vegacervera LE 27 Uc 91
24888 Vega de Almanza, La LE 28 Uf 92
24281 Vega de Antoñán LE 26 Ua 93
33892 Vega de Anzo AS 14 Tf 88
24852 Vega de Boñar, La LE 27 Ue 91
34485 Vega de Bur P 29 Vd 92
34115 Vega de Doña Olimpa P 28 Vc 93
24430 Vega de Espinareda LE 25 Tc 92
33814 Vega de Hórreo AS 13 Tb 90
24346 Vega de Infanzones LE 27 Uc 94
23487 Vega de la Higuera J 153 Wf 122
09640 Vega de Lara BU 49 Wd 96
38293 Vega de las Mercedes TF 181 Ie 177
49341 Vega del Castillo ZA 45 Td 96
16150 Vega del Codorno, La CU 89 Ya 106
14240 Vega del Fresno CO 135 Ue 119
24219 Vega de los Árboles LE 27 Ue 93
10317 Vega de Mesillas CC 99 Ub 108
24940 Vega de Monasterio LE 28 Ue 92
49524 Vega de Nuez ZA 44 Td 98
33770 Vegadeo AS 13 Sf 88
37451 Vega de Olleros SA 82 Ua 104
39685 Vega de Pas CB 18 Wb 90
33519 Vega de Pola AS 15 Uc 88
47151 Vega de Porras, La VA 66 Vb 99
33875 Vega de Rey AS 14 Tc 89
33637 Vega de Rey AS 15 Ub 90
34878 Vega de Riacos P 28 Vb 92
35637 Vega de Río Palmas GC 183 Lf 178
47609 Vega de Ruiponce VA 47 Uf 95
35320 Vega de San Mateo GC 184 Kc 180
05292 Vega de Santa María AV 84 Vc 103
49331 Vega de Tera ZA 45 Tf 97
37170 Vega de Tirados SA 64 Ua 102
24520 Vega de Valcarce LE 25 Ta 93
47133 Vega de Valdetronco VA 47 Uf 99
49133 Vega de Villalobos ZA 46 Ud 97
40220 Vegafría SG 67 Vf 100
38811 Vegaipala TF 184 He 180
47290 Vegalatorre VA 47 Vc 98
49542 Vegalatrave ZA 45 Tf 98
02448 Vegallera AB 139 Xe 117
39686 Vegaloscorrales CB 18 Wb 90
39686 Vegalosvados CB 18 Wb 90
29510 Vega Malilla MA 166 Vb 128
40395 Veganzones SG 67 Wa 101
24152 Vegaquemada LE 27 Ud 92
29500 Vega Redonda MA 166 Vb 127
24132 Vegarienza LE 26 Tf 92
33554 Vegas, Las AS 16 Vb 89
14900 Vegas, Las CO 151 Vd 120
38594 Vegas, Las TF 180 Ic 180
06731 Vegas Altas BA 118 Uc 114
13412 Vega San Ildefonso CR 135 Va 116
23630 Vega San Miguel J 152 Wb 121
29569 Vega Santa María MA 166 Vb 128
23440 Vega Santa María, La J 153 Wd 121
41470 Vegas de Almenara SE 150 Ud 122
10623 Vegas de Coria CC 82 Te 106
37510 Vegas de Domingo Rey SA 82 Td 106
24153 Vegas del Condado LE 27 Ud 92
18101* Vegas del Genil GR 168 Wb 125
40423 Vegas de Matute SG 85 Ve 104
35571 Vegas de Tegoyo GC 182 Mb 175
23747 Vegas de Triana J 152 Vf 120
24386 Vegas de Yeres LE 25 Tb 94
47359 Vega Sicilia VA 48 Vd 99
45691 Vegas y San Antonio, Las TO 101 Vb 109
10848 Vegaviana CC 97 Tb 108
45250 Vega Vieja TO 102 Wb 109
09344 Veguecilla BU 48 Wa 96
24397 Veguellina, La LE 26 Tf 93
24323 Veguellina, La LE 27 Ue 95
24359 Veguellina de Fondo LE 27 Ua 94
24350 Veguellina de Órbigo LE 27 Ua 94
35016 Vegueta GC 184 Kd 180
35560 Vegueta, La GC 182 Mc 174
39538 Veguilla CB 17 Vf 88
39808 Veguilla CB 18 Wc 89
19238 Veguillas GU 69 Wf 103
37454 Veguillas, Las SA 83 Ub 104
44134 Veguillas de la Sierra TE 106 Yd 108
27517 Veiga LU 24 Sb 93
32817 Veiga, A OR 42 Sa 96
32360 Veiga, A OR 44 Sf 95
27671 Veiga de Brañas LU 25 Sf 93
32311 Veiga de Cascallá, A OR 25 Ta 94
27112 Veiga de Logares, A LU 13 Sf 89
32626 Veiga de Nostre OR 43 Se 96
27614 Veiga de Sarria LU 24 Sd 92
15169 Veigue C 11 Re 88
11150 Vejer de la Frontera CA 172 Ua 131
39577 Vejo CB 16 Vb 90
39689 Vejorís CB 18 Wa 89
14850 Vela CO 151 Ve 123
45612 Velada TO 100 Uf 109
40134 Velagómez SG 66 Vd 103
42210 Velamazán SO 69 Xb 100
47463 Velascálvaro VA 66 Va 101
42193 Velasco SO 50 Xa 99
05292 Velayos AV 84 Vc 103
24715 Veldedo LE 26 Te 93
04212 Velefique AL 170 Xd 125
04830 Vélez Blanco AL 155 Xf 122
18670 Vélez de Benaudalla GR 168 Wc 127
29700 Vélez-Málaga MA 167 Vf 128
04820 Vélez Rubio AL 155 Xf 123
26133 Velilla RI 51 Xd 95
37882 Velilla SA 83 Ud 104
45270 Velilla TO 102 Wa 109
47114 Velilla VA 66 Uf 99
24127 Velilla, La LE 26 Ua 92
40173 Velilla, La SG 67 Wb 102
22528 Velilla de Cinca HU 55 Ab 99
50760 Velilla de Ebro Z 73 Zd 100
34869 Velilla de la Peña P 28 Vc 92
24392 Velilla de la Reina LE 27 Ub 93
42189 Velilla de la Sierra SO 51 Xd 98
42225 Velilla de los Ajos SO 70 Xe 100
24224 Velilla de los Oteros LE 27 Ud 94
34886 Velilla del Río Carrión P 28 Va 92
42257 Velilla de Medinaceli SO 70 Xd 102
28891 Velilla de San Antonio MD 86 Wd 106
24327 Velilla de Valderaduey LE 28 Va 93
22122 Velillas HU 54 Ze 96
34114 Velillas del Duque P 28 Vb 94
18612 Velilla-Taramay GR 168 Wc 128
32960 Velle OR 24 Sa 94
37427 Vellés, La SA 65 Uc 102
42320 Vellilla de San Esteban SO 49 We 99
16510 Vellisca CU 104 Xb 108
47131 Velliza VA 47 Va 99
28722 Vellón, El MD 86 Wc 104
40312 Vellosillo SG 68 Wb 101
42172 Vellosillo SO 51 Xd 96
32860 Venceáns OR 42 Rf 97
22535 Vencillón HU 55 Ab 98
32611 Vendas da Barreira OR 43 Se 97
39572 Vendejo CB 17 Vc 90
43700 Vendrell, El T 76 Bd 101
05100 Venero Claro AV 84 Vc 106
33929 Veneros AS 15 Ub 89
24858 Veneros LE 27 Ue 91
49153 Venialbo ZA 65 Uc 100
25220 Vensilló L 56 Ae 99
39518 Venta CB 17 Ve 90
21760 Venta H 163 Td 128
23250 Venta J 138 We 119
41730 Venta SE 163 Ua 127
09491 Venta, La BU 49 Wc 99
14813 Venta, La CO 152 Vf 124
13250 Venta, La CR 121 Wc 114
18800 Venta, La GR 169 Xa 124
50792 Venta, La Z 73 Ze 101
50130 Venta Alta, La Z 72 Zb 100
29713 Venta Baja MA 167 Vf 127
04117 Venta Balsaseca AL 171 Xe 127
23280 Venta Cabrera J 138 Xa 119
30195 Venta Casa Blanca MC 155 Xf 120
30850 Venta Chicharra MC 156 Yc 122
23689 Venta de Agramaderos J 167 Wa 124
41410 Venta de Alcaudete SE 149 Ub 124
02696 Venta de Alhama AB 124 Yc 115
41210 Venta de Ana Vázquez SE 148 Tf 123
18567 Venta de Andar GR 152 Wc 124
22210 Venta de Ballerías HU 54 Zf 97
34200 Venta de Baños P 47 Vd 97
23280 Venta de Beas J 138 Xa 119
12185 Venta de Blanco CS 92 Aa 106
13250 Venta de Borondo CR 121 Wc 115
18698 Venta de Cabramontés GR 168 Wb 127
46192 Venta de Cabrera V 126 Zc 112
29150 Venta de Cadenas MA 167 Vd 127
29150 Venta de Cadenas o Barrio de la Hornilla MA 167 Vc 127
44709 Venta de Cadurro TE 91 Zb 103
10550 Venta de Calleja CC 116 Tc 113
18820 Venta de Campillejos GR 154 Xd 121
29679 Venta de Candelas MA 174 Uf 129
41659 Venta de Cañete SE 166 Uf 125
04550 Venta de Cañicas AL 170 Xd 126
13760 Venta de Cárdenas CR 137 Wd 118
31312 Venta de Chiquito NC 33 Yd 94
19326 Venta de Conejo GU 89 Yc 104
41880 Venta de Curro Fal SE 148 Te 122
45820 Venta de Don Quijote TO 103 Xa 111
45820 Venta de Don Quijote TO 103 Xa 111

310 | Valle del Robledillo

44610 Venta de Ejerique TE 74 Aa 102
21609 Venta de Eligio H 161 Tb 123
45470 Venta de Enmedio TO 121 Wb 112
44370 Venta de Follante TE 90 Ye 106
46199 Venta de Gaeta V 125 Za 113
02600 Venta de Gómez AB 123 Xb 113
50660 Venta de Íñigo Z 53 Ye 96
11510 Venta de la Catalana CA 172 Tf 129
18615 Venta de la Cebeda GR 168 Wc 127
23592 Venta de la Chata J 153 Wd 121
24275 Venta de la Cruz LE 27 Ub 92
43785 Venta de la Fam T 74 Ac 102
13459 Venta de la Inés CR 136 Vd 117
23268 Venta del Aire J 138 Xa 118
44477 Venta del Aire TE 107 Zb 108
14440 Venta de la Jara CO 135 Vb 119
04531 Venta del Almirez AL 170 Xc 126
09339 Venta del Alto BU 49 Wb 96
18127 Venta de la Mañana GR 168 Wa 127
50750 Venta de la María Z 73 Zd 99
04729 Venta de La Menea AL 170 Xc 127
18540 Venta del Amparo GR 153 We 124
18567 Venta de la Nava GR 168 Wc 124
05110 Venta de la Palomera AV 84 Vb 105
43559 Venta de la Punta T 93 Ab 105
50290 Venta de la Romera Z 71 Ye 99
28925 Venta de la Rubia MD 86 Wb 106
30890 Venta de las Cegarras MC 155 Ya 123
11540 Venta de la Serrana CA 163 Te 128
02600 Venta de las Madres AB 123 Xc 113
18614 Venta de las Monjas GR 168 Wd 128
30334 Venta de las Palas MC 157 Ye 122
33314 Venta de las Ranas AS 15 Uc 87
30410 Venta de las Revueltas MC 155 Ya 121
18511 Venta de la Trinidad GR 169 Wf 125
46630 Venta de la Vicenta V 126 Za 115
19223 Venta de la Vieja GU 68 Wd 102
30155 Venta de la Virgen MC 157 Yf 121
50530 Venta de la Virgen Z 52 Yd 97
44195 Venta del Barranco Hondo TE 90 Ye 106
44477 Venta del Barro TE 107 Zb 108
44193 Venta del Bobo TE 90 Yf 106
18891 Venta del Camacho GR 154 Xc 123
04271 Venta del Campico AL 171 Xf 125
14446 Venta del Cerezo CO 136 Ve 119
14446 Venta del Charco CO 136 Ve 119
41420 Venta del Cobre SE 150 Ud 124
11370 Venta del Cojo CA 173 Uc 131
50120 Venta del Coscón Z 53 Za 97
41130 Venta del Cruce SE 163 Tf 125
44490 Venta del Cuerno TE 71 Ye 102
06260 Venta del Culebrín BA 148 Te 120
18840 Venta del Cura GR 154 Xc 122
30178 Venta de Ledesma MC 156 Yc 121
04628 Venta del Empalme AL 171 Ya 125
30800 Venta del Estrecho MC 155 Yb 122
43593 Venta del Fangar T 74 Ac 103
50238 Venta del Feo Z 71 Ya 101
18640 Venta del Fraile GR 168 Wb 127
18891 Venta del Grullo GR 154 Xc 123
05141 Venta del Hambre AV 84 Va 104
06260 Venta del Helechoso BA 148 Te 121
45005 Venta del Hoyo, La TO 102 Vf 109
44549 Venta del Junco TE 72 Zb 102
44162 Venta del Lino TE 90 Yf 106
18820 Venta del Manco GR 154 Xd 121
26513 Venta del Monte, La RI 32 Xf 94
46310 Venta del Moro V 106 Yd 112
05123 Venta del Obispo AV 84 Uf 106
44313 Venta del Ojo de Mierla TE 90 Yd 104
18120 Venta de López GR 168 Wa 127
41450 Venta de los Ángeles SE 149 Ub 121
29391 Venta de los Arrieros MA 174 Ud 129
44600 Venta de los Caños TE 73 Zd 102
13210 Venta de los Poblillas CR 121 Wd 113
23265 Venta de los Santos J 138 Wf 118
18891 Venta del Peral GR 154 Xc 123
18820 Venta del Perdido GR 154 Xc 121
30439 Venta del Pino MC 156 Yb 120
04114 Venta del Pobre AL 171 Xf 127
43559 Venta del Polit T 93 Ac 105
43786 Venta del Pollo T 74 Ab 102
46649 Venta del Potro V 126 Zb 115
23410 Venta del Puente J 138 We 120
44192 Venta del Puente TE 90 Yf 107
02499 Venta del Puerto AB 141 Yc 118
18820 Venta del Puerto GR 154 Xd 120
18540 Venta del Puntal GR 169 We 124
44370 Venta del Ratón TE 90 Yd 106
50144 Venta del Relenco Z 72 Zb 102
22520 Venta del Rey HU 74 Aa 99
34491 Venta del Rojo P 29 Vd 94
30559 Venta del Tollo MC 141 Ye 119
02312 Venta del Vecino AB 139 Xc 116
18127 Venta del Vicario GR 168 Wa 127
50680 Venta del Zapato Z 34 Ye 94
41450 Venta de Majalimar SE 149 Uc 122
44368 Venta de Mal Abrigo TE 90 Yd 105
18659 Venta de Marina GR 168 Wb 127
02610 Venta de Marta AB 123 Xc 115
18120 Venta de Martín GR 167 Wa 127
18811 Venta de Mateo GR 154 Xa 123
18858 Venta de Micena GR 155 Xd 122
30528 Venta de Montesinos MC 141 Yd 117
19350 Venta de Montesoro GU 89 Yb 103
05540 Venta de Muñana AV 84 Uf 105
30535 Venta de Oliva MC 141 Yd 119
10590 Venta de Paco CC 98 Tf 109
18120 Venta de Palma GR 167 Wa 127
18810 Venta de Pepearo GR 154 Xb 123
02340 Venta de Pepés o Colonia AB 123 Xd 116
29160 Venta de Pinoda MA 167 Vd 127
05111 Venta de Pocapena AV 84 Vb 105
47116 Venta de Pollos VA 65 Ue 100
30528 Venta de Primitivo MC 141 Yd 118
05132 Venta de Raquilla AV 84 Uf 106
04131 Venta de Retamar AL 170 Xe 127
11160 Venta de Retín CA 173 Ub 131
43595 Venta de Roc T 74 Ac 103
02499 Venta de Rodrigo AB 141 Yc 117
43512 Venta de Roixa T 74 Ac 103
30559 Venta de Román MC 141 Yd 119
18840 Venta de Rosa GR 154 Xc 122
26509 Venta de Rufino RI 32 Xe 94
23250 Venta de San Andrés J 138 We 119
41730 Venta de San Antonio SE 164 Ua 127
29150 Venta de San Antonio o de la Leche MA 167 Vc 127
02161 Venta de San Miguel AB 123 Xd 115
31370 Venta de San Miguel NC 33 Yb 94
44548 Venta de San Pedro TE 72 Zc 102
12400 Venta de Santa Lucía CS 107 Zd 110
41740 Venta de Santa Lucía SE 164 Tf 127
50750 Venta de Santa Lucía Z 73 Zd 100
05289 Venta de San Vicente AV 85 Vc 104
02161 Venta de Segovia AB 123 Xe 115
30628 Venta de Soldado MC 141 Yf 120
05279 Venta de Tablada AV 85 Vd 106
34812 Venta de Valdemudo P 47 Vc 96
31312 Venta de Vicentico NC 33 Yd 94
31177 Venta de Zumbel NC 32 Xf 92
04619 Venta el Perejil AL 171 Ya 125
22559 Ventafarinas HU 55 Ac 98
10291 Venta la Barquilla CC 99 Ua 111
04117 Venta La Cepa AL 171 Xe 128
03560 Venta Lanuza A 143 Ze 118
11159 Venta La Rambla CA 172 Ua 131
11692 Venta Leches CA 166 Ue 127
43558 Ventalles, Les T 93 Ac 105
17473 Ventalló GI 59 Da 96
50140 Venta María Z 72 Za 101
21610 Ventanas H 161 Ta 125
30610 Ventanas, Las MC 141 Yd 119
34844 Ventanilla P 29 Vc 91
13343 Venta Nueva CR 138 Wf 118
18360 Venta Nueva GR 168 Vf 125
23213 Venta Nueva J 137 Wc 119
33811 Ventanueva AS 13 Tc 90
11580 Venta Nueva de Galiz CA 173 Uc 129
30612 Venta Puñales MC 141 Ye 120
10665 Venta Quemada CC 98 Tf 108
18800 Venta Quemada GR 154 Xa 124
18859 Venta Quemada GR 154 Xd 123
31796 Venta Quemada NC 21 Yc 90
46392 Venta Quemada V 126 Za 112
04500 Venta Ratonera AL 169 Xa 125
03409 Ventas, Las A 141 Za 117
33112 Ventas, Las AS 14 Tf 89
09620 Ventas, Las BU 30 Wb 95
18312 Venta Santa Bárbara GR 167 Ve 125
26131 Ventas Blancas RI 32 Xe 94
45127 Ventas con Peña Aguilera, Las TO 101 Ve 111
16612 Ventas de Alcolea CU 123 Xd 113
31797 Ventas de Arraiz NC 21 Yc 90
21668 Ventas de Arriba H 147 Tc 122
23615 Ventas de Doña María J 151 Vf 122
37607 Ventas de Garriel SA 82 Tf 105
47131 Ventas de Geria VA 66 Va 99
50150 Ventas de Herrera Z 72 Za 101
18131 Ventas de Huelma GR 168 Wb 126
31440 Ventas de Judas, Las NC 33 Yd 93
23693 Ventas del Carrizal J 152 Wa 123
14913 Ventas del Río Anzur CO 167 Vd 125
44780 Ventas de Muniesa TE 72 Zb 102
45710 Ventas de Pando TO 102 Wc 111
45183 Ventas de Retamosa, Las TO 85 Vf 108
45568 Ventas de San Julián, Las TO 100 Ue 108
26330 Ventas de Valpierre RI 31 Xb 94
18125 Ventas de Zafarraya GR 167 Vf 127
30179 Venta Seca MC 156 Yd 120
23689 Venta Valero CO 168 Vf 124
44780 Ventavieja TE 72 Zb 102
14112 Ventilla, La CO 150 Uf 122
13130 Ventillas CR 136 Ve 118
11130 Ventorrillo del Álamo CA 172 Tf 130
41560 Ventorrillo del Portichuelo SE 166 Va 125
39491 Ventorrillo CB 17 Vf 90
23130 Ventorrillo J 152 Wc 123
28491 Ventorrillo MD 86 Vf 104
02640 Ventorrillo, El AB 125 Yf 115
44500 Ventorrillo de Andorra TE 73 Zd 102
30420 Ventorrillo de Hondonera MC 140 Yc 119
11170 Ventorrillo de Rufino CA 172 Ua 130
29391 Ventorrillo Las Canillas MA 173 Uc 129
18120 Ventorrillo Nuevo GR 168 Vf 126
30849 Ventorrillos, Los MC 156 Yd 121
16340 Ventorro, El CU 105 Ya 108
19314 Ventorro del Chato GU 89 Ya 104
19141 Ventorro del Cojo GU 87 Wf 106
41899 Ventorro del Negro SE 148 Te 122
05132 Ventorro del Quinto AV 84 Uf 106
18312 Ventorros de Balerma GR 167 Ve 125
18312 Ventorros de la Laguna GR 167 Ve 125
18312 Ventorros San José GR 167 Vf 125
33829 Ventosa AS 14 Tf 88
19392 Ventosa GU 89 Ya 104
36529 Ventosa PO 23 Sa 92
26371 Ventosa RI 31 Xc 94
37410 Ventosa, La SA 65 Ud 102
42291 Ventosa de Fuentepinilla SO 50 Xb 99
47239 Ventosa de la Cuesta VA 66 Vb 100
42161 Ventosa de la Sierra SO 51 Xd 97
42230 Ventosa del Ducado, La SO 69 Xc 102
37329 Ventosa del Río Alnar SA 65 Ud 103
34405 Ventosa de Pisuerga P 29 Ve 93
42174 Ventosa de San Pedro SO 51 Xe 96
25528 Ventosa i Calvell L 37 Af 93
32415 Ventosela OR 23 Rf 95
25316 Ventoses, Les L 56 Ba 98
09443 Ventosilla BU 49 Wb 98
24687 Ventosilla LE 15 Ub 91
40165 Ventosilla SG 68 Wb 101
40389 Ventosilla, La SG 67 Wb 101
45161 Ventosilla, La TO 101 Ve 110
42189 Ventosilla de San Juan SO 51 Xd 98
23006 Ventosillas J 152 Wb 121
33776 Ventoso AS 13 Sf 89
26329 Ventrosa RI 50 Xa 96
28729 Venturada MD 86 Wc 104
27349 Ver LU 24 Sd 93
04620 Vera AL 171 Ya 125
23313 Veracruz J 153 We 120
38720 Verada, La TF 181 Hb 176
38729 Verada de las Lomadas TF 181 Hb 176
38685 Vera de Erque TF 180 Ib 179
50580 Vera de Moncayo Z 52 Yb 98
41660 Verbena, La SE 166 Ue 126
34828 Verbios P 29 Vd 91
32161 Verdefondo OR 24 Sb 94
35458 Verdejo GC 184 Kc 180
19324 Verdel, El GU 89 Yc 104
16146 Verdelpino de Cueva CU 105 Xf 108
16540 Verdelpino de Huete CU 104 Xc 108
34846 Verdeña P 17 Vd 91
24960 Verdiago LE 28 Uf 91
29011 Verdiales MA 167 Vd 128
33448 Verdicio AS 15 Ua 87
25340 Verdú L 56 Ba 99
32813 Verea OR 42 Sa 96
19223 Vereda, La GU 68 Wd 102
13459 Veredas CR 136 Vd 117
21342 Veredas H 147 Tb 121
16317 Veredilla, La CU 89 Yb 107
14729 Veredón CO 150 Va 121
31254 Vergalijo NC 33 Yb 94
12550 Verge de Gràcia, La CS 108 Zf 109
03770 Vergel A 127 Aa 115
07190 Verger, Es IB 110 Cd 111
17142 Verges GI 59 Da 96
25200 Vergós de Cervera L 56 Bb 99
25214 Vergós Garrejat L 57 Bc 98
42173 Verguizas SO 51 Xd 96
22470 Veri HU 36 Ad 94
27579 Verín LU 24 Sa 92
32600 Verín OR 43 Sd 97
43775 Verinxel T 75 Ae 102
15313 Verís C 11 Rf 89
25737 Vernet L 56 Ba 97
34219 Vertavillo P 48 Ve 98
08189 Verti B 58 Cb 98
18859 Vertiendes, Las GR 154 Xd 123
18530 Vertientes Altas GR 153 We 123
50592 Veruela Z 52 Yb 98
09249 Vesgas, Las BU 30 Wd 93
31473 Vesolla NC 33 Yd 92
43763 Vespella T 76 Bc 101
41730 Vetaherrado SE 164 Ua 126
33558 Veyos AS 16 Uf 89
49840 Vezdemarbán ZA 46 Ud 99
33585 Viabaño AS 16 Ue 88
22585 Viacamp HU 55 Ad 96
22585 Viacamp y Litera HU 55 Ad 96
24688 Viadangos de Arbás LE 15 Ub 91
39525 Viallán CB 17 Vf 88
27286 Vián LU 12 Sd 89
31230 Viana NC 32 Xd 93
47150 Viana de Cega VA 66 Vb 99
42218 Viana de Duero SO 69 Xd 99
19295 Viana de Jadraque GU 69 Xb 102
19492 Viana de Mondéjar GU 88 Xc 105
32550 Viana do Bolo OR 43 Sf 95
10492 Viandar de la Vera CC 99 Uc 108
15687 Viano Pequeno C 11 Rc 90
02315 Vianos AB 139 Xc 117
39511 Viaña CB 17 Ve 89
15687 Viaño Pequeno C 11 Rc 90
41319 Viar, El SE 149 Ua 123
24517 Viariz LE 25 Ta 93
04240 Viator AL 170 Xd 127
33746 Viavélez AS 13 Ta 87
33557 Viboli Alto AS 16 Uf 89
45700 Viborera, La TO 121 Wc 112
08500 Vic B 58 Cb 97
28052 Vicálvaro MD 86 Wc 106
04738 Vícar AL 170 Xc 128
06445 Vicaría, La BA 133 Ua 118
06292 Vicaría, La BA 148 Td 120
27860 Vicedo, O LU 10 Sb 86
03318 Vicentes, Los A 141 Za 119
04149 Vicentes, Los AL 171 Ya 126
30333 Vicentes, Los MC 156 Ye 122
15839 Viceso C 22 Rb 91
25211 Vicfred L 57 Bc 98
22190 Vicién HU 54 Zd 96
27157 Vicinte LU 12 Sb 90
05194 Vicolozano AV 84 Vc 104
02439 Vicorto AB 140 Xf 118
07009 Victoria IB 110 Ce 111
11130 Victoria, La CA 172 Tf 130
14140 Victoria, La CO 150 Va 122
38380 Victoria de Acentejo, La TF 180 Id 178
21320 Victoriana, La H 147 Ta 122
01207 Vicuña VI 32 Xd 91
09471 Vid, La BU 49 Wd 99
24670 Vid, La LE 27 Uc 91
27765 Vidal LU 13 Se 88
17401 Vidal, El GI 58 Cc 98
32790 Vidalén OR 24 Sc 95
30330 Vidales, Los MC 157 Yf 122
30730 Vidales, Los MC 157 Za 122
30593 Vidales, Los MC 157 Za 122
24950 Vidanes LE 28 Uf 92
31413 Vidángoz = Bidankoze NC 34 Yf 92
31176 Vidaurre NC 33 Ya 92
49135 Vidayanes ZA 46 Uc 97
09249 Vid de Bureba, La BU 30 We 93
32701 Vide OR 43 Sc 95
36446 Vide PO 42 Rd 96
27418 Vide, A LU 24 Sc 93
49541 Vide de Alba ZA 45 Tf 98
32613 Videferre OR 43 Sc 97
49164 Videmala ZA 45 Tf 99
33597 Vidiago AS 16 Vc 88
37214 Vídola, La SA 63 Td 102
33558 Vidosa = Veyos AS 16 Uf 89
17515 Vidrà GI 58 Cb 96
17411 Vidreres GI 59 Ce 98
34887 Vidrieros P 16 Vc 91
33792 Vidural AS 13 Tc 87
33558 Viego AS 16 Uf 89
24856 Viego LE 16 Ue 91
27869 Vieiro LU 10 Sc 87
27116 Vieiro LU 13 Sf 90
21239 Viejos, Los H 147 Ta 121
25530 Vielha L 37 Ae 92
25530 Vielha e Mijaran L 37 Ae 92
24916 Vierdes LE 16 Uf 90
09588 Viérgol BU 19 We 90
50513 Vierlas Z 52 Yb 97
39315 Viérnoles CB 17 Vf 89
33411 Viescas AS 14 Ua 87
24722 Viforcos LE 26 Te 93
33827 Vigaña AS 14 Te 89
33790 Vigo AS 13 Tc 87
15314 Vigo C 11 Rf 89
36211 Vigo PO 41 Rb 95
49361 Vigo ZA 44 Tb 96
26121 Viguera RI 32 Xc 95
31291 Viguria NC 33 Ya 92
19223 Vihuela, La GU 68 Wd 102
AD200 Vila ◘ AND 38 Bd 93
25537 Vila L 37 Ae 92
32311 Vila OR 25 Ta 94

32648 Vilá OR 42 Sa 97
32858 Vila, A OR 42 Rf 97
15684 Vilabade C 11 Rc 90
43886 Vilabella T 76 Bb 101
17760 Vilabertran GI 40 Cf 95
17180 Vilablareix GI 59 Ce 97
27721 Vilaboa LU 13 Se 89
32368 Vilaboa OR 25 Sf 95
36141 Vilaboa PO 22 Rc 94
27114 Vilabol de Suarna LU 13 Sf 90
27865 Vilabuín LU 12 Sc 87
25537 Vilac L 37 Ae 92
27546 Vilacaíz LU 24 Sc 92
27778 Vilacampa LU 12 Sc 87
27877 Vilachá LU 10 Sc 86
27190 Vilachá LU 12 Sd 91
27413 Vilachá LU 24 Sd 94
27663 Vilachá LU 25 Sf 91
27231 Vilachá de Mera LU 12 Sc 91
36750 Vilachán PO 41 Rb 97
25716 Vilaclreres L 57 Bd 95
15318 Vilacoba C 11 Re 89
15212 Vilacoba = Vilacova C 22 Rb 92
17474 Vilacolum GI 59 Da 95
15212 Vilacova C 22 Rb 92
08613 Vilada B 57 Bf 96
15530 Vila da Igrexa C 11 Sa 87
17137 Viladamat GI 59 Da 96
17833 Viladamí GI 59 Ce 96
17464 Viladasens GI 59 Cf 96
15819 Viladavil C 11 Rf 91
15592 Vila de Area C 11 Re 87
08275 Viladecaballs de Calders B 58 Bf 98
24550 Viladecanes LE 25 Tb 93
08840 Viladecans B 77 Ca 101
08232 Viladecavalls B 77 Bf 99
36590 Vila de Cruces PO 23 Re 92
17746 Vilademires GI 59 Ce 95
17468 Vilademuls GI 59 Cf 96
24565 Viladepalos LE 25 Tb 93
32334 Viladequinta OR 25 Ta 94
32696 Viladerrei OR 43 Sc 96
08680 Viladomiu Nou B 57 Bf 96
17513 Viladonja GI 58 Ca 96
17406 Viladrau GI 58 Cc 97
27466 Vilaescura LU 24 Sc 94
27889 Vilaestrofe LU 10 Sd 87
12192 Vilafamés CS 108 Zf 108
17740 Vilafant GI 59 Cf 95
27766 Vilafernando LU 13 Sf 88
38615 Vilaflor TF 180 Ic 180
27767 Vilaformán LU 13 Se 88
43850 Vilafortuny T 75 Ba 102
27797 Vilaframil LU 13 Sf 89
07250 Vilafranca de Bonany IB 111 Da 111
08720 Vilafranca del Penedès B 76 Be 100
03009 Vilafranquesa A 142 Zd 118
17468 Vilafreser GI 59 Cf 96
36539 Vilafrío PO 24 Sa 92
36611 Vilagarcía = Vilagarcia de Arousa PO 22 Rb 93
36611 Vilagarcia de Arousa = Vilagarcía PO 22 Rb 93
27375 Vila Grande LU 12 Sc 90
25330 Vilagrassa L 56 Ba 99
25217 Vilagrasseta L 56 Bb 99
17476 Vilajoan GI 59 Cf 95
03570 Vila Joiosa, La = Villajoyosa A 143 Ze 117
17493 Vilajuïga GI 40 Da 95
27800 Vilalba LU 12 Sb 89
43782 Vilalba dels Arcs T 74 Ac 102
43782 Vilalba la Vella T 74 Ac 101
08455 Vilalba Sasserra B 58 Cc 99
27367 Vilaleo LU 24 Sd 91
27124 Vilalle LU 12 Se 90
08504 Vilalleons B 58 Cb 97
25552 Vilaller L 36 Ae 94
17529 Vilallobent GI 38 Bf 94
43141 Vilallonga del Camp T 75 Bb 101
17869 Vilallonga de Ter GI 39 Cb 95
09001 Vilallonquejar BU 30 Wb 94
25748 Vilalta L 56 Bb 97
27299 Vilalvite LU 12 Sb 90
17474 Vilamacolum GI 59 Da 95
15847 Vilamaior C 10 Rb 90
15637 Vilamaior C 11 Rf 88
27111 Vilamaior LU 13 Sf 89
27613 Vilamaior LU 24 Sc 92
32633 Vilamaior da Boullosa OR 42 Sb 97
27233 Vilamaior de Negral LU 12 Sb 91
32627 Vilamaior do Val OR 43 Sd 97
25692 Vilamajor L 56 Ae 97
25749 Vilamajor d'Agramunt L 56 Bb 98
17469 Vilamalla GI 59 Cf 95
27663 Vilamane LU 25 Sf 91
17781 Vilamaniscle GI 40 Da 94
17534 Vilamanya GI 39 Ca 94
27798 Vilamar LU 13 Se 88
27415 Vilamarín LU 24 Sd 94
32101 Vilamarín OR 24 Sa 94
32340 Vilamartín de Valdeorras OR 25 Sf 94
46191 Vilamarxant V 107 Zc 111
15638 Vilamateo C 11 Rf 89
32870 Vilameá OR 42 Rf 97
27450 Vilamelle LU 24 Sc 94
25654 Vilamitjana L 56 Af 96
25632 Vilamolat de Mur L 56 Af 96
27325 Vilamor LU 24 Se 93
25551 Vilamòs L 36 Ae 92
17743 Vilanant GI 40 Cf 95
17162 Vilanna GI 59 Ce 97
27569 Vilanova LU 24 Sb 92
27611 Vilanova LU 24 Sc 92
27666 Vilanova LU 25 Sf 92
32366 Vilanova OR 25 Ta 95
32816 Vilanova OR 42 Sa 95
36945 Vilanova PO 22 Ra 95
27760 Vilanova (Lourenzá) LU 13 Se 88
12183 Vilanova d'Alcolea CS 92 Aa 107
36620 Vilanova de Arousa PO 22 Rb 93
25718 Vilanova de Banat L 38 Bd 94
25264 Vilanova de Bellpuig L 56 Af 99
25749 Vilanova de la Aguda = Vilanova de l'Aguda L 56 Bb 97
25690 Vilanova de la Barca L 56 Ae 98
25749 Vilanova de l'Aguda L 56 Bb 97
17492 Vilanova de la Muga GI 40 Da 95
25612 Vilanova de la Sal L 56 Ae 97
08788 Vilanova del Camí B 76 Bd 99
25612 Vilanova de les Avellanes L 56 Ae 97
08410 Vilanova del Vallès B 77 Cb 99
25736 Vilanova de Meià L 56 Ba 97
43439 Vilanova de Prades T 75 Af 100
08519 Vilanova de Sau B 58 Cc 97
43311 Vilanova d'Escornalbou T 75 Af 102
25133 Vilanova de Segrià L 55 Ad 98
08789 Vilanova d'Espoia B 76 Bd 99
32317 Vilanova de Valdeorras OR 25 Ta 94
08800 Vilanova i la Geltrú B 76 Be 101
36616 Vilanoviña PO 22 Rb 93
15819 Vilantime C 23 Rf 91
46312 Vilanueva V 106 Yf 110
27712 Vilaosende LU 13 Sf 88
27816 Vilapedre LU 12 Sc 88
27614 Vilapedre LU 24 Sd 92
43380 Vilaplana T 75 Ba 101
27531 Vilaquinte LU 24 Sb 94
27655 Vilaquinte LU 25 Ta 91
15293 Vilar C 22 Qf 91
15822 Vilar C 23 Rd 92
27632 Vilar LU 25 Se 92
32646 Vilar OR 42 Sa 97
32768 Vilar OR 43 Sd 95
32626 Vilar OR 43 Sd 96
36647 Vilar PO 22 Rb 92
36555 Vilar PO 23 Re 93
36436 Vilar PO 42 Rd 96
07470 Vilar, Es IB 111 Da 109
27328 Vilarbacú LU 25 Sf 93
27112 Vilarchao LU 13 Sf 89
32950 Vilarchao OR 24 Sa 94
32702 Vilar de Barrio OR 43 Sc 96
12162 Vilar de Canes CS 92 Zf 106
32899 Vilar de Cas OR 42 Sa 97
32706 Vilardecás OR 43 Sc 95
15845 Vilar de Céltigos C 10 Ra 90
Vilar de Cervos OR 43 Sd 97
15109 Vilar de Cima C 11 Rc 90
27216 Vilar de Donas LU 24 Sb 91
27668 Vilar de Frades LU 25 Sf 91
32695 Vilar de Lebres OR 43 Sc 97
36750 Vilardematos PO 41 Rb 97
32555 Vilardemilo OR 43 Sf 96
27329 Vilar de Mondelo LU 25 Se 94
15613 Vilar de Mouros C 11 Rf 88
27240 Vilar de Mouros LU 13 Se 89
27413 Vilar de Mouros LU 24 Sd 94
32650 Vilar de Santos OR 42 Sb 96
15839 Vilar de Suso C 10 Rb 91
32616 Vilardevós OR 43 Se 97
27112 Vilardíaz LU 13 Sf 89
43812 Vilardida T 76 Bc 101
27116 Vilardongo LU 13 Sf 90
27130 Vilar dos Adros LU 13 Se 90
17538 Vilar d'Urtx, El GI 38 Bf 94
12540 Vila-Real = Villarreal CS 108 Zf 109
27546 Vilarello LU 24 Sc 93
36516 Vilarello PO 23 Rf 93
32708 Vilarellos OR 24 Sb 95
27723 Vilargondurfe LU 13 Se 89
17741 Vilarig GI 40 Cf 95
15807 Vilariño C 11 Rf 90
15991 Vilariño C 22 Ra 93
27307 Vilariño LU 12 Sa 89
27120 Vilariño LU 12 Sd 90
27317 Vilariño LU 24 Se 94
36514 Vilariño PO 23 Rf 92
32611 Vilariño das Touzas OR 43 Se 97
32557 Vilariño de Conso OR 43 Se 96
32790 Vilariño Frío OR 24 Sc 95
27113 Vilarmeán LU 13 Sf 89
15823 Vilarmeao C 23 Re 91
32557 Vilarmeao OR 43 Se 95
27329 Vilarmel LU 25 Sf 94
27724 Vilarmide LU 13 Se 89
27363 Vilarmosteiro LU 24 Sc 91
17762 Vilarnadal GI 40 Cf 94
43814 Vila-rodona T 76 Bc 101
27788 Vilaronte LU 13 Se 87
43365 Vila Rosita T 75 Af 101
15688 Vilarromariz C 11 Rd 91
15554 Vilarrube C 10 Rf 87
32150 Vilarrubín OR 24 Sb 94
25793 Vilars, Els L 56 Bb 95
15128 Vilarseco C 10 Qf 90
25795 Vila-rubla L 37 Bb 94
27722 Vilarxuane LU 13 Sf 89
27112 Vilarxubín LU 13 Sf 89
36686 Vilas PO 23 Rd 92
17485 Vila-sacra GI 40 Da 95
15807 Vilasantar C 11 Rf 90
22451 Vilas de Turbón HU 36 Ad 94
25286 Vila-seca L 57 Bd 96
43480 Vila-seca T 75 Ba 102
32141 Vilaseco OR 23 Sa 94
32555 Vilaseco OR 44 Sf 96
36879 Vilasobroso PO 41 Rd 95
27345 Vilasouto LU 24 Sd 93
08339 Vilassar de Dalt B 77 Cc 99
08340 Vilassar de Mar B 77 Cc 99
32151 Vilasusa OR 24 Sb 94
08515 Vilatammar B 58 Ca 96
27840 Vilate LU 12 Sb 89
17484 Vilatenim GI 40 Cf 95
08779 Vilates, Les B 76 Bd 100
27787 Vilatuxe LU 12 Se 87
32164 Vilatuxe OR 24 Sc 94
36519 Vilatuxe PO 23 Re 93
17483 Vilaür GI 59 Cf 96
17494 Vilaüt GI 40 Da 95
27515 Vilaúxe LU 24 Sb 93
33769 Vilavedelle AS 13 Sf 88
32549 Vilavella OR 44 Sf 96
17833 Vilavenut GI 59 Ce 96
43490 Vilaverd = Vilavert T 75 Ba 100
15147 Vilaverde C 10 Rb 89
43490 Vilavert T 75 Ba 100
27180 Vilavite LU 12 Sc 91
36629 Vilaxoán PO 22 Rb 93
27240 Vilaxuso LU 13 Se 89
27177 Vilaxuste LU 24 Sb 91
32618 Vilaza OR 43 Sd 97
23220 Vilches J 137 Wc 119
42311 Vildé SO 69 Wf 100
48142 Vildosolo BI 19 Xb 90
27363 Vileiriz LU 24 Sc 92
27711 Vilela LU 13 Sf 87
27596 Vilela LU 24 Sb 92
27626 Vilela LU 25 Se 92
08699 Vilella B 57 Be 95
25555 Vilella L 37 Af 94
43375 Vilella Alta, La T 75 Ae 101
09249 Vileña BU 30 We 93
17462 Vilers GI 59 Cf 97
17832 Vilert GI 59 Ce 95
25343 Vilet, El L 75 Ba 99
22482 Vileta, La HU 36 Ad 95
25635 Vileta, La L 56 Ae 96
24219 Viligüer LE 27 Ud 93
33412 Villa AS 15 Ua 87
33537 Villa, La AS 15 Ud 89
46250 Villa Amparín V 126 Zc 113
49192 Villa Antonia ZA 64 Ub 99
09511 Villaba de Losa BU 19 Wf 91
33535 Villabajo AS 15 Ud 88
24191 Villabalter LE 27 Uc 93
24136 Villabandín LE 26 Tf 91
24393 Villabante LE 27 Ua 94
39660 Villabáñez CB 18 Wa 89
47329 Villabáñez VA 47 Vc 99
47815 Villabaruz de Campos VA 47 Va 96
09568 Villabáscones BU 18 Wb 90
09572 Villabáscones de Bezana BU 18 Wb 91
09510 Villabasil BU 18 We 90
34475 Villabasta P 28 Vc 93
34406 Villabermudo P 29 Vd 93
37450 Villa Bernardo SA 82 Ua 103
21590 Villablanca H 161 Sd 125
24100 Villablino LE 14 Te 91
33480 Villabona AS 15 Ub 88
20150 Villabona SS 20 Xf 89
47820 Villabrágima VA 47 Uf 98
24206 Villabraz LE 46 Ud 95
49770 Villabrázaro ZA 46 Ub 96
33826 Villabre AS 14 Tf 89
24548 Villabuena LE 25 Tb 93
42290 Villabuena SO 50 Xc 98
01307 Villabuena de Álava = Eskuernaga VI 31 Xb 93
49820 Villabuena del Puente ZA 65 Ud 100
24163 Villabúrbula LE 27 Ud 93
19274 Villacadima GU 68 We 101
24172 Villacalabuey LE 28 Uf 94
24234 Villacalbiel LE 27 Uc 94
22623 Villacampa HU 35 Ze 94
23569 Villacampo del Moral J 153 Wd 123
39210 Villacantid CB 17 Ve 90
45860 Villacañas TO 103 Wd 111
22483 Villacarlí HU 36 Ad 94
47609 Villacarralón VA 47 Uf 95
39640 Villacarriedo CB 18 Wb 89
23300 Villacarrillo J 138 Wf 120
40150 Villacastín SG 85 Vd 104
24234 Villacé LE 27 Uc 94
24391 Villacedré LE 27 Uc 93
24225 Villacelama LE 27 Ud 94
24344 Villacerán LE 28 Uf 93
24227 Villacete LE 27 Ud 93
09511 Villacián BU 19 Wf 91
34492 Villacibio P 29 Ve 92
34349 Villacidaler P 47 Va 95
24161 Villacidayo LE 28 Ue 93
47607 Villacid de Campos VA 46 Uf 96
09195 Villacienzo BU 30 Wb 95
42192 Villaciervitos SO 50 Xc 98
42192 Villaciervos SO 50 Xc 98
24228 Villacil LE 27 Ud 93
24344 Villacintor LE 28 Uf 94
47181 Villaco VA 48 Ve 98
34247 Villaconancio P 48 Ve 97
28360 Villaconejos MD 103 Wd 108
16860 Villaconejos de Trabaque CU 88 Xe 106
24219 Villacontilde LE 27 Ud 93
24882 Villacorta LE 28 Va 92
40512 Villacorta SG 68 Wd 101
19269 Villacorza GU 69 Xb 102
47609 Villacreces VA 28 Uf 95
34129 Villacuende P 28 Vb 94
34340 Villada P 47 Va 95
24392 Villadangos del Páramo LE 27 Ub 93
38589 Villa de Arico TF 180 Id 179
24530 Villadecanes LE 25 Tb 93
45850 Villa de Don Fadrique, La TO 103 We 111
10814 Villa del Campo CC 98 Td 108
28630 Villa del Prado MD 85 Ve 107
10960 Villa del Rey CC 97 Tb 111
14640 Villa del Río CO 151 Ve 121
38739 Villa de Mazo = El Pueblo TF 181 Hb 177
24237 Villademor de la Vega LE 27 Uc 95
49250 Villadepera ZA 64 Tf 99
36309 Villadesuso PO 41 Ra 96
28051 Villa de Vallecas MD 86 Wc 106
09120 Villadiego BU 29 Vf 93
24327 Villadiego de Cea LE 28 Va 93
34469 Villadiezma P 29 Vd 94
50490 Villadoz Z 71 Ye 102
33794 Villadún AS 13 Sf 87
34475 Villaeles de Valdavia P 29 Vc 93
09127 Villaescobedo BU 29 Vf 92
39213 Villaescusa CB 17 Ve 91
49430 Villaescusa ZA 65 Ud 101
39232 Villaescusa de Ebro CB 30 Wa 92
34486 Villaescusa de Ecla P 29 Vd 92
16647 Villaescusa de Haro CU 104 Xb 111
09559 Villaescusa del Butrón BU 30 Wc 92
19493 Villaescusa de Palositos GU 88 Xc 105
09314 Villaescusa de Roa BU 48 Vf 98
09292 Villaescusa la Solana BU 30 Wd 94
09292 Villaescusa la Sombría BU 30 Wd 94
09650 Villaespasa BU 49 Wd 96
47811 Villaesper VA 46 Uf 97
30815 Villaespesa MC 156 Yc 122
44190 Villaespesa TE 90 Yf 107
47112 Villaesteres, Los VA 65 Ue 99
33615 Villaestremerí AS 15 Ua 89
24791 Villaestrigo LE 46 Ub 95
49136 Villafáfila ZA 46 Uc 97
24219 Villafalé LE 27 Ud 93
24162 Villafañé LE 27 Ud 93
50391 Villafeliche Z 71 Yc 101
24145 Villafeliz de Babia LE 14 Ua 91
24195 Villafeliz de la Sobarriba LE 27 Ud 93
24236 Villafer LE 46 Uc 96
49695 Villaferrueña ZA 45 Ua 96
05357 Villaflor AV 84 Va 104
49165 Villaflor ZA 45 Ua 99
19139 Villaflores GU 87 Wf 105
37406 Villaflores SA 65 Ue 102
34131 Villafolfo P 47 Vc 95
47606 Villafrades de Campos VA 47 Va 96
31330 Villafranca NC 33 Yb 95
40318 Villafranca SG 68 Wb 101
14420 Villafranca de Córdoba CO 151 Vc 121
47529 Villafranca de Duero VA 65 Ue 100
50174 Villafranca de Ebro Z 53 Zc 99
05571 Villafranca de la Sierra AV 84 Ue 106
24500 Villafranca del Bierzo LE 25 Tb 93
44394 Villafranca del Campo TE 90 Yd 104
28692 Villafranca del Castillo MD 86 Wa 106
29570 Villafranca del Guadalhorce MA 175 Vb 128
06220 Villafranca de los Barros BA 133 Td 117
45730 Villafranca de los Caballeros TO 122 Wd 112
09257 Villafranca-Montes de Oca BU 30 We 94
12150 Villafrancia del Cid CS 92 Ze 106
06195 Villafranco del Guadiana BA 116 Tb 115
24913 Villafrea de la Reina LE 16 Va 91
47810 Villafrechos VA 46 Ue 97
33129 Villafría AS 14 Tf 87
09192 Villafría BU 30 Wc 94
01118 Villafría VI 32 Xc 93
34869 Villafría de la Peña P 28 Vb 92
01427 Villafría de San Zadornil BU 31 We 92
09344 Villafruela BU 48 Wa 97
34310 Villafruela P 47 Vc 95
47180 Villafuerte VA 48 Ve 98
09339 Villafuertes BU 49 Wb 95
39638 Villafufre CB 18 Wa 89
09268 Villagalijo BU 31 We 94
24250 Villagallegos LE 27 Uc 94
47840 Villagarcía de Campos VA 46 Ue 98
06950 Villagarcía de la Torre BA 133 Tf 119
16236 Villagarcía del Llano CU 124 Ya 113
24368 Villagatón LE 26 Tf 93
33116 Villagime AS 14 Ua 90
47608 Villagómez la Nueva VA 46 Uf 96
06473 Villagonzalo BA 117 Te 115
09001 Villagonzalo-Arenas BU 30 Wb 94
40496 Villagonzalo de Coca SG 66 Vc 101
37893 Villagonzalo de Tormes SA 65 Ud 103
09195 Villagonzalo-Pedernales BU 30 Wb 95
23630 Villagordo = Villatorres J 152 Wb 121
09230 Villagutiérrez BU 30 Wa 95
34257 Villahán P 48 Vf 96
14210 Villaharta CO 135 Va 120
26223 Villa Herminia RI 31 Xb 94
13332 Villahermosa CR 138 Xa 116
44494 Villahermosa del Campo TE 71 Ye 102
12124 Villahermosa del Río CS 91 Zd 107
09125 Villahernando BU 29 Wa 93
34469 Villaherreros P 29 Vd 94
24930 Villahibiera LE 28 Ue 93
09339 Villahizán BU 48 Wa 96
09128 Villahizán de Treviño BU 29 Vf 94
09343 Villahoz BU 48 Wa 96
33719 Villainclán AS 13 Tc 87
34115 Villaires P 28 Vb 93
34419 Villajimena P 48 Vd 96
03570 Villajoyosa = La Vila Joiosa A 143 Ze 117
02249 Villa Juana AB 125 Yd 114
34261 Villalaco P 48 Ve 96
09514 Villalacre BU 18 Wd 90
34115 Villalafuente P 28 Vb 93
09554 Villalaín BU 30 Wc 91
09511 Villalambrús BU 19 We 91
47675 Villalan de Campos VA 46 Ue 96
22822 Villalangua HU 34 Zb 94
47111 Villalar de los Comuneros VA 65 Uf 99
49158 Villalazán ZA 65 Uc 100
09569 Villalázara BU 18 Wd 90
10894 Villalba CC 97 Ta 108
42223 Villalba SO 69 Xd 100
44161 Villalba Alta TE 90 Za 105
44162 Villalba Baja TE 90 Yf 106
47237 Villalba de Adaja VA 66 Vb 100
13739 Villalba de Calatrava CR 137 Wc 117
09443 Villalba de Duero BU 49 Wb 98

312 | Vilá

34889 Villalba de Guardo P 28 Vb 92
49126 Villalba de la Lampreana ZA 46 Uc 98
21860 Villalba del Alcor H 162 Td 124
47689 Villalba de la Loma VA 46 Ue 95
16140 Villalba de la Sierra CU 89 Xf 107
47639 Villalba de los Alcores VA 47 Va 97
43782 Villalba de los Arcos = Vilalba dels Arcs T 74 Ac 102
06208 Villalba de los Barros BA 132 Tc 117
37451 Villalba de los Llanos SA 82 Ua 104
44359 Villalba de los Morales TE 90 Yd 103
16535 Villalba del Rey CU 88 Xc 106
50333 Villalba de Perejil Z 71 Yc 101
26292 Villalba de Rioja RI 31 Xa 93
47113 Villalbarba VA 46 Ue 99
34869 Villalbeto de la Peña P 28 Vb 92
16840 Villalbilla CU 88 Xe 107
28810 Villalbilla MD 87 We 106
09197 Villalbilla de Burgos BU 30 Wb 94
09453 Villalbilla de Gumiel BU 49 Wc 98
09125 Villalbilla de Villadiego BU 29 Vf 93
09141 Villalbilla-Sobresierra BU 30 Wc 93
09258 Villalbos BU 30 We 94
09199 Villalbura BU 30 Wd 95
49166 Villalcampo ZA 64 Tf 99
34449 Villalcázar de Sirga P 29 Vc 95
34347 Villalcón P 28 Va 95
34310 Villaldavín P 47 Vc 96
09227 Villaldemiro BU 29 Wa 95
24326 Villalebrín LE 28 Va 94
33410 Villalegre AS 15 Ua 87
50216 Villalengua Z 71 Ya 100
24711 Villalfeide LE 27 Uc 91
02636 Villalgordo del Júcar AB 124 Xf 113
16646 Villalgordo del Marquesado CU 104 Xc 110
09129 Villalibado BU 29 Wa 93
24766 Villalís LE 26 Tf 95
33695 Villallana AS 15 Ub 89
34815 Villallano P 29 Ve 92
24326 Villalmán LE 28 Uf 94
09390 Villalmanzo BU 49 Wb 96
09258 Villalmóndar BU 30 Wd 94
24233 Villalobar LE 27 Uc 94
26256 Villalobar de Rioja RI 31 Xa 94
34419 Villalobón P 48 Vc 96
23688 Villalobos J 152 Wa 124
49134 Villalobos ZA 46 Ud 97
02328 Villa Lola AB 124 Xf 114
12550 Villa Lola CS 108 Zf 109
09258 Villalómez BU 30 We 94
14129 Villalón CO 150 Uf 122
29560 Villalón MA 166 Vb 128
47600 Villalón de Campos VA 47 Uf 96
29430 Villalones MA 165 Ue 127
46720 Villalonga V 127 Ze 115
49860 Villalonso ZA 46 Ue 99
49630 Villalpando ZA 46 Ud 97
16611 Villalpardillo CU 123 Xe 113
16270 Villalpardo CU 105 Yc 112
24218 Villalquite LE 27 Ue 93
09559 Villalta BU 30 Wc 92
49539 Villalube ZA 46 Uc 99
47511 Villa Lucía VA 65 Ue 100
09512 Villaluenga BU 19 We 91
45520 Villaluenga de la Sagra TO 102 Wa 108
34111 Villaluenga de la Vega P 28 Vb 93
11611 Villaluenga del Rosario CA 173 Ud 128
34307 Villalumbroso P 47 Vb 95
47810 Villalumbrós o Villa Eulalia VA 46 Ue 97
09192 Villalval BU 30 Wc 94
42351 Villálvaro SO 49 We 99
49343 Villalverde ZA 45 Te 96
40542 Villalvilla de Montejo SG 68 Wb 100
01423 Villamaderne VI 31 Wf 92
02270 Villamalea AB 124 Yc 112
12224 Villamalur CS 108 Zd 109
24238 Villamandos LE 46 Uc 95
24687 Villamanín LE 15 Uc 91
24690 Villamanín de la Tercia LE 15 Ub 91
13343 Villamanrique CR 138 Xa 117
41850 Villamanrique de la Condesa SE 164 Te 125
28598 Villamanrique de Tajo MD 103 We 108
28610 Villamanta MD 85 Vf 107
28609 Villamantilla MD 85 Vf 106
24234 Villamañán LE 27 Uc 95
47132 Villamarciel VA 66 Va 99
24345 Villamarco LE 27 Ue 94
01427 Villamardones VI 31 We 91
49835 Villa María Luisa ZA 65 Ud 99
11650 Villamartín CA 165 Uc 127
34170 Villamartín de Campos P 47 Vc 96
24344 Villamartín de Don Sancho LE 28 Uf 93
24469 Villamartín de Sil LE 26 Tc 92
09568 Villamartín de Sotoscueva BU 18 Wb 90
09124 Villamartín de Villadiego BU 29 Vf 93
21400 Villa Matías H 161 Sd 125
33583 Villamayor AS 15 Ue 88
05301 Villamayor AV 66 Uf 103
37185 Villamayor SA 64 Ub 102
50162 Villamayor Z 53 Zb 98
13595 Villamayor de Calatrava CR 120 Vf 116
49131 Villamayor de Campos ZA 46 Ud 97
24155 Villamayor del Condado LE 27 Ud 93
09339 Villamayor de los Montes BU 49 Wb 96
09259 Villamayor del Río BU 31 Wf 94
31242 Villamayor de Monjardín NC 32 Xf 93
16415 Villamayor de Santiago CU 103 Xa 110
09128 Villamayor de Treviño BU 29 Vf 94
09258 Villambístia BU 30 We 94
34347 Villambrán de Cea P 28 Va 94
01423 Villambrosa VI 31 Wf 92
34113 Villambroz P 28 Vb 94
24397 Villameca LE 26 Tf 93
34239 Villamediana P 48 Vd 96
26142 Villamediana de Iregua RI 32 Xd 94
39232 Villamediana de Lomas BU 30 Wa 91
34260 Villamedianilla BU 48 Vf 96
24711 Villamejil LE 26 Tf 93
33114 Villamejín AS 14 Tf 89
28311 Villamejor MD 102 Wb 109
34475 Villamelendro P 29 Vc 93
18659 Villamena GR 168 Wc 127
34408 Villameriel P 29 Vd 93
10263 Villamesías CC 117 Ua 113
10893 Villamiel CC 97 Tb 107
09649 Villamiel de la Sierra BU 49 Wd 95
09239 Villamiel de Muñó BU 30 Wb 95
45594 Villamiel de Toledo TO 102 Vf 109
45440 Villaminaya TO 102 Wa 110
24344 Villamizar LE 28 Uf 93
24175 Villamol LE 28 Uf 94
24930 Villamondrín de Rueda LE 27 Ue 93
24765 Villamontán de la Valduerna LE 26 Ua 95
45400 Villamontiel TO 102 Wb 111
39250 Villamoñico CB 29 Vf 92
09512 Villamor BU 18 Wd 91
24339 Villamoratiel de las Matas LE 27 Ue 94
34127 Villamorco P 28 Vc 94
49211 Villamor de Cadozos ZA 64 Tf 101
24234 Villamor de Laguna o Villamorico LE 46 Ub 95
49215 Villamor de la Ladre ZA 64 Tf 100
49719 Villamor de los Escuderos ZA 65 Uc 101
24393 Villamor de Órbigo LE 27 Ua 94
09199 Villamorico BU 30 Wd 94
24888 Villamorisca LE 28 Va 92
09128 Villamorón BU 29 Vf 94
34126 Villamoronta P 28 Vb 94
24217 Villamoros de Mansilla LE 27 Ud 93
09269 Villamudria BU 30 We 95
45749 Villamuelas TO 102 Wb 110
34309 Villamuera de la Cueza P 28 Vb 95
24344 Villamuñio LE 28 Ue 94
47814 Villamuriel de Campos VA 46 Ue 97
34190 Villamuriel de Cerrato P 47 Vc 97
01426 Villanañe VI 31 Wf 91
47491 Villa Narcisa VA 66 Va 100
09258 Villanasur-Río de Oca BU 30 We 94
49697 Villanazar ZA 45 Ub 97
47131 Villán de Tordesillas VA 47 Va 99
09123 Villandiego BU 29 Vf 94
33610 Villandio AS 15 Ub 89
34407 Villaneceriel P 29 Vd 93
09339 Villangómez BU 49 Wb 95
24161 Villanófar LE 28 Ue 93
09128 Villanoño BU 29 Vf 94
22467 Villanova HU 36 Ac 93
22710 Villanovilla HU 35 Zd 93
34114 Villantodrigo P 28 Vc 94
22870 Villanúa HU 35 Zc 92
47620 Villanubla VA 47 Va 98
33776 Villanueva AS 13 Sf 89
33725 Villanueva AS 13 Tb 88
33115 Villanueva AS 14 Tf 89
33111 Villanueva AS 14 Tf 90
33591 Villanueva AS 16 Va 88
33590 Villanueva AS 17 Vc 88
39690 Villanueva CB 18 Wa 88
31438 Villanueva NC 20 Yd 91
31177 Villanueva NC 32 Ya 92
09572 Villanueva-Carrales BU 30 Wb 91
34878 Villanueva de Abajo P 28 Vb 92
31671 Villanueva de Aezkoa, Hiriberri/ NC 20 Ye 91
45810 Villanueva de Alcardete TO 103 Wf 110
19460 Villanueva de Alcorón GU 88 Xe 104
29310 Villanueva de Algaidas MA 167 Vd 125
09652 Villanueva de Argaño BU 29 Wa 94
19246 Villanueva de Argecilla GU 69 Xa 103
34879 Villanueva de Arriba P 28 Vb 92
05114 Villanueva de Avila AV 84 Vb 106
49699 Villanueva de Azoague ZA 46 Uc 97
45410 Villanueva de Bogas TO 102 Wc 110
26123 Villanueva de Cameros RI 50 Xc 96
49708 Villanueva de Campeán ZA 64 Ub 100
09611 Villanueva de Carazo BU 49 We 97
24270 Villanueva de Carrizo LE 27 Ub 93
46270 Villanueva de Castellón V 126 Zc 114
14440 Villanueva de Córdoba CO 135 Vc 119
47239 Villanueva de Duero VA 66 Va 99
50830 Villanueva de Gállego Z 53 Zb 98
05164 Villanueva de Gómez AV 84 Vb 103
42311 Villanueva de Gormaz SO 69 Wf 100
16531 Villanueva de Guadamajud CU 88 Xc 107
09450 Villanueva de Gumiel BU 49 Wc 98
34811 Villanueva de Henares P 29 Vf 91
50153 Villanueva de Huerva Z 72 Yf 100
50247 Villanueva de Jalón Z 71 Yc 100
24762 Villanueva de Jamuz LE 45 Ua 95
50370 Villanueva de Jiloca Z 71 Yd 102
28691 Villanueva de la Cañada MD 86 Vf 106
05212 Villanueva del Aceral AV 66 Va 102
29230 Villanueva de la Concepción MA 167 Vc 127
47608 Villanueva de la Condesa VA 47 Uf 96
13330 Villanueva de la Fuente CR 139 Xb 116
16230 Villanueva de la Jara CU 124 Ya 112
39250 Villanueva de la Nía CB 29 Vf 92
09294 Villanueva de la Oca BU 31 Xb 92
39509 Villanueva de la Peña CB 17 Ve 89
34859 Villanueva de la Peña P 28 Vc 92
24193 Villanueva del Árbol LE 27 Uc 93
23730 Villanueva de la Reina J 152 Wa 120
41808 Villanueva del Ariscal SE 163 Tf 124
23330 Villanueva del Arzobispo J 138 Wf 119
09226 Villanueva de las Carretas BU 48 Wa 95
21592 Villanueva de las Cruces H 147 Sf 123
06700 Villanueva de la Serena BA 118 Ub 115
10812 Villanueva de la Sierra CC 82 Td 107
49580 Villanueva de la Sierra ZA 44 Sf 96
24225 Villanueva de las Manzanas LE 27 Ud 94
49333 Villanueva de las Peras ZA 45 Ua 97
18539 Villanueva de las Torres GR 153 Wf 123
19310 Villanueva de las Tres Fuentes GU 89 Yb 106
19209 Villanueva de la Torre GU 87 We 105
34828 Villanueva de la Torre P 29 Vd 91
10470 Villanueva de la Vera CC 99 Ud 108
05591 Villanueva del Campillo AV 84 Ue 105
49100 Villanueva del Campo ZA 46 Ud 97
24391 Villanueva del Carnero LE 27 Uc 93
29230 Villanueva del Cauche MA 167 Vd 127
24154 Villanueva del Condado LE 27 Ud 93
37658 Villanueva del Conde SA 82 Tf 105
14250 Villanueva del Duque CO 135 Va 118
06110 Villanueva del Fresno BA 131 Sf 118
34115 Villanueva del Monte P 28 Vb 93
31481 Villanueva de Lónguida NC 33 Yd 92
47850 Villanueva de los Caballeros VA 46 Ue 98
21540 Villanueva de los Castillejos H 161 Se 123
49165 Villanueva de los Corchos ZA 45 Tf 99
16194 Villanueva de los Escuderos CU 104 Xe 108
13320 Villanueva de los Infantes CR 138 Wf 116
47174 Villanueva de los Infantes VA 47 Vd 98
09593 Villanueva de los Montes BU 30 Wd 92
34129 Villanueva de los Nabos P 28 Vc 94
37428 Villanueva de los Pavones SA 65 Ud 102
28229 Villanueva del Pardillo MD 85 Wa 106
34309 Villanueva del Rebollar P 47 Vb 95
44223 Villanueva del Rebollar de la Sierra TE 72 Yf 103
14230 Villanueva del Rey CO 135 Uf 119
41409 Villanueva del Rey SE 150 Uf 123
34131 Villanueva del Río P 28 Vc 95
30613 Villanueva del Río Segura MC 141 Ye 120
09197 Villanueva del Río Ubierna BU 30 Wb 94
41350 Villanueva del Río y Mina SE 149 Ub 123
41359 Villanueva del Río y Minas SE 149 Ub 123
29312 Villanueva del Rosario MA 167 Vd 127
29313 Villanueva del Trabuco MA 167 Vd 126
18369 Villanueva de Mesía GR 168 Vf 125
09128 Villanueva de Odra BU 29 Vf 93
24135 Villanueva de Omaña LE 26 Tf 92
33777 Villanueva de Oscos AS 13 Ta 89
28609 Villanueva de Perales MD 85 Vf 106
09125 Villanueva de Puerta BU 29 Wa 93
13379 Villanueva de San Carlos CR 137 Wa 117
41660 Villanueva de San Juan SE 166 Ue 126
47813 Villanueva de San Mancio VA 47 Uf 97
22231 Villanueva de Sigena HU 54 Zf 98
29315 Villanueva de Tapia MA 167 Vd 125
09219 Villanueva de Teba BU 31 Wf 93
09215 Villanueva de Tobera BU 31 Xb 92
01427 Villanueva de Valdegovía VI 31 Wf 91
24415 Villanueva de Valdueza LE 26 Tc 94
49337 Villanueva de Valrojo ZA 45 Te 97
12428 Villanueva de Viver CS 107 Zc 108
42128 Villanueva de Zamajón SO 51 Xe 99
09555 Villanueva la Blanca BU 18 Wc 91
09239 Villanueva-Matamala BU 49 Wb 95
44479 Villanuevas, Los TE 107 Zc 108
09214 Villanueva-Soportilla BU 31 Wf 92
34477 Villanuño de Valdavia P 29 Vc 93
09511 Villaño BU 19 Wf 91
49618 Villaobispo ZA 45 Ua 96
24007 Villaobispo de las Regueras LE 27 Uc 93
24719 Villaobispo de Otero LE 26 Tf 93
34879 Villaoliva de la Peña P 28 Vb 92
24222 Villaornate LE 46 Uc 95
39292 Villapaderne CB 17 Vf 90
24940 Villapadierna LE 28 Uf 92
02350 Villapalacios AB 139 Xc 117
09515 Villapanillo BU 30 Wd 91
23440 Villapardillo J 153 Wd 121
24175 Villapeceñil LE 28 Uf 94
33194 Villapérez AS 15 Ua 88
24124 Villapodambre LE 27 Ua 92
34491 Villaprovedo P 29 Vd 93
34128 Villaproviano P 28 Vc 94
34112 Villapún P 28 Vb 93
24235 Villaquejida LE 46 Uc 96
24008 Villaquilambre LE 27 Uc 93
09119 Villaquirán de la Puebla BU 29 Vf 95
09118 Villaquirán de los Infantes BU 48 Vf 95
33548 Villar AS 16 Ue 88
39210 Villar CB 17 Ve 90
39808 Villar CB 18 Wc 89
14115 Villar CO 150 Uf 123
40165 Villar SG 68 Wb 102
47140 Villar VA 47 Vb 99
02459 Villar, El AB 124 Ya 114
04813 Villar, El AL 155 Xe 123
13597 Villar, El CR 137 Vf 117
21649 Villar, El H 147 Tb 122
26586 Villar, El RI 51 Xe 96
49159 Villaralbo ZA 64 Ub 100
14490 Villaralto CO 135 Va 118
44509 Villa Ramón TE 73 Zc 103
09515 Villarán BU 30 Wd 91
41800 Villarán SE 148 Te 124
11500 Villarana CA 172 Te 129
12170 Villa Raquel CS 92 Aa 106
09556 Villarcayo BU 18 Wc 91
33584 Villarcazo AS 16 Ue 89
09556 Villarcyo de la Merindad de Castilla la Vieja BU 18 Wc 91
24511 Villar de Acero LE 25 Tb 92
37497 Villar de Argañán SA 81 Tb 104
26511 Villar de Arnedo, El RI 32 Xf 95
16709 Villar de Cantos CU 104 Xd 112
16433 Villar de Cañas CU 104 Xc 110
02695 Villar de Chinchilla AB 124 Yc 115
37488 Villar de Ciervo SA 81 Tb 104
24722 Villar de Ciervos LE 26 Te 94
49562 Villardeciervos ZA 45 Te 97
19444 Villar de Cobeta GU 88 Xe 104
05516 Villar de Corneja AV 83 Ud 106
23006 Villar de Cuevas J 152 Wb 121
16840 Villar de Domingo García CU 88 Xe 107
49132 Villardefallaves ZA 46 Ud 97
49330 Villar de Farfón ZA 45 Te 97
37524 Villar de Flores SA 81 Tb 106
47860 Villardefrades VA 46 Ue 98
33615 Villar de Gallegos AS 15 Ub 89
37320 Villar de Gallimazo SA 65 Ue 103
24721 Villar de Golfer LE 26 Te 94
33584 Villar de Huergo AS 16 Ue 88
16648 Villar de la Encina CU 104 Xc 111
16161 Villar del Águila CU 104 Xc 109
42165 Villar del Ala SO 50 Xc 97
46170 Villar del Arzobispo V 107 Zb 110
24458 Villar de las Traviesas LE 26 Td 92
16542 Villar de la Ventosa CU 104 Xd 108
37488 Villar de la Yegua SA 81 Tb 104
49240 Villar del Buey ZA 64 Te 101
42112 Villar del Campo SO 51 Xf 98
44114 Villar del Cobo TE 89 Yb 106

A B C D E F G H I J K L M N Ñ O P Q R S T U V W X Y Z

Villar del Cobo | 313

E

37766 Villar de Leche SA 83 Ub 105
16162 Villar del Horno CU 104 Xd 108
16370 Villar del Humo CU 105 Yc 109
16813 Villar del Infantado CU 88 Xd 106
16542 Villar del Maestre CU 104 Xd 108
24738 Villar del Monte LE 45 Te 95
28512 Villar del Olmo MD 87 We 106
37460 Villar de los Álamos SA 82 Tf 103
24414 Villar de Los Barrios LE 26 Tc 93
50156 Villar de los Navarros Z 72 Yf 102
10330 Villar del Pedroso CC 100 Ue 110
13431 Villar del Pozo CR 121 Wa 115
24836 Villar del Puerto LE 27 Uc 91
06192 Villar del Rey BA 116 Ta 114
42173 Villar del Río SO 51 Xd 96
44311 Villar del Salz TE 89 Yd 104
16123 Villar del Saz de Arcas CU 105 Xf 109
16190 Villar del Saz de Navalón CU 104 Xd 108
24249 Villar del Yermo LE 27 Ub 94
05220 Villar de Matacabras AV 66 Uf 102
24392 Villar de Mazarife LE 27 Ub 94
16196 Villar de Olalla CU 105 Xe 108
46351 Villar de Olmos V 106 Yf 111
37147 Villar de Peralonso SA 64 Te 102
10720 Villar de Plasencia CC 99 Tf 108
37609 Villar de Profeta SA 82 Tf 104
06716 Villar de Rena BA 117 Ub 114
37217 Villar de Samaniego SA 63 Td 102
33728 Villar de San Pedro AS 13 Ta 88
24138 Villar de Santiago, El LE 26 Te 91
40317 Villar de Sobrepeña SG 67 Wb 101
46351 Villar de Tejas V 106 Yf 111
26325 Villar de Torre RI 31 Xa 94
02213 Villar de Ves AB 125 Ye 113
33480 Villardeveyo AS 15 Ua 88
33842 Villar de Vildas AS 14 Td 90
49250 Villardiegua de la Ribera ZA 64 Te 99
49211 Villardiegua del Nalso ZA 64 Tf 101
49178 Villardiegua del Sierro ZA 64 Ub 101
49129 Villárdiga ZA 46 Ud 98
23659 Villardompardo J 152 Vf 121
49871 Villardondiego ZA 46 Ud 99
02139 Villarejo AB 140 Xf 117
05120 Villarejo AV 84 Vb 106
26325 Villarejo RI 31 Xa 94
37172 Villarejo SA 64 Te 101
37591 Villarejo SA 81 Td 106
40590 Villarejo SG 68 Wc 101
44120 Villarejo, El TE 90 Yc 107
16432 Villarejo de Fuentes CU 104 Xb 110
16541 Villarejo de la Peñuela CU 104 Xd 108
49342 Villarejo de la Sierra ZA 44 Td 96
16843 Villarejo del Espartal CU 88 Xd 107
44357 Villarejo de los Olmos, El TE 90 Ye 103
05413 Villarejo del Valle AV 84 Va 107
19445 Villarejo de Medina GU 70 Xd 103
45179 Villarejo de Montalbán TO 101 Vc 110
24358 Villarejo de Órbigo LE 27 Ua 94
28590 Villarejo de Salvanés MD 103 We 107
16771 Villarejo-Periesteban CU 104 Xd 109
16195 Villarejo Seco CU 104 Xd 109
16195 Villarejo-Sobrehuerta CU 104 Xd 108
02439 Villares AB 140 Xf 118
14811 Villares, Los CO 167 Ve 124
14800 Villares, Los CO 167 Ve 125
18181 Villares, Los GR 169 We 124
23650 Villares, Los J 152 Vf 122
23747 Villares, Los J 152 Wa 120
23160 Villares, Los J 152 Wb 122
44421 Villares, Los TE 107 Yf 108
19244 Villares de Jadraque GU 69 Wf 102
37184 Villares de la Reina SA 65 Uc 102
16442 Villares del Saz CU 104 Xc 109
24288 Villares de Órbigo LE 27 Ua 94
37267 Villares de Yeltes SA 82 Td 103
37217 Villargordo SA 63 Te 102
41898 Villargordo SE 148 Td 123
46317 Villargordo del Cabriel V 106 Yd 111
24144 Villargusán LE 14 Ua 91
09513 Villarías BU 30 Wc 91
04616 Villaricos AL 171 Yb 125
09195 Villariezo BU 30 Wb 95
42174 Villarijo SO 51 Xf 96
33778 Villarín AS 13 Ta 88
24127 Villarín de Riello LE 26 Ua 92
24741 Villarino LE 26 Tc 95
37160 Villarino SA 63 Td 101
24498 Villarino del Sil LE 26 Td 91
49521 Villarino de Manzanas ZA 44 Td 97
49358 Villarino de Sanabria ZA 44 Tc 96
49518 Villarino Tras la Sierra ZA 44 Td 98
49523 Villariño de Cebal ZA 45 Te 98
44559 Villarluengo TE 91 Zc 105
37130 Villarmayor SA 64 Ua 102
09131 Villarmentero BU 30 Wb 94
34447 Villarmentero de Campos P 29 Vd 95
47172 Villarmentero de Esgueva VA 47 Vc 98
24397 Villarmeriel LE 26 Tf 92
09197 Villarmero BU 30 Wb 94
34114 Villarmienzo P 28 Vb 93
37217 Villarmuerto SA 63 Td 102
24164 Villarmún LE 27 Ud 93
34813 Villarn de Valdivia P 29 Ve 92
24795 Villarnera LE 26 Ua 94
45311 Villa Román TO 103 Wc 109
37639 Villa Rosa SA 82 Te 105
44380 Villarquemado TE 90 Ye 105
34113 Villarrabé P 28 Vb 94
24238 Villarrabines LE 46 Uc 95
34350 Villarramiel P 47 Va 96
21850 Villarrasa H 162 Tc 124
42181 Villarraso SO 51 Xe 97
24165 Villarratel LE 27 Ud 93
06107 Villarreal BA 131 Se 116
30813 Villarreal MC 156 Yc 123
12540 Villarreal = Vila-Real CS 108 Zf 109
50490 Villarreal de Huerva Z 71 Ye 101
22771 Villarreal de la Canal HU 34 Za 93
10695 Villarreal de San Carlos CC 99 Tf 109
26313 Villarrica RI 31 Xb 94
49137 Villarrín de Campos ZA 46 Uc 98
24252 Villarrín del Páramo LE 27 Ub 94
24226 Villarroañe LE 27 Uc 94
34112 Villarrobejo P 28 Vb 94
02600 Villarrobledo AB 123 Xc 113
23393 Villarrodrigo J 139 Xc 118
24197 Villarrodrigo de las Regueras LE 27 Uc 93
34113 Villarrodrigo de la Vega P 28 Vb 94
24276 Villarrodrigo de Ordás LE 27 Ub 92
24273 Villarroquel LE 27 Ub 92
26587 Villarroya RI 51 Xf 96
50310 Villarroya de la Sierra Z 71 Yb 100
50368 Villarroya del Campo Z 71 Ye 102
44144 Villarroya de los Pinares TE 91 Zb 105
14711 Villarrubia CO 150 Va 121
13670 Villarrubia de los Ojos CR 121 Wc 113
45360 Villarrubia de Santiago TO 103 Wd 109
24566 Villarrubín LE 25 Sf 93
16420 Villarrubio CU 104 Xa 109
22471 Villarrué HU 36 Ad 94
16280 Villarta CU 124 Yc 112
45910 Villarta de Escalona TO 101 Vd 108
06678 Villarta de los Montes BA 119 Vb 113
13210 Villarta de San Juan CR 121 Wd 113
26259 Villarta-quintana RI 31 Wf 94
33718 Villartorey AS 13 Tb 88
42173 Villartoso SO 51 Xd 96
28370 Villas MD 103 Wd 107
24219 Villasabanego LE 27 Ud 93
34127 Villasabariego de Ucieza P 28 Vc 94
09580 Villasana de Mena BU 19 We 90
09109 Villasandino BU 29 Vf 94
09569 Villasante BU 18 Wd 90
34132 Villasarracino P 29 Vd 94
42214 Villasayas SO 69 Xc 100
37256 Villasbuenas SA 63 Tc 102
10858 Villasbuenas de Gata CC 98 Tc 107
37468 Villasdardo SA 64 Tf 102
16843 Villas de la Ventosa CU 88 Xd 107
16144 Villaseca CU 88 Xe 107
26212 Villaseca RI 31 Xa 93
40317 Villaseca SG 67 Wb 101
42173 Villaseca Bajera SO 51 Xd 96
42132 Villaseca de Arciel SO 51 Xf 99
42132 Villaseca de Arciel SO 70 Xd 102
19294 Villaseca de Henares GU 69 Xb 103
24140 Villaseca de Laciana LE 14 Te 91
45260 Villaseca de la Sagra TO 102 Wa 109
24228 Villaseca de la Sobarriba LE 27 Ud 93
19184 Villaseca de Uceda GU 87 Wd 104
42174 Villaseca Somera SO 51 Xd 96
49181 Villaseco ZA 64 Ua 100
37114 Villaseco de los Gamitos SA 64 Tf 102
37150 Villaseco de los Reyes SA 64 Te 102
24344 Villaselán LE 28 Uf 93
37129 Villaselva SA 64 Ub 102
45740 Villasequilla de Yepes TO 102 Wb 109
39698 Villasevil CB 18 Wa 89
47134 Villasexmir VA 47 Uf 99
09123 Villasidro BU 29 Vf 94
34475 Villasila de Valdavia P 29 Vc 93
09109 Villasilos BU 29 Vf 95
24670 Villasimpliz LE 27 Uc 91
24193 Villasinta de Torío LE 27 Uc 93
33611 Villasola AS 15 Ub 89
41410 Villasparra SE 149 Uc 123
37522 Villasrubias SA 81 Tc 106
44130 Villastar TE 90 Yf 107
34115 Villasur P 28 Vb 93
09199 Villasur de Herreros BU 30 Wd 95
39451 Villasuso CB 17 Vf 89
39407 Villasuso CB 17 Vf 89
09589 Villasuso de Mena BU 18 We 90
16441 Villas-Viejas CU 104 Xb 109
09512 Villate BU 18 Wd 91
33817 Villategil AS 14 Tc 90
46389 Villa Teresa V 126 Zb 112
34349 Villátima P 28 Va 95
45310 Villatobas TO 103 We 109
09512 Villatomil BU 18 Wd 91
34307 Villatoquite P 47 Vb 95
05560 Villatoro AV 84 Uf 105
09006 Villatoro BU 30 Wb 94
23630 Villatorres = Villagordo J 152 Wb 121
02215 Villatoya AB 125 Yd 113
21720 Villa Trene H 162 Tc 125
33879 Villatresmil AS 14 Td 88
09310 Villatuelda BU 48 Wa 98
31132 Villatuerta NC 32 Ya 93
34129 Villaturde P 28 Vb 94
24226 Villaturiel LE 27 Ud 93
34192 Villaumbrales P 47 Vc 96
43460 Villa Urrutia T 75 Ba 101
09125 Villaute BU 29 Wa 93
31195 Villava NC 33 Yc 91
33128 Villavaler AS 14 Te 88
02154 Villavaliente AB 125 Yd 114
47329 Villavaquerín VA 47 Vd 99
33889 Villavaser AS 14 Tc 89
09515 Villavedeo BU 30 Wd 91
09124 Villavedón BU 29 Vf 93
34478 Villavega P 29 Vd 94
34810 Villavega de Aguilar P 29 Ve 91
34485 Villavega de Ojeda P 29 Vd 92
24327 Villavelasco de Valderaduey LE 28 Va 93
26329 Villavelayo RI 50 Xa 96
47883 Villavellid VA 46 Ue 98
49870 Villavendimio ZA 46 Ud 99
24195 Villavente LE 27 Uc 93
09514 Villaventín BU 18 Wd 90
02340 Villaverde AB 123 Xd 116
33314 Villaverde AS 15 Uc 87
33557 Villaverde AS 16 Uf 89
05140 Villaverde AV 84 Va 104
35640 Villaverde GC 183 Ma 177
28021 Villaverde MD 86 Wb 106
28598 Villaverde MD 103 We 108
01118 Villaverde VI 32 Xc 93
24890 Villaverde de Abajo LE 27 Uc 92
24171 Villaverde de Arcayos LE 28 Uf 93
24890 Villaverde de Arriba LE 27 Uc 92
02460 Villaverde de Guadalimar AB 139 Xc 118
37428 Villaverde de Guareña SA 65 Uc 102
40219 Villaverde de Íscar SG 66 Vc 101
24390 Villaverde de la Abadia LE 25 Tb 93
24844 Villaverde de la Cuerna LE 15 Ud 90
19261 Villaverde del Ducado GU 69 Xd 102
09339 Villaverde del Monte BU 49 Wb 96
42145 Villaverde del Monte SO 50 Xb 98
41318 Villaverde del Río SE 149 Ua 123
47465 Villaverde de Medina VA 66 Uf 101
40542 Villaverde de Montejo SG 68 Wc 99
39793 Villaverde de Pontones CB 18 Wb 88
26321 Villaverde de Rioja RI 31 Xb 95
24217 Villaverde de Sandoval LE 27 Ud 93
39880 Villaverde de Trucios CB 19 We 89
34309 Villaverde de Volpejera P 47 Vc 95
24930 Villaverde la Chiquita LE 28 Ue 93
09226 Villaverde-Mogina BU 48 Vf 96
09591 Villaverde-Peñahorada BU 30 Wb 94
16111 Villaverde y Pasaconsol CU 104 Xe 110
09109 Villaveta BU 29 Vf 94
31481 Villaveta NC 33 Yd 92
49760 Villaveza del Agua ZA 46 Ub 97
49697 Villaveza de Valverde ZA 45 Ua 97
39776 Villaviad CB 18 Wd 88
47676 Villavicencio de los Caballeros VA 46 Ue 96
33300 Villaviciosa AS 15 Ud 88
05130 Villaviciosa AV 84 Va 105
14300 Villaviciosa de Córdoba CO 150 Uf 120
24271 Villaviciosa de la Ribera LE 27 Ua 93
28670 Villaviciosa de Odón MD 86 Wa 106
19413 Villaviciosa de Tajuña GU 87 Xa 104
24225 Villavidel LE 27 Uc 94
12526 Villavieja CS 108 Ze 109
47113 Villavieja del Cerro VA 66 Uf 99
28739 Villavieja del Lozoya MD 68 Wb 102
09239 Villavieja de Muñó BU 30 Wa 95
37260 Villavieja de Yeltes SA 81 Td 103
34249 Villaviudas P 48 Vd 97
24989 Villayandre LE 28 Uf 91
09191 Villayerno Morquillas BU 30 Wc 94
33717 Villayón AS 13 Tb 88
39407 Villayuso CB 17 Vf 89
24126 Villayuste LE 27 Ua 92
24328 Villazanzo de Valderaduey LE 28 Va 93
33868 Villazón AS 14 Te 88
09226 Villazopeque BU 48 Vf 95
25725 Villec L 38 Be 95
09128 Villegas BU 29 Vf 94
40496 Villeguillo SG 66 Vc 101
44131 Villel TE 90 Ye 107
34492 Villela BU 29 Ve 92
19332 Villel de Mesa GU 70 Ya 102
34349 Villelga P 28 Va 95
34349 Villemar P 28 Va 95
03400 Villena A 142 Za 117
42173 Viller de Maya SO 51 Xd 96
34305 Villerías de Campos P 47 Va 97
12594 Villes, Les CS 108 Aa 108
24324 Villeza LE 28 Ue 95
24250 Villibañe LE 27 Uc 94
09007 Villimar BU 30 Wc 94
24163 Villimer LE 27 Ud 93
22622 Villobas HU 35 Ze 94
34466 Villodre P 48 Ve 95
34257 Villodrigo BU 48 Wf 96
34131 Villoldo P 47 Vc 95
24218 Villomar LE 27 Ud 93
16371 Víllora CU 106 Yc 110
09133 Villorejo BU 29 Wa 94
12311 Villores CS 92 Ze 104
33986 Villoria AS 15 Uc 89
37339 Villoria SA 65 Ud 103
37281 Villoria de Buenamadre SA 82 Te 103
24358 Villoria de Órbigo LE 27 Ua 94
09199 Villorobe BU 30 We 95
34409 Villorquite de Herrera P 29 Vd 94
34117 Villorquite del Páramo P 28 Vb 93
09640 Villoruebo BU 49 Wd 95
37338 Villoruela SA 65 Ud 102
34111 Villosilla de la Vega P 28 Vb 93
37148 Villosino SA 64 Tf 102
40449 Villoslada SG 66 Vd 103
26125 Villoslada de Cameros RI 50 Xb 96
34118 Villota del Duque P 28 Vc 94
34112 Villota del Páramo P 28 Va 93
34129 Villotilla P 28 Vb 94
09310 Villovela de Esgueva BU 48 Wa 98
40393 Villovela de Pirón SG 67 Vf 102
09348 Villoviado BU 49 Wb 97
34449 Villovieco P 29 Vd 95
09124 Villusto BU 29 Vf 93
17184 Vilobí d'Onyar GI 59 Ce 97
17466 Vilopriu GI 59 Cf 96
31283 Viloria NC 32 Xe 92
47166 Viloria VA 67 Vd 100
01420 Viloria VI 31 Xa 92
09259 Viloria de Rioja BU 31 Wf 94
17462 Vilosa, La GI 59 Cf 96
25457 Vilosell, El L 75 Af 100
15687 Vilouchada C 11 Rc 91
15806 Vilouriz C 12 Sa 91
32160 Vilouriz OR 24 Sb 94
27694 Vilouta LU 25 Se 91
08735 Viloví = Vilobí del Penedès B 76 Be 100
50219 Vilueña, La Z 71 Yb 101
37258 Vilvestre SA 63 Tb 102
42153 Vilviestre de los Nabos SO 50 Xc 97
09690 Vilviestre del Pinar BU 50 Wf 97
09230 Vilviestre de Muñó BU 29 Wa 95
43430 Vimbodí T 75 Ba 100
15129 Vimianzo C 10 Qf 90
44591 Vinaceite TE 73 Zc 101
05216 Vinaderos AV 66 Vb 102
25440 Vinaixa L 75 Af 100
46114 Vinalesa V 108 Zd 111
43517 Vinallop T 93 Ad 104
12500 Vinaròs CS 93 Ac 106
36389 Vincios PO 41 Rb 96
16812 Vindel CU 88 Xd 105
43792 Vinebre T 74 Ad 101
43750 Vingalis T 74 Ad 101
26329 Viniegra de Abajo RI 50 Xa 96
26329 Viniegra de Arriba RI 50 Xa 96
15819 Vinos C 23 Re 91
07440 Vin Roma IB 111 Da 110
36687 Vinseiro PO 23 Rd 92
42150 Vinuesa SO 50 Xb 97
08509 Vinyoles d'Orís B 58 Cb 96
43391 Vinyols i Arcs T 75 Ba 102
15313 Viña C 11 Rf 89
11400 Viña de Dios CA 163 Tf 128
30879 Viña de Raja MC 156 Ye 123
05410 Viñaesquinade AV 84 Uf 107
32537 Viñao OR 23 Rf 94
49517 Viñas ZA 44 Td 98
18870 Viñas, Las GR 154 Wf 124
01308 Viñaspre VI 32 Xd 93
05147 Viñegra AV 84 Uf 104
05309 Viñegra de Moraña AV 84 Va 103
33310 Viñón AS 15 Ud 88
39584 Viñón CB 16 Vc 89
13460 Viñuela CR 136 Ve 116
29712 Viñuela MA 167 Vf 127
14430 Viñuela, La CO 136 Vc 120
23590 Viñuela, La J 153 We 122
49177 Viñuela de Sayago ZA 64 Ua 101
19184 Viñuelas GU 87 Wd 104
46199 Viñuelas V 125 Yf 113
10691 Viñuelas de Enmedio CC 98 Te 109
22375 Vío HU 35 Aa 93
39479 Vioño CB 17 Wa 88
30876 Viquejos MC 156 Yc 123
01129 Virgala Mayor VI 32 Xd 92
01129 Virgala Menor VI 32 Xd 92
23748 Virgen de la Cabeza J 136 Vf 119
50730 Virgen de la Columna Z 72 Zb 99
23711 Virgen de la Encina J 137 Wb 119
44432 Virgen de la Vega TE 91 Zb 106
24198 Virgen del Camino, La LE 27 Uc 93
41410 Virgen del Rocío SE 149 Ub 124
43762 Virgili T 76 Bc 102
27373 Virís LU 12 Sb 90
03409 Virtudes, Las A 142 Za 117
09213 Virués BU 30 Wd 92
33559 Vis AS 16 Uf 89
22484 Visalibons HU 36 Ad 94

314 | Villar de Leche

15689 Visantoña C 11 Re 90
15808 Visantoña C 23 Rf 91
31695 Viscarret NC 21 Yd 91
15124 Viseo C 10 Qe 90
44164 Visiedo TE 90 Yf 104
36691 Viso PO 23 Rc 95
02155 Viso, El AB 124 Yb 114
02510 Viso, El AB 124 Yb 116
02214 Viso, El AB 125 Ye 113
14470 Viso, El CO 135 Va 118
32811 Viso, O OR 42 Rf 95
41520 Viso del Alcor, El SE 165 Ub 124
13770 Viso del Marqués CR 137 Wc 117
45215 Viso de San Juan, El TO 102 Wa 108
21660 Vista Alegre H 147 Tc 122
07839 Vista Alegre IB 109 Bb 115
23214 Vista Alegre J 137 Wc 119
03319 Vistabella A 157 Zb 120
43154 Vistabella T 75 Bb 101
50482 Vistabella Z 72 Yf 101
12135 Vistabella del Maestrazgo CS 91 Ze 107
03559 Vista Hermosa A 142 Zd 118
11500 Vistahermosa CA 172 Te 129
37008 Vistahermosa SA 64 Ub 103
37479 Vista-Hermosa SA 81 Td 104
02155 Vistalegre AB 124 Ya 114
05146 Vita AV 84 Uf 104
33549 Vita, La AS 16 Ue 88
30610 Vite MC 141 Yd 120
23296 Vites J 139 Xd 120
37210 Vitigudino SA 63 Td 102
01059 Vitoria-Gasteiz VI 31 Xb 91
01130 Vitoriano VI 19 Xb 91
22378 Viu HU 35 Zf 93
22450 Viu HU 36 Ac 94
04240 Viudas, Las AL 170 Xd 127
25556 Viu de Llevata L 37 Ae 94
09587 Vivanco de Mena BU 18 Wd 90
30335 Vivancos, Los MC 156 Ye 123
40236 Vivar de Fuentidueña SG 67 Vf 100
06412 Vivares BA 117 Ua 114
39314 Viveda CB 17 Vf 88
27850 Viveiro LU 10 Sc 87
32816 Viveiro OR 42 Sa 95
27837 Viveiró, O LU 12 Sc 88
44740 Vivel del Río Martín TE 90 Za 103
15380 Vivente C 11 Re 89
32411 Vivenzo OR 23 Re 95
12460 Viver CS 107 Zc 109
50249 Viver de la Sierra Z 71 Yc 100
25216 Viver de Segarra L 57 Bc 98
50332 Viver de Vicort Z 71 Yd 100
08673 Viver el Castellot B 57 Be 97
02310 Viveros AB 123 Xc 116
28830 Viveros, Los MD 86 Wc 106
41240 Viveros, Los SE 148 Ua 122
49514 Vivinera ZA 45 Te 98
15967 Vixán C 22 Qf 93
04600 Vizcaíno AL 155 Yb 124
09613 Vizcaínos BU 49 We 96
46178 Vizcota V 106 Yf 109
34260 Vizmalo BU 48 Vf 96
42173 Vizmanos SO 51 Xd 96
18179 Víznar GR 168 Wc 125
15318 Vizoño C 11 Re 89
24444 Voces LE 25 Tb 94
23380 Voladores, Los J 139 Xd 119
25794 Voloriu L 57 Bc 95
43390 Voltes, Les T 75 Af 102
24859 Vozmediano LE 28 Ue 91
42107 Vozmediano SO 52 Ya 97
24859 Voznuevo LE 27 Ue 91
39688 Vozpornoche CB 18 Wa 90
38870 Vueltas TF 184 He 180
05134 Vueltas, Las AV 84 Va 106
17111 Vullpellac GI 59 Da 97

W

47190 Wamba VA 47 Va 98
17310 Water World Parc GI 59 Ce 98

X

32373 Xaba OR 25 Sf 95
07640 Xabarlinar, Es IB 111 Da 112
03730 Xàbia = Jávea A 127 Ab 116
43512 Xalamera T 74 Ac 103
15838 Xallas C 22 Ra 91
03727 Xaló = Jalón A 143 Zf 116
15685 Xanceda C 11 Re 90
03709 Xara, La A 127 Aa 116
32365 Xares OR 44 Ta 95
13250 Xarrié CR 121 Wb 114
46800 Xàtiva V 126 Zc 115
15687 Xavestre C 11 Rc 91
15122 Xaviña C 10 Qf 90
46770 Xeraco V 127 Ze 114
43791 Xercuns T 74 Ad 101
46790 Xeresa V 127 Ze 114
27833 Xermade LU 12 Sb 88
27377 Xermar LU 12 Sc 89
32898 Xermeade OR 42 Sa 97
12360 Xert, Chert/ CS 92 Aa 105
43592 Xerta T 74 Ac 103
36836 Xesta PO 23 Rd 94
36515 Xesta PO 23 Rf 93
15315 Xestal C 11 Rf 89
15186 Xesteda C 11 Rc 90
36859 Xesteira, A PO 23 Rc 94
27250 Xesto LU 12 Sd 89
32930 Xestosa OR 23 Sa 95
27306 Xestoselo LU 12 Sb 89
27329 Xestoso LU 24 Se 93
36548 Xestoso PO 23 Rd 93
15315 Xestoso (Santa María) C 12 Sa 88
36151 Xeve PO 22 Rc 94
27227 Xiá LU 12 Sa 90
27557 Xián LU 24 Sb 92
36968 Xil PO 22 Rb 94
07872 Xindri, La IB 109 Bd 116
03640 Xinorla A 142 Za 118
03649 Xinorlet A 141 Za 118
15258 Xinzo C 22 Qf 91
36678 Xinzo PO 23 Rc 93
32706 Xinzo da Costa OR 43 Sc 95
32630 Xinzo de Limia OR 42 Sb 96
30890 Xiquena MC 155 Ya 122
32520 Xirazga OR 23 Re 94
46950 Xirivella = Chirivella V 107 Zd 112
03520 Xirles A 143 Zf 117
32688 Xironda OR 43 Sc 97
12160 Xisquerol CS 92 Ze 106
12314 Xiva de Morella CS 92 Zf 105
33206 Xixón = Gijón AS 15 Uc 87
03100 Xixona = Jijona A 142 Zc 117
32701 Xocín OR 43 Sc 95
12134 Xodos CS 91 Ze 107
15110 Xornes C 10 Rb 89
27870 Xove LU 10 Sc 86
15805 Xubial C 11 Rf 91
32459 Xubín OR 23 Rf 95
27723 Xudán LU 13 Se 89
15996 Xufres C 22 Ra 93
15520 Xuncedo C 11 Re 88
32671 Xunqueira de Ambía OR 42 Sb 95
32730 Xunqueira de Espadanedo OR 24 Sc 95
15995 Xuño = Santa Mariña de Xuño C 22 Qf 93
27692 Xusaos LU 24 Se 92
36827 Xustáns PO 23 Rc 94
27377 Xustás LU 12 Sd 89
27547 Xuvencos LU 24 Sc 93

Y

35570 Yaíza GC 182 Mb 175
31790 Yanci NC 21 Yb 89
42172 Yanguas SO 51 Xd 96
40493 Yanguas de Eresma SG 67 Ve 102
33557 Yano AS 16 Ue 89
31470 Yárnoz NC 33 Yc 92
22141 Yaso HU 54 Zf 95
18448 Yátor GR 169 Wf 127
46367 Yátova V 126 Zb 112
35541 Ye GC 182 Md 173
22375 Yeba HU 35 Aa 93
45470 Yébenes, Los TO 102 Wa 111
19141 Yebes GU 87 Wf 105
19111 Yebra GU 87 Xa 106
24388 Yebra LE 25 Tb 94
22610 Yebra de Basa HU 35 Ze 94
30850 Yéchar MC 156 Yc 122
30510 Yecla MC 141 Yf 117
37219 Yecla de Yeltes SA 63 Td 103
01322 Yécora VI 32 Xd 93
04271 Yedra, La AL 171 Xf 125
35333 Yedra, La GC 184 Kc 180
23160 Yedra, La J 152 Wa 123
18460 Yegen GR 169 Wf 127
04813 Yegua Alta, La AL 155 Xe 123
02448 Yeguarizas, Las AB 139 Xe 117
23770 Yegüerizas J 151 Ve 120
19413 Yela GU 87 Xb 104
19143 Yélamos de Abajo GU 87 Xa 105
19143 Yélamos de Arriba GU 87 Xa 105
06411 Yelbes BA 117 Tf 115
45220 Yeles TO 102 Wb 108
42230 Yelo SO 70 Xc 101
31485 Yelz NC 33 Yc 92
16373 Yémeda CU 105 Yb 110
45313 Yepes TO 102 Wc 109
22193 Yéqueda HU 54 Zd 95
39685 Yera CB 18 Wb 90
33826 Yermes y Tameza AS 14 Tf 89
39460 Yermo CB 17 Vf 89
33826 Yernes AS 14 Tf 89
31410 Yesa NC 34 Ye 93
46178 Yesa, La V 107 Za 109
26527 Yesal, El RI 51 Ya 96
02155 Yesares, Los AB 124 Yb 114
04200 Yesos, Los AL 170 Xe 126
18713 Yesos, Los GR 169 Wf 128
22622 Yéspola HU 35 Zd 94
02480 Yeste AB 139 Xe 118
22820 Yeste HU 34 Zb 94
02536 Yetas de Abajo AB 139 Xd 119
22370 Yosa HU 35 Zf 93
42248 Yuba SO 70 Xd 101
09123 Yudego BU 29 Vf 94
11630 Yugo, El CA 163 Ua 128
24879 Yugueros LE 28 Ue 92
45529 Yuncler TO 102 Wa 108
45591 Yuncillos TO 102 Wa 108
45210 Yuncos TO 102 Wa 108
29410 Yunquera MA 174 Va 128
02161 Yunquera, La AB 123 Xe 115
19210 Yunquera de Henares GU 87 Wf 104
19361 Yunta, La GU 71 Yb 103

Z

31292 Zábal NC 32 Xf 92
48383 Zabala-Belendiz BI 19 Xc 89
31422 Zabalceta NC 33 Yc 92
31699 Zabaldika NC 33 Yc 91
31470 Zabalegui NC 33 Yc 92
09511 Zaballa BU 19 Wf 91
48180 Zabaloetxe BI 19 Xa 89
31174 Zabalza NC 33 Yb 92
31472 Zabalza NC 33 Yc 92
31448 Zabalza NC 34 Ye 92
24396 Zacos LE 26 Tf 93
46176 Zaé V 106 Yf 110
09339 Zael BU 49 Wb 96
30441 Zaén de Abajo MC 140 Xf 119
30441 Zaén de Arriba MC 140 Xf 119
49214 Zafara ZA 64 Te 100
18128 Zafarraya GR 167 Vf 127
03640 Zafra A 142 Za 118
06300 Zafra BA 133 Td 118
03408 Zafra, La A 142 Za 116
10182 Zafra, La CC 117 Te 113
16771 Zafra de Záncara CU 104 Xc 109
16317 Zafrilla CU 89 Yc 107
37130 Zafrón SA 64 Tf 102
37116 Zafroncino SA 64 Tf 102
18311 Zagra GR 167 Ve 125
23790 Zahán, El J 152 Ve 121
11688 Zahara CA 165 Ud 127
11393 Zahara de los Atunes CA 173 Ua 132
41410 Zahariche SE 149 Ud 124
06380 Zahínos BA 132 Ta 119
11159 Zahora CA 172 Tf 131
18329 Zahora, La GR 168 Wa 126
50784 Zaida, La Z 73 Zd 101
22530 Zaidín HU 55 Ab 99
01138 Zaitegui VI 19 Xb 91
31789 Zalain NC 21 Yb 89
06430 Zalamea de la Serena BA 134 Uc 117
21640 Zalamea la Real H 147 Tc 122
24207 Zalamillas LE 46 Ud 95
31484 Zalba NC 33 Yd 91
48250 Zaldibar BI 20 Xc 89
20247 Zaldibia SS 20 Xf 90
26289 Zaldierna RI 31 Wf 95
20247 Zaldivia = Zaldibia SS 20 Xf 90
09199 Zalduendo BU 30 Wd 94
01208 Zalduondo VI 32 Xd 91
29569 Zalea MA 166 Vb 128
47810 Zalengas VA 46 Ue 97
48860 Zalla BI 19 Wf 89
47009 Zamadueñas VA 47 Vb 98
42128 Zamajón SO 51 Xd 99
36310 Zamáns PO 41 Rb 96
37591 Zamarra SA 81 Td 105
41780 Zamarra SE 165 Ud 127
40196 Zamarramala SG 67 Vf 103
37110 Zamayón SA 64 Ub 102
14950 Zambra CO 167 Vd 124
01212 Zambrana VI 31 Xa 93
24249 Zambroncinos LE 27 Ub 95
37110 Zamocino SA 64 Ua 101
23569 Zamora J 153 Wd 123
49001* Zamora ZA 64 Ub 99
14814 Zamoranos CO 151 Vf 123
48170 Zamudio BI 19 Xa 89
30840 Zancarrones, Los MC 156 Yd 121
31799 Zandio NC 33 Yc 91
10815 Zangajito CC 98 Td 108
09211 Zangandez BU 30 We 92
31400 Zangoza = Sangüesa NC 33 Ye 93
04887 Zanjas, Las AL 170 Xc 124
11370 Zanona CA 173 Ub 131
33490 Zanzabornín AS 15 Ub 87
19495 Zaorejas GU 88 Xe 104
05154 Zapardiel de la Cañada AV 83 Ud 105
05631 Zapardiel de la Ribera AV 83 Ue 106
05514 Zapata AV 83 Ue 106
06475 Zapatera, La BA 117 Te 116
02315 Zapateros AB 139 Xc 117
21840 Zapillo, El H 147 Tb 124
41429 Zapillo, El SE 149 Ud 123
42127 Zárabes SO 70 Xe 99
50001* Zaragoza Z 53 Za 99
50709 Zaragozeta Z 73 Zf 102
48820 Zaramillo BI 19 Wf 89
37170 Zarapicos SA 64 Ua 102
48480 Zaratamo BI 19 Xa 89
37170 Zaratán SA 64 Ub 102
47610 Zaratán VA 47 Vb 99
20800 Zarautz SS 20 Xe 89
30810 Zarcilla de Ramos MC 155 Ya 121
03409 Zaricejo, El A 142 Za 117
20530 Zarimutz SS 20 Xc 90
31190 Zariquiegui NC 33 Yb 92
31481 Zariquieta NC 33 Ye 92
46621 Zarra V 125 Yf 114
32839 Zarracós OR 42 Sa 95
26291 Zarratón RI 31 Xa 93
31869 Zarrautz NC 21 Yb 91
02327 Zarza, La AB 124 Xf 116
05621 Zarza, La AV 83 Uc 107
06830 Zarza, La BA 117 Te 116
14550 Zarza, La CO 151 Vb 123
30529 Zarza, La MC 141 Yf 119
30179 Zarza, La MC 156 Yd 121
37290 Zarza, La SA 82 Te 104
38579 Zarza, La TF 180 Id 179
47452 Zarza, La VA 66 Vb 101
06611 Zarza-Capilla BA 119 Ue 116
37173 Zarza de Don Beltrán SA 63 Td 101
10710 Zarza de Granadilla CC 82 Tf 107
10189 Zarza de Montánchez CC 117 Tf 113
37253 Zarza de Pumareda, La SA 63 Tc 102
16470 Zarza de Tajo CU 103 Wf 108
30814 Zarzadilla de Totana MC 156 Yb 121
23610 Zarzaíca J 152 Wa 123
10880 Zarza la Mayor CC 97 Ta 109
28293 Zarzalejo MD 85 Ve 105
04213 Zarzales AL 170 Xe 125
29197 Zarzo MA 175 Ve 128
26586 Zarzosa RI 51 Xd 95
09108 Zarzosa de Riópisuerga BU 29 Ve 93
37621 Zarzosilla SA 82 Tf 105
10670 Zarzoso CC 98 Te 108
37621 Zarzoso SA 82 Tf 105
16146 Zarzuela CU 89 Xf 107
11393 Zarzuela, La CA 173 Ub 132
19238 Zarzuela de Galve GU 68 We 102
19237 Zarzuela de Jadraque GU 69 Wf 102
40152 Zarzuela del Monte SG 85 Vd 104
40293 Zarzuela del Pinar SG 67 Ve 101
15850 Zas C 10 Ra 90
15805 Zas de Rei C 11 Rf 91
01139 Zátrate VI 19 Xb 91
42351 Zayas de Báscones SO 49 We 98
42329 Zayas de Torre SO 49 We 98
42351 Zayuelas SO 49 We 98
31438 Zazpe NC 33 Yd 92
09490 Zazuar BU 49 Wc 98
48144 Zeanuri BI 19 Xb 90
48499 Zeberio BI 19 Xb 90
20215 Zegama SS 20 Xe 91
48278 Zeinka BI 20 Xc 89
48140 Zelaia BI 19 Xb 90
48289 Zelaia = Celaya o San Pedro de Mendeja BI 20 Xd 88
48314 Zelaieta (Gautegiz Arteaga) BI 19 Xc 88
30588 Zeneta MC 157 Za 120
26131 Zenzano RI 32 Xd 95
20214 Zerain SS 20 Xe 90
01192 Zerio = Cerio VI 31 Xc 91
20740 Zestoa SS 20 Xe 89
31639 Zibelti NC 21 Yd 91
48500 Zierbena BI 19 Wf 88
31796 Zigaurre NC 21 Yc 90
01138 Zigoitia VI 19 Xb 91
31809 Ziordia NC 32 Xe 91
48278 Ziortza BI 20 Xc 89
20159 Zizurkil SS 20 Xf 89
23749 Zocueca J 137 Wa 120
04890 Zoilas, Los AL 170 Xc 124
31192 Zolina NC 33 Yc 92
48499 Zollo BI 19 Xa 89
44707 Zoma, La TE 91 Zc 104
16193 Zomas, Las CU 105 Xf 109
27730 Zoñán LU 12 Sd 89
10130 Zorita CC 118 Ub 113
37116 Zorita SA 64 Tf 102
37116 Zorita SA 64 Ub 102
37408 Zorita de la Frontera SA 65 Ue 102
47609 Zorita de la Loma VA 47 Uf 95
12311 Zorita del Maestrazgo CS 92 Ze 104
19119 Zorita de los Canes GU 87 Xa 106
05163 Zorita de los Molinos AV 84 Vb 104
34407 Zorita del Páramo P 29 Vd 93
50020 Zorongo, El Z 53 Za 98
26288 Zorraquín RI 31 Wf 95
28292 Zorreras, Las MD 85 Vf 105
29718 Zorrillas, Las MA 167 Ve 128
24791 Zotes del Páramo LE 27 Ub 95
18858 Zoya, La GR 155 Xd 123
02270 Zua, La AB 125 Yd 112
24249 Zuares del Páramo LE 27 Ub 95
01477 Zuaza VI 19 Wf 90
01208 Zuazo VI 32 Xd 91
01430 Zuazo de Cuartango VI 31 Xa 91
31421 Zuazu NC 33 Yd 92
48380 Zubero BI 20 Xc 89
18140 Zubia, La GR 168 Wc 126
48499 Zubialde BI 19 Xa 90
48130 Zubiaur BI 19 Xb 88
31241 Zubielqui NC 32 Xf 92
48192 Zubieta BI 19 Wf 89
31746 Zubieta NC 21 Yb 90
31630 Zubiri NC 33 Yc 91
12125 Zucaina CS 107 Zd 108
31272 Zudaire NC 32 Xf 92
01409 Zudibiarte Ugalde VI 19 Xa 89
50800 Zuera Z 53 Zb 97
31241 Zufía NC 32 Xf 92
21210 Zufre H 148 Td 122
31710 Zugarramurdi NC 21 Yc 89
01195 Zuhatzu = Zuazo de Vitoria VI 31 Xb 91
14870 Zuheros CO 151 Ve 123
18291 Zujaira GR 168 Wa 125
18811 Zújar GR 154 Xa 123
02214 Zulema AB 125 Yd 113
28810 Zulema MD 86 Wd 106
31470 Zulueta NC 33 Yc 92
20750 Zumaia SS 20 Xe 89
29566 Zumaque MA 166 Vb 128
20700 Zumarraga SS 20 Xe 90
09150 Zumel BU 30 Wb 94
01211 Zumento VI 31 Xb 93
31484 Zunzarren NC 33 Yd 91
09245 Zuñeda BU 31 We 93
31284 Zúñiga NC 32 Xe 92
30814 Zúñiga y La Juncosa MC 156 Yb 122
01520 Zurbao = Zurbano VI 31 Xc 91
06720 Zurbarán BA 118 Ub 114
09294 Zurbitu BU 31 Xb 92
33629 Zureda AS 15 Ua 90
04650 Zurgena AL 171 Xf 124
31699 Zuriáin NC 33 Yc 91
39479 Zurita CB 17 Wa 88
22569 Zurita HU 55 Ac 97
22728 Zuriza HU 34 Zb 91
30889 Zurraderas, Las MC 156 Yc 124
31292 Zurucuáin NC 32 Xf 92
09491 Zuzones BU 49 Wd 99

Zuzones | 315 E

AC	Açores	E	Évora	PT Portalegre
AV	Aveiro	FA	Faro	SA Santarém
BE	Beja	GD	Guarda	SE Setúbal
BN	Bragança	L	Lisboa	VC Viana de Castelo
BR	Braga	LE	Leiria	VR Vila Real
C	Coimbra	MA	Madeira	VS Viseu
CB	Castelo Branco	P	Porto	

A

5000-014 Abaças VR 61 Sb 101
4750-009 Abade de Neiva BR
    60 Rc 99
4860-011 Abadim BR 61 Sa 99
5370-010 Abambres BN 62 Se 99
4950 Abedim VC 41 Rc 97
7000 Abegoaria E 130 Sa 116
7240-201 Abegoaria E 131 Se 118
2985 Abegoaria SE 129 Rc 116
7540-011 Abela SE 144 Rc 120
7540 Abela, Estação Ferroviária
    de SE 144 Rc 121
8100 Abelheira FA 159 Re 125
2530-059 Abelheira L 112 Qe 113
6320-591 Abitureira GD 80 Sf 106
2005-129 Abitureiras SA 113 Rb 113
3100-012 Abiúl LE 95 Rc 109
4600-500 Aboadela P 61 Sa 101
5400 Abobeleira VR 43 Sd 98
2785 Abóboda L 128 Qd 116
6120-111 Aboboreira SA 95 Rf 111
4820-011 Aboim BR 61 Rf 99
4600-510 Aboim P 61 Rf 101
4730-010 Aboim da Nóbrega BR
    41 Rd 98
4970 Aboim das Chocas VC
    41 Rd 97
4750-020 Aborim BR 41 Rc 99
2025-011 Abrã SA 113 Rb 112
4560-015 Abragão P 60 Re 102
2200 Abrantes SA 114 Re 112
2200 Abrantes, Estação
    Ferroviária de SA
    114 Re 112
3515 Abravesses VS 79 Sa 104
5370-021 Abreiro BN 62 Se 100
2580-001 Abrigada L 112 Qf 114
6005-250 Abrunhal CB 96 Sd 109
3140-011 Abrunheira C 94 Rb 108
3530-011 Abrunhosa-a-Velha VS
    79 Sc 105
3530-050 Abrunhosa do Mato VS
    79 Sb 105
8550 Abutareira FA 158 Rb 125
9630 Achada AC 177 Ze 121
9240 Achada da Madeira MA
    178 If 152
9230 Achada do Cedro Gordo
    MA 178 Ka 152
7750-401 Achada do Gamo BE
    146 Sc 123
9630 Achadinha AC 177 Ze 121
9225 Achadinha MA 178 Kb 152
2000-321 Achete SA 113 Rb 113
5160-011 Açoreira BN 62 Sf 102
6360 Açoreira GD 80 Se 105
2605 A-da-Beja L 112 Qe 116
4755 Adães BR 60 Rc 99
2510-011 A-da-Gorda LE 112 Qf 112
6300 Adão GD 80 Se 106
2550 Adão L 112 Qf 113
4710 Adaúfe BR 41 Rd 99
6355-010 Ade GD 81 Ta 105
3640-160 A-de-Barros VS 62 Sc 103
5160-002 Adeganha BN 62 Sf 101
7750 A-de-Lede BE 145 Sb 123
2135-001 Adema SA 129 Ra 115
3025 Adémia de Cima C
    78 Rd 107
6185-402 Adgiraldo CB 96 Sb 108
2590 A-do-Baço L 128 Qe 115
6420-501 A-do-Cavaio GD 80 Se 103
7830-011 A-do-Pinto BE 146 Sd 121
5120-011 Adorigo VS 61 Sc 102
2405 A-dos-Barbas LE
    94 Ra 110

3630 A-dos-Bispo VS 62 Sd 103
7670 A-dos-Calças BE
    145 Re 122
2560-005 A-dos-Cunhados L
    112 Qe 114
3750-801 A-dos-Ferreiros AV
    78 Rd 105
6420-351 A-dos-Ferreiros GD
    80 Se 104
2500-001 A-dos-Francos LE
    112 Qf 113
7700 A-dos-Grandes BE
    159 Sa 124
2510-321 A-dos-Negros LE
    112 Qf 112
5000 Adoufe VR 61 Sb 100
2680 Adrião L 112 Qf 116
2000-322 Advagar SA 113 Rb 112
4900-011 Afife VC 41 Ra 98
2525 Afonguia da Baleia LE
    112 Qe 112
5450-100 Afonsim VR 61 Sb 99
8970-011 Afonso Vicente FA
    146 Sc 124
3750 Agadão AV 78 Re 105
4615 Agilde BR 61 Rf 100
2420-169 Agodim LE 94 Rb 110
2100-011 Agolada SA 129 Rc 114
8100 Agostas FA 159 Re 126
4850 Agra BR 42 Rf 99
5400 Agreia VR 43 Sd 98
4820 Agrela BR 61 Re 99
4825 Agrela P 60 Rd 101
3360-051 Agrelo C 78 Rd 107
5460 Agrelos VR 42 Sb 99
5070 Agrelos VR 62 Sc 101
5350 Agrobom BN 63 Ta 100
5335-011 Agrochão BN 44 Sf 98
2305 Água Boa SA 113 Rc 115
7630 Água Branca BE
    144 Rd 122
3750-031 Aguada de Baixo AV
    78 Rd 105
3750-041 Aguada de Cima AV
    78 Rd 105
4840 Água da Pala BR 42 Rf 98
3600 Água de Alte VS 79 Sa 104
2445-011 Água de Madeiros LE
    94 Qf 110
9560 Água de Pau AC
    177 Zc 122
7920 Água de Peixe BE
    130 Sa 119
9200 Água de Pena MA
    178 Kb 152
7570 Água de Porco SE
    144 Rb 119
7570-101 Água Derramada SE
    144 Rd 119
9680 Água do Alto AC
    177 Zd 122
7090 Água Doce E 130 Re 118
8800 Água dos Fusos FA
    160 Sb 125
4825-063 Água Longa P 60 Rd 101
4940-011 Agualonga VC 41 Rc 97
9760 Agualva AC 176 Xe 116
9650 Água Retorta AC
    177 Zf 122
5430 Água Revés VR 62 Sd 99
6090-011 Águas CB 97 Se 108
7750-011 Água Salgada BE
    145 Sb 122
6320-011 Águas Belas GD 80 Sf 106
2240 Águas Belas SA 95 Re 110
2100-301 Águas Belinhas SA
    129 Rd 115
3560-010 Águas Boas VS 80 Sc 103

2965-520 Águas de Moura SE
    129 Rb 117
2965 Águas de Moura,
    Estação Ferroviária de
    SE 129 Rb 117
8800 Águas de Tábuas FA
    159 Sb 125
5400-601 Águas Frias VR
    43 Sd 98
9100 Águas Mansas MA
    178 Kb 152
4830 Aguas Santas BR
    42 Rf 99
4425 Águas Santas P
    60 Rc 101
5000-732 Águas Santas VR
    61 Sc 100
5225 Aguas Vivas BN
    63 Td 100
2205-161 Água Travessa SA
    114 Re 113
4490 Aguçadoura P
    60 Rb 100
3260-021 Aguda LE 95 Re 109
3750-101 Águeda AV 78 Rd 105
4970-051 Aguiã VC 41 Rd 97
4750 Aguiar BR 41 Rc 99
7090 Aguiar E 130 Sa 118
3570-010 Aguiar da Beira GD
    80 Sc 104
4585-009 Aguiar de Sousa P
    60 Rd 102
3750 Aguieira AV 78 Rd 105
3525-501 Aguieira VS 79 Sa 105
3780-621 Aguim AV 78 Rd 106
4870 Aguinchos VR 61 Sa 100
2970 Aiana de Baixo SE
    128 Qf 117
4650-011 Aião P 61 Re 101
4650 Airães P 61 Re 101
4805 Airão (Santa Maria) BR
    60 Rd 100
4805 Airão (São João Batista)
    BR 60 Rd 100
7780-010 Aivados BE 145 Re 122
8365 Aivados e Fontes FA
    159 Rd 125
7080 Ajuda Velha E
    129 Rd 117
4830 Ajude BR 42 Re 99
5340-011 Ala BN 44 Sf 99
6320-051 Alagoas GD 80 Sf 107
7300 Alagoinha PT
    115 Sd 113
7600 Alamo BE 145 Re 121
7750 Alamo BE 146 Sb 123
7750 Álamo BE 146 Se 120
7000 Álamo E 130 Rf 118
7250-101 Alandroal E 131 Sd 116
5400-646 Alanhosa VR 43 Sd 98
4810 Albaçã (São Tomé) BR
    60 Re 100
6300-015 Albardo GD 80 Sf 105
2635 Albarraque L
    128 Qd 116
2005-113 Albergaria SA
    113 Ra 113
3850-501 Albergaria-a-Nova AV
    78 Rd 104
3850-001 Albergaria-a-Velha AV
    78 Rd 104
3850-001 Albergaria-a-Velha e
    Valmaior AV 78 Rd 104
4540 Albergaria das Cabras
    AV 79 Re 103
3100-081 Albergaria dos Doze LE
    94 Rc 110
7940 Albergaria dos Fusos BE
    130 Sa 119

7580-302 Alberge SE 129 Rc 118
7800-601 Albernoa BE 145 Sa 121
6110 Albrunheiro Grande CB
    95 Re 110
8200 Albufeira FA 159 Re 126
2490-001 Alburitel SA 95 Rc 111
2645 Alcabideche L 128 Qd 116
7580 Alcácer do Sal SE
    129 Rc 118
7090-010 Alcáçovas E 130 Rf 118
3530 Alcafache VS 79 Sa 105
6060-011 Alcafozes CB 97 Sf 109
6230 Alcaide CB 96 Sd 108
2640 Alcainão Grande L
    128 Qe 115
6005-001 Alcains CB 96 Sd 109
8500 Alcalá FA 158 Rc 125
7050 Alcalva E 130 Rf 117
2025-030 Alcanede SA 113 Rb 112
2380-011 Alcanena SA 113 Rb 112
2000 Alcanhões SA 113 Rc 113
8365-009 Alcantarilha FA 159 Rd 126
2230 Alcaravela SA 95 Rf 111
7700 Alcaria BE 159 Re 124
6230-022 Alcaria CB 80 Sc 107
8100 Alcaria FA 159 Rf 125
8800 Alcaria FA 160 Sb 125
8970 Alcaria FA 160 Sc 124
8950 Alcaria FA 160 Sd 125
2480-011 Alcaria LE 94 Rb 111
8970 Alcaria Alta FA 146 Sb 124
8800 Alcaria Alta FA 159 Sb 125
7960-111 Alcaria da Serra BE
    145 Sb 119
7780-501 Alcaria do Coelho BE
    145 Sa 123
7750 Alcaria Longa BE
    160 Sa 123
8970-322 Alcaria Queimada FA
    160 Sc 124
7750-013 Alcaria Ruiva BE
    145 Sb 122
7670-011 Alcarias BE 145 Re 122
8970 Alcarias FA 160 Sb 125
8950 Alcarias FA 160 Sc 125
7750 Alcarias de Javazes BE
    160 Sc 123
6430 Alcarva GD 62 Sd 102
2460-001 Alcobaça LE 94 Ra 111
2040-011 Alcobertas SA 113 Ra 112
2890-001 Alcochete SE 128 Ra 116
    Alcofra VS 79 Re 105
2645 Alcoitão L 128 Qd 116
6230-040 Alcongosta CB 96 Sd 108
3450-012 Alcordal VS 79 Re 106
8800 Alcornicosa FA 159 Sb 125
7480 Alcorrego PT 114 Sa 114
8800 Alcorvel FA 160 Sb 125
8970-051 Alcoutim FA 146 Sd 124
6300 Aldeia Viçosa GD
    80 Se 105
4755 Aldeia BR 60 Rc 100
4640 Aldeia P 61 Sa 101
4950 Aldeia VC 41 Rc 96
3660 Aldeia VS 79 Rf 103
3320-152 Aldeia Cimeira C
    95 Sa 108
7200 Aldeia da Barrada E
    131 Sd 118
7630 Aldeia da Bemposta BE
    158 Rc 123
6320-211 Aldeia da Dona GD
    81 Ta 106
2025 Aldeia d'Além SA
    113 Rb 112
    Aldeia da Mata PT
    114 Sb 113
6230 Aldeia da Mata da Rainha
    CB 96 Se 108

7150 Aldeia da Nora E
    115 Sc 116
6320-031 Aldeia da Ponte GD
    81 Ta 106
6100-602 Aldeia da Ribeira CB
    95 Rf 110
6320-041 Aldeia da Ribeira GD
    81 Ta 106
7630-513 Aldeia das Amoreiras BE
    144 Rd 122
3400-201 Aldeia das Dez C
    79 Sa 107
7040 Aldeia da Serra E
    114 Sa 116
7200-012 Aldeia das Pias E
    131 Sd 117
7200-011 Aldeia da Venda E
    131 Sd 117
    Aldeia de Ana de Avis LE
    95 Re 109
6120-151 Aldeia de Eiras SA
    95 Rf 111
7250 Aldeia de Faleiros E
    131 Sd 117
7250 Aldeia de Ferreira E
    131 Sd 117
6230-045 Aldeia de Joanes CB
    96 Sc 108
6090-151 Aldeia de João Pires CB
    97 Sf 108
7100-041 Aldeia de Mourinhos E
    115 Sc 116
3620-010 Aldeia de Nacomba VS
    61 Sc 103
2840 Aldeia de Paio Pires SE
    128 Qf 117
7900-113 Aldeia de Ruins BE
    145 Re 120
6300-255 Aldeia de Santa Madalena
    GD 80 Se 106
6060-021 Aldeia de Santa Margarida
    CB 97 Se 108
6320-050 Aldeia de Santo António GD
    80 Sf 106
6355 Aldeia de São Sebastião
    GD 81 Ta 105
8100-381 Aldeia de Tor FA
    159 Rf 125
7460 Aldeia de Vale de Maceiras
    PT 115 Sc 114
6090-071 Aldeia do Bispo CB
    97 Sf 108
6300 Aldeia do Bispo GD
    80 Se 106
6320 Aldeia do Bispo GD
    81 Ta 107
7555-012 Aldeia do Cano BE
    144 Rc 122
6200 Aldeia do Carvalho CB
    80 Sd 107
7570 Aldeia do Futuro SE
    144 Rc 119
2200-601 Aldeia do Mato SA
    95 Re 111
2970-051 Aldeia do Meco SE
    128 Qe 118
7200 Aldeia do Outeiro E
    131 Sd 118
3100-013 Aldeia do Rio LE
    95 Rc 109
7600-301 Aldeia dos Elvas BE
    145 Re 122
7700-301 Aldeia dos Fernandes BE
    159 Re 123
7670 Aldeia dos Grandaços BE
    145 Re 123
8200 Aldeia dos Matos FA
    159 Re 125

7700 Aldeia dos Neves BE 159 Rf 123
7200 Aldeia dos Orvalhos E 131 Sd 117
6200-501 Aldeia do Souto CB 80 Sd 106
7670-202 Aldeia dos Palheiros BE 159 Re 123
2925 Aldeia dos Pinheiros SE 128 Qf 117
3405-391 Aldeia Formosa C 79 Sa 106
2580-081 Aldeia Galega da Merceana L 112 Qf 114
2580-101 Aldeia Gavinha L 112 Qf 114
5210 Aldeia Nova BN 64 Te 99
6420 Aldeia Nova GD 80 Sd 104
6350 Aldeia Nova GD 81 Ta 104
3560 Aldeia Nova VS 79 Sc 104
5470 Aldeia Nova de Montalegre VR 42 Sb 97
7830 Aldeia Nova de São Bento BE 146 Sd 121
5470-062 Aldeia Nova do Barroso VR 42 Sb 98
6230-050 Aldeia Nova do Cabo CB 96 Sc 108
6360-011 Aldeia Rica GD 80 Se 105
7960 Aldeias BE 131 Sb 120
6290-012 Aldeias GD 80 Sc 106
5110 Aldeias VS 61 Sb 102
7200 Aldeias do Montoito E 131 Sc 117
6320 Aldeia Velha GD 81 Ta 106
7480 Aldeia Velha PT 114 Rf 114
2100-300 Aldeia Velha SA 113 Re 115
7200 Aldeios dos Marmelos E 131 Sd 117
4905 Aldreu BR 41 Rb 99
7830 Alecrinais BE 146 Sd 121
7300 Alegrete PT 115 Se 113
Alegria-Estação BN 62 Sd 101
3230-201 Além de Água C 95 Rd 108
4900 Além do Rio VC 41 Ra 98
3130 Alençarce de Cima C 94 Rc 108
2580-012 Alenquer L 112 Qf 114
7350 Alentisca PT 115 Se 115
5300-401 Alfaião BN 44 Tb 98
6320-081 Alfaiates GD 81 Ta 106
1170 Alfama L 128 Qf 116
5350 Alfândega da Fe BN 62 Ta 100
8400-550 Alfanzina FA 158 Rd 126
5450-120 Alfarela de Jales VR 62 Sc 100
3130 Alfarelos C 94 Rc 108
2970-004 Alfarim SE 128 Qf 118
7800 Alfarrobeira de Baixo BE 145 Sa 121
7800 Alfarrobeira de Cima BE 145 Sa 121
8375 Alfarrobeiras FA 159 Re 125
7580 Alfebre do Mato SE 129 Rd 118
7580 Alfebrinho SE 129 Rd 118
8100 Alfeição FA 159 Rf 126
2460-101 Alfeizerão LE 94 Qf 112
4445-001 Alfena P 60 Rc 101
8550-011 Alferce FA 158 Rd 125
2200-454 Alferrarede SA 95 Re 112
8100-062 Alfontes FA 159 Rf 126
2005 Alforgemel SA 113 Ra 113
2040 Alfovês SA 113 Rb 113
6030 Alfrivida CB 96 Sc 110
7900-011 Alfundão BE 130 Rf 120
7750 Algodor BE 145 Sb 122
2950-051 Algeruz SE 129 Rb 117
7300 Algoa PT 115 Sc 112
7630-013 Algoceira BE 158 Rb 123
6440 Algodres GD 62 Sf 103
6370 Algodres GD 80 Sc 105
5200-351 Algosinho BN 63 Tc 101
5230 Algóso BN 63 Tc 100
8365-055 Algoz FA 159 Re 126
2550-012 Alguber L 112 Qf 113
2725-003 Algueirão L 112 Qd 116
3090 Alhadas C 94 Rb 107
3650-010 Alhais VS 80 Sb 103
3650 Alhais de Cima VS 80 Sb 103
2600-401 Alhandra L 112 Qf 115
4750-057 Alheira BR 41 Rc 99
Alheiro Negro SA 113 Rd 114
4690 Alhões VS 61 Rf 103
2860-004 Alhos Vedros SE 128 Qf 117
5070 Alijo VR 62 Sd 101
5300 Alimonte BN 44 Ta 98
3780 Aljaraz AV 78 Rd 106
8670 Aljezur FA 158 Rb 125
2460-601 Aljubarrota LE 94 Ra 111
7600 Aljustrel BE 145 Rf 121
2065 Alkoentre L 112 Ra 113
3450 Almaça VS 79 Re 106
6000-001 Almaceda CB 96 Sc 108
2800-001 Almada SE 128 Qf 116
8950-012 Almada de Ouro FA 160 Sd 125
8600 Almadena FA 158 Rb 126
9580 Almagreira AC 177 Zf 127
Almagreira LE 94 Rc 109
3040 Almalaguês C 95 Rd 108
8135 Almancil FA 159 Rf 126
3515 Almargem VS 79 Sa 104
2715-210 Almargem do Bispo L 112 Qe 115
8800 Almarginho FA 160 Sa 125
8300-010 Almarjão FA 158 Rd 125
6350 Almeida GD 81 Ta 104
6300-210 Almeidinha GD 80 Sf 105
7780-101 Almeirim BE 145 Rf 122
2380 Almeirim SA 113 Rb 112
2080 Almeirim SA 113 Rc 113
5150-011 Almendra GD 62 Sf 103
Almendra-Estación BN 62 Sf 102
7000 Almendres E 130 Rf 117
7700 Almodôvar BE 159 Rf 123
7700 Almodôvar-a-Velha BE 159 Rf 123
6440 Almofala GD 81 Ta 103
2500-331 Almofala LE 112 Qf 112
3600 Almofala VS 61 Sb 103
4640-101 Almofrela P 61 Rf 101
7630-017 Almograve BE 144 Rb 123
2970-001 Almoinha SE 128 Qf 118
2715-244 Almornos L 112 Qe 116
3250-021 Almoster LE 95 Rd 109
2005-111 Almoster SA 113 Rb 113
7750 Almuinha Velha BE 160 Sc 123
6050-011 Alpalhão PT 115 Sc 112
6230-056 Alpedrinha CB 96 Sd 108
2460-231 Alpedriz LE 94 Ra 111
4575 Alpendurada P 60 Re 102
2090 Alpiarça SA 113 Rc 113
8150-014 Alportel FA 160 Sa 125
8200-552 Alpouvar FA 159 Re 126
3090 Alqueidão C 94 Rb 108
2460 Alqueidão LE 94 Ra 111
2350 Alqueidão SA 94 Rc 111
2300 Alqueidão SA 95 Re 111
2480-013 Alqueidão da Serra LE 94 Rb 111
2480 Alqueidão de Arrimal LE 94 Ra 111
2025-140 Alqueidão do Mato SA 113 Rb 112
3850-301 Alquerubim AV 78 Rc 105
7220 Alqueva E 131 Sc 119
9700 Altares AC 176 Xe 116
8100-012 Alte FA 159 Re 125
7440 Alter do Chão PT 115 Sc 113
8600 Alto da Cerca FA 158 Rb 126
2040-063 Alto da Serra SA 112 Ra 112
8100 Alto do Serra FA 159 Rf 126
8100-154 Alto Fica FA 159 Rf 125
8950-414 Altura FA 160 Sc 125
5460-010 Alturas do Barroso VR 42 Sb 98
3600-394 Alva VS 79 Sa 103
5030 Alvacões do Corgo VR 61 Sb 101
5050 Alvações do Tanha VR 61 Sb 101
4870-011 Alvadia VR 61 Sb 100
2480-032 Alvados LE 94 Rb 111
6030-151 Alvaiade CB 96 Sb 110
3250-100 Alvaiázere LE 95 Rd 110
2495 Alvaijar SA 94 Rc 111
7565-011 Alvalade SE 144 Rd 121
7830 Alvarão BE 131 Sc 120
4960 Alvaredo VC 42 Re 96
5320-010 Alvaredos BN 44 Sf 98
4745 Alvarelhos P 60 Rc 101
5430 Alvarelhos VR 43 Sd 98
4540 Alvarenga AV 61 Rf 103
7750-501 Álvares BE 145 Sb 123
3330 Álvares C 95 Rf 108
3750-361 Alvarim AV 78 Rc 105
6160 Álvaro CB 95 Sa 109
4905-300 Alvas VC 41 Rb 99
2205-101 Alvega SA 95 Rf 112
Alveite Grande C 79 Re 107
4755 Alvelos BR 60 Rc 99
6300-030 Alvendre GD 80 Se 105
3350-202 Alve Peq C 79 Re 107
6400-101 Alverca da Beira GD 80 Se 104
2615-001 Alverca do Ribatejo L 128 Qf 115
7750-402 Alves BE 146 Sc 123
4540-293 Alviada AV 60 Rd 103
2305-061 Alviobeira SA 95 Rd 110
4860 Alvite BR 61 Rf 100
4870 Alvite VR 61 Sb 100
3620-021 Alvite VS 61 Sb 103
5370-030 Alvites BN 62 Sf 99
7920 Alvito BE 130 Sa 119
4750 Alvito BR 41 Rc 99
7920 Alvito, Estação Ferroviária de BE 130 Rf 119
6150-011 Alvito da Beira CB 96 Sb 110
6270-012 Alvoco da Serra GD 80 Sb 107
3400-301 Alvoco das Várzeas C 79 Sa 107
3420-161 Alvoeira C 79 Rf 107
8500-002 Alvor FA 158 Rc 126
4970 Alvora VC 41 Rd 97
2350-011 Alvorão SA 95 Rc 111
3240-402 Alvorge C 95 Rd 109
2500-330 Alvorninha LE 112 Qf 112
4585 Alvre P 60 Rd 102
4900 Amada VC 41 Ra 98
2700 Amadora L 128 Qe 116
4600-001 Amarante P 61 Rf 101
8100 Amarela FA 159 Rf 125
7885-011 Amareleja BE 131 Se 119
4640-102 Amarelhe P 61 Rf 102
4720 Amares BR 42 Rd 99
8800 Amaro FA 160 Sb 126
4935 Amarosa VC 41 Ra 99
3045 Ameal C 95 Rc 107
5140 Amedo BN 62 Se 101
4960 Ameijoeira VC 42 Re 97
7570-104 Ameiras de Baixo SE 144 Rc 119
8100-050 Ameixial FA 159 Sa 124
6120 Amêndoa SA 95 Rf 111
8365-231 Amendoais FA 159 Re 125
7750 Amendoeira BE 145 Sa 122
7750 Amendoeira BE 146 Sb 122
5340-021 Amendoeira BN 62 Ta 99
8100 Amendoeira FA 159 Sa 125
8800 Amendoeira FA 160 Sb 125
2025 Amiães de Cima SA 113 Rb 112
2025-300 Amiais de Baixo SA 113 Rb 112
5470-402 Amiar VR 42 Sa 98
7220 Amieira E 131 Sc 119
2430 Amieira LE 94 Ra 110
7425 Amieira PT 114 Re 114
2965 Amieira SE 129 Rb 116
Amieira, Estação Ferroviária de C 94 Rb 108
3090 Amieira Calvete C 94 Rb 108
6040 Amieira Cova PT 114 Sa 112
6050-103 Amieira do Tejo PT 96 Sb 111
6160 Amieira-Oleiros CB 96 Sa 109
3140-021 Amieiro C 78 Rc 107
5070 Amieiro VR 62 Sd 101
3330 Amioso C 95 Rf 108
6100-609 Amioso CB 95 Rf 109
4925 Amonde VC 41 Rb 98
2400-759 Amor LE 94 Ra 110
2845-125 Amora SE 128 Qf 117
7630 Amoreiras-Odemira, Estação Ferroviária de BE 144 Rd 122
8200 Amoreira FA 159 Re 126
8800 Amoreira FA 160 Sb 124
6355 Amoreira GD 81 Sf 105
2620 Amoreira L 112 Qe 116
2510 Amoreira LE 112 Qe 112
2200-752 Amoreira SA 95 Re 112
3780-011 Amoreira da Gândara AV 78 Rc 106
7630 Amoreiras BE 144 Rd 122
4495-101 Amorim P 60 Rb 100
4495 Amorim de Cima P 60 Rb 100
3780-200 Anadia AV 78 Rd 106
3040 Anaguéis C 95 Rd 108
4990 Anais VC 41 Rc 98
6090 Anascer CB 80 Se 107
3060-070 Ança C 78 Rc 107
3780-051 Ancas AV 78 Rc 106
4640-003 Ancede P 61 Rf 102
3305-010 Anceriz C 79 Sa 107
2480-072 Andam LE 94 Ra 111
3025-329 Andorinha C 78 Rc 107
Andrães VR 61 Sb 101
2230-101 Andreus SA 95 Rf 111
7960 Andreza BE 130 Sb 120
5425-011 Anelhe VR 43 Sc 98
4455 Angeiras P 60 Rb 101
3850-401 Angeja AV 78 Rc 104
9701 Angra do Heroismo AC 176 Xe 117
5230-020 Angueira BN 45 Td 99
4935 Anha VC 41 Rb 99
4850 Anissó BR 42 Rf 99
9580 Anjos AC 177 Zf 126
4850 Anjos BR 42 Rf 99
3150-012 Anobra C 95 Rc 108
Anreade VS 61 Sa 102
3240-101 Ansião C 95 Rd 109
6350 Ansul GD 81 Ta 105
4500 Anta AV 60 Rc 102
3040-557 Antanhol C 95 Rd 107
4740-011 Antas BR 41 Rb 99
2500 Antas LE 112 Qf 112
7425 Antas PT 114 Re 114
4940 Antas VC 41 Rc 97
5060-421 Antas VR 61 Sc 101
3630 Antas VS 61 Sa 102
3630 Antas VS 62 Sd 103
3550 Antas VS 80 Sc 105
3680-171 Antelas VS 79 Re 104
5470 Antigo VR 42 Sa 98
5470 Antigo de Arcos VR 43 Sc 98
4820-005 Antime BR 61 Rf 100
7300 Antiqueira PT 115 Sd 112
3105 Antões LE 94 Rb 109
3025 Antuzede C 78 Rd 107
7700 Apariça BE 130 Sa 120
Apaúlinha SE 144 Rc 119
2970-145 Apostiça SE 128 Qf 117
8100 Apra FA 159 Sa 126
4740-030 Apúlia BR 60 Rb 100
8100 Águas Frias FA 159 Re 125
3885-002 Arada AV 60 Rc 103
3830 Aradas AV 78 Rc 105
6090-211 Aranhas CB 97 Sf 108
2205 Aranhas SA 114 Re 113
8500 Arão FA 158 Rc 125
4930-001 Arão VC 41 Rc 96
3140-022 Arazede C 78 Rc 107
4990 Arca VC 41 Rc 98
3475 Arca VS 79 Re 105
5060 Arça VR 61 Sc 101
5340 Arcas BN 44 Sf 99
Arcas VS 61 Sb 102
3630 Arcas VS 62 Sd 102
2640 Archada L 128 Qd 115
9270 Archadas de Cruz MA 178 Ie 151
2460 Arcipreste LE 94 Qf 111
5360 Arco BN 62 Sf 101
9370 Arco da Calheta MA 178 If 152
4860 Arco de Baúlhe BR 61 Sa 100
9230 Arco de São Jorge MA 178 Ka 152
7100 Arcos E 115 Sc 115
4480-011 Arcos P 60 Rb 100
4990 Arcos VC 41 Rc 98
5470 Arcos VR 43 Sb 98
5120 Arcos VS 62 Sc 102
7100 Arcos, Estação Ferroviária de E 115 Sc 116
4970 Arcos de Valdevez VC 41 Rd 97
5425-021 Arcossó VR 43 Sc 99
4730 Arcozelo BR 41 Rc 99
4750 Arcozelo BR 60 Rc 99
6290 Arcozelo GD 80 Sc 105
4410 Arcozelo P 60 Rc 102
4990 Arcozelo VC 41 Rc 98
3680 Arcozelo das Maias VS 79 Re 104
3620 Arcozelos VS 61 Sc 103
5460-100 Ardãos VR 43 Sc 98
4820-007 Ardegão BR 61 Rf 100
4990-535 Ardegão VC 41 Rc 99
2460-817 Ardido LE 94 Ra 112
8200 Areeiro FA 159 Re 125
8100 Areeiro FA 159 Rf 126
3260-070 Arega LE 95 Re 109
2560 Areia L 112 Qd 114
4485 Areia P 60 Rb 101
6040 Areia PT 95 Sa 111
2530-065 Areia Branca L 112 Qe 113
3860 Areia de Gonde AV 78 Rc 104
5140 Areias BN 62 Se 101
4750 Areias BR 60 Rc 99
8700 Areias FA 160 Sb 126
2240 Areias SA 95 Rd 110
9950 Areie Larga AC 176 Wc 117
2510-191 Arelho LE 112 Qe 112
2440 Arengões LE 94 Rb 111
4705-472 Arentim BR 60 Rc 100
6050-201 Arez PT 96 Sb 112
4910-035 Arga de Baixo VC 41 Rb 97
4910-040 Arga de Cima VC 41 Rb 97
4910 Arga de São João VC 41 Rb 97
5340-171 Argana BN 43 Sf 98
3300-011 Arganil C 79 Rf 107
6120-211 Arganil SA 95 Sa 110
2350 Argea SA 95 Rd 111
4910 Argela VC 41 Rb 97
5400 Argenil VR 43 Se 97
5445 Argeriz VR 43 Sd 99
6400-601 Argomil GD 80 Se 105
4505-001 Argoncilhe AV 60 Rc 102
5230-025 Argozelo BN 44 Tc 99
3610-101 Arguedeira VS 61 Sb 102
7700 Arharrua BE 159 Rf 124
5110 Arícera VS 61 Sc 102
3620-080 Ariz VS 61 Sc 103
8365 Armação de Pera FA 159 Rd 126
3320-101 Armadouro C 96 Sa 108
5110 Armamar VS 61 Sb 102
4820-010 Armil BR 61 Re 100
5140 Arnal BN 62 Sd 101
3640-011 Arnas VS 80 Sd 103
2755 Arneiro L 128 Qd 116
7520 Arneiro SE 144 Rb 121
2000 Arneiro das Milharicas SA 113 Rb 112
2120 Arneiros SA 129 Rb 114
2565 Arneirós L 112 Qe 114
4890-051 Arnoia BR 61 Rf 100
4820 Arnosela BR 61 Rf 100
4775 Arnoso BR 60 Rc 100
4770 Arnoso BR 60 Rd 100
8950 Aroeira FA 160 Sc 125
2130 Aroeira SA 129 Rb 115
3100-017 Aroeiras LE 95 Rc 109
3730 Arões AV 79 Re 104
4820 Arões BR 60 Re 100
4800 Arosa BR 60 Re 99
4860 Arosa BR 61 Sa 99
4540-098 Arouca AV 60 Re 103
7580 Arouca SE 144 Rd 119
2420-001 Arrabal LE 94 Rb 110
2950 Arraiados SE 129 Rb 117
6060 Arraial da Poupa CB 97 Sf 110
7040 Arraiolos E 130 Sa 116
3750 Arrancada AV 78 Rd 105
3105 Arrancada LE 94 Rc 109
2630-011 Arranhó L 128 Qf 115
7425 Arrão de Baixo PT 113 Re 114
4595 Arreigada P 60 Rd 101
2840-142 Arrentela SE 128 Qf 117
3700 Arrifana AV 60 Rc 103
5340 Arrifana BN 62 Ta 99
3150 Arrifana C 95 Rc 108
6300 Arrifana GD 80 Se 105
6320 Arrifana GD 81 Ta 105
2065-311 Arrifana L 113 Ra 113
Arrifana de Cima C 79 Re 107
9500 Arrifes AC 177 Zb 122
9930 Arrife Terras AC 177 We 118
2480-043 Arrimal LE 94 Ra 112
8970 Arrisada FA 159 Sb 124
8300 Arrochela FA 158 Rd 125
8800 Arroios FA 160 Sb 126
5000 Arroios VR 61 Sb 101
7340 Arronches PT 115 Se 114
7340 Arronches, Estação Ferroviária de PT 115 Sd 114
Arroteia LE 94 Rc 109
2040-031 Arrouquelas SA 113 Ra 113
2040 Arruda dos Pisões SA 113 Ra 113
2630-110 Arruda dos Vinhos L 128 Qf 115
4480-046 Árvore P 60 Rb 100
7670 Arzil BE 144 Rd 122
3045-319 Arzila C 95 Rc 107
4905 Aslvarães VC 41 Rb 99
Asnela BR 61 Sa 99
3040-657 Assafarge C 78 Rd 108

Assafarge | 317 P

8800 Carne Cerva FA 160 Sb 125
Carneiro P 61 Sa 101
8800-152 Carneiros FA 160 Sb 125
6420-321 Carnicães GD 80 Se 104
3060 Carniceira C 78 Rb 106
7630-518 Carniceiro BE 144 Rd 123
Carnide L 128 Qe 116
3105 Carnide LE 94 Rb 109
2580 Carnota L 128 Qf 114
5320 Caroceiras BN 43 Sf 97
3050 Carquejo AV 78 Rd 107
4660 Cárquere VS 61 Sa 102
5300 Carragoosa BN 44 Tb 97
6270 Carragozela GD 79 Sb 106
4970 Carralcova VC 42 Rd 97
Carrapatal SE 129 Rb 116
5340-070 Carrapatas BN 62 Ta 99
Carrapateira FA 158 Ra 125
8800 Carrapateira FA 160 Sc 125
6360-040 Carrapichana GD 80 Sd 105
7665 Carrascal BE 158 Rc 123
7040 Carrascal E 130 Rf 118
7090 Carrascal E 130 Rf 118
Carrascal, Estação Ferroviária de SA 95 Rd 111
8670-417 Carrascalinho FA 158 Rb 124
3105 Carrascos LE 94 Rb 108
3330 Carrasqueira C 95 Rf 108
8375 Carrasqueira FA 159 Re 125
8200 Carrasqueiro FA 159 Re 125
8100 Carrasqueiro FA 159 Sa 125
5140 Carrazeda de Ansiaes BN 62 Se 101
5300 Carrazedo BN 44 Ta 98
Carrazedo BR 41 Rd 99
4860 Carrazedo BR 42 Rf 99
5120 Carrazedo VS 61 Sc 102
5450-181 Carrazedo da Cabugueira VR 43 Sc 99
5445-151 Carrazedo de Montenegro VR 62 Sd 99
5450-262 Carrazedo do Alvão VR 61 Sb 100
4900 Carreço VC 41 Ra 98
2580-463 Carregado L 128 Ra 114
2600 Carregado, Estação Ferroviária de L 128 Ra 115
6150 Carregais CB 96 Sb 110
2100 Carregais SA 129 Re 115
6000 Carregal CB 96 Sd 110
3640 Carregal VS 62 Sc 103
2205 Carregal Cimeiro SA 114 Sa 112
3430-001 Carregal do Sal VS 79 Rf 106
2100 Carregoiceira SA 129 Rd 115
3840 Carregosa AV 78 Rc 105
3720 Carregosa AV 78 Rd 103
6120 Carregueira SA 95 Rf 111
2140 Carregueira SA 113 Rd 112
2135 Carregueira SA 129 Ra 115
7600 Carregueiro BE 145 Rf 122
2305-204 Carregueiros SA 95 Rd 111
4775 Carreira BR 60 Rc 100
4765 Carreira BR 60 Rd 100
2425-251 Carreira LE 94 Ra 109
4825 Carreira P 60 Rd 101
7300 Carreiras PT 115 Sd 112
3105 Carriço LE 94 Rb 109
2300 Carril SA 95 Rd 111
2460-480 Carris LE 94 Ra 112
3070 Carromeu P 78 Rb 106
7750-805 Carros BE 160 Sb 123
3100 Cartaria LE 95 Rc 110
2070-003 Cartaxo SA 113 Rb 114
3105-310 Caruncho LE 94 Rc 109
5090-031 Carva VR 62 Sc 100
6100 Carvahal CB 95 Rf 109
6100 Carvaihos CB 95 Re 109
3650 Carvalha VS 61 Sb 103
5370 Carvalhais BN 62 Sf 99
3090 Carvalhais C 94 Rb 108
3660 Carvalhais VS 79 Rf 104
5160 Carvalhal BN 62 Ta 101
4755 Carvalhal BR 60 Rc 99
6250 Carvalhal CB 80 Se 107
6100 Carvalhal CB 95 Sa 109
8100 Carvalhal FA 159 Sa 125
8800 Carvalhal FA 160 Sb 125
6430 Carvalhal GD 80 Se 103
6400 Carvalhal GD 80 Se 105

6400 Carvalhal GD 81 Sf 104
6320 Carvalhal GD 81 Ta 106
2460 Carvalhal LE 94 Ra 112
2540-327 Carvalhal LE 112 Qf 113
7330-307 Carvalhal PT 115 Sd 112
7300-562 Carvalhal PT 115 Sd 113
7300 Carvalhal PT 115 Se 113
2230-862 Carvalhal SA 95 Re 111
7570 Carvalhal SE 144 Rb 119
3460 Carvalhal VS 79 Rf 105
3600-394 Carvalhal VS 79 Sa 103
3515 Carvalhal VS 79 Sa 104
3560 Carvalhal VS 80 Sb 104
2500-404 Carvalhal Benfeito LE 112 Qf 112
2350-693 Carvalhal da Aroeira SA 95 Rc 111
6270 Carvalhal da Loiça GD 79 Sb 106
7300 Carvalhal das Vinhas PT 115 Sd 113
3130 Carvalhal de Azóia C 94 Rb 108
3670 Carvalhal de Vermilhas VS 79 Rf 105
6300-055 Carvalhal Meão GD 80 Sf 106
4540-369 Carvalhal Redondo AV 60 Rd 103
3525-401 Carvalhal Redondo VS 79 Sa 105
5300 Carvalhas BN 44 Tc 98
3885 Carvalheira AV 60 Rc 103
7900 Carvalheira BE 145 Rf 120
4840 Carvalheira BR 42 Re 98
5460-130 Carvalhelhos VR 42 Sb 98
8950 Carvalhinhos FA 160 Sc 125
3880 Carvalho AV 78 Rc 103
4890 Carvalho BR 61 Rf 100
3360 Carvalho C 78 Rd 107
3320 Carvalho C 95 Sa 108
8550 Carvalho FA 158 Rc 124
5460 Carvalho VR 42 Sb 98
5070 Carvalho VR 62 Sd 100
5360-050 Carvalho de Egas BN 62 Se 101
4600-570 Carvalho do Rei P 61 Rf 101
4755 Carvalhos BR 60 Rc 100
4415-130 Carvalhos P 60 Rc 102
4590 Carvalhosa P 60 Rd 101
3600 Carvalhosa VS 61 Sa 103
Carvalhos de Figueiredo, Estação Ferroviária de SA 95 Rd 111
5090 Carvas VR 62 Sd 100
5160-069 Carviçais BN 63 Ta 101
2425-334 Carvide LE 94 Ra 109
2655 Carvoeira L 112 Qd 115
2565 Carvoeira L 112 Qf 114
3320-302 Carvoeiro C 95 Sa 108
8400 Carvoeiro FA 158 Rd 126
6120 Carvoeiro SA 96 Sa 111
4905 Carvoeiro VC 41 Rb 99
7050-520 Casa Branca E 130 Rf 117
7470 Casa Branca PT 114 Sb 115
7595 Casa Branca SE 144 Rd 119
2005 Casa da Charneca SA 113 Rb 113
2500 Casa da Marina LE 112 Ra 112
9760 Casa da Ribeira AC 176 Xf 116
4820-573 Casadela BR 61 Rf 100
2970 Casa do Infantado SE 128 Qe 117
4620 Casais P 60 Re 101
2305 Casais SA 95 Rd 111
5470 Casais VR 42 Sa 99
2435-033 Casais da Abadia SA 95 Rc 110
2460 Casais da Charneca LE 94 Ra 112
7885 Casais da Freixeira BE 131 Se 119
3240 Casais da Granja C 95 Rd 109
2500-535 Casais da Serra LE 112 Ra 113
2050 Casais de Monte Godelo L 112 Ra 114
2200-458 Casais de Revelhos SA 95 Re 111
2460-715 Casais de Santa Teresa LE 94 Ra 111
3130 Casais de São Jorge C 95 Rc 109
2640-206 Casais de São Lourenço L 128 Qd 114

3025-341 Casais de Vera Cruz C 78 Rc 107
2480 Casais do Chão da Mendiga LE 94 Ra 111
3600-454 Casais do Monte VS 79 Sa 104
3140 Casais dos Faiscas C 78 Rb 107
2070-367 Casais dos Penedos SA 113 Ra 114
7885 Casais dos Trincalhos BE 131 Sd 119
2350-223 Casais Martanes SA 94 Rc 111
2040-015 Casais Monizes SA 113 Ra 112
2380-562 Casais Robustos SA 94 Rb 111
3060 Casal C 78 Rc 107
4660 Casal VS 61 Sa 102
2200 Casalão SA 114 Re 112
3050-151 Casal Comba AV 78 Rd 106
6100-017 Casal Cutelo CB 95 Rf 109
6300 Casal da Cinza GD 80 Sf 105
3220-406 Casal da Senhora C 78 Re 108
3200 Casal de Ermio C 95 Re 108
5085-010 Casal de Loivos VR 62 Sc 101
3300-129 Casal de São José C 79 Rf 107
3070-041 Casal de São Tomé C 78 Rb 106
3300 Casal do Frade C 79 Rf 107
6060 Casal do Meio CB 97 Se 109
3130-002 Casal do Redinho C 94 Rc 108
2200-631 Casal do Rei SA 95 Re 111
2435-522 Casal do Ribeiro SA 95 Rc 110
3130 Casal dos Barcelos C 94 Rb 108
2435-001 Casal dos Bernardos SA 95 Rc 110
3090 Casal dos Cunhas C 78 Rb 107
3060 Casal dos Netos C 78 Rb 106
2090 Casalinho SA 113 Rc 113
2560 Casalinho de Alfaiate L 112 Qd 114
2495-353 Casalinho Farto SA 94 Rc 111
2400-763 Casalito LE 94 Ra 110
3720 Casal Nova AV 60 Rc 103
6110 Casal Nova CB 95 Rf 111
2530 Casal Nova L 112 Qe 113
3330 Casal Novo C 95 Rf 108
2425 Casal Novo LE 94 Rb 109
6370-021 Casal Vasco GD 80 Sc 105
2460-199 Casal Velho LE 94 Qf 112
2230-002 Casal Velho SA 95 Rf 111
3090-433 Casal Verde C 94 Rb 108
3080 Casa Nova C 78 Rb 107
6120 Casa Nova de São Bento SA 95 Rf 110
8550 Casa Queimada FA 159 Rd 125
4860 Casares BR 61 Rf 99
2705 Casas L 112 Qd 116
8800 Casas Atlas FA 160 Sb 125
8800-016 Casas Baixas FA 160 Sb 124
6120-218 Casas da Ribeira SA 95 Rf 110
8500 Casas da Senhora do Verde FA 158 Rc 125
6185-401 Casas da Zebreira CB 96 Sb 108
5400 Casas de Monforte VR 43 Sd 98
6420 Casas de Moreira GD 80 Se 104
7555-025 Casas Grandes SE 144 Rb 122
3240 Casas Novas C 95 Rd 108
7050 Casas Novas E 113 Rd 116
7340 Casas Novas PT 115 Sd 114
7555 Casas Novas SE 144 Rc 122
7200 Casas Novas dos Mares E 131 Sd 117
7670 Casas Velhas BE 144 Re 123
7750 Casa Velha BE 159 Sa 123
2495 Casa Velha SA 94 Rc 111

7700 Casa Velha da Botelha BE 159 Sa 123
2750 Cascais L 128 Qd 116
9900 Cascalho AC 176 Wb 117
4585-685 Casconha P 60 Rd 102
7580 Casebres SE 129 Rd 117
6225-101 Casegas CB 96 Sb 107
8550 Caseis FA 158 Rc 125
7780 Casével BE 145 Re 122
7780 Casével BE 145 Re 122
3150-255 Casével C 95 Rc 108
2000-460 Casével SA 113 Rc 112
3560 Casfreiras VS 80 Sb 104
3150-272 Casmilo C 95 Rd 108
3630-070 Castainço VS 62 Sd 103
5200 Castanheira BE 63 Tc 100
3320 Castanheira C 96 Sa 107
6150 Castanheira CB 96 Sa 110
6420 Castanheira GD 80 Sd 103
6300 Castanheira GD 80 Sf 105
2240-332 Castanheira SA 95 Re 110
4940 Castanheira VC 41 Rc 97
5470 Castanheira VR 42 Sb 98
6200 Castanheira de Cima CB 80 Sd 107
3280 Castanheira de Pêra LE 95 Re 108
2600-600 Castanheira do Ribatejo L 128 Ra 115
3750-373 Castanheira do Vouga AV 78 Rd 105
3750 Castanheira do Vouga AV 78 Rd 105
7520 Castanheiro SE 144 Rb 121
5130-021 Castanheiro do Sul VS 62 Sc 102
7750-602 Castanhos BE 160 Sa 123
5160-071 Castedo BN 62 Se 101
5070 Castedo VR 62 Sd 101
6430-041 Casteição GD 80 Se 103
7670 Castelão BE 145 Re 123
8800 Castelão FA 160 Sa 125
5340-082 Castelãos BN 63 Ta 99
5400-609 Castelãos VR 43 Sc 98
6320-121 Casteleiro GD 80 Se 107
7750 Casteleja BE 160 Sa 124
7670 Castelejo BE 145 Re 123
6230-152 Castelejo CB 96 Sc 108
3440 Castelejo VS 79 Rf 106
3105-159 Castelhanas LE 94 Rb 109
8970 Castelhanos FA 160 Sb 124
8950 Castelhanos FA 160 Sd 125
5350 Castelo BN 63 Ta 100
4890 Castelo BR 61 Rf 100
6100 Castelo CB 95 Re 109
6120 Castelo SA 95 Rf 111
5090 Castelo VR 62 Sd 100
3620 Castelo VS 61 Sc 102
3475 Castelo VS 79 Re 105
3660 Castelo VS 79 Rf 104
6355-042 Castelo Bom GD 81 Ta 105
9900 Castelo Branco AC 176 Wb 117
5200-130 Castelo Branco BN 63 Tb 101
6000 Castelo Branco CB 96 Sd 104
4475 Castêlo da Maia P 60 Rc 101
4550 Castelo de Paiva AV 60 Re 102
3550 Castelo de Penalva VS 79 Sc 105
7320-101 Castelo de Vide PT 115 Sd 112
7320 Castelo de Vide, Estação Ferroviária de PT 115 Sd 112
4935 Castelo do Neiva VC 41 Rb 99
3730 Castelões AV 78 Rd 104
3465 Castelões VS 79 Rf 105
5150-101 Castelo Melhor GD 62 Sf 102
6355-051 Castelo Mendo GD 81 Ta 105
6230-160 Castelo Novo CB 96 Sd 108
2300-226 Castelo Novo SA 95 Rf 111
Castelo-Novo, Estação Ferroviária de CB 96 Sd 108
6440-031 Castelo Rodrigo GD 81 Ta 103
7000 Castelos E 130 Rf 117
7630 Castelo Velho BE 144 Rd 121

3040-713 Castelo Viegas C 78 Rd 108
4630-158 Castilho P 61 Rf 102
5300-471 Castrelos BN 44 Ta 97
5430 Castro VR 62 Se 99
3600-069 Castro Daire VS 61 Sa 103
5300 Castro de Avelãs BN 44 Tb 98
4960 Castro Laboreiro VC 42 Rf 96
8950-121 Castro Marim FA 160 Sd 125
5340-520 Castro Roupal BN 63 Tb 99
7780-090 Castro Verde BE 145 Rf 122
5350-201 Castro Vicente BN 63 Ta 100
3140-032 Catarruchos C 78 Rb 107
7555-030 Catifarras SE 144 Rc 122
6290-061 Cativelos GD 80 Sb 105
3740-034 Catives AV 78 Re 104
6150-116 Catraia Cimeira CB 96 Sb 110
2705-569 Catribana L 112 Qd 115
8550 Causino FA 158 Rd 124
3060 Cavadas C 78 Rb 106
6300 Cavadoude GD 80 Se 105
7160 Cavaleira E 131 Sd 116
7630 Cavaleiro BE 158 Rb 123
3050 Cavaleiros AV 78 Rd 107
2100-650 Cavaleiros SA 113 Rc 115
3350 Cavalho C 78 Re 107
3140 Cavalinha C 94 Rb 107
8100 Cavalos FA 159 Sa 125
7780 Cavandela BE 145 Rf 122
9970 Caveira AC 176 Tf 112
7570 Caveira SE 144 Rb 120
4950-200 Cavenca VC 42 Re 96
3505-111 Cavernães VS 79 Sb 104
4860 Cavez BR 61 Sa 99
2420 Cawieira LE 94 Rb 110
2435-019 Caxarias SA 95 Rc 110
2760 Caxias L 128 Qe 116
4480 Caxinas P 60 Rb 100
6030-114 Cebolais de Baixo CB 96 Sc 110
6000-500 Cebolais de Cima CB 96 Sc 110
5370-101 Cedães BN 62 Sf 100
5370 Cedainhos BN 62 Sf 100
5155-006 Cedovim GD 62 Se 102
3740-014 Cedrim AV 78 Rd 104
9970 Cedro AC 176 Tf 112
9900 Cedros AC 176 Wb 117
6060 Cegonhas Novas CB 97 Se 110
3030-848 Ceira C 95 Rd 107
3320-078 Ceiroquinho C 95 Sa 108
4950 Ceivães VC 42 Rd 96
2460 Cela LE 94 Qf 111
4960 Cela VC 42 Re 96
5400 Cela VR 43 Sd 98
5320-021 Celas BN 44 Ta 98
3300-204 Celavisa C 95 Rf 107
5430 Celeiros VR 43 Sd 99
5060 Celeiros VR 62 Sc 101
4705 Celeirós BR 60 Rd 99
6360 Celorico da Beira GD 80 Sd 105
4890-209 Celorico de Basto BR 61 Rf 100
2305-417 Cem Soldos SA 95 Rd 111
8200-465 Centieira FA 159 Re 126
4820 Cepães BR 61 Re 100
5470 Cepeda VR 43 Sb 98
4600-591 Cepelos P 61 Rf 101
4990 Cepões VC 41 Rc 98
5100-344 Cepões VS 61 Sb 102
3505 Cepões VS 79 Sb 104
3300-222 Cepos C 79 Sa 108
7800 Cerca BE 145 Sa 122
6110 Cercadas CB 96 Se 111
8670 Cerca dos Pomares FA 158 Rb 125
3130 Cercal C 94 Rc 108
2550-210 Cercal L 112 Ra 113
2490-101 Cercal SA 94 Rc 110
7555 Cercal SE 144 Rb 122
8200 Cerca Velha FA 159 Re 126
7520-038 Cerca Velha SE 144 Rb 121
5210-041 Cércio BN 63 Te 100
3450 Cercosa VS 79 Re 106
5460 Cerdedo VR 42 Sa 99
3305 Cerdeira C 79 Sa 107
3330 Cerdeira C 95 Rf 108
5450 Cerdeira VR 61 Sc 100
3650 Cerdeira VS 61 Sb 103
3450 Cerdeira VS 78 Re 106
6320 Cerdeora GD 81 Sf 105

5350-220 Cerejais BN 63 Ta 101
3040-757 Cernache C 95 Rd 108
6100 Cernache do Bomjardim CB 95 Re 110
8800 Ceróis FA 160 Sb 125
3360-019 Cerquedo C 78 Rd 106
6150 Cerrejeita CB 96 Sb 110
8100 Cerro FA 159 Re 125
Cerro FA 159 Rf 125
8800 Cerro FA 160 Sb 125
7665 Cerro das Pedras BE 158 Rd 123
8125 Cerro da Vila FA 159 Rf 126
8970 Cerro da Vinha FA 146 Sc 124
8100 Cerro de Alganduro FA 159 Rf 125
8950 Cerro do Anho FA 160 Sc 125
8200-468 Cerro do Ouro FA 159 Re 126
7200 Cerros E 131 Sc 118
4870-042 Cerva VR 61 Sa 100
4730 Cervães BR 41 Rc 99
5470-057 Cervos VR 43 Sb 98
3700 Cesar AV 60 Rd 103
4580-309 Cete P 60 Rd 101
2435 Chã SA 94 Rc 111
5470 Chã VR 42 Sb 98
5070 Chã VR 62 Sd 101
8670 Chabouco FA 158 Rb 125
8550-248 Chã da Casinha FA 158 Rc 124
4935 Chafé VC 41 Rb 99
3230 Chainça C 95 Rd 108
2480 Chainça LE 94 Rb 111
5335 Chairos Carrica BN 43 Se 98
7630 Chaissa Madriz BE 144 Rd 123
7630 Chalé BE 144 Rd 122
3440-007 Chamadouro VS 79 Rf 106
7630 Chaminé BE 146 Se 120
2205 Chaminé E 114 Rf 115
7350 Chaminé PT 115 Se 115
2205 Chamiré SA 114 Rf 113
4840 Chamoim BR 42 Re 98
3405-251 Chamusca C 79 Sb 106
2140-051 Chamusca SA 113 Rd 112
7440-201 Chança PT 114 Sb 113
7440 Chancelaria PT 114 Sb 113
2350-073 Chancelaria SA 95 Rc 111
7800 Chancuda BE 145 Sa 121
2500 Chão da Parada LE 94 Qf 112
8500 Chão das Donas FA 158 Rc 126
6030-153 Chão das Servas CB 96 Sb 110
Chão da Vã CB 96 Sc 109
6050-472 Chão da Velha PT 96 Sb 111
6120-114 Chão de Codes SA 95 Rf 111
3240-462 Chão de Couce C 95 Rd 109
6150 Chão de Galego CB 96 Sb 110
6120 Chão de Lopes Grande SA 95 Rf 111
4910-188 Chão do Porto VC 41 Rb 97
9900 Chão Frio AC 176 Wc 117
3450 Chão Miudo VS 79 Re 106
2480 Chão Padro LE 94 Ra 111
6300 Chãos GD 80 Se 105
6430 Chãos GD 62 Se 103
2565 Chãos L 128 Qe 114
3260-305 Chãos LE 95 Re 109
4640 Chãos P 61 Rf 102
2240 Chãos SA 95 Rd 110
7540 Chãos SE 144 Rb 121
3400-260 Chão Sobral C 79 Sb 107
4600 Chapa Fridão P 61 Rf 101
7555 Chaparral SE 144 Rb 121
7830 Charneca BE 146 Sd 121
7050 Charneca E 129 Re 117
2620 Charneca L 112 Qf 116
3100 Charneca LE 94 Rc 109
3105 Charneca LE 94 Rc 109
2000 Charneca SA 113 Rb 112
2829-503 Charneca da Caparica L 128 Qe 117
8375 Charneca da Velha FA 159 Re 125
7630 Charnequinha BE 145 Re 121
7555 Charnequinha Silveiras SE 144 Rc 122
5150 Chãs GD 62 Se 103
2415 Chãs LE 94 Rb 110

6285-012 Chãs de Égua C 79 Sb 107
3530 Chãs de Tavares VS 80 Sc 105
4640-383 Chavães P 61 Rf 101
5120 Chavães VS 62 Sc 102
4540-264 Chave AV 60 Rd 103
6120-219 Chaveira SA 95 Sa 110
6350 Chavelhas GD 81 Ta 105
5400 Chaves VR 43 Sd 98
4960 Chaviães VC 42 Re 96
4940-104 Chavião VC 41 Rc 97
6400 Cheiras GD 80 Sf 105
5070-342 Cheires VR 62 Sc 101
2640-112 Cheleiros L 128 Qe 115
3360-103 Chelo C 79 Re 107
5470 Chelo VR 42 Rf 98
8550-249 Chilrão FA 158 Rc 125
2460 Chiqueda de Cima LE 94 Ra 111
8950 Choça FA 160 Sc 125
3840 Choca do Mar AV 78 Rb 106
4840 Chorense BR 42 Re 98
4755 Chorente BR 60 Rc 100
9350 Choro MA 178 If 152
3640-042 Chosendo VS 62 Sd 103
7920 Chouriço BE 130 Sa 119
2140-211 Chouto SA 113 Rd 113
4840 Cibões BR 42 Re 98
7050-611 Ciborro E 114 Re 116
5210-020 Cicouro BN 45 Te 99
2500-717 Cidade LE 112 Qe 112
6400-191 Cidadelhe GD 62 Sf 103
5040 Cidadelhe VR 61 Sa 101
5450 Cidadelhe VR 61 Sc 99
5450 Cidadelhe de Jales VR 62 Sc 100
4785-098 Cidai P 60 Rc 101
6060 Cidral CB 97 Sf 108
3025 Cidreira C 78 Rd 107
7160 Ciladas E 115 Se 116
5160 Cilhade BN 62 Ta 101
7570 Cilha do Centeio SE 144 Rd 119
7570 Cilha do Pascoal SE 144 Rd 119
7160 Cilidas E 115 Se 116
2200 Cima da Igreja SA 95 Rf 111
8550-251 Cimalhas FA 158 Rc 124
2205 Cima Ventoso SA 114 Rf 112
5110-167 Cimbres VS 61 Sb 102
6100 Cimo da Ribeira CB 95 Rf 109
3880 Cimo de Vila AV 78 Rc 103
5400 Cimo de Vila da Castanheira VR 43 Se 98
6440-051 Cinco Vilas GD 81 Ta 104
4690-022 Cinfães VS 61 Rf 102
8800 Cintados FA 160 Sc 125
5320-131 Cisterna BN 43 Se 97
8100 Clarianes FA 159 Sa 125
8970 Clarines FA 146 Sc 124
7040 Claros Montes E 114 Sa 115
5370-110 Cobro BN 62 Se 100
3060-587 Cochadas C 78 Rb 106
2125-012 Cocharro SA 113 Rc 114
5090 Codaval VR 62 Sd 100
5140 Codeçais BN 62 Se 101
3600-312 Codeçais VS 61 Sa 103
4730 Codeceda BR 41 Rd 98
4890 Codeçoso BR 61 Rf 100
5470 Codeçoso VR 42 Sa 98
6300-085 Codesseiro GD 80 Se 105
5470 Codessoso VR 42 Sb 98
5460 Codessoso VR 43 Sb 99
7800 Coelheira BE 145 Rf 121
3660-043 Coelheira VS 79 Rf 104
7555 Coelheiras SE 144 Rc 122
2100 Coelhos SA 113 Rb 115
5300 Coelhoso BN 44 Tc 99
3280 Coentral LE 95 Rc 108
6420-341 Cogula GD 80 Se 104
3330 Coiços C 95 Rf 108
3000 Coimbra C 78 Rd 107
Coimbra „A", Estação Ferro-viária de C 78 Rd 107
Coimbra „B", Estação Ferro-viária de C 78 Rd 107
2425-452 Coimbrão LE 94 Ra 109
5460 Coimbró VR 42 Sa 98
2830 Coina SE 128 Qf 117
8970 Coito FA 146 Sc 124

3305-090 Coja C 79 Sa 107
3570 Coja GD 80 Sc 104
2705-140 Colares L 112 Qd 116
2565-297 Colaria L 128 Qe 114
3600 Cole de Pito VS 61 Sa 103
8600 Colégio FA 158 Rb 126
5140-231 Coleja BN 62 Se 102
7750-209 Colgadeiros BE 160 Sc 123
3330 Colmeal C 95 Rf 108
6250 Colmeal CB 80 Se 106
7250 Colmeal E 131 Se 117
6440 Colmeal GD 81 Sf 103
5350-432 Colmeias BN 62 Sf 100
2420 Colmeias LE 94 Rb 110
6320 Cólonia Agricola de Martim Rei GD 80 Sf 107
7570 Colónia Penal SE 144 Rb 119
7630 Colos BE 144 Rd 122
8800 Colos FA 160 Sc 125
7580 Colos SE 129 Rd 118
6040 Comenda PT 114 Sb 112
2000 Comenda SA 113 Rc 113
7040 Comenda Grande E 130 Sa 116
9930 Companhia de Ca. AC 176 Wd 118
7580 Comporta SE 129 Rb 118
5340 Comunhas BN 44 Ta 99
7490 Conçala E 114 Rf 115
7670-021 Conceição BE 145 Re 122
8005 Conceição FA 159 Sa 126
8800 Conceição FA 160 Sc 126
3150 Condeixa-a-Nova C 95 Rd 108
3150-220 Condeixa-a-Velha C 95 Rd 108
7490 Condes E 114 Sa 115
4935 Conehada VC 41 Rb 98
5180 Congira BN 63 Tb 102
5300-473 Conlelas BN 44 Ta 98
6150 Conqueiros CB 96 Sa 110
2525 Consolação LE 112 Qd 113
Constance P 61 Rf 101
2250 Constância SA 95 Re 112
5210 Constantim BN 45 Te 99
5000-081 Constantim VS 61 Sb 101
3360-284 Contenças C 78 Rd 107
3530-344 Contenças de Baixo VS 80 Sb 105
5320-151 Contim BN 43 Sf 97
5470 Contim VR 42 Sa 98
5110-575 Contim VS 61 Sc 102
2140 Conventa SA 113 Rd 112
7425 Corças PT 113 Re 114
7750-604 Corcha BE 160 Sa 124
8100-129 Corcitos FA 159 Sa 125
7050 Cordiçadas do Lavre E 113 Rd 116
3060-232 Cordinhã C 78 Rc 106
4505 Corga AV 60 Rd 103
4760 Corga BR 60 Rc 100
6270 Corga GD 79 Sb 106
6150 Corgas CB 96 Sa 110
8150 Corgas FA 159 Sa 125
4890 Corgo BR 61 Sa 100
6430-051 Coriscada GD 80 Se 103
4920 Cornes VC 41 Rb 97
4745 Coronado P 60 Rc 101
8150-029 Corotelo FA 159 Sa 126
7750 Corredoura BE 160 Sa 123
2040-172 Correias SA 113 Rb 112
2970 Corroios SE 128 Qe 118
2855 Corroios SE 128 Qf 117
8550-118 Corsino FA 158 Rb 125
3330 Corte C 95 Rf 109
8800 Corte António Martins FA 160 Sc 125
7750-101 Corte Azinha BE 146 Sd 122
Corte Cobres BE 145 Sa 122
7800 Corte Condessa BE 146 Sb 121
8970-019 Corte das Donas FA 160 Sd 124
8970-018 Corte da Seda FA 160 Sd 124
8800 Corte de Besteiros FA 160 Sc 125
8100 Corte de Ouro FA 159 Sa 124
8950 Corte de São Tomé FA 160 Sc 124
7700 Corte de Cabo BE 159 Rf 124
8950 Corte do Gago FA 160 Sc 125
7750-102 Corte do Pinto BE 146 Sd 122

7700 Corte Fugueira BE 159 Rf 124
3885 Cortegaça AV 60 Rc 103
3450 Cortegaça VS 79 Re 106
3610-070 Cortegada VS 61 Sb 102
7750-308 Corte Gafo de Cima BE 146 Sb 122
7750 Corte Garfo de Baixo BE 146 Sb 122
8100 Corte João Marques FA 160 Sa 124
8100 Cortelha FA 159 Sa 125
8800 Cortelha FA 159 Sb 125
8950 Cortelha FA 160 Sc 125
2500 Cortém LE 112 Qf 112
7630-521 Corte Malhão BE 159 Rd 123
7800 Corte Negra BE 145 Sa 120
8950-322 Corte Nova FA 160 Sc 124
7750-502 Corte Pão e Água BE 145 Sb 123
8375 Corte Paral FA 159 Re 124
7750 Corte Pequena BE 145 Sa 122
7700 Corte Pequena BE 146 Sc 122
7700 Corte Pinheiro BE 159 Rf 124
7830 Corte Poço BE 146 Sc 120
7670 Corte Preta BE 144 Rd 122
3330 Corterredor C 95 Rf 108
7800 Cortes BE 145 Sa 120
8375 Cortes FA 159 Re 125
2410-501 Cortes LE 94 Rb 110
4950 Cortes VC 41 Rd 96
7960 Cortes de Baixo BE 130 Sa 120
7960 Cortes de Cima BE 130 Sb 120
6215 Cortes de Meio CB 80 Sc 107
8970 Corte Serranos FA 159 Sb 124
7595 Cortes Grandes SE 145 Re 119
7750-311 Corte Sines BE 146 Sc 122
7665-859 Cortes Pereiras BE 159 Rd 123
8970 Cortes Pereiras FA 146 Sc 124
8970 Corte Tabelião FA 146 Sc 124
7750 Corte Velha BE 145 Sb 122
7600-161 Corte Vicente Anes BE 145 Rf 121
7700-204 Corte Zorrinho BE 159 Rf 123
6230-788 Cortiçada CB 96 Sd 108
3570 Cortiçada GD 80 Sc 104
3465 Cortiçada VS 79 Rf 105
7000 Cortiçadas E 130 Rf 117
8100-171 Cortiçadas FA 159 Sa 125
2025-014 Cortiçal SA 94 Rb 112
3070-631 Corticeiro de Baixo C 78 Rb 106
3060-752 Corticeiro de Cima C 78 Rb 106
2080 Cortiçóis SA 113 Rb 114
5340-102 Cortiços BN 62 Sf 99
7630 Cortinhas BE 144 Rb 122
5090 Cortinhas VR 62 Sc 100
5370 Cortins BN 62 Se 99
3570-120 Coruche GD 80 Sc 104
2100-057 Coruche SA 113 Rc 115
2425 Coruchu LE 94 Ra 109
5340-110 Corujas BN 44 Ta 99
6300 Corujeira GD 80 Sd 105
3560 Corujeira VS 80 Sb 104
3070 Corujeiras C 78 Rb 106
8950 Corujos FA 160 Sc 125
5470 Corva VR 42 Sa 99
7200 Corval E 131 Sd 118
3465-014 Corveira VS 79 Rf 105
3420 Corvelo C 79 Rf 107
4600 Corvelo do Monte P 61 Sa 101
7750 Corvos BE 159 Sa 124
8150 Corxo FA 159 Sb 125
4750-842 Cossourado BR 41 Rc 99
4940-132 Cossourado VC 41 Rc 97
7750 Costa BE 146 Sc 123
4810 Costa BR 60 Re 100
4595 Costa P 60 Rd 101

7500 Costa SE 144 Rb 120
4920 Costa VC 41 Rb 97
4925 Costa VC 41 Rb 98
4880 Cota VR 61 Sa 100
2825-283 Costa da Caparica SE 128 Qe 117
7570 Costa da Galé SE 129 Ra 118
3090-458 Costa de Lavos C 94 Ra 108
3600 Costilhão VS 61 Sa 103
3505 Cota VS 79 Sb 104
5070-252 Cotas VR 62 Sd 101
3600-373 Cotelo VS 61 Sa 102
8600-077 Cotifo FA 158 Rb 126
6420-351 Cótimos GD 80 Se 104
2500-432 Coto LE 112 Qf 112
8200 Cotovio FA 159 Re 126
8800 Cotovio FA 160 Sc 125
4730 Couceiro BR 41 Rd 98
2400-768 Coucinheira LE 94 Ra 110
2100-305 Couço SA 113 Re 115
4940 Coura VC 41 Rc 97
5110 Coura VS 61 Sc 102
3600 Coura VS 79 Sa 104
4755 Courel BR 60 Rc 100
7555 Courela SE 144 Rc 121
7800 Courelas BE 145 Sa 121
6420-586 Courelas GD 80 Sd 104
7005-127 Courelas da Azaruja E 130 Sb 116
7005-753 Courelas da Toura E 130 Sb 117
7170 Courujeira E 131 Sc 117
4960 Cousso VC 42 Re 96
6215 Coutada CB 96 Sc 107
8900 Coutada FA 160 Sc 125
2140 Coutadas SA 113 Rd 112
4750 Couto BR 41 Rc 99
6060 Couto CB 97 Se 110
4780 Couto P 60 Rd 101
4970 Couto VC 41 Rc 97
3510-582 Couto de Baixo VS 79 Rf 105
3510-602 Couto de Cima VS 79 Rf 104
3740 Couto de Esteves AV 78 Re 104
6060 Couto do Cabeludo CB 97 Se 109
7460 Coutos (Paragem) PT 115 Sc 114
6060 Couto Velho CB 96 Sd 109
7050 Couvela de São Mateus E 130 Re 117
6100 Couxaria CB 95 Rf 109
4850 Cova BR 42 Rf 98
3090-706 Cova C 94 Ra 108
5300 Cova da Lua BN 44 Tb 97
2565-839 Cova da Moura L 112 Qd 114
8150-030 Cova da Muda FA 160 Sa 125
7630-442 Cova da Zorra BE 144 Rc 122
3670 Cova de Lobishomen VS 79 Rf 104
2825 Cova de Vapor SE 128 Qe 117
7540 Cova do Gato SE 144 Rc 120
7470 Covães PT 114 Sa 115
3300 Covais C 79 Rf 107
3440 Coval VS 79 Rf 105
3100-285 Covão da Silva LE 94 Rc 109
Covão do Coelho SA 94 Rb 111
2380 Covão do Feto SA 94 Rb 112
3840-126 Covão do Lobo AV 78 Rc 106
3420 Covas C 79 Sa 106
4620 Covas P 60 Re 101
4920 Covas VC 41 Rb 97
5450 Covas VR 62 Sc 100
3670 Covas VS 79 Rf 104
2715-260 Covas de Ferro L 128 Qe 115
5085-203 Covas do Douro VR 61 Sc 101
3660-094 Covas do Rio VS 61 Rf 103
5470-091 Covelães VR 42 Sa 98
4540 Covelas AV 60 Rd 103
5350 Covelas BN 62 Ta 100
4830 Covelas BR 42 Rd 99
4640 Covelas P 61 Sa 102
5050 Covelinhas VR 61 Sb 102
4515 Covelo P 60 Rd 102
Covelo VS 79 Re 104
3475 Covelo VS 79 Re 105

3830-469 Gafanha da Encarnação AV 78 Rb 105
3830-551 Gafanha da Nazaré AV 78 Rb 105
3840-253 Gafanha da Vagueira AV 78 Rb 105
3830-013 Gafanha de Aquém AV 78 Rb 105
3840 Gafanha do Areão AV 78 Rb 105
3830-401 Gafanha do Carmo AV 78 Rb 105
3600-345 Gafanhão VS 61 Rf 103
7430 Gafete PT 114 Sb 112
7700 Gagos BE 159 Rf 124
4890 Gagos BR 61 Rf 100
6300 Gagos GD 80 Sf 105
6250 Gaia GD 80 Se 106
4640 Gaia P 61 Rf 102
3220-414 Gaiate C 95 Re 108
2510 Gaieiras LE 112 Qf 112
4990-635 Gaifar VC 41 Rc 99
2460-771 Gaio LE 94 Qf 112
2860 Gaio SE 128 Qf 116
8970-334 Galachos FA 160 Sc 124
5050 Galafura VR 61 Sb 101
5000 Galçada VR 61 Sb 101
7240 Galeana E 131 Sf 119
8670 Galé de Baixo FA 158 Rb 124
8670 Galé de Cima FA 158 Rb 124
8970 Galego FA 160 Sb 125
4750 Galegos BR 60 Rc 99
4830 Galegos BR 60 Re 99
4560 Galegos P 60 Re 102
7330-063 Galegos PT 115 Se 112
7780 Galequinha Grande BE 145 Sa 122
7630 Galharda BE 144 Rd 122
3515 Galifonge VS 79 Sa 104
6000 Galisteu CB 96 Se 111
5100-453 Galvã VS 61 Sb 102
7400-001 Galveias PT 114 Sa 114
2100 Gamas SA 129 Rc 115
2910 Gambia SE 129 Rb 117
6400 Gamelas GD 81 Sf 104
4880 Gampahó VR 61 Sa 101
2025-601 Gançaria SA 113 Ra 112
4930 Gândara VC 41 Rc 96
3840 Gândara AV 78 Rb 106
2415 Gândara dos Olivais LE 94 Rb 110
4835 Gandarela BR 60 Rd 100
4890 Gandarela BR 61 Rf 100
3360 Gandelim C 79 Re 107
4740 Gandra BR 60 Rb 99
4585 Gandra P 60 Rd 101
4990 Gandra VC 41 Rc 98
4950 Gandrachão VC 41 Rc 97
4930-355 Ganfei VC 41 Rc 96
4970 Garcão VC 42 Rd 98
5300 Garcãosinho BN 44 Tb 99
8800 Garcia FA 160 Sb 124
2430-014 Garcia LE 94 Ra 110
6030-013 Gardete CB 96 Sb 111
4830 Garfe BR 60 Re 99
5060-422 Garganta VR 61 Sc 101
9230 Garnal MA 178 Ka 152
6030 Garreta CB 96 Sc 110
8800-025 Garrobo FA 160 Sb 125
7885 Garrochais BE 131 Se 120
7670-121 Garvão BE 144 Rd 122
7900 Gasparões BE 145 Re 121
6300-070 Gata GD 80 Se 105
4600 Gatão P 61 Rf 101
6430 Gateira GD 62 Se 103
7750 Gato BE 159 Sb 123
7050 Gato E 130 Re 117
3140 Gatões C 78 Rb 107
9100 Gaula MA 178 Kb 152
4960 Gave VC 42 Re 96
4920 Gavea VC 41 Rb 97
2140 Gaviao SA 113 Re 113
7600 Gavião BE 145 Rf 122
4760 Gavião BR 60 Rc 100
6030 Gavião CB 96 Sb 110
6040 Gavião PT 95 Sa 112
2140 Gavião SA 113 Rd 113
8375-040 Gavião de Baixo FA 159 Re 125
8375-155 Gavião de Cima FA 159 Re 125
6000 Gaviãosinho CB 96 Sb 110
4970 Gavieira VC 42 Re 97
3400 Gavinhos de Baixo C 79 Sa 106
5350-250 Gebelim BN 63 Ta 100
4900 Gelfa VC 41 Ra 98
4730 Geme BR 41 Rd 99
4890 Gémeos BR 61 Rf 100
4740 Gemezes BR 60 Rb 99
8100-389 Gemica FA 159 Rf 125
4475 Gemunde P 60 Rc 101
5210-090 Genísio BN 63 Td 99
4820 Gens BR 61 Rf 100
4515 Gens P 60 Rd 102
2525-511 Geraldes LE 112 Qe 113
4830 Geraz do Minho BR 42 Re 99
5470 Gerês VR 42 Sa 98
3550-093 Germil VS 79 Sb 105
4980 Germill VC 42 Re 98
4640 Gestaçô P 61 Sa 101
3060 Gesteira C 78 Rb 107
3130 Gesteira C 94 Rc 108
5320 Gestosa BN 43 Sf 97
3440-128 Gestosa VS 79 Rf 106
3730-061 Gestoso AV 78 Rd 104
3660-139 Gestoso VS 79 Re 103
4525 Gião AV 60 Rd 103
8700 Gião FA 160 Sb 126
4485-171 Gião P 60 Rb 101
4970 Giela VC 41 Rd 97
3750 Giesteira AV 78 Rd 105
7000 Giesteira E 130 Rf 117
2495 Giesteira SA 94 Rb 111
6150-721 Giesteiras Cimeiras CB 96 Sb 110
8550-289 Gil Bordalo FA 158 Rc 125
4755 Gilmonde BR 60 Rc 99
8100 Gilvrazino FA 159 Rf 126
5300-553 Gimonde BN 44 Tb 98
9555 Ginetes AC 176 Za 121
9240 Ginjas MA 178 If 152
8970 Giões FA 146 Sb 124
6270-051 Girabolhos GD 79 Sb 105
7800 Giralda BE 145 Sb 121
8550-135 Giraldo FA 158 Rb 124
2140 Giraldo SA 113 Rd 113
7780 Giraldos BE 145 Rf 122
7100 Glória E 115 Sc 116
2125-021 Glória do Ribatejo SA 113 Rc 114
4730 Goães BR 41 Rc 98
4720 Goães BR 42 Re 99
2705-784 Godigana L 112 Qd 115
5050-059 Godim VR 61 Sb 101
4730 Godinhaços BR 41 Rd 98
7100 Godinheira E 114 Sb 115
3220-112 Godinhela C 95 Rd 108
4755 Góios BR 60 Rc 100
7750 Góis BE 159 Sb 123
4740 Góis BR 60 Rb 99
3330-209 Góis C 95 Rf 108
4820 Golães BR 61 Re 100
2150 Golegã SA 113 Rd 112
6420-504 Golfar GD 80 Sd 104
5370-553 Golfeiras BN 62 Se 100
7700-222 Gomes Aires BE 159 Re 123
4730 Gomide BR 42 Rd 98
4800-190 Gonça BR 60 Re 99
6300-115 Gonçalo GD 80 Sd 106
6300-120 Gonçalo Bocas GD 80 Se 105
8700 Gonçalves FA 160 Sb 126
8100 Goncinha FA 159 Rf 126
4580-402 Gondalães P 60 Rd 101
4835-537 Gondar BR 60 Rd 100
4600 Gondar P 61 Rf 101
4920 Gondar VC 41 Rb 97
4910 Gondar VC 41 Rb 98
4860-137 Gondarém BR 61 Rf 99
4920 Gondarém VC 41 Rb 97
2490-135 Gondemaria SA 94 Rc 110
5300-561 Gondesende BN 44 Ta 97
4860 Gondiães BR 42 Sa 99
4475 Gondim P 60 Rc 101
4930 Gondim VC 41 Rc 97
4730 Gondomar BR 42 Rd 98
4800 Gondomar BR 60 Re 99
4420 Gondomar P 60 Rc 102
3610 Gondomar VS 61 Sb 102
4930 Gondomil VC 41 Rc 96
4840 Gondoriz BR 42 Re 98
4970 Gondoriz VC 41 Rd 97
4990 Gondufe VC 41 Rc 98
Gondufe VC 41 Rc 98
6285-068 Gondufo GD 79 Sb 107
4820-485 Gontim BR 61 Rf 99
7700 Gorazes BE 159 Rf 123
5430-230 Gorgoço VR 43 Se 98
7580 Gorgolim SE 129 Rd 117
2140 Gorjão SA 114 Re 113
4640 Gosende P 61 Rf 102
3600-374 Gosende VS 61 Sa 102
5300-574 Gostei BN 44 Tb 98
5110-373 Goujoim VS 61 Sc 102
5450-210 Gouvães da Serra VR 61 Sb 100
5085-242 Gouvães do Douro VR 62 Sc 101
5350-262 Gouveia BN 62 Ta 101
6290 Gouveia GD 80 Sc 106
2705-409 Gouveia L 112 Qd 115
3610-033 Gouviães VS 61 Sb 102
5060-052 Gouvinhas VR 61 Sc 101
4640-264 Gove P 61 Rf 102
3270-022 Graça LE 95 Re 109
3100 Gracieira LE 94 Rc 110
2510 Gracieira LE 112 Qf 113
3780 Grada AV 78 Rd 106
4970 Grade VC 42 Rd 97
2665-101 Gradil L 112 Qe 115
3570-160 Gradiz GD 80 Sc 103
5450 Graheira VR 61 Sc 100
8800-027 Grainho FA 160 Sb 125
5470-160 Gralhas VR 43 Sb 97
Gralheira VS 61 Sa 102
8550 Gralhos FA 158 Rc 125
5340 Gralhós BN 63 Tb 99
3400-263 Gramaça C 79 Sa 107
7350 Gramicha PT 115 Sf 115
5300-482 Grandais BN 44 Tb 98
7900 Grandão BE 130 Rf 120
7570 Grândola SE 144 Rc 119
Granho SA 113 Rc 114
2125 Granho Novo de Magos SA 129 Rb 114
9900 Granja AC 176 Wc 117
5160 Granja BN 62 Ta 102
5200 Granja BN 63 Tc 100
5225 Granja BN 63 Td 99
3130 Granja C 78 Rc 108
3360 Granja C 78 Rd 107
7100 Granja E 115 Sc 115
7240 Granja E 131 Se 119
6420 Granja GD 80 Se 104
6300 Granja GD 80 Sf 105
3100 Granja LE 94 Rc 109
4410 Granja P 60 Rc 102
7340 Granja PT 115 Se 114
4950 Granja VC 42 Rd 96
5460 Granja VR 43 Sc 98
5450 Granja VR 62 Sc 100
5070 Granja VR 62 Sd 101
3600 Granja VS 61 Sa 103
3630 Granja VS 62 Sd 102
3060 Granja de Ança C 78 Rd 107
3810-818 Granja de Baixo AV 78 Rc 105
3810-811 Granja de Cima AV 78 Rc 105
5120-161 Granja do Tedo VS 61 Sc 102
3640 Granjal VS 62 Sc 103
Granja Nova VR 61 Sb 99
3610-042 Granja Nova VS 61 Sb 102
5120 Granjinha VS 62 Sc 102
3570 Gravaca GD 80 Sc 104
3610 Gravaz VS 61 Sb 102
5000-027 Gravelos VR 61 Sb 100
8300 Gregórios FA 159 Rd 125
5200-382 Gregos BN 63 Tc 100
4415 Grijó P 60 Rc 102
5300-582 Grijó de Parada BN 44 Tb 98
5340-152 Grijó de Vale Benfeito BN 62 Ta 100
4640 Grilo P 61 Rf 102
4775 Grimancelos BR 60 Rc 100
3230-020 Grocinas C 95 Rd 109
2425 Grou LE 94 Ra 109
4925 Grovas VC 41 Rb 98
4980 Grovelas VC 41 Rd 98
2040 Gruta de Alcobertas SA 112 Ra 112
8500 Grutas de Ibne Ammar FA 158 Rc 126
5225 Grutas de Santo Adrião BN 63 Td 99
9880 Guadalupe AC 176 Wf 114
5300-822 Guadramil BN 44 Tc 97
4505 Gualtar AV 60 Rc 103
4710 Gualtar BR 60 Rd 99
3240-671 Guarda C 95 Rd 109
6300 Guarda GD 80 Se 105
3105 Guarda do Norte LE 94 Ra 109
6300 Guarda-Gare GD 80 Se 105
3475 Guardão VS 79 Rf 105
4765-401 Guardizela BR 60 Rd 100
7700 Guedelhas BE 159 Sa 124
7700 Guedelhinhas BE 159 Rf 123
5120-350 Guedieiros VS 62 Sc 102
8550-137 Guena FA 158 Rb 125
4755-251 Gueral BR 60 Rc 100
7780 Guerreiro BE 145 Sa 122
Guia BN 94 Rb 109
8200 Guia FA 159 Re 126
Guia, Estação Ferroviária de LE 94 Rb 109
5000-111 Guiães VR 61 Sc 101
4745 Guidões P 60 Rc 101
4485-001 Guilhabreu P 60 Rc 101
4970 Guilhadeses VC 41 Rd 98
5450-080 Guilhado VR 61 Sc 100
6300 Guilhafonso GD 80 Se 105
3640-700 Guilheiro GD 62 Sd 103
4850-188 Guilhofrei BR 42 Rf 99
4560-144 Guilhufe P 60 Re 101
4810 Guimarães BR 60 Re 100
4825 Guimarei P 60 Rd 101
4950-207 Guimil VC 41 Rd 96
4525-310 Guisande AV 60 Rd 103
4705 Guisande BR 60 Rd 100
4405 Gulpilhares P 60 Rc 102
3515-789 Gumiei VS 79 Rf 104

H

6150 Herdade CB 96 Sb 109
7000 Herdade da Mitra (Escola Agrícola) E 130 Rf 117
7875-101 Herdade da Negrita BE 146 Se 120
7750 Herdade de Santa Maria BE 159 Sb 123
7200 Herdadinha E 131 Sc 118
3360-249 Hombres C 79 Re 107
9900 Horta AC 176 Wc 117
5155 Horta GD 62 Se 102
7220 Horta da Quinta E 130 Sa 118
5160-101 Horta da Vilariça BN 62 Sf 101
7340-111 Hortas de Baixo PT 115 Se 114
7340-113 Hortas de Cima PT 115 Se 113
8650-281 Hortas do Tabual FA 158 Ra 126
7250-069 Hortinhas E 131 Sd 117

I

6060 Idanha-a-Nova CB 97 Se 109
6060-041 Idanha-a-Velha CB 97 Sf 109
5210-101 Ifanes BN 45 Te 99
3670-172 Igarei VS 79 Rf 104
4750 Igreja Nova BR 41 Rc 99
2640-300 Igreja Nova L 128 Qe 115
2240 Igreja Nova do Sobral SA 95 Re 110
7040 Igrejinha E 130 Sa 116
9230 Ilha MA 178 Ka 152
3830 Ílhavo AV 78 Rb 105
2135 Infantado SA 129 Rb 115
4810 Infantas BR 60 Re 100
4890 Infesta BR 61 Rf 100
4940 Infesta VC 41 Rc 97
4815 Infias BR 60 Re 100
4640-175 Ingilde P 61 Rf 102
6250-162 Inguias CB 80 Se 107
4940 Insalde VC 41 Rc 97
6230 Ínsuas da Ponte CB 96 Sd 107
3740 Irijó AV 78 Re 104
4560 Irivo P 60 Re 101
5300-591 Izeda BN 63 Tb 99

J

2240-300 Jamprestes SA 95 Rd 110
8950 Janaqueira FA 160 Sd 125
4540-402 Janarde AV 61 Rf 103
3730 Janardo AV 78 Rd 104
2415 Janardo LE 94 Rb 110
2710-007 Janas L 112 Qd 116
3320-105 Janeiro de Baixo C 96 Sb 108
6185-102 Janeiro de Cima CB 96 Sb 108
9350 Jardim da Serra MA 178 If 152
9370 Jardim do Mar MA 178 Ie 152
6355-151 Jardo GD 81 Ta 105
8970-336 Jardos FA 160 Sb 125
8150-040 Javali FA 160 Sa 125
4600 Jazente P 61 Rf 101
2665 Jerumelo, Estação Ferroviária de L 112 Qe 115
4770-160 Jesufrei BR 60 Rc 100
4770 Joane BR 60 Rd 100
8100 João Andrês FA 159 Re 125
6300-066 João Antão GD 80 Se 106
7480-057 João Galego PT 114 Rf 114
7750-032 João Serra BE 145 Sa 122
8375-210 Joios FA 159 Rd 124
4970 Jolda VC 41 Rc 98
4970 Jolda (São Paio) VC 41 Rd 98
2490 Jorja SA 94 Rc 110
5000 Jorjais VR 61 Sb 101
5070 Jorjais VR 62 Sc 100
5090-076 Jou VR 62 Sd 100
4510-001 Jovim P 60 Rc 102
3475 Juens VS 79 Re 105
4610 Jugueiros P 60 Re 100
4860-426 Juguelhe BR 61 Sa 99
6400-145 Juizo GD 80 Sf 103
6350-072 Junça GD 81 Ta 104
6370-332 Juncais GD 80 Sc 105
2480-065 Juncal LE 94 Ra 111
2100-627 Juncal SA 129 Rd 114
6000-541 Juncal do Campo CB 96 Sc 109
7100 Junceira E 115 Sb 116
2300-024 Junceira SA 95 Rd 111
2140 Junco SA 113 Rd 113
3730 Junqueira AV 78 Re 104
5160 Junqueira BN 62 Sf 101
5230 Junqueira BN 63 Tc 100
4480 Junqueira P 60 Rb 100
5445 Junqueiro VR 43 Sd 99
7600 Junqueiros BE 145 Re 121
7250-242 Juromenha E 131 Se 116
3720 Jusã AV 78 Rc 103
5000-121 Justes VR 61 Sc 100

L

5300-422 Labiados BN 44 Tc 97
8970-208 Laborato FA 160 Sb 124
7670 Laborela BE 144 Rd 122
3360 Laborino C 79 Re 107
4485-293 Labruge P 60 Rb 101
2580 Labrugeira L 112 Qf 114
2150 Labruja SA 113 Rd 112
4990-655 Labruja VC 41 Rc 97
4990-660 Labrujó VC 41 Rc 97
4970 Laceiras VC 41 Rd 97
3430-690 Laceiras VS 79 Sa 106
5000 Ladares VR 61 Sc 101
7630 Ladeira BE 159 Rd 123
6030 Ladeira CB 96 Sb 110
8550 Ladeira FA 158 Rc 125
6120 Ladeira SA 96 Sa 111
8550-299 Ladeira de Cima FA 158 Rc 124
6060-201 Ladoeiro CB 97 Se 109
Ladrugães VR 42 Sa 98
5320-242 Lagarelhos BN 44 Sf 97
5400 Lagarelhos VR 43 Sd 98
3405 Lagares C 79 Sa 106
4560 Lagares P 60 Rd 102
4610 Lagares P 60 Re 100
6290-091 Lagarinhos GD 80 Sb 106
7630 Lagarteira BE 144 Rc 122
3240 Lagarteira C 95 Rd 109
6050 Lage da Prata PT 114 Sb 112
4720 Lago BR 41 Rd 99
9560 Lagoa AC 177 Zc 122
7800 Lagoa BE 145 Rf 121
5340 Lagoa BN 63 Tb 100
4820 Lagoa BR 61 Rf 99
3070 Lagoa C 78 Rb 106
6110 Lagoa CB 95 Rf 110
8400 Lagoa FA 158 Rd 126
8950 Lagoa FA 160 Sc 125
2640 Lagoa L 128 Qd 114
5180-201 Lagoaça BN 63 Tb 101
2965 Lagoa da Palha, Estação Ferroviária de SE 129 Ra 117
2970 Lagoa de Albufeira SE 128 Qe 117
7570 Lagoa de Melides SE 144 Rb 120
2460-613 Lagoa do Cão LE 94 Ra 111
7700 Lagoa do Soeiro de Cima BE 159 Rf 123
2495-024 Lagoa Ruiva LE 94 Rb 111
3060 Lagoas C 78 Re 106
5430-406 Lagoas VR 43 Se 99
5450-134 Lago Bom VR 61 Sc 99
5300-514 Lagomar BN 44 Tb 98
8600 Lagos FA 158 Rb 126
8005 Lagos FA 159 Sa 126
3405-254 Lagos da Beira C 79 Sb 106
2965 Lagou do Calvo SE 129 Rb 116
4730 Laje BR 41 Rd 99

324 | Gafanha da Encarnação

9960 Lajedo AC 176 Te 112
3405-301 Lajeosa C 79 Sa 106
6320 Lajeosa GD 81 Tb 106
3460-153 Lajeosa VS 79 Sa 105
6360-492 Lajeosa do Mondego GD 80 Sd 105
9760 Lajes AC 176 Xf 116
7670 Lajes BE 159 Re 123
7005 Lajes E 130 Sb 117
8150 Lajes FA 159 Sb 125
6270 Lajes GD 80 Sb 106
9960 Lajes das Flores AC 176 Te 112
9930 Lajes do Pico AC 177 We 118
7555 Lajinha SE 144 Rc 122
5100-550 Lalim VS 61 Sb 102
4750 Lama BR 60 Rc 99
4780 Lama P 60 Rd 100
9270 Lamaceiros MA 178 Ie 151
9225 Lamaceiros MA 178 Ka 152
2240 Lamaceiros SA 95 Re 110
Lama Chã VR 42 Sb 98
5400-636 Lama de Arcos VR 43 Sd 98
5340 Lamalonga BN 43 Sf 98
5000-132 Lamares VR 61 Sc 101
3025-385 Lamarosa C 78 Rc 107
Lamarosa, Estação Ferroviária de SA 95 Rc 111
3220 Lamas C 95 Rd 108
2550-366 Lamas L 112 Qf 113
5470 Lamas VR 42 Sa 98
4870 Lamas VR 61 Sb 100
3600 Lamas VS 79 Sa 104
3560 Lamas de Ferreira VS 80 Sb 104
4960-170 Lamas de Mouro VC 42 Re 96
5000-142 Lamas de Olo VR 61 Sb 100
5370-152 Lamas de Orelhão BN 62 Se 100
5340 Lamas de Podence BN 44 Ta 99
3750-551 Lamas do Vouga AV 78 Rd 105
6200 Lamçais CB 80 Sd 107
Lamedo BR 42 Rf 99
6400-232 Lamegal GD 80 Sf 105
5100 Lamego VS 61 Sb 102
4820 Lameira BR 61 Rf 100
3420 Lameiras C 79 Sa 106
6320 Lameiras GD 80 Se 106
6400 Lameiras GD 80 Sf 104
2420 Lameiras LE 94 Rb 109
9240 Lameiros MA 178 If 152
4825 Lamelas P 60 Rd 101
3640-140 Lamosa VS 61 Sc 103
5200 Lamoso BN 63 Tc 101
4590 Lamoso P 60 Rd 101
5430 Lampaca VR 43 Se 98
2205-135 Lampreia SA 114 Rf 112
2870 Lancada SE 128 Ra 116
5300-902 Lanção BN 44 Ta 98
2500-530 Landal LE 112 Qf 113
5320-084 Landedo BN 44 Sf 97
2965-401 Landeira E 129 Rc 117
3660-248 Landeira VS 79 Rf 104
4770-300 Landim BR 60 Rd 100
4730 Lanhas BR 41 Rd 98
4910-202 Lanhelas VC 41 Rb 97
4925 Lanheses VC 41 Rb 98
4830 Lanhoso BR 42 Re 99
3060 Lapa C 78 Rc 106
6270 Lapa GD 79 Sb 106
2070-352 Lapa SA 113 Ra 114
4950 Lapa VC 41 Rd 96
3640 Lapa VS 80 Sc 103
3525-601 Lapa do Lobo VS 79 Sa 106
6270-651 Lapa dos Dinheiros GD 80 Sb 106
2350-085 Lapas SA 95 Rc 112
Lapeiras MA 179 Kd 150
4860-140 Lapela BR 61 Rf 99
4950 Lapela VC 41 Rc 96
5470-019 Lapela VR 42 Sa 98
4950 Lara VC 41 Rc 96
4520 Laranjeira AV 60 Rc 103
8950 Laranjeiras FA 160 Sd 124
8700 Laranjeiro FA 159 Sb 126
3020-522 Larçã C 78 Rd 107
6005-193 Lardosa CB 96 Sd 109
3090-648 Lares C 94 Rb 108
5160-001 Larinho BN 62 Sf 101
2100 Latadas SE 113 Rc 116
2950-065 Lau SE 129 Rb 117
4570 Laundos P 60 Rb 100
6230-500 Lavacolhos CB 96 Sc 108
4415 Lavadores P 60 Rb 102
3770 Lavandeira AV 78 Rd 105
5140 Lavandeira BN 62 Se 101
5460 Lavaradas VR 42 Sb 98
3350 Lavegadas C 79 Re 107
2425-614 Lavegadas LE 94 Rb 109
3090 Lavos C 94 Rb 108
4455-001 Lavra P 60 Rb 101
4980 Lavradas VC 41 Rd 98
2835 Lavradio SE 128 Qf 116
7050-467 Lavre E 129 Rd 116
5100-582 Lazarim VS 61 Sa 102
4540-580 Lázaro AV 60 Rd 103
7830 Lebre BE 146 Sd 122
5430-149 Lebução VR 43 Se 98
4450 Leça da Palmeira P 60 Rb 101
4465 Leca do Bailio P 60 Rc 101
4635-605 Légua P 61 Rf 101
2740-004 Leião L 128 Qe 116
Leiradas BR 41 Sa 99
2400 Leiria LE 94 Rb 110
5000 Leirós VR 61 Sc 100
3090 Leirosa C 94 Ra 108
6090 Leitoa CB 97 Se 107
3070 Leitões C 78 Rb 106
3060-211 Lemede C 78 Rc 107
4775-400 Lemenhe BR 60 Rc 100
3050-181 Lendiosa AV 78 Rd 106
4480 Lente P 60 Rb 100
6000 Lentiscais CB 96 Sd 110
8200-483 Lentiscais FA 159 Re 125
3070-231 Lentisqueira C 78 Rb 106
6350-081 Leomil GD 81 Ta 105
3620 Leomil VS 61 Sc 103
4415-402 Lever P 60 Rd 102
3780-174 Levira AV 78 Rc 106
3140-146 Liceia C 78 Rb 107
5180 Ligares BN 62 Ta 102
4750 Lijó BR 60 Rc 99
5430-201 Lilela VR 62 Se 99
5340-400 Limãos BN 63 Ta 99
5400 Limãos VR 43 Sd 98
4870 Limões VR 61 Sb 100
1495 Linda-a-Velha L 128 Qe 116
4980 Lindoso VC 42 Re 97
7800 Linhares BE 145 Sa 121
5140 Linhares BN 62 Sd 101
6360 Linhares GD 80 Sd 105
4940 Linhares VC 41 Rc 97
5000 Linhares VR 61 Sc 100
2710-001 Linhó L 128 Qd 116
1150 Lisboa L 128 Qf 116
6000 Lisga CB 96 Sa 109
2350-487 Liteiros SA 94 Rc 112
9500 Livramento AC 177 Zc 122
2480 Livramento LE 94 Rb 111
4615 Lixa P 61 Rf 101
5450 Lixa de Alvão VR 61 Sb 99
4505-422 Lobão AV 60 Rd 103
3460 Lobão da Beira VS 79 Rf 105
7830 Lobata BE 146 Sc 121
3320-168 Lobatos C 95 Sa 108
3530-090 Lobelhe do Mato VS 79 Sa 105
2530 Lobos L 112 Qe 113
5030 Lobrigos VR 61 Sb 101
4620-210 Lodares P 60 Re 101
5360 Lodões BN 62 Sf 101
4920-070 Loivo VC 41 Rb 97
4640 Loivos P 61 Sa 101
5470 Loivos VR 42 Sa 98
5425 Loivos VR 43 Sc 99
4640 Loivos da Ribeira P 61 Sa 102
4705 Lomar BR 60 Rd 99
9960 Lomba AC 176 Tf 112
3840 Lomba AV 78 Rb 105
3730 Lomba AV 79 Re 104
6320 Lomba GD 80 Sf 106
4515 Lomba P 60 Rd 102
4600 Lomba P 61 Rf 101
6000 Lomba Chão CB 96 Sc 110
9360 Lombada MA 178 If 152
9240 Lombada MA 178 If 152
Lombada dos Marinheiros MA 178 Ie 152
9630 Lomba da Fazenda AC 177 Zf 121
9625 Lomba da Maia AC 177 Zd 122
9630 Lomba da Pedraira AC 177 Zf 122
9600 Lombadas AC 177 Zd 122
9385 Lombada Velha MA 178 Ie 152
7780-403 Lombador BE 159 Sa 123
7750-314 Lombardos BE 146 Sc 123
9900 Lombega AC 176 Wb 117
5340-190 Lombo BN 63 Ta 100
Lombo C 95 Re 108
9360 Lombo de S. João MA 178 If 152
9230 Lombo Galego MA 178 Ka 152
3840 Lombomeão AV 78 Rb 105
8400 Lombos FA 158 Rd 126
3020 Lomeiro C 78 Rd 107
5120-221 Longa VS 61 Sc 102
7400-454 Longomel PT 114 Sa 112
4805-192 Longos BR 60 Rd 99
4950 Longos Vales VC 41 Rd 96
6160 Longra CB 95 Sa 109
6430-071 Longroiva GD 62 Se 103
4815 Lordelo BR 60 Rd 100
4580 Lordelo P 60 Rd 101
4930 Lordelo VC 41 Rc 96
4950 Lordelo VC 41 Rd 96
5000 Lordelo VR 61 Sb 101
3515 Lordosa VS 79 Sa 104
9370 Loreto MA 178 If 152
6270-072 Loriga GD 80 Sb 107
3360-106 Lorvão C 78 Re 107
8970-209 Lotão FA 146 Sb 124
8100 Loulé FA 159 Rf 126
3050 Louredo AV 60 Rd 103
4850 Louredo BR 42 Rf 98
4830 Louredo BR 60 Re 99
4580 Louredo P 60 Rd 101
4600 Louredo P 61 Rf 101
5030 Louredo VR 61 Sb 101
4730 Loureira BR 41 Rd 99
2495 Loureira LE 94 Rb 111
3250 Loureira LE 95 Rd 110
3720 Loureiro AV 78 Rc 104
3040 Loureiro C 95 Rd 108
5050 Loureiro VR 61 Sb 101
3500 Loureiro de Silgueiros VS 79 Sa 105
2710-009 Lourel L 112 Qd 116
4970 Lourenda VC 41 Rd 97
2670 Loures L 112 Qe 116
3105-165 Louriçal LE 94 Rb 108
Louriçal, Estação Ferroviária de LE 94 Ra 108
6005-210 Louriçal do Campo CB 96 Sc 108
3270 Louriceira LE 95 Rf 109
6120 Louriceira SA 95 Rf 111
2380 Louriceira SA 113 Rb 112
4980 Lourido VC 42 Re 98
2530-126 Lourinhã L 112 Qe 113
3360-021 Lourinhal C 78 Re 106
4760-530 Louro BR 60 Rc 100
4535 Lourosa AV 60 Rc 103
3400-404 Lourosa C 79 Sa 107
4540-649 Lourosa de Matos AV 60 Re 103
Lousa BN 62 Se 101
6110 Lousa CB 95 Rf 111
6005-232 Lousa CB 96 Sd 109
2670-742 Lousa L 128 Qe 115
3200 Lousã C 95 Re 108
4620-009 Lousada P 60 Re 101
4760 Lousado BR 60 Rc 100
7780 Louseira BE 145 Sa 122
7595 Louseira SE 144 Rd 119
8600 Louzeira FA 158 Rb 126
4920-075 Lovelhe VC 41 Rb 97
8135-021 Ludo FA 159 Rf 126
4600 Lufrei P 61 Rf 101
4900 Lugar do Meio VC 41 Ra 98
5110-617 Lumiares VS 61 Sb 102
3550-182 Lusinde VS 79 Sb 104
3050-221 Luso AV 78 Rd 106
4620 Lustosa P 60 Re 100
3515 Lustosa VS 79 Sa 104
9880 Luz AC 176 Xa 114
7240 Luz E 131 Sd 118
8600 Luz FA 158 Rb 126
8800 Luz FA 160 Sb 126
7665-891 Luzianes BE 158 Rd 123
4560 Luzim P 60 Re 102

M

6250 Macainhas CB 80 Se 106
6300 Macainhas de Baixo GD 80 Se 105
6420-792 Maçal da Ribeira GD 80 Se 104
6360-090 Maçal do Chão GD 80 Se 104
6120-720 Mação SA 95 Sa 111
2460 Macarea LE 94 Qf 111
8550-302 Maçarotal FA 158 Rc 125
5300 Maçãs BN 44 Ta 97
3250 Maças de Caminho LE 95 Rd 109
3250 Maçãs de Dona Maria LE 95 Re 109
3885-701 Maceda AV 60 Rc 103
5360-201 Macedinho BN 62 Sf 100
5340-193 Macedo de Cavaleiros BN 62 Ta 99
5300-663 Macedo do Mato BN 44 Tb 99
5200-401 Macedo do Peso BN 63 Tc 100
5335 Maceira BN 43 Sf 98
6370 Maceira GD 80 Sd 104
2715 Maceira L 112 Qe 115
2405-018 Maceira LE 94 Ra 110
7580 Maceira SE 129 Rd 119
2405-026 Maceirinha LE 94 Ra 110
7860 Machados BE 131 Sd 120
8150 Machados FA 160 Sa 126
7005 Machede E 130 Sb 117
8100 Macheira BE 158 Rd 124
9200 Machico MA 178 Kb 152
3320 Machio, Portela do Fojo- C 95 Rf 108
2140 Machuqueira do Grou SA 113 Rd 114
6100 Macieira CB 95 Rf 109
4870 Macieira VR 61 Sb 100
3640 Macieira VS 62 Sd 103
4485 Macieira da Maia P 60 Rb 100
3750-561 Macieira de Alcoba AV 79 Re 105
3730-220 Macieira de Cambra AV 78 Rd 103
4755-260 Macieira de Rates BR 60 Rc 100
3720 Macinhata de Seixa AV 78 Rd 104
3750 Maçinhata do Vouga AV 78 Rd 105
5160-141 Maçores BN 62 Sf 102
5400-651 Maços VR 43 Sd 98
2065-601 Maçussa L 113 Ra 113
3720 Madail AV 78 Rc 103
9950 Madalena AC 176 Wc 117
6400 Madalena GD 80 Sf 103
4405 Madalena P 60 Rc 102
4580 Madalena P 60 Rd 101
4600 Madalena P 61 Rf 101
2305-425 Madalena SA 95 Rd 111
4970 Madalena VC 41 Rd 98
9360 Madalena do Mar MA 178 If 152
Madeirã CB 95 Rf 109
8970-337 Madeiras FA 160 Sb 124
4925 Madorra VC 41 Rb 98
2640 Mafra L 112 Qe 115
8970 Mafrade FA 160 Sb 124
5000-013 Magalhã VR 61 Sc 101
4785-520 Maganha P 60 Rc 100
8950-332 Magoito FA 160 Sc 125
3320 Mahada de Serra C 95 Rf 108
9625 Maia AC 177 Zd 122
Maia AC 177 Zf 127
4470 Maia P 60 Rc 101
6320 Maimão CB 80 Sf 107
3090-476 Maiorca C 94 Rb 107
2460-531 Maiorga LE 94 Ra 111
5400-640 Mairos VR 43 Sd 98
3050-182 Mala AV 78 Rd 106
2040-535 Malaqueijo SA 113 Rb 113
7490-406 Malarranha E 114 Sa 115
7630 Malavado BE 158 Rb 123
9580 Malbusca AC 177 Zf 127
6320-181 Malcata GD 80 Sf 107
7750 Malhada BE 145 Sb 122
3330 Malhada C 95 Sa 108
2125 Malhada SA 113 Rb 114
3600-429 Malhada VS 79 Sa 103
8800 Malhada de Santa Maria FA 160 Sb 125
8800 Malhada de Santa Maria FA 160 Sc 125
6000-694 Malhada do Cervo CB 96 Sc 109
8800-166 Malhada do Judeu FA 159 Sb 125
8800 Malhada do Peres FA 160 Sc 125
3320-363 Malhada do Rei C 96 Sa 108
8800 Malhada do Rico FA 160 Sb 125
6150-342 Malhadal CB 95 Sa 110
5210 Malhadas BN 63 Te 99
6355-080 Malhada Sorda GD 81 Ta 105
7645 Malhadinha BE 144 Rb 122
8550 Malhão FA 158 Rb 125
7630-382 Malhão BE 144 Rc 122
8365 Malhão FA 159 Rd 125
8800 Malhão FA 160 Sb 126
3475 Malhapão VS 79 Re 105
6270 Malho Pão GD 80 Sb 106
3100-348 Malhos LE 94 Rb 109
2380-502 Malhou SA 113 Rb 112
6100-873 Maljoga CB 95 Sa 110
6350 Malpartida GD 81 Ta 104
6000-560 Malpica do Tejo CB 96 Sd 110
9370 Malseira MA 178 Ie 152
5340-371 Malta BN 63 Ta 100
6400 Malta GD 80 Sf 104
4485-431 Malta P 60 Rb 101
2665-185 Malveira L 112 Qe 115
2755 Malveira de Serra L 128 Qd 116
3770-033 Mamarrosa AV 78 Rc 106
3810-731 Mamodeiro AV 78 Rc 105
3600 Mamouros VS 79 Sa 103
9800 Manadas AC 177 Wf 117
4605 Mancelos P 61 Rf 101
6400-272 Mangide GD 81 Ta 104
3530-092 Mangualde VS 79 Sb 105
6290-111 Mangualde da Serra GD 80 Sc 106
Manhenhas AC 177 Wf 118
4750 Manhente BR 60 Rc 99
2955 Manhoso SE 128 Ra 117
3660-144 Manhouce VS 79 Re 104
Manhufe P 61 Rf 101
4630-168 Manhuncelos P 61 Rf 102
6400-251 Manigoto GD 80 Sf 104
2710-036 Manique de Cima L 128 Qd 116
2065-315 Manique do Intendente L 113 Ra 113
4540 Mansores AV 60 Rd 103
6260-014 Manteigas GD 80 Sc 106
7750-614 Manuel Galo BE 159 Sb 123
5100 Maqueija VS 61 Sa 102
4740 Mar BR 41 Rb 99
8700-078 Maragota FA 160 Sb 126
7480-373 Maranhão PT 114 Sa 114
8600 Marateca FA 158 Rb 126
2965 Marateca SE 129 Rb 117
7630 Maravilha BE 144 Rd 123
3810 Marco AV 78 Rc 105
8800 Marco FA 160 Sb 126
4630 Marco de Canaveses P 61 Rf 101
3550 Mareco VS 80 Sc 105
4560 Marecos P 60 Re 101
2640 Marfa, Estação Ferroviária de L 112 Qe 115
7830 Margaleas BE 146 Sc 120
7480 Margem PT 114 Rf 114
6040 Margem PT 114 Sa 112
6430-081 Marialva GD 62 Se 103
2300-178 Marianaia SA 95 Rd 111
8670-430 Maria Vinagre FA 158 Rb 124
8970-105 Marim FA 146 Sc 124
8200 Marina de Vilamoura FA 159 Rf 126
3880 Marinha AV 78 Rc 103
2425 Marinha da Carpalhosa LE 94 Rb 109
3090-001 Marinha das Ondas C 94 Rb 108
2430-034 Marinha Grande LE 94 Ra 110
2125-101 Marinhais SA 113 Rb 114
4820-537 Marinhão BR 61 Rf 100
4740 Marinhas BR 60 Rb 99
4750 Mariz BR 60 Rb 99
6030-016 Marmelal CB 96 Sb 110
7960-011 Marmelar BE 131 Sc 119
2040 Marmeleira SA 113 Ra 113
3450-095 Marmeleira VS 79 Re 106
6100-427 Marmeleiro CB 95 Rf 110
8970 Marmeleiro FA 146 Sd 124
8550-145 Marmelete FA 158 Rb 125
5370-160 Marmelos BN 62 Se 100
6300 Marmoleiro GD 80 Sf 106
7630-088 Marofanha BE 158 Rb 123
3250 Marques LE 94 Qf 111
4730 Marrancos BR 41 Rc 99
2415 Marrazes LE 94 Rb 110
8950 Marroquil FA 160 Sc 125
3885 Marteira AV 60 Rc 103
2530-338 Marteleira L 112 Qe 113
6230-511 Martianas CB 96 Se 108
2100 Martianes SA 114 Re 116
4755 Martim BR 60 Rc 99
3240 Martim C 95 Rd 109
5090 Martím VR 62 Sd 100
7570 Martim Afonso SE 144 Rb 119
6000-003 Martim Branco CB 96 Sc 109

Martim Branco | 325 P

6320-521 Martim da Pega GD 80 Sf 106
8970 Martim Longo FA 160 Sb 124
7340 Martim Tavares PT 115 Se 114
2200-638 Martinchel SA 95 Re 111
2420 Martinela LE 94 Rb 98
2445-701 Martingança LE 94 Ra 110
7750-506 Martinhanes BE 145 Sa 123
3060 Marvão C 78 Rc 106
7330 Marvão PT 115 Sd 112
7330 Marvao-Beira, Estação Ferroviária de PT 115 Sd 112
3260 Marvila LE 95 Re 109
2140 Marvila SA 113 Re 113
5140 Marzagão BN 62 Se 101
5370-173 Mascarenhas BN 62 Sf 99
7555 Mascarenhas SE 144 Rd 120
4835 Mascotelos BR 60 Re 100
3240 Mata C 95 Rc 109
6005 Mata CB 96 Sd 109
7040 Mata E 114 Rf 116
2580 Mata L 112 Qf 115
7300 Mata PT 115 Sd 112
2435 Mata SA 95 Rc 110
2350 Mata SA 95 Rc 111
Mata, Estação Ferroviária de PT 114 Sb 113
2565-352 Matacães L 112 Qe 114
3320 Mata Cartomil C 95 Sa 107
6440-211 Mata de Lobos GD 63 Ta 103
2025-157 Mata do Rei SA 113 Ra 112
3800 Mataduços AV 78 Rc 105
2140 Mata Forme SA 113 Rd 113
3105 Mata Mourisca LE 94 Rb 108
3105 Mata Mourisca LE 94 Rb 109
6370-353 Matança GD 80 Sc 104
2530 Matas L 112 Qe 113
2490 Matas SA 94 Rc 111
5230-153 Matela BN 63 Tc 99
3550 Matela VS 80 Sc 104
5000-268 Mateus VR 61 Sb 101
4990 Mato VC 41 Rc 99
2150-062 Mato de Miranda SA 113 Rc 112
8800 Mato do Santo Espírito FA 160 Sc 126
3090 Matos C 94 Ra 108
2240 Matos SA 95 Rd 110
2260 Matos SA 95 Rd 111
4454-510 Matosinhos P 60 Rb 101
2500 Matueira LE 112 Qf 112
3850 Mauquim AV 78 Rd 104
4630 Maureles P 61 Re 101
6215 Ma Velha CB 80 Sb 107
6150 Maxiais CB 96 Sb 110
6000 Maxiais CB 96 Sc 110
6100 Maxial CB 95 Rf 109
6185 Maxial CB 96 Sb 108
6000 Maxial CB 96 Sb 109
2565 Maxial L 112 Qe 114
2230-837 Maxial SA 95 Re 111
3320-106 Maxialinho C 96 Sb 108
6120 Maxieira SA 95 Sa 111
4935 Mazarefes VC 41 Rb 98
4950-275 Mazedo VC 41 Rd 96
5100-583 Mazes VS 61 Sa 102
5180-320 Mazouco BN 63 Tb 102
3600 Meã VS 61 Rf 103
7240 Meada E 131 Se 119
7320 Meada PT 96 Sd 111
4900 Meadela VC 41 Rb 98
8800 Mealha FA 160 Sa 124
3050-382 Mealhada AV 78 Rd 106
3320 Meãs C 96 Sb 108
3140 Meãs do Campo C 78 Rc 107
2580 Meca L 112 Qf 114
7750 Meceares BE 145 Sb 122
7800 Mechão BE 146 Sb 121
3140-037 Meco C 78 Rc 107
6430 Meda GD 62 Se 103
3420-121 Meda de Mouros C 79 Rf 107
4515-344 Medas P 60 Rd 102
7830 Medeiros BE 146 Sc 121
8300 Medeiros FA 159 Rd 125
5470 Medeiros VR 42 Sb 98
6060 Medelim CB 97 Se 108
4820 Medelo BR 61 Rf 100
3465 Medorno VS 79 Rf 105
2200-601 Medroa SA 95 Re 111
5030 Medrões VR 61 Sb 101

6060 Medronheira CB 97 Sf 110
8800 Medronheira FA 159 Sa 124
3330-141 Mega Cimeira C 95 Rf 108
3330 Mega Fundeira C 95 Rf 109
4970 Mei VC 41 Rd 97
8600 Meia Praia FA 158 Rb 126
2350-625 Meia Via SA 95 Rc 112
8550-307 Meia Viana FA 158 Re 125
5100-630 Meijinhos VS 61 Sa 102
6090-381 Meimoa CB 80 Se 107
4620 Meinedo P 60 Re 101
6300-135 Meios GD 80 Sd 106
3105 Meirinhas LE 94 Rb 109
5200-160 Meirinhos BN 63 Tb 101
5300-673 Meixedo BN 44 Tb 97
4925 Meixedo VC 41 Rb 98
5470 Meixedo VR 42 Sb 97
3610-071 Meixedo VS 61 Sb 102
5470-180 Meixide VR 43 Sc 98
4595 Meixomil P 60 Rd 101
5100 Melcões VS 61 Sb 102
2605 Meleças L 112 Qe 116
5340-014 Meles BN 44 Sf 99
4960-578 Melgaço VC 42 Re 96
4870-214 Melhe VR 61 Sb 99
5320 Mêlhe BN 44 Ta 98
7570-600 Melides SE 144 Rb 120
6290-121 Melo GD 80 Sc 105
4515-461 Melres P 60 Rd 102
3240-689 Melrica C 95 Rc 109
6110 Melrica CB 95 Rf 110
6160 Melrico CB 96 Sa 109
2725-001 Mem Martins L 112 Qd 116
2420-227 Memória LE 94 Rc 110
7200-053 Mencoca E 131 Sc 117
6000-696 Mendares CB 96 Sc 109
3100-563 Mendes LE 94 Rb 109
2480-215 Mendiga LE 94 Ra 112
6420-641 Mendo Gordo GD 80 Sd 103
6300-160 Menoita GD 80 Se 105
4920 Mentrestido VC 41 Rb 97
8800 Mercador FA 160 Sb 125
2580-087 Merceana L 112 Qf 114
2635 Merces L 112 Se 101
7230 Mercês BE 132 Sf 120
4700 Merelim BR 41 Rd 99
7750 Mértola BE 146 Sc 123
4950 Merufe VC 42 Rd 96
3405-350 Meruge C 79 Sb 106
4810 Mesão Frio BR 60 Re 100
5040 Mesão Frio VR 61 Sa 102
4640-360 Mesquinhata P 61 Rf 102
7750 Mesquita BE 160 Sc 123
8970 Mesquita FA 146 Sb 124
8365 Mesquita FA 159 Rd 125
6360 Mesquitela GD 80 Sd 105
6355 Mesquitela GD 81 Ta 105
3530 Mesquitela VS 79 Sb 105
7830 Messangil BE 146 Sd 121
4950 Messegães VC 42 Rd 96
7600-310 Messejana BE 145 Re 122
8375-046 Messines de Baixo FA 159 Re 125
3330 Mestras C 95 Rf 108
8970 Mestras FA 160 Sa 124
2525 Mestre Mendo LE 112 Qe 112
8500-132 Mexilhoeira Grande FA 158 Rc 126
3600 Mezio VS 61 Sa 103
6355-100 Mido GD 81 Ta 105
4755 Midões BR 60 Rc 99
3360 Midões C 78 Rd 107
3420 Midões C 79 Sa 106
5445 Midões VR 62 Sd 99
2415-020 Milagres LE 94 Rb 110
4950-104 Milagres VC 41 Rd 96
5370-023 Milhais BN 62 Se 100
5300-682 Milhão BN 44 Tc 98
8670 Milharada FA 158 Ra 126
2665-307 Milharado L 112 Qe 115
4755 Milhazes BR 60 Rc 100
6440-062 Milheiro GD 81 Sf 104
2240 Milheiros SA 95 Rd 110
3700 Milheirós de Poiares AV 60 Rd 103
7750 Milhoro BE 145 Sb 123
6110 Milreu CB 95 Rf 111
7570 Mina da Caveira SE 144 Rc 120
7800-731 Mina da Juliana BE 145 Rf 121
7230 Mina de Apariz BE 131 Sf 120
7780 Mina de Ferragudo BE 145 Rf 123
7580 Mina de Jungeis SE 129 Rd 118

7750-120 Mina de São Domingos BE 146 Sd 122
7250-053 Mina do Bugalho E 131 Se 116
7570 Mina do Lousal SE 144 Rd 120
5300-494 Minas da Ribeira BN 44 Tc 98
4870 Minas de Adoria VR 61 Sa 100
4870-031 Minas de São João VR 61 Sa 100
5070 Minas de Vinheiros VR 62 Sc 101
7670 Minas do Montinho BE 144 Re 122
5470 Minas dos Carris VR 42 Rf 98
2395 Minde SA 94 Rb 111
4485-469 Mindelo P 60 Rb 101
6360-110 Minhocal GD 80 Sd 104
4775 Minhotães BR 60 Rc 100
3560-085 Mioma VS 80 Sd 104
3070-301 Mira C 78 Rb 106
2485 Mira d'Aire LE 94 Rb 111
5370-660 Miradeses BN 62 Se 99
6400 Miragaia GD 80 Sf 105
2530-403 Miragaia L 112 Qe 113
4970 Miranda VC 41 Rc 97
3220-116 Miranda do Corvo C 95 Re 108
5210-190 Miranda do Douro BN 63 Te 99
5370 Mirandela BN 62 Se 100
3360-073 Miro C 79 Re 107
6355-110 Miuzela GD 81 Sf 105
6300 Mizarela GD 80 Sd 105
2005-095 Moçarria SA 113 Rb 113
2910 Mocho SE 129 Ra 117
7250 Mocissos E 131 Se 117
4590 Modelas P 60 Rd 101
4485-572 Modivas P 60 Rb 101
3600 Mões VS 79 Sa 103
5320-060 Mofreita BN 44 Ta 97
5200 Mogadouro BN 63 Tb 100
5140-171 Mogo de Malta BN 62 Se 101
3780-453 Mogofores AV 78 Rd 106
5340 Mogrão BN 44 Sf 99
5320 Moimenta BN 44 Ta 97
4690 Moimenta VS 61 Re 102
3600 Moimenta VS 61 Rf 103
3620-300 Moimenta da Beira VS 61 Sc 103
6290-141 Moimenta da Serra GD 80 Sc 106
3530-310 Moimenta de Maceira Dão VS 79 Sb 105
6420-491 Moimentinha GD 80 Se 104
7700-260 Moimentos BE 159 Rf 124
8500-140 Moinho da Rocha FA 158 Rc 125
3140 Moinho de Almoxarife C 94 Rb 108
7750 Moinho de Vento BE 146 Sb 123
7700 Moinho de Vento BE 159 Rf 123
8670 Moinho do Sogro FA 158 Rb 124
2965 Moinhola E 129 Rc 117
2425 Moinhos LE 94 Ra 109
3090 Moinhos da Gândara C 78 Rb 107
3780 Moita AV 78 Rd 106
6320 Moita GD 80 Se 107
2445 Moita LE 94 Ra 110
3280 Moita LE 95 Re 109
2495 Moita SA 94 Rb 111
2860 Moita SE 128 Ra 117
3600 Moita VS 79 Sa 103
2425-508 Moita da Roda LE 94 Rb 110
3420-034 Moita da Serra C 79 Rf 107
2495-028 Moita do Martinho LE 94 Rb 111
2530 Moita dos Ferreiros L 112 Qe 113
6150 Moitas CB 96 Sa 110
2380-563 Moitas Venda SA 94 Rc 112
7580-709 Moitinha SE 129 Rb 118
7665-803 Moitinhas BE 158 Rc 124
4890 Molares BR 61 Sa 100
4540 Moldes AV 60 Re 103
2530-514 Moledo L 112 Qe 113
4910 Moledo VC 41 Ra 97
3600-460 Moledo VS 79 Sa 104
3460-009 Molelos VS 79 Rf 105
7800-641 Mombeja BE 145 Rf 120
4950 Monção VC 41 Rd 96

8700-081 Moncarapacho FA 160 Sb 126
8550 Monchique FA 158 Rc 125
8970 Monchique FA 160 Sb 124
3610-049 Mondim da Beira VS 61 Sb 102
4880-231 Mondim de Basto VR 61 Sa 100
5000 Mondrões VR 61 Sb 101
5090-013 Monfebres VR 62 Sd 100
7450 Monforte PT 115 Sd 114
5470 Monforte VR 43 Sd 98
6000-580 Monforte da Beira CB 97 Se 110
6060-071 Monfortinho CB 97 Ta 108
3320-170 Moninho C 95 Sa 108
3260-042 Moninhos Fundeiros LE 95 Re 109
6060-085 Monsanto CB 97 Sf 108
2380-575 Monsanto SA 113 Rb 112
7200-175 Monsaraz E 131 Sd 118
3780-563 Monsarros AV 78 Rd 106
7090 Monsarves E 130 Re 118
4830 Monsul BR 42 Re 99
7040 Monta dos Abelhões E 114 Sb 115
5470 Montalegre VR 42 Sb 98
6050-431 Montalvão PT 96 Sc 111
7860 Montalvo BE 131 Sd 120
7750 Montalvo BE 146 Sc 122
2250-220 Montalvo SA 95 Re 112
7425 Montargil PT 114 Re 114
4925 Montaria VC 41 Rb 98
6005 Mont de São Luís CB 96 Sd 109
9950 Monte AC 176 Wc 118
Monte AV 78 Rc 104
4840 Monte BR 42 Re 98
4820 Monte BR 61 Re 99
9050 Monte MA 178 Ka 152
8800 Monte Agudo FA 160 Sb 126
7670 Monte Alto BE 145 Re 122
7750 Monte Alto BE 146 Sc 123
7750 Monte Alto BE 146 Sc 123
8375 Monte Alto FA 159 Re 125
7670 Monte Arriba BE 159 Re 123
2640-066 Monte Bom L 128 Qd 115
7830 Monte Branco BE 146 Sd 120
Monte Branco BE 160 Sa 124
7040 Monte Branco E 114 Sb 116
7250 Monte Branco E 131 Se 116
8375 Monte Branco FA 159 Rd 125
7670 Monte Branco da Serra BE 146 Se 120
6000 Monte Brito CB 96 Sd 109
8100 Monte Brito FA 159 Re 125
6050-474 Monte Claro PT 96 Sb 111
4825 Monte Córdova P 60 Rd 101
7630-355 Montecos BE 144 Rc 122
7200 Monte da Azinheira E 131 Sc 118
7170 Monte da Capitoa E 131 Sc 117
8100 Monte da Charneca FA 159 Re 125
7630 Monte da Estrada BE 144 Rc 122
7050 Monte da Estrada E 114 Sb 115
7750-039 Monte da Légua BE 145 Sa 122
7320 Monte da Meada PT 96 Sd 112
7480 Monte da Ordem PT 114 Rf 115
7900 Monte da Panasqueira BE 130 Sa 120
7430 Monte da Pedra PT 114 Sb 112
7580 Monte da Pedra SE 129 Rc 118
7780 Monte da Perdigova BE 145 Rf 122
2100-500 Monte das Figueiras SA 113 Rc 116
Monte das Flores E 130 Sa 117
6000 Monte das Lameiras CB 96 Sd 109
6040 Monte das Lameiras PT 114 Sb 112

7800 Monte das Pereiras BE 145 Rf 121
7080 Monte das Piçarras E 129 Rc 117
7780 Monte das Sorraias BE 145 Sa 123
6060 Monte da Toula CB 97 Sf 109
6355-020 Monte da Velha GD 81 Ta 105
7430 Monte da Velha PT 115 Sc 113
7700 Monte da Vinha BE 159 Sa 123
7480 Monte da Vinha PT 114 Rf 114
7580 Monte da Volta SE 129 Rc 118
7320 Monte de Adelina PT 96 Sc 111
7595-022 Monte de Algalé SE 144 Re 119
8970 Monte de Argil FA 160 Sb 124
8950 Monte de Baixo Grande FA 160 Sc 125
6000 Monte de Goula 96 Sb 109
7600 Monte de São João BE 145 Re 121
7220-201 Monte de Trigo E 130 Sb 118
7750 Monte de Viegas BE 145 Sa 122
6000 Monte do Barata CB 96 Se 110
6250 Monte do Bispo CB 80 Se 107
7005 Monte do Bussalfão E 130 Sb 117
7900 Monte do Corvo BE 159 Sa 123
7430 Monte do Gamito PT 115 Sc 113
6040 Monte do Pereiros PT 114 Sa 112
6050 Monte do Pombo PT 96 Sc 111
4900-279 Montedor VC 41 Ra 98
2130 Monte dos Condes SA 113 Rb 115
7700 Monte dos Corvos BE 146 Sc 123
7050-640 Monte dos Frades E 113 Rc 116
7450-100 Monte dos Francos PT 115 Sd 114
7220 Monte dos Hospitais E 130 Sb 118
7425 Monte dos Leões PT 114 Re 114
6050-475 Monte dos Matos PT 96 Sb 111
7700 Monte dos Mestres BE 159 Sa 123
7220 Monte dos Pernes E 131 Sc 119
7600-171 Monte dos Poços BE 145 Rf 122
6030-052 Monte Fidalgo CB 96 Sc 110
6005 Monte Fidalgo CB 96 Sd 109
8950-201 Monte Francisco FA 160 Sd 125
6000 Monte Gordo CB 96 Sb 110
8900 Monte Gordo FA 160 Sd 125
6000 Monte Grande CB 96 Sb 110
8300 Monte Grandes FA 159 Rd 126
3600-474 Monteiras VS 61 Sa 103
6300 Monteiros GD 80 Sf 105
5450-183 Monteiros VR 43 Sb 99
7700 Monte João Dias BE 159 Sa 124
8600 Monte Judeu FA 158 Rb 126
2715-615 Montelavar L 112 Qe 115
6300-145 Monte Margarida GD 80 Sf 106
Montemor, Estação Ferroviária de C 78 Rb 108
7050 Montemor-O-Novo E 130 Re 117
3140-249 Montemor-o-Velho C 94 Rb 107
2665-410 Montemuro L 128 Qe 115
5450-264 Montenegrelo VR 61 Sc 100

8005 Monte Negro FA 159 Sa 126
7670 Montenegro, Estação Ferroviária de BE 144 Rd 122
7780-305 Monte Nobre BE 145 Sa 122
7830 Monte Nova de Ferradura BE 146 Sd 121
7700 Monte Novo BE 159 Sa 124
8670 Monte Novo FA 158 Ra 125
8670 Monte Novo FA 158 Rb 124
8670 Monte Novo FA 158 Rb 125
6320 Monte Novo GD 80 Se 106
Monte Novo SE 129 Rc 118
7780 Monte Novo das Janelas BE 145 Rf 122
7630 Monte Novo de Troviscais BE 144 Rb 123
Monte Novo-Palma, Estação Ferroviária de SE 129 Rc 118
6355 Monte Perebolso GD 81 Ta 105
2425 Monte Real LE 94 Ra 109
7300 Monterecos PT 115 Se 113
3360 Monte Redondo C 78 Rd 107
2565-518 Monte Redondo L 112 Qe 114
2425-617 Monte Redondo LE 94 Rb 109
4970 Monte Redondo VC 41 Rd 98
8670 Monte Ruivo FA 158 Rb 125
6300 Montes GD 80 Sf 105
6150-128 Montes da Senhora CB 96 Sb 110
8500-059 Montes de Alvor FA 158 Rc 126
8500 Montes de Cima FA 158 Rc 125
7250 Montes Juntos E 131 Sd 117
7430 Montes Novos PT 115 Sc 113
8100 Montes-Novos FA 160 Sa 125
8970 Monte Vascão FA 160 Sc 123
6300-155 Monte Vasco GD 80 Se 106
7630 Monte Velho BE 144 Rd 122
7830 Monte Velho BE 146 Sd 120
7750 Monte Velho BE 160 Sa 123
6060 Monte Velho CB 97 Sf 109
7580-321 Montevil SE 129 Rc 118
7170 Monte Virgem E 131 Sc 116
2460 Montez LE 94 Ra 111
5300 Montezinho BN 44 Tb 97
2870 Montijo SE 128 Ra 116
4820-580 Montim BR 61 Rf 100
7665 Montinho BE 144 Rc 123
7700 Montinho BE 159 Rf 124
3060-502 Montinho C 78 Rc 106
8950 Montinho FA 160 Sc 125
7480 Montinho PT 114 Sa 114
7300 Montinho PT 115 Se 113
2100 Montinho SA 113 Rd 115
2910 Montinho SE 129 Ra 117
7750 Montinho ale de Camelos BE 145 Sa 122
7780 Montinhos BE 145 Rf 122
8600-119 Montinhos da Luz FA 158 Rb 126
7200 Montoito E 131 Sc 117
3060-292 Montouro C 78 Rc 106
5320-085 Montouto BN 44 Ta 97
5230-231 Mora BN 63 Tc 100
7490 Mora E 114 Rf 115
5340-351 Morais BN 63 Tb 100
7750-409 Moreanes BE 146 Sc 123
5300-844 Moredo BN 44 Tb 99
4470 Moreira P 60 Rc 101
4950 Moreira VC 41 Rd 96
5450 Moreira VR 62 Sc 100
3520 Moreira VS 79 Sa 105
4815-253 Moreira de Cónegos BR 60 Rd 100
4905 Moreira de Geraz do Lima VC 41 Rb 98

6420 Moreira de Rei GD 80 Se 104
4890 Moreira do Castelo BR 61 Rf 100
4990-670 Moreira do Lima VC 41 Rc 98
4820 Moreira do Rei BR 61 Rf 100
5400-643 Moreiras VR 43 Sd 99
2350 Moreiras Grandes SA 95 Rc 111
6420-507 Moreirinhas GD 80 Se 103
4485 Moreiró P 60 Rb 101
7340 Moreiros PT 115 Sd 114
2715-011 Morelena L 112 Qe 115
2710-007 Morelinho L 112 Qd 116
7750-379 Morena BE 145 Sb 123
6060 Morena CB 97 Sf 110
8800 Morenos FA 160 Sb 125
5470 Morgade VR 42 Sb 98
4860 Morgado BR 61 Sa 100
2070 Morgado SA 113 Rb 104
3140 Morraça C 78 Rc 107
4705-481 Morreira BR 60 Rd 100
3450-120 Mortágua VS 79 Re 106
7300 Mortais PT 115 Sc 113
3450-338 Mortazel VS 79 Re 106
Mós BR 41 Rd 98
5155 Mós GD 62 Se 102
4905 Mós VC 41 Rb 98
1885-001 Moscavide L 112 Qf 116
4860-430 Moscoso BR 42 Sa 99
5300 Mós de Rebordãos BN 44 Tb 98
8200-562 Mosqueira FA 159 Re 126
7570 Mosqueirão SE 144 Rc 120
3475-060 Mosteirinho VS 79 Re 105
Mosteiro AC 176 Te 112
4520 Mosteiro AV 60 Rc 103
7750 Mosteiro BE 146 Sb 122
5385 Mosteiro BN 43 Sf 99
4850 Mosteiro BR 42 Rf 99
6100 Mosteiro CB 95 Rf 110
6160 Mosteiro CB 95 Sa 109
3270-077 Mosteiro LE 95 Re 109
3640 Mosteiro VS 62 Sc 103
3600 Mosteiro VS 79 Sa 103
5430-125 Mosteiró de Cima VR 43 Sd 98
3460 Mosteiro de Fráguas VS 79 Rf 105
2440 Mosteiro de Santa Maria da Vitória LE 94 Rb 111
9555 Mosteiros AC 176 Zb 121
7340 Mosteiros PT 115 Se 113
2025-158 Mosteiros SA 113 Ra 112
4485 Mosteirós P 60 Rb 101
7200-177 Motrinos E 131 Sd 118
5000 Mouçós VR 61 Sb 101
6100-670 Mougueira CB 95 Rf 110
6160 Mougueiras de Cima CB 96 Sb 109
2560 Mougueles L 112 Qd 114
4660-145 Moumis VS 61 Sa 102
7860 Moura BE 131 Sd 120
3305-224 Moura da Serra C 79 Sa 107
5050 Moura Morta VR 61 Sb 101
3600-480 Moura Morta VS 61 Sa 103
7780 Mourão BE 145 Rf 122
5360 Mourão BN 62 Se 101
7240 Mourão E 131 Sd 118
3460-330 Mouraz VS 79 Rf 106
4730 Moure BR 41 Rd 99
4830 Moure BR 42 Rf 99
4755 Moure BR 60 Rc 99
6005 Mourela CB 96 Sc 108
5470 Mourilhe VR 42 Sa 97
4970 Mourisca VC 41 Rd 97
3105 Mourisca de Baixo LE 94 Rb 109
3750-776 Mourisca do Vouga AV 78 Rd 105
2200-683 Mouriscas SA 95 Rf 111
Mouriscas, Estação Ferroviária de SA 95 Rf 112
Mourisca-Sado, Estação Ferroviária de SE 129 Sd 119
3305-225 Mourisia C 79 Sa 107
4580-590 Mouriz P 60 Rd 101
3420 Mouronho C 79 Rf 107
3750-825 Mouteado AV 78 Rd 105
5320 Moz de Celas BN 44 Ta 98
3515 Mozelos VS 79 Sa 104
3465 Múceres VS 79 Rf 105
7540-068 Muda SE 144 Rb 121
2125-312 Muge SA 113 Rb 114
2125 Muge, Estação Ferroviária de SA 113 Rb 114
3465-154 Muna VS 79 Rf 105

3505-352 Mundão VS 79 Sa 104
7300 Muralha PT 115 Sd 113
5155 Murça GD 62 Se 102
5090 Murça VR 62 Sd 100
2755-002 Murches L 128 Qd 116
5340 Murçós BN 44 Ta 98
3300 Murganheira C 79 Rf 107
2640 Murgueira L 112 Qe 115
5385 Múrias BN 43 Sf 99
6090 Muro CB 97 Se 108
4745 Muro P 60 Rc 101
7580 Murta SE 129 Rb 118
3060 Murtede C 78 Rc 106
7750 Murteira BE 160 Sa 123
2670 Murteira L 112 Qe 115
2550 Murteira L 112 Qf 113
6150-616 Murteirinha CB 96 Sb 110
3870-103 Murtosa AV 78 Rc 104
5150 Muxagata C 62 Sf 102
6370 Muxagata GD 80 Sd 105

N

6290 Nabais GD 80 Sc 105
2000-344 Nabais SA 113 Rb 112
5360-101 Nabo BN 62 Sf 101
2500-542 Nadadouro LE 112 Qe 112
2530 Nadrupe L 112 Qe 113
3620-400 Nagosa VS 61 Sc 102
3440-631 Nagosela VS 79 Rf 106
5130-221 Nagoselo do Douro VS 62 Sd 101
7780 Namorados BE 145 Rf 123
7750 Namorados BE 145 Sb 123
3460-355 Nandufe VS 79 Rf 105
5400-581 Nantes VR 43 Sd 98
3810-559 Nariz AV 78 Rc 105
7630 Nascedios BE 144 Rb 122
7630 Nascedios BE 158 Rc 123
4495-073 Navais P 60 Rb 100
5370-601 Navalho BN 62 Se 100
6440 Nava Redona GD 81 Ta 103
4710 Navarra BR 42 Rd 99
7750-046 Navarro BE 145 Sb 122
8550 Nave FA 158 Rc 125
6320 Nave GD 81 Ta 106
6355 Nave de Haver GD 81 Ta 105
8100-188 Nave do Barão FA 159 Rf 125
7340-115 Nave Fria PT 115 Se 113
7665 Nave Redonda BE 158 Rd 124
6150 Naves CB 96 Sb 111
6350 Naves GD 81 Ta 105
4990-675 Nazaré LE 94 Qf 111
2450 Nazaré LE 94 Qf 111
7750 Negas BE 160 Sa 124
2715-313 Negrais L 112 Qe 115
5320-023 Negreda BN 44 Ta 98
4775-190 Negreiros BR 60 Rc 100
7780 Negrões BE 145 Rf 123
5470 Negrões VR 42 Sb 98
4935 Neiva VC 41 Rb 99
3505 Nelas VS 79 Sa 104
3520 Nelas VS 79 Sa 105
6100-459 Nesperal CB 95 Rf 110
4835-468 Nespereira BR 60 Re 100
6290 Nespereira GD 80 Sc 105
4620 Nespereira P 60 Re 101
4690 Nespereira VS 61 Rf 102
3090-448 Netos C 78 Rb 107
3105 Netos LE 94 Rc 108
7750-047 Neves BE 146 Sb 123
4730 Nevogilde BR 41 Rd 99
4620 Nevogilde P 60 Re 101
2965 Nicolau L 112 Qe 117
7540 Nicolau SE 144 Rc 120
4775-440 Nine BR 60 Rc 100
6000-590 Ninho do Açor CB 96 Sc 109
6050 Nisa PT 96 Sc 111
5300 Nogueira BN 44 Tb 98
3300 Nogueira C 79 Rf 107
6090 Nogueira CB 97 Sf 107
4920 Nogueira VC 41 Rb 97
4925 Nogueira VC 41 Rb 98
4980 Nogueira VC 41 Rd 98
5460 Nogueira VR 43 Sc 98
5000 Nogueira VR 61 Sb 101
3505-234 Nogueira VS 79 Sa 104
5400-652 Nogueira da Montanha VR 43 Sd 99
4500-691 Nogueira da Regedoura AV 60 Rc 102
3700 Nogueira do Cravo AV 78 Rd 103
3400-427 Nogueira do Cravo C 79 Sa 106
7050 Nogueirinha E 130 Rf 117

4540-039 Noninha AV 61 Rf 103
8375 Nora FA 159 Rd 125
8800 Nora FA 160 Sc 125
8900 Nora FA 160 Sc 125
9630 Nordeste AC 177 Zf 122
9630 Nordestinho AC 177 Ze 121
8300-036 Norinha FA 159 Rd 125
9800 Norte Grande AC 177 Wf 116
Norte Pequeno AC 176 Wb 117
9850 Norte Pequeno AC 177 Wf 117
7000-013 Nossa Senhora da Boa Fé E 130 Rf 117
7320 Nossa Senhora da Graça de Póvoa e Meadas PT 96 Sc 111
7000 Nossa Senhora da Graça do Divor E 130 Sa 117
7370 Nossa Senhora da Graça dos Degolados PT 115 Sf 114
7800-651 Nossa Senhora das Neves BE 145 Sb 120
7005-672 Nossa Senhora de Machede E 130 Sb 117
9700 Nossa Senhora do Pilar AC 176 Xe 116
7450 Nossa Senhora dos Prazeres PT 115 Sd 115
9650 Nossa Senhora dos Remedios AC 177 Ze 122
7230 Noudar BE 132 Sf 119
5090-200 Noura VR 62 Sd 100
8670 Nova FA 158 Rb 125
5400 Nova de Veiga VR 43 Sd 98
4765 Novais BR 60 Rd 100
5400 Noval VR 43 Sc 98
7630 Nova Reguengo Pequeno BE 144 Rc 122
2705 Novas L 112 Qd 116
4560-262 Novelas P 60 Re 101
5445-082 Nozedo VR 43 Sd 99
5340 Nozelos BN 44 Sf 99
5160 Nozelos BN 62 Sf 101
5430-180 Nozelos VR 43 Se 98
5155-610 Numão GD 62 Se 102
5320 Nunes BN 44 Ta 98
5320 Nuzedo BN 43 Sf 97

O

2510 Óbidos LE 112 Qe 112
8670-320 Odeceixe FA 158 Rb 124
8950-351 Odeleite FA 160 Sd 124
8300-037 Odelouca FA 158 Rd 125
7630 Odemira BE 158 Rc 123
7630 Odiáxere FA 158 Rc 126
7900-360 Odivelas BE 145 Rf 119
2675 Odivelas L 112 Qe 116
2780 Oeiras L 128 Qa 116
3680 Oestriz VS 79 Re 105
4740-405 Ofir BR 60 Rb 99
3770-059 Oiã AV 78 Rc 105
3750 Óis da Ribeira AV 78 Rc 105
3780-502 Óis do Bairro AV 78 Rd 106
2350 Olais SA 95 Rd 111
2300-088 Olalhas SA 95 Re 111
5130 Olas VS 62 Se 102
4575 Oldrões P 60 Re 102
6060-621 Oledo CB 97 Se 109
5300-674 Oleirinhos BN 44 Tb 97
7040 Oleirita E 130 Sa 116
5300 Oleiros BN 44 Ta 97
4730 Oleiros BR 41 Rd 99
4805 Oleiros BR 60 Rd 100
6160 Oleiros, Amieira- CB 96 Sa 109
2580-191 Olhalvo L 112 Qf 114
8700 Olhão FA 159 Sb 126
7900 Olhas BE 145 Re 120
6000 Olheirão CB 96 Sc 109
7050 Olheiro E 130 Re 117
2510-511 Olho Marinho LE 112 Qe 113
3060 Olhos da Fervença C 78 Rb 106
8200 Olhos d'Água FA 159 Re 126
2950-554 Olhos de Água SE 128 Ra 117
1990 Olivais L 128 Qf 116
2495 Olivais LE 94 Rb 110
4415 Olival P 60 Rc 102
2435 Olival SA 94 Rc 110
4750 Oliveira BR 41 Rc 99

4830 Oliveira BR 42 Re 99
4770 Oliveira BR 60 Rd 100
4605 Oliveira P 61 Re 101
5040 Oliveira VC 41 Sa 101
3720-001 Oliveira de Azeméis AV 78 Rd 103
3500-892 Oliveira de Barreiros VS 79 Sa 105
3680 Oliveira de Frades VS 79 Re 104
3770 Oliveira do Bairro AV 78 Rd 105
3430-341 Oliveira do Conde VS 79 Sa 106
4430 Oliveira do Douro P 60 Rc 102
4690-420 Oliveira do Douro VS 61 Rf 102
3400-056 Oliveira do Hospital C 79 Sa 106
Oliveira do Mondego C 79 Re 107
7040 Oliveiras E 130 Rf 116
3810 Oliveirinha AV 78 Rc 105
3430-151 Oliveirinha VS 79 Sa 106
5340-372 Olmos BN 63 Ta 100
4600 Olo P 61 Rf 101
2420-122 Opeia LE 94 Rb 110
7830 Orada BE 131 Sc 120
7150-308 Orada E 115 Sd 115
4910 Orbacém VC 41 Rb 98
6230-512 Orca CB 96 Sd 108
7960 Ordem BE 130 Sb 120
4620 Ordem P 60 Re 101
5040 Ordem P 61 Sa 101
4560-192 Ordins P 60 Rd 102
5060 Ordonho VR 61 Sc 101
5150-145 Orgal GD 62 Sf 102
7220-301 Oriola E 130 Sa 119
6200-580 Orjais CB 80 Sd 106
5400 Orjais VR 43 Se 98
5470-382 Ormeche VR 42 Sa 98
6120 Ortiga SA 95 Rf 112
7540 Ortiga SE 144 Rb 121
2425-664 Ortigosa LE 94 Ra 110
3450 Ortigosa VS 79 Re 106
6185-269 Orvalho CB 96 Sb 108
3720 Ossela AV 78 Rd 104
3105 Osso da Baleia LE 94 Ra 108
2580-243 Ota L 112 Ra 114
3840-302 Ouca AV 78 Rc 105
5400-658 Oucidres VR 43 Sd 98
7370-200 Ouguela PT 116 Sf 114
8200 Oura FA 159 Re 126
5425-201 Oura VR 43 Sc 99
2490-201 Ourém SA 94 Rc 111
3060 Ourenta C 78 Rc 106
4890 Ourilhe BR 61 Rf 100
7780 Ourique BE 145 Re 122
7670 Ourique BE 158 Rc 123
6230-900 Ourondo CB 96 Sb 108
3630-135 Ourozinho VS 62 Sd 103
5320 Ousilhão BN 44 Ta 98
2900 Outão SE 128 Ra 118
4850 Outeiro BR 61 Rf 99
4760 Outeirinho BR 60 Rc 100
3720 Outeiro AV 78 Rc 104
5300 Outeiro BN 44 Tc 98
4740 Outeiro BR 41 Rb 99
4740 Outeiro BR 60 Rb 99
4860 Outeiro BR 61 Rf 99
3420 Outeiro C 79 Rf 107
3090 Outeiro C 94 Rb 108
3240 Outeiro C 95 Rd 109
7490 Outeiro E 114 Rf 115
2835 Outeiro SE 128 Qf 117
4920 Outeiro VC 41 Rb 97
4925 Outeiro VC 41 Rb 98
5470 Outeiro VR 42 Sa 98
5450 Outeiro VR 61 Sb 100
5450 Outeiro VR 61 Sc 99
6040 Outeiro Cimeiro PT 96 Sa 112
2565-590 Outeiro da Cabeça L 112 Qe 113
2040-174 Outeiro da Cortiçada SA 113 Rb 113
6430-312 Outeiro de Gatos GD 62 Se 103
7300 Outeiro do Alho PT 115 Sd 113
2300-241 Outeiro do Forno SA 95 Re 111
5400 Outeiro Seco VR 43 Sd 98
3060-491 Outil C 78 Rc 107
4760-692 Outiz BR 60 Rc 100
7580 Ouvidor SE 129 Rc 118
4660 Ovadas VS 61 Sa 102
3880-001 Ovar AV 78 Rc 103
2100-407 Ovelhas SA 113 Rc 114
3440 Óvoa VS 79 Rf 106

2240 Pessegueiro SA 114 Rf 112
6300-070 Pessolta GD 80 Se 105
4860-024 Petimão BR 61 Rf 100
5300-502 Petisqueira BN 44 Tc 97
6350-331 Peva GD 81 Ta 105
3620-441 Peva VS 80 Sb 103
2480-140 Pia Carneira LE 94 Rb 112
3330-205 Piães C 95 Rf 107
Pia Furada C 95 Rc 109
7750 Pias BE 146 Sc 122
7830 Pias BE 146 Sd 120
2240-566 Pias SA 95 Re 110
4950 Pias VC 41 Rc 96
7800 Pica Milho BE 146 Sb 121
3600-540 Picão VS 61 Sa 103
7780 Piçarras BE 145 Rf 123
4730 Pico BR 41 Rd 98
8100 Pico Alto FA 159 Re 125
9600 Pico da Pedra AC 177 Zc 122
4730 Pico de Regalados BR 41 Rd 98
5350 Picões BN 62 Ta 101
7750-410 Picoitos BE 146 Sc 123
5225-072 Picote BN 63 Td 100
4505 Picoto AV 60 Rc 102
9930 Piedade AC 177 Wf 118
3750-406 Piedade AV 78 Rd 105
4505 Pigeiros AV 60 Rd 103
2430-321 Pilado LE 94 Ra 110
4690 Pimeiro VS 61 Rf 102
5470 Pinças VR 42 Rf 98
2100-300 Pinçais SA 129 Re 115
2100-300 Pinçalinhos SA 129 Re 115
2640 Pincanceira L 128 Qd 114
3090-421 Pincho C 78 Rb 107
8600 Pincho FA 158 Rb 125
3720 Pindelo AV 78 Rd 103
3500-543 Pindelo VS 79 Sa 105
3660-170 Pindelo dos Milagres VS 79 Sa 104
5300-751 Pinela BN 44 Tb 98
5230-181 Pinelo BN 44 Tc 99
8100 Pinhal FA 159 Re 126
5140-270 Pinhal do Douro BN 62 Se 101
5140-205 Pinhal do Norte BN 62 Sd 101
2955-001 Pinhal Novo SE 128 Ra 117
6270-141 Pinhanços GD 80 Sb 106
5085 Pinhão VR 62 Sc 101
5060 Pinhão Cel VR 61 Sc 100
3850 Pinheira AV 78 Rc 105
7630 Pinheiro BE 144 Rb 122
7600 Pinheiro BE 145 Re 121
4850 Pinheiro BR 42 Rf 99
8800 Pinheiro FA 160 Sb 126
3570 Pinheiro GD 80 Sc 104
9350 Pinheiro MA 178 If 152
4575 Pinheiro P 60 Re 102
7580 Pinheiro SE 129 Rb 118
3600 Pinheiro VS 61 Sa 103
3680 Pinheiro VS 79 Re 104
3430 Pinheiro VS 79 Rf 106
Pinheiro, Estação Ferroviária de SE 129 Rb 118
3720 Pinheiro da Bemposta AV 78 Rd 104
3440 Pinheiro de Ázere VS 79 Rf 106
3420-192 Pinheiro de Coja C 79 Sa 107
2140-307 Pinheiro Grande SA 113 Rd 112
5320-121 Pinheiro Novo BN 43 Sf 97
2440 Pinheiros LE 94 Rb 110
4950 Pinheiros VC 41 Rc 96
5320 Pinheiro Velho BN 43 Sf 97
6400 Pinhel GD 81 Sf 104
5460 Pinho VR 43 Sc 99
3660 Pinho VS 79 Rf 104
2530 Pinhôa L 112 Qe 113
Pinhovelo BN 62 Ta 99
6400-069 Pínzio GD 81 Sf 105
6285 Piódão C 79 Sb 107
4880-084 Pioledo VR 61 Sa 100
8500 Pirra FA 158 Rc 126
3050 Pisão AV 78 Rd 107
3305 Pisão C 79 Sa 107
7480 Pisão PT 114 Sa 114
7430 Pisão PT 115 Sc 114
7860 Pisões BE 131 Sd 120
7800 Pisões BE 146 Sb 121
6100 Pisões CB 95 Rf 110
2445 Pisões LE 94 Ra 111
5470 Pisões VR 42 Sa 98
7050 Pitamariça de Baixo E 129 Rd 116
5470 Pitões das Júnias VR 42 Sa 97

6185-141 Pizoria CB 96 Sa 109
Pó LE 112 Qe 113
3060 Pocariça C 78 Rc 106
2200 Pocariça SA 95 Re 111
2200-721 Poçarrão SA 95 Rf 112
2965-214 Poceirão SE 129 Rb 117
7170 Pocinho E 131 Sc 117
8900 Pocinho FA 160 Sc 125
5150 Pocinho GD 62 Sf 102
3070 Poço da Cruz C 78 Rb 106
1950 Poço do Bispo L 128 Qf 116
6430-335 Poço do Canto GD 62 Se 103
3240 Poço dos Cães C 95 Rc 109
8300-044 Poço Fundo FA 158 Rd 126
2300 Poço Redono SA 95 Re 111
7670 Poço Seco BE 159 Rf 123
6355-131 Poço Velho GD 81 Tb 105
4950-670 Podame VC 42 Rd 96
5340-392 Podence BN 44 Ta 99
3230-521 Podentes C 95 Rd 108
5180-340 Poiares BN 63 Ta 102
4990 Poiares VC 41 Rc 99
5050 Poiares VR 61 Sb 101
8500-149 Poio FA 158 Rc 125
4835-445 Polvoeira BR 60 Re 100
6040 Polvorão PT 114 Sa 112
6040 Polvorosas PT 114 Sa 112
8900 Pomar FA 160 Sc 125
7750-411 Pomarão BE 160 Sc 123
3305 Pomares C 79 Sa 107
7540 Pomar Grande SE 144 Rb 120
7000 Pomarinho E 130 Sa 117
8550-035 Pomba FA 158 Rc 124
5140 Pombal BN 62 Sd 101
5350 Pombal BN 62 Sf 101
3100 Pombal LE 94 Rc 109
7340 Pombal PT 115 Se 113
3130-096 Pombalinho C 95 Rd 108
2150 Pombalinho SA 113 Rc 112
5300-761 Pombares BN 44 Ta 99
6100-682 Pombas CB 95 Rf 110
2140 Pombas SA 114 Re 113
2240-372 Pombeira SA 95 Re 110
3300-318 Pombeiro da Beira C 79 Rf 107
4610 Pombeiro de Riba Vizela P 60 Re 100
7800 Pombeiros BE 145 Sa 121
5460 Pomer da Rainha VR 42 Sa 99
5470-384 Pondras VR 42 Sa 98
9970 Ponta AC 176 Te 97
9400 Ponta MA 179 Kd 150
9970 Ponta Delgada AC 176 Te 102
9504 Ponta Delgada AC 177 Zb 122
9240 Ponta Delgada MA 178 Ka 152
8200 Ponta do Castelo FA 159 Re 126
9385 Ponta do Pargo MA 178 Ie 152
9360 Ponta do Sol MA 178 If 152
9680 Ponta Garça AC 177 Zd 122
4730 Ponte BR 41 Rd 98
4730 Ponte BR 60 Rd 100
4910 Ponte VC 41 Ra 98
4980-610 Ponte da Barca VC 41 Rd 98
3350 Ponte da Mucela C 79 Re 107
Ponte de Assamassa LE 94 Rc 109
4990-011 Ponte de Lima VC 41 Rc 98
4880 Ponte de Olo VR 61 Sa 100
7400-201 Ponte de Sor PT 114 Sa 113
3840 Ponte de Vagos AV 78 Rb 106
3640-202 Ponte do Abade VS 80 Sd 103
2560-106 Ponte do Rol L 112 Qe 114
5470-363 Ponteira VR 42 Sa 98
Ponte romano VR 43 Sd 98
Pontes VS 79 Re 104
Pontével SA 113 Ra 114
3200-037 Ponte Velha C 95 Re 107
7330 Ponte Velha PT 115 Sd 112
5450 Pontido VR 61 Sb 100
Pontinha L 128 Qe 116
5070-313 Pópulo VR 62 Sc 100
2420 Porcejal LE 94 Rb 110

8400-455 Porches FA 159 Rd 126
7580 Porches SE 144 Rd 119
5350-202 Porrais BN 63 Tb 100
5090-014 Porrais VR 62 Sd 100
4940 Porreiras VC 41 Rc 97
4970 Porta Cova VC 42 Rd 97
7300-002 Portalegre PT 115 Sd 113
7300 Portalegre, Estação Ferroviária de PT 115 Sd 113
2600 Portas do Capitão Mór L 112 Ra 115
2600 Portas do Mar de Caes L 128 Qf 115
2600 Portas do Mouchão da Cabra L 128 Qf 115
7700-212 Porteirinhos BE 159 Rf 123
7220 Portel E 130 Sa 118
9900 Portela AC 176 Wb 117
5300 Portela BN 44 Ta 97
4770 Portela BR 60 Rd 100
3140 Portela C 78 Rb 106
6100 Portela CB 95 Rf 110
6110 Portela CB 95 Rf 110
8550 Portela FA 158 Rc 125
8375 Portela FA 159 Re 125
8100 Portela FA 159 Sa 124
8800 Portela FA 160 Sb 125
4575 Portela P 60 Re 102
2250 Portela SA 113 Re 112
4970 Portela VC 41 Rd 97
4950 Portela VC 41 Rd 97
5000 Portela VR 61 Sb 101
3510 Portela VS 79 Rf 104
4730 Portela das Cabras BR 41 Rc 98
4870-129 Portela de Santa Eulália VR 61 Sb 99
3320 Portela do Fojo-Machio C 95 Rf 109
6120 Portela dos Colos SA 95 Rf 110
8600 Portelas FA 158 Rb 126
4905 Portela Susã VC 41 Rb 98
7555 Portelinha SE 144 Rc 122
4960 Portelinha VC 42 Re 96
5300 Portêlo BN 44 Tb 97
8500 Portimão FA 158 Rc 126
Portinho da Arrábida SE 128 Ra 118
4000-008* Porto P 60 Rb 101
2135-015 Porto Alto SA 129 Ra 115
2825 Porto Brandão SE 128 Qe 116
2405 Porto Carro LE 94 Ra 111
8800 Porto Carvalhoso FA 160 Sa 125
4525 Porto Carvoeiro AV 60 Rd 102
7520 Porto Covo da Bandeira SE 144 Rb 121
6300-170 Porto da Carne GD 80 Se 105
9225 Porto da Cruz MA 178 Kb 152
7330 Porto da Espada PT 115 Sd 112
7630 Porto das Barcas BE 158 Ra 123
6000 Porto da Vila CB 96 Sc 109
8500 Porto de Lagos FA 158 Rc 125
8600 Porto de Mós FA 158 Rb 126
2480-006 Porto de Mós LE 94 Rb 111
6355 Porto de Ovelha GD 81 Ta 105
7520 Porto de Sines SE 144 Ra 121
6230-753 Porto dos Asnos CB 96 Sc 108
Porto dos Boscoitos AC 176 Xe 116
9625 Porto Formosa AC 177 Zd 122
9700 Porto Judeu AC 176 Xf 117
9760 Porto Martins AC 176 Xf 116
9270 Porto Moniz MA 178 Ie 151
7900 Porto Mouro BE 144 Rd 120
3730-301 Porto Novo AV 78 Rd 103
2560-100 Porto Novo L 112 Qe 113
2740 Porto Salvo L 128 Qe 116
9700 Porto Santo AC 176 Xe 116
3060 Portunhos C 78 Rc 107
4925 Portuzelo VC 41 Rb 98
5430-191 Possacos VR 62 Sc 100
7830 Posto Fiscal de Penalva BE 146 Se 121

7830 Posto Fiscal de Sopos BE 146 Sd 121
7830 Posto Fiscal de Val Covo BE 146 Sd 122
7350 Posto Fiscal do Caia PT 116 Sf 115
7370 Posto Fiscal do Retiro PT 116 Sf 115
3130-541 Pouca Pena C 94 Rc 108
4755-411 Pousa BR 60 Rc 99
4710 Pousada BR 42 Rd 99
4640 Pousada P 61 Rf 102
5000 Pousada VR 61 Sa 101
3405 Pousada de Santa Barbara C 79 Sb 106
4770-400 Pousada de Saramagos BR 60 Rd 100
3105 Pousadas Vedras LE 95 Rc 109
3420-172 Pousadouros C 79 Rf 107
3240-610 Pousaflores C 95 Rd 109
6320-233 Pousafoles do Bispo GD 80 Se 106
4960 Pousios VC 42 Re 97
2410 Pousos LE 94 Rb 111
3780-594 Poutena AV 78 Rc 106
2460 Povoa LE 94 Ra 111
5160 Póvoa BN 62 Sf 101
5210 Póvoa BN 63 Te 99
3320 Póvoa C 95 Sa 108
2565 Póvoa L 112 Qf 113
4415 Póvoa P 60 Re 102
2000 Póvoa SA 113 Rc 112
5470 Póvoa VR 42 Sa 99
5070 Póvoa VR 62 Sc 101
5430 Póvoa VR 62 Se 99
5100 Póvoa VS 61 Sa 102
3650 Póvoa VS 61 Sb 103
9650 Povoação AC 177 Ze 122
2665-300 Póvoa da Galega L 112 Qe 115
2005 Povoa da Isenta SA 113 Rb 113
3060-213 Póvoa da Lomba C 78 Rc 107
3780-525 Póvoa da Palmeira AV 78 Rd 106
3430-565 Póvoa da Pegada VS 79 Sa 106
6290 Póvoa da Rainha GD 80 Sb 105
5425 Póvoa de Agrações VR 43 Se 99
6230-600 Póvoa de Atalaia CB 96 Sd 108
3770 Póvoa de Carreco AV 78 Rc 106
3530-320 Póvoa de Cervães VS 80 Sb 105
4830-191 Póvoa de Lanhoso BR 42 Re 99
6400 Póvoa d'El-Rei GD 80 Se 104
3420 Póvoa de Midões C 79 Sa 106
3440 Póvoa de Mosqueiros VS 79 Rf 106
2560-046 Póvoa de Penafirme L 112 Qd 114
3630-350 Póvoa de Penela VS 62 Sd 102
3780 Póvoa de Pereira AV 78 Rd 106
6000-610 Póvoa de Rio de Moinhos CB 96 Sc 109
2625-002 Póvoa de Santa Iria L 112 Qf 115
2000-531 Póvoa de Santarém SA 113 Rb 113
2620 Povoa de Santo L 112 Qf 116
3430-771 Póvoa de Santo Amaro VS 79 Rf 106
3405-115 Póvoa de São Cosme C 79 Sa 106
7885 Póvoa de São Miguel BE 131 Se 119
3060-471 Póvoa do Bispo C 78 Rc 106
6420-531 Póvoa do Concelho GD 80 Se 104
3800-550 Póvoa do Paço AV 78 Rc 104
3810-756 Póvoa do Valado AV 78 Rc 105
3750 Póvoa do Vale do Trigo AV 78 Rd 105
7320 Póvoa e Meadas PT 96 Sc 111
6270-221 Póvoa Nova GD 79 Sc 106
2040-154 Póvoas SA 113 Ra 112
Povoinha CB 96 Sb 109

3505-247 Povolide VS 79 Sb 104
2910 Praça do Quebedo, Estação Ferroviária de SE 129 Ra 117
5320-221 Prada BN 44 Ta 97
4730 Prado BR 41 Rd 98
4730 Prado BR 41 Rd 98
3570 Prado GD 80 Se 105
4960 Prado VC 42 Re 96
3620 Prado de Baixo VS 62 Sc 103
5225-041 Prado Gatão BN 63 Td 100
6360 Prados GD 80 Sd 105
6400 Prados GD 80 Se 104
2550-371 Pragança L 112 Qf 113
9880 Praia AC 176 Xa 114
2430 Praia LE 94 Ra 109
4410 Praia da Aguda P 60 Rc 102
2530-209 Praia da Areia Branca L 112 Qd 113
2705-061 Praia das Maçãs L 112 Qd 116
Praia da Vitoria AC 176 Xf 116
4910 Praia de Âncora VC 41 Ra 98
3885 Praia de Cortegaça AV 60 Rc 103
3885 Praia de Esmoriz AV 60 Rc 103
3070 Praia de Mira C 78 Rb 106
8670 Praia de Odeceixe FA 158 Rb 124
2525 Praia de São Bernardino LE 112 Qd 113
3870 Praia de Torreira AV 78 Rb 104
Praia do Almoxarife AC 176 Wc 117
9900 Praia do Norte AC 176 Wb 117
2260 Praia do Ribatejo SA 95 Rd 112
2910 Praia do Sado SE 129 Rb 117
9580 Praia Formosa AC 177 Zf 127
9940 Prainha AC 177 We 118
2910 Praixa-Sado, Estação Ferroviária de SE 129 Rb 117
9370 Prazeres MA 178 Ie 152
4800 Prazins BR 60 Re 100
4800 Prazins BR 60 Re 100
8970 Preguiça FA 160 Sc 125
8970 Preguiças FA 160 Sc 124
Preguinho VS 79 Re 104
3070 Presa C 78 Rb 106
3150 Presa C 95 Rc 108
2230-010 Presa SA 95 Rf 111
3750-679 Préstimo AV 78 Rd 105
5100-740 Pretarouca VS 61 Sa 102
5070 Prezandães VR 62 Sd 101
4705-555 Priscos BR 60 Rd 100
6150 Proenca-a-Nova CB 96 Sa 110
6060 Proença-a-Velha CB 97 Se 108
6430-341 Prova GD 62 Sd 103
7520 Provença SE 144 Rb 121
5060 Provensende VR 62 Sc 101
4540-486 Provezende AV 60 Re 103
Prozelo BR 42 Rd 99
4970 Prozelo VC 41 Rd 97
3250-389 Pussos LE 95 Rd 110

Q

3840 Qinta AV 78 Rb 105
5320-195 Quadra BN 44 Sf 97
6320-242 Quadrazais GD 81 Ta 107
6320 Quarta-Feira GD 80 Se 106
8125 Quarteira FA 159 Rf 126
2550 Quartel L 112 Qf 113
8700 Quatrim FA 160 Sb 126
8700-128 Quatrim do Sul FA 160 Sb 126
3130-083 Quatro Lagoas C 95 Rd 108
9760 Quatro Ribeiras AC 176 Xe 116
2065-110 Quebradas L 112 Ra 113
4990-685 Queijada VC 41 Rc 98
9800 Queimada AC 177 We 116
8950 Queimada FA 160 Sc 125
5110 Queimada VS 61 Sb 102
4820-560 Queimadela BR 61 Rf 99
5110 Queimadela VS 61 Sb 102
7665 Queimado BE 158 Rc 123

3670-174 Queirã VS 79 Rf 104
3515-500 Queirela VS 79 Sa 104
3650-051 Queiriga VS 79 Sb 104
6370 Queiriz GD 80 Sd 104
8700 Quelfes FA 159 Sb 126
6090 Quelhinhas CB 80 Sf 108
2735 Queluz L 128 Qe 116
4785-064 Quereledo P 60 Rc 101
8100 Querença FA 159 Sa 125
3080-516 Quiaios C 78 Ra 107
4640 Quinta P 61 Sa 102
5450 Quinta VR 61 Sc 100
7750 Quintã BE 146 Sc 123
7750 Quintã BE 160 Sa 124
8100 Quintã FA 159 Sa 125
5000 Quintã VR 61 Sa 101
5130 Quinta da Cascalheira VS 62 Sc 101
7540-021 Quinta da Corona SE 144 Rd 121
3560 Quinta da Deguedinha VS 80 Sc 104
3570-074 Quinta da Estrada GD 80 Sc 103
8100 Quinta da Quarteira FA 159 Rf 126
5200 Quinta das Quebradas BN 63 Tb 101
5160 Quinta de Martin Tirado BN 63 Tb 102
3640 Quinta de Paulo Lopes VS 80 Sd 103
6440 Quintã de Pêro Martins GD 80 Sf 103
6320-125 Quinta de Santo Amaro GD 80 Se 107
2825 Quinta de Santo António SE 128 Qe 117
2000 Quinta de São João SA 113 Rc 113
5230 Quinta de Vale de Peña BN 44 Tc 98
2950-532 Quinta do Anjo SE 128 Ra 117
2925 Quinta do Conde SE 128 Qf 117
7090 Quinta do Duque E 145 Rf 119
7800 Quinta do Estácio BE 145 Sb 121
3810 Quinta do Gato AV 78 Rc 105
8135 Quinta do Lago FA 159 Rf 126
6090 Quinta do Major CB 80 Sf 107
6230 Quinta do Monte Leal CB 96 Sd 108
6320 Quinta do Passarinho GD 81 Ta 107
2350 Quinta do Paul SA 113 Rc 112
6270 Quinta do Rio GD 80 Sb 106
6400 Quinta dos Bernardos GD 81 Sf 104
7000 Quinta de Sousa E 129 Rc 117
3870 Quinta dos Ricos AV 78 Rb 104
9300 Quinta Grande MA 178 If 153
2100-056 Quinta Grande SA 129 Rc 115
5180 Quintana da Ribeira BN 63 Ta 102
5160 Quintana das Centieras BN 62 Ta 102
Quintana de Alva BN 63 Ta 102
5300-772 Quintanilha BN 44 Tc 98
2140 Quinta Nova SA 113 Rc 113
3050 Quintas AV 78 Rd 107
6230 Quintas CB 80 Se 107
2665 Quintas L 128 Qe 115
2040 Quintas SA 113 Ra 113
3830 Quintas AV 78 Rc 105
6230 Quintas da Feijoeira CB 96 Se 108
6320-251 Quintas de São Bartolomeu GD 80 Sf 106
3870 Quintas do Norte AV 78 Rb 104
5320 Quintela BN 44 Ta 97
5430 Quintela VR 43 Sd 98
3670 Quintela VS 79 Rf 104
3640 Quintela VS 80 Sc 103
3530-334 Quintela de Azurara VS 80 Sb 105
5300 Quintela de Lampacas BN 44 Ta 99

4750 Quintiães BR 41 Rc 99
7800-661 Quintos BE 146 Sb 121
5320 Quirás BN 43 Sf 97

R

6300-075 Rabaça GD 81 Sf 105
7300-467 Rabaça PT 115 Se 113
3230-544 Rabaçal C 95 Rd 108
7050 Rabaçal E 130 Re 116
6430 Rabaçal GD 80 Se 103
2500 Rabaceiro LE 112 Qf 112
6150-127 Rabacinas CB 96 Sb 110
5300-791 Rabal BN 44 Tb 97
7040 Rabasqueira E 130 Rf 116
7555 Rabo do Lobo SE 144 Rb 122
7080 Rádio Marconi E 129 Rd 116
4590 Raimonda P 60 Rd 101
4550-247 Raiva AV 60 Rd 102
3360 Raiva C 79 Re 107
5450-344 Raiz do Monte VR 61 Sc 100
5040 Ramadas VR 61 Sa 101
7960 Ramado BE 131 Sc 120
Ramalhais de Cima LE 95 Rc 109
2565-646 Ramalhal L 112 Qe 114
3250-422 Ramalhal LE 95 Rd 110
2305 Ramalheira SA 95 Rd 110
2500-377 Ramalhosa LE 112 Qf 112
9700 Raminho AC 176 Xe 116
4690 Ramires VR 61 Rf 102
8375 Ramos FA 159 Rd 124
2580 Rancas L 112 Qf 114
4650 Rande P 60 Re 100
7330 Ranginha PT 115 Sd 112
3100-362 Ranha de Baixo LE 94 Rb 109
3105 Ranha de São João LE 94 Rb 109
6430 Ranhados GD 62 Se 103
3660 Ranhados VS 79 Sa 105
6360-130 Rapa GD 80 Sd 105
2080-701 Raposa SA 113 Rc 114
8650 Raposeira FA 158 Ra 126
2420-218 Raposeira LE 94 Rb 110
2100-650 Raposeira SA 113 Rc 115
9370 Raposeiro do Logarinho MA 178 Ie 152
6000 Rapoula CB 96 Sb 109
6300 Rapoula GD 80 Se 105
6320-261 Rapoula do Côa GD 81 Sf 106
4560 Rãs P 60 Re 101
3560 Rãs VS 79 Sc 104
7330 Rasa PT 115 Sd 112
4570-410 Rates P 60 Rb 100
8900 Rato FA 160 Sc 126
6360-140 Ratoeira GD 80 Sd 105
2350 Reais SA 113 Rc 112
4550-250 Real AV 60 Re 102
4605 Real P 61 Re 101
3550 Real VS 80 Sb 105
6100 Rebaixia CB 95 Rf 110
2460-362 Rebelos LE 94 Qf 111
6420-541 Reboleiro GD 80 Sd 104
3150-258 Rebolia C 95 Rc 108
6320-271 Rebolosa GD 81 Ta 106
5300 Rebordainhos BN 44 Ta 98
5300-811 Rebordãos BN 44 Tb 98
4525 Rebordelo AV 60 Rd 103
5335 Rebordelo BN 43 Sf 98
4600 Rebordelo P 61 Sa 100
5470 Rebordelo VR 43 Sb 98
3670 Rebordinho VS 79 Re 105
4795 Rebordões P 60 Rd 100
4990 Rebordões VC 41 Rc 98
3360 Rebordosa C 79 Re 107
4585-305 Rebordosa P 60 Rd 101
4920 Reboreda VC 41 Rb 97
5450 Reboredo VR 62 Sc 100
3750-726 Recardães AV 78 Rd 105
4585-594 Recarei P 60 Rd 102
4560 Recezinhos P 61 Re 101
5400 Redial VR 43 Sc 98
3105-321 Redinha LE 94 Rc 108
6150 Redonda CB 96 Sa 111
Redonda FA 160 Sa 124
5400 Redondelo VR 43 Sc 98
7170 Redondo E 131 Sc 117
3100 Redondos LE 94 Rc 109
5425 Redondos VR 43 Sd 98
4825-286 Redundo P 60 Rd 101
5300 Reféga BN 44 Tc 98
4990 Refóios do Lima VC 41 Rc 98
4860 Refojos de Basto BR 61 Sa 99

4825-292 Refojos de Riba de Ave P 60 Rd 101
4610 Refontoura P 61 Re 101
4820 Regadas BR 61 Rf 100
4815 Regilde P 60 Re 100
4820 Rego BR 61 Rf 100
3250 Rego da Murta LE 95 Rd 110
5385 Regodeiro BN 43 Sf 99
5370-110 Rego de Vide BN 62 Se 100
2415 Regueira de Pontes LE 94 Rb 110
4825-360 Reguenga P 60 Rd 101
7600 Reguengo BE 145 Re 121
7780 Reguengo BE 145 Rf 122
7490 Reguengo E 114 Rf 115
7300 Reguengo PT 115 Sd 113
7340 Reguengo PT 115 Se 114
2070 Reguengo, Estação Ferroviária de SA 113 Rb 114
2440-208 Reguengo do Fetal LE 94 Rb 111
2530-564 Reguengo Grande L 112 Qe 113
7630 Reguengo Pequeno BE 144 Rc 123
7200-200 Reguengos de Monsaraz E 131 Sc 118
2500 Reguenho LE 112 Qe 112
6440 Reigada GD 81 Ta 104
6400 Reigadinho GD 80 Se 104
5470 Reigoso VR 42 Sa 98
3680-192 Reigoso VS 79 Re 104
3250 Reivas LE 95 Rd 109
8550 Relém FA 158 Rc 125
7630-392 Relíquias BE 144 Rd 122
9360 Relogio do Poiso MA 178 If 152
9500 Relva AC 177 Zb 122
6110 Relva CB 95 Rf 110
6060 Relva CB 97 Sf 108
7330 Relva PT 115 Sd 112
3600-475 Relva VS 61 Sa 103
6150-501 Relva da Louça CB 95 Sa 110
3300 Relvas C 95 Sa 107
6230 Relvas CB 80 Sb 108
2500-796 Relvas LE 112 Qf 112
7540-240 Relvas Verdes SE 144 Rb 121
3305-227 Relva Velha C 79 Sa 107
3020 Relvinha C 78 Rd 107
7540 Relvinhas SE 144 Rc 120
9545 Remédios AC 177 Zb 121
2520 Remédios LE 112 Qd 112
4755-010 Remelhe BR 60 Rc 100
4960 Remoães VC 42 Re 96
5200-370 Remondes BN 63 Tb 100
3420-415 Remouco C 79 Rf 106
6320 Rendo GD 81 Sf 106
4800 Rendufe BR 60 Re 100
Rendufe VR 62 Sd 99
4830 Rendufinho BR 42 Re 99
4720 Rendute BR 41 Rd 99
6000-620 Represa CB 96 Sc 110
7050 Represa E 130 Rf 116
3800-861 Requeixo AV 78 Rc 105
4770 Requião BR 60 Rd 100
4660-211 Resende VS 61 Sa 102
3140 Resgatados C 78 Rd 107
6000-621 Retaxo CB 96 Sc 110
7830 Retorta BE 146 Sc 121
7050 Retorta E 129 Rc 117
4480-350 Retorta P 60 Rb 100
5450-294 Revel VR 62 Sc 100
7330-336 Reveladas PT 115 Sd 112
3140 Reveles C 94 Rb 108
4820-630 Revelhe BR 61 Rf 100
7340 Revelhos PT 115 Se 114
8100 Reveses FA 159 Sa 124
4650 Revinhade P 60 Re 100
2350-290 Riachos SA 113 Rc 112
2350 Riachos, Estação Ferroviária de SA 113 Rc 112
5100-330 Ribabelide VS 61 Sa 102
4910 Riba de Âncora VC 41 Rb 98
2425 Riba de Aves LE 94 Rb 110
4950 Riba de Mouro VC 41 Re 96
4640 Ribadoura P 61 Rf 102
3515 Ribafeita VS 79 Sa 104
2525 Ribafria LE 112 Qe 113
2475 Ribafria LE 112 Ra 112
2565-173 Ribaldeira L 112 Qe 114
5140-224 Ribalonga BN 62 Sd 101
5070-322 Ribalonga VR 62 Sd 100
2530 Ribamar L 112 Qe 113
2640 Ribamar L 128 Qd 114

6290-251 Ribamondego GD 80 Sc 105
4890 Ribas BR 61 Rf 100
3090 Ribas C 78 Rb 107
3220 Ribas C 95 Re 107
3880 Ribeira AV 78 Rc 103
4840 Ribeira BR 42 Re 98
3200 Ribeira C 95 Re 108
2240 Ribeira SA 95 Re 110
4990 Ribeira VC 41 Rc 98
8365 Ribeira Alta FA 159 Re 125
2350-396 Ribeira Branca SA 94 Rc 112
9350 Ribeira Brava MA 178 If 152
Ribeira Cha AC 177 Zd 122
9800 Ribeira da Areia AC 177 Wf 117
8900-055 Ribeira da Gafa FA 160 Sc 125
9270 Ribeira da Janela MA 178 If 151
8550-366 Ribeira das Canas FA 158 Rc 125
9680 Ribeira dasTainhas AC 177 Zd 122
8200-501 Ribeira de Alte FA 159 Re 125
3045 Ribeira de Frades C 78 Rd 107
3850 Ribeira de Fráguas AV 78 Rd 104
7300 Ribeira de Nisa PT 115 Sd 113
7700 Ribeira de Odelouca BE 159 Re 124
4870-150 Ribeira de Pena VR 61 Sb 99
2040-511 Ribeira de São João SA 113 Ra 113
3505 Ribeira de Sátão VS 79 Sb 104
Ribeira de Seiça, Estação Ferroviária de C 94 Rb 108
6230 Ribeira de Ximassa CB 96 Sc 108
3680 Ribeiradio VS 78 Re 104
9900 Ribeira do Cabo AC 176 Wb 117
2205-291 Ribeira do Fernando SA 114 Rf 112
9930 Ribeira do Meio AC 177 We 118
9800 Ribeira do Nabo AC 177 Wf 117
7630-394 Ribeira do Salto BE 144 Rc 122
6300-185 Ribeira dos Carinhos GD 80 Sf 105
7630-357 Ribeira do Seissal BE 144 Rc 122
9700 Ribeira do Testo AC 176 Xf 117
9900 Ribeira Funda AC 176 Wb 117
Ribeira Grande AC 177 Zc 122
4760-266 Ribeirão BR 60 Rc 100
9675 Ribeira Quente AC 177 Ze 122
9930 Ribeiras AC 177 We 118
9700 Ribeira Seca AC 176 Xf 116
9850 Ribeira Seca AC 177 Xa 117
9600 Ribeira Seca AC 177 Zc 122
9900 Ribeirinha AC 176 Wc 117
9880 Ribeirinha AC 176 Wf 114
9700 Ribeirinha AC 176 Xe 117
9930 Ribeirinha AC 177 Wf 118
9600 Ribeirinha AC 177 Zd 122
8800 Ribeirinha FA 160 Sb 125
7330 Ribeirinha PT 115 Sd 112
5450 Ribeirinha VR 62 Sc 100
4940 Ribeirinho VC 41 Rc 97
8950 Ribeiro FA 160 Sc 125
8375 Ribeiro de Arade FA 159 Re 125
4960 Ribeiro de Cima VC 42 Re 97
7430 Ribeiro de Freixo, Estação Ferroviária de PT 115 Sc 113
3320 Ribeiro do Soutelinho C 95 Rf 109
9230 Ribeiro Frio MA 178 Ka 152
4820 Ribeiros BR 61 Rf 100
3600 Ribolhinhos VS 79 Sa 103
3600-623 Ribolhos VS 79 Sa 103

6230 Rio CB 96 Sb 108
4950 Rio Bom VC 41 Rd 97
5445 Rio Bom VR 43 Sd 99
4970 Rio Cabrão VC 41 Rd 98
4845 Rio Caldo BR 42 Re 98
3050 Rio Coro AV 78 Rd 107
4755 Rio Covo BR 60 Rc 100
5130-287 Riodades VS 62 Sd 102
2435-530 Rio de Couros SA 95 Rd 110
5320-279 Rio de Forn BN 44 Sf 97
4540-243 Rio de Frades AV 79 Re 103
3040-488 Rio de Galinhas C 95 Rd 108
4630 Rio de Galinhas P 61 Rf 101
6420 Rio de Mel GD 80 Sd 104
3660-191 Rio de Mel VS 79 Sa 104
7600 Rio de Moinhos BE 145 Re 121
7150-361 Rio de Moinhos E 115 Sc 116
4575 Rio de Moinhos P 60 Re 102
7595 Rio de Moinhos SE 144 Re 119
4970 Rio de Moinhos VC 41 Rd 97
3560 Rio de Moinhos VS 80 Sb 104
2200 Río de Moinhos SA 95 Re 112
2635 Rio de Mouro L 128 Qe 116
5300 Rio de Onor BN 44 Tc 97
4860 Rio Douro BR 61 Sa 99
5300-831 Rio Frio BN 44 Tc 98
2955 Rio Frio SE 129 Ra 116
4970 Rio Frio VC 41 Rd 97
2040-092 Rio Maior SA 112 Ra 112
4730 Rio Mau BR 41 Rc 98
4575 Rio Mau P 60 Rd 102
4520-467 Rio Meão AV 60 Rc 103
3450-341 Rio Milheiro VS 79 Rf 106
6420 Rio Moinhos GD 80 Sd 104
8950 Rio Saco FA 160 Sd 125
7920 Rio Seco BE 145 Rf 119
8005 Rio Seco FA 160 Sa 126
7900 Rio Seco da Estrada BE 145 Re 119
3840-303 Rio Tinto AV 78 Rc 106
4740 Rio Tinto BR 60 Rb 100
4435 Rio Tinto P 60 Rc 101
6290 Rio Torto GD 79 Sc 105
5430 Rio Torto VR 62 Se 99
3220 Rio Vide C 95 Re 108
5060-423 Roalde VR 61 Sc 101
6120-167 Robalo SA 95 Rf 111
6300-190 Rocamondo GD 80 Se 105
3740-182 Rocas do Vouga AV 78 Rd 104
8100 Rocha FA 159 Rf 125
4925 Rocha VC 41 Rb 98
8400 Rocha Bravo FA 158 Rd 126
2550 Rocha Forte L 112 Qf 113
6000-007 Rochas de Baixo CB 96 Sc 109
6000-008 Rochas de Cima CB 96 Sc 108
6300-195 Rochoso GD 80 Sf 105
4850 Roda BR 61 Rf 99
6120 Roda SA 95 Rf 110
3530 Roda VS 79 Rf 104
3330-108 Roda Cimeira C 95 Rf 108
3330-109 Roda Fundeira C 95 Rf 108
2305-121 Roda Grande SA 95 Rd 112
6030-115 Rodeios CB 96 Sc 110
4960 Rodeiro VC 42 Rf 96
3730 Roge AV 78 Rd 103
8670-440 Rogil FA 158 Rb 124
5360 Róios BN 62 Sf 101
3440 Rojão Grande VS 79 Rf 106
6100 Rola CB 95 Rf 110
7780-408 Rolão BE 145 Sa 122
8500 Rolhão FA 158 Rc 125
Roliça LE 112 Qe 113
9100 Roma MA 178 Kb 152
4940 Romarigães VC 41 Rc 97
3700-808 Romariz AV 60 Rd 103
3560 Romãs VS 79 Sc 104
7700 Romba BE 159 Sa 124
2005-076 Romeira SA 113 Rb 113
7750 Romeiras BE 159 Sb 123
8550 Romeiras FA 158 Rf 125
5370 Romeu BN 62 Sf 99
7750 Roncão BE 160 Sc 123
7750 Roncão BE 159 Sb 124
7200 Roncão E 131 Sd 119
7540 Roncão SE 144 Rc 120

4805-354 Ronfe BR 60 Rd 100
6400 Roque GD 80 Sf 104
6160 Roqueiro CB 96 Sa 109
4750 Roriz BR 41 Rc 99
4795 Roriz P 60 Rd 100
5400 Roriz VR 43 Se 98
3550-252 Roriz VS 79 Sb 104
9800 Rosais AC 177 We 116
7830 Rosal BE 146 Sc 120
7700 Rosário BE 159 Rf 123
7250-203 Rosário E 131 Sd 117
9240 Rosário MA 178 If 152
2860-626 Rosário SE 128 Qf 116
4625 Rosem P 61 Re 102
6060-185 Rosmaninhal CB 97 Sf 110
7400 Rosmaninhal PT 114 Sa 113
6120 Rosmaninhal SA 95 Sa 111
2140 Rosmaninhal SA 113 Re 113
3600-377 Rossão VS 61 Sa 103
4540 Rossas AV 60 Re 103
4850 Rossas BR 42 Rf 99
4660 Rossas VS 61 Sa 102
2205-062 Rossio ao Sul do Tejo SA 114 Re 112
4970 Roucas VC 42 Re 97
4960 Roussas VC 42 Re 96
3510-816 Routar VS 79 Rf 105
3360-109 Roxo C 78 Rd 107
3620 Rua VS 62 Sc 103
7600 Ruas BE 145 Rf 121
4940 Rubiães VC 41 Rc 97
3100 Ruge Água LE 94 Rc 110
4705 Ruilhe BR 60 Rd 100
7670 Ruínas Romanas BE 159 Re 123
4765 Ruivães BR 60 Rd 100
4820 Ruivães BR 61 Rf 100
6320 Ruivina GD 81 Sf 106
8600 Ruivo FA 158 Rb 125
6320 Ruivos GD 81 Ta 106
4980 Ruivos VC 41 Rd 98
2565-710 Runa L 112 Qe 114

S

4990 Sá VC 41 Rc 98
4970 Sá VC 41 Rd 97
4950 Sá VC 42 Rd 96
5430 Sá VR 43 Sd 98
3660-074 Sá VS 79 Rf 104
2305-622 Sabacheira SA 95 Rd 110
4970 Sabadim VC 41 Rd 97
4730 Sabariz BR 41 Rd 99
7665-819 Sabóia BE 158 Rd 124
5060 Sabrados VR 61 Sc 101
5060 Sabrosa VR 62 Sc 101
5450 Sabroso VR 43 Sc 99
5000 Sabroso VR 61 Sb 101
6320 Sabugal GD 80 Sf 106
2715-006 Sabugo L 112 Qe 116
3460 Sabugosa VS 79 Rf 105
3130-098 Sabugueiro C 95 Rc 109
7040 Sabugueiro E 130 Rf 116
6270 Sabugueiro GD 79 Sc 106
5470 Sabuzedo VR 42 Sa 97
2685 Sacavém L 112 Qf 116
5300-433 Sacoias BN 44 Tb 97
5470-125 Sacoselo VR 42 Sa 98
7875-051 Safara BE 131 Se 120
7050 Safira E 129 Rd 117
Safres VR 62 Sd 101
6090 Safurdão CB 97 Sf 108
6400-621 Safurdão GD 80 Sf 105
4950 Sago VC 41 Rd 96
8650-317 Sagres FA 158 Ra 126
8670 Saiceira FA 158 Rb 124
3780 Saide AV 78 Re 106
3300-365 Sail C 79 Rf 107
5350 Saladonha BN 63 Ta 100
4850 Salamonde BR 42 Rf 98
9900 Salão AC 176 Wc 117
9100 Salão MA 178 Kb 152
Salavessa PT 96 Sc 111
5200-383 Saldanha BN 63 Tc 100
8650 Salema FA 158 Rb 126
9630 Salga AC 177 Ze 121
7555-260 Salgadinho SE 144 Rc 122
6360 Salgueirais GD 80 Sd 105
3050-265 Salgueiral AV 78 Rd 106
6030 Salgueiral CB 96 Sc 111
6400 Salgueiral GD 80 Sf 105
3510 Salgueiral VS 79 Rf 105
3840 Salgueiro AV 78 Rc 105
5200 Salgueiro BN 63 Tb 100
6230 Salgueiro CB 80 Se 107
2540 Salgueiro LE 112 Qf 113
7425 Salgueiro PT 114 Rf 114
6000-631 Salgueiro do Campo CB 96 Sc 109
7750 Salgueiros BE 146 Sc 123
5320 Salgueiros BN 44 Sf 97
2100 Salguirinha (Paragem) SA 113 Rc 115
8400-422 Salicos FA 158 Rd 126
8100-202 Salir FA 159 Rf 125
2500-637 Salir de Matos LE 112 Qf 112
2500-651 Salir do Porto LE 94 Qf 112
3865-176 Salreu AV 78 Rc 104
5300-845 Salsas BN 44 Tb 99
5340-400 Salselas BN 63 Ta 99
7780 Salto BE 145 Sa 122
5470-430 Salto VR 42 Sa 99
7800 Salvada BE 145 Sb 121
6090 Salvador CB 97 Sf 108
7450 Salvador PT 115 Sd 114
2140 Salvador SA 113 Rd 113
4600 Salvador do Monte P 61 Rf 101
2205-536 Salvadorinho SA 114 Re 112
2120-051 Salvaterra de Magos SA 129 Rb 114
6060 Salvaterra do Extremo CB 97 Ta 109
3610-073 Salzedas VS 61 Sb 102
5200 Samaio BN 63 Tb 100
4860-221 Samão BR 61 Sa 99
5000 Samardã VR 61 Sb 100
5350-312 Sambade BN 62 Ta 100
6270 Sameice GD 79 Sb 106
6260 Sameiro GD 80 Sd 106
3780-596 Samel AV 78 Rc 106
5300 Samil BN 44 Tb 98
5100-758 Samodães VS 61 Sb 102
5360 Samões BN 62 Se 101
5400-580 Samoiões VR 43 Sd 98
2135 Samora Correira SA 113 Ra 115
5140 Samorinha BN 62 Se 101
2890-201 Samouco SE 128 Qf 116
8670-152 Samouqueira FA 158 Ra 124
5360 Sampaio BN 62 Sf 101
2970 Sampaio SE 128 Qf 118
3130-126 Samuel C 94 Rb 108
4600 Sanche P 61 Rf 101
2510 Sancheira LE 112 Qf 112
2510 Sancheira-Grande-Pequena LE 112 Qf 112
4805 Sande BR 60 Rd 100
4805 Sande BR 60 Rd 100
4805 Sande BR 60 Rd 99
5100 Sande VS 61 Sb 102
4730 Sande Oriz BR 41 Rd 98
4990 Sandiães VC 41 Rc 99
5320 Sandim BN 43 Se 97
4415-405 Sandim P 60 Rc 102
2435-531 Sandoeira SA 95 Rd 110
6270-174 Sandomil GD 79 Sb 106
5430 Sanfins VR 43 Sd 99
5400 Sanfins VR 43 Se 98
4595 Sanfins de Ferreira P 60 Rd 101
5070-351 Sanfins do Douro VR 62 Sc 101
4520 Sanfis AV 60 Rc 103
3780-111 Sangalhos AV 78 Rd 106
4505-578 Sanguedo AV 60 Rc 102
3300 Sanguinhedo C 79 Rf 107
5000 Sanguinhedo VR 61 Sc 100
3505 Sanguinhedo VS 79 Sa 104
3060 Sanguinheira C 78 Rb 107
3060-353 Sanguinheira C 78 Rc 106
7425 Sanguinheira PT 114 Rf 114
6120 Sanguinheira SA 96 Sa 111
2100 Sanguinheira Velha SA 113 Re 114
5200-384 Sanhoane BN 63 Tc 100
5030 Sanhoane VR 61 Sb 101
5400-578 Sanjurge VR 43 Sc 98
3600 San Martinho das Moitas VS 61 Rf 103
9270 Santa MA 178 Ie 151
3660-075 Santa VS 79 Rf 104
3420 Santa Amara C 79 Sa 106
9700 Santa Bárbara AC 176 Xd 116
9930 Santa Bárbara AC 177 We 118
9600 Santa Bárbara AC 177 Zc 122
9580 Santa Bárbara AC 177 Zf 127
2530 Santa Bárbara L 112 Qe 113
3610 Santa Bárbara VS 79 Sb 104
8005 Santa Bárbara de Nexe FA 159 Sa 126
7780 Santa Barbara de Padrões BE 145 Sa 123
9900 Santa Catarina AC 176 Wb 117
3840 Santa Catarina AV 78 Rc 106
2500-768 Santa Catarina LE 112 Qf 112
2910 Santa Catarina SE 129 Rb 118
7580 Santa Catarina SE 129 Rd 118
2495-186 Santa Catarina da Serra LE 94 Rb 110
2305-123 Santa Cita SA 95 Rd 111
Santa Cita, Estação Ferroviária de SA 95 Rd 111
3040 Santa Clara C 78 Rd 107
2230-011 Santa Clara SA 95 Rf 111
7700 Santa Clara-a-Nova BE 159 Rf 124
7665-880 Santa Clara-a-Velha BE 158 Rd 123
7800 Santa Clara de Louredo BE 145 Sa 121
5150 Santa Comba GD 62 Sf 103
6270 Santa Comba GD 80 Sb 106
4585 Santa Comba P 60 Rd 102
4990 Santa Comba VC 41 Rc 98
3440 Santa Comba Dão VS 79 Rf 106
5360-170 Santa Comba da Vilariça BN 62 Sf 100
5300 Santa Comba de Roça BN 44 Tb 99
5340-410 Santa Combinha BN 44 Ta 99
3450-062 Santa Cristina VS 79 Re 106
7700 Santa Cruz BE 159 Sa 124
5320 Santa Cruz BN 44 Ta 97
2560 Santa Cruz L 112 Qd 114
9100 Santa Cruz MA 178 Kb 152
7540 Santa Cruz SE 144 Rb 120
9880 Santa Cruz da Graciosa AC 176 Wf 114
9970 Santa Cruz das Flores AC 176 Tf 112
3660-252 Santa Cruz da Trapa VS 79 Rf 104
5110 Santa Cruz de Lumiares VS 61 Sb 102
4640 Santa Cruz do Douro P 61 Rf 102
4990 Santa Cruz do Lima VC 41 Rd 98
6400 Santa Eufémia GD 80 Se 104
2420-354 Santa Eufémia LE 94 Rb 110
5070 Santa Eugénia VR 62 Sd 100
4540 Santa Eulália AV 60 Re 103
6270 Santa Eulália GD 79 Sb 106
2625 Santa Eulália L 112 Qe 115
7350 Santa Eulália PT 115 Se 114
7830 Santa Íria BE 146 Sc 121
2690-143 Santa Iria de Azóia L 128 Qf 115
5350-232 Santa Justa BN 62 Sf 101
8970 Santa Justa FA 146 Sb 124
2100-376 Santa Justa SA 129 Re 114
4905 Santa Leocádia VC 41 Rc 98
5400 Santa Leocádia VR 43 Sd 99
5120 Santa Leocádia VS 61 Sc 102
5320-153 Santalha BN 43 Sf 97
4710 Santa Lucrécia de Algeriz BR 41 Rd 99
9940 Santa Luzia AC 176 Wd 117
7670 Santa Luzia BE 144 Rd 122
8800 Santa Luzia FA 160 Sc 126
4900 Santa Luzia VC 41 Ra 98
8100 Santa Margarida FA 159 Re 125
8800 Santa Margarida FA 160 Sb 126
2305 Santa Margarida SA 113 Re 112
2250-350 Santa Margarida da Coutada SA 113 Re 112
7570-777 Santa Margarida da Serra SE 144 Rc 120
7900 Santa Margarida do Sado BE 144 Rd 120
4905 Santa Maria VC 41 Rb 98
4990 Santa Maria VC 41 Rc 98
4520 Santa Maria da Feira AV 60 Rc 103
6440 Santa Maria de Aguiar GD 81 Ta 103
4805 Santa Maria de Airão BR 60 Rd 100
4720 Santa Maria de Bouro BR 42 Re 98
5445-052 Santa Maria de Emeres VR 62 Sd 99
4535-340 Santa Maria de Lamas AV 60 Rc 103
4550 Santa María de Sardoura AV 60 Re 102
Santa Marinha BR 42 Rd 98
6270 Santa Marinha GD 79 Sc 106
4950 Santa Marinha VC 42 Rd 96
Santa Marinha VR 61 Sb 99
4640 Santa Marinha do Zêzere P 61 Sa 102
8970 Santa Marta FA 146 Sc 124
5450-240 Santa Marta da Montanha VR 61 Sb 99
4720 Santa Marta de Bouro BR 42 Re 99
5030-381 Santa Marta de Penaguião VR 61 Sb 101
9940 Santana AC 176 Wd 117
9630 Santana AC 177 Ze 121
7830 Santana BE 146 Sc 121
3090 Santana C 78 Rb 107
7040 Santana E 114 Sa 116
7220 Santana E 130 Sb 119
9230 Santana MA 178 Ka 152
6050 Santana PT 96 Sb 111
2970-002 Santana SE 128 Qf 118
2070 Santana Cartaxo, Estação Ferroviária de SA 113 Rb 114
6300 Santana da Azinha GD 80 Se 106
7670-613 Santana da Serra BE 159 Re 123
7750-413 Santana de Cambas BE 146 Sc 123
7040-130 Santana do Campo E 130 Rf 116
3400-591 Santa Ovaia C 79 Sa 107
7670 Santa Pequena BE 159 Re 124
3520-121 Santar VS 79 Sa 105
2005 Santarém SA 113 Rb 113
7050-349 Santa Sofia E 130 Rf 117
7700 Santa Susana BE 159 Re 124
7580-713 Santa Susana SE 129 Rd 118
7005 Santa Susana, Estação Ferroviária de E 130 Sb 117
5430-232 Santa Valha VR 43 Se 98
7100 Santa Victória do Amixial E 115 Sb 115
7800 Santa Vitoria BE 145 Rf 121
Santa Vitória-Ervidel, Estação Ferroviária de BE 145 Sa 121
4515 Sante P 60 Rd 102
8800 Sant Estêvão FA 160 Sb 126
5200 Santiago BN 63 Tc 100
6270 Santiago GD 79 Sb 106
5400 Santiago VR 43 Sd 98
5110 Santiago VS 61 Sb 102
Santiago da Guarda C 95 Rd 109
3465-157 Santiago de Besteiros VS 79 Rf 105
4785 Santiago de Bougado = Bougado P 60 Rc 100
4785 Santiago de Bougado = Bougado (Santiago) P 60 Rc 100
3530 Santiago de Caçurraes VS 80 Sb 105
3100-682 Santiago de Litém LE 94 Rc 109
2230-062 Santiago de Montalegre SA 95 Rf 111
4690-439 Santiago de Piães VS 61 Rf 102
3720 Santiago de Riba-Ul AV 78 Rd 103
5445 Santiago de Ribeira de Alhariz VR 43 Sd 99
7540 Santiago do Cacém SE 144 Rb 120
7050 Santiago do Escoural E 130 Re 117
2630-501 Santiago dos Velhos L 128 Qf 115
7200 Santiago Maior E 131 Sd 117
3100-683 Santiais LE 95 Rc 110
6100 Santinha CB 95 Sa 110
7450 Santo Aleixo PT 115 Sd 115
7875-150 Santo Aleixo da Restauração BE 146 Sf 120
4870 Santo Aleixo de Além VR 61 Sb 99
7875-250 Santo Amador BE 131 Se 120
9800 Santo Amaro AC 177 We 116
Santo Amaro AC 177 We 118
3770 Santo Amaro AV 78 Rc 105
5155 Santo Amaro GD 62 Se 102
7470 Santo Amaro PT 115 Sd 115
3090 Santo Amaro de Bouça C 94 Rb 107
Santo Amaro-Veiros, Estação Ferroviária de PT 115 Sc 114
5200 Santo André BN 63 Ta 101
7425 Santo André PT 114 Re 114
2830 Santo André SE 128 Qf 117
4950 Santo André VC 41 Rd 96
5470 Santo André VR 43 Sc 97
6000-656 Santo André das Tojeiras CB 96 Sb 110
9875 Santo Antão AC 177 Xb 117
6355 Santo Antão GD 81 Ta 105
2660-099 Santo Antão do Tojal L 128 Qf 115
9800 Santo Antonio AC 177 Wf 116
9940 Santo António AC 176 Wd 117
9545 Santo António AC 177 Zb 121
8650 Santo António FA 158 Ra 126
9325 Santo António MA 178 Ka 152
7330 Santo António das Areias PT 115 Sd 112
9100 Santo António da Serra MA 178 Kb 152
7450 Santo António das Paredes PT 115 Sc 114
2835 Santo António de Charneca SE 128 Qf 117
5400 Santo António de Monforte VR 43 Sd 98
7200 Santo António do Baldío E 131 Sd 118
7830 Santo António Velho BE 146 Sc 121
4455 Santo Cruz do Bispo P 60 Rb 101
4830 Santo Emilião BR 60 Re 99
6320-511 Santo Estêvão GD 80 Sf 107
2130 Santo Estêvão SA 113 Rb 115
5400 Santo Estêvão VR 43 Sd 98
2665 Santo Estêvão das Galés L 128 Qe 115
Santo Evos VS 79 Sb 105
7350 Santo Ildefonso PT 115 Sf 116
2640-039 Santo Isidoro L 128 Qd 115
4635-248 Santo Isidoro P 61 Rf 101
3130-064 Santo Isidro C 94 Rb 108
2985 Santo Isidro de Pegões SE 129 Rc 116
2590-265 Santo Quintino L 128 Qf 114
9760 Santo Rita AC 176 Xf 116
6120 Santos SA 95 Sa 111

Santos I 331

2025 Santos SA 113 Rb 112
4780 Santo Tirso P 60 Rd 100
3140-401 Santo Varão C 94 Rc 107
5230-200 Santulhão BN 63 Tc 99
4905 San Vicente BR 41 Rb 99
7700-263 São Barnabé BE 159 Rf 124
7340 Sao Bartalomeu PT 115 Se 114
8950 São Bartolomeu FA 160 Sd 125
São Bartolomeu PT 114 Sa 112
7540-321 São Bartolomeu da Serra SE 144 Rc 120
9700 São Bartolomeu de Regatos AC 176 Xe 116
7750 São Bartolomeu de Vio Glória BE 146 Sb 123
7220-521 São Bartolomeu do Outeiro E 130 Sa 118
2530 São Bartolomeu dos Galegos L 112 Qe 113
7005 São Benta do Mato E 130 Sb 116
9700 São Bento AC 176 Xe 117
2480 São Bento LE 94 Rb 111
7595 São Bento SE 144 Rd 119
4940 São Bento da Porta Aberta VC 41 Rc 97
7100 São Bento de Ana Loura E 115 Sc 115
7100-610 São Bento do Ameixial E 115 Sc 115
7100-630 São Bento do Cortiço E 115 Sc 115
9760 São Bras AC 176 Xf 116
7830 São Brás BE 146 Sc 121
7670 São Brás BE 159 Re 123
7000 São Brás da Regedoura E 130 Rf 118
8150-101 São Brás de Alportel FA 160 Sa 126
7920 São Brissos BE 130 Rf 119
7800 São Brissos BE 145 Sa 120
9950 São Caetano AC 176 Wd 118
3060-739 São Caetano C 78 Rb 106
5400 São Caetano VR 43 Sc 98
5320-024 São Cibrão BN 44 Ta 98
5000-039 São Cibrão VR 61 Sc 101
4660 São Cipriano VS 61 Sa 102
3510 São Cipriano VS 79 Sa 105
5300 São Ciriaco BN 44 Tb 99
5110 São Cosmado VS 61 Sc 102
4970 São Cosme e São Damião VC 41 Rd 97
7050 São Cristóvão E 129 Re 118
3660 São Cristóvão de Lafões VS 79 Re 104
4690 São Cristóvão de Nogueira VS 61 Rf 102
5085 São Cristóvão do Douro VR 62 Sc 102
6000 São Domingos CB 96 Sc 109
2230-063 São Domingos SA 95 Re 111
7540 São Domingos SE 144 Rc 121
7005 São Domingos da Ordem E 131 Sb 117
7100 São Domingos de Ana Loura E 115 Sc 115
2785-289 São Domingos de Rana L 128 Qd 116
2205 São Facundo SA 114 Rf 112
3660 São Félix VS 79 Rf 104
4410-005 São Félix da Marinha P 60 Rc 102
6005 São Fiel CB 96 Sc 108
2890 São Francisco SE 128 Ra 116
7540-555 São Francisco da Serra SE 144 Rc 120
3030-884 São Frutuoso C 95 Rd 107
3460-158 São Gemil VS 79 Sa 105
7050 São Geraldo E 130 Re 116
3400-571 São Gião C 79 Sb 106
9060 São Gonçalo MA 178 Ka 153
7040 São Gregório E 114 Sa 116
2500 São Gregório LE 112 Qf 112
3800 São Jacinto AV 78 Rb 105
5230-251 São Joanico BN 44 Td 99
3600 São Joaninho VS 61 Sa 103

3440 São Joaninho VS 79 Rf 106
9930 São João AC 176 Wd 118
3780-140 São João da Azenha AV 78 Rd 106
3420-227 São João da Boa Vista C 79 Rf 106
5445-084 São João da Corveira VR 43 Sd 99
6370 São João da Fresta VS 80 Sc 105
3700 São João da Madeira AV 60 Rd 103
5130-321 São João da Pesqueira VS 62 Sd 102
2040-460 São João da Ribeira SA 113 Ra 113
São João das Craveiras, Estação Ferroviária de E 129 Rc 116
3680-264 São João da Serra VS 79 Re 104
2705-411 São João das Lampas L 112 Qd 115
2695-081 São João da Talha L 112 Qf 116
8135 São João da Venda FA 159 Sa 126
3440-465 São João de Areias VS 79 Rf 106
4660-343 São João de Fontoura VS 61 Sa 102
3850-771 São João de Loure AV 78 Rc 105
3850-771 São João de Loure e Frossos AV 78 Rc 105
3500-618 São João de Lourosa VS 79 Sa 105
7600 São João de Negrilhos BE 145 Re 121
4830 São João de Rei BR 42 Re 99
3610-082 São João de Tarouca VS 61 Sb 103
4520 São João de Ver AV 60 Rc 103
3025-415 São João do Campo C 78 Rc 107
3475-072 São João do Monte VS 79 Re 105
6110-055 São João do Peso CB 95 Rf 110
7750-513 São João dos Caldeiros BE 159 Sb 123
2600-767 São João dos Montes L 112 Qf 115
5320-160 São Jomil BN 43 Se 98
7005 São Jordão E 130 Sb 118
4505 São Jorge AV 60 Rc 103
2480-062 São Jorge LE 94 Ra 111
9230 São Jorge MA 178 Ka 152
4970 São Jorge VC 42 Rd 98
6225-251 São Jorge da Beira CB 96 Sb 107
6120-069 São José das Matas SA 96 Sa 111
2100 São José de Lamarosa SA 113 Rd 114
5300 São Julião BN 44 Tc 98
4575 São Julião P 60 Rd 102
7300 São Julião PT 115 Se 113
4930 São Julião VC 41 Rc 97
5400-754 São Julião de Montenegro VR 43 Sd 98
5300 São Julião de Palácios BN 44 Tc 98
2660-355 São Julião do Tojal L 112 Qf 115
5400 São Lourenço VR 43 Sd 98
7100 São Lourenço de Mamporção E 115 Sc 115
5060-405 São Lourenço de Ribapinhão VR 62 Sc 101
3780-179 São Lourenço do Bairro AV 78 Rd 106
7800 São Luís BE 130 Sb 120
7630 São Luís BE 144 Rc 122
2495 São Mamede LE 94 Rb 111
2510 São Mamede LE 112 Qf 113
5130 São Mamede VS 62 Sd 101
4730-500 São Mamede de Escariz BR 41 Rc 99
4465 São Mamede de Infesta P 60 Rc 101
4795 São Mamede de Negrelos P 60 Rd 100
5070-471 São Mamede de Ribatua VR 62 Sd 101

7570 São Mamede do Sádão SE 144 Rd 120
7005-720 São Manços E 130 Sb 118
7830 São Marcos BE 146 Sd 122
8800 São Marcos FA 160 Sc 126
São Marcos da Ataboeira BE 145 Sa 122
8375-250 São Marcos da Serra FA 159 Rd 124
3750 São Martinho AV 78 Rd 105
6230 São Martinho CB 96 Sb 108
6270 São Martinho GD 80 Sb 106
6420 São Martinho GD 80 Se 104
9020 São Martinho MA 178 Ka 153
7480 São Martinho PT 114 Rf 114
3620 São Martinho VS 61 Sb 103
4785 São Martinho = Bougado P 60 Rc 101
3300-367 São Martinho da Cortiça C 79 Rf 107
3720 São Martinho da Gândara AV 78 Rc 103
7630-536 São Martinho das Amoreiras BE 144 Rd 123
5110 São Martinho das Chãs VS 61 Sc 102
5210 São Martinho de Angueira BN 45 Td 99
5060-425 São Martinho de Antas VR 61 Sc 101
4785 São Martinho de Bougado = Bougado (São Martinho) P 60 Rc 101
4660 São Martinho de Mouros VS 61 Sa 102
4550-233 São Martinho de Sardoura AV 60 Re 102
3020 São Martinho do Bispo C 78 Rd 107
5200-403 São Martinho do Peso BN 63 Tc 100
2460-083 São Martinho do Porto LE 94 Qf 111
9950 São Mateus AC 176 Wd 118
9700 São Mateus AC 176 Xe 117
7800 São Matias BE 130 Sa 120
6050 São Matias PT 96 Sb 111
7630 São Miguel BE 158 Rb 124
2425-516 São Miguel LE 94 Rb 109
6060-511 São Miguel de Acha CB 96 Se 108
7005-760 São Miguel de Machede E 130 Sb 117
3560 São Miguel de Vila Boa VS 79 Sb 104
4540 São Miguel do Mato AV 60 Rd 103
3515 São Miguel do Mato VS 79 Sa 104
3460-451 São Miguel do Outeiro VS 79 Rf 105
7750 São Miguel do Pinheiro BE 160 Sa 123
2205 São Miguel do Rio Torto SA 114 Re 112
3280 São Nicolau LE 95 Re 109
6290 São Paio GD 80 Sc 105
4960 São Paio VC 42 Re 96
3360 São Paio de Farinha Podre C 79 Rf 107
3400-003 São Paio de Gramaços C 79 Sa 106
4970 São Paio de Jolda VC 41 Rd 98
4535 São Paio de Oleiros AV 60 Rc 103
3360 São Paulo C 78 Re 107
3020 São Paulo de Frades C 78 Rd 107
3090-662 São Pedro C 94 Ra 108
9580 São Pedro AC 177 Zf 127
7800 São Pedro BE 145 Sb 120
4850 São Pedro BR 42 Rf 99
6050 São Pedro PT 96 Sb 111
5470 São Pedro VR 42 Sa 98
4400 São Pedro da Afurada P 60 Rc 102
2560-180 São Pedro da Cadeira L 112 Qd 114
4510-164 São Pedro da Cova P 60 Rc 102

7040 São Pedro da Gafanhoeira E 130 Rf 116
4930-515 São Pedro da Torre VC 41 Rc 97
5400 São Pedro de Agostém VR 43 Sd 98
3360-258 São Pedro de Alva C 79 Rf 107
3505 São Pedro de France VS 79 Sb 104
2430-476 São Pedro de Muel LE 94 Qf 110
6355 São Pedro de Rio Seco GD 81 Ta 105
5300 São Pedro de Serracenos BN 44 Tb 98
7750 São Pedro de Solis BE 160 Sa 124
2300 São Pedro de Tomar SA 95 Re 111
5370-160 São Pedro de Vale do Conde BN 62 Se 100
5430 São Pedro de Veiga de Lila VR 62 Se 100
6150 São Pedro do Esteval CB 96 Sa 111
3660-426 São Pedro do Sul VS 79 Rf 104
4425 São Pedro Fins P 60 Rc 101
5385-057 São Pedro Velho BN 43 Sf 98
7050 São Romão E 129 Rd 117
6270 São Romão GD 80 Sb 106
5110 São Romão VS 61 Sb 102
4660 São Romão de Aregos VS 61 Sa 102
7670 São Romão de Panoias BE 144 Rd 122
7595 São Romão do Sadão SE 144 Rd 119
9500 São Roque AC 177 Zc 122
9225 São Roque MA 178 Ka 152
9020 São Roque MA 178 Ka 153
9940 São Roque do Pico AC 177 We 117
5370 São Salvador BN 62 Sf 100
2065 São Salvador L 112 Ra 113
4970 São Salvador VC 41 Rd 98
7330 São Salvador da Aramenha PT 115 Sd 112
7630 São Salvador e Santa Maria BE 144 Rc 123
3510 São Salvator VS 79 Sa 105
9700 São Sebastião AC 176 Xf 116
3230 São Sebastião C 95 Rd 108
3400 São Sebastião da Feira C 79 Sa 107
7750-811 São Sebastião dos Carros BE 160 Sb 123
3025-539 São Silvestre C 78 Rc 107
3870 São Simão AV 78 Rc 104
São Simão PT 96 Sc 111
2305 São Simão SA 95 Rd 111
4600 São Simão de Gouveia P 61 Rf 101
3100-724 São Simão de Litém LE 94 Rc 110
7595 São Soeiro SE 145 Re 118
7630 São Teotónio BE 158 Rb 123
9875 São Tomé AC 177 Xa 117
4810 São Tomé de Abaçao = Albaçã (São Tomé) BR 60 Re 100
5000-731 São Tomé do Castelo VR 61 Sb 100
4800-294 São Torcato BR 60 Re 100
São Torcato CB 96 Sb 109
2100 São Torcato, Estação Ferroviária de SA 129 Rd 115
7900 São Vicente BE 145 Rf 120
8650 São Vicente FA 158 Ra 126
9240 São Vicente MA 178 If 152
5400 São Vicente VR 43 Se 97
6005-270 São Vicente da Beira CB 96 Sc 108
3680 São Vicente de Lafões VS 79 Rf 104
2000 São Vicente de Paúl SA 113 Rc 112
3880 São Vicente de Pereira AV 78 Rc 103
7350 São Vicente e Ventosa PT 115 Se 115
9545 São Vicente Ferreira AC 177 Zc 122
4920 Sapardos VC 41 Rc 97

2590-401 Sapataria L 128 Qe 115
8375-222 Sapeira FA 159 Rd 124
5460-501 Sapelos VR 43 Sc 98
5460-502 Sapiãos VR 43 Sc 98
7750 Sapos BE 146 Sb 123
7750 Sapos BE 146 Sc 123
2230 Saramaga SA 95 Rf 111
4550 Saravigões AV 60 Re 103
6160 Sardeiras de Baixo CB 96 Sa 109
6160 Sardeiras de Cima CB 96 Sa 109
2230-121 Sardoal SA 95 Rf 111
8600 Sargaçal FA 158 Rb 126
3020 Sargento Mór C 78 Rd 107
2870 Sarilhos Grande SE 128 Qf 116
2860-641 Sarilhos Pequenos SE 128 Qf 116
6100 Sarnadas CB 95 Rf 110
8100 Sarnadas FA 159 Rf 125
6160 Sarnadas de Baixo CB 95 Sa 109
6030 Sarnadas de Rodão CB 96 Sc 110
6160 Sarnadas de São Simão CB 96 Sb 109
3300-325 Sarnadela C 79 Rf 107
6030 Sarnadinha CB 96 Sb 110
8100 Sarnadinha FA 159 Rf 125
8375 Sarnim FA 159 Re 125
5470-465 Sarraquinhos VR 43 Sc 98
3800-592 Sarrazola AV 78 Rc 104
5300 Sarzeda BN 44 Tb 98
3640-180 Sarzeda VS 62 Sd 103
6000-708 Sarzeda CB 96 Sb 109
6150-504 Sarzedinha CB 95 Sa 110
5130-141 Sarzedinho VS 62 Sc 102
3300-401 Sarzedo C 79 Rf 107
6200 Sarzedo CB 80 Sd 106
3620-480 Sarzedo VS 61 Sc 102
3280-100 Sarz São LE 95 Re 109
3560-150 Sátão VS 79 Sb 104
6270-351 Sazes da Beira GD 79 Sb 106
3360 Sazes do Lorvã C 78 Rd 107
6110 Seada CB 95 Re 110
4845 Seara BR 42 Re 98
4990 Seara VC 41 Rc 98
4960 Seara VC 42 Rf 96
5400-780 Seara Velha VR 43 Sc 98
5155-701 Sebadelhe GD 62 Se 102
6420-612 Sebadelhe da Serra GD 80 Sd 103
3150 Sebal Grande C 95 Rc 108
6060 Sebes Rotas CB 97 Sf 108
4575-541 Sebolido P 60 Rd 102
5460 Sebradelo VR 43 Sc 99
3300-450 Secarias C 79 Rf 107
5460-370 Secerigo VR 43 Sb 99
7440-225 Seda PT 114 Sb 113
7750-226 Sedas BE 160 Sc 123
5040 Sedielos VR 61 Sa 101
3750 Segadães AV 78 Rd 105
3560 Segoes VS 80 Sb 103
4950 Segude VC 42 Rd 96
6060-521 Segura CB 97 Ta 110
6270-374 Seia GD 80 Sb 106
2435-545 Seiça SA 95 Rc 110
7330 Seiçal PT 115 Sd 112
Seiça-Ourém, Estação Ferroviária de SA 95 Rc 110
8375 Seiceira FA 159 Rd 125
8375 Seiceiro FA 159 Rd 124
4770 Seide BR 60 Rd 100
4820 Seidões BR 61 Rf 100
4870-024 Seirós VR 42 Sb 99
2705 Seixal L 112 Qd 115
2530 Seixal L 112 Qe 113
9270 Seixal MA 178 If 152
2840 Seixal SE 128 Qf 117
5320 Seixas BN 43 Sf 97
3405-396 Seixas C 79 Sa 106
5155 Seixas GD 62 Se 102
4910 Seixas VC 41 Rb 97
4415-403 Seixezelo P 60 Rc 102
7780 Seixo BE 145 Sa 122
5385 Seixo BN 43 Sf 99
3070 Seixo C 78 Rb 106
6100 Seixo CB 95 Re 109
7005 Seixo E 130 Sb 117
7200 Seixo E 131 Sd 117
Seixo LE 94 Rb 109
5425 Seixo VR 43 Sc 99
3640 Seixo VS 62 Sd 103
4415-735 Seixo Alvo P 60 Rc 102
6300-215 Seixo Amarelo GD 80 Sd 106
3405-388 Seixo da Beira C 79 Sa 106

A B C D E F G H I J L M N O P Q R S T U V X Z

5450-167 Tinhela de Cima VR 62 Sc 99
7370 Tinoca PT 115 Sf 114
2785-051 Tires L 128 Qd 116
7630-360 Tisnada BE 144 Rd 122
5200-422 Tó BN 63 Tc 101
3060-702 Tocha C 78 Rb 107
5110 Toês VS 61 Sb 102
6300-185 Toito GD 80 Sf 105
7090 Tojais Novos E 130 Rf 118
7000 Tojal E 130 Rf 118
8550 Tojeira FA 158 Rb 125
3140 Tojero C 78 Rb 107
9800 Toledo AC 177 Wf 116
9950 Toledos AC 176 Wc 117
Tolões P 61 Sa 101
6050-501 Tolosa PT 114 Sb 112
5150 Tomadias GD 62 Sf 103
2300 Tomar SA 95 Rd 111
7875 Tomina BE 147 Sf 120
3460 Tonda VS 79 Rf 106
3460 Tondela VS 79 Rf 105
9875 Topo AC 177 Xb 117
5000-747 Torgueda VR 61 Sb 101
2500-315 Tornada LE 112 Qf 112
4860 Torneiro BR 42 Sb 99
8970 Torneiro FA 160 Sd 124
5460 Torneiros VR 43 Sb 98
4620 Torno P 61 Re 101
4650 Torrados P 60 Re 100
8500 Torralta FA 158 Rc 126
7595 Torrão SE 145 Re 119
3880 Torrão Lameiro AV 78 Rb 104
4720 Torre BR 42 Rd 99
3420 Torre C 79 Rf 106
6060 Torre CB 97 Ta 109
8600 Torre FA 158 Rc 126
6320 Torre GD 81 Sf 106
2750 Torre L 128 Qd 116
2440-210 Torre LE 94 Rb 111
2305 Torre SA 95 Rd 111
2100 Torre SA 113 Rc 115
7580 Torre SE 129 Rb 118
4925 Torre VC 41 Rb 98
8500 Torre Alcala FA 158 Rc 125
7800 Torre da Cardeira BE 146 Sb 121
7050-601 Torre da Gadanha E 129 Rd 117
8800 Torre de Ares FA 160 Sb 126
7005-776 Torre de Coelheiros E 130 Sa 118
5385 Torre de Dona Chama BN 43 Sf 99
7450 Torre de Frade PT 115 Sd 115
3510-843 Torredeita VS 79 Rf 105
5160 Torre de Moncorvo BN 62 Sf 101
8005 Torre de Natal FA 160 Sa 126
Torre de Todos C 95 Rd 109
3240 Torre de Vale de Todos C 95 Rd 109
Torre do Bispo SA 113 Rc 112
5060-565 Torre do Pinhão VR 61 Sc 100
7800 Torre do Pinto BE 130 Sa 120
6420 Torre do Terrenho GD 62 Sd 103
4720 Torre Portela BR 42 Rd 99
6420 Torres GD 80 Se 104
3030 Torres de Montego C 78 Rd 107
2350 Torres Novas SA 95 Rc 112
2560 Torres Vedras L 112 Qe 114
7670-407 Torre Vã BE 144 Rd 122
4860-015 Torrinheiras BR 42 Sa 99
7580 Torroal SE 144 Rb 119
3300-123 Torrozelas C 79 Sa 107
6270-555 Torrozelo GD 79 Sb 106
6200-254 Tortosendo CB 80 Sc 107
6030-162 Tostão CB 96 Sb 110
7665 Totenique BE 158 Rc 123
5090-081 Toubres VR 62 Sd 100
6230-123 Touca CB 96 Sd 108
5155 Touça GD 62 Se 102
2490 Toucinhos SA 95 Rc 111
4480-480 Tougues P 60 Rb 100
6060 Touril CB 97 Sf 109
6270-586 Tourais GD 79 Sb 106
7040 Tourega E 114 Sa 115
5470-490 Tourém VR 42 Sa 97
5450-287 Tourencinho VR 61 Sb 100
3465-195 Tourigo VS 79 Re 106

7875 Touril BE 146 Se 120
7630 Touril BE 158 Rb 123
8100 Touris FA 159 Rf 125
3650-081 Touro VS 61 Sb 103
4635-518 Toutosa P 61 Rf 101
2825 Trafaria SE 128 Qe 116
2785-007 Trajouce L 128 Qd 116
5140 Tralhariz BN 62 Sd 101
7400-604 Tramaga PT 114 Rf 113
2205-387 Tramagal SA 114 Re 112
7490 Tramagueira E 114 Rf 115
6420 Trancoso GD 80 Sd 104
3550 Trancozelos VS 80 Sb 105
4705-631 Trandeiras BR 60 Rd 100
5450-103 Trandeiras VR 61 Sb 99
4925 Trás Âncora VC 41 Rb 98
2510 Tras do Outeiro LE 112 Qe 112
4520 Travanca AV 60 Rc 103
3720 Travanca AV 78 Rd 104
5340 Travanca BN 62 Ta 99
5200 Travanca BN 63 Tc 100
4605 Travanca P 61 Re 101
4690 Travanca VS 60 Re 102
3405-478 Travanca de Lagos C 79 Sa 106
Travanca do Mondego C 79 Re 107
4640 Travanca do Monte P 61 Rf 101
5400-798 Travancas VR 43 Se 98
6270-601 Travancinha GD 79 Sb 106
5320 Travanco BN 44 Ta 97
3750 Travasso AV 78 Rc 105
4860 Travasso BR 61 Sa 99
3100 Travasso VC 41 Re 109
3050-402 Travassô AV 78 Rd 106
4820 Travassos BR 61 Re 100
4830 Travassos BR 61 Re 99
5470 Travassos VR 42 Sa 98
5470 Travassos VR 42 Sa 98
4880 Travassos VR 61 Sa 100
4820 Travassos VR 61 Rd 99
3505-562 Travassós de Cima VS 79 Sa 105
3150 Traveira C 95 Rd 108
5110 Travanca VS 61 Sb 102
4905 Tregosa BR 41 Rb 99
3440-510 Treixedo VS 79 Rf 106
6060 Tremal CB 97 Sf 110
8970 Tremelgo FA 160 Sa 124
2025 Tremêz SA 113 Rb 112
2480-113 Tremoceira LE 94 Ra 111
8550-160 Três Figos FA 158 Rb 125
5450-296 Tresminas VR 62 Sc 100
Tresouras P 61 Sa 102
6230 Três Povos BE 80 Se 107
5130 Trevões VS 62 Sd 102
3450-386 Trezoi VS 78 Rd 106
7800-771 Trigaches BE 145 Sa 120
6250 Trigais CB 80 Se 106
7800 Trindade BE 145 Sa 121
5360-202 Trindade BN 62 Sf 100
3320-338 Trinhão C 95 Rf 109
6300-225 Trinta GD 80 Sd 105
6005-271 Tripeiro CB 96 Sc 109
6100 Trisio CB 95 Re 110
3750-791 Trofa AV 78 Rd 105
4785 Trofa P 60 Rc 100
4990 Trogal VC 41 Rb 98
7570-789 Tróia SE 129 Ra 118
7940 Trolho BE 145 Rf 119
5400-800 Tronco VR 43 Se 98
4540-604 Tropeço AV 60 Re 103
4920 Troporiz VC 41 Rc 96
6110 Trotas CB 95 Re 110
3025 Trouxemil C 78 Rd 107
7630 Troviscais BE 144 Rb 123
3770 Troviscal AV 78 Rc 106
6100 Troviscal CB 95 Rf 109
4900-281 Troviscoso VC 41 Ra 98
2430 Trutas LE 94 Ra 110
4950 Trute VC 41 Rd 96
5130 Tua VS 62 Sd 101
2205 Tubaral SA 114 Rf 112
4630 Tuias P 61 Rf 101
5320 Tuizelo BN 44 Sf 97
3330-115 Tulhas C 95 Rf 108
8365 Tunes Gare FA 159 Re 126
2565-791 Turcifal L 112 Qe 114
4730 Turiz BR 41 Rd 99
2460-806 Turquel LE 112 Ra 112

U

3610 Ucanha VS 61 Sb 102
4750-761 Ucha BR 41 Rc 99
4950 Ucha Anhões VC 41 Rd 97
2140-364 Ulme SA 113 Rd 113
7800 Ulmo BE 145 Rf 121
8800 Úmbria FA 160 Sb 125

8800 Umbrias de Camacho FA 160 Sc 125
6215-513 Unhais da Serra CB 80 Sc 107
3320-368 Unhais-o-Velho C 96 Sb 108
4650 Unhão P 60 Re 101
2680-374 Unhos L 112 Qf 116
4810 Urgeses BR 60 Re 100
3300-370 Urgueira C 79 Rf 107
2435-681 Urqueira SA 94 Rc 110
7300-565 Urra PT 115 Sd 113
4540 Urrô AV 60 Re 103
4560 Urrô P 60 Re 101
5160-401 Urros BN 62 Sf 102
5200-461 Urrós BN 63 Td 100
9800 Urzelina AC 177 Wf 117
5230-232 Uva BN 63 Tc 100
4860-482 Uz BR 42 Sa 99

V

5110-662 Vacalar VS 61 Sb 102
4890 Vacaria BR 61 Rf 100
4905 Vacaria VC 41 Rb 98
3050-511 Vacariça AV 78 Rd 106
4980 Vade VC 41 Rd 98
3840-001 Vagos AV 78 Rb 105
7450-260 Vaiamonte PT 115 Sc 114
4485-051 Vairão P 60 Rb 101
7340 Valada PT 115 Se 114
2070-506 Valada SA 113 Rb 114
2965 Vala da Asseiceira SE 129 Rb 117
4405 Valadares P 60 Rc 102
4640 Valadares P 61 Sa 102
4925 Valadares VC 41 Rb 98
4950 Valadares VC 42 Rb 96
3660-673 Valadares VS 79 Re 104
6110 Valadas CB 95 Re 111
7425 Vala da Vaca PT 114 Rf 114
2460 Valado de Santa Quitéria LE 94 Qf 112
2450-301 Valado dos Frades LE 94 Qf 111
7630 Valas BE 158 Rb 123
4730 Valbom BR 42 Rd 98
6000 Valbom CB 96 Sc 109
6400 Valbom GD 80 Sf 104
4420 Valbom P 60 Rc 102
5200-404 Valcerto BN 63 Tc 100
5460-473 Valdegas VR 43 Sc 98
2965 Valdera, Estação Ferroviária de SE 129 Rb 117
5100-837 Valdigem VS 61 Sb 102
4845 Valdozende BR 42 Re 99
4730 Valdreu BR 42 Re 98
5340-400 Valdrez BN 63 Ta 99
6420-662 Valdujo GD 80 Se 103
4525 Vale AV 60 Rd 103
8375 Vale FA 159 Re 125
Vale LE 95 Rc 109
4970 Vale VC 42 Rd 97
5450 Vale VR 62 Sc 100
3465 Vale VS 79 Re 106
4770 Vale (São Cosme) BR 60 Rd 100
4770 Vale (São Martinho) BR 60 Rd 100
3600-405 Vale Abrigoso VS 61 Sa 103
Vale Alto SA 94 Rc 111
8950 Vale Andreu FA 160 Sc 125
7630 Vale Bacias BE 144 Rc 122
5340 Vale Benfeito BN 62 Ta 100
7595-191 Vale Bom SE 130 Re 119
6000-715 Vale Bonito CB 96 Sc 109
3140 Vale Canosa C 78 Rc 107
7200 Vale Carneiro E 131 Sd 118
6000-660 Vale Chiqueiro CB 96 Sb 110
Vale Covo FA 159 Rf 126
2540 Vale Covo LE 112 Qe 113
7630 Vale da Beja BE 144 Rb 122
6040 Vale da Feiteira PT 114 Sb 112
2240 Vale da Figueira SA 113 Rc 113
6120-030 Vale da Gama SA 96 Sa 111
8550 Vale da Horta FA 158 Rb 125
2205-410 Vale da Horta SA 114 Rf 113
6100-889 Vale da Junça CB 95 Rf 110

2140 Vale da Lama SA 113 Rc 113
5200-500 Vale da Madre BN 63 Tb 100
3780 Vale da Mó AV 78 Rd 106
8700 Vale da Mó FA 160 Sa 126
8100 Vale da Moita FA 159 Sa 124
7005 Vale da Moura E 130 Sa 117
6150 Vale da Mua CB 96 Sb 110
6350-235 Vale da Mula GD 81 Tb 104
6120 Vale da Mura SA 95 Sa 111
8670 Vale da Nora das Arvores FA 158 Rb 125
8200 Vale da Parra FA 159 Re 126
2070-704 Vale da Pedra SA 113 Rb 114
6000 Vale da Pereira CB 96 Sb 110
7040 Vale da Pinta E 114 Sa 115
2070-554 Vale da Pinta SA 113 Rb 113
5340-470 Vale da Porca BN 63 Ta 99
7520 Vale da Roca SE 144 Rb 121
8100 Vale da Rosa FA 159 Sa 125
8970 Vale da Rosa FA 160 Sb 125
6320-551 Vale das Éguas GD 81 Sf 106
6060 Vale das Eiras CB 97 Ta 109
6090 Vale da Senhora da Póvoa CB 80 Se 107
5335-134 Vale das Fontes BN 43 Sf 98
2230-014 Vale das Onegas SA 95 Rf 111
3100-059 Vale das Velhas LE 95 Rc 109
6005-196 Vale da Torre CB 96 Sd 108
2025-171 Vale da Trave SA 113 Rb 112
6150 Vale da Ursa CB 96 Sa 110
8200-426 Vale da Ursa FA 159 Re 126
8800 Vale da Vaca FA 160 Sb 125
8135-032 Vale da Venda FA 159 Sa 126
8300 Vale da Vila FA 159 Rd 125
5130 Vale da Vila VS 62 Sd 102
7750 Vale de Açor BE 145 Sa 122
7400 Vale de Açor PT 114 Sa 113
2205-409 Vale de Açor SA 114 Rf 112
7630 Vale de Agrilhão BE 144 Rb 122
8550 Vale de Água FA 158 Rb 125
2205 Vale de Água SA 114 Rf 112
7555 Vale de Água SE 144 Rc 121
5210-173 Vale de Águia BN 64 Te 99
6440-251 Vale de Alfonsinho GD 62 Sf 103
5230 Vale de Algóso BN 63 Tc 100
5335 Vale de Almeiro BN 43 Sf 98
7050 Vale de Ancho E 129 Rc 117
5400-360 Vale de Anta VR 43 Sc 98
7400 Vale de Arco PT 114 Sa 112
7050 Vale de Asna E 129 Rd 117
5370-652 Vale de Asnes BN 62 Sf 100
3780-481 Vale de Avim AV 78 Rd 106
6360 Vale de Azares GD 80 Sd 105
2425 Vale de Bajouca LE 94 Rb 109
4890 Vale de Bouro BR 61 Rf 100
7860 Vale de Calvão BE 131 Sd 120
2305 Vale de Calvo SA 95 Rd 111
3730-200 Vale de Cambra AV 78 Rd 104
3450 Vale de Carneiro VS 78 Re 106

5430 Vale de Casas VR 43 Se 99
7630 Vale de Casca BE 144 Rc 122
2140-405 Vale de Cavalos SA 113 Rc 113
6350-351 Vale de Coelha GD 81 Tb 104
3220-442 Vale de Colmeias C 95 Rd 107
6160 Vale de Cuba CB 96 Sa 109
5070 Vale de Cunho VR 62 Sd 100
8800 Vale de Ebros FA 160 Sc 125
Vale de Égua VR 62 Sd 99
7000 Vale de El-Rei de Baixo E 130 Rf 117
6320 Vale de Espinho GD 81 Ta 107
7700-207 Vale de Estacas BE 159 Rf 124
6300-230 Vale de Estrela GD 80 Se 105
7750-389 Vale de Évora BE 145 Sb 122
7630 Vale de Ferro BE 144 Rc 122
7630 Vale de Figueira BE 158 Rb 123
6050 Vale de Figueira PT 96 Sc 111
6050 Vale de Figueira PT 96 Sd 111
5120 Vale de Figueira VS 61 Sc 102
7630 Vale de Figueiras BE 144 Rc 123
2140 Vale de Flor SA 113 Rd 113
5230-253 Vale de Frades BN 44 Td 99
6090 Vale de Freixo CB 97 Se 107
5385-133 Vale de Gouvinhas BN 43 Se 99
7875 Vale de Grou BE 146 Se 121
6120 Vale de Grou SA 95 Sa 111
7580 Vale de Guiso, Estação Ferroviária de SE 144 Rc 119
7580 Vale de Guizo SE 144 Rd 119
7700 Vale de Hortas BE 159 Re 124
3830-270 Vale de Ílhavo AV 78 Rc 105
2080 Vale de Inferno SA 113 Rc 114
5335-136 Vale de Janeiro BN 43 Sf 98
8100 Vale de Juden FA 159 Rf 126
2715 Vale de Labos L 112 Qe 116
5370 Vale de Lagôa BN 44 Sf 99
5300 Vale de Lamas BN 44 Tb 98
5370-102 Vale de Lobo BN 62 Sf 99
2460 Vale de Maceira LE 94 Qf 112
6400-671 Vale de Madeira GD 81 Sf 104
6040 Vale de Madeira PT 114 Sa 112
3525-350 Vale de Madeiros VS 79 Sa 106
6150 Vale de Matos CB 96 Sb 111
5085-100 Vale de Mendiz VR 62 Sc 101
5070-304 Vale de Mir VR 62 Sd 100
5210-060 Vale de Mira BN 63 Te 100
7630 Vale de Moinhos BE 158 Rc 123
7050 Vale de Mós E 130 Re 117
2205 Vale de Mós SA 114 Rf 112
5000 Vale de Negueiras VR 61 Sb 101
5300 Vale de Nogeira BN 44 Ta 99
2040 Vale de Óbidos SA 112 Ra 113
8800 Vale de Odre FA 159 Sb 124
2445 Vale de Paredes LE 94 Qf 110
8950 Vale de Pinheiro FA 160 Sc 124
5200-510 Vale de Porco BN 63 Tb 101

6430 Vale de Porço GD 62 Se 102
6030 Vale de Pousadas CB 96 Sc 110
5340 Vale de Pradinhos BN 44 Sf 99
5385 Vale de Prados BN 43 Sf 99
5340 Vale de Prados BN 63 Ta 99
6230 Vale de Prazeres CB 96 Sd 102
3450 Vale de Rémígio VS 79 Re 106
7800 Vale de Rocins BE 145 Sb 121
5370 Vale de Salgueiros BN 43 Se 99
5370-137 Vale de Sancha BN 62 Sf 100
2005-029 Vale de Santarém SA 113 Rb 113
6120-782 Vale de São Domingos SA 95 Sa 111
6040 Vale de São João PT 114 Sa 112
6420 Vale de Seixo GD 80 Se 104
2240 Vale de Serrão SA 95 Re 110
6060 Vale de Sobral CB 97 Sf 110
6160 Vale de Souto CB 95 Sa 109
5385-140 Vale de Telhas BN 43 Se 99
Vale de Todos C 95 Rd 109
5360 Vale de Torno BN 62 Se 101
3305 Vale de Torno C 79 Sa 107
6230-740 Vale de Urso CB 96 Sc 108
7830-469 Vale de Vargo BE 146 Sd 121
2460 Vale de Ventos LE 94 Ra 112
7800 Vale de Vinagre BE 146 Sb 120
2205 Vale de Zebrinho SA 114 Rf 112
4440 Vale Direito P 60 Rd 101
5130 Vale do Figueira VS 62 Sd 102
2400 Vale do Horto LE 94 Ra 110
8135 Vale do Lobo FA 159 Rf 126
2050 Vale do Paradíso L 113 Ra 114
6100 Vale do Pereiro CB 95 Rf 110
7040 Vale do Pereiro E 130 Sb 116
7430-351 Vale do Peso PT 115 Sc 112
7430 Vale do Peso, Estação A PT 115 Sb 112
7430 Vale do Peso, Estação Ferroviária de PT 115 Sc 112
3260 Vale do Rio LE 95 Re 109
8005 Valedos FA 159 Sa 126
7800 Valefanado BE 145 Rf 122
6060 Vale Feitoso CB 97 Ta 108
8375 Vale Figueira FA 159 Re 125
6430-371 Vale Flor GD 62 Se 103
2810 Vale Flor SE 128 Qe 117
3240 Vale Florido C 95 Rd 109
2025 Vale Florido LE 94 Rb 112
2300 Vale Florido SA 95 Rb 111
8375 Vale Fontes FA 159 Re 124
6200 Vale Formosa CB 80 Sd 106
8100 Vale Formoso FA 159 Rf 126
5360-220 Vale Frechoso BN 62 Sf 100
2445 Vale Furado LE 94 Qf 110
8375-082 Vale Fuzeiros FA 159 Rd 125
3880-463 Válega AV 78 Rc 103
7780 Vale Gonçalo BE 145 Rf 122
3750 Vale Grande AV 78 Rd 105
3320 Vale Grande C 96 Sa 108
8375 Vale Grou FA 159 Rd 124
7000 Valeira E 130 Rf 117
7100 Valeja E 115 Sc 115
7630 Vale Juncalinho BE 158 Rb 124
7630 Vale Longo BE 144 Rd 122
6320 Vale Longo GD 81 Sf 106

7800 Vale Loução de Baixo BE 145 Sb 121
7555 Vale Manhãs SE 144 Rb 121
7000 Vale Maria E 130 Rf 117
7540 Vale Miguel SE 144 Rb 121
6320-014 Vale Mourisco GD 80 Sf 106
2100 Vale Mouro SA 113 Rd 115
4930-587 Valença VC 41 Rc 96
5120-500 Valença do Douro VS 62 Sd 102
5335 Valepaço BN 43 Sf 98
9050 Vale Paraiso MA 178 Ka 152
5370 Vale Pereiro BN 62 Sf 99
5350 Vale Pereiro BN 63 Ta 100
7540 Vale Pereiro SE 144 Rc 121
2120 Vale Queimado SA 113 Rd 114
7630 Vales BE 144 Rc 122
5350 Vales BN 62 Sf 100
6200 Vales CB 80 Sc 107
8670 Vales FA 158 Ra 125
8800 Vales FA 160 Sa 125
6440 Vales GD 62 Ta 103
5430 Vales VR 62 Sd 100
2405-035 Vale Salgueiro LE 94 Ra 110
7630 Vale Santiago BE 144 Rd 122
7565 Vale Santiago SE 144 Rd 121
6120 Vales de Cardigos SA 95 Sa 110
6230-584 Vales de Pêro Viseu CB 80 Sd 107
7300 Vale Serrão PT 115 Sc 112
7830 Vales Mortos BE 146 Sd 122
7750 Vale Travessos BE 146 Sc 122
5370 Vale Verde BN 62 Se 100
6350 Vale Verde GD 81 Ta 104
5200 Valeverde BN 63 Tb 101
2125-202 Vale Zebro SA 129 Rb 114
6270-621 Valezim GD 80 Sb 106
2230-180 Valhascos SA 95 Rf 111
6300-235 Valhelhas GD 80 Sd 106
4920 Valinho VC 41 Rb 97
3850-835 Valmaior AV 78 Rd 104
4730 Valões BR 41 Rd 98
3040 Valongo C 95 Rd 107
8800 Valongo FA 160 Sc 126
2420 Valongo LE 94 Rb 110
4440 Valongo P 60 Rc 101
7480 Valongo PT 114 Sa 113
5430 Valongo VR 43 Sd 99
5370-070 Valongo das Meadas BN 62 Se 99
5090-224 Valongo de Milhais VR 62 Sd 100
5130 Valongo dos Azeites VS 62 Sd 102
3750-836 Valongo do Vouga AV 78 Rd 105
5450-300 Valoura VR 62 Sc 99
5430-407 Valpaços VR 43 Se 99
4575-588 Valpedre P 60 Re 102
9950 Valverde AC 176 Wc 117
5300 Valverde BN 44 Tb 98
5350 Valverde BN 62 Ta 101
6230 Valverde CB 96 Sd 108
3570 Valverde GD 80 Sc 104
2655 Valverde L 112 Qd 115
2025 Valverde SA 94 Ra 112
5430 Valverde VR 43 Se 99
4585-761 Vandoma P 60 Rd 101
8970-351 Vaqueiros FA 160 Sb 124
2000-791 Vaqueiros SA 113 Rc 112
6060 Vaquilha CB 97 Ta 108
6100-368 Vaquinhas CB 95 Rf 110
Varadoura AC 176 Wb 117
7350-422 Varche PT 115 Se 115
5300-412 Varge BN 44 Tb 97
5130 Vargelas VS 62 Se 102
7750-812 Vargens BE 160 Sb 123
5090-210 Varges VR 62 Sd 100
5200-312 Variz BN 63 Tc 100
4540 Várzea AV 60 Re 103
4755 Várzea BR 60 Rc 99
3420 Várzea C 79 Sa 106
8970 Várzea FA 160 Sc 125
4610 Várzea P 61 Re 100
4600 Várzea P 61 Sa 101
2005-001 Várzea SA 113 Rb 113
4970 Várzea VC 42 Re 97
3660 Várzea VS 79 Rf 104
3510 Várzea VS 79 Rf 105
3515 Várzea VS 79 Sa 104
4820-820 Várzea Cova BR 61 Rf 99

8800-025 Várzea da Azinheira FA 160 Sb 125
3610-187 Várzea da Serra VS 61 Sb 103
5100-879 Várzea de Abrunhais VS 61 Sb 102
6270-631 Várzea de Meruge GD 79 Sb 106
6100-327 Várzea de Pedro Mouro CB 95 Re 110
3530 Várzea de Tavares VS 80 Sc 105
5130 Várzea de Trevões VS 62 Sd 102
6100-894 Várzea dos Cavaleiros CB 95 Rf 110
2120 Varzea Fresca SA 129 Rb 115
7540-025 Várzea Nova SE 144 Rc 120
7050 Várzeas E 113 Re 116
2425 Várzeas LE 94 Ra 109
3060-215 Varziela C 78 Rc 106
4650 Varziela P 61 Re 100
Varzielas VS 79 Re 105
4940 Vascões VC 41 Rc 97
6270-015 Vasco Esteves de Baixo GD 80 Sb 107
6270-014 Vasco Esteves de Cima GD 80 Sb 107
3670 Vasconha VS 79 Rf 104
7750-517 Vasco Rodrigues BE 160 Sb 123
6400-681 Vascoveiro GD 80 Sf 104
5430-603 Vassal VR 43 Sd 99
2510-665 Vau LE 112 Qe 112
7800 Vau de Cima BE 146 Sb 121
5430-620 Veiga de Lila VR 62 Se 99
5300 Veigas BN 44 Tc 98
3860-274 Veiros AV 78 Rc 104
7100 Veiros E 115 Sc 115
6300 Vela GD 80 Se 108
Velas AC 177 We 116
8970-106 Velhas FA 146 Sc 124
6360-190 Velosa GD 80 Se 105
4910 Venade VC 41 Rb 97
4940 Venade VC 41 Rc 97
7750 Venda BE 145 Sb 122
4850 Venda BR 42 Rf 98
6150 Venda CB 96 Sb 110
7340 Venda PT 115 Sd 113
6400-242 Vendada GD 80 Sf 104
2500-386 Venda da Costa LE 112 Ra 112
3105-296 Venda da Cruz LE 94 Rc 109
3420-069 Venda da Esperança C 79 Sa 107
2100-407 Venda da Lamarosa SA 113 Rc 114
2475-043 Venda das Raparigas LE 112 Ra 112
3400-434 Venda de Galizes C 79 Sa 107
6420-579 Venda do Cepo GD 80 Sd 104
7040 Venda do Dugue E 114 Sb 116
2665-498 Venda do Pinheiro L 128 Qe 115
3060 Venda Nova C 78 Rc 106
3130 Venda Nova C 95 Rc 108
8300 Venda Nova FA 158 Rd 125
6120 Venda Nova SA 96 Sa 111
5470 Venda Nova VR 42 Sa 98
2605 Venda Seca L 112 Qe 116
7080-011 Vendas Novas E 129 Rd 116
7200 Vendinha E 131 Sc 118
4850 Ventosa BR 42 Re 99
2530 Ventosa L 112 Qe 113
2565 Ventosa L 112 Qe 114
2550 Ventosa L 112 Qf 113
2580 Ventosa L 112 Qf 113
3670-223 Ventosa VS 79 Rf 104
3050-554 Ventosa do Bairro AV 78 Rd 106
5400 Ventoselos VR 43 Sc 98
5200 Ventozelo BN 63 Tc 101
7220 Vera Cruz de Marmelar E 131 Sb 119
3810-596 Verba AV 78 Rc 105
6200 Verdelhos CB 80 Sd 106
4930 Verdoejo VC 41 Rc 96
2100 Verdugos SA 129 Rd 115
6150 Vergão CB 95 Rf 110
3840-555 Vergas AV 78 Rb 105
8700 Vergílios FA 160 Sa 126
Verigo LE 94 Rc 109
4830 Verim BR 42 Re 99

2550-504 Vermelha L 112 Qf 113
8100 Vermelhos FA 159 Rf 124
4805-546 Vermil BR 60 Rd 100
6440 Vermiosa GD 81 Ta 104
Vermoil LE 94 Rc 109
4770 Vermoim BR 60 Rd 100
4470 Vermum P 60 Rc 101
6030-024 Vermum CB 96 Sb 111
3140-601 Verride C 94 Rb 108
2435-804 Vesparia SA 94 Rb 110
2460-743 Vestiaria LE 94 Ra 111
Vesúvio, Estação BN 62 Se 102
4890 Viade BR 61 Sa 100
5470-528 Viade de Baixo VR 42 Sa 98
6040 Viale da Vinha PT 114 Sa 112
2625 Vialonga L 128 Qf 115
2300-108 Vialonga SA 95 Re 111
7090 Viana do Alentejo E 145 Rf 118
4900 Viana do Castelo VC 41 Rb 98
4640 Viariz P 61 Sa 101
4775-250 Viatodos BR 60 Rc 100
7750 Vicentes BE 160 Sc 123
8970 Vicentes FA 146 Sc 124
8100 Vicentes FA 159 Rf 125
2100-407 Vicentinhos SA 113 Rc 114
Viçosa E 130 Sb 118
8970 Vidago FA 146 Sb 124
5425-301 Vidago VR 43 Sc 99
2500-749 Vidais LE 112 Qf 112
6285 Vide GD 79 Sb 107
6360-200 Vide entre Vinhas GD 80 Sd 105
3070 Videira C 78 Rb 106
6300-245 Videmonte GD 80 Sd 105
7050 Vidigal E 130 Re 116
2410 Vidigal LE 94 Rb 110
7960 Vidigueira BE 130 Sb 119
3220 Vidual C 95 Re 108
3320 Vidual, Fajão- C 96 Sa 108
5200-010 Viduedo BN 63 Tb 100
2025-251 Viegas SA 113 Ra 112
2430-592 Vieira de Leiria LE 94 Ra 109
4850-506 Vieira do Minho BR 42 Rf 99
3105-069 Vieirinhos LE 94 Rb 108
5360 Vieiro BN 62 Se 100
6400 Vieiro GD 80 Se 104
4860 Viela BR 61 Sa 99
5445 Viela VR 43 Sd 99
7940 Vila Alva BE 130 Sa 119
7800 Vila Azeda BE 145 Sb 120
9400 Vila Baleira MA 179 Kd 150
5300 Vila Boa BN 44 Tb 99
5370 Vila Boa BN 62 Sd 100
4860 Vila Boa BR 42 Rf 99
4750 Vila Boa BR 60 Rc 99
6320 Vila Boa GD 81 Sf 106
4970 Vila Boa VC 42 Rd 97
3450 Vila Boa VS 79 Re 106
3600 Vila Boa VS 79 Sa 103
3560 Vila Boa VS 79 Sc 104
5320-210 Vila Boa de Ousilhão BN 44 Ta 98
4635 Vila Boa de Quires P 61 Re 101
4625-640 Vila Boa do Bispo P 61 Re 102
6360-210 Vila Boa do Mondego GD 80 Sd 105
7350-501 Vila Boim PT 115 Se 115
4705-651 Vilaça BR 60 Rd 99
5470 Vilaça VR 42 Sa 98
3100 Vila Cã LE 95 Rc 109
4600 Vila Caiz P 61 Rf 101
4540 Vila Chã AV 60 Rd 103
3730 Vila Chã AV 78 Rd 103
4740 Vila Chã BR 41 Rb 99
3350 Vila Chã C 79 Re 107
6370 Vila Chã GD 80 Sd 105
4485 Vila Chã P 60 Rb 101
2835-462 Vila Chã SE 128 Qf 117
5070 Vila Chã VR 62 Sd 101
4980 Vila Chã (Santiago) VC 42 Re 98
4980 Vila Chã (São João Baptista) VC 42 Re 98
3610-210 Vila Chã da Beira VS 61 Sb 102
5230 Vila Chã da Ribeira BN 63 Tc 99
5210-335 Vila Chã de Braciosa BN 63 Td 100
2070-611 Vila Chã de Ourique SA 113 Rb 113
3510 Vila Chã de Sá VS 79 Sa 105

3720 Vila Chã de São Roque AV 78 Rd 103
3610 Vila Chã do Monte VS 61 Sb 103
3510 Vila Chã do Monte VS 79 Rf 105
4990 Vila Chão VC 41 Rd 98
4600 Vila Chão do Marão P 61 Rf 101
6290 Vila Cortês da Serra GD 80 Sc 105
6300-250 Vila Cortês do Mondego GD 80 Sd 105
4820 Vila Cova BR 60 Rb 99
4560 Vila Cova BR 61 Re 99
5000 Vila Cova P 60 Re 101
6270 Vila Cova VR 61 Sa 101
6270 Vila Cova a Coelheira GD 79 Sb 106
3650 Vila Cova a Coelheira VS 79 Sb 103
3305-285 Vila Cova de Alva C 79 Sa 107
3730 Vila Cova de Perinho AV 60 Rd 103
3550 Vila Cova do Covelo VS 80 Sc 105
3640-307 Vila da Ponte VS 62 Sc 103
3130 Vila da Rainha C 94 Rb 108
5200-544 Vila de Ala BN 63 Tc 101
3440-138 Vila de Barba VS 79 Rf 106
3720 Vila de Cucujães AV 78 Rd 103
5400 Vila de Frade VR 43 Sd 98
7960-421 Vila de Frades BE 130 Sb 119
4905-641 Vila de Punhe VC 41 Rb 99
6110 Vila de Rei CB 95 Rf 110
2140 Vila de Rei SA 113 Rd 113
3505-238 Vila de Um Santo VS 79 Sb 104
8650-405 Vila do Bispo FA 158 Ra 126
4480 Vila do Conde P 60 Rb 100
5450 Vila do Conde VR 43 Sc 99
3420-149 Vila do Mato C 79 Sa 106
9580 Vila do Porto AC 177 Zf 127
5200-571 Vila dos Sinos BN 63 Tc 101
6320-592 Vila do Touro GD 80 Sf 106
2565-642 Vila Facaia L 112 Qe 114
3270 Vila Facaia LE 95 Re 109
Vila Fernando GD 80 Sf 106
7350-511 Vila Fernando PT 115 Se 115
5360-301 Vila Flor BN 62 Sf 101
4970 Vila Fonche VC 41 Rd 97
7440 Vila Formosa PT 114 Sb 113
5300 Vila Franca BN 44 Ta 99
3405 Vila Franca C 79 Sa 106
4905 Vila Franca VC 41 Rb 98
3600-435 Vila Franca VS 79 Sa 103
6290-622 Vila Franca da Serra GD 80 Sc 105
6420-692 Vila Franca das Naves GD 80 Se 104
2600-002 Vila Franca de Xira L 128 Ra 115
Vila Franca do Campo AC 177 Zd 122
6300-260 Vila Franca do Deão GD 80 Se 105
2665-418 Vila Franca do Rosário L 128 Qe 115
2925 Vila Fresca do Azeitão SE 128 Ra 117
4750-833 Vila Frescainha BR 60 Rc 99
4610-864 Vila Fria P 60 Re 100
4935 Vila Fria VC 41 Rb 99
6420 Vila Garcia GD 80 Se 105
6300 Vila Garcia GD 80 Se 105
4600 Vila Garcia P 61 Rf 101
3560-220 Vila Longa VS 80 Sc 104
4525-480 Vila Maior AV 60 Rd 102
3660 Vila Maior VS 79 Rf 104
3060-761 Vilamar C 78 Rc 106
5040 Vila Marim VR 61 Sa 101
5000 Vila Marim VR 61 Sb 101
5300 Vila Meã BN 44 Tc 97
4920 Vila Meã VC 41 Rb 97
5450 Vila Meã VS 79 Re 106
3450 Vila Meã VS 79 Re 106
6300 Vila Mendo GD 80 Se 106
3530 Vila Mendo de Tavares VS 80 Sc 105
4640 Vila Monim P 61 Rf 102

A B C D E F G H I J L M N O P Q R S T U V X Z

2380-634	Vila Moreira SA 94 Rb 112		
4925	Vila Mou VC 41 Rb 98		
8125	Vilamoura FA 159 Rf 126		
2925-007	Vila Nogueira de Azeitão SE 128 Qf 117		
9760	Vila Nova AC 176 Xf 116		
5340	Vila Nova BN 43 Sf 98		
5300	Vila Nova BN 44 Tb 98		
5370	Vila Nova BN 62 Se 99		
5350	Vila Nova BN 62 Ta 100		
3060	Vila Nova C 78 Rc 107		
3220	Vila Nova C 95 Re 108		
5445	Vila Nova VR 43 Sd 99		
3450	Vila Nova VS 79 Re 106		
3140-651	Vila Nova da Barca C 94 Rb 108		
7920	Vila Nova da Baronia BE 130 Rf 119		
2260-368	Vila Nova da Barquinha SA 95 Rd 112		
2050-501	Vila Nova da Rainha L 128 Ra 114		
3460-712	Vila Nova da Rainha VS 79 Rf 106		
3130-400	Vila Nova de Anços C 94 Rc 108		
8900-067	Vila Nova de Cacela FA 160 Sc 125		
4920-201	Vila Nova de Cerveira VC 41 Rb 97		
9980-024	Vila Nova de Corvo AC 176 Tf 110		
4760	Vila Nova de Famalicão BR 60 Rc 100		
4400	Vila Nova de Gaia P 60 Rc 102		
7645-211	Vila Nova de Milfontes BE 144 Rb 122		
4980	Vila Nova de Muía VC 42 Rd 98		
3420	Vila Nova de Oliveirinha C 79 Sa 106		
2490	Vila Nova de Ourém SA 94 Rc 111		
3650	Vila Nova de Paiva VS 79 Sb 103		
3350-151	Vila Nova de Poiares C 79 Re 107		
7500	Vila Nova de Santo André SE 144 Rb 120		
6290	Vila Nova de Tazém GD 80 Sb 105		
3330-407	Vila Nova do Ceira C 95 Rf 107		
2005	Vila Nova do Couto SA 113 Rb 113		
2065	Vila Nova do São Pedro L 113 Ra 113		
4485	Vila Nova Telha P 60 Rb 101		
6420-553	Vila Novinha GD 80 Sd 104		
5460-418	Vila Pequena VR 42 Sa 99		
4820	Vila Pouca BR 61 Rf 100		
3045	Vila Pouca C 78 Rc 107		
3610	Vila Pouca VS 61 Sb 102		
3440	Vila Pouca VS 79 Rf 106		
3400-755	Vila Pouca da Beira C 79 Sa 107		
5450-001	Vila Pouca de Aguiar VR 61 Sc 99		
4910-384	Vila Praia de Âncora VC 41 Ra 98		

4840	Vilar BR 42 Re 98
2550-069	Vilar L 112 Qf 113
3280	Vilar LE 95 Re 108
5460	Vilar VR 42 Sb 98
3600	Vilar VS 61 Sa 103
3620	Vilar VS 62 Sc 103
5430	Vilaranda Boa VR 43 Sd 99
5430-630	Vilarandelo VR 43 Se 99
6185-460	Vilar Barroco, Estreito- CB 96 Sb 109
5350-402	Vilar Chão BN 63 Ta 100
4690	Vilar da Arca VS 61 Re 102
6120-036	Vilar da Lapa SA 96 Sa 111
5320	Vilar da Lomba BN 43 Se 98
4990-790	Vilar das Almas VC 41 Rc 99
4845	Vilar da Veiga BR 42 Re 98
6440-271	Vilar de Amargo GD 62 Sf 103
4430	Vilar de Andorinho P 60 Rc 102
3465	Vilar de Besteiros VS 79 Rf 105
4860-483	Vilar de Cunhas BR 61 Sa 99
4880	Vilar de Ferreiros VR 61 Sa 100
4755	Vilar de Figos BR 60 Rc 100
5370-088	Vilar de Ledra BN 62 Sf 99
4425	Vilar de Luz P 60 Rc 101
5070-576	Vilar de Maçada VR 62 Sc 101
4910	Vilar de Mouros VC 41 Rb 97
4925	Vilar de Murteda VC 41 Rb 98
5400	Vilar de Nantes VR 43 Sd 98
5320-243	Vilar de Ossos BN 44 Sf 97
5385	Vilar de Ouro BN 43 Sf 98
5470-461	Vilar de Perdizes VR 43 Sc 97
5470-480*	Vilar de Perdizes e Meixide VR 43 Sb 97
5320	Vilar de Peregrinos BN 44 Sf 98
4970	Vilar de Suento VC 42 Re 97
6030-025	Vilar do Boi CB 96 Sb 111
4850	Vilar do Chão BR 42 Rf 99
5340-490	Vilar do Monte BN 62 Ta 99
4750	Vilar do Monte BR 60 Rc 99
4990	Vilar do Monte VC 41 Rc 97
3515-771	Vilar do Monte VS 79 Sa 104
4405	Vilar do Paraíso P 60 Rc 102
5200	Vilar do Rei BN 63 Tb 101
6110-023	Vilar do Ruivo CB 95 Re 110
2490	Vilar dos Prazeres SA 95 Rc 111
4620	Vilar do Torno e Alentém P 61 Re 101
5000	Vila Real VR 61 Sb 101
8900-201	Vila Real de Santo António FA 160 Sd 125
5450	Vilarelho VR 62 Sc 99

5400-813	Vilarelho da Raia VR 43 Sd 97
5350-420	Vilarelhos BN 62 Sf 100
5385	Vilares BN 43 Sf 99
6420	Vilares GD 80 Se 104
5090	Vilares VR 62 Sc 100
	Vilares de Baixo CB 96 Sc 109
5350	Vilares de Vilariça BN 62 Sf 100
6355	Vilar Formoso GD 81 Tb 105
5200-313	Vilariça BN 63 Tc 100
8670-238	Vilarinha FA 158 Ra 126
3700	Vilarinho AV 60 Rd 103
3800	Vilarinho AV 78 Rc 104
7800	Vilarinho BE 145 Sa 120
5320	Vilarinho BN 43 Sf 99
5300	Vilarinho BN 44 Ta 97
4730	Vilarinho BR 41 Rd 98
3020	Vilarinho C 95 Re 108
4485	Vilarinho P 60 Rb 100
4795	Vilarinho P 60 Rd 100
4910	Vilarinho VC 41 Ra 98
4920	Vilarinho VC 41 Rb 97
32698	Vilarinho VR 43 Sd 98
4880	Vilarinho VR 61 Sa 100
3610	Vilarinho VS 61 Sb 103
3660	Vilarinho VS 79 Re 104
	Vilarinho VS 79 Re 104
5140-275	Vilarinho da Castanheira BN 62 Sf 100
5460-165	Vilarinho da Mó VR 42 Sb 98
5360-470	Vilarinho das Azenhas BN 62 Se 100
4760-739	Vilarinho das Cambas BR 60 Rc 100
5425-401	Vilarinho das Paranheiras VR 43 Sc 99
5340-500	Vilarinho de Agrochão BN 44 Sf 98
5085-120	Vilarinho de Cotas VR 62 Sc 101
5000-781	Vilarinho de Samardã VR 61 Sb 100
5450-204	Vilarinho de São Bento VR 43 Sc 99
3720	Vilarinho de São Luís AV 78 Rd 104
5060-630	Vilarinho de São Romão VR 62 Sc 101
3780-599	Vilarinho do Bairro AV 78 Rc 106
5340-510	Vilarinho do Monte BN 43 Sf 99
5050	Vilarinho dos Freires VR 61 Sb 101
5200	Vilarínho dos Galegos BN 63 Tc 101
4970-140	Vilarinho do Souto VC 42 Re 97
5460-030	Vilarinho Seco VR 42 Sb 98
6320-601	Vilar Maior GD 81 Ta 106
8500	Vila Romana FA 158 Rc 126
8005	Vila Romana FA 159 Sa 126
5130-557	Vilarouco VS 62 Sd 102
5350	Vilar Seco BN 63 Ta 100
5230	Vilar Seco BN 63 Td 99

3520-225	Vilar Seco VS 79 Sa 105
5320-263	Vilar Seco de Lomba BN 43 Se 97
6440	Vilar Torpim GD 81 Ta 104
	Vila Ruiva BE 145 Sa 119
6370-401	Vila Ruiva GD 80 Sc 105
3520-224	Vila Ruiva VS 79 Sb 105
5360-493	Vilas Boas BN 62 Se 100
5425-502	Vilas Boas VR 43 Sc 99
3260-224	Vilas de Pedro LE 95 Re 109
4755	Vila Seca BR 60 Rb 99
3150-318	Vila Seca C 95 Rd 108
5050	Vila Seca VR 61 Sb 101
5110	Vila Seca VR 61 Sc 102
6300-270	Vila Soeiro GD 80 Sd 105
6030	Vilas Ruivas CB 96 Sb 111
6030	Vila Velha de Ródão CB 96 Sb 111
5320	Vila Verde BN 44 Ta 97
5370	Vila Verde BN 62 Sf 100
4730	Vila Verde BR 41 Rd 99
3025	Vila Verde C 78 Rc 107
3090	Vila Verde C 94 Rb 108
6270	Vila Verde GD 80 Sc 105
2715	Vila Verde L 128 Qd 115
2500	Vila Verde LE 112 Qf 113
4650	Vila Verde P 61 Re 101
4910	Vila Verde VC 41 Rb 98
5425	Vila Verde VR 43 Sc 99
5070	Vila Verde VR 62 Sc 100
5400-805	Vila Verde da Raia VR 43 Sd 98
2580-442	Vila Verde dos Francos L 112 Qf 114
7160	Vila Viçosa E 115 Sd 116
3025-622	Vil de Matos C 78 Rc 107
3510	Vil de Souto VS 79 Sa 104
4910	Vile VC 41 Ra 98
4720	Vilela BR 42 Rd 98
4830	Vilela BR 60 Re 99
4820	Vilela BR 61 Rf 100
4580	Vilela P 60 Rd 101
4970	Vilela VC 41 Rd 97
4970	Vilela VC 42 Rd 98
5450	Vilela VR 43 Sc 99
5400	Vilela do Tâmega VR 43 Sc 98
4970	Vilela Seca VC 42 Rd 97
5400	Vilela Seca VR 43 Sd 98
2530	Vimeiro L 112 Qe 113
2460-781	Vimeiro LE 94 Qf 112
3050-187	Vimieira AV 78 Rd 106
7040	Vimieiro E 114 Sa 116
2200-733	Vimieiro SA 95 Rf 111
7040	Vimiero, Estação Ferroviária de E 114 Sb 116
5230	Vimioso BN 44 Tc 99
5320-326	Vinhais BN 44 Sf 97
3460-161	Vinhal VS 79 Sa 105
5340	Vinhas BN 63 Tb 99
4630-776	Vinheiros P 61 Rf 101
3305	Vinho C 79 Sa 107
6290	Vinhó GD 80 Sc 106
4820	Vinhos BR 61 Re 100
5050	Vinhos VR 61 Sa 101
6005-273	Violeiro CB 96 Sc 108
4960-120	Virtelo VC 42 Re 96
2050-040	Virtudes L 113 Rb 114
3500	Viseu VS 79 Sa 105

7780-491	Viseus BE 145 Sa 123
4910	Viso VC 41 Ra 98
3830-292	Vista Alegre AV 78 Rb 105
9880	Vitória AC 176 Wf 114
4990-800	Vitorino das Donas VC 41 Rc 98
4990-810	Vitorino dos Piães VC 41 Rc 98
7700	Viúvas BE 159 Sa 123
5460-495	Viveiro VR 42 Sb 98
4815	Vizela BR 60 Re 100
3670-231	Vouzela VS 79 Rf 104
5450-345	Vreia de Jales VR 61 Sc 100

X

7595	Xarraminha SE 144 Re 119
5470-025	Xertelo VR 42 Rf 98
8100-053	Ximeno FA 159 Sa 124
4905	Xisto VC 41 Rb 99

Z

7750	Zambujal BE 160 Sc 123
3060	Zambujal C 78 Rc 107
3150	Zambujal C 95 Rd 108
8970	Zambujal FA 146 Sb 124
8100	Zambujal FA 159 Rf 125
2660	Zambujal L 112 Qf 115
2710	Zambujal L 128 Qd 116
3250	Zambujal LE 95 Rd 110
2500	Zambujal LE 112 Qf 112
2965	Zambujal SE 129 Rb 117
2970-140	Zambujal de Baixo SE 128 Qf 118
7005	Zambujal do Conde E 130 Sa 118
7630	Zambujeira BE 144 Rb 122
7630	Zambujeira BE 144 Rd 123
7630-761	Zambujeira do Mar BE 158 Rb 123
7630	Zambujeiras BE 144 Rc 122
3140	Zambujeiro C 78 Rc 107
7170	Zambujeiro E 131 Sc 117
7220	Zambujeiro E 145 Sb 118
8670	Zambujeiro FA 158 Rb 124
5200-286	Zava BN 63 Tb 101
8650	Zavial FA 158 Ra 126
5470-466	Zebral VR 43 Sb 98
6230-513	Zebras CB 96 Sd 108
5430-302	Zebras VR 62 Sd 100
6060-186	Zebreira CB 97 Sf 109
2100-407	Zebrinho SA 113 Rc 114
8550	Zebro FA 158 Rb 125
5140-300	Zedes BN 62 Se 101
5300-742	Zeive BN 44 Ta 97
7400	Zézere PT 114 Rf 113
2590	Zibreira L 128 Qe 114
2350-826	Zibreira SA 94 Rc 112
5320-244	Zido BN 44 Sf 97
5450-283	Zimão VR 61 Sc 100
8800	Zimbral FA 160 Sb 125
6120-037	Zimbreira SA 96 Sa 111
5300-911	Zoio BN 44 Ta 98
3505-240	Zonho VS 79 Sb 104

Every edition is always revised to take into account the latest data and having regard to the current political de facto administrations (or allegiances). This may lead to discrepancies towards the international legal situation. Nevertheless, despite every effort, errors can still occur. Should you find an error, we would be grateful if you could forward the relevant information to us.